THE
INTERNSHIP
BIBLE

THE PRINCETON REVIEW

THE INTERNSHIP BIBLE

MARK OLDMAN
AND
SAMER HAMADEH

RANDOM HOUSE, INC.
New York
2001 EDITION

www.randomhouse.com/princetonreview

Princeton Review Publishing, L. L. C.
2315 Broadway
New York, NY 10024
E-mail: comments@review.com

Published in the United States by Random House, Inc. New York, and simultaneously in Canada by Random House of Canada Limited, Toronto.

ISBN 0-375-75638-8
ISSN 1073-5801

Account Manager: Amy Kinney

Manufactured in the United States of America on partially recycled paper.

9 8 7 6 5 4 3 2 1

2001 Edition

The Independent Education Consultants Association recognizes The Princeton Review as a valuable resource for high school and college students applying to college and graduate school.

ACKNOWLEDGMENTS

Our gratitude goes to: John Katzman, whose support made this book a reality. Jeanne Krier, a supernatural wellspring of publicity and good cheer. Hilary Abramson, for her editing expertise and grace under pressure, Amy Bryant and Kristen Azzara for making sure the book looked great. John Bergdahl, for his scintillating illustrations.

The other TPR essentials: Bruno Blumenfeld, Jeff Grollo, Brenda Campbell, Stephanie Silverman, and the self-cleaning Tor. Our own interns, the dedicated Erik Neuenschwander, Maureen Reilly, and Barbara Chai.

Special thanks to the production crew of Julieanna Lambert, Scott Harris, Greta Englert, Melissa Fernandez, Chris Blazier, Michael Palumbo, and Heather Smith.

Mucho gratitude to our farm-based research assistant, Erik Neuenschwander.

Our tip of the hat to: (in no particular order) Dan Duff & Jeannie Higgins & the "1-day Hotdogger Internship," Marie Eliezer, The NYC Meat-Eaters (you know who you are), Jen Eng, The Great Jane Emery, Laura Locke, Elaine Gayle, Sidney Goldman, Jason Linn and Chris Otto, Heather Holtman, Chris McGee and all at John's Westside, Tom "Nellie" Nelson & the Cabo Compound, Joan "Our Archivist" Saylor, Marc Fioravanti, Brandon McKinney, Jason Schroedl, The Texans, Urge Overkill, Simon "1-night internship at the Buddah" Allen, Neighborly Jane Levine, Ola Oxing & the Swedes, Nascar C. Philips, Mary Radford, Geoff Martz, Betty Wang, Andrew Frutkin, Elena Reilly, Karyn Goodman, Frankie Simmons, Rachel Zalis, Jose Castellote, M. Alexander Hoye, Tuc Watkins, Baluchis, Mike Fee, Michelle Brown, Rob "Full" Nelson, Cindy Ortegon, Roger Kuhn, Denise Kite, Sue Gray, Carroll E. Bronson, Alexandra Lee, Christopher McNally, Doug Mollenauer, Dan Ewert, Glenn Jones, and Janet Keller.

Our continuing appreciation to all Oldmans and Hamadehs.

"Check it, bleed!"

CONTENTS

Information You Need

Miscellaneous Features

Fascinating Lists and Information

Brief Profiles of Prominent Former Interns and Apprentices

Appendix

INTRODUCTION

How This Book Came About

After the publication of *America's Top Internships*, it was obvious we had created a stir in the stagnant field of career education. Visiting over 22 campuses on an 11-city book tour, we met countless students and recent grads who were using internships to launch their careers or to find out what fires their vocational passion. Over and over, they told us there were few good resources to guide them in their internship searches. "Boring," "incomplete," and "out-of-touch" was how they described the one or two internship directories previously available.

It soon became clear that we should put together a second book to include the hundreds of rewarding internships that just missed the cut for *America's Top Internships*. We initiated the most thorough research effort ever performed on the subject of internships, reassessing the programs we already knew about and searching intensively for new internship opportunities. We collected every bit of information on internships we could find, and conducted hundreds of student surveys at colleges across the country. We also hit up dozens of internship coordinators and career center experts for recommendations about plum internships they knew of, and we received hundreds of leads from readers via our mailbox and a specially created online bulletin board.

Why This Book Isn't an "Internship Directory"

This book is not what most people are used to—that is, stale, phonebook-like guides that offer only a random sampling of internships. These "internship directories" spit their information into standardized, generic listings. Pick one up and you will see superficial and useless phrases appearing again and again: "possibility of full-time employment" (really!), "sponsor is willing to complete any necessary paperwork for intern to receive credit" (what good sponsor isn't?), "sponsor is willing to write letters of recommendation" (again, what good sponsor isn't?). What they are doing is the textual equivalent of using meat by-products—inserting low-quality filler to make their product seem more complete.

There's a Latin expression we love—*experto credite*, "trust those who've had experience." When looking for our own internships as Stanford students, the last thing we wanted was an internship book compiled by out-of-touch, professional fact-collectors. But that is exactly who writes internship directories: older, institutional data-collectors with no practical experience in the field. To use their books was as useful as having Uncle Bob or Grandma Gertrude pick out our clothes for us.

The Internship Bible breaks from this tradition of mediocrity. It springs from real experience, benefiting from our work as internship experts as well as our position as recent grads who together served eleven internships in eight different fields. Unlike those responsible for internship directories, we have spent the last few years interviewing a steady stream of internship coordinators and former interns, shaping their remarks into individually crafted entries on specific internship programs. This has been our full-time job.

Not Just "Internships"

The word "internship" is tricky. An "internship" to one organization is a "volunteer position" to another, whereas a third might call it a "fellowship," another might say "apprenticeship," and still another might say "externship." The lines of distinction blur into a "You say tomato, I say too-maw-tow" situation. The word "internship," while common, is just not universally used.

We therefore decided to include in *The Internship Bible* not only internships labeled as such, but internship-like programs that are titled otherwise. To be sure, most of the programs we describe follow the traditional format of an internship, running the length of a semester and open to college students. But you will also find programs such as the Peace Corps, which lasts for over two years, as well as specialized opportunities like the one at William Morris Agency, which bills itself as a "training program" open only to college grads. The book also contains programs that are like old-time apprenticeships in which participants learn a trade; Tracy Watts Millinery, for example, teaches interns the art of hat making.

So what characteristics are common to every program in this book? Well, we made sure every program included in *The Internship Bible* met two criteria. First of all, the program had to be temporary, whether it ran for two weeks or two years. So long as the program had an end point, it was eligible for inclusion. The other prerequisite was that the program had to include something that distinguished it from entry-level or staff positions. Are there specific learning goals? Are there special mentoring or networking opportunities? Do special intern meetings or seminars exist? Are program participants taken on field trips or given tours of facilities? If so, the program was ripe for our picking.

The First Ever Blockbuster Guide

In addition to providing a goldmine of excellent programs, we wanted this book to educate and inspire readers. To this end we included essential advice on the internship application process, covering everything from writing effective resumes to securing visas and work permits for overseas internships. Where possible, we sought the advice of experts, asking, for example, an image consultant to comment on how to dress for success for internship interviews and a law professor (and former internship coordinator) to reveal how best to apply to highly selective programs like the internship at the US Supreme Court.

Moreover, we wanted to provide inspirational proof of an internship's ability to launch a successful career. Not only did we intersperse throughout the book profiles of accomplished former interns, but we included over 30 exclusive interviews with such former interns as actress Jodie Foster, publisher Grace Mirabella, Broadway director Harold Prince, and Senator Kay Bailey Hutchison. You'll learn why George Plimpton calls himself "Mr. Intern," where Nora Ephron thinks "Harry & Sally" would have worked had they done internships, and why Tabitha Soren earned the nickname "Boots" from Peter Jennings during her internship. It's all here—the first-ever blockbuster guide to everything relevant to internships.

We hope that this book inspires you to pursue your grandest vocational dreams. Internships can be a springboard to a satisfying and successful career, and with *The Internship Bible* in hand, you've begun the journey.

—Mark Oldman and Samer Hamadeh
The Internship Informants™ and
Founders of Vault.com

New York, NY
August 2000
www.vault.com

HOW TO READ AN ENTRY

SELECTIVITY

Selectivity measures the approximate applicant pool and number of interns accepted annually. Selectivity (i.e., percentage of interns accepted) is rated as follows:

🔍🔍🔍🔍🔍	<5%
🔍🔍🔍🔍	5 – <10%
🔍🔍🔍	10 – <20%
🔍🔍	20 – <30%
🔍	≥30%

COMPENSATION

Compensation measures the payment interns receive, as well as any housing, transportation, and food allowances. Compensation is rated as follows:

💲💲💲💲	≥ $500
💲💲💲💲	$400 – $499
💲💲💲	$300 – $399
💲💲	$200 – $299
💲	None – $199

LOCATION(S)

Location(s) lists the cities and/or states and/or countries in which the internship is located. "HQ" (when indicated) denotes an organization's headquarters, which is usually where the majority of interns work.

FIELD(S)

Field(s) defines the primary vocational disciplines associated with the organization. For other areas interns are exposed to at the organization, see The Work. For example, an organization whose field is pharmaceuticals, such as Merck, also offers opportunities in marketing, finance, human resources, and sales.

DURATION

Duration provides time parameters for the internship. Most internships are offered year-round and parallel academic semesters, denoted in this book by "Summer, Fall, Spring." Other internships follow no seasonal schedule and use interns on a rolling basis, denoted in this book as "ongoing." Some internships that describe their duration as "Summer, Fall, Spring" also accept interns between these periods or during these periods for shorter lengths of time (e.g., August–October or January–March).

Some internship programs permit interns to work part time, especially during the academic year. Many internship programs also permit interns to work for longer or shorter periods than the number of weeks prescribed. Always contact the coordinator before you start the internship if you want any special arrangements.

DEADLINE(S)

Deadline(s) states when to submit application materials. Because some deadlines change without notice, always confirm the dates with the organization's internship coordinator before you apply. It's best to submit your materials at least one month before the deadline but no later than four days before the deadline. If you cannot make the deadline or the deadline has passed, contact the internship coordinator to see if he or she will accept applications after the deadline.

THE WORK

The Work provides a general description of the organization and lists the departments that accept interns and/or the duties required of interns.

PERKS

Perks are the benefits available to interns at the organization. These include brown-bag luncheons with executives, intern receptions, planned social activities, employee discounts, field trips, access to fitness centers, and company culture.

FYI

FYI provides any additional enlightening information on the internship program and/or the organization. This includes what percentage of interns are offered permanent employment, when the internship program was founded, noteworthy internship alumni, and other bits of advice and trivia. The ellipses (. . .) that sometimes appear in these sections are used to separate disparate ideas.

TO APPLY

To Apply describes who qualifies for the internship, the required application materials, and the contact information.

Class levels are defined as follows:

- "High school students" refers to students in high school during the internship.

- "Undergrads" refers to college freshmen through seniors; "college seniors" refers to students who have completed their junior year by the start of the internship; "college juniors" refers to students who have completed their sophomore year by the start of the internship; "college sophomores" refers to students who have completed their freshman year by the start of the internship; "college freshmen" refers to students currently in their freshman year and, in a few cases, incoming freshman.

- "Recent college grads" refers to college grads within three years of graduation, unless otherwise noted.

- "Grad students" are JD, MBA, MD, MS, MA, PhD, etc., candidates unless otherwise noted.

- "High school grads" refers to anyone with a high school degree.

- "College grads of any age" refers to anyone with a college degree.

- "International applicants eligible" indicates that the internship program is open to non-US citizens, providing they obtain the proper visa and/or work permit (see "How to Obtain a Visa/Work Permit for Overseas Internships"). Moreover, the criteria for international applicants are the same, with rare exceptions, as those for US citizens.

- "Must receive academic credit" indicates that you must secure academic credit from your school. In most cases, you will need to submit written verification that your school is granting credit for the internship.

Application materials:

- "Cover letters" should always describe your qualifications, educational and professional interests, and, if applicable, the department(s) in which you wish to intern (see "The Great Cover Letter").

- "Recommendations" refers to two letters of recommendation, unless otherwise noted.

- "References" refers to a list of at least three people (with addresses and phone numbers) who can vouch for your abilities.

And BEAR IN MIND:

- If no phone and/or fax number is given, the organization has requested that all inquiries and applications be sent by mail.

- Many organizations will assist interns in finding housing by providing a list of local college dorms, apartment complexes, and/or employees willing to sublet.

THE INTERNSHIPS

A&M RECORDS

See Polygram

ABBOTT LABORATORIES

SELECTIVITY 🔍🔍🔍🔍🔍
Approximate applicant pool: 4,000–5,000; Interns accepted: 200–300

COMPENSATION 💲💲💲💲
$340–$625/week for undergrad students; $490–$1,250/week grad students; round trip travel; housing for nonlocal students

LOCATION(S)
Lake County, IL

FIELD
Health care products and services

DURATION
12 weeks: Summer

DEADLINE(S)
Resumes and cover letters accepted between September and March 1

THE WORK
Founded in 1888, Abbott Laboratories is a center for cutting edge medical research as well as a manufacturer of a broad range of health care products that are used to prevent, diagnose, and treat medical conditions. Their pioneering advances include the production of commercial penicillin and the first US Food and Drug Administration–licensed test to screen blood for HIV. Interns may support one of Abbott's varied business and product lines: pharmaceuticals, diagnostics, nutritionals, or hospital-related products. In each of these areas, interns may work in Research and Development, Production/Operations Management, Sales and Marketing, Engineering, Information Technology/Statistics, Finance and Accounting, or Human Resources Management.

PERKS
Free college housing for nonlocal students; well-organized seminars; social/networking activities.

FYI
Before they arrive, interns receive a handbook in the mail. Contains program background such as a calendar of events, maps of the surrounding area and of Abbott facilities, a description of housing accomodations, suggestions for what to bring, and reference phone numbers; the handbook prepares interns for the vast range of experiences in store for them at Abbott.

TO APPLY
Open to college sophomores, juniors, and seniors, as well as grad students. International applicants authorized to work in the US are eligible. Candidates should see us when we visit their campus in the fall or e-mail a resume (indicating GPA and field of interest) through www.abbott.com/career. Applications are completed at time of interview.

(847) 935-3888
www.abbott.com

ABRAMS ARTISTS AGENCY

ABRAMS ARTISTS AGENCY

SELECTIVITY 🔍
Approximate applicant pool: 10; Interns accepted: 5

COMPENSATION 💲
None

LOCATION(S)
Los Angeles, CA; New York, NY

FIELD
Talent agencies

DURATION
12 weeks: Summer, Fall, Spring, 15 hours/week minimum

DEADLINE(S)
Rolling

THE WORK
Established in 1977, Abrams Artists Agency is a large full-service, bicoastal talent agency representing adult and child actors and actresses in feature film, television, legitimate theatre, and radio & television advertising (commercials). We offer vast experience/training to anyone interested in pursuing a career in the business side of the entertainment industry. We help the studios, networks, and casting directors acquire employment for actors. During the course of the internship the intern will work out of the mail room and will assist with general operations which includes screening phones, covering scripts, pulling submissions, routing mail/faxes, assisting agents, etc.

PERKS
Free tickets to film, theater, and television screenings; invitations to industry-wide social functions.

FYI
An internship is an excellent way to determine if the full-time Agent Trainee Program is a career path the candidate wants to pursue after graduation. Half of our talent agents rose up through our Agent Trainee Program.

TO APPLY
Open to high school juniors and seniors, high school grads, undergrads, college grads, and grad students. International applicants eligible. Submit resume, cover letter, and recommendations.

Internship Coordinator
Abrams Artists Agency
9200 Sunset Boulevard, 11th Floor
Los Angeles, CA 90069
(310) 859-0625
(310) 276-6193 (Fax)

Internship Coordinator
Abrams Artists Agency
275 Seventh Avenue, 26th Floor
New York, NY 10001
(646) 486-4600
(646) 486-0100 (Fax)

Image and career consultant Camille Lavington offers this advice for college students interviewing for jobs: "[They should make sure] that their teeth are in good condition and that they take a breath mint…Most of the kids today drink too much, and they have this terrific hangover breath…These kids go into interviews not only looking hungover but smelling it."

ASA
ACADEMIC STUDY ASSOCIATES

SELECTIVITY 🔍🔍🔍
Approximate applicant pool: 500; Interns accepted: 60

COMPENSATION 🔍🔍🔍
$300/week; free room and board

LOCATION(S)
Amherst, MA; Stanford, CA; and Oxford, England

FIELD
Education

DURATION
5–8 weeks: Summer

DEADLINE(S)
April 1

THE WORK
Founded in 1983, Academic Study Associates (ASA) offers summer programs for high school and junior high students at three universities—Stanford, Massachusetts at Amherst, and Oxford. Each program includes classroom instruction in such topics as theater, art, writing, psychology, business, law, computers, physics, and the SAT, balanced with field trips, a weekend excursion, sports, and recreation. Interns work as resident advisors.

PERKS
Local field trips with students; college facilities (swimming pool, gym, tennis courts, etc.); free staff t-shirt.

FYI
ASA's philosophy: "Students are encouraged to make choices between activities and ways to spend their free time. Ideally, students will learn to use less structured time to their advantage."

TO APPLY
Open to college juniors and seniors as well as grad students. International applicants eligible. Write for application.

Internship Coordinator
Academic Study Associates
355 Main Street
P.O. Box 800
Armonk, NY 10504-0038
(914) 273-2250 or (800) 752-2250
(914) 273-5430 (Fax)
E-mail: summer@asaprograms.com
www.ASAPrograms.com

SELECTIVITY 🔍🔍🔍🔍🔍
Approximate applicant pool: 100; Interns accepted: 7

COMPENSATION 💲💲💲
$500–$1,000 stipend; free room and board

LOCATION(S)
Washington, DC

FIELD
Public policy

DURATION
15 weeks–1 year: Summer, Fall, Spring

DEADLINE(S)
Rolling

THE WORK
Established in 1969, The Academy for Advanced and Strategic Studies is a small future-oriented think tank fostering exploration of issues that are strategic to social and personal progress. It studies a variety of current issues: small community and economic developments; arts and the media; religion and corporate cultures; global culture wars and defense industry right-sizing; policy analysis and researchable libraries; new patterns for organizing education, health care, and transportation; and the governance of cities. Assigned their own research counselors, interns serve as researchers on one or more team projects, "thoroughly engaged in the work of the Academy."

PERKS
Receive detailed and constructive criticism of projects; mentors; access to multi-server computer network and a 250,000-item library; the challenge to help achieve creative excellence with world class clients.

FYI
According to the internship coordinator: "This is neither a job nor exploratory employment, but a full-time learning and developmental experience that you should approach with the intensity of graduate training. Productive internships can lead to paid residencies."

TO APPLY
Open to undergrads, recent college grads, college grads of any age, and grad students. International applicants eligible. Submit cover letter and resume.

Internship Coordinator
The Academy for Advanced and Strategic Studies
1647 Lamont Street NW
Washington, DC 20010-2796

ACADEMY OF TELEVISION ARTS & SCIENCES

SELECTIVITY 🔍🔍🔍🔍🔍
Applicant pool: 1,600; Interns accepted: 30

COMPENSATION 💲💲💲
$2,500 stipend; $500 disbursement for students residing outside of Los Angeles County

LOCATION(S)
Los Angeles, CA

FIELD
Television

DURATION
8 weeks: Summer

DEADLINE(S)
March 15

THE WORK
The Academy has a membership of over 10,000. The Academy is responsible for the Emmy Awards, television's highest honor, and also holds competitions for student filmmakers. Internships exist in twenty-seven categories: Agency, Animation-Traditional, Animation-Computer Generated, Art Direction, Broadcast Advertising & Promotion, Business Affairs, Casting, Children's Programming/Development, Cinematography, Commercials, Costume Design, Development, Documentary, Editing, Entertainment News, Episodic Series, Movies for TV, Music, Network Programming Management, Production Management, Public Relations and Publicity, Sound, Syndication/Distribution, Television Directing–Single Camera, Television Directing–Multi-Camera, Television Scriptwriting, and Videotape Post Production.

PERKS
Intern party, mentors, Academy activities/seminars, screenings

FYI
Says the internship director: "Our interns perform as much 'hands-on' as possible and have special contact with top industry professionals . . . We make it clear to the hosts that the internships must include very little gofer, filing, or photocopying work . . . There's no guarantee of job placement, but having been an Academy intern sends a very positive message to people in this town."

TO APPLY
Open to undergrads, recent college grads, and graduate students. American and international students are eligable only if they are pursuing a degree from a college or university in the United States. Write or call for application requirements or look on the Academy's web site form January 1 through March 10. (Fax entries not accepted).

Academy of Television Arts & Sciences
Student Internship Program
5220 Lankershim Boulevard
North Hollywood, CA 91601-3109
(818) 754-2830
www.emmys.org

ACCURACY IN ACADEMIA

SELECTIVITY 🔍🔍
Approximate applicant pool: 50; Interns accepted: 10

COMPENSATION 💲
$125/week

LOCATION(S)
Washington, DC

FIELD
Education

DURATION
6–12 weeks: Summer, Fall, Spring

DEADLINE(S)
Summer: March 15; Fall: August 15; Spring: November 15

THE WORK
Founded in 1985, Accuracy in Academia (AIA) is a conservative, nonprofit organization dedicated to documenting and publicizing political bias within the academic system. AIA publishes a monthly newsletter, *Campus Report*, and interns work in Research and Writing as well as for the annual Conservative University, which AIA sponsors.

PERKS
Attendance welcome at various conferences and conventions; attendance welcome at meetings on Captiol Hill.

FYI
Thomas Sowell of the Hoover Institution writes: "If sanity ever returns to the academic world, part of the credit will go to a small newspaper called *Campus Report*, which has exposed innumerable incidents of brainwashing replacing education on college campuses."

One of the most successful producers in television history, **Steven Bochco** (third from left) spent the summer of 1965 overseeing an internship program for aspiring screenwriters at Universal Studios. Bochco went on to develop a number of critically acclaimed television programs, including *Hill Street Blues* and *L.A. Law*, which together captured the Emmy Award for best dramatic series seven times in the 1980s.

TO APPLY

Open to high school seniors (summer only), high school students, undergrads, grads, and grad students. International applicants eligible. Submit resume, cover letter, and writing samples.

Internship Coordinator
Accuracy in Academia
4455 Connecticut Avenue NW, Suite 330
Washington, DC 20008
(202) 364-3085
(202) 364-4098 (Fax)

ACCURACY IN MEDIA

SELECTIVITY 🔍 🔍 🔍 🔍
Approximate applicant pool: 60; Interns accepted: 5

COMPENSATION Ⓢ
$125/week

LOCATION(S)
Washington, DC

FIELD
Journalism; Marketing; Strategic planning

DURATION
2–12 months: Summer, Fall, Spring

DEADLINE(S)
Summer: March 15; Fall: August 15; Spring: November 15

THE WORK

Columnist Victor Lasky deemed AIM "a modern-day David fighting Goliath—the most powerful institution in America today—the media." Accuracy in Media (AIM) is a conservative, nonprofit, nonpartisan organization promoting fairness, balance, and accuracy in news reporting. In its quest to expose serious media abuses, AIM publishes a newsletter, produces a radio program, arranges speaking engagements, and sponsors several conferences. Interns work on web page story content, marketing, and strategic business plans.

PERKS

Attendance welcome at various conferences and conventions; opportunity to visit television news programs based in DC.

FYI

The internship program has been in existence since 1974, five years after AIM's founding.

TO APPLY

Open to high school students, high school seniors (summer only), undergrads, recent college grads, college grads of any age, and grad students. International applicants eligible. Submit resume, cover letter, and one writing sample on a political or current event topic.

Internship Coordinator
Accuracy in Media
4455 Connecticut Avenue NW, Suite 330
Washington, DC 20008
(202) 364-4401
(202) 364-4098 (Fax)
E-mail: intern@aim.org

ACKERMAN MCQUEEN

SELECTIVITY 🔍 🔍 🔍
Approximate applicant pool: 100; Interns accepted: 10

COMPENSATION Ⓢ
None

LOCATION(S)
Fairfax, VA ; Irving, TX; Oklahoma City and Tulsa, OK

FIELD
Advertising

DURATION
12–15 weeks: Summer, Fall, Spring

DEADLINE(S)
Rolling

THE WORK

Founded in 1934, Ackerman McQueen is a full-service advertising agency with expertise in food, outdoor and recreational products, high-technology, high-volume retail sales outlets, and national associations. Its clients have included Pizza Hut, Hitachi computer products, the National Rifle Association, Southwestern Bell, and Brunswick bowling products. Interns work in Advertising and Information Services.

PERKS

Attendance welcome at some client meetings; new, state-of-the-art office in VA.

FYI

According to the internship coordinator: "[Ackerman McQueen] is heavily into computers—by the time they leave, interns will have been exposed to just about every type of software used in advertising."

TO APPLY

Open to high school students, high school grads, undergrads, recent college grads, college grads of any age, and grad students. International applicants eligible. Submit resume, cover letter, and recommendations.

Internship Coordinator
Ackerman McQueen
11250 Waples Mill Road, Suite 350
Fairfax, VA 22030
(703) 352-6400
(703) 352-6408 (Fax)

Internship Coordinator
Ackerman McQueen
1100 Equity Tower
1601 NW Expressway
Oklahoma City, OK 73118
(405) 843-7777
(405) 848-8034 (Fax)

Internship Coordinator
Ackerman McQueen
600 Commerce Tower
545 East John Carpenter Freeway
Irving, TX 75062
(214) 444-9000
(214) 869-4363 (Fax)

Internship Coordinator
Ackerman McQueen
320 South Boston
Suite 1200
Tulsa, OK 74103
(918) 582-6200
(918) 582-4512 (Fax)

SELECTIVITY 🔍🔍🔍🔍🔍
Approximate applicant pool: 1,000; Interns accepted: 40–45

COMPENSATION 💲
None

LOCATION(S)
Louisville, KY

FIELD
Theater

DURATION
10 months: August to June; Some half-season and summer positions available

DEADLINE(S)
April 15 for Acting Apprenticeships; Rolling for Internships

THE WORK
Founded in 1963, the Actors Theatre of Louisville (ATL) is one of the nation's major regional theaters, where, according to *The Charlotte Observer*, "everyone who is anyone in the American theatre comes to see what's new." Performing annually to an audience of over 250,000, ATL stages over thirty productions a year in three theaters and on international tours as well as produces three festivals—the critically acclaimed Humana Festival of New American Plays, the Classics in Context Festival, and The Flying Solo and Friends Festival. Twenty to twenty-five interns work in stage management, directing, literary management, arts administration, production management, casting, public relations and marketing, festival management, community relations and company management, development, lighting, properties, costumes, sound, and scenic design.

PERKS
Mentors; training sessions; opportunity to audition for New York agents and casting directors (Apprentices: see FYI).

FYI
For those interested in acting, ATL offers twenty-two positions per year in its Apprentice Company . . . Working from August to June, apprentices attend classes on such topics as audition training, scene study, script analysis, and improvisation; listen to agents, casting directors, and directors at seminars; and stage four productions during the ATL season—a showcase of monologues, a performance for young audiences, a bill of short original scripts, and a final production . . . Apprenticeships are open to undergrads, grads, and grad students who are not members of acting unions . . . Write ATL for more information (deadline: April 15) . . . Apprentice Company alumni include actors Timothy Busfield, Jenny Robertson, and Danny Jenkins.

TO APPLY
Open to high school students, high school grads, undergrads, recent college grads, college grads of any age, and grad students. International applicants eligible. Write for application.

Apprentice/Intern Office
Actors Theatre of Louisville
316 West Main Street
Louisville, KY 40202-4218
(502) 584-1265

Interning on Capitol Hill

Since the establishment of Congress in 1789, Members of the House and Senate have supplemented their staffs with temporary assistants—referred to as pages, volunteers, and interns—who help in research and in communicating with constituents. Although nearly all such positions are unpaid, some interns receive modest stipends out of their Member's general office accounts. Since each congressional office and committee has its own intern selection process, prospective applicants should contact offices of interest directly.

1. For the names of specific caucuses and committees, consult the *Congressional Yellow Book* in your local library's reference section or ask your Congressman or Senator for an updated copy of the *CRS Report for Congress—Internships and Fellowships: Congressional, Federal, and Other Work Experience Opportunities* (also lists colleges and private organizations offering programs that place interns in congressional offices).

2. For the phone numbers of specific Members, committees, and caucuses, call the congressional switchboard at (202) 224-3121.

3. Address your cover letter to:
The Honorable (Name)
United States Senate
Washington, DC 20515

The Honorable (Name)
United States House of Representatives
Washington, DC 20515

(Name of committee or caucus)
United States Congress
Washington, DC 20515

4. The salutation on your cover letter should read as follows:
Dear Senator (Last name)
Dear Representative (Last name)

SELECTIVITY 🔍🔍🔍🔍
Approximate applicant pool: 100; Interns accepted: 6

COMPENSATION 💲
None

LOCATION(S)
New York, NY

FIELD
Clothing; Women's fashion design

DURATION
8 weeks: ongoing

DEADLINE(S)
Rolling

THE WORK
Founded in 1987, Adrienne Vittadini is a clothing company specializing in women's sportswear. Sold in major department and specialty stores as well as free-standing Vittadini boutiques, the Vittadini collection focuses on sportswear but has expanded to include scarves, swimwear, eyewear, shoes, gloves, luggage, and bed & bath products. Interns work in collections, and sports lines, where they assist staff in sketching, coloring, executing layouts, and office work.

PERKS
Forty-five percent discount on clothing; flexible hours; close interaction with design staff who always have time for questions and advice.

FYI
Famous for making knitwear fashionable, the Eastern Europe-born Adrienne Vittadini always includes a range of casual and elegant knitwear in her collection.

TO APPLY
Open to undergrads, recent college grads, college grads of any age, and grad students. Must have fashion or art background. International applicants eligible with suitable visa. Submit resume and cover letter.

Internship Coordinator
Adrienne Vittadini
575 Seventh Avenue, 21st Floor
New York, NY 10018
(212) 921-2510
(212) 398-1448 (Fax)

ADVERTISING CLUB OF NEW YORK

SELECTIVITY 🔍🔍🔍
Approximate applicant pool: 200–300; Interns accepted: 25–30

COMPENSATION 💲💲💲
$300/week

LOCATION(S)
New York City, NY

FIELD
Advertising and Publishing (sales and marketing)

DURATION
10 weeks

DEADLINE(S)
March 15

THE WORK
Since 1990, the Advertising Club of New York has offered summer internships at local ad agencies, publications, and client companies; past employers have included Young & Rubicam, Grey Advertising, TBWA/Chiat Day, and Mad Dogs & Englishmen. Available positions include Account Management, Media, Creative, Production, Publishing, and Sales. Detailed descriptions of each area are available upon request.

PERKS
Frequent social and networking opportunities; lunch seminars with ad gurus; honorary summer membership in the Advertising Club of NY.

FYI
According to the internship coordinator, "In the past two years, approximately half of our interns have gone on to positions with their summer employer. Some juniors receive standing offers to return after graduation . . . "

TO APPLY
Open to college juniors and seniors. Write for application. Applicants selected for a phone interview will be notified by April 1.

Advertising Club of NY
Attn: Internship Chair
235 Park Avenue South
New York, NY 10003
(212) 533-8080

ADVOCATES FOR CHILDREN OF NEW YORK

SELECTIVITY 🔍🔍🔍🔍🔍
Approximate applicant pool: 250; Interns accepted: 6–8

COMPENSATION 💲
Unpaid internship students should come in with their own funding.

LOCATION(S)
New York, NY

FIELD
Education; Law; Public policy

DURATION
8–10 weeks: Summer, Fall, Spring

DEADLINE(S)
Rolling

THE WORK
Established in 1970, Advocates for Children of New York (AFC) is a nonprofit organization working to ensure a quality education for New York City public school students, particularly those at greatest risk due to poverty, discrimination, disability, limited English proficiency, and immigrant status. AFC has provided individual assistance to over 35,000 children and families, participated in 10 precedent-setting class action lawsuits, and trained tens of thousands of parents to be effective advocates for their own children. Interns work in education advocacy, research, and legal.

PERKS
Extensive training in education law and advocacy; opportunity to represent clients; opportunities to publish educational research.

FYI
In existence since 1985, the internship program counts among its alumni the assistant coordinator of AFC's Early Intervention Program . . . According to the internship coordinator: "Several interns achieve their first publications through researching and writing reports for AFC."

TO APPLY
Open to grad students. International applicants eligible. Submit resume, cover letter, and writing samples.

Internship Coordinator
151 West 30th Street, 5th Floor
New York, NY 10001
(212) 947-9779
(212) 947-9790 (Fax)

A.E. SCHWARTZ & ASSOCIATES

SELECTIVITY 🔍 🔍
Approximate applicant pool: 800; Interns accepted: 20

COMPENSATION 💲
$25/week contingent upon project and quality of contribution

LOCATION(S)
Boston, MA

FIELD
Management training; Consulting

DURATION
16 weeks–1 year: ongoing

DEADLINE(S)
Rolling

THE WORK
Founded in 1985, A.E. Schwartz & Associates is a comprehensive training organization offering over forty management training programs and practical solutions to organizational problems. The firm's programs range from topics such as time management, team building, and long-term planning to stress management, decision making, motivation, and conflict resolution. Interns work in Publishing, Writing/Editorial, Public Relations, Graphic Design, Sales and Marketing, Internet Development, and Special Projects.

PERKS
Hands-on attendance welcome at training programs, sales/client meetings, and various industry events; detailed evaluations upon completion of internship.

FYI
Firm president, Andrew E. Schwartz, writes: "Since we are a small and growing organization, we can ensure that our interns do not spend the majority of their time on mind-numbing office work." . . . A.E. Schwartz hires approximately 25 percent of its interns for contract employment.

TO APPLY
Open to undergrads, recent college grads, college grads of any age, and grad students. International applicants eligible. Submit resume, cover letter, writing samples, recommendations, and references.

Internship Coordinator
A.E. Schwartz & Associates
P.O. Box 79228
Waverley, MA 02149-0228
(617) 926-9111
(617) 926-0660 (Fax)
E-mail: aes@aeschwartz.com
www.aeschwartz.com
www.trainingconsortium.com

AETNA LIFE INC.

SELECTIVITY 🔍 🔍 🔍
Approximate applicant pool: 3,000; Interns accepted 100

COMPENSATION 💲 💲 💲 💲
$6–$6.25/hour for high school students; $9–$12/hour for undergrads; $12–$14/hour for grad students

LOCATION(S)
Corporate home office: Hartford, CT
Regional home offices: Aetna US Healthcare: Blue Bell, PA; Middletown, CT; Atlanta; Dallas; Chicago; Walnut Creek, CA
Field Offices in most states

FIELD
Health care; Investment management; International

DURATION
12–14 weeks: Summer

DEADLINE(S)
March 1

THE WORK
Founded in 1853, Aetna is one of the nation's leading health care benefits companies and a global insurance and financial services organization. Through Aetna US Healthcare, Aetna Retirement Services, and Aetna International, the company provides millions of customers worldwide with the best-value products, information and expert advice to meet their changing needs. Aetna US Healthcare provides a full spectrum of managed care, indemnity, and group insurance products on a risk and non-risk basis to more than 23 million Americans.   Aetna Retirement Services markets a wide array of life insurance, retirement, and investment products to individuals and small businesses. Aetna International primarily sells life insurance and financial products, along with some health care products, in selected emerging markets. Previous interns have majored in the following: CIS & MIS, Business Administration, Insurance, Health Sciences, Computer Sciences, Finance, Marketing/Sales, Statistics, Accounting, Actuarial Science, and Mathematics.

PERKS
Free educational coursework; access to Aetna gym; classes in computers, diversity issues, and other work-related topics.

FYI
Since the internship program's start in 1979, numerous interns have returned to Aetna as regular employees. Their time spent as interns is applied toward pensions, vacations, and benefits.

TO APPLY
Open to college juniors, senior, and grad students. Minimum GPA 3.0. International applicants studying in the US are eligible. Submit resume, cover letter, and transcript.

College Relations
Attn: RSAA
Aetna Life & Casualty
151 Farmington Avenue
Hartford, CT 06156
(860) 273-0123
(800) 872-3862
(860) 273-1757 (Fax)
www.aetna.com

AFFILIATED SANTE GROUP

SELECTIVITY 🔍🔍
Approximate size of applicant pool: 500; Interns accepted: 100

COMPENSATION 💲
Sometimes partial parking/reimbursement for all expenses related to actual job duites.

LOCATION(S)
Silver Spring, MD/ accessible to all public transportation

FIELD
Mental health care; Community rehabilitation for adults with disabilities

DURATION
At least one semester (3 months), for at least one day (2 half days) weekly

DEADLINE(S)
Rolling

THE WORK
Founded in 1973, the Affiliated Sante Group are not-for-profit community rehabilitation statewide services that help people with developmental disabilities and mental health needs become members of everyday community life. Their holistic philosophy has garnered the Student Volunteer Service numerous awards and recognition as a model for experiential learning and rehabilitation. To support this multi-dimensional approach, interns work in a variety of fields, including Counseling, Life Skills Instruction, Clinical, Administration, Marketing/PR, Recreation, Social Work, and Service Learning.

PERKS
The Affiliated Sante Group is a national model for experiential learning. Sophomore Reena Metzer explains, "The volunteer experience is a two-way street. A college student in this program learns about himself as well." Staff member Jeff Carswell states, "I developed marketable skills here and then they hired me." Americorps volunteer Steve Order says, "I developed a civic culture while making a difference in someone's life."

FYI
Working in conjunction with 100 universities nationwide, interns work with Director students to have their job descriptions tailored individually for university curriculum fulfilling credit requirements. We assist volunteers, interns, Americorps, K–12, business—all sectors of the community.

TO APPLY
Undergraduate and graduate students and/or volunteers should send resume, cover letter, and a request for an application. A phone meeting to gather more information is welcome.

Beth Albaneze, Director
Student/Volunteer Service
1107 Spring St. Suite C
Silver Spring MD 20910
(301) 589-8303 Ext 834
(301) 588-1567 (Fax)

OPERA GREATS: CARMEN, DON GIOVANNI, MADAME BUTTERFLY, AND JOHN, THE APPRENTICE?

In Act II, Scene 2 of Benjamin Britten's opera *Peter Grimes*, fisherman Peter Grimes instructs his apprentice, John, to prepare for the morning boat ride.

Nigerian music groups adhere to an informal apprenticeship system in which a young, aspiring musician will serve as a band's gofer, hoping to land a position as a back-up musician and eventually as a main player. **King Sunny Adé**, one of the greatest musicians ever to emerge from Africa, spent his teenage years completing such an apprenticeship with the dance band Moses Olaiya and his Rhythm Dandies. By his nineteenth birthday in 1965, Adé had achieved the position of guitarist with the band, giving him the confidence to launch his own band a year later.

THE AFRICA FUND

See American Committee on Africa/The Africa Fund

AFS INTERCULTURAL PROGRAMS

SELECTIVITY 🔍
Approximate applicant pool: 150; Interns accepted: 50 (Internship), 50 (Team Mission)

COMPENSATION 💲
Internship: stipend covering daily carfare and lunch. Team Mission: $3,000–$3,700 fee (includes orientation, insurance, round-trip travel, room and board).

LOCATION(S)
Internship: CA, IL, MA, MD, MN, NY (HQ), OR, TX; Team Mission: varies yearly, but 1995 included Bolivia, China, Costa Rica, Czech Republic, England, Ghana, Hong Kong, Hungary, Panama, Russia

FIELD
Education; Public service

DURATION
Internship:10–16 weeks: Summer, Fall, Spring; Team Mission: 3 weeks: Summer

DEADLINE(S)
Summer: February 28; Fall: June 30; Spring: December 31; Team Mission: May 1

THE WORK
Tracing its history back to 1914, AFS Intercultural Programs is one of the world's largest student-exchange organizations, operating programs in over fifty countries for 10,000 high school students and teachers annually. Interns work in Marketing/Communications, Finance, US Travel Documents, Systems, and US Programs. AFS also runs the Team Mission Program, through which young students travel overseas to participate in three-week community-service projects.

PERKS
Orientation, awards, calculator with AFS's logo.

FYI
AFS hires approximately 15 percent of its interns for full-time positions . . . Former interns include: Bob Stableski, AFS's Senior Vice President . . . AFS Intercultural Programs is a division of the American Field Service, a volunteer organization founded during World War I by volunteers who drove ambulances for the allied forces in France.

EXCLUSIVE INTERVIEW WITH TABITHA SOREN

As a former MTV News reporter and anchor, Tabitha Soren was responsible for developing and writing news stories, conducting interviews, producing and editing, and on-camera hosting. She was the news reporter for MTV's "Choose or Lose" election '92 coverage in which she interviewed President Bill Clinton, Vice President Al Gore, and President George Bush. She graduated with a B.A. from New York University in 1987. During her years at NYU, Soren served no less than four internships, logging time at CNN, MTV, ABC, and NBC. In an interview with The Internship Informants, she elaborated on:

Interning at CNN:
It was very valuable because CNN wasn't union—it was understaffed and underpaid, so they were all too willing to give away important assignments to interns. I was out field producing. I was editing. Basically, if it wasn't for interns, the channel wouldn't have been on the air 24 hours a day. So in terms of hands-on experience, it was invaluable.

Making the late rock promoter Bill Graham feel like cattle:
One day at CNN, Bill Graham was supposed to be the live guest. I picked him up from his hotel in a limo, and I brought him up to the studio, but I didn't ask him if he wanted water or coffee. I just sort of put him in the green room, and said "We'll be with you in a couple of minutes." He felt like he wasn't treated importantly enough. As an intern, I thought things were supposed to be more egalitarian. Once I got him [to CNN], I thought my job with him was over. He said he felt like he had been treated like cattle. And he almost walked out. The producers had to chase him down the elevator and convince him to come back.

Where interning at CNN led:
A great part of the internship, like many internships, was networking. The executive producer [at CNN] referred me to an old friend of his at MTV, who hired me as a production assistant for [MTV's] "The Year in Rock" in 1986. I think they paid me minimum wage. Now when executives at MTV talk about me...they'll say I was a former intern, but I was actually getting paid. Maybe in their minds it was so little that it didn't really count. But in my mind, it was good to be paid anything for journalism work.

Moving from CNN to MTV to ABC:
From there, an executive producer at MTV recommended me to somebody at ABC's *World News Tonight with Peter Jennings*. So I got an internship there, which was also paid. Basically, I was a desk assistant. It was a big contrast with my internship at CNN because it was union. There were computers I couldn't touch. There was equipment I couldn't touch. They just wanted me to answer the phones, put mail into [mail] slots, and run script changes up [to the studio] during commercials. Not that exciting work, but nonetheless I got to transcribe a script on the phone from Beirut, which made a lot of the stuff I had done in the past feel pretty trivial. And it was good to make connections as well and get to know Peter Jennings.

"The girl with the boots":
I went to school full time, and then at two o'clock I would go over to *World News Tonight*, change into a suit and [put on] pantyhose. But I always refused to wear heels. I would have my combat boots on, because we had to do a lot of running up and down stairs, and damned if I was going to trip, just so I could look nice. As a result, Peter [Jennings] always called me "the girl with the boots."

Moving from ABC to NBC:
My senior year, I got another paid internship, [this one] at WNBC [television news], as [reporter] Gabe Pressman's assistant. I covered the mayoral election with him. The election was between [Ed] Koch and [David] Dinkins—it was really exciting. I learned a lot in terms of local news. [Reporters] Magee Hickey and Jack Cafferty took me under their wings. They'd let me come in on days I wasn't supposed to, or on weekends. If I was willing to come in at six in the morning to go out on a shoot with Magee, I could do that.

Life after graduation:
I went to Vermont and became a State House correspondent for an ABC affiliate up there. I stayed up there a year and a half and started anchoring, but I decided I wanted to go back to New York. Back in New York, I became a producer at VH-1 and then [sister channel] MTV hired me away to be a producer for MTV News. [MTV] had been looking for a woman to be on the air for like two years, and they hadn't found anybody yet. [Anchor Kurt Loder] wanted to go on vacation, and his normal substitute, John Norris, had switched over to being a VJ, so Kurt didn't have a sub. They pulled me out of an edit room and asked me to do an audition. That led to my anchor [position at MTV News].

TO APPLY

Interns: open to high school juniors and seniors, under-grads, and grad students; international applicants (grad students) eligible. Team Mission: open to high school students and under-grads up to twenty years of age. Interns: submit resume and cover letter directly to office of interest; addresses and phone numbers may be obtained from headquarters. Team Mission: write for application.

Internship Coordinator or Team Mission Coordinator
AFS Intercultural Programs/USA
220 East 42nd Street, 3rd Floor
New York, NY 10017
(800) AFS-INFO or
(212) 949-5100

AGENCY FOR TOXIC SUBSTANCES AND DISEASE REGISTRY

See Oak Ridge Institute for Science and Education

As a senior at George Washington University in 1951, the late **Jackie Bouvier (Kennedy)** won *Vogue*'s Prix de Paris contest (defunct since 1969), which offered the winner a one-year editorial internship—six months at *Vogue*'s office in New York followed by another six months at the magazine's offices in Paris. One of her six essays described "People I Wish I Had Known," where she named the Russian ballet impresario Serge Diaghileff, a choice *Time* magazine recently called "shrewd, sophisticated . . . bound to knock the glossy's one-upping editors back on their heels."

AGORA PUBLISHING

AGORA

SELECTIVITY   🔍🔍🔍🔍
Approximate applicant pool: 400+; Interns accepted: 25–30

COMPENSATION $
Hourly stipend or for college credit and housing available

LOCATION(S)
Baltimore, MD (mostly); also Ireland

FIELD
Publishing

DURATION
Flexible: Summer, Fall, Spring

DEADLINE(S)
Rolling

THE WORK
Founded in 1979, Agora, Inc. creates and markets international newsletters on health, travel, and finance. Interns work in Editorial and Marketing.

PERKS
Housing available; real hands-on experience in a publishing company; informal atmosphere.

FYI
In ancient Greece "agora" meant "community center," a lively place where people came, not only to buy and sell goods, but also to meet and exchange news and ideas.

TO APPLY
Open to undergrads, recent college grads, and grad students. International applicants eligible. Send cover letter and resume.

Internship Coordinator
Agora, Inc.
14 W. Mt. Vernon Place
Baltimore, MD 21201
(410) 230-1263
(410) 783-8455 (Fax)

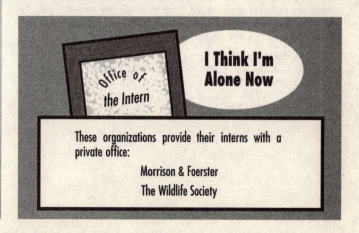

I Think I'm Alone Now

Office of the Intern

These organizations provide their interns with a private office:

Morrison & Foerster

The Wildlife Society

AIESEC

SELECTIVITY N/A
Approximate applicant pool: N/A; Interns accepted: 5,000 (200 Americans)

COMPENSATION $
Stipend starting at $175/week

LOCATION(S)
Internships abroad in over 80 countries

DURATION
2–18 months: ongoing

FIELD
Business, Management, Technology, Engineering, Language

DEADLINE(S)
Rolling

THE WORK
Founded in 1948, AIESEC is the world's largest student-run educational organization, dedicated to increasing international understanding and cooperation. Seeking to develop professional and management skills within its 50,000 members, AIESEC offers training seminars and paid business and technical internships. Under the auspices of the International Traineeship Exchange Program, interns work overseas at nearly 200 companies including: American Express, IBM, Draft, and UPS—in such areas as marketing, finance, economics, management, sales, accounting, computer programming, languages, and human resources.

PERKS
Aide in finding housing, transportation, help securing visa/work permit, management and leadership seminars, cultural learning, AIESEC member network near internship location, alumni network.

FYI
Although membership is not required, we do encourage interns to be active in AIESEC activities abroad and at home to help increase international understanding, cooperation, and education.

TO APPLY
Traineeships are open to all students of higher education and recent graduates. The application fee of $500 covers predeparture cultural preparation, help in obtaining a visa, a personalized traineeship search, and includes a $50 refund upon successful completion of your traineeship.

AIESEC United States
135 West 50th Street, 13th Floor
New York, NY 10020
(212) 757-3774
(212) 757-4062 (Fax)

AIESEC International
40 Rue Washington
B-1050 Brussels, Belgium
E-mail: aiesec@aiesec.org
www.aiesec.org

aigner associates inc.
PUBLIC RELATIONS • SPONSORSHIPS • EVENTS

SELECTIVITY 🔍🔍🔍🔍🔍
Approximate applicant pool: 250 per session; Interns accepted: 2 per session

COMPENSATION $
Credit

LOCATION(S)
Brighton, MA

FIELD
Public relations; Special events and promotions

DURATION
12 weeks: Summer, Fall, Spring, Winter

DEADLINE(S)
Rolling

THE WORK
Founded in 1984, Aigner Associates is one of Boston's top Public Relations and marketing agencies, specializing in the production and promotion of special events, and promotional partnerships. Clients include: British Airways, WellsPark Group malls (including CambridgeSide Galleria, Arsenal Mall, and many others) TNT Vacations, WJMN-FM, and the Boston Center of Adult Education as well as major special events. Interns work in Public Relations, Special Events, and Business.

PERKS
Attendance welcome at client meetings: opportunity to work at special events and brainstorming meetings; gain portfolio materials.

FYI
Approximately 40 percent of interns are hired for or referred to full-time positions.

TO APPLY
Open to undergrads and grad students. International applicants eligible. Submit resume and cover letter.

Internship Coordinator
Aigner Associates
250 Everett
Brighton, MA 02134
(617) 254-9500
(617) 254-3700 (fax)

SELECTIVITY
Approximate applicant pool: 20; Interns accepted: 3–6

COMPENSATION
None

LOCATION(S)
Dayton, OH

FIELD
Teaching; Recreation; the Disabled

DURATION
15 weeks: ongoing

DEADLINE(S)
Rolling

THE WORK
Founded in 1958, AIM for the Handicapped is a nonprofit organization providing free exercise and rehabilitation programs to individuals with visual handicaps, hearing impairments, emotional or learning disabilities, and orthopedic or coordination problems. Exercises emphasize fine and gross motor skills done rhythmically to music. Volunteer positions include assistants to the Education director, and teachers, who learn the AIM exercises at the AIM Workshop and teach handicapped children a minimum of one hour each week.

PERKS
Certification as an AIM teacher; alumni newsletter.

FYI
The late actor Gene Kelly was AIM's Honorary Chairman. Tennis legend Billie Jean King, golf pro Nancy Lopez, baseball hall of famer Joe Morgan, and TV/Radio celebrity Bob Braun are all National Ambassadors for AIM.

TO APPLY
Open to high school students, high school grads, undergrads, college grads, and grad students. International applicants eligible. Submit resume and cover letter.

Education Department
AIM
945 Danbury Road
Dayton, OH 45420
(937) 294-4611
(937) 294-3783

SELECTIVITY
Approximate applicant pool: 300; Interns accepted: 40

COMPENSATION
$50–$75/week stipend; shared, rustic housing

LOCATION(S)
25 locations throughout Alaska

FIELD
Parks management; Recreation; Archaeology

DURATION
8–16 weeks: Summer

DEADLINE(S)
April 1

THE WORK
The largest state park system in the United States, Alaska State Parks comprises over 3 million acres of scenic land. Volunteer positions are available in twenty-five different locations, from the rain forests and fjords of southeast Alaska, to the salmon streams of the Kenai Peninsula, to the rolling hills and birch forests of the interior. Volunteers work as ranger assistants, backcountry hosts, natural history interpreters, and trail crew assisting the staff with regular duties and special projects. There are several positions with the Office of History and Archaeology as archaeological assistants.

PERKS
Diverse wildlife, vast wilderness of Alaska.

FYI
The Alaska State Parks comprise a virtual Noak's Ark, home to bears, moose, beavers, caribou, Dall sheep, mountain goats, wolves, swans, bald eagles, and willow ptarmigans (the state bird).

TO APPLY
Open to undergrads, recent college grads, and grad students. Must be 18 or older and a U.S. citizen. Call or write for addresses and information about sites throughout Alaska or visit their website at www.dnr.state.ak.us/parks/vip.

Volunteer Coordinator
Alaska State Parks
550 West 7th Avenue, Suite 1380
Anchorage, AK 99501-3561
(907) 269-8708
(907) 269-8907 (Fax)
E-mail: volunteer@dnr.state.ak.us

See Westin Hotels and Resorts

SELECTIVITY 🔍🔍🔍
Approximate applicant pool: 20; Interns accepted: 2

COMPENSATION Ⓢ
None (stipend at completion)—Budget pending

LOCATION(S)
New York, NY

FIELD
Arts administration

DURATION
12 weeks: Summer, Fall, Spring

DEADLINE(S)
Rolling

THE WORK
The Alliance of Residence Theaters/New York (A.R.T./NY) is a service organization for over 350 not-for-profit theaters in New York City. A.R.T. members range from the Lincoln Center Theater and the New York Shakespeare Festival, to the newest and most innovative Off-Off-Broadway Theaters. Interns provide support as need warrants in the following areas: Adminstration, Marketing, Development, and Member Services.

PERKS
Complimentary tickets to Off-Broadway theater; access to workshops with theater professionals; small staff.

FYI
Alumni of the 26-year-old program include A.R.T.'s Deputy Director.

TO APPLY
Open to undergrads, recent college grads, college grads of any age, and grad students. Submit resume and cover letter.

Internships
A.R.T./New York
575 8th Avenue
Suite 17S
New York, NY 10018
questions@art-newyork.org

See National Public Radio

SELECTIVITY 🔍🔍
Approximate applicant pool: 25; Interns accepted: 5

COMPENSATION Ⓢ
None

LOCATION(S)
New York, NY

FIELD
Clothing

DURATION
6–24 weeks: Summer, Fall, Spring

DEADLINE(S)
Rolling

THE WORK
Founded in 1981, Alper International is a textile and trimming buying office, focused on locating and buying all the components relating to the manufacture of ready-to-wear garments. Servicing a national and international roster of clients, Alper is involved in all phases of garment buying, such as negotiating transactions, shipping garments, and tracking current and future market trends; it also arranges appointment schedules and hotel reservations for clients visiting New York. Interns work with textile buyers as well as garment buyers.

PERKS
National and international networking opportunities; opportunity to learn sourcing for garments and textiles.

FYI
According to the internship coordinator: "From here, interns can go anywhere, either in the textile market (manufacturing) or garment market (retail)."

TO APPLY
Open to undergrads, recent college grads, college grads of any age, and grad students. International applicants eligible. Submit resume and cover letter.

Internship Coordinator
Alper International
1412 Broadway, Suite 1610
New York, NY 10018
(212) 840-1580
(212) 840 1356 (Fax)

SELECTIVITY 🔍 🔍 🔍
Approximate applicant pool: 1,000; Interns accepted: 105 annually

COMPENSATION $ $
Most positions are compensated with a housing stipend as follows:
$225 weekly housing stipend plus two free meals per day
(Other positions are compensated with an hourly wage)

LOCATION(S)
Amelia Island, FL

FIELD
Hotels/Resorts

DURATION
A 16-week minimum commitment is required based on the semester system. Some students perform two or more semesters back-to-back.

DEADLINE(S)
Open

THE WORK
Amelia Island Plantation is a 1,350-acre internationally recognized, gated resort/residential community located on the state's only barrier island just 45 minutes from Jacksonville. Please view our web site for a glimpse of the beautifully preserved natural setting of our resort, including miles of sandy beach and many amenities!

Internships are offered in many different areas including Commercial Recreation, Golf, Tennis, Theme Parties, Recreation Rental & Retail, Aquatics, Lodging, Rooms Management, Turf Management, Culinary, Marketing, and Environmental Education!

PERKS
Leisure-time access to all recreational facilities; 20 percent discount in AIP shops and restaurants; 50 percent discount on dinner; free uniform in most departments; assistance in locating housing.

melia Island Plantation

FYI
In existence since 1981, the internship program counts among its alumni many current managers. Interns are considered as potential job candidates. Preference is given to seniors, and those who express the desire and are able to seek a permanent position with the company after their internship.

TO APPLY
Applicants must be current students who require the internship to graduate. Applicants must be fluent in conversational English (speaking, reading, writing, and understanding). Applicants must provide their own reliable transportation. A car is recommended for all, and some internship positions require one. Applicants should call or e-mail for an application packet, indicating their area of interest and the semester(s) they are interested in applying for.

Barbara Ross - Internship Coordinator
Amelia Island Plantation
P.O. Box 3000
Amelia Island, FL 32035-3000
(904) 277-5904
(904) 277-5994 (Fax)
www.aipfl.com
intern@aipfl.com

SELECTIVITY 🔍
Approximate applicant pool: 60; Interns accepted: 25–30

COMPENSATION $
Paid/unpaid, $6.75 for undergrads, $9.01 for Master's students

LOCATION(S)
Phoenix, AZ

FIELD
Airline transportation

DURATION
12–16 weeks: Summer, Fall, Spring

DEADLINE(S)
Rolling, As-needed basis—resumes held for 3 months

THE WORK
Founded in 1981, America West Airlines is the nation's ninth-largest airline, with 11,000 employees and nearly $1.5 billion in annual sales. Providing service throughout the United States and Mexico, America West flies an average of 15 million passengers per year. Interns work in Marketing, Finance, Safety Engineering, and other administrative positions.

PERKS
Two discount travel passes (space available)

FYI
Subject to normal guidelines mandated by local, state, and federal law, as well as company policy

TO APPLY
Open to undergrads and grad students. International applicants eligible. Submit resume and cover letter.

Internship Coordinator
Connie Razza
America West Airlines
Sky Harbor International Airport
4000 East Sky Harbor Boulevard
Phoenix, AZ 85034
(480) 693-8813 (Fax, no phone calls)

AMERICAN & INTERNATIONAL DESIGNS, INC.

SELECTIVITY
Approximate applicant pool: 30; Interns accepted: 4–8

COMPENSATION
Lunch and travel expenses

LOCATION(S)
Staten Island, NY

FIELD
Interior design; Space planner and product designers; Photography

DURATION
8–14 weeks: Summer, Fall, Spring

DEADLINE(S)
Rolling

THE WORK
Founded in 1980, American & International Designs (A&ID) is an interior design firm specializing in the health care and hospitality industries. Focusing on all aspects of space planning, from carpeting and wallcovering to furniture and accessories, A&ID designs restaurants, lobbies, waiting and exam rooms, executive offices, and back office facilities. Clients have included: Integrated Gulf Oil Resources; Integrated Resources, Ramada Inn, and New York City's Mezzaluna Restaurants. Interns work in Purchasing, Project Management, Expediting, Design, Specifications, Rendering, Library, and as assistants to the head designer, CAD operators, and Web Designers.

PERKS
Mentors; attendance welcome at trade shows in New York and New Jersey.

FYI
Launched in 1982, A&ID's internship program leads to permanent employment for one or two interns a year.

TO APPLY
Open to recent college grads. Submit resume and cover letter; please do not call.

Internship Coordinator
American & International Designs, Inc.
Executive Suite
900 South Ave.
Staten Island, NY 10314
(718) 983-7395
(718) 370-2705 (Fax)
e-mail: susanharrann@aol.com
website: designamericanyc.com

AMERICAN-ARAB ANTI-DISCRIMINATION COMMITTEE

SELECTIVITY
Approximate applicant pool: 100; Interns accepted: 15–20

COMPENSATION
$800 Legal and graduate students, $500 stipend for summer program, $800 for graduate students

LOCATION(S)
Washington, DC

FIELD
Civil rights; Middle East

DURATION
Semester/quarter: Summer

DEADLINE(S)
Summer: March 30

THE WORK
Founded in 1980, the American-Arab Anti-Discrimination Committee (ADC) defends the rights and promotes the ethnic heritage of Arab Americans. Interns are assigned to work with senior staff members in the Community Organizing, Educational Outreach, Media Publications, and Legal departments, government affairs, American Committee on Jerusalem, and sometimes with congressional offices.

PERKS
Attend weekly lectures, films or conferences, or meetings with government offices and embassies. Interns publish *Intern Perspective II* each year (summer program only).

FYI
A significant number of former interns return to ADC for full-time employment; former interns include ADC's Director of Publications, Internship Coordinator, and Director of Computer Services . . . One former intern writes: "We . . . had a chance to participate in discussions with ambassadors and their aides, and eat some amazing Arabic food!"

Interns at the American-Arab Anti-Discrimination Committee met with Senator Paul Simon during one of ADC's Friday sessions.

TO APPLY

Open to college sophomores, juniors, and seniors, recent college grads, college grads of any age, and grad students. International applicants eligible. Year-round positions for work-study or college credit available. Contact:

Intern Coordinator
ADC Research Institute
4201 Connecticut Avenue NW
Suite 300
Washington, DC 20008
(202) 244-2990
(202) 244-3196 (Fax)

AMERICAN ASSOCIATION FOR THE ADVANCEMENT OF SCIENCE

SELECTIVITY 🔍 🔍 🔍
Approximate applicant pool: 200; Interns accepted: 25

COMPENSATION 💲 💲
Weekly stipend

LOCATION(S)
Nationwide

FIELD
Science or Engineering

DURATION
10 weeks: ongoing

DEADLINE(S)
January 15

THE WORK
Increasing public understanding of science and technology is one of the principal aims of the AAAS. AAAS has improved coverage of science and technology in the mass media through the Mass Media Science and Engineering Fellows Program. Fellows assist media professionals at radio and television stations, newspapers, and magazines. Fellows are provided a weekly stipend as well as travel expenses. The program is competitive and the program is designed to seek out all qualified candidates including African American, Hispanic, and Native American students. (Note: Applicants *must* be enrolled as students in the natural or social sciences, mathematics, or engineering to qualify.) Now in its 23rd year, the program has supported a total of 359 fellows.

PERKS

Occasional luncheons and seminars; free copies of *Science*.

FYI

AAAS launched its internship program in 1975.

TO APPLY
Open to undergrads, recent grads, and grad students. International applicants eligible. Submit name and address.

Internship Coordinator
Human Resources
American Association for the Advancement of Science
1200 New York Avenue, NW
Washington, DC 20005
(202) 326-6760
(202) 371-9849 (Fax)
E-mail: aking@aaas.org

AMERICAN ASSOCIATION OF ADVERTISING AGENCIES

SELECTIVITY 🔍 🔍
Approximate applicant pool: 200; Interns accepted: 75-100

COMPENSATION 💲 💲 💲 💲
$350/week, 60 percent of housing and transportation costs

LOCATION(S)
Nationwide

FIELD
Advertising

DURATION
10 weeks: Summer

DEADLINE(S)
January 21

THE WORK

Since 1973, the American Association of Advertising Agencies (AAAA), which is the national trade association for ad agencies, has run the Multicultural Advertising Intern Program (MAIP). Placing multicultural students in major advertising agencies across the country, MAIP offers its participants the chance to gain practical work experience, establish contacts, and prepare for a career in advertising. Recent years have seen a wide variety of sponsoring agencies, such as BBDO Worldwide, Saatchi & Saatchi, Young & Rubicam, and Leo Burnett. At each agency interns are placed in specific departments: Account Management, Creative (Copywriting, Art Direction) or Broadcast Production, Interactive Technologies, Media Research, Traffic, Print Production, or Digital Media job responsibilities include everything from administrative to long- and/or short-term projects.

PERKS
Seminars; agency tours.

FYI
The American Association of Advertising Agencies is dedicated to providing multicultural students with a valuable advertising experience. In recent years, some former interns have accepted career positions in advertising agencies, or have related jobs in the communications industry.

TO APPLY
Open to multicultural college juniors, seniors, recent college grads, and grad students. Minimum GPA: 3.0. The application process includes submitting the application, resume, two essays, two recommendations (professor and employer), recent transcript, and creative samples (for art direction or copywriting only).

Multicultural Advertising Intern Program
American Association of Advertising Agencies
405 Lexington Avenue, 18th Floor
New York, NY 10174-1801
(800) 676-9333
(212) 573-8968 (Fax)

AMERICAN ASSOCIATION OF OVERSEAS STUDIES

SELECTIVITY   N/A
Approximate applicant pool: N/A; Interns accepted: 100

COMPENSATION $
$1,000 fee; room and board for $600–$1,000/month

LOCATION(S)
New York, NY; London, England

FIELD
Over 25 different fields (see THE WORK)

DURATION
Four weeks minimum: Summer, Fall, Spring

DEADLINE(S
Rolling

THE WORK
Founded in 1984, the American Association of Overseas Studies (AAOS) is a private organization providing students with internships and study courses. Internships are tailored to the requirements of the intern and may be arranged in several industries, including: architecture, art, banking, business, community service, computer science, economics, engineering, fashion, film, geology, government, journalism, languages, law, marketing, museum, music, physical and life sciences, politics, public relations, publishing, sports, stock market trading, theater, and women's studies.

PERKS
Field trips to cultural sites (e.g., Parliament); club and theater nights; AAOS receptions (London); access to sports facilities.

FYI
Former interns include senior executives in investment banks, partners in law firms, film producers, a White House aide, and an assistant producer of Broadway's *Damn Yankees* . . . In London, AAOS operates a company called Lox, Stock, & Bagel, which provides interns with catered food (e.g., spinach rolls, smoked salmon, bagels) and has a trendy coktail bar called *Janet's Bar* which is frequented by English celebs in media, business, and politics. For a list of participating organizations in your field of interest, call AAOS's director in London collect.

TO APPLY
Open to high school students, high school grads, undergrads, recent college grads, college grads of any age, and grad students. International applicants eligible. Write for application.

American Association of Overseas Studies
151 West 82nd Street
Suite 4E
New York, NY 10024-5534
(212) 724-0804

American Association of Overseas Studies
51 Drayton Gardens (Suite 4)
London SW10 9RX
England
44-171-835-2143
011-44-171-244-6061 (Fax)
e-mail: aaos@hotmail.com
website: www.worldwide.edu/uk/aaos

AMERICAN ASSOCIATION OF UNIVERSITY WOMEN EDUCATIONAL FOUNDATION

AAUW
EDUCATIONAL
FOUNDATION

SELECTIVITY   🔍
Approximate applicant pool: 30; Interns accepted: 15

COMPENSATION $
$50 stipend per week

LOCATION(S)
Washington, DC

FIELD
Women's Studies; Education; Business; Management; Public policy; Politics; Diversity initiatives

DURATION
4 weeks to 1 year: Summer, Fall, Spring

DEADLINE(S)
Rolling

THE WORK
The American Association of University Women (AAUW) Educational Foundation awards $2.5 million each year to support women participating in scholarly research, advanced graduate study, community action projects, and public school teacher fellowships. It also publishes research concerning the status of girls in public schools, such as "Shortchanging Girls, Shortchanging America," a nationwide poll on girls and self-esteem. Departments accepting interns include: Foundation Director, Research, Higher Education, International, Multicultural Initiatives, Community Action, Development, Information Systems, and Communications.

CHIEF JUSTICE WARREN BURGER'S TAKE ON INTERNSHIPS

According to *The Washington Post*, the late Chief Justice **Warren Burger** proposed that law students devote their third and final year to a legal internship, where they would be immersed in "every phase of the litigation process," from initial interviews with clients to the preparation of trial briefs. Addressing the 1978 conference of the American Law Institute, Burger said such internships would be an indispensable way for law students to "[wed] theory and practice."

PERKS
Mid-term catered luncheon honoring interns; attendance welcome at departmental meetings; career development lunches for interns, mentoring opportunities, and networking with other DC organizations and interns. The foundation also pays for interns to attend a seminar at the Institute for Policy Studies.

FYI
AAUW Educational Foundation offers permanent employment to many of its interns.

TO APPLY
Open to high school grads, undergrads, recent college grads, college grads of any age, and grad students. International applicants eligible. Submit resume, cover letter, two writing samples, and two recommendations.

Internship Coordinator
AAUW Educational Foundation
1111 16th Street NW
Washington, DC 20036-4873
(202) 785-7700
(202) 872-1425 (Fax)

AMERICAN BAR ASSOCIATION

SELECTIVITY
Approximate applicant pool: 2,000; Interns accepted: 30

COMPENSATION ⑤
None for most positions

LOCATION(S)
Chicago, IL (HQ); Harlingen, TX; Washington, DC

FIELD
Law

DURATION
12–16 weeks: Summer, Fall, Spring

DEADLINE(S)
Rolling

THE WORK
Founded in 1878, the American Bar Association (ABA) is the national organization of the legal profession. It is also the world's largest voluntary professional association, with 400,000+ members—half of all lawyers in the United States. Its goals include improving the American legal system, creating easier access to legal representation for all people, increasing respect for the law, and enhancing members' legal knowledge through educational programs. Interns in DC work in Children and the Law, Immigration Law and Representation, Central and East European Law, Mental and Physical Disability Law, Governmental Affairs, Government and Public Sector Lawyers, Individual Rights and Responsibilities, International Law, Post-Conviction Penalty Representation, Public Services, Dispute Resolution, and Law and National Security. Departments in Illinois accepting interns include: Communications, Administration, Meeting Planning and Association Management, Legal Services, Technical Services, Marketing, Public Education, and Center for Professional Responsibilty. Interns in Texas work for Immigration Law and Representation only and must be law students.

PERKS
Brown-bag lunches with department attorneys; summer softball league.

FYI
Intern duties include helping to plan legal education courses, conducting research on legal issues relevant to their assigned departments, and responding to member inquiries.

TO APPLY
Open to undergrads, recent college grads, and grad students. International applicants eligible. Submit resume and cover letter. Texas applicants should submit materials to DC office.

Internship Coordinator   *Internship Program*
American Bar Association   *Information Services*
750 North Lake Shore Drive   *American Bar Association*
Chicago, IL 60611   *740 15th Street, NW*
(312) 988-5177 (Fax)   *Washington, DC 20005*

AMERICAN CIVIL LIBERTIES UNION

SELECTIVITY 🔍🔍🔍🔍🔍
Approximate applicant pool: 100 for summer, less for Fall and Spring; Interns accepted: 1–3 nationwide

COMPENSATION ⑤
None

LOCATION(S)
New York, NY (HQ); Denver, CO; Atlanta, GA; Washington, DC; and over 50 affiliate offices in all 50 states

FIELD
Law; Public policy

DURATION
10–12 weeks; Summer, Fall, Winter/Spring

DEADLINE(S)
Summer: March 1; Fall: September 1; Spring: November 1

THE WORK
The American Civil Liberties Union (ACLU) was founded in 1920 to preserve and expand Americans' rights and freedoms. The ACLU files more lawsuits than any other organization in the United States except the Federal Government. Internship opportunities are available at nearly every ACLU office. In New York and Washington, interns work in the Legal Department on many of the ACLU's projects and in Public Affairs, Field/Legislative, and Development. Other offices accept fewer interns in legal or administrative capacities.

PERKS
Brown-bag luncheons with ACLU directors; casual dress.

FYI
One intern felt the ACLU is "the best place to be—at the forefront of a lot of the legal issues of today, improving society." Another intern had the opportunity to meet ACLU supporters Michelle Pfeiffer and Tom Skerritt.

TO APPLY
Open to undergrads, and grad students. There is no application. Send resume, cover letter, and a five-page, or less, non-fiction writing sample. Note: The following address is applicable to

applicants interested in New York **only**. Those seeking internships in other states should contact those offices directly.

Internship Coordinator
ACLU National Headquarters
125 Broad Street
18th Floor
NY, NY 10004
(212) 549-2610
E-mail: vvela@aclu.org

AMERICAN COMMITTEE ON AFRICA/THE AFRICA FUND

SELECTIVITY 🔍 🔍 🔍 🔍 🔍
Approximate applicant pool: 200; Interns accepted: 4

COMPENSATION 🅂
None

LOCATION(S)
New York, NY

FIELD
Foreign affairs; Human rights; Public policy; Women's issues

DURATION
One month minimum: ongoing

DEADLINE(S)
Summer: April 1; Fall: July 1; Rolling the rest of year

THE WORK
The American Committee on Africa (ACOA) is devoted to supporting African people in their struggle for freedom, independence, and economic justice. ACOA organizes programs and projects to inform and mobilize Americans in support of these aims. It organizes campaigns on key policy issues and assists an extensive US network to lobby on such issues. The Africa Fund (AF) is an educational humanitarian organization associated with ACOA. AF research publications and public education projects provide critical information, particularly on southern Africa and Nigeria and the US. ACOA and AF have complementary programs, sharing office and staff.

PERKS
Mentors; self-designed research projects; receptions; lectures; meetings with diplomats and African and US political leaders.

FYI
Past projects include an analysis of new labor laws in South Africa, which was published by the United Nations; the design of a campaign poster, which was reproduced in a book of political posters; the coordination of a national Anti-Apartheid Conference, which President Nelson Mandela attended; and the compilation of a data fact sheet, which reviewed human rights and social issues in post-1990 South Africa.

TO APPLY
Open to undergraduate and graduate students of any age. International applicants eligible. Submit resume, cover letter, writing samples, and references.

Internship Coordinator
The Africa Fund/American Committee on Africa
50 Broad Street
Suite 711
New York, NY 10004
(212)785-1025
(212)785-8570 (Fax)
E-mail: africafund@igc.apc.org or acoa@igc.apc.org

AMERICAN CONSERVATORY THEATER

SELECTIVITY 🔍 🔍 🔍
Approximate applicant pool: 75; Interns accepted: 9–13

COMPENSATION 🅂
Some stipends available

LOCATION(S)
San Francisco, CA

FIELD
Theater production

DURATION
August/September to June/July (Theater Season)

DEADLINE(S)
April 15

THE WORK
San Francisco's American Conservatory Theater is one of the nation's largest regional companies, performing nine productions each season, utilizing around fifty actors. In recent years, shows have included *Uncle Vanya*, *Rosencrantz and Guildenstern Are Dead*, *Pygmalion*, and both parts of *Angels in America*. Interns find positions in Stage Management, Properties Construction, Stage Technician, Scenic Design, Sound Design, Lighting Design, Makeup and Wig Construction, Costume Rentals, Costume Construction, Production Management, and Production.

PERKS
Theater tickets; comfortable offices. State-of-the-art theater facility.

FYI
This internship, with its long work days and eight to ten-month duration, requires a serious commitment. ACT's actors include William Hurt, John Turturro, and Jean Stapleton . . . The performances returned to Geary Theater in 1996 after damages from an earthquake were repaired.

TO APPLY
Open to undergrads and college grads of any age. International applicants eligible. Write for application.

American Conservatory Theater
Susan West, Internship Coordinator
30 Grant Avenue
San Francisco, CA 94108
(415) 834-3200
(415) 834-3326 (Fax)

SELECTIVITY 🔍🔍
Approximate applicant pool: 60–70; Interns accepted: 15

COMPENSATION $
$950 and $1,100 stipend/summer

LOCATION(S)
Durham, NC

FIELD
Dance; Arts administration

DURATION
9 weeks: Summer

DEADLINE(S)
February 15

THE WORK
Established in 1934 by American dance pioneers Martha Graham, Hanya Holm, Charles Weidman, and Doris Humphrey, the American Dance Festival (ADF) is a nonprofit organization promoting dance in the United States. The ADF community—consisting of dancers, choreographers, body therapists, dance medical specialists, arts managers, teachers, and critics—presents performances by such renowned modern-dance artists as Merce Cunningham, Paul Taylor Dance Co., Pilobolus Dance Theatre, Laura Dean, and Eiko & Koma, and offers educational programs to an international group of nearly 600 students at the ADF School. Interns work in Archives, Box Office, Press and Publications, Finance, Merchandising, Performances, School, Special Projects, and Support Services and Production.

PERKS
Weekly intern seminar on issues in the arts with special guests; one free dance class per day; attendance welcome at discussions, seminars, and lectures; complimentary tickets to more than a dozen dance performances.

FYI
Intern duties include scheduling performers, managing the ADF Store, assisting with the administrative coordination of performances, creating press packets, and publishing daily and weekly calendars for the ADF School.

TO APPLY
Open to undergrads, recent college grads, college grads of any age, and grad students. International applicants eligible. Write for application.

Intern Program
American Dance Festival
Duke University, Box 90772
Durham, NC 27708-0772
(919) 684-6402
(919) 684-5459 (Fax)
E-mail: adfnc@acpub.duke.edu
www.AmericanDanceFestival.org

Tip

Interviewing Tips

1. **Sell yourself only after you know what the company is looking for**. Employers hire people to solve problems. Your first task, then, is to determine the employer's problem (see the job description) and then offer yourself as the solution. Play up your strengths but anticipate and carefully rebut objections to your weaknesses. And don't falsify: most employers can sniff out exaggeration.

2. **Be ready for standard as well as off-the-wall questions**. Employers will naturally ask you about your past jobs, personal interests, and education. But some employers also want to evaluate how you would handle certain job situations and will make up scenarios for you to analyze. For example, a consulting firm may describe a business looking to expand and ask you to develop a strategy; an advertising agency may present a fictional client for whom you must outline a marketing plan.

3. **Display your knowledge of the company**. Libraries, government offices, professional associations, and the company's own public affairs department are good places to find out what products and services the company offers. If the interviewer asks you what you think of the company's new line, a knowledgeable answer will significantly enhance your standing.

4. **Prepare questions**. Because most interviewers will invite you to ask questions about the organization, it's wise to have some ready in advance. Asking the interviewer what he or she does at the organization works especially well; people love to talk about themselves.

5. **Look and act like a professional**. You get only one shot at a first impression. Be on time (10–15 minutes early) and dressed and groomed appropriately. When you meet the interviewer, smile, shake his or her hand firmly, and commit his or her name to memory (to use at the end of the interview).

6. **Practice**. Ask a friend or someone at the career center to take you through a mock interview or two. Sometimes it is also advisable to interview for jobs you do not want just to get the hang of it.

SELECTIVITY
Approximate applicant pool: 300; Interns accepted: 40–55

COMPENSATION
None

LOCATION(S)
Washington, DC

FIELD
Public policy; Think tank

DURATION
12 weeks; Summer, Fall, Spring

DEADLINE(S)
Summer: April 1; Fall: September 15; Spring: January 1

THE WORK
Founded in 1943, the American Enterprise Institute, (AEI), is a think tank committed to research on government policy, economics, and American politics. Interns are assigned to a "resident scholar," a member conducting research in one of three policy areas: economic policy, foreign and defense policy, or social politics. Positions are also available in Marketing, Public and Media Relations, Publications, Seminars and Conferences, and *The American Enterprise* magazine.

PERKS
Access to more than 2,000 conferences a year, Friday Forums, Informal Dining Room, complimentary tickets to our largest formal dinner of the year (2,000 guests)—the annual Francis Boyer Award Lecture and Dinner, intern dinners, free lunch every day in the informal dining room for interns only.

FYI
Interns enjoy the proximity to renowned scholars at this open, nonpartisan think tank and have a role in formulating public policy. Interns may also attend the Bradley Lecture Series, a set of evening lectures given by "non-AEI people who are influential in the world of ideas": Stanley Crouch and Michael Medved are but a few of the recent distinguished Bradley Lecturers.

TO APPLY
Open to undergraduates of any level, recent graduates, and graduate students. Candidates from any academic background are welcome to apply. Submit cover letter, resume, transcript, and a writing sample of roughly 500 words.

American Enterprise Institute
Director of Human Resources—Internships
1150 Seventeenth Street NW
Washington, DC 20036
(202) 862-5800
www.aei.org

SELECTIVITY
Approximate applicant pool: 100; Interns accepted: 5–10

COMPENSATION
$280/week

LOCATION(S)
Washington, DC

FIELD
Education; Social policy; Politics; Labor

DURATION
Varies, 12 weeks–1 year: ongoing

DEADLINE(S)
Rolling, February 28 for summer

THE WORK
Founded in 1916, the American Federation of Teachers AFL-CIO (AFT) is a union representing the interests of K-12 teachers, school support staff, public and municipal employees, college faculty, and healthcare employees. Through education programs to members and affiliates and through lobbying initiatives, AFT advocates national health care reform, national education standards, the professionalism of teaching, and the right of students and teachers to work together in a safe environment. Interns may work in different departments depending on need and appropriate fit.

PERKS
Participation in meetings and seminars, attendance at conferences representing the AFT.

FYI
The membership of AFT has included such notables as Albert Einstein, John Dewey, Elie Wiesel, Hubert Humphrey, Ralph Bunche, Christa McAuliffe, and Frank McCourt.

TO APPLY
Open to undergrads and grad students. International applicants eligible. Submit resume, cover letter, and writing samples.

Internship Coordinator
American Federation of Teachers
555 New Jersey Avenue NW
Washington, DC 20001
(202) 393-3443
E-mail: tolshefs@aft.org

SELECTIVITY
Approximate applicant pool: 500; Interns accepted: 20–25

COMPENSATION
$50/week

LOCATION(S)
Jacksonville, FL; Washington, DC

FIELD
Environment

DURATION
3–6 months: ongoing

DEADLINE(S)
Rolling

THE WORK

Founded in 1875 as the American Forestry Assocation, American Forests (AF) is a national citizens conservation organization with 100,000 members dedicated to protecting trees and forests. Each year, approximately twenty interns and three Fellows work in Advertising and Marketing, Communications, Education, Global ReLeaf, Global ReLeaf International, Management, Policy, Publications (including opportunities to write for *American Forests*, published since 1894), Research, and Urban Forestry.

PERKS

Brown-bag seminars with senior staff; tours of National Wildlife Foundation, urban tree-planting sites, etc.; free t-shirt.

FYI

A pioneer in the urban forestry movement, AF is one of the world's oldest conservation organizations.

TO APPLY

Open to college sophomores, juniors, and seniors, recent college grads, college grads of any age, and grad students. International applicants eligible. Write for flier.

Intern Coordinator
American Forests
P.O. Box 2000
Washington, DC 20013
(202) 955-4500
(202) 955-4588 (Fax)
E-mail: lurose@amfor.org

AMERICAN FRIENDS SERVICE COMMITTEE

American Friends
Service Committee

SELECTIVITY
Approximate applicant pool: 200; Interns accepted: 90–115

COMPENSATION
PA: occasional carfare and lunch money; Regional offices: none; Cuba: $400 fee; Mexico: $900 fee (includes room, board, and transportation)

LOCATION(S)
Atlanta, GA; Baltimore, MD; Cambridge, MA; Chicago, IL; Des Moines, IA; New York, NY; Oakland and Pasadena, CA; Philadelphia, PA (HQ); Seattle, WA; Cuba; Mexico

FIELD
Peace studies; Human rights

DURATION
US: 4 weeks minimum: ongoing; Mexico: 7 weeks: Summer

DEADLINE(S)
US: Rolling; Mexico: April 1

THE WORK

Part of the Religious Society of Friends (Quakers), the American Friends Service Committee (AFSC) is a nonprofit organization committed to the principles of nonviolence and justice. Through education programs, worldwide development projects, policy papers, lobbying efforts, and its Quaker United Nations Office (see separate entry), AFSC seeks to end war and poverty, improve conditions in mental hospitals and prisons, and achieve racial equality. Volunteers work in all capacities, including doing administrative tasks, folding clothing in the Material Aids warehouse (PA only), and writing for the Information Services Department. Volunteers in

AFSC's Mexico Program, placed in villages throughout Mexico, complete projects involving construction, reforestation, gardening, health, and nutrition. Volunteers live in a diverse community with others their age.

PERKS

Orientation; programs in music and culture; local dances and fiestas (Mexico).

FYI

There are about 200,000 Quakers worldwide . . . In 1947, AFSC and the British Friends Service Council shared a Nobel Peace Prize for their "silent help from the nameless to the nameless." . . . AFSC offers some scholarships for its Mexico programs.

TO APPLY

Volunteer: open to anyone over the age of 15. Mexico: open to 18- to 26-year olds; must be proficient in Spanish. International applicants eligible. Write Philadelphia headquarters for Volunteer, Mexico application. Contacts in regional offices may be obtained from Philadelphia.

Personnel Department-Helene Pollock
American Friends Service Committee
1501 Cherry Street
Philadelphia, PA 19102
(215) 241-7295
E-mail: hpollock@afsc.org
www.afsc.org

THE AMERICAN GEOGRAPHICAL SOCIETY

SELECTIVITY
Approximate applicant pool: 40; Interns accepted: 4–6

COMPENSATION
None

LOCATION(S)
New York, NY; Milwaukee, WI; Reno, NV; Lexington, KY

FIELD
Geography

DURATION
10 weeks minimum

DEADLINE(S)
Rolling

THE WORK

Founded in 1851, The American Geographical Society (AGS) is a nonprofit organization seeking to increase worldwide knowledge of geography. It sponsors conferences, grants awards to explorers and scholars, conducts research on geographical topics, performs specialized research under contract for government agencies, and publishes journals and books. Departments accepting interns include: the Office of the Chief Executive, Teacher Services, Fundraising, Business, Geographers Volunteer Teaching Program, Educational Travel Program, the scholarly journal *Geographical Review*, *Focus* magazine, and *Ubique* newsletter.

EXCLUSIVE INTERVIEW WITH JANE PRATT

Jane Pratt founded Sassy, *the highly successful magazine for teens, where she served as editor-in-chief until 1993. She graduated from Oberlin College in 1984 with a double major in theater/dance and communications.*

The Internship Informants: Let's hear about your internships.
Pratt: I've done many internships. First, I interned at a magazine called *Sportstyle*, which is owned by Fairchild, the people who do *Womens Wear Daily*. Then I interned at *Rolling Stone*. And then I went back to Oberlin for a year, and after I graduated, I interned at *McCall's* magazine.

The Internship Informants: It sounds like interning gave you some great experience.
Pratt: Well, one of the best things about internships is that because you don't get paid much or at all, your supervisor often feels like he or she has to throw in some good opportunities with the typing and the filing. So sometimes you get better opportunities as an intern than if you were in an entry-level position. At *Rolling Stone*, for example, I did a lot of cleaning out the record library and sorting through old newspapers (which coated my hands and arms with black ink). But because I was doing all that junk, [my supervisor] would also throw me little bones—like getting to interview Julia Child for a celebrity round-up piece. It got published—my mini-interview with Julia Child—and for a long time I remember mentioning it on my resume.

The Internship Informants: Organizations are increasingly accepting teenagers as interns. As someone who has been involved with writing about teenage issues, what do you think about internships and teenagers?
Pratt: I think it's so important for people to intern as young as they want to. At *Sassy*, we always took high school interns as well as college interns. It's great experience for high school students—when I was in high school, I would have loved to have had the opportunity to intern at a magazine.

PERKS
Free copies of publications; special emphasis on providing job and graduate school recommendation; small, tight-knit office.

FYI
AGS has used interns since 1988 . . . Interns working for Publications proofread, edit, and collect data, help organize events, recruit volunteer teachers, input computer data, do library research, write press releases, etc.

TO APPLY
Open to undergrads, recent college grads, college grads of any age, and grad students. International applicants eligible. Submit resume, cover letter, and writing samples. "Distance Internships" available—inquire for details.

Internship Coordinator
The American Geographical Society
120 Wall Street, Suite 100
New York, NY 10005
(212) 422-5456
(212) 422-5480 (Fax)

AMERICAN HOCKEY LEAGUE

SELECTIVITY 🔍 🔍 🔍
Approximate applicant pool: 40; Interns accepted: 3–4

COMPENSATION 💲
None

LOCATION(S)
Springfield, MA

FIELD
Sports—Professional Hockey

DURATION
15 weeks: Summer, Fall, Spring

DEADLINE(S)
Rolling

THE WORK
Started in 1936, the American Hockey League (AHL) serves as the National Hockey League's (NHL) premiere development league. seventy percent of NHL players during the 1999–2000 season developed their skills in th AHL. The AHL consists of 19 member clubs in the U.S. and Canada. Interns work in Marketing, Public Relations, and Hockey Operations.

PERKS
Tickets to AHL games; opportunity to attend the AHL All-Star Game (January); opportunity to work at AHL games.

FYI
According to the internship coordinator: "This is a tremendous opportunity for interns to learn from and network with professionals in the business."

TO APPLY

Open to undergrads, recent grads, and grad students. Submit resume, cover letter, writing samples, and recommendations.

Chris Nikolis
Internship Coordinator
AHL
1 Monarch Place, Suite 2400
Springfield, MA 01144
(413) 781-2030
(413) 746-0408 (Fax)

AMERICAN INDIAN SCIENCE & ENGINEERING SOCIETY

SELECTIVITY
Approximate applicant pool: 150; Interns accepted: 75

COMPENSATION
$450/week for undergrads; $550/week for grad students

LOCATION(S)
Washington, D.C. and various other locations in the US

FIELD
Engineering; Business

DURATION
10 weeks: Summer

DEADLINE(S)
Mid-February (contact AISES for the exact date)

THE WORK
Established in 1995, the American Indian Science & Engineering Society (AISES) Summer Work Experience Program places Native American students in science, engineering, and business related internships within federal government agencies. The program is designed to "bridge science and technology with traditional Native values" and to develop technologically informed professionals to become leaders within American Indian communities. The program draws students from a variety of majors, including Law, Economics, Physical Sciences, Mathematics, Computer Science, and Psychology. Participating agencies have included the U.S. Department of Commerce, the U.S. Department of Energy, the National Resource Conservation Service, the National Institute of Health, the Central Intelligence Agency, and the Federal Aviation Administration.

PERKS
Round-trip travel; free housing (Washington, D.C. only); mentors; several cultural and social activities, including an opening reception and local pow wow.

FYI
According to one program participant, "The program helps dispel the notion that there are very few American Indian students around with advanced skills and education." A $1,000 scholarship is awarded each year to one program participant.

TO APPLY

Open to American Indian/Alaskan Native college sophomores, juniors, seniors, and grad students with at least a 2.5 GPA. Write for application or download from web site (www.colorado.edu/AISES/intern).

AISES-Jobs
Internship Coordinator
566 Airport Blvd.
Boulder, CO 80301
(303) 939-0023 ext. 31
(301) 939-8150
www.coloradu.edu/AISES/intern

AIFS–FLORENCE

AMERICAN INSTITUTE
FOR FOREIGN STUDY

SELECTIVITY
Approximate applicant pool: 100; interns accepted: 25

COMPENSATION
Unpaid internships. Semester program fees are approximately $12,000 for room, board, insurance, one-way flight to Florence with three-day stopover in London, three-week orientation in Siena, field trips to Venice, Ravenna and Rome, on-going social and cultural activities and services of on-site resident director. Scholarships available.

LOCATION(S)
Florence, Italy

FIELD
Business administration; Social science

DURATION
15 week semesters

DEADLINE(S)
Fall: May 15; Spring: November 1

THE WORK
This AIFS internship sees students working part time in local companies or small businesses in or near Florence a minimum of 130 hours. Placement is determined after application, interviews and competitive selection by the director and faculty. Students must have a good working knowledge of Italian. Three hours credit can be earned for an internship along with credit for an Italian language course and another course from among offerings in history, fine arts, art history, economics, and social sciences. Social science placements may be in elementary education, assistance to the elderly, or healthcare assistance.

PERKS
Field trips to Rome, Venice, and Ravenna included in fee as well as ongoing social and cultural activities organized by the AIFS Resident Director and staff. Flight to Italy includes three-day stopover in London.

FYI
The program is offered by AIFS through Richmond, The American International University in London, a private, independent nonprofit institution licensed to award BA, BS, MA, MS, and

MBA degrees by the Department of Public Instruction of the state of Delaware. It is accredited by the Commission on Higher Education of the Middle States Association of Colleges and Schools.

The American Institute For Foreign Study (AIFS) has sent 950,000 participants in its educational and cultural exchange programs since its founding over 35 years ago.

TO APPLY
Open to college sophomores, juniors, and seniors with minimum 2.5 GPA. Must be fluent in Italian. Students can apply at www.aifsabroad.com or contact AIFS:

American Institute For Foreign Study
River Plaza
9 West Broad Street
Stamford, CT 06902
E-mail: college.info@aifs.com
www.aifs.com/java/US/aifsay_s/italy/italy.htm

AIFS—LONDON

SELECTIVITY
Approximate applicant pool: 250; interns accepted: 100-150

COMPENSATION
Unpaid internships. Program fees are approximately $7,000 for summer including tuition, room, board, and round trip flight and approximately $12,000 for semester tuition, room, board, insurance, and one-way flight to London. Scholarships available.

LOCATION(S)
London, England

FIELD
More than 30 fields (see THE WORK)

DURATION
11 weeks: Summer, 15 weeks: semesters

DEADLINE(S)
Summer: March 15; Fall: May 15; Spring: November 1

THE WORK
The AIFS International Internship Program in London combines a rigorous academic program and 10 weeks working in major British and international institutions. Semester students earn up to 18 credits (12 in summer) by study of contemporary British culture, an internship workshop throughout the semester and 10 weeks on a full-time unpaid internship.

In addition students can choose one or two semester-long three-credit courses taught weekday evenings or Fridays by Richmond faculty, many of whom are practicing experts in their fields. Placements may be in the fields of politics and social sciences, fine arts, theater, business and economics, computer science, and communications.

An intern sponsored by the American Institute For Foreign Study at work in the CNN bureau in London.

PERKS
Optional orientation tour of Europe. Individual attention to clarify and set goals, preparation for the British workplace and support throughout the placement.

FYI
The program is offered by the American Institute For Foreign Study through Richmond, The American International University in London, a private, independent nonprofit institution licensed to award BA, BS, MA, MS, and MBA degrees by the Department of Public Instruction of the state of Delaware. It is accredited by the Commission on Higher Education of the Middle States Association of Colleges and Schools. Like London itself, Richmond provides a diverse and multicultural environment in which to study. With a full-time student body of 1,300 from more than 100 countries, Richmond makes global culture part of your internship experience. The American Institute For Foreign Study (AIFS) has sent 950,000 participants in its educational and cultural exchange programs since its founding over 35 years ago.

TO APPLY
Open to college juniors and seniors and graduate students with minimum 2.5 GPA. Must be fluent in English. International students are eligible. Students can apply at:

American Institute For Foreign Study
River Plaza
9 West Broad Street
Stamford, CT 06902
(800) 727-2437
E-mail: college.info@aifs.com
www.aifs.com/java/US/aifsay_s/ukintem/int.htm; summer,
www.aifs.com/java/US/aifscss/ukintem/sint.htm

AMERICAN ISRAEL PUBLIC AFFAIRS COMMITTEE

SELECTIVITY
Approximate applicant pool: 300; Interns accepted: 50

COMPENSATION
Possible stipends for undergrads

LOCATION(S)
Chicago, IL; Houston, TX ; Los Angeles and San Francisco, CA; Missoula, MT; Washington, DC (HQ); Jerusalem, Israel; Fort Lauderdale, FL; Seattle, WA; New York, NY

FIELD
Foreign affairs

DURATION
8–10 weeks: Summer, Fall, Spring

DEADLINE(S)
Summer: April 1; Fall: September 15; Winter: December 1; Spring: January 15

THE WORK
Established in 1954, the American Israel Public Affairs Committee (AIPAC) is the only American organization registered to lobby on behalf of the US-Israel relationship. Its mission is to nurture and advance the US-Israel relationship so as to assure that the ties are continuing and solid. Interns work in Legislative, Foreign Policy Issues, Political Affairs, Development, and Political Leadership Development.

INTERNS OF A FEATHER
SHOOT HOOPS TOGETHER

Mutombo interned with Rep. Robert Matsui (D-CA) while at Georgetown (Summer 1989).

Ewing interned with the Senate Finance Committee while at Georgetown (Summer 1983).

Three New York Knicks players—Bill Bradley, Patrick Ewing, and Greg Anthony—and Denver Nuggets center Dikembe Mutombo all interned on Capitol Hill during their college years.

Former Sen. Bradley (D-NJ) interned with former Rep. Richard Schweiker (R-PA) while at Princeton (Summer 1964).

Anthony interned with Rep. Barbara Vucanovich (R-NV) while at UNLV (Summer 1989).

PERKS
Planning and participating in AIPAC's National Political Leadership Training seminar; brown-bag luncheons with execs; attendance welcome at out-of-office briefings; developing relationships on Capitol Hill

FYI
In existence since 1979, the internship program counts among its alumni AIPAC's Director of Defense and Strategic Affairs and the Director of its Jerusalem office.

TO APPLY
Open to undergrads, recent college grads, and grad students. International applicants eligible. Write for application. Call DC headquarters for contacts in other cities.

Joel Barkin
Internship Coordinator
American Israel Public Affairs Committee
440 First Street NW Suite 600
Washington, DC 20001
(202) 639-5200
(202) 347-4918 (Fax)

AJCongress

★ ★ ★

SELECTIVITY 🔍 🔍 🔍
Approximate applicant pool: 350; Interns accepted: 60

COMPENSATION Ⓢ
None

LOCATION(S)
Baltimore, MD; Beachwood, OH; Boston, MA; Chicago, IL; Dallas, TX; East Orange, NJ; Great Neck, NY; Los Angeles and San Francisco, CA; New York, NY (HQ); Miami Beach, FL; Philadelphia, PA; St. Louis, MO; Washington, DC; Jerusalem, Israel

FIELD
Civil rights; Public policy

DURATION
6–14 weeks: Summer, Fall, Winter

DEADLINE(S)
Rolling

THE WORK
Founded in 1916, the American Jewish Congress (AJC) is a nonprofit membership organization promoting social and economic justice, religious freedom, and human rights for Jewish communities throughout the world. Issues on AJC's agenda include anti-Semitism, US-Israel relations, civil and constitutional rights, separation of church and state, reproductive freedom and women's equality, homelessness, Israel-Middle East relations, human rights, immigration, and health care. Interns work in Legal, Domestic Policy, and Programming, where they participate in Jewish community work, organize coalitions, initiate letter-writing campaigns, and research issues; interns in Legislative (DC only) attend and report on Congressional committee meetings as well as interest-group coalition meetings.

PERKS
Orientation; occasional seminars; occasional opportunities to attend White House and Congressional events (DC).

FYI
AJC calls itself the "attorney general of the Jewish community," pursuing the First Amendment's promise of religious accommodation in the private workplace.

TO APPLY
Open to undergrads, recent grads, and grad students. Submit resume and cover letter directly to office of interest; for DC office, write for application. Applicants are required to submit a cover letter, resume, the names and phone numbers of three references, and a writing sample to:

Internship Coordinator
American Jewish Congress
15 East 84th Street
New York, NY 10028
(212) 879-4500
(212) 249-3672 (Fax)
E-mail: ai835@lafn.org (Los Angeles); ajc-ny@shamash.nysernet.org (New York City); ajcstl@aol.com (MO); sfcongl@aol.com (PA); ajc-dc@clark.net or ajc-dc@israel.nysernet.org (DC)

SELECTIVITY 🔍🔍🔍
Approximate applicant pool: 50; Interns accepted: 1–2

COMPENSATION $
None

LOCATION(S)
Chicago, IL

FIELD
Law; Politics

DURATION
12–16 weeks: Summer, Fall, Spring

DEADLINE(S)
Rolling

THE WORK
The American Judicature Society is an independent nonprofit organization that works to improve the operation of the courts and increase public understanding of the justice system. AJS offers two different types of unpaid internships for undergraduate and graduate students interested in the administration of justice, the improvement of the courts, and law and society issues. Many interns have earned academic credit for their experiences.

Program Internship: Working with AJS programs staff members, the intern helps research and organize information that will be used for educational programs, court improvement projects, and grant proposals. The intern may conduct computer-based and library research, draft reports, develop and maintain contacts with members of the judiciary and legal profession, and perform an array of other tasks as they arise in the implementation of AJS programs.

PERKS
Free one-year membership in AJS; training in research techniques.

FYI
According to the internship coordinator: "Interning here is quite beneficial to aspiring law students and others interested in working in courts because they are exposed to the issues you don't see that much in school. They don't learn so much about the justice system as they do about the administration of the justice system."

TO APPLY
Open to undergrads, recent grads, and grad students. Candidates should have strong writing, research, computer, and telephone skills. Submit resume, cover letter, writing samples, and three academic or professional references.

Seth Andersen
Director, Hunter Center for Judicial Selection
American Judicature Society
180 N. Michigan Ave., Suite 600
Chicago, IL 60601
(312) 558–6900 x105
E-mail: sandersen@ajs.org

SELECTIVITY 🔍🔍
Approximate applicant pool: 300; Interns accepted: 60

COMPENSATION $
$8.00/hour

LOCATION(S)
New York, NY

FIELD
Management

DURATION
2–4 months

DEADLINE(S)
Spring and Fall: Rolling; Summer: April 7

THE WORK
Founded in 1923, the American Management Association (AMA) is a nonprofit organization that provides educational training forums worldwide where members and their colleagues learn, discover, and improve their practical business skills. AMA also has a publishing program that provides tools individuals use to extend learning beyond the classroom and covers the latest trends in business. Interns work in Training and Development, Human Resources, Publishing, General Management, Marketing, and Market Research.

PERKS
Intern luncheon with CEO; choice of two complimentary AMA seminars, intern mixers; attendance at departmental meeting and AMA social functions.

FYI
Recent years have found interns creating a supervisory training video for new managers at AMA, analyzing evaluations of AMA's Annual Human Resources Conference, creating a statistical analysis of a customer service survey, and researching new ways of marketing AMA's international courses.

TO APPLY
Open to high school students, undergrads, and grad students. International applicants eligible. Submit resume, cover letter, and two letters of reference (one academic and one employment).

Internship Coordinator
American Management Association
1601 Broadway, 11th Floor
New York, NY 10010
(212) 903-8021
(212) 903-8163 (Fax)

SELECTIVITY 🔍🔍🔍
Approximate applicant pool: 100; Interns accepted: 10

COMPENSATION 💲
Travel money or stipend

LOCATION(S)
New York, NY

FIELD
Theater

DURATION
8 weeks–1 year: ongoing

DEADLINE(S)
Rolling

THE WORK
Founded in 1963, The American Place Theatre (APT) produces new plays by living American playwrights. Winner of over thirty Obie awards, APT has staged such originally produced plays as Sam Shepard's *States of Shock* with John Malkovich, Bill Irwin's *Regard of Flight* and John Legizamo's *Mambo Mouth,* and has hosted such actors as Michael Douglas, Faye Dunaway, Raul Julia, and Sigourney Weaver.   Interns work in Education, Production, Literary, and Administration.

PERKS
Free tickets to all performances; free tickets to other theaters, performances, and readings; course credit.

FYI
According to the internship coordinator: "Our literary interns read the scripts which are submitted here, so it's up to them what plays get read by our artistic directors."

TO APPLY
Open to undergrads, recent college grads, and grad students. International applicants eligible. Submit resume and cover letter.

Internship Coordinator
The American Place Theatre
111 West 46th Street
New York, NY 10026
(212) 840-2960 ext. 10
(212) 391-4019 (Fax)

One of the country's best known comic journalists, **Erma Bombeck** launched her career in 1944 as a copy girl with the *Journal-Herald* in Dayton, Ohio.

American Red Cross ✚

SELECTIVITY 🔍🔍
Approximate applicant pool: 200; Interns accepted: 20

COMPENSATION 💲💲💲
$376/week

LOCATION(S)
Washington, DC metropolitan area

FIELD
Public service; Health care

DURATION
10 weeks: Summer

DEADLINE(S)
May 1

THE WORK
Chartered by Congress in 1905, the American Red Cross (ARC) is a humanitarian organization that provides relief to victims of disasters and helps people prevent, prepare for, and respond to emergencies. It runs organ-donor programs, collects blood, raises money for charity, teaches HIV/AIDS classes, and funds medical research. ARC's Presidential Internship Program (PIP) places students at headquarters in Development, Human Resources, Information Services, Policy, Procedures and Training, Health and Safety Services, International Services, Finance, and Biomedical Services.

PERKS
Meetings with senior management; breakfast with ARC President; opportunities to take Red Cross training; opportunities to travel to conferences and ARC chapters.

FYI
PIP began in June 1993 under the auspices of "The President's Agenda for Cultural Diversity," an ARC-wide program . . . President Elizabeth Dole writes: "[W]e have a moral obligation, as well as a very practical duty, to ensure that the American Red Cross is as diverse as the nation and the people we serve." . . . Those interested in interning at one of ARC's over 1,300 chapters nationwide should call the chapter directly (consult your phonebook); each chapter is autonomous and may or may not have an internship program.

TO APPLY
Open to minority undergrads, and grad students (or who have just graduated the spring immediately prior to their appointment). Write for application.

Internship Coordinator
Corporate Diversity JP-6
American Red Cross National Headquarters
8111 Gatehouse Road, 2nd Floor
Falls Church , VA 22042
(703) 206 8819
(703) 206-8572 (Fax)

American Repertory Theatre
and Institute for Advanced Theatre Training

SELECTIVITY 🔍🔍🔍
Approximate applicant pool: 100+; Interns accepted: 10–20

COMPENSATION 💲
Some compensation available to full year Stage Management interns.

LOCATION(S)
Cambridge, MA

FIELD
Theater

DURATION
10 weeks minimum: ongoing; No summer internships in artistic or production

DEADLINE(S)
Rolling

THE WORK
Established in 1979, the American Repertory Theatre (ART) produces a five-play mainstage season, a New Stages series, and a variety of special events. Based in Harvard University's Loeb Drama Center, ART has hosted such celebrated directors as Anne Bogart, Ron Daniels, Michael Kahn, Peter Sellars, Susan Sontag, and Robert Wilson. Interns work in Voice Coaching, Movement Coaching, Artistic Management, Box Office, Financial Management, Fundraising, House Management, Literary Management, Marketing and Public Relations, Production Management, Running Crew, Scene Shop, Paint Department, Costume Shop, Prop Shop and Stage Management.

PERKS
Free tickets; "curtain comps" to ART productions; occasional tickets to other theaters.

FYI
The internship program has been in existence since 1979 . . . ART is one of the few resident theater companies in the country performing in rotating repertory.

TO APPLY
Open to undergrads, recent college grads, grad students, high school grads, and college grads of any age. International applicants eligible. Write for application or send resume and cover letter with a list of three references to:

How to Marry a Senator

- Senator Strom Thurmond (R-SC) married his intern, a former Miss South Carolina, when he was 66 and she was 22.

- Senator Edward M. Kennedy (D-MA) married his former intern, Victoria Reggie, now a partner at a Washington law firm.

Internship Coordinator
American Repertory Theatre
64 Brattle Street
Cambridge, MA 02138
(617) 495-2668
(617) 495-1705 (Fax)
Website: www.amrep.org

American Rivers

SELECTIVITY 🔍🔍
Approximate applicant pool; 100; Interns accepted: 16

COMPENSATION 💲💲
$1,000 for three months

LOCATION(S)
Washington, DC

FIELD
Environment

DURATION
3 months: Winter, Spring, Summer, Fall

DEADLINE(S)
Rolling

THE WORK
American Rivers is a national nonprofit river conservation organization, which since 1973 has addressed river protection issues across the country. The organization's mission is to preserve and restore America's river systems and to foster a river stewardship ethic. Policy work covers nationally significant rivers, hydropower policy reform, western water issues, urban rivers, and clean water issues. Departments accepting interns include Conservation, Development, and Communications.

PERKS
Casual dress, a flexible schedule, and a downtown location near the White House enhance the American Rivers experience.

FYI
American Rivers' Director of Floodplain Programs and Grants Coordinator both started as AR interns.

TO APPLY
Open to undergrads, college grads, and grad students. International students are eligible. Submit cover letter, resume, a brief writing sample, and a list of three references.

Internship Coordinator
American Rivers
1025 Vermont Ave, NW
Suite 720
Washington, DC 20005
(202) 347-7550
(202) 347-9240 (Fax)
E-mail: ahoffert@amrivers.org

SELECTIVITY 🔍

Approximate applicant pool: 600; Interns accepted: 300–500 total (25–30 Americans)

COMPENSATION 💲💲

Sufficient to cover living expenses; varies by assignment.

LOCATION(S)

Americans: Denmark, Finland, Iceland, Norway, Sweden; Scandinavians: all 50 states in the US

FIELD

5 fields (See THE WORK)

DURATION

2–18 months: Start date depending on position

DEADLINE(S)

Americans: January 1 for technical positions, February 1 for TOEFL positions. Scandinavians: Rolling.

 THE WORK

Founded in 1910, The American-Scandinavian Foundation (ASF) is a nonprofit organization promoting cultural and educational exchange between the US and Scandinavia. The 3,500-member group offers a Fellowship program funding graduate and postgraduate study and research, publishes *Scandinavian Review*, administers a training program, and sponsors Scandinavian cultural events like film screenings, art exhibitions, an annual winter Skating Party at Central Park's Wollman Rink, theater performances, and poetry readings. Under the auspices of ASF's Training Program, interns arrange their own work assignments, receiving assistance from ASF in obtaining work permits, visas, and housing. A few placements in Scandinavia exist for Americans studying chemistry, computer science, agriculture, or engineering (chemical, civil, electrical, and mechanical), TOEFL, and business.

PERKS

Vary with placement.

FYI

Participating companies in the US include Ericsson, Inc., ABB, SKF, Inc., Alger Farms, Finnair, Volvo, Pharmacia, and Mid-America Overseas . . . Housing in Scandinavia, arranged by ASF and the participating companies, costs interns $150–$200/month.

TO APPLY

For Americans: open to college juniors, seniors, and recent graduates (within 2 years). Minimum GPA: 2.5. Write for application. Application fee: $50. Minimum age: 21.

For Americans:
Technical Training Program
The American-Scandinavian Foundation
15 East 65 Street
New York, NY 10021
(212) 879-9779
(212) 249-3444 (Fax)
E-mail: training@amscan.org

For Scandinavians:
Denmark: The Denmark-American Foundation (45-33-1282-23)
Finland: The League of Finnish-American Societies (358-9-4133-3700)
     or The Centre for International Mobility (358-9-7747-7033)
Iceland: The Icelandic-American Society, P.O. Box 320, 121 Reykjavik, Iceland
Norway: The Norway-American Assoc. (47-2-335-7160)
Sweden: The Sweden-American Foundation (46-08-611-4611)
     or The International Employment Office (46-08-406-5728)

FOUNDED IN 1817

SELECTIVITY 🔍🔍

Approximate applicant pool: 30; Interns accepted: 6

COMPENSATION 💲💲

Free room & board

LOCATION(S)

West Hartford, CT

FIELD

Education

DURATION

8 weeks: Summer, Fall, Spring

DEADLINE(S)

Rolling

THE WORK

Founded in 1817, the American School for the Deaf (ASD) is the oldest school of its kind in the United States. Serving students age 3 to 21, ASD operates educational and vocational programs for the deaf and hard of hearing. Interns assist teachers in classroom instruction and recreational activities.

PERKS

Free classes in sign language; housing in private dormitory rooms; 13 free meals per week.

FYI

The internship program has been running since 1984 . . . Says an ASD staff member: "For those interested in becoming a teacher of the deaf, this is an ideal internship. [Interns] are totally immersed in deaf culture."

TO APPLY

Open to undergrads. International applicants eligible. Write for application.

Internship Coordinator
American School for the Deaf
139 North Main Street
West Harford, CT 06107
(860) 570-2300
(860) 570-2801 (Fax)

SELECTIVITY 🔍🔍
Approximate applicant pool: 175; Interns accepted: 45

COMPENSATION 💲💲💲
Minimum $325/week for undergrads

LOCATION(S)
New York, NY; Washington, DC

FIELD
Magazine

DURATION
10 weeks: Summer

DEADLINE(S)
December 15

THE WORK
The American Society of Magazine Editors (ASME) arranges summer internships for college seniors at leading consumer and business magazines. Interns work in the editorial department, and at some magazines there are writing opportunities. Past magazine placements include: *National Geographic*, *Sports Illustrated*, *Business Week*, *Life*, *Glamour*, *Essence*, and *Esquire*.

PERKS
Three-day orientation; weekly luncheons with top editors; field trips to publishing companies.

FYI
Each spring ASME distributes a "Book of Resumes" of the prior summer's interns to about 850 editors . . . ASME currently has 375 names on its active alumni list, with 150 working in the New York area.

TO APPLY
Open to college juniors. Must have taken academic courses in journalism, participated in campus journalism, and/or previous journalism-oriented internships. Applicants are typically nominated by the department of journalism or an appropriate dean at their college. Write for application.

Internship Program
American Society of Magazine Editors
919 Third Avenue
New York, NY 10022
(212) 872-3700
(212) 906-0128 (Fax)

> Each spring, the American Society of Magazine Editors distributes a "Book of Resumes" of the prior summer's interns to about 850 editors nationwide.

SELECTIVITY 🔍🔍🔍🔍
Approximate applicant pool: 50; Interns accepted: 3–5

COMPENSATION 💲
$1,000 stipend

LOCATION(S)
Washington, DC

FIELD
Orchestra; Education

DURATION
12 weeks: Summer, Fall, Spring

DEADLINE(S)
Summer: April 15; Fall: July 15; Spring: November 15

THE WORK
Founded in 1942 and chartered by Congress in 1962, the American Symphony Orchestra League (ASOL) is a service organization for over 1,600 symphony and chamber orchestras in the United States. To ensure orchestras' artistic, organizational, and financial strength, ASOL provides such services as the Orchestra Management Seminars, Employment Search and Referral Service, *SYMPHONY* magazine, and Conducting Workshops. Departments accepting interns include Information Resources Center, Orchestra Services, Meetings, Government Affairs, Marketing, Fundraising, Research and Library Science, Magazine Production, Communications/Development, and Finance and Administration.

PERKS
Biweekly workshops on word processing and spreadsheets; possible orchestra tickets; attendance welcome at national conference (Portland, OR in the past).

FYI
An ASOL brochure states: "We are American orchestras working in concert.". . . American orchestras perform more than 20,000 concerts per year in the United States.

TO APPLY
Open to undergrads and recent college grads. International applicants eligible. Write for application.

Intern Coordinator
American Symphony Orchestra League
33 W. 60th St., 5th Floor
New York, NY 10023
Fax: (212) 262-5298
E-mail: League@Symphony.org

SELECTIVITY 🔍🔍🔍
Approximate applicant pool: 100; Interns accepted: 10

COMPENSATION 💲
None

LOCATION(S)
Washington, DC

FIELD
Education; Business; Culture

DURATION
12–15 weeks: Summer, Fall, Spring

DEADLINE(S)
Rolling

THE WORK
Founded in 1980 as the Andrei Sakharov Institute, the American University in Moscow (AUM) is a private educational institution providing college instruction to 300 international students annually and promoting Russian-American cooperation in education, business, politics, and culture. Interns work at AUM's DC office in Administration, Telecommunications, and Liaison; at AUM's Russia House, a DC-based consulting firm that assists Western companies seeking to penetrate developing free markets throughout Russia and the Newly-Independent States.

PERKS
Attendance welcome at all receptions for visiting foreign dignitaries; possibility of attending International Congresses in Moscow (all expenses paid).

FYI
AUM hires approximately 10 percent of its interns for full-time administrative positions at its offices in DC.

TO APPLY
Open to undergrads, recent grads, recent college grads, college grads of any age, and grad students. International applicants eligible. Submit resume and cover letter.

Internship Coordinator
American University in Moscow
1800 Connecticut Avenue NW
Washington, DC 20009
(202) 986-6010
(202) 667-4244 (Fax)
E-mail: aum@russiahouse.org

SELECTIVITY 🔍🔍
Approximate applicant pool: 50; Interns accepted: 10

COMPENSATION 💲💲
$240–$320/week

LOCATION(S)
Washington, DC

FIELD
Environment

DURATION
12 weeks: Summer, Fall, Spring

DEADLINE(S)
Rolling

THE WORK
Founded in 1974, the American Wind Energy Association (AWEA) works to advance the development of wind energy as an economically and technically viable energy alternative. It serves its members with publications on wind energy, legislative and regulatory representation, a monthly newsletter entitled *Windletter*, and a variety of conferences and seminars. Interns work in Administration, Finance, Legislative, International, Membership, and Meetings.

PERKS
Free t-shirts, posters, and books; occasional free lunches; "casual, fun" work environment.

FYI
The members of AWEA include wind turbine and accessory part manufacturers, wind-power plant developers and operators, energy consultants, repair and maintenance companies, electric utilities, and research centers.

TO APPLY
Open to undergrads, recent grads, and grad students. International applicants eligible. Submit resume and cover letter.

Internship Coordinator
American Wind Energy Association
122 C Street NW, 4th Floor
Washington, DC 20001
(202) 383-2500
(202) 383-2505 (Fax)

SELECTIVITY 🔍🔍🔍
Approximate applicant pool: 50; Interns accepted: 6–8

COMPENSATION ⑤
None

LOCATION(S)
New York, NY

FIELD
Women's Entrepreneurship; Business

DURATION
6–12 weeks: ongoing

DEADLINE(S)
Rolling

THE WORK
Founded in 1976, American Women's Economic Development Corporation (AWED) is a nonprofit educational organization providing training, counseling, and technical assistance to women who own or would like to own a business. Programs include classes, seminars, and workshops on such topics as networking, marketing, finance, and business planning run by successful entrepreneurs and business professionals. Interns work in training, counseling, and development, where they assist with marketing and research (i.e., responding to public inquiries, marketing AWED programs, registering clients for classes, researching and preparing resource grant applications).

PERKS
Attendance welcome at AWED programs free of charge; small office staff.

FYI
" . . . AWED provides scholarships to cover the cost of some of its programs . . . Approximately 50 percent of women who enroll in AWED's programs are minorities.

TO APPLY
Open to undergrads, recent grads, and grad students. International applicants eligible. Submit resume, cover letter, and writing samples directly to:

Chief Operating Officer
American Women's Economic
Development Corp.
216 East 45th Street, 10th Floor
New York, NY 10017
(917) 368-6120
(212) 986-7114 (Fax)

Even trouble-making Russian politician **Vladimir Zhirinovsky** once served an internship. While enrolled at Moscow State University's prestigious Institute for Oriental Languages in the late 1960s, he spent several months interning as an interpreter in the Turkish city of Iskenderun. During his time in Turkey, Zhirinovsky was arrested by Turkish police, purportedly for distributing Soviet pins. His swift release from jail was widely suspected to have been engineered by the KGB.

SELECTIVITY 🔍
Approximate applicant pool: 10; Interns accepted: 4

COMPENSATION 🔍🔍
$5.75/hour

LOCATION(S)
Washington, DC

FIELD
Public policy; Newspaper

DURATION
8–12 weeks: ongoing

DEADLINE(S)
Rolling (2 months before start date)

THE WORK
Founded in 1984, the American Youth Work Center (AYWC) is a nonprofit organization advocating improved services for children. AYWC activities include: publishing *Youth Today*, a free, bimonthly newspaper on domestic and international work opportunities for those in the youth-service field; running international conferences on juvenile justice and troubled youth; distributing videos and booklets on issues such as missing children, child safety, and child abuse; and providing technical assistance to youth-service agencies in government relations and fundraising. Interns research and write for *Youth Today*, maintain files on youth issues, respond to public inquiries, and assist with production.

PERKS
Attendance welcome at Capitol Hill hearings; small, friendly office.

FYI
Launched in 1992, *Youth Today* reaches over 44,000 after-school youth-services agencies, from adolescent health clinics to juvenile correctional facilities . . . Articles focus on proven methods for adolescent development, including work training and health.

TO APPLY
Open to undergrads, recent college grads, and grad students. Submit resume, cover letter, writing sample, and three references.

Internship Coordinator
American Youth Work Center
1200 17th Street NW, 4th Floor
Washington, DC 20036
(202) 785-0764
(202) 728-0657 (Fax)
E-mail: HN2759@HandsNet.org

See National Aeronautics and Space Administration

You know you've made it when your picture is snapped by **Yousuf Karsh**, one of the world's most celebrated portrait photographers. Way before he began photographing statesmen, oil mavens, and celebrities, Karsh apprenticed in his late teens under John H. Garo, a noted painter and photographer based in Boston. Said Karsh in an interview with the *Saturday Review*: "My job was not only mixing the chemicals for photography, but also for the drinks."

AMNESTY INTERNATIONAL

SELECTIVITY 🔍🔍
Approximate applicant pool: 100; Interns accepted: 15–17

COMPENSATION Ⓢ
Usually unpaid

LOCATION(S)
Washington, DC (HQ); Egypt; Jordan; Kuwait; Lebanon; Morocco; Syria; Tunisia; United Arab Emirates; West Bank/Gaza; Yemen

FIELD
Public service; Foreign affairs; Educational and cultural exchange

DURATION
8–16 weeks: Summer, Fall, Spring, Winter

DEADLINE(S)
Rolling

SELECTIVITY 🔍🔍🔍🔍
Approximate applicant pool: 400; Interns accepted: 35

COMPENSATION Ⓢ
Varies, depending on internship

LOCATION(S)
Chicago, IL; Culver City and San Francisco, CA; Nederland, CO; New York, NY; Somerville, MA; Washington DC; Atlanta, GA

FIELD
Human rights

DURATION
4 weeks to 1 year

DEADLINE(S)
Rolling

THE WORK
Founded in 1951, AMIDEAST (America-Mideast Educational and Training Services) is a private, nonprofit organization promoting educational and cultural exchange between Americans and the people of the Middle East and North Africa. Its services include free educational advising and testing (TOEFL, SAT, GRE, etc.); publications and videos on teaching, study, and research opportunities in the United States, Middle East, and North Africa; and technical assistance to support the building of Arab educational institutions, health-care facilities, and small businesses. Interns work in Information Services, Resources and Research, Public Relations, and Fundraising and Democratic Development.

PERKS
Attendance welcome at staff meetings and social functions; occasional brown-bag lunches.

FYI
AMIDEAST occasionally offers stipends ($100 per week) for certain projects and departments . . . AMIDEAST also designs and manages training programs in the United States for sponsors of Middle Eastern students, trainees, and visitors; programs include Fulbright Foreign Student Program, Ford Foundation Scholarships, and Yemen Ministry of Oil and Mineral Resources Training Project.

TO APPLY
Open to undergrads, recent college grads, and grad students. International applicants eligible. Submit resume, cover letter, and two recommendations directly to office of interest. Call DC headquarters for contacts in other cities.

Personnel Director
AMIDEAST
1730 M Street, NW. #1100
Washington, DC 20036-4505
(202) 776-9600
(202) 776-7000 (Fax)
E-mail: Personnel@Amideast.org

THE WORK
The world's best-known human rights organization, Amnesty International (AI) works to free prisoners of conscience and abolish torture and capital punishment worldwide. Internship areas include: Casework/Country Actions, Death Penalty, Legal Internship, Press/Video/Country Actions, Press Assistant, Membership, Communications, and Board Liaison.

PERKS
Use of extensive video library and AI reports; brown-bag lunches with guest speakers; attendance welcome at staff meetings.

FYI
Casual dress is the name of the game at Amnesty.

TO APPLY
Open to undergrads, college grads, and grad students. International applicants eligible with prior work authorization. Submit resume and cover letter directly to office of interest. Call relevent office for further information and details. Call or write the national office for internships in New York.

Internship Coordinator
Amnesty International
322 Eighth Avenue
New York, NY 10001
(212) 807-8400
(212) 627-1451 (Fax)

Amtrak®

SELECTIVITY 🔍

Approximate applicant pool: 80; Interns accepted: 35

COMPENSATION 💲 💲 💲

Many positions pay $10–15/hour

LOCATION(S)

Chicago, IL; Los Angeles, CA; Washington, DC

FIELD

Transportation

DURATION

15 weeks: Summer, Fall, Spring

DEADLINE(S)

Rolling

THE WORK

Established by Congress in 1971, Amtrak is the only nationwide passenger railroad, providing 50 million riders per year with service to over 500 cities in 45 states. Interns work in: Public and Government Affairs, Planning, Finance and Administration, Customer Services, Human Resources, and Information Systems, performing such tasks as writing press releases, helping plan staff and special events, and conducting research for special projects.

PERKS

Access to Amtrak fitness facilities; invitations to special events (e.g., train exhibits, service launches); two free round-trip tickets on Amtrak.

FYI

In existence since 1980, the internship program counts among its alumni Amtrak's Communications Director.

TO APPLY

Open to undergrads and grad students. Must receive academic credit (unpaid positions only). International applicants eligible (undergrads only). Submit resume, cover letter, and writing samples (public and government affairs only).

Internship Coordinator
Human Resources Department
Amtrak
800 North Alameda Street
Los Angeles, CA 90012
(213) 683-3516

Internship Coordinator
Human Resources Department
Amtrak
210 South Canal Street, Room 229
Chicago, IL 60606
(312) 655-2402

Internship Coordinator
Human Resources Department
Amtrak
60 Massachusetts Avenue NE
Washington, DC 20002
(202) 906-3860
(202) 906-3865 (Fax)

Amway®

SELECTIVITY 🔍 🔍 🔍

Approximate applicant pool: 400; Interns accepted: 45

COMPENSATION 💲 💲 💲

$475/week for undergrads; $520/week for grad students; round-trip travel

LOCATION(S)

Ada, MI

FIELD

Consumer goods

DURATION

16 weeks: Summer

DEADLINE(S)

January 31

THE WORK

Founded in 1959, Amway is one of the world's largest network-marketing companies, with 12,000 employees worldwide and operations in over 60 countries. Its 2 million disbributors market 400 Amway health, beauty, fitness, consumer, and industrial goods as well as 6,500 brand-name goods and services like MCI Long Distance and Franklin Day Planner in Amway's "Personal Shoppers" catalog. Interns work in Accounting, Data Processing, Engineering, Marketing, Financial Services, Purchasing, Research and Development, and Information Services.

PERKS

Discount on Amway products, lodging at Amway Grand Plaza Hotel, and gas at Amway service station; orientation and monthly employee/intern meetings; access to gym; shuttle service to buildings at the Amway complex.

FYI

Intern projects include testing skin and hair care products, conducting experiments on household cleaners and laundry detergents in pilot plants, writing computer programs in COBOL and CICS, developing chemical methods for raw material analysis, redesigning air and water purification systems, and creating packaging using graphic arts software . . . Seven miles east of Grand Rapids, Ada is a small community, with many opportunities for hiking, boating, swimming, and canoeing.

TO APPLY

Open to college seniors and grad students. Minimum GPA 2.7 (cumulative), 3.0 (major). International applicants studying in the United States are eligible. Submit resume, cover letter, and official transcript.

Sr. Advisor, College Relations (78-1C)
Amway Corporation
7575 Fulton Street East
Ada, MI 49355-0001
(616) 676-6000
(616) 676-5675 (Fax)

An Amway intern using the latest microbiological techniques to evaluate preservative systems.

ANACOSTIA MUSEUM

See Smithsonian Institution

ANASAZI HERITAGE CENTER

ANASAZI HERITAGE CENTER

SELECTIVITY 🔍🔍🔍
Approximate applicant pool: 30; Interns accepted: 4

COMPENSATION 💲💲
$50/week; free housing

LOCATION(S)
Dolores, CO

FIELD
Archaeology; Museums; Native American studies

DURATION
8 weeks: year round

DEADLINE(S)
January 15 (Spring); April 15 (Summer); July 15 (Fall); October 15 (Winter)

THE WORK
Established in 1985, the Anasazi Heritage Center is a museum dedicated to the interpretation and study of cultures from Colorado's Four Corners region. The Center houses almost 3 million records and artifacts from southwest Colorado; it also offers exhibits, films, and special programs on archaeology, public lands, and the Pueblo, Ute, and Navajo cultures. Interns work in Collections Management, Exhibit Development, and Archives Management.

PERKS
Access to exhibits, films, and special programs; housing in a 3-bedroom house; spectacular hilltop views of McPhee Lake, Mesa Verde, Southwest Colorado mountain ranges, and the Four Corners country.

FYI
Dolores is about 45 miles west of Durango, a lively college town. The Center's exhibits allow visitors to grind corn, weave on a loom, use microscopes, and hold artifacts.

TO APPLY
Open to college juniors and seniors, recent grads, college grads, and grad students. Submit resume and cover letter.

Internship Coordinator
Anasazi Heritage Center
27501 Highway 184
Dolores, CO 81323
(970) 882-4811

ANCHORAGE DAILY NEWS

SELECTIVITY 🔍🔍🔍🔍🔍
Approximate applicant pool: 300; Interns accepted: 3

COMPENSATION 💲💲💲
$380/week

LOCATION(S)
Anchorage, AK

FIELD
Newspapers

DURATION
12 weeks: Summer

DEADLINE(S)
January 1

THE WORK
Founded in 1946, the *Anchorage Daily News* has a daily circulation of over 75,000 and is the largest newspaper in Alaska. More than 300 employees work at the paper, which averages nearly 100 pages daily. Interns work in Local News, Features, Photo, Art, or Copy Editing.

PERKS
Mentors; possible roadtrips; sunlight virtually 24 hours a day; terrific fishing and other outdoor opportunities.

FYI
A $1,000 scholarship is available for minority undergrad interns enrolled at the University of Anchorage . . . The Photo Editor has been named the best newspaper photo editor in the country.

TO APPLY
Open to undergrads, recent college grads, and grad students. International applicants eligible. Submit resume, cover letter, and at least a half dozen writing samples/clips; applicants interested in the Photo department must submit a portfolio of about twenty slides. No electronic applications.

Newsroom Intern Coordinator
Anchorage Daily News
P.O. Box 149001
Anchorage, AK 99514-9001
(907) 257-4300
(907) 257-2157 (Fax)
Job Line: (907) 257-4402

THE ANDY WARHOL MUSEUM

SELECTIVITY 🔍🔍🔍
Approximate applicant pool: 50; Interns accepted: 2–3

COMPENSATION
None

LOCATION(S)
Pittsburgh, PA

FIELD
Museums

DURATION
Year-round

DEADLINE(S)
Rolling

THE WORK
Established in 1994 by the Carnegie Institute, The Andy Warhol Museum is the first and only museum devoted exclusively to the late Andy Warhol, one of the most influential American artists of the twentieth century. Displaying everything from Warhol's famous silkscreens of Marilyn Monroe and Campbell's soup cans to rare Warhol-produced films and celebrity photographs, the Museum contains an awesome variety of drawings, prints, paintings, and sculpture as well as extensive archives. Interns work in Curatorial, Administration, Education, Media Relations, Museum Shop, Archives, Director's Office, Development, and Film and Video.

PERKS
Attendance welcome at museum seminars and educational events; 20 percent discount in all gift shops of the Carnegie Institute; free admission to other museums of the Carnegie Institute.

FYI
The Museum's vast collection of art and archives make it the most comprehensive single-artist museum in the world . . . Former interns give high ratings to the Museum's cafeteria.

TO APPLY
Open to undergrads, recent grads, college grads, and grad students. International applicants eligible. Send resume and cover letter..

Rachel Baron
Administrative Assistant
The Andy Warhol Museum
117 Sandusky Street
Pittsburgh, PA 15212

ANGEL RECORDS

See EMI Records Group North America

ANHEUSER-BUSCH

SELECTIVITY 🔍🔍🔍🔍🔍
Approximate applicant pool: 700; Interns accepted: 20–25

COMPENSATION 💲💲💲
Est.: $400–$500/week for undergrads; Est.: $450–$600/week for grad students

LOCATION(S)
St. Louis, MO

FIELD
Consumer goods (beer and foods)

DURATION
Intern: 12 weeks, Summer; Co-op: one or two 5- to 8-month sessions; June/August–December or January– June/August

DEADLINE(S)
Intern: Rolling; Co-op: January start date (September 1); June or August start date (February 1)

THE WORK
Founded in 1852, Anheuser-Busch (A-B) is the world's largest beer company, with 16 subsidiaries, 43,000 employees, and over $13 billion in sales annually. In addition to producing, marketing, and distributing such beers and beverages as Budweiser, Bud Light, Bud Dry, King Cobra, Michelob, and O'Doul's, A-B manufactures such foods as Eagle chips, IronKids bread, and Cape Cod popcorn; owns and operates entertainment properties like the St. Louis Cardinals baseball team and Sea World (see separate entry); produces metal cans; and develops real estate. Summer interns (8–15) work in Corporate Research and Development, Budget Analysis, and Sales Analysis. Ten co-op interns work in Corporate Engineering, which coordinates the design and construction of A-B properties.

PERKS
Mentors; attendance welcome at staff meetings; discount on A-B paraphernalia.

FYI
The internship coordinator writes: "Anheuser-Busch does not have a formal internship program and does not wish to give the impression that we do . . . [We provide internships] on an as-needed basis.". . . 44 percent of all beer sold in the United States is made by A-B.

TO APPLY
Internship: open to college juniors and seniors as well as grad students; must be majoring in chemistry, biology, or computer science. Co-op: open to college juniors and seniors; must be majoring in electrical, mechanical, plant, construction, chemical, or environmental engineering. Submit resume and cover letter.

Internship or Co-op Program
Employment Services
Anheuser-Busch Companies
One Busch Place
St. Louis, MO 63118
(314) 577-2000

ANOTHER WORLD

See Procter and Gamble Productions

THE ANTARCTICA PROJECT

SELECTIVITY 🔍 🔍
Approximate applicant pool: 100; Interns accepted: 20

COMPENSATION 💲
None

LOCATION(S)
Washington, DC

FIELD
Environment

DURATION
12–15 weeks: Summer, Fall, Spring

DEADLINE(S)
Rolling

THE WORK
Founded in 1982, The Antarctica Project (TAP) is the world's only conservation organization dedicated exclusively to protecting the natural resources of Antarctica and the Southern Ocean. Working with members and governments worldwide, TAP has lobbied to retain Antarctica as the planet's only nuclear-free continent, supported scientific research in global warming and ozone depletion, campaigned successfully to ban Antarctic mining and oil drilling, and helped establish the Southern Ocean Whale Sanctuary. Assisting TAP's Director, interns conduct research, write fact sheets, and attend conferences.

PERKS
Attendance welcome at congressional hearings; free Antarctica poster.

FYI
The waters surrounding Antarctica absorb more carbon dioxide from the atmosphere than all of the earth's rainforests combined . . . Antarctica's ecosystem supports the world's largest populations of penguins, albatrosses, petrels, seals, and great whales.

TO APPLY
Open to college juniors and seniors, recent grads, and grad students. Minimum GPA: 3.0. International applicants eligible. Submit resume, cover letter, and one three-page writing sample.

Internship Coordinator
The Antarctica Project
P.O. Box 76920
Washington, DC 20013
(202) 234-2480
(202) 234-2482 (Fax)
E-mail: antarctica@igc.apc.org

APERTURE FOUNDATION

SELECTIVITY 🔍 🔍 🔍 🔍 🔍
Approximate applicant pool: 500; Interns accepted: 20

COMPENSATION 💲 💲
$250/month

LOCATION(S)
New York, NY and Millerton, NY

FIELD
Photography; Publication

DURATION
6 months minimum

DEADLINE(S)
None

THE WORK
The Aperture Foundation is a not-for-profit organization devoted to photography and the visual arts. Its mission is to promote photography as one of the most powerful forms of human expression and to further the unique capabilities of photography to illuminate important social, environmental, and cultural issues. Positions are available in the following departments: Editorial, Production, Development, Circulation, Marketing, Publicity, Foreign Rights, Director's Office, Burden Gallery, Traveling Exhibition, and Paul Strand Archive, Image Bank, Information Technology/Systems.

PERKS
Access to darkroom; discount on books; limited edition print upon completion of the internship.

FYI
The Aperture publishes around 20 books a year as well as the magazine *Aperture*, a quarterly. Aperture's Burden Gallery hosts four shows a year and organizes traveling exhibitions both in the United States and internationally.

TO APPLY
Open to college students and grads. International applicants eligible. Submit resume and cover letter to:

Work-Scholar Coordinator
Aperture Foundation
20 East 23 Street
New York, NY 10010-4463
(212) 505-5555, x336
(212) 475-8790 (Fax)
E-mail: mdecsey@aperture.org

BUSYWORK. GRUNTWORK.
SLAVE LABOR.
BABYSITTING MR. COFFEE.
PHOTOCOPY PURGATORY.

It has many names, but we all know what it is—menial, mind-numbing work that make some internships a real drag. But there's a way of knowing what to expect before you start work. Consult **The Busywork Meter**, the only device ever created to reveal how much slave labor is required at the nation's best internships. Guaranteed to be accurate within 500 photocopies, 10 pots of coffee, or 400 envelope stuffings. Only in *The Best 106 Internships* by The Internship Informants—Mark Oldman and Samer Hamadeh (Princeton Review Books/Random House).

SELECTIVITY 🔍🔍🔍🔍🔍
Approximate applicant pool: 2,000; Interns accepted: 100-200

COMPENSATION 💲💲💲💲
$600–$1,100/week depending on education and work experience; round-trip travel

LOCATION(S)
Santa Clara Valley, CA

FIELD
Computers; Servers; Peripheral; Software; Personal digital assistants

DURATION
12 weeks: Summer

DEADLINE(S)
Rolling

THE WORK
In 1976, Steven Jobs and Stephen Wozniak founded Apple Computer, Inc. to produce affordable, innovative computers. Apple revolutionized the home computing industry in 1984 with the introduction of the Macintosh, and became one of the era's legends—and then, one of its horror shows. Poor management, failed products, and a certain little company in Redmond, Washington have plagued Apple throughout the 90s, leading it to the brink of extinction several times. Lately, though, the company has once again come out kicking, with sales of its new G3 line and its OS8 operating system taking off and its "Think Different" ad campaign generating media buzz. Internships exist in both technical and nontechnical positions in Hardware, Software, Sales & Marketing, Advanced Technology, and Administration.

PERKS
Stunning offices; fitness center; intern workshops; picnic lunches; progressive spirit.

FYI
Business trips for interns are possible. Destination for some have included Las Vegas, Boston, and San Francisco. Many interns participate in company intramural sports.

TO APPLY
Open to undergrads and grad students. International applicants eligible. Submit resume and cover letter.

Apple Computer, Inc.
Internship Program
1 Infinite Loop, MS 75-2HR
Cupertino, CA 95014
(800) 331-4496
(408) 974-5691 (Fax)
www.apple.com

SELECTIVITY 🔍
Approximate applicant pool: 20; Interns accepted: 6–8

COMPENSATION 💲💲
$280/week

LOCATION(S)
Washington, DC

FIELD
Public policy

DURATION
10–12 weeks: Summer, Fall, Spring

DEADLINE(S)
Rolling

THE WORK
A nonprofit, bipartisan organization, the Arab American Institute (AAI) was founded in 1985 "to nurture and encourage the direct participation of Arab Americans in political and civic life in the United States." The organization plans political events, mobilizes the Arab-American vote, publishes two newsletters, briefs foreign visitors, and develops election resources. Interns work in Organizing and Public Affairs.

PERKS
Intern meeting with AAI President and Director; welcome at meetings and parties hosting visiting dignitaries.

FYI
AAI President Dr. James Zogby hosts *A Capital View*, a weekly television talk show in English, broadcast on the Arab Network of America.

TO APPLY
Open to undergrads. International applicants eligible. Submit resume and cover letter.

Internship Coordinator
Arab American Institute
918 16th Street NW, #601
Washington, DC 20006
(202) 429-9210
(202) 429-9214 (Fax)

SELECTIVITY 🔍🔍🔍
Approximate applicant pool: 75–100; Interns accepted: 10

COMPENSATION 💲
Daily transportation stipend

LOCATION(S)
New York, NY

FIELD
Film; Television

DURATION
6–12 weeks: ongoing

DEADLINE(S)
Rolling

THE WORK

Founded in 1979, Archive Films/Photos is a leading international supplier of film and photo stock footage for television shows, news broadcasts, documentaries, commercials, films, and educational videos. Archive's collections date back to 1890 and include news footage on virtually every twentieth-century famous event and personality, documentaries, and over 10,000 films. Departments accepting interns include: Film and Photo Research, Film Sales, Marketing, and Acquisitions/Duplication.

PERKS

Occasional luncheons with department heads; training on complex film and video equipment.

FYI

Intern duties include preparing tape retransfers to NTSC, PAL, and VHS formats, repairing and splicing 35mm and 16mm original film, and searching Archive's computer database to answer client questions.

TO APPLY

Open to high school grads, undergrads, recent college grads, college grads, and grad students. International applicants eligible. Submit resume and cover letter.

Internship Coordinator
Archive Films
530 West 25th Street
New York, NY 10001
(212) 645-2137 (Fax)

ARDEN THEATRE COMPANY

SELECTIVITY 🔍🔍🔍
Approximate applicant pool: 75; Interns accepted: 10

COMPENSATION 💲
Limited stipend for some production internships

LOCATION(S)
Philadelphia, PA

FIELD
Theater

DURATION
12–45 weeks; minimum 15 hours/week; some flexible schedules

DEADLINE(S)
Rolling

THE WORK

WCHS-TV and WVAH-TV are two of the 61 television stations owned or operated by Sinclair Broadcast Group Inc. We produce 24 hours of news a week on our two ABC and FOX affiliate channels. Interns get a broad base of experience from working the assignment desk to working with individual "show" producers to assisting video tape editors to working with sports and weather. Basic work includes research for producers and reporters. It also includes taking satellite feeds and doing other basic news gathering research in this union shop.

PERKS

Free tickets to all performances; free tickets to local theaters.

FYI

For undergrads and college grads, ATC offers the Arden Professional Apprentice Program, in which apprentices work at the theater for the entire season (August through June) . . . Apprentices participate in every department of the theater, and receive $250 per week plus health and dental benefits.

TO APPLY

Open to high school students, high school grads, undergrads, recent college grads, college grads, and grad students. International applicants eligible. Submit letter and resume.

Internship Coordinator
Arden Theatre Company
40 N. 2nd Street
Philadelphia, PA 19106
(215) 992-8900 ext. 30
(215) 992-7011 (Fax)

ARENA STAGE

SELECTIVITY 🔍🔍🔍
Approximate applicant pool: 300; Interns accepted: 15–25

COMPENSATION 💲
$120/week

LOCATION(S)
Washington, DC

FIELD
Theater

DURATION
16–44 weeks (though some internships follow a production cycle of 6–12 weeks): Summer, Fall, Spring, Seasonal

DEADLINE(S)
Summer: March 1 (Administrative, Literary Management, Living Stage only); Fall, Seasonal: May 1; Spring: October 1

THE WORK

Founded in 1950, Arena is an internationally respected resident theater. Its three-theater complex houses the 800-seat Arena, the 500-seat Kreeger Theater, and the 150-seat Old Vat Room, as well as various shops and offices. Interns work in Accessibility, Artistic Administration, Arts in Education, Audience Enrichment Programs, Casting/Production, Communications/Marketing/Media Relations, Costumes, Development/Fundraising, Directing, Graphic Design, Operations/House Management, Executive Director, Finance/Personnel, Information Systems, Lighting, Literary Management, Properties, Set Construction/Paints, Sound, Stage Management, Sales Office and in production or administration with Living Stage (our social outreach theater).

PERKS

Monthly intern seminars covering an array of theater topics; guest speakers; monthly luncheon; field trips; free tickets to all performances; free tickets to local theaters. In existence since 1959, the internship program counts among its alumni the theater's former Artistic Director and Director in Residence, guest directors,

EXCLUSIVE INTERVIEW WITH JEAN FUGETT, JR.

A former All-Pro tight-end for the Dallas Cowboys and Washington Redskins, Jean Fugett, Jr. is the founder and CEO of IVR Research & Development, senior partner at his law firm Fugett & Associates, former chairman and CEO of TLC Beatrice International Food Company, journalist, and former sports announcer. During his years at Amherst College, from which he graduated in 1972, and in the NFL, he served three internships—the Baltimore Orioles, The Baltimore Sun, and The Washington Post.

The Internship Informants: What did you do as an intern for the Orioles?
Fugett: I was there in [1970]. I split my responsibilities between Public Relations and the Farm Department. For the Farm Department, I kept track of all the statistics of the minor-league teams, which would be released on a weekly basis. I would compile them, keep them posted in the department, and maintain the files—it was a lot of paper. This was pre-computer, so I did it manually. Earl Weaver [the Orioles coach at the time] was one of the first to keep statistics of his hitters against opposing pitchers.... He wanted to know who hit well against a certain pitcher.

The Internship Informants: This work landed you in *Sports Illustrated*. How did that happen?
Fugett: I went back to college not finishing all the stats for the year. But it wasn't a top priority because the baseball schedule has each team finishing the season with the other teams in its division. I was behind on the Western Division, but it wasn't important until next year, so I promised [Weaver] that I would finish it later and took it with me. Of course I got to college, threw it in the closet, and forgot about it. Well, it turned out the Orioles ended up in the World Series [against Cincinnati] facing a pitcher who had, at the end of the season, been traded from the Western Division to Cincinnati. So [Weaver] needed to know who had hit well against this pitcher. I had to go into my closet and dig out the stats. I gave him the name of the player [who had hit well against this guy]—Chico Salmon. So [Salmon] gets to pinch hit; he hits a single and then scores the winning run. And [*Sports Illustrated*] said Earl Weaver's secret weapon was a little, brainy kid at Amherst.

The Internship Informants: Did you hang out much that summer with your friend David Eisenhower, who was interning for the Washington Senators?
Fugett: Sure. We were in Washington. He came up one time when the Senators were playing [the Orioles], and I bought him some crab cakes from the Orioles press box. Then when [the Orioles] played Washington, I got to go to the White House after that game—a little better than the Orioles press box [Eisenhower's father-in-law is the late President Nixon].

The Internship Informants: How did you come to do the newspaper internships?
Fugett: I was always interested in journalism, and I was vice chairman of Amherst's student newspaper.

The Internship Informants: How did you juggle classes, internships, and football?
Fugett: I went to a Division III school, so it really wasn't juggling any more than someone in the Glee Club. I would maybe be a little more bruised physically than they were, but as far as the time commitment, believe it or not it was very similar.

The Internship Informants: But for Division I athletes, it would be difficult to manage internships with practice. Nonetheless, would you advise athletes to intern?
Fugett: I advise people in sports to do something that's not sports-related. The biggest problem that athletes have is that sports have become a year-round commitment, whereas that wasn't the case when I was playing. Anyone who is serious about sports from high school on would want to stay in shape and stay close to their sport 365 days a year. But they need to broaden their experience background because the chances are that they won't eventually end up doing something in their sport. So to the extent that they have other experiences via internships or more education, it will help them.

The Internship Informants: You certainly took your own advice to heart, even in the NFL. Not only did you enroll in law school, you interned at *The Washington Post*.
Fugett: Yeah, that's right. While I was in Washington [in 1976], the year before I signed with the Redskins, I did the *Post* internship ... It was specially arranged during the off-season, from February to June, right after I played in Super Bowl X [which the Cowboys lost]. That year I also started studying law at Georgetown, part-time at night.

The Internship Informants: Did you yearn as a football player to get back into journalism?
Fugett: When I was in Dallas, I did a radio show, and I was also a columnist in the *Dallas Cowboy Weekly*. So I stayed in journalism even as a football player. As far as the *Post* is concerned, I simply grabbed an opportunity to write for one of the nation's great newspapers and the chance to work for Ben Bradlee and Bob Woodward.... And I didn't work in sports. I worked in the News department.

The Internship Informants: Even with all the internships that you did, is there somewhere you would intern now if you could?
Fugett: I would love to go back to Amherst College and be an intern professor. Being able to work with young, inquisitve minds in an academic and intellectual environment would be very stimulating to me.

Casting Director, Administrative Director, Business Manager, Technical Director, Associate Director of I.S., Production Coordinator, Publications Manager, Marketing Associate, and the Fellows and Intern Program Coordinator.

FYI
Arena Stage also runs the Allen Lee Hughes Fellows Program, a season-long theater apprenticeship for minority theater professionals.

TO APPLY
Open to undergrads, college grads, grad students, and career changers. International applicants eligible, if they have a visa. Write for brochure/application.

Internship Coordinator
Arena Stage
1101 Sixth Street, SW
Washington, DC 20024
(202) 554-9066
(202) 488-4056 (Fax)
Email: lrobinson@arenastage.org
www.arenastage.org

ARGONNE NATIONAL LABORATORY

SELECTIVITY
Approximate applicant pool: 1,200; Interns accepted: 175

COMPENSATION
$250/week; free housing; round-trip travel

LOCATION(S)
Argonne, IL

FIELD
Science; Engineering research

DURATION
11–15 weeks: Summer, Fall, Spring

DEADLINE(S)
Summer: February 1; Fall: March 15; Spring: October 20

THE GREAT COVER LETTER

A resume is a wonderful tool to show employers just what you've done so far—but only if they bother to read it.

Many employers admit that an unsolicited resume *usually* goes straight into the garbage. After all, a resume by itself has no context. "What job is this person interested in? Who recommended her? I wonder what's for lunch?"—and before you know it, "swishhhh," it's in the circular file. Ah, but I said *usually*. There is one way to get that resume read. One way to open doors. One way to communicate with someone you've never met and with whom you have no connection:

A Great Letter.

You were expecting something more profound? Believe me, this is plenty profound. For one thing, letter-writing is a dying art. A typical boss may receive 50 e-mails a day, even more phone calls, but an actual letter? It's getting rare.

I cannot begin to tell you how important a Great Letter can be. It can change everything. It can make mediocre grades superfluous. It can make irrelevant work experience seem relevant. It can get you in to see someone who is impossible to see. The Great Letter is the beginning of everything.

☞ What makes a Great Letter Great?

All employers are looking for *passion*. A Great Letter conveys your passion to work for them. It should also demonstrate your intelligence, with just a touch of humor thrown in for good measure. If you can combine these three elements in a one-page letter, you are halfway in the door already.

Like any cover letter, a Great Letter should be laid out in business format, single spaced, with a line between each paragraph. It should never exceed one page, never contain a typo, and never be mass-produced. While you may be able to use some of the ideas again, the important point is that *this* letter could only have been written to this one prospective employer about *this* one job.

Thus, you may not be able to write a Great Letter to every employer. Why? Simply because you won't feel passionate about every job possibility, and *you can't fake passion*. They'll know if you try.

☞ So What Happens When I Can't Write A Great Letter?

You write a good one. A good letter is the next best thing. It conveys all the same things: your interest in the job, a brief summary of your credentials, an understanding of the industry. In fact, you may not even know when you've written a good letter and when you've written a Great Letter. But you'll find out when the phone rings.

Source: Geoff Martz, author of *How to Survive Without Your Parent's Money* (Princeton Review Books/Random House), which provides terrific advice for college students entering the "real world," including a section on how to write an effective cover letter.

THE WORK

Chartered in 1946 as a research facility of the US Department of Energy (see separate entry), Argonne National Laboratory (ANL) is involved in studies of linear accelerators, nuclear reactors, medical hazards of energy, fuel cells, superconductors, climate, and other energy-related areas. Interns (some under the auspices of Argonne's Co-op program) do basic research in physical and life sciences, math, computer science, and all areas of engineering (including architecture) as well as applied research in coal, conservation, fission, fusion, and environmental technology.

PERKS

Seminars in science and engineering; opportunity to take Argonne university-level courses for credit; field trips to the Planetarium, Art Institute of Chicago, and other cultural sites.

FYI

Some interns publish their research and/or are selected for an expense-paid trip to present their research at the annual undergrad conference of the National Council on Undergraduate Research.

TO APPLY

Open to college juniors and seniors as well as recent college grads (within one year of graduation) and first-year grad students. ANL's co-op program is open to students who have completed at least four semesters of study. Minimum GPA: 3.0. Write for application.

Student Research Programs
Division of Educational Programs
Argonne National Laboratory
Argonne, IL 60439-4845
(630) 252-4495
(630) 252-3193 (Fax)

ARISTA RECORDS

See Bertelsmann Music Group

THE ARIZONA REPUBLIC

See Central Newspapers/The Indianapolis News

The next time you slide on a pair of Calvins, consider this: after graduating from the Fashion Institute of Technology in 1962, the great **Calvin Klein** launched his career with an apprenticeship, working in New York's garment district with garment designer Dan Millstein.

ARMS CONTROL ASSOCIATION

SELECTIVITY 🔍 🔍 🔍 🔍
Approximate applicant pool: 200; Interns accepted: 8–10

COMPENSATION 💲
$25/week and daily commuting expenses

LOCATION(S)
Washington, DC

FIELD
Foreign affairs; International arms control policy; National security policy

DURATION
12 weeks: Summer, Fall, Spring

DEADLINE(S)
Summer: mid-May; Fall: mid-August; Spring: mid-December

THE WORK

The Arms Control Association (ACA) is a nonprofit, nonpartisan organization dedicated to increasing public understanding of the contribution arms control can make to national security. Interns help research and write about national security, assist in preparing and editing ACA's monthly journal *Arms Control Today*, and monitor activity on Capitol Hill.

PERKS

Attendance welcome at press conferences; attendance welcome at Board of Directors luncheons; occasional trips to meetings and hearings on Capitol Hill.

FYI

Alumni of the intern program typically go on to graduate school, jobs on Capitol Hill and the Executive Branch, or positions at defense contractor organizations . . . Presidential advisor George Stephanopoulos was an intern at ACA before joining the White House. . . The intern coordinator says: "Initiative is rewarded with substantive assignments and strong recommendations from the staff—a boon for job placement and graduate school admissions, as ACA has an excellent reputation in the governmental and educational fields of foreign affairs."

TO APPLY

Open to undergrads, recent college grads, and grad students. Submit a resume, a cover letter, and a three- to five-page writing sample.

Internship Coordinator
The Arms Control Association
1726 M Street NW
Suite 201
Washington, DC 20036
(202) 463-8270
(202) 463-8273 (Fax)

"I believe it is impossible for students to understand how the US government works on foreign affairs these days without some time in Washington, "on the firing line." With its focus on international security policy, on experts and reporters covering foreign affairs and on government officials responsible for arms control, **ACA** is an excellent place to learn how Washington works."

—George Bunn
Consulting Professor
Institute of International Studies,
Stanford University

ARTHRITIS FOUNDATION
NORTHERN CALIFORNIA CHAPTER

ARTHRITIS FOUNDATION®

SELECTIVITY 🔍🔍🔍
Approximate applicant pool: 80; Interns accepted: 7 or 8

COMPENSATION 💲💲
$1,500 stipend for high school juniors and seniors; $2,000 stipend for undergrads and recent college grads

LOCATION(S)
Throughout Northern California

FIELD
Medical research

DURATION
8 weeks: Summer (June 1–September 15)

DEADLINE(S)
Mid-February

WORK
Since 1948, the Arthritis Foundation (AF) has been supporting research to find a cure for arthritis and to improve the quality of life for people with arthritis, a disease that affects 40 million Americans. Interns work under the auspices of the George Hagan Memorial Summer Science Fellowship Program in various Bay Area labs (e.g., Stanford, UCSF) under the supervision of scientists.

PERKS
Presentation of final paper to Board of Directors; interns profiled in foundation's local newsletter, *Joint Efforts*.

FYI
The program has been in existence since 1989, but funding remains tenuous from year to year . . . An intern once appeared on local television during AF's international telethon.

TO APPLY
Open to high school students (at least 17 years old by June 1) and college undergrads. Must reside or study in California. International applicants eligible. Write for application.

Internship Coordinator
Arthritis Foundation
657 Mission Street, Suite 603
San Francisco, CA 94105
(800) 464-6240 or (415) 356-1230

ARTHUR ANDERSEN

ARTHUR ANDERSEN
ARTHUR ANDERSEN & CO, SC

SELECTIVITY 🔍🔍🔍
Approximate applicant pool: 5,772; Interns accepted: 1–465

COMPENSATION 💲💲💲
$2,500-$3,500/week on average

LOCATION(S)
Most offices have programs nationwide

FIELD
Assurance and Business Advisory; Economic and Financial

DURATION
10–12 weeks: Summer, Winter

DEADLINE(S)
Summer: February 15; Winter: October 31

"Mr. Andrews, I'm not having any fun."

THE WORK

Established in 1913, the Arthur Andersen Worldwide Organization has grown to be the world's largest professional services company with more than 104,00 personnel in more than 79 countries. Among the Big Six accounting firms, Arthur Andersen is the largest both in the United States and worldwide. The internship program offers entry-level positions in both Audit & Business Advisory Services and Tax & Business Advisory Services.

PERKS

Exceptional training course; mentors; professional atmosphere. Opportunity to network with people worldwide.

FYI

The program has been running since 1950 . . . interns are trained at Arthur Andersen's Center for Professional Education or at the office. . . Says the internship coordinator: "The office's goal . . . is to replicate the same experiences and situations that a new hire would have during their first year."

TO APPLY

Open to college juniors and seniors. Must have minimum of 12 units of accounting. International applicants eligible. Submit resume and cover letter to your office of interest. A list of offices can be found on the website.

Arthur Andersen
Internship Program
(312) 580-0069
www.arthurandersen.com/offices/index.htm

ARTISTS SPACE

ARTISTS SPACE

SELECTIVITY   🔍🔍🔍
Approximate applicant pool: 160; Interns accepted: 30

COMPENSATION   Ⓢ
None

LOCATION(S)
New York, NY

FIELD
Museums/Galleries/Art Institutions

DURATION
2–6 months; At least 16 hours per week

DEADLINE(S)
Rolling

THE WORK

Founded in 1973, Artists Space is a nonprofit institution supporting contemporary art and artists in fine art, video, performance, architecture, and design. In addition to providing exhibition space for new art and artists, the organization maintains a computerized slide file of 2,500 contemporary artists for artists, curators, and the public. Internships focus on the operations and/or curatorial aspects of gallery work. There is also a computer-oriented internship in the slide file. More information is available at www.artistsspace.org.

PERKS

Invitations to Artists Space openings and events; location in Manhattan's chic, art-oriented SoHo district; invitations to events at nearby galleries; complimentary books, catalogs, and t-shirts. Interns have the opportunity to participate in intern programming as well as to undertake long-term and independent projects with curatorial themes.

FYI

In existence since 1973, the internship program counts among its alumni: the former director of Artists Space, a curator at the Metropolitan Museum of Modern Art, and the director of the UCLA/Hammer Museum.

TO APPLY

Open to undergrads, recent college grads, college grads, and grad students. International applicants eligible. Submit resume and cover letter.

Internship Coordinator
Artists Space
38 Greene Street, 3rd Floor
New York, NY 10013
(212) 226-3970
(212) 966-1434 (Fax)

THE ARTS & EDUCATIONAL COUNCIL OF GREATER ST. LOUIS

SELECTIVITY   🔍
Approximate applicant pool: 5; Interns accepted: 1

COMPENSATION   Ⓢ
None

LOCATION(S)
St. Louis, MO

FIELD
Fundraising/Public Relations/Marketing

DURATION
6 weeks or more ongoing

DEADLINE(S)
Rolling

THE WORK

Established in 1963, The Arts & Education Council of Greater St. Louis is a nonprofit fundraising organization for arts, cultural, and arts education organizations in the St. Louis area. Seeking funding through corporations, workplace giving campaigns, and private donors, the Council provides annual operating support to nine principal beneficiaries and over 160 grants-pool members. Interns work on a variety of projects.

PERKS

Free tickets to arts performances; attendance welcome at staff meetings.

FYI

The Council's funded organizations are Craft Alliance, Dance St. Louis, KETC-TV/Channel 9, Opera Theatre of St. Louis, St. Louis Black Repertory Company, St. Louis School Partnership Program, St. Louis Symphony Community Music School, and Young Audiences of St. Louis.

TO APPLY

Open to undergrads, recent college grads, and grad students. International applicants eligible. Submit resume and cover letter.

Internship Coordinator
The Arts & Education Council of Greater St. Louis
3526 Washington Avenue
St. Louis, MO 63103
(314) 535-3600
(314) 535-3606 (Fax)

AS THE WORLD TURNS

See Procter & Gamble Productions

ASHOKA: INNOVATORS FOR THE PUBLIC

SELECTIVITY
Approximate applicant pool: 50; Interns accepted: 6–8

COMPENSATION S
None

LOCATION(S)
Arlington, VA

FIELD
International nonprofit; Public entrepreneurial ASSN

DURATION
Summer, Fall, Spring

DEADLINE(S)
Flexible

THE WORK

Ashoka is an international, nonprofit organization that helps find and invest in social entrepreneurs in Asia, Latin America, Africa, and East and Central Europe. Social entrepreneurs are people whose creativity and drive open up major possibilities in various fields of human need and drive social change. We invest in social entrepreneurs because we believe that is the most leveraged way to promote positive social change. Ashoka has formed an association of social entrepreneurs that we call a "Fellowship." We invest in our "Fellows" financially through a living stipend and professionally through Ashoka's value-added services and global network of social entrepreneurs. Ashoka Fellows work in serving the public in many areas including health, environment, education, legal rights, women's and children's issues, and microenterprise, among others. Currently, more than 1,000 social entrepreneurs are making lasting impacts in their fields and are earning reputations as pioneers at regional, national, and international levels.

PERKS

Brown-bag luncheons with Fellows; attendance welcome at seminars and workshops.

FYI

Overseas experience and proficiency in any of the following languages are desirable, but not required: Spanish, French, Portuguese, Bahasa Indonesian, Thai, Nepali, Bengali, Polish, and Hungarian.

TO APPLY

Open to undergrads, recent college grads, and grad students. International applicants eligible. Submit resume, cover letter, and writing samples (if available). Include information on background, international travel and/or work, languages (and level of proficiency), interests, experience, etc.

Internship Coordinator
ASHOKA: Innovators for the Public
1700 North Moore Street, Suite 1920
Arlington, VA 22209-1903
(703) 527-8300
Website: www.ashoka.org

ASIAN AMERICAN ARTS CENTRE

SELECTIVITY
Approximate applicant pool: 70; Interns accepted: 15

COMPENSATION S
None

LOCATION(S)
New York, NY

FIELD
Performing Arts

DURATION
12 weeks: Summer, Fall, Spring

DEADLINE(S)
Rolling

THE WORK

Established in 1974, the Asian American Arts Centre sponsors exhibitions in visual arts, folk arts, contemporary dance, video documentation, and other performing arts. Situated in New York's Chinatown, the Arts Centre maintains the nation's largest archive of documents and slides on Asian-American artists. Interns organize and update the archives, conduct research on Asian-American artists, plan and supervise exhibitions, work on publications and video documentation, and carry out administrative work.

PERKS

Attendance welcome at all exhibition openings; opportunity to "meet artists."

FYI

The internship coordinator advises: "Demonstrate a seriousness of purpose in your application. We want applicants who are interested in Asian-American art and who want to learn how a community organization operates."

TO APPLY

Open to high school students, high school grads, undergrads, recent college grads, college grads, and grad students. International applicants eligible. Submit resume, cover letter, and any samples of art work or writing.

Internship Coordinator
Asian American Arts Centre
26 Bowery Street, 3rd Floor
New York, NY 10013
(212) 238-2154
(212) 766-1287 (Fax)

Asian American Journalists Association

SELECTIVITY 🔍
Approximate applicant pool: 25; Interns accepted: 1–2

COMPENSATION 💲
None

LOCATION(S)
San Francisco, CA

FIELD
Journalism; Nonprofit

DURATION
8–16 weeks: Summer, Fall, Spring

DEADLINE(S)
Rolling

THE WORK
Founded in 1981, the Asian American Journalists Association (AAJA) is a nonprofit organization seeking to promote and provide support for Asian-American journalists. With 17 chapters across the United States, AAJA is responsible for educational programs, scholarships and fellowships, a newsletter, and a national convention. Interns assist staff in coordinating scholarships and fellowships, job services, and mentor programs.

PERKS
Access to job services information; opportunity to volunteer at local events (scholarship fundraisers, etc.); possible travel to national convention in August.

FYI
Says the internship coordinator: "We are a small organization, but we have high visibility and are well respected by professionals. Interning here often leads to good employment opportunities at other nonprofits, journalism organizations, and in Asian-American communities."

TO APPLY
Open to undergrads, recent college grads, college grads, and grad students. International applicants eligible. Submit resume and cover letter.

Internship Coordinator
Asian American Journalists Association
1182 Market Street, Suite 320
San Francisco, CA 94102
(415) 346-2051
(415) 346-6343 (Fax)

During the summer before his senior year at Notre Dame, **Phil Donahue** worked as a gofer for South Bend's WNDU-TV. These days he has not only hosted his own award-winning talk show, but is married to none other than "That Girl," Marlo Thomas.

Tips for Snagging 'Ships

1. **Fantasize.** Think about careers that fire your passion, regardless of whether you know of internships in those fields. Advertising? Law? Comic Books? Space travel?

2. **Scrap.** Research your career possibilities. Consult every possible resource—family connections, college alumni, career centers, classmates, professors, and the library. Once you've identified companies, call and ask for an internship application.

3. **Don't procrastinate.** Check deadlines (some hit as early as November, others as late as May, and many have rolling deadlines). Early applications increase your chances of securing an internship.

4. **Materialize.** Get a range of application materials ready—resume, cover letter, recommendations, transcripts, samples of your work.

5. **Customize.** Write a special cover letter for each application. Organizations want to know why you are interested in them. Customize your resume, too.

6. **Personalize.** If possible, visit the internship sites for an interview, or make a personal call to the internship coordinator. Your enthusiasm will show.

7. **Energize.** Passion and persistence pay off. Follow up your cover letters with phone calls and your interviews with thank you notes.

8. **It's never too late.** Most organizations offer internships throughout the year. If you've missed a deadline, apply now for next year, and ask to be considered if something opens up sooner. And don't be discouraged by your age: internships are available for high school, college, and grad students as well as recent graduates—even career changers.

SELECTIVITY
Approximate application pool: 150; Interns accepted: 12

COMPENSATION
$125/week plus housing

LOCATION(S)
Aspen, CO

FIELD
Environment/nature

DURATION
12 weeks: early June to early September

DEADLINE(S)
March 1

THE WORK
The Aspen Center for Environmental Studies (ACES) is a private nonprofit environmental learning center located within the 25-acre Hallam Lake nature preserve, immediately adjacent to the City of Aspen. Our mission is to inspire a life-long commitment to the preservation of the natural world by educating for environmental stewardship, conserving and restoring the balance of natural communities, and advancing the ethic that the earth must be respected and nurtured. Interns' responsibilities include almost every aspect of operating the center; teaching environmental education programs, maintaining trails, caring for resident birds of prey, and leading off-site interpretive hikes at the Maroon Bells, Snowmass, and on top of Aspen Mountain.

PERKS
Housing provided; participation in Naturalist Field School course; mountain surroundings.

FYI
The city of Aspen provides interns with endless activities and cultural events, while the surrounding Wilderness Areas offer plenty of peace and quiet.

TO APPLY
Open to college juniors, seniors, recent college grads, and grad students. International applicants encouraged. Write, call, or e-mail for application. Or obtain the application from our website: www.aspen.com/aces.

Aspen Center for Environmental Studies
Internship Coordinator
100 Puppy Smith Street
Aspen, CO 81611
(970) 925-5756
(970) 925-4819 (Fax)
E-mail: acesone@rof.net

AMERICAN SLAVIC STUDENT INTERNSHIP
SERVICE AND TRAINING CORPORATION

SELECTIVITY
Approximate applicant pool: 60–75; Interns accepted: 50

COMPENSATION
$1,800 (1 month); $6,800 (1 year) fee covering airfare, visa fees, housing, and monthly food stipend

LOCATION(S)
Russia

FIELD
Advertising; Banking; Journalism; Publishing; Sports; Tourism

DURATION
1 month–1 year: ongoing

DEADLINE(S)
Rolling

THE WORK
Founded in 1992, ASSIST (the American Slavic Student Internship Service and Training Corp.) is a clearinghouse placing students in internships in Russia. Depending on their interests, interns work in one of a range of areas (see Field) at assigned enterprises, joint-ventures, cooperatives, small businesses, universities, institutes, schools, and camps. Completely immersed in Russian culture, interns participate in all aspects of Russian life, "from dealing with office politics and bureaucracies to standing in long lines to enjoying pleasant, carefree times at friends' homes and dachas."

PERKS
Orientation; ongoing support and guidance from ASSIST representatives; special emphasis on providing valuable letters of recommendation.

FYI
The majority of interns work in Moscow and St. Petersburg. A former intern says: "Having spent the summer in a real Russian work environment is one of the best things I have done to enhance my personal experience. Everyone has worked at home and many have studied abroad—working abroad, however, is defining." . . . Interns are housed in private homes, dormitories, apartments, hotels, and cabins.

TO APPLY
Open to undergrads, recent college grads, grad students, high school grads 18 years and older, and college grads of any age. Russian language skills preferable but not required. International applicants eligible. Write for application.

Internship Coordinator
ASSIST
399 Ringwood Road
Freeville, NY 13068
(607) 539-6145

ASSISTANT DIRECTORS TRAINING PROGRAM

SELECTIVITY
Approximate applicant pool: 1,200; Interns accepted: 8–20

COMPENSATION
$487–$598/week

LOCATION(S)
Los Angeles, CA

FIELD
Film; Television

DURATION
400 working days, starting early Summer

DEADLINE(S)
November 12

THE WORK
Established in 1965 and sponsored by the Directors Guild of America and the Alliance of Motion Picture and Television Producers, the Assistant Directors Training Program seeks to "train Second Assistant Directors for the motion picture and television industry." Interns work on episodic television shows, television movies, pilots, mini-series, and feature films with studios and production companies.

PERKS
Health Plan; seminars on the motion picture and television industry; occasional travel out-of-state or overseas to work on films.

FYI
Trainees work with cast and crew members and learn about set operations and the collective bargaining agreements of more than twenty entertainment guilds and unions . . . Upon completion of the program, interns' names are placed on the Southern California Area Qualification List for employment as assistant directors.

TO APPLY
Open to recent college grads (including those who will receive their associate's or bachelor's degree by June 30), grad students, and college grads of any age. International applicants with the right to work in the United States are eligible. For those who have done little or no college work, relevant work experience alone may satisfy the program's requirements. Write or phone for application or visit our website at: www.dgptp.org.

Administrator
Directors Guild-Producer Training Plan
14724 Ventura Boulevard, Suite 775
Sherman Oaks, CA 91403-3522
(818) 386-2545
www.dgptp.org

ASSOCIATION FOR INTERNATIONAL PRACTICAL TRAINING

SELECTIVITY   N/A
Approximate applicant pool: N/A; Interns accepted: N/A

COMPENSATION
The employer is required to provide living expenses. Trainees are expected to cover all international and domestic travel costs to and from the training location, as well as personal expenses.

LOCATION(S)
Worldwide

FIELD
Varies

DURATION
12 weeks—18 months

DEADLINE(S)
Rolling

THE WORK
Founded in 1950, The Association for International Practical Training (AIPT) is a nonprofit international educational exchange organization that sponsors and facilitates on-the-job practical training exchanges for students and professionals between the United States and more than 70 other countries in many fields. AIPT is also the U.S. affiliate of the International Association for the Exchange of Students for Technical Experience (IAESTE), which provides international training opportunities for university students in the fields of engineering, architecture, agriculture, computer science, mathematics, and the natural/physical sciences as well as hospitality and tourism. AIPT's new online placement service, www.pinpointtraining.org, matches individuals seeking training opportunities with appropriate training positions in their field of education or experience. In addition, AIPT offers short-term experiential learning programs for students and professionals from many fields and countries. AIPT's client list includes Amoco, Disney Corp., The Gillette Co., Marriott Corp., and IBM Corp.

PERKS
Varies with assignment.

FYI
The most common destinations for U.S. participants have been the United Kingdom, France, and Germany.

TO APPLY
Open to college juniors and seniors, graduate students, and professionals. International applicants are eligible.

Association for International Practical Training
10400 Little Patuxent Parkway, Suite 250
Columbia, MD 21044-3510
(410) 997-2200
(410) 992-3924 fax
E-mail: aipt@aipt.org
www.aipt.org

SELECTIVITY 🔍🔍
Approximate applicant pool: 25; Interns accepted: 6

COMPENSATION 💲
Stipend of $7 per hour

LOCATION(S)
New York, NY

FIELD
Performing arts

DURATION
6–12 weeks

DEADLINE(S)
Rolling

THE WORK
Founded in 1975, the Association of Hispanic Arts (AHA) is a nonprofit organization serving Latino artists and arts organizations as well as the general public. Through its publications, technical assistant program, and information and advocacy service, AHA works with artists and organizations to strengthen Latino cultural institutions and bring artistic works to the public. Interns assist staff with handling requests for information and updating AHA's Artists Opportunity Bank.

PERKS
Free tickets to arts events (e.g., poetry readings, concerts, dance events); "very cooperative and energized" work environment.

FYI
According to the internship coordinator: "Whether they're artists or just interested in the art world, interns will get incredible amounts of exposure to the Latino arts community, both in New York and nationally."

TO APPLY
Open to high school students, undergrads, recent college grads, grad students, high school grads, and college grads of any age. International applicants eligible. Submit resume and cover letter.

Internship Coordinator
Association of Hispanic Arts
250 West 26th Street 4th Floor
New York, NY 10001
(212) 727-7227
(212) 727-0549 (Fax)

Between her junior and senior years at Duke University, **Judy Woodruff** interned with Rep. Robert G. Stephens, Jr., the representative from her home district in Georgia. She went on to become an accomplished broadcast journalist, serving as a White House correspondent for NBC News, a Washington correspondent for NBC's *Today Show*, the anchor of her own public television documentary-series, *Frontline with Judy Woodruff*, and an anchor on CNN.

For The People

SELECTIVITY 🔍🔍🔍🔍🔍
Approximate applicant pool: 300; Interns accepted: 10

COMPENSATION 💲💲💲
$8.50/hour (H.S); $10/hour (college); $12/hour (post college); $12.50/hour (law students)

LOCATION(S)
Washington, DC

FIELD
Law

DURATION
10 weeks: Summer

DEADLINE(S)
March 1

THE WORK
As the world's largest trial bar with nearly 60,000 members, ATLA is the preeminent organization advancing the mission of trial lawyers. Established in 1946, ATLA safeguards victims' rights and strengthens the civil justice system through education and disclosure of information critical to the health and safety of the American public. ATLA serves the professional needs of trial lawyers through publications, continuing legal education, sale of products, legal research, legislative support, public relations, and other member services. Interns work in Public Affairs, State Affairs, Legal Affairs, Media Relations, Meetings & Conventions, Continuing Legal Education, Publications, Production, and Foundations. Positions are clerical in nature.

PERKS
Prime location; Georgetown Public Transportation subsidy.

FYI
The third floor of ATLA's offices contains an exercise room, and snack bar machines.

TO APPLY
Open to high school seniors, undergrads, recent college grads, and grad students. Submit resume and cover letter.

After one year of college at the University of Illinois, **John Chancellor** dropped out in 1948 to become a copy boy at the *Chicago Sun-Times*. Within two years, he had worked his way up to a position at the newspaper's rewrite desk. A few years later he joined NBC News, where he went on to serve as reporter, foreign bureau chief, anchor, and commentator.

Internship Coordinator
Association of Trial Lawyers of America
1050 31st Street NW
Washington, DC 20007
(202) 333-2861 (Fax)

ASYLUM RECORDS

See Elektra Entertainment Group

AT&T BELL LABORATORIES

SELECTIVITY
Approx. applicant pool: 500 (SRP)/ 2,700 (UR)
Interns accepted: 80 (SRP)/ 250 (UR)

COMPENSATION
Est. $430–$520/wk for undergrads;
Est. $550–$620/wk for grad students; round trip travel

LOCATION(S)
NJ and PA (see brochure)

FIELD
Telecommunications research

DURATION
10–12 weeks: Summer

DEADLINE(S)
SRP: December 1
UR: January 31

 THE WORK
AT&T Bell Labs is known the world over as a center for research and product development. Since its founding in 1925, Bell Labs has been awarded patents for inventions like the transistor, liquid crystal displays, lasers, and touch-tone phones. Interns are able to work in the Basic Research department and Product Development (UR interns only).

PERKS
Excellent mentors; science seminars; dorm housing.

FYI
The Summer Research Program for Minorities and Women (SRP) was established in 1972 to attract minority undergraduate students to Ph.D. programs in the sciences . . . The laboratory created the University Relations Summer Program (UR) in 1945 . . . Interns are assigned mentors, some who are world-renowned, such as Jum West, inventor of the modern telephone microphone.

TO APPLY
SRP: Open to college sophomores, juniors, and seniors. UR: Open to undergrads and grad students, provided they are available for permanent employment within 2 years after the internship. Minimum GPA: 3.0. International applicants eligible. SRP candidates should write for application. For UR internships, submit resume, cover letter, and transcript.

AT&T Bell Laboratories
University Relations
Rochelle Richardson
101 Crawfords Corner Road, Rm. 222
Holmdel, NJ 07733
(908) 949-1377

ATLANTA BALLET

SELECTIVITY
Approximate applicant pool: 15; Interns accepted: 6

COMPENSATION
None

LOCATION(S)
Atlanta, GA

FIELD
Arts administration

DURATION
8–12 weeks: Summer, Fall, Spring

DEADLINE(S)
Rolling

THE WORK
Under the artistic leadership of John McFall, Atlanta Ballet presents a seven performance season of theatrical full-length ballets and cutting-edge new work. In addition, this internationally known company has toured throughout the Southeast and as far away as Korea. The Ballet houses the Atlanta Ballet Centre for Dance Education, the official school of the Company. In addition to classes for both students and adults, the Centre participates in educational outreach activities for local youth. Interns work in Marketing, Public Relations, and Development.

PERKS
Free tickets to all ballets; passes to performances of local arts groups; free dance classes.

FYI
The internship program has been in existence since 1979.

TO APPLY
Open to undergrads, recent college grads, and grad students. International applicants eligible. Write for application.

Internship Coordinator
Atlanta Ballet
1400 W. Peachtree Street, NW
Atlanta, GA 30309
(404) 873-5811
(404) 874-7905 (Fax)

ATLANTA JUNIOR GOLF ASSOCIATION

See PGA Tour

EXCLUSIVE INTERVIEW WITH ROALD HOFFMAN

A professor of chemistry at Cornell University, Dr. Roald Hoffman won the Nobel Prize in Chemistry in 1981 for his contribution to the Woodward-Hoffman rule, a breakthrough principle on the reactivity of molecules. He has also published three books of essays and poetry—The Metamict State, Gaps and Verges, and Chemistry Imagined. Hoffman graduated summa cum laude with a degree in chemistry from Columbia in 1958 and a Ph.D. from Harvard in 1962.

The Internship Informants: You interned at the National Bureau of Standards during the summers of 1955 and 1956. Tell us about your experience.
Hoffman: The first summer, I worked on a project that was not terribly exciting, but it did give me an introduction to science. I studied the heat released in various cement compounds reacting with water, and I worked with a man named Edwin Newman. It was a wonderful introduction to real science research. The second summer, I did some very interesting work with "cool flames"—where you heat up hydrocarbons, like the components of petroleum, at relatively low temperatures until they begin to burn. That was frontline research at the time.

The Internship Informants: Did you get published?
Hoffman: From that first summer's research, I did actually publish my first scientific paper, in the *Journal of Research of the National Bureau of Standards*. For an 18-year old kid to get published was really great.

The Internship Informants: You matriculated to Columbia in the fall of 1955. Having already served one science internship, did you know immediately that you wanted to become a chemist?
Hoffman: I was a pre-medical student, and I took a lot of chemistry courses. But I eventually decided to major in chemistry and drop the pre-medical ambitions. However, the chemistry courses I took at Columbia were pretty standard. What kept me interested in research were the internships—the two at the National Bureau of Standards and another one at Brookhaven [National Laboratory in the summer of 1957]. And even though I didn't wind up working in the fields that I researched during the internships, they gave me a feeling for the excitement of research.

The Internship Informants: What research did you do as an intern at Brookhaven?
Hoffman: I worked with a wonderful nuclear chemist named Jim Cumming, my mentor there. I did research on radiochemistry, and that work also led to a scientific paper. I have one vivid memory of rushing on a bicycle from [Brookhaven's] big cyclotron, called the Cosmotron, down to the chemistry lab, carrying a sample of a thousand atoms of a certain isotope of carbon, and they were disappearing with a half-life of twenty minutes. We had to get them on a counter, which we had to build very carefully from lead that was not exposed to the atmosphere [to prevent contaminating the counter with atmospheric radioactivity]. We rushed the apparatus down to the lab, stuck [the sample] in, and the carbon atoms were dying away, but we caught a few of them.

The Internship Informants: Weren't you afraid of not getting there quickly enough or of dropping the sample?
Hoffman: Yes. It took ten minutes to get the sample out of the place where they were made. It took another ten minutes to bike down, another ten minutes to put it into the counter. In those thirty minutes, the atoms were down from 1,000 to under 400. There wasn't much time, and it all had to be done very efficiently. It was just exciting.

The Internship Informants: Do you still keep in touch with some of the other interns from that time?
Hoffman: I lived in a temporary barracks of sorts with other interns and met interns in the Brookhaven cafeteria or at various social activities we arranged for ourselves. Some of them I still talk to—Pradip Bakshi, a physicist at Boston College, and Robert Socolow, an applied physicist and environmental scientist at Princeton.

The Internship Informants: Would you attribute some of your interest in chemistry to the internships?
Hoffman: I don't think I would have become a chemist if it weren't for those internships … I think I would have gone into something else, probably in the humanities. I think the internships … really awakened a love for research and at a critical time, when my courses were not as inspiring as they should have been.

SELECTIVITY 🔍🔍🔍
Approximate applicant pool: 300; Interns accepted: 45

COMPENSATION $
None

LOCATION(S)
Washington, DC

FIELD
Foreign affairs; Public policy

DURATION
10 weeks minimum: Summer, Fall, Spring

DEADLINE(S)
Rolling

THE WORK
Founded in 1961, the Atlantic Council of the United States (ACUS) is a nonprofit, nonpartisan public policy center addressing American interests in Europe, North America, Slavic and Eurasian states, and Asian and Pacific nations. Serving as an adviser to the White House, Congress, businesses, academics, and diplomats, ACUS identifies challenges and opportunities in US foreign, security, and international economic policies. Interns work in the following areas: Atlantic Cooperation, NATO Information Office, Harriman Chair for East-West Studies, Atlantic-Pacific Interrelationships, Energy and Environment, Collective Security, Education, Peace and Conflict Resolution, Operations and Planning.

PERKS
Brown-bag luncheons with policymakers; weekly Intern Discussion Series (IDS) on public and foreign policy issues; attendance welcome at ACUS policy meetings and seminars.

FYI
ACUS interns spend most of their time assisting program and office directors in organizing and executing the Council's public affairs and education programs . . . Former IDS speakers include Secretary of State Madeline Albright, former Secretary of State Lawrence Eagleburger, and former Secretary of Defense Frank Carlucci.

TO APPLY
Open to college juniors and seniors, recent college grads, and grad students. International applicants eligible. Submit resume, cover letter, brief writing sample, transcript, and two recommendations.

Internship Coordinator
Atlantic Council of the United States
910 17th Street NW, Suite 1000
Washington, DC 20006
(202) 778-4964
(202) 463-7241 (Fax)
E-mail: internships@acus.org

SELECTIVITY 🔍🔍🔍🔍
Interns: Approx. applicant pool: 50 (Fall & Spring) 750 (summer); accepted: 15–20 (Fall & Spring); 30–40 (Summer)
College Reps: Approx. applicant pool: 250–500; Accepted: 40–50

COMPENSATION $
Interns: None—must receive college credit;
College Reps: None—must qualify for college credit

LOCATION(S)
Interns: New York City & Los Angeles
College Reps: Colleges around the country

FIELD
Music

DURATION
Interns: 8–16 weeks: Summer, Spring, Fall
College Reps: 1 year minimum (10–20 hours/week)

DEADLINE(S)
Rolling

THE WORK
Founded in 1948, Atlantic Records, part of the Warner-Elektra-Atlantic (WEA) partnership, is a record company embracing several smaller labels. Atlantic's artists include legends such as Ray Charles and Led Zeppelin and newcomers like Hootie and The Blowfish and Jewel. Interns have the opportunity to work within various creative departments in the company and learn the "ins and outs" of the music industry. Interns in the College Marketing program serve as Reps at their college campuses promoting Atlantic artists on a local level through retail stores, college radio, media/press, and tour support.

PERKS
Free CDs and concert tickets; possible travel on concert tours (Reps); flexible hours (Reps).

FYI
Atlantic internships are a great way to get your foot in the door of the music industry and provide the opportunity to work with industry professionals.

TO APPLY
Internships are open to college students who are able to earn academic credit from their school. The College Marketing Program is open to college students with at least one-and-a-half years left in school. Submit resume and cover letter directly to area you wish to work.

Internships: *Internship Coordinator*   *Internship Coordinator*
                Atlantic Records   *Atlantic Records*
                1290 Avenue of the Americas   *9229 Sunset Blvd.*
                28th Floor   *Los Angeles, CA 90069*
                New York, NY 10104   *www.atlantic-records.com*
                www.atlantic-records.com

College Reps: *College Marketing Department*
                Atlantic Records
                1290 Avenue of the Americas-24th Floor
                New York, NY 10104
                (212) 405-5469 (Fax)
                www.atlantic-records.com

SELECTIVITY
Approximate applicant pool: 30–50; Interns accepted: 6–8

COMPENSATION
None

LOCATION(S)
Washington, DC

FIELD
Government

DURATION
12–16 weeks: Summer, Fall, Spring, Winter

DEADLINE(S)
Summer: April 1; Fall: August 1; Spring: January 1; Winter: November 1

THE WORK
The Australian Embassy serves as the official diplomatic office of the Australian Ambassador to the United States. Working to protect and advance Australian interests in the United States, the Embassy sponsors social and educational events with United States officials, provides information on political, trade and strategic developments in Australia, coordinates immigration and education programs, and distributes a variety of publications. Interns work in the Congressional Liaison, Public Affairs, and Cultural Relations offices.

PERKS
Intern receptions; attendance welcome at embassy happy hours; "friendly Australian atmosphere."

FYI
The internship program has been in existence since 1992 . . . In the words of the internship coordinator, the mission of the Embassy is "to win a future for Australia in the world."

TO APPLY
Open to college juniors and seniors, recent college grads, and grad students. International applicants eligible. Submit resume and cover letter.

Internship Coordinator
Australian Embassy
1601 Massachusetts Avenue NW
Washington, DC 20036
(202) 797-3071
(202) 797-3414 (Fax)

See Random House

SELECTIVITY
Approximate applicant pool: 50; Interns accepted: approximately 9 per year

COMPENSATION
$20/week; free parking

LOCATION(S)
Columbus, OH

FIELD
Ballet

DURATION
10 weeks: Summer, Fall, Winter, Spring

DEADLINE(S)
Rolling

THE WORK
Founded in 1978, BalletMet is one of the top fifteen professional dance companies in the United States. Operating on a budget of over $4.8 million, BalletMet performs in Columbus's historic Ohio Theater, participates in national and international tours, and runs community and educational outreach programs. Interns work in Marketing/Public Relations and Development.

PERKS
Free tickets to all performances; attendance welcome at parties and other events; free parking.

FYI
The internship program has been running since 1991 . . . BalletMet's production of *The Nutcracker* is the only one in the country that is designed and choreographed to evoke the original production premiered in 1892 at the Maryinksy Theatre in St. Petersburg, Russia.

TO APPLY
Open to undergrads. International applicants eligible. Submit resume, cover letter, and writing samples.

Internship Coordinator
BalletMet
322 Mount Vernon Avenue
Columbus, OH 43215
(614) 229-4860
(614) 229-4858 (Fax)

The long-time US Senator from Hawaii, **Daniel Inouye**, gained some hands-on political experience while he was a law student at George Washington University. In the summer of 1951, he served as a volunteer for the Democratic National Committee.

SELECTIVITY
Approximate applicant pool: 50; Interns accepted: 20

COMPENSATION
None

LOCATION(S)
Baltimore, MD

FIELD
Zoos

DURATION
10 weeks: Summer, Fall, Spring; 4-week break in January

DEADLINE(S)
Rolling; 3 weeks before intended starting date.

THE WORK
Dating back to 1876, the Baltimore Zoo is situated in an urban and wildlife park of 760 acres. In addition to offering a variety of educational and recreational programs, the zoo's work includes international breeding programs for the lion-tailed macaque and the black-footed penguin. Interns work in Aviculture, Education, Financial Analysis, Herpetology, Horticulture, Marketing, Membership, Public Relations, Special Events, and Veterinary Medicine, Animal Behavior, Intro to Zoo Field. All positions are entry level.

PERKS
Luncheons and field trip (summer); discounts in zoo store and concession stands; uniform provided if needed, free parking.

FYI
Interns in the Intro to Zoo Field had better like the rugged side of zookeeping; according to the internship bulletin, their work involves "clean[ing] animals' quarters and exhibits by raking, hosing, scrubbing, bleaching, or disinfecting as needed."

TO APPLY
Open to undergrads, recent college grads, grad students, high school grads of any age, and college grads of any age. Must have proof of a negative TB test. Write for application and enclose a self-addressed stamped envelope.

Internship Coordinator
Education Department
Baltimore Zoo
Druid Hill Park
Baltimore, MD 21217
(410) 396-6013
(410) 396-6464 (Fax)

BARNEYS NEWYORK

SELECTIVITY
Approximate applicant pool: 200; Interns accepted: 20

COMPENSATION
Stipend; Course credit; Store discount

LOCATION(S)
New York, NY (HQ)

FIELD
Retail

DURATION
Semester; Fall, Spring, Summer

DEADLINE(S)
Rolling

THE WORK
Barneys New York is an upscale specialty retailer featuring high quality merchandise in stores across the U.S. Interns gain hands-on experiences in Buying, Advertising, Graphic Design, Marketing, Publicity, Merchandise Planning, Fashion Merchandising, Store Design/Display, Personal Shopping, Studio Services, and Human Resources.

PERKS
Possible employment opportunities.

FYI
Barneys New York was founded in 1923 by Barney Pressman who pawned his wife's engagement ring (at her suggestion) to rent a small store and stock it with forty suits. Since then, the retailer has rapidly grown into an emporium of luxury selling high-end fashion while offering unsurpassed quality and service. Barneys New York is notorious for its cutting edge fashion assortments and its uniquely creative storefront windows.

TO APPLY
Open to undergrads and graduate students. International applicants eligible with correct paperwork for work authorization. Submit resume and cover letter.

Internship Coordinator
Human Resources
Barneys New York
575 Fifth Avenue 11th Floor
New York, NY 10017
(212) 450-8731
(212) 450-8489 (Fax)

> **B**arneys New York was founded in 1923 by **Barney Pressman** who pawned his wife's engagement ring—at her suggestion—to raise the $500 to cover the rent and the initial inventory of 40 suits. Barneys is now one of the preeminent specialty stores in the United States.

BARRY-HAFT-BROWN ARTISTS AGENCY

SELECTIVITY 🔍
Approximate applicant pool: 10; Interns accepted: 4

COMPENSATION 💲
$5 a day for lunch and transportation

LOCATION(S)
New York, NY

FIELD
Talent agency

DURATION
12 weeks: Summer, Fall, Winter, Spring

DEADLINE(S)
Rolling

THE WORK
Founded in 1991, Barry-Haft-Brown (BHB) Artists Agency is a mid-sized talent agency representing nearly 100 theater and film actors. Clients include John Spencer (of *L.A. Law* fame), Katherine Wallach, Teresa Hughes, and Louise Sorel. Interns assist BHB's agents, including preparing agents' submissions to casting directors.

PERKS
Occasional complimentary tickets to film screenings and plays.

FYI
Co-founder Bob Barry started his career as an agent in the early 1960s.

TO APPLY
Open to high school grads, undergrads, recent college grads, college grads of any age, and grad students. Must be proficient in English. International applicants eligible. Submit resume and cover letter.

Internship Coordinator
Barry-Haft-Brown Artists Agency
165 West 46th Street, Suite 908
New York, NY 10036
(212) 869-9310
(212) 398-1268 (fax)

BARWOOD PRODUCTIONS

SELECTIVITY 🔍🔍🔍🔍
Approximate applicant pool: 70; Interns accepted: 4

COMPENSATION 💲
Daily free lunch

LOCATION(S)
New York, NY

FIELD
Film; Television

DURATION
12 weeks–6 months; ongoing

DEADLINE(S)
Rolling

THE WORK
Founded in 1979, Barwood Productions is Barbra Streisand's official production company. It is responsible for most of Streisand's films, including *The Main Event*, *Yentl*, *The Prince of Tides*, and *The Mirror Has Two Faces*. Interns work in the Development department.

PERKS
Free passes for movie screenings; small, intimate office environment.

FYI
In addition to producing movies in which Streisand stars, Barwood has begun pursuing non-Streisand projects such as the 1995 made-for-television movie *Serving in Silence* starring Glenn Close.

TO APPLY
Open to undergrads, recent college grads, college grads of any age, and grad students. International applicants eligible. Submit resume and cover letter.

Internship Coordinator
Barwood Productions
330 West 58th Street, Suite 301
New York, NY 10019
(212) 765-7191
(212) 765-6988 (Fax)

BATES USA

SELECTIVITY 🔍🔍🔍🔍
Approximate applicant pool: 75; Interns accepted: 5–10

COMPENSATION 🔍
None; Possible bonus stipend

LOCATION(S)
New York, NY

FIELD
Advertising

DURATION
10–12 weeks; Summer, Fall, Spring; 2 to 4 days/week

DEADLINE(S)
Rolling

THE WORK
Bates USA is the world's fifth largest advertising agency, having a client roster including Wendy's, Magnavox, Campbell's Soup, and Hyundai Motor America. All interns at Bates USA are placed in Strategic Planning, the department that researches consumer attitudes and trends.

PERKS
Chrysler building; quality cafeteria; two interns to an office; Intern Answer Book.

FYI
Every intern receives a helpful and official "Intern Answer Book" . . . interns are only two to an office and have a stunning view of New York from the Chrysler Building.

TO APPLY
Open to college juniors and seniors, grad students. Minimum GPA 3.0. International applicants eligible. Submit resume and writing sample.

Bates USA
Internship Program
The Chrysler Building
405 Lexington Avenue
New York, NY 10174
(212) 297-7000

BATH & BODY WORKS

See The Limited

BAXTER INTERNATIONAL

Baxter

SELECTIVITY 🔍🔍🔍
Approximate size of applicant pool: 750; Interns accepted: 50-75

COMPENSATION $
Varies depending on function and year in school

LOCATION(S)
Northern Illinois; California

FIELD
Healthcare

DURATION
12 weeks

DEADLINE(S)
resumes only accepted from January 1–March 1

THE WORK
Baxter International Inc. is a global leader in delivering critical therapies for life-threatening conditions. All of our technologies are related to the blood and circulatory system. Baxter's products are sold in more than 112 countries and more than 50 percent of our sales come from outside the United States and represent our fastest-growing markets. Departments hiring interns include engineering, finance, human resources, R & D, information technology, and marketing. The internship program involves challenging, real work. At the end of the internship, students from the different functions generate a report detailing their contribution and experience acquired during the summer and they make a presentation to other interns and to the management staff.

PERKS
Intern orientation, Welcome Reception, Conference, Spirit of Chicago Boat Cruise, Farewell Picnic.

FYI
An American student who is presently doing an internship in Brazil said: "At first I did not know what to expect from this internship, but as time passes I have come to realize that I am getting hands on experience in my job with another culture—an awesome, unforgettable experience."

TO APPLY
Open to college juniors and seniors and graduate students. International applicants eligible. Submit tesumes to:

Baxter International
Summer Internship Program
One Baxter Parkway
Deerfield, IL 60015

BAYWATCH

SELECTIVITY 🔍🔍🔍
Approximate applicant pool: 20; Interns accepted: 3–4

COMPENSATION $
None

LOCATION(S)
Honolulu, HI

FIELD
Television

DURATION
16–22 weeks; ongoing

DEADLINE(S)
Rolling

THE WORK
Produced by The Baywatch Production Company, a division of the film and television distribution house Pearson Television, *Baywatch* is a hit syndicated television show about five lifeguards patrolling a Southern California beach. Cast members include Jason Brooks and Brande Roderick. Ranked by Nielsen as one of America's top-ten shows, *Baywatch Hawaii* was recently dubbed the most popular television series in history by *Entertainment Weekly*. Interns work in Production, Casting, and Post Production (i.e. Editing).

PERKS
Invitations to company parties; attendance welcome at production meetings.

FYI
Baywatch has hired approximately 70 percent of its interns for full-time work as production assistants and runners since the show's first season in 1990.

TO APPLY
Open to undergrads for college credit only, International applicants eligible. Submit resume, cover letter, and recommendations.

Internship Coordinator
The Baywatch Production Company
510 18th Avenue
Honolulu, HI 96816
(808) 733-4142 (Fax)

EXCLUSIVE INTERVIEW WITH MARK McCORMACK

Widely credited with founding the athlete-representation business, former lawyer and college-golf champion Mark McCormack started International Management Group in 1960 by signing up Arnold Palmer as his first client. Over 30 years later, his creation—IMG—is the world's largest and most influential sports-marketing firm, with 64 offices in 25 countries. McCormack is also the author of five books, including the bestselling *What They Don't Teach You at Harvard Business School*. He holds a B.A. from the College of William & Mary and a J.D. from Yale Law School.

The Internship Informants: What is your view on internships?

McCormack: I started offering internships in 1961 in order to find the best people. At IMG, we are deluged with resumes—thousands worldwide ... Some of the resumes are incredible, and you think somewhere there is a great superstar of the future. How do you tell from a piece of paper whether you want to hire somebody? Unfortunately, timing is the key to it. For example, a fellow resigned in one of our divisions last week, and so now we have a need ... for someone of a certain caliber. What happens is that the resumes that come in during the next week or two are the people that get thought of, and the ones that we received in the last six months are sitting in some personnel file somewhere. So the internship program alleviates that problem. It gives us an opportunity to look at a face compared to a resume, and it gives the intern an inside track if they later want to come work for us.

The Internship Informants: You've made the IMG internship more formal in the last few years. How has it improved?

McCormack: It used to work that your next door neighbor had a son who wanted to do something for the summer, and you'd have them help out with a golf tournament.... Now we have the departments put in requests, and we try to assign each intern to a specific place. In addition, we develop some social programs for them and try to get to know them better.

The Internship Informants: Some of them, at least the ones in Cleveland, get to meet you. What do you tell them?

McCormack: I ask them about themselves ... tell them that they have an inside track here based on the reviews they get from the people they work with and that they go in a separate file of people [considered for permanent positions].

The Internship Informants: Why do you think that so many people want to work at IMG?

McCormack: Our business—sports, fashion, and classical music—is perceived by a lot of people as a very glamorous business. If you were a ball-bearing manufacturer in Toledo, Ohio, I think it would be much harder to attract people to you.

BEACH ASSOCIATES

SELECTIVITY
Approximate applicant pool: 30; Interns accepted: 6

COMPENSATION $
None

LOCATION(S)
Arlington, VA; Washington, DC

FIELD
Video/visual communications

DURATION
12 weeks: Summer, Fall, Spring

DEADLINE(S)
Rolling

THE WORK
In existence since 1983, Beach Associates is a media production company providing comprehensive production services for videotape, special event, and live business-television program- ming, interactive, multi-media and web site development. Clients include United Way of America, Hospice Foundation or America, Wyncom, Inc., FDA, and American Speech Language Hearing Association, to name a few. Three; internship positions are available. One each in Production, Marketing, and New Media.

PERKS
Use of kitchen, occasional opportunities to go on field shoots; small, team-oriented staff; free parking, metro nearby.

FYI
Beach Associates was one of the first programmers of satellite-assisted video conferencing and distance learning.

TO APPLY
Open to college juniors and seniors as well as recent college grads. International applicants eligible. Submit resume and cover letter.

Internship Coordinator
Beach Associates
200 North Glebe Road, Suite 720
Arlington, VA 22203-3728
(703) 812-8813 (703) 812-9710 (Fax)
E-mail: thebeach@beachassociates.com

SELECTIVITY 🔍🔍🔍
Approximate applicant pool: 150; Interns accepted: 16–20

COMPENSATION 💲
Modest stipend Fall and Spring

LOCATION(S)
Boston, MA

FIELD
Publishing

DURATION
12 weeks: Fall, Spring; positions starting in January

DEADLINE(S)
Summer: April 1; Fall: September 1; Spring: January 1; Winter break: November 1

THE WORK
An independent, nonprofit publishing house established in 1854, Beacon Press specializes in nonfiction books focusing on social issues. Beacon titles include educator Deborah Meier's *The Power of Their Ideas*, poet Sonia Sanchez's *Wounded in the House of a Friend*, ecologist Stephanie Mill's *In Service of the Wild*, journalist Ben Bagdikian's *The Media Monopoly*, and Geoffrey Canada's *Fist Stick Knife Gun: A Personal History of Violence in America*. Interns work in Business, Administration, Editorial, Marketing, Publicity, and Production.

PERKS
Intern luncheon with entire staff; mentors; free books.

FYI
Beacon hires approximately 15 percent of interns for full-time positions . . . Former interns include one of the publishing house's Acquisition Editors.

TO APPLY
Open to high school grads, undergrads, recent college grads, college grads of any age, and grad students. Fall and spring internshpis are for people of color. Write for application.

Internship Coordinator
Beacon Press
25 Beacon Street
Boston, MA 02108
(617) 742-2110, x553
(617) 742-2290 (Fax)

What is the SF-171?

Until 1995, applicants for Federal Government positions (including internships) were required to submit an SF-171, a form which requested information on the applicant's qualifications and work history and often took several hours to complete. Why is the form no longer used? Says a staffing assistant in the Personnel department of the Office of Personnel Management, "It was simply too bulky." Agencies are now forbidden to ask for the form, which is no longer being printed, and must instead accept a detailed resume or the optional (2-page) OF-612.

SELECTIVITY   N/A
Approximate applicant pool: N/A; Interns accepted: 30–60

COMPENSATION 💲💲💲💲
Est. $300-$500/week

LOCATION(S)
Los Angeles and San Francisco CA (HQ); Gaithersburg, MD; Houston, TX; London, England

FIELD
Architecture; Construction

DURATION
Varies, flexible

DEADLINE(S)
Rolling

THE WORK
Bechtel is a global engineering-construction organization providing premier technology, management, and directly related services to develop, manage, engineer, build, and operate installations for customers worldwide. Founded in 1898, Bechtel is a privately held company that has been under the leadership of its founding family for four generations. Through Bechtel's Cooperative Education Program, students enrolled in their college's co-op program can work at Bechtel to fulfill part of their curriculum requirements. Depending on the program needs of individual schools, students may work at Bechtel a few days a week or work full-time for several months. Bechtel's program is flexible to meet the needs of each college or university. The purpose of these programs is to provide participants with practical, hands-on experience and exposure to Bechtel, while giving the company an opportunity to evaluate a student's professional potential.

PERKS
Mentors; attendance welcome at planning and strategy meetings.

FYI
At any given time, Bechtel is working for over 500 clients on more than 1,000 projects worth an estimated $7-$12 billion.

TO APPLY
Open to undergrad and grad students enrolled in a cooperative education program. Students must have satisfactorily completed at least one year of study in engineering or in a professional acadmic discipline such as business, accounting, finance, or computer science. Submit resume and cover letter.

Bechtel Corporation
College Relations – SATT
P. O. Box 36359
Phoenix, AZ 85067-6359
Email: staffpx@bechtel.com
Website: www.bechtel.com

BELLEVUE HOSPITAL CENTER

SELECTIVITY   N/A
Approximate applicant pool: N/A; Interns accepted: N/A

COMPENSATION $
Free meal from employee cafeteria each day

LOCATION(S)
New York, NY

FIELD
Health care

DURATION
3 consecutive months, 9 hrs/week positions available on an ongoing basis

DEADLINE(S)
Rolling; PHC: February 1

THE WORK
Dating back to 1736, Bellevue Hospital Center is the oldest public hospital in the US. An average of 10,000 patients, visitors, and employees move through its modern, 25-story building each day. Volunteers of all ages are accepted for the following programs: General Volunteers (computer skills), Bellevue Emergency Explorers Program (for high school students only), Volunteer Friendly Visitors Program (work with patients), Rape Crisis Program (work with sexual assault victims), hospitality program (assist throughout the hospital) interpreters, PAVERS and Project Health Care (see FYI).

PERKS
Opportunity to ride in ambulance, observe an autopsy, and witness childbirth at OB/GYN (Project Health Care).

FYI
An ideal program for aspiring doctors and nurses, Project Health Care (PHC) enables twenty college students to spend ten weeks (June 1 to mid-August) rotating through various areas of the Emergency Services Department. PHC volunteers assist doctors, nurses, social workers, patients, and administrators.

TO APPLY
Open to high school students, high school grads, undergrads, recent college grads, college grads of any age, and grad students. The minimum age is 16 years old. Must have had medical examination within 12 months prior to service. International applicants eligible. Write for PHC application only. Specify program of interest.

MWM. From Arkansas. Won a Rhodes Scholarship. Completed an Internship. Achieved High Elected-Office. Named "Bill."

Who is this man? The description actually applies to two men. The first, President **Bill Clinton**, spent the summer of 1967 serving an internship in the US Senate before heading to Oxford on a Rhodes Scholarship. The other, the legendary Senator from Arkansas, **J. William Fulbright**, interned in the antitrust division of the Justice Department in 1934 after returning from his Rhodes Scholarship experience.

Where did the "first Bill" intern? As fate would have it, in the office of the "second Bill," Senator J. William Fulbright.

Department of Volunteer Services
Bellevue Hospital Center
First Avenue and 27th Street
New York, NY 10016
(212) 562-4858

THE TRAPPER JOHN TRIPLE-PLAY

Participants in Bellevue Hospital Center's Project Health Care have the opportunity to take an ambulance ride, observe an autopsy, and witness childbirth at the hospital.

BENETTON USA CORP.

UNITED COLORS OF BENETTON.

SELECTIVITY   🔍
Approximate applicant pool: N/A; Interns accepted: 4

COMPENSATION $
None

LOCATION(S)
New York, NY

FIELD
Apparel

DURATION
6–8 weeks; ongoing

DEADLINE(S)
Rolling

THE WORK
Founded in 1965 in Ponzano Veneto near Treviso, Italy, Benetton is a global apparel company with 7,000 retail stores in over 120 countries. Its clothing lines include United Colors of Benetton, Sisley, and 012. The New York office oversees its operations in North America, as well as its flagship store on Fifth Avenue. Interns work in Public Relations, Accounting, Advertising, and Customer Service.

PERKS
Up to five complete Benetton outfits free; attendance welcome at press conferences and events.

FYI
Benetton is also well-known for its *COLORS* magazine and controversial ad campaigns emphasizing multiculturalism.

TO APPLY
Open to high school students, high school grads, undergrads, recent college grads, college grads of any age, and grad students. International applicants eligible. Knowledge of Italian is preferred. Submit resume and cover letter.

Internship Coordinator
Benetton USA Corporation
597 Fifth Avenue
New York, NY 10017
(212) 593-0290
(212) 371-1438 (Fax)

HOW TO WRITE A

TRASHPROOF RESUME

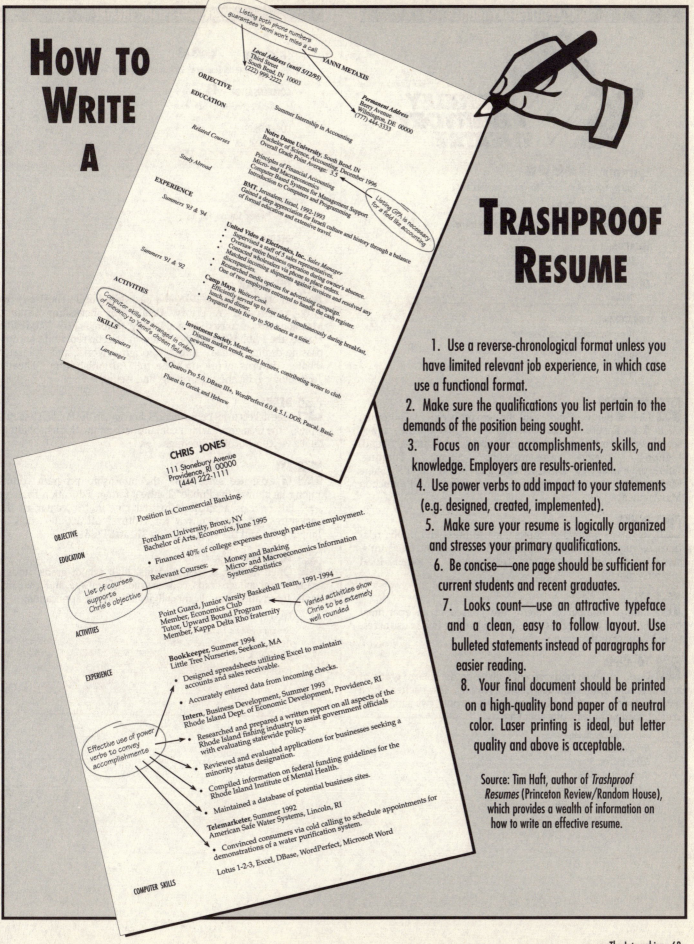

Resume 1 — Yanni Metaxis

Listing both phone numbers guarantees Yanni won't miss a call

YANNI METAXIS

Local Address (until 5/12/95)
Third Street
South Bend, IN 10003
(222) 999-2222

Permanent Address
Berry Avenue
Wilmington, DE 00000
(777) 444-3333

OBJECTIVE
Summer Internship in Accounting

EDUCATION
Notre Dame University, South Bend, IN
Bachelor of Science, Accounting, December 1996
Overall Grade Point Average: 3.5

Listing GPA is necessary for a field like accounting

Related Courses
Principles of Financial Accounting
Micro- and Macroeconomics
Computer Based Systems for Management Support
Introduction to Computers and Programming

Study Abroad
BMT, Jerusalem, Israel, 1992-1993
Gained a deep appreciation for Israeli culture and history through a balance
of formal education and extensive travel.

EXPERIENCE
Summers '93 & '94
United Video & Electronics, Inc., *Sales Manager*
• Supervised a staff of 5 sales representatives.
• Oversaw entire business operation during owner's absence.
• Contacted wholesalers via phone to place orders.
• Matched incoming shipments against invoices and resolved any discrepancies.
• Researched media options for advertising campaign.
• One of two employees entrusted to handle the cash register.

Summers '91 & '92
Camp Maya, *Waiter/Cook*
• Efficiently served up to four tables simultaneously during breakfast, lunch, and dinner.
• Prepared meals for up to 500 diners at a time.

ACTIVITIES
Investment Society, Member
• Discuss market trends, attend lectures, contributing writer to club newsletter.

Computer skills are arranged in order of relevancy to Yanni's chosen field

SKILLS
Computers
Quattro Pro 5.0, DBase III+, WordPerfect 6.0 & 5.1, DOS, Pascal, Basic

Languages
Fluent in Greek and Hebrew

Resume 2 — Chris Jones

CHRIS JONES
111 Stonebury Avenue
Providence, RI 00000
(444) 222-1111

OBJECTIVE
Position in Commercial Banking.

EDUCATION
Fordham University, Bronx, NY
Bachelor of Arts, Economics, June 1995
• Financed 40% of college expenses through part-time employment.

Relevant Courses:
Money and Banking
Micro- and Macroeconomics
Information Systems
Statistics

List of courses supports Chris's objective

ACTIVITIES
Point Guard, Junior Varsity Basketball Team, 1991-1994
Member, Economics Club
Tutor, Upward Bound Program
Member, Kappa Delta Rho fraternity

Varied activities show Chris to be extremely well rounded

EXPERIENCE
Bookkeeper, Summer 1994
Little Tree Nurseries, Seekonk, MA
• Designed spreadsheets utilizing Excel to maintain accounts and sales receivable.
• Accurately entered data from incoming checks.

Intern, Business Development, Summer 1993
Rhode Island Dept. of Economic Development, Providence, RI
• Researched and prepared a written report on all aspects of the Rhode Island fishing industry to assist government officials with evaluating statewide policy.
• Reviewed and evaluated applications for businesses seeking a minority status designation.
• Compiled information on federal funding guidelines for the Rhode Island Institute of Mental Health.
• Maintained a database of potential business sites.

Telemarketer, Summer 1992
American Safe Water Systems, Lincoln, RI
• Convinced consumers via cold calling to schedule appointments for demonstrations of a water purification system.

COMPUTER SKILLS
Lotus 1-2-3, Excel, DBase, WordPerfect, Microsoft Word

Effective use of power verbs to convey accomplishments

---

1. Use a reverse-chronological format unless you have limited relevant job experience, in which case use a functional format.

2. Make sure the qualifications you list pertain to the demands of the position being sought.

3. Focus on your accomplishments, skills, and knowledge. Employers are results-oriented.

4. Use power verbs to add impact to your statements (e.g. designed, created, implemented).

5. Make sure your resume is logically organized and stresses your primary qualifications.

6. Be concise—one page should be sufficient for current students and recent graduates.

7. Looks count—use an attractive typeface and a clean, easy to follow layout. Use bulleted statements instead of paragraphs for easier reading.

8. Your final document should be printed on a high-quality bond paper of a neutral color. Laser printing is ideal, but letter quality and above is acceptable.

Source: Tim Haft, author of *Trashproof Resumes* (Princeton Review/Random House), which provides a wealth of information on how to write an effective resume.

SELECTIVITY
Approximate applicant pool: 230; Interns accepted: 6–12

COMPENSATION
$300/month; free housing for limited number of interns

LOCATION(S)
Berkeley, CA

FIELD
Theatre

DURATION
10 months: starting August/September

DEADLINE(S)
April 15

THE WORK
One of the most successful theater companies in California, the Berkeley Repertory Theatre attracts over 20,000 subscribers each season to its stage. Interns work in Properties, Costumes, Sound, Lighting, Scenic Construction, Scenic Painting, Literary/Dramaturgy, Development and Marketing/PR, Stage Management, Theatre Administration, Education, and Production Management.

PERKS
Regular seminars on topics such as press and public relations, costuming, casting, and personnel management; free admission to all BRT productions; free passes to other local theaters/movies.

FYI
Limited number of interns are housed in an apartment building within walking distance of "the Rep" or in a house accessible by subway about a mile away.

TO APPLY
Open to undergrads, recent college grads, college grads of any age, and grad students. Submit resume, cover letter, three recommendations, and for literary applicants only, two samples of critical writing, at least one about a play.

Internship Coordinator
Berkeley Repertory Theatre
2025 Addison Street
Berkeley, CA 94704
(510) 204-8901 Administration
(510) 845-4700 Box Office
(510) 841-7711 Fax

SELECTIVITY
Approximate applicant pool: 200; Interns accepted: 24

COMPENSATION
Housing provided for $25/week

LOCATION(S)
Pittsfield, MA

FIELD
Theater

DURATION
12 weeks: Summer, Fall, Spring

DEADLINE(S)
Rolling

THE WORK
In existence since 1976, the Berkshire Public Theatre is the only year-round repertory theater in Berkshire County, Massachusetts. Housed in a partially restored 1912 Vaudeville House, the Public Theatre performs an eclectic repertoire encompassing drama, comedy, musicals, original works, and children's theater. Interns work in Theatre Administration, Theater Technology, Education, Directing, and Acting.

PERKS
Free tickets to all performances; housing in the Public Theatre's annex, "the Octagon," which contains a communal kitchen; attendance welcome at staff meetings.

FYI
In existence since 1983, the internship program counts among its alumni the Public Theatre's former Education Director . . . Pittsfield is a small industrial city in the center of the Berkshires, an area known for cultural attractions such as Tanglewood and the Williamstown Theatre Festival.

TO APPLY
Open to high school students, high school grads, undergrads, recent college grads, college grads of any age, and grad students. International applicants eligible. Write for application.

Internship Coordinator
Berkshire Public Theatre
P.O. Box 860
30 Union Street
Pittsfield, MA 01202-0860

BERMUDA BIOLOGICAL STATION FOR RESEARCH

SELECTIVITY 🔍🔍🔍
Approximate applicant pool: 200 (VIP), 10 (GIP); Interns accepted: 10–20 (VIP), 12 (GIP)

COMPENSATION 💲💲
VIP: free room and board

LOCATION(S)
St. George's, Bermuda

FIELD
Marine and atmospheric science research, Human/Ocean health

DURATION
VIP: 16 weeks: Summer, Fall, Winter; GIP: 3 months–1 year, ongoing

DEADLINE(S)
VIP: Summer: February 1, Fall: June 1, Winter: October 1; GIP: rolling

THE WORK
Founded in 1903, the Bermuda Biological Station for Research (BBSR) is a research and education institute involved in studies of the atmosphere and marine life, from coral reef ecology to oceanography. Its facilities include ten labs for visiting scientists, a radioisotope lab, a 20,000-volume library, vessels for ocean research, and lecture halls and classrooms. Under the auspices of the Volunteer Internship Program (VIP), interns conduct research on such topics as global climate change, use of optics for sea study, ocean carbon, nitrogen cycling, coral symbiosis, effects of oil spills and smoke stack emissions on tropical environments, and larval marine animals. Grad students are accepted to the Graduate Intern Program (GIP), in which they conduct independent research for their dissertations in exchange for teaching and lecturing.

PERKS
Free monthly scuba dives; access to 16-foot boat for marine data collection (GIP); mild climate year-round.

INTERNSHIP = JOB OR $5,000 BACK

In 1994, St. John Fisher College of Rochester, New York unveiled a revolutionary plan. The school decided to guarantee students a job within six months of graduation, provided they complete an internship as well as participate in campus activities, map out career goals, and maintain a GPA of at least 2.75. Those who failed to land employment at the end of the prescribed period would receive $400 per month until they found a job or collected $5,000 in payments from the college.

FYI
BBSR also sponsors a volunteer program in which participants are involved in the daily operations of the station, from conducting weekly guided tours to stuffing envelopes.

TO APPLY
VIP: open to college juniors and seniors as well as recent college grads. GIP: open to grad students in marine biology, marine chemistry, carbonate geology, and oceanography. International applicants eligible. Write/e-mail or visit website for an application.

Education Officer
Bermuda Biological Station for Research
Ferry Reach, St. George's
GE01, Bermuda
(441) 297-1880
(441) 297-1919 (Fax)
E-mail: education@bbsr.edu
www.bbsr.edu

BERNSTEIN-REIN

B E R N S T E I N – R E I N

SELECTIVITY 🔍🔍🔍🔍🔍
Approximate applicant pool: 200; Interns accepted: 9

COMPENSATION 💲💲💲
$300/week

LOCATION(S)
Kansas City, MO

FIELD
Advertising

DURATION
10 weeks: Summer

DEADLINE(S)
February 1

THE WORK
Founded in 1964, Bernstein-Rein (B-R) is the largest advertising agency in Kansas City and, according to *ADWEEK*, one of the top 50 full-service ad agencies in the country. Providing services in advertising as well as marketing, and promotion, B-R handles such companies as Bayer, Thrifty Car Rentals, Russell Stovers, Shoney's, and WalMart. Interns work in Account Service, Creative, Media, and Research.

PERKS
Brown-bag luncheons with executives; round-table discussions with CEO; attendance welcome at agency meetings; positive, friendly, and fun working environment.

FYI
In existence since 1970, the internship program leads to permanent employment at B-R for about 20 percent of interns . . . B-R's interns work together on a group project and make a final presentation to the company's CEO, Robert Bernstein . . . B-R created McDonald's legendary Happy Meal promotion in 1976.

TO APPLY
Open to college seniors with one to two semesters undergraduate work left. Write for application.

Internship Coordinator
Bernstein-Rein
4600 Madison, Suite 1500
Kansas City, MO 64112
(816) 756-0640
(816) 531-5708 (Fax)
E-mail: human_res@bradv.com

BERTELSMANN MUSIC GROUP

SELECTIVITY ⌕ ⌕ ⌕ ⌕
Approximate applicant pool: 360; Interns accepted: 30

COMPENSATION $ $
$5/hour and $220/month for field expenses

LOCATION(S)
Cities in CA, CO, FL, GA, IL, MA, MI, MN, MO, NC, OR, PA, TX, WA, Washington, DC

FIELD
Music

DURATION
1 year to 2–1/2 years; ongoing, 20 hours/week

DEADLINE(S)
Rolling

THE WORK
Owned by the German entertainment empire Bertelsmann, the Bertelsmann Music Group is composed of a variety of record labels, such as Arista Records, Zoo Entertainment, and RCA Records, as well as BMG Distribution, one of the world's most powerful record distribution systems. Interns have the opportunity to work as regional marketing representatives, in BMG Direct, or for one of the record labels.

PERKS
Promotional freebies; meetings and conferences; possible tour work.

FYI
The program has been running since 1989 . . . Interns sometimes accompany a band on a leg of its tour . . . Says an intern: "There's always plenty of goodies left over after you distribute some to stores and radio stations."

TO APPLY
Open to undergrads and grad students. Others eligible, see brochure. International applicants eligible. Submit resume and cover letter.

Bertelsmann Music Group
Alternative Marketing Program or BMG Direct or RCA/Arista/Zoo Records
Manager of Recruiting & Development
1540 Broadway, 38th Floor
New York, NY 10036
(212) 930-4000
(212) 930-4862 (Fax)

Intern in a Benetton Ad

These internships typically have a high proportion of international participants:

Camp Counselors USA
Caux Scholars Program
Creamer Dickson Basford
Hawk Mountain Sanctuary
Human Service Alliance
Institute of Cultural Affairs
Interlocken
Intelsat
International Volunteer Projects
Manhattan Theater Club
Southface Energy Institute
TBWA
Vereinsbank Capital Corp.
Volkswagen
Volunteers for Peace
Volunteers in Asia
Women's International League for Peace and Freedom

BEST BUDDIES INTERNATIONAL

SELECTIVITY ⌕ ⌕ ⌕
Approximate applicant pool: 140; Interns accepted: 14

COMPENSATION $
None

LOCATION(S)
Santa Monica, CA; New Haven, CT; Fort Lauderdale, Orlando, and Miami, FL; Atlanta, GA; Chicago, IL; Bethlehem and Philadelphia, PA; Dallas, TX; Washington DC; Baltimore and Silver Spring, MD; Salt Lake City, UT

FIELD
Public service; The disabled

DURATION
12–24 weeks: Summer, Fall, Spring

DEADLINE(S)
Rolling

THE WORK
Founded in 1987, Best Buddies International is the first recreational and social program to pair college students, high

school students, and citizens with people with mental retardation. A nonprofit organization, it operates out of 230 college chapters in the US, Canada, and Greece. Interns work in Public Relations, Marketing, and Development.

PERKS
Attendance welcome at parties and other events; friendly, casual offices; creative flexibility, program projects rather than clerical work available.

FYI
Anthony Shriver Kennedy, nephew of the late John F. Kennedy, founded Best Buddies while he was an undergrad at Georgetown; he currently serves as Best Buddies' president.

TO APPLY
Open to undergrads and grad students. International applicants eligible. Submit resume, cover letter, and writing samples. Call DC office for contacts in other cities.

Internship Coordinator, Holly Snyder
Best Buddies International, Eastern Regional Office
1325 G Street NW #500
Washington, DC 20005
(202) 347-7265
(202) 824-0200 (Fax)

SUMMER JOBS WITH THE FEDERAL GOVERNMENT

Summer internships are offered throughout the US at many Federal agencies and departments, usually in larger cities. There are four ways to find out about available positions:

1. Contact the agency of interest directly.

2. Call Career America Connection at (912) 757-3000, a recorded job-listing compiled by the Office of Personnel Management (OPM).

3. Log on to one of OPM's 24-hour-a-day electronic bulletin boards, which provide the same information as Career America Connection but allow you to download information to your computer:

WASNET	(202) 606-1113	FJIC	(313) 226-4423
OPM MAINSTREET	(202) 606-4800	FederalJobLine	(818) 575-6521
PayPerNet	(202) 606-2675	FJOB	(912) 757-3100
OPM Express	(214) 767-0565	FedJobs	(215) 580-2216

4. Visit your local Federal Job Information Center (FJIC), staffed with counselors who can help you identify and apply for summer jobs. FJIC addresses and phone numbers are listed in the OPM brochure, "General Information About Summer Job Opportunities With The Federal Government." To obtain this brochure, contact:

US Office of Personnel Management
Career Entry Group
Theodore Roosevelt Building
1900 E Street, NW
Washington, DC 20415-0001
(202) 606-2700

GENERAL INFORMATION
ABOUT
SUMMER JOB OPPORTUNITIES
WITH THE
FEDERAL GOVERNMENT

United States / Career Entry Group / Theodore Roosevelt Building, 1900 E Street, NW, Washington, DC 20415-0001
Office of Personnel Management

SELECTIVITY 🔍🔍🔍
Approximate applicant pool: 150; Interns accepted: 50

COMPENSATION 💲
None; Summer stipends for needy law clerks

LOCATION(S)
Los Angeles, CA

FIELD
Law

DURATION
12 weeks: Summer, Fall, Spring

DEADLINE(S)
Summer: April 14; Academic year: rolling

THE WORK
Established in 1974 to provide legal services to poor and elderly, Bet Tzedek serves people of every race, religion, and ethnicity on issues such as landlord/tenant, consumer protection, and bankruptcy. Every summer seven undergrads are chosen to serve as Legal Assistants under the direction of litigation attorneys.

PERKS
References for applications to law or paralegal schools; orientation and training.

FYI
Bet Tzedek has been taking interns since 1988 . . . Its motto: "Together, we can protect the legal rights of the poor."

TO APPLY
Open to recent high school grads, undergrads, law and paralegal students, and college grads of any age. International applicants eligible. Submission of cover letter serves as an application.

Volunteer Coordinator
Bet Tzedek Legal Services
145 South Fairfax Avenue, Suite 200
Los Angeles, CA 90036
(213) 939-1040 ext. 814

BETSEY JOHNSON.

SELECTIVITY 🔍🔍🔍🔍🔍
Approximate applicant pool: 180; Interns accepted: 7

COMPENSATION 💲
None

LOCATION(S)
New York, NY

FIELD
Clothing

DURATION
6 weeks–5 months; 20 hours/week

DEADLINE(S)
Rolling

THE WORK
Interns work in Sales/Merchandising, Design and Public Relations. An average day would include assisting in departmental projects, running errands throughout the city and working with the fashion line. Interns are needed the most six weeks prior to the fashion shows that take place in February and September. Internship alumni include several Betsey Johnson account executives, production and design assistants.

PERKS
Attendance an/or help welcome at fall and spring fashion shows; possible discounts on Betsey Johnson clothes; "casual, funky" work atmosphere.

FYI
Founded in 1979 by Betsey Johnson herself, this women's apparel company operates 35 retail outlets across the country. The company is known for its youthful and highly creative designs. Betsey Johnson epitomizes "rocker chic" meets SoHo chic."

TO APPLY
Open to high school students, undergrads, and grad students. International applicants eligible. Submit resume and cover letter.

Internship Coordinator
Betsey Johnson
498 Seventh Avenue, 21st Floor
New York, NY 10018

Bike-Aid cyclists celebrate their arrival in Washington, DC after 3,000 miles and two months of riding.

SELECTIVITY 🔍
Approximate applicant pool: 200; Interns accepted per year: 75

COMPENSATION 💲
Some scholarships available

LOCATION(S)
San Francisco, CA; Mexico City, Mexico; Montreal, Canada. All routes end in Washington, D.C.

FIELD
Social and economic justice; International relations; Environmental issues; Education; and Community development

DURATION
9 weeks

DEADLINE(S)
Rolling for office interns; April 1 for the ride

THE WORK
Bike-Aid is a project of JustAct-Youth (ACTion for Global JUSTice). JustAct works to develop in young people a life-long commitment to social and economic justice around the world. We provide a network that links students and youth to educational opportunities and to grassroots movements working for equitable, sustainable and self-reliant communities locally and globally. Bike-Aid participants meet with local community groups and grassroots organizations across the country learning how local citizens are making their communities more livable and sustainable. Once a week, cyclists take part in community service projects such as painting a house, striping bike lanes, or lending a hand at a local food shelter.

PERKS
Global Education: International partner riders from Africa, Asia, and Latin America join the participants sharing stories of their communities and work. Community Living: Live in a "community on wheels" with 25 riders from around the world. Service Learning: Participate in community service projects once a week. Enjoy educational presentations to and from communities. Physical Challenge: Ride an average of 70 miles a week! Fundraising: Raise $1/mile. Cyclists decide which organizations receive 25 percent of the net proceeds.

FYI
Since 1986 over 1,000 people have "pedaled for the planet" with Bike-Aid and raised more than $1.7 million for locally initiated, sustainable projects in over 30 countries around the world.

TO APPLY
Contact us at 1-800-RIDE-808 for an application, or download one off our website at www.bikeaid.org. Bike-Aid is open to anyone at least 16 years old and in good physical condition. (If you're under 18, you must have an adult mentor).

BikeAid/JustAct
333 Valencia St #101
San Francisco, CA 94103
415-431-4480; 1-800-RIDE-808 (tel)
415-431-5953 (fax)

Exclusive Interview with Betsey Johnson

A fashion designer of international repute, Betsey Johnson owns the $18 million (sales) women's apparel company and thirty-five retail outlets which bear her name. Johnson's highly imaginative designs have been worn by the likes of Brigitte Bardot, Raquel Welch, Twiggy, and the late Jacqueline Kennedy Onassis. Johnson graduated Phi Beta Kappa with a B.A. in art from Syracuse University in 1964.

The Internship Informants: Upon graduation from Syracuse, you were invited to be a "guest editor" at *Mademoiselle*. Tell us more about this internship.
Johnson: Because I did so many fabric designs at Syracuse, they put me in the department of DJ White, who headed *Mademoiselle*'s fabric library. In those days, fashion magazines all had fabric libraries, where they cataloged the full range of American and European fabrics. It was great, I looked through all the files and books. There were fabrics from a million places—from Yankee baseball-team striped-flannels to the felt on billiard tables to all the plastics, all the metallics, all the day-glows you could imagine. I learned a ton about the fabrics out there.

The Internship Informants: We read that you really made the most of your time at *Mademoiselle*.
Johnson: DJ took time off to have a baby, so my internship in the fabric library lasted longer than the month it was supposed to. I took the fabrics that no one was using and started a little business making clothes.

The Internship Informants: A business? How did you manage that and work at the magazine at the same time?
Johnson: Well, the building we were in not only housed the offices of Mademoiselle, but also all the other women's magazines owned by Condé Nast, like *Vogue* and *Glamour* and *Brides*. So I thought, "Hey, girls from all these magazines go to the ladies room here." So I made a little catalog of the clothes I was designing, like little t-shirts and t-shirt dresses made out of hand-crochet fabrics and velvets. And I sold my clothes out of the ladies room.

The Internship Informants: They must have loved you there. Did any other interesting things happen at *Mademoiselle*?
Johnson: Well, during the internship, I had met Betsy Blackwell, who was then the editor [of *Mademoiselle*]. When she had a dinner party that summer, she invited me because she had a grandson who was about my age coming to the party. It was fun, and I sent her a thank you note, [on which] I drew a picture of a shoe. I had known that she was a shoe nut—there were shoes all over her office. She had shoe collections coming out of her ears. The next day, she goes to the Art Director and says, "Betsey can draw!" *Mademoiselle* then started giving me a lot of freelance artwork to do. That's how I really started to like fashion. I drew with felt tip magic markers, and I could make a thing too unattractive to photograph look really great in a drawing. It was so funny because I ended up throwing away my college portfolio when my first drawing was published. I xeroxed [the drawing] to poster size and that was my portfolio. I started doing other little jobs. And people would call the Art Department and say, "I'd like to reach this Betsey Johnson illustrator." And I'd think, oh that's me, the intern!

The Internship Informants: For those who want to break into the fashion business, how important are internships?
Johnson: I think they're crucial. You learn so much, especially if it's a good internship, not one where you're stuck in a corner and trace collars all day. Even if you just intern for a month, you can see how a whole business works—you can get the A through Z of it. My wonderful design assistant started as an intern with me while she was at Pratt [Institute] and after that I hired her. Because she needed an assistant, we just hired someone who was once an intern here. So I look to my interns when I need to hire new staff people.

BLACK ENTERPRISE

SELECTIVITY 🔍🔍🔍🔍🔍
Approximate applicant pool: 300; Interns accepted: 6

COMPENSATION 💲
Amount to be decided

LOCATION(S)
Internships are availabe in the New York City location only

FIELD
Magazines

DURATION
10 weeks

DEADLINE(S)
February 1

THE WORK
Founded in 1970, *Black Enterprise* is the premier business-service magazine for African-American entrepreneurs, corporate executives, professionals, and decision makers. Every issue covers business trends, profiles of business leaders, tips for emerging businesses, investment strategies for building personal wealth, networking techniques, and advice on mastering the rules of the workplace. Most interns work in Editorial, although any department may request an intern.

PERKS
Weekly roundtable discussions with staff; tours of other companies (*Business Week*, *The New York Times*, etc.); attendance welcome at company picnic (summer); free copies of magazine.

FYI
Black Enterprise publishes a variety of special issues, including: "The B.E. 100s: The Nation's Largest Black Businesses," "Career & Business Opportunities," "Money Management," "Franchising," and "Small Business Management."

TO APPLY
Open to undergrads and grad students with a GPA of 3.0 or better. Submit cover letter and resume. Students interested in internships in the Editorial Department should provide writing samples as part of their application materials.

Natalie M. Hibbert
Employment & Benefits Programs Manager
Earl G. Graves, Ltd.
130 Fifth Avenue
New York, NY 10011

BLACK ENTERTAINMENT TELEVISION

SELECTIVITY   🔍 🔍 🔍
Approximate applicant pool: 500; Interns accepted: 60

COMPENSATION $
None

LOCATION(S)
Washington, DC

FIELD
Television production; Magazines; Restaurant development

DURATION
12–16 weeks: Summer, Fall, Spring

DEADLINE(S)
Rolling

THE WORK
Launched in 1980, Black Entertainment Television (BET) is the nation's first and only Black-owned cable television network, featuring quality Black entertainment, music, sports, and public affairs. In addition to the cable network, BET operates Action Pay-Per-View, a national pay-per-view movie channel, and BET on Jazz, an advertiser-supported network featuring a variety of jazz productions. BET also publishes *Emerge*, a news magazine targeting Black America. Interns work in Production, News, Sports, Programming, Public Relations, International, Legal, and the Editorial departments within BET.

PERKS
Informal meetings with department heads; occasional opportunities to watch tapings; possible star gazing.

FYI
Says the internship coordinator: "Entertainment is the first thing people think of with BET, but the people here are [BET's] best asset. Everyone is outgoing and upbeat—making for a great environment to work in." . . . In 1991, BET, through its parent company

BET Holdings, Inc., became the first black-owned company to be traded on the New York Stock Exchange.

TO APPLY
Open to high school students, undergrads, and grad students. Must receive academic credit. International applicants eligible. Submit cover letter and resume along with academic transcripts and a letter of certification from your school verifying that you will receive academic credit for the internship.

Teion Van Damm
Internship Coordinator
Black Entertainment Television
One BET Plaza
1900 W Place, NE
Washington, DC 20018
(202) 608-2020
(202) 608-2589 (Fax)

THE BLADE

SELECTIVITY   🔍 🔍 🔍 🔍 🔍
Approximate applicant pool: 300; Interns accepted: 4

COMPENSATION $ $ $
$474/week

LOCATION(S)
Toledo, OH

FIELD
Newspapers

DURATION
12 weeks: Summer

DEADLINE(S)
January 15

THE WORK
Founded in 1835, *The Blade* is Toledo's only newspaper. It is owned and managed by the Block family, who also own cable television franchises and the *Pittsburgh Post-Gazette* (see separate entry). Serving northwestern Ohio and southeastern Michigan, the newspaper posts a daily circulation of 150,000 during the week and over 200,000 on Sundays. Interns work in Editorial, where they help research, write, and edit stories.

PERKS
Mentors; occasional luncheons with senior editors to discuss newspaper issues; tour of city.

FYI
On average, one intern each year is hired as a full-time junior reporter.

TO APPLY
Open to undergrads, recent college grads, college grads of any age, and grad students. International applicants eligible. Submit resume, cover letter, writing samples, and recommendations.

Assistant Managing Editor/Administration
The Blade
541 North Superior Street
Toledo, OH 43660
(419) 724-6127

BLAIR
TELEVISION

SELECTIVITY 🔍🔍🔍🔍
Approximate applicant pool: 100; Interns accepted: 6

COMPENSATION $
$6/hour & reimbursement for lunch and commutation

LOCATION(S)
New York, NY

FIELD
Television

DURATION
12 weeks: Summer, Fall, Spring

DEADLINE(S)
Rolling

THE WORK
Founded in 1948, Blair Television (BT) is the nation's oldest independently owned and operated sales and marketing firm for television stations. Representing 145 stations—those owned by broadcast groups like Gannett, LIN, and Media General—Blair generates nearly $1 billion annually in advertising billings for its clients. Blair also assists 6,000 spot television advertisers and 2,000 advertising agencies in finding sponsorship opportunities and buying television advertising. Interns work in Sales, Research, or Programming. Blair is a subsidiary company of Petry Media Corporation.

PERKS
Mentors; attendance welcome at staff meetings; and special programs to learn about the industry.

FYI
The television stations Blair represents, taken together, broadcast to over 75 percent of US households.

TO APPLY
Open to college juniors and seniors, recent college grads, and college grads of any age. Must have completed at least one communications course. Submit resume and cover letter directly to office of interest.(If interested in an internship at a regional office, you can obtain addresses and home numbers from NY headquarters or website—www.petrymedia.com.)

Internship Coordinator
Blair Television
3 East 54th Street
New York, NY 10022
(212) 603-5000
(212) 603-5712 (Fax)

SELECTIVITY 🔍
Approximate applicant pool: 10; Interns accepted: 5

COMPENSATION $
College credit; Possible royalties or commissions

LOCATION(S)
Culver City, CA (interns accepted nationwide as this is a virtual internship)

FIELD
Comics; Publishing

DURATION
3 months—1 year

DEADLINE(S)
Rolling

THE WORK
A start-up publishing venture, Blue Corn publishes the Native American comic series Peace Party. Interns at Blue Corn work on every step of the comic book publishing process, and the company values interns from almost all educational backgrounds. Students of business and marketing, multicultural studies, public relations, communications, publishing, education, and media are sought, though anyone with a strong desire to work on comics is encouraged to apply. Interns work as editorial assistants who research and write business plans, do background research for stories, and identify book printers and potential distribution channels.

PERKS
Free Comics; free T-shirts; free posters; possible royalties; "Editorial Assistant" credit in comics and on website; write-up in the personnel section of the webpage; career and writing guidance

FYI
Blue Corn Comics is the vision of Robert Schmidt, a freelance business and technology writer who has read comics since 1967.

TO APPLY
Send resume and cover letter to (E-mail applications are encouraged):

Robert Schmidt, Publisher
Blue Corn Comics
6150 Buckingham Parkway #204
(310)-641-8931
E-mail: 73472.324@compuserve.com
http://members.xoom.com/peaceparty

BOEING

SELECTIVITY 🔍🔍🔍🔍🔍

Approximate applicant pool: 10,000; Interns accepted: 150–400 annually

COMPENSATION 💲💲💲💲

Varies by location: Students may receive salary, relocation assistance, housing services, commuter assistance programs, learning centers, recreation, employee credit union, employee benefits

LOCATION(S)

Houston, TX; Huntsville, AL; Kennedy Space Center, FL; Mesa, AZ; Philadelphia, PA; Seattle, WA; St. Louis, MO; Wichita, KS; and various Southern California locations.

FIELD

Business, Computer Science, Engineering, Engineering Technology, and Mathematics

DURATION

8–12 weeks: Summer (internships)
6 months: year round (co-ops)

DEADLINE(S)

Summer: January 31
Co-ops: Continual review

THE WORK

The Boeing Company is the largest aerospace company in the world: a global enterprise that designs, produces and supports commercial airplanes, defense systems, and civil and defense space systems. We are one of the largest U.S. exporters with customers in 145 countries. We have major operations in 27 U.S. States with approximately 190,000 employees.

Our goal is to remain the number-one aerospace company in the world and one way we are working toward this goal is by recruiting bright people and giving them the opportunity to develop to their full potential. The Boeing Company offers a dynamic, exciting environment, one that affords many opportunities.

PERKS

Life-long learning opportunities; recreational opportunities and on-site health and fitness centers, off- and on-hour training, and social activities.

FYI

"Among the 'nirvana' internships . . . Apple, Boeing, Intel, Microsoft . . ." – *The Wall Street Journal*

TO APPLY

Interested students should check our intern web site for application instructions specific to their area of interest: www.boeing.com/employment. Summer internship activities usually begin the previous fall, while co-op work experience activities are year round.

Boeing College Recruiting
Internship Coordinator
P.O. Box 3707l; M/S 6H-PR
Seattle, WA 98124
(425) 234-1957
(206) 234-2568 (fax)
www.boeing.com/employment

THE BOSTON GLOBE

SELECTIVITY 🔍🔍🔍

Approximate applicant pool: 400–500; Interns accepted: approximately 20

COMPENSATION 💲💲💲💲💲

$430/week for co-ops; $580/week for undergrads (summer interns); $580–$740/week for grad students (1-year interns).

LOCATION(S)

Boston, MA; Washington, DC (one position)

FIELD

Newspapers

DURATION

Summer: 13 weeks; One-Year internship; Co-op: 6 months full time (January–June or July–December)

DEADLINE(S)

Editorial Summer: November 1; Business: Summer; One-Year: February 10; Co-op: rolling

THE WORK

A subsidiary of The New York Times Company, The *Boston Globe* was founded in 1872 and is New England's largest newspaper. Two interns in the Business Summer Program work in Accounting and Advertising. Three interns in the One-Year Business Program work in Advertising, Advertising Design, and Circulation; 18 interns in the Editorial Summer Program work in Editorial (sports, living/arts, business, photography, and Washington bureau); and 40 interns work year-round under the auspices of the Co-op Program in Editorial, Advertising, Accounting, and Personnel.

PERKS

Weekly seminars on issues in journalism (e.g. libel law); informal gatherings with Globe editors and columnists; access to company gym; one-year interns are eligible for health insurance benefits.

FYI

The Editorial Summer and Co-op programs are both well established: the former dates back to 1966, the latter to the 1940s.

TO APPLY

Summer programs: open to college sophomores and juniors; One-Year Business Program: open to recent college grads and grad students; Co-op Program: open to undergrads. International applicants eligible. Call or write for an application.

Assistant Manager, HR
The Boston Globe
P.O. Box 2378
Boston, MA 02107-2378
(617) 929-2795
(617) 929-3376 (fax)

SELECTIVITY 🔍🔍
Approximate applicant pool: 100; Interns accepted: 20

COMPENSATION 💲
None

LOCATION(S)
Boston, MA

FIELD
Magazines

DURATION
12–15 weeks: Summer, Fall, Spring

DEADLINE(S)
Summer: May 1; Fall: August 1; Spring: January 1

THE WORK
The nation's second largest city magazine, *Boston Magazine* has been keeping Bostonians abreast of the city's latest cultural and political trends since 1963. Departments accepting interns include: Editorial, Advertising, Art, Accounting, Marketing, and Production.

PERKS
Marketing interns attend special events like the annual Best of Boston™ Party. Art interns often go on photo shoots.

FYI
The intern coordinator estimates that over a quarter of the staff is made up of former *Boston Magazine* interns; this group includes the Manager of Research and the Associate Art Director.

TO APPLY
Open to undergrads and recent college grads. International applicants eligible. Submit resume and cover letter. Writing samples only necessary if applying for editorial. Please specify the department you're applying for in cover letter.

Internship Coordinator
Boston Magazine
Horticultural Hall
300 Massachusetts Avenue
Boston, MA 02115
(617) 262-9700
(617) 262-4925 (Fax)

LAWYER TURNED HOLLYWOOD SCREENWRITER

After graduating from law school in 1984, **Paul Attanasio** spurned an offer at the prestigious law firm Cravath, Swain, & Moore to intern as a film critic for *The Washington Post*. Solidifying a love for film during the internship, he decided on a career in filmmaking and a few years later wrote the scripts for the hit movies *Quiz Show* and *Disclosure*.

SELECTIVITY 🔍
Approximate applicant pool: 900; Interns accepted: 700

COMPENSATION 💲
None; internships for academic credit

LOCATION(S)
Beijing, China; Dresden, Germany; Dublin, Ireland; London, England; Haifa, Israel; Madrid, Spain; Moscow, Russia; Paris, France; Sydney, Australia; Washington, DC

FIELD
Advertising or Public relations; Arts and arts administration; Economics; Health and human services; Hospitality administration; Management and finance; The Media; Journalism; Film and television; Politics; and Prelaw

DURATION
8–20 weeks: Fall, Spring, and Summer semesters

DEADLINE(S)
Fall: March 15; Spring: October 15; Summer: March 1. Applications are reviewed on a rolling basis.

THE WORK
Boston University's Division of International Programs offers global internship programs that combine academic coursework in language and liberal arts with an internship experience. Internship placements are available in the following fields: Advertising or Public Relations; Arts and Arts Administration; Film and Television; Health and Human Services; Hospitality Administration; Journalism; Management and Finance; Politics; and Prelaw. Courses and internships are conducted exclusively in the local language. Summer programs are available in London, Madrid, Sydney, and Washington, D.C., only.

PERKS
In-country orientation and field trips to cultural sites; 16 semester-hour credits.

FYI
Past internship placements include: AIDS/Infoshare Russia, Baker & McKenzie, Amtrak, Guiness, Estée Lauder, Marriott, IBM, Sotheby's, Chemical Bank, *International Herald Tribune*, Goldman Sachs, Hard Rock Cafe, American Airlines, BBC, Amnesty International, The Cassel Hospital, World Wildlife Fund, *Vogue*, Sheraton, Coca-Cola, and the Australian Stock Exchange . . . BUIP offers a few study abroad grants and merit scholarships, from $200 to $1,000 for fall and spring, $100 to $1,000 for summer.

TO APPLY
Write for application. Application fee: $45.

Boston University International Programs
232 Bay State Road
Boston, MA 02215
(617) 353-9888
(617) 353-5402 (Fax)
E-mail: abroad@bu.edu
www.bu.edu/abroad

BOYS HOPE

GIRLS HOPE

SELECTIVITY
Approximate applicant pool: 65; Volunteers/Interns accepted: 35–40

COMPENSATION
$50/week; round-trip travel; free room and board; eligible to apply for medical benefits, Americorps Education Assistance Only Award

LOCATION(S)
Phoenix, AZ; Orange County, CA; Denver, CO; Jacksonville, FL; Chicago, IL; Baton Rouge and New Orleans, LA; Detroit, MI; St. Louis, MO (HQ); New York, NY; Cincinnati, and Cleveland, OH; Pittsburgh, PA; Las Vegas, NV; San Antonia, TX; San Francisco, CA

FIELD
Education; Social service; Recreation

DURATION
1 year

DEADLINE(S)
Rolling

THE WORK
Founded in 1975, Boys Hope Girls Hope (BHGH) is a non-profit, nondenominational organization providing family-like homes, counseling, and college-preparatory educational activities for at-risk yet academically capable boys and girls between the ages of 10 and 17. Children are allowed to stay in residence until they graduate from high school and are provided with financial assistance to attend college. Volunteers assist staff in maintaining a stable home environment, assume a "Big Brother/Sister" role, and provide tutoring and mentoring.

PERKS
One-week orientation and mid-year "renewal" in St. Louis; housing in one of BHGH's group homes for children.

FYI
Approximately 30 percent of BHGH volunteers are later hired by the organization for full-time positions .

TO APPLY
Open to grads and grad students (part-timers only). Must pass police background check and physical examination. Write for application.

Volunteer Coordinator, Stephanie Welberg
Boys Hope Girls Hope
12120 Bridgeton Square Drive
Bridgeton, MO 63044
(800) 545-2697 or (314) 298-1250
(314) 298-1251 (Fax)
E-Mail: hope@bhgh.org
www.BoysHopeGirlsHope.org

SELECTIVITY
Approximate applicant pool: 150; Interns accepted: 6–8

COMPENSATION
$7 an hour

LOCATION(S)
Omaha, NE

FIELD
Public relations; Advertising, Copywriting, Art direction, Interactive, Media planning

DURATION
12 weeks: Summer

DEADLINE(S)
January 31

THE WORK
Founded in 1921, in Omaha, Bozell is a full-service advertising and public relations agency. Its diverse client base includes Mutual of Omaha, First National Bank, and American Tool Companies. Interns are involved in all areas of the agency work.

PERKS
Attendance at company events; occasional travel to off-site client meetings.

FYI
Approximately 25 percent of interns are hired for full-time employment.

TO APPLY
Open to undergrads, recent college grads, and grad students. Application can be found at:

www.bozell-omaha.com/summerintern.

BP

SELECTIVITY
Approximate applicant pool: 500; Interns accepted: 30

COMPENSATION
$450–$650/week; round-trip travel; medical insurance

LOCATION(S)
New Orleans, LA; Lima and Toledo, OH; Marcus Hook, PA; Green Lake, TX

FIELD
Oil and gas; Chemicals

DURATION
At least two 4-month sessions: Fall, Spring

DEADLINE(S)
Rolling

We Know How You Feel.

Naked. Here you are a year from graduation and what do you have to show for it? No work. No experience. Nothing that sets you apart from the hundreds of soon-to-be job hunters. Well, fear not. Once again Bozell Omaha will be hiring a team of summer interns. Students doing real work alongside advertising professionals for a whopping $5 an hour. Alright. So the salary isn't that great. But think of it. While all your classmates are working on their tan this summer, you'll be working on your book. And that just might give you the edge you need to land that job of your dreams. Hey, it worked for the seven former interns now on Bozell's full-time staff. Of course, they were wearing business suits when we interviewed them. For an application package, see:

Bozell
O M A H A

> Two of the advertisements created by the Omaha headquarters of Bozell Public Relations to publicize its internship program. The posters feature former interns.

Our boss is looking for someone to take our jobs.

We were both in your shoes a couple years ago. No real experience and graduation right around the corner. Luckily, we applied for the Bozell Summer internship. Three months of working in the real world on real projects with real clients. We even got real paychecks (they weren't real big, but they were real). It gave us the experience we needed to land bitchin' jobs. Of course, we're not the only ones. The fact is, five other former interns are currently on Bozell's staff and countless others are working for other agencies. Now Bozell's looking to hire someone to fill our old jobs. There are internship positions available in the Account Service, Media and Creative Departments. Apply. Take it from a couple guys who know. it's worth it. Because while the pay is only $5 an hour, the experience is priceless. For more information, pick up an internship curriculum and application package at

Bozell
O M A H A

THE WORK

Tracing its history back to 1870, BP (for British Petroleum) is one of the world's largest petroleum companies, with over $75 billion in annual sales and a product mix that includes oil, gasoline, plastics, high-tech ceramics, and basic chemicals. In the US, BP America is the nation's biggest domestic crude-oil producer, churning out 700,000 barrels a day, most of which is refined into gasoline sold out of over 7,500 service stations in 25 states. Under the auspices of BP America's Co-op Program, interns (who may stay on for the summer) work in Development and in Processing at four refineries (in LA, OH, and PA) and two chemical plants (in OH and TX).

PERKS

Occasional training workshops (e.g. safety, refining methods); access to fitness facilities (varies with location).

FYI

BP owns 50 percent of the 800-mile-long trans-Alaska pipeline, which it co-established . . . BP America pays 90 percent of tuition expenses for co-op interns taking evening/weekend classes at local universities during their internship.

TO APPLY

Open to college sophomores and juniors in chemical engineering only. Submit resume and cover letter.

Co-op Coordinator
BP America
200 Public Square, Room 11-B
Cleveland, OH 44114
(216) 586-4141

BRECKENRIDGE OUTDOOR EDUCATION CENTER

BRECKENRIDGE
OUTDOOR
EDUCATION
CENTER

SELECTIVITY
Approximate applicant pool: 70–100; Interns accepted: 10

COMPENSATION
$50/month; free room and board

LOCATION(S)
Breckenridge, CO

FIELD
Outdoor Recreation; Adventure Therapy; Recreation Therapy

DURATION
4–6 months: May–September; November—May

DEADLINE(S)
Summer: March 20; Winter: September 15

THE WORK

Established in 1976, the Breckenridge Outdoor Education Center (BOEC) empowers people through outdoor experiences. The population that we serve includes people of all abilities, ranging from people with cognitive, physical, emotional, and/or psychological disabilities, "at risk" youth, people with chronic illnesses, and/or professional challenge groups. Operating out of an alpine lodge at the base of Breckenridge mountain, the BOEC offers specialized programs in skiing, rock climbing, camping, canoeing, rafting, ropes course, climbing wall, team-building, etc. Interns are involved in all aspects of the BOEC. They are the wheels that make the BOEC move. Time and time again our clients comment that the energy, professionalism, and expertise of the BOEC staff is the center's greatest asset.

PERKS
Three- to six-week training in the operation of BOEC's programs; free ski pass (winter); limited pro-deals on outdoor gear; free room and board; personal fulfillment and enrichment.

TO APPLY
Open to high school grads 21 and over, college grads 21 and over, grad students, and anyone else looking to gain experience in the outdoors or with special populations. Look on our website for an application or write:.

Internship Coordinator
Breckenridge Outdoor Education Center
P.O. Box 697
Breckenridge, CO 80424
(970) 453-6422
(970) 453-4676 (Fax)
www.boec.org

> "Interns are the life blood of the Breckenridge Outdoor Education Center. They are 'where the rubber meets the road.'"
> —Internship Coordinator, Breckenrige Outdoor Education Center

BRETHREN VOLUNTEER SERVICE

SELECTIVITY
Approximate applicant pool: 150; Interns accepted: 100

COMPENSATION
$50–$70/month; round-trip travel to and from project; free room and board (community housing, apartment, or homestay); medical insurance

LOCATION(S)
23 states in the US, Washington, DC; 21 countries overseas and Central America (See Appendix)

FIELD
Public service in 20 fields (see THE WORK)

DURATION
US: 1 year minimum, ongoing; Overseas: 2 years minimum, ongoing

DEADLINE(S)
Rolling

THE WORK
Founded in 1948, Brethren Volunteer Service (BVS) is a non-profit organization of volunteers working to "help a world in need." Sponsored by the Church of the Brethren, BVS seeks to promote justice and peace, serve basic human needs, and maintain "the integrity of creation." Volunteers "examine and study the

Christian faith" by working on over 130 community-service projects in the following categories: Children, Youth/Young Adults, Senior Citizens, General Community Services, Farmworkers, Disabled Persons, Agriculture, Hunger/Homelessness, Prisoners and the Prison System, Refugees, Peace/Justice, Domestic Violence, Housing, Health Care, Outdoor Ministries, Community Organizing/Development Advocacy, Education/Teaching, Environment, Congregations, and Miscellaneous.

PERKS
Three-week orientation in the US (determines placement); deferment of educational loans; possibility of receiving Americorp Education award.

FYI
BVS's motto: "Sharing God's love through acts of service." Current volunteers are caring for children, tending to patients at hospices, organizing activities at churches, feeding the homeless, visiting with victims of the Hiroshima atomic bomb, organizing protests, teaching English, building houses, and much more. The design of the Peace Corps (see separate entry) was based in part on BVS.

TO APPLY
Anyone 18 years of age and over. Open to high school grads, undergrads, recent college grads, college grads of any age, and grad students. Must be at least 21 to serve overseas. International applicants eligible. Write for application and project booklet.

Recruitment Division
Brethren Volunteer Service
1451 Dundee Avenue
Elgin, IL 60120
(800) 323-8039 or (847) 742-5100
E-mail: bvs_gb@brethren.org
www.brethrenvolunteerservice.com
(847) 742-0278 (Fax)

BRICK WALL MANAGEMENT

SELECTIVITY
Approximate applicant pool: 60; Interns accepted: 10–12

COMPENSATION
None

LOCATION(S)
New York, NY

FIELD
Record Industry

DURATION
12–16 weeks (flexible): Summer, Fall, Spring

DEADLINE(S)
Rolling

THE WORK
Founded in 1996, Brick Wall Management represents a variety of artists in the music industry, both signed and unsigned. Its small staff is involved in all aspects of running the company, and interns get an unusually hands-on experience at Brick Wall—duties include everything from office clerical work and concert promotion to "in the field" work, such as attending soundchecks, stocking CDs at local record stores, helping bands prepare for shows, and attending to the merchandise stand at concerts.

PERKS
Frequent contact with Brick Wall Management's bands; free concert tickets; small office environment; exposure to all aspects of the music industry

FYI
Although the internships are unpaid, the internship coordinator says, "Whenever there is paying work available with one of our acts, the interns are our first choice."

TO APPLY
Open to high school students, college undergrads, recent grads, grad students, and high school or college graduates of any age. Submit resume by fax, e-mail (paul@brickwallmgmt.com), or regular mail.

Brick Wall Management
Attn: Internship Coordinator
648 Amsterdam Avenue
Suite 4A
New York, NY 10025
(212) 501-0748
(212) 724-0849 (Fax)
brickwallmgmt.com
E-mail: bweast@brickwallmgmt.com

BROOKFIELD ZOO

Chicago Zoological Society
Brookfield Zoo

SELECTIVITY
Approximate applicant pool: 100 (Summer); 50 (Fall, Winter); Interns accepted: 20 (Summer); 20 (Fall, Winter)

COMPENSATION
None

LOCATION(S)
Brookfield, IL

FIELD
Zookeeping/Animal management Conservation

DURATION
6–12 weeks: Summer, Fall, Winter

DEADLINE(S)
Summer: February 1; Winter: December 1; Fall: August 1

THE WORK
Internationally renowned Brookfield Zoo's mission, "helping people develop a sustainable and harmonious relationship with nature," is served by the Intern Program. Experiential learning opportunities for students pursuing conservation-related careers are available in many animal departments: Seven Seas Panorama, The Living Coast, Australia House, Department of Animal Health, Reptile House, Children's Zoo, Bird Department, Habitat Africa, Tropic World, The Fragile Kingdom, The Swamp, Department of Nutrition Services, and Conservation Biology. Zookeeper interns gain valuable hands-on experience working with the zoo's diverse animal collection, containing over 2,000 specimens of over 400 species. Internships in nonanimal departments, such as Environmental Education, Water Quality, Human Resources, Exhibit Design, Development, Public Relations, Marketing, Life Safety, and Horticulture are also available.

PERKS
Animals aplenty; down and dirty; interns receive a group tour of all the animal areas; all interns receive an employee pass, which grants them special opportunities.

FYI
Along with keeping a daily journal, interns particpate in research projects involving many aspects of captive animal management. Zookeeping is a physically demanding profession, and physical strength is required. Housing is not provided. All internships are unpaid unless otherwise indicated.

TO APPLY
Open to college juniors and seniors, recent grads, grad students, college grads of any age. Minimum 2.5 GPA. International applicants eligible with appropriate documentation. Write for application.

Jan Rizzo
Coordinator, Intern Program
Brookfield Zoo
3300 South Golf Road
Brookfield, IL 60513
(708) 485-0263 ext.459
(708) 485-0986 (Fax)
E-mail: jarizzo@brookfieldzoo.org

BROOKHAVEN NATIONAL LABORATORY

SELECTIVITY
Approximate applicant pool: 1,500; Interns accepted: 125

COMPENSATION
$225/week; round-trip travel; free housing

LOCATION(S)
Upton, NY

FIELD
Science; Engineering research

DURATION
10 weeks: Summer; 16 weeks: Fall, Spring

DEADLINE(S)
Summer: January 31; Fall: March 15; Spring: October 20

THE WORK
Established in 1947 as a research facility of the US Department of Energy (see separate entry), Brookhaven National Laboratory (BNL) conducts fundamental studies in such fields as energy technology, solid-state physics, environmental sciences, and nuclear reactor safety. Specialized BNL research facilities include the Alternating Gradient Synchrotron and the National Synchrotron Light Source. Interns—under the auspices of the Summer Student Program—work on research projects in chemistry, physics, biology, nuclear medicine, engineering, computer science, applied mathematics, high and low energy particle accelerators, and science writing.

PERKS
Attendance welcome at lectures and seminars; subsidized food at cafeteria; access to recreational facilities.

FYI
BNL's summer internship was started in 1949 . . . Former BNL interns include BNL Director Dr. N.P. Samios, who participated in 1952, and Dr. Roald Hoffman, a 1957 intern and winner of the Nobel Prize in Chemistry (1981). (See Exclusive Interview with Roald Hoffman.)

TO APPLY

Open to college juniors and seniors as well as college grads within six months of graduation (fall and spring only). Minimum GPA: 3.0. Write for application.

Summer Student Program
Office of Educational Programs, Building 438
Brookhaven National Laboratory
P.O. Box 5000
Upton, NY 11973-5000
(516) 282-4385
(516) 282-5832 (Fax)
E-mail: thomas@bnlarm.bln.gov

> **Michael Otto**, the German billionaire whose family owns Spiegel, the US catalog company, once interned in Munich at Merck Finck & Co., the second-largest private bank in Germany.

THE BROOKINGS INSTITUTION

SELECTIVITY
Approximate applicant pool: 75; Interns accepted: 10

COMPENSATION
None

LOCATION(S)
Washington, DC

FIELD
Public policy; Think tank

DURATION
12 weeks: Summer, Fall, Winter/Spring; Part-time available

DEADLINE(S)
Summer: April 1; Winter/Spring: Dec. 1; Fall: August 1

THE WORK

Founded by woodenware tycoon Robert Brookings in 1916, the Brookings Institution espouses a decades-old mission—that is, "to bring knowledge to bear on the current and emerging public policy problems facing the American people." The Institution offers students formal internships in Governmental Studies, Foreign Policy Studies, Economic Studies, Center for Public Policy, Education, Public Affairs, Brookings Press Marketing and Information Technology Services

PERKS

Intellectual environment; access to political conferences; seminars.

FYI

All of Brookings' resources are open to interns—such as Brookings' library, the Library of Congress, and the National

Archives . . . Scholars seem surprisingly "relaxed and informal, frequently available to answer questions about research, graduate schools, or political issues" . . . Brookings is considered predominantly liberal in ideology.

TO APPLY

Open to college juniors and seniors, grad students. International applicants eligible. Submit resume, cover letter, transcript plus course descriptions of all political science credits, writing sample (3 to 5 pages) preferably from a political science course, and two letters of recommendation.

The Brookings Institution
Internship Coordinator
(Name of Program)
1775 Massachusetts Avenue NW
Washington, DC 20036-2188
Job line: (202) 797-6096
(202) 797-24779 (fax)
www.brook.edu

BROOKLYN BOTANIC GARDEN

SELECTIVITY
Approximate applicant pool: 40; Interns accepted: 10

COMPENSATION
$7/hour

LOCATION(S)
Brooklyn, NY

FIELD
Horticulture

DURATION
Varies according to internship: Summer and Spring

DEADLINE(S)
Varies according to internship

THE WORK

Founded in 1910 on a reclaimed waste dump, the Brooklyn Botanic Garden (BBG) features over 12,000 kinds of plants on 52 acres. One of the country's leading urban gardens, it includes a Children's Garden where young people ages three to 17 learn hands-on gardening techniques. Interns work in Education and Horticulture.

PERKS

Brown-bag luncheon lectures; lunch with BBG's president; field trips to other gardens; free passes to other NY cultural institutions.

FYI

In existence since 1944, the internship program counts among its alumni BBG's Vice President of Education, and the Gardener-in-Charge of the Desert Collection.

TO APPLY

Open to high school juniors and seniors, college juniors and seniors, recent college grads, college grads of any age, and grad students. International applicants eligible. Send resume and cover letters.

Internship Coordinator
Brooklyn Botanic Garden
1000 Washington Avenue
Brooklyn, NY 11225-1099
(718) 622-4433 x216
(718) 857-2430 (Fax)

EXCLUSIVE INTERVIEW WITH RICHARD HIEB

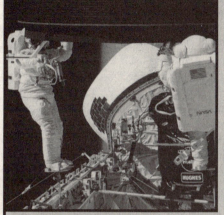

After graduating in 1979 from the University of Colorado with an M.S. in aerospace engineering, Richard Hieb, a North Dakota native, worked at NASA in crew procedures development and crew activity planning. He then applied to the NASA Astronaut Program, to which he was admitted in 1985, becoming an astronaut one year later. An alumnus of three Space Shuttle missions, Hieb participated in the first-ever three-person space walk and has logged over 750 hours in space. He graduated with a B.A in math and physics from Northwest Nazarene College in 1977. At left, Richard Hieb (far left) and other Endeavour crew members successfully capture the Intelsat VI satellite for later deployment.

The Internship Informants: You served an internship at NASA's Johnson Space Center during the summer of 1978. Where were you assigned?

Hieb: I was in the engineering side of the house here. We're divided roughly into two big groups at Johnson Space Center, between engineering and operations…but the engineering side does all the design stuff, and my particular area was in the Design group, focused on mechanical parts and in particular, space craft.

The Internship Informants: What did you do?

Hieb: One of our biggest customers was the TDRS [Tracking Data and Relay Satellite], which was mounted on the Inertial Upper Stage [IUS]. Like a lot of satellites we deploy, we only get up a couple hundred miles above the earth. Most satellites, to do their job, have to be up at 25,000 miles, so they need another booster to get them up there and the IUS booster for this satellite was the biggest one that we flew on shuttle. The problem was that it was mounted in the very back of the bay, which is good for putting the center of gravity aft but you had the big booster plus the satellite cantilevered off the end of this thing. The big concern was, if you have to abort and bring the thing back, now you're landing like an airplane, and the weight is being carried differently. So there was interest in looking into some sort of energy-absorbing mechanism—springs, dampers, whatever—to keep this from basically bouncing around on the end of this long cantilever and shaking itself loose from the payload bay [during landing, if NASA had to abort]. So my job for the summer was to investigate the possibilities of such a damping system and basically determine some characteristics of it—how well could it damp, how heavy would it have to be, what would be the cost associated with some sort of damper.

The Internship Informants: As an intern, did you ever meet any astronauts?

Hieb: I did…. In fact, before I left, my second-level supervisor walked over to the Astronaut Office with me, and he walked into John Young's office, who was the chief, and said, "Hey, I wonder if you could sign a picture for Mr. Hieb here," and John said, "Sure, I'd be glad to." So I met John at that point … sort of my hero [John Young made five space trips, including an Apollo moon walk and the first shuttle flight]…. I was very impressed to meet John and interested to see what this hero was like in person. I was astonished to find that John is a pretty shy person.

The Internship Informants: What role did the NASA internship play in your becoming an astronaut?

Hieb: I can't imagine how I would have got here without that internship. I grew up in North Dakota, in a blue-collar family. The only guy I knew that worked for the Federal Government was the mailman … so the chances of my finding my way into government service were practically zilch…. [As an intern], I'm not sure I produced a whole lot for NASA, but I learned an awful lot about real life and discovered, hey, I can do this work.

The Internship Informants: How did you find out about the internship?

Hieb: I went to a small undergraduate school … then I went on to the University of Colorado at Boulder, and it was there that—one day I was walking down the hall, and I saw this little flyer up on the bulletin board that said "Summer Jobs with NASA"… I picked it up and discovered that the deadline was two or three days away, so I made a mad scramble to put everything together … Then I truthfully forgot about it because, I figured, there's no way. One morning, I got a phone call, and my landlady came pounding on my door. I come out, and the guy on the other end of the phone is speaking Texan, and I almost couldn't understand him. I ended up working for him.

The Internship Informants: Did you have a lot of engineering experience up to that point?

Hieb: No, I mean I was laughing at myself because my experience prior to that point had been working at truck stops, picking cherries, being a dorm assistant, and stuff like that.

Hieb interview continued . . .

The Internship Informants: Did you decide, as an intern, that you were going to become an astronaut?

Hieb: I was not entertaining the notion then.... I grew up needing glasses to be able to see, so I knew I couldn't be a pilot, and in the old days, to be an astronaut, you had to be a pilot. The summer I [interned] here, all the new guys—the first sort of modern-era class of astronauts from 1978—came aboard, and that was the first time they ever had what they called mission specialists. I thought to myself—mission specialist—that'd be the perfect job for me. But I couldn't see well enough to qualify, so I never even thought about it.

The Internship Informants: But then after the internship, you did get an entry-level job with NASA. How did the astronaut position come about?

Hieb: In about '83, they reduced the vision requirement for mission specialist, slightly—enough to get me in the window. So I applied and didn't get selected the first time, which is pretty typical, and got picked the next time around. Here I was, to my great astonishment, and it had everything to do with seeing that little ad one day walking down the hallway in Boulder.

The Internship Informants: What did it feel like to be up in space, wear the space suit, and float around up there?

Hieb: If I start with probably the number-one highlight that I'm sure I'll take with me forever, it's when I went out the hatch on my first spacewalk.... our field of view is sort of limited to being straight ahead. If you turn your head, the helmet stays in place, so you see the side of the helmet eventually, and you're always facing whichever direction your hands are pointed because the suit is not terribly flexible. I was working around on the front face of the Orbiter, and I got to a point where all of a sudden I came up over the edge ... and there was the earth in front of me ... for the first time in my career, suddenly I could see the whole earth laid out below me ... this huge, broad picture of the earth that I'd never seen looking out the window, and it was all I could do to bite my tongue.

The Internship Informants: And what about the launch phase? What does that feel like?

Hieb: If you're not scared, then you're probably too stupid to be flying in space because there's a certain element of risk associated with every launch. You feel it all the way to the tips of your toes because you're shaken around pretty good for the first couple of minutes while the solids burn. Then it gets smooth under the main engines, but until they cut off, you're in an environment that's purely test and always risky. Then the engines shut off, and you're in free fall. It takes a few days to really appreciate that, but to be able to float is just as good as anybody ever thought it would be.... It's a marvelous experience.

THE BROOKLYN MUSEUM

THE BROOKLYN MUSEUM

SELECTIVITY 🔍🔍🔍🔍🔍
Between 75–100 applicants. Accepted: 5–7 in Education. Other internships vary by department.

COMPENSATION 💲💲
$13,500 stipend. Other internships vary by department. Some volunteer internships opportunities in curatorial departments.

LOCATION(S)
Brooklyn, New York

FIELD
Museums

DURATION
Education: 10 months beginning in September; Other departments: vary

DEADLINE(S)
Application for Education internships: March 31; Other departments: vary

THE WORK
Opened to the public in 1893, the Brooklyn Museum of Art is the second-largest art museum in New York State. The Museum possesses encyclopedic collections ranging from the arts of ancient Egypt to the most recent examples of contemporary art. Internships at the Brooklyn Museum of Art offer graduate and undergraduate students entry-level experience in the various aspects of museum work. The Brooklyn Museum of Art offers paid and volunteer internships in curatorial departments and the Education Division.

PERKS
Intensive four-week orientation/training; tours of the Museum; attendance welcome at Museum events; employee discounts at the Museum shops and cafe; free admission to other NY museums.

FYI
In the last ten years more than five hundred interns have successfully trained at the Brooklyn Museum of Art and gone on to positions in prestigious institutions around the world. The museum offers a limited number of shorter, credit-only internships in Planning, Design, Development, the Libraries, Archives, and registrar's Office. Call for more details.

TO APPLY
Open to recent college graduates and graduate students. Submit resume, cover letter with statement of interest, and two recommendations.

Education
The Brooklyn Museum of Art
200 Eastern Parkway
Brooklyn, NY 11238
(718) 638-5000 x230
(718) 783-6301 (Fax)

SELECTIVITY 🔍 🔍 🔍 🔍 🔍
Approximate applicant pool: 100; Interns accepted: 4

COMPENSATION $
All expenses reimbursed

LOCATION(S)
Martinez, CA

FIELD
Public relations

DURATION
12–16 weeks: Summer, Fall, Spring

DEADLINE(S)
Summer: May 20; Fall: August 20; Spring: January 20

THE WORK
Brown·Miller Communications is a full-service public relations agency specializing in the food, beverage, and agriculture industries. Its clients include Livermore Valley Winegrowers Association, California Department of Health Services, The American Society for Enology and Viticulture, Seguin Moreau USA, the Unified Wine and Grape Symposium, and California Canning Peach Association. Interns serve as account coordinators, helping to write press releases, track press coverage, and coordinate events.

PERKS
Hands on experience; close supervision by the entire staff; access to industry Professional Societies; (PRSA, IABC); and industry educational seminars.

FYI
The offices of Brown·Miller Communications are located one-half hour east of San Francisco.

TO APPLY
Open to college juniors and seniors, recent college grads, college grads of any age, and grad students with college related course experience in public relations, journalism, English or communications. International applicants eligible. Submit resume, cover letter, writing samples, and recommendations.

Internship Coordinator Amy Woodman
Brown·Miller Communications
1114 Jones Street
Martinez, CA 94553
(925) 370-9777
(800) 710-9333
(925) 370-9811 (Fax)
E-mail: amy@brownmillerpr.com

SELECTIVITY 🔍 🔍 🔍 🔍 🔍
Approximate applicant pool: 100; Interns accepted: 5

COMPENSATION $ $
$365/week; reimbursement for daily car expenses

LOCATION(S)
Levittown and Richboro, PA

FIELD
Newspapers

DURATION
12 weeks: Summer

DEADLINE(S)
February 1

THE WORK
Founded in 1910, the *Bucks County Courier Times* is a daily newspaper serving the Philadelphia suburb of Bucks County. With a daily circulation of over 80,000, the *Courier Times* covers news, sports, business, and lifestyle and consumer issues. Interns work as news reporters, bureau reporters, copy desk assistants, photographers, sports writers, and features writers.

PERKS
Orientation luncheon with publisher; mentors; opportunity to work on a professional level.

FYI
The *Courier Times* internship program began in the late 1980s, was discontinued in 1990 because of cutbacks, and re-emerged in 1992 as a minority program.

TO APPLY
Open to minority undergrads. Submit resume, cover letter, and writing samples.

Internship Coordinator
Bucks County Courier Times
8400 Route 13
Levittown, PA 19057
(215) 949-4177 (Fax)

BUFFALO BILL HISTORICAL CENTER

BUFFALO BILL HISTORICAL CENTER

SELECTIVITY 🔍
Approximate applicant pool: 30; Interns accepted: 8–15

COMPENSATION 💲💲
Varies, unpaid to $250/week

LOCATION(S)
Cody, WY

FIELD
Museums; Print media; Website

DURATION
3 months minimum, year round

DEADLINE(S)
Four months before start date

THE WORK
Located in the heart of the American West and just 50 miles from Yellowstone National Park, the Buffalo Bill Historical Center is an internationally acclaimed complex of four museums pertaining to the culture, history, and art of the American West and to the technological development of firearms. The center attracts over 280,000 visitors annually. Interns work in Curatorial, Collections, Registration, Library, Education, Public Relations, Development/Membership, Accounting, Photography, and Publications.

PERKS
Attendance welcome at various educational programs; attendance welcome at all staff functions (parties, picnics, etc.); discounts in museum gift shop and restaurant; close proximity to Yellowstone National Park.

FYI
The Center also offers a Native American Internship

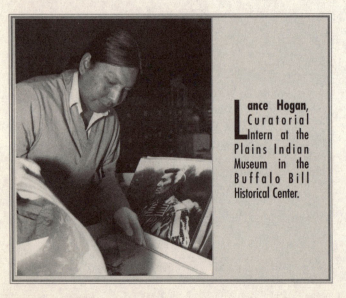

Lance Hogan, Curatorial Intern at the Plains Indian Museum in the Buffalo Bill Historical Center.

Program in which interns spend three to six months working under the curator of the Plains Indian Museum. The internship is open to members of American Indian tribes who have completed at least their second year of college.

TO APPLY
Open to undergrads, recent college grads, college grads of any age, and grad students. International applicants eligible. Write for application.

Internship Coordinator/Director of Education
Buffalo Bill Historical Center
720 Sheridan Avenue
Cody, WY 82414
(307) 578-4005, ext. 215
(307) 587-5714 (Fax)

B.U.G.

SELECTIVITY 🔍🔍🔍🔍
Approximate applicant pool: 40; Interns accepted: 1–3

COMPENSATION 💲💲💲💲
$350/week; round-trip travel

LOCATION(S)
Sapporo, Japan

FIELD
Computers

DURATION
12 weeks–6 months; ongoing

DEADLINE(S)
Rolling

THE WORK
Established in 1989, B.U.G. designs and manufactures creative, state-of-the-art software and hardware. With 100 employees and three branch offices, the company specializes in graphic design, image processing, media storage, digital prepress, input-output devices, and network and communication. Interns work in Research & Development and Business Development.

PERKS
Mentors; subsidized meals in company cafeteria; subsidized housing ($100/month); social and sports activities.

FYI
In existence since 1990, the internship program leads to permanent employment at B.U.G. for approximately 20 percent of interns . . . B.U.G. has partnerships with Canon, Apple Computer, Dai Nippon Printing, and Radius & SuperMac.

TO APPLY
Open to undergrads, recent college grads, and grad students. Must have at least one year of coursework in Japanese. Must have background in engineering, computer science, or business. International applicants eligible. Submit resume and cover letter.

Internship Coordinator
B.U.G.
1-14 Technopark 1-Chome
Atsubetsu-ku
Sapporo 004 Japan
81-11-807-6666
81-11-807-6646 (Fax)
E-mail: JUN@BUG.CO.JP

BUICK

See General Motors

BUREAU OF ECONOMIC ANALYSIS

See US Department of Commerce

BUREAU OF ENGRAVING AND PRINTING

See Oak Ridge Institute for Science and Education

BUREAU OF EXPORT ADMINISTRATION

See US Department of Commerce

Burson-Marsteller

SELECTIVITY 🔍🔍🔍🔍
Approximate applicant pool: 150–200; Interns accepted: 20–25 in New York; 4–6 in Chicago

COMPENSATION 💲💲
$275/week

LOCATION(S)
Chicago, IL; New York, NY; Wasington DC

FIELD
Public relations

DURATION
10 weeks: Summer

DEADLINE(S)
Mid-February

THE WORK
One of the world's largest public relations firms, Burson-Marsteller has 63 offices in 32 countries throughout the world. Among its 400 clients are Coca-Cola, Du Pont, and General Electric. Interns are assigned to a supervisor in one of the following service areas: Corporate, Public Affairs, Marketing, Technology/Telecommunications, Healthcare, and Creative Services.

PERKS
Weekly seminars with senior executives; team competition with final presentation to senior managers and client; possible participation in client meetings and press conferences.

FYI
Alumni of the internship program include the Director of Corporate Practice (Singapore office) and a Managing Director in Marketing (New York office).

TO APPLY
Open to college seniors and recent grads. Minimum GPA: 3.0. International applicants eligible. Write for application.

Internship Coordinator
Burson-Marsteller
230 Park Avenue South
New York, NY 10003
(212) 614-4000
(212) 598 6964 (Fax)

Internship Coordinator
Burson-Marsteller
One East Wacker Drive
Chicago, IL 60601
(312) 329-9292

SELECTIVITY 🔍🔍🔍🔍
Approximate applicant pool: 175; Interns accepted: 10

COMPENSATION 💲💲
$200/week

LOCATION(S)
Washington, DC (HQ)

FIELD
Public policy; Defense

DURATION
8–16 weeks: Summer, Fall, Spring

DEADLINE(S)
Summer: April 1; Fall: July 31; Spring: December 1

THE WORK
In existence since 1982, Business Executives for National Security (BENS) is a national, nonpartisan organization of business leaders promoting better defense management, economic and military strength, and practical ways to stop the proliferation of nuclear chemical and biological weapons. BENS's work has included helping establish commissions for closing unnecessary military bases, supplying political candidates with information on national security issues, helping enact legislation calling for a one-year moratorium on nuclear testing, and pushing for changes to make the Pentagon more business-like. Interns work in Policy.

PERKS
Attendance welcome at seminars and luncheons with key policy-makers, government officials, and Pentagon brass; opportunity to work and receive citation on published papers and articles.

FYI
Many interns have found themselves studying legislative and national security issues or researching US international economic competitiveness and economic security.

TO APPLY
Open to undergrads, recent college grads, and grad students. International applicants eligible. Submit resume, cover letter, and writing samples.

Internship Coordinator
Business Executives for National Security
1717 Pensylvania Ave. Suite 350
Washington, DC 20006-4603
(202) 296-2125
(202) 296-2490 (Fax)
E-mail: bens@access.digex.net

Fine Art Auctioneers and Appraisers since 1865

SELECTIVITY 🔍🔍🔍
Approximate applicant pool: 300; Interns accepted: 35–45

COMPENSATION Ⓢ
$10/day stipend

LOCATION(S)
San Francisco and Los Angeles, CA; and Chicago, IL

FIELD
Auction and appraisal

DURATION
12–15 weeks
Summer, Fall, Spring; 15 hours/week

DEADLINE(S)
Summer: March 30; Fall: July 30; Spring: December 15

THE WORK
Founded in 1865 on the present site of San Francisco's Transamerica Building, Butterfield & Butterfield is the largest and oldest full-service auction house in western America. It also offers a host of appraisal services. A range of departments accepts interns: Painting, Asian Art, Prints, Furniture and Decorative Arts, American Indian/Ethnographic Art, Oriental Rugs, Catalogues/Marketing, Public Relations, and Marketing.

PERKS
Previews and appraisal clinics; free parking; hands-on contact with objects.

FYI
One intern notes: "It sounds funny, but you get to play with wonderful objects. It's the ultimate hands-on experience for someone interested in art." . . . Bidding at auctions is allowed for interns; the insider tips put them ahead of other bidders.

TO APPLY
Open to junior and senior undergrads, grad students, and college grads of any age. International applicants eligible. international students must also have either a B-1 visa or an H-3 visa to be eligible. Write for application. Personal interviews are required.

Butterfield & Butterfield
Internship Program
220 San Bruno Avenue
San Francisco, CA 94103
(415) 861-7500 ext. 359
(415) 861-8486 (Fax)

Butterfield & Butterfield
Internship Program
7601 Sunset Blvd
Los Angeles, CA 90046
(213) 850-7500 ext. 219

Butterfield & Butterfield
Internship Program
441 West Huron Street
Chicago, IL 60610
Fax: (312) 377-7501

SELECTIVITY 🔍
Approximate applicant pool: 10; Interns accepted: 6

COMPENSATION Ⓢ
None

LOCATION(S)
San Diego, CA

FIELD
Parks management

DURATION
13 weeks: Summer, Fall, Spring

DEADLINE(S)
Summer: May 1; Fall: September 1; Spring: January 1

THE WORK
Established in 1913, Cabrillo National Monument (CNM) is a 144-acre memorial park commemorating Juan Cabrillo's 16th century exploration of the western coast of California and his discovery of "San Miguel," the site of modern San Diego. A unit of the National Park Service (see separate entry), CNM receives over 1.1 million visitors annually. Interns rotate through all of CNM's divisions, including, Interpretation, Visitor Center, Resource Protection, Fee Collection, Planning, Resources Management, Maintenance, and Administration. In addition, the intern completes a project under supervision within one of these divisions.

PERKS
Mentors; access to NPS job listings; opportunities for gray whale watching (late December to late February).

FYI
Established in 1989, CNM's internship program provides its participants with a "behind the scenes look at a park ranger career." . . . Intern duties include running film programs, talks, and nature walks; providing visitors with information on the park; maintaining trails; and writing reports and letters.

TO APPLY
Open to undergrads, recent college grads, college grads of any age, and grad students. Write for application.

Internship Coordinator
National Park Service
Cabrillo National Monument
1800 Cabrillo Memorial Drive
San Diego, CA 92106-3601
(619) 557-5450
(619) 557-5469 (Fax)
(619) 222-8211 (TTY)
Website: www.nps.gov/cabr

See General Motors

CAIRNS & ASSOCIATES

SELECTIVITY
Approximate applicant pool: 35–50; Interns accepted: 3–5 per semester

COMPENSATION
$5.15/hour

LOCATION(S)
New York, NY

FIELD
Public relations

DURATION
12 weeks: Summer, Fall, Spring

DEADLINE(S)
Summer: April 30; Fall: July 31; Spring: December 29

THE WORK
Founded in 1983, Cairns & Associates (C&A) is an independently-owned, full-service public relations and marketing agency with $3 million in annual billings. Recognized as a leader in fashion and cosmetics, C&A represents clients such as Vaseline, Elizabeth Arden, Helene Curtis, Smarovski, Six Flags, Rave, Fabergé, Ponds, Frito-Lay, Scholastic Books, Brut, Cotex, The Thymes Limited, Volvo, and Waterman Pens. Interns assist account teams in preparing media lists, contacting media, clipping articles, preparing client reports, developing story ideas, coordinating press events, and writing photo captions, pitch letters, and releases.

PERKS
Weekly workshops with senior management; mentoring program; certificate of completion; free promotional products; in-office manicure available every Monday ($9).

FYI
C&A's internship program was launched in 1988 . . . Of the agency's 48 employees, three started as interns at C&A . . . C&A

sums up its philosophy in a phrase first used by tarot-card readers: "Head in the sky, feet on the ground."

TO APPLY
Open to undergrads and grads. Submit resume and cover letter.

Internship Coordinator
Cairns & Associates
3 Park Avenue, 14th Floor
New York, NY 10016
(212) 413-0516
(212) 413-0799 (Fax)

CALIFORNIA GOVERNOR'S OFFICE

SELECTIVITY
Approximate applicant pool: 400 (Interns), 500 (Fellows); Interns accepted: 150 (Interns), 15 (Fellows)

COMPENSATION
Interns: None; Fellows: $400/week, health insurance

LOCATION(S)
Interns: CA (Fresno, Los Angeles, Orange County, Sacramento, San Diego, and San Francisco); Washington, DC; Hong Kong; Frankfurt; London; Mexico City; Tokyo; Fellows: Sacramento, CA

FIELD
Government

DURATION
Interns: 10–12 weeks: Summer, Fall, Spring; Fellows: 10 months: September–July

DEADLINE(S)
Interns: Rolling; Fellows: March 1

MAXIMIZING THE UNPAID INTERNSHIP

1. **Knock on doors.** At most organizations, higher-ups are willing to grant a few minutes of their time to an inquisitive intern. Ask top-level employees how they spend a typical day, what other opportunities exist in the field, and who else you should talk to. Seek a mentor. You want to leave the internship with at least a handful of contacts whom you can call on later.

2. **Get credit.** To get academic credit for your internship, it's in your best interest to treat the position as a course (an end-of-internship paper is usually the only assignment). In fact, some employers who offer unpaid internships require that you receive academic credit. To assist you, most campuses have internship or co-op offices which grant college credit for unpaid internships. Unfortunately, the student often has to pay for each unit. If your school will not grant credit for internships and the employer demands it, you can usually satisfy the employer by asking a relevant department or faculty member to write a letter that fudges the issue; the letter should indicate that the internship you are seeking qualifies for academic credit.

3. **Go behind the scenes.** The action at an organization often occurs behind closed doors. Ask to sit in on strategy sessions and office meetings. If you intern at a TV station, ask to watch tapings of various programs. At a news show, ask to accompany correspondents on interviews. At a magazine, ask to observe editors interacting with writers. What you learn about the lifeblood of an organization will not only allow you to decide whether its industry is right for you but also put you on firm footing if you later want to get hired there.

THE WORK

Founded in 1850, the year California was admitted into the Union, the California Governor's Office (CGO) heads the Golden State's executive branch. Interns work in Overseas Trade Offices, Planning and Research, Community Relations, Child Development & Education, Executive, Communications, Constituent Affairs, Legislative, Legal, Scheduling, Advance Special Projects, Cabinet Appointments, International Trade, Administration, and MIS. In 1986, CGO and the Center for California Studies, a public service and research institute at California State University, Sacramento (CSUS), established the State of California Executive Fellowship Program, which places Fellows in Health and Welfare; Finance; Child Development and Education; Environmental Protection; State Treasurer; Food and Agriculture; Legal Affairs; Air Resources; and Business, Transportation, and Housing.

PERKS

Brown-bag luncheons with Governor and/or senior staff; attendance welcome at Governor's speaking engagements; weekly seminars featuring guest speakers and 12 graduate units from CSUS (Fellows); photo-ops with VIPs.

FYI

Says CGO's internship coordinator: "The Governor's Office expects interns to perform on par with its staff; consequently, the work is challenging." . . . Former Fellows include several deputy directors in the Administration of Governor Pete Wilson.

TO APPLY

Internship: open to high school grads, undergrads, recent college grads, college grads of any age, and grad students. Fellowship: open to college grads. Must be proficient in local language. International applicants eligible. Write for application.

Internship or Executive
Fellowship Coordinator
The Governor's Office
State Capitol
Sacramento, CA 95814
(916) 445-2841
(916) 445-4133 (Fax)

Executive Fellowship Program
The Center for California Studies
CSU Sacramento
6000 J Street
Sacramento, CA 95819-6081
(916) 278-6906

THE WORK

Established in 1850, the California State Assembly (CSA) is the 80 member "Lower House" of California's bicameral legislature. In 1957, CSA started the country's first legislative fellowship program. In 1987, the Assembly Fellowship was renamed the Jesse Marvin Unruh Assembly Fellowship Program to honor the former Speaker of the Assembly and California State Treasurer. The program is run jointly by the CSA and the Center for California Studies, a public service and research institute at California State University, Sacramento. Fellows serve as legislative assistants and committee consultants, developing and researching legislative proposals, analyzing bills, and writing press releases and speeches.

PERKS

Academic Seminars; publication of research/project papers in Assembly Fellowship Journal; 12 graduate units from CSUS Government Department.

FYI

Former Fellows include, in part, Rose Elizabeth Bird, former California Supreme Court Chief Justice; Howard Berman, Member of Congress; Dotson Wilson, Chief Clerk of the CSA; and Bill Leonard and Dean Florez, current Members of the CSA.

TO APPLY

Open to all University and four-year college grads. International applicants are eligible. Visit the website http://www.csus.edu/calst/program/jesse unruh.html, or write:

The Jesse Marvin Unruh Assembly Fellowship Program
Legislative Office Building
1020 N Street
Sacramento, CA 9584
(916) 319-3753

Center for California Studies
The Jesse Marvin Unruh Assembly Fellowship Program
California State University, Sacramento
6000 J Street
Sacramento, CA 95819-6081
(916) 278-6906
(916) 278-5199 (Fax)
www.csus.edu/calst/program/jesse_unruh.html

CALIFORNIA STATE ASSEMBLY

SELECTIVITY
Approximate applicant pool: 300; Fellows accepted: 18

COMPENSATION
$1,800/month; Comprehensive medical, dental, and vision benefits

LOCATION(S)
California State Capitol, Sacramento, CA

FIELD
Government

DURATION
11 months: October–September

DEADLINE(S)
March 1

CALIFORNIA STATE SENATE

SELECTIVITY
Approximate applicant pool: 500; Interns accepted: 18

COMPENSATION
$400/week; health insurance

LOCATION(S)
Sacramento, CA

FIELD
Government

DURATION
11 months: October–September

DEADLINE(S)
February 16

THE WORK
Established in 1850, the California State Senate (CSS) is the forty-member "upper house" of California's bicameral legislature. In 1972, CSS established the California Senate Fellow Program, recently renamed the California Senate Associates Program. Now jointly run with the Center for California Studies, a public service and research institute at California State University Sacramento (CSUS), the program places associates with senators and committees, where they work as professional staffers, helping to develop legislative proposals, researching and analyzing bills, answering constituent inquiries, and writing press releases and speeches.

PERKS
Four-week orientation featuring talks with staff, journalists, and lobbyists; two 3-month seminars with key figures in government and the press; twelve graduate units from CSUS Government Department.

FYI
Former interns include congressman Xavier Becerra (D-CA).

TO APPLY
Open to college grads. International applicants eligible. Write for application to one of the offices below or any State Senator's office.

California Senate Associates Program
Senate Rules Committee
California State Senate
State Capitol, Room 500 A
Sacramento, CA 95814
(916) 322-7563

Center for California Studies
CSU Sacramento
6000 J Street
Sacramento, CA 95819-6081
(916) 278-7681

THE CALLAGHAN GROUP

SELECTIVITY
Approximate applicant pool: 200; Interns accepted: 3

COMPENSATION
$50/week

LOCATION(S)
New York, NY

FIELD
Public relations

DURATION
12 weeks: Summer, Fall, Spring

DEADLINE(S)
Summer: March 30; Fall: August 1; Spring: February 1

THE WORK
Founded in 1991, The Callaghan Group is a public relations firm specializing in the entertainment industry. Its client roster ranges from personalities such as talk show host Rolanda Watts, author Sydney Biddle Barrows, and drag superstar Jem Jender to legendary girl group The Shirelles, jeweler to the stars Harry Winston, and destination restaurants like Fashion Cafe and Commonwealth Brewing Company. Assisting account executives, interns perform clerical work, make calls to media contacts, and write press releases.

PERKS
Free passes to "virtually every movie that opens"; attendance welcome at occasional fundraisers, concerts, press events, etc.; star gazing galore.

FYI
Says firm president Edward Callaghan: "We are a small shop, but our clients are very high-profile. As a result, interns wind up having incredible amounts of direct contact with clients. This could mean escorting Claudia Schiffer over to the *Today Show* for an interview or attending a staff meeting for the *Rolanda Show*."

TO APPLY
Open to college seniors, recent college grads, and grad students. Submit resume, cover letter, and writing samples.

Internship Coordinator
The Callaghan Group
219 East 31th Street
New York, NY 10016
(212) 685-5520
(212) 685-5549 (Fax)

During his internship with The Callaghan Group, Fordham University grad Leroy Bradley helped coordinate media interviews at a party introducing the Fashion Café, a bar created by supermodels Naomi Campbell, Elle Macpherson, and Claudia Schiffer. At the end of the evening, Bradley was given another assignment: "[Claudia Schiffer] asked if I had a problem helping her to her car. I said no, not at all. So I had to hold her a little by her waist and escort her down the red carpet and into her limo. She is absolutely gorgeous. It was a big thrill for me . . . so much so that I got in trouble with my girlfriend."

CALLAWAY ADVANCED TECHNOLOGY

CALLAWAY
POWERFULLY ENGINEERED AUTOMOBILES

SELECTIVITY
Approximate applicant pool: 90; Interns accepted: 4

COMPENSATION
None

LOCATION(S)
Old Lyme, CT

FIELD
Automobiles

DURATION
12 weeks: Summer, Fall, Spring

DEADLINE(S)
Rolling

THE WORK

Established in 1987, Callaway Advanced Technology is an automotive engineering firm specializing in the design and manufacture of ultra-high-performance cars. Working with companies like Porsche, Mercedes-Benz, Alfa Romeo, Aston Martin, and Chevrolet, Callaway has produced high-performance engines, turbocharger systems, completely re-engineered cars, and Indy Car engines. It has also developed its own car, the Callaway C-7, a 560 horsepower ultra-high-performance sports roadster. Interns work in Engineering, Marketing, and Sales.

PERKS

Possible travel to car races; discounted Callaway paraphernalia (t-shirts, caps, mini maglites).

FYI

In existence since 1992, the internship program leads to permanent employment at Callaway for about 50 percent of interns . . . Callaway is best known for helping develop the Callaway Twin Turbo Corvette, the fastest street-driveable car in the United States, recording speeds of over 250 mph.

TO APPLY

Open to undergrads and grads. International applicants eligible. Submit resume and cover letter.

Internship Coordinator
Callaway Advanced Technology
3 High Street
Old Lyme, CT 06371
(860) 434-9002
(860) 434-1704 (Fax)

> Interns at Callaway Advanced Technology have the opportunity to help design parts of ultra-high performance cars. Callaway helped develop the country's fastest street-driveable car, the Twin Turbo Corvette, which has recorded speeds of over 250 mph.

CALLAWAY GARDENS

SELECTIVITY 🔍 🔍
Approximate applicant pool: 50; Interns accepted: 5

COMPENSATION 💲 💲
$5.67/ per hour; free housing

LOCATION(S)
Pine Mountain, GA

FIELD
Horticulture; Education

DURATION
Summer: 12 weeks; Spring/Summer: 6 months (March–August)

DEADLINE(S)
Summer: February15; Spring/Summer: January 15

THE WORK

Established in 1952, Callaway Gardens is a display garden and recreational center in West Central Georgia. Spread over 2,500 intensively managed acres, Callway offers a horticultural center, a conservatory, a butterfly center, a 40-acre azalea garden, a white sand beach, a chapel, scenic walking trails, bicycle trails, and drives. Interns work in Education and Horticulture.

PERKS

Access to Education Department library for research and reading; access to recreation and sports facilities (golf, tennis, beach); employee discounts in restaurants and gift shop.

FYI

Pine Mountain is a rural agricultural community of 1,500 located 75 miles southwest of Atlanta . . . The internship program has been offered since 1960.

TO APPLY

Open to college juniors and seniors. Write for application.

Internship Coordinator
Callaway Gardens
Ida Cason Callaway Foundation
Pine Mountain, GA 31822
(706) 663-5146
(706) 663-6720 (Fax)

CAMP COUNSELORS USA

SELECTIVITY 🔍
Approximate applicant pool: 100–400; Interns accepted: 200+

COMPENSATION 💲 💲 💲
Small stipend; free room and board

LOCATION(S)
Youth Campus in Russia

FIELD
Any

DURATION
June–August

DEADLINE(S)
April 15

THE WORK

Camp Counselors USA (CCUSA) places Americans in Russian Summer Youth Camps all across Russia and Venezuela. Camps vary from General Recreational Camps to Specific Sports, Drama, English Language/American Culture Camps. The daily routine depends on whether one is a specialist or general camp counselor, but everyone will be acting as a cultural ambassador.

PERKS

The opportunity to visit another country and to experience a culture first-hand; orientation; supportive home office; emergency hotline; and the great outdoors.

FYI

Camp Counselors USA is designated an Exchange Visitor Program sponsored by the United States Information Agency.

TO APPLY

Open to undergrads, recent college grads of any age, and grad students, average group age range 18–30 years old. E-mail or call for an application. Information available on our website.

CCUSA, Outbound Program
2330 Marinship Way, Suite 250.
Sausilito, CA 94965
(800) 999-2267
E-mail: outbound@campcounselors.com
www.campcounselors.com

> **R**eal estate mogul **Donald Trump** spent his summers as a high school and college student interning for the Trump Corporation, his father's construction company in Brooklyn, New York.

CAMPHILL SOLTANE

SELECTIVITY
Approximate applicant pool: 25; Interns accepted: 5–10

COMPENSATION
$25/week; free room and board

LOCATION(S)
Glenmoore, PA

FIELD
Education; Special education

DURATION
6 months–1 year

DEADLINE(S)
Rolling

THE WORK

Established in 1988, Camphill Soltane is an educational center designed to develop the emotional and intellectual potential of mentally handicapped people ages 18 to 25. A community sharing meals and household chores, Camphill has its students participate in academic college sessions, life-skills training, and a range of work opportunities. Interns are involved in all aspects of the center, such as assisting in the orchard, the pottery studio, and the weaving studio, as well as working in Development/Fundraising.

PERKS

Attendance welcome in educational seminar; participation welcome in all community festivals and celebrations; visits to sister communities in the area; lovely rural setting featuring rolling fields, woodlands, gardens, and orchards.

FYI

The internship program has been in existence since 1988 . . . Life at Camphill is based on the community-oriented principle of "anthroposophy," described as an "awareness of one's humanity," leading "from the spirit in the human being to the spirit in the universe."

TO APPLY

Open to high school grads, undergrads, recent college grads, college grads of any age, and grad students. International applicants eligible. Write for application.

Internship Coordinator
Camphill Soltane
224 Nantmeal Road,
Glenmoore, PA 19343
(610) 469-0933
(610) 469-1054 (Fax)

CANAAN PUBLIC RELATIONS

SELECTIVITY
Approximate applicant pool: 50; Interns accepted: 6

COMPENSATION
$75/week

LOCATION(S)
New York, NY

FIELD
Public relations

DURATION
16 weeks: Summer, Fall, Spring

DEADLINE(S)
Rolling

THE WORK

Founded in 1977, Canaan Public Relations is a public relations firm specializing in the business, entertainment, fashion, and hospitality industries. Its eclectic client list ranges from the Santa Fe Jazz Festival, the Linda Evans Tennis Tournament in Florida, and Club Beverly Hills to the Jerry Lewis Muscular Dystrophy Telethon, the National Black Enterprise Council, and the Glenn Miller Orchestra. Interns work in Publicity and Event Planning.

PERKS

Direct interaction with the president; free tickets to theatre.

FYI

Says the president: "Our interns learn the ropes of public relations through a small firm with a truly diversified clientele. We handle everyone from restaurants to plastic surgeons. By the end of their [internship], interns will see all the different types of PR out there."

A MASCOT FOR NASCAR
The most successful stock-car racer in history, **Richard Petty** learned the ropes of stock car maintenance in the early 1950s by serving as an apprentice mechanic to his father Lee, himself a stock-car champion. According to his autobiography *Grand National*, Petty became "sort of the NASCAR mascot," working in the pit and helping out at races in Greensboro, North Carolina.

Canadian Embassy /
Ambassade du Canada

SELECTIVITY 🔍 🔍 🔍 🔍
Approximate applicant pool: 450; Interns accepted: 38

COMPENSATION Ⓢ
None

LOCATION(S)
Washington, DC

FIELD
Government

DURATION
16 weeks: Summer, Fall, Spring

DEADLINE(S)
Summer: March 15; Fall: July 15; Spring: November 15

THE WORK
Established in 1927, the Canadian Embassy serves as the official chancery of the Canadian Ambassador to the United States. Working to protect and advance Canadian interests in the United States, the Embassy performs such functions as providing information on trade and tourism opportunities in Canada, hosting trade fairs for Canadian corporations, and monitoring compliance with NAFTA. Interns work in Public Affairs, Trade, Environment, Congressional Relations, Travel & Tourism, and Office Liaison of International Financial Institutions (OLIFI).

PERKS
Attendance welcome at meetings with US policymakers; intern seminars featuring department heads and Q and A with Ambassador; access to embassy gym; half-day off per week.

FYI
According to the internship coordinator, interns receive the training similar to a first-year foreign service officer.

TO APPLY
Open to college juniors and seniors, recent college grads, college grads of any age, and grad students. Minimum GPA: 3.5. Eligibility limited to Canadian and US citizens. Write for application.

Internship Coordinator
Public Affairs
Canadian Embassy
501 Pennsylvania Avenue NW
Washington, DC 20001
(202) 682-1740 Ext. 7530
(202) 682-7791 (Fax)
E-mail: ingrid.summa@dfait.maeci.gc.ca

CARE

SELECTIVITY N/A
Approximate applicant pool: N/A; Interns accepted: 50–70

COMPENSATION Ⓢ
None

LOCATION(S)
Atlanta, GA (HQ); Chicago, IL; Concord, MA; Dallas and Houston, TX; Denver, CO; Kansas City, MO; Los Angeles and San Francisco, CA; Minneapolis, MN; New York, NY; Philadelphia, PA; Seattle, WA; Washington, DC; 51 countries overseas (see Appendix)

FIELD
Public service in at least 10 fields (see THE WORK)

DURATION
3 months–2 years: ongoing

DEADLINE(S)
Rolling

THE WORK
Founded in 1945, CARE is an international relief and development organization working to improve lives in developing nations throughout the world. Projects include rehabilitating and building infrastructure, training local community leaders to run government agencies, starting businesses, and providing technical assistance on matters in agriculture, banking, family planning, and health care. Volunteers work in the areas of finance, government relations, fundraising, construction, human resources, internal audit, health care, agriculture, food security, population, and small enterprise development. As CARE is highly decentralized, positions vary from site to site and may not be available at some sites.

PERKS
Varies with placement.

FYI
Today's "care packages" trace their roots to the post-World War II CARE Packages—plain, brown boxes, each containing a blanket, food, and socks—that were delivered to some 100 million WWII refugees.

TO APPLY
Open to high school grads with at least five years of field experience in a developing country and college grads with at least two years of field experience in a developing country. International applicants eligible. Submit resume and cover letter directly to office of interest. Call headquarters for addresses and phone numbers.

Human Resources
CARE
151 Ellis Street NE
Atlanta, GA 30303-2439
(404) 681-2552
(404) 577-7418 (Fax)

SELECTIVITY 🔍 🔍 🔍
Approximate applicant pool: 150; Interns accepted: up to 11

COMPENSATION 💲 💲 💲
$1,912/month plus medical, life, and business travel insurance; round-trip travel reimbursed

LOCATION(S)
Washington, DC

FIELD
International relations; Foreign policy; Magazine

DURATION
1 year: Summer, Fall, Winter, Spring

DEADLINE(S)
January 15

THE WORK
The Carnegie Endowment for International Peace (CEIP) is an educational organization devoted to international affairs research. Its Junior Fellows Program assigns interns as editorial assistants to CEIP's *Foreign Policy* magazine or to specific areas of research, such as arms control, nuclear non proliferation, Middle East, use of force, multilateralism, and immigration.

PERKS
Intern lunches with speakers; interaction with top players in foreign affairs research; opportunities to attend Foreign Policy press briefings.

FYI
Says a former intern: "Although this program lasts only six months, you meet enough well-connected researchers that it's an easy transition from here to a permanent position at a think tank."
(Currently this position lasts for 12 months.)

TO APPLY
Open to graduating seniors and those who have graduated during past academic year with significant coursework in international politics or economics. No one who has started graduate studies will be considered. Applications accepted only through invitation by designated offices at participating colleges and universities.

Carnegie Endowment for International Peace
1779 Massachusettes Avenue, NW
Washington, DC 20036
(202) 483-7600

> The late **Lee Atwater**, Republican National Committee Chairman and strategist for Presidents Reagan and Bush, got his start in politics as an intern for Sen. Strom Thurmond (R-SC).

CAROLYN RAY
CAROLYN RAY

SELECTIVITY 🔍 🔍 🔍
Approximate applicant pool: 20; Interns accepted: 2

COMPENSATION 💲 💲
Travel stipend

LOCATION(S)
Yonkers, NY

FIELD
Wallcovering and fabric design; hand productions for interiors

DURATION
4–12 weeks: Summer, Fall, Spring, Winter

DEADLINE(S)
Rolling

THE WORK
Established in 1977, Carolyn Ray is an internationally recognized innovator in the interior design industry. Fabric production is the name of the game at Carolyn Ray. Owned and operated by a team of artists, it specializes in producing high quality and unusual fabrics and wall coverings. Interns work in the Production Studio, Office, Sample Department, and Warehouse.

PERKS
Learn design trade and make contacts, free pass to Manhattan Design showrooms: "no free t-shirts, but students will learn enough printing processes to print their own."; free pieces of fabric.

FYI
In existence since 1978, the internship program leads to permanent employment at Carolyn Ray for some interns.

TO APPLY
Open to high school juniors and seniors, undergrads, grad students, high school grads of any age, and college grads. International applicants eligible. Submit resume, cover letter, transcript, recommendations, and slides of artwork (if possible).

Internship Coordinator
Carolyn Ray
578 Nepperhan Avenue
Yonkers, NY 10701
(914) 476-0619
(914) 476-0677 (Fax)

> "We don't have 'free t-shirts' [for interns], but interns will learn enough printing processes to print their own!"
> —internship coordinator at Carolyn Ray

EXCLUSIVE INTERVIEW WITH TIPPER GORE

The wife of Vice President Al Gore, Tipper Gore currently serves as Mental Health Advisor to the President and Special Advisor to the Interagency Council on the Homeless. A well known advocate of children and the mentally impaired, Tipper founded Tennessee Voices for Children, a coalition to promote the development of services for children with serious behavioral, emotional, substance abuse, or other mental health problems. She received a B.A. in psychology from Boston University in 1970 and an M.A. in psychology from George Peabody College in 1975.

The Internship Informants: How important are interns to the White House?
Gore: Frankly, we couldn't get along without the help of interns. I can speak to you out of direct knowledge of the interns that have worked here in my office and my husband's office. You'll find interns [who are] energized and committed young people all around this administration.

The Internship Informants: Were you ever an intern?
Gore: Well, I never did an internship per se. I did do a work-study program when I was at [Boston University]. I worked at Boston State Hospital. It was similar to an internship, I suppose . . . And my daughters have interned in fields ranging from medicine to journalism . . . My oldest daughter completed an environmental internship in Costa Rica and then did an internship in journalism. So has my second daughter, who is a senior in high school.

The Internship Informants: Good to hear. We like to stress the value of students interning while they are still in high school.
Gore: In fact, [my second daughter] interned last summer, which was between her junior and senior year. Even though a lot of organizations will say they prefer somebody older (college age), I find that they are taking them younger these days, probably because they understand that if a kid is that committed, it's good for them to help that kid along. They seem to be breaking their own rule in letting younger and younger kids take advantage of interning. Around the OVP [Office of the Vice President], even the younger [interns] are given a lot of responsibility. I think they gain valuable work experience.

The Internship Informants: Do you interact much with the White House interns?
Gore: I make a practice of talking to the interns in this office as they are leaving. We usually have a good-bye party. And I ask them about their experience . . . and they really express the fact that it has been a meaningful experience for them and they appreciate the responsibility that they've been given. I think it's very sincere. They feel like it's a meaningful entry on their budding resumes.

The Internship Informants: What are some of your words of encouragement to White House interns?
Gore: I tell them that I want them to take the experience that they've had and build on it and incorporate it into their studies. [I tell them that] I hope they've learned something about themselves . . . I also tell them to stay in touch, and they do. They write us, they call, and they let us know where they are from year to year. And I've had a couple of them come back and intern for me again, which is of course very nice.

The Internship Informants: It sounds like you have a family atmosphere in the office.
Gore: Exactly. I think that's one reason why people like our office as much as they do. We try to impart [a friendly feeling]. We work hard, but we also try to have some fun.

THE CARTER CENTER

SELECTIVITY
Approximate applicant pool: 450 (100 per semester);
Interns accepted: 100 (30 per semester)

COMPENSATION S
None; Financial aid may be available

LOCATION(S)
Atlanta, GA

FIELD
Foreign affairs; Health; Public policy

DURATION
12 weeks: Summer, Fall, Spring

DEADLINE(S)
Fall: June 15; Spring: October 15; Summer: March 15

THE WORK
In 1982, James Earl "Jimmy" Carter founded The Carter Center, a public policy institute to improve the quality of life for people around the world. Guided by Carter, the Center works with world leaders and dignitaries to promote democracy, protect human rights, eradicate disease—in general, to improve the quality of life. Interns work in one of the Center's many programs: Latin American and Caribbean, Human Rights, Global 2000, Mental Health, the Global Development Initiative, and Conflict Resolution. Positions are also available in administrative departments.

PERKS
Japanese garden; access to exercise room; access to high-level meetings; intellectual atmosphere.

FYI
An official internship program has been in place since 1984 . . . By the director's estimate, filing and photocopying absorb only 30 percent of interns' time . . . Interns feel that this internship involves them in the world events: "I learned a lot about conflicts and became an expert on the things going on in the countries I researched."

TO APPLY
Open to college juniors and seniors, recent college grads, grad students. International applicants eligible. Write for application.

The Carter Center
Internship Program
One Copenhill Avenue
Atlanta, GA 30307
(404) 420-5151
(404) 420-5196 (Fax)

THE CARTOON NETWORK
See Turner Broadcasting System

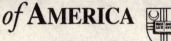

THE CATHOLIC UNIVERSITY of AMERICA

SELECTIVITY
Approximate applicant pool: 500; Interns accepted: 25

COMPENSATION S
Tuition fee ($2,400 for summer, $4,800–$6,000 for fall and spring); $1,500–$2,500 cost for housing and food

LOCATION(S)
London, England; Dublin, Ireland

FIELD
Government

DURATION
12–16 weeks: Summer, Fall, Spring

DEADLINE(S)
Summer: February 1; Fall: April 15; Spring: October 15

THE WORK
The Catholic University of America (CUA), incorporated in 1887, is a 13-college university of 10,000 students. Since 1979, CUA has offered semester-abroad programs that complement coursework in politics and government with internships in legislative branches—British House of Commons, British Parliament, and Irish Parliament. Interns take three courses (no courses in summer) and work for members as legislative aides, answering constituent letters, researching legislation, and helping to draft speeches and articles. CUA's summer program is available in London only.

PERKS
Orientation on local culture and political traditions; weekly seminars on government and politics; tours of local political institutions.

FYI
Interns receive grades on an oral exam and a journal they keep . . . The summer program grants six semester units of credit while fall and spring programs provide 12 to 15 units.

TO APPLY
Open to college juniors and seniors as well as grad students. Minimum GPA: 3.0. Write for application.

Internship Coordinator
The Catholic University of America
Box 20 Cardinal Station
Washington, DC 20064
(202) 319-5128 (Fax)

CBS News's *60 Minutes* correspondent **Mike Wallace** interned at the now-defunct weekly newspaper, the *Brookline Citizen*, during his years at Massachusetts's Brookline High School.

SELECTIVITY
Approximate applicant pool: 250; Interns accepted: 15

COMPENSATION
Free parking

LOCATION(S)
Cleveland, OH

FIELD
Sports; Entertainment

DURATION
12–15 weeks: Summer, Fall, or Winter/Spring

DEADLINE(S)
Rolling

THE WORK
Founded in 1994, the CAVS/Gund Arena Company owns the NBA Cleveland Cavaliers and WNBA Cleveland Rockers basketball teams and operates the Gund Arena, Cleveland's multimedia entertainment facility. Gund Arena hosts over 200 events a year, including CAVS and Rockers basketball, Lumberjacks hockey, rock concerts, ice shows, rodeos, and track and field meets. Interns work for the Cleveland Cavaliers (only 3 interns a year) and/or for the Arena in various areas of Administration, Building and Event Operations, and Marketing and Sales. Interns also lend support to the Cleveland Rockers of the WNBA.

PERKS
Occasional stipends for game-night set-up or promotions work. Free indoor parking. Free tickets to basketball games.

FYI
The number of requests for summer internships far exceeds the number for other periods. Therefore, when possible, we encourage students to apply for a fall or winter internship. The Arena is centrally located in the city's center, easily accessible to buses and rapids.

TO APPLY
Open to undergrads and grad students. Must receive academic credit. International applicants eligible. Submit resume, cover letter, personal essay describing interest in sports management and/or building operations, and two recommendation letters.

Internship Coordinator
Human Resources
CAVS/Gund Arena Company
One Center Court
Cleveland, OH 44115-4001
(216) 420-2214
(216) 420-2223 (Fax)

SELECTIVITY
Approximate applicant pool: 1,000; Interns accepted: 150–200

COMPENSATION
None; college credit

LOCATION(S)
Atlanta, GA; New York, NY (HQ); Washington, DC

FIELD
Television

DURATION
12–16 weeks: Summer (full-time), Fall, Spring (2–3 days)

DEADLINE(S)
Summer: February 28; Fall: June 15; Spring: October 1

THE WORK
A division of the CBS television network, CBS News produces a mix of radio and television news programs, including *CBS Evening News*, *60 Minutes*, and *Up to the Minute*. Broadcasting since 1928, CBS News has featured such beloved journalists as Walter Cronkite, Edward Murrow, Mike Wallace, Dan Rather, Lesley Stahl, and Ed Bradley. Interns are placed in *CBS This Morning*, *CBS Evening News*, *48 Hours*, *60 Minutes*, *Face the Nation*, Public Relations, CBS Promotions, CBS Production, *Sunday Morning*, Weekend News, *Up to the Minute*, and NewsPath (a satellite newsgathering system providing news feeds as well as editorial and technical support to CBS affiliates).

PERKS
Intern luncheons with CBS News executives (summer only); attendance welcome at most staff meetings; occasional opportunities to accompany reporters on shoots.

FYI
According to the internship brochure: "Due to contractual agreements with several unions, interns are not allowed to use equipment. However, the equipment will be demonstrated by station personnel, and interns are encouraged to watch and ask questions."

TO APPLY
Open to college juniors, seniors, and grad students. Must receive academic credit. International applicants eligible. Submit resume, cover letter, personal essay describing your interest in news, transcript, and two recommendations. Must have 3.0 GPA. Send resumes to:

Director of Internships, News Division
CBS News
2020 M Street, N.W.
Wahington, D.C. 20036
(202) 973-0768
(202) 331-1791 (Fax)

SELECTIVITY 🔍
Approximate applicant pool: 500; Interns accepted: 175

COMPENSATION $ $ $
Variable

LOCATION(S)
Primarily Germany; France; Great Britain; Italy; Netherlands; Spain

FIELD
Over 12 fields (see THE WORK)

DURATION
3–18 Months

DEADLINE(S)
Vary; typically 4–6 months prior to start of internship

THE WORK
Tracing its history back to the 1920s, CDG is a German government–financed organization promoting worldwide exchange and professional development for citizens of Europe and developing countries through internships, exchange programs, study tours, and seminars. Its American counterpart, CDS International, handles exchange and development opportunities for US citizens wishing to work in Germany. Together, CDG and CDS offer over 60 internship, fellowship, and training programs. Placements span several fields, including accounting, agriculture, arts, business, design, education, engineering, hospitality, hotel management, journalism, law, medicine, public policy, and science.

PERKS
Alumni association; other perks vary with placement.

FYI
CDS interns have worked at such organizations as Avon Cosmetics, Robert Bosch, Coca-Cola, BMW, Steinway & Sons, Kodak, Deutsche Bank, and Siemens; CDG interns have been assigned to BMG Music, Citicorp, Honeywell, Lockheed, Lost Trails Hot Springs Resort, Nutrasweet, and Sprint . . . Interns may be required to take a one-month language course depending on ability. A limited number of stipends are available.

TO APPLY
Open to high school grads, undergrads, recent college grads, college grads of any age, and grad students. Most positions for Americans require proficiency in German; many positions for non-Americans require proficiency in English. Write for application. Most programs have an administrative fee of $200-$400 and a non-refundable application fee of $50.

For US citizens:
CDS International
330 Seventh Avenue
New York, NY 10001
(212) 497-3500
(212) 497-3535 (Fax)

For nonUS citizens:
Carl Duisberg Gesellschaft e.V. (CDG)
Weyerstreasse 79-83
50676 Cologne, Germany
49-221-209-80

See US Department of Commerce

SELECTIVITY 🔍🔍🔍🔍🔍
Approximate applicant pool: 100; Interns accepted: 3–10

COMPENSATION $
$500/month

LOCATION(S)
Provincetown, MA

FIELD
Marine mammal research

DURATION
3 sessions: January–mid-May; June–August; September–November

DEADLINE(S)
January 31

THE WORK
The Center for Coastal Studies (CCS) was founded in 1976 to conduct research, education, and conservation programs on coastal and marine environments, with an emphasis on regional whale populations. Interns work in Field Biology and Conservation, where they learn biological research techniques, and may include one or more of the following: data gathering, report writing, plankton analysis, and computer data entry.

PERKS
Intern research projects; free T-shirt and discount at CCS's gift shop.

FYI
Started in 1979, CCS's internship program is one of the few "designed to help fill the need for students to get field research experience in marine and coastal sciences."

TO APPLY
Open to college juniors and seniors, recent college grads, and grad students with backgrounds in biology, zoology, or wildlife ecology. Non-US citizens who are US residents eligible. Please submit resume, unofficial transcript, letter of intent, and a $10 nonrefundable application fee.

Internship Review Committee
Center for Coastal Studies
59 Commercial Street
P.O. Box 1036
Provincetown, MA 02657
(508) 487-3622
(508) 487-4495 (Fax)

SELECTIVITY 🔍🔍🔍🔍
Approximate applicant pool: 100; Interns accepted: 4 per semester

COMPENSATION $
$700/month

LOCATION(S)
Washington, DC

FIELD
Defense; Foreign affairs; Public policy, Broadcast journalism

DURATION
12–20 weeks: Summer, Fall, Spring

DEADLINE(S)
Summer: March 15; Fall: July 1; Spring: October 15

THE WORK
Founded in 1972 by retired military officers, the Center for Defense Information (CDI) is a research organization opposing excessive expenditure for military weapons and policies increasing the danger of nuclear war. CDI publishes the monthly newsletter *The Defense Monitor*, produces the weekly national television show *America's Defense Monitor*, and answers written and phone inquiries from the press, government offices, and the public. Interns work in Research and Television.

PERKS
Attendance welcome at tapings of *America's Defense Monitor*; opportunities to attend television interviews with US Senators, Ambassadors, and other officials.

FYI
In existence since 1976, the internship program counts among its alumni the Deputy Assistant Secretary of Defense for Peacekeeping and Peace Enforcement, the Principal Deputy to the Assistant Secretary of Defense for Strategy and Requirements, and the Foreign Affairs Officer with the Arms Control and Disarmament Agency.

TO APPLY
Open to undergrads, recent college grads, college grads of any age, and grad students. International applicants eligible. Submit resume, cover letter, writing sample, transcript, and recommendations.

Internship Coordinator
Center for Defense Information
1500 Massachusetts Avenue NW, Suite 24
Washington, DC 20005
(202) 862-0700
(202) 862-0708 (Fax)
E-mail: info@cdi.org
www.cdi.org

Center for Investigative Reporting, Inc.

SELECTIVITY 🔍🔍🔍🔍🔍
Approximate applicant pool: 250 annually; Interns accepted: 8 annually

COMPENSATION $
$200/month

LOCATION(S)
San Francisco, CA

FIELD
Investigative journalism

DURATION
Six months: Winter/Spring, Summer/Fall; Part time available

DEADLINE(S)
Winter/Spring: December 1; Summer/Fall: May 1

THE WORK
In 1977, freelance journalists Lowell Bergman, Dan Noyes, and David Weir founded the Center for Investigative Reporting (CIR) with the belief that the media needed a nonprofit, independent organization committed to investigative reporting. It is no surprise that media outlets such as *Frontline*/PBS rely upon the CIR to produce stories for them. Interns get the chance to moonlight as journalists for a minimum of 20 hours per week with the CIR.

PERKS
Seminars; meetings with journalists.

FYI
The CIR founded the program in 1977. . . CIR's brochure lists the internship's primary objective as "to teach investigative reporting skills to novice reporters." . . . Interns also are able to attend seminars. The list of past speakers reads like a who's who in American journalism.

TO APPLY
Open to high school students, undergrads, grad students, college grads of any age. International applicants eligible. Submit resume, cover letter, and several writing samples or published clips.

Center for Investigative Reporting
c/o internship Coordinator
500 Howard Street, Suite 206
San Francisco, CA 94105-3000
(415) 543-1200
(415) 543-8311 (Fax)
E-mail: center@cironline.org
www.muckraker.org

CENTER FOR MARINE CONSERVATION

SELECTIVITY 🔍🔍🔍
Approximate applicant pool: 150; Interns accepted: 15

COMPENSATION $
None for undergrads; $200–$1,000 stipend for grad students; reimbursement of daily transportation costs

LOCATION(S)
Hampton, VA; Marathon and St. Petersburg, FL; San Francisco, CA; Washington, DC (HQ)

FIELD
Environment

DURATION
3 months minimum: Summer, Fall, Winter, Spring

DEADLINE(S)
Summer: May 17; Fall: August 2; Winter: December 7; Spring: March 8

THE WORK
Founded in 1972, the Center for Marine Conservation (CMC) is a private, nonprofit environmental organization dedicated to protecting marine life and their habitats through public education and lobbying efforts. DC interns work in Press Relations, Art/Publications, and Finance and Administration; for CMC's newsletters *Marine Conservation News*, *Coastal Connections*, and *Sanctuary Currents*; and in the following programs: Communications and Media Department, Marine Debris and Entanglement, Sea Turtle Conservation, Marine Habitat Conservation, Marine Mammal Conservation, Fisheries Conservation, and Marine Biological Diversity. Interns in the regional offices work on similar projects.

PERKS
Orientation; attendance welcome at Capitol Hill hearings (DC); seasonal beach cleanups (regional offices); attendance welcome at staff meetings.

FYI
Intern duties include responding to public requests for information, making local presentations, researching and writing educational materials, and summarizing legislation.

TO APPLY
Open to undergrads and grad students. International applicants eligible. Submit resume, cover letter, and writing sample (two-five pages) directly to office of interest. Call DC headquarters for contacts in regional offices.

Internship Coordinator
Center for Marine Conservation
1725 DeSales Street NW, Suite 500
Washington, DC 20036
(202) 429-5609

Dream Internships

Can you believe these places take interns?

Barneys New York
Baywatch
Callaway Advanced Technology
Christian Dior
Dallas Cowboys
Forty Acres and a Mule
Hanna-Barbera
Howard Stern Show
Jim Henson Productions
The Juilliard School
Late Show with David Letterman
Lucasfilm
Miller Brewing Company
MTV
NBA
NFL
Nike
Oscar Mayer Wienermobile
Peggy Guggenheim Collection
Playboy
Polo Ralph Lauren
Rush Limbaugh Show
Saks Fifth Avenue
San Francisco 49ers
Sesame Street
Sports Illustrated
Virgin Records

SELECTIVITY 🔍🔍
Approximate applicant pool: 800; Interns accepted: 200

COMPENSATION 💲
Two interns receive Anne Armstrong Leadership Awards (AALA) of $3,000

LOCATION(S)
Washington, DC

FIELD
Foreign affairs; Public policy

DURATION
16 weeks: Summer, Fall, Spring

DEADLINE(S)
Rolling; AALA: April 1 and November 1

THE WORK
Founded in 1962, the Center for Strategic & International Studies (CSIS) is a public policy research institute providing US policymakers with strategic perspectives on issues of international security, politics, economics, and business. CSIS projects focus on areas like AIDS, arms control, conflict resolution, NATO, the environment, immigration, intelligence, trade, health care, OPEC, space policy, and terrorism. Interns work in six regional programs (African, Americas, Asian, European, Middle East, and Russian), six functional programs (Domestic Policy, Energy/Environment, International Communications, International Business & Economics, and Political-Military), and in administrative areas (Government Affairs, Public Affairs, Publications & Marketing and Finance & Accounting).

PERKS
Attendance welcome at seminars with high-ranking officials; invitations to CSIS monthly parties; tours of DC cultural sites and brown-bag luncheons with staff; summer softball league.

FYI
CSIS projects often receive substantive input from outside experts in government, academia, and business, who have included Senator Sam Nunn, Procter & Gamble President John Pepper, former Secretary of State Henry Kissinger, and Glaxo Chairman Charles Sanders.

TO APPLY
Open to undergrads, recent college grads, college grads of any age, and grad students. If applying to a regional program, proficiency in region's language is helpful. AALA applicants must be college sophomores, juniors, or seniors with a minimum GPA of 3.5 in their major (write for application). International applicants eligible. Submit resume, cover letter, and writing sample.

Intern Program
Center for Strategic & International Studies
1800 K Street NW
Washington, DC 20006
(202) 887-0200

SELECTIVITY 🔍
Applicant Pool: 12; Applicants Selected: 4

COMPENSATION 💲
College credit; No pay

LOCATION(S)
Baltimore, MD

FIELD
Conflict resolution; Academia; Fundraising

DURATION
3 months or more

DEADLINE(S)
Rolling

THE WORK
The Center for the Study of Conflict dedicates itself to examining ways to control violence at the individual, group, and international levels. Areas of study have included Switzerland's social policies and Baltimore's fight against crime. Interns at the Center do library research in social science and history, and some interns also do writing, editing, and fundraising.

PERKS
"Great" letters of recommendation from the director

FYI
Some of the former donors to the Center have been such notables as a former president of the Women's International League for Peace and Freedom as well as a U.S. Air Force chief of staff, and a former president of the American Association for the Advancement of Science.

TO APPLY
Open to all undergraduate graduate students, and recent college grads. Send resume and cover letter to:

Dr. Richard Wendell Fogg
Director
5846 Bellona Avenue
Baltimore, MD 21212
410-323-7656

SELECTIVITY 🔍 🔍 🔍
Approximate applicant pool: 2,000; Interns accepted: 50–60

COMPENSATION 💲 💲 💲
$440–$640/wk (undergrad); $640–$840/wk (grad); round-trip travel

LOCATION(S)
Langley, VA; Washington, DC; and other sites

FIELD
Government

DURATION
Fall, Spring, Summer

DEADLINE(S)
Undergrad: November 1; Grad: 6–9 months prior to work

THE WORK
The Central Intelligence Agency is charged with guarding America's national security. With this responsibility comes the necessary secrecy and security precautions. For this reason, one of an intern's first activities will be a lie detector test. Interns may apply under three programs: The Undergraduate Student Trainee Program, the CIA Summer Internship Program, and the Graduate Studies Program. They will be assigned to one of three divisions: the Directorate of Science and Technology, the Directorate of Intelligence, or the Directorate of Administration.

PERKS
Tight-knit culture; speaker series; Co-op Association; employee benefits.

FYI
If interns find their assignments unrewarding, chances are they will have the opportunity to switch jobs or offices . . . Interns have to get used to the fact that the nature of their work is almost always secret . . . Housing assistance is available through Student Programs. Upward of 72 percent of all interns are offered jobs at the CIA.

TO APPLY
The Undergraduate Student Trainee Program is open to sophomores and juniors. The CIA Summer Internship is open to sophomores, juniors, and seniors, predominantly for minority and disabled students. The Graduate Studies Program is available for minority and nonminority students entering their first or second years of graduate study. Applicants must be US citizens and over 17 1/2 years of age at time of application, have a minimum GPA of 3.0 for both undergrads and grads, and successfully pass medical and security screening. Apply six to nine months prior to the desired work period. Submit resume, cover letter, and transcript.

Central Intelligence Agency
CIA Recruitment Center
P.O. Box 4090
Reston, VA 20195

SELECTIVITY 🔍 🔍 🔍
Approximate applicant pool: 140; Interns accepted: 20

COMPENSATION 💲 💲 💲 💲
$577/week

LOCATION(S)
Indianapolis, IN; Phoenix, AZ

FIELD
Newspapers

DURATION
10 weeks: Summer

DEADLINE(S)
Early Application Deadline: October 15; Final Postmark Deadline: March 1

THE WORK
Since 1974, Central Newspapers has chosen college students and recent college graduates from throughout the country for internships at its newspapers. Interns work as reporters, feature writers or copy editors, depending on their areas of interest and experience. Starting with the Summer 2001 program, competition will be open to college sophomores, juniors, seniors, grad students and working journalists. Four of the 20 interns will have an opportunity to work an additional nine months for us after the internships end in mid-August. After that nine-month period, there may be the chance of permanent employment with our newspapers.

PERKS
Twice-weekly luncheons with guest speakers and in-house executives.

FYI
Started in 1974, the internship program includes among its alumni four Pulitzer Prize winners.

TO APPLY
International applicants eligible. Write for application or request one by e-mail.

Russell B. Pulliam, Editor
The Pulliam Fellowships
P.O. Box 145
Indianapolis, IN 46206-0145
(317) 633-9121
(317) 630-9549 (Fax)
E-mail: rpulliam@starnews.com

CIA INTERN BECOMES WORST SPY IN CIA HISTORY

Aldrich Ames, the CIA spy turned traitor, committed what Ted Koppel calls the "most devestating betrayal in the history of espionage." Secretly allied with the former Soviet Union, he leaked to the Soviets some of America's most critical secrets, including information that led to the execution of several CIA informants. Guess where the "worst spy in CIA history" got his start? The CIA Summer Internship program!

SELECTIVITY 🔍🔍🔍🔍
Approximate applicant pool: 50; Interns accepted: 4

COMPENSATION 💲
None

LOCATION(S)
New York, NY

FIELD
Performing arts

DURATION
10–15 weeks: Summer, Fall, Spring

DEADLINE(S)
Rolling

THE WORK
Established in 1986 by the City Parks Foundation and the New York City Department of Parks and Recreation, Central Park SummerStage (CPSS) is a summertime outdoor performing arts festival featuring music, dance, literary readings, and video. Concerts are on weekends, and admission is always free. Featured artists have included Joan Baez, Bo Diddley, the Lounge Lizards, the New York Grand Opera, Gipsy Kings, Los Lobos, Ivo Papasov and His Bulgarian Wedding Band, Joyce Carol Oates, Oscar Hijuelos, Carl Bernstein, Amiri Baraka, Lou Reed, and Jump Sister Jump. Interns work in Production and Publicity.

PERKS
Free concerts (summer only); small, friendly staff; free t-shirts.

FYI
CPSS is known for embracing multiculturalism, showcasing artists and work from all over the world . . . Says the internship coordinator: "Interns work extensively with artists and the media and gain an intimate sense of New York City arts."

TO APPLY
Open to high school grads, undergrads, recent college grads, college grads of any age, and grad students. International applicants eligible. Submit resume, cover letter, and writing samples.

Internship Coordinator
Central Park SummerStage
830 Fifth Avenue
New York, NY 10021
(212) 360-2756
(212) 360-2754 (Fax)

SELECTIVITY 🔍
Approximate applicant pool: 15; Interns accepted: 4–12

COMPENSATION 💲
Free housing at CASA hospital for interns with considerable clinical experience

LOCATION(S)
San Miguel de Allende, Mexico

FIELD
Health care; Public service

DURATION
8 weeks minimum: ongoing

DEADLINE(S)
Rolling

THE WORK
Founded in 1981, Centro para los Adolescentes de San Miguel de Allende (CASA) is a nonprofit health and social-service agency serving indigents of Guanajuato, Mexico. With a staff of 80 doctors, nurses, and social workers tending to over 50,000 people per year, CASA offers such services as general medicine, reproductive health care, family planning, sex education, adolescent peer counseling, day care, and dental care. Interns work in one or more of the following programs: Peer Counselor Program in Rural Areas, Day Care for Children of Adolescent Mothers, Out-Patient Medical Services, Maternity Hospital (including dental clinic, pharmacy, and laboratory), Psychological Services, Research, Administrative, Library, Grant Writing/Fundraising, and School Program for Students, Teachers, and Parents.

PERKS
Attendance welcome at births, surgeries, staff meetings, and training sessions; time off to take Spanish classes; "colonial, artistic town of San Miguel de Allende."

FYI
The state of Guanajuato has been designated by the Mexican Government as one of five "priority states" because of the poor health status of most of the state's 4 million residents and one of the highest infant mortality rates in Mexico . . . Says the clerkship bulletin: "The vast majority of CASA's work happens out in the field! There is often need to walk considerable distances, make home visits, sit on dirt floors, etc."

TO APPLY
Open to high school students, high school grads, undergrads, recent college grads, college grads of any age, and grad students (especially medical students). Must be proficient in Spanish. International applicants eligible. Submit resume, cover letter, and recommendations.

Clerkship Program
Centro para los Adolescentes de San Miguel de Allende
Umaran 62
San Miguel de Allende
Guanajuato, Mexico 37700
52-415-2-26-88 or 2-20-54 or 2-61-81
52-415-2-01-21 (Fax)

An intern at Centro para los Adolescentes de San Miguel de Allende (CASA) in Mexico shows two CASA visitors her favorite condom.

THE CENTURY PLAZA HOTEL

See Westin Hotels & Resorts

CHAMBER MUSIC AMERICA

SELECTIVITY
Approximate applicant pool: 20; Interns accepted: 1–3

COMPENSATION
None

LOCATION(S)
New York, NY

FIELD
Chamber music

DURATION
9–16 weeks: Summer, Fall, Spring

DEADLINE(S)
Rolling

THE WORK
Created in 1977, Chamber Music America (CMA) is a membership service organization devoted to professional chamber musicians. With over 4,200 members, CMA publishes the quarterly magazine *Chamber Music*, and organizes various conferences, seminars, and technical assistance programs. Interns work in Fundraising, Conference Planning, Marketing, and Publishing.

PERKS
Attendance welcome at board meetings; occasional free tickets to music events; small staff.

FYI
Recent interns have found themselves researching potential fundraising sources, helping prepare a survey of the chamber music field, helping organize a directory of summer chamber music programs, and writing articles for *Chamber Music*.

TO APPLY
Open to undergrads, recent college grads, college grads of any age, and grad students. Submit resume and cover letter.

Internship Coordinator
Chamber Music America
545 Eighth Avenue
New York, NY 10018
(212) 244-2772
(212) 244-2776 (Fax)

CHANTICLEER FILMS

SELECTIVITY
Approximate applicant pool: 40–50; Interns accepted: 20

COMPENSATION
None

LOCATION(S)
Los Angeles, CA

FIELD
Film

DURATION
Ongoing

DEADLINE(S)
Rolling

THE WORK
Founded in 1986 by three film industry veterans, Chanticleer Films has produced over 60 half-hour films and 10 feature length films, as well as the television series "The ShowTime Thirty-Minute Movie" and "Directed By." Chanticleer's short films include the Academy Award-winning *Ray's Male Heterosexual Dance Hall* and *Session Man*. Interns work in Production and Post-Production.

PERKS
Attendance welcome at film screenings; intern seminars with department heads; opportunities to be "on set"; attendance welcome at various parties.

FYI
Alumni of the program include the Executive in Charge of Production at New Line Cinema.

TO APPLY
Open to high school grads, undergrads, recent college grads, college grads of any age, and grad students. International applicants eligible. Submit resume and recommendations.

Internship Coordinator
Chanticleer Films
1680 North Vine Street, #1212
Hollywood, CA 90028

SELECTIVITY 🔍🔍🔍
Approximate applicant pool: 100; Interns accepted: 10

COMPENSATION ⑤
None, but credit may be obtained from school

LOCATION(S)
Watertown, MA

FIELD
Publishing

DURATION
12 weeks: Summer, Fall, Spring

DEADLINE(S)
Rolling

THE WORK
Founded in 1989, Charlesbridge Publishing publishes educational materials and children's books. Interns work as editorial assistants in the school division. For more information refer to the online catalog at www.charlesbridge.com.

PERKS
Small, friendly office; easy access to managing editor.

FYI
Says the internship coordinator: "Interns do real editorial work (no typing and filing) on real books. Responsibilities include editing text and art, researching, fact-checking, and communicating with authors and illustrators. Each intern has primary responsibility for all phases of the development of a book project."

TO APPLY
Open to college juniors and seniors, recent college grads, college grads of any age, and grad students. The intern should have a strong background in English. Submit resume, cover letter, and writing samples.

Elena Dworkin Wright
Managing Editor
Charlesbridge Publishing
85 Main Street
Watertown, MA 02472
(617) 926-0329
(617) 926-5720 (Fax)
www.charlesbridge.com

FROM INTERN TO RIVAL CANDIDATE

Adam Clayton Powell IV, the son of former Congressman Adam Clayton Powell, Jr., interned during the summer of 1981 for Representative **Charles Rangel** (D-NY), who had defeated the elder Powell in the 1970 congressional race. Thirteen years after the internship, the younger Powell made an unsuccessful run at reclaiming his father's seat, losing to Rangel in the 1994 congressional election.

CHARLIE ROSE

SELECTIVITY 🔍🔍🔍
Approximate applicant pool: 70; Interns accepted: 6–8

COMPENSATION ⑤
None

LOCATION(S)
New York, NY

FIELD
Television

DURATION
3–6 months: ongoing

DEADLINE(S)
Rolling

THE WORK
Charlie Rose is a nightly one-hour talk show that airs on over 200 PBS stations throughout the United States. Making its nationwide debut in January 1993, the show is anchored by Charlie Rose, an Emmy Award-winning journalist and a correspondent for *60 Minutes II* on CBS. Interns work in Production/Research, where they "learn how to produce a nightly talk show—pitching ideas, booking guests, producing segments, and getting the product on the air."

PERKS
Occasional opportunities to travel with crews on local shoots; free snack foods (e.g., cereal, fruits, and soups).

FYI
During an interview Mr. Rose did in 1993, when asked why he chooses a big round table for the program's set, he said: "It says to the audience, 'This is the table at which you are invited to sit.' I want every member of my audience to essentially come sit at my table for a good conversation." . . . Of *Charlie Rose's* twelve-member staff, eight are former interns at the show.

TO APPLY
Open to undergrads, grad students, and college grads. Submit resume, cover letter, and one recommendation.

Internship Coordinator
Charlie Rose
499 Park Avenue, 15th Floor
New York, NY 10022
(212) 940-1600
(212) 940-1909 (Fax)

SELECTIVITY
Approximate applicant pool: 500; Interns accepted: 15

COMPENSATION
$400/week; $300 travel allowance

LOCATION(S)
Research Triangle Park, NC

FIELD
Biomedical research

DURATION
10–12 weeks: Summer

DEADLINE(S)
March 1

THE WORK
Established in 1974 by 11 chemical companies, the Chemical Industry Institute of Toxicology (CIIT) is a nonprofit research institute conducting cutting-edge toxicological research and promoting the professional development and training of toxicologists. Seeking to assess the health risks of exposure to chemicals, CIIT research projects have investigated the effects of dioxin on hepatic enzymes, pharmacokinetic models of inhaled methanol, formaldehyde-induced nasal lesions, and the effects of unleaded gasoline on tumor promotion. Assigned to various CIIT labs, interns design and perform experiments in carcinogenesis, inhalation toxicology, developmental toxicology, and neurotoxicology.

PERKS
Likely publication in major toxicology or cancer journal; presentation of research at CIIT's Summer Intern Research Symposium; mentors.

FYI
Launched in 1989, CIIT's internship program, according to a CIIT brochure, is "central to achieving the overall research mission of the Institute and often forms the basis of many presentations at national scientific meetings and ultimately publications."

TO APPLY
Open to college juniors and seniors, recent college grads, college grads of any age, and grad students. Write for application.

Internship Coordinator
Chemical Industry Institute of Toxicology
6 Davis Drive
P.O. Box 12137-2137
Research Triangle Park, NC 27709
(919) 558-1200
(919) 558-1300 (Fax)

CHEVROLET
See General Motors

SELECTIVITY
Approximate applicant pool: 1,000; Interns accepted: 100

COMPENSATION
$400–$700/wk for undergrads; $800/wk for grad students; round-trip travel; temporary-lodging allowance

LOCATION(S)
Bakersfield, Concord, El Segundo, Richmond, San Francisco (HQ), & San Ramon, CA; New Orleans, Lafayette, LA; Pascagoula, MS; Houston and Midland TX.

FIELD
Chemicals; Oil & gas

DURATION
Intern: 12 weeks, Summer
Co-op: at least two 3-month sessions, ongoing

DEADLINE(S)
Rolling (until on-campus interviews in January)

THE WORK
Chevron is the largest refiner and marketer of petroleum products in the United States and one of the world's largest petroleum companies. Headquartered in San Francisco, Chevron employs 35,000 people worldwide in over 100 countries. The company offers internships in many areas: Upstream Operations (exploration and production), Downstream Operations (refinery products), Refining, Finance (MBAs only), Human Resources (grad students only), Computer Science, and Accounting.

PERKS
Orientation; Chevron fitness centers & cafeterias; summer Intern Day; special tours.

FYI
Each year, up to 50 percent of new hires are former Chevron interns . . . Interns from around the country have the opportunity to visit the corporate headquarters in San Francisco and attend presentations given by senior managers . . . The atmosphere is supportive. "Everybody always took an interest in me and in what I did. I was always included," said one intern.

TO APPLY
Open to undergrads, recent grads, grad students, and college grads of any age. International applicants with F-1 visas are eligible. Submit resume, cover letter, and transcript.

Chevron Recruiting Team
12th Floor
575 Market Street
San Francisco, CA 94105
www.chevron.com

SELECTIVITY 🔍🔍🔍
Approximate applicant pool: 100; Interns accepted: 17–22

COMPENSATION 💲💲
$230/week

LOCATION(S)
Glencoe, IL

FIELD
Horticulture

DURATION
12 weeks–1 year: ongoing

DEADLINE(S)
Rolling

THE WORK
The Chicago Botanic Garden (CBG) was established in 1965 to provide a permanent site for the Chicago Horticultural Society's flower shows, gardens, lectures, and research programs. Besides maintaining twenty-one different gardens for the public's viewing pleasure, the 300-acre CBG offers courses in botany and gardening and runs day camps for kids. Interns work in Administration, Horticulture, Education, Integrated Pest Management, Research and Conservation Ecology, Public Relations, Graphic Design, and Horticultural Therapy (i.e., the benefits of horticulture in promoting physical and mental well-being).

PERKS
Seminars, workshops, and weekly staff meetings; classes and field trips to Chicago's horticultural institutions; opportunity to publish at least one article in CBG's intern newsletter or a garden magazine.

FYI
Started in 1978, CBG's internship program rotates interns from one department to another once a month, thus providing a broad overview of horticulture, public garden management, botany, and landscaping. By the end of the internship, interns will have washed pots, taught classes, mapped out gardens, cleaned walkways, weeded, planted, pruned, and answered questions from the public.

TO APPLY
Open to college students, recent college grads, college grads of any age (within two years of graduation), and grad students (in horticulture, botany, plant sciences, etc.). International applicants eligible. Write for application.

Aviva Levavi
Internship Coordinator
Chicago Botanic Garden
1000 Lake Cook Road
Glencoe, IL 60022
(847) 835-8263
E-mail: alevavi@chicagobotanic.org

SELECTIVITY 🔍🔍🔍🔍🔍
Approximate applicant pool: 500; Interns accepted: 10

COMPENSATION 💲💲
100 percent commission for sales

LOCATION(S)
Chicago, IL

FIELD
Sports management

DURATION
16 weeks, June 1 to October 1, Monday to Friday from 9 to 5

DEADLINE(S)
April 15

THE WORK
In 1966, the NBA added "Da Bulls" to its roster. Since then, the Bulls and the NBA have grown to national and global prominence. Interns sell season tickets and program ads and are paid on commission. The positions are 100 percent cold-call telemarketing through an in-house database and the yellow pages to Chicagoland businesses.

PERKS
Catered lunch daily; free parking.

FYI
The Bulls' internship program was founded in 1986, and eight former interns currently work at the organization. According to the coordinator, interns work long hours to help achieve the organization's goals "to win championships and to maximize the sales potential of our product."

TO APPLY
Open to recent college graduates only. No phone calls of any kind, please. Submit resume, cover letter, and recommendations. No faxes, please. Recent college writing samples are helpful but not required.

Internship Coordinator
Chicago Bulls
1901 West Madison Street
Chicago, IL 60612

CHICAGO CHILDREN'S MUSEUM

SELECTIVITY 🔍🔍
Approximate applicant pool: 200;   Interns accepted: 45–50

COMPENSATION 💲
Travel stipend of up to $100

LOCATION(S)
Chicago, IL

FIELD
Museums; Education

DURATION
12–15 weeks: Summer, Fall, Spring

DEADLINE(S)
Summer: May 15; Fall: August 15; Spring: December 15

THE WORK
Founded in 1982, the Chicago Children's Museum strives to "activate the intellectual and creative potential of children by being a catalyst for the process of learning." The museum has gained worldwide recognition for its innovative, hands-on exhibits as well as its educational outreach programs. Interns work in Education, Exhibits, Development, Marketing, Human Resources, Community Outreach, and Volunteer Services.

PERKS
Orientation; Professional brown bag lunch series; family passes for museum admission; attendance welcome at staff meetings, conferences, etc.; travel stipend of up to $100 and parking discount; 10 percent discount at Museum Gift Shop and various vendors on Navy Pier.

FYI
The Chicago Children's Museum has a staff of one hundred and twenty. Interns are given significant projects, often working on teams with professional staff, and have the chance to gain meaningful work experience.

TO APPLY
Open to college juniors and seniors, recent college grads of any age, and grad students. International applicants eligible. Write for application.

Director of Internships
Chicago Children's Museum
445 East Illinois Street, #352
Chicago, IL 60611-3428
(312) 464-7652
(312) 527-9082 (Fax)

CHILDREN'S DEFENSE FUND

SELECTIVITY 🔍🔍🔍
Approximate applicant pool: 500; Interns accepted: 50–75

COMPENSATION 💲
Reimbursement for daily, local travel

LOCATION(S)
Washington, DC

FIELD
Public policy; Public service

DURATION
3 months–1 year: Summer, Fall, Spring; also weekly or monthly externships are available

DEADLINE(S)
Summer: February 28; Fall: August 15; Spring: December 31

THE WORK
Founded in 1968 by activist Marian Wright Edelman, the Children's Defense Fund (CDF), formerly the Washington Research Project, is a nonprofit child advocacy organization, serving as a "strong and effective voice for American children who cannot speak, vote, or lobby for themselves." CDF monitors federal and state programs like Head Start and provides technical assistance to child advocates, organizations, and public officials in the areas of health, education, child welfare, adolescent pregnancy prevention, and youth employment. Departments accepting interns include Intergovernmental Relations, Family Income, Health, Black Community Crusade for Children, Policy (e.g., Child Care, Child Welfare), Communications.

PERKS
Orientation, where interns receive handbook and introductory packet; attendance welcome at congressional hearings, press conferences, and briefings; attendance welcome at staff meetings.

FYI
A graduate of Yale Law School, Edelman was the first black woman admitted to the Mississippi bar and in 1990 was named one of America's fifty most powerful women by *Ladies Home Journal*.

TO APPLY
Open to undergrads, recent college grads, college grads of any age, and grad students. International applicants eligible. For an application, visit the website.

Internship Coordinator
Children's Defense Fund
25 E Street NW
Washington, DC 20001
(202) 628-8787
www.childrensdefense.org

The Children's Museum
of Indianapolis

SELECTIVITY 🔍🔍🔍
Approximate applicant pool: 400; Interns accepted: 75

COMPENSATION Ⓢ
None

LOCATION(S)
Indianapolis, IN

FIELD
Museums

DURATION
10–16 weeks: Summer, Fall, or Spring

DEADLINE(S)
Rolling

THE WORK
The largest children's museum in the world, the Children's Museum of Indianapolis houses five stories of galleries exploring the physical and natural sciences, history, foreign cultures, and the arts. The museum includes a sweeping atrium entrance complete with a unique water clock, an education center, and a world-class planetarium. Departments hiring interns include Education, Programs, Collections, Exhibits, Finance, Marketing, Public Relations, Fundraising, Information Systems, Multi-media Technology, and the President's Office.

PERKS
Orientation; field trips to area and regional arts institutions; appreciation luncheon; resume and interview workshops, Myers Briggs profiling, reciprocal admission to Indianapolis arts organizations, and restaurant/store discounts.

FYI
Crows the internship coordinator, "I would put our program and the types of experiences our interns have against any other museum program in the nation."

TO APPLY
Open to undergrads, recent college grads, college grads of any age, and grad students. International students eligible. Send resume to:

Manager of Recruiting Services
Children's Museum of Indianapolis
P.O. Box 3000
Indianapolis, IN 46206
(317) 334-3302
(317) 920-2047 (Fax)

SELECTIVITY 🔍🔍
Approximate applicant pool: 300; Interns accepted: 60

COMPENSATION Ⓢ
None, travel/lunch stipend

LOCATION(S)
New York, NY

FIELD
Television

DURATION
12 weeks: Summer, Fall, Spring

DEADLINE(S)
Rolling

THE WORK
Since 1968, the Children's Television Workshop (CTW) has dedicated itself to using television as a medium to educate children, particularly those from poor and minority households. In addition to producing the childhood staple *Sesame Street* (see separate entry), CTW is responsible for children's programming such as *Ghostrider* as well as children's magazines, merchandise, games, and software. Interns work in a variety of internships including Production, Research, International, Publishing, Community Education Service, New Show Projects, Human Resources, etc.

PERKS
Attendance welcome at staff meetings; opportunities to watch show tapings; possible travel stipend; attendance welcome at occasional social events (e.g., holiday parties); possible job opportunities

FYI
CTW's headquarters is located in the heart of New York's trendy Upper West Side, across the street from the majestic Lincoln Center.

TO APPLY
Open to undergrads, recent college grads, college grads of any age, and grad students able to commit to a minimum of 3 work days. International applicants eligible. Submit resume and cover letter.

Internship Coordinator, CT
Children's Television Workshop
One Lincoln Plaza, 8th Floor
New York, NY 10023
(212) 875-6640
(212) 875-6088 (Fax)
E-mail: human.resources@ctw.org

David Peterson (left), the twentieth premier of Ontario, Canada, got his first taste of public service while pursuing a B.A. in philosophy and political science. During the summer of 1962, he served as a volunteer teacher in an adult education program in Saskatchewan.

SELECTIVITY 🔍🔍
Approximate applicant pool: 50; Interns accepted: 8–12

COMPENSATION 💲
Free lunch; daily transportation expenses covered

LOCATION(S)
Chicago, IL

FIELD
Theater

DURATION
8 weeks: ongoing

DEADLINE(S)
Rolling

THE WORK
Founded in 1978, the Child's Play Touring Theatre (CPTT) is the premier theater in the United States dedicated exclusively to performing pieces written by children. Visiting cities across the United States, two full-time troupes of professional actors and musicians present several short plays and songs at each show. Interns work in Development, General Administration, Public Relations, Story Selection, and Technical Production.

PERKS
Free tickets to all CPTT performances; attendance welcome at master classes and workshops; intimate, upbeat office environment.

FYI
In existence since 1987, the internship program leads to permanent employment at CPTT for 10 percent of interns . . . Says a former intern: "How can anyone judge a piece of art created with the delicate heart and highly impressionable mind of a second grader? I had to ask this question objectively every time I curled up with 75 new stories—fresh from the souls of their creators, eager to be chosen."

TO APPLY
Open to high school students, high school grads, undergrads, recent college grads, college grads of any age, and grad students. International applicants eligible. Write for application.

Internship Coordinator
Child's Play Touring Theatre
2518 West Armitage
Chicago, IL 60647
(773) 235-8911
(773) 235-5478 (Fax)

> "How can anyone judge a piece of art created with the delicate heart and highly impressionable mind of a second grader? I had to ask this question objectively every time I curled up with 75 new stories — fresh from the souls of their creators eager to be chosen . . ."
> —former intern, Child's Play Touring Theatre

SELECTIVITY 🔍🔍🔍🔍🔍
Approximate applicant pool: 100; Interns accepted: 1–5 within each category

COMPENSATION 💲💲
$100/week; free housing

LOCATION(S)
Assateague Island, VA

FIELD
Wildlife management; Environmental education, interpretation, and field research

DURATION
12–16 weeks: Summer, Fall, Spring

DEADLINE(S)
Summer: March 15; Fall: July 3 and August 1; Spring: January 15

THE WORK
Located on Assateague Island, a 14,000-acre island off Virginia's eastern shore, Chincoteague National Wildlife Refuge (CNWR) is one of 500 national wildlife refuges operated by the US Fish and Wildlife Service. Created in 1943, it serves as a wintering ground and migratory stopover for waterfowl, a protected area for endangered and native species, and a wildlife-oriented recreation and education center. Interns work in Visitor Services, where they staff the visitor center, write brochures and design exhibits, and educate visitors on the refuge's various species; in Biology, where they monitor bird populations, conduct vegetation transects, and repair nests; and in Law Enforcement, where they assist with dispatching duties.

PERKS
Excellent bird- and wildlife-watching opportunities; extensive system of walking and biking trails; access to swimming, surfing, and fishing.

FYI
Interns live in a former lighthouse-keeper's home next to Assateague Lighthouse or a mobile home, two miles from the beach . . . The intern coordinator describes CNWR as "one of the most complex, highly visited, and beautiful refuges in the country."

TO APPLY
Open to college juniors and seniors as well as grads and grad students. Submit resume and cover letter.

Volunteer Coordinator
Chincoteague National Wildlife Refuge
P.O. Box 62
Chincoteague, VA 23336
(757) 336-6122
(757) 336-5273 (Fax)

Interns at Chincoteague National Wildlife Refuge live in Assateague Island's historic lighthouse-keepers' home, next to Assateague Lighthouse.

SELECTIVITY 🔍 🔍 🔍
Approximate applicant pool: 175–200; Interns accepted: 30

COMPENSATION 💲 💲 💲
$400/week for undergrads; $420/week for grad students; free room and board

LOCATION(S)
Wallingford, CT

FIELD
Education; Liberal arts

DURATION
5 weeks: Summer

DEADLINE(S)
February 1

THE WORK
Located two hours from New York, Choate Rosemary Hall is a prestigious prep school spread over 400 acres in Connecticut. Employed during Choate's Summer Session for high school and middle school students, interns serve as teaching assistants in two major courses, in subjects ranging from English to economics. Interns also serve as resident-house advisers, afternoon-recreation coaches, and field-trip chaperones.

PERKS
Superb campus facilities, including a $14 million science center designed by I.M. Pei; use of athletic facilities (twenty-seven tennis courts, three basketball ball courts, twenty-five-meter pool, track, and gym); 4th of July celebration, talent show, reggae dance, and barbecues; trips to nearby beaches, sporting events, and amusement parks.

FYI
The Summer Session began in 1916, only three decades after the founding of The Choate School in 1896. The intern program has been in existence since the 1970s.

TO APPLY
Open to college juniors and seniors, recent college grads, college grads of any age, and grad students. International applicants eligible. Write for application or complete from website.

Teaching Intern Program
Choate Rosemary Hall Summer Session
333 Christian Street
Wallingford, CT 06492
(203) 697-2365
(203) 697-2519 (Fax)
E-mail: jirzyk@choate.edu
www.choate.edu/summer

Did world renowned film director **Brian DePalma** get his start interning for a movie house? Nope. The man responsible for such classic films as *Carrie, Dressed to Kill,* and *Scarface* spent a few high school summers working part time in a hospital laboratory in Philadelphia. It was only later when he was an undergrad at Columbia that his interests switched from science to film.

CHRISTIE'S

SELECTIVITY 🔍 🔍 🔍
Approximate applicant pool: 300; Interns accepted: 50

COMPENSATION 💲
Fall and Spring: $6 daily stipend

LOCATION(S)
New York, NY

FIELD
Auction house

DURATION
August–December, January–May

DEADLINE(S)
Fall and Spring: Rolling

THE WORK
Founded in 1766, Christie's is the world's oldest fine-art auctioneer. With seventy-seven offices in thirty countries, the publicly traded company auctions everything from paintings, furniture, and jewelry to comic books, wine, and sports memorabilia. Interns work with specialists in over a dozen Fine and Decorative Art departments as well as in Marketing, Public Relations, Human Resources, and Information Systems.

PERKS
Weekly round-table luncheons with Christie's specialists; field trips to museums as well as corporate and private art collections; mentors; orientation and farewell parties.

FYI
Christie's has retained approximately 15 percent of its former interns for full-time positions since starting the internship program in the mid-1970s, and at least a dozen former interns, including John Hays, Senior VP and auctioneer of American Furniture and Decorative Arts, fill Christie's hallowed halls as auctioneers, senior specialists, and managers of departments . . . Christie's offers a few scholarships.

TO APPLY
Open to college juniors and seniors as well as grads. Include cover letter and resume. Indicate internship desired, availability, and interests.

Laura Weissenberger
Internship Coordinator, HR
1230 Avenue of the Americas
New York, NY 10020

I WAS AN INTERN-SPY FOR PLAYBOY!

*While completing his B.A. in communications from Fordham University, **John Champion** spent part of 1991 interning in the New York office of Playboy magazine. Champion worked in various departments, including the Publisher's Office and Public Relations. The Internship Informants interviewed him about a secret spying mission he undertook during his internship.*

Background:
[The office] had been getting a lot of grief from this guy Reverend Donald Wildmon. Wildmon is the president and founder of the American Family Association [AFA] . . . a radically conservative organization which is against even pretty innocent [television] shows like *Seinfeld* because they refer to sexual subjects. So naturally when it comes to *Playboy,* they want it banned. How they go about it is that they try to pressure the advertisers to drop out. And [during my internship] I had been working on campaigns to get Wildmon off the back of our car advertisers.

The plan:
I was planning to go down South [to my family's home] for a few weeks of summer vacation, and AFA's base in Tupelo, Mississippi, is just a few hours' drive from where I was going. So I worked it out that I would pay [AFA's national conference] a visit while I was down there . . . For me, it was a chance [to get material] to possibly write a major article for *Playboy.* I arranged it carefully so that I wouldn't get found out—I made sure to pre-register [for the conference].

Infiltration:
I got to the conference, and I saw that I was about 40 years younger than the average person there. It was kind of funny—I got immediately taken in because I guess I was young and enthusiastic. So here are the heads of other chapters of AFA taking me out to dinner and loaning me books about how America is going to hell.

Exposed:
I had already gone to some meetings the night before, but the Saturday morning meeting was the big event. It was about an hour into the program when Donald Wildmon himself interrupted the speaker and announced that they had a special guest in the audience—and it was me. He asked me to come up on stage with him, and at that point he announced that I was a spy from *Playboy.* He told me to leave . . . to get out and come back when I had found God. He then instructed the audience to pray for me as I was leaving. There were a few gasps [in the audience] and a lot of stares. It was the longest walk I've ever made. I had been told before that they probably wouldn't hurt me if they found me out, but it was still really unnerving. I went over to get my notes, and they told me very forcefully to leave them there, even though I legally had the right to take my notes. I sort of trotted to the backdoor and got out of there.

How did it happen?
When I got back to New York, I dedicated myself to figuring out how in the world [the AFA] found out about me. I kept thinking—maybe they tapped my phone, because they used to brag about how they had plants in the Justice system. It turns out that a few years later I found out that there was another journalist [undercover] at the meeting. My best guess is that this journalist found out that I was there [from a mutual friend at *Playboy*] and turned me in so that he would have an exclusive story for another magazine. That was my first run-in with highly unethical journalists. [laughs]

After graduating from Beverly Hills High School in 1965, **Rob Reiner** served an apprenticeship for two summers in regional theater on the East Coast. He went on to play Mike "Meathead" Stivic on *All in the Family* and then direct such award-winning films as *This Is Spinal Tap, The Sure Thing, Stand By Me,* and *The Princess Bride.*

SELECTIVITY 🔍🔍🔍
Approximate applicant pool: 25–30; Interns accepted: 3

COMPENSATION $
$227.50/week

LOCATION(S)
Middleburg, VA

FIELD
Magazines

DURATION
16–18 weeks: Summer, Fall, Spring

DEADLINE(S)
Rolling (at least 3 months prior to desired term)

THE WORK
In existence since 1937, *The Chronicle of the Horse* is a weekly magazine covering English riding and horse sports. Serving approximately 22,000 subscribers, it features news, rider profiles, and how-to articles pertaining to fox hunting, combined training, dressage, hunters and jumpers, steeplechase racing, trail riding, and equine activities for youth. Interns work in the Editorial department, but are also welcome to spend time in Advertising, Lay out, and Circulation.

PERKS
Contribution welcome in all meetings and inter-office decisions; possible travel to cover news events.

FYI
Approximately 25 percent of interns are offered permanent employment at the magazine.

TO APPLY
Open to undergrads, recent college grads, college grads of any age, and grad students. Must have knowledge of equestrian sports. Submit resume, cover letter, and writing samples.

Internship Coordinator
The Chronicle of the Horse
P.O. Box 46
Middleburg, VA 20118
(540) 687-6341
(540) 687-3937 (Fax)
www.chronofhorse.com

EMI Records

See EMI Records Group North America

CHRYSLER CORPORATION

SELECTIVITY N/A

COMPENSATION $ $ $ $
$340–740/wk for undergrads, $595-1000/wk for graduate students; $700 housing stipend & round-trip travel for out-of-towners

LOCATIONS
Detroit, MI (HQ); Wittmann, AZ; Carlsbad, CA; plus plants and sales offices throughout US (see brochure)

FIELD
Automobiles; Finance

DURATION
10–14 weeks (mid-May to mid-August)

DEADLINES
Undergrads: end of fall semester; Grads: March 1

THE WORK
Founded in 1925, Chrysler is the third-largest automaker in the US (behind GM and Ford) with nearly $61.4 billion in yearly revenue. Its three divisions—Chrysler/Plymouth, Dodge Car/Truck, and Jeep/Eagle—pump out popular cars like Cirrus, Town & Country, Neon, Voyager, Cherokee, Wrangler, Ram Pickup, and Viper. The company's summer internship program was started in the 1950s but only in 1992 did the program become formalized, serving as an organized preview of full-time employment. Departments available to interns include Vehicle Engineering, Manufacturing, Procurement & Supply, Finance, Human Resources & Employee Relations, Information Services, Facilities & Services, and Chrysler Financial.

PERKS
Tours of assembly plants; test rides at Chelsea Proving Grounds; intern meeting with a Chrysler VP; computer software training; tickets to social events.

FYI
Forbes magazine named Chrysler 1996's "Company of the Year," citing its "Hot cars. Great managers. Financial strength. And a spirit more like Silicon Valley than the Rust Belt."

TO APPLY
Open to college juniors and seniors as well as graduate students with "innovative problem solving ability." Minimum GPA: 3.0. A majority of interns are mechanical and electrical engineering majors, with much of the remainder comprising business, computer science, and logistics majors. Submit resume and cover letter or sign up for an interview at your career center.

Summer Internship Program
Chrysler Corporation
CIMS 485-01-99
1000 Chrysler Drive
Auburn Hills, MI 48326-2766
(248) 576-5741

Jeffrey Katzenberg, the former Disney Studios executive and current partner at DreamWorks SKG, spent much of his time between 1966 and 1973 volunteering for New York City Mayor John Lindsay. Commenting on his City Hall experience, Katzenberg told *Playboy* recently : "It was better than college. I was in a structured environment. I worked. I had responsibilities. I learned about people and had the most extraordinary experience in my life."

CINEMAX

See Home Box Office

CITIBANK

SELECTIVITY
Approximate applicant pool: 1,500; Interns accepted: 100

COMPENSATION
$500–$700/week for undergrads; $800–$1,000/week for grads

LOCATION(S)
New York, NY; Chicago, IL; Los Angeles, CA; Atlanta, GA; Houston and Dallas, TX

FIELD
Banking

DURATION
Summer: 10–13 weeks

DEADLINE(S)
April 1

THE WORK
Citibank is a premier global financial services organization. With a network linking almost 100 countries, Citibank is the only international bank with a significant presence in so many markets. For the Consumer, Institutional, Corporate or Private customers, this means worldwide access to Citibank's products and services, supported by the diversity of Citibankers' experience, skills and talent. As the world's economies become increasingly interrelated and integrated, the ability to deliver services globally will be an important competitive advantage. Interns may be placed in the following areas: Corporate Finance, Sales & Trading, Global Transaction Services, Consumer Banking, Corporate Audit, Financial Control and Real Estate.

PERKS
Orientation with chairman; entry-level responsibility; professional atmosphere; good cafeterias.

FYI
Interns are encouraged to participate in Citibank organized public service projects. Citibank was the first bank to offer compound interest on savings accounts.

TO APPLY
Internships are open to college juniors and grad students one year from graduation.

Citibank
Summer Associate Programs
575 Lexington Avenue
12th Floor/Zone 3
New York, NY 10043
(800) 442-CITI (2484)
www.citibank.com/hr/mg programs

THE CITIZENS NETWORK FOR FOREIGN AFFAIRS

SELECTIVITY
Approximate applicant pool: 300; Interns accepted: 12

COMPENSATION
$250/week

LOCATION(S)
Washington, DC

FIELD
Foreign affairs; Public policy

DURATION
10–16 weeks: Summer, Fall, Spring

DEADLINE(S)
Summer: April 1; Fall: July 1; Spring: November 1

THE WORK
Founded in 1986, The Citizens Network for Foreign Affairs is a nonprofit organization focusing on the United States' role in promoting global economic growth, particularly in the emerging economies and democracies. Through various programs and conferences, The Citizen's Network works to promote sustainable economic development in the former Soviet Union and Africa, mobilize the expertise and human resources of US agriculture to farmers, stimulate dialogue on the US stake in emerging democracies, and promote economic cooperation between the US and developing countries. An Internship with The Citizens Network is a unique opportunity to explore international issues from several different perspectives: that of community, multinational corporations, and the legislative and policy-making side of the government. Interns research US foreign policy and international economic issues, prepare briefs, and assist staff in program operations.

PERKS
Attendance welcome at staff luncheons, meetings on Capitol Hill, and seminars on relevant issues; access to kitchen and gym; "surplus of free coffee."

FYI
In existence since 1987, the internship program leads to permanent employment at The Citizen's Network for about 15 percent of interns.

TO APPLY
Open to college juniors and seniors, recent college grads, and grad students. Minimum GPA: 3.0. International applicants

How to Obtain A Visa/Work Permit for Overseas Internships

Obtaining authorization to intern in a country in which you do not have citizenship is an involved process, taking anywhere from several hours to six months. Often an organization will not even consider offering an internship to a foreigner who has not already initiated the process or who has not allowed for the time it takes to fill out the necessary paperwork. And there's no way to skirt this requirement—no one can lawfully enter and work in a foreign country without the proper documentation.

US CITIZENS WISHING TO INTERN OUTSIDE OF THE US

Before you can travel abroad, you must possess a valid US passport (exceptions: Canada, Mexico, and certain Caribbean islands). To intern in a foreign country, you must hold a valid US passport as well as a special work permit. Because each country's rules regarding the employment of foreigners vary, it is advisable to contact that country's nearest consulate office well in advance of your intended start date for the specific requirements (consulate offices are located in most major cities; to find out where the nearest regional office is, contact that country's embassy in Washington, DC).

Before contacting the consulate, however, consider the following. According to Christopher McNally at the Council on International Educational Exchange (CIEE), most countries are very protective of their jobs (including internships) and guard their work permits closely. As is usually the case, unless a prospective employer can show that you are not taking a job away from a citizen, your request to work there will be denied. Happily, says McNally, some countries have specific internship regulations that make it easier for Americans to obtain the necessary permit. In Germany, for example, you will usually be allowed to intern if you can show that the internship you are seeking is a required part of your coursework and is related to your field of study. In Britain, unpaid interns acting merely as observers do not even need a work permit. And in most European countries, students entering the country as part of a study-abroad program usually have an easier time obtaining permission to intern either part time while taking courses or for a few months afterwards.

For full-time students (wishing to intern during the summer or during a semester off) and recent graduates (within one semester of graduation), several organizations are available to help you through this confusing and time-consuming process. For a $160 fee at CIEE, for example, you can obtain a work permit in four weeks or less. Contact the following organizations (see separate entries in this book) for more information on fees, eligibility, etc.: AIESEC, The American-Scandinavian Foundation, CDG/CDS International, Council on International Educational Exchange (CIEE), IAESTE, and AIPT Hospitality/Tourism Exchange Program.

NON-US CITIZENS WISHING TO INTERN IN THE US

Before you can enter the US, you must hold a valid passport from your home country. And before you can begin an internship, whether paid or unpaid, you must secure the appropriate visa.

STUDENTS ENROLLED IN US SCHOOLS

As a non-US citizen studying in the US, you already hold an F-1 or M-1 visa (a few of you hold a special type of visa called the J-1 "student" visa). Each of these visas allows off-campus employment (including internships) related to your course of study. While the amount of time you spend serving internships is limited (a total of 12 months for an F-1 student, 6 months for an M-1 student, and 18 months for a J-1 student), your internships may be undertaken at any time—during the academic year, over several summers, and/or immediately after graduation. Before commencing work, you must submit several different forms to the nearest Immigration & Naturalization Service (INS), which will then issue the work permit, called an Employment Authorization Document (EAD). See your Designated School Official, or DSO—the person designated on your campus by the INS to help international students apply for EADs. "Once directed by your DSO," says Doug Mollenauer at the National Association of Foreign Student Advisors in Washington, DC, "you should have no problem obtaining the necessary work permit, but apply well in advance—[the application process] varies from walk-in service to a several-month wait through the mail."

PEOPLE LIVING OUTSIDE THE US

Contact the local US consulate for information on Q, B-1, and H-3 visas, which allow non-US citizens to work for US employers as "cultural exchange visitors," "visitors for business," and "trainees," respectively. Q visas are applicable to internship programs that seek non-US citizens highly proficient in English to teach their culture to Americans (according to Dan Ewert at the Association for International Practical Training, employers who could use Q visas include Disney's EPCOT center and some of the Smithsonian museums). B-1 visas, good for up to six months, cover unpaid training experiences (e.g., seminars, courses, internships), sometimes sponsored by an employer abroad. H-3 visas apply to established, formal training programs; in such cases, the employer must demonstrate that a similar training program is not available in the trainee's home country ("It's such a lengthy and involved process," says Ewert, "that anyone seeking this visa should consult a lawyer."). If you are a student enrolled in a school outside the US, your school's international career services office can assist you in securing Q, B-1, H-3, or other types of visas.

Despite the availability of these visas, the most prevalent type of visa covering internships is the J-1 "trainee" visa. Only students and professionals (e.g., businesspeople, scientists, doctors) are eligible for this visa, issued under the auspices of US Information Agency-approved exchange programs. For a fee, these international exchange organizations can possibly arrange an internship for you and/or help you secure the J-1 "trainee" visa, which allows you to "train" in the US for up to 18 months. Contact the following organizations (see separate entries in this book) for more information on fees, eligibility, etc.: AIESEC, The American-Scandinavian Foundation, CDG/CDS International, Council on International Educational Exchange (CIEE), IAESTE, and AIPT Hospitality/Tourism Exchange Program.

eligible. Application requirements: resume, three letters of recommendation, and a writing sample of under five pages. Write for application.

Internship Coordinator
The Citizens Network for Foreign Affairs
1111 19th Street NW, Suite 900
Washington, DC 20036
(202) 296-3920
(202) 296-3948 (Fax)
E-mail: bkramer@cnfa.org or deleam@cnfa.org
www.cnfa.com

CITY LIMITS

City Limits
NEW YORK'S URBAN AFFAIRS NEWS MAGAZINE

SELECTIVITY 🔍🔍🔍🔍
  Approximate applicant pool: 50; Interns accepted: 2–3

COMPENSATION Ⓢ
  None

LOCATION(S)
  New York, NY

FIELD
  Magazines

DURATION
  10–12 weeks: Summer, Fall, Spring

DEADLINE(S)
  Rolling

THE WORK
In print since 1976, *City Limits* magazine is a nonprofit monthly magazine devoted to covering issues important to New York City's low- and moderate-income neighborhoods. Read by community activists, public officials, journalists, scholars, and concerned citizens, *City Limits* features articles on housing, community development, the urban environment, crime, public health, and labor. Interns work in the Editorial department, where their responsibilities include research and writing, proofreading, and assisting with marketing, distribution, and fundraising.

PERKS
Cover City Hall; meetings with activists and local politicians; casual office; young staff; opportunities to get published clips.

FYI
Writes the internship coordinator: "[Not only] is the internship a good introduction to magazine journalism, it is a valuable introduction to urban affairs, politics, and the world of grassroots community advocacy and organizing."

TO APPLY
Open to college juniors and seniors, recent college grads, college grads of any age, and grad students. International applicants eligible. Submit resume, cover letter, and writing samples (journalism only).

Internship Coordinator
City Limits
120 Wall Street
20th Floor
New York, NY 10005

An Intern by Any Other Name is Also an Intern

"Interns," that is, people undertaking supervised practical experience, are not always called "interns." Some alternatives we have encountered:

Apprentice
Assistant
Copy boy/girl
Dewey
Errand boy/girl
Extern
Fellow
Gofer
Helper
Learner
Mentee
Office boy/girl
Property boy/girl
Researcher
Rookie
Servant-learner
Studente (Italian)
Tea boy/girl
Trainee
Volunteer
Cabana boy (just kidding)

SELECTIVITY 🔍🔍

Approximate applicant pool: 500; Interns accepted: 100

COMPENSATION $

40 paid positions; some stipends for Federal work-study participants

LOCATION(S)

New York, NY; Queens,NY; Brooklyn, NY; Bronx, NY; Staten Island, NY

FIELD

City government

DURATION

Flexible: Summer, Fall, Winter, Spring

DEADLINE(S)

Rolling

THE WORK

City of New York/Parks & Recreation is responsible for New York City's "Emerald Empire"—28,000 acres of green space, including 2.5 million trees, 14 miles of beaches, hundreds of tennis courts, 950 playgrounds, 34 major recreation centers, and 13 golf courses. Parks also oversees an astounding number of cultural, athletic, and social events, such as nature walks, concerts, puppet shows, learn-to-swim classes, tennis clinics, and historic house tours. Internships are available in a wide variety of areas, including public administration, recreation, environmental science, computer operations, photography, architecture, landscape architecture, engineering, urban planning, revenue, accounting, and forestry.

PERKS

Parks offers a customer driven internship program, with tailor made positions to suit the skill level, schedule, and interest of each intern. Parks & recreation interns receive on-the -job training and may participate in a monthly speaker series and an end of term appreciation ceremony.

FYI

Recent intern projects have included writing press releases and speeches for the Commissioner, inspecting concessions in Central Park to ensure compliance with contracts, providing capital project status reports on a quarterly basis to Community Boards and Council Members, installing Parks Local Area Networks (LANs), and planning for Parks special events such as the Great Halloween Party, the Easter Eggstravaganza, and 1999 Youth Games.

TO APPLY

Open to high school, college, and graduate students. Candidates should send a cover letter and resume to:

Internship Coordinator
City of New York Parks & Recreation
830 Fifth Avenue
New York, NY 10021
(212) 360-1349
(212) 360-1387 (Fax)

SELECTIVITY 🔍

Approximate applicant pool: 75; Interns accepted: 50

COMPENSATION $

None

LOCATION(S)

New York, NY

FIELD

Arts management; Public service

DURATION

12–16 weeks: Summer, Fall, Spring

DEADLINE(S)

Rolling

THE WORK

Since 1968, CityArts has been dedicated to creating public art and to fostering cultural and educational development in New York City. It has pioneered and inspired collaborations between professional artists, businesses, schools, and community organizations to involve over 10,000 youths, senior citizens, and neighborhood dwellers in the creative process. To date, over 190 CityArts sculptures, mosaics, and site-specific murals have enlivened New York's urban landscape. Interns are assigned to the following departments: Development/Fundraising, Public Relations/Communications, Exhibition, Marketing/Promotion, Clerical, Programs, and Artist Assistant.

PERKS

Flexible hours; free t-shirts, postcards, and catalogs.

FYI

Says a former intern, "Not only have I learned a great deal about what is involved in doing public relations work, but I have learned how a nonprofit organization gets the funding it needs to continue in its artistic endeavors."

TO APPLY

Open to high school seniors, undergrads, and grads. International applicants eligible. Submit resume and cover letter.

Internship Coordinator
CityArts, Inc.
525 Broadway, Suite 700
New York, NY 10012
(212) 966-0377
(212) 966-0551 (Fax)

NYC Parks & Recreation Commissioner Henry Stern, intern Paul Narain, and Chief of Staff Ian Shapiro at the opening ceremonies for a Learn-to-Swim Program.

CLARKE & COMPANY

SELECTIVITY 🔍🔍🔍🔍
Approximate applicant pool: 150–175; Interns accepted: 9–10

COMPENSATION $ $
$7/hour

LOCATION(S)
Boston, MA

FIELD
Public relations

DURATION
12–20 weeks: Summer, Fall, Spring

DEADLINE(S)
Summer: April 1; Fall: June 1; Spring: November 1

THE WORK
Founded in 1977, Clarke & Company is one of New England's leading public relations and communications consulting firms, specializing in strategic planning, employee relations, community relations, crisis control, trade shows, new product launches, investor relations, and lecture tours. Clients have included IBM, Polaroid, Locate in Scotland, Blue Cross & Blue Shield Massachusetts, and Stevens Roofing Systems. Assisting account coordinators, interns write press releases, generate media lists, conduct research for specific clients, set up for events, archive client files, and deliver packages to the media.

PERKS
Breakfast or luncheon meeting with chairperson; attendance welcome at internal tutorials (e.g., computer skills); small, close-knit office.

FYI
Approximately 25 percent of interns are hired for full-time positions at Clarke & Co.

TO APPLY
Open to college juniors and seniors as well as first-year grad students. Must be very computer literate and familiar with Word for Windows. International applicants eligible. Submit resume and cover letter and a typed essay answering: "Why I want to intern at Clarke & Company."

Clarke & Company Public Relations
535 Boylston Street
Boston, MA 02116
Attn: Vice president of Human Resources
No phone calls please.
(617) 536-8524 (Fax)
clarkeco@clarkeco.com

> "I can't imagine how I would have [become an astronaut] without [my NASA internship]."
> — *Astronaut Richard Hieb*

SELECTIVITY 🔍🔍
Approximate applicant pool: 50; Interns accepted: 10

COMPENSATION $
None

LOCATION(S)
New York, NY

FIELD
Performing arts

DURATION
12-15 weeks: Summer, Fall, Spring

DEADLINE(S)
Rolling

THE WORK
Founded in 1967, the Classic Stage Company (CSC) is an award-winning Off-Broadway theater dedicated to reimagining classic theater. It is a place where "old and new, foreign and familiar, meet on equal terms to create original work that is highly theatrical, multicultural, and intellectually challenging." Interns work in Development, Marketing, Production, Dramaturgy, and Audience Services.

PERKS
Free tickets to all performances; attendance welcome at rehearsals; passes to other Off-Broadway theaters.

FYI
Among CSC's awards are two *Village Voice* Obies for outstanding achievement in the Off-Broadway theater, an Outer Critics Circle Citation for Sustained Excellence, and a Rosetta LeNoire Award for Nontraditional casting.

TO APPLY
Open to undergrads, recent college grads, college grads of any age, and grad students. Submit resume and cover letter.

Internship Coordinator
Classic Stage Company
136 East 13th Street
New York, NY 10003
(212) 677-4210
(212) 477-7504 (Fax)

CLEVELAND CAVS

See CAVS/Gund Arena Company

See The Metropolitan Museum of Art

See Turner Broadcasting System

COLLEGE LIGHT OPERA COMPANY

SELECTIVITY
Approximate applicant pool: 350; Interns accepted: 70

COMPENSATION
Free room and board; stipend or salary for all except vocal company

LOCATION(S)
Falmouth on Cape Cod, MA

FIELD
Theater; Musicals and operettas

DURATION
11 weeks: Summer

DEADLINE(S)
Rolling: starting March 15

THE WORK
Founded in 1969, the College Light Opera Company (CLOC) is the largest resident theater company in the United States. With eighty-six performers and staff members, CLOC stages nine operettas and musicals each season with full orchestral accompaniment. Almost half of all interns work as singers/actors or orchestra musicians; the rest serve as stage and costume staff, chorus masters, piano accompanists, lead coaches, set designers, costume designers, choreographers, box office treasurers, publicity directors, assistant business managers, cooks, and co-op work directors.

PERKS
Housing on country estate, 500 yards from the beach; family-style dining facilities; relaxed and informal atmosphere.

FYI
Alumni of the program include John Lee Beatty, a Broadway set designer; Stephen Lord, General Director of the Boston Lyric Opera Company; Maryanne Telese, an opera star with the NYC Opera and other companies; and Will Chase, the current male lead in *Miss Saigon*.

TO APPLY
Open to high school seniors, undergrads, recent college grads, college grads of any 116age, and grad students. International applicants eligible. Write for application.

Off-season address:
Internship Coordinator
College Light Opera Company
162 South Cedar Street
Oberlin, OH 44074
(440) 774-8485

COLUMBIA JOURNALISM REVIEW

SELECTIVITY
Approximate applicant pool: 75; Interns accepted: 6

COMPENSATION
None

LOCATION(S)
New York, NY

FIELD
Magazines

DURATION
12–16 weeks: Summer, Fall, Spring

DEADLINE(S)
Rolling

THE WORK
In existence since 1961, the *Columbia Journalism Review* (CJR) is one of the nation's largest and most respected magazines dedicated to monitoring print and electronic news. Affiliated with Columbia University's prestigious Graduate School of Journalism, CJR provides a "forum for journalists to examine and question their own practices and principles." Interns work in the Editorial department.

PERKS
Compensation for writing published in the magazine; some free books; free t-shirt.

FYI
Alumni of the program, started in 1981, include Laurence Zuckerman, business writer for *The New York Times*, and Andy Court, editor of *American Lawyer*.

TO APPLY
Open to undergrads, recent college grads, college grads of any age, and grad students. International applicants eligible. Submit resume, cover letter, writing samples (clips preferred), and recommendations.

Internship Coordinator
Columbia Journalism Review
Journalism Building, Room 700A
New York, NY 10027
(212) 854-2716

COLUMBIA PICTURES

See Sony Pictures Entertainment

COLUMBIA RECORDS

See Sony Music Entertainment

EXCLUSIVE INTERVIEW WITH JODIE FOSTER

Jodie Foster began her acting career at the age of three as "The Coppertone Girl" in the suntan lotion's tv commercial. Some thirty years later, she has appeared in over 30 films, including Taxi Driver (1976), Contact (1997), The Accused (1988), and The Silence of the Lambs (1991), the last two garnering her two Academy Awards (aka "Oscars") for Best Actress. In 1992, she started a production company, Egg Pictures, whose film credits so far include Nell and Home for the Holidays. Foster graduated with honors from Yale in 1984, earning a B.A. in literature.

The Internship Informants: We heard that you did an internship at Esquire magazine in the summer of 1982. How did that come about?

Foster: I had written a piece [for Esquire] that [the magazine's editorial advisor] had solicited from me about going to college. This was in 1980 as I was about to graduate from high school. I had met him a few months before that, and we started corresponding by letter—quippy, little faxy type letters. He said, "Why don't you write a little piece for us," which I did, and they published it. Then I went to college, and I continued to correspond with him—the same quippy, little, facile pieces. We became friends, and he said, "I have a great idea for you if you're up for the challenge to become an intern [at Esquire]." So I met with all of the appropriate people [at Esquire], and I guess I passed muster.

The Internship Informants: What did the internship involve?

Foster: Once a week, someone new was supposed to take me out to lunch and tell me how they became who they were.

The Internship Informants: They probably had to twist some arms to get people to do that.

Foster: [laughs] Well, all the interns had to go through it. We'd spend a couple weeks at one desk, then another week at another desk, then another week at another desk, and then each person was supposed to basically tell you what they did . . . This was something that all the interns went through and that the editors found really boring.

The Internship Informants: Besides lunching with editors, what did you do for the magazine?

Foster: I went through all the unsolicited fiction—the "slush piles"—opening letters, taking out the unsolicited fiction, and reading them all through. Then I'd send a lot of letters saying, "I'm sorry, the magazine does not accept unsolicited fiction. Thank you very much."

The Internship Informants: Did you ever read anything good?

Foster: Actually, no, but fascinating. I think that was the best part of the job.

The Internship Informants: But did you have the power to say, "I really like this. I think you should look at it"?

Foster: Yes. Magazines, especially then, were different. [Esquire] still had a lot of these old, liberal, martini-drinking, fiction-loving guys...there was a lot of reading books and saying, "This is a great novel." So, yes, I passed a couple of things on to people's desks that they did or didn't like. They also asked me questions about [stories] they had bought—for example, what do you think of this, and do you like this guy.

The Internship Informants: Did you work on any specific projects?

Foster: I did research for a big piece on "The 100 Best Bars in the Country." Of course I couldn't drink [because I was under 21], but I combed everyone I knew, everyone I could think of around the country and got them to figure out, without my ever going to any of these places, which were the hundred best bars.

The Internship Informants: What about busywork?

Foster: I did the secretarial/assistant work, a lot of copying and collating, which at the time was not as easy as it is now.

The Internship Informants: Because you were already a famous person, were you treated any differently than other interns?

Foster: No, not at all.

The Internship Informants: At the time, what was your impression of the internship?

Foster: It was my first brush with the 9-to-5 job, with going to work at a certain time and staying in an office all day and then leaving at 5:30. And I had never done that. I have always been on movie sets, where you're committed for fourteen hours a day, and you're obsessed with whatever it is that you're doing, and you're constantly stuck with people. I realized that I really don't like the 9-to-5 gig. I spent a lot of time during my internship just really having a great time in New York City. That was fun. But I thought at the time that what I really wanted to do was maybe write for magazines, and I realized by the end of it that I didn't.

Foster interview continued . . .

The Internship Informants: Write for magazines? But you were already a successful actress at that point.

Foster: I was, but my career was in a strange spin, and it had been a weird time in my life [A year earlier, John Hinckley, Jr. had attempted to assassinate President Ronald Reagan in hopes of impressing her]. I definitely was thinking about what I would ultimately end up doing because I didn't believe I would ever end up being an actress when I grew up . . . I didn't think it would last, and it wasn't a particularly stellar time in my career. The kinds of movies that I could look forward to doing were not really earth-shaking, and the industry at the time was in a strange slump. I was at a weird age, and I didn't quite look the way I was supposed to look. I would say it was one of the most unhappy moments of my life. I really was searching for something that was going to make it better.

The Internship Informants: And an unpaid internship was the answer?

Foster: Actually, no, this was a paid internship. I made $125 or $100 a week . . .I just wanted to see if maybe [a career] was somewhere lodged in there, and I quickly realized it wasn't. But I did write a piece for *Esquire* when I left that they published ["Why Me?" describing the personal details of her life surrounding the John Hinckley, Jr. episode] . . . [The internship] made me realize that I wanted to be on the artistic end of things. I didn't want to be on the managerial or the editing side, which is the great frustration of working at a magazine. You go there to be with writers and have more contact with them and with the writing process and what you end up doing is proofreading, cutting things out, and going to meetings and trying to sell ideas.

The Internship Informants: Were there any redeeming qualities to the internship at all?

Foster: When I was doing unsolicited fiction, I started making two piles. I would cover up the page, and I wouldn't look to see whether [the writer] was a man or a woman. Usually, these unsolicited pieces are just people's fantasies . . . and they kind of fell into two categories. One was, and I'm paraphrasing them, my wife walks through the door, only she's wearing black garter belts. She doesn't ask me what movie we are going to see or did I take the kids to gymnastics. It is just pure and total lust, and she treats me like a sex object, and then, guess what, she's my wife again. That was the men's fantasy. The women's fantasy—I'm on a train, and I see some guy I don't know, and he comes up to me. We're caught between two cars, and he says with tears in his eye, "I've loved you your entire life, and I know everything about you," and he's the most intimate person you've ever met. Then the train stops, and he gets off. I swear to God, virtually every piece that I saw fell into these two categories . . . I thought it was really fascinating that I could just cover up the names and put them into two different categories and find that [the distinction between the male and female stories] would work out. That's how I amused myself.

The Internship Informants: What advice do you have for young people today? Should they do internships?

Foster: Absolutely. The best thing you can do before you enter the job force is to find out what are the things that make you happy and scintillated and make you want to come into work everyday . . . Ultimately, somewhere down the line, if your personal life, or your personal habits, or your personal way of being—your psyche—just doesn't fit in to what you're doing you're going to end up being a miserable person. I learned that very quickly. I like to be around a lot of people, and that's key. I cannot sit in a room, alone, by myself and do what I do. I like collaborating with a lot of people, and I like being on the artistic end.

The Internship Informants: What qualities do you look for in your own interns, at Egg Pictures?

Foster: Since it's going to be only a couple months out of your life, you'd better commit to it one-hundred percent because there's nothing worse than somebody walking in and being half-assed about it and saying what they really want to do is go out and get milkshakes and maybe stroll in and do the work, maybe make the call but not make the second call. Even if you hate it, do it to the nth degree.

The Internship Informants: What do your interns do?

Foster: They read, and they do a lot of computer stuff, which was not around when I was in college. They understand it, and we don't, so we're often asking, "Hey, can you help me with this?" We basically let them in on everything. If we've picked the right people, they'll be interested in that.

The Internship Informants: Do you ever meet with them or address them?

Foster: Sure, all the time.

The Internship Informants: Think back to some of the characters you've played in the movies, perhaps Agent Starling from *The Silence of the Lambs*. Where would she have interned?

Foster: She would have been the superstar intern of the century. Besides the FBI, she would have interned as a page in Congress . . . because she would need to do something that had a moral bent, that served the good of mankind, and that was highly ethical.

SELECTIVITY 🔍 🔍 🔍 🔍
Approximate applicant pool: 300; Interns accepted: 25

COMPENSATION 💲
Generous travel stipend

LOCATION(S)
New York, NY; Los Angeles, CA

FIELD
Television

DURATION
8–12 weeks: Summer, Fall, Spring

DEADLINE(S)
Summer: April 1; Fall, Spring: Rolling

THE WORK
The only all-comedy cable network, Comedy Central (CC) was formed in 1991 through a merger between Viacom and HBO. Comedy Central's internship program provides an exciting opportunity to experience first-hand what it is like to work at a cable TV network. Interns work in Marketing, Talent & Development, Programming Online, Corporate Communication, Affiliate Relations, Finance, Human Resources, Sales Research, On-Air Promotions, Off-Air Creative, and Production.

PERKS
Breakfast meetings with company executives; field trips to studios and the Museum of Television/Radio; social events (Yankees game, company summer picnic, boat trip, etc.).

FYI
Students have been tuning in to CC's internship program since the channel's founding; about 10 percent of former interns are hired for full-time positions.

TO APPLY
Open to undergrads. Must receive academic credit. International applicants eligible. Submit resume and cover letter.

Human Resources Administrator
Comedy Central
1775 Broadway, 10th Floor
New York, NY 10019
(212) 767-8600
(212) 767-4257 (Fax)

SELECTIVITY 🔍
Approximate applicant pool: 100; Interns accepted: 40

COMPENSATION. 💲
Reimbursement for daily round-trip travel

LOCATION(S)
Washington, DC

FIELD
Public policy

DURATION
10–12 weeks: Summer, Fall, Spring

DEADLINE(S)
Rolling

THE WORK
Common Cause is a nonpartisan, nonprofit lobbying organization, founded in 1970 by John Gardner, former Secretary of Health, Education, and Welfare. Working to make government more efficient, responsive, and honest, the 250,000-member organization has influenced such reforms as public financing of presidential elections, strengthened congressional ethics, and "sunshine" laws. Interns work in Grassroots and Legislative Policy, Media Communications, Membership, Campaign Finance Research, and Web Design.

PERKS
Intern seminars and briefings; softball team; frequent social outings.

FYI
As old as the organization itself, CC's intern program provides students with a broad education in the workings of Congress and the Executive branch.

TO APPLY
Open to undergrads. International applicants eligible. For application and/or more information, write or call.

Volunteer Office
Common Cause
1250 Connecticut Ave., NW
Washington, DC 20036
(202) 833-1200

Common Cause interns lobbying on Capitol Hill.

WINNING ADMISSION TO A TOP INTERNSHIP

To get an insider's view of what it takes to win admission to a top internship, we consulted an expert, **Professor Mary Radford**, who chose interns for the US Supreme Court's Judicial Internship Program during her 1990–91 tenure as one of the Court's Judicial Fellows. Graduating Phi Beta Kappa with a BA from Tulane in 1974 and with top honors with a JD from Emory School of Law in 1981, Radford is a Professor of Law at the Georgia State University College of Law. Here are her thoughts on what constitutes the "right stuff" for internship applicants to the Supreme Court and in general:

Choosing from the "Cream of the Crop"

In early August 1990, I began a year-long term as a Judicial Fellow, working in the office of the Administrative Assistant to the Chief Justice of the United States. Even before I officially began the duties of my new job, I was sent a packet containing the applications of a variety of college juniors and seniors who wished to spend a quarter working at the Court. I was struck immediately with the thought that I would never be able to make choices among this very talented group. The outgoing Fellow had winnowed down the selection and had sent me only the "cream of the crop." My assignment was to call these finalists and conduct telephone interviews whereby I would somehow discern which two students would be hired. As I was not yet really sure what my own job entailed, I relied primarily on my instincts when making the choice. In the course of my interviews with the students, I made observations on a variety of levels: Did the student seem enthusiastic about the prospect of working at the Court? Was the student self-confident without being arrogant, outgoing without being pushy? Had the student devoted much thought to why this particular internship would be good for him or her? Most importantly, was the student excited about learning? In the long run, the interns with whom I worked who had the best experiences were those who made every day a learning experience.

The Application: It Carries a Subliminal Message

For the next round of internship applications, I was able to observe the process from the outset. One tip I would pass on to the students applying for internships is this: don't underestimate the importance of the impression that your application will make. Take time preparing your application and make sure it is complete, orderly, and polished. As with many internships, the Judicial Intern application form requires the student to send in a writing sample, including a personal statement. I was surprised to find some of the writing samples and statements filled with typographical and grammatical errors. Others were so poorly written that I doubted whether I would be able to delegate writing jobs to those students. The solution to this problem is really a quite simple one: ask someone you trust to read and give you an honest assessment of your application before you send it in! This is sometimes hard to do, particularly with personal statements, because most of us don't like to reveal ourselves to people we know, let alone subject ourselves to criticism. It also may seem ridiculous to think that your application could be screened out because of a few careless errors. But remember that the persons who read these applications are looking for interns who are meticulous and who pay attention to detail. The subliminal message sent out by the form of your application can at times be as compelling as the substance of the application itself.

Recommendations: Be Cautious of the Congressional Letterhead

Applicants for the Judicial Internship often asked me, "What kinds of recommendations are you looking for?" The answer was simple: a recommendation that tells me something important about the writer's experience with the applicant. If your mother's best friend's mother-in-law happens to be a Congressman, you may think that a letter on US House of Representatives stationery will be key for you. While this may be minimally helpful in some offices, the far more impressive recommendations are those written by people who have had the opportunity to observe you in action. Choose a favorite teacher or an employer. Tell the recommender of situations in which he or she may have observed you performing similar tasks. Supply the recommender with a copy of your resume and ask that person whether it would be helpful to have a discussion with you about the particular application and about your general career and educational aspirations. In my own experience of writing letters of recommendation for students at my law school, I find that my letters are most effective if I have had a chance to sit down with the student to discuss the student's goals and to think through how the job in question might fit in with those goals.

The Personal Statement: Creativity and Reality

As I mentioned before, one component of the Judicial Internship application is the personal statement. This type of statement gives you a chance to tell your potential employer what makes you uniquely qualified for the job in question. When reviewing these statements, I looked for signs of creativity and versatility in the applicant. The statements that told me something concrete about the applicant (for example, about a public service project in which the applicant was involved or a particular course in which the applicant had made some unusual contribution) were much more effective than those that spoke in abstracts. I also looked for a realistic attitude about the internship. Some applicants wrote about how they planned to influence the Justices in their decision-making process or to make the appropriate contacts so that they would be chosen to serve on the Supreme Court in the future. These overblown notions indicated to me that the applicant not only had no idea what the internship entailed but probably would be profoundly disappointed to discover how mundane an intern's tasks can be. The more successful applicants were those who told me how they planned to profit from the opportunity to observe the Court in action, to absorb the rich history of the environment, and to use each job assignment, no matter how ordinary, as a chance to improve themselves in some way. When these applicants became interns, their positive attitudes served them well. They made beneficial contributions to the program and (hopefully!) took from the program a rare perspective on one of the most important institutions in the country.

COMMUNITY SERVICE VOLUNTEER PROGRAMME

SELECTIVITY   N/A
Approximate applicant pool: N/A; Interns accepted: 3,000 (90–100 US citizens)

COMPENSATION $
$1,650 placement fee, includes stipend of £22/week (Approximately $35/week), immigration papers, room and board, all work-related travel within UK

LOCATION(S)
Cities and towns throughout England, Scotland, and Wales

FIELD
Working with the disabled; Education; Psychology; Public service

DURATION
4–12 months: ongoing

DEADLINE(S)
Rolling

THE WORK
A registered UK charity, Community Service Volunteer Programme (CSV) encourages citizens worldwide to perform public service in order to enable and help people in need, learn practical skills, and gain exposure to careers in human services. It was founded in 1961 by Alec Dickson, an expert in volunteerism who advised President John F. Kennedy on the establishment of the Peace Corps. CSV volunteers work in institutions, hospitals, day centers, schools, and private homes with homeless people, the disabled, the elderly, and youth.

PERKS
One week paid vacation for every four months of service; free tickets to cultural events, paid travel within United Kingdom; national health insurance while in service.

FYI
Some of CSV's projects, particularly those working with children or vulnerable populations, require a "police check," a statement from participants' local or state police department indicating whether they have ever been convicted of a crime.

TO APPLY
Open to individuals 18 to 35 years of age. International applicants fluent in English are eligible. CSV has a nonrejection policy, but requires personal interviews arranged in the United States. Contact for further information and application:

*US and Candian citizens based
in North America contact:
Worldwide Internships
& Service Education
303 South Craig Street, Suite 202
Pittsburgh, PA 15213
(412) 681-8120
(412) 681-8187 (Fax)
E-mail: wiset@pitt.edu*

*Non-US citizens contact:
Community Service
Volunteer Programme
237 Pentonville Road
London, England N1 9NJ
44-171-278-6601*

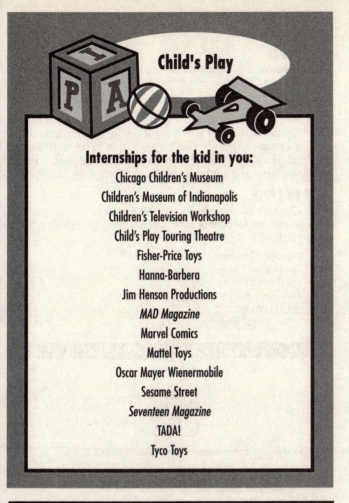

Child's Play

Internships for the kid in you:

Chicago Children's Museum

Children's Museum of Indianapolis

Children's Television Workshop

Child's Play Touring Theatre

Fisher-Price Toys

Hanna-Barbera

Jim Henson Productions

MAD Magazine

Marvel Comics

Mattel Toys

Oscar Mayer Wienermobile

Sesame Street

Seventeen Magazine

TADA!

Tyco Toys

CONCRETE MARKETING

SELECTIVITY 🔍 🔍
Approximate applicant pool: 50; Interns accepted: 12

COMPENSATION 💲
$50/week

LOCATION(S)
New York, NY

FIELD
Marketing (hard rock music)

DURATION
12 weeks: Summer, Fall, Spring

DEADLINE(S)
Rolling

THE WORK
Founded in 1983, Concrete Marketing designs marketing programs to increase the exposure of hard rock bands. Working with record stores, radio stations, music magazines, and direct-to-

consumer mailings, it has contributed to the success of such bands as Pearl Jam, Nirvana, Soundgarden, Tool, Alice in Chains, and White Zombie. Interns work in Marketing, Radio, and Video Department.

PERKS
"More free rock 'n' roll shows than interns can possibly see"; free CDs, t-shirts, and other promotional items; casual atmosphere.

FYI
Says the internship coordinator: "Our interns learn a lot about marketing and make major music industry connections." ... Alumni have gone on to positions at major record labels, including Sony, Columbia, Warner Brothers, and Elektra.

TO APPLY
Open to high school grads, undergrads, and grads. International applicants eligible. Submit resume, cover letter.

Internship Coordinator
Concrete Marketing
1133 Broadway, Suite 1220
New York, NY 10010
(212) 645-2607 (Fax)
E-mail: concrete6@aol.com

> "Everything in life is part busywork."
>
> —*Senator Kay Bailey Hutchison*

CONGRESSIONAL HISPANIC CAUCUS INSTITUTE

SELECTIVITY 🔍 🔍 🔍 🔍
Approximate applicant pool: 500 (Interns), 100 (Fellows); Interns accepted: 30 (Interns), 16 (Fellows)

COMPENSATION 💲 💲 💲
Interns: $2,000; Fellows: $1,550/month

LOCATION(S)
Washington, DC

FIELD
Public policy

DURATION
Internship: 2 months, Summer; Fellowship: 9 months, September–May

DEADLINE(S)
Interns: January 28; Fellows: March 17

THE WORK
Established in 1978, the congressional Hispanic Caucus Institute (CHCI) is a nonprofit organization offering programs that heighten the Hispanic community's awareness of the US political system. CHCI's Internship Program places interns in Congressional offices, while its Fellowship Program assists Fellows in finding nine-month internships in government and other public policy agencies.

PERKS
Weekly workshops on leadership skills; orientation.

FYI
In addition to sponsoring its Internship and Fellowship Programs, CHCI publishes a newsletter on education issues and conducts scholarship searches for Hispanic students . . . The Internship and Fellowship Programs have been offered since 1978.

TO APPLY

Internship: open to undergrads. Fellowship: open to grads within one year of graduation and grad students. International applicants selected must be eligible for employment. Write for application.

Internship or Fellowship Coordinator
Congressional Hispanic Caucus Institute
504 C Street NE
Washington, DC 20002
(202) 543-1771
(202) 546-2143 (Fax)
www.chci.org

CONGRESSIONAL MANAGEMENT FOUNDATION

SELECTIVITY 🔍🔍🔍🔍
Approximate applicant pool: 150; Interns accepted: 10

COMPENSATION Ⓢ
None

LOCATION(S)
Washington, DC

FIELD
Public policy; Management

DURATION
8–12 weeks: Summer, Fall, Spring

DEADLINE(S)
Summer: March 31; Fall and Spring: Rolling

THE WORK

The Congressional Management Foundation (CMF) is a nonprofit, nonpartisan organization established in 1977 to help members of Congress and their staffs better manage their workloads. CMF's services include seminars and workshops for Congressional staff, detailed studies of members' offices, and publications on management issues. Interns assist staff in research, writing, and analysis.

PERKS

Attendance welcome at meetings with members of Congress; small staff.

FYI

Writes a former intern: "When trying to decide where to apply for an internship, I was wary at first of CMF because of the small staff size. I thought that bigger equals better equals more important. However, this illusion was quickly shattered . . . I did important work and got lots of feedback."

TO APPLY

Open to undergrads, recent college grads, college grads of any age, and grad students. International applicants eligible. Write for application.

Internship Coordinator
Congressional Management Foundation
513 Capitol Court NE, Suite 300
Washington, DC 20002
(202) 546-0100
(202) 547-0936 (Fax)

CONGRESSIONAL RESEARCH SERVICE

CONGRESSIONAL RESEARCH SERVICE

SELECTIVITY 🔍🔍🔍🔍
Approximate applicant pool: 1,000; Interns accepted: 70

COMPENSATION Ⓢ
None; school credit

LOCATION(S)
Washington, DC

FIELD
Research and analysis for US Congress and Committees

DURATION
3–4 months

DEADLINE(S)
Rolling

THE WORK

Created in 1914, the Congressional Research Service (CRS) is a division of the Library of Congress (see separate entry), providing objective and nonpartisan research, legislative analysis, and reference services to members and committees of Congress. Departments accepting interns include: American Law, Economics, Education and Public Welfare, Environment and Natural Resources Policy, Foreign Affairs and National Defense, Government, Science Policy Research, Congressional Reference and Library Services, Special Programs, and Administration.

PERKS

Attendance welcome at CRS seminars, briefings, and hearings.

FYI

CRS handles over 600,000 congressional requests annually.

David Eisenhower, grandson of President Dwight D. Eisenhower, interned for the Washington Senators baseball team (now the Texas Rangers) in the summer of 1970. The young man and then-President Richard M. Nixon, who happened to be Eisenhower's father-in-law, would occasionally get together at games to talk baseball trivia.

TO APPLY

Open to college seniors as well as grads, grad students. Must be fluent in English. Submit resume, cover letter.

Warren Lenhart
Congressional Research Service
LM-203, Library of Congress
Washington, DC 20540-7000
(202) 707-7641
(202) 707-2615 (Fax)
www.loc.gov/crsinfo

CONNECTICUT JUDICIAL BRANCH

SELECTIVITY

Approximate applicant pool: 900; Interns accepted: 800

COMPENSATION

Insurance, references, reimbursement for mileage and parking and a half day of orientation. The Office of Adult Probation requires an additional half day of training.

LOCATION(S)

Cities throughout CT

FIELD

Law

DURATION

By Semester: Spring, Summer, Fall

DEADLINE(S)

Rolling (preferably a semester in advance)

THE WORK

The Judicial Branch of the State of Connecticut consists of twenty-two courts and approximately 2,400 employees. There are Internships and Volunteer placements available in Adult Probation, Juvenile Matters, Family Division, State Attorney, and Public Defender's Offices statewide. Opportunities and duties may include: court coverage, including contacts with clients; working with court personnel such as prosecutors and Judges, acquiring inside knowledge of criminal court process and the legal system; assisting probation officers in the supervision of cases, completing investigations for the court; field duty, including exposure to the correctional and therapeutic modalities within the community.

Under the auspices of the Judicial Volunteer and Intern Program, interns are assigned to Adult Probation, Juvenile Matters, Family Division, State's Attorney and Public Defender's Offices statewide. Duties may include researching court records, assisting prosecutors and judges, interviewing juvenile offenders and crime victims, or visiting correctional facilities.

PERKS

Orientation and formal training program; insurance coverage; possibility of inclusion in job pool after completion of internship.

FYI

The internship program began in 1976 with one student from the University of Connecticut; it now accepts over 800 interns from all parts of the country, as well as overseas.

TO APPLY

Open to college juniors and seniors, law students, graduates, with interest in the Criminal Justice system. Students with F-1 Visa may apply. Call or write for application and information.

Ms. Claire Collings
Program Director
Connecticut Judicial Branch
2275 Silas Deane Highway
Rocky Hill, CT 06067
(860) 563-5797
(860) 721-9474 (Fax)

CONNECTICUT MAGAZINE

CONNECTICUT®
M A G A Z I N E

SELECTIVITY

Approximate applicant pool: 40; Interns accepted: 10

COMPENSATION

None

LOCATION(S)

Trumbull, CT

FIELD

Magazines

DURATION

12–20 weeks: Summer, Fall, Spring

DEADLINE(S)

Rolling

THE WORK

Founded in 1972, *Connecticut Magazine* is a general-interest magazine covering the arts, politics, people, and business of Connecticut. It has a paid circulation of 85,000 readers and an average reader age of 48. Interns work in the Editorial department.

PERKS

Daily contact with the editor; intern lunch at end of internship; free copies of magazine; small, friendly office.

FYI

Says the internship coordinator: "One of the great things about this internship is that interns get to read the manuscripts that are sent in. They get to see why certain stories are accepted and why others are not. It's great training for budding writers."

TO APPLY

Open to undergrads, recent college grads, college grads of any age, and grad students. Submit resume, cover letter, and writing samples.

Internship Coordinator
Connecticut Magazine
35 Nutmeg Dr.
Trumbull, CT 06611
(203) 380-6600 ext. 329
(203) 380-6612 (Fax)

CONSERVATION ANALYTICAL LABORATORY

See Smithsonian Institution

SELECTIVITY 🔍🔍🔍🔍🔍
Approximate applicant pool: 25; Interns accepted: 1

COMPENSATION Ⓢ
None

LOCATION(S)
Vienna, VA

FIELD
Public policy

DURATION
8–12 weeks: Summer, Fall, Spring

DEADLINE(S)
Summer: March 15; Fall: July 15; Spring: November 15

THE WORK
Founded in 1974, The Conservative Caucus (TCC) is a grass-roots lobbying organization with a conservative position on fiscal, social, and foreign policy issues. TCC supports lower taxes, budget cuts, US military bases in Panama, and the deployment of Strategic Defense Initiative (SDI), and opposes the United Nations and other multinational organizations, socialized medicine, DC statehood, and the current system of pay and pensions for Congress. Its opinions are disseminated through Congressional Testimony, a weekly cable-television show (Conservative Round-table), a monthly audio tape, and the TCC newsletter, *Member's Message*. Interns research Congressional legislation, help obtain and review government documents through the Freedom of Information Act, write issue papers, help with the TV program, and do other assignments, as needed.

PERKS
Attendance welcome at DC meetings; opportunity to work at TCC Phone Bank for wages and commissions.

FYI
By its own description, TCC is devoted solely to conservative principle and not to any political party or leader.

TO APPLY
Open to high school students, high school grads, undergrads, recent college grads, college grads of any age, and grad students. Write for application.

Internship Coordinator
The Conservative Caucus
450 Maple Avenue East
Vienna, VA 22180
(703) 281-4108 (Fax)
E-mail: corndorf@cais.com

CONSUMERS FOR WORLD TRADE

SELECTIVITY 🔍🔍🔍🔍
Approximate applicant pool: 80–100; Interns accepted: 6

COMPENSATION Ⓢ
None

LOCATION(S)
Washington, DC

FIELD
Trade

DURATION
3–5 months: ongoing

DEADLINE(S)
Rolling

THE WORK
A national, nonprofit group founded in 1978, Consumers for World Trade (CWT) supports trade expansion and liberalization to promote healthy economic growth and provide choices in the marketplace for consumers. Governed by a board of trade experts, economists, and academics, CWT publishes newsletters and bulletins, organizes conferences, lobbies Congress, and consults organizations on trade issues. Interns assist staff in Research, Fundraising, and Membership development.

PERKS
Attendance welcome at monthly breakfast meetings; free publications.

FYI
The internship program has been running since CWT's founding in 1978 . . . CWT was created "because of the need for the consumer's voice to be represented in trade policy and the need to defeat the Burke-Hartke bill, a controversial protectionist proposal."

TO APPLY
Open to undergrads, recent college grads, college grads of any age, and grad students. International applicants eligible. Submit resume, cover letter, and writing samples.

Before her senior year at the University of Maryland, news anchor **Connie Chung** (here posing with a CBS News intern) worked as a summer intern to Seymour Halpern, a Republican congressman from New York. The thrilling experience of writing press releases for the Senator prompted Chung to switch her major from biology to journalism.

Internship Coordinator
Consumers for World Trade
2000 L Street NW, Suite 200
Washington, DC 20036
(202) 785-4835
(202) 785-0175 (Fax)
E-mail: cwt@ids.2.idsonline.com

CONTINUOUS ELECTRON BEAM ACCELERATOR FACILITY

See Oak Ridge Institute for Science and Education

COOPER-HEWITT MUSEUM

See Smithsonian Institution

THE CORO FOUNDATION

SELECTIVITY
Approximate applicant pool: 300–400; Interns accepted: 60

COMPENSATION
$3,500 tuition; grants, scholarships, installment plans, and tuition loans are available

LOCATION(S)
San Francisco, CA; Los Angeles, CA; St. Louis, MO; New York, NY; Pittsburgh, PA

FIELD
Public service

DURATION
9 months: September–June

DEADLINE(S)
Mid-January; call to verify

THE WORK

According to its promotional literature, the 58-year-old Coro Foundation "offers the kind of hands-on experience that most graduate schools only talk about." Every year, each of the five regional Coro centers picks twelve college graduates and subjects them to a rigorous nine-month series of internships, interviews, public service projects, and seminar meetings. By the end of the internship, Fellows will have interned in a government agency, a corporation, a community organization, a media organization, a labor union, and a political campaign.

JERRY SEINFELD'S DAD, "INTERN"

On an episode of *Seinfeld*, Elaine hires Jerry Seinfeld's dad to work at her place of employment, J. Peterman's. When an angry Mr. Peterman asks Elaine if she hired the irritating senior Seinfeld, she replies: "Well, he's more like an intern."

PERKS

Variety of organizations; focus weeks; weekly seminars.

FYI

The participants are a source of learning to each other. Said a Fellow: "Coro carefully selects its Fellows from a highly qualified pool of applicants—and it shows. Each of the twelve Fellows has done something special to get selected." . . . A recent Coro class included a professional dancer, a speech and debate champion, and a third degree black belt in Chinese boxing . . . The Coro network is among the nation's most productive and prestigious, including Senator Dianne Feinstein, an associate justice of the California Supreme Court, and a member of the California State Assembly.

TO APPLY

Open to college grads of any age, or equivalent experience. Candidates must apply to only one Coro center. Write for application.

The Coro Fellows Program
Northern California Center
690 Market Street, 11th Floor
San Francisco, CA 94104
(415) 986-0521

The Coro Fellows Program
Midwestern Center
1730 South 11th Street
St. Louis, MO 63104
(314) 621-3040

The Coro Fellows Program
Southern California Center
811 Wilshire Boulevard
Suite 1025
Los Angeles, CA 90017-2624
(213) 623-1234

The Coro Fellows Program
Eastern Center
42 Broadway 18th Floor
New York, NY 10005
(212) 248-2935 ext.230
(212) 248-2970 (Fax)
E-mail: ynorthern@coro.org

The Coro Center for Civic Leadership
425 6th Avenue, 17th Floor
Pittsburgh, PA 15222
(412) 201-5772
(412) 201-0672 (Fax)

THE CORPORATE RESPONSE GROUP

SELECTIVITY
Approximate applicant pool: 50; Interns accepted: 5

COMPENSATION
None

LOCATION(S)
Washington, DC

FIELD
Management consulting; Crisis management

DURATION
12 weeks: Summer, Fall, Spring

DEADLINE(S)
Rolling

THE WORK

Founded in 1986, the Corporate Response Group (CRG) is a crisis-management consulting firm in the business of enhancing its clients' ability to anticipate, prepare for, respond to, and recover from crises ranging from natural disasters to man-made catastrophes. CRG's clients range from major petrochemical corporations and nuclear power facilities to the US Department of Health and the US Department of State. Interns work as Research Assistants.

PERKS
Authorship of case studies on environmental/industrial incidents.

FYI
The internship program has been in existence since CRG's founding . . . CRG is one of the few crisis management firms in the world that constructs a crisis-management program from the perspective of the client's CEO, Board of Directors, and other senior management.

TO APPLY
Open to college juniors and seniors, recent college grads, college grads of any age, and grad students. International applicants eligible. Submit resume and cover letter.

Internship Coordinator
The Corporate Response Group
1101 17th Street, NW
Suite 1200
Washington, DC 20036
(202) 973-0319
(202) 467-0513 (Fax)

CORPORATION FOR NATIONAL SERVICE

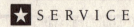

CORPORATION

FOR NATIONAL

★ SERVICE

SELECTIVITY 🔍 🔍 🔍
Approximate applicant pool: 250; Interns accepted: 35

COMPENSATION $
None

LOCATION(S)
Washington, DC

FIELD
Public service

DURATION
12–16 weeks: Summer, Fall, Spring; Part-time available

DEADLINE(S)
Summer: March 15; Fall and Spring: Rolling

THE WORK
Founded in 1993 by the Clinton administration, the Corporation for National Service (CNS) is an amalgam of four groups—ACTION, the Commission on National and Community Service, the White House Office of National Service, and the National Civilian Community Corps (NCCC). CNS administers AmeriCorps, Learn and Serve America (LSA), and the National Senior Service Corps (NSSC). CNS Interns work in the Office of the CEO, Office of Management and Budget, Federal Agency Liaison, Congressional Liaison, General Counsel, Public Affairs, Public Liaison, VISTA Recruitment, LSA Administration, NCCC Management, and NSSC Quantitative Research.

PERKS
Brown-bag luncheons with CNS executives; speaker series; community service days in the field.

FYI
Created by the executive director and considered to be one of the corporation's youth development initiatives, the internship program provides substantive opportunities for students to gain a greater understanding of national service.

TO APPLY
Open to college undergrads and grad students. Submit resume and cover letter.

Internship Program
Corporation for National Service
1201 New York Ave. NW
Washington, DC 20525
(202) 606-5000

COUNCIL OF ENERGY RESOURCE TRIBES

SELECTIVITY 🔍 🔍 🔍
Approximate applicant pool: 100; Interns accepted: 10–14

COMPENSATION $ $ $ $ $
$400/week; free housing; round-trip travel

LOCATION(S)
Denver, CO and local tribal locations in CO

FIELD
Environment; Public policy; Science; Native American studies

DURATION
10 weeks: Summer

DEADLINE(S)
March 15

THE WORK
Founded in 1975, the Council of Energy Resource Tribes (CERT) is a tribal organization governed by the elected tribal leadership of fifty-two federally recognized Indian tribes in the US and four affiliated Canadian bands. The CERT Tribal Internship Program provides students with the opportunity to work alongside senior CERT staff, tribal leaders, and host companies on technical and scientific issues, policies, and projects. Past projects have focused on tribal water quality studies, tribal/state and local government cooperative planning on environmental issues, hazardous waste operations training, and biodiversity.

PERKS
Culture Camp out with high school participants and tribal leaders; pizza party with executive director; pot-luck dinners and barbecues.

FYI
Says a former CERT participant whose company hosts the National Conference of State Legislatures: "My main project was to research and prepare a state legislative report . . . [which summarized] all of the American Indian legislation examined by the states this year . . . [It] was a great learning experience [which helped make] me a positive role model for other Indian youth."

TO APPLY
Open to college sophomores, juniors, and seniors, as well as grads and grad students. Native American applicants preferred. Submit resume, cover letter, writing samples, college transcript, recommendations (from tribal officials, employers, or professors), and tribal affiliation documentation (if applicable).

Internship Coordinator
Council of Energy Resource Tribes
1999 Broadway, Suite 2600
Denver, CO 80202
(303) 297-2378
(303) 296-5690 (Fax)
www.everettinternships.org

COUNCIL ON ECONOMIC PRIORITIES

CEP
COUNCIL ON
ECONOMIC
PRIORITIES

SELECTIVITY 🔍 🔍 🔍
Approximate applicant pool: 200; Interns accepted: 20

COMPENSATION $
Fall and Spring: Variable; Summer: $200/week

LOCATION(S)
New York, NY

FIELD
Corporate Responsibility (Environmental and Social)

DURATION
10–12 weeks: Summer, Fall, Spring

DEADLINE(S)
Rolling; March 31 for Summer

THE WORK

The Council on Economic Priorities (CEP) defines, measures, and promotes excellence in corporate citizenship to improve the environment and society, both locally and globally. The Council on Economic Priorities' mission is to improve corporate performance through the leverage of public exposure and through consumer and investor pressure. CEP believes that the underlying logic of its mission is that public access to information is the critical element for generating corporate environmental and social change. Internships are available in CEP's three main departments: Research (Environmental and Social); Marketing & Communications; and Finance & Administration. Interns participate in all activities of CEP, working directly with the staff. Applicants should have excellent research, communication, and writing skills, as well as solid computer experience.

TIME, INC.—
THE FANTASTIC 4 START AT TIME PUBLICATIONS AND RISE TO THE TOP

1) **Henry Grunwald**, former editor-in-chief of Time, Inc., interned at *Time* in 1945.
2) **Jason McManus**, former editor-in-chief of Time, Inc., interned at *Sports Illustrated* in 1957.
3) **Henry Muller**, editorial director of Time, Inc., interned at *Life* in 1960.
4) **Loudon Wainwright**, renowned *Life* writer and columnist, interned at *Time* in 1945.

PERKS

Course credit; work-study experience; attendance aged at weekly department meetings; summer lecture serie ous intern social activities.

FYI

CEP's programs are designed to provide incentives for superior corporate responsibility performance. Corporate responsibility issue areas analyzed by CEP include the following: environment; women's advancement; minority advancement; charitable giving; community outreach; family benefits; workplace issues; social disclosure; international sourcing; military contracts; and animal testing.

TO APPLY

Internships are available throughout the year. During the summer, CEP participates in the Everett Public Service Internship program. See www.everettinternships.org for additional information. Prospective interns are required to submit a cover letter outlining their interest in CEP's work (including which department they seek an internship), a current resume, and a three-page writing sample. There is no separate application form. Interns will be contacted by CEP if an interview is granted. No phone calls please. All materials should be sent to:

Nicholas J. Puma
Director of Finance and Administration
Council on Economic Priorities
30 Irving Place
Ninth Floor
New York, NY 10003-2386
www.everettinternships.org

COUNCIL ON FOREIGN RELATIONS

SELECTIVITY 🔍 🔍 🔍
Approximate applicant pool: 200; Interns accepted: 20–25

COMPENSATION $
None

LOCATION(S)
New York, NY, Washington, DC

FIELD
Foreign affairs

DURATION
13–15 weeks: Summer, Fall, Spring

DEADLINE(S)
Rolling

THE WORK

Founded in 1921, the Council on Foreign Relations is a nonprofit and nonpartisan membership organization dedicated to improving the understanding of U.S. foreign policy and international affairs through the free exchange of ideas. Its 3,400 members include nearly all past and present Presidents, Secretaries of State, Defense and Treasury, other senior U.S. government officials, renowned scholars, and major leaders of business, media, human rights, and other nongovernmental groups. Each year the Council sponsors several hundred meetings and publishes Foreign Affairs, the preeminent journal in the field. (See separate entry.) As a leader in the community of institutions concerned with American foreign policy, the Council conducts a comprehensive Meetings Program. The meetings sponsored by the Council reflect the issues of current concern in international affairs, and are led by top foreign policy officials and experts who are critical to the discussion of policy. The Council is also host to one of the country's largest foreign policy think tanks with a widely respected and influential research staff of over 65 Fellows. Known as its Studies department, this area aims to produce insights into international affairs and U.S. foreign policy through its research, programs, and publications.

PERKS
Attendance welcome at events sponsored by Meeting Program; participation welcome at Council on Foreign Relations intramural sports teams.

FYI
Council on Foreign Relations hires approximately 5 percent of its interns for full-time positions.

TO APPLY
Open to all undergrads and grads in International Relations, Government, Political Science, and related fields. International applicants eligible. Submit resume and cover letter later as application to program.

Human Resources
Council on Foreign Relations
58 East 68th Street
New York, NY 10021
(212) 434-9400
(212) 734-1493 (Fax)

COUNCIL ON HEMISPHERIC AFFAIRS

SELECTIVITY 🔍🔍🔍🔍🔍
Approximate applicant pool: 484; Interns accepted: 24

COMPENSATION $
None

LOCATION(S)
Washington, DC; Canada; Latin America

FIELD
Foreign affairs; Think tank; Canada and Latin America

DURATION
18 weeks: Summer; 14 weeks: Fall, Spring

DEADLINE(S)
Rolling

THE WORK
A nonprofit, hard-hitting liberal think tank and advocacy group, the Council on Hemispheric Affairs (COHA) was founded in 1975 to encourage good relations and monitor policies among the US, Latin America, and Canada. Issues of concern to COHA include diplomacy, human rights, freedom of the press, economics and development, and free trade. Interns (called research associates) write articles for COHA's distguished biweekly publication *Washington Report on the Hemisphere*, interview policymakers and journalists, conduct research for position papers, write press releases, and respond to public inquiries.

PERKS
Periodic free lunches and after-work food money; frequent opportunities to publish op-ed pieces in journals and newspapers;

occasional opportunities to appear on network television and radio shows in English and Spanish; attendance welcome at press briefings and Congressional hearings.

FYI
COHA's rigorous and prestigious internship program was started in 1975; approximately one to two interns are eligible for hiring every semester for full-time positions. Former interns include reporters for *The New York Times*, the heads of two Associated Press bureaus, and career diplomats in the Foreign Service.

TO APPLY
Open to high school students, undergrads, recent college grads, college grads of any age, and grad students. International applicants eligible. Write for application or e-mail

Secretary for Internships
Council on Hemispheric Affairs
1444 I Street, NW, Suite 211
Washington, DC 20005
(202) 216-9201
(888) 922-9261 (Fax)
E-mail: coha@coha.org
www.coha.org

COUNCIL ON INTERNATIONAL EDUCATIONAL EXCHANGE

SELECTIVITY N/A
Approximate applicant pool: N/A; Interns accepted: 3,000–3,500 (1,200 US citizens)

COMPENSATION $ $ $
Program fee: $200 (US citizens), $200–$600 (nonUS citizens)
Salary: $175–$600/week

LOCATION(S)
US citizens: Canada, Costa Rica, England, France, Germany, Ireland, Jamaica, New Zealand; NonUS citizens: all 50 states of the US

FIELD
Several fields (See Appendix)

DURATION
US citizens: 3–6 months, ongoing;
NonUS citizens: 3 months–1 year, ongoing

DEADLINE(S)
Rolling

THE WORK
Founded in 1947, the Council on International Educational Exchange is a private, nonprofit organization of over 200 colleges, universities, and international exchange organizations. Striving to make international learning a part of every student's experience, Council provides counseling and information services, publishes reports and books, organizes workshops, and offers work-abroad programs, including Work Exchanges and International Volunteer Projects. Under the auspices of Work Exchanges (WE), 22,000 students a year (5,500 US citizens) work as secretaries and office assistants, waiters and caterers, bartenders, shop salespeople, nannies,

hotel bellhops, and interns (approximately 15 percent of non-US citizens and 25 percent of US citizens). Council does not make any placements, but instead provides students with visas, work permits, advice on employment, and access to employment listings that enable them to locate work, which nearly all students pursuing internships do before arriving in their host country.

PERKS
Arrival orientation; housing listings; arranged social activities with other interns (varies).

FYI
Past interns have worked at such organizations as Citibank, Amnesty International, British Telecom, Merrill Lynch, Societe Generale Banque, KPMG Peat Marwick, EDS, Lloyd's of London, CNN, Gap, Siemens, Volkswagen, BMW, and Sanyo . . . CIEE provides up to ten $500 scholarships for minority interns.

TO APPLY
Open to undergrads and grad students from Canada, Costa Rica, England, France, Ireland, Italy, Germany, Jamaica, New Zealand, Spain, and to students and recent grads in the United States. Write for application.

Work Exchanges Department
Council on International Educational Exchange
205 East 42nd Street
New York, NY 10017
(212) 661-1414, x1130
E-mail: WABrochure@ciee.org (include name, address, phone, school, major)
For Minority Scholarship: call (212) 661-1414, x1139 for an application.

CREAMER DICKSON BASFORD

CREAMER DICKSON BASFORD
A EURO RSCG AGENCY

SELECTIVITY
Approximate applicant pool: 400
Interns accepted: 10–15 (NY); 2–4 (MA); 2–4 (PA)

COMPENSATION
$250/week

LOCATION(S)
Westwood, MA; New York, NY (HQ); Pittsburgh, PA

FIELD
Public relations

DURATION
12 weeks; Summer, Fall, Spring

DEADLINE(S)
Summer: March 1; Fall/Spring: Rolling

THE WORK
The North American anchor of Eurocom Corporate & PR, a US/Pan-European group that ranks among the top five international public relations firms, Creamer Dickson Basford is one of the top ten public relations firms in the nation. They handle such products as Coors beer, Skippy peanut butter, and Pizza Hut pizza. Interns are assigned to one or more business accounts and placed in all of CDB's operating groups: Creative Services, Food & Consumer, Corporate Financial, Business-to-Business, Healthcare, ChemTech, and International.

PERKS
Private workspace; professional development seminars; lunch with CDB's chairman; casual dress on Fridays.

FYI
CDB established its internship program in 1987 . . . The program seeks to "take a leading role in training the next generation of public relations practitioners. . . . The company subscribes to an "open door" policy allowing interns to interact freely with seasoned employees.

TO APPLY
Open to college seniors, recent grads, grad students, college grads of any age. Submit resume, cover letter, writing samples, recommendations, and "anything else that will persuade us to hire you," says the coordinator.

Internship Program
Creamer Dickson Basford
350 Hudson Street, 5th Floor
New York, NY 10014
(212) 367-6800
(212) 367-7154 (Fax)

CREATIVE TIME

SELECTIVITY
Approximate applicant pool: 80; Interns accepted: 15–20

COMPENSATION
Academic credit only

LOCATION(S)
New York, NY

FIELD
Fine arts; Performing arts; Public art

DURATION
12 weeks: Summer, Winter, Fall, Spring

DEADLINE(S)
Rolling

THE WORK
Since 1973, Creative Time has sponsored projects by visual and performing artists in public locations throughout New York City. It is "interested in projects that challenge viewers, defy categories, and might normally fall between the cracks." Interns work in Public Relations, Development, Administration, Website Design, or as on-site assistants, helping artists in the creation and instillation of site-specific projects.

PERKS
Access to all projects; direct contact with a range of professional artists; occasional passes to other performances and programs.

FYI
The internship program has been in existence since 1973 . . . Works sponsored by Creative Time have often appeared in unlikely locations, including the Battery Park City Landfill, US Customs House, the Russian Baths, subways, the Brooklyn Bridge Anchorage, Times Square, milk cartons, and now the internet (www.creativetime.org).

TO APPLY
Open to undergrads, recent college grads, college grads of any age, and grad students. International applicants eligible. Submit resume and cover letter.

Internship Coordinator
Creative Time
307 Seventh Ave.
Suite 1904
New York, NY 10001
(212) 206-6674
(212) 255-8467 (Fax)
Email: staff@creativetime.org
www.creativetime.org

CREEDE REPERTORY THEATRE

SELECTIVITY   🔍 🔍 🔍 🔍
Approximate applicant pool: 500; Interns accepted: 10

COMPENSATION $ $
$130/week; free housing

LOCATION(S)
Creede, CO

FIELD
Theater

DURATION
15 weeks: Summer

DEADLINE(S)
March 1

THE WORK
Founded in 1966, Creede Repertory Theatre (CRT) performs four mainstage productions, a children's show, and a one-act play every season. The largest summertime employer in its county, CRT has a loyal following of patrons who regularly fill the theater to capacity. Interns work in Set Construction, Light/Sound, Costume Construction, Stage Management, and Business Management.

PERKS
Housing, book of eight free tickets; spectacular scenery; hiking; fishing; rafting, on-the-job training.

FYI
The internship program has been running since 1974 . . . Once a silver mining town, Creede (pop. 400) is located at the headwaters of the Rio Grande River in the San Juan Mountains of Colorado.

TO APPLY
Open to high school grads, undergrads, recent college grads, college grads of any age, and grad students. International applicants eligible. Write for application.

Internship Coordinator
Creede Repertory Theatre
P.O. Box 269
Creede, CO 81130
(719) 658-2541
(719) 658-2343 (Fax)
E-mail: CRT@CreedeRep.com
www.creederep.com

CROMARTY & CO.

Cromarty & Co.

SELECTIVITY   🔍 🔍 🔍 🔍
Approximate applicant pool: 200; Interns accepted: 10

COMPENSATION $
$42.50/week

LOCATION(S)
New York, NY

FIELD
Theater (publicity)

DURATION
15 weeks: Summer, Fall, Spring

DEADLINE(S)
Summer: April 15; Fall: August 1; Spring: December 15

THE WORK
Founded in 1987, Cromarty & Co. is a theatrical publicity agency promoting a variety of Broadway and Off-Broadway shows. Its roster of clients has included *Damn Yankees*, *The Sound of Music*, and *Victor/Victoria*. Interns assist publicists in all aspects of their work, including compiling press kits, coordinating performers' schedules, attending photo shoots, and arranging television and radio interviews.

PERKS
Free tickets to Broadway and Off-Broadway shows as well as some cabaret and dance events; star gazing.

FYI
Says a former intern: "As an aspiring actress, the marketing skills I learned working on the different shows at Cromarty & Co. will come in very handy for my acting career. From accompanying stars to television interviews and sitting in on press conferences to working with directors and choreographers and choosing photos, my many experiences will be invaluable for my career."

TO APPLY
Open to undergrads, recent college grads, college grads of any age, and grad students. Write for application.

Internship Coordinator
Cromarty & Co.
110 West 40th Street, Room 405
New York, NY 10018
(212) 944-8191
(212) 302-1257 (Fax)

CROSSFIRE

See Turner Broadcasting System

CROW CANYON
ARCHAEOLOGICAL CENTER

SELECTIVITY 🔍🔍🔍
Approximate applicant pool: 130; Interns accepted: 10–12

COMPENSATION 💲💲
Room, board, and stipend (approximately $50/week); maximum $350 travel reimbursement

LOCATION(S)
Cortez, CO

FIELD
Archaeology

DURATION
10–12 weeks

DEADLINE(S)
Early March (may vary)

THE WORK
Organized in 1984, Crow Canyon Archaeological Center is dedicated to exploring the Ancestral Pueblo culture of the Mesa Verde region. For its research efforts, Crow Canyon was the recipient of the President's Award for Historic Preservation in 1992. Interns are utilized as field interns, as researchers in the laboratory, and in Environmental Archaeology.

PERKS
Beautiful location; Tex-Mex meals; seminars.

FYI
Housing is in tents or rustic cabins on an embankment affectionately know as "intern hill" . . . Winter month participants are housed indoors . . . Interns get the weekends off . . . The organization is located 10 miles from the entrance to Mesa Verde National Park, in one of the most pristine natural areas in America.

TO APPLY
Open to college juniors and seniors, and grad students. International applicants eligible. Write for application or download application from website: www.crowcanyon.org.

Crow Canyon Archaeological Center
Internship Program
23390 County Road K
Cortez, CO 81321
(970) 565-8975
(970) 565-4859 (Fax)
www.crowcanyon.org

CROWN BOOKS

See Random House

CROWN ⬧ CAPITAL
Financial

SELECTIVITY 🔍🔍🔍🔍🔍
Approximate applicant pool: 200; Interns accepted: 1–2

COMPENSATION 💲
$500/month

LOCATION(S)
San Francisco, CA

FIELD
Commercial real estate; investment and mortgage banking

DURATION
8 weeks–6 months: ongoing—state your availablilty

DEADLINE(S)
Rolling

THE WORK
In business for over 25 years, Crown Capital is a commercial real estate investment and mortgage banking firm performing debt and equity placements, acquisitions, sales, and management and advisory services. Crown owns and manages in excess of $70 million in real estate, including apartments, condominiums, offices, and agricultural properties in the western U.S. Interns assist in all aspects of real estate work, with opportunities to "work with principals of the company on sophisticated real estate deals."

PERKS
Daily interaction with company president; prime location in San Francisco's financial district.

FYI
As a mortgage banker, Crown has made or arranged in excess of $600 million in commercial real estate loans.

TO APPLY
Open to college juniors and seniors from top academic institutions. Minimum GPA: 3.5. Submit resume GPA, SAT scores, and cover letter.

Internship Coordinator
Crown Capital
540 Pacific Avenue
San Francisco, CA 94133
(415) 398-6330
(415) 398-6057 (Fax)

C-SPAN

SELECTIVITY
Approximate applicant pool: 200; Interns accepted: 60/year

COMPENSATION S
None

LOCATION(S)
Washington, DC

FIELD
Television

DURATION
12 weeks: Summer, Fall, Spring

DEADLINE(S)
Rolling

THE WORK
C-SPAN, the Cable Satellite Public Affairs Network, is located in Washington, D.C., one block from the Capitol. The cable television industry created C-SPAN in 1979 to provide live, gavel-to-gavel coverage of the U.S. House of Representatives. C-SPAN interns arrive from colleges and universities worldwide with majors ranging from communications and political science to marketing and American studies. Intern classes are small, between 1 to 4 students per department, providing an opportunity for a hands-on, real-life experience.

The C-SPAN Internship Program seeks to utilize the talents and education of students like yourself who are interested in communications and politics. During your internship you will become familiar with the workings of a cable television network and you'll get a front row seat to the political process. You will assist in research, writing and/or production for a specific unit or department. This may include learning aspects of print and video production; technical, promotional and public relations techniques; or program production.

FYI
C-SPAN offers a minority scholarship for one United Negro College Fund Student per year.

TO APPLY
Open to college juniors and seniors. International applicants eligible. Submit resume and cover letter.

"It's an apprenticeship that never stops."

Guitarist **Ron Wood**, on having joined the Rolling Stones after they were already established.

(*Rolling Stone* magazine, January 1995)

Internship Coordinator
C-SPAN
400 North Capitol Street NW, Suite 650
Washington, DC 20001

CUSHMAN SCHOOL

The Cushman School · Established 1924 ·

SELECTIVITY
Approximate applicant pool: 20; Interns accepted: 2–4

COMPENSATION S
$118/week for US citizens; $175/week for nonUS citizens

LOCATION(S)
Miami, FL

FIELD
Education

DURATION
17 weeks: Fall, Spring

DEADLINE(S)
Rolling

THE WORK
Established in 1924, the Cushman School is an independent elementary school for boys and girls of average and above-average learning ability. Located in the heart of Greater Miami, the School enrolls 350 students from neighborhoods throughout Miami. Interns assist staff in grading papers, supervising students, and performing administrative work.

PERKS
Training seminars; field trips; free parking, coffee, and t-shirts.

FYI
In existence since 1985, the internship program leads to permanent employment at Cushman for about 25 percent of interns . . . The Cushman building has been designated an historic site.

TO APPLY
Open to undergrads, recent college grads, college grads of any age, and grad students. International applicants eligible. Submit resume and cover letter.

Internship Coordinator
Ann Gorman
The Cushman School
592 North East 60th Street
Miami, FL 33137
(305) 757-1966
(305) 757-1632 (Fax)

SELECTIVITY 🔍🔍
Approximate applicant pool: 200; Interns accepted: 25

COMPENSATION $
None

LOCATION(S)
New York, NY

FIELD
New media; Marketing; Publishing

DURATION
4–6 months (flexible): Summer, Fall, Spring

DEADLINE(S)
Rolling

THE WORK
As the name implies, Cybergrrl's goal is "to empower women to integrate technology into their personal and professional lives." The company was founded in January of 1995 just as the internet was catapulting into the national consciousness. Cybergrrl, Inc. is a media and entertainment company, featuring a network of women's websites that specialize in online content, resources, sites and communities for women and girls. The company's three sites (Cybergrrl.com, Webgrrls.com, and Femina.com) offer a network of services to women, including content and community, networking opportunities, and a search directory, all with a focus on women and things of interest to women. Intern projects include, but are not limited to, web production, marketing support, editorial research, community moderating, building databases, writing and designing content, and more.

PERKS
The benefits of working with this dedicated team of professionals include the opportunity of learning any and all aspects of the new media business that interest interns; networking opportunities with some of the top women in the industry; small office environment; exposure to new technologies.

FYI
Several interns have gone on to paid full- and part-time positions with Cybergrrl. Additionally, many former interns have gone on to hold prominent positions with many companies in the new media industry.

TO APPLY
Open to college and undergraduates and graduates. Submit a resume and cover letter indicating what type of internship you are seeking, what you hope to learn, and what you can contribute, as well as your availability. Electronic submissions are preferred.

Internship Coordinator
Cybergyrrl
50 Broad Street, Suite 1614
New York, NY 10004
www.cgim.com

Lights... Camera... *Intern!*
Interns in film and on television:

While interning at the Arms Control Association, **George Stephanopoulos** appeared on *Nightline* to relate his experience with a man who threatened to blow up the Washington Monument.

COWBOYS

SELECTIVITY 🔍🔍🔍🔍🔍
Approximate applicant pool: 450; Interns accepted: 16

COMPENSATION $
$300–$500 stipend

LOCATION(S)
Irving, TX

FIELD
Sports

DURATION
10–14 weeks: Summer, Fall, Spring

DEADLINE(S)
Rolling

THE WORK
Founded in 1960, the Dallas Cowboys is one of the most successful and admired football teams in the NFL. The Cowboys' blue-and-silver jersey has been worn by such legends as running back Tony Dorsett, wide receiver Drew Hill, and quarterback Roger Staubach. The Cowboys' current roster features such stars as quarterback Troy Aikman, running back Emmitt Smith, wide receiver Michael Irvin, and defensive lineman Leon Lett. Interns work in Public Relations, Marketing, Television, Sales and Promotion, Ticket Office, and Administration.

PERKS
Free Cowboys paraphernalia; attendance welcome at social events; "Can-do, upbeat, and very Texan" work environment.

FYI
Although Cowboys internships used to be limited to the summertime, the organization has recently expanded its program to include internship opportunities during the season. Interns working during the season may work at home games, helping out

in the press box, on the field, or in the Stadium Club . . . The Cowboys have won five Super Bowls.

TO APPLY
Open to undergrads, recent college grads, college grads of any age, and grad students. International applicants eligible. Submit resume and cover letter.

Internship Coordinator
Dallas Cowboys
1 Cowboys Parkway
Irving, TX 75063
(972) 556-9900
(972) 556-9304 (Fax)

DAVID LEADBETTER GOLF ACADEMY

See International Management Group

DAVIS HAYS AND CO.

SELECTIVITY 🔍🔍🔍🔍🔍
Approximate applicant pool: 125; Interns accepted: 1–2

COMPENSATION 💲💲
$240/week

LOCATION(S)
River Edge, NJ

FIELD
Communications consulting

DURATION
6 weeks: ongoing

DEADLINE(S)
Rolling

THE WORK
A communications consulting firm founded in 1984, Davis Hays and Co. has a national reputation for quality implementation of public relations and corporate communications programs. Its client list includes Aetna, Becton Dickinson, Booz Allen & Hamilton, Raytheon, Bellcone, The Money Store, Janssen Pharmaceutica, and Oxford Health Plans. Interns assist account executives in all aspects of their work.

PERKS
Attendance welcome at client meetings; possible travel to seminars; small, tight-knit environment.

FYI
Says the internship coordinator: "Our interns don't just do filing and make lists. They're involved in everything, from preparing press releases to writing short articles to coordinating special events, like the opening of a new building." . . . Davis Hays' motto is: "We get it, and we get the job done."

TO APPLY
Open to undergrads, recent college grads, college grads of any age, and grad students. Submit resume and cover letter.

Internship Coordinator
Davis Hays and Co.
80 Grand Avenue
River Edge, NJ 07661
(201) 342-7288
(201) 342-7701 (Fax)

D.C. BOOTH HISTORIC FISH HATCHERY

SELECTIVITY 🔍🔍🔍
Approximate applicant pool: 10; Interns accepted: 1–2

COMPENSATION 💲
Free housing or stipend, if funding permits

LOCATION(S)
Spearfish, SD

FIELD
Museums

DURATION
6 weeks minimum: Summer, Fall, Spring

DEADLINE(S)
Summer: March 1; Fall and Spring: rolling

THE WORK
Established in 1896, the D.C. Booth Historic Fish Hatchery (HFH) is one of the nation's oldest fish hatcheries, its original purpose to introduce trout into the streams of the surrounding Black Hills. Part of the US Fish and Wildlife Service, HFH was transformed in 1983 into a museum and educational center in order to increase respect for fish and natural resources. Over 150,000 visitors tour the site each year. Interns work in the museum, cataloging the collection, preserving historic pieces, processing archives, taking photographs, and upgrading exhibits.

PERKS
Orientation; discount at HFH gift shop; on-site housing near the Booth House, if available.

FYI
The Booth House, built in 1905, was home to the first HFH superintendent, Mr. D.C. Booth, and subsequent superintendents until 1983 . . . The National Fish Culture Hall of Fame, which recognizes contributions to the advancement of fish culture in the US, is located at HFH.

TO APPLY

Open to undergrads, recent college grads, college grads of any age, and grad students. International applicants eligible. Submit resume and cover letter.

Internship Coordinator
D.C. Booth Historic Fish Hatchery
423 Hatchery Circle
Spearfish, SD 57783
(605) 642-7730
(605) 642-2336 (Fax)
E-mail: r6ffa_dcb@mail.fws.gov

DEATH VALLEY NATIONAL PARK

See National Park Service

DECATUR HOUSE MUSEUM

SELECTIVITY
Approximate applicant pool: 100; Interns accepted: 10–12

COMPENSATION
None

LOCATION(S)
Washington, DC

FIELD
Museum

DURATION
6–8 weeks: Summer, Fall, Spring

DEADLINE(S)
Rolling

THE WORK

Owned by the National Trust for Historic Preservation, the Decatur House Museum is a nineteenth century historic house in the heart of downtown Washington, DC. Its mission is to "preserve the buildings, grounds, and collections of the site and to interpret to the public the architectural and social development of Washington, DC from 1818 to the present." Interns work in the following departments: Curatorial/Collections Management, Education, Research, and Administration.

PERKS

Breakfast with vice presidents and roundtable with National Trust president; attendance welcome at National Trust summer picnic; career planning/resume session with the Human Services Department; field trips to local museums and historical sites.

FYI

Recent intern projects include researching the Civil War's impact on Washington, designing an architecture education program for local elementary school students, and researching early Washington, DC census records for information about the nineteenth century African American population.

TO APPLY

Open to undergrads, recent college grads, college grads of any age, and grad students. Write for application.

Internship Program
Decatur House Museum
748 Jackson Place, NW
Washington, DC 20006
(202) 842-0920
(202) 842-0030 (Fax)

DEF JAM RECORDS

See Polygram

DELL COMPUTER

SELECTIVITY
Approximate applicant pool: 800; Interns accepted: 75

COMPENSATION
$350–$480/week for undergrads; $500–$650/week for grad students; round-trip travel (some positions)

LOCATION(S)
Austin, TX

FIELD
Computers

DURATION
10–14 weeks: Summer, Fall, Spring

DEADLINE(S)
Rolling (until April 1 for summer)

Dick Cavett the Copy Boy: "A Marshmallow Lightly Haired Over"

Television personality **Dick Cavett** launched his career in the media as a copy boy with *Time* in 1960. In the October 30, 1970 issue of *Life*, journalist Brad Darrach recalls his experience supervising Cavett the copy boy, whom Darrach likened to "a marshmallow lightly haired over." Darrach went on to provide an excerpt of the evaluation he wrote of Cavett in 1960:

INTERN EVALUATION
CAVETT, Richard

• Initiative and Resourcefulness	Adequate
• Cooperation with others	Rational
• Dependability	Tedious but worth bearing
• Overall job summary	3 on a scale of 5
• Would you hire this person to work for you again	No

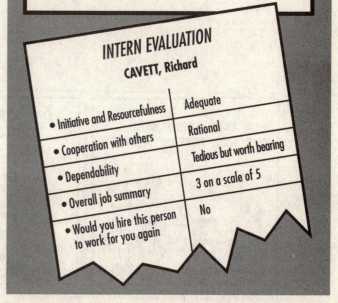

THE WORK

Founded in 1984, Dell Computer Corporation has grown from a small start-up run out of a dorm room at the University of Texas-Austin to a $3.5-billion-a-year international company with nearly 7,500 employees. Its products include notebook computers (e.g., Latitude XP), desktop computers (e.g., Dimension XPS and OptiPlex), and network servers (e.g., PowerEdge XE). Interns work in Product Development, Technical Support, Marketing, Manufacturing, Finance, Human Resources, and International.

PERKS

Monthly meetings featuring top management as guest speakers, including founder and CEO Michael Dell; occasional Texan activities (e.g., hay ride, barnyard dance); youthful, progressive environment.

FYI

The internship program was started in 1992 . . . Dell's University Relations staff works closely with interns to identify suitable projects, rotate interns through various assignments, and provide career counseling . . . Nearly 90 percent of interns are offered full-time employment at Dell.

TO APPLY

Open to undergrads and grad students. For fall and spring, students must be enrolled in at least nine semester units (undergrads) or six semester units (grad students) during internship. International applicants eligible. Submit resume and cover letter.

Internship Coordinator
University Relations
Dell Computer Corporation
2214 West Braker Lane
Austin, TX 78758
(512) 728-3330 (Fax)

Deloitte & Touche

SELECTIVITY 🔍 🔍 🔍 🔍
Approximate applicant pool: 5,000; Interns accepted: 350 (US), 25 (overseas) (See Appendix)

COMPENSATION 💲 💲 💲 💲
$600–$850/week for undergrads; $700–$950/week for grad students

LOCATION(S)
38 offices in 21 states: CA, CT, FL, GA, IL, MA, MI, MN, MO, NC, NE, NV, NJ, NY, OH, OR, PA, TX, UT, VA, WA; Washington, DC; 120 countries overseas (See Appendix)

FIELD
Professional services

DURATION
8–12 weeks: Summer, Fall, Spring

DEADLINE(S)
Rolling

THE WORK

Founded in 1895, Deloitte and Touche (D & T) is one of the world's largest Professional Services firms consulting firms, with 90,000 employees in over 130 countries worldwide and over $7.4 billion annually in revenues. Providing service in assurance and advisory services, tax, and consulting services, D & T audits nearly one-fifth of the world's largest companies. Interns work in Assurance and Advisory Services, Enterprise Risk Services, Human Capital Advisory Services, Management Solutions and Services, and Tax Services.

PERKS

Training in assurance and advisory services, taxation, and specialized software application; former interns as mentors; three-day Summer Intern Conference featuring firm leaders; planned social activities.

DILBERT reprinted by permission of United Feature Syndicate, Inc.

TO APPLY
Open to college juniors (second-semester) and seniors as well as grad students (MBA, JD, and Master of Accounting or Taxation). Must be fluent in local language. Minimum GPA (in major): 3.0. International applicants eligible. Submit resume and cover letter directly to office of interest. Addresses may be obtained from campus career centers or headquarters; contact nearest D & T office for information on overseas positions).

National Campus Recruiting
SELECT Internship Program
Deloitte and Touche
P.O. Box 820
Wilton, CT 06897
(203) 761-3000
(203) 834-2294 (Fax)

DENVER ART MUSEUM

SELECTIVITY   N/A
Approximate applicant pool: N/A, Interns accepted: N/A

COMPENSATION $
None

LOCATION(S)
Denver, CO

FIELD
Museums

DURATION
Program duration varies from a minimum of one month on a full-time basis to as long as a year on a part-time or full-time basis, depending upon project requirements and intern availability.

DEADLINE(S)
Rolling

THE WORK
Dating back to 1893, the Denver Art Museum is dedicated to the enrichment of the lives of Coloradans through the acquisition, presentation, and preservation of works of art, supported by a variety of education and outreach programs. The museum's permanent collections are particularly strong in Pre-Columbian, Spanish Colonial, American Indian, and American art. Interns work in Education, Curatorial, Conservation, and Administration. The Education Department participates in the interpretation of exhibitions by labels, audiovisual and printed guides (in collaboration with curators, editors and designers), implementation of school, family and adult programs, and visitor research.

PERKS
Attendance welcome at exhibition openings; attendance welcome at educational seminars; 10 percent discount in museum shop.

FYI
The internship program has been in existence since 1986 . . . The Denver Art Museum is the largest regional art museum between St. Louis and the West Coast.

TO APPLY
Open to college seniors, recent college grads, college grads of any age, and grad students. Preference given to candidates with an interest in museum education, experience with teaching, and art history or studio art coursework. International applicants eligible. Write for application.

Christine Deal
Attn: Education Department
Denver Art Museum
100 West 14th Avenue Parkway
Denver, CO 80204
(720) 913-0065
(720) 913-0005 (Fax)
www.denverartmuseum.org

DESIGNTECH INTERNATIONAL

SELECTIVITY   🔍🔍🔍🔍🔍
Approximate applicant pool: 100–300; Interns accepted: 8–15

COMPENSATION $ $
$125/week for undergrads; $200/week for grad students and apartment; free company apartment with gym and pool

LOCATION(S)
Springfield, VA

FIELD
Consumer goods

DURATION
12 weeks–1 year

DEADLINE(S)
Rolling

THE WORK
Situated near Washington, DC, DesignTech International is a small consumer electronics company that develops products focusing on safety, security, and convenience. From remote control gadgets to remote car starters, DesignTech products are found in stores such as Sharper Image, Radio Shack, Brookstone, Kmart and Target. Departments hiring interns include Marketing, Sales, International Sales, Public Relations, Consumer Relations/Database Development, and Operations.

PERKS
Travel to trade shows; high level of interaction with President and Vice President; interns are eligible for bonus at end of internships.

FYI
Says a former intern, "The defining characteristics of a DesignTech internship are freedom and responsibility. Interns are given a rough list of projects based on their personal interests, but they have the liberty to trade jobs as well as create their own projects."

TO APPLY

Open to college juniors and seniors, recent college grads, college grads of any age, and grad students (preferably MBAs). International applicants eligible. Submit resume and cover letter.

Internship Program
DesignTech International
7955 Cameron Brown Court
Springfield, VA 22153
(703) 866-2000
(703) 866-2001 (Fax)

DHL WORLDWIDE EXPRESS

SELECTIVITY 🔍🔍🔍
Approximate applicant pool: 20; Interns accepted: 3

COMPENSATION Ⓢ
None

LOCATION(S)
Redwood City, CA

FIELD
Transportation

DURATION
12–20 weeks: Summer, Fall, Spring

DEADLINE(S)
Rolling

THE WORK

Spanning the globe with 160 aircraft and 38,000 employees, DHL Worldwide Express is the world's largest air express network. Based 30 minutes south of San Francisco, DHL's network is linked to 80,000 destinations in more than 220 countries. Interns are assigned to Marketing, where they help plan promotions, do research for marketing projects, and work with production vendors.

PERKS

Casual working environment, DHL promo items, meaningful work assigments based on intern performance.

FYI

DHL is named after the company's founders—Dalsey, Hillblom, and Lynn—who started things off in 1969 by shuttling bills of lading between San Francisco and Honolulu.

TO APPLY

Open to college juniors, and seniors as well as grad students. International applicants residing in the USA eligible. Submit resume, cover letter, and writing samples.

Marketing Dept. MS 639
DHL Worldwide Express
333 Twin Dolphin Drive
Redwood City, CA 94065

THE DISCOVERY CHANNEL

See Discovery Communications

DISCOVERY COMMUNICATIONS

DISCOVERY COMMUNICATIONS, INC.

SELECTIVITY 🔍🔍🔍
Approximate applicant pool: 400; Interns accepted: 50

COMPENSATION Ⓢ Ⓢ
Undergrads $7/hour; grads $10/hour

LOCATION(S)
Bethesda, MD; New York, NY; Los Angeles, CA;; Detroit, MI; Chicago, IL; Miami, FL

FIELD
Television

DURATION
10 weeks: full time

DEADLINE(S)
March 1

THE WORK

Anchored by cable television's The Discovery Channel and The Learning Channel, Discovery Communications is a privately held multimedia company that also operates businesses in home entertainment, interactive multimedia, publishing, merchandising, and international sales and distribution. Departments hiring interns include The Learning Channel (Production), The Discovery Channel (Production), Consumer Marketing, International Marketing, Program Information, Program Evaluation, Destination Discovery Magazine, Human Resources, Program Editing, Communications, International, Educational Relations, Ad Sales, and Media Careers.

PERKS

Weekly brown-bag luncheons with executives; tour of offices and field trips to post-production houses; Intern Orientation and New Hire Orientation.

FYI

The Discovery Communications internship was established in 1986.

TO APPLY

Open to college juniors and seniors as well as grad students. Minimum GPA: 3.0. Must receive academic credit. International

---

It seems appropriate that **Tom Wolfe**, the brilliant writer responsible for such works as *The Electric Kool-Aid Acid Test*, *The Right Stuff*, and *Bonfire of the Vanities*, would have served an internship at a top publishing house. Or considering his penchant for dapper white suits, perhaps he would have spent some time apprenticing in a haberdashery. In actuality, Wolfe spent six months in 1959 apprenticing as a general assignment reporter with the *Springfield Union* in Massachusetts. His apprenticeship led to jobs with *The Washington Post* and the *New York Herald Tribune*'s Sunday magazine *New York*, where he developed the unorthodox and provocative writing style that would later imbue his books.

applicants eligible. Write for application. Submit application with resume, cover letter, and current official college transcript.

Internship Coordinator
Discovery Communications
Human Resources
7700 Wisconsin Avenue
Bethesda, MD 20814
(301) 986-1999
www.discovery.com

DONNA MAIONE

SELECTIVITY 🔍🔍
Approximate applicant pool: 30; Interns accepted: 3–6

COMPENSATION 💲
None

LOCATION(S)
New York, NY

FIELD
Clothing

DURATION
12 weeks: Summer, Fall, Spring

DEADLINE(S)
Rolling

THE WORK
In operation since 1988, Donna Maione is a small women's clothing company producing casual and evening wear in knitted fabrics. Lauded by magazines such as *Women's Wear Daily* and *Fashion Watch*, Maione's clothes are known for their fine yarn construction and innovative designs. Interns work in Design, Marketing, and Production.

PERKS
Critique from designer on personal portfolio sketches; attendance welcome at company dinners and parties; extra fabric remnants and color swatches.

FYI
Says a former intern: "This has been one of the most rewarding experiences of my education . . . I have learned pattern making, sewing, and how to weigh and measure garments . . . I have also [learned] the fashion design operation from concept, to sketch, to design, to production, to sales."

TO APPLY
Open to high school students at least 17 years old, high school grads of any age, undergrads, recent college grads, college grads of any age, and grad students. International applicants eligible. Submit resume, cover letter, and any portfolio sketches.

Internship Coordinator
Donna Maione
525 Seventh Avenue, 19th Floor
New York, NY 10019
(212) 730-6701
(212) 730-6704 (Fax)

DOW CHEMICAL COMPANY

SELECTIVITY 🔍
Approximate applicant pool: 300–400; Interns accepted: 100 (Interns), 45 (ATCs)

COMPENSATION 💲💲💲💲
$2,100–3,400/undergrad; $3,300–5,500/grad student; round-trip travel; furnished housing available at $12/day;

LOCATION(S)
Midland, MI (HQ), OH; Freeport, TX;

FIELD
Chemicals

DURATION
Interns: 12 weeks: Summer, Fall, Spring; ATCs: at least three 3–6 month sessions

DEADLINE(S)
Interns: October 31; ATCs: rolling

THE WORK
Dow is a leading science and technology company that provides innovative chemical, plastic and agricultural products and services to many essential consumer markets. With annual sales of $19 billion, Dow serves customers in 162 countries and a wide range of markets that are vital to human progress, including food, transportation, health and medicine, personal and home care, and building and construction, among others. Committed to the principles of sustainable development, Dow and its 39,000 employees seek to balance economic, environmental, and social responsibilities. Opportunities for both alternating term co-ops and interns include Manufacturing, Research, Information Systems, Accounting, Sales, and Human Resources (MS only). For students pursuing an MBA, opportunities are available in Finance, Treasury, and Marketing.

PERKS
Subsidized Housing; Tours of Dow facilities; access to fitness centers.

FYI
Launched in 1970, Dow's student programs offer opportunity for permanent employment consideration.

TO APPLY
Interns: open to college juniors and seniors as well as grad students. ATCs: open to college sophomores and juniors at 40 participating schools. Minimum GPA: 3.0. International applicants studying in the US are eligible. Submit resume and cover letter. For more information, contact your campus Cooperative Education Coordinator or the placement office to find out when a Dow representative will be visiting your campus.

A luxurious knit-turtleneck and pom-pom hat from Donna Maione clothing company.

National Student Program
Dow Chemical Company
P.O Box 1655
Midland, MI 48641-1655
(877) 623-8079
www.careersatdow.com

THE DOW JONES NEWSPAPER FUND

DOW JONES
DJNF
NEWSPAPER FUND INC.

SELECTIVITY 🔍 🔍
Approximate applicant pool: 550; Interns accepted: 120

COMPENSATION 💲 💲 💲
Average of $300/week ($275–$800/week); some travel

LOCATION(S)
Over 90 newspapers in AR, AZ, CA, CO, CT, FL, ID, IN, KY, MA, MI, MN, MO, NE, NJ, NY, OH, OR, PA, SC, SD, TN, TX, UT, VA, WA, WY, Washington, DC

FIELD
Newspapers, Online newspapers and real-time financial information newswires

DURATION
10 weeks: Summer

DEADLINE(S)
November 15

THE WORK
The Dow Jones Newspaper Fund (DJNF) was founded in 1965 to encourage people to consider careers in journalism. Its Editing Internship Programs allow students to work as copy editors at daily newspapers, online newspapers, and real-time financial newswires. Among the more than 100 participating media are: *The Boston Globe, The Wall Street Journal, The Indianapolis Star, The Detroit News, The Washington Post, The Houston Chronicle, Dow Jones News Service, New York Times Electronic Media Co., Access Atlanta,* and *Bloomberg Business News.*

PERKS
One or two-week training (layout, libel law, etc.) in CA, FL, MO, NE, NY, PA, or TX,; $1,000 scholarship for students returning to undergrad or grad studies; other perks vary with assignment.

FYI
DJNF interns are highly sought after by news organizations once they graduate from school (over half of interns receive full-time copy editor jobs or reporting offers). Former interns include the editor of News Bureau International at *The Wall Street Journal,* the executive news editor at *St. Paul Pioneer Press,* the vice president for News Knight Ridder, and senior project manager for Time Inc. New Media.

TO APPLY
Open to college juniors and seniors as well as grad students. For an application contact:

Dow Jones Newspaper Fund
P.O. Box 300
Princeton, NJ 08543-0300
(609) 452-2820 or (800) DOW-FUND
(609) 520-5804 (Fax)
E-mail: newsfund@wsj.dowjones.com
www.dowjones.com/newsfund

The Intern Library

Apprentices mentioned in the classics:

A Connecticut Yankee in King Arthur's Court (1889) by Mark Twain
When Hank Morgan, a 19th-century "Connecticut Yankee," is transported to the 6th century and jailed, he recruits a "page" (the medieval version of a gofer) named Clarence to deliver messages to the Court.

The Canterbury Tales (c. 1390) by Geoffrey Chaucer
The chapter "The Cook's Tale" describes an apprentice cook, Perkin Reveler, whose drunken merrymaking gets him fired.

The Good Earth (1931) by Pearl Buck
Protagonist Wang Lung's second son progresses from an apprenticeship in the grain merchant's business to become the steward over Wang's growing estate.

Gulliver's Travels (1726) by Jonathan Swift
While in school in Nottinghamshire, Lemuel Gulliver serves as an apprentice, proving his competence before journeying to Lilliput.

The House of the Seven Gables (1850) by Nathaniel Hawthorne
Mentions "Domdaniel Cavern," a mythological place where a wizard meets with his apprentices.

Johnny Tremain (1943) by Esther Forbes
Follows the adventures of a young apprentice silversmith in Boston just before the Revolutionary War.

The Old Man and the Sea (1952) by Ernest Hemingway
The "old man," Santiago, is aided by Manolin, a loyal teenager who has apprenticed with the fisherman since the age of five.

Tess of the D'Urbervilles (1891) by Thomas Hardy
In disgrace at having a child out of wedlock, Tess hires herself out as a dairymaid at the faraway Talbothays Dairy. There, she falls in love with Angel Clare, an apprentice dairyman.

SELECTIVITY
Approximate applicant pool: 75; Interns accepted: 15

COMPENSATION
None

LOCATION(S)
New York, NY

FIELD
Museums

DURATION
12 weeks: Summer, Fall, Spring

DEADLINE(S)
Rolling

THE WORK
In existence since 1976, The Drawing Center is the only museum in the country to focus solely on the exhibition of drawings, both contemporary and historic. In addition to its exhibitions, the Center presents a wide variety of public programs including panel discussions, lectures, and Line Reading, a literary series of new prose and poetry. Interns work in Exhibitions, School Programs, Viewing Program, Development, Publications, and Special Events.

PERKS
Invitations to all openings and events (panel discussions, lectures, and performances); placement on mailing list.

FYI
The Drawing Center accepts students participating in the Federal Work-Study Program and shares wages with those students' schools . . . The program has been running since 1977.

TO APPLY
Open to undergrads, recent college grads, and grad students. International applicants eligible. Write for application.

Internship Coordinator
The Drawing Center
35 Wooster Street
New York, NY 10013
(212) 219-2166
(212) 966-2976 (Fax)

The spare elegance of The Drawing Center.

SELECTIVITY
Interns placed in appropriate internships: 100%

COMPENSATION
None

LOCATION(S)
Dublin, Ireland

FIELD
Internships include all majors, minors and career options, e.g. business, marketing, human resources, financial services, communications, education, teaching, psychology, sociology, health, environmental studies.

DURATION
Fall and Spring: 15 weeks, September–December and January–April
Summer: 10 weeks, June–August
Other terms available as required.

DEADLINE(S)
A minimum of three months prior to arrival in Dublin is recommended

THE WORK
Dublin Internships is a professional organization specializing in the provision of quality work experience. Interns are assigned a site supervisor and engage in professional-level work. Interns attend an orientation at the work site and on-the-job-training as appropriate. Flexibility, enthusiasm, and a willingness to learn are among qualities that characterize successful interns. Placements are selected in line with the specific requirements of each intern.

PERKS
Vary from site to site.

FYI
Interns are given an orientation to Dublin and Ireland during the initial days, accompanied by an Information Pack. A family stay is arranged with a host family before arrival. Interns seeking other living arrangements are given information and advice, and accommodation is reserved in a Dublin hostel for the initial days. Interns' colleges/universities set out the eligibility and criteria required for participation in the internship which is generally full time. An optional seminar on Irish culture is available and the colleges/universities award credit for participation.

"My mind and my resume have both benefited in ways unattainable at home," says one former intern.

TO APPLY
Open to college juniors and seniors, and grad students. If academic credit is required the interns must secure it from their college/university.   Application materials include: completed Application Form; resume; copy of transcript; letter of recommendation from two faculty members; a cover letter; a one-page, typed statement setting out the preferred area of internship along with the reason for selecting Dublin/Ireland; and a deposit of $200. A scale of fees applies to semester and summer internships.

For further information please contact the appropriate office/faculty on campus or send an e-mail to:

mhrieke@lircom.net
011-353-1-4945277
homepage.lircom.net/~dublininternships

DUFFEY COMMUNICATIONS

SELECTIVITY 🔍🔍🔍
2–4 interns accepted per semester

COMPENSATION 💲
Hourly wage commensurate with experience

LOCATION(S)
Atlanta, GA

FIELD
Public relations; Marketing; Public affairs

DURATION
12 weeks

DEADLINE(S)
Rolling

THE WORK
Since its inception in 1984, Duffey Communications has grown into the Southeast's largest independent, full-service public relations, business marketing, and public affairs firm. Duffey Communications has served a wide variety of clients, including Kinko's, CenturyTel, Atlantic Southeast Airlines, Navision Software Worldwide, the Centers for Disease Control and Prevention, Kroger, PricewaterhouseCoopers, and Matria Healthcare. Interns work directly with account personnel on many aspects of client accounts, as well as special projects.

PERKS
Monthly professional development sessions with executives, participation in creative and planning meetings, extensive writing and research experience, exposure to media, mentor program.

FYI
Duffey Communications has received more than 300 national and international awards, including several Silver Anvil awards – the highest honor for public relations service. Also named one of the nation's 12 Hot Creative Shops, Best Strategic Counseling Firms and Top New Media Pioneers.

TO APPLY
Open to college students who are pursuing a career in public relations/marketing, have worked on publications in some capacity and have a college G.P.A. of at least 2.5. Recent graduates also are invited to apply. All resumes should be accompanied by a cover letter and writing samples. Please do not call before sending your resume.

Duffey Communications, Inc.
Peachtree Lenox Building
7th Floor
3379 Peachtree Road NE
Atlanta, GA 30326
(404) 266-2600
(404) 262-3198 (Fax)
info@duffey.com

DU PONT

SELECTIVITY 🔍🔍🔍🔍🔍
Approximate applicant pool: 2,500; Interns accepted: 100

COMPENSATION 💲💲💲💲
Est. $450–$880/week; round-trip travel

LOCATION(S)
Wilmington, DE; U.S. region plants and research laboratories are predominantly in the Mid-Atlantic, Mid-South, Southeast, and Gulf Coast

FIELD
Specialty polymers; Pigments and chemicals; Specialty fibers; Performance coatings and polymers; Nylon enterprise; Agriculture and nutrition

DURATION
10–16 weeks: Summer

DEADLINE(S)
December 31

THE WORK
DuPont, one of the best-known names in industry, is a science company, delivering science-based solutions that make a difference in people's lives in food and nutrition; health care; apparel; home and construction; electronics; and transportation. Committed to The miracles of science, DuPont operates in 65 countries, has nearly 95,000 employees and generates sales of about $30 billion. Revered as an innovator, DuPont's portfolio of 2,000 trademarks and brands include such well-known names as Lycra, Teflon, Stainmaster, Kevlar, Nomex, Tyvek‚ Dacron, Cordura,, Corian, Silverstone, and Mylar. As it approaches its 200th birthday, DuPont is transforming itself yet again to take a leadership position in biotechnology, investing heavily in life sciences, while nourishing traditional businesses with a special emphasis on new biotechnology approaches to making chemicals, polymers, and fibers.

PERKS
Orientation; mentors.

FYI
DuPont is dedicated to certain values that have characterized its operations for nearly 200 years. It recognizes that people are its greatest resource; safety is the highest priority; ethical business practices are fundamental; environmental responsibility is a corporate-wide concern; quality is an unending quest; and customer satisfaction is a must.

TO APPLY
Open to rising college juniors/seniors and recent college graduates who will be attending graduate school in the fall. Must be majoring in engineering (primarily ChE, ME, and EE), science (including chemistry, biological sciences, physics, and computer science), or business (accounting, finance, logistics, MIS, and marketing at the MBA level). Send resume with cover letter.

DuPont Resume Processing Center
P.O. Box 540177
Waltham, MA 02453-0117
E-mail: Jobs@dupont.com
www.dupont.com/careers/apply
(800) 774-2271
(800) 978-9774 (Fax)

DUKE UNIVERSITY TALENT IDENTIFICATION PROGRAM

SELECTIVITY 🔍
Approximate applicant pool: 500; Interns accepted: 300

COMPENSATION 💲 💲 💲
$1,000 per term; free room and board

LOCATION(S)
Lawrence, KS; Durham, Davidson, Boone, and Beaufort, NC; MT; NM; Mountain Lake, VA; England; Italy; Greece; Costa Rica

FIELD
Teaching/Education

DURATION
3–7 weeks: Summer

DEADLINE(S)
February 28

THE WORK
Founded in 1980, the Duke University Talent Identification Program (TIP) runs several programs designed to nurture academically talented youth. Its Summer Residential Programs offer students in grades seven through eleven intensive, fast-paced courses in the humanities, social sciences, natural sciences, mathematics, and computer sciences. Most interns are assigned to Summer Studies Programs held on college campuses, but positions are also available in Pre-College Programs, Scientific and Humanities Field Studies, and TIP International Programs. Interns are employed as teaching assistants, resident advisors, and instructors.

PERKS
Use of campus facilities; summer camp atmosphere.

FYI
Interns with Summer Studies Programs receive a comprehensive handbook discussing the ins and outs of working with TIP participants; topics include "Balancing Residential and Instructional Time," "Counseling the Gifted," and "Conflict Intervention."

TO APPLY
Open to undergrads, recent college grads, grad students, and career changers of any age. International applicants eligible. Submit resume, cover letter, and transcript, and TIP application (available on website).

Duke University Talent Identification Program
Duke University
P.O. Box 90747
Durham, NC 27708-0747
(919) 684-3847
(919) 681-7921 (Fax)
www.tip.duke.edu

DYKEMAN ASSOCIATES

SELECTIVITY 🔍 🔍 🔍 🔍 🔍
Approximate applicant pool: 85; Interns accepted: 2–3

COMPENSATION 💲 💲
"Barter money" for use at participating restaurants, entertainment, gifts, dry cleaning, etc.

LOCATION(S)
Dallas, TX

FIELD
Public relations; Marketing; Advertising; Aide production

DURATION
12 weeks–6 months: Summer, Fall, Spring

DEADLINE(S)
2–3 months before expected internships

THE WORK
Founded in 1974, Dykeman Associates Inc., is known for its creativity. Clients include a wide range of companies and nonprofit organizations, from financial and professional services to health, sports and hospitality. Interns receive a variety of hands-on public relations and marketing experience. They may also have an opportunity to work on video productions and websites.

PERKS
Weekly staff meetings to brainstorm client projects; attendance welcome at client meetings; opportunities to accompany CEO Alice Dykeman in attending community and civic group meetings.

FYI
Interns are responsible for compiling a scrapbook of work performed for clients; according to the internship coordinator, the scrapbooks "give us a chance to analyze interns' organizational abilities as well as their ability to grasp the strategy and methodology that goes into a public relations program."

TO APPLY
Open to college juniors and seniors, recent college grads, college grads of any age, and grad students. International applicants eligible. Submit resume and cover letter.

Internship Coordinator
Dykeman Associates
4115 Rawlins
Dallas, Texas 75219-3661
(214) 528-2991
(214) 528-0241 (Fax)
E-mail: adykeman@airmail.net
www.dykemanassc.com

THE ENVIRONMENTAL MAGAZINE

SELECTIVITY

Approximate applicant pool: 500+/semester; Interns accepted: 20+/semester

COMPENSATION

None; school credit only

LOCATION(S)

Los Angeles; New York

FIELD

Cable television network

DURATION

Minimum 12 weeks: Summer, Fall, Spring

DEADLINE(S)

Summer: June 1; Fall: September 30; Spring: January 15

SELECTIVITY

Approximate applicant pool: 100; Interns accepted: 12

COMPENSATION

None

LOCATION(S)

Norwalk, CT

FIELD

Magazines

DURATION

Quarterly

DEADLINE(S)

Rolling

THE WORK

Founded in 1990, E! Entertainment Television is a 24-hour cable television network offering entertainment news reports, original programs such as *Talk Soup* and *True Hollywood Stories* and exclusive live coverage of major awards shows and celebrity events. A majority interest of E! is owned by Comcast Communications Corporation and the Walt Disney Company. E! is managed by C3, the programing arm of Comcast. E! has 54 million subscribers and a target audience between 18 and 49 years of age. Interns work in Programing (LA & NY), Advertising Sales (NY only), Marketing, Talent/Booking & Casting, International Development, On-Air Design & Promotions, Duplications, and Closed-Captioning.

PERKS

Team environment with "prime networking potential"; valuable "hands on" experience; free parking (Los Angeles).

FYI

In existence since 1992, the internship program leads to permanent employment at E! for approximately 35 percent of interns.

TO APPLY

Open to college juniors and seniors as well as grad students who are able to earn school credit. Submit resume and cover letter to:

Internship Coordinator
E! Entertainment Television
5750 Wilshire Boulevard
Los Angeles, CA 90036
(323) 954-2710
(323) 954-2888 (Fax)

THE WORK

E magazine was founded in 1989 to provide information, news, and commentary on environmental issues to the general public and professional environmentalists. Posting a national circulation of 50,000, the bimonthly magazine has been recognized as a promising newcomer, winning The Alternative Press Award for New Titles and the Ozzie Silver Award (for design). Interns work in the Advertising and Editorial departments.

PERKS

Luncheons with staff, editors, publisher; occasional free review copies of books and product samples; Ecotourism trips.

FYI

E was conceived during the "Greenhouse Summer" of 1988, amid reports of medical waste on New Jersey shores, fires in Yellowstone National Park, and increased public awareness of the environment . . . Half of *E*'s current employees were once interns at the magazine.

TO APPLY

Open to undergrads, recent college grads, college grads of any age, and grad students. International applicants eligible. Submit resume, cover letter, and writing samples.

Internship Coordinator
E Magazine
P.O. Box 5098
Westport, CT 06881
(203) 854-5559 ext. 107
(203) 866-0602 (Fax)
E-mail: jimm@emagazine.com

E-SYSTEMS

SELECTIVITY   🔍🔍🔍🔍

Approximate applicant pool: 500; Interns accepted: 30–50

COMPENSATION   💲💲💲💲

$300–$420/week for Accounting and HR; $400–$520/week for Engineering

LOCATION(S)

Dallas (HQ) and Greenville, TX; Falls Church and Vienna, VA; Linthicum, MD;
St. Petersburg, FL; State College, PA

FIELD

Defense

DURATION

At least three semester- or summer-long sessions: ongoing

DEADLINE(S)

Rolling

THE WORK

Founded in 1964, E-Systems manufactures and distributes electronic systems and communications networks, including electronic warfare equipment, navigation and reconnaissance machinery, and highly sophisticated spying devices. Employing 16,000 people worldwide and generating over $2 billion annually in sales (85 percent of which is classified), the company has outfitted such military projects as the Doomsday Plan (the system that allows the President to manage a nuclear war) and Operation Desert Storm. Interns are placed in seven of E-System's nine operating units in such areas as engineering, engineering development, accounting, and human resources.

PERKS

Co-op club at each site; softball leagues, picnics, trips to sporting events, etc.; access to workout facilities at some sites.

FYI

Launched in 1985, E-System's co-op program offers permanent employment to over 50 percent of interns. During their first co-op session, interns working in technical areas (approximately 75 percent of interns) apply for a security clearance, requiring four to ten months to obtain . . . According to a recent *60 Minutes* investigation, many of E-Systems' employees are former and possibly current CIA agents.

TO APPLY

Open to college sophomores (second semester) and juniors. Must be majoring in engineering (aeronautical, civil, electrical, mechanical, and software), math, physics, accounting, or business administration. Contact campus co-op office for information on application procedure.

Manager of Staffing
Corporate Offices
E-Systems
P.O. Box 660248
Dallas, TX 75226
(214) 661-1000

SELECTIVITY   🔍🔍🔍🔍

Approximate applicant pool: 800; Interns accepted: 63–88

COMPENSATION   💲💲💲

$10/day

LOCATION(S)

Bethesda, MD; New York, NY; Philadelphia, PA; Richmond, VA; St. Petersburg, FL

FIELD

Advertising agency

DURATION

12–17 weeks: Summer, Fall, Spring

DEADLINE(S)

Rolling

THE WORK

Founded in 1952 by newspaper publisher Earle Palmer Brown, Earle Palmer Brown (EPB) is the nation's 21st largest full-service marketing communications company. Its clients include CoreStates, DuPont, Omni Hotels, Pizza Hut, Turner Broadcasting, USAir, and Wawa Food Markets. Interns work in Account Services, Advertising, Broadcast Production Creative, Direct Marketing, Human Resources, Media, New Business, Public Relations, Research, Sales Promotions (PA and MD only), Traffic, and Yellow Pages Advertising (PA only). Bethesda interns work as part of EPB teams for specific clients.

PERKS

On-site seminars conducted by department heads; opportunities to attend trade shows (Public Relations interns); client promo materials (t-shirts, etc.).

FYI

EPB has offered internships since 1979 . . . According to one EPB internship coordinator: "Your supervisors will rely on you for various tasks and will give you as much responsibility as you can handle."

TO APPLY

Open to college juniors and seniors, recent college grads, college grads of any age, and grad students. International applicants eligible. Submit resume and cover letter indicating top three department choices.

Internship Program
Earle Palmer Brown
One Liberty Place
1650 Market Street
Philadelphia, PA 19103
(215) 851-9505

Internship Program
Earle Palmer Brown
345 Hudson Street
New York, NY 10014-4502
(212) 463-6900

Internship Program
Earle Palmer Brown
Public Relations
1 East Cary Street
Richmond, VA 23219
(804) 343-2300

Internship Program
Earle Palmer Brown
6935 Arlington Road
Bethesda, MD 20814
(301) 657-6219

Internship Program
Earle Palmer Brown
1710 East Franklin Street
Richmond, VA 23223
(804) 775-0700

Internship Program
Earle Palmer Brown
260 First Avenue South, Suite 300
St. Petersburg, FL 33701
(813) 821-5155

EASTMAN KODAK COMPANY

SELECTIVITY 🔍 🔍 🔍 🔍
Approximate applicant pool: 2,200; Interns accepted: 200

COMPENSATION 💲 💲 💲 💲
$400–$700/week for undergrads; $550–$800/week for grad students; Round-trip travel; Co-op benefits (e.g., paid holidays, vacation pay, bonus, health and life insurance)

LOCATION(S)
Rochester, NY

FIELD
Consumer goods (imaging)

DURATION
Interns: 10 weeks–1 year: Summer, Fall, Spring; Co-ops: minimum of three 3–4-month sessions (at least one must be during academic year)

DEADLINE(S)
Summer: February 1; Fall and Spring: Rolling

THE WORK
Founded in 1880, the Eastman Kodak Company (EKC) is the world's largest imaging company, with over $13 billion in annual sales and nearly 100,000 employees worldwide. Its 20,000 consumer and industrial products include Kodak and Ektar films, medical and dental x-ray films, chemicals, cameras, photocopiers, and computer disks. Summer interns and co-op interns work in such areas as Research, Manufacturing, Business Research, Product & Process Development, and Design at three facilities—Kodak Office, Kodak Park, and Kodak Equipment Manufacturing Division.

PERKS
Housing search assistance; student council plans social activities; regularly scheduled info sharing sessions with fellow students.

FYI
In recent years, up to 70 percent of co-op interns have been hired for full-time positions at EK . . . According to company history, founder George Eastman decided to call his company "Kodak" simply because he liked the letter "K."

TO APPLY
Open to undergrads and grad students. Most openings are technical in nature, therefore, majors in engineering and science are appropriate. Majors such as MBA are also considered for business openings, minimum GPA: 2.8. Submit resume and cover letter.

Student Programs
Eastman Kodak Company
343 State Street
Rochester, NY 14650-1139
(716) 724-4000

EASTWEST RECORDS

See Elektra Entertainment Group

THE ECCO PRESS

SELECTIVITY 🔍 🔍
Approximate applicant pool: 50; Interns accepted: 1–2

COMPENSATION 💲
None

LOCATION(S)
New York City, NY

FIELD
Publishing; Magazines

DURATION
12 weeks: Summer, Fall, Spring

DEADLINE(S)
Rolling

THE WORK
In existence since 1969, The Ecco Press is a small, high-quality publishing house that handles approximately forty titles a year. Its catalogue runs the gamut, from travel books to top-flight novels. Interns do everything from answering telephones to evaluating unsolicited manuscripts. Ecco was acquired in 1999 by HarperCollins Publishing and continues to operate as an independent imprint.

PERKS
Brown-bag luncheons with executives; daily phone conversations with authors; free books; "There is no dress code."

FYI
The offices are located at 10 East 53rd Street in the HarperCollins building.

TO APPLY
Open to undergrads, recent college grads, college grads of any age, and grad students. International applicants eligible. Submit resume, cover letter, and recommendations (if available).

Internship Coordinator
The Ecco Press
HarperCollins Publishers
10 East 53rd Street
New York, NY 10022
(212) 207-7847
(212) 702-2460 (Fax)

> "There is no dress code. Suits are almost never seen—we will think you are selling something if you show up in one."
> —Internship Coordinator, *The Ecco Press*

EXCLUSIVE INTERVIEW WITH GEORGE PLIMPTON

Editor of the literary quarterly Paris Review, George Plimpton has had an extraordinary career as a writer and journalist. A self-described "Mr. Intern," Plimpton has written about his experiences sampling dozens of careers. His "internships" include sitting in as a percussionist with the New York Philharmonic, playing a game with the Detroit Lions, fighting a bullfight staged by Ernest Hemingway, losing a tennis match to Pancho Gonzales, conducting the Cincinnati Symphony Orchestra, playing golf in three Pro-Am tournaments, serving as a trapeze artist and lion-tamer for the Clyde Beatty-Cole Brothers Circus, and boxing heavyweight Archie Moore. Plimpton holds a B.A. from Harvard University (1950) and an M.A. from King's College, Cambridge (1954). At left, a young Plimpton samples pro football.

The Internship Informants: Tell us about your experience at *Time* magazine.
Plimpton: It was the summer when I was 20 years old. I was going into my senior year at Harvard. I was an intern from June until late August. I was actually a "copy boy," which is what interns at *Time* were called then.

The Internship Informants: Just from the sound of it, it seems as a "copy boy" you weren't exactly writing articles for the magazine.
Plimpton: My job was to wander around and fill and empty in-and-out baskets. I remember filling the inkwell of Whittaker Chambers, who was the religion editor. Then once a week, I used to carry part of the issue down to Philadelphia where the magazine was put together. If I didn't get it successfully to wherever I took it in Philadelphia, there was the end of the issue. So it was the most important thing I think I've ever done in my life. I carried it down there in an envelope; I often wanted to get a handcuff and have it handcuffed to my hand because I had been warned that if I lost it, it would be the end of *Time* for that week.

The Internship Informants: How many other copy boys worked with you?
Plimpton: There were about eight of us. We all sat together in one room, sort of like bellhops in a hotel. From there, we were sent to various offices to deliver packages and so forth.

The Internship Informants: Did anything else happen during your tenure at *Time*?
Plimpton: Well, part of the summer I spent in [*Time's*] library. I was the president of the *Harvard Lampoon* at the time, and we were doing a parody of *Esquire* magazine. I decided to write an exposé of Yale's secret societies. That year Levi Jackson had been tapped for Skull & Bones, the ultra-secret society, and so there was a lot of materials on the secret societies [in the library] sent in by the stringers in New Haven which I shamelessly plundered. The story I wrote became the best known exposé on Yale's secret societies, probably to this day...

The Internship Informants: It sounds like writing the article was a great success for you.
Plimpton: The article had a profound effect on my life . . . Back at Harvard, I submitted the story (which eventually appeared in the *Lampoon*) in a writing class called "English S" taught by the poet Archibald McLeash, and he gave it an A. When the Korean War started, I was an infantry officer in the reserves; the only way to keep from being called back in was to continue my education. In desperation, I wrote to three colleges at Oxford and three at Cambridge along with a wonderful letter of recommendation by Archibald McLeash, who said I had written this powerful piece of journalism about the secret societies at Yale. By the luck of the stars, I was accepted at King's College, Cambridge, where I spent two splendid years. So in a sense, the resources I had as an intern at *Time* had these repercussions.

The Internship Informants: What do think about the interns you now have at *The Paris Review*?
Plimpton: The interns are treated like staff. They see something about the workings of the magazine, and they attend the meetings that we have every Wednesday. Most of them are people who want to be in publishing or want to write, so there is a lot of interaction with the staff—they're certainly not "copy boys" or "copy people" as I guess one would say today.

Plimpton interview continued . . .

The Internship Informants: Where do your interns work?
Plimpton: Interns are down in the "cellar," a rather murky part of the building reachable by a circular staircase. But the entire office is small, and we're all in here together—it's like an anthill.

The Internship Informants: What is the George Plimpton view on the importance of internships?
Plimpton: I think they are important if you are given something more to do than fill inkwells. Our interns [at *The Paris Review*] are not moving packages around; they are here to learn to write, which our editors can help them with. They read submissions. That's why we like to find people who are writing novels or poems or at least are very interested in writing. If they're not, they might as well work at the Central Park Zoo filling water troughs for the animals.

The Internship Informants: Referring to the incredible number of professions you've sampled as a journalist, someone once said of you, "He enjoys what it feels like to be a participant." Do you see a parallel between internships and the multitude of temporary vocational experiences you've had and written about?
Plimpton: Certainly. All through my participatory life I've had internships. You can say I was an intern with the Detroit Lions, an intern with the New York Philharmonic, an intern with the Boston Bruins, and an intern with all the other organizations I sampled as a journalist. I am "Mr. Intern."

The Internship Informants: How did you convince these organizations, especially the sports teams, to take you on?
Plimpton: Each was different, but I was tremendously helped by the fact that I was working for *Sports Illustrated*. I had a specific and serious purpose when I approached the sports teams—to find out as much as I could about the inner workings of the teams and then write about it.

The Internship Informants: Was there ever something you said or an attitude you conveyed which brought about one of these experiences?
Plimpton: An important moment came with football, when I spent a month at the training camp of the Detroit Lions. When the time came [for the players] to go to the first class meeting, each player had to pick up a playbook. We were all in line, and when I got up to receive my playbook, the coach said, "No. You can't go in there." And I said, "But Coach, don't you understand what it is I want to do?" The coach stood there for what seemed like an eternity, and he finally said OK and gave me a playbook. That was a pivotal moment, because had he not given me a playbook, I would have been an outsider. But the fact that he did give me one put me right there in the classroom and made me part of the team.

ECONOMIC DEVELOPMENT ADMINISTRATION

See US Department of Commerce

ECONOMIC RESEARCH SERVICE

SELECTIVITY 🔍🔍🔍
Approximate applicant pool: 150; Interns accepted: 10–15

COMPENSATION 💲💲💲
$350–$400/week for undergrads; $450–$820/week for grad students

LOCATION(S)
Washington, DC

FIELD
Economic research

DURATION
8–12 weeks

DEADLINE(S)
March 1

THE WORK
An agency of the US Department of Agriculture, the Economic Research Service (ERS) develops economic and other social science information and analysis to assist in public and pri-
vate decision making on issues relating to agriculture, food, natural resources, and rural America. The information is provided to policymakers in the executive and legislative branches, and to environmental, consumer, farm, industry, and other public policy organizations, as well as international entities, universities, and the general public. Interns work directly with researchers to develop and disseminate research and analysis.

PERKS
Commuter transit subsidies; ERS reception; orientation; USDA reception featuring Secretary of Agriculture and all USDA interns; intern seminars on ERS research topics and techniques; day on Capitol Hill.

FYI
Says the internship coordinator: "Students pursuing graduate work gain access to invaluable resources—both data and professional expertise—for use in developing dissertation proposals or carrying them out."

TO APPLY
Submit resume cover sheet (application form), resume, and transcript. Application information, including resume cover sheet, available beginning in January at: www.ers.usda.gov (Jobs). Open to undergrads and grad students, US citizens only.

Summer Intern Program
Economic Research Service
US Deptartment of Agriculture
1800 M Street NW, Rm. 4151
Washington, DC 20036-5831
(202) 694-5004
(202) 694-5757 (Fax)
E-mail: rsmith@ers.usda.gov
www.ers.usda.gov

The Economist

SELECTIVITY 🔍🔍🔍🔍
Approximate applicant pool: 5,000; Interns accepted: 3

COMPENSATION 💲💲💲
Est. £200–£300/week (approximately $325–$500/week)

LOCATION(S)
London, England

FIELD
Magazines

DURATION
12 weeks: Summer

DEADLINE(S)
March 1

THE WORK
Founded in 1843, *The Economist* is a weekly magazine featuring news and analysis of international current events, politics, business, finance, arts, sports, science, and technology. Advocating free trade, minimum interference with market forces, and individual responsibility, it reaches 700,000 subscribers worldwide. Interns write articles for three sections of the magazine: Science and Technology (under the auspices of the Richard Casement Internship), Business, and, depending on need, International or Britain.

PERKS
Mentors; attendance welcome at editorial meetings; occasional luncheons with editors.

FYI
According to an editorial assistant, interns are "treated like members of the staff." Although *The Economist* is based in London, over 80 percent of its subscribers live outside of the UK.

TO APPLY
Open to college seniors as well as grad students under 24 years of age. International applicants eligible. Submit resume and cover letter.

Editorial Manager
The Economist
25 St. James's Street
London SW1A 1HG
England
44-171-839-7000

EDELMAN
Public Relations Worldwide

SELECTIVITY 🔍🔍🔍🔍🔍
Approximate applicant pool: 600; Interns accepted: 25 in Chicago and New York—varies by office

COMPENSATION 💲💲
$400/week (Chicago and New York); pay varies by office

LOCATION(S)
Chicago and New York (Co–HQs); and 36 other offices worldwide

FIELD
Public relations

DURATION
12 weeks: Summer; Flexible Fall/Spring

DEADLINE(S)
March 1: Summer; Rolling: Fall/Spring

THE WORK
Founded in 1952, Edelman Public Relations Worldwide is the largest independent and the fifth largest public relations firm in the world, with 38 offices and over 1,800 employees worldwide. Dedicated solely to the practice of public relations, Edelman Worldwide creates and directs highly effective PR programs for many of the world's leading companies. Practice areas hiring interns include Consumer Marketing, Crisis Communications, Financial Services, Healthcare, Investor Relations, New Media, Professional Services, Public Affairs, Special Event Marketing, and Technology.

PERKS
Interns work on an "Edel-Project," which allows students to work together to develop a comprehensive public relations program for a hypothetical client. Interns present their programs to an internal review committee at the end of the summer. In addition, interns attend weekly "Edel-U" classes, Edelman's exclusive in-house public relations training program (varies by location).

FYI
Edelman is known as a "front-page firm" because of its ability to generate headline news . . . Edelman-spun stories include the StarKist/Heinz announcement of "dolphin safe" tuna; the acquisition of Saks Fifth Avenue by Investcorp; the launch of the recyclable ketchup bottle from Heinz; and the World Chess Championship match between Kasparov and Karpov.

TO APPLY
Open to students of current junior, senior, or post-graduate status as well as international applicants. For more information, or to apply online, please look at our website at www.edelman.com

SELECTIVITY N/A

Approximate applicant pool: N/A; Interns accepted: 95–135

COMPENSATION $

None. Students pay $4,100–$7,500 program fee covering internship, classes, room, and some food

LOCATION(S)

Brussels; Edinburgh; London; Paris; Bonn; Cologne; Berlin; Madrid; Melbourne

FIELD

Over 15 fields (see THE WORK)

DURATION

Spring or Fall semester, 2-month summer term

DEADLINE(S)

Summer: March 1; Fall: May 1; Spring: November 15

THE WORK

Established in 1971, Educational Programs Abroad (EPA) organizes internship-based study abroad programs for American universities and for individual students. European Program internships are available in a variety of fields, including advertising, art galleries, banking, business, computers, education, environment, government, graphic design, health care, journalism, law, medical research, museums, politics and pressure groups, public policy, publishing, psychology, social sciences and theater. EPA's Australia Program places students in parliamentary internships. Summer internships are available in London, Bonn, Brussels, and Edinburgh.

PERKS

Orientation and extensive language instruction; courses in a range of subjects (offered fall and spring only) taught by university faculty; field trips to local cultural sites.

FYI

Past participants have interned with such organizations as the House of Commons, House of Lords, Greenpeace, the Institute for Public Policy Research, the Museum of London, St. George's Hospital, J. Walter Thompson, Lehman Brothers, Reader's Digest, CNN, Merrill Lynch, and the European Parliament . . . Students seeking academic credit, but whose school will not grant credit for the program, can receive credit from the University of Rochester.

TO APPLY

Open to college juniors and seniors as well as grads. Must be proficient in language of host country. For more information contact:

Educational Programs Abroad
137 North Park Street
Kalamazoo, MI 49007
(616) 382-0139
(616) 382-5222 (Fax)
E-mail: EPAinterns@aol.com

Center for Study Abroad
Lattimore 206/P.O. Box 270376
University of Rochester
Rochester, NY 14627-0376
(716) 275-7532
(716) 461-5131 (Fax)
E-mail: csaip@cc.rochester.edu

SELECTIVITY 🔍🔍🔍🔍

Approximate applicant pool: 700 (Interns), 350 (Reps); Interns accepted: 80 (Interns), 15–20 (Reps)

COMPENSATION $

Interns: daily travel allowance; Reps: reimbursement of expenses such as gas, phone, photocopies

LOCATION(S)

Interns: Los Angeles, CA; Nashville, TN; New York, NY; Reps: Atlanta, GA; Austin, TX; Boston, MA; Buffalo, NY; Chicago, IL; Denver, CO; Detroit, MI; Los Angeles and San Francisco, CA; Madison, WI; Minneapolis, MN; Philadelphia, PA; Providence, RI; Seattle, WA; Washington, DC

FIELD

Record labels

DURATION

Interns: 8–14 weeks, Summer, Fall, Spring; Reps: 2 years minimum, ongoing

DEADLINE(S)

Rolling

THE WORK

A division of Warner Music, the Elektra Entertainment Group comprises Asylum, EastWest, and Elektra record labels. The labels handle such artists as En Vogue, AC/DC, Bryan White, Emmylou Harris, Anita Baker, The Cure, The Breeders, Anthrax, Tracy Chapman, and Da Lench Mob, as well as new acts like Buffalo Tom, Clutch, Opus III, and The Dambuilders. Forty to 50 NY interns work in Publicity, Artist Relations, Sales, Marketing, Video, Promotion, and Art. Twenty CA interns work in Promotion, Publicity, Artists & Repertoire, and Video. Twelve TN interns work in Artists & Repertoire, Publicity, Promotion, and Marketing & Creative Services for Asylum's country music bands. Under the auspices of the College Marketing Internship, college marketing reps promote EastWest's and Elektra's alternative and metal acts.

PERKS

Free CDs and cassettes; free stickers, t-shirts, posters, and pins; planning of and attendance at after-concert parties (reps).

FYI

EEG's college-rep program was started in 1993. Reps perform such tasks as escort bands to college radio stations, monitor record stock at local stores, arrange awareness campaigns for concerts, and put up posters.

TO APPLY

Interns: open to undergrads; must receive academic credit. Reps: open to college freshmen and sophomores. International applicants eligible. Submit resume and cover letter (Interns). Write for application (Reps).

Internship Coordinator
Elektra Entertainment Group
75 Rockefeller Plaza, 16th Floor
New York, NY 10019
(212) 275-4490

Internship Coordinator
(Name of Department)
Elektra Entertainment Group
345 North Maple Drive, Suite 123
Beverly Hills, CA 90210
(310) 288-3800

Office Manager
Asylum Records
1906 Acklen Avenue
Nashville, TN 37212
(615) 292-7990

College Marketing Internship
Elektra Entertainment Group
75 Rockefeller Plaza
New York, NY 10019
(212) 275-2500

ELEKTRA RECORDS

See Elektra Entertainment Group

ELITE MODEL MANAGEMENT

SELECTIVITY 🔍 🔍
Approximate applicant pool: 100; Interns accepted:13–18

COMPENSATION Ⓢ
None; Bonus possible

LOCATION(S)
New York, NY; Chicago, IL; Los Angeles, CA; Atlanta, GA; Miami, FL; overseas (see TO APPLY)

FIELD
Model management

DURATION
At least 3 months; Year-round; Part time available

DEADLINE(S)
Rolling

 THE WORK
In 1971, John Casablancas opened his first Elite in Paris to train fledgling models to become Europe's stars. Today Elite continues to attract the industry's creme de la creme. No fewer than six of the world's top ten models, featured on the cover of Vogue's April 1992 "100th Anniversary Special" worked for Elite. Interns for Elite work in Scouting.

PERKS
Casual dress; friendly atmosphere; fun.

FYI
Elite has had an internship program since 1985 . . . Claims one intern: "Elite is the most influential agency in the business, representing the most famous models" . . . All say that they will never forget the experience. "I would love to be an Elite intern forever," concluded one.

TO APPLY
Open to undergrads. International applicants eligible. Send a resume and cover letter, but be personal.

Elite Model Management
111 East 22nd Street
New York, NY 10010
(212) 529-9700

Elite Los Angeles
345 North Maple Drive #397
Beverly Hills, CA 90210
(310) 274-9395

Elite Chicago
58 West Huron Street
Chicago, IL 60610
(312) 943-3226

Elite Atlanta
181 14th Street #325
Atlanta, GA 30309
(404) 872-7444

Elite Miami
1200 Collins Avenue
Miami Beach, FL 33139
(305) 674-9500

Overseas:
Rio de Janeiro, Brazil: 55-21-511-3437
São Paulo, Brazil: 55-11-210-6019
Toronto, Canada: (416) 369-9395
London, England: 44-171-333-0888
Paris, France: 33-1-4044-3222
Hamburg, Germany: 49-40-440-555

ESTIMATED STARTING SALARIES FOR NEW COLLEGE GRADS

Chemical engineering	$40,689
Mechanical enginering	$35,713
Electrical engineering	$35,302
Industrial engineering	$33,593
Computer science	$32,762
Nursing	$30,078
Civil engineering	$29,838
Geology	$28,689
Chemistry	$28,551
Accounting	$28,022
Physics	$27,330
Financial administration	$26,838
Mathematics	$26,630
Sales	$24,790
Marketing	$24,780
Agriculture	$24,455
Business administration	$23,950
Hotel/Restaurant management	$23,855
Education	$22,898
Human resources	$22,760
Natural resources	$22,760
Social science	$22,600
Retailing	$22,195
Advertising	$21,870
Communications	$21,860
Human ecology	$21,353
Home economics	$21,252
Liberal arts	$21,124
Journalism	$20,837
Telecommunications	$20,821

Source: College Placement Council of Bethlehem, PA, "Salary Survey for 1993-94."

Munich, Germany: 49-89-341-336
Hong Kong: 85-2-285-05550
Milan, Italy: 39-2-481-4704
Tokyo, Japan: 81-3-3587-0200
Amsterdam, the Netherlands: 31-20-627-9929
Barcelona, Spain: 34-3-418-8099
Madrid, Spain: 34-1-310-2777
Fribourg, Switzerland: 41-37-224-815

ELIZABETH DOW

SELECTIVITY 🔍 🔍 🔍 🔍
Approximate applicant pool: 500; Interns accepted: 20–30 per year

COMPENSATION 💲 💲
Some paid positions (summer only)

LOCATION(S)
New York, NY

FIELD
Art and design; Interior design

DURATION
3–12 weeks: Summer, Fall, Spring

DEADLINE(S)
Rolling

THE WORK
Established in 1982, Elizabeth Dow is a paint and design studio specializing in custom paint finishes for walls and furniture, trompe l'oeil, murals, and hand-painted wall coverings. Written up in such magazines as *House and Garden*, *Interior Design*, and *Architectural Digest*, the work of Elizabeth Dow has been used in private homes, retail stores, and public centers nationally. Interns work in Art and Design, or Business and Marketing.

PERKS
Possible travel opportunities to on-site painting jobs; "tremendously fun, music-filled environment"; attendance welcome at company parties.

FYI
Says president Elizabeth Dow, "Each of our interns works in a variety of areas of the business, from designing new wall coverings to actually naming the product and assessing salability and marketing techniques; interns also participate in areas of customer service, shipping and handling, project management, ordering, and production."

TO APPLY
Open to high school students, high school grads, undergrads, recent college grads, college grads of any age, and grad students. International applicants eligible. Submit resume, cover letter, recommendations.

Internship Coordinator
Elizabeth Dow
155 Ave. of the Americas, 4th Floor
New York, NY 10013
(212) 463-0144
www.elizabethdow.com

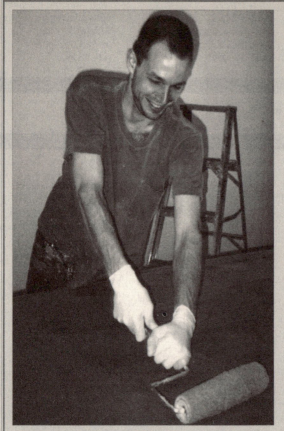

An intern at Elizabeth Dow design studio working some magic with a roller brush.

> "Looking back, if I had had the opportunity to intern during my college education, I think my comprehension of the business world would have certainly fine-tuned far sooner than it did."
> —Elizabeth Dow, founder and president,
> Elizabeth Dow Paint and Design

ELIZABETH GLASER PEDIATRIC AIDS FOUNDATION

SELECTIVITY 🔍
Approximate applicant pool: 100; Interns accepted: up to 50

COMPENSATION 💲 💲
$2,000 award

LOCATION(S)
Intern's home campus; all 50 states and Puerto Rico or sponsor's institution; internationally

FIELD
Pediatric AIDS research

DURATION
320 hours: minimum of 4 hours/week

DEADLINE(S)
End of March

THE WORK

The Pediatric AIDS Foundation (PAF) is a nonprofit organization addressing the medical problems unique to children infected with HIV/AIDS. Its Student Intern Awards are designed to encourage students to enter clinical and research programs related to pediatric AIDS. Working with sponsors recognized for their contributions to pediatric AIDS, interns conduct basic research or clinical research and care.

PERKS

Vary with lab.

FYI

Several of PAF's interns have gone on to pursue higher level research in pediatric AIDS.

TO APPLY

Open to high school seniors, undergrads, grad students, and medical students. Minimum GPA for undergrads: 3.0. International applicants eligible. Write for application, which must be completed by the student's sponsor and the student.

Chris Hudmall
Elizabeth Glaser Pediatric AIDS Foundation
2950 31st St. Suite 125
Santa Monica, CA 90405
(310) 314-1459
(310) 314-1469 (Fax)
E-mail: chris@pedaids.org

ELKMAN ADVERTISING & PUBLIC RELATIONS

ELKMAN
ADVERTISING & PUBLIC RELATIONS

SELECTIVITY
Approximate applicant pool:100; Interns accepted: up to 4 each semester

COMPENSATION $
None

LOCATION(S)
Bala Cynwyd, PA

FIELD
Advertising; Public relations

DURATION
12 weeks: Summer, Fall, Spring

DEADLINE(S)
Summer: May 15; Fall: September 15; Spring: January 15

THE WORK

Founded in 1955, Elkman Advertising and Public Relations is an independently owned full-service marketing-communications firm. Its staff of 30 employees service over twenty-five accounts, including Montifore Medical Center. VoiceNet, Price Automotive Group, Chilton Research Services, and PA Dutch Convention & Visitors Bureau.

PERKS

Brown-bag luncheons with executives; attendance welcome at firm-wide educational meetings; Cross pen as end-of-internship gift.

FYI

Elkman started its internship program in the early 1970s . . . A group of interns who recently helped K'Nex market its toy building blocks ended up constructing a miniature roller coaster out of K'Nex blocks that was used in a K'Nex television commercial.

TO APPLY

Open to college juniors and seniors, recent college grads, college grads of any age, and grad students. International applicants eligible. Submit resume, cover letter, writing samples (for Public Relations and Copywriting), and portfolio (for Art Direction).

Internship Coordinator
Elkman Advertising & Public Relations
150 Monument Road
Bala Cynwyd, PA 19004-1777
(610) 668-1100

EMERGE

See Black Entertainment Television

EMI RECORDS GROUP NORTH AMERICA

EMI Records

SELECTIVITY
Approximate applicant pool: 350; Interns accepted: 50

COMPENSATION $
College credit only

LOCATION(S)
Interns: New York, NY; Los Angeles, CA

FIELD
Record label, Corporate entertainment

DURATION
Interns: 12–16 weeks: Summer, Fall, Spring

DEADLINE(S)
Rolling

THE WORK

EMI is one of the largest international companies in the music industry with a line-up of artists covering every music genre. We are dedicated to sharing our music with the world. EMI also has the largest music publishing company worldwide and manufactures and distributes its own music.

EMI often hires their intern participants for full-time positions. The internship coordinator writes, "We make all efforts to ensure that interns receive bona fide on-the-job experience and that they participate in projects."

PERKS

Orientation; informal luncheons with EMI executives; free t-shirts and CDs.

FYI

EMI often hires their intern participants for full-time positions. The internship coordinator writes, "We make all efforts to ensure that interns receive bona fide on-the-job experience and that they participate in projects."

TO APPLY

Open to undergrads and grad students. Must receive academic credit. International applicants eligible (college-level interns only). Submit resume and cover letter.

EMI Recorded Music, North America
Human Resources
1290 Avenue of the Americas, 38th Floor
New York, NY 10104
(212) 492-5448
(212) 492-1720 (Fax)

EMILY'S LIST

 EMILY'S LIST

SELECTIVITY
Approximate applicant pool: 150; Interns accepted: 5

COMPENSATION
$500/month

LOCATION(S)
Washington, D.C.

FIELD
Politics

DURATION
4 months: Fall, spring, summer

DEADLINE(S)
1 month before internship starts

THE WORK

EMILY's List assists pro-choice, Democratic women running for the House, Senate, and governorship through raising money, giving political support, and mobilizing women voters through EMILY's List WOMEN VOTE! The membership of EMILY's List has increased dramatically from 3,000 members in 1990 to more than 40,000 in 1997. Departments accepting interns include Communications, Development, Political, and Research.

PERKS

Within walking distance of the White House, the Smithsonian, and other DC landmarks.

FYI

In 1985, when EMILY's List was founded, there were only twelve Democratic women serving in the House of Representatives; EMILY's List has since helped to elect thirty-four women to the House, five to the Senate, and two to governor's mansions.

TO APPLY

College students of all ages with good oral and written skills should call for an application or submit a cover letter and resume. Knowledge of WordPerfect for Windows is required.

EMILY's List
Attn: Internship Coordinator
805 15th St. NW
Suite 400
Washington, DC 20005
(202) 326-1400
(202) 426-1415 (Fax)

ENERGY RECORDS

 Energy Records

SELECTIVITY
Approximate applicant pool: 10–20; Interns accepted: 6–8

COMPENSATION
$5/day

LOCATION(S)
Interns: New York, NY; Street Reps: CA, IL, MA, MN, NY, OH, OR, TX, WA

FIELD
Record labels

DURATION
12 weeks: Summer, Fall, Spring

DEADLINE(S)
Rolling

THE WORK

Founded in 1992, Energy Records is a record label focusing on industrial, gothic, electro, and some metal music. It's roster of acts includes Pro-pain, Hanzel und Gretyl, Bile, Sunshine Blind, Heavy Water Factory, and fueled. Interns work in publicity, retail, radio, artist & repertoire, and tour promotion.

PERKS

Free CDs, tapes, and t-shirts; cool, "music-filled" office environment.

FYI

Energy Records also runs the Street Rep Program, where regionally based interns visit local clubs, radio stations, and record stores to promote and monitor interest in Energy acts. Call for more details.

TO APPLY

Open to high school grads, undergrads, recent college grads, college grads of any age, and grad students. International applicants eligible. Submit resume and cover letter.

Internship Coordinator
Energy Records
545 Eighth Avenue, 17th Floor
New York, NY 10018
(212) 695-3000
(212) 695-5584 (Fax)
E-mail: energyearec@aol.com

ENTENMANN'S

See Kraft General Foods

ENTERTAINMENT DESIGN/LIGHTING DIMENSIONS

SELECTIVITY 🔍🔍🔍🔍🔍
Approximate applicant pool: 50; Interns accepted: 1

COMPENSATION 💲
$10/hour

LOCATION(S)
New York, NY

FIELD
Magazines

DURATION
8–12 weeks: Summer only

DEADLINE(S)
Rolling

THE WORK
Published by Intertec Publishing Corp., *Entertainment Design* and *Lighting Dimensions* magazines are theatrical trade publications. *ED* specializes in the business of entertainment technology in theatre, film, video, clubs, architecture, theme parks, and concert tours. *Lighting Dimensions* is published for the lighting design professional who works in architecture, film, television, concert tours, and clubs. Etecnyc.net is their web site, featuring articles and information on all aspects of ED/LD and the Lighting Dimensions International Trade Show. Interns work in both Editorial and Advertising departments.

FYI
Writes the internship coordinator: "Interns have the opportunity to research, investigate, and report on selected areas of production techniques, resources, and administration in theater, dance, opera, film, and television, and learn trade magazine marketing methods."

TO APPLY
Open to high school seniors, undergrads, recent college grads, college grads of any age, and grad students. Submit resume, cover letter, and recommendations.

Internship Coordinator
Intertec Publishing
32 West 18th Street
New York, NY 10011-4612
(212) 229-2084 (Fax, no calls please)

ENTERTAINMENT WEEKLY

Entertainment WEEKLY

SELECTIVITY 🔍🔍🔍🔍🔍
Approximate applicant pool: 400; Interns accepted: 4 per session (3 sessions/year)

COMPENSATION 💲💲
$8/hour and overtime

LOCATION(S)
New York, NY

FIELD
Magazines

DURATION
12–18 weeks: Summer, Fall, Spring

DEADLINE(S)
Summer: February 15; Fall: June 1 ; Spring: October 15

THE WORK
Established in 1990, *Entertainment Weekly* (EW) is a magazine providing "an informative, inside look at the people, motives, and ideas that shape the increasingly influential world of entertainment." Each month, EW provides readers with over 250 reviews on movies, television, music, and video. Interns work in Editorial, Photo, and Design.

PERKS
Occasional movie passes; summer softball league.

FYI
In existence since 1991, the internship program counts among its alumni James Earl Hardy, author of *Ringmaster* and *B-Boy Blues* . . . Proclaims the internship coordinator: "We love our interns to death!"

TO APPLY
Open to college juniors and seniors and students who have received their degrees in the past 12 months. Submit resume, cover letter, and, three to four writing samples, preferably published clips.

Internship Coordinator
Entertainment Weekly
1675 Broadway
New York, NY 10019
(212) 522-5600
(212) 522-6104 (Fax)

THE ENVIRONMENTAL CAREERS ORGANIZATION

SELECTIVITY 🔍🔍🔍🔍🔍
Approximate applicant pool: 30,000; Interns accepted: 600

COMPENSATION 💲💲💲
$400–$600/week

LOCATION(S)
Nationwide (see Appendix)

FIELD
Environment

DURATION
12 weeks–2 years: Year-round

DEADLINE(S)
Rolling

THE WORK
In 1972, the Environmental Careers Organization (ECO) was founded to "protect and enhance the environment through the development of professionals, the promotion of careers, and the inspiration of individual action. Interns may apply to one of two programs: Diversity Initiative (DI) and Environmental Placement Services (EPS).

EXCLUSIVE INTERVIEW WITH HAROLD PRINCE

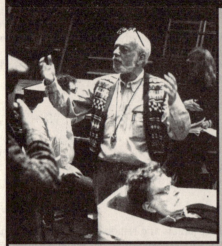

Harold Prince has directed and/or produced over 50 musicals, plays, and operas throughout the world, including The Phantom of the Opera, Show Boat, Kiss of the Spider Woman, Evita, Candide, Follies, Fiddler on the Roof, Madama Butterfly, Damn Yankees, *and* West Side Story. *He has won 19 Tony Awards and was a 1994 Kennedy Center Honoree. In 1948, after graduating from the University of Pennsylvania, Prince worked as an intern for the late George Abbott—the legendary Broadway director whose 75-year career produced such hits as* Three Men on a Horse, Boy Meets Girl, Room Service, *and* On Your Toes.

The Internship Informants: How did you get the internship with Abbott and what was it like meeting him?
Prince: I was actually hired by someone else to be an office boy. It was very informal, unpaid…I ran the plug-in telephone, filled the water cooler, opened the windows, that sort of stuff. I met him a couple weeks into the internship. He was a towering figure, both by reputation and physically. He was a big, tall, very imposing man. He very quickly took a liking to me, and after about four months, he began to pay me $25 a week to cover subways and lunches.

The Internship Informants: Then he later hired you to work backstage?
Prince: After about six months, I replaced the assistant stage manager on *Touch and Go*, a revue written by Jean and Walter Kerr, for which I got paid $75 a week. Technically, I was still an intern, because I continued to work days in the Abbott office, observing Abbott casting, Abbott working with designers, and ultimately, Abbott in rehearsal.

The Internship Informants: It sounds like the internship sparked your interest in the theater.
Prince: Actually, I was interested in theater from the age of eight on. Theater is an escapist pursuit for many of the people who choose to make a life in it. As a kid, I would go to theater with my parents every Saturday…I had a puppet stage at home, and I used these pin figures I bought at the five-and-dime, and I would make up plays, all for myself. [Directing] is very much a loner's pursuit. You put your life very much into imagination and fantasy. Scratch the surface of any actor, playwright, or director, and you're likely to find a lonely kid with a toy stage somewhere.

The Internship Informants: But the internship did give you some confidence to actually give directing a try.
Prince: Yes. [Abbott] encouraged me to make a career in it, registered intelligent responses to the work I was doing, and sort of put a guiding arm around me. The imprimatur of somebody very successful, celebrated, and—much more importantly—qualified is a thing a young person needs. You're scared to death, and at the same time, eager to venture forth. You need the encouragement of somebody whose opinion you really respect.…These days, there's not a lot of encouragement out there for people who are ambitious and striving. And because there's a lot of competition, you're more likely to be discouraged then encouraged. So all you really need is one formidable, qualified human being to say, "you're good, go for it," and I found that person.

The Internship Informants: Are you that kind of person with your own interns?
Prince: Once I was established enough to arrange internships on each show I did, I hired people to get coffee or take notes or make phone calls. But then it became more structured, and I started accepting letters from interested people.… Now I think I provide a good mentoring experience. I'm anxious to repay what was so generously given to me, but also, the theater is not the healthy place it used to be. There used to be 30 directors, dozens of playwrights, and a dozen production companies working all the time. Now, there are very few people who work regularly—maybe only 5 percent of what used to be there. So I feel an obligation to expose people to the experience.

The Internship Informants: Have any of your past interns become really successful?
Prince: Andy Cadiff was an apprentice on *On The Twentieth Century*, a show I directed. He turned out to be so good that when we released a stage manager, we put Andy in and gave him a salary, which is exactly what had happened to me all those years earlier. Andy is now director and producer for *Home Improvement*, a top television show. Luke Yankee is another. He apprenticed for me… He's now the managing director of the Long Beach Theater, a 3,000-seat theater in Long Beach, California.

The Internship Informants: Do you think that internships are as important now as ever?
Prince: I'm absolutely convinced that it's harder now to make a career, not just in the theater but almost anywhere. It's almost as if the world is that much larger, and the whole intrusion of computerization has, in a terrible, soulless way, made [getting a job] that much more competitive.… If you can somehow work for someone who is truly qualified, from whom you can really learn, and if you can … afford to work, at first, without a salary for that person, then you're way ahead. But most kids can't do that. I was lucky that my parents backed me. Most kids have to work as unpaid interns and juggle several jobs, like waiting tables. But if you want to make it, I'm afraid that that's what you have to do.

PERKS
Social events; *Connections* magazine; networking opportunities.

FYI
ECO's main business is finding and creating environmental internships . . . The program has nearly 7,000 alumni . . . Says ECO president John Cook, "We're specialized . . . We can place a student who wants to work in wetlands ecology with a position in wetlands ecology." . . . Over half of all interns work for local, state, and federal agencies.

TO APPLY
All internships are posted on ECO's website at www.eco.org. DI: open to minority undergrads, recent grads, grad students. EPS: open to college juniors and seniors, grad students, college grads any age.

The Environmental Careers Organization
179 South Street
Boston, MA 02111
(617) 426-4375
(617) 423-0998 (Fax)
www.eco.org

EPIC RECORDS

See Sony Music Entertainment

ERNST &° YOUNG

SELECTIVITY   N/A
Approximate applicant pool: N/A; Interns accepted: 300–400

COMPENSATION $ $ $ $
$400–$550/week for undergrads; $550–$700/week for grad students

LOCATION(S)
US: 101 cities in 37 states, DC, Puerto Rico, and Virgin Islands; Overseas: major cities in Argentina, Australia, Austria, Belgium, Brazil, Canada, China, Denmark, Egypt, England, Finland, France, Germany, Greece, Hong Kong, India, Italy, the Netherlands, New Zealand, Norway, Poland, Portugal, Russia, Saudi Arabia, South Africa, Spain, Sweden, Switzerland

FIELD
Accounting; Management consulting

DURATION
10–12 weeks: Summer

DEADLINE(S)
January 15

THE WORK
With 64,000 employees in over 120 countries, Ernst & Young (E & Y) is one of the world's largest accounting and management consulting firms. Generating over $6 billion in annual revenues, E & Y assists corporations with preparing corporate tax returns and annual reports, improving business operations, and utilizing information technology more effectively. Clients include American Express, Time Warner, Mobil, McDonald's, Reebok, Coca-Cola, Harley-Davidson, the PGA Tour, and Silicon Graphics. Interns work in Audit and Tax and in Management Consulting Groups (e.g., Human Resources, Performance Improvement, Information Technology).

PERKS
Development seminars; mentors; organized social activities (e.g., trips to sporting events, concerts, dinners).

FYI
E & Y's internship program is a major source for hiring entry-level accountants and consultants—an estimated 50 percent of all interns are hired for full-time positions.

TO APPLY
Open to college seniors as well as grad students. Must be fluent in local language. International applicants eligible. Submit resume and cover letter directly to office of interest. Contact NY headquarters for addresses and phone numbers.

Campus Recruiting
Ernst & Young
(212) 773-3000

ESPN

SELECTIVITY   🔍 🔍 🔍 🔍 🔍
Approximate applicant pool: 1,500; Interns accepted: 15 Spring, 35 Summer, 15 Fall

COMPENSATION $ $
$7/hour undergrad; $9/hour grad

LOCATION(S)
Bristol, CT; New York, NY

FIELD
Television; Sports

DURATION
12 weeks: Summer, Fall, Spring

DEADLINE(S)
Summer: March 1; Fall and Spring: Rolling

THE WORK
A subsidiary of Disney Capital Cities/ABC, ESPN comprises eight distinct businesses: ESPN, a 24-hour sports channel and America's largest cable television network; ESPN2, a sports channel aimed at 18-34 year olds; ESPN International, broadcasting ESPN in 120 countries; ESPN Radio Network, delivered to over 275 radio stations; ESPN Enterprises, offering pay-per-view services, online sports services, and video games; OCC and Creative Sports, two television sports production companies; and Sportsticker, a sports wire service. Interns work in CT, and NY in Production, Programming, Broadcast Promotions, Communications sales and Marketing.

PERKS
Mentors; intern party; discount on ESPN paraphernalia; networking factor.

FYI
ESPN's internship program places students in one of the company's businesses: ESPN, ESPN2, ESPN Radio, ESPN Classic, ESPN .Com, and Administrative Services. . . Founded in 1979, ESPN reaches over 60 million households in the US and televises coverage of 65 sports . . . Says the internship coordinator: "[Interns] participate in entry-level responsibilities, learning about the cable television industry first-hand."

CELEBRITY OFFSPRING WHO HAVE UNDERTAKEN INTERNSHIPS

Name	Relation	Where and When Interned
Billy Boesky	*Son of convicted inside trader Ivan Boesky*	*Late Night with David Letterman*
Adam Clayton Powell IV	*Son of former Cong. Adam Clayton Powell, Jr.*	Rep. Charles Rangel, D-NY (Summer 1981)
Jim Cooper	*Son of former Tenn. Gov. Prentice Cooper*	Former Sen. Jim Sasser, D-TN (1980)
David Eisenhower	*Grandson of Pres. Dwight D. Eisenhower*	Washington Senators baseball team (Summer 1970)
Catherine Forbes	*Daughter of Forbes pres. Malcolm Forbes, Jr.*	American Enterprise Institute (Winter 1994)
Victoria Gifford	*Daughter of NY Giants great Frank Gifford*	Sen. Edward M. Kennedy, D-MA (late 1970s)
Karenna Gore	*Daughter of Tipper and VP Al Gore*	environmental org. in Chile (Summer 1993) & Memphis's WREG-TV (Summer 1994)
Marin Hopper	*Daughter of actor Dennis Hopper*	*Mirabella*
Karis Jagger	*Daughter of Rolling Stones' Mick Jagger*	*The Young Indiana Jones* TV show (Summer 1990)
Holly Kirkland	*Daughter of AFL-CIO head Lane Kirkland*	AFL-CIO headquarters (Summer 1974)
Gwynneth Paltrow	*Daughter of actress Blythe Danner*	Williamstown Theatre Festival (Summer 1994)
Jennifer Philbin	*Daughter of talk-show host Regis Philbin*	*Seventeen Magazine*
Melissa Rivers	*Daughter of comedienne Joan Rivers*	CBS News and *Rescue 911* TV show
Meile Rockefeller	*Granddaughter of former VP Nelson Rockefeller*	Battery Park City Authority (Summer, mid-1970s)
Tracee Ross	*Daughter of singer Diana Ross*	*Mirabella* (Summer, 1994)
P.D. Tyrrell	*Son of American Spectator founder R. Emmett Tyrrell*	*American Spectator* (Summer 1994)

TO APPLY

Open to undergrads. International applicants eligible. Submit resume and cover letter.

Internship Coordinator
Human Resources Department
ESPN
ESPN Plaza
Bristol, CT 06010-9454
No phone calls please

ESSENCE

ESSENCE.

SELECTIVITY 🔍🔍🔍
Approximate applicant pool: 50; Interns accepted: 8

COMPENSATION 💲💲
$275/week

LOCATION(S)
New York, NY

FIELD
Magazines

DURATION
6 weeks: Summer

DEADLINE(S)
November 30

THE WORK

Founded in 1970, *Essence* is the nation's pre-eminent magazine for black women. With a circulation exceeding 1 million readers, *Essence* covers contemporary issues, fashion and cultural trends, and profiles of accomplished African Americans; it also markets *Essence*-brand eyeglasses, hosiery, and fabric patterns. Interns work in Editorial, Research, Fields Promotion, and Advertising.

PERKS

Outings to other publishing businesses; talks with department heads.

FYI

Writes *The New York Times*: "Essence has built a kind of cult following, not only among blacks but among people who deal with the extraordinary problems faced by many black women."

TO APPLY

Open to college juniors and seniors. International applicants eligible. Submit resume, cover letter, and writing samples.

Essence Internship Coordinator
1500 Broadway, Suite 600
New York, NY 10036
(212) 642–0700
(212) 921-5173 (Fax)

 ucia A. Noto, Chairman and CEO of Mobil Corp., started at Mobil as a summer intern in 1961 after his first year at Cornell University's business school.

EVERGLADES NATIONAL PARK

See National Park Service

EXXON

SELECTIVITY 🔍🔍🔍🔍
Approximate applicant pool: 2,500; Interns accepted: 300

COMPENSATION 💲💲💲💲
Compensation is competitive; Round-trip travel; Interim (1 week) living expenses

LOCATION(S)
Baton Rouge, New Orleans, LA; Florham Park, NJ; and Baytown, Houston, TX

FIELD
Oil and gas; Chemicals

DURATION
Interns: 10–14 weeks, Summer

DEADLINE(S)
Rolling (until on-campus interviews in October and November)

THE WORK

Dating back to 1882, Exxon is one of the world's largest oil and gas companies, engaged in the exploration, production, transportation, and sale of crude oil, natural gas, chemicals, coal, copper, minerals, and petroleum products. Employing nearly 79,000 people in more than 100 countries, Exxon generates annual revenues in excess of $130 billion. Summer interns work in Production, Refining, Chemicals, Research & Engineering, Office of Controllers, Accounting, and MIS.

PERKS
Exxon-organized social activities

TO APPLY

Open to college juniors as well as grad students. Most internships are filled through on-campus interviews. Resumes may be mailed to:

Campus Recruiting
Exxon
P.O. Box 2180
Houston, TX 77252-2180
(713) 656-3636

FABER AND FABER

SELECTIVITY 🔍🔍🔍
Approximate applicant pool: 40; Interns accepted: 4

COMPENSATION 💲
None

LOCATION(S)
Winchester, MA

FIELD
Publishing

DURATION
10–16 weeks: Summer, Fall, Spring, Winter

DEADLINE(S)
Rolling

THE WORK
A subsidiary of England's Faber and Faber, Ltd., Faber and Faber is a small trade publisher located 7 miles north of Boston. Its catalog of fiction and nonfiction titles include *Duplex Planet*, edited by David Greenberger, *Living with the Animals*, edited by Gary Indiana, and *The Gutenberg Elegies* by Sven Birkerts. Interns work in either Editorial or Marketing. Please state preference.

PERKS
Free books; flexible hours; small office.

FYI
Fifty percent of entry-level hirings come from past or present interns.

TO APPLY
Open to undergrads and grads. Submit resume, cover letter, and writing sample.

Internship Coordinator
Faber and Faber
53 Shore Rd.
Winchester, MA 01890
(781) 721-1427
(781) 729-2783 (Fax)

FACE THE NATION

See CBS News

FAIR (FAIRNESS AND ACCURACY IN REPORTING)

FAIR

SELECTIVITY
Approximate size of applicant pool: N/A; Interns accepted: N/A

COMPENSATION 🅂
None

LOCATION(S)
New York, NY

FIELD
Media

DURATION
8–12 weeks (varies with length of student's semester and summer vacation): Summer, Fall, Winter, Spring

DEADLINE(S)
Rolling

> "I did research for a big piece on 'The 100 Best Bars in the Country.'"
> —Jodie Foster, on her internship at *Esquire* magazine

THE WORK
FAIR is a media-watch group that attempts to correct bias in the media. FAIR advocates for greater media pluralism and against the narrow, corporate ownership of the press. Interns commonly do research, proofreading, fact checking, media monitoring, and administrative tasks. Interns must work a minimum of twelve hours per week during the school year, and twenty-five hours per week during the summer.

PERKS
Possible recognition in FAIR's magazine; FAIR gives its full cooperation to students who wish to obtain college credit for their work.

FYI
FAIR's magazine—*Extra!*—and their nationally syndicated radio program—CounterSpin—are produced without funds from corporate sponsors.

TO APPLY
College students should write for an application.

FAIR
Attn: Peter Hart
130 W. 25th Street
New York, NY 10001

FAMILIES USA FOUNDATION

SELECTIVITY
Approximate applicant pool: 500; Interns accepted: 18

COMPENSATION 🅂
$400/week

LOCATION(S)
Washington, DC

FIELD
Health care; Public policy

DURATION
10–20 weeks: Summer, Fall, Spring

DEADLINE(S)
Rolling

Renowned fashion designer **Diane Von Fürstenberg** owes her start to an apprenticeship she served in 1969 with Italian textile manufacturer Angelo Ferretti. Spending three months learning every aspect of dress making from Ferretti, Von Fürstenberg gained the confidence to begin her own line of dresses, which she would eventually parlay into a clothing empire.

THE WORK

A national consumer group founded in 1982, Families USA Foundation (FUSA) works to achieve affordable health and long term care for all American families. "Wield[ing] extraordinary influence in national health-care debate," according to *The Wall Street Journal*, FUSA engages in public education, policy research, organizing at state and local levels, and advocacy. Internships now include health policy and government affairs (in addition to media and field departments).

PERKS

Attendance welcome at all staff meetings and select client meetings; field trips to Washington agencies, newspapers, and attractions; visits to Capitol Hill hearings; access to all staff, including executive director.

FYI

In existence since 1994, the internship program counts among its alumni a current policy analyst . . . Says one former intern: "The internship program is designed to train and motivate the public advocates and activists of the future."

TO APPLY

Submit resume, cover letter, three to five-page writing sample, and three references. (Academic transcript no longer required.)

Internship Coordinator
Families USA Fondation
1334 G Street NW
Washington, DC 20005
(202) 628-3030
(202) 347-2417 (Fax)
E-mail: info@familiesusa.org

FANTAGRAPHICS BOOKS

SELECTIVITY
Approximate applicant pool: 100; Interns accepted: 2–3

COMPENSATION
None

LOCATION(S)
Seattle, WA

FIELD
Comics

BOOKLETS FOR BUDDING JOURNALISTS

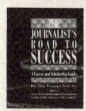 

The Dow Jones Newspaper Fund publishes two guides for aspiring journalists: *Newspapers, Diversity, and You* (for minorities, free of charge) and *The Journalists' Road to Success* ($3). Both provide information on careers, graduate schools, training programs, grants, scholarships, and internships (for undergrads and grad students) in journalism and communications. They may be ordered by calling 1-800-DOW-FUND.

It was sometime in April 1983, and actress **Brooke Shields** was on the phone with her good friend Joan Embery. The high school senior was wondering whether Embery, the San Diego Zoo's goodwill ambassador, could arrange an internship for her at the Zoo. "We had worked together on a couple of TV shows before," Shields told us, "and she said to me that if I ever needed work, she would get me a position." Shields started the first week of May, working primarily with primates in the Zoo's nursery. "I would get up in the dark and drive an hour from La Jolla," Shields explained. "My day would start at 6 am and end at 3 pm, and I would clean cages and pens, cut up fruits and vegetables for the animals, prepare bottles, and assist the doctors in emergencies." Feeding times fell every hour, but because each animal had a different feeding schedule, Shields "was feeding [the animals] every 15 minutes. It was messy and a lot of hard work."

Even draped in a khaki, mud-stained Zoo uniform, Brooke Shields was still, well, Brooke Shields. Did her presence at the Zoo cause a commotion? Employees at the time reported that after Shields threw away three of the four shots that the Zoo took for her i.d. badge, a few office workers immediately retrieved the photos from the waste basket and asked her to autograph them. The actress obliged. Despite all the attention, Shields says, she remained focused on deepening her knowledge of animals, "which have always been [her] escape." At least one person—friend Embery—noticed. "Her attitude was wonderful," Embery told us. "She didn't come in as a know-it-all or expecting to be treated any differently . . . I remember she worked very hard, and I was impressed and pleased . . . with how much effort she put into it."

DURATION
10 weeks: Summer, Fall, Spring

DEADLINE(S)
Rolling

THE WORK

Founded in 1976, Fantagraphics Books publishes underground comic books, book collections of classic comic strips, and a trade magazine of comic news and criticism, *The Comics Journal*. Its roster of over twenty underground comic book titles includes the well-regarded *Love and Rockets*, *Jim*, and *Omaha the Cat Dancer*. Interns work in Editorial (*Comics Journal* only), Production, and Marketing/Promotions.

PERKS

Free comic books; employee discount on books and memorabilia; casual work environment.

Dressing for the Job Interview

According to behavioral scientists, people's impressions of one another are based 60 percent on appearance, 33 percent on speaking style, and 7 percent on content. So no matter what your age, says career and image consultant Camille Lavington, you must be dressed and groomed impeccably for the interview. "You're either well-groomed or you're not," she explains. "There's no excuse for being naive and unpolished." This is true, she adds, whether you're interviewing with a Fortune 500 company or a small nonprofit. To maximize your appearance in formal interviews, Ms. Lavington offers the following recommendations.

MEN

Do's

Hair
Short sideburns and haircut

Shirts
White shirt, stiff collar

Neckties
Small, repeating, geometric patterns

Suspenders or belts
Understated, but never wear both
No flashy belt buckles

Pocket squares (optional)
White or complementary to suit or tie

Suits
Single-breasted (CL: "Double-breasted is fine if you're tall and slender")
Solid or pin-stripe
Navy blue or gray

Socks
Calf-high

Shoes
Black or cordovan lace-ups or tasseled loafers (CL: "Be sure they're polished")

Dont's

Hair
Long hair, beards, moustaches
The exception: artistic or creative fields (CL: "Only those people who are on the leading edge of the music industry or the creative arts should flaunt ... a more fashion-forward look")

Shirts
Bright collars
Button-down collar (CL: "A button-down always looks sloppy with a necktie")

Neckties
Loud or bold patterns (CL: "It's dangerous stuff to try to call attention to your necktie instead of your brains")
The exception: artistic or creative fields (CL: "Then you can be a little more flamboyant")

Suits
Bold patterns like plaid or houndstooth check
Bright colors

Socks
Ankle-length

Shoes
Penny loafers

Fragrance
Musk

WOMEN

Do's

Hair
At or above the collar; longer hair should be put in a chignon

Jewelry (optional)
Button earrings, simple watch or bracelet

Suits
Single color, skirts no higher than knee-length

Dresses
One-piece (CL: "You can accessorize it with either a pin or a necklace or a scarf but not all three— just one of those things")

Makeup
Natural looking, subtle

Nails
Clear or light-colored polish

Fragrance
Minimum or none

Hosiery
Milky or semi-opaque (CL: "Like the male, you want the leg covered")

Shoes
Low-heeled pumps

Dont's

Hair
Ponytails (CL: "OK, but it suggests that you're an ingénue"), Big hair

Jewelry
Tear-drop earrings, dangling bracelets (CL: "Anything that moves is distracting")
More than one ring per hand

Blouses
Revealing necklines (Adds CL: "The blouse collar should not come out over the collar of the suit unless it has exactly the same structural design line")

Suits
Blazer jackets, short skirts (CL: "Try not to cross your legs during an interview. Keep both feet flat on the floor and in a parallel line")

Dresses
Prints, stripes, plaids; sheer, see-through fabrics

Nails
Long talons; bright polish

Makeup
Heavy eye makeup

Hosiery
Clear or bright colors

Shoes
High heels

FYI

Alumni of the ten-year-old program include the internship coordinator, the production manager, and the editor . . . Says the internship coordinator: "Fantagraphics offers a healthy alternative to corporate America, stressing artistic integrity over commercial success. The relative smallness of our company ensures more hands-on experience in the publishing industry than larger companies can offer."

TO APPLY

Open to undergrads, recent college grads, college grads of any age, and grad students. Submit resume and cover letter ("indicate familiarity and/or interest in alternative media").

Internship Coordinator
Fantagraphics Books
7563 Lake City Way NE
Seattle, WA 98115
(206) 524–1967
(206) 524–2104 (Fax)

FARM SANCTUARY

SELECTIVITY
Approximate applicant pool: 200; Interns accepted: 70

COMPENSATION
Free housing

LOCATION(S)
Orland, CA; Watkins Glen, NY

FIELD
Agriculture; Animal rights

DURATION
4–12 weeks: ongoing

DEADLINE(S)
Rolling

THE WORK

Founded in 1986, Farm Sanctuary is a national, nonprofit organization dedicated to ending farm animal abuse. Operating a 175-acre farm in New York and a 300-acre farm in California, the sanctuary provides care and shelter for hundreds of abused and neglected farm animals. It also runs educational programs promoting the protection of farm animals and initiates investigative, legal, and legislative campaigns to prevent cruelty to farm animals. Interns are involved in all aspects of the farms' work, from feeding animals to performing office duties to conducting educational tours.

PERKS

Twenty-four hour access to kitchen facilities; weekly grocery trip for interns without transportation.

FYI

The animals sheltered by the sanctuary range from veal calves to turkeys . . . According to the internship bulletin: "Since the Sanctuaries are volunteer-based shelters, the interns are a vital

part of this important work and directly contribute to our efforts to stop farm animal abuse. Sanctuary interns literally save lives, and teach hundreds of people that farm animals are animals too."

TO APPLY

Open to high school students age 16 and up, undergrads, and grad students. Must "have a personal commitment to vegetarianism." International applicants eligible. Write for application.

Internship Coordinator   *Internship Coordinator*
Farm Sanctuary   *Farm Sanctuary*
P.O. Box 1065   *P.O. Box 150*
Orland, CA 95963   *Watkins Glen, NY 14891*
(530) 865–4617   *(607) 583–2225*

> "Imagine waking up each morning to the sound of roosters crowing back and forth between the barn and the chicken house just a few yards from where you are lying in your trailer. Imagine it's time to fling on your bathrobe, steal out into the cool morning air and unlatch the barn doors so that the farm animals—tucked inside by you the night before—can come outside and start to enjoy their day. A pastoral fantasy, you say? Not unless I dreamed the five weeks I spent last summer working as a volunteer intern at the unique haven for farm animals . . . called the Farm Sanctuary."
>
> —Karen Davis, former intern, Farm Sanctuary

FARRAR STRAUS & GIROUX

SELECTIVITY   N/A
Varies

COMPENSATION
None

LOCATION(S)
New York, NY

FIELD
Publishing

DURATION
Varied periods, 4-week winter-break positions sometimes available

DEADLINE(S)
Rolling

THE WORK

A small but distinguished publishing house owned by the German publisher Holtzbrinck, Farrar Straus & Giroux (FSG) publishes fiction, nonfiction, and children's books. Its well-regarded catalog includes books by Tom Wolfe, Scott Turow, and Jamaica Kincaid. Interns work in various departments according to their needs.

PERKS

Free books on occasion; informal, noncorporate office atmosphere.

FYI

FSG has been accepting interns since the mid-1970s . . . Says a former intern: "You really sense here that [FSG] is committed to publishing works of quality, not just those of mass-market appeal."

TO APPLY

Open to undergraduates, recent college grads, and grad students. International applicants eligible. Submit resume and call for appointment.

Internship Coordinator–Peggy Miller
Farrar Straus & Giroux
19 Union Square West
New York, NY 10003
(212) 741–6900

The publishing house Farrar Straus & Giroux owes much to the influence of co-founder **Roger W. Straus, Jr.,** (left) whose commitment to publishing books of the highest quality has helped make FSG a publisher of worldwide repute. The seed of Straus's literary interest was planted when he spent the summer of 1932 as a copyboy with the *Daily Reporter* in White Plains, New York. Here he hugs Nobel Prize-winning poet Joseph Brodsky.

FEDERAL BUREAU OF INVESTIGATION

SELECTIVITY
Approximate applicant pool: 2,000; Interns accepted: 75–100

COMPENSATION
$390/week

LOCATION(S)
Washington, DC; Quantico, VA

FIELD
Domestic intelligence; Criminal investigation

DURATION
10 weeks: Summer (June–August)

DEADLINE(S)
November 1

THE WORK

Since its founding in 1908, the FBI has been tracking down and arresting criminals, including guys Al Capone, Pretty Boy Floyd, Baby Fa Machine Gun Kelly. Today the men and women FBI still hold the lofty ideal emblazoned on the Bravery, and Integrity—to lead them in their mission. work in units such as Behavioral Science Services, Criminal Informant, Accounting and Budget Analysis, Legal Forfeiture, European/Asian/Money Laudering, Undercover and Sensitive Operations, and Audit.

PERKS

Lunch with FBI director; firearms training; field trips.

FYI

The FBI Honors Internship Program was started in 1985 . . . Interns whose hearts are set on brandishing a gun receive a half-day of firearms training . . . At the end of the summer, interns pose for a photograph with the FBI director and are given this with a yearbook and a certificate.

TO APPLY

Open to college juniors, grad students. A minimum 3.0 GPA and US citizenship are required. Candidates undergo a background check. Write for application. For more information, contact the FBI office nearest your school.

Jobs hotline: (202) 324-3674

FEDERAL BUREAU OF PRISONS

SELECTIVITY
Approximate applicant pool: 400; Interns accepted: 120

COMPENSATION
Discounted meals at some locations

LOCATION(S)
All 50 states

FIELD
Corrections

DURATION
12 weeks–6 months: ongoing

DEADLINE(S)
Rolling

THE WORK

Founded in 1930, the Federal Bureau of Prisons (FBP) operates federally sponsored correctional facilities across the country. Under its jurisdiction are over 85 penitentiaries and detention centers as well as over 250 contract halfway houses. Assigned to the DC administrative headquarters or directly to a FBP facility, interns work in such departments as Community Corrections, General Counsel (Legal), Public Affairs, Health Services, Administration, Program Development, Human Resources, and Program Review.

PERKS

Brown-bag lunches with executives (DC); tours (DC); other perks vary with placement.

FYI

Says the internship coordinator: "Internships truly count towards employment here. We document all internship experiences, and we consider them as valuable as regular work experi-

...hen we hire permanent employees.". . . The FBP's famous
...rectional facilities include US Penitentiary Leavenworth in
...nsas, US Penitentiary Marion in Illinois, and the US Penitentiary
...n Atlanta.

TO APPLY
Open to high school students age 16 and older, undergrads, grads, grad students. Submit resume and cover letter. Applicants interested in working at a FBP facility must apply to the DC headquarters.

Internship Coordinator
Federal Bureau of Prisons
National Office of Citizen Participation
320 First Street NW
Washington, DC
(202) 307–3998
(202) 514–7940 (Fax)

FEDERAL EMERGENCY MANAGEMENT AGENCY

SELECTIVITY 🔍 🔍 🔍 🔍

COMPENSATION 💲 💲 💲 💲

LOCATION
Summer in Washington, D.C. followed by two semesters of research in city chosen by FEMA

DURATION
Summer, Fall academic semester, Spring academic semester

DEADLINES:
January 10

THE WORK
Though FEMA's name might make you think this Federal agency only manages disasters, the agency's Hazard Mitigation Directorate tries to prevent them, too. Hazard Mitigation specialists study the damage that potential earthquakes, floods or other natural disasters can wreak and then make recommendations on land use, construction techniques, and building designs. FEMA's Hazard Mitigation Planning Fellowship is an effort to integrate the lessons of hazard mitigation into the broader, more traditional fields. Fellows will work in Washington during the summer, preparing for a two-day workshop they will host for a selected community in America. Over the next two semesters, the fellows continue to work with FEMA and the selected community on hazard mitigation projects.

THE PERKS
Each fellow is paid at least $25,000 ($6,600 salary during the summer, $3,000 for summer lodging expenses, $6,000 in tuition and fees over two semesters , and a $9,400 stipend over the two semesters).

FYI
Forms of hazard mitigation can include sound land-use management based on known natural threats, purchase of flood insurance, moving out of floodplains, installing hurricane straps between house roofs and walls, and developing and enforcing effective building codes.

TO APPLY
FEMA picks two (2) Hazard Mitigation fellows, who must have finished at least one year of grad school and completed most of their core courses in urban, regional, or environmental planning. Applicants must be U.S. citizens or permanent residents who plan on receiving no other forms of financial aid during the school year, except for GI Bill benefits. Applicants must include an application form, academic transcripts for their graduate work and last two undergraduate years, a personal statement, and a faculty recommendation letter.

For more information, check the FEMA website at www.fema.gov or write:
Thomas Hollenbach
National Institute of Building Sciences
Mulithazard Mitigation Council
1090 Vermont Avenue NW, Suite 700
Washington, DC 20005-4905
Email: thollenbach@nibs.org
202-289-7800, ext. 131

FEDERAL RESERVE BANK OF NEW YORK

SELECTIVITY 🔍 🔍 🔍 🔍 🔍
Approximate applicant pool: 900; Interns accepted: 12

COMPENSATION 💲
Varies

LOCATION(S)
New York, NY

DURATION
10–12 weeks: Summer

FIELD
Banking

DEADLINE(S)
January 31

THE WORK
The Federal Reserve Bank of New York (FRB-NY) is one of twelve branches of the Federal Reserve System (FRS), which also includes the Federal Reserve Board in Washington, DC. The Reserve Banks act collectively to regulate and supervise the US banking system. Because of its location in the world's financial center, FRB-NY also implements US monetary policy, buys and sells foreign currencies for the US Treasury and FRS, and stores 25 percent of the free world's official gold reserves. Interns work in Research, Bank Supervision, and Systems Development.

PERKS
Weekly seminars/luncheons with bank executives; workshops on resume writing and interviewing techniques; field trips to FRB-NY operations centers; tour of New York Stock Exchange.

FYI
The internship program was started in 1988, and an impressive 50 percent of interns are hired for full-time positions.

TO APPLY
Open to high school students from the New York area, college seniors, and grad students. Submit resume, cover letter, transcript, and writing samples.

Internship Coordinator
Federal Reserve Bank of New York
59 Maiden Lane, 39th Floor
New York, NY 10038
(212) 720–6922

FEDERAL RESERVE BOARD

SELECTIVITY 🔍 🔍 🔍 🔍
Approximate applicant pool: 400; Interns accepted: 25

COMPENSATION 💲
$300/week for high school students; $300–$425/week for undergrads;
$550–$700/week for grad students; some positions unpaid

LOCATION(S)
Washington, DC

FIELD
Banking

DURATION
12 weeks: Summer, Fall, Spring

DEADLINE(S)
Summer: March 15; Academic year: rolling

THE WORK
Established in 1913 as an independent agency, the Federal Reserve Board holds sole power to set US monetary policy. Its duties include supervising the twelve Federal Reserve Banks, setting stock market margin requirements, and protecting consumers' rights in borrowing transactions. Interns, including those in a Minority Cooperative Education Program, work in Research & Statistics, Monetary Affairs, International Finance, Banking Supervision & Regulation, Information Resources Management, and Legal.

PERKS
Weekly seminars and conferences; subsidized cafeteria; access to on-site gym.

FYI
Alumni of the 50-year-old internship program include over 250 current employees . . . Approximately 30 percent of interns come back to the board as permanent employees.

TO APPLY
Open to high school students, undergrads, and grad students. International applicants eligible. Write for application.

Board of Governors of the Federal Reserve System
20th and Constitution NW
Division of Human Resources Management
Stop #129
Washington, DC 20551
(800) 448–4894 or (202) 452–3038

FELLOWSHIP OF RECONCILIATION

SELECTIVITY 🔍 🔍 🔍 🔍
Approximate applicant pool: 50; Interns accepted: 4

COMPENSATION 💲
NY: $650/month, 4 weeks paid vacation, free housing; health insurance;
Overseas: none

LOCATION(S)
Nyack, NY (US HQ); Argentina; Bolivia; Brazil; Chile; Colombia; Ecuador; Nicaragua; Panama; Paraguay; Peru; the Netherlands (International HQ)

FIELD
Peace studies

DURATION
NY: 1 year, starting in September; Overseas: 1 month–1 year

DEADLINE(S)
US: March 15; Overseas: rolling

THE WORK
An international, spiritually based movement of people of all religious affiliations, the Fellowship of Reconciliation (FOR) was founded in 1914 to promote nonviolence as a way to effect personal, social, and political change. Offering seminars, conferences, and position papers, FOR's chapters and affiliates in over forty countries seek racial and economic justice, worldwide disarmament, and the growth of the nonviolent activist movement. New York interns work in Programs (including the Racial and Economic Justice program, Youth Nonviolence training program, International/Interfaith program and local group organizing) and in Communications for FOR's bimonthly magazine, *Fellowship*. Interns in the Netherlands work on the publication *RI* (which stands for "Reconciliation International") and the Nonviolence Training and Education Project. Latin American volunteers are placed with organizations that are part of Servicio Paz y Justicia, a network of peace activists, where they write for publications, translate documents, produce radio programs, and teach workshops.

PERKS
Possible travel opportunities to US conferences (NY only); occasional workshops and seminars.

FYI
New York offices and interns' bedrooms are ensconced in a forty room mansion situated on the banks of the Hudson River. The oldest peace organization in the US, FOR worked with Martin Luther King Jr. during the Montgomery bus boycott.

TO APPLY
Open to college grads. Write for application directly to office of interest; contact CA office for Latin American positions.

Voluntarios Solidarios
Task Force on Latin America and the Caribbean
995 Market St., Suite 801
San Francisco, CA 94103
(415) 495–6334
(415) 495–5628 (Fax)
email: For/atom@igo.org

Internship Coordinator	*Internship Coordinator*
Fellowship of Reconciliation	*International Fellowship of Reconciliation*
Box 271	*Spoorstraat 38*
Nyack, NY 10960	*1815 BK Alkmar*
(914) 358–4601	*the Netherlands*
(914) 358–4924 (Fax)	*31–72–123–014*
email: pti@forusa.org	*email: office@ifor.org*

Interns at the Fellowship of Reconciliation live free of charge at Shadowcliff, a 40-room mansion on the banks of the Hudson River.

THE FEMINIST MAJORITY

THE FUND FOR THE
FEMINIST MAJORITY

SELECTIVITY 🔍 🔍 🔍 🔍
Approximate applicant pool: 300; Interns accepted: 20

COMPENSATION 💲
None

LOCATION(S)
Los Angeles, CA; Arlington, VA

FIELD
Women's rights; Think tank

DURATION
Two months minimum: Year-round; Part time available

DEADLINE(S)
Rolling

THE WORK
Founded by TV producer and philanthropist Peg Yorkin and former National Organization for Women president Eleanor "Ellie" Smeal in 1987, the Feminist Majority's purpose was to encourage more women to run for public office. In more recent years it has added to its agenda an Empowering Women campaign, a Rock for Choice project, an abortion clinic defense project, lobbying, and women's rights research. Interns will work on the Feminist Majority's research project that best matches their interests.

PERKS
Substantive projects; lobbying on Capitol Hill (DC).

FYI
Internships have existed since 1987, the Feminist Majority's founding year . . . Most interns are women, but men are welcome, and a few have served as interns . . . In DC, the interns occasionally organize intern lobby days for important legislation . . . The organization is very intimate. "The executive director and the chair of the board were always available if I had questions or needed advice," said an intern.

TO APPLY
Open to high school students, undergrads, and grad students. International applicants eligible. Submit resume, cover letter, and writing sample of two to ten pages (an academic paper is sufficient).

The Feminist Majority
8105 West Third Street, Suite 1
Los Angeles, CA 90048
(213) 651-0495

The Feminist Majority
1600 Wilson Boulevard, Suite 801
Arlington, VA 22209
(703) 522-2214

FENTON COMMUNICATIONS

SELECTIVITY 🔍 🔍 🔍 🔍
Approximate applicant pool: 150–175; Interns accepted: 12–15

COMPENSATION 💲 💲
$200/week

LOCATION(S)
Washington, DC; New York, NY

FIELD
Public relations

DURATION
3 months in the Summer; 4 months in the Fall or Spring

DEADLINE(S)
Summer: February 1; Fall: July 1; Spring: November 1

THE WORK
In operation since 1981, Fenton Communications is a public relations firm committed to representing only clients with "a progressive social perspective." Among its "socially responsible" clients are The Body Shop, the Natural Resources Denfense Council, Rock Against Drugs, and Greenpeace. Interns assist account executives with all aspects of their work, including developing media lists, monitoring media coverage, and distributing press materials.

PERKS
Attendance welcome at press conferences and staff meetings; enables interns to work on media campaigns on a variety of interesting issues.

FYI
Interns go to most staff meetings. They are not included in senior staff meetings. Internship coordinator is willing to send interns copies of the *Washington Post's* classified ads to aid in housing searches.

By turns an engineer, inventor, architect, and philosopher, **Buckminster Fuller** is best known for dreaming up the geodesic dome, a remarkable structure comprised of honeycombed triangles. What most people do not know is that Fuller gained some practical experience in 1914 when he served as an apprentice mechanic at a textile mill in Sherbrooke, Canada.

TO APPLY

Open to undergrads, recent college grads, college grads of any age, and grad students. Minimum GPA: 3.0. Send cover letter with dates of availability and resume.

Internship Coordinator
Fenton Communications
1320 18th Street NW Fifth Floor
Washington, DC 20036
(202) 822–5200
(202) 822–4787 (Fax)
E-mail: fenton@fenton.com

Internship Coordinator
Fenton Communications
260 Fifth Avenue 10th Floor
New York, NY 10001
(212) 584-5000
(212) 584-5045 (Fax)

FIRST BUSINESS

See United States Chamber of Commerce

FISHER-PRICE TOYS

See Mattel Inc.

FLORIDA GRAND OPERA

SELECTIVITY

Approximate applicant pool: 400; Interns accepted: 15

COMPENSATION

$180/week; free housing including electricity; round-trip travel; health insurance

LOCATION(S)

Fort Lauderdale and Miami, FL

FIELD

Opera

DURATION

35 weeks: starts September

DEADLINE(S)

Singers and coach/accompanists: October of preceding year; Technical positions: August 2

THE WORK

The premier opera company in the Southeast, Florida Grand Opera comprises the Greater Miami Opera and Opera Guild of Ft. Lauderdale. Recent productions include *The Barber of Seville*, *Il Trovatore*, and *The Coronation of Poppea*. Accepted to the Opera's Young Studio and Technical Apprentice Program, interns are used as singers, coach/accompanists, or assistants in stage management, properties, costume, and lighting design.

PERKS

Vocal coaching, acting/body movement classes (singers and coach/accompanists); seminars on technical theater, Italian language, etc.

FYI

Applicants interested in singing and coach/accompanists positions must attend an audition; see application for more audition dates and locations.

TO APPLY

Open to college grads. Write for application. Application fee: 25.

Frank Ragsdale
Florida Grand Opera
1200 Coral Way
Miami, FL 33145
(305) 854–1643
(305) 856–1042 (Fax)

FOCUS ON WOMEN

SELECTIVITY

Approximate applicant pool: 8; Interns accepted: 1–2

COMPENSATION

None

LOCATION(S)

Dearborn, MI

FIELD

Women's issues

DURATION

12–17 weeks: Summer, Fall, Winter, Spring

DEADLINE(S)

Rolling

THE WORK

Founded in 1974, Focus on Women Program is an educational center offering courses, noncredit seminars, and special events in women's studies to assist women in setting goals, examining their values, training for careers, and enrolling in degree programs. Located at Dearborn's Henry Ford Community College, the organization also houses books, pamphlets, and journals dealing specifically with women's issues. Interns assist staff with coordinating programs, interviewing clients, and maintaining resource files.

PERKS

Attendance welcome at seminars and luncheons; access to resource files; networking opportunities with sister organizations.

FYI

Focus on Women Program has been using interns since 1988 . . . Says the internship coordinator: "We are an umbrella program designed primarily to assist women to move from dependence to independence, to help them re-enter education or the workforce, and to educate the community on women's issues."

TO APPLY

Open to college juniors and seniors, recent college grads, college grads of any age, and grad students. International applicants eligible. Submit resume and cover letter.

Focus on Women
Henry Ford Community College
5101 Evergreen Road
Deerborn, MI 48128–1495
(313) 845–9629
(313) 845–9852 (Fax)
E-mail: grace@mail.henryford.cc.mi.us

Food for the Hungry

Meeting physical and spiritual needs worldwide

SELECTIVITY
Approximate applicant pool: 150; Interns accepted: 1–25

COMPENSATION
Deputation—raise support through your church, families, and friends

LOCATION(S)
Bangladesh; Bolivia; Brazil; Cambodia; China; Dominican Republic; Guatemala; Japan; Kenya; Laos; Malaysia; Mexico; Mongolia; Myanmar; Nicaragua; Honduras; Peru; Romania; Tajikistan; Uganda; and Uzbekistan.

FIELD
Public service in approximately 10 fields (see THE WORK)

DURATION
2–24 months; 3 years–lifetime

DEADLINE(S)
Rolling

THE WORK
Often described as the "Christian Peace Corps," Food for the Hungry (FH) is a nonprofit relief and development agency founded in 1971 to meet both the physical and spiritual needs of the poorest people in the world. Food for the Hungry promotes "Christ's love" while facilitating emergency relief and community development in over 20 countries worldwide. Community projects focus on agriculture, business, computers, engineering, health care, teaching, water resources and general development.

PERKS
Initial One-Week Training course to be held in Phoenix, AZ five times a year. A follow-up three week training course for individuals who wish to serve longer than one year with Food for the Hungry.

TO APPLY
Open to most individuals who wish to help the physically and spiritually poor overseas. Must be at least 21 years old. For more information, please contact:

Food for the Hungry: Hunger Corps Department
7729 East Greenway Road
Scottsdale, AZ 85260
1-877-780-4261 x208
(602) 998–9448 (Fax)
E-mail: go_now@fh.org
www.fh.org
AOL search keyword:FFH

FONTANA RECORDS

See PolyGram

SELECTIVITY
Approximate applicant pool: 300; Interns accepted: 20–25

COMPENSATION
None

LOCATION(S)
New York, NY

FIELD
Television

DURATION
12–16 weeks: ongoing (Fall, Spring, and Summer)

DEADLINE(S)
Rolling

THE WORK
Launched in November 1993, Food Network is the first and only 24-hour television network devoted to all things related to food, cooking and entertainment. Food Network is one of the world's leading resources on food and nutrition, with lifestyle programming that covers everything from gourmet dishes and healthy diet, to quick weeknight meals and wine selection. Food Network's internship program allows students to see what goes on behind the scenes. Interns spend the semester in a particular department of interest and are able to explore other areas of the company. Activities and programs are held throughout the semester. Internships are available in the following departments: Advertising Sales, Chef Events, Creative Services, Marketing/PR, Studio Operations, Programming, Production, and New Media. Bring an appetite!

PERKS
Opportunity to meet celebrities, on-air talent, and famous chefs; free recipes, etc.; occasional free network merchandise (e.g., aprons, t-shirts) and sometimes free food; attendance welcome on shoots with reporters.

Food Network intern Ari Ariel reviews a script with sous chef Lauren Deen.

Forbes

SELECTIVITY 🔍🔍🔍🔍🔍
Approximate applicant pool: 150; Interns accepted: Varies

COMPENSATION 💲
NY: $330/week

LOCATION(S)
New York

FIELD
Magazines

DURATION
NY: 12–14 weeks, Summer; Other times possible

DEADLINE(S)
April 15

THE WORK
Founded in 1917, *Forbes* is one of the world's leading business magazines. And in 1998, *Forbes Global* debuted to provide subcribers overseas with the high-quality coverage of of business topics, high technology, global investment and leisure opportunities that *Forbes* gives the American business reader. Interns will work in editorial on one of the above publications, researching and writing alongside with reporters.

PERKS
Fitness center, possible intern acknowledgement in editors letter, "unbureaucratic environment", and access to leading business and investment people."

FYI
Forbes Inc. has been taking interns since 1984 . . . Over 47 percent of the magazine's readers have a net worth of over $1 million . . . In 1997, *Forbes* ranked first among all American magazines in advertising pages (first among all from 1991-1996)...*Forbes Global* is now extendingthe Forbes name overseas with both original content and articles adapted from *Forbes*.

TO APPLY
Open to undergrads and grad students. Foreign languages a plus for *Forbes Global* Submit resume, cover letter, writing samples, and recommendations.

Internship Coordinator
Human Resources Deparment
60 Fifth Avenue
New York, NY 10011
Fax 212 505 5105

Manfred Schumacher, Editor-in-Chief
Forbes von Burda
Focuf Magazin Verlag.
Postfach 810164
81901 Munich, Germany
49–89–9250–0
49–89–9250–2203 (Fax)

SELECTIVITY 🔍🔍🔍🔍🔍
Approximate applicant pool: 1,200; Interns accepted: 17

COMPENSATION 💲💲💲💲
$35,000/year; assistance with costs for relocation to New York, medical and dental insurance, vacation, sick leave, and a savings plan.

LOCATION(S)
New York, NY

FIELD
Human development and reproductive health; Community and resource development; Economic development; Human rights and international cooperation; Education, Knowledge and religion; and Media, arts, and culture.

DURATION
Two years beginning Fall 2001

DEADLINE(S)
Late Fall 2000

THE WORK
Founded in 1936, the Ford Foundation's purpose is to strengthen democratic values, reduce poverty and injustice, promote cooperation, advance human achievement in an attempt to aid every society in facing the challenges of creating a political, economic, and social system that promotes peace, human welfare, and the sustainability of the environment on which life depends

The foundation works mainly by making grants or loans that create awareness and encourage initiatives towards problems faced by individuals across the world; to strengthen organizations to create a collaboration among the nonprofit, government and business sectors; and build networks of individuals from diverse cultures and societies that work together to solve problems of public interest and to share lessons learned across social groups and national boundaries.

Program Assistants will work in programs focusing on human development and reproductive health; community resource development, economic development; human rights and international cooperation; education knowledge and religion; and media arts and culture. They will assist program staff in a wide range of grant making activities.

PERKS
Attendance welcome at in-house meetings and major conferences worldwide; exposure to influential leaders, ideas, and programs worldwide; access to fitness facility.

FYI
FF has provided an annual average of $400 million worth of grants.

TO APPLY
Must have master's or law degree conferred within two years of the start of the Program Assistantship. In the case of international applicants, proof of authorization to work within the United States for the entire two year period is required. An interactive online application is located at our website at http://www.fordfound.org. While this is the preferred method of aplication, those without access to the Web may obtain a hard copy of the application through graduate schools offices or by written request.

Program Assistantship/Human Resources
The Ford Foundation
320 East 43rd Street
New York, NY 10017
www.fordfound.org

EXCLUSIVE INTERVIEW WITH JOAN EMBERY

Best known for some 75 appearances on The Tonight Show *as "that blonde woman who shared animals with Johnny Carson," Joan Embery is the goodwill ambassador for the San Diego Zoo and San Diego Wild Animal Park. She speaks on wildlife conservation at zoos and animal organizations nationwide, leads expeditions of wild animal habitiais in countries like Kenya and China, and trains and handles such animals as elephants and orangutans. Embery studied zoology and telecommunications at San Diego State University and completed a B.A. in communications from Eastern Illinois University.*

The Internship Informants: Where did you intern in your youth?
Embery: With my uncle, who was a veterinarian, from about junior high school through high school. I would spend summers out in his truck on ranch calls with him, go through his veterinary clinic, and watch treatments. That triggered my interest from a relatively young age into thinking in terms of veterinary medicine, which is what led me to the [San Diego] Zoo.

The Internship Informants: Describe what you did with your uncle.
Embery: My uncle was a large-animal veterinarian, and he had a clinic, but he also went out on emergency, or ranch, calls. He handled horses [on the ranches] and the small animals one sees in the clinic—dogs and cats. Of course, I was most fascinated with horses at that time, so I loved to go out on the ranch calls. I was very impressed with his work and what he was able to do, to the point that I would bring home all his veterinary books and read about canine surgery and equine lameness.

The Internship Informants: How did you solidify this interest once you got to college?
Embery: I applied right out of high school to the San Diego Zoo, Sea World, and a few veterinary clinics to get some practical experience because women were not readily accepted into veterinary programs, nor were they accepted in zoos in any abundance. I mean, you could be a secretary or you could work with baby animals. But I was finally hired for a part-time job [at the Children's Zoo in 1968], where I was on call day and night.

The Internship Informants: How did you get the spokesperson job?
Embery: Talk about perserverence. [The zoo] developed a job similar to one that Disneyland had as goodwill ambassador for the Zoological Society's fiftieth anniversary of the zoo, and they were in the process of building a major new 1,800-acre wild animal park. They thought it would be a good idea to have somebody to go out and speak on behalf of the organization... The zoo advertised the job in the newspaper, and it was perceived by many people as the ultimate job because it meant handling animals, possibly working to some degree in television, and people saw animals and TV and thought, that's it. They interviewed 600 people. I was working part-time at the zoo ... [but] I did not get much consideration, and in fact, they hired a very pretty model for the job.

The Internship Informants: How did the model make out?
Embery: Eventually, they realized there was more to the job than looking pretty. [The spokesperson] had to be able to handle animals, think on his or her feet, drive heavy equipment, be self-sufficient, know San Diego, know the zoo and its history, know every aspect of zoos and animal life. So the first person they hired was not well-equipped, and in the second year, they questioned whether to continue the position. Well, they kept it and decided to emphasize animal expertise. Then I was given the opportunity for the job, and the rest is history. My interest at the time was elephants, and it was the elephant work that I did that led to my first appearance on *The Tonight Show.*

The Internship Informants: Were you prepared to handle this sudden success?
Embery: Not really. The next thing I knew, without much television training, I was in front of three cameras live in front of Johnny Carson. I was like, "Oh, my God, what do I do?" It was very much sink or swim. Talk about challenging.

The Internship Informants: Do you take on interns now?
Embery: [The San Diego Zoo] has had programs on and off. I've had an intern or two work with me, but it's very selective because I'm on the road a lot, and I'm moving around, and I don't have a lot of time to spend with people. We've had interns in our Veterinary program at the zoo, in our Research program at the zoo. We have on occasion had summer school programs that involved ... exploring what zoos are all about and spending a couple of days with a keeper. The programs vary year to year.

Embery interview continued . . .

The Internship Informants: How do people go about getting an internship with you?
Embery: Somebody may write me, and if I see that they have the credentials and I'm not going to be out of the country or something, and it works for a summer program, and they can find themselves a place to stay, then that can work out. In fact, one of the interns I brought in one summer went on to become an employee at the zoo . . . We don't have a system for taking applications and evaluating people, but situations come up where we work with a college or we're working on a particular behavioral project. Then we open up for people to come in on an internship basis and help with behavioral work.

The Internship Informants: What advice do you have for college students thinking about careers?
Embery: You have to be focused. Students today think that when they finish their education that they should be able to name their career and walk right into their ultimate job. But the people who tend to get ahead are the people who work hard and are willing to take whatever opportunity and turn that into a positive direction. I started at $2.19 an hour, on call, basically babysitting baby elephants and from there jumped into representing the zoo as its spokesperson and from there to television work.

The Internship Informants: Do you advise students interested in animals to do internships?
Embery: Definitely, because for careers working with animals, so much of it is experience and practical work. So if you can, get your feet wet any way possible—volunteering at a humane society or an animal clinic or zoo. It will give you insight into whether this is something you really want to do. It will introduce you to people and situations. That is the key to opening doors.

FORD MODELS

SELECTIVITY   N/A
Approximate applicant pool: N/A; Interns accepted: 20–40

COMPENSATION $
Lunches; subway fare

LOCATION(S)
Los Angeles, CA; Miami, FL; New York, NY; Scottsdale, AZ; Buenos Aires, Argentina; Paris, France; São Paulo, Brazil; Toronto, Canada

DURATION
4 weeks minimum: ongoing

FIELD
Model management

DEADLINE(S)
Rolling

THE WORK
Founded in 1946, Ford Models is one of the world's largest and most prestigious modeling agencies, representing such models as Naomi Campbell, Rachel Hunter, Stephanie Seymour, Vendela, and Patricia Velasquez. Known for discovering many of the world's top female models, Ford also represents children, men, and actors, and sponsors an annual Supermodel of the World contest. Interns (ten to fifteen in NY) work in Accounting, Runway, Women's, Men's, Television, Commercial Print, Children's, and 12+ Women (full-sized models).

PERKS
Invitations to parties and fashion shows; possible travel for Supermodel of the World contest (NY); fast-paced, energetic atmosphere.

FYI
Former Ford models include Hollywood stars Candace Bergen, Lauren Hutton, Kim Basinger, Melanie Griffith, Kelly Le Brock, and Sharon Stone, as well as legendary models Christie Brinkley, Jerry Hall, Suzy Parker, Jean Shrimpton, and Cheryl Tiegs . . . Founder Eileen Ford often talks of being able to spot star quality within beautiful faces—an elusive quality she calls "the X factor."

TO APPLY
Open to undergrads. International applicants eligible. Submit resume and cover letter directly to office of interest.

New York, NY: (212) 219-6500
Chicago, IL: (312) 707-9000
Los Angeles, CA: (310) 276-8100
Miami, FL: (305) 534-7200
Cleveland, OH: (216) 522-1300
Scottsdale, AZ: (602) 966-2537
Buenos Aries, Argentina: 5411-4815-3565
Paris, France: 331-5305-2525
Sao Paulo, Brazil: 55-11-884-5920
Toronto, Canada: 416-362-9208

FORD MOTOR COMPANY

SELECTIVITY 🔍 🔍 🔍 🔍
Approx. applicant pool: 10,000; Interns accepted: 1,000–1,200

COMPENSATION 💲 💲 💲 💲
$2,235–2,890/month for undergrads; $3,470–$5,325/month for grad students; return travel; free housing and transportation (Dearborn) or housing allowance (non-Dearborn)

LOCATION(S)
Southeast Michigan and throughout the U.S.

FIELD
Automomotive; Finance

DURATION
14 weeks: Summer

DEADLINE(S)
April 1

THE WORK
It was 1908 when Ford produced the Model T, one of the first automobiles produced using standardized parts and assembly-line methods. These days Ford is transforming itself into the world's leading consumer company for automotive products and services. Many internships are for engineers. However, internships are also in: Product Engineering, Manufacturing, Finance, Purchasing, Marketing, Sales & Service, Human Resources, Process Leadership, Technical Affairs, Quality, Ford Land, and Ford Motor Credit.

PERKS
Orientation & seminars with division heads; job counseling; plant tours; social functions, and challenging work assignments.

FYI
Ford views its summer internship program as a major source of full-time hires for its exclusive Ford College Graduate program. Established in 1953, the program was recently revamped to ensure that each participant receives valuable experience under professional management. Located just 20 minutes from downtown Detroit, Dearborn provides easy access to many of Detroit's attractions.

TO APPLY
Open to undergrads and grad students. International applicants may be eligible. Submit resumes to:

Ford Motor Company
Salaried Recruiting - ATS
HR Customer Operations
PO Box 0520
Allen Park, MI 48101-0520
E-mail: career@ford.com

FOREIGN AFFAIRS

SELECTIVITY 🔍 🔍 🔍 🔍
Approximate applicant pool: 150; Interns accepted: 4

COMPENSATION 💲
None: Fall and Spring; $300/week: Summer; $450/week: academic year

LOCATION(S)
New York, NY

FIELD
Magazines; Foreign Affairs

DURATION
10 weeks: Summer (full time), Fall, Spring (1 day/week; 10 months: academic year (September–June/full-time)

DEADLINE(S)
Summer: March 15; Fall: September 5; Spring: December 1; Academic year: March 15

THE WORK
Published by the Council on Foreign Relations (see separate entry) since 1922, *Foreign Affairs* is a bimonthly magazine featuring articles by politicians and academics on issues concerning US foreign policy. Recent contributors include Samuel Huntington, Strobe Talbott, Paul Krugman, Zbigniew Brzezinski, Nelson Mandela, and Fritz Stern. Interns are involved in every stage of the editorial process. They read and evaluate manuscripts, do research and layout, proofread, and edit.

PERKS
Attendance welcome at council meetings and council-sponsored speeches; full-time interns acknowledged in magazine's masthead.

FYI
Since the internship program was started in 1989, two interns have returned to the magazine as full-time editors.

TO APPLY
Open to college juniors, seniors, grad students, recent grads. International applicants eligible. Submit resume, cover letter, and writing sample (Fall and Spring). Submit resume, cover letter, three writing samples, and three recommendations (academic year and summer).

Editorial Internships
Foreign Affairs
58 East 68th Street
New York, NY 10021
(212) 434-9508
(212) 861-1849 (Fax)

FOREIGN POLICY

See Carnegie Endowment for International Peace

SELECTIVITY 🔍 🔍 🔍
Approximate applicant pool: 100; Interns accepted: 10–15

COMPENSATION 💲
None

LOCATION(S)
Philadelphia, PA

FIELD
Foreign affairs; Magazines

DURATION
15 weeks: Summer, Fall, Spring

DEADLINE(S)
Rolling (Preferably 2 months prior to start date)

 THE WORK
The Foreign Policy Research Institute, founded in 1955, is an independent, nonprofit organization devoted to scholarly research and public education on international affairs. Current research focuses on American foreign policy; American defense and national security issues; the future of NATO; East Asia, particularly the role of the People's Republic of China in the region; the transition to free markets and pluralism in the ex-Soviet bloc; the Arab-Israeli peace process; South Asian energy and environmental issues; and emerging markets.

PERKS
Attendance welcome at institute lectures; access to gym.

FYI
In addition to performing scholarly research, FPRI publishes the quarterly journal *Orbis*, operates the Middle East Council and Asia Program, and administers the Marvin Wachman Fund for International Education.

TO APPLY
Open to high school seniors, undergrads, recent college grads, college grads of any age, and grad students. International applicants eligible. Submit resume, cover letter, writing samples, and two recommendations.

Internship Coordinator
Foreign Policy Research Institute
1528 Walnut Street, Suite 610
Philadelphia, PA 19102–3684
(215) 732-3774 ext. 302
(215) 732-4401 (Fax)
E-mail: fpri@aol.com

FSSC
Foreign Student
Service Council

SELECTIVITY 🔍
Approximate applicant pool: 10–20; Interns accepted: 6

COMPENSATION 💲
None

LOCATION(S)
Washington, DC

FIELD
Education

DURATION
12–16 weeks: Summer, Fall, Spring

DEADLINE(S)
Four to six weeks prior to applicant's intended start date

THE WORK
Founded in 1956, the Foreign Student Service Council (FSSC) is a nonprofit organization operating educational and social programs for local and traveling international students. Among its services are a housing referral service, a resource center, student social activities, short-term homestays, an international student speakers bureau, and international leadership workshops. Interns help plan social and education programs, greet and advise international students, and provide administrative support.

PERKS
Attendance welcome at meetings with government and business leaders; attendance welcome at leadership workshops; participation in a wide range of social activities with foreign students.

Lights... Camera... *Intern!*
Interns in film and on television:

The 1995 CBS television series, *Clarissa*, follows the life of an 18-year-old intern at a New York newspaper.

The internship program has been in existence since 1988 . . . Student participants in FSSC represent nearly every area of the world, even such remote places as Trinidad, the Ivory Coast, and Malawi.

TO APPLY
Open to undergrads, recent college grads, college grads of any age, and grad students. International applicants eligible. Submit resume, cover letter, and writing samples.

Internship Coordinator
Foreign Student Service Council
Friendly House
1930 18th Street NW #21
Washington, DC 20009
(202) 232–4979
(202) 667–9305 (Fax)
E–mail: fssc@clark.net

FORTY ACRES AND A MULE FILMWORKS

SELECTIVITY
Approximate applicant pool: 600; Interns accepted: 15

COMPENSATION $
None

LOCATION(S)
Brooklyn, NY

FIELD
Motion picture production

DURATION
8–11 weeks: Coincides with production dates

DEADLINE(S)
Rolling

THE WORK
When Spike Lee needed a name for his film company, Forty Acres and a Mule seemed like the logical choice. It underscored his intention to reclaim, through film, the power that had been denied African Americans. Since his first movie release in 1986, Spike's films have changed the face of American cinematography, creating features in which blacks are the main characters and no longer just bit players in the white story. Interns work (only when a movie is in production) in Wardrobe, Props, Extras Casting, Accounting, Director's Assistant, Production, and Editing.

PERKS
Parties; Spike's Joint discount.

FYI
If they play their cards right, interns may be used as extras; a few were placed in the background of a dance scene in *Malcolm X* . . . One intern noted, "There are a lot of filmmakers out there who will be impressed that you worked for Spike, no matter what you did."

TO APPLY
Open to high school, undergrad, and grad students. International applicants eligible. Submit resume and cover letter. Prospective interns must take an admissions test.

Forty Acres and a Mule Filmworks, Inc.
Internship Program
124 Dekalb Avenue
Brooklyn, NY 11217

48 HOURS

See CBS News

FOUNDATION FOR CONTEMPORARY MENTAL HEALTH

SELECTIVITY
Approximate applicant pool: 100; Interns accepted: 15

COMPENSATION $
None

LOCATION(S)
Rockville, Bethesda and Chevy Chase, MD; Falls Church, VA; Washington, DC

FIELD
Mental health care

DURATION
8 weeks: Summer

DEADLINE(S)
March 1

THE WORK
The nonprofit Foundation for Contemporary Mental Health was founded in 1967 to further understanding of mental health through educational programming. Interns are placed in psychiatric inpatient settings and at day treatment programs at such facilities as Suburban Hospital, Psychiatric Institute of Washington, and Dominion Hospital.

Spike Lee's career in filmmaking, which includes such acclaimed films as *She's Gotta Have It, Do the Right Thing,* and *Malcolm X,* was prefaced by an internship. After graduating from Morehouse College in 1979 and before enrolling in NYU's Institute of Film and Television, Lee spent a summer interning at the Columbia Pictures studio in Burbank, California.

PERKS
Supervision of work by licensed mental health professionals; inclusion in staff planning meetings; weekly two-hour seminar on mental health issues.

FYI
FCMH's internship program was started in 1969 . . . Interns work as psychiatric technicians alongside psychiatrists, psychologists, nurses, social workers, and therapists.

TO APPLY
Open to college seniors with previous coursework in abnormal psychology and grad students studying mental health or social work. International applicants eligible. Write for application.

Summer Mental Health Internship Program
Foundation for Contemporary Mental Health
2112 F Street NW, Suite 404
Washington, DC 20037
(202) 296-7100
(202) 296–5455 (Fax)

FOURTH WORLD MOVEMENT

SELECTIVITY
Approximate applicant pool: 80; Interns accepted: 10–15

COMPENSATION
$300/month and free housing (after first 15 weeks); $540/month (after first year)

LOCATION(S)
Covington and New Orleans, LA; New York, NY; Washington, DC; Belgium; Benin; Burkina Faso; Canada; Central African Republic; France; Germany; Great Britain; Guatemala; Haiti; Honduras; Ivory Coast; Luxembourg; Madagascar, Mauritius; The Netherlands; Philippines; Portugal; Reunion Island; Senegal; Spain; Switzerland; Taiwan; Thailand

FIELD
Education; Public service; Social justice

DURATION
15 weeks–2 or more years; 2 weeks–2 months in summer

DEADLINE(S)
Rolling

THE WORK
The International Fourth World Movement (FWM) was founded in 1957 in a camp for homeless families outside Paris, by the late Joseph Wresinski, a Catholic priest who himself grew up in poverty and exclusion. Gathering men and women of different faiths, nationalities, ages, and backgrounds, the FWM undertakes three major lines of action: grassroots presence and involvement among very poor families and communities; research into poverty, undertaken with the poor themselves; and campaigning and mobilizing public opinion at various levels. The nonprofit organization's projects are run by the members of the FWM Volunteer Corps, emphasize education and citizenship, and include pre-school activities, family centers, artistic and cultural programs, and discussion forums in which poor families can voice their concerns.

PERKS
For US citizens, three-month internships available; possibility to join the long-term Volunteer Corps. (two-year commitment, at least); sense of community encouraged; after first year, all Volunteer Corps members receive same minimal stipend, regardless of position or time involved; daily writing to build qualitative histories of very poor families is essential; regular training sessions.

FYI
A commemorative stone dedicated by FWM's founder and laid in on the Human Rights Plaza in Paris reads: "Wherever men and women are condemned to live in extreme poverty, human rights are violated. To come together to ensure that these rights be respected is our solemn duty" . . . Replicas of this commemorative stone exists in several other countries, including at the United Nations' Plaza in New York City. US citizens who train with FWM/USA stay in North America for up to a year before going to FWM's international center. There they join a wider group of trainee volunteers and are placed with FWM projects in aforementioned countries. Short term programs in Europe occur each summer. Ask for a summer brochure. (Int'l Center address: ATD Quart Monde, 8 rue des Vaux a Epluches, 95540 Mery s/ Oise, France.)

TO APPLY
Open to those 19 years and older, with High school education and 1 year work, and/or college experience. Please send SASE requesting more information.

Fourth World Movement
7600 Willow Hill Drive
Landover, MD 20785
(301) 336–9489
(301) 336–0092 (Fax)
E-mail: fourthworld@erols.com
www.atd-fourthworld.org

FOX

SELECTIVITY
Approximate applicant pool: 800; Interns accepted: 60–90

COMPENSATION
$300/week for undergrads; $450/week for grad students

LOCATION(S)
Dallas, TX (see FYI); Los Angeles, CA; New York, NY

FIELD
Film; Television; Sports; Video games

DURATION
8–16 weeks: Summer, Fall, Spring

DEADLINE(S)
Rolling

THE WORK
Established in 1986, Fox is a conglomerate of 19 entertainment companies, including Fox Broadcasting, the television network; cable channels fX and fXM (see separate entry); Twentieth Television, which syndicates Fox television shows; Morning Studios, which produces live programming for fX; Fox Sports,

which broadcasts NFL and NHL games; Fox Children's Network; Fox Latin America Channel; Twentieth Century Fox, producer of such blockbusters as *Big*, *Speed*, *True Lies*, *Wall Street*, and the *Star Wars* trilogy; Twentieth Century Fox TV, which produces shows like *Picket Fences*, *NYPD Blue*, and *The Simpsons* for ABC, CBS, NBC, and Fox; Twentieth Century Fox Licensing and Merchandising; Fox Animation Studios; Fox Video; Fox Interactive (video games); and Fox Searchlight Pictures, whose film credits include *The Brothers McMullen*. Interns work in all the aforementioned companies in such departments as Production, Programming, Legal, Accounting, Research, Finance, and Sales & Marketing.

PERKS
Invitations to Fox movie screenings; free videotape of a Twentieth Century Fox movie.

FYI
According to personnel, internships in television divisions are rarely available during the summer . . . Twentieth Century Fox offers a one-year sales trainee program for recent college grads, starting in June; trainees work in Los Angeles, Dallas, and New York and receive $450/week . . . Fox is a subsidiary of News Corp., the global news and entertainment company owned by Australian billionaire Rupert Murdoch . . . The oldest Fox company is Twentieth Century Fox, founded in 1915 as Fox Film Corp., which merged with Twentieth Century Pictures in 1935.

TO APPLY
Open to undergrads and grad students. Must receive academic credit for unpaid positions. International applicants studying in the US are eligible. Submit resume and cover letter.

Personnel Department
(Name of Fox Company)
P.O. Box 900
Beverly Hills, CA 90213
(310) FOX–1000

FOX FX

SELECTIVITY
Approximate applicant pool: N/A; Interns accepted: 30–40

COMPENSATION
Travel stipend

LOCATION(S)
New York, NY

FIELD
Television

DURATION
8–16 weeks; Fall, Winter, Spring, Summer

DEADLINE(S)
Rolling

THE WORK
Fox Studios East is an entertainment and sports basic cable network presenting original programming plus timeless TV favorites, all hosted from its unique apartment home base in New York. Fox Studios East and FX are a unit of Fox Television, A News Corporation Company, producing two full-time networks, FX and FXM: Movies from FOX. FX is a national general entertainment basic cable network from FOX Television and Liberty Media, featuring marquee sports events produced by FOX Sports, distinctive original programming, hit series, and Twentieth Century Fox films. Interns work for Fox After Breakfast, Backchat, Personal FX, Publicity, On-Air Promotions, Human Resources, General Business & Administration, Operations, Publicity, Sales/Marketing, & Tape Library.

PERKS
Orientation; mentors; intern seminars/luncheons featuring department heads and show producers.

FYI
In the spirit of "family" the internship coordinators "believe it is important for you to feel comfortable and to ask any questions that you might have . . . We welcome your ideas and want you to help make FX the best entertainment cable network."

TO APPLY
Open to college juniors and seniors. Must receive academic credit. International applicants studying in the United States are eligible. Submit resume and cover letter to:

Internship Coordinator
Fox Studios East, Inc.
212 Fifth Avenue
New York, NY 10010
(212) 802-4000
(212) 802-4206 (Fax)
(212) 802-4082 (Fax)

FRANKLIN D. ROOSEVELT LIBRARY

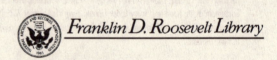

SELECTIVITY
Approximate applicant pool: 50; Interns accepted: 6–8

COMPENSATION
$200/week

LOCATION(S)
Hyde Park, NY

FIELD
Libraries

DURATION
6–7 weeks between mid-May and the end of August

DEADLINE(S)
April 1

THE WORK
Opened in 1941, the Franklin D. Roosevelt Library houses artifacts from the lives of President Roosevelt and Eleanor Roosevelt, documents of FDR when he was governor of New York and president, and materials belonging to those who served him in

Albany and Washington. It also hosts a variety of special events, including a birthday ceremony and World War II living-history weekends. Interns work in the archives department, where they assist the archives staff.

PERKS
Attendance welcome at special events; free museum tour; discounts at museum shop.

FYI
Past projects have found interns creating a computerized chronology of FDR's life to be included on the Internet, developing educational programs for teachers and students of all grade levels, and carrying out computer projects to help streamline the research process.

TO APPLY
Open to undergrads and grad students. International applicants eligible. Write for application.

Internship Coordinator
Franklin D. Roosevelt Library
511 Albany Post Road
Hyde Park, NY 12538
(914) 229–8114
(914) 229–0872 (Fax)
E-mail: library@roosevelt.nara.gov
www.fdrlibrary.marist.edu/summer.html

THE FRANKLIN LIFE INSURANCE CO.

AMERICAN GENERAL FINANCIAL GROUP

The Franklin Life Insurance Company

SELECTIVITY
Approximate applicant pool: 400; Interns accepted: 80

COMPENSATION $
Based on activity and results. Interns can earn $20 for each sales interview during the 12-week period, up to $600, and 20 percent of submitted core production credit, up to $1,000 per case.

LOCATION(S)
Varies with the location of the field associate working with the intern (within the US)

FIELD
Sales of life insurance and financial products

DURATION
12 weeks

DEADLINE(S)
Rolling

THE WORK
Founded in 1884, The Franklin Life Insurance Company has nearly 3,000 associates serving approximately 800,000 policyowners in 49 states, the District of Columbia, the Virgin Islands and Puerto Rico. The Franklin is part of the American General Financial Group, one of the nation's largest diversified financial services organizations, with assets of more than $100 billion. A number of The Franklin's most successful associates entered the business through the Career Internship Program for College Undergraduates and New Graduates.

PERKS
Based on performance; honor club awards, recognition in company publications and convention trips are among the many incentives offered to Franklin associates.

FYI
If an intern meets certain criteria and signs a full-time contract, The Franklin will donate $1,000 to the former intern's educational institution the following year.

TO APPLY
Seniors and recent graduates should write for an application. This opportunity is not open to international students.

The Franklin Life Insurance Co.
attn: Darrell Malano
#1 Franklin Square
Springfield, IL 62713
(800) 528-2011 Ext. 2913
(217) 753-8414 (Fax)

FREEDOM THEATRE

Walter Dallas, *Artistic Director*
Donald O. H. Brown, *Managing Director*

SELECTIVITY
Approximate applicant pool: N/A; Interns accepted: 2

COMPENSATION $
$150/week

LOCATION(S)
Philadelphia, PA

FIELD
Performing Arts

DURATION
1 year: September to September

DEADLINE(S)
August 15

THE WORK
Founded over 30 years ago, Freedom Theatre is Pennsylvania's oldest and best-known African American Theatre. The institution operates as both a theatrical organization and training school; since its founding, it has staged over 300 productions and trained 10,000 students. The internship program, begun in 1996, offers two positions, in Research & Writing and Professional Development. The Research intern is responsible for drafting correspondence, grant proposals, and summary memos, and for investigating corporate, government, and private funding opportunities. The Professional Development intern rotates through every area of the theatre's Development office, working with corporate sponsors by attending events and monitoring packages, writing grant proposals and identifying prospects, and making presentations for membership donations.

PERKS
Free shared Freedom Theatre apartment in an historic mansion; contact with prominent playwrights, actors, and directors.

FYI
Freedom Theatre's alumni include *Living Single's* Erika Alexander, Wanya Morris of Boyz II Men, and Samm-Art Williams, producer of *The Fresh Prince of Bel Air, Martin,* and *Hangin' with Mr. Cooper*... The theatre's high-school education programs are extremely successful: over 98 percent of the program participants graduate from high school, and 85 percent go on to higher education.

TO APPLY
Open to college juniors and seniors, recent college grads (preferred), grad students, and college grads of any age. Submit resume, cover letter, and writing sample.

Freedom Theatre
Attn: Internship Coordinator
1346 N. Broad Street
Philadelphia, PA 19121
(215) 765-2793
(215) 765-4191 (Fax)

FREER GALLERY OF ART

See Smithsonian Institution

THE FRENCH–AMERICAN CENTER

SELECTIVITY 🔍
Approximate applicant pool: 150; Interns accepted: 40 (Americans), 70 (French)

COMPENSATION 💲
Fees: $120 (membership) and $300 (placement)

LOCATION(S)
US citizens: Avignon, Aix-en-Provence, Lyon, Marseille, and Montpellier, France; French citizens: San Diego, CA; NJ; New York, NY

FIELD
Several fields: (see THE WORK)

DURATION
4–12 weeks: ongoing

DEADLINE(S)
Rolling

THE WORK
Founded in 1985, The French-American Center (FAC) is a nonprofit educational organization that sponsors a variety of language courses and cultural exchange programs, including internships, for US and French citizens. Internship placements span a wide range of technical and nontechnical fields, with most placements occurring in business, communications, film, journalism, and social work.

PERKS
Free membership in local FAC; in-country orientation and discounted language courses ($6/hour); organized social events.

FYI
Participating organizations in France include the newspaper *Midi-Libre*; the French-American Film Workshop, and Open City Films. Participating organizations in the United States include The Kitchen, Guerlain, Air France, and the Brooklyn Botanic Garden.

TO APPLY
Open to undergrads, recent college grads, college grads of any age, and grad students. Americans must be fluent in French; French citizens must be fluent in English. Write for application.

US citizens:
The French-American Center
198 Avenue of the Americas
New York, NY 10013
(212) 343-2675

French citizens:
The French-American Center
10, montée de la Tour
30400 Villeneuve-les-Avignon, France
33–90–25–93–23

FRENCH EMBASSY

SELECTIVITY 🔍🔍
Approximate applicant pool: 100; Interns accepted: 20

COMPENSATION 💲
None

LOCATION(S)
Washington, DC

FIELD
Government

DURATION
10–14 weeks: Summer, Fall, Spring

DEADLINE(S)
Rolling

THE WORK
The French Embassy serves as the official diplomatic office of the French Ambassador to the United States. Working to protect and advance French interests in the United States, the Embassy provides general information on France, coordinates immigration and travel, hosts trade fairs for French companies, and publishes a quarterly magazine and a biweekly newsletter. Interns work in Cultural Service and Press & Information Service (e.g., *FRANCE* magazine and The Documentation Center).

PERKS
Invitations to some Embassy events.

FYI
The internship program has been offered since 1987. Distributed to 61,000 readers across the United States, *FRANCE* magazine is an English language magazine designed to showcase France to an American audience ... The Documentation Center is a public information and research center located within the Embassy.

TO APPLY
Open to undergrads, recent college grads, college grads of any age, and grad students. Must be proficient in French. International applicants eligible. Submit resume and cover letter.

Internship Coordinator
French Embassy
4101 Reservoir Road NW
Washington, DC 20007
(202) 944–6093
(202) 944–6072 (Fax)

FRIENDS COMMITTEE ON
FCNL
NATIONAL LEGISLATION

SELECTIVITY 🔍 🔍 🔍 🔍
Approximate applicant pool: 40; Interns accepted: 3

COMPENSATION 💲 💲 💲
$305/week; health coverage; vacation; sick leave

LOCATION(S)
Washington, DC

FIELD
Public policy

DURATION
11 months: starts in September

DEADLINE(S)
March 1

THE WORK
Founded in 1943, the Friends Committee on National Legislation (FCNL) is a lobbying organization working to bring Quaker values to bear on national policy. Through Congressional testimony, Capitol Hill visits, educational activities, grass roots lobbying, and publications such as the monthly FCNL Washington Newsletter, FCNL addresses a wide range of peace and social justice issues (e.g., ending the arms race, strengthening international cooperation, reducing poverty, supporting rights of conscience, and supporting civil rights of all people). Interns participate in advocacy, research, writing, and other work to support the legislatives advocacy process.

PERKS
Attendance welcome at seminars related to FCNL work; visits to committee hearings and meetings of relevant interest groups; limited financial support to enable participation in relevant workshops and conferences is possible.

FYI
FCNL's internship program was established after young Friends attending the 1970 annual meeting convinced the committee of their desire to participate in the work of FCNL through an internship program.

TO APPLY
Open to individuals with a college degree or equivalent experience. Please request application packet January–March 1 only.

Internship Coordinator
Friends Committee on National Legislation
245 Second Street NE
Washington, DC 20002
(202) 547–6000
(202) 547–6019 (Fax)

World-renowned photographer **Francesco Scavullo** got his start as an apprentice for the now-defunct William Becker Studio.

SELECTIVITY 🔍 🔍 🔍 🔍
Approximate applicant pool: 300–400; Interns accepted: 25

COMPENSATION 💲 💲 💲 💲
$375–$649/wk for undergrads; $649-$953/wk for grads;
up to $500 relocation assistance

LOCATION(S)
Dallas, TX (HQ) various locations nationwide

FIELD
Consumer goods (snack food)

DURATION
10–12 weeks: Summer

DEADLINE(S)
May 1

THE WORK
Frito-Lay is the world's largest snack-food company, with yearly sales of nearly $7 billion. Every year, its factories churn out a couch potato's fantasy menu: Doritos tortilla chips, Fritos corn chips, Lay's and Ruffles potato chips, and Chee-tos snacks. Interns are placed in Sales, Marketing, Operations, Finance, Purchasing, Service and Distribution, Engineering, Management Information Systems, Research and Development, and Human Resources.

PERKS
Three-day intern conference; team of mentors; chip heaven.

FYI
Frito-Lay started the Minority Intern Program in 1990, but opened up the program to include all students in 1994 . . . "There are bags of chips everywhere," remarked an intern, "We eat them at meetings, during lunch, on breaks, and for dinner." . . . Many of our summer interns are offered permanent jobs with Frito-Lay.

TO APPLY
Open to college juniors and seniors, grad students. Minimum GPA: 3.0. International applicants eligible. Submit resume (GPA included) and cover letter indicating a preference for position and location.

Frito-Lay, Inc.
Staffing Department
Dept: Intern
P.O. Box 225458
Dallas, TX 75222-5458

Disappointed by your internship? Treated unfairly? Bored to tears?

or just generally

WRONGED BY YOUR INTERNSHIP?

Now you have a place to turn...

TELL THE INTERNSHIP WATCHDOG™!

Through our Internship Watchdog, we record and monitor complaints about internship programs. Your feedback is very important, because it helps us decide which programs to include in future editions of upcoming books.

Just tell us (one) your name, address, and (optional) phone number, (two) the organization at which you interned, (three) the date of your internship, and (four) why you were dissatisfied with your internship.

Address:
The Internship Watchdog
c/o The Internship Informants
150 West 22nd Street
Fifth Floor
New York, NY 10011

E-mail:
InternInfo@aol.com

Exploitative internships, beware: The Internship Watchdog is on guard!

SELECTIVITY 🔍🔍
Approximate applicant pool: 15; Interns accepted: 4

COMPENSATION 💲
$250 covers room and board for 3 months upon acceptance

LOCATION(S)
Wendover, KY

FIELD
Rural health care, education

DURATION
12 weeks minimum: Year-round

DEADLINE(S)
Rolling

THE WORK
The Frontier Nursing Service (FNS) was created in 1925 by Mary Breckinridge after she lost both of her children. Her goal was to reduce the maternal and infant mortality rates in Leslie County, Kentucky—located in the Appalachian mountains. Today the FNS still provides quality health care. Interns, known as "couriers" shadow and assist in one or more of the following areas: Women's Health Care, FNS Outpost Clinics, Mary Breckinridge Hospital, and Home Health Agency. Opportunities also exist in adult literacy, public health education, and assisting in the public school system. Couriers help transport supplies and host functions of the FNS.

PERKS
Immersion in Appalachian culture; volunteers live on the grounds of the beginnings of the FNS—now a National Historic Landmark.

FYI
The Courier Program can be tailored to meet the needs of each individual volunteer. Those who are motivated self-initiators will find the opportunities vast.

TO APPLY
Open to high school grads at least 18 years old. Driver's license, vehicle, and ability to operate a standard transmission vehicle required. International applicants eligible. Write for application.

Frontier Nursing Service
Courier Program
Wendover, KY 41775
(606) 672-2317

GAP

SELECTIVITY 🔍
Approximate applicant pool: N/A; Interns accepted: N/A

COMPENSATION 💲
$6–$14/hour; benefits package (medical/dental, bonus, 401K, stock purchase plan, union reimbursement)

LOCATION(S)
Approximately 950 stores in the US; Puerto Rico; Canada

FIELD
Retail

DURATION
12–15 months: beginning March 1

DEADLINE(S)
January 31

THE WORK
Founded in 1969, Gap, Inc. is one of America's largest retailers of casual clothing, operating nearly 1,800 Gap, GapKids, Gap Outlet, Gap Shoes, Banana Republic, and Old Navy Clothing Co. stores, in the US, UK, Puerto Rico, France, Germany, Japan, and Canada. Under the auspices of the company's Work Study Program, college students with 12–15 months of school remaining on March 1 work in retail management at Gap and GapKids stores near their campus. Undergoing four phases of training, interns learn management skills such as how to generate sales, prepare operational reports, present merchandise, handle inventory, recruit employees, and plan holiday business.

PERKS
Group workshops and meetings with senior managers; Prepare for a management position upon graduation.

FYI
Gap hires all qualified Work Study interns for full-time management positions at Gap stores . . . The Work Study Program is one of the only long-term, formal retail management internships in the country . . . Gap-name clothing sells more units than any other brand except Levi.

TO APPLY
Open to college students with 12–15 months of school remaining on March 1. International applicants studying in the United States and Canada are eligible. Apply in person at a nearby Gap or GapKids store. Please note: The Work Study Program is not a Corporate internship program.

Work Study Program
Training Department
Gap, Inc.
900 Cherry Avenue
San Bruno, CA 94066
(800) 333-7899, ext. 44183 or (650) 874–4183

Behold Zonk, the intern!

From Doonesbury by G. B. Trudeau

THE GAZETTE COMPANY

SELECTIVITY 🔍🔍🔍
Approximate applicant pool: 150; Interns accepted: 1

COMPENSATION 💲
$6.50–7.50/hour (Cedar Rapids Gazette only)

LOCATION(S)
Cedar Rapids, IA

FIELD
Newspapers; Television; Marketing; Advertising

DURATION
12–16 weeks: Summer, Fall, Spring

DEADLINE(S)
Summer: December 1; Fall: May 1; Spring: October 1

THE WORK
Founded in 1883, The Gazette Company is an information-services corporation that owns the *Cedar Rapids Gazette*, a daily newspaper reaching nearly 200,000 readers in sixteen counties in eastern Iowa; other publications, such as *Penny Saver* and *Iowa Farmer Today*; KCRG-TV; KCRG-AM radio; Interactive Media, which provides computer- and telephone-accessed information on car sales, weather, news, sports, and stocks; and Decisionmark, which develops software that analyzes demographic data. Interns work at the *Cedar Rapids Gazette* (in Newsroom, Photo, Sports, and Advertising departments), KCRG-TV (summer only in Community Affairs and News), *Iowa Farmer Today* (for agricultural journalists), and Decisionmark (in Data Development and Programming).

PERKS
Opportunity to accompany reporters on assignment (Gazette); use of top-notch camera equipment (Photo and Television interns); discounted newspaper subscription.

FYI
The *Gazette* prides itself on promoting conservation: it uses over 50 percent recycled paper in each issue and prints with soybean oil-based ink only.

TO APPLY
Open to college sophomores, juniors, and seniors. International applicants eligible. Submit resume, cover letter, references, up to six published clips (Newsroom only), and slide portfolio (Photo only).

Employment Coordinator
Human Resources
The Gazette Company
P.O. Box 511
500 Third Avenue SE
Cedar Rapids, IA 52406
(800) 397-8211 (in Iowa) or (319) 398-5845
(319) 368-8834 (Fax)
E-mail: gazcohr@fyiowa.infi.net

GEFFEN RECORDS

GEFFEN

SELECTIVITY 🔍🔍
Approximate applicant pool: 120; Interns accepted: 32

COMPENSATION 💲
$25/Day

LOCATION(S)
Los Angeles, CA; New York, NY

FIELD
Record labels

DURATION
12–16 weeks: Summer, Fall, Spring

DEADLINE(S)
Summer: May 15; Fall: August 31; Spring: January 15

THE WORK
A division of Universal (see separate entry), Geffen Records was founded in 1980 by music and film mogul David Geffen. Artists featured on the revered label (and its subsidiary, DGC Records) include Days of the New, She Moves, Lisa Loeb, The Sundays, the Eels, 10,000 Maniacs, Counting Crows, Veruca Salt, and Beck. Interns work in Alternative Music, Publicity, International, Promotion/Album-Oriented Rock, Marketing, Sales, Information Technology, and Video Promotion.

PERKS
Orientation with director of human resources; luncheon with president of Geffen Records; attendance welcome at weekly department and marketing meetings; free concert tickets, posters, CDs, etc.

FYI
Approximately 25 percent of interns are hired by Geffen for full-time positions . . . Intern duties include promoting artists on college radio stations and arranging concert appearances (Alternative Music), contacting the press, setting up artist interviews, planning radio contests, tracking sales, coordinating budgets, writing marketing plans, and updating company information on the "information superhighway."

"I thought 'I want to be around this. I want to be near it. It's so exciting. I would pay them to be here.'"—**David Geffen**, on starting his career as an usher at *The Judy Garland Show*, *The Danny Kaye Show*, *The Red Skelton Show*, and *The Carol Burnett Show* (ABC News 20/20, November 11, 1994)

TO APPLY

Open to college juniors and seniors as well as grad students. Must receive academic credit. Submit resume and cover letter.

Internship Coordinator
Geffen Records
9130 Sunset Boulevard
Los Angeles, CA 90069
(310) 285-2779
(310) 271-2706 (Fax)

GENENTECH

Genentech, Inc.
Genentech, Inc.
Genentech, Inc.
Genentech, Inc.
Genentech, Inc.

SELECTIVITY 🔍 🔍 🔍 🔍
Approximate applicant pool: 1,700; Interns accepted: 100

COMPENSATION 💲 💲 💲
$475/week for undergrads; $575/week for grad students

LOCATION(S)
South San Francisco, CA

FIELD
Biotechnology

DURATION
10–12 weeks: Summer

DEADLINE(S)
March 15

THE WORK

In 1976, Genentech was born from a desire to explore the commercial potential of biotechnology. Within a year, company employees had created a human protein using recombinant DNA technology—the first demonstration of its kind. Today, Genentech upholds its mission "to diagnose, treat and cure serious human disease—and create a better way of life for millions of people." Positions are available in Manufacturing, Business, Quality Control, Medical Affairs, Marketing, Corporate Communications, Research, Engineering, Development, Human Resources, and Process Sciences.

GEFFEN RECORDS' "TIPS FOR A SUCCESSFUL INTERNSHIP"

1. Maintain good attendance and punctuality.
2. Be cooperative.
3. Ask questions.
4. Accept criticism as a way of learning.
5. Maintain a positive attitude.
6. Admit a mistake to your supervisor. Better your supervisor finds out from you instead of from someone else.
7. Keep a sense of humor and don't be afraid to let it show.
8. Do not use the office phone for excessive personal calls.
9. Be patient. Don't expect too much too soon.
10. Dress in a professional manner; casual is OK, sloppy is not.
11. Show initiative. Volunteer for assignments if your work is completed.
12. Learn from the internship.
13. Establish and maintain good business relationships.

Source: Geffen Records' internship packet

PERKS

Bay view; Friday parties (Ho Ho's); daily science lectures; social activities.

FYI

The Summer Internship Program was started in 1987 . . . Interns work diligently to make a final presentation or provide a manuscript to be considered for publication . . . Managers assign interns to laboratories; they do not choose their own projects.

TO APPLY

Open to college sophomores, juniors, seniors, and grad students. Must be returning to school in the fall. International applicants eligible. Submit resume detailing relevant laboratory and/or business skills, a cover letter.

Genentech
Human Resources
Summer Internship Program
PO Box 1950
South San Francisco, CA 94083–1950
E-mail: jobs@gene.com
www.gene.com

GENERAL FOODS

See Kraft General Foods

GENERAL MILLS

General Mills

SELECTIVITY 🔍 🔍 🔍
Approximate applicant pool: 1,000; Interns accepted: 70–75

COMPENSATION 💲 💲 💲 💲
$500–$700/week for undergrads; $800–$1,000/week for grad students

LOCATION(S)
Albuquerque, NM; Buffalo, NY; Cedar Rapids, IA; Chicago, IL; Covington, GA; Lodi, CA; Minneapolis, MN (HQ); Toledo, OH; and various sales locations

FIELD
Consumer goods (foods)

DURATION
10–14 weeks: Summer

DEADLINE(S)
February 1

THE WORK

Tracing its history back to 1866, General Mills is one of America's largest food companies, employing 10,000 people worldwide and generating over $5 billion in sales annually. Responsible for some of America's best-known foods, General Mills manufactures and distributes such staples as Cheerios and Wheaties cereals, Betty Crocker cake mix, Gold Medal flour, Bisquick pancake mix, Yoplait yogurt, and Popsecret Popcorn. Interns at headquarters work in Marketing Research, Brand Management, Promotions, Sales, Human Resources, Food Science, Research and Development, and Product Development. At the plants, interns work in Manufacturing, Engineering, and Human Resources. Graduate-level internships only in Brand Management and Market Research.

PERKS
Frequent meetings, luncheons and social activities; attendance welcome at department meetings; access to General Mills Fitness Center (HQ).

FYI
General Mills offers permanent employment to over 50 percent of its interns.

TO APPLY
Open to college sophomores, juniors, and seniors as well as grad students. Submit resume and cover letter. To research background info before you apply, check out www.vaultreports.com

Internship Program, Recruiting
General Mills
P.O. Box 1113
Minneapolis, MN 55440
(763) 764-2311

GENERAL MOTORS MARKETING INTERNSHIP (GMMI)

SELECTIVITY
Interns accepted: 3,500 (15–20 per college)

LOCATION(S)
Approximately 200 colleges and universities in AZ, AL, AR, CA, CO, FL, GA, ID, LA, MN, MO, MS, MT, NV, NM, NC, OK, OR, SC, TN, TX, UT, WA, WY

FIELD
Marketing

DURATION
One academic term (quarter or semester); Fall and Spring

DEADLINE(S)
Rolling

THE WORK
EdVenture Partners (EVP), a marketing firm, founded the General Motors Marketing Internship (GMMI) program in 1991. College students, in a marketing course or business club form their own marketing team for a specific GM Brand and a local GM dealership. Student interns research, design, implement, and analyze a promotional campaign to market GM vehicles to the college population.

PERKS
While earning academic credit and building resume experience, each team receives a $2,500 budget not only to design and present their plan, but to put their ideas into action. Working under a faculty advisor and EVP Field Associate, interns are also provided all necessary GM collateral, GMMI tee shirts, support materials, and a post-program wrap-up party.

FYI
Over 17,000 students have gone through the GMMI program since its inception. Many have been hired by EdVenture Partners and General Motors straight out of the program. Dozens of other Fortune 500 companies recognize GMMI as one of the leading internships leading to entry level employment.

TO APPLY
Open to undergrads. Check with your Business/Marketing Department Chair or contact EdVenture Partners for a list of participating schools.

General Motors Marketing Internship
c/o EdVenture Partners
ATTN: GM Account Manager
809 Heinz Avenue
Berkeley, CA 94710
(800) 783-9464
www.edventurepartners.com

GENSLER

Gensler

SELECTIVITY
Approximate applicant pool: 450–500; Interns accepted: 35–40

COMPENSATION
$10–$15/hour; Possible scholarship

LOCATION(S)
New York, NY; Washington, DC; San Francisco and Los Angeles, CA; Denver, CO; Houston, TX

FIELD
Architecture; Interior design; Graphic design

DURATION
2 months to 1 year: Summer, Fall, Spring

DEADLINE(S)
Summer: February 1; Fall and Spring: Rolling

THE WORK
Founded in 1965, Gensler is one of the leading international architectural and interior architectural firms. Its designs are fixtures on the American landscape: GAP stores, Apple Computer buildings, NASA headquarters in Washington, and many more. Most interns are assigned to an architect or team of architects in one of the office's design studios, though some are placed in support departments such as the library.

PERKS
Educational and cultural programs; airy offices.

FYI
Some interns leave with a love for their work. Said one: "That's the thrill of architecture—when you feel like you're affecting the lives of people for years down the road." . . . Projects are available for experienced applicants and beginners with no previous design experience . . . The San Francisco office runs an "ad-hoc art gallery" in its lobby to provide its employees with a "creative stimulus."

TO APPLY
Open to college sophomores, juniors, seniors as well as grad students. International applicants eligible. Submit resume, cover letter, and if possible, "a photocopy of one's best design-oriented work, such as working drawings or a design project."

Gensler
Intern Coordinator
600 California Street
San Francisco, CA 94108
(415) 627-3577

GEORGETOWN UNIVERSITY LAW CENTER

SELECTIVITY 🔍🔍🔍🔍

Approximate applicant pool: 400–500; Interns accepted: 30

COMPENSATION 💲

Parking; Business mileage

LOCATION(S)

Washington, DC

FIELD

Criminal law

DURATION

12–14 weeks: Summer, Fall, Spring

DEADLINE(S)

Summer: April 1; Fall: Round 1—March 15, Round 2—July 1; Spring: December 1

THE WORK

In 1960, the Criminal and Juvenile Justice Clinics at Georgetown University Law Center were founded to help indigent criminal defendants. The mission of the Clinics has been to give those persons charged with criminal offenses representation by high-quality, energetic attorneys who can provide the best legal services. Interns work in the Criminal and Juvenile Justice Clinics, supervised by attorneys and assisting them in every aspect of a criminal case.

PERKS

Brown-bag lunch with the Dean of Admissions; tour of a maximum security prison; ride-alongs with police officers; other field trips. Discounts on Kaplan and Princeton Review LSAT prep courses.

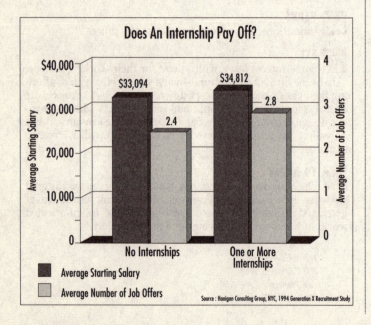

Does An Internship Pay Off?

No Internships: Average Starting Salary $33,094; Average Number of Job Offers 2.4

One or More Internships: Average Starting Salary $34,812; Average Number of Job Offers 2.8

■ Average Starting Salary
■ Average Number of Job Offers

Source : Hanigan Consulting Group, NYC, 1994 Generation X Recruitment Study

FYI

The Clinics have been accepting interns since 1985 . . . Admissions for fall and spring are rolling, so apply early . . . Applicants should have a general understanding of the workings of the American criminal justice system . . . Former interns have been hired by the FBI or have entered the nations' prestigious law schools and law firms.

TO APPLY

Open to college juniors and seniors as well as recent college grads, college grads of any age, and grad students. International applicants eligible. Write for application.

Creecy Chandler
Investigations Supervisor
The Criminal and Juvenile Justice Clinic
Georgetown University Law Center
111 F Street NW
Washington, DC 20001-2095
(202) 662-9575
(202) 662-9681 (Fax)
E-mail: accs@law.georgetown.edu

GEORGIA GOVERNOR'S OFFICE

SELECTIVITY 🔍

Approximate applicant pool: 600; Interns accepted: 300

COMPENSATION 💲

$75/week for undergrads; $100/week for grad students

LOCATION(S)

Cities throughout Georgia

FIELD

Several fields (see The Work)

DURATION

10–13 weeks: Summer, Fall, Winter, Spring

DEADLINE(S)

Summer: April 15 (February 1 for law students); Fall: July 15; Spring: October 15

THE WORK

Established in 1776, the Georgia Governor's Office heads the Peach State's executive branch. The Governor's Intern Program, founded in 1971 by then-governor Jimmy Carter, places interns in governmental and nonprofit agencies throughout the state, including theaters, museums, health care organizations, and environmental groups (e.g., Department of Natural Resources, Department of Corrections, City of Atlanta, The Nature Conservancy, Solicitor General's offices). Law students are placed in the Legal departments of the aforementioned organizations (summer only).

PERKS

Intern reception with Governor; other perks vary with placement.

According to the internship brochure, the internship program seeks to "provide college students with professional experience before they enter the working world" . . . Former interns include numerous judges, lawyers, agency directors, and legislative assistants.

TO APPLY

Open to college juniors and seniors as well as grad students. Must be a Georgia resident or attending a school in Georgia. Minimum GPA: 2.75. International applicants eligible. Write for application.

Governor's Intern Program
Office of the Governor
245 State Capitol
Atlanta, GA 30334
(404) 656-3804
(404) 651-5110 (Fax)
E-mail: rachel@gov.state.ga.us

THE GESHER SUMMER INTERNSHIP PROGRAM

SELECTIVITY 🔍
Approximate applicant pool: 90–100; Interns accepted: 40

COMPENSATION 💲 💲 💲
$550/month for undergrads; $750/month for holders of BA degree; $950/month for grad students

LOCATION(S)
Israel (Tel Aviv, Jerusalem, Haifa)

FIELD
Finance; Marketing; Computer science; Engineering; Information systems

DURATION
June–August (minimum 8 weeks)

DEADLINE(S)
February 28

THE WORK

For the past 9 years, the Israeli Forum, a nonpolitical volunteer organization has been placing students for a paid summer internship in Israel's leading companies and corporations. Interns are placed in marketing, computers, business, and economic divisions of the top banks, The Israel Electric Company, Teva Pharmaceuticals, Venture Capitals, and more. Students work as full-time employees and are provided with a structured social program throughout the summer.

PERKS

The social program includes: Cross cultural seminar preparing the student for work in an Israeli business environment; weekend trips and hikes throughout Israel; lectures by top executives; seminar at the Foreign Ministry office and more.

FYI

"Gesher" is the Hebrew word for "bridge," symbolizing The Forum's commitment to fostering closer relations between American students and the Israeli business community.

TO APPLY

Open to undergrads with at least sophomore standing and grad students. Application form as well as all information can be found on our website.

Yael Shapira, Project Coordinator
972-3-9063668
972-3-9063667 (Fax)
E-mail: if_yael@netvision.net.il
www.intournet.co.il/gesher

GLEN HELEN OUTDOOR EDUCATION CENTER

SELECTIVITY 🔍 🔍 🔍
Approximate applicant pool: 150; Interns accepted: 20

COMPENSATION 💲
$250/month; room and board; academic credit through Antioch University

LOCATION(S)
Yellow Springs, OH

FIELD
Environment; Education

DURATION
16–20 weeks: Fall and Spring

DEADLINE(S)
Rolling

THE WORK

The Glen Helen Outdoor Education Center is a nonprofit, residential environmental education center founded in 1956 and owned by Antioch University. Situated on a 1,000-acre nature preserve, Glen Helen operates educational programs for school children and their teachers, a summer ecology camp for young people ages 5 to 17, and a variety of adult workshops relating to the environment. Interns lead hikes, work with injured birds of prey, and participate in evening educational/recreational programs.

PERKS

Two-week orientation and weekly training sessions with staff and guest speakers; field trips and one free workshop on an environmental topic; access to campus library, pool, gym, and racquetball/tennis courts; access to darkroom.

FYI

In existence since 1957, the internship program counts among its alumni Glen Helen's interim director and the director of the Cape Cod Environmental Center . . . Each intern is required to portray a character from the 1700s during one hike.

TO APPLY

Open to college juniors and seniors, recent college grads, college grads of any age, and grad students. International applicants eligible. Write for application.

Assistant Director
Glen Helen Outdoor Education Center
1075 SR 343
Yellow Springs, OH 45387
(937) 767-7648
(937) 767-6655 (Fax)
E-mail: ghelen@antioch-college.edu

> Interns at Glen Helen Outdoor Education Center are required to lead visiting school children on hikes into the wilderness. During one of these hikes, interns must portray characters from the late 1700s.

GLOBAL ⊕ EXCHANGE

SELECTIVITY 🔍
Approximate applicant pool: 100; Interns accepted: 24

COMPENSATION 💲
Public transit voucher

LOCATION(S)
San Francisco, CA

FIELD
Human rights/social justice

DURATION
One month minimum: Summer, Fall, Spring

DEADLINE(S)
Summer: April 1; Fall/ Spring: rolling

THE WORK
Global Exchange (GX) was founded in 1988 to promote social justice and to forge closer ties between US and third world citizens. GX works to link North Americans with grassroots groups struggling for social justice around the world. Its campaigns include a program to end the Cold War against Cuba; support the democracy movement in Mexico; and promote Corporate Accountability of US firms manufacturing overseas. GX also arranges speaking tours for staff and prominent international Human Rights and Social Justice activists operates Fair Trade craft stores, publishes educational resources, and organizes Reality Tours—one to two week trips to foreign lands, including Ireland, Cuba, China, Palestine, and Israel, South Africa, Haiti, Brasil, Mexico, amd more. Interns work in the following areas; Reality Tours, Fundraising, Fair Trade, Campaign Programs, Publications, Research, and Speakers Bureau.

PERKS
Discounts on GX Reality Tours and crafts and other merchandise from our Fair Trade stores.

FYI
Depending on their position, interns develop information packets, write articles and press releases, recruit speakers, or create in-store displays and learn organizing skills.

TO APPLY
Open to high school grads, undergrads, recent college grads of any age, and grad students. International applicants proficient in English are eligible. Application available at: www.globalexchange.org.

Internship Coordinator
Global Exchange
2017 Mission, #303
San Francisco, CA 94110
(800) 497-1994
E-mail: globalexchange.org

GLOBAL volunteers ™

SELECTIVITY N/A
Approximate applicant pool: N/A; Interns accepted: N/A

COMPENSATION 💲
None. Volunteers pay a tax-deductible fee (includes training, an experienced team leader, ground transportation, food, and lodging)

LOCATION(S)
Locations around the world: China; Cook Islands; Costa Rica; Ecuador; Ghana; Greece; India; Indonesia; Ireland; Italy; Jamaica; Mexico; Poland; Romania; Spain; Tanzania; Turkey; USA; and Vietnam.

FIELD
Public service in agriculture; Construction; Health care; Teaching, Child care

DURATION
9 days–3 weeks: ongoing

DEADLINE(S)
Rolling

THE WORK
Founded in 1984, Global Volunteers is a private nonprofit organization sponsoring short-term work opportunities worldwide. Working with villagers in rural communities, volunteers (called "servant-learners") build schools and community centers, paint health-care clinics, dig wells, erect street signs, install playground equipment, construct homes and water systems, work with health care professionals, plant crops, and teach students of all ages a variety of basic subjects.

PERKS
Orientation manuals and on-site leadership; language training for assignments where little English is spoken; access to beaches, historical sites, hiking, etc. (varies with placement).

FYI
According to Global Volunteers, its program "departs from conventional adventure travel and cultural immersion experiences in one very important way . . . [you] serve, and thereby, learn firsthand about the host community."

TO APPLY
Open to all ages including high school students, undergrads, recent college grads, and grad students. Minors must be accompanied. International applicants eligible. Write or call for application and catalogue.

Global Volunteers
375 East Little Canada Road
St. Paul, MN 55117-1628
(800) 487-1074 or (651) 407-6100
E-mail: globalvolunteers.org
www.globalvolunteers.org

GMC TRUCK

See General Motors

See National Aeronautics and Space Administration

GOLF DIGEST

See PGA Tour

GOOD MORNING AMERICA

SELECTIVITY
Approximate applicant pool: 100 (Summer); Interns accepted: 25

COMPENSATION
None

LOCATION(S)
New York, NY

FIELD
Television

DURATION
10–16 weeks: Summer, Fall, Spring

DEADLINE(S)
Summer: January 31

THE WORK
A production of ABC News, *Good Morning America* (GMA) is a two-hour, live news and information show, hosted by Charles Gibson and Lisa McRee and airing six days a week—two hours on weekdays and one hour on Sundays. Segments involve news, consumer information, health issues, film reviews, and celebrity interviews. Working in "production support" capacities (e.g., answering phones, filing, researching story ideas, screening tapes), interns are assigned to nearly fifteen departments, including Entertainment, Booking, Promotion, Consumer, Home Improvement, Production Management, Tape, Science, Medical, and Research.

PERKS
Attendance welcome at production meetings; opportunities to observe show from the control room.

FYI
First broadcast in 1975. . . According to the internship coordinator, fall and spring may be preferable times to intern because "sweeps" weeks during those periods ensure that there is a lot of activity at GMA.

TO APPLY
Open to college sophomores, juniors, and seniors as well as grad students (in summer, only college seniors are eligible). Must receive academic credit. International applicants eligible. Please send cover letter and resume to:.

Internship Coordinator
Good Morning America
147 Columbus Avenue
New York, NY 10023
(212) 456-5900

GOODMAN THEATRE

Goodman
The Theatre

SELECTIVITY
Approximate applicant pool: 150; Interns accepted: 30–40

COMPENSATION
Selected fellowships

LOCATION(S)
Chicago, IL

FIELD
Theater

DURATION
12–20 weeks: one season, two seasons

DEADLINE(S)
Summer: March 9; Fall: June 16; Winter: November 3

THE WORK
Chicago's oldest and largest resident company, the Goodman Theatre was established in 1925 as a gift to the Art Institute of Chicago. Recent productions include *Death of a Salesman* (winner of four 1999 Tony Awards), *Floyd Collins*, and *Jitney*. Internships are offered in Arts in Education, Business Administration, Casting, Development, Dramaturgy, Literary Management, Production, Stage Management, Ticket Services, and Public Relations.

PERKS
Brown-bag forums with staff; free tickets to all productions; passes to Art Institute of Chicago and other city museums; discount in gift shop.

TO APPLY
Open to college seniors, recent college grads, college grads of any age, and grad students. International applicants eligible. Write for application. Application also available on website: www.goodman.theatre.org

Internship Coordinator
Goodman Theatre
200 South Columbus Drive
Chicago, IL 60603

SELECTIVITY 🔍🔍🔍🔍
Approximate applicant pool: 25–50; Interns accepted: 2

COMPENSATION Ⓢ
Est. $4.25–$6/hour

LOCATION(S)
Miami, FL

FIELD
Public relations agencies

DURATION
12 weeks: Summer, Fall, Spring

DEADLINE(S)
Rolling

THE WORK
Founded in 1988, The Gothard Group (GG) is a public relations agency specializing in multicultural public relations, advertising, and special events. Clients have included Blockbuster Entertainment, McDonald's, Philip Morris, Port of Miami, Aruba Jazz & Latin Music Festival, the Florida Marlins, Joe Robbie Stadium, Black Archives Research Foundation, and the Royal Visit of England's Queen Elizabeth II to Miami. Interns assist staff with all aspects of PR and special events coordination, from contacting media to helping write press releases.

PERKS
Access to GG seminars on facets of public relations; attendance welcome at client and staff meetings; free tickets to sporting events.

FYI
Approximately 35 percent of interns return to GG for full-time positions. GG is a member of IPREX, a worldwide network of 46 owner-operated PR firms, that was founded by Makovsky & Company (see separate entry).

TO APPLY
Open to college juniors and seniors as well as college grads. Must have taken at least one public relations, communications, or marketing course. International applicants eligible. Submit resume, cover letter, and writing sample.

Internship Coordinator
The Gothard Group
4100 NE Second Avenue, #305
Miami, FL 33137
(305) 576-4914
(305) 576-4829 (Fax)

SELECTIVITY 🔍
Approximate applicant pool: 30–40; Interns accepted: 10–12

COMPENSATION Ⓢ Ⓢ
$57/week; free room and board; medical benefits for 1-year commitment

LOCATION(S)
Lincoln and Monterey, MA

DURATION
Preference given to one-year commitment

FIELD
Health care; Human service; Social work; Psychology

DEADLINE(S)
Rolling

THE WORK
Founded in 1913, Gould Farm is a residential treatment program for adults with mental illnesses. Situated on a 600-acre farm in the Berkshire Hills, the farm offers a variety of work, recreational, and social activities designed to rehabilitate people with emotional and psychiatric difficulties. Interns work in the following areas: kitchen, recreation, gardens/grounds, farm (dairy and other livestock care) forestry, business office, child care, residential support, and maintenance.

PERKS
Close-knit community of staff and guests; extensive recreational opportunities (e.g., maple syrup production, wood cutting, pottery, weaving, furniture making); use of art room and weaving studio; close proximity to skiing and Tanglewood and other music festivals. This is an invaluable hands-on experience!

FYI
In existence since 1913, Gould Farm began with 100 percent volunteer staff . . . The farm is located about 130 miles from both New York and Boston, and 40 miles from Hartford, CT . . . The farm owns and operates The Roadside Store & Café, featuring vegetables, bread, and dairy products produced on the farm. All staff and interns live on the property.

TO APPLY
Open to undergrads, recent college grads, grad students, and college grads of any age. International applicants with proper visa or "green card" eligible. Submit resume, cover letter, and three references.

Internship Coordinator
Gould Farm
Box 157
Monterey, MA 01245-0157
(413) 528-1804 ext.17
(413) 528-5051 (Fax)
www.gouldfarm.org

> In the movie *Reality Bites*, when the disillusioned character played by Winona Ryder is about to leave her job, the show's host says to his producer: "I can find an intern who will do her job for free."

SELECTIVITY 🔍
Approximate applicant pool: 30; Interns accepted: 10

COMPENSATION 💲💲
None

LOCATION(S)
Arlington, VA; Washington, DC

FIELD
Government

DURATION
4 weeks minimum: ongoing

DEADLINE(S)
Rolling

THE WORK
Established in 1965, the Government Affairs Institute (GAI) is a training division of the US Office of Personnel Management. Through Capitol Hill courses—which include lectures by members of congress and their staffs, lobbyists, academics, and journalists—GAI educates members of the executive branch about congressional processes, procedures, and practices as well as current legislative policy issues. Interns research and write issue briefs and fact sheets, summarize legislation, and write major policy papers to be used in GAI courses.

PERKS
Attendance welcome at GAI seminars and Capitol Hill briefings; session on how to use Legis-Slate, an online database on congress; special office for interns.

FYI
GAI launched its internship program in 1975 . . . The internship coordinator writes: "Because [issue briefs] are written under considerable time constraints and then updated for each new course, they must be written quickly, concisely, and accurately by interns."

TO APPLY
Open to undergrads and grad students. Submit resume, cover letter, writing sample, and transcript.

Internship Coordinator
The Government Affairs Institute
US Office of Personnel Management
P.O. Box 988
Washington, DC 20044
(703) 312-7267
(703) 235-1495 (Fax)

See National Park Service

GREAT PROJECTS
Film Company, Inc.

SELECTIVITY 🔍🔍🔍
Approximate applicant pool: 40; Interns accepted: 1–4

COMPENSATION 💲
$50–$200/week, full time

LOCATION(S)
New York, NY

FIELD
Documentary film

DURATION
12–20 weeks: ongoing

DEADLINE(S)
Rolling

THE WORK
Emmy-winning film producers Daniel B. Polin and Kenneth Mandel founded Great Projects Film Company (GPFC) in 1988 to produce television programming that explores history, politics, and culture with a focus on American achievements. Created for PBS and the Discovery Channel, GPFC documentaries include *George Marshall and the American Century* (1993), *He Conquered Space* (1996), *An Essay on Matisse* (1996), *Media Matters* (1999), *The Trial of Adolf Eichmann* (1997), *The Empire State Building* (1999), and *Picasso Paints Picasso* (1998). Interns are involved in all aspects of the company, from answering phones, typing, and logging tapes to doing research, writing proposals, editing film, and providing general office support. Attention to detail and initiative are essential for the intern to remain on staff when the internship is over.

PERKS
Attendance welcome at parties and luncheons.

FYI
Says Daniel Polin, "This is a small operation—two to ten people, depending on projects in-house. If someone wants to get an inside look at how documentaries are produced, from research and fundraising to production and promotion, this is an ideal placement.". . . Approximately 50 percent of interns are hired for full-time positions.

TO APPLY
Open to recent college grads, college grads of any age, and grad students. International applicants eligible. Submit resume, cover letter, and five- to ten-page writing sample "not about films, preferably a history or English paper or research summary." Apply anytime as it is impossible to know when a position will open up. Full time or near full time preferred.

Internship Program
Great Projects Film Company
584 Ninth Avenue
New York, NY 10036
(212) 581-1700
(212) 581-3157 (Fax)
greatproj@aol.com

Greater Media Cable
WGMC-TV **3**
CENTRAL MASS

SELECTIVITY
Approximate applicant pool: 50; Interns accepted: 5–8

COMPENSATION $
None

LOCATION(S)
Worcester, MA and 20 other central MA towns

FIELD
Television

DURATION
16 weeks: Summer, Fall, Spring

DEADLINE(S)
Summer: April 30; Fall: August 1; Spring: December 31

THE WORK
A subsidiary of Greater Media Inc.—a radio, cable television, and newspaper corporation based in New Jersey—Greater Media Cable (GMC) is a cable company serving the second largest city in New England and 20 surrounding towns; it produces the only local newscast for central Massachusetts. Interns work in News, Production, and Advertising.

PERKS
Participation in live productions using GMC's mobile production vans; full access to camera and production equipment; free tickets to events.

FYI
The coordinator writes: "The interns get to do more television production here than any other television production internship that I know of." . . . About 30 percent of interns return for full-time positions.

TO APPLY
Open to college and grad students as well as grads in communications or related majors. Interns must have a vehicle in order to travel to various locations for productions. Write for application.

Internship Coordinator
Greater Media Cable
95 Higgins Street
Worcester, MA 01606
(508) 853-1515

SELECTIVITY   N/A
Approximate applicant pool: N/A; Interns accepted: 30–50

COMPENSATION $
None

LOCATION(S)
Atlanta, GA; Austin, Dallas, and Houston, TX; Boston, MA; Cleveland, OH; Chicago, IL; Denver, CO; Detroit, MI; Los Angeles, San Diego, and San Francisco (HQ), CA; Miami, FL; New York, NY; Phoenix and Tuscon, AZ; Portland, OR; Philadelphia, PA; Seattle, WA; Washington, DC

FIELD
Real estate

DURATION
4 weeks minimum: ongoing

DEADLINE(S)
Rolling

THE WORK
Founded in 1958, Grubb & Ellis (G&E) is one of the nation's largest independent real estate companies, offering services in commercial and mortgage brokerage, property and facilities management (through its subsidiary, Axiom), appraisal, auction services, and consulting. With 55 offices and over 4,000 employees nationwide, G&E handles sales of hotels, office buildings, shopping complexes, and industrial parks for a broad range of clients, from private investors to corporations. Interns at headquarters work in Legal, Human Resources, MIS, Accounting, and Marketing. Interns in the commercial brokerage offices work as assistants to real estate agents.

PERKS
Mentors; opportunities to accompany real estate agents on appraisals.

FYI
G&E pioneered the concept of requiring its salespeople to specialize by real estate product type and market area . . . G&E's Auction Services alone manages over $1.5 billion worth of transactions annually.

TO APPLY
Open to high school students, undergrads, recent college grads, college grads of any age, and grad students. International applicants studying in the United States are eligible. Submit resume and cover letter directly to office of interest. Call headquarters for addresses and phone numbers.

Human Resources
Grubb & Ellis
One Montgomery Street
Telesis Tower, 9th Floor
San Francisco, CA 94104
(415) 956-1990

EXCLUSIVE INTERVIEW WITH GEORGE STEPHANOPOULOS

George Stephanopoulos was previously the Senior Advisor to the President for Policy and Strategy. During the 1992 presidential election, he served on the Clinton/Gore Campaign as the Deputy Campaign Manager and Director of Communications. He holds a Masters in theology from Balliol College, Oxford University, where he studied as a Rhodes Scholar, and a B.A. in political science from Columbia University.

The Internship Informants: Where did you intern and what did you do?

Stephanopoulos: My first internship was the summer of 1981, and it was in the office of Congresswoman Mary Rose Oakar, here in Washington, DC It was just about six weeks. That was interesting—it was a split summer. The second six weeks I interned with the Cleveland Electric Illuminating Company. They were both great, but it helped me figure out what I wanted to do—I liked the political work, the congressional work much more.

The Internship Informants: Did you intern anywhere else?

Stephanopoulos: Right after I graduated I interned with the Arms Control Association. It was terrific; it was in association with the Carnegie Endowment for International Peace.

The Internship Informants: Was this when you appeared on "Nightline"?

Stephanopoulos: Right, it was crazy. This guy from off the street would always come in [to the Arms Control Association] and offer $10,000 to anyone who could prove that nuclear weapons deterred war. Since I was the intern, I was the one who talked to him. So when he tried to blow up the Washington Monument, I called the police, and from then on I was the guy who knew the guy who wanted to blow up the Washington Monument.

The Internship Informants: Are you still in touch with some of the people you interned with?

Stephanopoulos: Sure . . . [they are] some of my best friends.

The Internship Informants: If you had to distill out the most important things you learned as an intern, what would they be?

Stephanopoulos: The biggest thing is that you learn what you're suited for. It's a great chance to experiment and see what kind of work you want to do and whether you're interested in it. And secondly, you learn, simply, how to work your way around an office . . . it's a great transition.

The Internship Informants: Do you realize that you may be the only former intern we're interviewing who has a fan club?

Stephanopoulos: [chuckles] No comment.

GTE

SELECTIVITY 🔍🔍🔍🔍🔍
Approximate applicant pool: 5,000; Interns accepted: 350

COMPENSATION 💲💲💲💲
$400–$600/week for undergrads; $750/week for grad students; round-trip travel

LOCATION(S)
Atlanta, GA; Irving and Dallas/Forth Worth Airport, TX; Needham and Waltham, MA; Oak Brook, IL; Tampa and Temple Terrace, FL; Thousand Oaks, CA; Westfield, IN

FIELD
Telecommunications; Defense

DURATION
12 weeks: Summer

DEADLINE(S)
April 15

THE WORK
With annual sales of $21 billion and 100,000 employees, GTE is one of the world's fourth largest publicly owned telecommunications company and a leader in local and cellular telephone services, government and defense communications systems, satellite and air-to-ground telecommunications, and telephone directories (Yellow Pages). Interns work in the areas of computer science, engineering, finance/accounting, human resources, marketing, sales, operations, public affairs, mathematics, materials management, and logistics in the following divisions: Telephone Operations, Data Services, Supply, Cellular Operations, Government Systems, Spacenet, Airfone, Industry Products & Services, Directories, and Laboratories.

PERKS
Intern Day featuring lunch and executive presentations; summer picnic (barbecue and t-shirt giveaway); access to GTE gyms; video conference with CEO broadcast nationwide to all interns.

FYI
Perhaps a first among internship programs, a group of GTE interns recently banded together to write an official Intern Mission Statement: "Although our assignments are only temporary, we, GTE Summer Interns, will add value and enthusiasm to the tasks at hand, realizing that our diverse backgrounds and experiences will promote teamwork, efficiency, quality and integrity in all that we do, while strengthening our educational foundations for the future."

TO APPLY
Open to undergrads and grad students (MBA, MA, MS, and PhD). Minimum GPA: 3.0. Submit resume and cover letter directly to division of interest. The Summer Intern Program brochure, which briefly describes the program and provides a list of GTE addresses, may be obtained from college career centers or by according to the company's website.

Manager—College Relations
GTE Service Corporation
700 Hidden Ridge Drive-HQW01J85
Irving, TX 75038
www.GTE.com

> **P**erhaps a first among internship programs, a group of GTE interns recently banded together to write an official Intern Mission Statement: "Although our assignments are only temporary, we, GTE Summer Interns, will add value and enthusiasm to the tasks at hand, realizing that our diverse backgrounds and experiences will promote teamwork, efficiency, quality and integrity in all that we do, while strengthening our educational foundations for the future."

GUIDING LIGHT

See Procter & Gamble Productions

GUND ARENA

See CAVS/Gund Arena Company

HABITAT FOR HUMANITY INTERNATIONAL

SELECTIVITY 🔍
Approximate applicant pool: 100; Interns accepted: 30

COMPENSATION 💲💲
$56/week for 3 month commitments; free furnished housing; medical reimbursement

LOCATION(S)
Americus, GA

FIELD
Public service

DURATION
3 months–3 years: Summer, Fall, Spring

DEADLINE(S)
Summer: March 30; Fall: July 30; Spring: December 30

THE WORK
A nonprofit, ecumenical Christian ministry, Habitat for Humanity International (HFHI) renovates impoverished housing and fights poverty and homelessness by building affordable homes for families in need. Since its founding in 1976, the organization has built over 30,000 homes worldwide. Interns all over the

world work in the areas of finance, communications, human resources, construction, information systems, legal services, graphic arts, photography, and language translation.

PERKS
Possible overseas travel; possible meetings with international diplomatic figures.

FYI
Since 1980, interns have assisted HFHI in its dream: "A decent house in a decent community for God's people in need." . . . Approximately 50 percent of interns return to HFHI full time.

TO APPLY
Open to high school seniors, high school grads, undergrads, recent college grads, college grads of any age, and grad students. International applicants eligible. Write for application.

Director of Human Resources
Habitat for Humanity International
121 Habitat Street
Americus, GA 31709-3498
(912) 924-6935, x124

> "There are lots of days I feel like I am just working with a construction company, only building houses. Then an older woman comes to my door to [make a payment] on her house. I invite her in and she talks about how God helped her to have this house . . . She moved into her house last month and is paying for it by selling [produce] from her garden. Yes, God is at work here, in other folks' lives and in mine."
> —An International Partner in Zaire with Habitat for Humanity International

HAFT/NASATIR

SELECTIVITY 🔍🔍🔍
Approximate applicant pool: 80; Interns accepted: 9

COMPENSATION 💲
None

LOCATION(S)
Los Angeles, CA; New York, NY

FIELD
Film; Television

DURATION
4–6 months: Summer, Fall, Spring

DEADLINE(S)
Summer: May 1; Fall: August 1; Spring: December 1

THE WORK
An independent film production company, Haft/Nasatir (HN) was founded in 1989. At a rate of about four films per year, HN has produced such memorable movies as *Dead Poets Society* starring Robin Williams and *Hocus Pocus* with Bette Midler. Interns work as assistants for the producers, helping out with budgets, casting, and development.

PERKS
Networking opportunities with writers, directors, and actors; invitations to movie premieres; attendance welcome at screenwriters' readings; small office.

FYI
The story editor for Scott Rudin Productions once worked as an HN intern . . . Says a former intern: "It's kind of an unwritten rule here that if you do a good job, [a producer] will write you a glowing recommendation. They realize how important recommendations can be for getting jobs in the entertainment industry."

TO APPLY
Open to high school grads, undergrads, recent college grads, college grads of any age, and grad students. International applicants fluent in English are eligible. Submit resume and cover letter.

Internship Coordinator
Haft/Nasatir
26 East 93rd Street #2E
New York, NY 10128
(212) 534-6764
(212) 534-7061 (Fax)

Internship Coordinator
Haft/Nasatir
1440 South Sepulveda Boulevard
Los Angeles, CA 90025
(310) 444-8415

HALLMARK CARDS

SELECTIVITY 🔍🔍🔍🔍🔍
Approximate applicant pool: 2,000; Interns accepted: 30–70

COMPENSATION 💲💲💲💲
$2,500–$3,000/month for undergrads; $3,800–$5,200/month for grad students

LOCATION(S)
Kansas City, MO (HQ); Plant locations in KS

FIELD
Greeting card; Personal communications products

DURATION
10–12 weeks; Summer

DEADLINE(S)
January 15

THE WORK
Hallmark is the world's largest greeting card company. From its persuasive advertising slogan, "When you care enough to send the very best," to its 665-person creative staff, Hallmark is the gold standard in greeting cards. Interns choose from a variety of business or technical positions like Accounting/Finance, Business Research, Engineering, Human Resources, Business Services, Manufacturing, Marketing, and Information Technology.

PERKS
Friendly culture; luncheon seminars; emplyee discount; social activities; fitness center.

FYI
To the disappointment of many students, interns in Hallmark's Corporate Intern Program do not write Hallmark cards . . . The word hallmark dates back to 18th-century England when official marks were stamped on gold and silver articles to dignify their purity.

TO APPLY

Open to students entering the final year of their undergrad or grad program. Submit resume and cover letter.

Hallmark Cards
Corporate Staffing/Internship Program
Mail Drop #112
P.O. Box 419580
Kansas City, MO 64141-6580
(816) 274-5111
E-mail: hcolle1@hallmark.com
www.hallmark.com

HALSTEAD COMMUNICATIONS/COLLEGE CONNECTIONS

SELECTIVITY 🔍 🔍
Applicant pool: 250; interns accepted: 1

COMPENSATION 💲 💲 💲
$300–$400/week and college credit

LOCATION(S)
New York, NY

FIELD
Public relations

DURATION
8–12 weeks: ongoing

DEADLINE(S)
Rolling

THE WORK

Founded in 1980, Halstead Communications/College Connections is among the oldest public relations and marketing communications firms to specialize in representing educational and nonprofit organizations. Its clients have included Agnes Scott College, Sarah Lawrence College, The College Board, Duke University, *Rolling Stone*, Rutgers University, UCLA, Vassar College, and UNICEF. Interns assist the staff in writing press releases, pitching stories to various media, and conducting mass mailings and research projects.

PERKS

Attendance welcome at client meetings and staff parties; small, close-knit office; backyard garden.

FYI

According to the internship coordinator, CC's internship is more than stuffing envelopes and filing. "As a case in point," she elaborates, "a recent intern wrote an entire news release on a program sponsored by her college and promoted the release to several different media. In the end, *USA Today* picked it up."

TO APPLY

Open to undergrads and grads. Submit resume and cover letter.

Internship Coordinator
College Connections
329 East 82nd Street
New York, NY 10028
(212) 734-2190
(212) 517-7284 (Fax)
E-mail: halstead@halsteadpr.com

HALT: AN ORGANIZATION OF AMERICANS FOR LEGAL REFORM

SELECTIVITY
Interns accepted: 4 Summer (full time), 6 Fall (part time), 6 Spring (part time)

COMPENSATION 💲
Varies

LOCATION(S)
Washington, DC

FIELD
Law; Public policy; Legislative

DURATION
10–15 weeks: Summer, Fall, Spring

DEADLINE(S)
Rolling

THE WORK

In existence since 1978, HALT: An organization of Americans for Legal Reform is a nonprofit organization dedicated to making the civil legal system more accessible, less costly, and more equitable to the average person. With a membership of approximately 50,000 people, HALT produces educational material on the legal system; works with member activists legislators, bar associations, and coalition groups; and publishes a newsletter on legal reform. Interns work on all aspects of the organization's operations.

PERKS

Field trips to related organizations; small staff; casual work environment.

FYI

Says a former intern: "Given the green light to pursue topics which I found exciting, I got to work on various writing assignments which required extensive research; the most important factor about the process is that the tasks always required some form of critical thinking or analysis. Not just any internship will allow you to [do this]."

TO APPLY

Open to high school seniors, high school grads, undergrads, and grads and law students. International applicants eligible. Submit resume, cover letter, and writing sample.

Internship Coordinator
HALT
1612 K Street NW, Suite 510
Washington, DC 20006
(202) 887-8255
(202) 887-9699 (Fax)

GOVERNOR'S OFFICE CONTACTS

The governments of virtually every state and US territory use interns in their Governors' offices. Here are the contacts:

Alabama
Gov. Don Siegelman (D)
State Capitol
600 Dexter Avenue
Montgomery, AL 36104
(205) 242-7100

Alaska
Gov. Tony Knowles (D)
P.O. Box 110001
Juneau, AK 99811-0001
(907) 465-3500

Arizona
Gov. Jane Dee Hull (R)
State Capitol
1700 W. Washington
Phoenix, AZ 85007
(602) 542-4331

Arkansas
Gov. Mike Huckabee (R)
250 State Capitol
Little Rock, AR 72201
(501) 682-2345

California (see separate entry)
Gov. Gray Davis (D)
State Capitol
Sacramento, CA 95814
(916) 445-2841

Colorado
Gov. Bill Owens (R)
136 State Capitol
Denver, CO 80203-1792
(303) 866-2471

Connecticut
Gov. John G. Rowland (R)
210 Capitol Avenue
Hartford, CT 06106
(203) 566-4840

Delaware
Gov. Tom Carper (D)
Tarnall Building
Dover, DE 19901
(302) 739-4101

Florida
Gov. Jeb Bush (R)
The Capitol
Tallahassee, FL 32399-0001
(904) 488-2272

Georgia (see separate entry)
Gov. Roy Barnes (D)
203 State Capitol
Atlanta, GA 30334
(404) 656-1776

Hawaii
Gov. Benjamin J. Cayetano (D)
State Capitol
235 S. Beretania Street
Honolulu, HI 96813
(808) 586-0034

Idaho
Gov. Dirk Kempthorne (R)
State House
Boise, ID 83720-0034
(208) 334-2100

Illinois
Gov. George H. Ryan (R)
State Capitol, Room 207
Springfield, IL 62706
(217) 782-6830

Indiana
Gov. Frank O'Bannon (D)
State House, Room 206
Indianapolis, IN 46204
(317) 232-4567

Iowa
Gov. Tom Vilsack (D)
State Capitol
Des Moines, IA 50319-0001
(515) 281-5211

Kansas
Gov. Bill Graves (R)
State Capitol, Second Floor
Topeka, KS 66612-1590
(913) 296-3232

Kentucky
Gov. Paul E. Patton (D)
State Capitol
700 Capitol St.
Frankfort, KY 40601
(502) 564-2611

Louisiana
Gov. Mike Foster (R)
P.O. Box 94004
Baton Rouge, LA 70804-9004
(504) 342-7015

Maine
Gov. Angus S. King Jr. (I)
State House, Station 1
Augusta, ME 04333
(207) 287-3531

Maryland
Gov. Parris N. Glendening (D)
State House
100 State Circle
Annapolis, MD 21401
(410) 974-3901

Massachusetts
Gov. Argeo Paul Cellucci (R)
State House, Room 360
Boston, MA 02133
(617) 727-9173

Michigan
Gov. John Engler (R)
P.O. Box 30013
Lansing, MI 48909
(517) 373-3400

Minnesota
Gov. Jesse Ventura (Reform)
75 Constitution Avenue
130 State Capitol
St. Paul, MN 55155
(612) 296-3391

Mississippi
Gov. Ronnie Musgrove (D)
P.O. Box 139
Jackson, MS 39205
(601) 359-3100

Missouri
Gov. Mel Carnahan (D)
P.O. Box 720
Jefferson City, MO 65102
(314) 751-3222

Montana
Gov. Marc Racicot (R)
Governor's Office
State Capitol
Helena, MT 59620-0801
(406) 444-3111

Nebraska
Gov. Mike Johanns (R)
P.O. Box 94848
Lincoln, NE 68509-4848
(402) 471-2244

Nevada
Gov. Kenny C. Guinn (R)
State Capitol
Carson City, NV 89710
(702) 687-5670

New Hampshire
Gov. Jeanne Shaheen (D)
Office of the Governor
State House, Room 208
Concord, NH 03301
(603) 271-2121

New Jersey
Gov. Christine T. Whitman (R)
125 W. State St., CN-001
Trenton, NJ 08625
(609) 292-6000

New Mexico
Gov. Gary E. Johnson (R)
Office of the Governor
State Capitol, Suite 400
Santa Fe, NM 87503
(505) 827-3000

New York
Gov. George E. Pataki (R)
State Capitol
138 Eagle Street
Albany, NY 12202
(518) 474-7516

North Carolina
Gov. James B. Hunt Jr. (D)
State Capitol
116 W. Jones St.
Raleigh, NC 27603-8001
(919) 733-4240

North Dakota
Gov. Edward T. Schafer (R)
600 E. Boulevard Avenue
Bismarck, ND 58505
(701) 328-2200

Ohio
Gov. Bob Taft (R)
77 S. High Street, 30th Floor
Columbus, OH 43266-0601
(614) 466-3555

Oklahoma
Gov. Frank Keating (R)
State Capitol Bldg., Suite 212
Oklahoma City, OK 73105
(405) 521-2342

Oregon
Gov. John A. Kitzhaber (D)
254 State Capitol
Salem, OR 97310
(503) 378-3111

Pennsylvania
Gov. Tom Ridge (R)
Main Capitol Bldg., Room 225
Harrisburg, PA 17120
(717) 787-2500

Rhode Island
Gov. Lincoln Almond (R)
222 State House
Providence, RI 02903
(401) 277-2080

South Carolina
Gov. Jim Hodges (D)
P.O. Box 11369
Columbia, SC 29211
(803) 734-9818

South Dakota
Gov. William J. Janklow (R)
500 E. Capitol
Pierre, SD 57501
(605) 773-3212

Tennessee
Gov. Don Sundquist (R)
State Capitol, 1st Floor
Nashville, TN 37423-0001
(615) 741-2001

Texas
Gov. George W. Bush (R)
P.O. Box 12428
Austin, TX 78711
(512) 463-2000

Utah
Gov. Mike Leavitt (R)
State Capitol, Suite 210
Salt Lake City, UT 84114
(801) 538-1500

Vermont
Gov. Howard Dean, MD (D)
Pavilion Office Bldg.
109 State Street
Montpelier, VT 05609
(802) 828-3333

Virginia
Gov. James S. Gilmore III (R)
State Capitol
Richmond, VA 23219
(804) 786-2211

Washington
Gov. Gary Locke (D)
Legislative Building
Olympia, WA 98504-0002
(360) 753-6780

West Virginia
Gov. Cecil H. Underwood (R)
State Capitol Complex
Charleston, WV 25305-0370
(304) 558-2000

Wisconsin
Gov. Tommy G. Thompson (R)
State Capitol
P.O. Box 7863
Madison, WI 53707
(608) 266-1212

Wyoming
Gov. Jim Geringer (R)
Office of the Governor
State Capitol Building
Cheyenne, WY 82002
(307) 777-7434

Territories:

American Samoa
Tause P.F. Sunia (D)
Office of the Governor
Pago Pago, AS 96799
684-633-4116

Guam
Gov. Carl T.C. Gutierrez (D)
Executive Chambers
P.O. Box 2950
Agana, GU 96910
671-472-8931

Northern Mariana Islands
Gov. Pedro P. Tenorio (R)
P.O. Box 10007 CK
Saipan, MP 96950
670-322-5091

Puerto Rico
Gov. Pedro Rossello (D)
La Fortaleza
San Juan, PR 00901
(809) 721-7000

Virgin Islands
Gov. Charles W. Turnbull (D)
20-21 Government House
St. Thomas, VI 00801
(809) 774-0001

Courtesy of: National Governors' Association
Hall of the States, 444 N. Capitol Street, Suite 267
Washington, DC 20001-1512
(202) 624-5330

"GOOD MORNING, INTERN!"

Adrian Cronauer, a Washington communications lawyer and former military DJ whose wartime experiences formed the basis for the movie *Good Morning, Vietnam*, was once an intern at the Federal Communications Commission under George Bush.

THE HANSARD SOCIETY FOR PARLIAMENTARY GOVERNMENT

SELECTIVITY
Approximate applicant pool: 65; Interns accepted: 45 per annum

COMPENSATION
£4,600 fee/semester (approximately $7,500) includes tuition, LSE registration, London travelpass, a series of study visits and cultural activities

LOCATION(S)
London, England

FIELD
Government; Public policy

DURATION
12 weeks semester program available: Fall, Spring; 10 weeks: Summer; Two semester program available

DEADLINE(S)
Rolling; applications accepted until semester is full

THE WORK
Internships take place in the House of Commons or the House of Lords, where students are assigned to work for an individual Member of Parliament, or within other political organizations such as party headquarters, media organizations, or interest groups. Students spend three days per week undertaking specific research tasks, speech writing, tabling questions, responding to constituent queries, attending meetings and briefings, and monitoring the press. Scholars are also expected to undertake some routine office tasks when at work. One day per week is spent at the London School of Economics, where students attend the Hansard Scholars courses on the structure and workings of Parliament, and current issues in public policy. Each student also undertakes an individual research project of their own choosing.

PERKS
The program includes a series of study visits and cultural activities, such as day trips and theater trips. Each semester includes a three-day study visit to a city outside England, such as Edinburgh, Scotland; Cardiff, Wales; or Bruges, Belgium. Other perks include access to all LSE facilities, and the opportunities available through working in the Parliamentary environment

At The Hansard Society for Parliamentary Government, intern Joshua Rosenstock (right) confers with his mentor, Martyn Jones, a Member of the British Parliament.

FYI
The Hansard Society is an independent, nonprofit organization which works to promote knowledge and understanding of Parliamentary Government. Highly respected in the British political world, they are responsible for placing the largest number of interns into U.K. Parliament. Many past students continue to keep in touch with the MP or Lord they worked for, and Hansard Scholars have gone on to hold key positions in the political arena of their home countries after graduation.

TO APPLY
Open to both undergraduates and recent graduates. Minimum GPA of 3.0 required. For an application and more information visit www.hansardsociety.org.uk/scholars or E-mail study@hansard.lse.ac.uk.

Programme Coordinator
Hansard Scholars Programme
The Hansard Society for Parliamentary Government
St. Philips Building North
Sheffield Street
London WC2A 2EX
England
44-171-955-7478
44-171-955-7492 (Fax)
E-mail: study@hansard.lse.ac.uk
www.hansardsociety.org.uk

HARLEY-DAVIDSON

SELECTIVITY
Approximate applicant pool: 200; Interns accepted: 10

COMPENSATION
$8.50–$13/hour; Grad students pay scale is based on market

LOCATION(S)
Milwaukee, WI; York, PA

FIELD
Motorcycles

DURATION
15 weeks: Summer, Fall, Spring

DEADLINE(S)
Summer: March 31; Fall: July 31; Spring: November 30

THE WORK
Based in Milwaukee, Harley-Davidson (H-D) has been revving its engines in motorcycle manufacturing since 1903. The industry leader in the heavyweight motorcycle market, the company also manufactures leather apparel and motorcycle accessories and parts. Interns work in Distribution & Logistics, Marketing, Human Resources, and Engineering.

PERKS
Possible travel opportunities to other H-D sites (WI, PA); access to company fitness center; tickets to Brewers baseball, Milwaukee Summerfest, etc.

FYI
Despite H-D's image as purveyor to burly toughs wrapped in leather jackets, fewer than 1 percent of all Harley-Davidson riders embrace the "outlaw" lifestyle.

TO APPLY
Open to high school students in the Milwaukee area; college sophomores, juniors, and seniors from across the country; and grad students in manufacturing management at MIT and Northwestern University. Submit resume.

Internship Coordinator
Harley-Davidson
P.O. Box 653
Milwaukee, WI 53201-0653
(414) 343-4621 (Fax)

HARPER'S MAGAZINE

SELECTIVITY
Approximate applicant pool: 100; Interns accepted: 12 (four interns each term)

COMPENSATION
None

LOCATION(S)
New York, NY

FIELD
Magazines

DURATION
12–20 weeks: Summer, Fall, Spring

DEADLINE(S)
Summer: February 15; Fall: July 15; Spring: October 15

THE WORK
First published in 1850, *Harper's Magazine* dedicates itself to covering a mix of political, literary, cultural, and scientific affairs. Renowned for its journalistic quality and sophistication, *Harper's* has been called "eclectic and bright and unusually rich with surprises and enlightenment" by the *Pittsburgh Post-Gazette*. Interns work in the Editorial and Marketing departments.

PERKS
Attendance welcome at editorial meetings; end-of-internship luncheon; attendance welcome at occasional author readings and parties.

FYI
Alumni of the program have gone on to positions at Random House, *Esquire*, *Details*, *New York Review of Books*, and *The New York Times Magazine*.

TO APPLY
Open to undergrads, college grads of any age, and grad students. International applicants eligible. Write for application.

Internship Coordinator
Harper's Magazine
666 Broadway
New York, NY 10012
(212) 614-6500

THE HASTINGS CENTER

SELECTIVITY
Approximate applicant pool: 15–20; Interns accepted: 5–10

COMPENSATION
None

LOCATION(S)
Briarcliff Manor, NY

FIELD
Public policy; Ethics

DURATION
2–6 weeks: Summer, Fall, Winter, Spring

DEADLINE(S)
None

THE WORK
Dedicated to the debate and study of biomedical, professional, and environmental ethics, The Hastings Center is a research organization that hosts foreign and American scholars and practitioners from academia, medicine, law, and the media. Recent projects and programs have focused on such issues as care of the dying, animal welfare, resource allocation, genetic screening, justice in health care, and long-term contraceptives. Interns carry out research projects on an ethical issue of interest to the center's research.

PERKS
Daily luncheons where interns discuss their research; mentors; access to visiting scholars.

FYI
Briarcliff Manor is a suburban town located 30 miles north of New York City.

TO APPLY
Open to undergrads and grad students. International applicants eligible. Write for application.

Director of Education
The Hastings Center
255 Elm Road
Briarcliff Manor, NY 10510
(914) 762-8500
(914) 962-2124 (Fax)

Lights... Camera... *Intern!*
Interns in film and on television:

In the film *Billy Bathgate*, Billy (**Loren Dean**) apprentices himself to the 1920s gangster Dutch Schultz (**Dustin Hoffman**). He secures the apprenticeship by bribing Schultz and Schultz's bookmaking cohorts with a bag of cupcakes.

HAWK MOUNTAIN

SELECTIVITY 🔍🔍🔍
Approximate applicant pool: 80; Interns accepted: 10

COMPENSATION 💲💲
$500/month; free housing

LOCATION(S)
Kempton, PA

FIELD
Conservation biology; Science education

DURATION
16 weeks: Fall (August–December); Spring (April–July)

DEADLINE(S)
Rolling

THE WORK
Hawk Mountain Sanctuary was founded in 1934 to stop the shooting of hawks migrating along an eastern ridge of the Appalachian Mountains in Pennsylvania. Today it is a nonprofit organization of more than 10,000 members devoted to the conservation of birds of prey and the central Appalachian environment through programs in education, research, and monitoring. Interns work in Research (carrying out various ecological studies in the field), Education (guiding field trips and presenting interpretive programs to the public), and Monitoring (assist once with biological inventories).

PERKS
Field trips; travel to important conservation venues; spectacular views of the Appalachian Mountains and of bird migration (an average of 20,000 hawks, eagles, and falcons pass over the Sanctuary's North Lookout in autumn).

FYI
Because many biologists, writers, and artists have walked its trails, the Sanctuary is known as the "Crossroads of Naturalists" . . . One third of Hawk Mountain's interns come from countries outside the US . . . In existence since 1974, the internship program counts among its alumni conservation leaders on four continents.

TO APPLY
Open to undergrads, recent college grads, college grads of any age, and grad students. International applicants eligible. Write for application.

Internship Coordinator
Hawk Mountain Sanctuary
1700 Hawk Mountain Road
Kempton, PA 19529
(610) 756-6961
(610) 756-4468 (Fax)

> Interns at Hawk Mountain Sanctuary have the opportunity to watch thousands of hawks, eagles, and falcons fly over the Sanctuary's North Lookout.

SELECTIVITY 🔍
Approximate applicant pool: 30; Interns accepted: 4–6

COMPENSATION 💲💲💲
Interns: $200/week; free room and board; Camp counselors: $1,000

LOCATION(S)
Ghent, NY

FIELD
Farm; Nature

DURATION
12 weeks–9 months: Summer, Fall, Spring

DEADLINE(S)
Rolling

THE WORK
Founded in 1972, HVF Visiting Students Program is a resident farm and nature experience for elementary school classes. Set on 400-acres in the eastern hills of Columbia County, New York, Hawthorne Valley is a biodynamic dairy farm. Classes come from Waldorf schools and other schools in the northeast. Biodynamic agriculture and Waldorf education are initiatives coming from the philosophy of Rudolf Steiner at the turn of the century. Interns work with small groups of children in activities such as bread baking, animal feeding, barn cleaning, horseback riding, gardening, hiking, and seasonal activities. There is a summer camp with similar activities with 12 counselors.

PERKS
Room and board plus $200 per month stipend; $1,000 for 8 weeks in the summer. Hawthorne Valley is a rural, farming, and education center. Food is organic or biodynamic. There is a cultural community with young people working on the farm. There is a full health food store on the premises.

FYI
Writes a former visitor to Hawthorne Valley Farm: "The abundance of good, healthy food, clean water, fresh air, physical activity, and a regular yet relaxed schedule were very healing for all of us."

TO APPLY
Camp counselor positions are open to high school graduates over 18. Internships are for individuals over 21 with some experience and background in working with groups of elementary age children.

Internship Coordinator–USP
Hawthorne Valley Farm, Main House
327 CR 21 C
Ghent, NY 12075
(518) 672-4790
(518) 672-7608 (Fax)
E-mail: VSP@taconic.net
www.camppage.com/hawthorne

EXCLUSIVE INTERVIEW WITH MARK GREEN

As New York City's Public Advocate, Mark Green is next-in-line to the Mayor and is charged with monitoring and investigating public complaints against City agencies and programs. A tireless advocate for consumer rights, he has appeared over 200 times on CNN's "Crossfire" and PBS's "Firing Line" and has written or edited fifteen books on government, law, and business. In the summer of 1967, after graduating magna cum laude from Cornell, Green secured an internship with New York Republican Senator Jacob Javits. During the internship, he rallied the support of about 20 other Congressional interns and sent President Lyndon Johnson a petition protesting U.S. involvement in the Vietnam War. The letter created a firestorm of controversy, giving some Washington bigwigs the impression that Javits' interns were drafting his foreign policy positions. As a result of Green's actions, Javits was publicly denounced by a conservative congressman and Green was deemed one of "the 10 most radical students in America" by the Chicago Tribune. President Johnson let his anger at the letter be known by canceling his annual address to Congressional interns at the Washington Monument, which then led the House of Representatives to temporarily suspend the entire Congressional Intern Program. At left, a young Green prepares himself to ruffle the feathers of Capitol Hill.

The Internship Informants: What prompted you to draft the infamous letter?

Green: It was right after a lot of Rhode Scholars and others had signed petitions to [President] Johnson about the war, so I thought of organizing summer interns [to do the same]. I showed the Administrative Assistant of the Javits office what I was doing, and he said, "Fine, go ahead and organize, but keep the Senator out of it." This man was Richard Aurelio, who now runs the cable system for Time Warner in New York. I started getting signatories. We had a meeting of anti-war people, but one of them was a staffer from a pro-war congressman named Robert Michel. He took my document, gave it to [Representative] Michel, who denounced me on the floor of the House of Representatives. Then the s--- hit the fan. Articles and interviews came. Javits was not happy that his colleagues were laughing about how his intern was determining foreign policy for him. Dick Aurelio was not a happy puppy that week.

The Internship Informants: How did other people react to the letter?

Green: Cornell University called and told me to keep their name out of it. [New York Congressman] Jacob Gilbert remarked to a colleague, "I'd like to beat the s--- out of the kid who started this." The result: My letter ended not the war but the intern program. The House Intern Program was abolished for three years for what I did.

The Internship Informants: Were there other consequences of your actions?

Green: The good news was that there was an outbreak of democracy. After I did this, that same summer, a group of pro-war interns got people to sign petitions. And then there was a group of no-petition interns who got people to sign a petition saying interns shouldn't take positions. It was great.

The Internship Informants: How do you view the controversy now?

Green: For me, it was a very informative and formative experience which left an indelible mark on me. I met a ton of people because I stumbled into a controversy I never intended. Now that I think about what I do on a daily basis, twenty-eight years later, I'm not much different. I'm the Public Advocate of New York City, and I investigate and rock the boat and raise consciousness and issues. It started with the internship letter. So that summer and that episode were about the most important political thing that happened to me early in my public career.

HBO

See Home Box Office

HEADLINE NEWS

See Turner Broadcasting System

HEALTH & ENVIRONMENTAL SCIENCES GROUP

SELECTIVITY
Approximate applicant pool: 50; Interns accepted: 2–4

COMPENSATION
$300/week

LOCATION(S)
Washington, DC

FIELD
Public health

DURATION
6 months or longer

DEADLINE(S)
Rolling

THE WORK
Since 1984, the Health Risk Management Group (HRM Group) has been conducting research on high-profile, policy-setting health and environmental issues. The HRM Group's projects include toxicological studies, risk assessments, epidemiological studies, clinical studies, technology assessments, and risk management. Interns are assigned multiple projects, for which they may conduct literature searches, review articles, write reports, make presentations, or work with scientists.

PERKS
Opportunities to attend conferences; possibility of staying on as a part-time research assistant; location.

FYI
Says the internship coordinator: "Interns will have the opportunity to work on cutting-edge public health questions, such as silicone breast implants, cellular telephones, AIDS treatments."

TO APPLY
Open to college juniors and seniors, recent college grads, college grads of any age, and grad students. Must be studying biology, public health, epidemology, or related subject areas. Minimum GPA: 3.0. US applicants only. Submit resume, cover letter, one writing sample (two pages on a science topic), and transcript.

Internship Coordinator
Health Risk Management Group, Inc.
1711 N Street NW, Suite 200
Washington, DC 20036
(202) 296-7000
(202) 296-7576 (Fax)

HEALTHY MOTHERS, HEALTHY BABIES

healthy mothers, healthy babies

SELECTIVITY
Approximate applicant pool: 60; Interns accepted: 1–3

COMPENSATION
None

LOCATION(S)
Alexandria, VA

FIELD
Health care; Education

DURATION
3 months or 1 year: Summer, Fall, Spring; 10–40 hours per week

DEADLINE(S)
Rolling

THE WORK
Healthy Mothers, Healthy Babies (HMHB) is a nonprofit, informal association of 80 organizations seeking to improve the health of mothers and children in the United States. HMHB develops educational materials and tools for our constituencies, and provides an innovative forum for collaborative partnerships among the public and private sectors. Our primary initiatives include breast-feeding, folic acid, adolescent health, immunization, and community outreach. Interns are assigned to a specifically federally funded project, working as a team member to assist with administrative and program support. We try to accommodate students with special projects when at all possible. Through our collaborative relations, interns also have the opportunity to cultivate and develop networks, interact with staff, and develop leadership skills.

PERKS
Attendance welcome at hearings on Capitol Hill.

FYI
HMHB's internship program was founded in 1989 . . . Approximately 30 percent of interns' time is spent on clerical duties.

TO APPLY
Open to undergrads, recent college grads, college grads of any age, and grad students. International applicants eligible. Submit resume and cover letter.

Laquitta Bowers
Internship Coordinator
Healthy Mothers, Healthy Babies Coalition
121 North Washington Street, Suite 300
Alexandria, VA 22314
(703) 836-6110 ext. 225
(703) 836-3470
lbowers@hmhb.org
www.hmhb.org

SELECTIVITY
Approximate applicant pool: 30; Interns accepted: 9–12

COMPENSATION S
One free meal per day

LOCATION(S)
New York, NY

FIELD
Performing arts; Museums

DURATION
12 weeks–1 year: Summer, Fall, Spring

DEADLINE(S)
Rolling

THE WORK
One of the largest arts centers in lower Manhattan, HERE presents the works of a variety of resident theater companies and artists. HERE's facilities include three theaters and an exhibition space; it also offers support programs to benefit the arts community. Interns work in General Management, House Management, Marketing, Development, Press/Publicity, Production, and Gallery.

PERKS
Free tickets to all events.

FYI
Just west of New York's chic SoHo district, HERE encompasses 13,000 square feet of space . . . In early 1995, HERE established a café called HEREfood.

TO APPLY
Open to high school juniors and seniors, high school grads, undergrads, recent college grads, college grads of any age, and grad students. International applicants eligible. Submit resume and cover letter.

Internship Coordinator
HERE
145 Avenue of the Americas
New York, NY 10013
(212) 647-0202
(212) 647-0257 (Fax)

SELECTIVITY   Q Q Q
Approximate applicant pool: 500; Interns accepted: 45

COMPENSATION S S
Summer: $250/week; School year: $40/week

LOCATION(S)
Washington, DC

FIELD
Public policy; Think tank

DURATION
10–15 weeks: Summer, Fall, Spring

DEADLINE(S)
Summer: March 1; Fall: August 1; Spring: December 1

THE WORK
Founded in 1973, The Heritage Foundation is a conservative think tank dedicated to the principles of free enterprise, limited government, individual freedom, traditional American values, and a strong national defense. Heritage's products include publications, articles, lectures, conferences, and meetings. Departments accepting interns include Asian Studies Center, Domestic Policy, Lectures and Educational Programs, Executive Offices, Foreign Policy, Government Relations, Town Hall, *Policy Review*, Public Relations, and Special Events.

PERKS
Educational seminars for interns; attendance welcome at Heritage lectures and meetings; invitations to seminars and lectures on Capitol Hill; intern alumni network.

FYI
Although Heritage is unabashedly conservative in ideology, the intern coordinator says: "Interns need not plan to be lifelong conservatives, but they must be open and interested in the ideas of conservatism."

TO APPLY
Open to undergrads, recent college grads, college grads of any age, and grad students. International applicants eligible. Call Intern hotline for application or find online at www.heritage.org.

Internship Coordinator
The Heritage Foundation
214 Massachusetts Avenue NE
Washington, DC 20002
Intern hotline: (202) 526-4400, x556
www.heritage.org

THE HERMITAGE

THE HERMITAGE
HOME OF ANDREW JACKSON

SELECTIVITY   🔍🔍🔍
Approximate applicant pool: 200; Interns accepted: 16

COMPENSATION   💲💲💲
$250/week, free room and board

LOCATION(S)
Hermitage, TN

FIELD
Archaeology; History

DURATION
Summer: 2 weeks, 5 weeks, or 10 weeks

DEADLINE(S)
April 10

THE WORK
Since 1987 archaeological fieldwork has been performed on the grounds of the Hermitage. By exploring the foundations and other subsurface artifacts adjacent to the Jackson family mansion, archaeologists and interns reconstruct what plantation life was like at the Hermitage of Jackson's time. Interns work at the Hermitage for a two-week or a five-week session, beginning an adventure in historical archaeology.

PERKS
Farmhouse residences; earthwatch meals; sweltering weather.

FYI
Life on the job is gritty and exhausting. However one intern noted: "physical discomfort is offset by the thrill of discovery" . . . The Hermitage is preserved by the Ladies' Hermitage Association . . . Many tourists visit the grounds every day and it is up to the interns to answer any questions they have about the excavation.

TO APPLY
Open to college juniors and seniors, recent grads, grad students. Previous field training required. International applicants eligible. Submit a letter summarizing education and field experience, and a statement explaining interest in the program. Specify a session preference. Applicant must also have a professor or previous employer send a letter of recommendation directly to the Hermitage.

The Hermitage
Internship Program
4580 Rachels Lane
Hermitage, TN 37076-1331
(615) 889-2941

HEWITT ASSOCIATES

SELECTIVITY   N/A
Approximate applicant pool: N/A; Interns accepted: N/A

COMPENSATION   💲💲💲💲
Competitive pay

LOCATION(S)
Lincolnshire, IL (HQ)

FIELD
Human resources consulting

DURATION
10–16 weeks: Summer

DEADLINE(S)
March 1

THE WORK
Hewitt Associates is a management consulting firm specializing in human resources. Founded in the 1940s, the firm now has over 7,000 employees and represents 2,800 clients. Interns work as Business Analysts, Programmer Analysts, or Actuarial Consultants, and are involved in a variety of projects, including testing computer systems, researching client problems, performing benefit calculations, developing programs, and analyzing merger and acquisition strategies.

PERKS
Frequent social activities, including field trips; housing assistance; seminars with Hewitt management (often including the President, Dale Gifford).

FYI
According to a former intern, Hewitt "does everything first class: I have interned with others in the past, but Hewitt provided a more organized and intellectually fulfilling experience." Another added, "I would love to obtain permanent employment at Hewitt based solely on my internship experience, and remain awed by how friendly and accessible everyone was whom I encountered throughout my experience."

TO APPLY
Open to college juniors and seniors with at least a 3.0 GPA. Submit resume and cover letter.

Hewitt Associates
Attn: Internship Coordinator
100 Half Day Road
Lincolnshire, IL 60069
(847) 295-5000
(847) 295-1178 (Fax)
www.hewitt.com

HEWLETT® PACKARD

SELECTIVITY
Approximate applicant pool: 5,000; Interns accepted: 600–900

COMPENSATION
$450–$700/week for undergrads; $1,000–$1,300/week for grad students; round-trip travel; relocation allowance

LOCATION(S)
CA, CO, DE, GA, ID, MA, NH, NJ, OR, WA

FIELD
Computers; Electronics

DURATION
10–14 weeks: Summer

DEADLINE(S)
Rolling

THE WORK

For over a half century, Hewlett-Packard has manufactured a diverse line of products that includes everything from high-speed frequency counters and fetal heart monitors to the world's first scientific handheld calculator. HP now offers 23,000 electronic products and dominates its industry in several areas. Interns may be offered positions in a wide variety of areas, including Research & Development, Manufacturing, Marketing, Field Sales, Quality, Materials, Facilities, Information Technology, Finance, and Personnel.

PERKS

"Management by Objectives;" beer busts; free HP calculator; social activities.

FYI

Hewlett-Packard's Student Employment and Educational Development (SEED) Program was formed in the early 1970s . . . Nearly 70 percent of eligible interns receive offer of permanent employment . . . Interns may also purchase products at employee cost. LaserJets at 40 percent off the retail price, for example, are common.

TO APPLY

Open to college sophomores, juniors, and seniors, and grad students. International applicants eligible. Submit resume and cover letter.

SEED Program
Hewlett-Packard
3000 Hanover Street
Mail Stop 20-AC
Palo Alto, CA 94304-1181
(415) 857-2092
www.hp.com

SELECTIVITY
Approximate applicant pool: 100; Interns accepted: 2 every 4 months

COMPENSATION
Free housing; $125 every 2 weeks

LOCATION(S
Paonia, CO

FIELD
Newspapers; Environment

DURATION
4 months: January 1–May 1, May 1–September 1, September 1–January 1

DEADLINE(S)
Rolling

THE WORK

Published every other week since 1970, the *High Country News* is a newspaper covering environmental issues in California, Wyoming, Montana, Idaho, Utah, Arizona, New Mexico, Nevada, Oregon, and Washington. Recent stories have covered ancient forests, Pacific salmon, and the future of Yellowstone National Park. Interns work in Editorial, and write intensively.

PERKS

Ample amounts of editorial feedback; "small town funkiness;" free t-shirts.

FYI

The motto on the masthead reads: "A Paper for People who Care about the West." . . . Paonia is a rural fruit-growing, coal-mining and ranching community. . . Free housing is available 5 blocks from the office.

TO APPLY

Open to college juniors and seniors, recent college grads, college grads of any age, and grad students. International applicants eligible. Write or e-mail for application.

Julie Nelson, intern at *High Country News*, relaxing on the porch of "Intern Acres."

Internship Coordinator
High Country News
P.O. Box 1090
Paonia, CO 81428
(970) 527-4898
www.hcn.org
E-mail: rebecca@hcn.org

"Intern Acres" is the place to be/Farm livin' is the life for me!

A small, environmentally oriented newspaper, the High Country News is based in the tiny mountain town of Paonia, Colorado, a place with little more than a natural foods market and a local movie theater. Where can a High Country intern find housing? Interns may reside at "Intern Acres," a small house on the edge of an orchard.

HIGH MUSEUM OF ART

SELECTIVITY
Approximate applicant pool: 50; Interns accepted: 25

COMPENSATION
None

LOCATION(S)
Atlanta, GA

FIELD
Museums

DURATION
12 weeks: Summer, Fall, Spring

DEADLINE(S)
Rolling

THE WORK
Founded in 1926, the High Museum of Art displays European and American painting and sculpture, as well as outstanding collections of African, contemporary, and decorative art. Departments accepting interns include: Curatorial, Exhibitions, Registrar, Development, Communications, Library, Student Programs, and Education.

PERKS
Discount in museum shop; complimentary tickets to occasional theater and symphony performances.

FYI
"The High," as it is commonly called, is housed in an ultra-modern white building in the heart of Atlanta's midtown arts district.

TO APPLY
Open to high school seniors, high school grads, undergrads, recent college grads, college grads of any age, and grad students. International applicants eligible. Submit resume and cover letter.

Internship Coordinator
High Museum of Art
1280 Peachtree Street NE
Atlanta, GA 30309
(404) 733-4462
E-mail: hma.internship@woodruffcenter.org

HILL AND KNOWLTON

HILL AND KNOWLTON

SELECTIVITY
Approximate applicant pool: 500; Interns accepted: 10–12

COMPENSATION
$400/week

LOCATION(S)
New York, NY

FIELD
Public relations

DURATION
10 weeks (full time): Summer; Fall and Spring, as needed

DEADLINE(S)
Summer: February 28, Fall: July 30, Winter: October 15

THE WORK
Founded in 1927, Hill and Knowlton is a world renowned international public relations firm. H&K's client list reads like Gordon Gekko's ideal stock portfolio, with such heavy-hitters as GAP, and Bell Atlantic. Interns are assigned to work with one or two supervisors and matched with exciting accounts in the areas of media, marketing, travel, healthcare, finance, and corporate.

PERKS
Seminars and field trips; company outing; Yankees game

FYI
Said an intern who attended a brainstorming session where shots of tequila were available: "You've got to know a product before you sell it." . . . H&K was the first American public relations firm to have offices in Europe. It now has offices on every continent except Africa and Antarctica.

TO APPLY
Open to college juniors and seniors, and grad students with preference given to seniors. International applicants eligible. Submit resume with department preference, cover letter, and writing sample ("any paper demonstrating one's proficiency in writing" says the brochure).

Hill and Knowlton
Internship Coordinator
466 Lexington Avenue
New York, NY 10017
(212) 885-0410
(212) 885-0570 (Fax)
E-mail: rmoatz@hillandknowlton.com

HILL|HOLLIDAY

SELECTIVITY
Approximate applicant pool: 700; Interns accepted: 15–35 per internship program

COMPENSATION $ $ $
$300/week (summer only); Course credit

LOCATION(S)
Boston, MA

FIELD
Advertising; Communications

DURATION
8 weeks (full time): Summer; 12 weeks (part time): Fall or Spring

DEADLINE(S)
Summer: March 1; Fall: July 1; Spring: November 1

THE WORK
Founded in 1968, Hill, Holliday is one of the country's leading midsize advertising agencies. It provides a full range of communications services to a variety of local and national clients including Dunkin' Donuts, Marshalls, anyday.com, and Fidelity Investments. Interns are placed in the following departments: Accounting, Account Service, Art Buying, Broadcast Production, Community Relation, Interactive, Direct Marketing, Human Resources, Market Research, Media, New Business, and Traffic.

PERKS
Friendly environment; breathtaking views; cafeteria/fitness room; seminars.

FYI
Hill, Holliday is located 40 stories above Boston in the John Hancock Building, the city's tallest skyscraper . . . Interns are welcome to accompany staff to the studio to watch a television or radio commercial being made.

TO APPLY
Open to college sophomores, juniors, seniors, grad students. Must receive credit (Fall, and Spring). International applicants eligible. Submit resume and cover letter (with a list of department preferences).

Hill, Holliday, Connors, Cosmopulos, Inc. Advertising
Internship Coordinator
200 Clarendon Street
Boston, MA 02116
(617) 585-3715
(617) 859-4279 (Fax)

SELECTIVITY
Approximate applicant pool: 350; Interns accepted: 60 (Corps); 4 (Fellows)

COMPENSATION $ $ $ $
$390/week; health insurance

LOCATION(S)
United States, Israel, Canada

FIELD
Jewish Communal Service; Public service; Public policy

DURATION
10–11 months

DEADLINE(S)
February 21 for Corps

THE WORK
Established in 1923, Hillel is the largest Jewish campus organization in the world. Maintaining a presence on over 400 college campuses, Hillel works with students to coordinate educational and social programs that advance the interests of Judaism. Under the auspices of Hillel's Steinhardt Jewish Campus Service Corps, recent college grads are assigned to a college campus to engage students in a variety of Jewish activities. Corps Fellows' duties include working with fraternity and sorority members, developing contacts with student government leaders, and encouraging participation from college freshman.

PERKS
Two five-day national training conferences; weekly guidance from trained supervisor; meetings with leaders in the Jewish community.

FYI
Hillel also offers four year-long fellowships beginning March 1, for recent college grads who wish to work in its DC headquarters. The Bittker Fellow's duties include building an Internet database, managing student task forces, and coordinating grant selection; the Public Policy Fellow helps plan policy forums and implement campus projects. The Soref Fellow works with student leaders on campuses with small Jewish populations or emerging Hillels. The Bronfman Fellow works in the Executive Office. Compensation and eligibility requirements parallel those of the Service Corps. Call for more details.

TO APPLY
Open to college grads (within one year of graduation). International applicants eligible. Write for application.

Jewish Campus Service Corps
Hillel
900 Hilgard Avenue
Los Angeles, CA 90024
(310) 208-1291
(310) 208-9642 (Fax)
E-mail: rweisman@hillel.org

HIRSHHORN MUSEUM AND SCULPTURE GARDEN

See Smithsonian Institution

HISPANIC ASSOCIATION OF COLLEGES AND UNIVERSITIES

SELECTIVITY 🔍🔍
Approximate applicant pool: 1,000–1,500; Interns accepted: 250–300+

COMPENSATION 💲💲💲
$370–$410/week for undergrads; $490/week for grad students; round-trip travel

LOCATION(S)
Washington, DC; all 50 states (locations vary yearly)

FIELD
Over 25 fields (see Appendix)

DURATION
10 weeks: Summer

DEADLINE(S)
March 1

THE WORK
Established in 1986, the Hispanic Association of Colleges and Universities (HACU) is a nonprofit organization representing over 120 "Hispanic-Serving Institutions" (i.e., institutes of higher learning with at least 25 percent Hispanic enrollment). HACU's goals involve developing member institutions, improving the quality of post-secondary educational opportunities for Hispanics, and helping to formulate national education policies. In order to "diversify the governmental work force," HACU places interns in dozens of departments within the following federal agencies: US Department of Agriculture, US Department of Commerce, US Department of Energy, US Department of the Interior, US Department of Labor, US Department of Transportation, Public Health Service, and Pension Benefit Guarantee Corporation.

PERKS
Seminars on professional development; brown-bag luncheons with HACU staff; intern-organized social community service activities; field trips; certificate and reception at completion of program.

FYI
In 1992, HACU and the Miller Brewing Co. started the Hispanic Education Leadership Fund, which provides scholarships, leadership training, mentors, and summer internships with Fortune 500 companies to eight promising Hispanic undergrads every year. For more information, contact your HACU member-school's financial aid office.

TO APPLY
Open to college sophomores, juniors, and seniors as well as grad students. Minimum GPA: 3.0. Write for application.

HACU National Internship Program
One Dupont Circle NW
Suite 425
Washington, DC 20036
(202) 467-0893
(202) 496-9177 (Fax)

HISTORIC DEERFIELD

SELECTIVITY 🔍🔍
Approximate applicant pool: 50; Interns accepted: 6–10

COMPENSATION 💲
Tuition, books, room & board; a limited number of awards to offset lost summer income ($500–$1,500) are awarded to students of exceptional promise and with demonstrated financial need

LOCATION(S)
Deerfield, MA

FIELD
Historic preservation; Museums

DURATION
9 weeks: Summer

DEADLINE(S)
March 1

THE WORK
Over 300 years old, Deerfield, Massachusetts is an agricultural community in Western Massachusetts with an unusually large number of eighteenth- and nineteenth-century houses. Established "to promote the causes of education and appreciation of the rich heritage of the original colonies," Historic Deerfield restores and oversees twelve of these historic houses and their collections of decorative arts. Its Summer Fellowship Program provides fellows with an intensive examination of early American history, architecture, decorative arts, museum interpretation, and museum operations.

PERKS
Intern lunches with museum staff and visiting lecturers; field trips to other museums, including Old Sturbridge Village, Plymouth Plantation, Hancock Shaker Village, and the Yale University Art Gallery, end-of-internship trip to Colonial Williamsburg and Winterthur.

FYI
Alumni of the program include: the Vice President for Museum Services at Christie's, the Director of American Furniture at Sotheby's, the President of Leigh Keno American Furniture, an Associate Professor of History at Amherst College, and the Director at Amon Carter Museum in Fort Worth, TX.

TO APPLY
Open to college sophomores, juniors, and seniors. International applicants eligible. Write for application.

Director of Academic Programs
Historic Deerfield
Deerfield, MA 01342
(413) 774-5581
(413) 773-7415 (Fax)
E-mail: sfp@historic-deerfield.org
www.deerfield-fellowship.org

SELECTIVITY
Approximate applicant pool: 25; Interns accepted: 8–10

COMPENSATION ⑤
None

LOCATION(S)
East Hampton, NY

FIELD
Film and Video

DURATION
6–12 weeks: Summer, Fall, Spring, Winter

DEADLINE(S)
Rolling

THE WORK
Founded in 1991, Historic Films is an archival motion picture library that supplies footage to feature films, documentaries, television shows, industrial films, CD-Roms, commercials, etc. Its clients include Ken Burns, Woody Allen, and Martin Scorsese. Interns carry out video research, film editing and dubbing, and archival library maintenance.

PERKS
Small staff; close proximity to beach.

FYI
Historic Films is not a production house, but a service-oriented business.

TO APPLY
Open to college students, college grads, and grad students, and other interested parties. Submit a resume and a cover letter.

Kevin Rice
Internship Coordinator
Historic Films
12 Goodfriend Drive
East Hampton, NY 11937
(516) 329-9200
(516) 329-9260 (Fax)

SELECTIVITY 🔍 🔍 🔍
Approximate applicant pool: 50; Interns accepted: 2–4/year

COMPENSATION ⑤ ⑤
Varies according to experience

LOCATION(S)
Chantilly, VA (suburban Wasington DC)

FIELD
History; Archives

DURATION
10–12 weeks: Spring, Summer, Fall, Winter

DEADLINE(S)
Spring; January 31; Summer: April 30; Fall: August 1; Winter: October 31

THE WORK
Founded in 1979, The History Factory (THF) advises businesess and associations on how to better utilize an important asset—their history—to enhance their corporate image and plan for the future. THF creates and manages coporate archives; researches and produces publications; conducts oral history interviews; design exhibits; plans anniversary celebrations; and manages media relations for their clients. Recent clients include international Paper Company, Kimberly Clark, Sears, Boeing, Sara Lee corporation, fireman's Fund Insurance, and Shell Oil. Internships are available in the interpretive (historical) and archival services deparments. Pior course in American history, archival management, and/or business administration on THF's programs clientele, and staff is available at our website.

PERKS
Research visits to Library of Congress and National Archives; access to rare corporate documents and memorabilia.

FYI
One of few organizations of its kind, THF contends that "history does more than define a company's history . . . it substantiates the firm's unique reputation and track record, a vital distinction in an increasingly competitive world."

TO APPLY
Open to college juniors and seniors, recent college grads, college grads of any age, and grad students. International applicants eligible. Submit resume and cover letter.

Internship Coordinator
The History Factory
14140 Parke Long Court
Chantilly, VA 22021
(703) 631-0500
(703) 631-1124 (Fax)

EXCLUSIVE INTERVIEW WITH JOHN HAYS

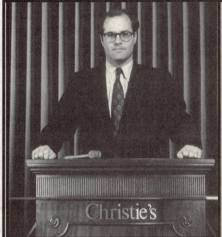

John Hays, the Sr. VP in charge of American Decorative Arts at Christie's New York, is responsible for the appraising and selling of American art made before 1850 for the venerable auction house. As part of his duties, he wields the auctioneer's gavel several times per year. After graduating from Ohio's Kenyon College in 1981 with degrees in English and art history, Hays served three different internships—the Metropolitan Museum of Art in New York (summer 1982), the Peggy Guggenheim Museum in Venice (summer 1983), and Christie's New York (October 1983) in the department he now runs.

The Internship Informants: Why did you intern at Christie's?
Hays: I came to Christie's as a 23-year-old after having completed my education at Kenyon and an intensive year in the Christie's Fine Arts Course in London…I interned for a month while I was looking for a job and looking at graduate schools, to see if I could meet people who had done graduate programs in American art, which was always my interest. I didn't feel that my year in London was a very extensive year in art history above and beyond what I had done as an undergraduate.

The Internship Informants: How much responsibility did you get?
Hays: I got to travel quite a bit. I remember we did a collection in Boston. We cataloged and photographed an on-site collection, a classical furniture collection…I was actually on the ground working with the art specialists.

The Internship Informants: And at the end of the month, did you find a job?
Hays: I was hired by Christie's in the American Furniture Department…Christie's sort of created a job for me, and 12 years later now, I run the department.

The Internship Informants: How would you describe your internship at Peggy Guggenheim?
Hays: It was a great experience, not only because I was in a different country working in Venice but as an American, you have an opportunity to be paid…They had about 14, maybe 12, interns or students. We guarded galleries, we moved works of art, we shuttled around visitors, we were paid 1,700 liras to the dollar, which was pretty good, about $750 a month…in Venice, you could exist on it and more…[The Peggy Guggenheim specializes in] American contemporary art and European contemporary art, so it gave me a chance to work in an area I was accustomed to…They had 14 Jackson Pollocks in a gallery there. It's at the Palazzo Venier dei Leoni right on the Grand Canal. It's a home turned into a museum, featuring American art in Venice.

The Internship Informants: You said you guarded galleries. Do you mean with weapons?
Hays: No weapons…Guarding galleries is really just many hours of standing around, answering visitors' questions.

The Internship Informants: You interned at two museums. What at those internships steered you toward a career in selling art?
Hays: As a young student [of art history], museums are the first thing that you think of because, unless you grew up in the art market, museums are probably the greatest exposure that you have to art…But I learned about the art market from those internships, and that had even more appeal. The auction world is a museum where the art is for sale, and your contact with the objects is a lot closer often than in a museum. It was a perfect match for me because it fulfilled a business interest of mine—the ability to work with clients in a business environment. It also allowed me the opportunity to work with the art that I was very interested in—American art. And it provided the opportunity to spread my wings a little bit further than I thought I would be able to in a museum. The requirements for being a curator of a major museum in the American wing really meant getting my Master's degree and a PhD, but I was hungry to jump into work.

The Internship Informants: What sort of internships do you recommend for people studying art?
Hays: I encourage people who are getting into the art world to try internships across the spectrum. They should know what the museum field is like. They should know what the art market is like…as an intern, you explore and learn without actually being labelled as someone from the art market or someone who's an academic from the museum field. So it allows you to explore without having to worry about the labelling. At Christie's, we look for people here who have had experience in the museum and academic world because we think that people over the long haul should have that experience under their belt.

The Internship Informants: Is an internship an important start to an art career, or any career for that matter?
Hays: As I look back on my life, I did a lot of art sculpture [in school] and worked with wood. And my internships were all in American art, so ending up at the American Furniture Department now makes perfect sense…[An internship] is a chance to ask questions without having to worry about showing your naiveté. It gives you a chance to live in a different environment under the wing of, hopefully, a sheltered nest of contacts…I encourage people to fill their hat with as many things as they can. The only thing that you can say is that you might learn something about something that you didn't know, at worst. And at best, you might find that, 12 years later, you're deeper involved in that area than you ever thought you would be.

Hays interview continued . . .

The Internship Informants: What's being an auctioneer like?
Hays: Department heads have a right to try to sell their art. When I became head of the department, or even slightly before, I began taking some minor sales. There are only about nine active auctioneers in the company. Many people try it but don't like it. I didn't have any great acting background. That was something that just occurred while at Christie's...It's something I enjoyed doing, and I think others enjoyed my style, so I was asked to do sales in other areas, and I am one of the principal auctioneers of the firm now.

The Internship Informants: How would you characterize your style?
Hays: I think it's a little more folksy...an American style, very different from someone who's French or English...I try for a little levity. But it's a major business transaction, so one has to have the proper decorum as well...I try to be upbeat and use my personality.

The Internship Informants: What do you tell your own interns about this business?
Hays: Starting off as an intern, I am acutely aware of what people who are starting out will feel they are up against, so I try very hard to show them both the good and the bad. It would be wrong to gild the lily and make it appear that this is all just fun and laughter. People work like investment bankers here and get paid far less. Someone once described Christie's as like a swan—it's serene and beautiful above the water, but down below, the little feet are going like that [makes a rapid paddling motion with his hands]. That describes the art world. It's glitzy, we get far more press than most companies our size, but there's tremendous amounts of research and travel, and it all seems romantic and exotic when you're first starting out...That picture you try to portray is an accurate one. For some it's very appealing; for others, it's not.

HOFFMANN-LA ROCHE

SELECTIVITY
Approximate applicant pool: 2,000; Interns accepted: 40–60

COMPENSATION
Commensurate with experience

LOCATION(S)
Nutley, NJ

FIELD
Pharmaceuticals; Health care

DURATION
10–12 weeks: Summer

DEADLINE(S)
February 15

THE WORK
Owned by Swiss-based Roche Holding Ltd., Hoffmann-La Roche is a leading research-intensive health care company. Roche discovers, develops, and markets prescription drugs in key therapeutic areas such as virology, infectious diseases, cardiology, oncology, transplantation and obesity. Roche's drug innovations include Valium (antianxiety), Accutane (antiacne), Invirase (the first protease inhibitor to reach the market, used for treatment of HIV & AIDS), Rocephin (antibiotic), and Xenical (antiobesity). Departments accepting interns include Research & Development, Quality Management, Technical Operations, Engineering, Marketing, Finance, Information Systems, and Law.

PERKS
Mentors, weekly speaker series, tours of facilities, workshops.

FYI
To meet the challenges of the dynamic and competitive pharmaceutical industry, Hoffmann-La Roche is planning for the future. The Roche Intern Program propels participants from the classroom into our world of science and business. Our company offers students considering careers within our industry the opportunity to experience personal development while they learn about our business, the pharmaceutical industry and the world of health care; handle challenging projects and assignments; attend a variety of seminars and educational events; and gain a glimpse of working for a global leader. Hoffmann-La Roche is mobilizing all of its talent, including interns. No matter what project you work on, we look to you to achieve meaningful results, to challenge us, to provide good ideas, and to add to the vitality of our project teams.

TO APPLY
Open to graduate and undergraduate college students. Minimum 3.0 GPA required. Submit resume and cover letter.

Internship Coordinator
University Relations
Hoffmann-La Roche
340 Kingsland Street
Nutley, New Jersey 07110-1199

H.O.M.E.

SELECTIVITY N/A
Approximate applicant pool: N/A; Interns accepted: 1,000

COMPENSATION
Free housing (farm or St. Francis Inn); free daily lunch and weekly dinner; free daily transportation

LOCATION(S)
Orland, ME

FIELD
Construction; Public service

DURATION
1 month–2 years: ongoing

DEADLINE(S)
Rolling

THE WORK
Homeworkers Organized for More Employment (H.O.M.E.) is a nonprofit cooperative community in rural Maine, dedicated to empowerment through economic and social reconstruction. Since its inception in 1970, H.O.M.E. has expanded its outlet for craftworkers to better "serve first those who suffer

most." Volunteers gain valuable experience by working in the soup kitchen and food bank, constructing low-income housing for the Covenant Community Land Trust, tutoring/mentoring persons with learning disabilities, GED tutoring, and English as a Second Language in the Learning Center, assisting in day care, and through craft training in pottery, stitchery, weaving, and carpentry. Assistance in the recovery barn, green house, auto shop, and saw/shingle mills needed as well. H.O.M.E. is in solidarity with Emmaus: San Juan, Comalapa in Guatemala, and volunteers gather donations to send to this impoverished community.

PERKS
Free training in areas of interest to gain new experience or build on existing skills; access to free horse riding lessons, Toddy Pond, and the 300-acres of woods at St. Francis Community/Mandala Farm.

FYI
In the county in which H.O.M.E. is located, nearly 35 percent of the population lives in poverty and 25 percent is illiterate . . . H.O.M.E. housing costs each family less than $35,000 . . . H.O.M.E. is part of Emmaus, a worldwide, nondenominational religious movement founded in 1949 by a French priest.

TO APPLY
Open to high school students, undergrads, recent college grads, college grads of any age, and grad students. International applicants eligible. Write for application.

Volunteer Coordinator
H.O.M.E.
P.O. Box 10
Orland, ME 04472
(207) 469-7961

HOME BOX OFFICE

SELECTIVITY 🔍🔍🔍
Approximate applicant pool: 850 Interns accepted: 150

COMPENSATION Ⓢ
None

LOCATION(S)
New York, NY

FIELD
Television; Film

DURATION
10 weeks: Summer, Fall, Spring

DEADLINE(S)
Summer: March 1; Fall: June 1; Spring: November 1

THE WORK
Founded in 1972, Home Box Office is the world's oldest and largest pay-television company. Reaching 24 million subscribers, its programming ranges from movies and boxing to comedy and music, on two 24-hour channels (HBO and Cinemax). Interns work in Original Programming, Marketing, Production, Media Relations, Finance, Accounting, Human Resources, and Film Programming.

PERKS
Orientation and luncheons with supervisors; tour of operations facility; interviewing workshop; speakers (including some former interns later hired as full-time employees); party attended by senior management

FYI
Owned by Time Warner, Home Box Office comprises such businesses as Time Warner Sports, Citadel Pictures, and HBO Video and has major equity stakes in Comedy Central, E!, BET, and Savoy Pictures. Over the course of the internship program's roughly 15-year history, approximately 10 percent of interns have been hired full-time.

TO APPLY
Open to undergrads. Must receive academic credit. International applicants eligible. Submit resume and cover letter.

Internship Program
Home Box Office
1100 Sixth Avenue, H3–33A
New York, NY 10036
H3 - 37A
(212) 512-1000

HOSTELLING INTERNATIONAL: AMERICAN YOUTH HOSTELS

HOSTELLING INTERNATIONAL

SELECTIVITY 🔍🔍🔍
Approximate applicant pool: 100; Interns accepted: 18

COMPENSATION Ⓢ Ⓢ
$100/week for undergrads; $150/week for grad students; free housing at local hostel when available.

LOCATION(S)
Washington, DC, Boston, Los Angeles, Seattle, Orleans, New York, and more

FIELD
Travel; Hotels; Intercultural education; Youth programs

DURATION
12–16 weeks

DEADLINE(S
Summer: May 15; Fall: August 15; Winter/Spring: February 1

THE WORK
Part of the International Youth Hostel Federation's (IYHF) worldwide network of 5,000 hostels, Hostelling International: American Youth Hostels (HI-AYH) organizes bargains for over 150 US hostels. The hostels provide dormitory-style bedrooms, separate for males and females, at $8 to $20 per night with such amenities as kitchens and libraries. Interns work in Programs and Education, Marketing, Hostel Development, and Resource Development at national office or on specific projects at local councils and hostels around the United States.

PERKS
Attendance welcome at DC hostel's social programs (tours, talks, etc.); membership card (reduced rates at 5,000 hostels worldwide and discounts on car rentals, restaurants, museum admissions, ski lift tickets, etc.); friendly, supportive atmosphere.

FYI

HI-AYH's mission is "to help all, especially the young, gain a greater understanding of the world and its people through hostelling."

TO APPLY

Open to undergrads, recent college grads, college grads of any age, and grad students. Must be fluent in English. International applicants eligible with J–1 visa. Submit resume, cover letter, transcript, and three recommendations.

Internship Program c/o Rose Colby
Hostelling International-American Youth Hostels
733 15th Street NW, #840
Washington, DC 20005
(202) 783-6161
(202) 783–6171 (fax)
E-mail: rcolby@hiayh.org
www.hiayh.org (internships listed on Internet)

HOUGHTON MIFFLIN COMPANY

SELECTIVITY   🔍 🔍 🔍 🔍
Approximate applicant pool: 300; Interns accepted: 20

COMPENSATION   💲 💲 💲
$8.50/hour

LOCATION(S)
Boston, MA

FIELD
Publishing

DURATION
12 weeks: Summer

DEADLINE(S)
April 15

THE WORK:

Founded in 1832, Houghton Mifflin (HM) publishes textbooks, educational software, fiction, nonfiction, and reference works. Its books include Curious George stories, Peterson Field Guides, and the *American Heritage Dictionary*, and its author list includes both the time-honored (Stowe, Longfellow, Emerson, and Twain), and the contemporary (Louis Auchincloss, Tracy Kidder, and Al Gore). Interns work in HM's College and School Divisions in: Rights & Permissions, Art & Design, Production, Software Development, Technology Services, Marketing, and Editorial areas (e.g., Business, Communication, English Literature, Foreign Language, Psychology, History & Political Science, Social Sciences and Humanities, Math, and Science).

PERKS

Lunches with department managers and editors; attendance at sales conferences, meetings, and demonstrations; 50 percent discount on book purchases and summer book sale ($1–$1.50/book).

FYI

Houghton Mifflin is pronounced HO-tin MIF-lin . . . Says the intern coordinator: "Interns can expect to gain considerable knowledge and skills of how textbooks are developed, produced, and marketed."

TO APPLY

Open to undergrads, recent college grads, college grads of any age, and grad students. International applicants eligible.

Submit resume and cover letter.

Intern Coordinator
Houghton Mifflin Company
College Division or School Division
222 Berkeley Street
Boston, MA 02116-3764
(617) 351-3893

HOUSTON INTERNATIONAL PROTOCOL ALLIANCE

Houston
INTERNATIONAL
PROTOCOL
ALLIANCE

SELECTIVITY   🔍 🔍
Approximate applicant pool: 50; Interns accepted: 10

COMPENSATION   💲
Parking reimbursed

LOCATION(S)
Houston, TX

FIELD
International affairs

DURATION
12–18 weeks: Summer, Fall, Spring

DEADLINE(S)
Rolling

THE WORK

In existence since 1983, the Houston International Protocol Alliance is a nonprofit organization serving as the official office of protocol and international affairs of the city. A resource for city government, international service organizations, and local businesses, the Protocol Alliance coordinates the visits of foreign dignitaries to Houston, acts as the city's liaison to local consular offices, advises the Mayor and other officials on protocol matters, and serves as a liaison to the city's thirteen sister-city organizations. Interns work in all areas of the organization, assisting staff with such tasks as conducting research, writing newsletters, and drafting correspondence.

PERKS

Opportunity to work at events involving government officials and foreign dignitaries; small, friendly staff.

FYI

In existence since 1987, the internship program counts among its alumni the Protocol Alliance's Director of Protocol Affairs . . . In addition to assisting staff, interns each complete a special project typically involving surveys, research, or event planning . . . Among the more illustrious dignitaries working with the Protocol Alliance has hosted in recent years are the President of Venezuela, Crown Prince of Norway, and the Prime Minister of Cameroon.

TO APPLY

Open to undergrads and grads. International applicants eligible. Send a cover letter, resume, and writing sample.

Internship Coordinator
Houston International Protocol Alliance
901 Bagby, Suite 100
Houston, TX 77002
(713) 227-3395
(713) 227-3399 (Fax)
ssposeep@ghcvb.org

HOWARD HUGHES MEDICAL INSTITUTE

SELECTIVITY 🔍 🔍

Approximate applicant pool: over 200 for RSP; Medical Students accepted: 42 for RSP, 45 for RTF

COMPENSATION 💲 💲 💲

Research Scholars Program (RSP): $17,800 salary; Research Training Fellowship (RTF): $15,000 stipend

LOCATION(S)

RSP-NIH: Bethesda, MD; RTF: any US academic or nonprofit research institution (except NIH)

FIELD

Biomedical research

DURATION

RSP: 9 months–1 year; RTF: 1 year

DEADLINE(S)

RSP: January 10; RTF: December 2

THE WORK

The Howard Hughes Medical Institute (HHMI) is a non-profit medical research organization, started in 1953 by billionaire Howard Hughes, the filmmaker, industrialist, and founder of Hughes Aircraft Company. The world's largest philanthropic organization, with $11 billion in assets, HHMI underwrites medical research to the tune of $300 million per year. Medical students conduct research in such fields as structural biology, cell biology, genetics, immunology, and neuroscience under the auspices of two programs: HHMI-NIH Research Scholars Program (RSP) and HHMI Research Training Fellowships for Medical Students Program (RTF).

PERKS

Certain HHMI fringe benefits (RSP); possible health insurance (RTF); access to NIH cafeteria, gym, library (RSP).

FYI

HHMI also offers 5-year fellowships for study toward a PhD or ScD in biological sciences ($15,000 annual stipend and $15,000 annual allowance for tuition, fees, and books).

TO APPLY

Open to U.S. medical students. International applicants attending medical school in United States are eligible (RTF only). Write for application.

HHMI-NIH Research Scholars Program
Howard Hughes Medical Institute
One Cloister Court
Bethesda, MD 20814-1460
(800) 424-9924
E-mail: research_scholars@hhmi.org
www.hhmi.org/cloister

Research Training Fellowships for Medical Students
Howard Hughes Medical Institute
Office of Grants and Special Programs
4000 Jones Bridge Road
Chevy Chase, MD 20815-6789
(301) 215-8889
(301) 215-8888 (Fax)
E-mail: fellows@hhmi.org
www.hhmc.org/fellowships

THE HOWARD STERN SHOW

SELECTIVITY 🔍 🔍 🔍 🔍

Approximate applicant pool: 300; Interns accepted: 10 each semester

COMPENSATION 💲

None

LOCATION(S)

New York, NY

FIELD

Radio; Television

DURATION

12 weeks: Summer, Fall, Spring

DEADLINE(S)

Rolling

THE WORK

With an estimated 7 million listeners tuning in across the country, *The Howard Stern Show* is one of the most successful and controversial radio programs in broadcasting history. Irreverent, bawdy, and often hilarious, *The Howard Stern Show* broadcasts every weekday morning from the studios of WXRK in New York City. Interns work in Production (where they serve as gofers and are exposed to every part of the show) or News (where they scan AP copy, research stories, edit sound tape, and assist in the organization of the newscast).

PERKS

Occasional travel to off-site interviews; occasional opportunities to appear on air with Stern; star-gazing opportunities.

FYI

For better or for worse, these days Howard Stern spends endless hours on the radio talking about, poking fun at, and even (in a few cases) lusting after his interns. Not only did he dedicate his second book, *Miss America*, to his interns, but he recently held an "Intern Beauty Contest," in which his female interns were judged for their talent, poise, and ability to wear a bikini. Said Stern, "I want you to know, our interns are hired on ability, not on their looks." Alumni include celebrity interviewer "Stuttering John" Melendez and Stern whipping-boy Steve Grillo.

TO APPLY

Open to undergrads and grad students. Must receive academic credit. International applicants eligible. Submit resume and cover letter.

Internship Coordinator
The Howard Stern Show
WXRK-KROCK
40 West 57th Street, 14th Floor
New York, NY 10019
(212) 314-9296

HOWARD TALENT WEST

SELECTIVITY
Interns accepted: 3

COMPENSATION
None

LOCATION
Toluca Lake, CA

FIELD
Talent agency

DURATION
Ongoing

DEADLINE
Rolling

THE WORK
Howard Talent West was founded in 1987, specializing in character actors of all ages. They have since expanded to include all types of entertainment talent. The internship is designed to expose those interested in "the Biz" to the inner workings of an agency. Serious interns may view the program as training to become a franchised agent. Responsibilities will include general office duties, heavy phone, fax, and taking audition appointments.

PERKS
Invitations to industry functions, star gazing, insight into the inner workings of the entertainment industry

FYI
Great for actors interested in learning the ins and outs of the business! There is a possibility of compensation once the internship is completed.

TO APPLY
Open to high school students, undergrads, grad students, and recent college grads. International applicants eligible. Call to arrange an interview.

Bonnie Howard
Internship Coordinator
Howard Talent West
(818) 766-5300

H.S.I. PRODUCTIONS

SELECTIVITY 🔍🔍🔍
Approximate applicant pool: 40; Interns accepted: 5

COMPENSATION 💲
Free lunch; daily travel expenses reimbursed

LOCATION(S)
Los Angeles, CA; New York, NY

FIELD
Television

DURATION
8–14 weeks: Summer, Fall, Spring

DEADLINE(S)
Rolling

THE WORK
Founded in 1986, H.S.I. Productions is considered one of the top commercial production companies in the country. In addition to creating award-winning television commercials for such clients as Neutrogena, Bell Atlantic, Nike, and L'Oreal, H.S.I. has churned out music videos for such cutting edge artsits as Jennifer Lopez, Christina Aguilera, No Doubt, Smashing Pumpkins, Jay Z, Sisqo, DMX, and Will Smith. Interns work in Production.

PERKS
Opportunities to go on shoots; work with directors, producers, and advertising agencies.

FYI
Says the internship coordinator: "Interns learn a lot about production. They are thrown in at the deep end . . . and many have gone on to get paid work through H.S.I. on film shoots or paid summer jobs.". . . The internship program has been in existence since the company's founding in 1986 . . . H.S.I. is responsible for Nirvana's "Smells Like Teen Spirit" video.

TO APPLY
Open to undergrads and grad students. Fax or mail resumes.

Internship Coordinator
H.S.I. Productions
1611 Electric Avenue
Venice, CA 90291
(310) 396-2128 (fax)

Internship Coordinator
H.S.I. Productions
7 West 18th Street
New York, NY 10011
(212) 627-3600
(212) 627-5947 (Fax)

One of the top commercial/music video production houses in the country, H.S.I. Productions created the video for Nirvana's legendary grunge anthem, "Smells Like Teen Spirit."

SELECTIVITY 🔍🔍
Approximate applicant pool: 70–100; Interns accepted: 6–25

COMPENSATION ⑤
None

LOCATION(S)
Indianapolis, IN; Washington, DC

FIELD
Public policy; Think tank

DURATION
12 weeks: Summer, Fall, Spring

DEADLINE(S)
Four weeks before start date

THE WORK
In existence since 1960, the Hudson Institute is a conservative think tank praised by *National Journal* for "future-oriented research that crosses disciplinary and ideological boundaries." Among Hudson's research programs are the Joint Hungarian-International Blue Ribbon Commission (working to promote capitalism in Hungary), the Modern Red Schoolhouse (improving elementary and secondary school education), and the Competitiveness Center (promoting public debate on issues such as legal reform, trade and investment liberalization, and job training). Interns serve as research assistants with institute fellows in the areas of Economics, Political Institutions, Education, National Security, Foreign Affairs, Science & Technology, Health, or Urban Affairs; or interns may work in Personnel, Public Affairs, Development, or Editorial.

PERKS
Indianapolis headquarters located in a 76-year-old Gothic-style mansion; intern meetings with department heads and executive staff; intern briefings (past speakers include a former US Secretary of Education, a former Chief of Naval Operations, and Hudson Trustee Dan Quayle).

FYI
Intern projects have included researching and reporting on states' efforts on health care reform, researching developments in enterprise zones in US cities, and researching nuclear proliferation in the post-cold-war era.

TO APPLY
Open to undergrads, recent college grads, college grads of any age, and grad students. Submit resume, cover letter, and writing samples.

Internship Coordinator
Hudson Institute
Herman Kahn Center
P.O. Box 26-919
Indianapolis, Indiana 46226
(317) 545-1000

Human Service Alliance

SELECTIVITY 🔍
Approximate applicant pool: 30; Interns accepted: 20

COMPENSATION ⑤⑤
Free room and vegetarian meals; free medical care for illnesses and injuries

LOCATION(S)
Winston-Salem, NC

FIELD
Health care; Public service

DURATION
4–16 weeks: ongoing

DEADLINE(S)
Rolling

THE WORK
Founded in 1988, the Human Service Alliance (HSA) is a nonprofit organization of citizens who "serve humanity selflessly, in the spirit of love and joy." It is all-volunteer; no one is paid. Named one of the "Thousand Points of Light" by President George Bush, HSA provides free housing and care for the terminally ill, and assistance for families with developmentally disabled children. Interns work at the Center for the Care of the Terminally Ill, where they clean the facility, prepare meals, and tend to the patients. If they wish, interns may also work in Respite Care, Bookkeeping, Building Maintenance, Carpentry, Clerical/Filing, and Computer.

PERKS
"Host" family for each intern; training sessions; geographically diverse group of interns and volunteers.

FYI
Former volunteers include President George Bush, who spent a few hours providing his personal endorsement of HSA in a video documentary that aired on PBS in the spring of 1995 . . . 100 percent of the money HSA receives in grants and donations goes to its programs . . . Says the internship coordinator: "People here learn to view death as a natural part of life . . . It may seem unlikely that a place where people are terminally ill could be joyful, yet this is so, and it is a wonderful paradox."

TO APPLY
Open to high school students, high school grads, undergrads, recent college grads, college grads of any age, and grad students. International applicants eligible. Write for application.

Coordinator of Internships
Human Service Alliance
3983 Old Greensboro Road
Winston-Salem, NC 27101
(910) 761-8745
(910) 722-7882 (Fax)

SELECTIVITY
Approximate applicant pool: 30–50; Interns accepted: 3–6

COMPENSATION
None, except for grad students interning in operations

LOCATION(S)
Alameda, CA

FIELD
Publishing

DURATION
12 weeks: Summer, Fall, Spring

DEADLINE(S)
Rolling

THE WORK
Founded in 1978, Hunter House is a small, independent publishing house that publishes about eighteen books each year. Their books focus primarily on fitness, health, especially women's health; personal growth and family, including lifestyle and sexuality; and violence intervention and violence prevention. Current titles include *Menopause Without Medicine* and *Peak Performance Fitness*. Interns work in Editorial, Acquisitions, Production, Marketing/Publicity, Marketing/Sales, and Operations/Publisher's Assistant.

PERKS
"Informal, friendly office"; free books.

FYI
Alameda is a small city in the Bay Area located about 30 minutes east of San Francisco.

TO APPLY
Open to undergrads, recent college grads, college grads of any age, and grad students. International applicants welcome. Submit resume, cover letter, and writing samples.

Internship Coordinator
Hunter House
P.O. Box 2914
Alameda, CA 94501-0914
(510) 865-5282
(510) 865-4295 (Fax)
E-mail: hhi@hunterhouse.com
www.hunterhouse.com

SELECTIVITY
Approximate applicant pool: 300–400; Interns accepted: 75–200

COMPENSATION
"Living expenses covered"

LOCATION(S)
70 countries (see Appendix)

FIELD
Various technical fields (see THE WORK)

DURATION
8 weeks–12 months

DEADLINE(S)
January 1

THE WORK
Founded in 1948, IAESTE (the International Association for the Exchange of Students for Technical Experience) arranges paid, technical internships for students interested in working abroad. The world's largest practical training program of its kind, IAESTE places US students in hundreds of organizations abroad, from Northern Telecom and Siemens to Shell and Olympus; IAESTE also coordinates internships for foreign students, who are sent to organizations outside of their home country, including dozens of positions in the United States. Host organizations include companies, research institutes and universities, consulting firms, and labs in such fields as engineering, computer science, mathematics, natural/physical sciences, architecture, and agricultural sciences.

PERKS
Varies with assignment.

FYI
According to IAESTE's annual report, the most common destination for US participants, out of more than 70 countries, has been the United Kingdom.

TO APPLY
Open to college juniors and seniors as well as grad students. Must be between 19 and 30 years of age. International applicants eligible and should write the IAESTE office in their home country; contact IAESTE United States or directory assistance for phone number of local IAESTE office. US applicants contact IAESTE/US for application. Application fee: $50 plus placement fees if selected.

IAESTE United States
Association for International Practical Training
10400 Little Patuxent Parkway, Suite 250
Columbia, MD 21044-3510
(410) 997-3068
(410) 997-5186 (Fax)
E-mail: iaeste@aipt.org
www.aipt.org/iaeste.html

SELECTIVITY
Approximate applicant pool: 10,000; Interns accepted: 1,000–2,000

COMPENSATION
Pay scale based on the credit hours earned toward degree; relocation expenses; asssistance in locating housing

LOCATION(S)
Atlanta, GA; Austin and Dallas, TX; Bolulder, CO; Burlington, VT; Charlotte and Raleigh, NC; Endicott, Poughkeepsie, and White Plains, NY; Rochester, MN; San Jose, CA; Chicago IL; Detroit, MI; Tampa, FL.

FIELD
Information technology and services

DURATION
(Intern) 10–14 weeks: Summer; (Co-op) 6–7 month period

DEADLINE(S)
Rolling; Suggested: Summer- March 1; Fall- June 1; Spring- November 1

THE WORK
IBM creates and develops, and manufactures the industry's most advanced information technologies, including computer systems, sofware, networking systems, storage devices and micro-electronics

We have two fundamental missions: We strive to lead in the creation, development, and manufacture of the most advance information technologies. We translate advanced technologies into value for our costumers as the world's largest information services company. Our professionals worldwide provide expertise within specific industries, consulting services, systems integration, and solution development and technical suport.

PERKS
Orientation; informational interviews with executives; employee discounts on IBM products; intramural softball and basketball leagues.

FYI
Approximately 25 percent of interns are offered permanent employment by IBM . . . IBM also offers a few nontechnical internships in most major cities throughout the country in such areas as accounting, marketing, administration, sales, and consulting services.

TO APPLY
Open to college sophomores, juniors, and seniors as well as grad students. Must be majoring in computer engineering, electrical engineering, or computer science. Submit resume and cover letter. Include current GPA, graduation date, and availability date.

IBM Staffing Services
Dept. 1DPA
Source Code: IBMNICCOP
PO Box 12195
RTP, NC 27709
www.cybrblu.ibm.com

SELECTIVITY
Must be accepted to an IES academic program.

COMPENSATION
None, eligible to receive academic credit

LOCATION(S)
La Plata, Argentina; Adelaide, Australia; Vienna, Austria; Beijing, China; London, England; Dijon, France; Nantes, France; Paris, France; Berlin, Germany; Freiburg, Germany; Dublin, Ireland; Milan, Italy; Tokyo, Japan; Madrid, Spain; Salamanca, Spain.

FIELD
Business & Marketing; Communications & Journalism; Education & Teaching; Fine Arts; International Relations & Government; Science; Social and Political Activism

DURATION
IES Summer, Fall, Spring, and Full-year terms

DEADLINE(S)
Vary; Contact IES for specific program applications

THE WORK
IES, the Institute for the International Education of Students, fosters students' personal and academic goals by providing quality study abroad programs worldwide. We work with more than 500 colleges and universities to enroll more than 1,800 students in 16 academic centers throughout Asia, Australia, Europe, and South America. We offer a broad-based curriculum that encompasses the humanities, languages, fine arts, social and natural sciences, mathematics, music, business and pre-professional studies. IES students can take courses at the IES Center, enroll at local universities, or both. In addition, specialized seminars, tutorials, field study, and internships are incorporated into the curriculum.

For internships, students enroll in an Internship Seminar, led by an IES coordinator, in which they discuss their work experiences and cross-cultural differences. Interns keep a journal and write a final paper. Students receive credit and a grade for the seminar based on their performance in the assigned internship, participation in the seminar, and the quality of work submitted.

PERKS
Long-standing reputation and extensive contacts worldwide; potential to earn academic credit; in-country orientation program; full curriculum of course offerings; field trips to local points of interest

FYI
Past student intern placements have included IBM Deutschland, Citibank, Donna Karan, Merrill Lynch, Europa Air, NATO, Tokyo Journal, Royal College of Music, Royal Academy of Art, British Parliament, Irish Parliament, Fulbright Commission, Chinese Academy of Sciences, and UNICEF. IES Merit scholarships for semester and full year students are available.

TO APPLY
Open to undergraduate students who are enrolled in any one of IES's programs worldwide. Visit the IES website at www.iesabroad.org for more information or call 1-800-995-2300 to speak to an IES representative.

ILLINOIS GENERAL ASSEMBLY

SELECTIVITY 🔍🔍
Approximate applicant pool: 100; Interns accepted: 20

COMPENSATION 💲💲💲💲
$2,026/month; student health insurance

LOCATION(S)
Springfield, IL

FIELD
Government

DURATION
10 1/2 months

DEADLINE(S)
February 1

THE WORK
Established in 1818, the year Illinois was admitted into the Union, the Illinois General Assembly is the Prairie State's legislative branch, divided into a 118-member House and a 59-member Senate. Administered by University of Illinois–Springfield, the Illinois Legislative Staff Internship Program (ILSIP) places 16 interns with the legislative staffs of the Senate Republicans/Democrats or House Republicans/Democrats (Partisan Internship), and four with the Legislative Research Unit (LRU), the Assembly's bipartisan research agency. Partisan interns research issues, draft bills, and analyze bills and agency budget requests for committee and floor debate. LRU interns work as science writers, explaining in layperson's terms issues in energy, the environment, waste disposal, health, and AIDS; and as general researchers, researching questions on public issues for legislators.

PERKS
Basic training in the legislative process; mentors; eight semester hours of graduate credit from University of Illinois–Springfield.

FYI
ILSIP was founded in 1963 to "attract highly qualified students to public service." . . . Former interns include former Illinois Governor Jim Edgar, former Congressman Terry Bruce, State Auditor General Bill Holland, State Senator Kirk Dillard, former State Senator Prescott Bloom, State Representative Kurk Grandberg, and former State Representative Paul Williams . . . General Assembly legislators regularly accept undergrads as interns in their offices; contact their staffs directly.

TO APPLY
Open to grads of any age. Minimum GPA (Partisan Internship): 2.75. Minimum GPA (LRU): 3.0. International applicants eligible. Write for application.

Illinois Legislative Staff Internship Program
PAC 476
University of Illinois
PO Box 19243
Springfield, IL 62794-9243
(217) 206-6158
(217) 206-6542 (Fax)
E-mail: gsimm1@uis.edu
aldrich.ann@uis.edu
For specific legislators:
(217) 782-2000 (State operator)

THE INDIANAPOLIS NEWS

See Central Newspapers/*The Indianapolis News*

THE INDIANAPOLIS STAR

See Central Newspapers/*The Indianapolis News*

INDIANAPOLIS ZOOLOGICAL SOCIETY

INDIANAPOLIS
ZOOLOGICAL
S O C I E T Y

SELECTIVITY 🔍🔍🔍
Approximate applicant pool: 250; Interns accepted: 35

COMPENSATION 💲
None

LOCATION(S)
Indianapolis, IN

FIELD
Zoos and gardens (Zoology, Veterinary Medicine, Horticulture)

DURATION
8–14 weeks: Summer, Fall, Spring, Winter

DEADLINE(S)
Rolling

THE WORK
Founded in 1964, the Indianapolis Zoological Society is one of the few zoos in the United States that is entirely self-supporting, deriving its income from admissions, concessions, memberships, and special donations. Situated in downtown Indianapolis, the zoo includes among its animal collections a hoofed animal complex, a display garden, an education center, and a library. Interns work in Animal Care, Horticulture & Botany, Environmental Education, and Marketing & Development.

PERKS
Thirty percent discount in Lion's Pride Gift Shop; monthly newsletter with information on IZS activities; free admission tickets and discounted IZS membership.

FYI
In existence since 1989, the internship program leads to permanent employment at the IZS for about 20 percent of interns.

TO APPLY
Open to undergrads, recent college grads, college grads of any age, and grad students. International applicants eligible. For application procedures, visit our website at www.indianapoliszoo.com or write to:.

Internship Coordinator
Volunteer Services
Indianapolis Zoological Society
1200 West Washington Street
Indianapolis, IN 46222
(317) 630-2041
(317) 630-5114 (Fax)
E-mail: volunteer@indyzoo.com
www.indianapoliszoo.com

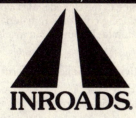

INROADS®

SELECTIVITY 🔍🔍
Approximate applicant pool: 5,500; Interns accepted: 1,000–1,200

COMPENSATION 💲💲💲
$240–$750/week

LOCATION(S)
Nationwide (see Appendix); Mexico City, Mexico; Toronto, Canada; Johannesburg

FIELD
Business; Engineering; Computer science; Applied sciences; and Liberal arts career development

DURATION
10–14 weeks: at least 2 Summers

DEADLINE(S)
January 31

THE WORK
Training talented students of color for professional careers, INROADS offers multi-year internships in various industries. Founded in 1970, the organization has grown from one office and seventeen sponsoring companies to fifty-two affiliates and a roster of corporate sponsors that includes most Fortune 1000 companies. Applicants officially become INROADS interns once they are accepted by a sponsoring company and offered a summer internship with that company until graduation.

PERKS
Business workshops, public service projects, mentors, and academic coaching.

FYI
INROADS alumni include bank presidents, corporate vice presidents, deputy commissioners, senior engineers, lawyers, and a number of thriving entrepreneurs. Anywhere from 70 to 90 percent of INROADS interns receive job offers from their sponsors and over half accept. Interns receive a substantial amount of career training from INROADS through the Leadership Development Institute, an annual four-day national business conference of workshops and corporate training attended by each intern.

TO APPLY
Open to minority high school and college students with a minimum B average, combined SAT score of 900 or composite ACT score of 20, or a top 10 percent ranking in their high school class. Interested students may apply via the Internet at www.inroadsinc.org or can write for an application.

INROADS, Inc.
10 South Broadway
Suite 700
St. Louis, MO 63102
(314) 241-7488
(314) 241-9325 (Fax)
www.inroadsinc.org

Institute for the Academic Advancement of Youth  The Johns Hopkins University
CTY   CAA

SELECTIVITY 🔍
Approximate applicant pool: 1,500; Interns accepted: 750

COMPENSATION 💲💲
RA, LA: $900/session; GA: $900/session
TA: $800/session; all positions include room and board

LOCATION(S)
MD, CA, PA, NY, CT, MA

FIELD
Education

DURATION
One or two 3-week sessions: Summer

DEADLINE(S)
January 31

THE WORK
Since 1980, the Institue for the Academic Advancement Youth (IAAY) of the Johns Hopkins University has been committed to nurturing academic talent in highly able young people. IAAY is comprised of two centers: the Center for Talented Youth (CTY) and the Center for Academic Advancement (CAA). IAAY runs summer programs with advanced courses at twelve college campuses around the country. CTY has two programs: one for students in grades 5 and 6, the other for grades 7 and above. CAA offers courses to students in grades 7–9. IAAY hires resident assistants (RAs), teaching assistants (TAs), laboratory assistants (LAs), general assistants (GAs) and office managers. Graduate students may be considered for instructional positions.

PERKS
Summer camp atmosphere; college facilities; field trips.

FYI
Interns are faced with extraordinary learners. One TA tutored a student who had published a chapbook on poetry at age 16 . . . Another "knew of a 14-year-old who mastered a pre-calculus book in 12 days" . . . TAs and LAs have the weekends off.

TO APPLY
Open to undergrad and grad students. Minimum GPA: 3.0. Applicants need not match the intellectual ability of IAAY students. International applicants eligible. Write, call, or E-mail for application.

IAAY - The Johns Hopkins University
Summer Programs Employment
3400 North Charles Street
Baltimore, MD 21218
(410) 516-0053
(410) 516-0804 (Fax)
E-mail: KAT@jhu.edu
www.jhu.edu/~gifted/acadprog/jobs.html

SELECTIVITY 🔍🔍🔍

Approximate applicant pool: 500; Interns accepted: 80

COMPENSATION 💲

Fee: $3,800–$5,500 (includes training, room and board, round-trip travel, vaccinations, and international health insurance)

LOCATION(S)

Angola, Mozambique, Zambia, Zimbabwe, Brazil, Nicaragua, India, Honduras, Guatemala, and El Salvador

FIELD

Education; Public health; Agriculture; Environment; Construction

DURATION

6–19 months, all programs have a preparation period in the U.S., an international period, and a follow-up period back in the U.S.

DEADLINE(S)

Rolling

THE WORK

Founded in 1986, the Institute for International Cooperation and Development (IICD) is a nonprofit organization dedicated to promoting global solidarity by improving living conditions in developing countries. Called "development instructors," volunteers educate people about nutrition and hygiene, teach classes in basic subjects (Angola); work in agriculture or organize vaccinations (Zimbabwe); teach troubled youth (Mozambique); and construct schools and day care centers, improve sanitation, and organize sports and cultural activities (Brazil and Nicaragua).

PERKS

Two to six months of preparation and language training in MI and MA (site features swimming pool, basketball court, skiing, and hiking); organized recreational and cultural activities; three-week study tours within the countries.

A volunteer with the Institute for International Cooperation and Development and an African plantation worker measure the height of a fledgling tree growing on a eucalyptus tree farm in Mozambique.

FYI

Upon returning to the United States, volunteers spend a few weeks in MA producing educational materials to educate people in North America. Limited financial aid available.

TO APPLY

Open to individuals 18 and up. International applicants eligible. Write for application.

Institute for International Cooperation and Development (IICD)
P.O. Box 520
Williamstown, MA 01267
(413) 458-9828
(413) 458-3323 (Fax)
iicd@berkshire.net
www.iicd-volunteer.org

INSTITUTE FOR POLICY STUDIES

SELECTIVITY 🔍🔍🔍

Approximate applicant pool: 300; Interns accepted: 35–50

COMPENSATION 💲

None

LOCATION(S)

Washington, DC

FIELD

Public policy

DURATION

10–15 weeks: Summer, Fall, Spring

DEADLINE(S)

Rolling

THE WORK

A liberal think tank founded in 1963, the Institute for Policy Studies (IPS) serves as one of the nation's leading formulators of progressive ideas. IPS fellows played key roles in the civil rights and anti-war movements of the 1960s, in the women's and environmental movements of the 1970s, and in the peace, anti-apartheid, and anti-intervention movements of the 1980s. Interns are assigned to: Biographical Researcher, Corporate Accountability/National Tax Policy/Feminist Agenda Projects, Global Communities Project, Global Economic Integration Project, Good Society Project, Hiroshima Study, Membership Development/Publications Promotions, New Immigrants Project, Newsletter, Pathways to the 21st Century, Press/Public Relations, Radio Project with *The Nation* magazine, and Technology Policy Project.

PERKS

Brown-bag lunches with speakers; free attendance at classes offered by IPS.

FYI

The IPS internship has been in existence for over a quarter century.

TO APPLY

Open to college juniors and seniors, recent college grads, college grads of any age, and grad students. International applicants eligible. Write for special application.

Internships Coordinator
Institute for Policy Studies
733 15th Street NW
Washington, DC 20005
(202) 234-9382
(202) 387-7915 (Fax)

THE INSTITUTE FOR UNPOPULAR CULTURE

SELECTIVITY 🔍🔍🔍
Approximate applicant pool: 200; Interns accepted: 20

COMPENSATION $
None

LOCATION(S)
San Francisco, CA; New York, NY; Los Angeles, CA

FIELD
Fine arts; Political science; Art history

DURATION
12–15 weeks: Summer, Fall, Spring, Winter

DEADLINE(S)
Rolling

THE WORK
We are a nonprofit organization that serves to promote artistic attempts to challenge and destabilize the status quo. We support alternative and censored artists through legal counsel, education, marketing and mentoring. Interns participate in the areas of graphic art, research, promotion, fundraising, artist assistance, marketing and administration.

PERKS
Exposure to artists, musicians, and poets; complimentary tickets to various performances.

FYI
The Institute's motto is "Aliquantum ex Ingenio Tuo, Sis," which means "a little originality, please."

TO APPLY
Open to undergrads, recent college grads, college grads of any age, and grad students. International applicants eligible. Please submit resume and cover letter.

Inside The Institute for Unpopular Culture. Note the book on blasphemy sitting on the desk.

Internship Coordinator
The Institute for Unpopular Culture
PMB #1523
1850 Union Street, Suite #4
San Francisco, CA 94123-4309
(415) 986-4382
(415) 986-4354 (Fax)
E-mail: rstlne@sirius.com

INSTITUTE OF CULTURAL AFFAIRS

SELECTIVITY 🔍🔍🔍
Approximate applicant pool: 120; Interns accepted: 15

COMPENSATION $
Limited number of volunteers (1 year full time) receive room and board. No compensation for short-term or part-time interns/volunteers.

LOCATION(S)
Chicago, IL; Denver, CO; Phoenix, AZ; Seattle, WA; Belgium; Canada; England; Egypt; Germany; Kenya; India; Malaysia; Mexico; Peru; Portugal; Zambia

FIELD
Public service

DURATION
13 weeks–1 year: ongoing

DEADLINE(S)
Rolling

THE WORK
Established in 1973, the Institute of Cultural Affairs in the U.S.A. (ICA) is a nonprofit organization promoting social innovation through participation and community building in organizations and neighborhoods. Through the Institute of Cultural Affairs International, ICA in the U.S.A. is connected with national ICA's in over 30 countries. Out of ICA's experience in working with communities, other non-profit organizations, public agencies and private companies, the organization has developed a set of basic group facilitation, called The Technology of Participation (ToP). ICA uses this Technology of Participation in short term facilitation of retreats and meetings, in long term partnerships with both local neighborhoods like the small communities in southwestern Arizona and national efforts like the Community Youth Development (CYD) movement. ICA also provides facilitator training courses across the nation. Apprentices and interns work with ICA staff and partners in both neighborhood and organizational settings to apply facilitation skills and support local leadership in both English and Spanish. They may take responsibility for the set up and implementation of programs and projects, assist with evaluation and documentation, participate in grassroots community development initiatives depending on their placement and the focus of their supervisor.

PERKS
Workshops on grassroots development and group facility; direct contact with senior staff; geographically and ethnically diverse group of interns; ICA alumni groups.

FYI
Says a former volunteer: "I came to the ICA to find out whether working in communities was the work I really wanted to do or if it was an idealistic dream of a socially conscious college student. ICA gave me the tools and hands-on experience that I needed to realize that my dreams were based in reality as well as theory."

TO APPLY

Open to high school grads, recent college grads, college grads of any age, and grad students. International applicants eligible. Submit resume, cover letter, and recommendations.

For placement in the US:
Volunteer Coordinator
Institute of Cultural Affairs
4220 North 25th Street
Phoenix, AZ 85016
(602) 955-4811
(602) 954-0563 (Fax)
E-mail: icaphoenix@lgc.org
www.ica-usa.org

For placement outside the US:
Volunteer Coordinator
Institute of Cultural Affairs
Rue Amedee Lynen 8
Brussels, Belgium B1030
Phone: 32-2-219-0087
Fax: 32-2-219-0406
E-mail: lcab@linkline.be
www.lcaworld.org

INSTITUTE OF GOVERNMENT

SELECTIVITY
Approximate applicant pool: 300–350; Interns accepted: 21

COMPENSATION
$270/week; dorm housing

LOCATION(S)
Raleigh, UNC Chapel Hill, and Research Triangle Park, NC

FIELD
All majors

DURATION
10 weeks: Summer

DEADLINE(S)
January 26, 2001

THE WORK

The Institute of Government places college students in government and arts-oriented internships throughout North Carolina, at organizations such as the State Bureau of Investigation, the Office of the Attorney General, the North Carolina Symphony, the Office of the Governor, and the Department of Parks and Recreation. Intern experiences vary considerably; past interns have done everything from writing public service announcements for television to writing text for museum exhibits.

PERKS

Local field trips; weekly seminars with government officials and corporate executives; some positions offer extensive travel.

FYI

Started in 1962, the program has an alumni list that includes NC Supreme Court Justice Willis Whichard, Congressman H. Martin Lancaster, David G. Martin, former Secretary of the University of North Carolina, Congressman Mel Watt and Current Secretary of the University of N. Carolina Rosalind Fuse-Hall.

TO APPLY

Open to college sophomores, juniors, and seniors. Must be a resident of North Carolina or an out-of-state resident attending college in North Carolina. Call for application.

Summer Intern Program
Institute of Government
The University of North Carolina at Chapel Hill
CB# 3330 Knapp Building
UNC-CH
Chapel Hill, NC 27599-3330
(919) 966-4347
www.iog.unc.edu/interns/

INSTITUTE OF INTERNATIONAL EDUCATION

SELECTIVITY
Approximate applicant pool: 30; Interns accepted: 6

COMPENSATION
$100/week

LOCATION(S)
Mexico City, Mexico

FIELD
International education; Educational counseling

DURATION
12 weeks: Summer, Fall, Winter/Spring

DEADLINE(S)
Changing

THE WORK

The Institute of International Education (IIE) is one of the world's largest overseas educational advising centers, providing information about US study to over 40,000 people per year. IIE advises the Mexican public on application procedures, admission tests, scholarship opportunities, conducts public information sessions, pre-departure programs and provides briefings for US university representatives among other activities. Interns work in the Educational Counseling center as student advisers, giving out information about US education and research on various projects.

PERKS

Orientation and training; occasional to take advantage of cultural activities.

FYI

IIE's internship program was started in 1979 . . . IIE is located in the Benjamin Franklin Library and operates as part of the U.S. Embassy in Mexico. In addition to counseling, IIE administers fellowship programs and is the computer based testing site where admissions exams such as the TOEFL, GRE, and the GMAT are administered

TO APPLY

Internship positions are open to college juniors and seniors, recent college grads, college grads of any age, and grad students. Must be proficient in Spanish and English. International applicants eligible. Write for application.

Internship Program
Institute of International Education
Educational Counseling Center
P.O. Box 3087
Laredo, TX 78044
(525) 703-0167 or (525) 209-9100 x 3510 and 4511
E-mail: iie@solar.sar.net
www.iie.org/latinamerica

SELECTIVITY 🔍 🔍 🔍 🔍 🔍
Approximate applicant pool: 250; Interns accepted: 8

COMPENSATION 💲 💲 💲 💲
$550–$600/week

LOCATION(S)
New York, NY

FIELD
Insurance

DURATION
12 weeks: Summer

DEADLINE(S)
February 1

THE WORK
Formed in 1971 by the property/casualty insurance industry, Insurance Services Office (ISO) provides over 1,500 participating insurance companies with statistical and actuarial information (helping them to set fair, competitive rates for their policies). Interns work in the following Actuarial departments: Data Management and Information Services, Actuarial Services and Research and Operations (where they apply math to make estimates of companies' future costs).

PERKS
Intern luncheon; weekly seminars on current events in the actuarial field; summer recreation program.

FYI
Property/casualty insurance includes personal auto insurance, business liability insurance, and homeowners insurance . . . Interns who pass the CAS exams during the summer receive a pay raise applied retroactively to the exam date or start date, whichever is later.

TO APPLY
Open to college juniors studying math, operations research, or statistics or those majoring in computer science, economics, or management with a minor in math. Minimum GPA: 3.0. Minimum SAT: 1300. International applicants studying in the United States are eligible. Submit resume and cover letter.

Actuarial Internship
Human Resources
Insurance Services Office
7 World Trade Center
New York, NY 10048
(212) 898-6084
(212) 898-6071
www.iso.com

SELECTIVITY 🔍 🔍
Approximate applicant pool: 4,000; Interns accepted: 950–1000

COMPENSATION 💲 💲 💲 💲
$450–$750/week (undergrads); $750–$1,000/week (grads);
$500–$700 relocation allowance; round-trip travel

LOCATION(S)
Phoenix, AZ; Folsom and Santa Clara, CA; Albuquerque, NM; Portland, OR

FIELD
Microprocessors/Computers

DURATION
8–15 weeks: Summer; 4–8 months: Fall, Spring

DEADLINE(S)
Rolling

THE WORK
Since its founding in 1968, Intel Corporation has grown increasingly more influential. In 1987, the company ranked tenth in chip production. Today, Intel's computer chips are currently inside three out of every four personal computers worldwide. Positions available to interns include Design Engineer, Product Engineer, Process Engineer, Software Engineer, Test Engineer, Quality/Reliability Engineer, Technical Sales Engineer, Application Engineer, Equipment Engineer, Financial Analyst, and Human Resources.

PERKS
Intel University; weekly brown-bags; social events; free rental car.

FYI
70 percent of all college graduates hired by Intel will be former Intel interns . . . Since Intel plans to hire at least 1,000 new college graduates annually for the next several years; interns are in prime position for a job . . . Intel used to release a new microprocessor every four years. To combat competition, that rate is now every two years, a pace that none of its rivals can match.

TO APPLY
Open to undergrads and grad students. Minimum 3.0 GPA. International applicants eligible. Submit resume and cover letter.

Intel Corporation
Staffing Department
FM4-145
P.O. Box 1141
Folsom, CA 95763-1141
(916) 356-8080

SELECTIVITY 🔍🔍🔍🔍
Approximate applicant pool: 300; Interns accepted: 1–3

COMPENSATION 💲
None

LOCATION(S)
San Francisco, CA

FIELD
High tech public relations

DURATION
Ongoing

DEADLINE(S)
Rolling

 THE WORK
InterActive specializes in launching start-ups and fast growth companies in the emerging technology markets of electronic commerce, infrastructure software and enterprise applications. Our internship programs introduce basic details of public relations such as editorial calendars, speaking opportunities, trade show assistance, press kit production, press release distribution, report writing, and the management of a wide range of logistic issues. Interns will also develop an understanding of a client's product and service offerings and be able to communicate key attributes and benefits. Time and priority management, the ability to move quickly, be resourceful and anticipate both agency and client needs is critical. A three month period is suggested.

PERKS
Small agency

FYI
Says the Vice President: "The goal of our program is to develop future employees. We count on each internship to either build our staff or at least build the reputation of the agency." . . . Interactive looks for "energetic people with theatrical finesse and brilliant creativity."

TO APPLY
Open to undergrads, recent college grads, college grads of any age, and grad students. International applicants eligible. Submit resume, cover letter, and writing samples.

Internship Coordinator
Interactive Public Relations
550 3rd Street
San Francisco, CA 94107
(415) 703-0400
(415) 703-0469 (Fax)

SELECTIVITY 🔍🔍🔍🔍
Approximate applicant pool: 50; Interns accepted: 4

COMPENSATION 💲💲
Free housing

LOCATION(S)
Albuquerque and Silver City, NM

FIELD
Foreign policy; U.S.-Mexico border

DURATION
12 weeks: Summer, Fall, Spring

DEADLINE(S)
Rolling

THE WORK
Since 1979 the Interhemispheric Resource Center (IRC), a private nonprofit research institute, has monitored, researched and analyzed worldwide events and provided people with the information they need to make informed decisions, to direct policy, and to be instruments for social change. The IRC currently has two main projects: the Foreign Policy in Focus project produces a series of policy briefs, a weekly ezine, special reports, and a biannual book to promote an alternative U.S. foreign policy agenda. The BIOS program produces borderlines, a monthly publication in Spanish and English, and maintains a bibliographic database and a contact database to provide information to U.S.-Mexico borderlands activists and policymakers. Interns work as researchers, with occasional writing assignments.

PERKS
Both IRC offices are small and friendly. The Silver City office is located in an especially beautiful, remote corner of New Mexico, with plenty of access to the Gila National Forest.

FYI
The IRC's mission is to provide information and analysis designed to drive U.S. foreign policy toward Mexico and across the globe in more responsible directions and to feed voices from the grassroots into debates on public policy.

TO APPLY
Open to undergrads, recent grads, and grad students. Submit resume, cover letter, 3 references, and writing sample.

Internship Coordinator
Interhemispheric Resource Center
P.O. Box 2178
Silver City, NM 88062
(505) 388-0208
(505) 388-0619 (Fax)
E-mail: irc@irc-online.org
www.irc-online.org

SELECTIVITY 🔍🔍🔍
Approximate applicant pool: 35; Interns accepted: 2–6

COMPENSATION 💲
None

LOCATION(S)
New York, NY

FIELD
Interior design; Sales

DURATION
6–12 weeks: Summer, Fall, Spring

DEADLINE(S)
Rolling

THE WORK
Interior Design Collections (IDC) is a multiline sales company offering high-end interior products sold to designers and architects. With a large portion of the business involving custom sales, IDC specializes in fabrics, furniture, wall coverings, and accessories. Interns work in Marketing & Sales and as Sample Coordinators and IDC Outside Representatives.

PERKS
Field trips to design/decorator markets and to trade shows; interaction with the "artists who design products and the designers who use them"; free samples of fabric, wall coverings, etc.

FYI
Established in 1993, President and founder Xenia Psihas is well known in design circles for her on going commitment to selling high quality products with high quality service says Psihas,"My interns get a practical, hands-on introduction to the business of selling interior design products. It is one thing to design a product, but IDC interns learn how to take the product to the marketplace."

TO APPLY
Open to all college level students. International applicants eligible, must speak English. Submit resume and cover letter.

Internship Coordinator
Interior Design Collections
39 East 12th Street, Suite 205
New York, NY 10003
(212) 995-9154
(212) 995-8288 (Fax)

SELECTIVITY 🔍🔍🔍
Approximate applicant pool: 500; Interns accepted: 50

COMPENSATION 💲💲💲
$150/week for undergrads; $225/week for grad students; free room and board

LOCATION(S)
Hillsboro, NH; or travel to other cities in the US or overseas (see Appendix)

FIELD
Recreation

DURATION
6–9 weeks: Summer

DEADLINE(S)
Rolling

THE WORK
In existence since 1961, Interlocken offers educational summer adventures for young people ages 9 to 18. Interns are hired as camp counselors at Interlocken's residential International Summer Camp in New Hampshire, where they lead recreational and cultural activities. Interns are also hired as group leaders for Crossroads Student Travel, a program that takes students on expeditions in cities in the US and Canada, Latin America, Europe, Africa, and Asia.

PERKS
Staff orientation; camp located on a 1,000-acre lakeside wilderness preserve.

FYI
Interlocken prides itself on being one of the first programs of its kind to bring together participants from a variety of ethnic, religious, socioeconomic, and national backgrounds.

TO APPLY
Camp Counselors: Open to undergrads, recent college grads, college grads of any age, and grad students. Travel Leaders: Open to anyone 24 years of age or older. International applicants eligible. Submit resume and cover letter.

Staff Coordinator
Interlocken Center for Experiential Learning
RR2, Box 165
Hillsboro, NH 03244
(603) 478-3166
(603) 478-5260 (Fax)

Mention the name **Ansel Adams**, and it might bring to mind Adams' celebrated photographs of the American West. Or it might recall his photographic portraits of celebrities like Georgia O'Keefe and John Marin. But most people won't remember Adams for apprenticeships, despite the fact that he advanced his boyhood interest in photography by apprenticing with Frank Dittman, the owner of a San Francisco photofinishing company.

🔍 🔍 🔍
pool: 500; Interns accepted: 20–25

...ION Ⓢ
...ne

LOCATION(S)
Washington, DC

FIELD
Foreign affairs

DURATION
12 weeks: Summer, Fall, Spring

DEADLINE(S)
Summer: March 31; Fall: June 30; Spring: November 30

📇 THE WORK
Founded in 1977, the International Center hosts foreign visitors, conducts programs of research, and publishes briefing books on the impact of American foreign policy. Interns work for one of the Center's divisions: the US-Vietnam Trade Council, the Commission on US-Russian Relations, or the New Forests Project.

🎭 PERKS
Brown-bag luncheons, seminars, and talks; attendance welcome at meetings with foreign officials.

🏛 FYI
Says Ken Meyer, a 1983 International Center intern who went on to become the Executive Director of the Wisconsin Democratic Party, "The Center taught me all the basics . . . to get me where I am today. It's small enough to allow the interns to really get involved in all aspects of the organization: from fundraising to research to policy work."

📦 TO APPLY
Open to college sophomores, juniors, and seniors as well as grads and grad students. International applicants eligible. Submit resume, cover letter, writing samples, and transcript.

Internship Coordinator
The International Center
731 8th Street SE
Washington, DC 20003
(202) 547-3800
(202) 546-4784 (Fax)

SELECTIVITY 🔍 🔍 🔍 🔍
Approximate applicant pool: 65; Interns accepted: 6

COMPENSATION Ⓢ
None

LOCATION(S)
New York, NY

FIELD
Museums; Photography

DURATION
12 weeks: Summer, Fall, Spring

DEADLINE(S)
Rolling

📇 THE WORK
The International Center of Photography (ICP) is New York City's only museum devoted exclusively to photography. The museum houses a collection of more than 50,000 photographs and mounts approximately twenty five exhibitions a year. Interns assist the curatorial staff in preparing exhibitions and publications, research and maintenance of the collection, and administrative duties.

🎭 PERKS
Attendance welcome at photography lectures, and special programs; discounts at ICP museum stores (uptown and midtown locations); free admission to many New York City museums.

🏛 FYI
Our interns are able to work with collections and exhibitions in all stages of development, and to take part in the daily operations of the museum. This is primarily an administrative position.

📦 TO APPLY
Open to college and graduate students. International applicants eligible. Applicants with background in art history preferred. Submit resume and cover letter.

Internship Coordinator
International Center of Photography
1133 Avenue of the Americas
New York, NY 10036
(212) 860-1777
(212) 768-4688 (Fax)

SELECTIVITY 🔍 🔍 🔍 🔍 🔍

Approximate applicant pool: 250 (interns), 1,000 (trainees);
Interns accepted: 40; trainees accepted: 16

COMPENSATION 💲 💲

None for interns; $300/week for agent trainees (mailroom)

LOCATION(S)

Beverly Hills, CA; New York, NY

FIELD

Talent agencies

DURATION

Interns: 4–16 weeks, ongoing; Agent trainees: 2–4 years, ongoing

DEADLINE(S)

April 8

THE WORK

Dating back to 1953, International Creative Management (ICM) is a talent and literary agency representing actors, producers, directors, and writers. Its 150 agents find work and handle negotiations for stars including Arnold Schwarzenegger, Denzel Washington, Richard Gere, Michelle Pfeiffer, Mel Gibson, Julia Roberts, Anthony Hopkins, INXS, LL Cool J, Rush, and Elvis Costello. Interns, used in CA only, are placed at various desks, including Motion Picture, Talent, Television, Literature, and New Technologies, where they help the assistants to the agents with administrative tasks such as sending out scripts. Agent Trainees work six months to one year in the mailroom, where they deliver mail, sort packages, run errands, and set up conference rooms, followed by one or more years of service as assistants to agents.

PERKS

Occasional opportunities to attend client meetings; star gazing.

FYI

According to a former intern, ICM interns are first in line for agent trainee positions.

TO APPLY

Interns: open to undergrads and grad students. Must receive academic credit. Agent trainees: open to all grads. Submit resume and cover letter.

Internship Coordinator or Agent Trainee Coordinator
International Creative Management
8942 Wilshire Boulevard
Beverly Hills, CA 90211
(310) 550-4000

Agent Trainee Coordinator
International Creative Management
40 West 57th Street
New York, NY 10019
(212) 556-5600

SELECTIVITY 🔍 🔍 🔍 🔍 🔍

Approximate applicant pool: 100; Interns accepted: 10

COMPENSATION 💲 💲 💲

$800/month; round-trip travel; health insurance

LOCATION(S)

Australia; Benin; Dominican Republic; Ethiopia; Gambia; Ghana; Guinea; Ivory Coast; Kenya; Malawi; Niger; Nigeria; Senegal; Sierra Leone; South Africa; Thailand; Zimbabwe

FIELD

Public service; Economic and social development

DURATION

Nine months: starts in August

DEADLINE(S)

February 28

THE WORK

A nonprofit charitable foundation, the International Foundation for Education and Self-Help (IFESH) supports grassroots development projects in Africa. Its International Fellows Program places students in administrative and development positions working in community development, health and eduation projects, agricultural projects, and other types of development activities.

PERKS

Pre-departure orientation; alumni network hosts a return convocation program; arranged housing; insurance coverage.

FYI

IFESH Fellows have gone on to staff positions with UNICEF, Save the Children, Technoserve, the Academy for Educational Development, the African Development Bank, and the US Department of Agriculture, CARE, Africare, and the International Foundation for Education and Self-Help (IFESH).

TO APPLY

Open to recent grads entering grad school, and grad students. Write for application.

International Fellows Program
The International Foundation for Education and Self-Help
5040 East Shea Boulevard, Suite 260
Phoenix, AZ 85254-4687
(480) 443-1800
(480) 443-1824 (Fax)

International Foundation
OF EMPLOYEE BENEFIT PLANS

SELECTIVITY 🔍 🔍
Approximate applicant pool: 860; Interns accepted: 200

COMPENSATION 💲 💲 💲
Approximately $350–$550/week

LOCATION(S)
Nationwide

FIELD
Human resources; Employee benefits

DURATION
10–12 weeks full time summer; part time during academic year also available

DEADLINE(S)
February 15

THE WORK
Founded in 1954, The International Foundation of Employee Benefit Plans (IFEBP) is a nonprofit association providing information on employee benefits through educational programs, publications, information services, research reports, an online database, and a certification program. IFEBP membership consists of over 7,800 multi-employer trust funds, corporations, public employee funds, and professional firms. Interns are recruited to work in the Human Resources and Employee Benefits departments of a wide range of companies and organizations nationwide.

PERKS
Opportunity to take courses leading to certification in the employee field; free use of IFEBP library services; other perks vary with placement.

FYI
Among the dozens of organizations sponsoring IFEBP interns are TIAA-CREF, AON Consulting, Towers Perrin, CIGNA, and CBS. IFEBP publishes *Measuring Up*, a newsletter for IFEBP interns, sponsors, and intern alumni.

TO APPLY
Open to students who have two summers available to work PRIOR to graduation. Some placements available for juniors with one summer available prior to graduation. Minimum GPA: 3.0 and business-related major. Strong communication and computer skills required. International applicants with proper work permits eligible. Write to headquarters or call regional director for applications.

Margie Trede, Administrative Supervisor
P.O. Box 69
Brookfield, WI 53008-0069
(262) 786-6710 x8218
(262) 786-8670 (Fax)

Dianne Fabii, Regional Director
P.O. Box 614
Marlton, NJ 08053
(856) 985-9599
(856) 985-9698 (Fax)
E-mail: Dfab3if@aol.com
www.ifebp.org

SELECTIVITY 🔍 🔍
Approximate applicant pool: 130; Interns accepted: 30–35

COMPENSATION 💲
Cost of local transportation reimbursed

LOCATION(S)
New York, NY; Washington, DC; Geneva, Switzerland

FIELD
Human rights; Women's issues; Public policy

DURATION
15 weeks: Summer, Fall, Spring

DEADLINE(S)
Rolling

THE WORK
The International Labor Organization (ILO) was founded in 1919 by an international group of governments, employers, and trade unions seeking to improve living and working conditions worldwide. Originally part of the League of Nations, ILO is now a specialized agency of the United Nations (see separate entry) and has over 170 member countries. ILO activities involve setting international labor standards, providing vocational and management training, and researching workplace issues, such as women's rights and the freedom to organize. DC interns work in Marketing and Publications, Technical Information/Library, and Recruitment (i.e., Personnel). Geneva interns work in over 40 branches, including Labor Law & Relations, Freedom of Association, Equality of Rights, Employment Strategies, Active Labor Markets Policies, and International Migration for Employment. NY interns (two to five per year) assist staff with research and cover meetings at the UN.

PERKS
Attendance welcome at UN meetings, IMF and World Bank seminars; intern acknowledgment in ILO newsletters.

FYI
ILO started its internship program in 1975 . . . Intern duties may include: editing speeches, writing articles for newsletters, compiling fact sheets on labor laws, and updating mailing lists.

TO APPLY
DC: open to undergrads and grad students. NY: open to college seniors, recent grads, and grad students. Geneva: open to recent grads and grad students. International applicants eligible. Submit resume and cover letter.

Internship Coordinator
International Labor Organization
1828 L Street NW, Suite 801
Washington, DC 20036

Internship Coordinator
International Labor Organization
4 Route des Morillons
CH-1211 Geneva 22, Switzerland
41-22-799-6111

Internship Coordinator
ILO Liaison Office with the UN
220 East 42nd Street, Suite 3101
New York, NY 10017
(212) 697-0150

INTERNATIONAL MANAGEMENT GROUP

SELECTIVITY 🔍🔍🔍🔍
Approximate applicant pool: 550; Interns accepted: 40

COMPENSATION 💲
None; £600 (S970) stipend for London

LOCATION(S)
Boston, MA; Chicago, IL; Cleveland, OH (HQ); Denver, CO; Detroit, MI; Kansas City, MO; Los Angeles and San Francisco, CA; Minneapolis, MN; New York, NY; Philadelphia, PA; San Antonio, TX; FL; NC; NJ; Argentina, Australia, Austria, Belgium, Canada, England, France, Germany, Hong Kong, Hungary, Ireland, Italy, Japan, Monaco, New Zealand, Norway, Scotland, Singapore, South Africa, Spain, Sweden, Switzerland, Thailand

FIELD
Sports management; Accounting; Finance; Law; Public relations

DURATION
Two sessions which run approximately six weeks each. Session dates vary from year to year; London's program will last 8 weeks during the summer

DEADLINE(S)
February 15; January 31 (London only)

THE WORK
Founded in 1960, International Management Group (IMG) is the world's largest sports marketing and management firm. Handling such areas as licensing, financing, and promotions, it represents athletes, television personalities, models, classical artists, writers, sports organizations, and companies. Clients include: Joe Montana, Wayne Gretzky, Lauren Hutton, Niki Taylor, Itzhak Perlman, the NFL, and the Mayo Clinic. IMG also manages events like tennis's Virginia Slims and golf's Australian Open, produces and distributes television sports programs, publishes books, operates golf courses, and runs tennis and golf academies. Departments accepting interns include: Golf, Team Sports, Racquet Sports, Marketing, Travel, Tax, Accounting, Human Resources, Information Systems, Trans World International, Modeling, Motorsports, Corporate Administration, Cleveland 500 Foundation, David Leadbetter Golf Academy, and Nick Bollettieri Tennis Academy.

PERKS
Senior Executive Luncheon; meeting with founder, CEO, and chairman Mark H. McCormack; attendance welcome at IMG-owned events (e.g., Cleveland Grand Prix, Detroit Grand Prix, World TeamTennis, Discover Card Stars on Ice).

FYI
Mark McCormack, author of the national bestselling *What They Don't Teach You at Harvard Business School*, is widely recognized as the founder of the sports-marketing industry (see Exclusive Interviews with Mark McCormack and Matt Stover) . . . Golf Division head Alastair Johnston served as an intern during the early 1960s.

TO APPLY
Open to undergrads and grad students. Must receive academic credit (US only). International applicants eligible. Submit resume and cover letter to Cleveland for US positions or to office of interest for overseas positions (addresses and phone numbers available at headquarters).

Internship Committee
IMG Center, Suite 100
1360 East 9th Street
Cleveland, OH 44114-1782
(216) 522-1200
(216) 522-1145 (Fax)

SELECTIVITY 🔍🔍🔍🔍
Approximate applicant pool: 500–600; Interns accepted: 35

COMPENSATION 💲💲
$300/week stipend; free housing; round-trip travel

LOCATION(S)
New York, NY

FIELD
Television; Radio; Advertising; Marketing; Public relations

DURATION
9 weeks: Summer

DEADLINE(S)
November 14

THE WORK
Founded in 1939, the International Radio and Television Society (IRTS) represents 1,000 members, who include, according to its brochure, "most of the top people in the world of electronic communications." Interns are assigned to New York-based corporations including all four major networks, local radio and television stations, national rep firms (which sell air time to advertisers), advertising agencies, and cable operations. At their assignments, interns work in the areas of broadcasting, commercials, advertising, news, radio, media planning, marketing, sales, and sports.

PERKS
One-week orientation on broadcasting, cable television, and advertising; field trips to IRTS members' organizations throughout NYC; attendance welcome at industry social functions.

FYI
Started in 1960, IRTS's internship program offers one of the best networking opportunities in the business . . . Dozens of former interns work as reporters, anchors, producers, managers, advertising account executives, and agents.

TO APPLY
Open to college juniors and seniors. International applicants eligible. Application available in September through our website www.irts.org

SELECTIVITY 🔍
Approximate applicant pool: 50
Interns accepted: 15 annually

COMPENSATION 💲💲
$8/hour plus academic credit if desired

LOCATION(S)
Website—SoHo in Lower Manhattan; Hamilton, NJ (HQ located near Princeton, NJ; 1 hour 30 minutes from Manhattan)

FIELD

Sculpture; Arts administration; Nonprofit management; Marketing; Website; Internet as an educational tool; Grant writing; Public programs

DURATION

12–16 weeks: Summer, Fall, Spring

DEADLINE(S)

Rolling, but most interns are selected by September 1, December 1, and May 1

THE WORK

The International Sculpture Center (ISC) is a not-for-profit organization founded in 1960. The ISC advances the creation and understanding of sculpture and its unique and vital contribution to society. The ISC publishes *Sculpture* magazine, the only international publication devoted exclusively to contemporary sculpture, which features criticism, reviews, studio visits, interviews, technical information, and *Opportunities*, a timely listing of commissions, calls for artists, grants and residencies. Other programs include the International Conferences, the ISC Resource Center, and web site (www.sculpture.org), awards programs for young professionals and K-12 art teachers, curriculum development.

PERKS

Opportunities to learn how a nonprofit arts service organization works! Strengthen skills in writing, fundraising, administration, information resources, website content development.

FYI

Alumni of the 10-year-old internship program include the managing editor of *Sculpture* magazine.

TO APPLY

Open to grad students, college seniors, and mature college juniors. Preferred majors: journalism, English, marketing, art history (including an interest in contemporary art), computer or library science, arts administration, and nonprofit management. Submit resume, cover letter, two references, and one one-page writing sample.

Carol Sterling, Director of Programs and
ISC Resource Center
International Sculpture Center
14 Fairgrounds Rd., Suite B
Hamilton, NJ 08619-3447
(609) 689-1051 ext. 107
(609) 689-1061 (Fax)
E-mail: carol@sculpture.org
www.sculpture.org

INTERNATIONAL TELECOMMUNICATIONS SATELLITE ORGANIZATION (INTELSAT)

SELECTIVITY

Approximate applicant pool: 400; Interns accepted: 70

COMPENSATION

$350/week for nonUS citizens (no taxes withheld); $440/week for US citizens

LOCATION(S)

East Windsor, NJ; Palo Alto, CA; Washington, DC; Munich, Germany

FIELD

Telecommunications

DURATION

10–15 weeks: Summer

DEADLINE(S)

March 15

THE WORK

Eleven countries founded INTELSAT in 1964 to provide satellite telecommunications services worldwide. With a system of 19 satellites, INTELSAT today links virtually every nation on the planet with telephone and television. Interns work in such departments as Sales, Spacecraft & Launch, Network Operations, Systems Engineering, Booking & Statistics, Corporate & Marketing Communications, Research & Development, Treasurer, and Human Resources.

PERKS

Computer classes and one-day time-management seminar; attendance welcome at INTELSAT social functions; access to INTELSAT fitness center.

FYI

INTELSAT's system was used on July 20, 1969 to broadcast, worldwide, the Apollo 11 moon landing and Neil Armstrong's first steps on the moon . . . Over half the interns each year are non-US citizens . . . Nearly 20 percent of interns later join the company as full-timers.

TO APPLY

Open to undergrads, recent college grads, college grads of any age (within one year of graduation), and grad students. International applicants eligible. Write for application.

Internship Coordinator
Human Resources Division
INTELSAT
Box 24-INT
3400 International Drive NW
Washington, DC 20008-3098
(202) 944-7243
(202) 944-7150 (Fax)

ETTA HULME reprinted by permission of NEA, Inc.

SELECTIVITY
Approximate applicant pool: 200; Interns accepted: 120

COMPENSATION
None

LOCATION(S)
Washington, DC

FIELD
Government

DURATION
8 weeks: ongoing

DEADLINE(S)
Rolling

THE WORK
An agency within the US Department of Commerce (see separate entry), the International Trade Administration (ITA) manages the nonagricultural trade operations of the US Government and assists the Office of the United States Trade Representative in coordinating trade policy. In order to increase American competitiveness abroad, open foreign markets, and eliminate unfair trade practices, ITA identifies trade and investment opportunities for US exporters, advises US businesses on overseas economic developments, monitors imports, and sponsors trade fairs and missions. Interns work in Trade Development, the Office of the Undersecretary, International Economic Policy, US and Foreign Commercial Service, and Import Administration.

PERKS
Occasional brown-bag luncheons featuring guest speakers; field trips to local cultural sites; access to fitness center (approximately $7/month).

FYI
ITA also offers a co-op internship program, allowing students to complete at least two semester-long internships at ITA during their undergraduate years.

TO APPLY
Open to undergrads and grad students. Write for application.

Personnel, Room 4814
International Trade Administration
US Department of Commerce
14th and Constitution Avenue NW
Washington, DC 20230
(202) 482-2262
(202) 482-1903 (Fax)

SELECTIVITY
Approximate applicant pool: 40; Interns accepted: 12 each year

COMPENSATION
Small stipend

LOCATION(S)
Washington, DC

FIELD
International development

DURATION
14 weeks: Summer, Fall, Spring

DEADLINE(S)
Summer: April 15; Fall: August 1; Spring: November 15

THE WORK
A private, nonprofit agency, International Voluntary Services (IVS) combats poverty, hunger, and economic inequality in third world communities in Bangladesh, Bolivia, Cambodia, Ecuador, Thailand, and Vietnam. Projects focus on transferring technical and managerial skills to villagers in the areas of animal husbandry, farming, small business, marketing, and health care. Since its founding in 1953, IVS has placed over 1,500 volunteers in more than 35 countries worldwide. Interns work in DC as project officers, performing such tasks as gathering data and drafting proposals, for the Andes Program, Bangladesh Program, AIDS-Prevention Program, and Public Outreach.

INTERNING OVERSEAS? TEN THINGS TO DO BEFORE YOU LEAVE

1. Obtain a work permit and visa.
2. Go to the local library or bookstore and bone up on your host country's history, politics, economy, traditions, music, food, etc.
3. Become familiar with the local language through language tapes or classes.
4. Purchase a round-trip ticket with a flexible return date (check the newspaper's travel section, 1-800-FLY-CHEAP, WORLDTEK TRAVEL at 1-800-247-0846, and Council Travel at 41 offices throughout the US or 1-800-2-COUNCIL).
5. Find out from the country's consulate if you need to obtain any vaccinations.
6. Clearly define your job duties and projects with the sponsoring organization.
7. Investigate any opportunities for scholarshiops or academic credit.
8. Ask the sponsoring organization for assistance in arranging housing.
9. Pack a basic medical kit (esp. if traveling to a third-world country or tropical region).
10. Bring a camera.

PERKS

Small staff; attendance welcome at staff and board meetings; attendance welcome at IVS-sponsored conferences.

FYI

IVS's program director once served as an intern in the DC office . . . Approximately 25 percent of interns are hired for full-time positions . . . Over 80 percent of IVS staff and volunteers come from third world countries.

TO APPLY

Open to college seniors as well as grads, and grad students. Must be fluent in English; must have proficiency in Spanish for Andes position. International applicants eligible. Submit resume and cover letter.

Internship Program
International Voluntary Services
1601 Connecticut Ave, NW Suite 402D
Washington, DC 20009
(202) 387-5533
(202) 387-4291 (Fax)
ivs.inc@erols.com

INTERNATIONAL VOLUNTEER PROJECTS

SELECTIVITY
Approximate applicant pool: 1,000–2,000; Interns accepted: 350–500

COMPENSATION
$195 placement fee (additional $30–$300 for Lithuania, Morocco, Russia, Ukraine, and Latin America; $2,350 placement fee in Ghana inclusive of international air travel); free room and board

LOCATION(S)
All 50 states in the US (varies yearly); Belgium, Canada, Czech Republic, Denmark, England, France, Germany, Ghana, India, Japan, Lithuania, Morocco, the Netherlands, Northern Ireland, Poland, Russia, Scotland, Slovakia, Slovenia, Spain, Tunisia, Turkey, Ukraine, Wales; Latin American countries (usually Bolivia, Brazil, Chile, Costa Rica, Mexico).

FIELD
Agriculture; Archaeology; Construction; Environment; Public service

DURATION
2–4 weeks (1–3 months for Ghana); Summer (January, February, April, and October for India)

DEADLINE(S)
Ghana: April 1; India: 2 months before start date; Others: rolling between April and June

THE WORK

Established in 1982, International Volunteer Projects (IVP) is a program of the Council on International Educational Exchange (see separate entry) and part of a network of organizations that has been coordinating workcamps since the early 1920s. Organized into workcamp groups of ten to twenty people from around the world, IVP volunteers work on over 600 projects (involving the environment, agriculture, archaeology, historic preservation, and public service) mostly in rural areas and typically in the summer.

PERKS

Organized leisure-time activities; geographically diverse group of interns.

FYI

CIEE provides several $500 scholarships for minority students who serve as IVP volunteers (deadline: April 1) . . . CIEE also offers round-trip travel grants to high school students and undergrads participating as IVP volunteers in Ghana, India, and Latin America . . . Past volunteers have found themselves drinking tea with Turkish villagers, riding bicycles to work in Holland, and toting buckets of water on their heads to replenish the water supply in a Ghanaian village.

TO APPLY

Open to anyone over age 18. US citizens and non-US citizens residing in the US: write CIEE for application, brochure, and directory of projects (published April 1, it costs $12, credited toward the placement fee). NonUS citizens living outside the US: contact CCIVS for address and phone number of organization in your country that runs workcamp programs.

International Volunteer Projects—CIEE
205 E. 42nd Street
New York, NY 10017
(212) 661-1414, ext. 1139
E-mail: ivpbrochure@ciee.org
(include name and address)

CCIVS
UNESCO
1 Rue de Miollis
75015 Paris, France
33-14-568-2731

For IVP Minority Scholarships, call:
(212) 661-1414, ext. 1139 for application

For Ghana, India, and
Latin America travel grants, call:
(212) 661-1414, ext. 1108 for application

INTERNSHIPS IN FRANCOPHONE EUROPE

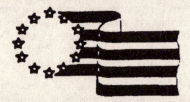

SELECTIVITY
Approximate applicant pool: 40; Interns accepted: 24–30

COMPENSATION
$5,950 tuition plus room/board with family $9,300 approx.

LOCATION(S)
Paris and its region

FIELD
Political science; French studies; Public policy; Art and culture; Media; Economics

DURATION
18 weeks: Fall, Spring

DEADLINE(S)
Fall: May 1; Spring: November 1

THE WORK

IFE is an academic internship program offered in both Spring and fall semesters in Paris, France. A full-time professional-level internship is the cornerstone of a 17-week experience that provides an immersion in European culture and society. Placements are in a wide array of public institutions and not-for-profit organizations and are arrange according to students back-

INTERNATIONAL RADIO AND TELEVISION SOCIETY INTERNS:

Interns meet with anchor **Peter Jennings** on the set of ABC's *World News Tonight.*

Interns listen to radio personality **Bruce Morrow** on the airwaves at WCBS-FM.

An IRTS Newsmaker Luncheon, held at the Waldorf-Astoria Hotel for over 600 media professionals, featured the interns (seated in first row) as the guests of honor. Panelists pictured (top row, second from left) are Videoware Corp. founder and CEO **Dick Hubert**, *Channels Magazine* founder **Les Brown**, and former NBC News President **Larry Grossman**.

ground and interest. Prior to the 12-week internship period students complete a rigorous 5-week preparatory session which integrates teaching (by French university professors and practitioners) in French society, politics, law, contemporary history, etc. The curriculum is designed to equip students to take full advantage of their internship as a result of their knowlege of contemporary France.

PERKS
Weekly seminars on French and European public policy issues; attendance welcome at host institution's staff meetings, receptions, and special events; possible travel throughout Europe on business for host institution.

FYI
IFE participants complete a research paper related to their work. IFE is recognized for university credit by a number of US institutions. Transfer credit can be arranged through out the University of Illinois. Write or email for details

TO APPLY
Open to college juniors and seniors, recent college grads, and grad students at American and Canadian colleges and universities. Must be proficient in French. Minimum GPA: 3.0. Write for application.

Internships in Francophone Europe
26, rue Ct Mouchotte 5108 #J.108
Paris 75014
France
33-1-43 21 7807
33-1-42 79 94 13 (Fax)
E-mail: IFEparis@worldnet.fr
www.ifeparis.org

INTERNSHIPS INTERNATIONAL

INTERNships
INTERNational —— *Quality work experiences abroad*

SELECTIVITY   N/A
Approximate applicant pool: N/A; Interns accepted: 100

COMPENSATION $
None. $700 placement fee

LOCATION(S)
Santiago, Chile; Dresden, Germany; Budapest, Hungary; Florence, Italy; London, England; Paris, France; Dublin, Ireland; Melbourne, Australia, Shanghai, China; Glasglow, Scotland; Ho Chiminh City, Vietnam

FIELD
Several fields (see Appendix)

DURATION
8 weeks–6 months: ongoing

DEADLINE(S)
Rolling

THE WORK
Founded in 1995, Internships International (II) is a not-for-profit internship placement service. Depending on their interests and needs, interns are placed at international businesses, government agencies, nonprofit groups, research institutes, think tanks, art institutes, fashion houses, and many other organizations. Sponsoring organizations include Citibank, British Labour Party, French fashion house, Institute Lorenzo de Medici, Nike. The intern defines the internship and Internships International funds it.

PERKS
Program representative in each city to provide guidance; "survival kit" with information on housing, cultural attractions, etc.; additional perks vary with placement.

FYI

According to II's director, the program is ideal for those who "realize that they need an international component in order to be competitive or those who simply wish to sample a career."

TO APPLY

Open to college grads or those seniors requiring an internship to graduate. Write for application.

Internships International
1612 Oberlin Rd. #5
Raleigh, NC 27608
(919) 832-1575
(919) 834–7170 (fax)
E-mail: intintl@AOL.com
rtpner.org/~intintl

INTERSCOPE RECORDS

See Atlantic Records

IOWA FILM OFFICE

IOWA FILM OFFICE

SELECTIVITY
Approximate applicant pool: 15; Interns accepted: 6

COMPENSATION
None

LOCATION(S)
Des Moines, IA

FIELD
Film

DURATION
12–16 weeks: Summer, Fall, Spring

DEADLINE(S)
Rolling

THE WORK

Founded in 1984, the Iowa Film Office (IFO) arranges the filming of motion pictures and advertising productions in Iowa. IFO has recruited over 56 feature films, including *Bridges of Madison County*, *Field of Dreams*, *Starman*, and *Twister*, and more than 1,500 internationally produced commercials, including those for Toyota Trucks, US West, and MCI. Interns assist staff in updating IFO's image database and in preparing photographic location packets for directors and producers.

PERKS

Attendance welcome on production sets; passes for movie screenings; opportunities to attend film events (Showcase Iowa, various speeches with directors/producers, etc.).

FYI

Says the internship coordinator: "I work hard to make sure that [interns] learn something and have the opportunity to make connections. I want my [interns] to remember me as someone who helped them rather than someone who held them back." . . . In existence since 1984, the internship program counts among its alumni the personal assistant to screenwriter and director Nora Ephron.

TO APPLY

Open to high school students, high school grads, undergrads, recent college grads, college grads of any age, and grad students. International applicants eligible. Submit resume and cover letter.

Internship Coordinator
Iowa Film Office
200 East Grand Avenue
Des Moines, IA 50309
(515) 242-4726
(515) 242-4809 (Fax)

ISLAND RECORDS

See PolyGram

IT'S YOUR BUSINESS

See US Chamber of Commerce

JACOB'S PILLOW DANCE FESTIVAL

SELECTIVITY
Approximate applicant pool: 100; Interns accepted: 26

COMPENSATION
$30/week stipend; free room and board

LOCATION(S)
Lee, MA

FIELD
Performing arts

DURATION
May 24–August 31

DEADLINE(S)
March 6

THE WORK

The oldest dance festival in America, Jacob's Pillow draws 40,000 people each summer for a 12-week performing season that includes modern and traditional ballet as well as the latest innovations in dance. Departments accepting interns include Business, Development, Marketing/Press, Education, Technical Theater/Production, Archives, Video, Operations, Programming/Special Projects, Box office.

PERKS

"Magical" small-town setting in Berkshires; housing with performers, artists-in-residence, dance students, and professional staff.

FYI

Started in 1983, the program offers about a quarter of its interns full-time employment . . . Says an intern: "This place is a treasure. It encourages self-growth and opens one to see more alternatives . . . No place else has such a supportive community feeling to it."

TO APPLY

Open to high school grads, undergrads, recent college grads, college grads of any age, and grad students. International applicants eligible. Submit resume, cover letter, writing samples, two letters of recommendations, tapes, and phone numbers of two work-related references. Applicants for Marketing-Press and Development should include at least two writing samples. If applying far more than one area, please list in order of preference.

Internship Coordinator
Jacob's Pillow Dance Festival
P.O. Box 287
Lee, MA 01238
(413) 637-1322
(413) 243-4744 (Fax)

Star Gazing

"Telescopes Recommended"

A partial list of organizations offering their interns opportunities for celebrity watching:

The Callaghan Group

Creative Artists Agency

Cromarty & Co.

Good Morning America

H.S.I. Productions

International Creative Management

International Management Group

Korff Enterprises

Late Show with David Letterman

MCT Management/Bold! Records

PMK

Roy A. Somlyo Productions

Saturday Night Live

Sesame Street

The Source

The Today Show

Tribeca Film Center

United Talent Agency

WGN-Chicago

William Morris Agency

Williamstown Theater Festival

JAPAN-AMERICA SOCIETY OF WASHINGTON

SELECTIVITY 🔍🔍
Approximate applicant pool: 40; Interns accepted: 8

COMPENSATION $
None

LOCATION(S)
Washington, DC

FIELD
U.S.–Japan relations; Culture, Education

DURATION
12–16 weeks: Summer, Fall, Spring

DEADLINE(S)
Rolling

THE WORK

Established in 1957, the Japan-American Society of Washington (JASW) is a nonprofit organization promoting understanding between America and Japan through cultural, public affairs, and educational programs. These programs include public affairs lectures, presentations of Japanese performing arts, an annual Japanese Festival, Japanese language instruction, educational seminars with local public schools, and sponsorship of newsletters, films, exhibits, and book signings. Interns assist staff in the preparation and execution of JASW's programs.

PERKS

Attendance welcome at all JASW programs; participation in receptions for visiting Japanese dignitaries; participation in Japanese language school courses.

FYI

To further its educational mission, JASW has partnered with the Capital Children's Museum to create a hands-on exhibit on Japan. Opens September 1999.

TO APPLY

Open to undergrads, and grad students. International applicants eligible. Submit resume and cover letter.

Internship Coordinator
Japan-America Society of Washington
1020 19th Street, LL#40
Washington, DC 20036
(202) 833-2210
(202) 833-2456 (Fax)

JCPENNEY

SELECTIVITY
Applicant Pool: 1,000; Interns accepted: 300

COMPENSATION Ⓢ Ⓢ Ⓢ
75 percent of the entry-level management salary
1999 rate: $10.10 per hour/40 hour work week

LOCATION(S)
Nationwide

FIELD
Retail

DURATION
10 weeks: Summer

DEADLINE(S)
April 1

THE WORK
Interns at JCPenney receive thorough training in merchandising, visual presentation, and customer service. While most interns are business, marketing, and merchandising majors, other students with strong leadership skills and a solid understanding of retail concepts are also encouraged to intern at JCPenney.

PERKS
Scholarship opportunities; discount privileges

FYI
Founder John Cash Penney got his start by founding a chain of stores on the frontier called the Golden-Rule stores. His first experience with free enterprise came at age eight when he saved up enough cash from odd jobs to start a small pig farm. As fate would have it, Penney returned to farming after having achieved his success in retail.

TO APPLY
Send resume and cover letter to:

College Relations Manager
JC Penney Company, Inc.
P.O. Box 10001
Dallas, TX 75301-8115
972-431-2316
972-431-2320 (Fax)

JET PROPULSION LABORATORY

See National Aeronautics and Space Administration

JEWISH VOCATIONAL AND CAREER COUNSELING SERVICE

SELECTIVITY
Approximate applicant pool: 110; Interns accepted: 30

COMPENSATION Ⓢ
$1,500/summer

LOCATION(S)
San Francisco Bay Area, CA

FIELD
Education; Health care; Finance; Journalism; Public policy and advocacy; Online services; Public service; Public relations

DURATION
8 weeks: Summer (mid-June to mid-August)

DEADLINE(S)
April 1

THE WORK
Jewish Vocational Services places college undergraduates in summer internships at various Jewish community agencies in the San Francisco Bay Area. Under the auspices of JVS's Kohn Summer Intern Program, interns work four days a week at agencies such as the American Israel Public Affairs Committee, the Anti-Defamation League, the Holocaust Oral History Project, Jewish Family and Children's Services, the Jewish Home for the Aged, and the Northern California Hillel Council.

PERKS
Orientation; weekly day-long seminars on topical issues every Friday (e.g., work place matters, Israeli politics, anti-Semitism on campus, intermarriage, AIDS crisis to the Jewish community); direct supervision with leading Jewish community agency executives and exposure to inner workings of foremost Jewish agencies.

FYI
Recent intern projects have included: conducting oral histories with Holocaust survivors; writing feature articles for the local *Jewish Bulletin of* Northern California; organizing Congressional caucuses; planning AIPAC's back to Campus Night; political advocacy; Online and website design; financial planning and resource allocation; case work with seniors.

TO APPLY
Open to college sophomores, juniors, and seniors. Must be Jewish. Must maintain residence in the Bay Area. Academic credit may be possible. Write/call for application.

Kohn Summer Intern Program
Jewish Vocational Service
77 Geary Street, Suite 401
San Francisco, CA 94108
(415) 391-3600
(415) 391-3617 (Fax)
E-mail: dlouria@jvs.org
www.jvs.org

THE JIM HENSON COMPANY

SELECTIVITY 🔍🔍🔍🔍🔍
Approximate applicant pool: 500; Interns accepted: 25

COMPENSATION Ⓢ
None

LOCATION(S)
New York, NY; Los Angeles, CA

FIELD
Office of the President (LA; Production (LA); Development (LA); Interactive media (LA); Production (NY); Publishing (NY); Public Relations (NY); Archives/Photo Library (NY); Jim Henson Foundation (NY); Licensing (NY); Exhibits (NY); Finance (NY), and Design services (NY). Not all internships are available at all times.

DURATION
12–16 weeks: Summer, Fall, Spring

DEADLINE(S)
Los Angeles: Applications are accepted November–January for Spring; March–May for Summer; July–August forFall

New York: November 30 for Spring; March 30 for Summer; July 30 for Fall

THE WORK
The Jim Henson Company, an established leader in family entertainment for more than forty years, is an independent multimedia production company, one of the top character licensers in the industry, a leading publisher of children's books, and home to Jim Henson Pictures and Jim Henson's Creature Shop. The Jim Henson Company is headquartered in Los Angeles, with offices in New York and London. Internships are available in a wide variety of departments in our Los Angeles and New York offices.

PERKS
Attendance welcome at studio tapings; friendly, energized work environment; close proximity to Muppets.

FYI
The Jim Henson Company (formerly Jim Henson Productions) has been accepting interns since the mid-1970s and has been running a structured internship program since 1992. According to the company's internship bulletin, intern duties include answering phones, making coffee, copying and faxing, assembling press kits, and "blowing bubbles."

TO APPLY
Internships are open to undergraduates and graduate students. You must receive credit for the internship from a college or university located in the United States to be considered. Please mail a cover letter and resume to:

Los Angeles:
Intern Progam-LA
Nicole Chiasson
The Jim Henson Company
5358 Melrose Avenue, Suite 300W
Hollywood, CA 90038
(323) 960-8053 (Fax)

New York:
Intern Coordinator
The Jim Henson Company
117 East 69th Street
New York, NY 10021
(212) 570-1147 (Fax)

JOHN WILEY AND SONS

WILEY

SELECTIVITY 🔍🔍🔍🔍🔍
Approximate applicant pool: 300; Interns accepted: 6–9

COMPENSATION Ⓢ Ⓢ Ⓢ
$300/week

LOCATION(S)
New York, NY

FIELD
Publishing

DURATION
9 weeks: Summer

DEADLINE
Febuary 15

THE WORK
John Wiley & Sons Inc., founded in 1807, is an independent publishing company in North America. Wiley textbooks are found in lecture halls, seminar rooms, and backpacks across the world. Wiley assigns interns to its Editorial, Sales, Corporate Communications, Marketing, New Media, or Production departments.

PERKS
Intern conferences; lunchtime lectures; departmental meetings; discounted books.

FYI
Wiley specializes in professional and consumer books and subscription services, textbooks and educational materials for colleges and universities, as well as scientific and technical books and journals. Some of their publications include *National Business Employment Guide*, *The Warren Buffet Way*, and *Anton's Calculus*.

TO APPLY
Open to college juniors (the summer between your junior and senior year). Submit resume and cover letter.

John Wiley & Sons, Inc.
Internship Program
605 Third Avenue
New York, NY 10158
(212) 850-6238

JOHNSON SPACE CENTER

See National Aeronautics and Space Administration

See US Department of Defense

JONES & BARTLETT

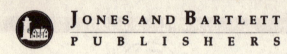

JONES AND BARTLETT
P U B L I S H E R S

SELECTIVITY N/A
Approximate applicant pool: N/A; Interns accepted: N/A

COMPENSATION
None

LOCATION(S)
Sudbury, MA

FIELD
Publishing

DURATION
8 or 12 weeks: Summer

DEADLINE(S)
Rolling

THE WORK
Founded in 1983 to publish textbooks, professional, and reference books, Jones & Bartlett is currently the tenth largest publisher of college textbooks in the nation, and the fastest growing one. The publisher's emphasis has been on the physical and medical sciences, such as nursing, mathematics, chemistry, computer science, and astronomy. The firm offers two different internship tracks: interns can either rotate through each of the company's departments—Sales/Marketing, Production, Editorial, and Customer Service—or concentrate in just one.

PERKS
Exposure to all aspects of the educational publishing industry.

FYI
Even if you haven't cracked a textbook in months, you've probably seen J&B's products: the company donated the books lining the shelves of the *Chicago Hope* sets . . . The company's rapid growth has led to what they're calling a period of "enormous expansion"—this is a good time to get your foot in the door.

TO APPLY
Open to college undergrads. Submit resume and cover letter.

Jones and Bartlett Publishers
Attn: Internship Coordinator
40 Tall Pine Drive
Sudbury, MA 01776
(508) 443-5000
(508) 443-8000 (fax)
www.jbpub.com

THE
J. PAUL
GETTY
TRUST

SELECTIVITY
Approximate applicant pool: 150 (undergrad), 150 (grad);
Interns accepted: 21 (undergrad), 21 (grad)

COMPENSATION
$300/week for undergrads; $350/week, $750 for travel and health benefits for grad students

LOCATION(S)
Los Angeles, CA

FIELD
Museums

DURATION
Undergrad: 10 weeks, Summer; Grad: 9 or 12 months, September—June

DEADLINE(S)
Undergrad: March 1; Grad: December 31

THE WORK
A private foundation devoted to the visual arts and the humanities, The J. Paul Getty Trust (JPGT) was founded in 1953 to oversee The J. Paul Getty Museum in Malibu, CA. Interns are assigned functions in administration, architecture, computers, conservation science, curatorial (e.g., Greek and Roman antiquities, European paintings, drawings, photographs, sculptures), education, grants, landscape, library, public affairs, and publications in one of seven programs—JPGT itself, the Museum, the Getty Center for the History of Art and the Humanities, Getty Conservation Institute, Getty Art History Information Program, Getty Center for Education in the Arts, and the Getty Grant Program.

FYI
The J. Paul Getty Trust was created to advance the enjoyment, understanding, and preservation of the world's artistic and cultural heritage. Internships are offered in various departments of the museum and other Getty programs.

TO APPLY
Undergraduate Internships at the Getty Center are intended specifically for outstanding students who are members of groups currently underrepresented in museum professions and fields related to the visual arts and humanities: individuals of African American, Asian, Latino/Hispanic, Native American, and Pacific Islander descent. Eligible applicants must be currently enrolled undergraduates who either reside or attend college in the Los Angeles area, will have completed at least one semester of college by June 2001, and will not graduate before December 2001. Candidates are sought from all areas of undergraduate study and are not required to have demonstrated a previous commitment to the visual arts. Graduate Internships are for those currently enrolled in a graduate course of study leading to an advanced degree in a field relevant to the internship which is being sought, or for those who have completed a relevant graduate degree since June 1999.

The J. Paul Getty Trust
Department of Education and Academic Affairs
P.O. Box 2112
Santa Monica, CA 90407-2112
(310) 451-6545 (undergrad internships)
(310) 459-7611 (grad internships)
www.getty.edu

EXCLUSIVE INTERVIEW WITH STUART FLACK

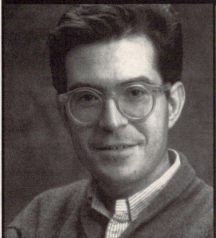

During the day, Stuart Flack serves as the Director of External Communications at the prestigious consulting firm McKinsey & Co. But at night and on weekends, he's a playwright. His plays, which include American Life & Casualty and Peaceful Creatures, have been staged at the Alleyway Theater in Buffalo, New York. Flack graduated with a BA in philosophy from Cornell University in 1982 and an MFA in Playwrighting from Columbia University in 1984.

The Internship Informants: How long have you been interested in the theater?
Flack: I have been writing plays, hanging out in theaters, building theaters, and doing tech work and design since junior high school…My high school in Evanston, Illinois had lavish, college-like theater facilities, and I wrote a couple of plays while in high school. Once at Cornell, I took one of the plays I had written in high school, shopped it around, and one of the student theater companies there read it and said let's do it. But I went to college not sure of whether or not I wanted to specialize in the hard sciences or in the theater.

The Internship Informants: Hard sciences?
Flack: That's what I studied in high school—physics, chemistry, and biology. Getting my play produced that first semester was a very gratifying experience and going to physics classes was not as immediately gratifying.

The Internship Informants: What internships did you do at Cornell?
Flack: Well, I started my own theater, the Whistling Shrimp Theatre Co. During the summers, I went back to Chicago, which has a very lively theater scene, and worked at some of the big theaters there. I did everything—building sets, doing lighting design, hanging lights—at places like Victory Gardens, the Organic, Perry Productions, and North Light Rep.

The Internship Informants: At Columbia in 1984, you served a 6-month internship with Arthur Kopit, author of the Broadway hit *Oh Dad, Poor Dad*. How did you hook up with him?
Flack: Kopit was teaching a graduate course in playwrighting at City University [in Manhattan]. As graduate students, we had teaching assistantships, some of which were outside of Columbia. Mine was with Arthur Kopit. So I started out as his TA. I was very lucky because Arthur and I had a great personal affinity toward each other, and we remain very good friends. He was a real mentor. In fact, he continues to be a mentor. But at that time, he was working on a musical, *Nine*, and on a show on Broadway [called *End of the World*], and he needed someone to work with him on those shows…I did everthing—held out-of-town tryouts in Washington, did rewrites, additional research, silly PR stuff. It was a look at what a playwright does in getting shows ready for big, commercial productions.

The Internship Informants: Did you make many contacts then?
Flack: The director of *Nine* was Tommy Tune. The other director was Harold Prince. So I worked with both of them.

The Internship Informants: What did the internship teach you?
Flack: It taught me what it's like to be a playwright in a real production—which is that it's enormously fun and gratifying, but it certainly is not easy. For example, Arthur's Broadway play, which is a wonderful play, got horrible reviews from [former New York Times theater critic] Frank Rich and closed very quickly…Arthur got in a fight with Frank on the street after the show; they were screaming at each other…So the plus side is that I got to see it, warts and all.

The Internship Informants: You obviously learned from Kopit that making a living out of playwrighting can be difficult. Is that why you became a reporter for *Forbes* a few months after graduating in 1984?
Flack: I could have become a literary manger or done some managerial work in the theater, but I really didn't want to do that. I wanted to get out in the world and do interesting stuff…[After Columbia], I teamed up with a stock trader that I used to play cards with, and through him, I helped run a hedge fund up in Vermont [where Flack also worked, in his free time, on *American Life & Casualty*]. Based on that and some people I knew, I was able to get an interview at *Forbes* because I was fluent in the markets and takeovers. This was in the mid-80s when financial journalism was very hot.

The Internship Informants: Does your job at McKinsey provide you with inspiration for your plays?
Flack: I wouldn't write plays about management consulting…but the work I do now is very intellectually demanding and the people I deal with are very intelligent, so it's stimulating…Writing is very closely linked to me to feeling like I'm intellectually alive and challenged and vibrant. My job provides me with that; I get to travel to interesting places—Europe and the Far East. It keeps me on my toes, and that's what I need to write plays. Plus the things I write about have elements of business in them. The people in the plays are people with jobs and the stories are about making a living and money and the world of finance and trade.

J.P. MORGAN AND CO.

JPMorgan

SELECTIVITY 🔍🔍🔍
Approximate applicant pool: 664; Interns accepted: 130

COMPENSATION 💲💲💲💲
Approximately $575/week

LOCATION(S)
New York, NY

FIELD
Commercial and investment banking

DURATION
8–12 weeks: Summer

DEADLINE(S)
March 1

THE WORK
JP Morgan is the nation's fourth largest bank and a veritable "superbank," having commercial and investment banking capabilities that render it the envy of Wall Street. The bank manages investment funds for corporate giants like McDonald's, PepsiCo, and United Airlines. Interns are hired for positions in the following departments: Management Services, Audit, Financial Management, Global Technology and Operations, Global Markets, Corporate Finance, and Human Resources.

PERKS
Free lunch; weekly training; trip to NYSE; professional atmosphere.

FYI
JP Morgan is one of the only Wall Street investment firms to offer a structured internship program for undergraduates . . . An employee and former intern says, "We train interns in order to make them Morgan material," hence the weekly training sessions . . . The bank's headquarters is known by employees as the "Taj Mahal" because it towers above nearby buildings.

TO APPLY
Open to college seniors who are returning to school in the fall. International applicants eligible. Submit resume, cover letter, and transcript.

JP Morgan & Co., Incorporated
60 Wall Street
New York, NY 10260
(212) 648-9909
www.jpmorgan.com

THE JUILLIARD SCHOOL

Professional Internships
TECHNICAL THEATER & ARTS ADMINISTRATION
The Juilliard SCHOOL

SELECTIVITY 🔍🔍🔍
Approximate applicant pool: 250; Interns accepted: 30

COMPENSATION 💲💲
$231/week

LOCATION(S)
New York, NY

FIELD
Performing arts

DURATION
9 months: September–May

DEADLINE(S)
June 1

THE WORK
A world renowned school of the arts, Juilliard sponsors a Professional Intern Program in both Technical Theater and Arts Administration. The program is designed to provide hands-on experience working with professionals and administrators in their respective fields. Technical Theater internships include Costumes, Wigs & Makeup, Electrics, Props, Stage Management, Scene Painting, Technical Direction. Arts Administration internships include Dance Division, Drama Division, Vocal Arts, Production Assistant, Facilities Management, Orchestra Library, Concert Office, Orchestra Management, Chamber Music Coordinator, Ensemble Operations, and Information Technology.

PERKS
Backstage tours of Broadway productions and Metropolitan Opera House; mini-seminars with professionals; extensive alumni network; basic student medical coverage.

BEYOND THE INTERNSHIP CHASE

Good internships are like good haircuts: easy to see but not so easy to come by. As internships are growing increasingly popular among college and grad students, the competition for intern positions at name organizations is becoming fierce. From the FBI to Hallmark Cards, top internship programs are now forced to choose from an ever expanding pool of applicants.

For those dissatisfied with the internship chase, there remains a long neglected but potentially winning route to a dream internship: make your own. Rather than apply only to pre-established programs, internship seekers should consider persuading an organization or an accomplished person who does not normally hire interns to offer an "ad hoc internship."

Here's how: think about six or so accomplished people whose shoes you would love to fill. It could be a bigwig advertising executive, a documentary filmmaker, a renowned park ranger, a compelling author—the sky's the limit. Just make sure it's not someone so famous that a letter from you would hit the trash before it ever reached your quarry's desk. Supercelebs like Oprah Winfrey, Bruce Springsteen, and H. Ross Perot fall into this class of virtual "unreachables."

After deciding upon a handful of people worth writing, it is time to research them thoroughly. Go to the local library and look up what that journalist (or cardiologist or ski racer or pilot) was doing last week, last month, and last year. Use biographies, databases, magazine indexes, annual reports, or anything else that will tell you exactly what your potential mentor is all about.

Then, write each figure an earnest letter that not only introduces you but convinces him or her that hiring you as an ad hoc intern would be mutally beneficial. Play up your best qualities—abilities either directly related to your potential mentor's work (e.g., your fluency in French if you are writing to the French ambassador) or traits suggesting that you would be a valuable assistant (emphasize your enthusiasm, discreetness, diligence, etc.) Be sure to customize each letter, showing each figure that you have done your homework by incorporating into the letter choice bits of information unearthed during your library resarch. Convey why his work is exactly what you want to be involved with or why her organization is singularly important to your career aspirations.

Chances are that your six letters, voraciously researched and carefully written, will yield at least one internship opportunity. If you think about it, this ad hoc internship may be more rewarding than a preestablished internship. There will be no preexisting limits to the internship, no areas where you are told "interns have never been allowed to do that." There probably will be no other interns, giving you the pick of possible projects and undivided accessibility to your mentor. It is not hard to see how the ad hoc internship will allow you to work closely with your mentor, forging a professional connection that may last a lifetime.

Some students have already discovered the rewards of the ad hoc internship. A few years ago, a sophomore at a university in California was paging through an issue of *Life* magazine that profiled the now late Albert P. Blaustein, a constitutional law professor at Rutgers University who had helped over forty countries draft their constitutions. His interest piqued, the student dashed off to the campus library and researched Blaustein's recent work. He then wrote this "modern-day James Madison" a detailed letter, introducing himself and offering his services as a summer research assistant. Within two weeks, Blaustein wrote back, informing the student that although no undergraduate had ever asked to be his assistant before, he would take a chance and hire the student for the summer.

When summer came, the student ended up researching constitutional histories for the professor's encyclopedic set of the world's constitutions. Importantly, the professor and his student assistant got along so well that at the end of the summer, when the government of Romania asked Blaustein to help it draft its new constitution, he invited the student to accompany him on a one-week trip to Bucharest. The following autumn found the two journeying to post-revolution Romania, where they met with the country's foreign minister, members of Parliament, and various other officials. Watching the professor advise government officials and academics, the student received a hands-on introduction to constitution-making that he will never forget.

When all was done, the student had created an ad hoc internship that rivalled anything he could have experienced at the best preestablished internships. It goes to show that it sometimes pays to look beyond the internship chase—and create an opportunity where none presently exists.

FYI

Several Juilliard staff members got their start in the internship program, including the Manager & Auditions Coordinator in the Drama Division, the production stage manager for the Fall Opera, the Master Electrician in the Juilliard Theater, and the Associate Production Manager in the Production Department.

TO APPLY

Open to high school grads, undergrads, recent college grads, college grads of any age, and grad students. Write for application.

Professional Internship Program
The Juilliard School
60 Lincoln Center Plaza
New York, NY 10023
(212) 799-5000 x7102
(212) 724-0263 (Fax)
E-mail: htaynton@juilliard.edu

JUSTACT: YOUTH ACTION FOR GLOBAL JUSTICE

SELECTIVITY 🔍🔍
Approximate applicant pool: 125; Interns accepted: 25 per year

COMPENSATION 💲
Some stipends available; mostly volunteer positions

LOCATION(S)
San Francisco, CA

DURATION
3 months minimum: Summer, Fall, or Winter/Spring

DEADLINE(S)
Rolling

THE WORK

JUSTACT is a national, student-based, nonprofit organization. Since its creation in 1983, JUSTACT has been a forum for thousands of young people to address global issues such as hunger, poverty, and social injustice. It runs four major programs: an Education program working with student groups on high school and university campuses throughout the United States to increase awareness around global issues; a Partnership program that supports grassroots alternatives to development around the globe; an Alternative Opportunities Clearinghouse, providing information on opportunities with international volunteer programs, alternative spring breaks, and community development organizations in various countries, and Bike-Aid, a cross-country cycling event that raises money and awareness of community-based approaches to development (see separate entry). Intern positions include Global Links Newsletter Co-Editor, Educational Resource Coordinator, Alternative Opportunities Clearinghouse Assistant, Bike-Aid Education Coordinator, Bike-Aid Public Relations & Media Intern, Webweaver, Graphic Designer, Alumni and Donor Relations Intern, and Office Operations Intern.

PERKS

Biweekly seminars featuring speakers on topics related to global justice issues; attendance welcome at staff meetings; friendly, supportive office atmosphere; opportunities to acquire valuable experience in the nonprofit field. We also have leadership training and workshops.

TO APPLY

Open to high school students, high school grads, undergrads, recent college grads, college grads of any age, and grad students. International applicants eligible. Call, write, or e-mail to request an application.

Internship Coordinator
JUSTACT
333 Valencia Street, Suite 330
San Francisco, CA 94103-3547
(415) 431-4204
(415) 431-5953 (Fax)
E-mail: info@justact.org

KARL LAGERFELD

SELECTIVITY 🔍🔍🔍
Approximate applicant pool: 50; Interns accepted: 8

COMPENSATION 💲
None

LOCATION(S)
New York, NY

FIELD
Womens clothing

DURATION
12–16 weeks: Summer, Fall, Spring

DEADLINE(S)
Rolling

THE WORK

Founded in 1984, Karl Lagerfeld is primarily known for its women's luxury ready-to-wear clothing, although it also manufactures men's ready-to-wear, furs, perfumes, and accessories. Owned by the luxury products empire Vendome Group, Lagerfeld distributes its line to about 230 boutiques and department stores worldwide. Interns assist staff with performing clerical work and drafting correspondence.

PERKS

Attendance welcome at industry events (e.g., Market Week); small, tight-knit office.

FYI

Lagerfeld's internship is not for those looking for hands-on, substantive experience in the clothing business. It involves mostly, if not total, busywork, but former interns report that it can lead to great connections and a powerful name on the resume.

TO APPLY

Open to undergrads, recent college grads, and grad students. International applicants eligible. Submit resume and cover letter

Internship Coordinator
Karl Lagerfeld
730 Fifth Avenue, Suite 1601
New York, NY 10019
(212) 586-8400
(212) 586-8486 (Fax)

KCSA

SELECTIVITY ⊠ ⊠ ⊠ ⊠ ⊠
Approximate applicant pool: 100; Interns accepted: 4

COMPENSATION ⑤
None

LOCATION(S)
New York, NY

FIELD
Public relations

DURATION
12 weeks: Summer, Fall, Spring

DEADLINE(S)
April 1

THE WORK
In existence since 1969, KCSA is the nation's eighteenth largest independent public relations firm. Its clients include a cross section of corporations, consumer products, and professional services. Interns work in Business to Business PR Group, Investor Relations Group, and Professional Services PR Group.

PERKS
Contact with clients and all levels of management; attendance welcome at some client luncheons (especially in Investor Relations); occasional opportunities to attend press conferences; attendance welcome at parties and social events.

FYI
The program has been running since 1987 . . . Says the internship coordinator: "The internship was created to educate students in the techniques of public relations from a practical standpoint."

TO APPLY
Open to college sophomores, juniors, and seniors. International applicants eligible. Submit resume and cover letter.

Joseph A. Mansi
KCSA Public Relations
800 Second Avenue
New York, NY 10017
(212) 682-6300 ext. 205
(212) 697-0910 (Fax)

The career of prolific photographer **Horst**, who over the decades photographed everyone from Bette Davis to Duran Duran, began with an apprenticeship to the legendary architect Le Corbusier in 1929. The opportunity came about when Horst, then a 23-year-old student in Hamburg, Germany, wrote Le Corbusier to ask if he could apprentice in the architect's Paris studio. Miraculously, Le Corbusier wrote back and offered him an unpaid apprenticeship. Commented Horst in *Coronet* magazine, "Everyone in Hamburg thought I had drawn a sweepstakes ticket."

The Kennedy Center

SELECTIVITY ⊠ ⊠ ⊠ ⊠
Approximate applicant pool: 500; Interns accepted: 30 (semester)

COMPENSATION ⑤
$650/month

LOCATION(S)
Washington, DC

FIELD
Arts management and performance

DURATION
12–16 weeks

DEADLINE(S)
Summer: March 1; Fall: June 23; Winter/Spring: November 1

THE WORK
Founded in 1971, The Kennedy Center is one of the country's foremost performing arts institutions. It attracts the country's finest talent while also providing a home to the National Symphony Orchestra, the American Film Institute, and the Washington Opera. Internship positions are available in a whopping twenty departments: Advertising, Alliance for Arts Education, Kennedy Center American College Theater Festival, Development, Education, Events for Teachers, Government Liaison, Grants, Marketing, National Symphony Orchestra, Performance Plus, Press Office, Production, Programming, Special Events, Theater for Young People, External Affairs, Member Services, Volunteer Management, and Management Information Services.

PERKS
Tickets to performances; weekly seminars; local tours.

FYI
Interns have has the opportunity to escort all sorts of VIPs, from Matthew Broderick to the head of the Joffrey Ballet . . . Internship alumni include a talent coordinator for Disney World, the general manager of New York's Ice Theater, the operations manager of the Arlington Symphony, a cultural affairs officer in San Juan, Puerto Rico, and the booking coordinator for The Kennedy Center.

TO APPLY
Open to undergrads who have completed 2 years of school, recent grads, and grad students. International applicants eligible. Submit resume, cover letter (stating your career goals, areas of interest, and computer experience), official transcript, brief writing sample, and two letters of recommendation.

Ms. Amanda L. Perry
Internship Program Coordinator
The Kennedy Center
Washington, DC 20566-0001
(202) 416-8821
(202) 416-8853 (Fax)
E-mail: alperry@kennedy-center.org
www.kennedy-center.org/internships

See National Aeronautics and Space Administration

KGO-TV

KGO-TV

SELECTIVITY 🔍 🔍 🔍
Approximate applicant pool: 300; Interns accepted: 30–45

COMPENSATION Ⓢ
CA prevailing minimum wage: Currently $5.15/hour

LOCATION(S)
San Francisco, CA

FIELD
Television

DURATION
1–2 Semesters (12–24 weeks); Summer, Fall, Spring

DEADLINE(S)
May 1; August 1; December 1

THE WORK
Channel 7/ABC in San Francisco is owned by ABC, Inc., a wholly owned subsidiary of the Walt Disney Company. Channel 7 is the #1 television station in the Bay Area, broadcasting to the fifth largest market in the country with 2.2 million TV households. The Bay Area represents one of the most ethnically diverse areas in the

---

TO KENNEDY IS TO INTERN

JOSEPH P. KENNEDY & ROSE FITZGERALD

John F. Kennedy
■ JFK, Jr. (Center for Democratic Policy while at Brown U., '81)

Robert F. Kennedy
■ RFK, Jr. (Manhattan DA Robert Morgenthau, summer '81)
■ David (*Atlantic Monthly's* Boston office)
■ Douglas (Capitol Hill while at Georgetown Prep High School)
■ Kerry, Dir. of RFK Ctr. for Human Rights (Amnesty International, 1981)

Edward M. Kennedy
■ Edward, Jr. (Massachusetts state senator while at Wesleyan, summer '82)
■ Patrick, Rep. D-RI (Rhode Island statehouse)

Lights... Camera... *Intern!*
Interns in film and on television:

A recent television ad for Starburst candy features a bank manager who tries to recruit a college student to work at the bank. The manager breaks into a longwinded speech—"When I was your age, you know what I heard knocking? Opportunity. I was with the bank, interning . . . "—but the student tunes him out and daydreams about eating Starbursts.

nation and Channel 7 continues to respond to this evolving and diverse viewership by producing award-winning newscasts and quality local programming that have been recognized throughout the broadcast industry. Ten to fifteen interns per semester work in almost every department at the station, including News, Programming, Promotions, Marketing Research, Sports, Weather, Public Affairs, Graphics, Sales, Information Systems, Accounting/Finance, and Human Resources. Channel 7/ABC also offers a Newswriter/Producer Training Program, which is an eighteen-month opportunity for an applicant with at least two years of work experience in the broadcast industry to learn all aspects of news production.

PERKS
Welcome luncheon to meet station managers; attendance welcome at Channel 7/ABC social events and monthly employee luncheon, end-of-internship gifts (e.g., umbrellas, portfolio bags, polo shirts, mugs, and hats featuring the Channel 7/ABC logo).

FYI
Channel 7/ABC has the pre-eminent intern program for broadcasting in the Bay Area. Interns, through active participation and contribution to the shows or projects to which they are assigned, gain invaluable skills and practical experience that will serve as a foundation for further success in the industry.

TO APPLY
Open to college juniors and seniors as well as grad students in journalism, communications, and related fields. Must receive academic credit. Write for application.

KGO-TV/Channel 7
Personnel Department
900 Front Street
San Francisco, CA 94111
(415) 954-7222

KIRO NEWS
710 AM · TV 7 · 1007 FM

SELECTIVITY
Approximate applicant pool: 50; Interns accepted: 10–15

COMPENSATION
None

LOCATION(S)
Seattle, WA

FIELD
Television

DURATION
10–16 weeks: Summer, Fall, Winter, Spring

DEADLINE(S)
Summer: April 15; Fall: July 15; Winter: November 15; Spring: February 15

THE WORK
A CBS television affiliate, KIRO broadcasts in Seattle as Channel 7. Interns work on KIRO's news shows and talk shows, in the newsroom, on news weather, and in the areas of photojournalism, sports, television programming, field production, sales, marketing, public affairs, accounting, and editorial.

PERKS
Internship orientation; opportunities to accompany KIRO news crews on shoots.

FYI
Started in 1984, KIRO's internship program is special in that it affords some interns the rare chance to write stories and work with cameras.

TO APPLY
Open to college juniors and seniors as well as grad students who are residents of WA or attending school in WA. Must receive academic credit. International applicants eligible. Write for application.

Intern Coordinator
KIRO
2807 Third Avenue
Seattle, WA 98121
(206) 728-7777
E-mail: jkelsch@kirotv.com

THE KITCHEN

SELECTIVITY
Approximate applicant pool: 100; Interns accepted: 15

COMPENSATION
None

LOCATION(S)
New York, NY

FIELD
Performing arts

DURATION
8 weeks–9 months: Ongoing

DEADLINE(S)
Rolling

THE WORK
Founded in 1971, The Kitchen is a nonprofit organization staging avant-garde productions of dance, music, literature, and performance art. Over the years it has featured artists such as Laurie Anderson, Eric Bogosian, David Byrne with The Talking Heads, Brian Eno, Vernon Reid, and Philip Glass. Interns work in Curatorial, Technical, Publicity, Fundraising, Administrative, and Media departments.

PERKS
Free tickets to all performances; contact with artists; occasional passes to other theaters and shows.

FYI
The Kitchen's name comes from the fact that it began in the unused kitchen of the Mercer Arts Center.

TO APPLY
Open to college juniors and seniors, recent college grads, college grads of any age, and grad students. International applicants eligible. Submit resume and cover letter.

Internship Coordinator
The Kitchen
512 West 19th Street
New York, NY 10011
(212) 645-4258 (Fax)
E-mail: info@thekitchen.org
www.thekitchen.org

KNOPF BOOKS

See Random House

KOREAN AMERICAN COALITION

SELECTIVITY 🔍🔍🔍
Approximate applicant pool: 90; Interns accepted: 15

COMPENSATION 💲
$1,000 stipend (summer only)

LOCATION(S)
Los Angeles, CA; Washington, D.C.

FIELD
Public policy; Corporate, media, Legal

DURATION
9 weeks: Summer

DEADLINE(S)
Summer: February 14

THE WORK
Established in 1983, the Korean American Coalition (KAC) is a nonprofit membership organization facilitating the Korean American community's participation in civil, legislative, and political affairs in the United States. Its projects include publishing directories and newsletters, sponsoring political conferences, running programs to assist immigrants, and studying the portrayal of Korean Americans in the media. Departments accepting interns include Media, Legal, Political, and Corporate.

PERKS
Intern banquet at end of internship; attendance welcome at press conferences and community meetings; access to resource library of Korean American business and political contacts.

FYI
Says the internship coordinator: "There's ample opportunity here for interns to gain exposure to the range of issues facing the Korean American community . . . Interns are given a lot of flexibility in choosing what projects they want to work on, and they are encouraged to approach their projects with creativity."

TO APPLY
Open to college freshmen, sophomores, juniors, and seniors. International applicants eligible. Write for application.

Internship Coordinator
Korean American Coalition
3421 West 8th Street, 2nd Floor
Los Angeles, CA 90005
(213) 365–5999
(213) 380-7990 (Fax)

KORFF ENTERPRISES

SELECTIVITY 🔍🔍
Approximate applicant pool: 60; Interns accepted: 9–16

COMPENSATION 💲💲💲
$300/week for undergrads; $325/week for grad students

LOCATION(S)
Mahwah, NJ;

FIELD
Events management; Marketing; Sports

DURATION
12 weeks: Summer

DEADLINE(S)
Rolling

THE WORK
Founded in 1978, Korff Enterprises is a full-service special events marketing company. Featured in *Forbes*, *Money*, and other magazines, Korff operates professional tennis events. Interns work in Advertising, Facilities Operations, Promotions, Finance, and the President's Office.

PERKS
Tickets to all Korff events; staff outings; free t-shirts and other event-related merchandise.

FYI
Interns may be offered permanent employment. No local housing available, applicants should be from the Tri-state area. (NY, NJ, CT).

TO APPLY
Open to college juniors and seniors, recent college grads, and grad students. Submit resume and cover letter.

Internship Coordinator
Korff Enterprises
1 International Boulevard, Suite 303
Mahwah, NJ 07430
(201) 529-2200
(201) 529-2353 (Fax)

KPIX-TV

KPIX 5

SELECTIVITY 🔍🔍
Approximate applicant pool: 250; Interns accepted: 50

COMPENSATION 💲
$5.50/day to cover travel costs

LOCATION(S)
San Francisco, CA

FIELD
Television

DURATION
6 months: January–June and July–December

DEADLINE(S)
Fall: June 1; Spring: December 1

THE WORK
KPIX broadcasts throughout the San Francisco Bay Area as Channel 5. Interns work in Marketing Research, Art/Design, News Assignment Desk, News Sports, Bay Sunday (a community affairs show), Creative Services, Public Relations, News Production, and Special Projects.

PERKS
Opportunities to accompany reporters in the field; attendance welcome at KPIX parties; KPIX t-shirts.

FYI
Started in 1975, KPIX's internship program hires 20 percent of interns for full-time positions. While most interns perform basic duties—dubbing tapes, researching stories, fielding incoming phone calls, etc.—those in Creative Services write 10-second ID's and 30-second promos for KPIX late-night movies.

EXCLUSIVE INTERVIEW WITH NORA EPHRON

A prolific and witty writer, Nora Ephron is known for her journalistic essays and for writing the screenplays for You've Got Mail, Silkwood, Cookie, Sleepless in Seattle, *and* When Harry Met Sally. *She graduated from Wellesley College in 1962.*

The Internship Informants: We heard that you served as a copy girl at CBS.
Ephron: I had worked for two summers at CBS in Los Angeles doing all sorts of horrible things that needed to be done, like updating the database of advertising contacts. It was a classic college person's horrible summer job. It was a true nightmare, one of those things where toward the end you're in a little race against yourself of how many you can do in an hour.

The Internship Informants: Did you get anything at all out of the experience?
Ephron: Well, it was 1959, and I thought to myself that if I write a letter to the President of CBS News on CBS stationery, he will have to look at it; whereas if I go back to college and write him on my own stationery, he will throw it away. So I wrote the president a memo saying that I was on my college newspaper and I wanted to work as a copy girl at the [Democratic National] convention. He interviewed me in New York, and I got a two-week job [at the Convention] . . . It was very exciting to see . . . Kennedy was nominated. And Adlai Stevenson was a kind of phantom figure, and when he finally appeared at the convention the place went crazy . . .

The Internship Informants: Then in 1961 you had a full-fledged internship at the White House with JFK's press secretary Pierre Salinger?
Ephron: Yes, but I was deskless and functionless. I didn't do one thing for six weeks, except that I got to go to the President's press conferences and the daily briefings. And I got to see a little bit of how the White House press corps worked . . . Meanwhile, I literally spent every day standing around and looking through the files. [Once] I was standing nearby when Speaker of the House Sam Rayburn locked himself in the men's room . . . He began rattling the door, and I let him out. I'm sorry to say it was the high point of the summer.

The Internship Informants: So do you regret the internship?
Ephron: No. It taught me that there was no point in wanting a career in politics in 1961 because women weren't [doing substantive work in Washington]. There were just no good jobs for women . . . So to learn that Washington was not the place to go absolutely and definitively was a huge thing to learn. I'm very grateful to [my internship] for that reason because I could have wasted some time in Washington. I would have been a miserable young woman there.

The Internship Informants: We like to stress the ability of internships to provide a window onto another vocation, even for people long graduated from school. If, right now, Nora Ephron had the chance to do an internship outside of film, where would it be?
Ephron: I think it would be fun if I could intern at a theater. I'd like to see someone directing a play—that would be interesting to me. Now I could probably arrange to do that, but my point is that it would be very interesting to me because I don't really know how you do that.

The Internship Informants: Any particular theater in mind?
Ephron: Yeah, I would love to watch the New York Shakespeare Festival . . . One of my friends, a young woman I know at Brown [University], interned there last summer. She had a fabulous time.

The Internship Informants: Let's turn to your movie *When Harry Met Sally*. Had Harry and Sally done internships in college, where would they have interned?
Ephron: Harry would have interned for his local Congressman. And he would have had one summer working at a law firm which would have decided him completely against becoming a lawyer . . . Sally would have been a camp counselor and the person in charge of the camp newspaper, if there was one. She would have had a summer in some sort of quasi-teaching thing that would have decided her against becoming a teacher. And then she would have spent a summer interning for the woman's page editor at her local newspaper, before going to journalism school.

TO APPLY

Open to college sophomores, juniors, and seniors as well as grad students in communications. Minimum GPA: 2.5. Must receive academic credit. Write for application.

Human Resources
KPIX-TV
855 Battery Street
San Francisco, CA 94111
(415) 765-8741

KQED-FM

KQED 88.5FM

SELECTIVITY 🔍 🔍 🔍
Approximate applicant pool: 100–150; Interns accepted: 20

COMPENSATION ⑤
None

LOCATION(S)
San Francisco, CA

FIELD
Radio

DURATION
12–15 weeks: Summer, Fall, Spring, Winter

DEADLINE(S)
Rolling

"I can't go on with the presentation, Mr. Smathers, unless that office boy stops making snide remarks about the advertising business every time he passes the door."

Drawing by W. Miller; © 1961 The New Yorker Magazine, Inc.

THE WORK

As Northern California's premiere all-news public radio station, KQED-FM "emphasizes strong writing and creative use of sound to tell thoughtful, balanced news stories to an intelligent, literate audience." KQED-FM also produces "The California Report," a statewide news program, and interns may request assignment on the show in place of the newsroom. Interns work with staff reporters, assisting in research, reporting, sound gathering, and writing.

PERKS

Tutorials on the basics of public radio news gathering and production; "No busywork—ever!"

FYI

Reports the intern coordinator: "Promising and competent interns often wind up their program doing on-air reports of news stories; [this is] great for gaining real radio news experience and creating a resume tape of broadcast work."

TO APPLY

Open to college seniors, recent college grads, and grad students. International applicants eligible. See www.kged.org for internship details.

David Gorn, Deputy News Director
KQED-FM News
2601 Mariposa Street
San Francisco, CA 94110-1400
(415) 553-2361
E-mail: dgorn@kqed.org
www.kged.org

KRAFT FOODS, INC.

We know what you're hungry for.

SELECTIVITY 🔍 🔍 🔍
Approximate applicant pool: 3,000; Interns accepted: 50–100

COMPENSATION ⑤ ⑤ ⑤ ⑤
$400–$600/week for undergrads; $800–$1,200/week for grad students

LOCATION(S)
Glenview, IL; Northfield, IL; Rye Brook, NY; Tarrytown, NY; Madison, WI

FIELD
Foods

DURATION
12 weeks: Summer

DEADLINE(S)
February 1

THE WORK

Kraft Foods is North America's largest food company, churning out over 2,500 products. Among these are such household favorites as Oscar Mayer meats, Kool-Aid, Philadelphia Brand cream cheese, Post Grape-Nuts, Velveeta, and Jell-O. Departments vary by location, but include Oscar Mayer, Cheese, Beverages, Desserts, Dinners, Post Cereals, Maxwell-House Coffee, Sales, Finance, Human Resources, and Information Systems.

PERKS

Presentation skills workshop.

FYI

Kraft Macaroni and Cheese is eaten by 72 percent of US college students . . . One intern says of the internship: "A child's dream to see and work with goodies we've eaten all our lives." . . . About 45 percent of interns receive offers of permanent employment.

TO APPLY

Open to undergrads and grad students. International applicants eligible. Submit resume and cover letter.

Kraft Foods, Inc.
University Relations
Three Lakes Drive
Northfield, IL 60093
(847) 646-2000

Kraft Foods
University Relations
800 Westchester Avenue
Rye Brook, NY
10573-1301
(914) 335-2500

Oscar Mayer
University Relations
910 Mayer Avenue
Madison, WI 53704
608) 241-3311

> Interns at Kraft General Foods enjoy a field trip to a local Entenmann's Bakery, where they tour a complex of huge ovens, 12-foot blenders, and doughnut makers. At the end of the tour, they sample the gooey delights of just-baked Entenmann's cookies.

KRCB TV & RADIO

SELECTIVITY   🔍 🔍
Approximate applicant pool: 200; Interns accepted: 12

COMPENSATION   💲
None

LOCATION(S)
Rohnert Park, CA; 1 hour north of San Francisco

FIELD
Public television; National Public Radio

DURATION
1 month–1 year: Ongoing

DEADLINE(S)
Rolling

THE WORK

An affiliate of the Public Broadcasting System and National Public Radio, KRCB broadcasts on television's Channel 22 and radio's 91.1 FM in Northern California. Like all public stations, it emphasizes educational programming. Interns work in Membership, Production, Auction, Volunteer, and Radio, where they correspond with members, compose press releases, participate in fundraising, and assist with live broadcast.

PERKS

Opportunities to appear on air; free mug.

FYI

The small station affords interns easy access to department heads and sophisticated equipment . . . According to the internship coordinator, interns learn nearly every facet of operating a televi-

sion and radio station. There is a very limited amount of production work.

TO APPLY

Open to high school grads, undergrads, recent college grads, college grads of any age, and grad students. International applicants eligible. Submit resume and cover letter.

Internship Coordinator
KRCB
5850 LaBath Avenue
Rohnert Park, CA 94928
(707) 585-8522

LAKE CHARLES AMERICAN PRESS

SELECTIVITY   🔍 🔍 🔍 🔍 🔍
Approximate applicant pool: 30; Interns accepted: 1–2

COMPENSATION   💲 💲
$340/week

LOCATION(S)
Lake Charles, LA

FIELD
Newspapers

DURATION
14 weeks: Summer

DEADLINE(S)
March 30

THE WORK

Founded in 1895, the *Lake Charles American Press* is an independent, family-owned community newspaper. With a circulation of 40,000, the *Press* is known for its investigative projects and aggressive coverage of governmental issues. Interns work in the Editorial department.

PERKS

"Same responsibilities, scheduling, and treatment as our own staff;" direct interaction with top brass; numerous interns were eventual hires.

FYI

In existence since 1970, the internship program counts among its alumni the New Delhi bureau chief for *The Washington Post* and an editor at *Reader's Digest* . . . Says the internship coordinator: "The *Press* is a watchdog type of paper. Our coverage of government and gambling is aggressive."

TO APPLY

Open to undergrads and recent grads. Submit resume, cover letter, and writing samples.

Internship Coordinator
Lake Charles American Press
P.O. Box 2893
Lake Charles, LA 70602
(337) 494-4081
(337) 494-4070 (Fax)

Lamont-Doherty Earth Observatory of Columbia University

SELECTIVITY 🔍🔍🔍
Approximate applicant pool: 150; Interns accepted: 16–20

COMPENSATION 💲💲💲
$200/week; free housing; daily transportation to LDEO; round-trip travel reimbursed if more than 200 miles away

LOCATION(S)
Palisades, NY

FIELD
Earth and Ocean sciences research

DURATION
10 weeks: Summer

DEADLINE(S)
March 10

THE WORK
Affiliated with Columbia University, the Lamont-Doherty Earth Observatory (LDEO) was founded in the late 1940s to conduct research in earth and ocean sciences. Supervised by research scientists, interns work in a wide variety of subject areas, including marine geochemistry, geophysics, micropaleontology, petrology, marine biology, and environmental policy.

PERKS
Twice-weekly lectures by LDEO staff; occasional sea-going research trips; lunchtime volleyball, basketball, and soccer games.

FYI
Since 1982, nearly 150 students have participated in the program . . . Many interns co-author published papers describing their research projects.

TO APPLY
Open to college juniors and seniors studying oceanography, geology, physics, chemistry, math, biology, and engineering. Write for application.

Summer Internship Program for Undergraduates
Lamont-Doherty Earth Observatory
Palisades, NY 10964
E-mail: dallas@ldeo.columbia.edu
www.deo.lcolumbia.edu/~dallas/abbott_sum.html

Land Between The Lakes TVA

SELECTIVITY 🔍🔍
Approximate applicant pool: 50; Interns accepted: 10

COMPENSATION 💲💲
$125/week; free housing

LOCATION(S)
Golden Pond, KY

FIELD
Education; Environment; Recreation

DURATION
12–16 weeks: Summer, Fall, Spring

DEADLINE(S)
Rolling

THE WORK
Established by the Tennessee Valley Authority in 1963, Land Between The Lakes (LBL) operates programs in outdoor recreation and environmental education at a 170,000-acre inland peninsula in Western Kentucky and Tennessee. LBL also supervises camping along two large lakes, hunting and fishing, sight-seeing, and hiking on some 200 miles of trails. Interns work in Environmental Education, Recreation, Natural Resources, Communications, and Engineering.

PERKS
Intern luncheons with speakers; participation welcome in all recreational activities; field trips; free t-shirts.

Vickie Ludden monitors bald eagle nests during her internship at Land Between The Lakes.

TO APPLY

TO APPLY
Open to college juniors and seniors, recent college grads, college grads of any age, and grad students. Write for application.

Internship Coordinator
Land Between the Lakes
100 Van Morgan Drive
Golden Pond, KY 42211
(502) 924-2000
(502) 924-2060 (Fax)

LANGLEY RESEARCH CENTER

See National Aeronautics and Space Administration

LARRY KING LIVE

See Turner Broadcasting System

LATE NIGHT WITH CONAN O'BRIEN

See National Broadcasting Company

LATE SHOW WITH DAVID LETTERMAN

LATE SHOW
with
David Letterman

SELECTIVITY 🔍 🔍 🔍 🔍 🔍
Approximate applicant pool: 750; Interns accepted: 15 per semester

COMPENSATION Ⓢ
None

LOCATION(S)
New York, NY

FIELD
Television

DURATION
14–16 weeks: Summer, Fall, Spring

DEADLINE
Summer: March 1; Fall: June 1; Spring: October 1

 THE WORK
Edgier and sassier than competitor Jay Leno, David Letterman still hosts the coolest talk show on TV. Interns work in Talent, Research, Production, Writing, Music, Audience Development, and the Executive Producer's Office. One intern is assigned as a floater.

PERKS
Free "Late Show" paraphernalia; busy environment.

FYI
There are currently 28 staff members who were once interns with the show . . . If answering phones, running errands, and making copies are unacceptable, then it's time to look for another internship.

TO APPLY
Open to undergrads. Must receive academic credit. International applicants eligible. Submit resume and cover letter.

Janice Penino
Late Show with David Letterman
1697 Broadway
New York, NY 10019
(212) 975-5300

Most of our interns are runaways! —David Letterman, 1997

Congressional Intern Program Office

In 1973, the House launched the Lyndon Baines Johnson (LBJ) Congressional Internship Program, which provides each Representative's DC office with $2,500 to hire an "LBJ intern" for two months or two such interns for one month each. Due to budget constraints, the LBJ program was suspended indefinitely in 1994. However, the Congressional Intern Program Office (CIPO), which provided LBJ interns with support services, is still available to all House and Senate interns. Managed by the Committee on House Oversight, CIPO offers:

1) a list of available housing in the DC area
2) a schedule of its Summer Lecture Series, featuring over 40 lectures with Representatives, Senators, and Executive and Judicial branch officials
3) (available through your congressman or senator) a Congressional Intern Handbook, offering information on basic office procedures, how a bill becomes law, congressional food services, and points of interest in DC

—*Committee on House Oversight*
(202) 225-8281

LAWRENCE LIVERMORE NATIONAL LABORATORY

SELECTIVITY 🔍
Approximate applicant pool: 1,000; Interns accepted: 250–300

COMPENSATION 💲💲💲💲
Participants are paid at competitive rates based on job assignment, academic achievement, and relevant work experience. Travel experience can be reimbursed if applicable.

LOCATION(S)
Livermore, CA

FIELD
Science and Engineering research

DURATION
12 weeks: Summer

DEADLINE(S)
December 31

THE WORK
Since the founding of the Laboratory in 1952, research teams of scientists, engineers, and support people have worked together to solve some of the nation's most challenging scientific problems. Lawrence Livermore continues to serve the national interest and support global security through its application of innovative, groundbreaking science and technology. Lawrence Livermore National Laboratory offers full-time science and technology summer research appointments to undergraduate, graduate, and occasionally high school students. Participants in the Summer Employment Program come from academic institutions nationwide, both large and small, representing diverse cultural and academic backgrounds. The Program provides an opportunity for students to apply their academic background to practical research problems resulting in worthwhile and enriching work experience.

PERKS
LLNL offers a series of lectures and seminars for summer students. Summer students may also participate in the on-site exercise program. The on-site employee store offers discounts on merchandise and reduced-cost tickets to area theme parks and special events. An Olympic-size pool, picnic areas, and par course are also located on site.

FYI
For two weeks in August, about 30 outstanding science and engineering students entering their senior year at colleges and universities throughout the nation come to Lawrence Livermore National Laboratory for lectures, tours, and to carry out research projects under the guidance of leading University of California faculty and LLNL researchers. The Undergraduate Summer Institute in Applied Science provides participants with a unique opportunity to develop an understanding of the basic principles and state-of-the-art areas in applied science. The appointments cover travel and living expenses in addition to a $1,000 award. Application deadline: December 31st. Website: http://www.llnl.gov/usi/

TO APPLY
Open to undergrads, recent college grads, and grad students. International applicants eligible. Submit resume, cover letter, one short writing sample (3–5 pages), academic transcript, and two letters of recommendation. For Summer Employment Program only, complete "LLNL Summer Employment Program Interest Form" at http://www.llnl.gov/jobs/SEP.

Summer Employment Program, Recruitment and Employment Division
Lawrence Livermore National Library
P.O. Box 808, L725
Livermore, CA 94551-0808
(925) 424-321

LAWYERS ALLIANCE FOR WORLD SECURITY

SELECTIVITY 🔍🔍🔍🔍
Applicant pool: about 35–45 per semester; Applicants selected: 2–3

COMPENSATION 💲
None

LOCATION(S)
Washington, DC

FIELD
Foreign Affairs and International Security

DURATION
Summer: 3 months; Fall/Spring: 4 months

DEADLINE(S)
March 15

THE WORK
LAWS is a membership organization of legal professionals and other prominent individuals engaged in prudent and practical efforts to reduce the risks posed by weapons of mass destruction. LAWS is led by a Board of Directors, which includes many of the most important contributors to the study and practice of arms control, nonproliferation, and disarmament, including former senior executive branch officials, legislators, diplomats, and military officers, as well as influential academics, lawyers, and other professionals distinguished in the field. LAWS/CNS focuses on strengthening the Non-Proliferation Treaty (NPT) regime through its international and domestic programs to address the threats of proliferation in the post-Cold War era.

PERKS
Contact with experts in the field; organizing and attending briefings, conferences, and meetings; and fundraising.

FYI
LAWS/CNS has hired approximately 13 percent of its former interns for full-time positions.

TO APPLY
Open to undergrads, recent college grads, college grads of any age, and grad students. International students eligible. Submit resume, cover letter, one writing sample, academic transcript, and recommendations.

Leonor Tomero, Program Director
LAWS/CNS
1901 Pennsylvania Ave., NW Suite 201
Washington, DC 20006
(202) 745-2450
(202) 667-0444 (Fax)

See Discovery Communications

LEAVENWORTH PRISON

See Federal Bureau of Prisons

LEGACY INTERNATIONAL

SELECTIVITY 🔍🔍🔍
Approximate applicant pool: 75; Interns accepted: 5

COMPENSATION $
None; room and board provided

LOCATION(S)
Bedford, VA

FIELD
International relations; Education; Cross cultural communication

DURATION
9 weeks: summer

DEADLINE(S)
April 1 for summer internship in Bedford

THE WORK
Founded in 1979, Legacy International is an organization that promotes conflict resolution, leadership training, environmentally sound development, and curriculum design. It has implemented programs in Central Asia, Europe, the Middle East, North Africa, and North America. Summer interns work as live-in counselors and program assistants during Legacy's annual international youth training program.

PERKS
Interns participate in Legacy's Training in Intercultural Relations Program prior to field placement.

FYI
Interns work as part of Legacy International's Global Youth Village—a 9-week summer program for young people (ages 11–18) that hires cabin counselors, teaching assistants, and administrative workers. The program is located in Bedford, VA and provides room and board. Call (540) 297-5982 for more details.

TO APPLY
Open to undergrads, and recent college grads. International applicants eligible. Submit resume and cover letter or visit the website for online application.

Internship Coordinator
Legacy International
1020 Legacy Drive
Bedford, VA 24523
(540) 297-5982
(540) 297-1860 (Fax)
E-Mail: staff@legacyintl.org
www.legacy.intl.org

LEO CASTELLI

SELECTIVITY 🔍🔍
Approximate applicant pool: 40; Interns accepted: 9

COMPENSATION $
None

LOCATION(S)
New York, NY

FIELD
Art gallery

DURATION
16–20 weeks: Summer, Fall, Spring

DEADLINE(S)
Summer: April 1; Fall: August 1; Spring: December 1

THE WORK
Founded in 1957 by Leo Castelli, now one of the most recognized names in the art business, Leo Castelli Gallery exhibits and sells contemporary art by American and European artists. Through the years, the Gallery has represented the best of the changing movements in art, featuring painters Jasper Johns and Frank Stella, Pop artists Roy Lichtenstein and Andy Warhol, Minimalists Donald Judd and Robert Morris, Conceptual artists Joseph Kosuth and Laura Grisi, and Expressionists Meyer Vaisman and the Starn Twins. Interns work in Photo Archives, which maintains photos of art works for publicity and educational purposes.

PERKS
Invitations to exhibition preview parties; opportunities to meet artists; small staff (twelve people).

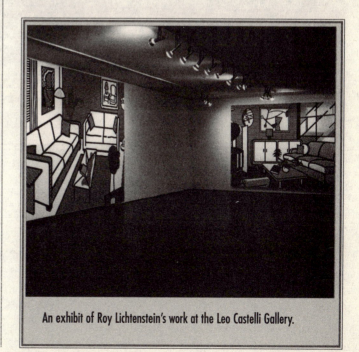

An exhibit of Roy Lichtenstein's work at the Leo Castelli Gallery.

Drawing by R. Chast ; © 1994 The New Yorker Magazine, Inc.

FYI

Leo Castelli's internship program was started in 1989 and offers interns exposure to the art business at its highest level.

TO APPLY

Open to undergrads, recent college grads, and grad students studying art history, arts management, studio art, and related arts disciplines. International applicants eligible. Submit resume and cover letter.

Leo Castelli Gallery
420 West Broadway
New York, NY 10012
(212) 431-5160
(212) 431-5361 (Fax)

LEVINE COMMUNICATIONS OFFICE, INC

SELECTIVITY
Approximate applicant pool: 200; Interns accepted: 35

COMPENSATION $
None

LOCATION(S)
Beverly Hills, CA; Las Vegas, NV; New York, NY; Washington DC ; London

FIELD
Public relations

DURATION
10–15 hours/week, 13 weeks: Summer, Fall, Spring, Winter

DEADLINE(S)
Rolling

THE WORK

One of the four largest entertainment public relations firms in the country, Levine represents approximately 90 celebrities ranging from Charlton Heston to Michael Jackson. It also boasts the largest music and comedy department of any public relations firm in the country. Interns work in Entertainment, Corporate, and Music.

PERKS

Attendance welcome at many client events; star-gazing opportunities.

FYI

Alumni of the internship program include executives at Motown Records, Capitol Records, Geffen Records, Warner Bros. Records, Creative Artists Agency, Touchstone Pictures, Showtime, and Keppler Associates. Says one intern, "I know for a fact that when I leave here, this experience will have an impact on what I do in the future."

TO APPLY

Open to high school seniors and undergrads. International applicants eligible. Write for application.

Internship Coordinator
Levine Communications
5750 Wilshire, Suite 555
Los Angeles, CA 90036
(323) 692-9999
E-Mail: action@levinepr.com
www.levinepr.com

LEWIS RESEARCH CENTER

See National Aeronautics and Space Administration

LIBERTY RECORDS

See EMI Records Group North America

THE LIBRARY OF CONGRESS

SELECTIVITY
Approximate applicant pool: 350; Interns accepted: 6–10

COMPENSATION $ $ $
$300/week

LOCATION(S)
Washington, DC

FIELD
Library

DURATION
8–12 weeks: Summer

DEADLINE(S)
April 1

THE WORK

When President Thomas Jefferson created the Library of Congress in 1800, he intended it to be a reference tool for congresspeople only. Today, its 105-million-item collection of books, manuscripts, maps, photographs, and films is open to anyone 18 years and older who is doing serious research. The intern class is divided among the following divisions: American Folklife Center, and Motion Picture, Broadcasting & Recorded Sound.

PERKS

Hands-on contact with artifacts; twice-weekly tours.

FYI

The Library of Congress started its Junior Fellows Program in the summer of 1991 . . . Some interns may publish articles on their work in journals like the Library of Congress' *Information Bulletin* and the American Library Association's *Meridian* . . . Interns may borrow books on their library card; apart from interns, only library employees, congresspeople, and congressional staffs are eligible for one.

TO APPLY

Open to college juniors and seniors, recent undergrads, grad students. International applicants eligible. Submit resume (including social security number, address, telephone number, date of birth, and citizenship), transcript, and a letter of recommendation from a professor or employer.

The Library of Congress
Junior Fellows Program Coordinator
Collection Services LM-642
Washington, DC 20540-4700
(202) 707-8253
lcmarvel.loc.gov

LIGHTHOUSE PRODUCTION

LIGHTHOUSE
P R O D U C T I O N S

SELECTIVITY 🔍🔍🔍
Approximate applicant pool: 85–100; Interns accepted: 5

COMPENSATION Ⓢ
None

LOCATION(S)
Beverly Hills, CA

FIELD
Film; Television

DURATION
16 weeks: Summer, Fall, Spring

DEADLINE(S)
Summer: April 1; Fall: August 1; Spring: December 1

THE WORK
Founded in 1990, Lighthouse Productions acquires, develops, and produces motion pictures and television movies. Headed by Academy Award-winning producer Michael Phillips, the company is responsible for films such as *The Eyes of an Angel* and *Don't Tell Mom the Babysister's Dead* as well as television movies such as *Jane's House* and *The Companion*. Interns receive a mix of formal instruction (assigned reading and weekly discussion meetings) and practical work experience (evaluating screenplays, developing story ideas, possible production work).

PERKS
Weekly intern meetings headed by the producer and featuring guest speakers (e.g., writers, producers, story consultants); occasional opportunities to work on production sets.

FYI
Founder Michael Phillips has produced such classics as *The Sting*, *Close Encounters of the Third Kind*, and *Taxi Driver*.

TO APPLY
Open to college juniors and seniors, recent college grads, and grad students. International applicants eligible. Write for application.

Internship Coordinator
Lighthouse Productions
120 El Camino Drive, Suite 212
Beverly Hills, CA 90212
(310) 859-4923
(310) 859-7511 (Fax)

LIGHTSTORM ENTERTAINMENT

L I G H T S T O R M
E N T E R T A I N M E N T

SELECTIVITY 🔍🔍🔍🔍
Approximate applicant pool: 250; Interns accepted: 15–20

COMPENSATION Ⓢ
None

LOCATION(S)
Los Angeles, CA

FIELD
Film

DURATION
12–18 weeks: Summer, Fall, Spring

DEADLINE(S)
Summer: May 1; Fall: August 15; Spring: December 15

THE WORK
Lightstorm Entertainment is the production company for films directed or produced by James Cameron, who directed *True Lies*, *The Terminator*, *Terminator 2: Judgment Day*, *The Abyss*, and *Aliens*. Interns work in the Development and Production departments.

PERKS
Biweekly company screenings of current and vintage films; attendance welcome at events and cast and crew screenings.

FYI
The internship program has been in existence since 1990 . . . Interns in Development spend much of their time reading and evaluating scripts. A former intern has created a ten-page intern manual that takes interns step-by-step through the process of reading, assessing, and summarizing scripts.

TO APPLY
Open to college juniors and seniors as well as grad students. Must receive academic credit. International applicants eligible. Submit resume, cover letter, and (for Development applicants) writing samples (one- to two- page sample script coverages or up to five pages of critical writing).

Internship Coordinator
Lightstorm Entertainment
919 Santa Monica Boulevard
Santa Monica, CA 90401
(310) 587-2500
(310) 393-3702 (Fax)

Lincoln Center for the Performing Arts, Inc.

SELECTIVITY 🔍 🔍 🔍 🔍 🔍
Approximate applicant pool: 75; Interns accepted: 2

COMPENSATION $ $ $ $
$500/week

LOCATION(S)
New York, NY

FIELD
Arts management

DURATION
12 weeks: Summer

DEADLINE(S)
February 9

THE WORK
The Lincoln Center is arguably the world's leading performing arts center. It is home to the New York State Theater, Alice Tully Hall, Avery Fisher Hall, the Metropolitan Opera House, the Beaumont Theater, the Mitzi Newhouse Theater, and the Juilliard School. Interns spend their first week interviewing with key staff members, with whom they develop a few projects meeting both the needs of the organization and the interests of the intern. The project will give interns a broad exposure to a range of departments, including Programming, Marketing, Finance, Operations, Planning and Development, and Education.

PERKS
Some free tickets available.

FYI
One notable intern is Bill Wingate, who recently served as executive director of the New York City Ballet.

TO APPLY
Open to grad students with one year of graduate coursework in arts administration or business. Must have a demonstrated interest in the arts. International applicants eligible. Submit resume and cover letter (describing qualifications and career goals).

Jay D. Spivack
Director of Human Resources and Labor Relations
Lincoln Center for the Performing Arts, Inc.
70 Lincoln Center Plaza
New York, NY 10023-6583
(212) 875-5000
(212) 875-5185 (Fax)

SELECTIVITY 🔍 🔍
Approximate applicant pool: 10; Interns accepted: 2

COMPENSATION $
None

LOCATION(S)
Keswick, VA

FIELD
Special education

DURATION
9 weeks: Summer, Fall, Spring

DEADLINE(S)
Summer: June 8; Fall: July 25; Spring: January 25

THE WORK
Founded in 1963, Little Keswick School (LKS) is a boarding school for emotionally disturbed and/or learning disabled boys from ages 7 to 18. Enrolling a total of 30 boys, the school strives to develop its students not only academically but through athletics, the arts, and vocational preparation. Interns work in all aspects of the school, from teaching to counseling to supervising recreational activities.

PERKS
Training in working with emotionally disturbed students; field trips to various museums, athletic events, etc.; free lunch; "warm, family atmosphere."

FYI
LKS is located 7 miles from the University of Virginia . . . The internship program has been in existence since 1978.

TO APPLY
Open to undergrads, recent college grads, and grad students. International applicants eligible. Write for application.

Internship Coordinator
Little Keswick School
P.O. Box 24
Keswick, VA 22947
(804) 295-0457
(804) 977-1892 (Fax)

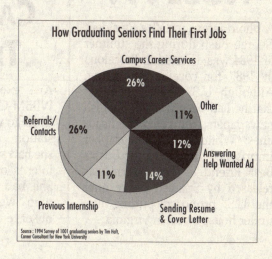

How Graduating Seniors Find Their First Jobs

Campus Career Services 26%
Other 11%
Answering Help Wanted Ad 12%
Sending Resume & Cover Letter 14%
Previous Internship 11%
Referrals/Contacts 26%

Source: 1994 Survey of 1001 graduating seniors by Tim Haft, Career Consultant for New York University

The INTERN TATTLER

Real Stories of Intern Controversy and Mayhem!

Steinbrenner To Intern: "Yerrr Out!"

At the New York Yankees' Fort Lauderdale stadium, an intern working for then Yankee publicist Harvey Green was sent from the press box to the downstairs offices to copy some documents. Before the intern could walk back upstairs, he was fired by Yankee owner George Steinbrenner for parking his car in such a way that Donald Trump, Steinbrenner's pal, had difficulty backing his own car out.

Biloxi Burning

In 1994, a former intern with the *Sun Herald* in Biloxi, Mississippi shot another former intern of that paper. Both men were reporters for the *Sun Herald*. Police said they didn't know the motive for the shooting.

Read My NOSE . . .

A photo intern for Vice President George Bush during the summer of 1984 was arrested in Barcelona in 1987 for cocaine smuggling. Although U.S. officials believed that he had been framed, Spanish newspapers trumpeted the headlines: "White House Photographer Imprisoned" and "George Bush's Best Friend." The intern was released by Spanish police after the U.S. proposed putting him under house arrest in Virginia.

Spin The Bottle?

An intern with *Spin* magazine was one of several female employees at the magazine who complained about a "hostile" work environment under publisher Bob Guccione, Jr. (son of *Penthouse* founder Bob Guccione, Sr.). The intern says she was in a room with Guccione and three other execs when he asked her, "If you were on a desert island, which of us would you pick to have sex with so you could procreate the human race?"

CANNED BY THE JUICE

An executive producer for WBBM-Ch. 2 "News Extra" in Chicago was forced to resign after station officials discovered that she had sent unsupervised college interns on a special assignment. She had dispatched the interns, who were only supposed to observe station doings, to the

CAPITOL TALES

Ousted By Rosty

After a summer intern in the office of former Rep. Dan Rostenkowsi (D-IL) told a Polish joke, Rostenkowsi picked him up and threw him out of the office. "Everyone thought he was going to kill the kid," a staffer recalled.

The Joker's Wild

A former intern in Senator Bob Packwood's office accused the Senator of reading sexually explicit jokes to her during her internship.

Chicago O'Hare Plaza Hotel to investigate where O.J. Simpson had been after his wife was murdered.

For more tantalizing tales... turn to page 434.

Liz claiborne

SELECTIVITY 🔍 🔍 🔍 🔍
Approximate applicant pool: 500–1,000; Interns accepted: 50 for summer

COMPENSATION 💲 💲
$9–$11/hour

LOCATION(S)
New York, NY; North Bergen, NJ

FIELD
Apparel and fashion accessories

DURATION
3–6 months: Summer, Fall, Winter/Spring; Part time available

DEADLINE(S)
Summer: March 15; Fall: August 1; Winter/Spring: December 1

THE WORK
Founded in 1976, Liz Claiborne, Inc., made the Fortune 500 list just 10 years later. It is today one of the largest marketers of women's apparel and accessories in the world, selling over $2 billion of products annually. The New York office offers internships in the Creative Resources, Marketing, Textile Design, Apparel Design, Merchandising, and Sales groups. At the New Jersey headquarters, interns work in administrative departments, such as Finance, Human Resources, Management Information Systems, and Production.

PERKS
Nurturing environment; garment district; 40 percent clothing discount, fast paced.

FYI
One intern produced a layout for a sweater idea—the shape, pattern, and colors . . . Employees go out of their way, as one intern put it, "to make sure students gain connections and experience— the two most valuable commodities in the fashion industry." . . . Liz Claiborne is one of only two companies founded by a woman to ever make the Fortune 500 list.

TO APPLY
Open to undergrads and grad students. International applicants eligible. Submit resume and cover letter indicating area of interest.

Liz Claiborne, Inc.
Attn: College Relations Coordinator
1440 Broadway, 2nd Floor
New York, NY 10018
(212) 626-5527 (Fax)

LOBSENZ**STEVENS**

SELECTIVITY 🔍
Approximate applicant pool: 15; Interns accepted: 6–7

COMPENSATION 💲
$2.50/hour plus daily travel reimbursement

LOCATION(S)
New York, NY

FIELD
Public relations

DURATION
8–14 weeks: Summer, Fall, Spring

DEADLINE(S)
Rolling

THE WORK
Founded in 1962, Lobsenz-Stevens (L-S) is a midsized, independent public relations agency whose clients are primarily pharmaceutical and health care companies. Interns work in Health Care, the agency's largest division, where they conduct research, develop media lists, and write press releases.

PERKS
Biweekly briefings on different aspects of public relations industry; interns assist account staff at client events; attendance welcome at L-S brainstorming sessions.

FYI
The intern coordinator writes: "Lobsenz-Stevens believes that the public relations industry owes college students the opportunity for hands-on experience in the workplace. The agency has one of the strongest, most flexible, year-round internship programs in the country."

TO APPLY
Open to college juniors and seniors. International applicants eligible. Submit resume and cover letter.

Internship Program
Lobsenz-Stevens
460 Park Avenue South
New York, NY 10016
(212) 684-6300

S(T)ING LIKE AN INTERN

In the song "Wrapped Around Your Finger," Sting sings the tune of many an intern: "You consider me a young apprentice. . . I have only come here seeking knowledge, that they would not teach me in college."

SELECTIVITY
Approximate applicant pool: 100; Interns accepted: 10/year

COMPENSATION
Free room and board plus $100/week

LOCATION(S)
Aitkin County, MN

FIELD
Education; Environment; Outdoor recreation

DURATION
16 weeks–9 months: Ongoing

DEADLINE(S)
Rolling

THE WORK
Established in 1963, the Long Lake Conservation Center (LLCC) is a residential environmental learning center offering students activities and classes in environmental and outdoor education. Serving students from the fourth grade through high school, LLCC offers instruction in canoeing, hiking, orienteering, wilderness cookery, snowshoeing, bog trekking, and other activities. Interns assist staff members in teaching classes, supervising activities, planning programs, and managing daily operations.

PERKS
Training in outdoor education; furnished housing in a dorm/classroom complex; scenic "bog country" location is home to "coyote and hare, pitcher plant and wild cranberry, bog copper butterfly and peat-producing sphagnum moss."

FYI
The internship program has been in existence since 1975 . . . Located in north-central Minnesota, Aitkin County is a rural area about the size of the state of Delaware but with a population of over 12,800.

TO APPLY
Open to high school grads, college sophomores, juniors, and seniors, recent college grads, college grads of any age, and grad students. Write for application.

Internship Coordinator
Long Lake Conservation Center
RR 2 Box 2550
Palisade, MN 56469
(218) 768-4653
(218) 768-2309 (Fax)
E-mail: llcc@mlecmn.net
Website: www.llcc.org

> Interns at the Long Lake Conservation Center are situated in rural Minnesota "bog country," home to "coyote and hare, pitcher plant and wild cranberry, bog copper butterfly and peat-producing sphagnum moss."

SELECTIVITY
Approximate applicant pool: 130; Interns accepted: 40

COMPENSATION
$5.18/hour; free housing

LOCATION(S)
Kennett Square, PA

FIELD
Horticulture; Education; Performing arts; Library science

DURATION
3–12 months: ongoing

DEADLINE(S)
November 1; February 1; May 1

THE WORK
Situated 30 miles east of Philadelphia, Longwood Gardens comprises 1,050 outdoor acres and 20 indoor gardens. Formerly the country estate of Pierre S. du Pont, Longwood offers 11,000 kinds of plants, spectacular illuminated fountains, and an outdoor theater amid ancient trees. Departments hiring interns include Arboriculture, Computer Graphics, Continuing Education, Curatorial, Greenhouse Production, Groundskeeping, Indoor Display, Integrated Pest Management, Landscape Design, Library Science, Nursery, Outdoor Display, Performing Arts (Arts Administration), Performing Arts (Technician), Research, Special Display, Student Programs, and Visitor Education.

PERKS
Field trips and lectures; free continuing education courses; paid holidays and one day off per month with pay.

FYI
One of the most prestigious internships in public horticulture, Longwood will provide prospective interns with a professionally produced video about the internship (on request).

TO APPLY
Open to undergrads and grads. International applicants eligible. Write for application.

Student Programs
Longwood Gardens
P.O. Box 501
Kennett Square, PA 19348-0501
(610) 388-100 ext.501/524
(610) 388-2908 (Fax)
E-mail: studentprograms@longwoodgardens.org
www.longwoodgardens.org

SELECTIVITY 🔍🔍🔍
Approximate applicant pool: 30–40; Interns accepted: 2–4

COMPENSATION 💲
None

LOCATION(S)
Inglewood, CA

FIELD
Sports

DURATION
6 months–1 year: Summer, Fall, Spring

DEADLINE(S)
Summer: May 1; Fall: September 1; Spring: before All-Star Break (mid-February)

THE WORK
Six-time NBA champs, the Los Angeles Lakers is one of the world's most prestigious sports franchises. The Lakers' purple and yellow uniform has graced the likes of Magic Johnson, Kareem Abdul Jabaar, and, yes, Chevy Chase in *Fletch*. These days, the Lakers' future looks as bright as the past, with Shaquille O'Neal leading a rejuvenated team. Interns work in the Public Relations office, at least one day a week as well as game nights, which occur about eight times a month.

PERKS
Work at all home Lakers games; dinner at arena on game nights; work at other Lakers functions (Stay in School, Jam Session, etc.).

FYI
Big networking potential: alumni include Lon Rosen (Magic Johnson's agent), Lorin Pullman (Kareem Abdul Jabaar's publicist), Jay Lucas (PR director, LA Dodgers), sportscaster Pat O'Brien's personal assistant, and employees at Upperdeck, World Cup Soccer, and Prime Ticket Network.

TO APPLY
Open to undergrads and grads (within two years of graduation). Must live in LA area. Submit resume, cover letter, and (if possible) recommendations.

Internship Program
Los Angeles Lakers
Great Western Forum
P.O. Box 10
Inglewood, CA 90306
(310) 419-3100

SELECTIVITY 🔍🔍
Approximate applicant pool: 70; Interns accepted: 12

COMPENSATION 💲
None

LOCATION(S)
Los Angeles, CA

FIELD
Magazines

DURATION
13 weeks: Summer, Fall, Spring

DEADLINE(S)
Summer: April 30; Fall: July 30; Spring: November 30

THE WORK
In print since 1960, *Los Angeles Magazine* covers the cultural life of the nation's second largest city. A division of Emmis Communications, it has a paid circulation of over 180,000 readers. Interns work in Editorial.

PERKS
Paid parking.

TO APPLY
Open to college juniors and seniors. Submit resume, cover letter, and writing samples (if possible).

Eric Mercado, Research Editor
Los Angeles Magazine
11100 Santa Monica Blvd. 7th Fl.
Los Angeles, CA 90025
(310) 312-2276
(310) 312-2285 (Fax)

SELECTIVITY 🔍
Approximate applicant pool: 20; Interns accepted: 15

COMPENSATION 💲
None

LOCATION(S)
Los Angeles, CA

FIELD
Museums

DURATION
15–20 weeks: Summer, Fall, Spring

DEADLINE(S)
Summer: May 1; Fall: August 1; Spring: December 1

THE WORK
Founded in 1951, the Los Angeles Municipal Art Gallery is a city-run gallery that focuses on contemporary art, particulary the work of living Southern California artists. Interns work in the Education department, where they serve as gallery educators and carry out other education projects.

PERKS
Training in leading tours; weekly group discussions with education coordinator; meetings with artists; field trips to local art galleries and studios; "exciting and creative" work environment.

FYI
The Gallery also supervises Hollyhock House, the first Los Angeles project completed by the great American architect Frank Lloyd Wright . . . The house and its surrounding 11 acres are open to the public for tours.

TO APPLY
Open to high school grads, undergrads, recent college grads, college grads of any age, and grad students. Must have background in art, education, or a related field. International applicants eligible. Write for application.

Internship Coordinator
LA Municipal Art Gallery
4800 Hollywood Boulevard
Los Angeles, CA 90027
(213) 485-4581
E-mail: cadmet@earthlink.net

LOS ANGELES TIMES

Los Angeles Times

SELECTIVITY
Approximate applicant pool: 200–800; Interns accepted: 20–50

COMPENSATION
Summer: $480/week; Fall and Spring: $6/hour

LOCATION(S)
L.A., Orange County., San Fernando Valley, San Gabriel Valley, San Diego, South Bay, and Ventura, CA; Washington DC

FIELD
Newspapers

DURATION
Summer: 11 weeks (full time); Fall and Spring: 17 weeks (part time)

DEADLINE
Summer: December 1; Fall: June 1; Spring: October 1

THE WORK
The *Los Angeles Times* is a top-flight national newspaper, admired as much for expert journalism as it is for meticulous local coverage. Indeed, *Time* magazine has praised the publication for its "packages of reporting, graphics, and presentation." Interns are sent to offices around the country, most of them working as business, news, or sports reporters, though positions are available in photojournalism, and, during summers, in copyediting and infographics (diagrams, charts, maps, etc.).

PERKS
Varies with site; generally comfortable; youthful culture.

FYI
The *LA Times* has the largest editorial department of any newspaper in the country and has won nineteen Pulitzer Prizes . . . One intern reports: "I was a bit embarrassed telling my journalist friends back home about how much responsibility I had." . . . Many interns report having written five or more front-page or front-section stories by the end of their internship.

TO APPLY
Open to undergrads. International applicants eligible. Submit resume, cover letter (noting which bureaus applicant prefers and any editorial interests, e.g., sports writing), and three telephone references. Other materials are needed for some positions. Write for more information.

Los Angeles Times
Editorial Internships
Times Mirror Square
Los Angeles, CA 90053
(800) 283-NEWS, Ext. 74487

LOVELACE RESPIRATORY RESEARCH INSTITUTE

Lovelace
Respiratory Research Institute

SELECTIVITY
Approximate applicant pool: 200; Up to 3 accepted depending on funding

COMPENSATION
$250/week; Possible travel allowances to $500

LOCATION(S)
Albuquerque, NM

FIELD
Science research

DURATION
10 weeks: Summer

DEADLINE(S)
March 15

THE WORK
This program was established in 1967 by the US Department of Energy (see separate entry) at the Inhalation Toxicology Research Institute (ITRI), a DOE contract organization operated by the Lovelace Institutes (TLI). On privatization of the institute in 1996, the educational programs of TLI were consolidated. LRRI research programs include health effects of inhaled toxic materials including bioassays, dosimetry and toxicokinetics of inhaled materials, aerosol technology and monitoring and control of airborne contaminants; molecular and genetic toxicology; pathobiology of disease; cardiopulmonary physiology, especially high altitude studies; immunotoxicology; thermoregulation; and population studies including substance abuse and efficacy of health interventions. Research projects are conducted under the supervision of a staff scientist in one of these areas. Interns design experiments, collect and analyze data, and make oral and written presentations.

PERKS
Weekly seminars with visiting scientists, workshops on computer skills, graduate school, and tools of the scientist.

FYI
This program is excellent experience for students considering advanced degrees in scientific research. LRRI is a highly multidisciplinary organization with expertise ranging from molecular biology through whole animal and human physiology, to aerosol science chemistry and Health physics.

EXCLUSIVE INTERVIEW WITH JULIE HANSON

Julie Hanson is the former Program Director of Outward Bound's Voyageur School in Minnesota and is currently a polar explorer with the International Arctic Project. In April 1995, she joined a team of seven explorers who accomplished the first dog-sled traverse of the Arctic Ocean in a single season. She graduated with a B.A. in biology and physical education from Concordia College in 1975.

The Internship Informants: You were an intern for Outward Bound. What did that involve?

Hanson: The internship provides on-the-job training for future instructors and people the School identifies as potentially good outdoor educators. When I was an intern in 1981, the assignments varied. Sometimes I'd spend the day on the ropes course, encouraging [Outward Bound students] and watching for misplaced carabiners. Or I'd help with a rock climbing session, again serving as extra eyes to watch for problems. Or I'd work in the trips house, where I'd help mix the dried foods for use on the trail and repair tents and pound out bent up pots. I'd also help drive students to various entry-points in the wilderness.

The Internship Informants: You've been on some major expeditions. How do they come about: does someone just ring you up on the phone and say, 'Hey, we're going to the South Pole, wanna go?'

Hanson: Yep, that's basically what happens [laughs]. Actually, being involved in Outward Bound is what made me an attractive candidate for being asked to join these expeditions. After my internship, I stayed at Outward Bound, working for their semester-long programs and helping start the dog-sledding program at the School. By 1989, I was the Program Director [at Outward Bound] and that's when the call came. I was sitting in the kitchen...and got a call from someone who had gotten my name because of my Outward Bound experience. She invited me on a Russian expedition to the South Pole in 1990-91. That's how it started. But it turns out that we didn't actually go to Antarctica, because it was the year the Soviet Union fell apart. But we did go to the Soviet Union . . . and explored the Arctic Circle . . . and the northeast tip of Siberia.

The Internship Informants: What's next on your plate?

Hanson: I'll be involved in the International Arctic Project, part of a team that will cross the Arctic Ocean. We are starting on the Siberian island of Severnaya Zemlya and then we will travel by dog team to the geographic North Pole. We plan to be there to celebrate the 25th anniversary of Earth Day on April 22nd. From there, we will continue towards Canada, and when we reach the magnetic North Pole . . . the dogs will be flown out and we will use specially-made canoe-sleds to travel to Resolute, which is the northernmost community in Canada's Northwest Territory. That's one of the things that makes this trip different from others—people have crossed the Arctic Ocean on skis before, but they have stopped and got picked up along the way. We're hoping to do it on our own power.

The Internship Informants: Besides teaching you skills and techniques, did your Outward Bound internship prepare you at all mentally for the expeditions you now do?

Hanson: Throughout my time at Outward Bound, I learned about the strengths and the depths of the human spirit, being out for long periods of time in all kinds of weather. It helped me cultivate a way of looking at things that are uncomfortable and learn how to get through them. The whole [Outward Bound] exercise of thinking through choices was important to me—a way of saying "Okay, if we allow these choices, what would be the worst thing that could happen and how would that affect the group experience and each individual experience" . . . It gave me a powerful way of looking at the world.

TO APPLY

Open to college juniors and seniors as well as recent grads. Eligible majors: Biology, Chemistry, Physics, Engineering and Math. Minimum GPA: 3.5 Write, call, or e-mail for application.

Jane painter, Employment Administrator
LRRI
PO Box 5890
Albuquerque, NM 87185-5890
(505) 845–1184
(505) 845–1035 (Fax)
E-mail: hrmail@LRRI.org
www.lrri.org

THE LOWELL WHITEMAN SCHOOL

SELECTIVITY

Approximate applicant pool: 100; Interns accepted: 3

COMPENSATION

$9,500/year; room and board; season ski pass; and medical benefits

LOCATION(S)

Steamboat Springs, CO

FIELD

Education

DURATION

One academic year: September–June

DEADLINE(S)

March 1

THE WORK

Nestled in the mountains five miles above Steamboat Springs, the Lowell Whiteman School is a college preparatory boarding/day school for grades 9-12 that combines a traditional classroom education with the excitement of wilderness and world exploration. Small classes, Rocky Mountain living, competitive skiing (10 years), foreign travel (40 years) and outdoor programs along with spirited, profound student-faculty relationships comprise the "Whiteman Experience."

An intern's primary responsibility is to serve as a surrogate parent in one of the school's three dorms. Interns also teach one class and lead student groups of mountain bikers, backpackers, skiers, rock-climbers and kayakers. Candidates should be comfortable and confident working with small groups of teenagers in a variety of settings.

PERKS

Quality of life!

FYI

The internship gives aspiring educators broad experience with high school students – in the classroom, in the dorm, on the slopes of the ski area, in foreign lands and in the wilderness.

TO APPLY

Open to recent college grads. International applicants eligible. Submit resume, cover letter, and recommendations.

Walt Daub
The Lowell Whiteman School
42605 RCR #36
Steamboat Springs, CO 80487
(303) 879-1350
(303) 879-0506 (Fax)

LPGA JUNIOR GOLF PROGRAM

See PGA Tour

LUCASFILM/LUCASDIGITAL

SELECTIVITY

Approximate applicant pool: 800–1,000; Interns accepted: 25–50 annually

COMPENSATION

Summer, Fall, and Spring: minimum wage

LOCATION(S)

San Rafael and Nicasio, CA

FIELD

Entertainment

DURATION

9–12 weeks: Summer, Fall, Spring

DEADLINE(S)

Summer: March 1; Fall: August 1; Spring: November 1

THE WORK

Lucasfilm is one of the world's leading motion picture production and entertainment companies, responsible for *American Graffiti*, the *Star Wars* trilogy, and the *Indiana Jones* series. LucasDigital is involved in film effect and post production sound, operating through its divisions Industrial Light and Magic (ILM) and Skywalker Sound, respectively. Departments accepting interns at Lucasfilm include THX, Information Systems, Library Archives, Skywalker Ranch Facility, Publicity, Finance/ Accounting, Merchandising/Licensing, and Human Resources. LucasDigital interns may work in Skywalker Sound as well as in the ILM division of Marketing & PR, Human Resources, Feature Post-Production Management, Art,Finance/Accounting, Technical Director, Animator, Computer Systems Engineering, Computer Graphics Software, web development and Editorial.

PERKS

Skywalker Ranch; fitness center; seminars; parties, screenings.

FYI

Apply early . . . The internship coordinator stresses that incomplete applications are not considered . . . We do not allow interns to repeat the internship program, despite their desire to do so . . . Interns can be invited to "dailies," the early morning screenings of the previous day's visual effects work.

TO APPLY

Open to college juniors and seniors as well as grad students. Must be returning to school after internship. Write for application.

Lucasfilm
Human Resources—Intern Department
P.O. Box 2009
San Rafael, CA 94912
(415) 662-1999
www.ilm-;gobs.com (to download the application)

LucasDigital
Internship Coordinator
P.O. Box 2459
San Rafael, CA 94912
(415) 258-2000
www.ilm.com

LUNAR AND PLANETARY INSTITUTE

SELECTIVITY 🔍 🔍 🔍 🔍
Approximate applicant pool: 100; Interns accepted: 12

COMPENSATION $ $ $ $
$350/week;and $1,000 maximum travel allowance

LOCATION(S)
Houston, TX

FIELD
Science research

DURATION
10 weeks: Summer

DEADLINE(S)
Early February

THE WORK

Founded in 1968, the Lunar and Planetary Institute (LPI) conducts research in lunar, planetary, and terrestrial sciences on behalf of university science departments and NASA. Each intern is paired with a research scientist on a science research project either at LPI or nearby NASA Johnson Space Center. Past projects have involved studies in planet formation, lunar sample characterization, planetary volcanism, remote sensing imagery, and impact cratering.

PERKS

Brown-bag seminars/lectures with staff and visiting scientists; access to gym at NASA Johnson Space Center; special tours of Johnson Space Center.

FYI

Over 268 interns have completed the program since its inception in 1977, and at least three dozen are now major players in planetary sciences . . . The intern coordinator writes: " [S]ome

students may be working . . . with lunar samples, rocks from Mars or meteorites of all kinds—some of the oldest material in the solar system!"

TO APPLY

Open to college sophomores, juniors, seniors, and grads (within one year of graduation). International applicants eligible. Write for application.

LPI Summer Internship Program
Lunar and Planetary Institute
3600 Bay Area Boulevard
Houston, TX 77058-1113
(281) 486-2180

> "[S]ome students may be working...with lunar samples, rocks from Mars or meteorites of all kinds—some of the oldest material in the solar system!"
> —intern coordinator, Lunar and Planetary Institute

LUTHERAN VOLUNTEER CORPS

SELECTIVITY 🔍
Approximate applicant pool: 150; Interns accepted: 85

COMPENSATION $ $
personal monthly stipend; rent and utilities, food, health insurance, transportation

LOCATION(S)
Baltimore, MD; Chicago, IL; Milwaukee, WI; Minneapolis, St. Paul, MN; Seattle, Tacoma, WA; Washington, DC ; Wilmington, DE

FIELD
Social work; Education; Advocacy; Public policy; Healthcare; Youth programs; Religious studies

DURATION
1 year: commences late August

DEADLINE(S)
February 1, March 1, May 1, April 1 (the earlier an application is received, the greater the variety of placement choices.)

THE WORK

The Lutheran Volunteer Corps places volunteers in urban areas across the country for a year of service with a nonprofit agency. Volunteer roles can include teaching in an inner-city school, counseling, staffing food banks, shelters for the homeless or after school programs for at-risk youth, lobbying on hunger issues, working to protect the environment and more. Volunteers live in groups of four to eight other volunteers, and share meals and household responsibilities.

PERKS

Two weeks paid vacation; four retreats per year; supportive staff; deferment of college loans. Many volunteers are eligible for up to $4,725 in loan/tuition reimbursement.

FYI

Says a former volunteer: "I wanted to learn how I could do meaningful work. I wanted to learn how to simplify my lifestyle—to learn to be more efficient about how I spend my time, money, and resources. The Lutheran Volunteer Corps offered me a year to experiment with new ways to pattern my lifestyle so that I could make a difference in the long run."

TO APPLY

Volunteers must be at least 21 years of age, there is no upper

GO GET 'EM, KID!
Exclusive advice from illustrious former interns

The great thing is to listen and not impose one's self. Being an intern is like being invited into someone's house; you shouldn't put your feet up on the sofa . . . Part of it is a matter of thinking of yourself as a privileged guest.

—George Plimpton, journalist and editor

A good intern is supposed to be like a good hairpiece: effective but unobtrusive.

—Mark Green, Public Advocate for New York City

Go out and experiment, try things, see what you like. Take a chance, don't think it's forever. Go out and try something different in an internship, because you might discover something you didn't know.

—George Stephanopoulos, senior advisor to President Clinton

Everybody's got to have a first [internship] somewhere. My advice is, hey, if you can find any way to afford it, try to work for free somewhere. Do anything to work in your field.

—Richard Hieb, astronaut

If you're going to intern, do it with the best. If you have a choice between getting paid at a second-rate place and not getting paid at a first-rate place, go with the first-rate place.

—Jo Maeder, radio personality

[An internship] is a chance to ask questions without having to worry about showing your naiveté. It gives you a chance to live in a different environment under the wing of a sheltered nest of contacts.

—John Hays, Christie's auctioneer

If your boss tells you that she wants you to do something, don't say to her, "How should I do that?" Leave the room, and call anyone you can think of to tell you how to do it.

—Nora Ephron, screenwriter

The most valuable thing you can get out of an internship is a mentor . . . so if you have a choice between a great institution and no mentor and an institution one-notch below in caliber offering you a chance to work with an outstanding person, take the latter.

—Stuart Flack, playwright

The more experience you can get doing internships early in life, the more options you keep open later in life.

—Jean Fugett, Jr., former All-Pro tight-end

Creativity and initiative [in interns] is so important. Doing the job, being available, being willing to say, "I have an idea, what do you think of it," or being willing to say, "Is there a chance I can come to this with you"—all lead to intern success.

—Senator Dianne Feinstein

If you have a little financial backing and you're adventuresome, you should go to where the action is. If you're interested in Russian studies, go to Moscow. If you've got an aptitude for Spanish, you could go to Central America. In journalism at least, you can usually do more work if you start where the action is, especially in some of the flowering democracies. Check out the international scene. The prospects are grand.

—Peter Arnett, veteran war correspondent

Write a good letter, and don't try to be too tricky. Some people think to get your attention, they should put the letter in a box of confetti, and when you open the box, the confetti goes flying. All that is intensely annoying. So what's impressive is a good, intelligent, earnest letter—a straightforward letter that seems to be truthful, that explains why you want the internship and what you seek to learn from it.

—Harold Prince, Tony-award winning director/producer

Science students should jump at the chance to do a summer research internship because it is such a wonderful antidote to large courses, which provide instruction, but not the social structure of a research group—people united in a search for knowledge, curious and interacting effectively. It opens up the world of what science is really like.

—Dr. Roald Hoffman, Winner of the Nobel Prize in Chemistry (1981)

The best intern I ever had didn't know s--- about news. She didn't read the paper. But she tried. And she was diligent. She came in on weekends. She was like this clean slate, this sponge that was soaking up every bit of information she could.

—Tabitha Soren, MTV News anchor

You have to have patience with the process of working. I used to think that if you don't like something, you should get out of it. But I don't think that is always a wise move. Especially today, when jobs aren't easy to come by, you've got to give things a chance. Sometimes you can turn things to your advantage.

—Grace Mirabella, founder of *Mirabella* magazine

The great thing about internships is they don't last, so it's not like you're going to be stuck there for the rest of your life. You can actually explore different parts of your personality, perhaps ones you never thought you had.

—Jodie Foster, actress

age limit. Volunteers are not required to be Lutheran. Applicants who are not U.S. citizens must obtain their own work VISA for the entire year of LVC. Contact the Lutheran Volunteer Corps office for an application, or download one from the website.

Lutheran Volunteer Corps
1226 Vermont Avenue NW
Washington, DC 20005
(202) 387-3222
E-mail: staff@lvchome.org
www.lvchome.org

MACDONALD COMMUNICATIONS CORP.

SELECTIVITY 🔍
Approximate applicant pool: 400; Interns accepted: 60

COMPENSATION ⑤
None

LOCATION(S)
New York, NY

FIELD
Magazines; Women's issues conferences, National Association for Female Executives (NAFE)

DURATION
12 weeks: Summer, Fall, Spring

DEADLINE(S)
Summer: May 30; Fall: June 30; Spring: October 30

THE WORK
Established in 1996, MacDonald Communications Corp. is the magazine publisher responsible for *Ms.*, *Working Mother*, and *Working Woman*. Departments at each magazine accepting interns include Editorial, Advertising, Marketing, Promotion, Production, Circulation, and Public Relations. *Ms.* magazine accepts for editorial only.

PERKS
Attendance welcome at staff meetings; free copies of magazines; other perks vary with magazine.

FYI
Ms., the woman's magazine co-founded by feminist Gloria Steinem in 1972, is the only major magazine besides *Consumer Reports* to operate without advertising.

TO APPLY
Open to undergrads and graduates. May receive academic credit. International applicants eligible. Submit resume, cover letter, and writing samples.

Internship Coordinator
[Name of Magazine]
c/o MacDonald Communications Corp.
135 W. 50th St., 16th Fl.
New York, NY 10020
(212) 446-6100

MAD MAGAZINE

TM and © E.C. Publications Inc., 1994

SELECTIVITY 🔍🔍🔍🔍
Approximate applicant pool: 35; Interns accepted: 2

COMPENSATON ⑤
None

LOCATION(S)
New York, NY

FIELD
Magazines

DURATION
9 weeks: two summer sessions (June–July; July–August)

DEADLINE(S)
May 1

THE WORK
Symbolized by the goofy gap-toothed grin of Alfred E. Neuman, *MAD* Magazine has been amusing legions of enthusiasts since 1952. It has a circulation of 500,000 readers, most of whom are adolescents with a taste for satire. Interns work in the Editorial department, where they participate in brainstorming sessions and work on article conception and development.

PERKS
"Free pinball instruction from a man who was once known as 'The Big Gun' and 'Gunther;'" free copies of the magazine.

FYI
The internship bulletin warns: "No phone calls, floral arrangements, candygrams, balloons, cold cut and cheese platters, etc.!"

TO APPLY
Open to college sophomores, juniors, and seniors. Must receive academic credit. International applicants eligible. Write for application. We are an equal opportunity employer.

Internship Program
MAD Magazine
485 Madison Avenue
New York, NY 10022
(212) 636-5051

The bulletin for *MAD Magazine*'s internship warns: "No phone calls, floral arrangements, candygrams, balloons, cold cut and cheese platters, etc.!"

MADISON SQUARE GARDEN

SELECTIVITY
Approximate applicant pool: 600; Interns accepted: 50

COMPENSATION
$125/week

LOCATION(S)
New York, NY; Hartford, CT

FIELD
Sports; Television; Music;

DURATION
12–16 weeks: Summer, Fall, Spring

DEADLINE(S)
Summer: April 15; Fall : October 15; Spring: January 17

THE WORK
In the words of the late sports journalist Red Smith, "Madison Square Garden is, very simply, the most famous and glamorous arena in creation." Hosting everyone from the New York Knicks to the Rolling Stones, the 20,000-seat Garden is New York's premiere sports and entertainment venue. Interns are assigned to the New York Knicks (Administration, Marketing/Promotions, Public Relations); the New York Rangers (Marketing/Promotions, Public Relations); MSG Network (Affiliate Services, Marketing, On-air Promotions, Production/Sports Desk, Programming, Research); Entertainment Division (Athletics, Concerts, Group Sales, Marketing); the Facilities Division (Event Presentation, Event Production).

PERKS
Complimentary tickets to some events; discounted passes to theme parks; and discounted MSG merchandise.

FYI
Madison Square Garden's Internship program offers students real business exposure within the various departments that incorporate the world's most famous arena.

TO APPLY
Open to undergraduates and graduate students. Must receive academic credit. International applicants eligible. For an application or further information, please write or call.

Madison Square Garden
Internship Coordinator
Human Resource Department
Two Pennsylvania Plaza
New York, NY 10001
(212) 465-6258

> Without any outside direction, interns at the Maine State Music Theatre produce their own show, which they present to the public at the end of the theater's season.

MAINE STATE MUSIC THEATRE

SELECTIVITY
Approximate applicant pool: 1,200; Interns accepted: 30

COMPENSATION
Performance Interns: $40/week; Production Interns: $60/week; free room and board

LOCATION(S)
Brunswick, ME

FIELD
Theater

DURATION
13 weeks: Summer

DEADLINE(S)
February 28

THE WORK
Established in 1958, the Maine State Music Theatre is the only professional, resident musical theater in the state of Maine. Situated on the campus of Bowdoin College, interns work in Costuming, Set Construction, Lighting, Props, Paints, Marketing, Management, Stage Management, and Performance.

PERKS
Weekly seminars on audition techniques, Equity rules, resume preparation, props, song interpretation, etc.; up to 13 Equity points awarded to performance and stage management interns; trips to beach and shopping center by theater volunteers; scenic, coastal New England town.

FYI
Company produces five shows in eleven weeks. Says the internship coordinator: "It's a unique opportunity for [interns] to apply everything they've learned during the summer to a live performance situation." . . . Interns live together in a rented fraternity house. All interns are required to work outside their focus area.

TO APPLY
Open to high school students 18 years and older, high school grads, undergrads, and college grads. International applicants eligible. Write or call for an application.

Company Manager
Kathi Kacinski
Maine State Music Theatre
14 Maine Street, Suite 109
Brunswick, ME 04011
(207) 725-8769
(207) 725-1199 (Fax)

> "Our interns live together in a rented-out fraternity house. Sure, it's a fraternity house . . . but we try to clean up a little before they move in."
>
> —intern coordinator, Maine State Music Theatre

MAKOVSKY

SELECTIVITY
Approximate applicant pool: 500; Interns accepted: 2–3 per semester

COMPENSATION S
$175/week

LOCATION(S)
New York, NY

FIELD
Public relations

DURATION
12–16 weeks: Summer, Fall, Spring

DEADLINE(S)
Spring: December 15; Summer: April 15; Fall: August 15

THE WORK
Founded in 1979, Makovsky & Company is a mid-size full-service public relations agency, specializing in financial and professional services, technology, investor relations, and health sciences. Makovsky was recently named in Inside PR's Report Card as one of the top agencies for "Business-to-Business Marketing" and "Investor Relations." Clients have included IBM, Dun & Bradstreet, Subaru, Security Pacific Bank, Prudential Securities, Abbott Laboratories, Pfizer, MetLife, Coopers & Lybrand, and Battelle Memorial Institute. Interns help plan campaigns, conduct research, write press releases, contact editors to generate publicity, and occasionally work with clients.

PERKS
Seminars in professional development; mentors.

FYI
The two facing heads in Makovsky's logo represent the partnership between the firm and its clients.

TO APPLY
Open to undergrads, recent college grads, and grad students. International applicants eligible. Submit resume, cover letter, writing sample, and references.

Internship Coordinator
Makovsky & Company
245 Fifth Avenue, 15th Floor
New York, NY 10022
(212) 508-9600
interns@makovsky.com

SELECTIVITY
Approximate applicant pool: 100; Interns accepted: 8–10

COMPENSATION S
None

LOCATION(S)
New York, NY

FIELD
Public relations

DURATION
4 weeks–1 year: ongoing

DEADLINE(S)
Rolling

THE WORK
Founded in 1976, Mallory Factor is a mid-size, full-service public relations firm known particularly for its strong investor relations department. Its clients have included National West Bank, Herbalife, Today's Man retail stores, Coopers & Lybrand, and Exide Corp. Interns work in Investor Relations, Marketing Communication, Issues Management, and Special Events.

PERKS
Intern luncheon; attendance welcome at client meetings and company parties.

FYI
In existence since 1988, the internship program leads to permanent employment at Mallory Factor for about 10 percent of interns.

TO APPLY
Open to undergrads, recent college grads, college grads of any age, and grad students. Submit resume and cover letter.

Internship Coordinator
Mallory Factor
275 Seventh Avenue, 19th Floor
New York, NY 10001
(212) 242-0000
(212) 242-0001 (Fax)

See Atlantic Records

MANHATTAN THEATRE CLUB

SELECTIVITY
Approximate applicant pool: 700; Interns accepted: 35 per year

COMPENSATION §
$120/week

LOCATION(S)
New York, NY

FIELD
Theater

DURATION
3 months–1 year: Summer, Fall, Winter/Spring

DEADLINE(S)
March 1 (Summer); July 1 (Fall); November 30 (Winter/Spring)

THE WORK
Founded in 1970, Manhattan Theatre Club has grown from a prolific Off-Broadway showcase into one of the country's most acclaimed theatre organizations. One of the only institutions in the U.S. solely dedicated to producing new plays and musicals, MTC develops and produces high-quality theatre that challenges, inspires, and entertains audiences. Significant past productions include Stephen Sondheim's *Putting It Together*; Jon Robin Baitz's *Mizlansky/Zilinsky* or "schmucks"; the Broadway production of *A Small Family Business*; Broadway and Off-Broadway transfers of *Lips Together Teeth Apart*, *Sight Unseen*, *Mass Appeal*, and *Loot*; the Tony Award-winning *Ain't Misbehavin'* and *Love! Valour! Compassion!*; and the Pulitzer Prize-winning *Crimes of the Heart* and *The Piano Lesson*. Interns work in Artistic Business, Casting, Development/Fundraising, General Management, Education, Information Systems, Literary, Marketing, Musical Theatre, Production Management, and Writers in Performance.

PERKS
Weekly intern seminars on artistic and management issues; free tickets to all performances; geographically diverse group of interns.

FYI
Located at the historic City Center Theater, MTC stages its performances in a 299-seat proscenium stage theater and in a 150-seat flexible black-box theater.

TO APPLY
Open to undergrads, recent college grads, early career professionals, and grad students. Submit resume, cover letter, and two letters of recommendation.

Paul A. Kaplan Theatre Management Program Coordinator
Manhattan Theater Club
311 West 43rd Street, 8th Floor
New York, NY 10036
(212) 399–3000
(212) 399–4329 (Fax)
www.mtc-nyc.org
E-mail: interns@mtc-nyc.org

SELECTIVITY
Approximate applicant pool: 50; Interns accepted: 8

COMPENSATION § § §
$170/week, room & board, some medical insurance & equipment discounts

LOCATION(S)
North Adams, MA

FIELD
Education; Environment; Recreation

DURATION
7–24 weeks, Spring, Summer, Fall

DEADLINE(S)
Summer: March 1; Fall: May 1; Spring: February 1

THE WORK
The nonprofit Manice Education Center provides urban youth with a breath of fresh air and stimulating learning experiences in the natural environment. Interns teach motivated students ecology and wilderness skills to increase knowledge, understanding, self-confidence, and leadership skills.

PERKS
Great opportunity to help enable a diverse group of interested students to achieve more of their potential in a breathtaking location; stimulating colleagues; great food; free sweatshirt.

FYI
Operated by Christodora, Inc., a nonprofit, nonsectarian foundation offering New York City's economically disadvantaged families a range of services and challenging education programs for 100 years.

TO APPLY
Open to undergrads, recent college grads, college grads of any age, and grad students. International applicants eligible. Submit resume and cover letter to receive an application.

One East 53rd Street
14th Floor
New York, NY 10022
(212) 371-5225
(212) 371-2111 (Fax)

According to Manice officials, in their youth music legends **George and Ira Gershwin** received free music lessons and gave their first piano recital at Christodora's settlement house on Manhattan's Lower East Side.

MANUS & ASSOCIATES LITERARY AGENCY

SELECTIVITY 🔍🔍🔍
Approximate applicant pool: 70; Interns accepted: 8

COMPENSATON Ⓢ
Expenses

LOCATION(S)
New York, NY; Palo Alto, CA

FIELD
Literary agency

DURATION
12 weeks–1 year: Summer, Fall, Spring

DEADLINE(S)
Rolling

 THE WORK
A bicoastal literary agency with offices in New York and Palo Alto, Manus & Associates represents fiction and nonfiction authors, 50 percent of books represented are sold into film and television markets. Interns spend much of their time screening submissions, communicating with writers, and analyzing manuscripts for content and marketability.

PERKS
Free books

FYI
A detailed "Intern Training Packet" is distributed to new interns; it covers everything from reviewing submissions to writing rejection letters.

TO APPLY
Open to undergrads, recent college grads, college grads of any age, and grad students. International applicants eligible. Submit resume and cover letter.

Internship Coordinator
Manus & Associates Literary Agency
417 East 57th Street
New York, NY 10022
(212) 644-8020
(212) 644-3394 (Fax)

Internship Coordinator
Manus & Associates Literary Agency
375 Forest Avenue
Palo Alto, CA 94301
(650) 470-5151
(650) 470-5159 (Fax)
Email: ManusLit@ManusLit.com
www.ManusLit.com

MARINA MAHER COMMUNICATIONS

SELECTIVITY 🔍🔍🔍
Approximate applicant pool: 80; Interns accepted: 6–8

COMPENSATION Ⓢ Ⓢ
$300/week; $6.50/hour

LOCATION(S)
New York, NY

FIELD
Public relations agencies

DURATION
8 weeks–1 year: Summer, Fall, Spring

DEADLINE(S)
Summer: May 1; Fall: August 1; Spring: December 1

 THE WORK
Founded in 1984, Marina Maher Communications (MMC) is the nation's leading public relations agency for products and services marketed to women. In addition to generating publicity for clients, MMC develops special events, promotional videos, trade campaigns, consumer brochures, and point-of-sale materials. Clients have included Benetton, Vidal Sassoon, Just for Men Haircolor, Hugo Boss, Cover Girl, Noxzema, Secret Deodorant, Max Factor Fragrances, and Wonderbra. Interns work in Accounting and Account Management.

PERKS
Free product samples; attendance welcome at MMC events.

FYI
Hired in 1994 by the Sara Lee Corporation to generate publicity for the upcoming Wonderbra, MMC created a "bra wars" pitch that challenged a rival bra's product launch, hyped Wonderbra, and resulted in a media blitz for what became known as "the cleavage weapon."

TO APPLY
Open to high school seniors, high school grads, undergrads, recent college grads, college grads of any age, and grad students. International applicants eligible. Submit resume, cover letter, writing samples (optional), and transcript.

Internship Coordinator
Marina Maher Communications
400 Park Avenue, 4th Floor
New York, NY 10022
(212) 759-7543
(212) 355-6318 (Fax)

MARION PENITENTIARY

See Federal Bureau of Prisons

See National Aeronautics and Space Administration

THE MARTIN AGENCY

The Martin Agency

SELECTIVITY
Approximate applicant pool: 100; Interns accepted: 15

COMPENSATION 🅢
None

LOCATION(S)
Richmond, VA

FIELD
Advertising

DURATION
8 days: June and January

DEADLINE(S)
June session: April 15; January session: December 1

THE WORK
The Martin Agency was founded in 1965, and has nine offices and more than 450 employees nationwide. Its clients have included Coca-Cola, GEICO, Kellogg, Marriott, Ping, Saab, Seiko, Timberland, Vassarette, and Yellow Pages Publishers Association. Interns participate in an eight-day student workshop that features seminars on issues in advertising as well as a case project for a Martin Agency client.

PERKS
Certificate of participation; video of final presentation.

FYI
Guided by two team heads from Account Management, each case project team of five interns "will concept, create and present a marketing and advertising program to agency executives and a client representative."...Only The Martin Agency's Richmond office offers this workshop.

Unique among advertising agency internships, The Martin Agency's Student Workshop offers undergraduates an eight-day experience at its Richmond, Virginia office. In between attending seminars on advertising, interns meet in project teams to create marketing and advertising programs they later present to Martin's clients.
As part of the Martin Agency's Student Workshop, groups of interns work on "real-life" case projects. Here a group puts together a marketing and advertising campaign for Wrangler.

TO APPLY
Open to undergrads. International applicants eligible. Write for application.

Student Workshop Committee
The Martin Agency
One Shockoe Plaza
Richmond, VA 23219-4132
(804) 698-8000
(804) 698-8244 (Fax)
www.martinagency.com

MARVEL COMICS

SELECTIVITY
Approximate applicant pool: 50; Interns accepted: 15–20

COMPENSATION 🅢
None

LOCATION(S)
New York, NY

FIELD
Comic books

DURATION
3 to 4 months: Summer, Fall, Spring

DEADLINE(S)
Rolling

THE WORK
According to Marvel Comics, 76 percent of American children between the ages of 6 and 17 have read Marvel comic books. Marvel cites one reason in particular for the success of its comic books: Marvel characters, who are bastions of unearthly brawn, suffer also from human concerns and conflicts. Regardless of the reason, Marvel creates Super Heroes who are understood and appreciated by children of all backgrounds. The Marvel College Internship program hires about 15–20 interns per session, each of whom is assigned to one of the company's 20 editors.

PERKS
Casual atmosphere; freebies galore.

FYI
No matter where an intern ends up, there is a lot of gofer work to be done . . . Interns should "be familiar with the Marvel universe of characters," in the words of the program's information sheet . . . Most of the interns in each session are male.

TO APPLY
Open to college juniors and seniors. Must receive academic credit. International applicants eligible. Submit resume, cover letter, and a letter from your college stating that you will receive credit for the internship.

Marvel Comics
Internship Program
attn: Kimberly Pecoraro
387 Park Avenue South
New York, NY 10016
(212) 696-0808

MASS MEDIA SCIENCE AND ENGINEERING FELLOWS PROGRAM

SELECTIVITY 🔍🔍🔍
Approximate applicant pool: 200; Interns accepted: 20–30

COMPENSATION 💲
$450 for 10 weeks; travel expenses

LOCATION(S)
Albuquerque, NM; Atlanta, GA; Chicago, IL; Columbus, OH; Dallas, TX; Detroit, MI; Greeley, CO; Milwaukee, WI; New York, NY; Raleigh, NC; Richmond, VA; Sacramento, CA; Seattle, WA; St. Louis, MO

FIELD
Health; Social, natural, and physical sciences; Engineering and mathematics

DURATION
10 weeks: Summer

DEADLINE(S)
January 15

THE WORK
The AAAS Mass Media Fellows work for 10 weeks during the summer as reporters, researchers, and production assistants in mass media organizations nationwide. The student-scientists and their host-journalists strive to make science news clear and comprehensive to the public.

PERKS
Three-day orientation and two-day wrap-up in Washington DC; mentors; published stories/articles with bylines.

FYI
According to the internship coordinator, the goal of the program is to "help improve coverage of science and technology in the mass media while sharpening interns' communication skills.". . . After graduating, approximately 50 percent of fellows become science journalists with organizations like *The New York Times*, *National Public Radio*, and *Science*.

TO APPLY
Open to advanced undergraduate, graduate students, and post-docs in the health, natural, social sciences, engineering and mathematics. International applicants are eligible.

Mass Media Science & Engineering Fellowship Program
American Association for the Advancement of Science
1200 New York Avenue, NW
Washington, DC 20005
(202) 326-6760
kmalloy@aaas.org

MATADOR RECORDS

See Atlantic Records

THE MATERNAL & CHILD HEALTH INSTITUTE

The Maternal & Child Health Institute

SELECTIVITY 🔍🔍
Approximate applicant pool: 10; Interns accepted: 2

COMPENSATION 💲
$125/week; free parking

LOCATION(S)
Atlanta, GA

FIELD
Health care

DURATION
12 weeks: Summer, Fall

DEADLINE(S)
Summer: April 1; Fall: July 1

THE WORK
The Maternal & Child Health Institute (MCHI) is a private, nonprofit health care advocacy organization. It was established in 1992 to help reduce Georgia's high rates of infant mortality and low birthweight. Through videos, issue papers, and media campaigns, MCHI educates the public about the need for early and regular prenatal care and lobbies the Georgia legislature for laws to improve health care for mothers and children. Interns conduct research on services to improve maternal and child health care in Atlanta, compile data, compose fact sheets, monitor Georgia legislation, and update MCHI's computer database of legislators and advocates.

PERKS
Field trips to community health departments.

FYI
MCHI's prenatal health education program, called "Healthy Mothers: Babies' Best Start," offers pregnant women a book containing health tips and free coupons worth $1,700 for such things as baby products, groceries, and clothing.

TO APPLY
Open to college juniors and seniors, recent college grads, college grads of any age, and grad students. Must be studying maternal and child health or public affairs. Must be fluent in English. International applicants eligible. Submit resume, cover letter, and recommendations.

Director of Communications/Assistant Project Director
The Maternal & Child Health Institute
1252 West Peachtree Street NW, Suite 551
Atlanta, GA 30350
(404) 875-5051
(404) 875-5085 (Fax)

SELECTIVITY 🔍🔍🔍🔍
Approximate applicant pool: 400–500; Interns accepted: 25–30

COMPENSATION 💲💲💲💲
$450–$600/week for undergrad
$700–$900/week for grad students

LOCATION(S)
Los Angeles, CA

FIELD
Consumer goods (toys)

DURATION
12 weeks: Summer

DEADLINE(S)
March 30

THE WORK
Mattel was founded in 1945 by Harold Mattson and Elliott Handler (the company name combines the first letters of their last and first names, respectively), two entrepreneurs who started out making doll furniture in a garage. Today, Mattel is an international corporation and, following its merger with Fisher-Price and Tyco, is the undisputed leader in the toy industry. Interns work in the following departments: Marketing, Finance, Design, and Information Systems.

PERKS
State-of-the-art gym; 25 percent discount at company store; half day on Friday (1:00 PM), fun-loving atmosphere.

FYI
One intern took advantage of the discount at the company store to start her own Barbie collection . . . Many interns have had opportunities to travel to places such as toy fairs and industry trade shows. Mattel offers a good shot at a permanent job offer to interns as well.

TO APPLY
Open to undergrads and grad students. International applicants eligible. Submit resume and cover letter.

Mattel, Inc.
Corporate Staffing-Internships
333 Continental Blvd.
El Segundo, CA 90245
(310) 252-2000
(310) 252-4423 (Fax)

MCA RECORDS

See MCA/Universal

SELECTIVITY 🔍🔍🔍🔍
Approximate applicant pool: 1,500; Interns accepted: 120

COMPENSATION 💲💲
$5–$7/hour for undergrads (a few positions)
$5–$7/hour for grad students (a few positions)

LOCATION(S)
Universal City, CA

FIELD
Film; Television; Music

DURATION
Summer, Fall, Spring; 10–12 weeks; Part-time available

DEADLINE(S)
Rolling

THE WORK
One of the largest and most successful entertainment companies in the world, Universal Studios, Inc. (formerly MCA, Inc.) was founded in 1924 by a Chicago doctor moonlighting as a booking agent for bands. Universal Studios is comprised of several diverse entities: Universal Pictures, Universal Television Group, Universal Music Group, Universal Studios Consumer Products Group, and Universal Home Entertainment Group. The internship program involves all the divisions outlined above. Interns can work for these divisions in production, publicity, casting, legal, marketing, promotions, and Human Resources/Labor Relations.

PERKS
Intern luncheon featuring Universal execs; free CDs and movie screenings; friendly, team-orientated atmosphere.

FYI
Interns have a good opportunity to find regular employment at Universal . . . interns at Universal Music Group "walk away from their internship with more free CDs than you can shake a stick at." Universal's main building is internally referred to as the "Black Tower," suggestive of the seriousness of the business evolving inside.

TO APPLY
Open to college juniors and seniors; grad students. Must receive academic credit for unpaid positions. International applicants eligible. Submit resume and cover letter.

Internship Program
Universal Studios
100 Universal City Plaza
Universal City, CA 91608
(818) 777-1000

EXCLUSIVE INTERVIEW WITH MATT STOVER

Drafted by the New York Giants in 1990, kicker Matt Stover became a free agent his second year, when he was signed by the Cleveland Browns. During the 1992 off-season, he interned at International Management Group (IMG), the sports management empire. Stover graduated with a degree in marketing from Louisiana Tech in 1990.

The Internship Informants: Why did you decide to do an internship when you already had a high-paying job kicking footballs?

Stover: Being that an NFL football player's career averages three years and four games, which is pretty short, I saw that there is not much security, even though a kicker's career length is, if you make it two years in the league, an average of six years. I had a degree, and I did take a couple of courses at Fairleigh Dickinson [in New Jersey, while I was with the Giants]. I had wanted to continue my degree even further . . . You hear about [NFL players like] Steve Young getting their law degree. I wanted to continue in my field. I wasn't very interested in getting a law degree or going to get a doctorate . . . so what I decided to do instead was to get some career experience.

The Internship Informants: So you just applied to IMG?

Stover: I had been talking to a career adviser for the Browns . . . who knew Peter Johnson, who is a top sports agent and represents individual players for IMG. [The advisor] had set up an interview with me because I was seeking an internship in marketing. She knew that IMG's world headquarters was here in Cleveland . . . and she had told me that they had a great internship program there. Due to that, we set up an interview with Peter Johnson, who gave me the opportunity.

The Internship Informants: What did they have you do?

Stover: They had an opening in Investments Advisory International . . . I learned all sorts of things, like how to manage the players' money, because [IMG provides] all [its players with] financial services . . . I gave the advisors a sounding board, some attitudes of the players, what [I thought] would be a good format for explaining investments to the players. Semi-annually, quarterly, whatever, they send out a report [to a player] . . . basically, they would show me a report and say, "Hey, what would you really want out of this report? What do you want to have explained to these guys?" I would sit down and say, "These numbers mean a lot to me, but I can tell you, basically, this, this, this, and this would be what the guy wants to see, and the rest of it they wouldn't even know what you're talking about."

The Internship Informants: Would you say that you brought a different perspective to how they report to their clients?

Stover: I gave them a sounding board of what attitude these guys have. Not that I'm typical, because I don't think I am, but at the same time, I do think that I understand the mentality and what it does take to communicate properly with an NFL player.

The Internship Informants: Did the IMG internship help you figure out your own finances?

Stover: They really helped me with my individual finances. They were willing to say, "Matt, here's what you need to do. It's to the point where we can't manage it for you." But they gave me some suggestions, and if I wanted to hire them, of course, they would manage it for me, and IMG is one of the best companies for that.

The Internship Informants: You still needed to train during the off-season, so how did you juggle the internship and training?

Stover: I worked out in the mornings and showed up [to IMG] at about 12 o'clock and continued to work through 5:30 every day. It wasn't a full-time thing for me . . . They knew my unique situation. Therefore, they were willing to do that for me. I was very appreciative of this.

The Internship Informants: As an NFL player, did you receive special treatment on the job?
Stover: No. In fact, I got into the filing side of it, too. I had to do some of the busywork, and of course, I wasn't going to argue about that. I was just glad that I had the opportunity . . . to really find out how [IMG] works.

The Internship Informants: Was this part of the NFL Players' Internship Program, which gives ball players resume-bolstering work during the off-season?
Stover: That was an opportunity brought up the year after I was in the system, which was the off-season in '93. It was not set up well enough for me to really take advantage of it in Cleveland. Now they have a network set up so well that [an NFL player] can go into any major city in the country and get an internship.

The Internship Informants: Where there other NFL players you knew of who did internships?
Stover: There were some guys [on the Browns] who wanted to be newscasters and went with the local TV stations. One guy did an internship in financial advising with McDonald & Co., a top financial agency here in Cleveland . . . But no more than three guys on each team would take advantage of something like this . . . out of 1,700 guys, maybe 170 [do internships].

The Internship Informants: Has the IMG internship given you any ideas of what you want to do after the NFL?
Stover: It turned me on to sports management, sports marketing. Let me tell you, that company has it all. I would love to work for IMG . . . They had definitely said, "Matt, when football's over, come talk to us." But they didn't do it on a serious note. I left the doors open. They left the doors open. In no way do I have a job definitely when I leave [the NFL] . . . Post-football will be a huge transition. In fact, the first six months after football's over is very difficult for most players, and knowing that I have something I can fall back on, with a degree and some work experience and what to expect, it will make the transition that much easier for me.

MCDONALD'S

SELECTIVITY N/A
Approximate applicant pool: N/A; Interns accepted: 30

COMPENSATION $ $ $
$8–$12/hour; health insurance; $1,000/year educational stipend

LOCATION(S)
San Franciscio, Los Angeles, San Diego, and Sacramento, CA; Phoenix, AZ

FIELD
Restaurant management

DURATION
16–24 weeks years

DEADLINE(S)
Rolling

THE WORK
Founded in 1955, McDonald's has grown from a single restaurant in Des Plaines, Illinois to over 14,000 restaurants worldwide, making the golden arches one of the most recognized corporate symbols on the planet. Generating over $25 billion in sales annually, "Mickey D's" has served over 80 percent of the world's population at least once. Interns work at McDonald's restaurants as manager trainees, learning how to operate work stations, plan and schedule shifts, order supplies, and keep the restaurant sanitized.

PERKS
Classes in management skills; extensive employee benefits (e.g., stock plan, profit sharing, paid vacations, matching gifts program, McSave program); occasional opportunities to attend training classes at McDonald's Hamburger University in Illinois.

FYI
Approximately 80 percent of interns are hired as full-time managers upon graduation from college . . . The Los Angeles area's program, started in 1985, is the oldest McDonald's internship . . . McDonald's corporate offices in Illinois hire summer interns through Inroads (see separate entry) . . . A new McDonald's restaurant is opened every eight hours.

TO APPLY
Open to college juniors. Minimum GPA: 2.0. Submit resume and cover letter directly to region of interest.

Internship Program
McDonald's
432 North 44th Street, Suite 250
Phoenix, AZ 85008
(602) 273-0230

Fresno & Sacramento:
Internship Program
McDonald's
1750 Howe Avenue, Suite 550
Sacramento, CA 95825
(916) 649-9797

Internship Program
McDonald's
4370 La Jolla Village Drive, Suite 800
San Diego, CA 92122
(619) 535-8900

Internship Program
McDonald's
21300 Victory Boulevard, Suite 800
Woodland Hills, CA 91367
(818) 594-0525

MCT MANAGEMENT/BOLD! RECORDS

SELECTIVITY
Approximate applicant pool: 50; Interns accepted: 5

COMPENSATION
Daily transportation costs covered

LOCATION(S)
New York, NY

FIELD
Record labels; Music management; Music promotion

DURATION
12 weeks: Summer, Fall, Spring

DEADLINE(S)
Rolling

 THE WORK
Founded in 1991, MCT Management/Bold! Marketing and Promotion is a music organization focusing on Electronic, Alternative, and R&B. MCT manages such acts as Moby and prominent producers/remixers including Rickidy Raw Productions and Phillip Steir. Bold! promotes electronic and alternative artists like Underworld, Aphex Twin, Fatboy Slim, Massive Attack, and Roni Size. Interns work in Management, Promotion, and Artists & Repertoire.

PERKS
Free CDs and concert tickets.

FYI
According to the internship coordinator: "Interns who work here are on the cutting edge of today's alternative scene . . . We have a less formal, less corporate environment here."

TO APPLY
Open to undergrads and grads. International applicants eligible. Submit resume and cover letter.

Internship Coordinator
MCT Management/Bold! Records
333 West 52nd Street, Suite 1003
New York, NY 10019
(212) 265-3740
(212) 315-4601 (Fax)

MERCK & COMPANY

SELECTIVITY
Approximate applicant pool: 5,000

COMPENSATION
$535/week for undergrads; $600/week for grad students;   free shuttle service to and from available housing (Whitehouse Station)

LOCATION(S)
Merck Research Labs: Rahway, NJ; West Point, PA; Manufacturing: Albany, GA; Danville and West Point, PA; Elkton, VA; Rahway and Whitehouse Station, NJ; Arecibo and Barceloneta, Puerto Rico; Human Health: West Point, PA; Whitehouse Station, NJ; Corp. staff: Whitehouse Station, NJ

FIELD
Pharmaceuticals

DURATION
Intern: 12–14 weeks: Summer; Co-op: one or two 6-month sessions, ongoing

DEADLINE(S)
February 15

THE WORK
Founded in 1892, Merck is the world's largest pharmaceutical company. It employs over 45,000 employees worldwide and generates nearly $11 billion in annual sales. It manufactures over 160 products, including Propecia chair regrowth treatment, Varivax (chickenpox vaccine), Proscar (prostate treatment), and Pepcid (anti-ulcer medication). Interns work in the following divisions: Merck Research Laboratories (conducting research on new therapeutic agents for humans, animals, and plants), Manufacturing (in Production, Technical Operations, Quality Control, Materials Management, Planning, Central Engineering [Somerset, NJ only], and Facility Engineering), Corporate Staff (in Computer Resources, Finance, Human Resources, and Public Affairs), Human Health (in Pharmacy Affairs, Sales & Marketing, and a minority program in Sales), and Agriculture & Veterinary (Agvet).

PERKS
Lunchtime intern seminars; attendance welcome at staff meetings and in-house seminars; planned social activities (e.g., picnics, trips to theme parks, barbecues); access to fitness center.

FYI
Merck's internship program commenced in 1951; former Merck CEO Dr. P. Roy Vagelos was the company's first intern . . . Assures Merck's internship bulletin: "[Interns] will face the same challenges, carry the same accountability, and have access to the same resources as full-time Merck professionals."

CHAINSAW BOB HATES BUSYWORK

CHAINSAW BOB ©1995 BRANDON McKINNEY

TO APPLY

Open to college seniors and grad students. International applicants eligible (Merck pays J-1 visa fee). Submit resume and cover letter.

Merck & Company
1 Merck Drive
P.O. Box 100
Whitehouse Station, NJ 08889-0100
(908) 423-1000 (Corporate Staff and Human Health)
(908) 594-4000 or (215) 652-5000 (Manufacturing & MRL)
(908) 855-3800 (Agvet)

Alexander Thweatt
Minority Sales
Field Sales
Merck & Company
WP39-244
West Point, PA 19486
(215) 652-3012

MERCURY RECORDS

See PolyGram

MERRILL LYNCH

SELECTIVITY ☷ ☷ ☷ ☷ ☷
Approximate applicant pool: 300; Interns accepted: 15

COMPENSATION $
None

LOCATION(S)
Oak Brook, IL and other offices nationwide

FIELD
Investment management; Financial planning

DURATION
12 weeks: Summer

DEADLINE(S)
March 1

THE WORK

Merrill Lynch is the world's largest provider of retail brokerage services—no small feat. However, it is also one of the world's most respected investment banks, advising companies and government institutions on how to raise equity and debt, hedge currency risk, or acquire a competitor, for example. Merrill Lynch also ranks number one worldwide in lead underwriting and total assets held in private accounts. Many of Merrill Lynch's US offices offer informal internships. The most structured program can be found at the Oak Brook, IL, office, where interns work as financial consultants in the Finance Department.

PERKS
Weekly speaker-luncheons; trips to financial institutions; intern parties; picnics, trips to sporting events.

FYI
Over 40 percent of interns are offered permanent employ-

ment upon graduation . . . Praised for its flexibility, Merrill Lynch's internship program is tailored to the specific interests of each intern . . . "The mentors can't pay us anything, so they show their appreciation with Sox and Cubs tickets, or gift certificates," one intern said.

TO APPLY

Open to college seniors in business and related majors. Minimum GPA: 3.3. International applicants eligible. Submit resume and cover letter to your local Merrill Lynch Office www.ml.com.

METLIFE

SELECTIVITY ☷ ☷ ☷
50 interns accepted

COMPENSATION $ $ $
Commission basis; State licensing and NASD registration fees

LOCATION(S)
Multiple locations throughout the US

FIELD
Personal financial services, including life and disability insurance

DURATION
1 semester–Graduation; Summers (year-round opportunities)

DEADLINE(S)
Rolling

THE WORK

Founded in 1868, MetLife prides itself on having more life insurance in force (over $1.2 trillion) than any other issuer in the US. The company has over $330 billion in assets under management and over 45,000 associates worldwide. The internship program officially began in January 1999, and it allows students to work closely with a mentor who is usually a full-time MetLife Account Representative. Once licensed and appointed, interns at MetLife learn about prospecting, selling, underwriting, and determining a client's long-range financial needs. Interns also learn about the specific products and services that MetLife offers.

PERKS

Financial support toward required state insurance licenses; financial support toward registering with the National Association of Securities Dealers (NASD); mentor program; standard training program; awards and recognition for high production.

FYI

Since 1985 MetLife has employed the Peanuts cartoon characters in its advertising campaigns. MetLife's auditorium in NY was used as a relief site for the survivors of the Titanic disaster in 1912.

TO APPLY

Open to undergrads with a minimum 2.2 GPA (juniors and seniors preferred) and grad students. MetLife is an equal opportunity employer. Submit resume and cover letter to:

MetLife
Internship/Recruiting Department
1 Madison Ave. Area 5D
New York, NY 10010
www.metlife.com
1-800-JOIN MET (Ext.41)

SELECTIVITY 🔍🔍
Approximate applicant pool: 150; Interns accepted: 30

COMPENSATION 💲💲
None; $125/month (Canada only)

LOCATION(S)
Los Angeles, CA; New York, NY; Calgary, Edmonton, Montreal, Ottawa, Toronto, Vancouver, and Winnipeg, Canada

FIELD
Film

DURATION
3–6 months: Summer, Fall, Spring

DEADLINE(S)
Rolling

THE WORK
With the verve of the roaring lion in its trademark, Metro-Goldwyn-Mayer/United Artists (MGM/UA) develops, promotes, publicizes, markets, and distributes motion pictures. Its repertoire of movies includes classics like *Rain Man* and *Rocky* as well as recent hits like *Stargate*, *Thelma and Louise*, *Six Degrees of Separation*, *Golden Eye*, and *Get Shorty*. Departments accepting interns include Story & Development (New York and Los Angeles only) and Publicity/Promotions.

PERKS
Attendance welcome at promotional parties in New York and Los Angeles; free movie soundtracks, t-shirts, and movie tickets; film screenings.

FYI
MGM/UA was created in 1981 through the merger of the venerable movie houses MGM and UA, founded in 1924 and 1919, respectively ... The Latin phrase on MGM/UA's logo—Ars Gratia Artis—means "Art for Art's Sake." ... Approximately 10 percent of interns return to MGM/UA as full-timers.

TO APPLY
New York and Los Angeles are open to undergrads and grad students. Canada is open to high school grads of any age, undergrads, recent college grads, college grads of any age, and grad students. Must receive academic credit (New York and Los Angeles only). International students eligible (Canada only). Submit resume and cover letter.

Internship Coordinator
Metro-Goldwyn-Mayer/United Artists
2500 Broadway Street
Santa Monica, CA 90404
(310) 449-3000

Internship Coordinator
Metro-Goldwyn-Mayer/United Artists
1350 Sixth Avenue, 24th Floor
New York, NY 10019
(212) 708-0300

Internship Coordinator
Metro-Goldwyn-Mayer/United Artists
720 King St. W., Suite 611
Toronto, ON M5V2T3
(416) 865-9579, x103
(416) 363-0535 (Fax)

SELECTIVITY 🔍🔍🔍🔍
Approximate applicant pool: 400 (undergrads), 120 (grads); Interns accepted: 30 (undergrads), 20 (grads)—varies

COMPENSATION 💲💲
$2,250 for Cloisters undergrads
$2,500 for Met undergrads; $2,750 for grad students

LOCATION(S)
New York, NY

FIELD
Art museum

DURATION
10 weeks: Summer

DEADLINE(S)
January–February. Inquiries, should be made in late fall

EMPLOYEE QUALIFICATIONS THAT MATTER TO EMPLOYERS

On behalf of the US Department of Education, the US Census Bureau recently asked over 4,000 employers nationwide: "When you consider hiring a new non-supervisory or production worker, how important are the following in your decision to hire?"

Ranked on a scale of 1 (not important or not considered) to 5 (very important)

Qualifications	Rank
Applicant's attitude	4.6
Applicant's communication skills	4.2
Previous work experience	4.0
Recommendations from current employees	3.4
Previous employer recommendation	3.4
Industry-based credentials (certifying applicant's skills)	3.2
Years of completed schooling	2.9
Score on tests administered as part of the interview	2.5
Academic performance (grades)	2.5
Experience or reputation of applicant's school	2.4
Teacher recommendations	2.1

Source: National Center on the Educational Quality of the Workforce, US Department of Education, "EQW National Employer Survey," February 21, 1995.

THE WORK

The Metropolitan Museum of Art, known as the Met, is the largest and most diverse museum in the Western Hemisphere, containing 2 million pieces that cover nearly 5,000 years of history. The internship places students in Conservation, Library, Education, Development, Communications, Merchandising, Human Resources, Registration, and 19 curatorial departments, including the Arts of Africa, Oceania, and the Americas; American Art; Ancient Near Eastern Art; Arms and Armor; Asian Art; the Costume Institute; European Paintings; Greek and Roman Art; Islamic Art; Musical Instruments; Photographs; Prints and Illustrated Books; and Twentieth Century Art.

PERKS

Orientaion and Monday field trips; exploratory environment.

FYI

The Met first offered summer internships in 1973 . . . The museum's logo is called the "Leonardo (da Vinci) M," but scholars dispute its origins . . . Undergraduate interns staff the Visitor Information Center's desk on a rotating schedule, ready to answer a wide variety of questions and give tours of the collection.

TO APPLY

The Met internship for grad students requires at least one year of graduate work in art history or a similar field. The undergraduate internship is open to students who are currently juniors, seniors, and to recent grads. International applicants eligible in certain cases. The Cloisters (the branch of the Museum dedicated to the art of the Middle Ages) is open to all undergrads. Write for application.

The Metropolitan Museum of Art
1000 Fifth Avenue
New York, NY 10028-0198
Attn: Education Dept.,
Internship Program
(212) 570-3882
www.metmuseum.org/education

The Cloisters
College Internship Program
Fort Tryon Park
New York, NY 10040
(212) 650-2280

MICROSOFT

Microsoft®

SELECTIVITY 🔍🔍🔍🔍
Approximate applicant pool: 8,000; Interns hired: 700

COMPENSATION 💲💲💲💲💲
$450–$650

LOCATION(S)
Redmond, WA

FIELD
Computer software

DURATION
10–12 weeks: Summer

DEADLINE(S)
Rolling

THE WORK

Founded in 1975 by Bill Gates and Paul Allen, Microsoft has grown to become the world's largest computer software provider. Its best known products, from an astonishing diverse line, include

Contrary to what you might expect, Microsoft CEO and multibillionaire **Bill Gates** never interned at a computer or electronics company. Instead, he served as a congressional page during a summer off from high school in 1972. The experience was valuable for honing Gates's entrepreneurial skills. While in Washington, he and a friend scooped up 5,000 George McGovern-Thomas Eagleton presidential-campaign buttons for a nickel apiece after Eagleton was dropped from the Democratic ticket. The buttons soon became collectors' items, and Gates and his buddy managed to resell them for as much as $25 each.

Windows '98, Windows NT, Microsoft Office, and Internet Explorer. Interns are assigned to positions in the areas of Product Development, Program Management, Software Testing, and Product Marketing.

PERKS

Beautiful campus; prime gym; flexible hours; casual dress; round-trip travel; rental car; subsidized housing; bike purchase plan.

FYI

Whatever they do, interns are treated like professional staff. "The permanent employees saw us as equals," said an intern . . . As far as amenities go, Microsoft is the closest one can get to on-the-job nirvana . . . The final round of interviews is no cakewalk. Recruiters spend a few minutes on pleasantries then launch into a battery of questions to test a student's problem-solving skills.

TO APPLY

Open to college freshman, sophomores, juniors, and seniors. Computer programming experience is preferred for most positions. Submit resume.

Microsoft Intern Program
Deborah Cragen/Program Manager
One Microsoft Way
Redmond, WA 98052-6399
Web site: www.microsoft.com/college

MIDDLE EARTH

SELECTIVITY 🔍
Approximate applicant pool: 12; Interns accepted: 6

COMPENSATION 💲
Free lunch

LOCATION(S)
Doylestown and Warminister, PA

FIELD
Education; Psychology; Criminal justice; Social work

DURATION
School year; semester or quarter, Fall and Spring

DEADLINE(S)
Rolling

THE WORK
Founded in 1973, Middle Earth is an alternative school and treatment center for at-risk youth ages 12 through 19. A community-based alternative to residential correctional facilities, it offers students academic classes, vo-tech training, rehabilitative treatment, and psychological services. Interns assist in classes, supervising recreational activities, and counseling students.

PERKS
Training seminars in teaching, communication skills, and conflict management; several field trips to local cultural and recreational sites; free t-shirts, free lunches.

FYI
Middle Earth hires approximately 25 percent of interns for permanent employment . . . Recreational activities supervised by interns include softball, bowling, deep-sea fishing, horseback riding, and skiing.

TO APPLY
Open to undergrads, recent college grads, college grads of any age, and grad students. International applicants eligible. Write for application.

Internship Coordinator
Middle Earth
299 Jacksonville Road
Warminster, PA 18974
(215) 443-0280
(215) 443-0245 (Fax)

MIDDLE EAST INSTITUTE

SELECTIVITY 🔍🔍🔍
Approximate applicant pool: 100; Interns accepted: 10

COMPENSATION 💲
Reimbursement of daily public transportation

LOCATION(S)
Washington, DC

FIELD
Foreign affairs; Public policy; Publishing

DURATION
10–16 weeks: Summer, Fall, Spring

DEADLINE(S)
Summer: April 1; Fall: August 1; Spring: December 1

THE WORK
A nonprofit center established in 1946, the Middle East Institute (MEI) seeks to educate and inform Americans about the cultures, religions, history, politics, economics, and languages of the Middle East, North Africa, the Caucasus, and Central Asia. MEI sponsors classes in Arabic, Hebrew, Persian, and Turkish; coordinates political and economic programs; maintains a 25,000-volume library; and publishes *The Middle East Journal*. Internships are available in the following departments. Program interns assist in administration, organization, and background research for MEI

conferences, seminars, brown-bag lunches, congressional briefings and other programs. Publications interns draft annotations of books and create a "Bibliography of Periodical Literature" for The Middle East Journal, update data bases, and correspond with Middle East specialists for reviews of books and articles. Development interns participate in prospect research on corporate and foundation donors, prepare correspondence, and maintain a database. Library interns catalogue materials, provide reference assistance to patrons, prepare bibliographies and correspondences, assist with circulation and bindery preparation, and organize materials. Language interns maintain relations between students and MEI, make contracts and certificates, mail brochures to prospective students, record finances, and maintain attendance rosters of teachers and students. All interns write articles for the MEI newsletter.

PERKS
Lunchtime guest lecturers; one free language course (worth $350); attendance welcomed at fall annual conference, and congressional briefing series.

FYI
A recent MEI annual conference—held at the National Press Club and attended by over 400 diplomats, business people, professors, and students—featured Central Asian cuisine, Turkish music, and discussions on issues such as the Israeli-Palestinian peace process and Middle East economic trends.

TO APPLY
Open to undergrads and grads. International applicants eligible. Submit resume, cover letter, transcript, five-page writing sample, and recommendation.

Internship Coordinator
Middle East Institute
1761 N Street NW
Washington, DC 20036
(202) 785-2710

MIDDLE EAST RESEARCH & INFORMATION PROJECT

SELECTIVITY 🔍🔍🔍🔍
Approximate applicant pool: 90; Interns accepted: 9

COMPENSATION 💲
None

LOCATION(S)
Washington, DC

FIELD
Foreign affairs; Magazines

DURATION
12 weeks: Summer, Fall, Spring

DEADLINE(S)
Rolling

THE WORK
For almost 30 years, the four-person staff at the Middle East Research & Information Project (MERIP) has published *Middle East Report*, a 48-page quarterly magazine analyzing the current event

and trends shaping the Middle East. Interns work in Editorial, Promotion, or Administration departments and also assist with general office work.

PERKS
Brown-bag luncheons with editors and journalists; attendance welcome at DC-area conferences on Middle East issues.

FYI
In addition to publishing *Middle East Report*, MERIP briefs reporters and delegations heading to the Middle East, organizes seminars, lectures, and films on the region, and sponsers academic workshops.

TO APPLY
Open to high school students, undergrads, recent college grads, college grads of any age, and grad students. International applicants eligible. Submit resume, cover letter, and writing sample.

MERIP Internship
1500 Massachusetts Avenue NW, Suite 119
Washington, DC 20005
(202) 223-3677
(202) 223-3604 (Fax)
E-mail: admin@merip.org

MILLER BREWING COMPANY

SELECTIVITY 🔍🔍🔍🔍🔍
Approximate applicant pool: 240; Interns accepted: 4–6

COMPENSATION 💲💲💲💲
$950/week; free housing

LOCATION(S)
Milwaukee, WI

FIELD
Consumer goods (beer)

DURATION
10–12 weeks: Summer

DEADLINE(S)
Rolling

THE WORK
Founded in 1855 by German brewmaster Frederick Miller, Miller Brewing Company (MBC) is the second largest brewer in the United States. A division of Philip Morris since 1969, MBC produces and distributes beer under several brand names, including Miller (Lite, Genuine Draft, GD Lite, High Life, and Ice House), Lite Ice, Miller Best, Miller Best Lite, Henry Weinhard's, Hamms, Olde English 800, Mickey's Malt Liquor, Meister Brau, Magnum, Red Dog, Molson, Foster's, Reserve Amber Ale, Leinenkugel's Red Lager, and Sharp's). Interns work in the Marketing, Finance, International, IS, Engineering and Category Management, Sales, Human Resources, Operations, and Corporate Affairs.

PERKS
Free beer (if 21 or older), promotional items (e.g., hats, t-shirts), access to company gym. Will have executive exposure through breakfast and reception.

FYI
Established in 1991, Miller's internship program hires many of its interns for full-time positions . . . Past interns have traveled all over the world—for example, Oregon, New York, Chicago, Istanbul, and Budapest—to assess possible joint ventures with various breweries.

TO APPLY
Open to college students with a 3.0 average or above. Submit resume and cover letter.

Miller Brewing Company
Corporate Staffing Department
Code: INT2000
3939 West Highland Boulevard
Milwaukee, WI 53208
E-mail: staffing@mbco.com
www.millerbrewing.com/career/employ/interns.asp

THE MILWAUKEE JOURNAL SENTINEL

SELECTIVITY 🔍🔍🔍🔍🔍
Approximate applicant pool: 500; Interns accepted: 12

COMPENSATON 💲💲💲
$450/week

LOCATION(S)
Milwaukee, WI

FIELD
Newspapers

DURATION
12 weeks: Summer

DEADLINE(S)
November 1

THE WORK
The Milwaukee Journal Sentinel is the largest newspaper in Wisconsin. Winner of five Pulitzer Prizes, it was created by the merger of the Milwaukee Sentinel and Milwaukee Journal in 1995. Interns work in Metro Desk, Features Department, Copy Desk, Sports, Photojournalism, and Graphics.

PERKS
Weekly meetings with editors; intern luncheons; mentor program.

FYI
In existence since 1966, the internship counts among its alumni an associate editor, a news editor, and a business editor. . . .The *Journal Sentinel* offers a special one-year internship for minority students interested in working on the Urban Affairs desk.

TO APPLY
Open to college juniors and seniors, recent college grads, college grads of any age, and grad students. International applicants eligible. Submit cover letter, resume, and eight to ten brief writing samples/clips.

Internship Coordinator—Paul Sevart
The Milwaukee Journal Sentinel
P.O. Box 371
Milwaukee, WI 53201-0371

SELECTIVITY
Approximate applicant pool: 12-15; Interns accepted: 3 each semester

COMPENSATON
Monthly stipend; free room and board; health insurance

LOCATION(S)
Shelby, MI

FIELD
Education, Psychology, Leisure Studies, Sociology

DURATION
Winter and/or Fall semester; Summer; year round

DEADLINE(S)
Summer: April 30; Fall: May 31; Spring: November 30

THE WORK
Interns prepare and implement programs for a wide age range of participants, design cirriculum, and facilitate high ropes and challenge course activities. The program gives interns a chance to gain skills in team and community building, program evaluation, budget preparation, public relations, meeting organization, conference hospitality, and developing marketing plans.

Established in 1925, Miniwanca is a division of the American Youth Foundation (AYF), a nonprofit organization dedicated "to developing leadership and education conferences; 360-acres of wooden Lake Michigan sand dunes, waterfront, and trails; major medical insurance; and laundry facilities.

PERKS
Regular meetings with supervisors; at staff training programs, management circles, and meetings; opportunities to attend nationwide leadership conferences; 360 acres of wooded sand dunes, waterfront, and secluded trails.

FYI
AYF offers similar internships at its headquarters in St. Louis, MO (314-646-6000) and its Merrowvista center in NH (603-539-6607) . . . AYF's motto: "My own self, at my very best, all the time." . . . AYF "dares" each individual to "live a balanced, four-fold life of mental, physical, social, and spiritual activity."

TO APPLY
Open to college juniors and seniors, recent college grads, college grads of any age, and grad students. Must be certified in first aid and CPR. International applicants eligible. Write for application.

Internship Coordinator
Miniwanca Education Center
8845 West Garfield Road
Shelby, MI 49455
(231) 861-2262
(231) 861-5244 (Fax)

UNITED STATES DEPARTMENT OF COMMERCE

MINORITY BUSINESS DEVELOPMENT AGENCY

See US Department of Commerce

SELECTIVITY
Approximate applicant pool: 1,000; Interns accepted: 3

COMPENSATON
Approximate $250/week; free room and board

LOCATION(S)
Farmington, CT

FIELD
Teaching

DURATION
9 months: September–June

DEADLINE(S)
March 31

THE WORK
Founded in 1843, Miss Porter's School is an independent boarding school for girls in grades 9 through 12. Committed to producing "resourceful, informed, responsible, and ethical young women," Miss Porter's admits 280 students from the United States and seventeen foreign countries. In addition to teaching courses in math, science, arts, classics, English, foreign languages, or history, each intern supervises a dormitory as an assistant to the House Director.

PERKS
Highly skilled teachers as mentors; weekly seminar on practical and theoretical issues in teaching; opportunities to coach or advise clubs and publications; access to libraries, fitness facilities, etc.

FYI
As its name suggests, Miss Porter's School was founded as a finishing school to shape girls into effective homemakers. Today, the only vestige of this curriculum that remains is the school's name . . . According to the intern coordinator, the course load for each teaching intern is not quite as heavy as that of staff teachers at Miss Porter's.

TO APPLY
Open to recent college grads. International applicants eligible. Submit resume, cover letter, transcript, and recommendations.

Director of New Teacher Program
Teaching Intern Program
Miss Porter's School
60 Main Street
Farmington, CT 06032
(203) 677-1321

SELECTIVITY 🔍
Approximate applicant pool: 10; Interns accepted: 2

COMPENSATON 💲
None

LOCATION(S)
Cranston, RI

FIELD
Public relations

DURATION
15 weeks: Summer; Fall; Winter; Spring

DEADLINE(S)
Summer: May 31; Fall : August 31; Spring: December 31

THE WORK
Founded in 1990, Mixed Media (MM) is a public relations firm specializing in the music industry. Clients have included Chubby Checker Management, Rounder Records, Wall Street Music, Lakewest Recording Studio, and Green Limet. Interns prepare press kits, arrange radio promotions, promote demo tapes for bands, and conduct follow up phone calls to newspapers, radio stations, TV and DJ pools and video channels.

PERKS
Frequent contact with artists; free CDs, cassettes, and concert tickets; small, comfortable office housing a roving cat ("the company mascot").

FYI
Cranston is a few miles from downtown Providence. Interns work out of the home office of MM's president, Ginny Shea.

TO APPLY
Open to undergrads and recent college grads. Company is unable to assist with accomodations. Area students preferred.

Internship Coordinator
20 Lockmere Road
Mixed Media
Cranston, RI 02910
(401) 942-8025
(401) 942-5487 (Fax)

SELECTIVITY 🔍🔍🔍
Approximate applicant pool: 20–40; Interns accepted: 2–5

COMPENSATON 💲
$125/month for interns committing to at least 6 months

LOCATION(S)
Eugene, OR

FIELD
People with disabilities; International education; Leadership development; Public relations

DURATION
3–6 months

DEADLINE(S)
Rolling

THE WORK
Founded in 1981, Mobility International USA (MIUSA) is a nonprofit organization running international exchange programs and leadership seminars for people with disabilities. The National Clearinghouse on Disability and Exchange (NCDE), funded by the United States Information Agency, provides information and referrals to individuals with disabilities as well as technical assistance to disability and exchange organizations. It also produces a variety of videos and publications on disability rights and issues. Interns work in Public Relations, Publications, Journalism, International Exchange, Research, Disability Issues, and Leadership Development.

PERKS
Activities with exchange groups (e.g., camping, whitewater rafting, and horseback riding); alumni newsletter; family-like office atmosphere.

FYI
MIUSA provides interns with information on apartments ranging in rent from $435 to $700 a month . . . MIUSA offers about 20 percent of interns employment.

TO APPLY
Open to high school grads, undergrads, recent college grads, college grads of any age, and grad students. International applicants eligible. Contact MIUSA for application. Submit with a resume, cover letter, and two letters of recommendation.

Internship Coordinator
Mobility International
P.O. Box 10767
Eugene, OR 97440
(541) 343-1284 (voice/TDD)
(541) 343-6812 (fax)
E-mail: exchange@miusa.org

SELECTIVITY 🔍
Approximate applicant pool: 80; Interns accepted: 30

COMPENSATON 💲💲💲
$100/week; free room and board

LOCATION(S)
Rockville, MD

FIELD
Corrections

DURATION
16 weeks–1 year: ongoing

DEADLINE(S)
Rolling

THE WORK
Nationally recognized as a model for community-based corrections, Montgomery County Community Corrections (MCCC) is one of the nation's only correctional systems independent of a local sheriff and managed by professionals in the correctional field. Interns work with one of the following: Pre-Release Center, a facility for adult offenders nearing release; Community Accountability, Reintegration, and Treatment Program; Intervention Program for Substance Abusers; and Pre-trial Services Unit, which determines the risk potential for pre-trial release of defendants and supervises those defendants granted pre-trial release. Depending on where they work, interns may participate in such activities as supervising residents, crisis intervention, urinalysis collection and testing, developing community service projects, and checking arrest histories.

PERKS
Weekly intern training sessions in CPR, first aid, etc. available; supportive network of supervisors.

FYI
In existence since 1975, the internship program counts among its alumni MCCC's supervisor of administration and training . . . Forty percent of MCCC staff are alumni of the internship program.

TO APPLY
Open to college juniors and seniors, recent college grads, college grads of any age, and grad students. International applicants eligible. Write for application.

Internship Coordinator
Montgomery County Community Corrections
11651 Nebel Street
Rockville, MD 20852
(301) 468-4200
(301) 468-4420 (Fax)

Morris Arboretum of the University of Pennsylvania
The official arboretum of the Commonwealth of Pennsylvania

SELECTIVITY 🔍🔍🔍
Approximate applicant pool: 55; Interns accepted: 7

COMPENSATON 💲💲
$235/week; health insurance and dental plan

LOCATION(S)
Philadelphia, PA

FIELD
Horticulture; Landscape design; Botany; Biology; Education; Plant pathology

DURATION
1 year: starts mid-June

DEADLINE(S)
February 15

THE WORK
Dating back to 1887, the Morris Arboretum is a recognized leader in horticultural display, public education, and botanical and horticultural research. Its 166-acres contain a Victorian temple with hidden grotto, a pond with Royal Swans, a rose garden, Japanese gardens, sculptures, meadows, woodlands, and an English landscape park with long vistas over rolling hills. Interns work in Horticulture, Education, Botany, Urban Forestry, Arboriculture, and Propagation.

PERKS
Practical sessions on tree pruning and planting, garden interpretation, resume writing, and identification of woody plants, etc.; attendance welcome at professional conferences and arboretum-sponsored classes and workshops; field trips to other arboreta, nurseries, and natural areas.

FYI
In existence since 1979, the internship program counts among its alumni the research/education manager at Briggs Nursery in Washington, the education manager at Philadelphia Green, and the development director at the North Carolina State University Arboretum . . . The arboretum is a University of Pennsylvania program.

Interns at the Morris Arboretum receiving a special lesson from Paul Meyer, the arboretum's director.

TO APPLY

Open to undergrads, recent college grads, college grads of any age, and grad students. International applicants eligible. Write for application.

Internship Coordinator
Morris Arboretum
9414 Meadowbrook Avenue
Philadelphia, PA 19118
(215) 247-5777, x 156
(215) 247-7862 (Fax)

MORRISON & FOERSTER

SELECTIVITY N/A
Approximate applicant pool: 300; Approximate Interns accepted: varies

COMPENSATON $ $ $ $ $
$2,750/month

LOCATION(S)
San Francisco, CA

FIELD
Law

DURATION
1 year (no summer positions)

DEADLINE(S)
Rolling

THE WORK

With 800 lawyers and 17 offices worldwide, Morrison & Foerster is a powerhouse law firm, arguably the most prestigious in San Francisco. More progressive than many law firms, Morrison & Foerster makes a strong commitment to performing pro bono work and hiring attorneys from a wide variety of backgrounds. Interns assist legal assistants and attorneys primarily in the litigation practice but assignments can extend to other areas such as labor, tax, and corporate work.

PERKS

Ongoing in-house training for paralegals, full benefits.

TO APPLY

Open to college grads. Submit resume, cover letter, and trancript directly to:

Internship/Paralegal Program
Morrison & Foerster
425 Market Street
San Francisco, CA 94105
(415) 268-7000

MOTE MARINE LABORATORY

SELECTIVITY 🔍
Approximate applicant pool: 250; Interns accepted: 75

COMPENSATON $
None (limited scholarship available)

LOCATION(S)
Sarasota, FL

FIELD
Environment; Oceanography

DURATION
8–16 weeks: Summer, Fall, Spring

DEADLINE(S)
Rolling

THE WORK

Established in 1955 by renowned shark biologist Dr. Eugenie Clark, Mote Marine Laboratory (MML) is a nonprofit institution engaged in marine research and education. MML's facilities consist of research laboratories, a 3,000-volume library, a conference center, a marine mammal research and rehabilitation center, a fleet of research vessels, and the Mote Aquarium. Interns work in Research (Biomedical, Chemical Fate & Effects, Environmental Assessment & Enhancement, Fisheries & Aquaculture, Marine Mammals, Sea Turtles, and Shark Biology) as well as Support Programs (Aquarium, Education, Communications, Graphics, and Business).

PERKS

Free admission to aquarium; attendance welcome at various lectures and seminars on marine sciences; discounts at gift shop.

FYI

MML is located on a site bordered by Sarasota Bay and New Pass, giving direct access to the Gulf of Mexico . . . The internship program has been offered since 1982.

The lushly landscaped entrance of Mote Marine Laboratory in Sarasota, Florida.

Open to undergrads, recent college grads. International applicants eligible. Write for application.

Internship Coordinator
Mote Marine Library
1600 Ken Thompson Parkway
Sarasota, FL 34236
(941) 388-4441
(941) 388-4312 (Fax)

MOTHER EARTH NEWS

See Sussex Publishers

MOTHER JONES

MOTHERJONES

SELECTIVITY
Approximate applicant pool: 600–700; Interns accepted: 10–12

COMPENSATON [S]
$100/month up to 4 months with possibility of $1,000 a month after 4 months

LOCATION(S)
San Francisco, CA

FIELD
Magazines

DURATION
16–32 weeks–1 year (16-week internship with possibility of 16-week fellowship)

DEADLINE(S)
Rolling

THE WORK
Named after a pioneer labor organizer known for her feisty spirit, *Mother Jones* is one of America's leading progressive magazines. Founded in 1976, it specializes in investigative reporting and political and cultural analysis. Interns initially work up to four months, then they may work up to an additional eight months and take on more substantive responsibilities. Departments accepting interns include Editorial, Art, and the Website.

PERKS
Brown-bag lunches with *Mother Jones* executives; opportunities for freelance fact checking; attendance welcome at editorial meetings; free promotional goodies (t-shirts, coffee mugs, etc.).

FYI
Says the intern coordinator: "We know clips are important to new journalists, so . . . we make sure everyone gets to write at least one short, bylined article in the magazine."

TO APPLY
Open to college juniors and seniors, recent college grads, college grads of any age, and grad students. International applicants eligible. Submit resume, cover letter, and at least three writing samples.

Internship Coordinator
Mother Jones
731 Market Street, Suite 600
San Francisco, CA 94103
(415) 665-6637
(415) 665-6696 (Fax)

MOTOWN RECORDS

See PolyGram

MS.

SELECTIVITY
Approximate application pool: 100; Interns accepted: 18

COMPENSATION [S]
None

LOCATION(S)
New York, NY

FIELD
Magazines; Women's Issues

DURATION
15–20 weeks: Summer (starting date June 1), Fall (September 1), Spring (January 1)

DEADLINE(S)
Summer: March 30; Fall: June 30; Spring: October 30

THE WORK
Ms. has had a tumultuous history: co-founded in 1972 by a group of women including Founding Editor Gloria Steinem, the magazine went nonprofit in 1979, only to be sold off to the Australian-based company John Fairfax Ltd. in 1987. Less than a year later, two of the magazine's journalists lead a successful management buyout, and in 1989, the magazine was purchased by its current owner, Lang Communications. The magazine suspended publication for seven months in 1990, and re-launched in 1991 — without advertising. The transition has been fairly successful: the magazine now has a circulation of over 200,000. Interns work in the editorial department; duties include answering phones, evaluating manuscripts, sorting mail, research, and collating survey results.

PERKS
Attendance and participation welcome at weekly editorial meetings; opportunity to write short news pieces for the magazine; small office environment

FYI
According to the intern coordinator, "We prefer journalism, women's studies, or communications majors . . . Generally, we are interested in candidates who are enthusiastic about the magazine itself, as they usually have positive experiences as interns." Ms. requires interns to work a minimum of 24 hours per week.

TO APPLY
Open to undergrads, recent graduates, and grad students. Submit resume, cover letter, writing samples (clips from a local/college or college-level newspaper), and at least two reference phone numbers.

Ms. Magazine Internship
Attn: Torang Sepah, Assistant Editor
135 W. 50th Street
New York, NY 10020
(212) 445-6162

MSG NETWORK

MADISON SQUARE GARDEN NETWORK

A Paramount Communications Company

See Madison Square Garden

MTV

MUSIC TELEVISION®

SELECTIVITY 🔍 🔍
Approximate applicant pool: 400–600; Interns accepted: 150

COMPENSATION $
None

LOCATION(S)
New York, NY; Los Angeles, CA; Orlando, Miami, FL; Atlanta, GA; Detroit, MI; Chicago, IL

FIELD
Television; Music

DURATION
10 weeks; Summer, Fall, and Spring; At least 2 days/week

DEADLINE(S)
Rolling

THE WORK
Since 1981, MTV's ongoing tapestry of music videos has not only defined how the young consume music, but how they talk, dress, and watch television. Despite those who blame MTV for corrupting the American mind, the network has attracted over 60 million subscribers and has even gained the respect of President Clinton, who participated in its "Choose or Lose" forum as a presidential candidate. Interns may be placed in a "business" department such as Marketing, Press and Public Relations, Programming, International Programming, and Advertising; a "creative" department such as Art Promotions, Talents Relations, Graphics, On-Air Talent, and Video Library; or a particular MTV program such as "MTV News," or "MTV Jams."

PERKS
Speaker luncheons; casual dress in some departments; possible promotional freebies.

FYI
MTV has been accepting interns since it hit the airwaves in the early 1980s . . . Said an intern: "With a little luck and a lot of initiative, the internship can be a perk-o-rama." . . . The MTV internship was written up in the *Seventeen* article "I Was an Intern at MTV."

TO APPLY
Open to high school students, undergrads, and grad students. Must receive academic credit. International applicants eligible. Submit resume, cover letter, and written verification of academic credit.

Suzanne Lumerman
MTV Networks Internship Program
Human Resources
1515 Broadway, 16th Floor
New York, NY 10036
(212) 846-1473

MUSEUM OF CONTEMPORARY ART, CHICAGO

SELECTIVITY 🔍 🔍 🔍
Approximate applicant pool: 350; Interns accepted: 55

COMPENSATION $
None

LOCATION(S)
Chicago, IL

FIELD
Museums

DURATION
12–16 weeks: Summer, Fall, Winter, Spring

DEADLINE(S)
Summer: March 15; Fall : July 15; Spring/Winter; November 15

THE WORK
Opened in 1967 by a "group of culturally concerned Chicagoans," the Museum of Contemporary Art (MCA), Chicago, has become one of the nation's leading forums for contemporary art. In addition to a diverse exhibition schedule, the MCA runs a range of courses, lectures, symposia, and gallery talks. Departments hiring interns include: Administration, Accounting, Development, Education, Graphic Design, Curatorial, Publications, Public Relations, Special Events, Membership, Information Systems, Photo Archives, Wholesale, Library, Registrar, Collections/Exhibitions, and Marketing.

Lights... Camera... *Intern!*
Interns in film and on television:

The closest MTV's **Beavis and Butt-head** have come to serving an internship is when the duo finds temporary employment at a real estate agency. On the job at Muller Real Estate, Beavis ends up short-circuiting his computer, only to be matched by Butt-head, who destroys his phone. When their supervisor arrives on the scene, Butt-head points to his partner-in-crime and explains: "Ma'am, this butt-munch broke your office!"

Special Interest Internships

Internships at African/African American Organizations

Organizations whose identity is primarily African/African American:
Africare
American Committee on Africa/The Africa Fund
Anacostia Museum
Black Enterprise
Black Entertainment Television
Essence
Forty Acres and a Mule Filmworks
Motown Records
National Museum of African Art
New Breed Entertainment
The Source
Tommy Boy Music
Washington Office on Africa

Internships at Asian/Asian-American Organizations

Organizations whose identity is primarily Asian or Asian American:
Asian American Arts Centre
Asian American Journalists Association
Japan-American Society of Washington
Korean American Coalition
Organization of Chinese Americans
National Asian Pacific American Legal Consortium
US-Asia Institute
Volunteers in Asia

Internships at Hispanic Organizations

Organizations whose identity is primarily Hispanic:
Association of Hispanic Arts
Congressional Hispanic Caucus Institute
Council on Hemispheric Affairs
Hispanic Association of Colleges and Universities
Washington Office on Latin America

Internships at Jewish Organizations

Organizations whose identity is primarily Jewish:
American Israel Public Affairs Committee
American Jewish Congress
Bet Tzedek Legal Services
Hillel
Jewish Vocational and Career Counseling Service
Volunteers in Israel
US Holocaust Museum

Internships at Middle Eastern Organizations

Organizations whose identity is primarily Middle Eastern:
American-Arab Anti-Discrimination Committee
AMIDEAST
Arab American Institute
Middle East Institute
Middle East Research & Information Project

Internships at Native American Organizations

Organizations whose identity is primarily Native American:
Anasazi Heritage Center
Council of Energy Resource Tribes
Navajo Nation

Internships at Conservative Organizations

Organizations whose identity is primarily Conservative:
American Enterprise Institute
The Conservative Caucus
The Heritage Foundation
Hudson Institute
Lake Charles American Press
The Ripon Society

Internships at Liberal Organizations

Organizations whose identity is primarily Liberal:
American Civil Liberties Union
Beacon Press
The Brookings Institution
The Carter Center
Council on Hemispheric Affairs
Hunter House
Mother Jones
The Nation
The Union Institute
Village Voice

Internships at Women's Organizations

Organizations whose identity is based primarily on Women's Issues:
American Association of University Women Educational Foundation
American Women's Economic Development Corp.
The Feminist Majority
Focus on Women
Healthy Mothers, Healthy Babies
International Planned Parenthood Federation
The Maternal & Child Health Institute
Ms.
My Sister's Place
National Association for Female Executives
National Organization for Women
NOW Legal Defense and Education Fund
Teen Voices
Women Express
Women's Institute for Freedom of the Press
Women's International League for Peace and Freedom
Women's Legal Defense Fund
Women's Project & Productions
Women's Sports & Fitness Magazine
Working Mother
Working Woman

PERKS

Intern lecture series featuring key staff; invitations to MCA events, member receptions, and parties; discount in MCA store, bookstore, and cafe; admission to Education programs and lectures.

FYI

Alumni of the program include the director of the Musee d'art Contemporain in Switzerland; Editor and Acting Executive Director of the *New Art Examiner*; Curator of Contemporary Art at the High Museum in Atlanta; and Assistant Vice President at Sotheby's, London, England.

TO APPLY

Open to high school grads, undergrads, recent college grads, college grads of any age, and grad students. International applicants eligible. Write for application.

Intern Coordinator
Museum of Contemporary Art
Office of Administration
220 East Chicago Avenue
Chicago, IL 60611
(312) 280–2660
(312) 397–4095 (Fax)

MUSEUM OF FINE ARTS, BOSTON

SELECTIVITY 🔍
Approximate applicant pool: 60; Interns accepted: 20

COMPENSATON 💲
None

LOCATION(S)
Boston, MA

FIELD
Museums

DURATION
10 weeks: Summer, Fall, Spring

DEADLINE(S)
Summer: April 1; Fall: September 1; Spring: January 1

THE WORK

Dating back to July 4, 1876, the Museum of Fine Arts, Boston, has a collection of art spanning every continent and epoch. It also runs a lecture series, a film program, chamber music concerts, studio art classes, and children's programs. Departments hiring interns include Education, Administration, Curatorial, Library, Publicity, and Marketing.

PERKS

Meetings with administrators and department directors; tours of "behind the scenes" areas.

FYI

The museum is renowned for its extensive array of educational programs, which, according to museum literature, "reach a larger audience than any arts organization in greater Boston."

TO APPLY

Open to undergrads, recent college grads, college grads of any age, and grad students. International applicants eligible. Write for application.

Internship Coordinator
Museum of Fine Arts, Boston
465 Huntington Avenue
Boston, MA 02115
(617) 369-3300

The Museum of Modern Art, N

SELECTIVITY 🔍🔍🔍🔍
Approximate applicant pool: 300–400 (HRF), 150 (AYP & TMI); Interns accepted: 25 (HRF), 30–50 (AYP), 3 (TMI)

COMPENSATON 💲💲
AYP: none; HRF: $225/week; TMI: $340/week plus health insurance

LOCATION(S)
New York, NY

FIELD
Museums

DURATION
HRF: 9 weeks, Summer; AYP: 12 weeks, Fall, Spring; TMI: 1 year, starting in September

DEADLINE(S)
Please see the education section of the museum's website for a complete listing of application deadlines

THE WORK

Founded in 1929, The Museum of Modern Art (MOMA) is one of the world's most comprehensive museums of twentieth-century art. Its collections include 100,000 paintings, sculptures, drawings, prints, photographs, architectural plans, and design objects. The Helena Rubinstein Foundation Summer Internship Program (HRF), the Academic-Year Program (AYP), and the Twelve-Month Internship (TMI) interns work in Architecture & Design, Drawings, Film & Video, Painting & Sculpture, Photography, Prints & Illustrated Books, Conservation, Exhibitions, Graphic Design, International Program, Library, Museum Archives, Publications, Registrar, Rights & Reproductions, Development, Finance, General Counsel, Personnel, Art Advisory, Education, Membership, Communications, and Marketing.

PERKS

Lecture program featuring department heads and curators; field trips to New York museums, galleries, and artists' studios.

FYI

The first art museum to recognize the motion picture as an art form, MOMA also owns 10,000 films and 4 million film stills.

TO APPLY

HRF: open to college juniors and seniors, grad students young professionals. AYP: open to college juniors and seniors, grad students, young professionals. TMI: open to college graduates. Visit the Education section of the Museum's Web site, www.moma.org, for a complete description of the program and an application form.

Internship Coordinator
Department of Education
The Museum of Modern Art
11 West 53rd Street
New York, NY 10019
(212) 708-9893
(212) 333-1118 (Fax)
www.moma.org

My Sister's Place
a shelter for battered women and their children

SELECTIVITY 🔍
Approximate applicant pool: 150; Interns accepted: 100

COMPENSATON 💲
None

LOCATION(S)
Washington, DC

FIELD
Public service; Women's issues

DURATION
4 weeks minimum: ongoing

DEADLINE(S)
Rolling

THE WORK
Established in 1979 by the Women's Legal Defense Fund, My Sister's Place (MSP) is a nonprofit shelter for battered women and their children. Committed to eradicating domestic violence, MSP provides shelter, and offers counseling and educational programs. Volunteers and interns work in Community Education/Speakers' Bureau, Children's Program, Development/Fundraising,Hotline, House Management, Office Work/Statistics, Transitional Housing, Transportation, Women's Advocacy, and Volunteer Program.

PERKS
Training in crisis counseling and legal issues of domestic violence; optional training in public speaking; attendance welcome at MSP seminars and court hearings; supportive, nurturing environment.

FYI
The name "My Sister's Place" was devised, in part, to provide a convenient answer for battered women and their families who were asked where they were staying. Intern duties include counseling callers and residents, preparing material for the public, giving speeches on domestic violence, conducting mailings, monitoring stock of food and supplies in the kitchen, and leading seminars.

TO APPLY
Open to high school grads, undergrads, recent college grads, college grads of any age, and grad students. International applicants eligible. Submit resume and cover letter.

Volunteer Coordinator
My Sister's Place
P.O. Box 29596
Washington, DC 20017
(202) 529-5261
(202) 529-5984 (Fax)

SELECTIVITY 🔍🔍
Approximate applicant pool: 50; Interns accepted: 12

COMPENSATON 💲💲
Limited stipends and furnished housing available

LOCATION(S)
Mystic, CT

FIELD
Museums

DURATION
10 weeks: Summer

DEADLINE(S)
April 14

THE WORK
In existence since 1929, Mystic Seaport is an internationally recognized maritime museum on 17 acres along the beautiful Mystic River. It features historic tall ships, nineteenth-century New England homes, sailors' arts and artifacts, and various maritime exhibitions. Interns spend their time on projects relating to museum collections, oral history, manuscripts, and exhibits; or also work in the Development, Public Affairs, or Education departments.

PERKS
Weekly college-level seminar in museum theory, procedures, and ethics; and field trips to other museums for behind-the-scenes tours and lectures.

FYI
Interns live in museum-owned, nineteenth-century homes about 200 yards from the river . . . Says the internship coordinator: "The interns are around for the liveliest time of the year; being an outdoor museum, [Mystic] sees a lot of visitors in July and August."

TO APPLY
Open to college juniors and seniors, college grads of any age, and grad students. International applicants eligible. Write for application.

Internship Coordinator
Mystic Seaport: The Museum of America & the Sea
P.O. Box 6000
Mystic, CT 06355-0990
(860) 572-5359 x4
(860) 572-5329 (Fax)
E-mail: munson@mysticseaport.org
www.mysticseaport.org

MYSTIC STUDIES
Interns at Mystic Seaport in Mystic, CT are treated to a college-level seminar in museum theory, procedures, and ethics. The seminar includes reading assignments, discussions, guest speakers, and visits to libraries and archives.

NABISCO

SELECTIVITY   🔍 🔍 🔍
Approximate applicant pool: 1,000; Interns accepted: 70

COMPENSATION   💲 💲 💲 💲
$400–$600/week for undergrads; $800–$1,000/week for grad students

LOCATION(S)
East Hanover and Parsippany, NJ

FIELD
Consumer goods (foods)

DURATION
14 weeks: Summer and Co-op

DEADLINE(S)
March 1 for summer

THE WORK
A subsidiary of RJR Nabisco, Nabisco is one of the world's largest food companies, with 49,000 employees, $8.3 billion in annual sales, and over 300 products. Its leading brands include Oreo cookies, Ritz crackers, Cream of Wheat cereals, A1 Steak Sauce, Grey Poupon mustard, Planters peanuts, and LifeSavers candies. Interns in New Jersey work in Marketing, Accounting-Finance, Logistics, and Information Services.

PERKS
Orientation; "Lunch and Learn" sessions with division heads; field trips to nearby bakeries.

FYI
Nabisco products constitute seven out of the top ten cookie and cracker brands . . . Approximately one-third of interns are hired by Nabisco for full-time positions . . . Past intern projects have involved performing P&L analyses for specific products, preparing cost-analysis studies of coupons and advertising, designing new information systems, evaluating software, and implementing consumer promotions.

TO APPLY
Open to undergrads and MBA students. Submit resume and cover letter.

Internship Coordinator
University Relations
Nabisco
100 De Forest Avenue
East Hanover, NJ 07936
(201) 503-2000

THE NATION

SELECTIVITY   🔍 🔍 🔍 🔍 🔍
Approximate applicant pool: 500; Interns accepted: 24

COMPENSATION   💲
$150/week

LOCATION(S)
New York, NY; Washington, DC

FIELD
Magazines

DURATION
12 weeks: Summer, Fall, Spring

DEADLINE(S)
Tentative; please contact for exact dates

THE WORK
America's oldest weekly magazine, *The Nation* is a progressive journal of politics and the arts that focuses primarily on foreign and domestic policy, civil liberties, and literature. Most interns are placed in the NY office, where they assist the advertising, circulation, and promotion staffs with day-to-day business, and help to create and carry out research projects.

PERKS
Biweekly seminars with journalists, activists, and political/cultural figures (recent years included Mario Cuomo and George McGovern); weekly editorial meetings with staff.

FYI
Alumni of the program, started in 1978, include *The Nation*'s editor, senior editor, and managing editor.

TO APPLY
Open to undergrads, recent college grads, college grads of any age, and grad students. International applicants eligible. Submit resume, cover letter, two recommendations, and two writing samples.

The Nation
Intern Program
33 Irving Place, 8th floor
New York, NY 10003
(212) 209-5400

"Young man, office boys are a dime a dozen."

Drawing by Ross; © 1967, 1995 The New Yorker Magazine, Inc.

SELECTIVITY N/A
Approximate applicant pool: N/A; Interns accepted: Est. 1,000

COMPENSATION 💲💲💲
$100–$400/week for undergrads; $400–$700/week for grad students

LOCATION(S)
AL, CA, FL, MD, MS, OH, TX, VA

FIELD
Aerospace and aeronautics

DURATION
6 weeks–4 months: Summer

DEADLINE(S)
Varies with program (see Application Procedure)

THE WORK
Since its inception, NASA has done much to advance America's mission "to plan, direct, and conduct aeronautical and space activities." Despite its share of setbacks, NASA has landed Americans on the moon, mapped the surfaces of every planet in the solar system except Pluto, and implemented the world's first reusable system of space shuttles. There are at least 200 different NASA programs for interns, including research projects in robotics, earth sciences, aerodynamics, biomedicine and biotechnology, materials processing, space propulsion, space structures, and satellite communications.

PERKS

Varies with location.

FYI
Of the approximately 100 active NASA astronauts, as many as five are former NASA interns . . . In the words of NASA's head of staffing policy, an experience at NASA is "a chance to work with cutting-edge technology and leading scientific experts." . . . Since 1959, only 214 individuals have been selected to become astronauts.

TO APPLY
Each NASA program has its own set of criteria. NASA has internships for virtually everyone, from high school students at least 16 years of age to college undergrads, grad students, and faculty members. Some programs require a minimum GPA of 3.0. International applicants eligible. The best source for information about NASA internships and application procedures and deadlines is at www.nasajobs.nasa.gov

NASA Headquarters
Educational Division
Mail Code FE
Washington, DC 20546
(202) 358-1110

NASA Kennedy Space Center
University Program Manager
Mail Code HM-CIU
KSC, FL 32899
(407) 867-7952

NASA Ames Research Center
University Affairs Office
Code 241-3
Moffett Field, CA 94035
(650) 604-6937

NASA Langley Research Center
Office of Education
Mail Stop 400
Hampton, VA 23681-0001
(804) 864-4000

NASA Goddard Space Flight Center
University Programs
Mail Stop 160
Greenbelt Road
Greenbelt, MD 20771
(301) 286-9690

NASA Glenn Research Center
Educational Programs
Mail Stop CP–1
21000 Brookpark Road
Cleveland, OH 44135
(216) 433-2956

Jet Propulsion Laboratory
Educational Affairs Office
Mail Stop 72-109
4800 Oak Grove Drive
Pasadena, CA 91109-8099
(818) 354-3274

NASA Marshall Space Flight
Center
University Affairs
Mail Stop CL01
MSFC, AL 35812
(256) 544-7604

NASA Johnson Space Center
University Programs
Mail Stop AP-2
Houston, TX 77058
(281) 483-4724

NASA Stennis Space Center
University Affairs Office
Mail Code AA10
SSC, MS 39529
(228) 688-3832

NATIONAL AIR AND SPACE MUSEUM

See Smithsonian Institution

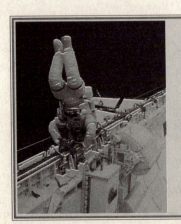

NASA Astronaut **Gregory Harbaugh**, who flew in the 1991 Space Shuttle Discovery mission, worked as an intern at NASA's Lewis Research Center in Cleveland the summer of 1977, after his junior year at Purdue.

SELECTIVITY 🔍🔍
Approximate applicant pool: 240; Interns accepted: 60

COMPENSATION $
None

LOCATION(S)
Baltimore, MD

FIELD
Aquariums

DURATION
120 hours: Summer, Fall, Winter, Spring

DEADLINE(S)
Summer: April 1; Fall: April 1; Winter: November 1; Spring: November 1

THE WORK
In operation since 1981, the National Aquarium in Baltimore is a stunningly modern institution, with five levels of aquatic life connected by a system of escalators, ramps, and bridges. More than 1.5 million visitors explore its galleries yearly, and over 150,000 school children participate in programs tailored for levels from pre-school through high school. Interns work in Audio-Visual Technology, Aquaculture, Aquarist, Aviculture, Development, Herpetology, Horticulture, Information Services, Library Science, Marine Education, Marine Mammal Training, Marketing, Membership, Public Relations, Publication, and Water Quality/Chemistry.

PERKS
Attendance welcome at seminars and workshops; 20 percent discount at gift shop and cafe; free uniform.

FYI
The internship has been in existence since 1981.

TO APPLY
Open to undergrads. International applicants eligible. Write for application.

Internship Coordinator
National Aquarium in Baltimore
Pier 3, 501 East Pratt Street
Baltimore, MD 21202-3194
(410) 576-8236
(410) 659-0116 (Fax)
intern@aqua.org
www.aqua.org

SELECTIVITY 🔍🔍🔍🔍
Approximate applicant pool: 50; Interns accepted: 4

COMPENSATION $
None

LOCATION(S)
Washington, DC

FIELD
Law; Public policy

DURATION
10–12 weeks: Summer, Fall, Spring

DEADLINE(S)
Fall: August 31; Spring: November 15; Summer: February 1

THE WORK
Founded in 1993, the National Asian Pacific American Legal Consortium (NAPALC) is a nonprofit, nonpartisan organization working to advance the legal and civil rights of the nation's Asian Pacific Americans. Focusing on the areas of voting rights, language rights, census, immigration, welfare reform, affirmative action, race relations, and anti-Asian violence, NAPALC is involved in litigation, advocacy, public education, and public policy development. Interns assist staff in conducting writing research, composing NAPALC's newsletter, tracking legislation, grassroots advocacy, participating in coalition meetings, and special events.

PERKS
Opportunity to work with national civil rights organizations, congressional staff, federal agencies; brown bag lunch discussions, busy, but "friendly, laid-back" office environment.

FYI
Says a former intern: "Interning [at NAPALC] is a great way to meet the people in public policy who are changing things for Asian people. There's a lot of field work. It was exciting—I met people I used to write reports on in school."

TO APPLY
Open to undergrads, recent college grads, law students, and grad students. International applicants eligible. Submit resume, cover letter, writing samples, and transcript.

Ronda Coleman, Program Assistant
NAPALC
1140 Connecticut Ave., NW, Suite 1200
Washington, DC 20036
(202) 296-2300
(202) 296-2318 (Fax)

SELECTIVITY 🔍🔍🔍
Approximate applicant pool: 45–50; Interns accepted: 5–7

COMPENSATION $
None

LOCATION(S)
Providence, RI

FIELD
Radio; Television

DURATION
6–36 weeks: Summer, Fall, Spring

DEADLINE(S)
Rolling

THE WORK
Established in 1988, the National Association of College Broadcasters (NACB) is a nonprofit organization dedicated to promoting the exchange of ideas, programming, and information among students involved in electronic media. Among the programs NACB sponsors are a national conference, The National College Radio Awards, The National College TV Programming Awards, and U Network, a student-produced, affiliate-run satellite network for college television. Interns work in Production, Publications, and Advertising/Sales.

PERKS
Possible travel opportunities to trade shows, etc.; miscellaneous merchandise (t-shirts, coffee mugs, key chains, etc.); small, casual office environment.

FYI
NACB interns have gone on to jobs in television and film production, radio sales and advertising, and television-oriented magazines.

TO APPLY
Open to high school juniors and seniors, undergrads, and grads. International applicants eligible. Submit resume, cover letter, and writing samples.

Internship Coordinator
National Association of College Broadcasters
71 George Street
Providence, RI 02912-1824
E-mail: NACB@aol.com

In 1963, between his junior and senior years at Denison University in Ohio, **Michael Eisner** sampled the entertainment business as a page with NBC. Eisner liked it and went on to become the president of Paramount Pictures and, currently, the chairman and CEO of The Walt Disney Company.

NATIONAL ASSOCIATION FOR FEMALE EXECUTIVES
When a woman succeeds, a company succeeds.™

SELECTIVITY 🔍
Approximate applicant pool: 10; Interns accepted: 3

COMPENSATION $
None

LOCATION(S)
New York, NY

FIELD
Women's studies; Marketing

DURATION
10–12 weeks: Summer, Fall, Spring

DEADLINE(S)
Rolling

THE WORK
Established in 1972, the National Association for Female Executives (NAFE) is the largest organization of businesswomen in the country. Through education, training, skill development, and networking, NAFE has supported thousands of women with the resources necessary to achieve success in the business world. Interns work in Marketing, Association Management, Satellite Conferences, and Chapter Management, and Customer Services.

PERKS
Attendance welcome at industry meetings and seminars; small, close-knit office.

FYI
NAFE has over 150,000 members; the average member supervises approximately five people at work, has at least a four-year college degree, and has a personal income of $42,280.

TO APPLY
Open to undergrads, recent college grads, college grads of any age, and grad students. International applicants eligible. Submit resume and cover letter.

Internship Coordinator
MacDonald Communications
135 West 50th Street
New York, NY 10020
(212) 425–6100

| NATIONAL ASSOCIATION OF PROFESSIONAL SURPLUS LINES OFFICES (NAPSLO) | NATIONAL AUDUBON SOCIETY |

SELECTIVITY 🔍🔍🔍

Approximate applicant pool: 100; Interns accepted: 8–10

COMPENSATION 💲💲💲💲

Up to $400/week; housing stipend; round-trip travel

LOCATION(S)

Chicago, IL; Denver, CO; Los Angeles, San Francisco, CA; New York, NY; Dallas, TX; Atlanta, GA; and various other metropolitan areas

FIELD

Insurance, Business, Finance

DURATION

9 weeks: Summer

DEADLINE(S)

February 1

THE WORK

NAPSLO is a trade association founded in 1975 to represent the surplus lines industry and the wholesale insurance marketing system. Its member firms write surplus lines insurance: insurance that covers "hard-to-place" risks (e.g. aviation, product liability, earthquake, amusement parks) that are not written by the standard insurance markets. Interns will be placed with member firms across the nation. Interns work with a Surplus Lines company member for five weeks and broker/agent member for four weeks. The program is designed so that interns experience all aspects of the business.

FYI

Up to four interns are selected to attend the NAPSLO Annual Convention in the fall (expenses paid); and, one intern will receive an additional internship in London (expenses paid plus stipend) the following summer. Many interns find permanent positions in the surplus lines industry due to their internship experience and networking opportunities.

TO APPLY

Fax or email request for application or apply online at www.napslo.org. Applicants must also submit a resume, two letters of recommendation, and a college transcript.

Jessica Free
Summer Internship Program
NAPSLO
6405 North Cosby Avenue, #201
Kansas City, MO 64151
(816) 741-3910
(816) 741-5409 (Fax)
E-mail: internship@napslo.org
www.napslo.org

SELECTIVITY 🔍🔍🔍🔍🔍

Approximate applicant pool: 100–200; Interns accepted: 8 (Summer), 3–8 (Fall, Winter)

COMPENSATION 💲

N/A

LOCATION(S)

Washington, DC and other cities (see Appendix)

FIELD

Environmental policy

DURATION

12 weeks: Summer; 12–20 weeks: Fall, Winter

DEADLINE(S)

Summer: April 1; Fall: August 1; Winter: January 1

THE WORK

Founded in 1905 as an organization to protect the lives of birds, the National Audubon Society now also defends wetlands, prairies, and ancient forests. Managing more than 100 sanctuaries nationwide, the society works to restore natural ecosystems "for the benefit of humanity and the Earth's biological diversity." The Government Affairs Internship Program exposes students to environmental policymaking, grassroots organizing, and lobbying in one of the following departments: Wetlands, Population, Agriculture, Refuges and Forests, and Ocean and Wildlife.

PERKS

Lobbying on Capitol Hill (DC); weekly softball games; intern alley; "free and easy" atmosphere.

FYI

Audubon established its internship program in the early 1980s . . . Interns occupy two rows of cubicles known in the office as "intern alley" . . . Part of an office culture that's "free and easy," interns frequently wear jeans and are even known to traipse around the office barefoot.

TO APPLY

Open to college juniors and seniors, recent grads, and grad students. International applicants eligible. Submit cover letter indicating an environmental issue of interest and a writing sample of fewer than ten pages on any subject.

National Audubon Society
1901 Pennsylvania Avenue, NW
Suite 1100
Washington, DC 20006
(202) 861–2242

EXCLUSIVE INTERVIEW WITH JANICE VOSS

While studying engineering science at Purdue University, Janice Voss spent five semesters as a co-op intern at NASA Johnson Space Center. From 1975, when she graduated from Purdue, until 1990, when she was selected by NASA to become an astronaut, Dr. Voss earned her M.S. in electrical engineering and Ph.D. in aeronautics/astronautics from MIT, taught navigation to Shuttle crew members at Johnson Space Center, and worked on satellites at Orbital Sciences Corporation. Dr. Voss has flown two Space Shuttle missions, logging over 400 hours in space. At left, she manipulates a video camera while in Spacehab-3 on board the Space Shuttle Discovery.

The Internship Informants: What made you want to become an astronaut?
Voss: I got interested in becoming an astronaut in sixth grade. I was at the library one day, and I picked up a child science-fiction book called *A Wrinkle in Time* by Madeleine L'Engle. I have always been a voracious reader, and it looked interesting. Well, it got me hooked on space programs.

The Internship Informants: So when you got to Purdue, you knew that space was in your future.
Voss: I was interested in working at NASA Johnson Space Center as soon as I arrived at Purdue . . . I was taking a class called "Freshmen Engineering," a program Purdue runs to orient freshmen to all its engineering departments. There was a lecture every week, and one week, the Cooperative Engineering organization came in. They talked about how you can get work experience while you study, and I was sitting there thinking, "My parents told me I probably shouldn't distract myself this way." Then [the lecturers] said, "One of the companies on our list is NASA Johnson Space Center." And immediately, my ears perked up. So I went and talked to them, and sure enough, there was an opening for that January.

The Internship Informants: What did you do during your internships?
Voss: I spent all five semesters in the Shuttle Avionics Integration Lab, or SAIL for short, which writes computer programs to study various aspects of the Shuttle program. It's a simulation facility, and my first assignment was to create a demo for lab visitors so that they could "fly" the shuttle—in essence, to build a shuttle model and connect it to a joystick device.

The Internship Informants: Wasn't this project extremely difficult?
Voss: I had a lot of reference manuals to turn to. I went to the library, checked out books, and found the equations I needed. Of course, I could also ask people. They also gave me a drawing of what they wanted so I could easily trace the points. It was a great learning experience because this was 1973 . . . It was my first exposure to computers.

The Internship Informants: So did your assignments become progressively more complex?
Voss: Yes. In fact, the last two work periods I did back to back, and because I was going to be there for a long stretch of time, they gave me a real program that was going into mainstream software being used at Johnson . . . They wanted to create a Shuttle simulator that's physically the same size as the real Shuttle—an exact model of the electrical set-up of the Shuttle. Then they would take this model and embed it in a computer model that feeds in data to simulate flying . . . I worked on the computer model that the Shuttle model was embedded in, writing real code in assembly language to help make it all work.

The Internship Informants: Did you meet any astronauts as an intern and if so, did any influence you to become an astronaut.
Voss: I did meet a few. I wrote to one of them, Story Musgrave, and he asked me to just come over and chat, which I did . . . I actually had many opportunities to speak to astronauts because they do public appearances all the time, and whenever there was one within fifty miles, I went to it . . . But the largest influence was just seeing how the space program works for real, which helped convince me that I was doing the right thing. The co-op experience confirmed that my dream could become a reality, that I wasn't fooling myself with a false perception of what NASA was all about, and because I worked in engineering, I was able to see that I would rather be in operations [i.e., the actual running of the Shuttle during the missions].

The Internship Informants: The first women astronauts didn't appear at NASA until 1978. Were you concerned during your internship that becoming an astronaut might be an elusive goal?
Voss: It never crossed my mind—probably because my parents were so supportive . . . What concerned me actually was that, because all of the astronauts up to this time were former pilots, I would need flying experience.

The Internship Informants: Thankfully, NASA added scientists to the Shuttle crews. What have been some of your highlights as a "mission specialist"?
Voss: The Astronaut Office always talks about the sight of the earth and the thunder of launch as being exciting, and they are, but I heard all of that before so I was ready for it. What really impressed me was the whole team—the astronauts, the ground crew at Johnson, the crew at Kennedy— coming together to pull off this tremendously complex launch.

The Internship Informants: Was there any specific event up in space that made an impression?

Voss: On my first flight, we rendezvoused with a spacecraft called EURECA. My assignment was to be back in a laboratory module called Spacehab, where I operated a laser device for measuring speed and distance as we got close [to EURECA] and fed that information back to the flight deck to help the pilots fly the approach . . . I had a headset on so I could hear the crew, but I felt very alone, as if I were in my own little spacecraft. As I sat in Spacehab, I watched EURECA out the overhead window as it slowly approached. It came in right over my window . . . Everyone on the Shuttle and on the ground worked together to pull it off, and it just went perfect.

The Internship Informants: Do you have any advice for today's twentysomethings seeking internships?

Voss: I usually repeat what I learned from Astronaut Randy Schweikart, who said something like, "Find what you do well and enjoy doing because then excellence will become a game and not a chore. Then you will be very competitive." The value of internships is that they give you a very well-organized way to find out what you like to do . . . Then once you've found your niche, companies will want to hire you.

NATIONAL BASKETBALL ASSOCIATION

SELECTIVITY ⬛⬛⬛⬛
Approximate applicant pool: 150; Interns accepted: 8–12

COMPENSATION $ $ $
$350/week stipend

LOCATION(S)
New York, NY; Secaucus, NJ

FIELD
Sports management

DURATION
12 weeks, Summer

DEADLINE(S)
December 15

THE WORK
At the time that the NBA was founded in 1946 as the Basketball Association of America, it had only eleven teams. Today, the organization has grown to include twenty-nine teams, and worldwide retail sales of NBA-licensed merchandise have reached $2 billion annually, a testament to the NBA's drawing power. Interns work in NBA Entertainment in Secaucus, NJ and in the following New York departments: Broadcasting, Consumer Products, Team Services (Marketing), and Public Relations. Interns work in NBA Entertainment in Secaucus, NJ and in the following New York departments: Global Merchandising, Marketing Partnerships, Team Operations, Internet Services, e-Commerce, and Public Relations.

PERKS
Lunches with NBA execs; travel opportunities; basketball mania.

FYI
The current internship was organized in 1988. Interns have the opportunity to attend WNBA games, meet with NBA executives, and gain exposure to the entire business. At the end of the summer, the coordinator puts together a going-away party for the interns.

TO APPLY
Open to undergraduates at any level. International applicants are eligible. Submit resume and cover letter outlining relevant background and indicating the department to which you are applying.

> National Basketball Association
> Intern Coordinator
> 645 Fifth Avenue
> New York, NY 10022
> (212) 407-8000

NATIONAL BROADCASTING COMPANY

SELECTIVITY ⬛
Approximate applicant pool: 1,000; Interns accepted: approximately 350

COMPENSATION $
None

LOCATION(S)
Burbank, CA; New York, NY

FIELD
Television; Sports

DURATION
8–14 weeks: Summer, Fall, Spring

DEADLINE(S)
Summer: April 15; Fall: September 15; Spring: December 15

THE WORK
Founded in 1926, the National Broadcasting Company (NBC) was the first permanent broadcasting network in the United States. From its early days in radio, NBC has evolved into one of America's primary television networks, airing top-rated shows like *ER, Frasier, Friends, Saturday Night Live, Law and Order,* and *The Tonight Show With Jay Leno.* NBC also owns and operates CNBC and, in a joint venture with Microsoft, owns 50 percent of and operates MSNBC. Interns work in News (including all of NBC's news shows like *The Today Show, Nightly News,* and *Dateline*), Sports, Marketing, Corporate Communications, Press & Publicity, Guest Relations, Sales, MIS, Talent Relations, WNBC-TV (New York), Daytime Casting (Burbank), Saturday Morning and Family Programming (Burbank).

PERKS
Vary with assignments (e.g., luncheons, t-shirts).

FYI
Interning at NBC's corporate headquarters significantly improves one's chances of being accepted to the 12-month NBC Page Program for college graduates (approximate pay: $10/hour). Pages conduct tours of NBC facilities, seat audiences at show tapings, and do administrative and production assistant work in various departments.

TO APPLY
Open to college sophomores (NY only), juniors, and seniors. Must receive academic credit. International applicants eligible. Submit resume, cover letter, and a letter on school letterhead acknowledging that you will receive course credit.

Internship Coordinator
NBC
30 Rockefeller Plaza, Rm. 1678 E
New York, NY 10112
(212) 664-5255

Internship Coordinator
NBC
3000 West Alameda Avenue, Room C-281
Burbank, CA 91523
(818) 840-4444

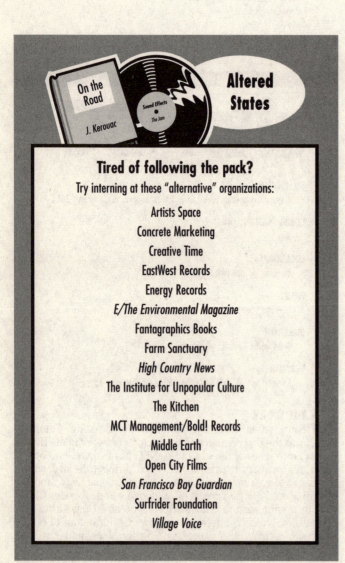

Tired of following the pack?

Try interning at these "alternative" organizations:

Artists Space

Concrete Marketing

Creative Time

EastWest Records

Energy Records

E/The Environmental Magazine

Fantagraphics Books

Farm Sanctuary

High Country News

The Institute for Unpopular Culture

The Kitchen

MCT Management/Bold! Records

Middle Earth

Open City Films

San Francisco Bay Guardian

Surfrider Foundation

Village Voice

NATIONAL CENTER FOR FAIR AND OPEN TESTING

SELECTIVITY
Approximate applicant pool: 50; Interns accepted: 1–2

COMPENSATION
$100/week

LOCATION(S)
Cambridge, MA

FIELD
Education

DURATION
10 weeks: Summer

DEADLINE(S)
March 20

THE WORK
Founded in 1985, the National Center for Fair and Open Testing (FairTest) is a public education and advocacy organization working to end the overuse and misuse of standardized testing. Focusing on testing for university admissions, public school, and employment, FairTest strives to ensure that evaluation methods are open, accurate, accountable, and educationally sound. Interns work as research assistants.

PERKS
Attendance welcome at occasional meetings with educational organizations; casual, comfortable office.

FYI
Past projects have found interns creating a bibliography of resources on bilingual assessment, preparing a report on test coaching, and researching challenges to tests and test misuses . . . The internship program was established in memory of Denise Carty-Bennia, a co-founder of FairTest, and "a dynamic and tireless advocate for the cause of testing reform."

TO APPLY
Open to undergrads, recent college grads, college grads of any age, and grad students. International applicants eligible. Submit resume, cover letter, and (optional) writing samples.

Internship Coordinator
National Center for Fair and Opening Testing
342 Broadway
Cambridge, MA 02139
(617) 864-4810
(617) 497-2224 (Fax)
E-mail: fairtest@aol.com
www.fairtest.org

NATIONAL CENTER FOR TOXICOLOGICAL RESEARCH

See Oak Ridge Institute for Science and Education

SELECTIVITY ⌕ ⌕ ⌕ ⌕ ⌕

Approximate applicant pool: 200; Interns accepted: 8

COMPENSATION $ $ $

$1,500/month; round-trip travel; health insurance; approx. $200 to cover health club membership

LOCATION(S)

Overland Park, KS; NCAA member conferences (see FYI)

FIELD

Sports

DURATION

1 year: Starting in September

DEADLINE(S)

February 15

THE WORK
Founded in 1906, the National Collegiate Athletic Association (NCAA) is a membership organization of over 900 colleges and universities competing in twenty-one different sports in three divisions (I, II, and III). In addition to administering seventy-nine national championships, NCAA formats rules-of-play for NCAA sports, adopts and enforces standards of eligibliity, and studies all phases of intercollegiate athletics, from graduation rates of athletes to revenues generated by college sports. NCAA places interns in Membership Services, Public Affairs (including Broadcast Services and *The NCAA News*), Championships, Finance & Business Services, and Education Services (including Sports Sciences and Youth programs).

PERKS
Mentors; weekly seminars on networking, resume writing, interviewing, etc.; at least two opportunities to travel nationwide on NCAA business; attendance welcome at NCAA seminars (e.g., Franklin Planning, NCAA rules, time management).

FYI
Started in 1989, the internship program has seen over 80 percent of former interns land jobs in athletics . . . Most of the NCAA's Division I conferences (e.g., Pac-10, Big East, Southwestern) also hire an intern or two (often recent college grads) for three months to one year, usually during the summer or starting in August; call NCAA for list of conference contacts . . . The NCAA Foundation offers eight $3,000 scholarships to college juniors who are campus-sports journalists or are majoring in journalism with a career interest in sports journalism; call NCAA for application (deadline: December 15).

TO APPLY
Open to minority and female college grads. Write for application.

Ethnic Minority and Women's Internship Programs
NCAA
6201 College Boulevard
Overland Park, KS 66211-2422
(913) 339-1906

SELECTIVITY ⌕ ⌕ ⌕ ⌕

Approximate applicant pool: 75; Interns accepted: 2–5

COMPENSATION $ $ $

$240/week; health insurance

LOCATION(S)

Washington, DC

FIELD

Philanthropy

DURATION

6 months–1 year: ongoing

DEADLINE(S)

Rolling

THE WORK
Founded in 1976, the National Committee for Responsive Philanthropy (NCRP) is a nonprofit organization dedicated to making philanthropy more responsive to socially, economically, and politically disenfranchised people. NCRP's work includes studies on profit-making corporations, research on community foundations' responsiveness to the disenfranchised, and a variety of conferences and lobbying initiatives. Interns assist staff in conducting research, seeking media coverage, fundraising, and coordinating conferences.

PERKS
Ideal "training ground for future activists"; attendance welcome at local conferences.

FYI
In existence since 1976, the internship program leads to full-time employment at NCRP for approximately 25 percent of interns . . . Writes the internship coordinator: "From international policy to a community soup kitchen, [former] interns have become activists, applying the skills and experience they learned as dreaded [watchdogs] of NCRP to every aspect of the struggle for social justice."

TO APPLY
Open to recent college grads. International applicants eligible. Submit resume and cover letter.

Internship Coordinator
National Committee for Responsive Philanthropy
2001 S Street NW, Suite 620
Washington, DC 20009
(202) 387-9177
(202) 332-5084 (Fax)

SELECTIVITY 🔍 🔍

Approximate applicant pool: 850; Interns accepted: 200–250

COMPENSATION 💲 💲 💲 💲

$500–$750/week and round-trip travel during internship; tuition, fees, and $6,000–$12,000 annual stipend

LOCATION(S)

All 50 states

FIELD

Engineering; Science

DURATION

12 weeks: Summer

DEADLINE(S)

December 1

 THE WORK

Organized in 1976, the National Consortium for Graduate Degrees for Minorities in Engineering and Science (GEM) is a non-profit partnership between universities and employers that seeks to increase the number of minorities pursuing engineering, science, math, and computer science graduate degrees. Under the auspices of three GEM programs (MS Engineering Fellowship, PhD Engineering Fellowship, and PhD Science Fellowship), Fellows alternate academic-year study with summer internships. Fellowships are applicable at seventy-five universities, and internships are available at over eighty Fortune 500 companies and government labs, including Argonne National Laboratory, BF Goodrich, Boeing, Chrysler, Dow Chemical, Eastman Kodak, GTE, IBM, Intel, Kraft General Foods, Merck, NASA, Schlumberger, 3M, and Xerox.

PERKS

Vary with placement.

FYI

GEM sells over a dozen publications and videos offering career advice, financial aid listings, and strategies on how to succeed in grad school and in an internship, including *Your Internship Is as Good as You Make It: A Practical Guide to Student Internships* ($2).

TO APPLY

Open to college juniors, seniors, and grads. Must be American Indian, African American, Mexican American, Puerto Rican, or other Hispanic American. Write for application.

GEM Central Office
P.O. Box 537
Notre Dame, Indiana 46556
(219) 631-7771
(219) 287-1486 (Fax)
E-mail: gem.1@nd.eds
www.hd.edu/~gem

SELECTIVITY 🔍 🔍 🔍 🔍 🔍

Approximate applicant pool: 400; Interns accepted: 12

COMPENSATION 💲 💲 💲

$360/week

LOCATION(S)

Washington, DC

FIELD

Government; Humanities (see THE WORK)

DURATION

11 weeks: Summer

DEADLINE(S)

March 3

THE WORK

Established in 1965, the National Endowment for the Humanities (NEH) is the Federal grant-making agency that funds US scholarship, research, education, and public programs in the humanities (e.g., history, philosophy, languages, linguistics, literature, archaeology, jurisprudence, art history, ethics, and comparative religions). Interns are placed in six divisions: Challenge Grants, Federal-State Partnership, Research and Education, Public Programs, and Preservation and Access.

PERKS

Mentors; weekly brown-bag luncheons featuring occasional speakers; field trips to National Archives, Holocaust Museum, etc.

FYI

NEH avoids funding projects that attempt to persuade an audience to a particular political, philosophical, religious, or ideological viewpoint, or ones involving the creative arts (e.g., music, dance, painting, sculpture, poetry), in the domain of the National Endowment for the Arts.

TO APPLY

Open to college juniors. Write for application.

Deputy Chairman
Summer Fellows Program
National Endowment for the Humanities
1100 Pennsylvania Avenue NW
Washington, DC 20506
(202) 606-8623
www.neh.gov/html/forms.html

SELECTIVITY 🔍🔍🔍🔍🔍
Approximate applicant pool: 1,000; Interns accepted: 6–10

COMPENSATION ⑤
$300/week

LOCATION(S)
New York, NY

FIELD
Sports management

DURATION
10–12 weeks: Summer

DEADLINE(S)
April 1

THE WORK
Since 1920, the National Football League (NFL) has represented football's greatest—from coaches such as Vince Lombardi, Tom Landry, Don Shula, and Bill Walsh to players like Bronko Nagurski, Dick Butkus, Joe Namath, Red Grange, Lawrence Taylor, and Joe Montana. Battling on the gridiron, the league's thirty teams attract 14 million spectators every fall, and its Super Bowl, nearly 1 billion television viewers worldwide. Interns work in Public Relations, Officiating, Finance, Legal, and Treasury.

PERKS
Intern lunch with Commissioner Paul Tagliabue; a few free tickets to NFL games; full-day visit of Jets training camp; free NFL t-shirts and hats.

FYI
Since the NFL's founding, students with a penchant for pigskin have worked at the league's headquarters . . . Former interns include the NFL's Executive Vice President of League and Football Development, Director of International Public Affairs and Senior Vice President of Communications and Government Affairs.

TO APPLY
Open to undergrads and grad students. International applicants eligible. Submit resume and cover letter.

Internship Coordinator
National Football League
280 Park Avenue
New York, NY 10017
(212) 450–2000

SELECTIVITY 🔍🔍
Approximate applicant pool: 10; Interns accepted: 2

COMPENSATION ⑤
None

LOCATION(S)
Washington, DC

FIELD
Education

DURATION
12 weeks: Summer

DEADLINE(S)
February 15

THE WORK
The National Foundation for the Improvement of Education (NFIE) is a nonprofit foundation created in 1969 by the National Education Association (NEA) and is dedicated to improving the quality of public education in the United States. NFIE works to ensure that America's teachers are able to meet the challenge of preparing students for the twenty-first century. A Change of Course, NFIE's initiative currently underway, has selected demonstration sites where strategies are being tested to make professional development a normal part of teachers' daily jobs. NFIE will provide the sites with grants and technical assistance to strengthen these efforts and extend their scope to reach larger numbers of students, teachers, and schools. NFIE also gives grants to provide educators with professional development opportunities that subsequently enable them to provide collegial leadership in their schools or institutions and to improve teaching and learning. Interns will assist in supporting the day-to-day operations of the Programs staff of the foundation. They may also assist staff in research and analysis as well as public relations and fundraising.

PERKS
Attendance welcome at staff meetings; free educational publications; informal office atmosphere.

FYI
Says the internship coordinator: "Our interns get to do substantive research on the professional development of teachers. We also encourage them to pick the brains of the staff so that they can further their background in educational issues as much as possible."

TO APPLY
Open to college juniors and seniors, and grads. International applicants eligible. Submit resume and cover letter.

Internship Coordinator
National Foundation for the Improvement of Education
1201 Sixteenth Street NW, Suite 416
Washington, DC 20036
(202) 822-7708
(202) 822-7779 (Fax)

See United States Department of Commerce

NATIONAL INSTITUTES OF HEALTH

SELECTIVITY
Approximate applicant pool: 3,000; Interns accepted: 800

COMPENSATION
Undergrads,$1,100–$1,400/month; grad students, $1,600–$2,000/month

LOCATION(S)
Bethesda, MD

FIELD
Biomedical research

DURATION
8-week minimum: Summer

DEADLINE(S)
February 15

THE WORK
From its humble beginnings as a one-person, one-laboratory operation in 1887 to its current status as the world's largest biomedical research institution, the NIH has made critical breakthroughs. It was the first to unravel the genetic code, to develop a vaccine against rubella, and to launch human gene therapy. Interns research within sixteen institutes including Aging; Alcohol Abuse and Alcoholism; Allergy and Infectious Diseases; Arthritis and Musculoskeletal and Skin Diseases; Child Health and Human Development; Deafness and Other Communication Disorders; Dental Research; Diabetes and Digestive and Kidney Diseases; Eye, Heart, Lung, and Blood; Mental Health; and Neurological Disorders and Intramural Research, the Warren Grant Magnuson Clinical Center, the Division of Computer Research and Technology, and the National Center for Research Resources.

PERKS
Seminars; cooperative atmosphere; athletic center.

FYI
In 1990 the NIH established the Office of Education to coordinate postdoctoral research and other educational programs, including a summer internship program . . . "You'd better read all the recent articles that your lab has published and ask lots of pertinent questions," advised one intern . . . Grant Falls Park, a favorite destination among hikers, canoers, and rock climbers, is near the NIH grounds.

TO APPLY
Open to high school students 16 years of age, undergrads, recent college grads, and grad students. International applicants eligible. Write for application.

Coordinator, NIH Summer
Internship Program
Office of Education
Building 10, Room 1C129
10 Center Drive, NSC 1158
Bethesda, MD 20892-1158
(301) 402-1907

Coordinator, Summer Research
Fellowship
Program for Medical and
Dental Students
Office of Education
Building 10, Room 1C129
10 Center Drive, NSC 1158
Bethesda, MD 20892-1158
(301) 402-1907

NATIONAL JOURNAL

SELECTIVITY
Approximate applicant pool: 400; Interns accepted: 3

COMPENSATION
$300/week

LOCATION(S)
Washington, DC

FIELD
Magazines

DURATION
5 months–1 year

DEADLINE(S)
Summer: March 15; Fall: July 15; Spring: November 15

THE WORK
Established in 1969, *National Journal* is a weekly magazine covering national politics and federal policy. The magazine features articles on members of Washington's community of lobbyists, political consultants, and journalists. Interns work in the Editorial Department.

PERKS
No busywork, only "research, reporting, and writing;" free copies of magazine.

FYI
Time magazine states that "*National Journal* makes sense out of government . . . Washington's shakers and movers, along with many of the shaken and the moved, read it scrupulously."

TO APPLY
Open to college seniors, recent college grads, college grads of any age, and grad students. International applicants eligible. Submit resume, cover letter, and six writing samples.

Internship Coordinator
National Journal
1501 M Street NW
Washington, DC 20036
(202) 739-8434

NATIONAL JOURNALISM CENTER

SELECTIVITY 🔍

Approximate applicant pool: 200; Interns accepted: 60–70

COMPENSATION 💲

$100/week

LOCATION(S)

Washington, DC

FIELD

Journalism

DURATION

12 weeks: Summer, Fall, Spring; 6 weeks: Winter

DEADLINE(S)

Summer: April 1; Fall: August 1; Spring: January 1

THE WORK
Established in 1977, the National Journalism Center places budding journalists in 12-week internships in Washington, DC. Interns spend the first six weeks at newspapers (e.g., *Northern Virginia Sun* and *Alexandria Gazette-Packet*), magazines (e.g., *Reader's Digest* and *Consumers' Research*), television and radio assignments are also available. Interns spend the remaining six weeks researching and writing an article on a topic suggested by NJC.

PERKS
Weekly seminars on journalism and the art of reporting; weekly seminars on topical issues (e.g., health care, the federal budget); occasional social events (e.g., softball games, trips to cultural sites).

FYI
In existence since 1977, the program counts among its alumni producers at CNN, seven journalists at Copley Newspapers, reporters with *The Washington Post*, and the chief editorial writer at *The Wall Street Journal*.

TO APPLY
Open to undergrads, recent college grads, college grads of any age, and grad students. International applicants eligible. Write for application.

> Internship Program
> National Journalism Center
> 800 Maryland Avenue NE
> Washington, DC 20002
> (202) 544-1333
> (202) 544-5368 (Fax)

NATIONAL MUSEUM OF AFRICAN ART

See Smithsonian Institution

NATIONAL MUSEUM OF AMERICAN ART

See Smithsonian Institution

NATIONAL MUSEUM OF AMERICAN HISTORY

See Smithsonian Institution

NATIONAL MUSEUM OF NATURAL HISTORY

See Smithsonian Institution

NATIONAL OCEANIC & ATMOSPHERIC ADMINISTRATION

See United States Department of Commerce

NATIONAL ORGANIZATION FOR WOMEN

SELECTIVITY 🔍🔍

Approximate applicant pool: 400; Interns accepted: 115–130

COMPENSATION 💲

None

LOCATION(S)

Washington, DC (HQ)

FIELD

Public polic; Field organizing; Accounting; Fundraising

DURATION

12–16 weeks: Summer, Fall

DEADLINE(S)

Summer: March 15; Fall: July 15; Winter or Spring: November 20

THE WORK
The National Organization for Women (NOW) was founded in 1966 by twenty-eight women. The largest feminist organization in the country, with over 500,000 contributing members, NOW strives to eliminate discrimination in all areas of life (e.g., citizenship, public service, employment, education, and reproduction) by lobbying legislators and sponsoring educational programs. In DC (75–90), interns and volunteers work in Political, Government Relations, Communications, International, Direct Mail/Marketing, Accounting, Field Organizing, and Special Projects.

PERKS
Weekly intern meetings with NOW staff and officers; trips to Capitol Hill hearings, including Intern Lobby Day (DC only); field trips exploring women's history.

FYI
NOW's political director and the press secretary for Representative Cynthia McKinney (D-GA) once served as interns in NOW's DC office.

TO APPLY
Open to high school juniors and seniors, high school grads, undergrads, recent college grads, college grads of any age, and grad students. International applicants eligible. Submit current resume and cover letter, and two letters of recommendation from professional reference. Write for application.

Intern/Volunteer Program Coordinator
National Organization for Women
733 15th Street NW
Second Floor
Washington, D.C. 20005
www.now.org/intern

National Organization for Women interns pose with Rep. Lynn Schenk (D-CA) at a NOW Press Conference on Violence Against Women.

NATIONAL PARK SERVICE

SELECTIVITY 🔍 🔍
Approximate applicant pool: 17,000; Interns accepted: 5,000

COMPENSATION 💲 💲 💲
$260–$350/week; free housing (a few positions)

LOCATION(S)
HQ in Washington, DC; regional offices in Atlanta, GA; Anchorage, AK; Boston, MA; Denver, CO; Omaha, NE; Philadelphia, PA; San Francisco, CA; Santa Fe, NM; Seattle, WA; centers in Denver, CO and Harpers Ferry, WV; over 350 parks in all 50 states, Guam, Puerto Rico, and Virgin Islands

FIELD
Park management

DURATION
12–16 weeks: Summer, Winter

DEADLINE(S)
Summer: January 15; Winter: July 15

THE WORK
Established in 1916 as a bureau of the US Department of the Interior, the National Park Service (NPS) is the Federal agency responsible for the preservation and management of America's natural, historical, and recreational areas. Parks under its jurisdiction include the Grand Canyon, Yellowstone, Death Valley, Joshua Tree, Everglades, Mesa Verde, the Statue of Liberty, Gettysburg Battlefield, Assateague Island, and Lake Mead. Under the auspices of the Seasonal Employment Program, interns (referred to as "seasonals") work as campground rangers, archaeologists, fee collectors, tour guides, naturalists, landscape architects, fire fighters, laborers, lifeguards, law enforcement rangers, carpenters, and historians.

PERKS
Park Service uniform; numerous opportunities for outdoor recreation.

FYI
Many NPS parks run independent internship programs (e.g., see separate entry for Cabrillo National Monument), placing interns in such areas as visitor services, interpretation, and administration. Contact parks of interest directly.

TO APPLY
Open to undergrads, recent college grads, college grads of any age, and grad students. Must be at least 18 years of age (21 for law enforcement positions). Write for "Seasonal Employment" brochure.

Seasonal Employment Unit, Room 2225
National Park Service
P.O. Box 37127
Washington, DC 20013-7127
(202) 208-5074

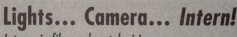

Lights... Camera... Intern!
Interns in film and on television:

In an episode of the tv sitcom *Taxi*, Alex Reeger (played by **Judd Hirsch**) attempts to realize a lifelong dream of working in the theater by serving as a gofer for two young, arrogant playwrights. To his frustration and Louie's delight, Alex ends up groveling in gruntwork, assigned such tasks as emptying garbage bins, washing a car, fetching coffee, and blowing air into a back cushion.

SELECTIVITY 🔍 🔍 🔍 🔍
Approximate applicant pool: 300; Interns accepted: 24

COMPENSATION $
None

LOCATION(S)
Washington, DC

FIELD
Law; Public policy; Women's issues; Employment; Health

DURATION
12–16 weeks: Summer, Fall, Spring

DEADLINE(S)
Fall and Spring: Rolling; Summer: March 1

THE WORK
Founded in 1971 as the Women's Legal Defense Fund, the National Partnership has grown from a small group of volunteers into one of the nation's most powerful and effective advocates for women and families. Working with business, government, unions, nonprofit organizations, and the media, the National Partnership is a voice for fairness, a source for solutions, and a force for change. The National Partnership offers internships to undergrads and grad students. The interns will be working in the fields of Work and Family, Workplace Fairness, Communications, Action Council and Membership, and aiding with the Annual Luncheon, the biggest fundraiser run by the National Partnership. Please visit the website at www.nationalpartnership.org for internship descriptions.

PERKS
Attendance welcome at WLDF news briefings and staff meetings; opportunity to attend congressional hearings.

FYI
Internship program was started in 1979 . . . Former interns include Harriet Harmon, a Member of British Parliament, and Neta Goldman, Director of the Association for Civil Rights in Israel.

TO APPLY
Open to undergrads, recent college grads, college grads of any age, grad students, and law students. International applicants eligible. Submit resume, cover letter, writing sample, transcript, and recommendations.

Volunteer Internship Coordinator
Women's Legal Defense Fund
1875 Connecticut Avenue NW, Suite 710
Washington, DC 20009
(202) 986-2600
(202) 986-2539 (Fax)
www.nationalpartnership.org

See Smithsonian Institution

SELECTIVITY 🔍 🔍 🔍
Approximate applicant pool: 200; Interns accepted: 20–30

COMPENSATION $ $
$5/hour stipend

LOCATION(S)
Washington, DC

FIELD
Radio

DURATION
8–12 weeks: Summer, Fall, Winter/Spring; 16–40 hours per week

DEADLINE(S)
Summer: March 30; Fall: August 15; Winter/Spring: December 15

THE WORK
Crackling to life in 1971, National Public Radio (NPR) is a radio network dedicated to providing its 14 million weekly listeners with lively news coverage and alternative cultural programming. NPR is out to prove that radio can be an exciting, provocative, and unpredictable source of information. Interns are placed either in a particular department—such as News, Cultural Programming, Promotion and Public Affairs, Development, Human Resources, Audience Research, Legal, Training, Marketing, Engineering and Operations, or Audio Engineering—or with one of NPR's programs—such as "Talk of the Nation."

PERKS
Creative environment; workshops and event lectures.

FYI
Sources say that the best position at NPR is with "All Things Considered." To many, the show is the "quintessential NPR experience" because it combines "informed journalism with a high degree of creativity . . . Dress is casual: "No one would blink if you wore cut-offs," according to one intern.

TO APPLY
Open to college juniors and seniors, and grad students. International applicants eligible. Write for application.

National Public Radio
Internship Coordinator
635 Massachusetts Avenue
Washington, DC 20001-3753
(202) 414-2909
(202) 414-3047 (Fax)

SELECTIVITY 🔍 🔍 🔍 🔍 🔍
Approximate applicant pool: 25; Interns accepted: 1

COMPENSATION 💲 💲 💲 💲
$400/week

LOCATION(S)
New York, NY

FIELD
Magazines

DURATION
12–14 weeks: Summer

DEADLINE(S)
December 1

THE WORK
Founded in 1955 by political commentator William F. Buckley, Jr., *National Review* is widely considered the nation's leading journal of conservative opinion. Covering national and international culture, economics, and politics, the biweekly magazine generates a paid circulation of over 250,000. The *Review's* intern works as editorial assistant, fact-checking, proofreading, as well as answering reader inquiries, and writing one paragraph in the Editorial section of the magazine.

PERKS
Attendance welcome at daily editorial meeting; attendance welcome at biweekly editorial luncheons.

FYI
The magazine's managing editor and senior editor got their starts at the *Review* as interns in 1969 and 1976, respectively . . . According to Pulitzer Prize-winning columnist George Will: "It is simply the case that *National Review* is the most consequential journal of opinion ever . . . It has changed first the ideas and then the politics and ultimately the policies of the most important nation the world has ever known."

TO APPLY
Open to college seniors and recent college grads (within 6 months of graduation). International applicants eligible. Submit resume and cover letter.

Summer Editorial Internship
c/o Managing Editor
National Review
150 East 35th Street
New York, NY 10016
(212) 679-7330

SELECTIVITY 🔍
Approximate applicant pool: 50; Interns accepted: 10

COMPENSATION 💲
Varies by department; some are $100/week

LOCATION(S)
Fairfax, VA

FIELD
Advocacy

DURATION
4–24 weeks, available on an ongoing basis

DEADLINE(S)
Rolling

THE WORK
The National Rifle Association (NRA) was created in 1871 to provide firearms training and encourage interest in the shooting sports. The organization has grown to include millions of members, drawing from every state in the union. Interns are placed in a number of departments and divisions: Institute for Legislative Action, Financial Services, Development, Recreational Shooting, General Counsel, Sales, Membership, Purchasing, Field Services, Security, Administrative Services, Community Services.

PERKS
Access to Association's gym; discounts at the NRA Café; discounts at the NRA Store.

FYI
The NRA is recognized by the U.S. Olympic Committee and the International Shooting Union as the National Governing Body for the shooting sports and oversees the US Olympic shooting effort.

TO APPLY
Open to college students, recent grads, college grads of any age, and grad students. International applicants eligible. Submit resume and cover letter.

Human Resources
National Rifle Association of America
11250 Waples Mill Road
Fairfax, VA 22030
(703) 267-1260
(703) 267-3938 (Fax)

NATIONAL SECURITY AGENCY

SELECTIVITY 🔍🔍🔍
Approximate applicant pool: 500; Interns accepted: 50

COMPENSATION 💲💲💲💲
All programs begin at approximately $500/week

LOCATION(S)
Fort Meade, MD

FIELD
Government; Defense

DURATION
SIP: 12 weeks, Summer; CEP: 52 weeks alternating between school and work schedule;
College Summer Emplyment Program (CSEP): 12 weeks during summer

DEADLINE(S)
CEP: Rolling; CSEP: November 15; Mathematics applications (SCEP and DSMP) must
be received by October 15th and must be accompanied by two letters of recommendation.

THE WORK
Established in 1952 as an agency of the US Department of
Defense (see separate entry), the National Security Agency (NSA)
is the Nation's cryptologic organization. It coordinates, directs,
and performs highly specialized activities to protect U.S. information systems and produce foreign intelligence information. A high
technology organization, NSA is on the frontiers of communications and data processing. It is also one of the most important centers of foreign language analysis and research within the
Government. The Agency offers programs such as the Co-op
Education Program (CEP), the Director's Summer Program (DSP),
a program specializing in mathematics, and the College Summer
Employment Program (CSEP), to college level students. These
programs provide students with an opportunity to work in the
areas of mathematics, engineering, and computer science. Since
the establishment of the CEP in 1952, NSA has experienced a high
success rate in offering full-time employment to Co-op students
who wished to work for the Agency after graduating from college.

PERKS
Mentors; access to NSA fitness center (approximate
$10/month); Co-op Association (arranges social activities and
tours of Federal agencies); affordable housing available
($200–$300/month); opportunity to take classes at NSA's National
Cryptological School.

FYI
All NSA interns must undergo a rigorous background investigation that includes a polygraph test . . . Since establishing CEP
in 1952, NSA has offered full-time employment to all Co-op interns
who have wished to work at the Agency after graduating from college . . . Fort Meade is located halfway between Baltimore and
Washington, DC.

TO APPLY
Applicants must be U.S. citizens. Applicants undergo a
comprehensive background investigation including a polygraph
examination. CEP: open to college freshman and sophomores. Co-
op applicants must be majoring in computer science, computer

engineering, or electrical engineering and have a minimum GPA of
3.0. CSEP: open to college juniors and seniors and grad students
in computer science, computer engineering, electrical engineering,
and mathematics. Minimum GPA for math majors: 3.5; all other
majors: 3.0. DSP: open to undergrad mathematics majors with a
minimum GPA of 3.5.

Department of Defense
9800 Savage Road
ATTN: S232 Co-op Education Program or Summer Intern Program
Fort Meade, MD 20755-6779
(800) 962-9398 (CEP)
(800) 669-0703 (CSEP, DSP)

NATIONAL SPACE SOCIETY

SELECTIVITY 🔍🔍🔍
Approximate applicant pool: 100; Interns accepted: 10–12

COMPENSATION 💲
None

LOCATION(S)
Washington, DC

FIELD
Advocacy management; Publications; Aerospace

DURATION
6 weeks: Summer, Fall, Spring

DEADLINE(S)
March 1

THE WORK
The National Space Society (NSS) is a nonprofit organization
promoting space exploration and colonization. NSS activities, which
are supported by 26,000 members in over seventy-five chapters worldwide, include publishing a bimonthly magazine *Ad Astra*, working
with Congress on the importance of space studies, and researching
and writing papers covering space science and the aerospace industry.
Interns work in Editorial, Political, Research, Association
Management, and Electronic Network (i.e., Internet services).

PERKS
Attendance welcome at annual conferences; invitations to
NSS events.

FYI
NSS's goals include a manned mission to Mars, another
manned mission to the moon, and a moon-based space station
capable of supporting human life indefinitely . . . *Ad Astra* means
"to the stars" in Latin . . . Individuals serving on NSS's various
boards include Buzz Aldrin, Hugh Downs, and Bob Hope.

TO APPLY
Open high school grads, undergrads, recent college grads,
college grads of any age, and grad students. International applicants eligible. Write for application.

Internship Coordinator
National Space Society
600 Pennsylvania Avenue SE
Washington, DC 20003
(202) 543-1900
(202) 546-4189 (Fax)

NATIONAL TECHNICAL INFORMATION SERVICE

See United States Department of Commerce

NATIONAL TELECOMMUNICATIONS & INFORMATION ADMINISTRATION

See United States Department of Commerce

NATIONAL TRUST FOR HISTORIC PRESERVATION

 National Trust for Historic Preservation

SELECTIVITY 🔍 🔍 🔍 🔍
Approximate applicant pool: 250; Interns accepted: 15–20

COMPENSATION 💲
None

LOCATION(S)
Washington, DC

FIELD
Architecture; Historic preservation; Law

DURATION
8 weeks: Summer

DEADLINE(S)
March 10

THE WORK
Chartered by Congress in 1949, the National Trust for Historic Preservation (NTHP) is a nonprofit organization committed to saving America's historic homes and to preserving and revitalizing the livability of communities nationwide. Owner of eighteen historic houses across the country, NTHP sponsors educational programs and technical workshops, advocates for the protection of historic sites, and publishes several magazines and books on preservation topics. Interns work in Public Policy, Law, Fundraising, Marketing, Publications, Public/Media Relations, Preservation Services, and National Conference Planning.

PERKS
Weekly seminars on NTHP, the preservation movement, and nonprofit management, etc.; free membership in NTHP; intern reception and staff picnic; tours of local historic sites.

FYI
The internship has been in existence since 1985 . . . Free membership in the NTHP gets interns a subscription to *Historic Preservation* and *Historic Preservation News*, a discount on books from Preservation Press, and free admission to most Trust properties.

TO APPLY
Open to college sophomores, juniors, and seniors, recent college grads, college grads of any age, and grad students. International applicants eligible. Submit resume and cover letter.

Internship Coordinator
National Trust for Historic Preservation
1785 Massachusetts Avenue, NW
Washington, DC 20036
(202) 673-4000
(202) 673-4038 (Fax)

NATIONAL WILDLIFE FEDERATION

SELECTIVITY 🔍 🔍 🔍 🔍 🔍
Approximate applicant pool: 300–400; Interns accepted: 10 (2–24week terms)

COMPENSATION 💲 💲
$275/week (includes some core benefits)

LOCATION(S)
Washington, DC

FIELD
Environmental policy

DURATION
24 weeks: January to June; July to December

DEADLINE(S)
January internship: September 15; July internship: March 15

THE WORK
The National Wildlife Federation, the nation's largest nonprofit conservation education organization, offers an internship program for college graduates and graduate students with an interest in environmental issues to work in Washington D.C. Much of an intern's time is spent researching environmental policy issues and covering congressional activity. Responsibilities may include attending congressional hearings, briefings, and seminars; drafting testimony to be presented by the Federation to congressional and executive panels; lobbying on environmental legislation. A small portion of an intern's time is spent on routine office work.

PERKS
Lobbying on Capitol Hill; brown-bags; environmentally conscious office.

FYI
Interns have been in NWF's program since 1980 . . . NWF is one of the few nonprofit environmental groups with a salaried internship program . . . As a group advocating conservation, NWF practices what it preaches. The environmentally conscious organi-

zation has done many things to cut down on use of materials, like using lights regulated by motion sensors.

TO APPLY
Open to grad students and college grads of any age. Submit resume, cover letter indicating areas of interest, names and telephone numbers of three to five academic or professional references, and a two- to four-page writing sample.

National Wildlife Federation
Resources Conservation Internship Program
1400 Sixteenth Street NW
Washington, DC 20036-2266
(202) 797-6800
(202) 797-6646
www.nfw.org

NATIONAL WOMEN'S HEALTH NETWORK

SELECTIVITY
Approximate applicant pool: 100; Interns accepted: 5 per semester/season

COMPENSATION $
Some weekly stipends available for fall and spring interns only

LOCATION(S)
Washington, DC

FIELD
Public policy; Health care; Women's issues

DURATION
12 weeks: Summer, Fall, Spring and Winter

DEADLINE(S)
Summer: March 15; All other times: Rolling

THE WORK
The only national public interest membership organization devoted solely to women and health, the National Women's Health Network (NWHN) was established in 1975 to give women a greater voice in the US health care system. NWHN researches and lobbies federal agencies on such issues as AIDS, reproductive rights, breast cancer, older women's health, and new contraceptive technologies. Interns work on federal health care projects, such as writing testimony for FDA hearings, and conduct research in response to written and telephone requests for information.

PERKS
Attendance welcome at staff meetings and staff lunches; attendance welcome at outside meetings (small coalitions, federal hearings, etc.).

FYI
The NWHN internship has been in existence for over 20 years.

TO APPLY
Open to undergrads, recent college grads, and grad students. International students eligible. Submit resume, cover letter, and writing samples.

Internship Coordinator
National Women's Health Network
514 10th Street NW
Suite 400
Washington, DC 20004
(202) 347-1140
(202) 347-1168
www.womenshealthnetwork.org

NATIONAL ZOO
See Smithsonian Institution

NATION'S BUSINESS
See United States Chamber of Commerce

THE NATURE CONSERVANCY

SELECTIVITY N/A
Approximate applicant pool: N/A; Interns accepted: 130–150

COMPENSATION
From $0–$12/hour and free housing for most positions on preserves

LOCATION(S)
Arlington, VA (HQ); 50 field and 8 regional offices and preserves in all 50 states

FIELD
Environment

DURATION
8 weeks–6 months: Summer and ongoing

DEADLINE(S)
Rolling

THE WORK
Founded in 1951, The Nature Conservancy (TNC) has over 1,000,000 members worldwide and owns and manages 9.3 million acres of land on 1,500 preserves. The organization is committed to preserving plants, animals, and natural communities that represent the biological diversity of the Earth. Interns work at headquarters in Botany, Fundraising, Communications, and Legal, in field offices in Stewardship, and as natural or environmental scientists on preserves nationwide.

PERKS
Careers-in-Conservation workshops (summer only in HQ only); brown-bag luncheons on international nature topics (HQ only); opportunity to network with ecologists.

FYI
TNC's strategy of buying lands to preserve them, rather than lobbying government to save them, is unique . . . Interns in preserve positions weed, monitor rare species, collect and analyze soil and groundwater, patrol for trespassers, clear trails, and prepare maps . . . Approximately 20 percent of interns are offered full-time positions.

TO APPLY
Open to undergrads, recent college grads, college grads of any age, and grad students (in biology, botany, etc.). Write for application directly to office of interest; write the Home Office for an address list and the pamphlet "Internships with The Nature Conservancy."

Internship Coordinator
The Nature Conservancy
Home Office
4245 N. Fairfax Dr. Suite 100
Arlington, VA 22203
(703) 841-5300
(703) 247-3721 (Weekly Employment Hotline)
(703) 841-1283
www.tnc.org/jobs (Click in "INTERNSHIPS")

NETWORK

SELECTIVITY 🔍

Approximate applicant pool: 20; Interns accepted: 3

COMPENSATION 💲

$140/week, some health benefits, daily transportation expense

LOCATION(S)

Washington, DC

FIELD

Public policy

DURATION

11 months: starts September

DEADLINE(S)

February 1

THE WORK

Founded in 1971, NETWORK is a nonprofit membership organization lobbying Congress to enact laws that provide economic justice for the poor, protect human rights at home and abroad, promote disarmament, and ensure world peace. A national Catholic social justice lobby, it focuses on the areas of housing, health care reform, welfare reform, the federal budget, and foreign policy. Interns and Associates assist lobbyists, monitor action on Captiol Hill, deliver NETWORK communications to Congressional offices, and communicate with NETWORK members.

PERKS

Attendance welcome at weekly legislative updates and strategy meetings; occasional lobbying experiences in Congressional offices.

FYI

The Internship program has been in existence since 1972.

TO APPLY

Open to recent college grads, college grads of any age, and grad students. International applicants eligible. Write for application.

Internship Coordinator
NETWORK
801 Pennsylvania Avenue SE, Suite 460
Washington, DC 20003
(202) 547-5556
(202) 547-5510 (Fax)
E-mail: network@networklobby.org
www.networklobby.org

NEW CANAAN COUNTRY SCHOOL

SELECTIVITY 🔍 🔍 🔍

Approximate applicant pool: 150; Interns accepted: 16

COMPENSATION 💲 💲 💲

$345/week; housing provided at $140/month

LOCATION(S)

New Canaan, CT

FIELD

Education

DURATION

10 months: starts September

DEADLINE(S)

March 15

THE WORK

Founded in 1916, New Canaan Country School (NCCS) is a prestigious private day school with approximately 550 students in grades Pre-K-9. NCCS's Teaching Fellowship Program provides recent college grads with on-the-job training at the kindergarten to grade-six levels. Supervised by an experienced teacher, Fellows help teach in the classroom; they also tutor students, supervise athletics and other recreational endeavors, head lunch tables, and participate in faculty meetings.

PERKS

Seminars on teaching led by NCCS staff and outside specialists; tuition subsidization for second-year interns enrolled at graduate school; access to all campus facilities, including gymnasium and hockey rink.

FYI

The school is within 50 miles of New York City and New Haven, CT . . . The Teaching Fellowship Program has been running since 1966.

TO APPLY

Open to recent college grads, college grads of any age, and grad students. International applicants eligible. Submit resume, cover letter, transcript, and recommendations.

Teaching Fellowship Program
New Canaan Country School
P.O. Box 997
New Canaan, CT
(203) 972-0771
(203) 966-5924 (Fax)

EXCLUSIVE INTERVIEW WITH LINDA KOCH LORIMER

Linda Koch Lorimer is the Secretary of Yale University, one of three senior officers at the university. She formerly served as the President of Randolph-Macon Woman's College and the Associate Provost of Yale. She graduated with a JD from Yale Law School in 1977 and an AB from Hollins College in 1974.

The Internship Informants: Let's hear about your internship.
Lorimer: I had the marvelous experience of being at NBC News's Washington bureau in the month of January 1971. My college had an intersession between the first and second semester, where all students could have an internship. So there I was in Washington, and I had the opportunity to go into work every morning and be surrounded by Paul Duke and by Barbara Walters (people forget that at one time she was with NBC News). I would go out with film crews to follow breaking stories and come back and do some research, which on some nights would actually get incorporated into stories that went on the nightly news.

The Internship Informants: What was the most memorable aspect of your NBC internship?
Lorimer: Well, the highlight was a three-day stint in the White House in which a one-hour documentary was being done on life in the White House. It gave me an opportunity to consider a career in journalism.

The Internship Informants: Were your classmates doing internships during the intersession as well?
Lorimer: I went to Hollins College, a woman's college in Virginia. And they were very supportive of internships at that time. As a woman's college, there was an institutional commitment to letting women get a sampling of what they might do in the workforce.

The Internship Informants: In your job, you are constantly interacting with students, some of whom may mention internships they've done. What's your take on the role of internships today?
Lorimer: Internships offer a fabulous opportunity for students to supplement their formal education with insights about the world in which we live and indeed careers they may want to pursue. It's often as important to pursue an internship and find out you do not want to be in a particular career as it to confirm your eagerness to pursue that career. For instance, I've had many students of mine who thought they wanted to be doctors, but after an internship in the emergency room they realized they didn't want that; it's certainly better to decide about your career aspirations before you go off to medical school than after. Similarly, I thought I had an interest in a career in journalism, and as much as I enjoyed my time at NBC News, I decided that was not for me.

The Internship Informants: Are there things you learned as an intern that help you today?
Lorimer: The [NBC internship] is serving me well in my current position because one of the areas of the university for which I'm responsible is the public relations department. So I have a much greater insight when we are working on stories that will be carried on "60 Minutes" or that are picked up by the national press. Even though my internship was almost a quarter century ago, I learned how that form of journalism works.

The Internship Informants: Did the internship enlighten you in any other way?
Lorimer: It gave me an appreciation for journalism at the highest level, as opposed to a local radio station, where I had worked previously. And it gave me an opportunity to sample what it is like to be in the workforce, which is very different from the daily rhythm of student life.

The Internship Informants: Did you do any other internships?
Lorimer: I also had an internship on Capitol Hill in my local congressman's office. It gave me the opportunity to see how our nation's government worked. And to the extent that I currently have responsibilities for some governmental relations, that internship serves me well now.

SELECTIVITY 🔍🔍🔍
Approximate applicant pool: 100; Interns accepted: 15–20

COMPENSATION 💲
$25/week

LOCATION(S)
New York, NY

FIELD
Theater

DURATION
20 weeks: Summer, Fall, Spring

DEADLINE(S)
Rolling

THE WORK
Founded in 1949, New Dramatists develops new playwrights through readings, workshops, grants, scholarships, and exchanges with theaters. Called "the Fort Knox of playwriting talent" by alumnus and playwright John Patrick Shanley, New Dramatists has served such playwrights as Robert Anderson, Israel Horowitz, Alice Childress, Maria Irene Fornes, and Paula Vogel. Interns work in Literary Management, Stage Management/Casting, Development, and Public Relations/Special Events.

PERKS
Free tickets to all performances; "meet the major players in the NY theater community"; offices located in the heart of NY's theater district.

FYI
Says the internship coordinator: "The internship is not a gofer position. Interns are given important projects . . . Interns must have a HUGE interest in new plays. They also must be able to deal well with people, especially those with enlarged egos."

TO APPLY
Open to high school students, high school grads, undergrads, college grads, and grad students. International applicants eligible. Submit resume and cover letter. Application may be downloaded from the website.

Internship Coordinator
New Dramatists
424 West 44th Street
New York, NY 10036
(212) 757-6960
(212) 265-4738 (Fax)
www.newdramatists.org

> "Interns must be able to deal well with people, especially those with enlarged egos."
> —intern coordinator, New Dramatists

THE NEW REPUBLIC

SELECTIVITY 🔍🔍🔍🔍🔍
Approximate applicant pool: 200–300; Interns accepted: 3–6

COMPENSATION 💲💲💲
$300/week

LOCATION(S)
Washington, DC

FIELD
Magazine

DURATION
12 weeks: Summer; 9 months: academic year

DEADLINE(S)
Summer: March 1; Academic Year: March 1

THE WORK
A weekly journal of political and cultural opinion founded in 1914, *The New Republic* is arguably the premier publication of its kind, with Charles Lane as editor. Interns work in the Editorial department.

PERKS
Luncheons with major Washington figures; small, "razor-sharp" editorial staff.

FYI
According to the internship coordinator, "while interns spend some time reading unsolicited manuscripts, checking facts, and running errands, they also write short articles, book reviews, and editorials."

TO APPLY
Open to college seniors, recent college grads, college grads of any age, and grad students. International applicants eligible. Submit resume, cover letter, two recommendations, and three to five writing samples.

Summer Intern Program or Academic Year Program
The New Republic
1220 19th Street NW, Suite 600
Washington, DC 20036
(202) 331-7494
(202) 331-0275 (Fax)

SELECTIVITY 🔍🔍🔍🔍🔍
Approximate applicant pool: 200; Interns accepted: 7

COMPENSATION 💲
Minimum wage

LOCATION(S)
Arlington, VA (HQ); Denver, CO

FIELD
Broadcast journalism

DURATION
6 months: Summer (starting end of July), Winter (starting February)

DEADLINE(S)
Summer: June 1; Winter: December 1

THE WORK

Established in 1975, *The NewsHour with Jim Lehrer* is broadcast on PBS every weekday evening, and attracts some 4.5 million viewers each night and over 12 million one or more times a week. According to a Times Mirror/Gallup Poll, the *NewsHour* is the "most believed" news program on American television. It has won seven National News Emmys and five Peabody Broadcast Awards. Desk Assistants in VA rotate shifts every six weeks. Desk Assistants in CO work part-time, researching stories.

PERKS

Orientation and tour; occasional opportunities to accompany reporters on shoots; brown-bag luncheons with staff members.

FYI

Depending on the shift, Desk Assistants answer producers' reporters', and correspondents' phones, run errands, handle guest transportation, respond to viewer mail, undertake research for stories, monitor news wires and help out in the tape library. Recent college grads are hired twice a year to work as entry-level Desk Assistants for six months . . . As of 1995, the NewsHour was no longer co-anchored by Robert MacNeil.

TO APPLY

Open to college seniors and grad students. International applicants eligible. Write for application (VA) or submit resume and cover letter (CO).

Desk Assistant Coordinator
The Newshour with Jim Lehrer
3620 27th Street South
Arlington, VA 22206
(703) 998-2150

Internship Coordinator
The Newshour with Jim Lehrer
2400 N. Syracuse Street
Denver, CO 80202
(303) 388-9100

NEW STAGE THEATRE

SELECTIVITY 🔍🔍🔍
Approximate applicant pool: 50–75; Interns accepted: 11

COMPENSATION 💲
$155/week and health insurance available

LOCATION(S)
Jackson, MS; acting interns visit other cities in MS

FIELD
Theater

DURATION
9 months: starts August

DEADLINE(S)
April 1

THE WORK

Founded in 1965, New Stage Theatre (NST) is Mississippi's only professional nonprofit theater, producing five mainstage shows during its regular season. Called "a center of the burgeoning American regional theater movement" by *The New York Times*, NST performs the classics, contemporary American theater, and new plays. Five Technical Interns work in Scenic Carpentry, Props/Sound/Lighting, and Scenic Painting/Carpentry; six Acting Interns are enlisted in the Acting Intern Company, which performs three different Arts-in-Education shows throughout the state of Mississippi.

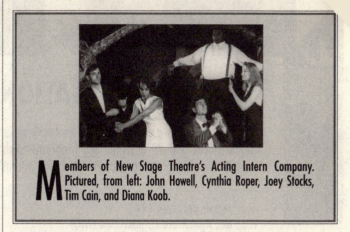

Members of New Stage Theatre's Acting Intern Company. Pictured, from left: John Howell, Cynthia Roper, Joey Stocks, Tim Cain, and Diana Koob.

PERKS

Each intern is salaried; attendance welcome at educational classes (Improvisation, Creative Drama, etc.); acting interns may earn points towards membership in Actor's Equity Association.

FYI

In existence since 1988, the internship program hires approximately 40 percent of interns for permanent employment . . . During their internship, Acting Interns visit approximately fifty towns throughout Mississippi.

TO APPLY

Open to undergrads, grads, and grad students. International applicants eligible. Submit resume, cover letter, recommendations, videotape of two monologues or arrange a personal audition (for Acting Interns), or arrange phone interview (for Technical Interns).

Internship Coordinator
New Stage Theatre
P.O. Box 4792
Jackson, MS 39296-4792
(601) 948-3533
(601) 948-3538 (Fax)

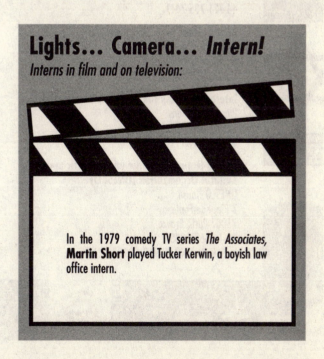

Lights... Camera... *Intern!*

Interns in film and on television:

In the 1979 comedy TV series *The Associates*, **Martin Short** played Tucker Kerwin, a boyish law office intern.

UNITED NATIONS INTERNSHIPS

The United Nations is organized into two headquarters locations—New York and Geneva—as well as 6 organizations and 29 agencies and programs, such as UNICEF, UNESCO, UNDP, IMF, and WHO. Each organization has its own procedures for hiring interns and must be contacted separately.

SPECIALIZED AGENCIES (14)

Food and Agriculture Organization (FAO)
Via delle Terme di Caracalla
00100 Rome, Italy
39-6-52-251

International Civil Aviation Organization (ICAO)
Place de l'Aviation Internationale
1000 Sherbrooke Street West
Montreal, Quebec H3A 2R2 Canada
(514) 285-8219

International Fund for Agricultural Development (IFAD)
Via del Serafico 107
00142 Rome, Italy
39-6-52-591

International Labor Organization (ILO)
4 Route des Morillons
CH-1211 Geneva 22, Switzerland
41-22-730-5111
(see separate entry in this book)

International Maritime Organization (IMO)
4 Albert Embankment
London, SE1 7SR United Kingdom
44-721-735-7611

International Monetary Fund (IMF)
700 19th Street, NW
Washington, DC 20431
(202) 623-7000

International Telecommunication Union (ITU)
Place des Nations
1211 Geneva 20, Switzerland
41-22-730-5111

United Nations Educational, Scientific and Cultural Organization (UNESCO)
UNESCO House
7 Place de Fontenoy
75007 Paris, France
33-14-568-1000
in New York: (212) 963-5995

United Nations Industrial Development Organization (UNIDO)
P.O. Box 300
Vienna International Centre
A-1400 Vienna, Austria
43-1-211-310

Universal Postal Union (UPU)
Union Postale Universelle
Weltpoststrasse 4
Berne, Switzerland
41-31-422-211

World Bank
1818 H Street, NW
Washington, DC 20433
(202) 477-1234
Note: The World Bank's internship program has been suspended indefinitely

World Health Organization (WHO)
20 Avenue Appia
1211 Geneva 27, Switzerland
41-22-791-2111

World Intellectual Property Organization (WIPO)
34 Chemin des Colombettes
CH-1211 Geneva 20, Switzerland
41-22-730-9111

World Meteorological Organization (WMO)
41, Avenue Giuseppe-Motta
Geneva, Switzerland
41-22-730-8111

SEPARATE AGENCIES (2)

World Trade Organization (WTO)
Centre William Rappard
154 Rue de Lausanne
1211 Geneva 21, Switzerland
41-22-739-5111
Note: This agency is the former GATT

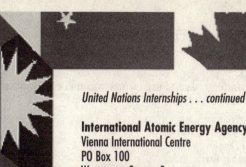

United Nations Internships . . . continued

International Atomic Energy Agency (IAEA)
Vienna International Centre
PO Box 100
Wargramer Strasse 5
A-1400 Vienna, Austria
43-1-23-600

PROGRAMS (13)
International Research and Training Institute for the Advancement of Women (INSTRAW)
P.O. Box 21747
Santo Domingo, Dominican Republic
500-809-685-2111
in New York: (212) 963-5684

Office of the High Commissioner for Refugees (UNHCR)
Centre William Rappard
154 Rue de Lausanne
1202 Geneva, Switzerland
41-22-739-8111
in New York: (212) 963-0032
in Washington, DC: (800) 220-1115

United Nations Children's Fund (UNICEF)
Three United Nations Plaza
New York, NY 10017
(212) 326-7000

UN Conference on Trade and Development (UNCTAD)
Palais de Nations, 8-14, Avenue de la Paix
CH-1211, Geneva 10, Switzerland
41-22-907-1234
in New York: (212) 963-6902

UN Development Fund for Women (UNIFEM)
304 E. 45th Street, 6th Floor
New York, NY 10017
(212) 906-6453

United Nations Development Programme (UNDP)
One United Nations Plaza
New York, NY 10017
(212) 906-5328

UN Environment Programme (UNEP)
P.O. Box 30552
Nairobi, Kenya
254-2-333-930
in New York: (212) 963-8093

UN Fund for Population Activities (UNFPA)
220 East 42nd Street, 19th Floor
New York, NY 10017
(212) 297-5000

UN Institute for Training and Research (UNITAR)
Palais de Nations
CH-1211, Geneva 10, Switzerland
41-22-798-5850

UN Relief and Works Agency for Palestine Refugees in the Near East (UNRWA)
Vienna International Centre
P.O. Box 500
A1400 Vienna, Austria
43-1-211-310
in New York: (212) 963-2255

UN University (UNU)
53-70, Jingumae 5-Chome
Shibuya-ku
Tokyo 150, Japan
81-3-3499-2811
in New York: (212) 963-6346

World Food Council (WFC)
Via delle Terme di Caracalla
00100 Rome, Italy
39-6-52-251
in New York: (212) 963-6036

World Food Programme (WFP)
Via Cristoforo Colombo 426
00145 Rome, Italy
39-6-57-971
in New York: (212) 963-8364

UN ORGANS (6)
International Court of Justice
Peace Palace
The Hague
2517 KJ The Netherlands
31-70-302-2323

Note: The other five UN organs—**Security Council, Economic and Social Council, Trusteeship Council, Secretariat, and General Assembly**—are located at United Nations headquarters and don't offer internships.
(please see United Nations entry for more information)

NEW YORK CITY GOVERNMENT

See Urban Fellows/Government Scholars Programs

NEW YORK KNICKS

See Madison Square Garden

NEW YORK PRESBYTERIAN HOSPITAL WESTCHESTER DIVISION

SELECTIVITY 🔍
Approximate applicant pool: 200; Interns accepted: 40–50

COMPENSATION Ⓢ
None

LOCATION(S)
White Plains, NY

FIELD
Heatlh care

DURATION
8 weeks: Summer

DEADLINE(S)
March 15

THE WORK
Established in 1894, The New York Presbyterian Hospital, Westchester Division, is the oldest psychiatric institution in New York State and the second oldest in the nation. The medical center's Pre-Career Practicum assigns participants to the following departments: Nursing, Therapeutic Activities, Social Services, Marketing, Psychology, and Research.

PERKS
Access to the hospital's swimming pool, tennis courts, nine-hole golf course, and medical library.

> The acclaimed documentary maker **Peter Davis** ushered in his career in 1958 as a copy boy at *The New York Times Magazine*. Ten years later he co-wrote the award-winning television documentary *Hunger in America* and then went on to write the Academy award–winning *Hearts and Minds* as well as the six-part television documentary *Middletown*.

FYI
All participants must provide their medical history prior to the start date of the program.

TO APPLY
Open to undergrads and grads. International applicants eligible. Write for application.

Pre-Career Practicum
The New York Presbyterian Hospital
Westchester Division
21 Bloomingdale Road
White Plains, NY 10605
(914) 682-6909 (Fax)

NEW YORK RANGERS

See Madison Square Garden

NEW YORK SHAKESPEARE FESTIVAL / PUBLIC THEATER

SELECTIVITY 🔍🔍🔍
Approximate applicant pool: 100–150; Interns accepted: 25

COMPENSATION Ⓢ
$62.50/week

LOCATION(S)
New York, NY

FIELD
Performing arts

DURATION
12 weeks; Sumer, Fall, Spring

DEADLINE(S)
Rolling

THE WORK
Since 1954, the Public Theater/NYSF has staged a rich variety of theatrical productions. In addition to running its Shakespeare Marathon, the Public Theater/NYSF has presented award-winning productions such as *A Chorus Line*, *Hair*, *The Pirates of Penzance*, *Twilight: Los Angeles, 1992*; and *Bring in Da' Noise, Bring in Da'Funk*. Departments hiring interns include Marketing, Community Affairs, Press, Producer's Office, Production, General Management, Development, and Casting.

PERKS
Access to productions, workshops, readings, and panel discussions at theater; invitations to social events.

FYI
Former interns have found permanent employment at the Public Theater/NYSF while others have gone on to jobs at Broadway and Off-Broadway productions (e.g., one became an assistant to the director of *The Merry Wives of Windsor*, another assisted the director of *Richard II* and another directed his own play).

Open to high school students, undergrads, recent college grads, college grads of any age, and grad students. International applicants eligible. Submit resume and cover letter.

Internship Coordinator
Public Theater/NYSF
425 Lafayette Street
New York, NY 10003
(212) 539–8659
(212) 539–8505 (Fax)

NEW YORK STATE BAR ASSOCIATION

SELECTIVITY 🔍🔍🔍🔍🔍

Approximate applicant pool: 30; Interns accepted: 1

COMPENSATION $ $

$280/week

LOCATION(S)

Albany, NY

FIELD

Public relations

DURATION

10 weeks: Summer

DEADLINE(S)

April 1

THE WORK

Dating back to 1876, the New York State Bar Association (NYSBA) is the oldest and largest voluntary state bar organization in the nation. With a membership of over 68,000 lawyers, NYSBA promotes legislation to simplify and update court procedures, encourages lawyers to provide pro bono legal services to the poor, and runs a variety of educational programs for the public. Interns work in the Media Services & Public Affairs department, where they create press releases, news articles, brochures, and other print or broadcast materials.

PERKS

Occasional travel to New York City to meet with outside public relations counsel; sleek offices with historical exhibits and galleries, a lounge, and a small research library.

FYI

The internship coordinator stresses that the internship program is only for students interested in public relations, not "for those who want to go to law school." Says a former intern: "I actually did stuff other than the usual intern activities like organizing files and coffee making. All the releases I worked on had a purpose other than being sent to the circular file."

TO APPLY

Open to college juniors and seniors. International applicants eligible. Submit resume, cover letter, and writing samples.

Bradley G. Carr
New York State Bar Association
One Elk Street
Albany, NY 12207
(518) 463-4276 (Fax)
E-mail: bcarr@nysba.org

NEW YORK STATE THEATRE INSTITUTE

SELECTIVITY 🔍

Approximate applicant pool: 50; Interns accepted: 20 per semester

COMPENSATION $

Fee: $250/semester; work study opportunities, limited scholarships available

LOCATION(S)

Troy, NY

FIELD

Performing arts

DURATION

1 or 2 semesters: Summer, Fall, Spring

DEADLINE(S)

Rolling

THE WORK

Located on the campus of Russell Sage College in the capital district region of New York State, the New York State Theatre Institute is a professional theater company whose schedule includes performing in New York City each year. Functioning as auxiliary staff members, interns rotate through the institute's departments, including Administration, Box Office, Costumes, Education, Electrics, Properties, Public Relations, and Scene Shop.

PERKS

Interns audition for possible peformance with the company productions; classes and workshops in acting, movement, voice, technical theater, arts management, and education; orientation and mentor program; complimentary tickets to every production; possible travel on tour with an institute production.

Interns and a teacher from the NYS Theatre Institute in the Institute's rehearsal room.

Says the intern coordinator: "We feel a strong accountability to the marketplace for our students. We are not training students to wait tables, and are committed to networking on behalf of our interns." . . . Alumni of the program, established in 1976, include performers on television and Broadway and in regional theaters and soap operas . . . Interns are sometimes cast in Institute productions.

TO APPLY
Open to high school seniors, high school grads, undergrads, recent college grads, college grads of any age, and grad students. International applicants eligible. Write for application.

Intern Director
New York State Theatre Institute
155 River Street
Troy, NY 12181-0028
(518) 274-3573
(518) 274-3815 (Fax)
E-mail: nysti@capitol.net
www.nysti.org

THE NEW YORK TIMES

SELECTIVITY
Approximate applicant pool: 400; Interns accepted: 8

COMPENSATION
$700/week; round-trip travel; $75/week housing allowance (housing available at New York University)

LOCATION(S)
New York, NY

FIELD
Newspapers

DURATION
10 weeks: Summer

DEADLINE(S)
November 15

THE WORK
Founded in 1851, *The New York Times* is one of the few daily newspapers that is a true American institution, covering international and national news as well as arts, business, education, fashion, health, science, and sports. Recently printing its 50,000th issue, *The Times* posts a paid nationwide circulation of 1.2 million copies on weekdays and 1.8 million on Sundays. Under the auspices of the paper's Summer Internship Program, interns work in Reporting (writing stories, some of which are published, for assigned sections of the paper including City Weekly/Metro, Science, or Culture), Copy Editing (editing stories), Design (rotating among art directors to learn how art is produced for the paper), Graphics (creating informational charts, diagrams, and graphs), and Photography (shooting photos for every section of the newspaper).

PERKS
Mentors; seminars featuring bureau chiefs, correspondents, columnists, and Pulitzer Prize–winning journalists: breakfasts/luncheons with reporters and editors.

FYI
At the end of the summer, at least one Reporting intern could be selected to serve a six-month internship. Working as staff reporters, six-month interns who impress the editors are hired as "intermediate reporters," *The Times* entry-level reporter position. *The New York Times* and its staff have won more prestigious journalism awards, including seventy-nine Pulitzers, than any other newspaper in the world.

TO APPLY
Open to college juniors, seniors, and grad students (for Graphics, Photo, and Design) and to seniors and grad students (for Reporting). Must have completed at least one internship at a daily newspaper. Submit resume, cover letter, eight to ten clips (for Reporting), portfolio (for Photography), and samples of graphic design work (for Graphics).

Sheila Rule
Summer Internship Program
The New York Times
229 West 43rd Street
New York, NY 10036
(212) 556-4143

NEWSDAY/NEW YORK NEWSDAY

SELECTIVITY
Approximate applicant pool: 700–800; Interns accepted: 42

COMPENSATION
$510/week

LOCATION(S)
Washington, DC; Long Island and Queens, NY

FIELD
Newspaper

DURATION
10 weeks: Summer

DEADLINE(S)
January 31; Fall: May 31; Spring: October 30

THE WORK
Winner of ten Pulitzer Prizes, *Newsday/New York Newsday*, a Times-Mirror newspaper, is the nation's fifth largest daily, with a circulation of over 700,000 and an editorial staff of over 700. Intern positions include Reporter (covering spot news and sports and writing features), Copy Editor (editing daily stories, features, and sports), Photographer, Artist (creating informational graphics, layout, and design), and Editorial Librarian.

PERKS
Experienced journalists as mentors; summer seminars on issues in journalism; free copies of newspaper.

FYI
The internship coordinator writes: "We think that this program, which has been in operation for more than 20 years and considered one of the best in the country, provides valuable opportunities, particularly for minority students ". . . The paper also offers 15–20 intern positions in fall and spring for New York–area students; these Academic Interns work as Reporters two days per week and receive $25/day plus expenses.

TO APPLY

Open to college sophomores, juniors, and seniors, as well as grad students. Must have car and valid driver's license. Must receive academic credit for fall and spring positions. International applicants eligible. Write for application.

Joyce Brown
Mgr. Editorial Staff
Development Newsday
235 Pine Lawn Raod
Melville, NY 11747-4250

NEWSWEEK

SELECTIVITY 🔍🔍🔍🔍🔍
Approximate applicant pool: 450; Interns accepted: 10–12

COMPENSATION 💲💲💲💲💲
$540/week

LOCATION(S)
New York, NY

FIELD
Magazines

DURATION
13 weeks: Summer

DEADLINE(S)
Early January

THE WORK

Founded in 1933 and acquired by The Washington Post Company in 1961, *Newsweek* is a weekly news magazine covering national and international affairs, business, society, science/technology, and arts. It boasts a worldwide circulation of over 4 million. Interns work in Editorial Research, where they research, fact-check, and report stories. In addition, the Photo Department hires two interns for the summer and the Communications Department has an opening for one intern interested in public relations.

PERKS

Meetings/luncheons with editors, including the editor-in-chief; tours of departments; free copies of magazine.

FYI

Newsweek has been running the program since the early 1960s . . . Typically, at least one intern every summer is retained for full-time work.

TO APPLY

Open to college seniors, college grads of any age, and grad students. International applicants eligible. Submit resume, cover letter stating reasons for applying and professional aspirations, and five published clips, and name and phone number of two references.

Abigail Kuflik, Deputy Chief of Correspondents
Newsweek
251 West 57th Street
New York, NY 10019-1894
(212) 445-5416

NICK BOLLETTIERI TENNIS ACADEMY

See International Management Group

NIGHTLINE

SELECTIVITY 🔍🔍🔍🔍🔍
Approximate applicant pool: 200/semester; Interns accepted: 4–5/semester
Post graduate internship selectivity: 600 : 1

COMPENSATION 💲
None; Post graduate internship compensation: salaried position

LOCATION(S)
Washington, DC

FIELD
Television news; Broadcast journalism

DURATION
12 weeks (flexible): Summer, Spring, Fall and Winter; Part time (3–4 days/week), full time (5 days/week)

DEADLINE(S)
Summer: March 15; Fall: July 1; Spring: November 15
Post graduate internship duration: 1 year (July 15–July 15)

THE WORK

Evolving in 1979 from the ABC News special broadcasts, "The Iran Crisis: America Held Hostage," "Nightline" has become an American institution. Broadcast each weekday evening from 11:35 p.m. to midnight, the show covers the major news stories through field correspondents and live interviews.

PERKS

Supportive staff; possible luncheon; transportation stipend; weekly speakers.

FYI

While "Nightline" provides little in the way of hands-on experience, it has much to offer in other areas. Says an intern: "The potential for networking is phenomenal at 'Nightline.' If you make a good effort and earn people's respect, they'll be there with valuable job recommendations later." . . . Interns report that the night shift is the key time to be at "Nightline." "Nightline" now offers a Post graduate internship open to recently graduated seniors.

TO APPLY

Open to college juniors and seniors. Must receive academic credit. International applicants eligible. Post graduate internship open to recently graduated seniors. Write or e-mail for internship applications to niteline@abc.com..

Nightline
Intern Coordinator
1717 DeSales Street NW, 3rd Floor
Washington, DC 20036
(202) 222-7000
E-mail: niteline@abc.com

SELECTIVITY 🔍🔍🔍🔍🔍
Approximate applicant pool: 1,000+; Interns accepted: 40+

COMPENSATION 💲💲💲
$1,000 living stipend; travel reimbursement; competitive salary

LOCATION(S)
Beaverton, OR

FIELD
Athletic shoes; Apparel; Accessories

DURATION
10 weeks; June–August

DEADLINE(S)
Mid-January

THE WORK
Bill Bowerman and Phil Knight joined forces in 1964, and together they parlayed a basement-based sneaker company into the world's first sports and fitness company to surpass $6.5 billion in annual total revenues. Their effort has made the name NIKE synonymous with the best aspects of athletics—vigorous competition, effective teamwork, and uncompromising performance. Internships are available in the following divisions: Sports Marketing, Information Technology, Finance, Apparel, Research, Design & Development, Retail, Customer Service, Sales, Human Resources, Legal, Marketing Communications, Equipment, Product Marketing, Logistics, Contract Manufacturing and Public Affairs.

PERKS
Awesome campus; immense gym; orientation; weekly speakers; career fair; employee store.

FYI
NIKE employees do not work at a complex, corporate headquarters, or industrial park; they work at the "NIKE World Campus" . . . For after-hours revelry, the place to go is the Boston Deli, a Cheers-style bar on the NIKE campus . . . Interns can shop at the employee store, which sells footwear, apparel, and accessories at or below cost.

TO APPLY
Open to college sophomores, juniors, seniors and graduate students. Call the toll-free NIKE intern hotline for application information, or see our web page.

Nike
Internship Program
One Bowerman Drive
Beaverton, OR 97005
(800) 890-6453
www.nikebiz.com

See PGA Tour

SELECTIVITY 🔍🔍🔍🔍
Approximate applicant pool: 150; Interns accepted: 3–8

COMPENSATION 💲💲💲
$100–$200/week; free housing and board

LOCATION(S)
Norfolk, CT

FIELD
Chamber music

DURATION
10 weeks: Summer

DEADLINE(S)
April 1

THE WORK
Established in 1941, the Norfolk Chamber Music Festival (NCMF) is an internationally known program providing training in, and performance of, the highest caliber chamber music. Sponsored by the Yale Summer School of Music, NCMF features concerts by faculty, guest artists, and students. Interns work in Box Office, Production, Marketing, and General Administration.

PERKS
Free tickets to all performances; attendance welcome at various music seminars; access to theater, library, dining hall, laundry room, and art gallery; recreational options include swimming at Toby Pond, hiking at Haystack Mountain, and frequent games of softball.

FYI
Describing its idyllic setting, the NCMF writes: "The lush gardens, gentle streams, and spacious meadows that inspired musicians and listeners of the past still delight."

TO APPLY
Open to college juniors and seniors, recent college grads, college grads of any age, and grad students. International applicants eligible. Submit resume, cover letter, and recommendations.

Internship Coordinator
Norfolk Chamber Music Festival
Box 208246
New Haven, CT 06520-8246
(203) 432-1966
(203) 432-2136 (Fax)
E-mail: norfolk@yale.edu
www.yale.edu/norfolk

north carolina botanical garden

NORTH CAROLINA BOTANICAL GARDEN

SELECTIVITY
Approximate applicant pool: 30; Interns accepted: 3

COMPENSATION
$300/week

LOCATION(S)
Chapel Hill, NC

FIELD
Horticulture; Botany; Conservation; Public garden education; Horticultural therapy

DURATION
Spring to Fall (April–October)

DEADLINE(S)
February 14

THE WORK
Established in 1960 as a division of The University of North Carolina at Chapel Hill, the North Carolina Botanical Garden (NCBG) is a regional center for research, conservation, and interpretation of plants. Occupying nearly 600 acres, NCBG comprises an arboretum, native plant displays, an herb garden, and a biological reserve. Working as gardeners, interns tend to native and exotic plants, keep records, learn propagation techniques, work with volunteers, and assist visitors.

PERKS
Trip to "Landscaping with Native Plants" conference at Western Carolina University; attendance welcome at NCBG public programs.

FYI
Says the internship coordinator: "This is a fairly small garden, which makes for a cozy, family type of atmosphere." NCBG has a particularly extensive collection of plants native to the southeastern United States, including a nationally prominent carnivorous plant display.

TO APPLY
Open to high school grads, undergrads, recent college grads, college grads of any age, and grad students. International applicants eligible. Write for application.

Internship Coordinator
North Carolina Botanical Garden
3375 Totten Center
University of North Carolina
Chapel Hill, NC 27599-3375
(919) 962-0522
(919) 962-3531 (Fax)

NORTH CASCADES INSTITUTE

SELECTIVITY
Approximate applicant pool: 50; Interns accepted: 20

COMPENSATION
Free room and board with some programs

LOCATION(S)
Sedro Woolley, WA

FIELD
Education; Environment; Recreation

DURATION
9–10 weeks: Summer, Fall, Spring

DEADLINE(S)
Summer: March 1; Fall: June 1; Spring: February 1

THE WORK
Founded in 1986, North Cascades Institute (NCI) is a nonprofit educational organization providing field-based environmental education to children and adults. At sites throughout the North Cascades ecosystem, it runs field seminars, teacher-training programs, watershed education programs, and outdoor school programs. Assigned to an NCI program or camp, interns assist with teaching, create educational materials, edit course proposals and newsletters, and participate in fundraising.

PERKS
Training in natural history, environmental education teaching methods, first aid, etc.; eligible for field seminar scholarships; spectacular natural scenery.

FYI
NCI's natural classroom comprises "a land of lush green forests, deep river valleys, rich marine shorelines, rugged mountains, and arid deserts."

TO APPLY
Open to undergrads, recent college grads, college grads of any age, and grad students. International applicants eligible. Submit resume, cover letter, and three references, as well as NCI's internship form. The form is available by contacting the institute at any of the following coordinates:

Internship Coordinator
North Cascades Institute
2105 Highway 20
Sedro Woolley, WA 98284–9394
(360) 856-5700 x209
(360) 856-1934 (Fax)
E-mail: nci@ncascades.org
www.ncascades.org/ncil

> Interns at the North Cascades Institute enjoy "a land of lush green forests, deep river valleys, rich marine shorelines, rugged mountains, and arid deserts."

SELECTIVITY 🔍 🔍 🔍
Approximate applicant pool: 200; Interns accepted: 35

COMPENSATION 💲 💲 💲 💲
$2,000/6 weeks; free room and board

LOCATION(S)
Northfield, MA

FIELD
Education

DURATION
6 weeks: Summer

DEADLINE(S)
February 21

THE WORK
Founded in 1879, Northfield Mount Hermon School (NMH) is a private boarding school located on the Connecticut River in Massachusetts, just south of the Vermont and New Hampshire state lines. The NMH Summer School offers a variety of classes to 400 junior and senior high school students. Assigned to a master teacher, the Summer School's Teaching Interns assist in planning and teaching a course; they also lead recreational activities and help supervise dormitories.

PERKS
Housing includes laundry service as well as linens and towels; access to all campus facilities; one weekend off; lovely rural campus.

FYI
The Teaching Intern Program has been running since 1964 . . . NMH is about an hour and a half drive north of Hartford, CT and two hours west of Boston . . . Says a former Teaching Intern: "Bring a fan. Bring your sense of humor and strong work ethic . . . This was an intense, learning, challenging work experience."

TO APPLY
Open to current college juniors and seniors, recent college grads, and grad students. International applicants eligible. Write for application.

Teaching Intern Program
Northfield Mount Hermon Summer School
206 Main Street
Northfield, MA 01360
(413) 498-3290
(413) 498-3112 (Fax)
E-mail: summer_school@nmhschool.org

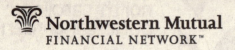

SELECTIVITY 🔍 🔍 🔍 🔍 🔍
Approx. applicant pool: 20,000; Interns accepted: 950–1,000

COMPENSATION 💲 💲 💲 💲
Commission basis; interns earn an average of $8–$12/hour; top ten interns average $26,214; leading intern earned $121,611

LOCATION(S)
350+ offices in all 50 states

FIELD
Life insurance; Financial services

DURATION
One semester–2 years
Summer: full time; School year: part time

DEADLINE(S)
Rolling

THE WORK
Founded in 1857, the Northwestern Mutual Financial Network is the fifth largest life insurance company in the United States, with $86 billion in assets and more than 7,000 agents based in over 350 offices across the country. The duties of a Northwestern Mutual intern are precisely those of their professional counterparts: Zeroing in on markets, finding and nurturing relationships with clients and achieving sales.

PERKS
Weekly classes in life insurance and financial planning; entrepreneurial spirit; annual meeting/party; College Awards Show.

FYI
In 1999 *Sales and Marketing Management* magazine ranked Northwest Mutual as "number one in the life insurance industry" in the country. Northwestern Mutual's internship program officially began in 1967, though they've recruited college students since the early 1930s.

TO APPLY
Open to undergraduates and graduate students. International applicants eligible. Submit resume and cover letter to:

E-mail: resume@northwesternmutual.com
www.northwesternmutual.com/sales

SELECTIVITY 🔍 🔍 🔍 🔍 🔍

Approximate applicant pool: 300; Interns accepted: 3–4

COMPENSATION 💲 💲

$150/week undergrad, grad students; $200/week for law students

LOCATION(S)

Washington, DC–Capitol Hill

FIELD

Women's issues; Legal; Legislative policy

DURATION

10–12 weeks: Summer, Fall, Spring; full time preferred

DEADLINE(S)

Summer: March 1, Fall: July 1, Spring: October 1

THE WORK

Established in 1970, the NOW Legal Defense and Education Fund (NOW LDEF) is a legal organization autonomous from the National Organization for Women (see separate entry). Seeking to define the agenda of the women's rights movement and bring women's issues to the public's attention, the Washington, D.C. office of NOW LDEF supports national legislation on issues including violence against women, child care, reproductive rights, and economic security for low-income women. Interns do both legal and policy-based work.

PERKS

Attending hearings on Capitol Hill, learning about the legislative process, and working with leading grassroots and national coalition groups.

FYI

Former NLDEF Legal interns include Catherine Weiss and Sarah Mandelbaum, legal directors of ACLU's Reproductive Freedom and Women's Rights Projects, respectively.

TO APPLY

Internships in DC are open to college juniors, seniors, graduate students, recent graduates, and law students. International applicants studying in the U.S. are eligible. Submit resume, cover letter, short writing sample, and reference to:

Pat Reuss, Senior Policy Analyst
NOW Legal Defense and Education Fund
119 Constitution Ave. NE
Washington, DC 20002
(202) 544-4470
(202) 546-8605 (Fax)
preuss@nowldefdc.org

SELECTIVITY 🔍 🔍

Approximate applicant pool: varies; Interns accepted: varies

COMPENSATION 💲 💲 💲

$200–$400/week for undergrads; $350–$550/week for grad students; round-trip travel; free housing (a few programs)

LOCATION(S)

Jefferson, AR; Orlando, FL; Atlanta, GA; Aberdeen Proving Ground, MD; Pittsburgh, PA; Aiken, SC; Oak Ridge, TN; Newport News, VA; Washington, DC; and any accredited US college or university (some graduate fellowship programs)

FIELD

Science; Engineering research

DURATION

4 weeks–4 years: Summer, Fall, Winter, Spring

DEADLINE(S)

Vary (see ORISE brochure)

THE WORK

Funded primarily by the US Department of Energy (see separate entry), the Oak Ridge Institute for Science and Education (ORISE), is a consortium of 86 research facilities and universities—among them the Oak Ridge National Laboratory (TN), the Pittsburgh Energy Technology Center, the Naval Air Warfare Center Training Systems Division (FL), the Bureau of Engraving and Printing (DC), and Savannah River Ecology Laboratory (SC). Under the auspices of internship and fellowship programs (some for minorities only), students participate in research projects, investigating such fields as materials science, nuclear waste management systems, engineering, architecture, lasers, computer science, low-energy physics, math, fossil energy, meteorology, environmental sciences, medicine, social science, and environmental and patent law.

FYI

Several ORISE (pronounced OH-rise) programs provide college and graduate school scholarships covering tuition, fees, and books.

TO APPLY

Open to undergrads and grad students (including second-year law students). Write for ORISE's brochure.

Education and Training Division, MS 36
Oak Ridge Institute for Science and Education
P.O. Box 117
Oak Ridge, TN 37831-0117
www.orau.gov/orise/resgd.htm

OAK RIDGE NATIONAL LABORATORY

See Oak Ridge Institute for Science and Education

OCTEL COMMUNICATIONS

SELECTIVITY
Approximate applicant pool: 600; Interns accepted: 20–30

COMPENSATION
$480–$640/week for undergrads; $720–$1,000/week for grad students

LOCATION(S)
Milpitas, CA

FIELD
Telecommunications

DURATION
10–12 weeks: Summer

DEADLINE(S)
May 15

THE WORK
Founded in 1982, Octel Communications is one of the world's top providers of voice information processing technology, with over $400 million in annual sales. Servicing clients that range from small businesses to multinational firms, Octel's voice-mail hardware and software allow users to send and receive voice-mail as well as receive, store, and forward faxes within one facility or among hundreds of locations. Customers include all seven of the Regional Bell Operating Companies and 70 percent of the Fortune 100, including General Electric, Hewlett-Packard, US WEST, McDonald's, New York Life, Prudential, and Amoco. Departments accepting interns include Manufacturing, Engineering, Finance, Marketing, Sales, Human Resources, and Public Relations.

PERKS
Brown-bag luncheons with executives; access to Octel fitness facility; planned social activities (e.g., ice cream social, picnics).

FYI
Launched in 1990, Octel's internship program leads to permanent employment for approximately 50 percent of interns . . . To date, Octel has sold and installed more than 35,000 voice-mail systems to over 20,000 customers worldwide . . . Octel is also developing voice-integrated E-mail (i.e., a product that translates E-mail messages into voice messages and vice versa).

TO APPLY
Open to college seniors and grad students. Must be majoring in a technical field or business. International applicants eligible. Submit resume and cover letter.

Internship Coordinator
Octel Communications
1001 Murphy Ranch Road
Milpitas, CA 95035
(408) 324-6847

The late Lebanese film director **Maroun Bagdadi**, whose films include *Little Wars* and *Hors La Vie*, which won a jury prize at the Cannes Film Festival in 1991, once worked as an intern with Francis Ford Coppola's studio American Zoetrope.

OFFICE OF THE CORPORATION COUNSEL FOR THE DISTRICT OF COLUMBIA

SELECTIVITY
Approximate applicant pool: 400; Interns accepted: 150

COMPENSATION
None

LOCATION(S)
Washington, DC

FIELD
Law: civil, criminal, family, mental health, personnel, finance, appellate, legislation, finance, economic development

DURATION
8–12 weeks (flexible)

DEADLINE(S)
Rolling

THE WORK
The Office of the Corporation Counsel (OCC) is one of the largest law offices in the District of Columbia. It is responsible for "all law business of the District of Columbia," according to the D.C. Code. Interns may work in different legal areas involving civil, family, mental health, personnel, finance, appellate, legislation or criminal law. Interns work directly with attorneys and assist them in all aspects of litigation and/or research of heavy caseloads.

PERKS
Attendance at court and related proceedings; speaker's series.

FYI
The OCC internship program has been around for 19 years. Numerous interns have gone on to law school and have been admitted to the Bar in various jurisdictions. Summer internships are generally full time, though part-time positions are available throughout the year.

TO APPLY
Open to college undergrads, college grads, and law and grad students. Submit resume, cover letter specifying terms of the internship and area of interest, writing sample of no more than ten pages, and two letters of recommendation.

Office of the Corporation Counsel
441 4th Street NW Rm 1060 North
Washington, DC 20001
Attention: Natalie Nash, Internship Coordinator
(202) 724-5648
(202) 347-8922 (Fax)
E-mail: nnash@occ.dcgov.org

OFFICE OF INSPECTOR GENERAL

See United States Department of Commerce

OFFICE OF JOB CORPS

SELECTIVITY 🔍 🔍 🔍
Approximate applicant pool: 50; Interns accepted: 6

COMPENSATION 💲 💲 💲 💲
$2,300–$3,300/month

LOCATION(S)
Washington D.C.

FIELD
Government; Public service

DURATION
12–18 months

THE WORK
Part of the US Department of Labor, the Office of Job Corps administers Job Corps, a program that helps economically disadvantaged youth gain employment in order "to become responsible adults." Servicing 60,000 students at 108 Job Corps centers nationwide, Job Corps provides academic and vocational training, work, counseling, housing, recreation, and health care. Interns work as skilled consultants at the National Office in DC in Academic Education, Vocational Education, and Human Resources.

PERKS
Possible travel to Job Corps centers and conferences; access to gym at US Department of Labor ($100/year).

FYI
Prior to reporting for work, interns must negotiate and sign a statement of work duties for which they are accountable . . . The intern coordinator writes: "[This is a] great opportunity for working toward improving youths' chances for a better tomorrow."

TO APPLY
Open to grads and grad students. International applicants eligible. Write for application. Opportunities for undergrads may exist at the ten Job Corps regional offices (call the National Office for contacts).

US Department of Labor
Office of Job Corps
200 Constitution Avenue NW Room N-4507
Washington, DC 20210
(202) 219-5559

OFFICE OF THE SPEAKER OF THE US HOUSE OF REPRESENTATIVES

SELECTIVITY 🔍 🔍 🔍 🔍
Approximate applicant Pool: 150 ; Interns accepted:15

COMPENSATION 💲
None

LOCATION(S)
Washington, DC

FIELD
Government

DURATION
At least 6 weeks: Spring, Summer, Fall

DEADLINE(S)
Summer: March 15; Fall: July 15; Spring: November 15

THE WORK
The Office of Speaker, currently held by Dennis Hastert, assigns interns to one of seven specialty areas: policy, press/communications, speaker's operations, information technology, office administration, planning, and speaker's prerogatives.

PERKS
Photo ops with big wigs; lecture series; opportunities to attend press conferences, sessions of Congress, and committee hearings.

FYI
A "Grappler in Government," Speaker Hastert is a former high-school wrestling coach.

TO APPLY
Applicants should submit cover letter stating why they want to work for the Office of the Speaker. Send resume and four references (one personal, three professional or educational) to:

Intern Coordinator
Office of the Speaker
H-326 Capitol
Washington DC 20515
(202) 225-0600

O K L A H O M A
REDHAWKS

SELECTIVITY 🔍 🔍 🔍 🔍 🔍
Approximate applicant pool: 100; Interns accepted: 4-6

COMPENSATION 💲 💲 💲
10 percent commission based on sales

LOCATION(S)
Oklahoma City, OK

FIELD
Sales and marketing; Events management

DURATION
9 months: January–September

DEADLINE(S)
End of November

THE WORK
As the Triple-A baseball club of the Texas Rangers franchise, the Oklahoma RedHawks are responsible for farming minor league players into major leaguers. The Oklahoma RedHawks will play in a new state-of-the-art stadium beginning in the Spring of 1998. The new ballpark in bricktown is considered the finest baseball facility in the United States, short of the major leagues.

PERKS
Opportunity to gain valuable experience in sports marketing; opportunity to network in the sports community; flexible work schedule in a fun atmosphere

FYI
Intern positions have potential for full-time employment within the organization.

TO APPLY
Open to college students and graduates. Submit resume, cover letter, and recommendation.

Internship Program
Oklahoma RedHawks
P.O. Box 75089
Oklahoma City, OK 73147
(405) 218-1000
(405) 218-1001 (fax)

OLDSMOBILE

See General Motors

SELECTIVITY 🔍 🔍 🔍 🔍 🔍
Approximate applicant pool: 400; Interns accepted: 15

COMPENSATION 💲
None

LOCATION(S)
New York, NY

FIELD
Film; Television

DURATION
12 weeks: ongoing

DEADLINE(S)
Rolling

THE WORK
Open City Films, founded by Jason Kliot and Joana Vicente in 1993, is a New York-based production company dedicated to advancing independent visions in film. Open City's *Three Seasons*, by Tony Bui, became the first film to win both the Grand Jury and Audience Awards at the Sundance Film Festival, and is being followed by the Miramax-financed *Down to You*, by Kris Isacsson. Jason Kliot and Joana Vicente were also the Associate Producers on *Welcome to the Dollhouse* and *The Incredibly True Adventure of Two Girls in Love*. Interns aid in daily office maintenance, operational projects, and, depending on desire and ability, development.

PERKS
Attendance welcome on sets; course credit where applicable; casual dress; open atmosphere.

FYI
Open City has been using interns since 1992 . . . In addition to its own production work, Open City lends itself to European production companies seeking assistance in their work in the United States. In 1993, for example, Open City served as the NY production office for Alain Corneau's *Tous Les Matins Du Monde*.

TO APPLY
Open to undergrads. Submit resume and cover letter.

Internship Coordinator
Open City Films
198 Avenue of the Americas
New York, NY 10013
(212) 343-1850
(212) 343-1849 (Fax)

ORACLE

SELECTIVITY N/A
Approximate applicant pool: N/A; Interns accepted: 100– 200

COMPENSATION N/A
Varies by position

LOCATION(S)
Redwood Shores, CA (HQ), and various other locations in New England, New York, and Oregon

FIELD
Computers

DURATION
12–16 weeks: Summer

DEADLINE(S)
Rolling

THE WORK
Oracle is the world's largest provider of database software and information management services, and its products—such as the Oracle 8 Universal Server—are nearly as famous as its flamboyant billionaire founder and CEO, Larry Ellison. Oracle's current crusade is the networked computer (NC), a low-cost, low-memory computer that runs software from a central server. Interns work on a variety of projects, principally in the Product Development department.

PERKS
Casual dress; free drinks; beautiful campus; excellent company gym; social atmosphere

FYI
Oracle's ever-growing campus includes gourmet cafes, a shopping center, a state-of-the-art gym, and a duck-infested saltwater lagoon nicknamed "Lake Larry."

TO APPLY
Open to college undergrads. To apply, submit resume. Oracle prefers to receive submissions electronically, by e-mail at college@us.oracle.com (include "INTERN" in the subject line) or on the web at www.oracle.com/college/jobs_res.html.

ORGANIZATION OF CHINESE AMERICANS

SELECTIVITY
Approximate applicant pool: 100; Interns accepted: 12

COMPENSATION
$200/week

LOCATION(S)
Washington, DC

FIELD
Public policy

DURATION
10 weeks: Summer, Fall, Spring

DEADLINE(S)
Summer: March 15; Fall : July 15; Spring: November 15

THE WORK
Founded in 1973, the Organization of Chinese Americans (OCA) strives to "cultivate leadership by providing opportunities for Asian Americans, students with a vested interest in the political process." Interns research background information for OCA's legislative meetings, help arrange legislative meetings, follow up on requests for information, and work on grant-related projects.

PERKS
Attendance welcome at meetings on Capitol Hill; travel to OCA National Convention (summer).

FYI
Says a former intern: "Everyone pitches in on eve[...] You really get to do a lot of substantive work here. And the [...]tor is very open to interns coming up with new projects to wo[...] on."

TO APPLY
Open to undergrads, recent college grads, college grads of any age, and grad students. International applicants eligible for non-paid positions. Write for application.

Internship Coordinator
Organization of Chinese Americans
1001 Connecticut Avenue NW, Suite #601
Washington, DC 20036
(202) 223-5500
(202) 296-0540 (Fax)
E-mail: oca@ocanatl.org
www.ocanatl.org

OSCAR MAYER

See Kraft General Foods

OSCAR MAYER WIENERMOBILE

SELECTIVITY
Approximate applicant pool: 1,000; Interns accepted: 12 for 1 year; 3–10 for 3 months

COMPENSATION
$425/week; food stipend: average $20/day; lodging stipend: average $60/day; benefits; expenses

LOCATION(S)
All 50 states; Canada; Mexico

FIELD
Consumer goods (meat products)

DURATION
3 months; June 1 with possibility to work year-round

DEADLINE(S)
February 1

THE WORK
Oscar Mayer is looking for outgoing, creative, enthusiastic graduating college seniors to represent Oscar Mayer as Hotdoggers – spokespeople/good-will ambassadors. Applicants typically have a BA or BS in journalism, public relations, advertising, or marketing, although all interested students are encouraged to apply. Hotdoggers drive the world famous Oscar Mayer

events across the country, spreading miles of ... ey may go. Along the way, Hotdoggers repre- ... public events and media interviews; they have ... ey role in major marketing and public relations ... the country. Hotdoggers have made promo- ... rything from supermarkets to the Super Bowl.

Ten-day training at "Hot Dog High" to learn Oscar Mayer history and products, special event procedures, and Wienermobile driving tips; "All the hotdogs you can eat," not to mention all the wienermobilia (promotional goodies) that you could imagine!

FYI
After Hotdogging, alumni have moved on to some really great opportunities including: Global Marketing Manager—Duke University Fuqua School of Business, Media Relations Manager—Special Olympics Inc., and On-Board Public Relations Director.

TO APPLY
Open to recent college grads and grad students. Submit resume and cover letter. Writing samples are accepted, but are not required.

Oscar Mayer Wienermobile Program
P.O. Box 7188
Madison, WI 53707
www.oscarmayer.com

WIENERMOBILE SPECIFICATIONS AT-A-GLANCE

Seating: six (driver's seat, "shot bun", and four passenger seats)
Furnishings: cellular phone, PA system, big-screen TV, front and back video cameras to guide parallel parking, VCR, sunroof, wrap-around windshield, storage hatch in tail of dog, and condiment control panel
Tunes: stereo system that can play "I wish I were an Oscar Mayer wiener" in 21 styles, including Cajun, rap, and bossa nova
Air conditioning: makes the cabin "chili"
Mileage: 10 miles/gallon
Engine: a "beefy" V-8
0 to 60 mph: 24 seconds
Top speed: 90 miles per hour
Weight: 10,000 lbs.
Length: 27 feet
Material: fiberglass
Cost: $100,000 per Wienermobile
Vehicles in operation: 6

OUTWARD BOUND-VOYAGEUR SCHOOL

OUTWARD BOUND
TO SERVE TO STRIVE AND NOT TO YIELD
VOYAGEUR

SELECTIVITY 🔍🔍🔍
Approximate applicant pool: 200; Interns accepted: 36

COMPENSATION 💲💲
$50/week; free room and board

LOCATION(S)
Minnesota and Montana

FIELD
Recreation

DURATION
8 weeks: Summer

DEADLINE(S)
March 1

THE WORK
Founded in 1941 to promote self-awareness and develop leadership skills, Outward Bound conducts wilderness expeditions for people of all ages. The Outward Bound Voyageur School arranges adventures focusing on backpacking (alpine, desert, or mountain), sea kayaking, canoeing, or dog sledding/cross-country skiing. In addition to assisting instructors, interns help prepare meals, drive

"The Oscar Mayer Company is looking for 12 recent college graduates to drive their Wienermobiles. Who says there aren't any good jobs for liberal arts majors?"
—Jay Leno, from the *Tonight Show* monologue, referring to the Oscar Mayer Wienermobile.

INTERVIEW WITH AN OSCAR MAYER "HOTDOGGER"

Without a doubt, the Oscar Mayer Wienermobile wins the award for the world's zaniest internship. Where else can one spend a year road-tripping across the land in a gigantic hot dog-on-wheels? To get the full "flavor" of this internship, we interviewed Dan Duff, one of 12 "Hotdoggers" who piloted the Wienermobile during 1995. At left, Dan Duff relaxes after a day of driving his Oscar Mayer Wienermobile.

What it takes to be a Hotdogger:
You have to be extroverted. You've got people coming up to you every day asking all sorts of questions. You can't be shy. Some people ask about the history of the Wienermobile, others ask about the specifications of the vehicle. Occasionally someone will ask if [the Wienermobile] floats, because the buns look like pontoons to some. Others ask what it runs on. I usually say, "High-octane mustard."

One of Dan's favorite memories:
On July 4th, we did a Fourth of July parade in upstate New York, and then we hauled our buns down to Washington, DC for the Fourth of July party at The White House. We actually didn't take the Wienermobile onto the driveway of The White House—we parked on the Ellipse. Then we went into the party and watched the fireworks display from the [White House's] South Lawn.

Whether hot dogs are actually available from the Wienermobile:
Although we have a microwave and a refrigerator, we don't go around grilling dogs in the Wienermobile. Sometimes we'll go to an event, and they'll have a grill for us and we'll actually work the grill.

Wienermobile license plates:
Our license plate is "OUR DOG," and the other ones are "HOT DOG," "BIG BUN," "YUMMY," "WIENER," and "OSCAR."

Brushes with the law:
We've been pulled over by policemen a lot. New Jersey and Pennsylvania State Troopers love to pull us over—just to see the inside of the Wienermobile. But I've never been pulled over for speeding or gotten into any accidents.

Whether the Wienermobile is a magnet for romance:
Well, sure. You meet all sorts of people. You definitely get people coming up and flirting with you. It's kind of funny, because my partner is a woman. We witness how guys will come up and talk to her, and girls will come up and talk to me. It's kind of funny to watch your partner when people start totally flirting.

Whether anyone has ever made love in the Wienermobile:
Hmm, I don't know. I'm asked this all this time. If somebody did, they kept it real quiet.

DANIEL H. DUFF

HUNGER:

Let's be frank, I would relish the opportunity to become an Oscar Mayer Hotdogger, travel the U.S.A., meet new people, have fun and get paid for it.

PREPARATION:

SYRACUSE UNIVERSITY - Syracuse, New York
Bachelor of Fine Arts, May 1994
Major: Advertising Design
• Deans List

FORDHAM UNIVERSITY - Bronx, New York
Major: Liberal Arts
• Transferred to Syracuse in 1991

ENTREES:

• Internship - Rhino Works Ad Agency, Solvay, New York - summer 1993
-worked on radio & tv copywriting, rough artwork (menus, flyers, print ads, billboards, etc...), planning promotions & press releases
• Production Assistant - The Wheetlay Company, Wilmette, Illinois
December 1993 - January 1994
-created computer illustrations on Adobe 5.0 to be used in grammar school textbooks for the state of Texas

DESSERTS:

• Member - SCABA (Syracuse's Creative Alternative to Boring Advertising)
• Fordham University Hockey Club
• Campus Tour Guide - Fordham University, Rose Hill Campus
• First Place Award - Southern Vermont Art Competition 1989
• Exhibiting Artist - Glencoe Art Fair 1988, 1989

SNACKS:

• House Painter - Summer 1993
L-M Painting
• Clerk - Summer 1993
Harris Bank Wilmette
• Camp Counselor, Arts & Crafts Teacher - Summers 1988, 1992
Glencoe Park District
• Clerk - Summer 1991
State Of Illinois, Secretary of States Office, Dept. of Motor Vehicles

TRAVEL HIGHLIGHTS:

• threw a curveball through four states (Arizona, Colorado, New Mexico, Utah)
• caught a 120 lb. Tarpon off the Florida Keys
• VIP guest at Norfolk Naval Base and Little Creek Marine & Amphibious Base
• jumped over the Mississippi River in Itasca, Minnesota
• went to the 1984 Olympic Games in Los Angeles, California (saw Carl Lewis win four gold medals)
• visited all but three of the Continental United States

INTERESTS:

Chicago Cubs, Puns, Domestic Travel, Acrylic and Airbrush Painting, Intramural Basketball, Piano and Spinach Lasagna.

The actual resume used by Dan Duff to win one of 12 places (out of 1,000 applicants) to the Oscar Mayer Wienermobile internship equipment to pick-up and drop-off destinations, manage expedition checkpoints, and participate in first-aid demonstrations.

PERKS
Field training in a group expedition with a senior instructor; professional discounts on outdoor gear; the great outdoors—superb white-water paddling and rock climbing; workshops offered by fellow interns on outdoor education topics.

FYI
Says the intern coordinator: "[Interning here] is one of the only entry-level routes into work at Outward Bound"; approximately 70 percent of interns are hired for instructional positions.

TO APPLY
Open to undergrads, recent college grads, college grads of any age, and grad students. Must have certification in CPR, Wilderness Advanced First Aid, and lifeguard training. International applicants eligible. Write for application.

Internship Coordinator
Outward Bound Voyageur School
P.O. Box 450
Ely, MN 55731
(218) 365-5761
(218) 365-5626 (Fax)

OVE ARUP & PARTNERS

SELECTIVITY 🔍🔍🔍🔍🔍
Approximate applicant pool: 2,000–2,500; Interns accepted: 70–100 (2–5 US citizens)

COMPENSATION 💲💲💲💲
£13,750–£15,000/year (approximately $450–$500/week); round-trip travel; 2-week interim dorm housing; end-of-fellowship bonus of £500 (approximately $800)

LOCATION(S)
London, England; Detroit, MI; San Francisco, CA

FIELD
Architecture; Engineering consulting

DURATION:
24 months: starting in September

DEADLINE(S)
December 31 in UK; April 1 in USA

THE WORK
Founded in 1946, Ove Arup & Partners (OA&P) is one of the world's leading independent engineering firms, specializing in design of stadiums, hospitals, recreation centers, museums, and offices for government and industry. It has done design work for the construction, renovation, or expansion of such sites as JFK International Airport, Sydney Opera House, Japan's Kansai Airport, Hong Kong/Shanghai Bank, France's Lille TGV Centre, Hong Kong's Central Plaza, Lloyd's of London, and the Pompidou Center in Paris. Under the auspices of the Graduate Intake Program and Arup Fellowship, fellows assist in-house engineers and architects with design work for local construction projects.

PERKS
Week-long orientation; seminars on engineering topics; geographically diverse group of interns.

FYI
Arup "scholars," the name for US participants, return to the US after their two-year stints to begin full-time jobs at one of OA&P's offices in Los Angeles, San Francisco, or New York City.

TO APPLY
Open to recent college grads. Must have a BS or MS in architectural, civil, electrical, mechanical, or structural engineering. International applicants eligible. Write for application.

US citizens or Resident Aliens:
Arup Fellowship
Ove Arup & Partners California
901 Market St. #260
San Francisco, CA 94103
(415) 957-9445
(415) 957-9096 (Fax)

NonUS citizens:
Graduate Intake Program
Ove Arup & Partners
13 Fitzroy
London, England W1P 6BQ
44-171-636-1531

OVERLAND ENTERTAINMENT

SELECTIVITY 🔍🔍
Approximate applicant pool: 15; Interns accepted: 2–4

COMPENSATION 💲
Commutation expense

LOCATION(S)
New York, NY

FIELD
Events management

DURATION
12–16 weeks: Summer, Fall, Spring

DEADLINE(S)
Rolling

THE WORK
Founded in 1983, Overland Entertainment stages and produces events for corporate clients. One of the East Coast's major event production firms, Overland is responsible for such events as Apollo Hall of Fame, Aretha Franklin Duets, EARTH 90, and Our Common Future GQ Men of the Year, Awards Movie Premiere Events. Interns work in Sales & Marketing and in overall management.

PERKS
Attendance welcome at client events (concerts, festivals, etc.); free passes to Broadway shows and other attractions; small, tight-knit office environment.

FYI
Overland's clients include AmFAR, Seagram Americas, Pfizer, Tropicana, Time Warner, Paine Webber, Conde Nast Publications, Dreamworks, France Telecom, Nomura Securities.

TO APPLY
Open to high school seniors, high school grads, undergrads, recent college grads, college grads of any age, and grad students. International applicants eligible. Submit resume and cover letter.

Internship Coordinator
Overland Entertainment
257 West 52nd Street
New York, NY 10019
(212) 262-1270
(212) 262-5229 (Fax)

OVERSEAS PRIVATE INVESTMENT CORPORATION

SELECTIVITY 🔍🔍
Approximate applicant pool: 500; Interns accepted: 40–46 each semester

COMPENSATION 💲
Usually paid during Summer; Unpaid Fall and Spring

LOCATION(S)
Washington, DC

FIELD
International business policy; Government

DURATION
Min-15 hrs/week for 3 months: Fall, Spring, Summer full-time

DEADLINE(S)
Rolling

THE WORK
Created by Congress in 1969, the Overseas Private Investment Corporation (OPIC) is the key federal agency encouraging US business investment in developing nations. OPIC provides qualified companies with investment insurance, project financing in the form of loans and loan guaranties, financing private investment funds, and a host of investor services. The projects supported by OPIC must improve US global competitiveness, create American jobs, and increase US exports. Interns work in Finance, Insurance, Investment Development, Environmental, Media Relations, Legal Affairs (law students only), Management Services, Financial Management and Statutory Review, and Investment Funds.

PERKS
Career panels, field trips to federal agencies, and softball league (summer only); language classes; reduced rates for fitness center (inexpensive parking, and metro subsidy, Summer only.)

FYI
Interns perform such tasks as assisting insurance officers with contracts, preparing country economic and political risk analyses, determining the impact of proposed overseas invest-

ments upon the US economy, researching worker rights issues, assisting in direct marketing, writing press releases, and monitoring Congressional activities . . . In the last 20 years, OPIC has supported $130 billion worth of investments, generated $61 billion in US exports, and helped create 242,000 US jobs.

TO APPLY
Open to undergrads and grad students. Write for application, or access website.

Intern Coordinator or Legal Affairs Internship Coordinator (for law students only)
Overseas Private Investment Corporation
1100 New York Avenue NW
Washington, DC 20527
(202) 336-8683
www.opic.gov

OVERSEAS SERVICE CORPS OF THE YMCA

SELECTIVITY 🔍
Approximate applicant pool: 30; Interns accepted: 20–25

COMPENSATION 💲💲💲💲
Return airfare, free housing, medical insurance, Reimburse airfare to Taiwan, (New Taiwanese Dollars) 26,000–31,000/month (approx. $850–$1,010 US).

LOCATION(S)
Taiwan

FIELD
Teaching conversational English

DURATION
1 year, starting in September

DEADLINE(S)
April 15; extension to May 15 available

RESOURCES TO HELP YOU FIND INTERNSHIPS IN INTERNATIONAL DEVELOPMENT

In addition to offering internships in its San Francisco office, the Overseas Development Network helps students locate internships with other international development organizations in the US and overseas through its own books and database. Ranging in price from $6 to $12, the books cover internship opportunities in California, New England, and Washington, DC as well as address how to create your own internship in international community development (see publications catalog).

Overseas Development Network (see separate entry)
333 Valencia Street, Suite 330
San Francisco, CA 94103-3547
(415) 431-4204
(415) 431-5953 (Fax)
E-mail: odn@igc.org

WORK

Established in 1974 in Taiwan, the Overseas Service Corps of the YMCA (OSCY) supplies the YMCAs (see separate entry) in Taiwan with English instructors. Referred to as OSCYs (pronounced AHS-kees), teachers (20-25 in Taiwan) provide 14-20 hours of conversation instruction and 10-15 office hours per week as well as administer tests, develop texts, record tapes for the language lab, judge oratorical contests, and staff summer English camps.

PERKS

Orientation; one-week paid vacation, financial bonuses, assistance with language study (Mandarin Chinese).

TO APPLY

Open to recent college grads and college grads of any age. Citizens of Canada and the United States who are native English speakers and will be reachable from the application deadline until the end of September are eligible. Write or call for application. Application fees: $50 (Taiwan).

OSCY Program
YMCA of the USA
101 N. Wacker Dr.
Chicago, IL 60606
(800) 872-9622 ext. 343
E-mail: jann.sterling@ymca.net

THE PARIS REVIEW

The Paris Review

SELECTIVITY
Approximate applicant pool: 200; Interns accepted: 9

COMPENSATION
None

LOCATION(S)
New York, NY

FIELD
Journals

DURATION
12 weeks: Summer, Fall, Spring

DEADLINE(S)
Rolling

THE WORK

Founded in 1953, *The Paris Review* is a literary quarterly publishing fiction, poetry, interviews with authors, and art portfolios. Edited by George Plimpton, the cutting-edge *Review* has included the work of authors such as John Updike, Henry Miller, Allen Ginsberg, Margaret Atwood, William Faulkner, Ezra Pound, and Norman Mailer. Interns work in the Editorial department, where they assist editors in all aspects of editing and publishing the journal.

PERKS

Attendance welcome at readings and other literary events; intimate office environment.

FYI

Alumni of the 40-year-old-program include the current managing editor, two associate editors, and the author Mona Simpson.

TO APPLY

Open to college juniors and seniors, recent college grads, college grads of any age, and grad students. International applicants eligible. Submit resume and cover letter.

Internship Coordinator
The Paris Review
541 East 72nd Street
New York, NY 10021
(212) 861-0016

THE PARTNERSHIP FOR SERVICE-LEARNING

The International PARTNERSHIP FOR SERVICE-LEARNING
Uniting Academic Studies and Community Service

SELECTIVITY
Approximate applicant pool: 200; Interns accepted: 160

COMPENSATION
Summer fee: $3,000–$5,600; Fall or Spring fee: $6,600–$8,900; all include room, tuition, internship placement, and orientation. Some include board

LOCATION(S)
England; France; India; Israel; Jamaica; Mexico; Philippines; Scotland; Czech Republic; Ecuador; South Dakota

FIELD
French; Spanish; Social sciences; Humanities; Environment; Business; International service

DURATION
3 months—1 year: Summer, semester, or year; also available is a 3-week January and August intersession in India

DEADLINE(S)
Two months before start of program; March 1st for Masters Degree

THE WORK

Founded in 1982, the International Partnership for Service-Learning (IPS-L) is a nonprofit consortium of colleges and service agencies linking academic study and public service in eleven countries. IPS-L participants take classes focusing on the local culture (e.g., history, literature, language, political science, sociology) and serve internships at agencies such as schools, orphanages, youth recreation

How did the legendary British filmmaker **David Lean**, the man responsible for such classics as *Passage to India*, *Doctor Zhivago*, and *Lawrence of Arabia*, get his start? As a "tea boy," of course. Graduating from high school in 1927, he found employment as a "tea boy" (the British term for "gofer") at London's Gaumont Studios. After completing this month-long unpaid internship, Lean was offered a job as a studio assistant. Within three years, he rose to the position of Editor of Newsreels, later leaving Gaumont to edit and ultimately produce major motion pictures.

centers, environmental organizations, women's groups, health care facilities, human rights institutes, Sioux Indian reservations, or community development projects.

PERKS
Field trips to local cultural attractions (e.g., pow wows, art centers, the Amazon); independent travel encouraged; geographically diverse group of interns; strong in-country support; and an active alumni association.

FYI
Classes are taught at nearby universities by local professors and grant six to fifteen semester credits for IPS-L work. Financial aid through the Federal Government or student's home college may be used.

TO APPLY
Open to high school graduates, college undergraduates, graduate students, and other college graduates of all ages. For Mexico, Ecuador, and France programs, previous language study is required. International applicants are encouraged to apply. Write or call for an application, or download from the Web:

The International Partnership for Service-Learning
815 Second Avenue, Suite 315
New York, NY 10017
212 986 0989
212 986 5039 (Fax)
E-mail: pslny@aol.com
www.ipsl.org

PATENT & TRADEMARK OFFICE

See United States Department of Commerce

PEACE CORPS

SELECTIVITY
Approximate applicant pool: 15,000; Interns accepted: 3,000

COMPENSATION
Monthly living stipend; medical and dental coverage; round-trip travel; 24 vacation days/year; $5,400 allowance upon completion; readjustment allowance of $200 per month of service

LOCATION(S)
Over 56 countries (see Appendix)

FIELD
Public service in 65 fields (see Appendix)

DURATION
27 months

DEADLINE(S)
Rolling (6–9 months before availability)

THE WORK
Founded in 1961 by President John F. [Kennedy?] renowned Peace Corps (PC) seeks to fight [war?] poverty, and lack of opportunity. To date, [volun]teers have served in over 100 countries. Volum[teers? PC] Corps refers to its workers, participate in communi[ty pro]jects in over sixty-five fields, including health, agricu[lture busi]ness, natural resources, skilled trades, education, and engine[ering.]

PERKS
Three-month language, cross-cultural, and technical training program; official training get-togethers during period of service abroad; grad school fellowships/scholarships.

FYI
Seventy-two percent of PC volunteers are age 20–29 . . . PC hires approximately 25 percent of its volunteers for full-time positions . . . Former volunteers include Carol Bellamy, current executive director of UNICEF; Senator Christopher Dodd (D-CT); Drew Days, Solicitor General; Robert Haas, chairman and CEO of Levi Strauss; Bob Vila, former host of "This Old House"; and Mike McCaskey, President and CEO of the Chicago Bears.

TO APPLY
Open to high school grads, college grads of any age, and grad students. Write for application.

Peace Corps
Recruitment
90 Church Street, Room 1317
New York, NY 10007
(800) 424-8580
(212) 606-4458 (Fax)

PEGGY GUGGENHEIM COLLECTION

SELECTIVITY
Approximate applicant pool: 800; Interns accepted: 90

COMPENSATION
1,200,000 lire/month ($650–$800/month)

LOCATION(S)
Venice, Italy

FIELD
Museum

DURATION
4–12 weeks: ongoing

DEADLINE(S)
November 15 for January–March; December 15 for April–December

THE WORK
The Italian sister of New York's Solomon R. Guggenheim Museum (see separate entry) and Italy's foremost modern art museum, the Peggy Guggenheim Collection opened in 1949 to showcase Peggy Guggenheim's American collection of paintings. Housed in the Palazzo Venier dei Leoni, an unfinished palace on the Grand Canal, the museum features over 300 objects and is renowned for its cubist, surrealist, and abstract masterpieces. Working four days a week, interns (called *studenti*) open and close the galleries, sell catalogs and tickets, check bags, guard works of art, staff the checkroom, help administrative staff in the offices, assist at special events, and work on special projects (prepare catalogs, install exhibits, etc.).

PERKS

...d Assistance welcome at Venice Biennale, the world's oldest ...event; twice-weekly discussions, lectures, and field trips on ...useology; intern acknowledgment in Guggenheim Foundation ...biennial report.

FYI
Intern activities are coordinated by a staff member, a chief intern appointed for up to six months, and a deputy chief intern appointed monthly . . . Says the coordinator: "The students leave impressed with the exciting contrast of modern masterpieces within the historical setting of Venice."

TO APPLY
Open to undergrads, recent college grads, and grad students. Must be fluent in English and have some Italian-language skills. International applicants eligible. Write for application.

Studentship Coordinator
Peggy Guggenheim Collection
Dursoduro 701
30123 Venezia, Italy
39-41-2405-411
E-mail: internship.pgc@interbusiness.it

PELLA CORPORATION

SELECTIVITY 🔍🔍🔍🔍🔍
Approximate applicant pool: 750–800; Interns accepted: 65

COMPENSATION 💲💲💲💲💲
75–85 percent of entry-level salary depending on year in college

LOCATION(S)
Various locations throughout Iowa: Pella, Carroll, Story City, Shenandoah

FIELD
Manufacturing; Home products (windows and doors)

DURATION
3–6 months; one semester

DEADLINE(S)
Rolling; however, interns are encouraged to apply two seasons before the semester during which they wish to intern

THE WORK
Pella is the second largest manufacturer of windows and doors. The company recently acquired Viking Windows and Doors as well as Cole Sewell Storm Doors, two of the leading window and door manufacturers in the world. Interns at Pella work closely with both a supervisor and a mentor. Supervisors assign work to interns on a weekly basis in a variety of departments including Engineering, Management/Marketing, and Accounting. Students can expect a supportive, educational work environment at Pella, where full-time jobs are typically extended to over 60 percent of interns.

PERKS
Supervisor and mentor programs; relocation expenses paid up to seven days lodging, meals, and local transportation; opportunities for medical coverage; opportunities for vacation time; paid holidays; opportunities for life insurance coverage; discounts on products; opportunities for profit sharing; opportunities to win grant money

FYI
The Pella Corporation is named after Pella, Iowa, the town where the company first opened offices.

Unique perks at selected internships:

- An engraved gold quill pen (American Association of University Women Educational Foundation)
- In-office manicure every Monday (Cairns & Associates)
- Two Q&A sessions with journalist Brian Lamb (C-SPAN)
- Espresso machine in the cafeteria (*The Seattle Times*)
- Free Playmate pictures (*Playboy*)
- Access to Muppets (The Jim Henson Company)
- Pinball instruction from "Gunther" (*MAD Magazine*)
- Operate a Zeiss sky projector (The Adler Planetarium)
- On-site chair massages (Southern Progress Organization)
- Excursion on the CEO's water-ski boat (Trilogy Development Group)
- Hot-air balloon rides (Korff Enterprises)
- Access to dark room, film, and photographic paper for personal projects (Francesco Scavullo studio)
- A half day of firearms training (Federal Bureau of Investigation)
- At least one free pair of sneakers (Reebok)
- Five free outfits (Benetton)
- Touring an Entenmann's Bakery (Kraft General Foods)
- Two tickets & free parking to every game (Chicago Bulls)
- Full day visit to the New York Jets training camp (National Football League)
- Free calculator (Hewlett–Packard)
- Fishing privileges (Wildlife Prairie Park)
- Mountain bikes available for use (Bike-Aid)
- Free cereal, fruits, and soup (*Charlie Rose*)
- Participation in a spring talent show (J. Walter Thompson-NY)
- Free language course worth $350 (Middle East Institute)
- Opportunity to observe a space shuttle launch (National Space Society)
- Free beer (Miller Brewing Company)
- Occasional appearances as an extra in skits (*Late Show with David Letterman*)
- Free dance class each day (American Dance Festival)
- Access to rare corporate documents and memorabilia (History Factory)
- Free canoeing or kayaking lesson (*Canoe & Kayak Magazine*)
- Two free round-trip train tickets (Amtrak)
- Free classes in sign language (American School for the Deaf)
- Traveling throughout the NY/NJ area reporting traffic from the "Shadow Van" (Shadow Broadcast Services)
- Unconditional, year-long fame (Oscar Mayer Weinermobile)
- Nurse and physician on call 24 hours a day (United States Senate Youth Program)
- Free acting classes (Arden Theatre)

Last year *Good Morning America* featured the Pella roll-screen window as a new product, despite the fact that Pella has had held the patent for it for several decades.

TO APPLY
Open to sophomores, juniors, and seniors. Submit a cover letter and resume to:

Tim Harn
Staffing Administrator
Pella Corporation
102 Main Street
Pella, Iowa 50219

PENDULUM RECORDS

See EMI Records Group North America

PENGUIN BOOKS

SELECTIVITY
Approximate applicant pool: 300; Interns accepted: 50–60

COMPENSATION
NY: $7–$8/hour for some positions (summer only); London: None

LOCATION(S)
New York, NY; London, England

FIELD
Publishing

DURATION
NY: 8–16 weeks, Summer, Fall, Spring; London: 2–3 weeks, ongoing

DEADLINE(S)
NY: Rolling (April 30 for Summer); London: Rolling

THE WORK
A subsidiary of Pearson, Inc., a diversified information services company, Penguin Books publishes fiction and nonfiction under more than a dozen imprints worldwide, including Viking, Plume, Dutton, Topaz (romance novels), Fredricke Warne (Peter Rabbit books), Puffin, Dial, Penguin Classics, and Signet Classics. Its catalog includes works by Stephen King, Terry MacMillan, Toni Morrison, and Don DeLillo. Departments accepting interns include Adult, Children, Editorial, Marketing, Publicity, Sales, Permissions, Art, Subsidiary Rights, and Contracts.

PERKS
Opportunities to read recently submitted manuscripts; free books.

FYI
According to a former intern and English major: "It was cool to be around all those Penguin Classics: I must have read half of them in college."

TO APPLY
Open to undergrads, recent college grads, college grads of any age (London only), and grad students (London only). International applicants eligible (must be studying in the United States to intern in NY). Must have a personal interview (London only). Submit resume and cover letter.

Internship Coordinator
Penguin USA
375 Hudson Street
New York, NY 10014
(212) 366-2000

Personnel
Penguin Books Ltd.
27 Wrights Lane
London, England W85TZ
44-171-416-3000

THE PENTAGON

See United States Department of Defense

PEOPLE TO PEOPLE INTERNATIONAL

SELECTIVITY
Approximate applicant pool: 100; Interns accepted: 50–95

COMPENSATION
None

LOCATION(S)
Rockhampton, Australia; Copenhagen, Denmark; Dublin, Ireland; Malaga, Spain; Recife and Sao Paulo, Brazil; London and Southampton, UK

FIELD
Open for all majors

DURATION
9 weeks, anytime

DEADLINE(S)
Rolling (applications must be submitted at least 3 months prior to internship)

THE WORK
We offer placement in virtually any field. Previous internships have included, but are not limited to: Investment Banking, International Relations, Museums, Theater, Human Resources, Marketing and Public Relations, International Business, Political Parties, Law, Radio, Travel, Journalism, Education, Community Service, Graphic Design.

PERKS
The internship program is co-sponsored by the University of Missouri—Kansas City. Interns can receive up to six hours of undergraduate and graduate credit. People to People works individually with applicants to customize internships according to their specific needs.

FYI
Founded in 1956 by President Dwight D. Eisenhower, People to People International is a nonpolitical, nonprofit organization dedicated to advancing international understanding and friendship through the exchange of ideas and experiences directly among peoples of different countries and cultures. President Bill Clinton is the eighth President serving as People to People's honorary chairman.

TO APPLY
Open to college juniors and seniors, college grads, and grad students. Language proficiency in all nonEnglish speaking countries (except Czech Republic and Denmark) is required. International applicants eligible. Please contact us for application forms or visit our website.

International Internship Program
People to People International
501 East Armour Boulevard
Kansas City, MO 64109-2200
(816) 531-4701 x113
(816) 561-7502 (Fax)
E-mail: internships@ptpi.org
www.ptpi.org/studyabroad

PERA CLUB

SELECTIVITY 🔍🔍🔍🔍
Approximate applicant pool: 50; Interns accepted: 4

COMPENSATION 💲
$75/week

LOCATION(S)
Tempe, AZ

FIELD
Recreation

DURATION
10–15 weeks: year round

DEADLINE(S)
Rolling

THE WORK
The PERA Club (short for Project Employees Recreation Association) is a private country club for employees and families of the Salt River Project, the major water and power utility in Phoenix and surrounding cities. The 83-acre club houses a social center, employee store, fitness center, swimming pool, game courts, and fields and offers children's programs, fitness classes, business meetings, sports leagues, and parties. Interns work in Recreation (i.e., Special Events, Food/Beverage, Aquatics [summer only], and the Employee Store), where they plan social activities, supervise part-time employees, and host at special events.

PERKS
Training in stress management and customer service; discount at the employee store; access to sporting events and PERA fitness center. Attend NESRA (National Employee Services and Recreation Association) meetings.

TO APPLY
Open to undergrads and grad students. International applicants 19 years of age and older are eligible. Write for application.

Internship Coordinator
PERA Club
PER 200
P.O. Box 52025
Phoenix, AZ 85072-2025
(602) 236-5782

PERFORMANCE TODAY
See National Public Radio

PERSPECTIVE RECORDS
See PolyGram

PFIZER

SELECTIVITY 🔍🔍🔍
Approximate applicant pool: 1,000–1,500; Interns accepted: 80–100

COMPENSATION 💲💲💲💲💲
$1,350/week

LOCATION(S)
Groton, CT; Terre Haute, IN; Lee's Summit, MO; Parsippany, Rutherford, and Clifton, NJ; Brooklyn and Manhattan, NY; Minneappolis, MN

FIELD
Pharmaceuticals; Health care

DURATION
12–15 weeks: Summer

DEADLINE(S)
Rolling

THE WORK
With sales topping $12.5 billion annually, Pfizer is a worldwide powerhouse in pharmaceuticals and health care. Its pharmaceutical products include the antidepressant Zoloft, the antibiotic Zithromax, and the cardiovascular agent Norvasc; Visine, Ben-Gay, Desitin, and Plax are among its consumer products. Departments accepting interns include Marketing Research, Legal, Medical Devices, Quality Control, Marketing, Human Resources, Tax, Licensing & Development, Sales, Public Affairs, Strategic Planning, Medical Affairs, Finance, Controllers, Engineering, Research & Development, CIT-Corporate Information Technology, and Treasury.

PERKS
Opening and closing luncheon with senior executives; intern projects presented to senior management; planned activities, including tours of plant facilities.

Intern Jason Whitt (holding paper) and other members of Pfizer's elite Strategic Development Group observe an X-ray diagnostic demonstration by urologist Andy Howenesian, MD (far right).

The Strategic Development Group (part of the Medical Devices department) offers a special research internship open to grad students and highly qualified college seniors and recent college grads. . . . Only the "cream of the crop" need apply: applicants must have at least a 3.8 GPA and a background in science, engineering, or medicine.

TO APPLY

Open to grad students. International applicants eligible. Submit resume and cover letter.

Internship Coordinator
Corporate Employee Resources
Pfizer Inc.
235 East 42nd Street, MS4-42
New York, NY 10017-5755
www.pfizer.com

PGA TOUR

SELECTIVITY 🔍🔍🔍🔍

Approximate applicant pool: 250; Interns accepted: 15–20

COMPENSATION 💲💲💲

$300/week; round-trip travel; housing available at $100/month at HQ

LOCATION(S)

Los Angeles, CA; St. John's County, FL, Philadelphia, PA; Ponte Vedra Beach, FL (HQ); Atlanta, GA; New York, NY; Chicago; IL Detroit; Myrtle Beach, SC; Palm Beach Gardens, FL

FIELD

Sports

DURATION

9 weeks: Summer

DEADLINE(S)

Minority program—March 15; General program—February 15

THE WORK

Tracing its history back to 1895, the PGA tour operates over 123 professional golf tournaments as part of the PGA, Senior PGA, and Buy.com tours, including the Kemper Open, Ford Senior Players Championship, and tour championships. Disbursing a purse of over $191 million annually, the three tours have featured such greats as Ben Hogan, Jack Nicklaus, Arnold Palmer, Al Geiberger, Ernie Els, Tom Lehman, Fred Couples, Nick Price, and most recently, wunderkind Tiger Woods. Interns in Florida (nine or ten) work in Communications, Corporate Marketing, Information Systems, Design Services, Onsite Promotions, PGA Tour Productions (i.e., TV shows and videos, based in St. John's County), Tournament Players Club (TPC) Food & Beverage, TPC Golf Operations/Professional Services, and TPC Golf Operations/Course Maintenance. Interns outside of Florida work for the Urban Youth Golf Program (CA), Golf Course Superintendents Association of America (GCSAA).

 PERKS

Orientation; discounts on 18 holes of golf at TPC in FL.

FYI

Depending on placement, interns conduct research for upcoming tournaments, assist with the architectural design of golf courses, contact corporate sponsors, arrange banquets at the TPC club, and collect Nielsen ratings data.

TO APPLY

Open to college juniors and seniors as well as grad students. Must be African, Asian, Hispanic, or Native American. International applicants eligible but must be able to work within the United States. Write for application.

Minority Internship Program
PGA Tour
112 TPC Boulevard
Ponte Vedra Beach, FL 32082
(800) 556-5400 x3520

THE PHILADELPHIA CENTER

 The Philadelphia Center

SELECTIVITY 🔍

Approximate applicant pool: 600; Students accepted: 200/year

COMPENSATION 💲

$8,150 tuition (00/01) (extra $175 for non-GLCA colleges); nonpaid internships

LOCATION(S)

Philadelphia, PA

FIELD

Several fields (see THE WORK)

DURATION

16 weeks: Fall, Spring

DEADLINE(S)

Rolling

THE WORK

The Philadelphia Center (TPC) is an off-campus program recognized by the Great Lakes Colleges Association, a consortium of 12 liberal arts colleges in the Midwest. In addition to completing a seminar and an elective course (e.g., finance, marketing, film, literature), students intern four days a week at any of 800 organizations within Philadelphia, including the Arden Theatre, the District Attorney's Office, the Federal Reserve Bank, H2L2 Architects, Jefferson Hospital, the Mayor's Office, the Philadelphia Museum of Art, the Philadelphia 76ers, PNC Bank, Prudential Securities, the US-Japan Institute, and the University of Pennsylvania. Additionally, students arrange their own housing and live independently within the city.

PERKS

One-week orientation; access to TPC Computer Center; access to TPC housing file listing local housing.

FYI

Participants receive sixteen semester credits from TPC. According to the internship coordinator, TPC is a national model for experiential learning programs . . . TPC's internships were first offered in 1969.

TO APPLY

Open to college sophomores, juniors, and seniors. International applicants eligible. Write for application.

The Philadelphia Center
121 South Broad Street, 7th Floor
Philadelphia, PA 19107
(215) 735-7300
(215) 735-7373 (Fax)
E-mail: wright@philactr.edu

THE PHILADELPHIA INQUIRER

SELECTIVITY
Approximate applicant pool: 250–300; Interns accepted: 28

COMPENSATION
$573/week

LOCATION(S)
Philadelphia, PA

FIELD
Newspapers

DURATION
10 weeks: Summer

DEADLINE(S)
November 15

THE WORK

Dating back to 1829, *The Philadelphia Inquirer* is considered Philadelphia's leading newspaper. A division of the Knight-Ridder Newspaper Group, it is renowned for its investigative and indepth coverage of local, national, and foreign issues. Accepted to the Art Peters Editing Program, interns are assigned to one of six desks at the paper: Metro, Neighbors, Foreign, National, Business News, and Features.

PERKS

Brown-bag lunches with speakers; orientation program; training workshops on all aspects of news gathering.

FYI

The *Inquirer* also runs a two-year Correspondent Program, a Minority Photojournalism Internship, and a Journalism Career Development Workshop for minority high school students; moreover, it selects two interns for the two-year Knight-Ridder Minority Development Program. Write for more information . . . In existence since 1979, the internship counts among its alumni Steve Twomey, a Pulitzer Prize winner and columnist for *The Washington Post*.

TO APPLY

Open to undergrads, recent college grads, college grads of any age, and grad students. Must have previous newspaper experience (campus or internship). International applicants eligible. Submit resume, cover letter, writing samples, and recommendations.

Internship Coordinator
The Philadelphia Inquirer
Suite 100
1100 East Hector Street
Conshohocken, PA 19428

PHILLIPS ACADEMY

SELECTIVITY
Approximate applicant pool: 350 (SS), 40–50 (MS) 2; Interns accepted: 25 (SS), 12–15 (MS) 2

COMPENSATION
$2,200 plus room & board (summer session)

LOCATION(S)
Andover, MA

FIELD
All disciplines

DURATION
6 Weeks: Summer

DEADLINE(S)
February 15: (Summer Session); February 15: (Math and Science for Minority Students). Applications received after February 15 will be considered only if openings occur.

THE WORK

Every summer, the Phillips Academy, a prestigious Massachusetts boarding school, runs innovative academic programs for high school students. The Summer Session Program (SS) enrolls over 600 students in a wide range of enriching classes designed to accelerate students' secondary education. Interns may participate in this program or Math and Science for Minority Students (MS²). Interns are hired as Teaching Assistants (TAs) in courses related to their field of study.

PERKS

College-caliber facilities; single rooms; meals included; weekend outings; lovely campus.

FYI

The Phillips Academy is commonly called "Andover" . . . Students of color are strongly urged to apply . . . Beyond their support duties, TAs are often given opportunities to teach. "How much you teach depends on the teacher and your experience," said a TA. "Most will let you teach at least a few classes alone; others are less willing to give you free rein."

TO APPLY

Open to college seniors, recent grads (you must have graduated by June, 2000), grad students. Write for application or visit the website.

Phillips Academy
Director, (MS)2
Andover, MA 01810
(508) 749-4402
E-mail: ms2@andover.edu

Phillips Academy
Director, Summer Session
Andover, MA 01810
(508) 749-4406
E-mail: summersession
@andover.edu

www.andover.edu/summersession/empopp/interns.html

THE PHOENIX GAZETTE

See Central Newspapers/The Indianapolis News

SELECTIVITY 🔍
Approximate applicant pool: 30; Interns accepted: 12–15/year

COMPENSATION 💲
None

LOCATION(S)
Boston, MA; Washington DC

FIELD
Human rights; International affairs

DURATION
Fall, Spring, Summer

DEADLINE(S)
Rolling

THE WORK

Founded in 1986, Physicians for Human Rights (PHR) is a nonprofit membership organization of health professionals, scientists, and concerned citizens. Using the knowledge and skills of the medical and forensic sciences, PHR investigates and helps prevent violations of international human rights. Interns assist staff in researching human rights violations in particular countries, writing governments to protest violations, researching selected human rights issues where medicine and law intersect, and organizing educational programs, working with media and website or working with advocacy campaigns.

PERKS

Attendance welcome at local meetings with human rights groups; free publications; prime downtown location near the State House, Boston Commons, or in D.C. near the senate.

FYI

Since its founding, PHR has worked to stop torture, disappearances, and political killings; improve health care in prisons and detention centers; investigate physical and psychological consequences of violations of international humanitarian law; defend medical neutrality and the delivery of health care in areas of armed conflict; protect health care professionals who are victims of violations; and prevent medical complicity in torture and other abuses. PHR shared the 1997 Nobel Peace Prize for its work as a founding member of the International Campaign to Ban Landmines.

TO APPLY

Open to college juniors and seniors as well as grads, grad students, and medical and nursing students. International applicants eligible. Submit resume, cover letter, and a three-page writing sample.

Internship Coordinator
Physicians for Human Rights
100 Boylston Street, Suite 702
Boston, MA 02116
(617) 695-0041
(617) 695-0307 (Fax)
E-mail: phrusa@phrusa.org

SELECTIVITY 🔍🔍
Approximate applicant pool: 300 per year; Interns accepted: 2 per term, 6 per year

COMPENSATION 💲💲
$200/week (DC only)

LOCATION(S)
Washington, DC (HQ); 88 chapters in 38 states (See Appendix)

FIELD
Public policy; Environment

DURATION
12–24 weeks: Summer, Fall, Spring

DEADLINE(S)
Summer: April 1; Fall: July 1; Spring: November 1

THE WORK

Founded in 1961, Physicians for Social Responsibility (PSR) is a nonprofit organization of 20,000 members advocating the control and elimination of weapons of mass destruction, promoting environmental protection, and seeking to reduce societal violence and its causes. Through speaking tours, congressional lobbying, and publications, PSR informs policymakers and the public about such issues as safe drinking water, lead poisoning, pesticides, global warming, ozone depletion, and the health impact of nuclear weapons production and testing. Interns work in Nuclear Weapons Complex and Environmental Policy & Programs, monitoring congressional legislation and writing fact sheets and position papers.

PERKS

Meetings with lobbyists on Capitol Hill; luncheons with directors; free publications.

FYI

PSR launched its internship program in 1985 . . . PSR is the US affiliate of International Physicians for the Prevention of Nuclear War, which won the 1985 Nobel Peace Prize for its work to stop the spread of nuclear weapons.

TO APPLY

Open to college juniors and seniors, recent college grads, college grads of any age, and grad students. Submit resume, cover letter, and writing samples (DC only) directly to office of interest. Call DC headquarters for addresses and phone numbers of chapter offices.

Internship Coordinator
Physicians for Social Responsibility
1101 14th Street, NW Suite 700
Washington, DC 20005
(202) 898-0150
E-mail: psrnatl@igc.dpc.org

See Oak Ridge Institute for Science and Education

PITTSBURGH POST-GAZETTE

SELECTIVITY 🔍🔍🔍🔍🔍
Approximate applicant pool: 300-500; Interns accepted: 8

COMPENSATION 💲💲💲
$480/week minimum, increase subject to Guild negotiation; reimbursement of daily travel expenses

LOCATION(S)
Pittsburgh, PA

FIELD
Newspapers

DURATION
13 weeks: ongoing

DEADLINE(S)
December 31

THE WORK
Founded in 1786, the *Pittsburgh Post-Gazette* is western Pennsylvania's largest daily newspaper. The PG is owned by Blade Communications, which also owns *The Blade* (see separate entry) and cable television franchises. Known for its hard-hitting investigative journalism, the PG has won numerous state and national awards. Interns work closely with senior editors who evaluate their work, offer suggestions for improvement and act as mentors. Interns are treated as full-time staff members and usually report or photograph or design the same assignments that any general assignment reporter, photographer, or artist would be given. Eight unpaid "academic" internships granted, too.

PERKS
The program is an intensive 3-month experience; exposure to the entire news room; excellent mentors.

FYI
Post-Gazette internships are designed to be learning experiences. Interns work in three distinct areas of the news room, including the news desk and the copy desk. Work in other departments is planned based on the candidates' ability and need. Alumni of the program include the paper's managing editor.

TO APPLY
Open to college juniors, seniors, recent college grads as well as grad students. International applicants encouraged. Submit resume, cover letter, 5-8 samples, and three references.

Todd Duncan
Assistant to the Editor
Pittsburgh Post-Gazette
34 Boulevard of the Allies
Pittsburgh, PA 15222
(412) 263-1297

THE CADDYSHACK INTERNSHIP

Like **Bill Murray** in *Caddyshack*, you can manage the "turf" as an intern for the PGA Tour. Some interns help maintain the Tour's two golf courses at the Tournament Players Club at Sawgrass, where their duties include trimming trees, planting flowers, and preparing the greens, roughs, and bunkers.

PLANNED PARENTHOOD
See International Planned Parenthood Federation

PLAYBOY

SELECTIVITY 🔍🔍
Approximate applicant pool: 20–40; Interns accepted: TBA

COMPENSATION 💲
None

LOCATION(S)
New York, NY

FIELD
Magazines

DURATION
8–12 weeks: Summer, Fall, Spring

DEADLINE(S)
Rolling

THE WORK
In print since 1953, *Playboy* magazine is one of the world's best known publications, featuring high-quality fiction, articles on current events, award-winning art, and celebrity interviews; it probably goes without saying that Playboy also includes, in the magazine's words, "pictorials of some of the world's most beautiful women." In addition to its magazine, Playboy Enterprises produces newsstand specials, calendars, and foreign editions as well as operating a television network and a direct marketing business. Interns work in Editorial, Art, Public Relations, and Marketing.

PERKS
Attendance welcome at promotional and publicity events; free t-shirts and mugs.

FYI
The internship program has been in existence since 1982 . . . *Playboy* founder Hugh Hefner originally planned to call his magazine *Stag Party*.

TO APPLY
Open to undergrads. Submit resume, cover letter, and writing samples.

Human Resource Manager
Playboy Enterprises
730 Fifth Avenue
New York, NY 10019
(212) 261-5000
(212) 957-2900 (Fax)

EXCLUSIVE INTERVIEW WITH PETER ARNETT

The only Western reporter based in Iraq for the duration of Operation Desert Storm, Peter Arnett is one of the world's leading war correspondents, having spent more than 35 years as a journalist covering the war zones from Vietnam to Baghdad. A CNN International Correspondent, Arnett landed an exclusive interview with Iraqi President Saddam Hussein during the Persian Gulf War. The full scope of his career is documented in Live from the Battlefield, an autobiography published by Simon and Schuster in 1994. He graduated from Waitaki College in Oamaru, New Zealand. During his early twenties, Arnett served an apprenticeship at the Southland Times, a daily newspaper in Invercargill, New Zealand. At left Arnett begins his career as an journalist. In an Interview with The Internship Informants, he elaborated on:

The supervisor of his apprenticeship:
I had a very tough city editor. He would say, "Now these are your three assignments for the day, plus these three," so I always had more work than I could possibly do. He was very gruff with me, and he pushed me around intellectually. He did not give me any favors. Now I was not the exception—he did this with every young journalist. I grew to dislike him because he intimidated me, but he was someone who impacted on my career in that he instilled in me standards of discipline and job performance. He was very important to me at a young age.

An unexpected dividend of his apprenticeship:
I found that when I was covering women's basketball, women would do a lot to get their picture in the paper. But those were innocent times. I mean, [I would] maybe go out on a date [with some of the basketball players] . . . After the game, they'd come up and say, "Aw, didn't you think I played well?" and "Will you put my picture in the paper?" I would probably go for a date with them or have a drink with them, I'll admit to that. It was a great way to meet women by writing about them in my column. In those days in New Zealand, a very conservative society, it was not easy to meet women. Today, you know, anyone can meet a girl. But in those days it was not easy, so I found that it was a way to meet women by saying nice things about them in the paper. But I assure you that it was a very limited usage of my journalist privilege, and after that apprenticeship, it did not work. I did not continue writing about sports . . . I [moved on] to doing much more responsible reporting, writing about wars and revolutions [in Southeast Asia].

What he learned about journalism:
I became excited about journalism [during the apprenticeship] because I realized that the whole community was very interested in what appeared in the local newspaper or on the local television (they didn't have television then). So I became conscious of the responsibility [of being a journalist]. Also, I became aware of how much people wanted to be in the paper—their desire to be well regarded, to be written about. I learned that the currency of information and news was valuable.

His big mishap:
Something that I'll never forget [during the apprenticeship] is that I missed a story. It's always haunted me. I was assigned to cover a rowing regatta, which is sort of equivalent to a college athletic meet in the States. It was held at a wonderful place called Queenstown, which is on a beautiful lake. [After the regatta] I had to head back about 60 miles to [the Southland Times] to file the story. I was traveling by bus, because nobody had much money then. [On the way] I went into a bar with some rowing friends of mine. I had a few drinks, and I missed the last bus. I tried to hitchhike back, but I got back too late for the edition of the paper. I was reamed; they wanted to kill me . . . My boss drummed me up and down. He jumped up and down and put on a tremendous performance . . . And [since then] I've never been late with a story. I have never allowed any personal consideration or personal pleasure to get in my way of getting a story back [to a news bureau]. I'm glad I learned that lesson in New Zealand.

The value of being an apprentice:
I had some acquaintances who [apprenticed] with me, and they got sick of it. They just did not enjoy the interview process, the writing process, or the real pressure of being a journalist. And they were able to drop out along the way. [Because they were doing an apprenticeship], they weren't committed irrevocably to a career in journalism. In my case, I realized that I was for this business, and each year reinforced my desire to stay in it. I realized [as an apprentice] that I had what a friend of mine calls "fire in the belly."

SELECTIVITY 🔍 🔍 🔍 🔍 🔍
Approximate applicant pool: 400–600; Interns accepted: 11–14

COMPENSATION 💲 💲
$100/week; free housing

LOCATION(S)
Memphis, TN

FIELD
Theater acting; Stage management; Technical; Props; Costumes; Administration; Electrics

DURATION
1 year: starts August

DEADLINE(S)
Rolling

THE WORK
Founded in 1969, Playhouse on the Square is a nonprofit professional theater organization comprising a 260-seat Playhouse and a 136-seat Circuit Playhouse. Offering about 16 productions yearly, Playhouse has recently staged such shows as *Swingtime Canteen*, *Old Wicked Songs*, *Peter Pan*, *Master Class*, and *Chess*. Interns work in Acting, Set Construction, Props, Sound, Lighting, Stage Management, Costumes, and Administration.

PERKS
Free tickets to all performances; departmental training seminars; opportunities to work off-hours with the Memphis Arts Council's Artist in the Schools program.

FYI
In existence since 1983, the internship program leads to permanent employment at the Playhouse for about 20 percent of interns . . . Says a former intern: "The long hours and taxing schedule of the intern program forced me constantly to find discipline, motivation, and co-operative attitude within myself . . . At the Playhouse, 'doing theater' can . . . be fun, but more than that, it is a job."

TO APPLY
Open to grads and grad students. Write for application.

Internship Coordinator
Playhouse on the Square
51 South Cooper
Memphis, TN 38104
(901) 725-0776
(901) 272-7530 (Fax)

> "Every actor should look upon interning as a prerequisite for life in the theater."
> —former intern, Playhouse on the Square

See Penguin Books

SELECTIVITY 🔍 🔍 🔍 🔍 🔍
Approximate applicant pool: 350; Interns accepted: 8

COMPENSATION 💲
None

LOCATION(S)
New York, NY

FIELD
Public relations

DURATION
12–18 weeks: Summer, Fall, Spring

DEADLINE(S)
Rolling

THE WORK
Established in 1980, PMK is one of the largest and most successful celebrity public relations agencies in the world. Its stellar roster of clients includes the likes of Robert Redford, Jodie Foster, Uma Thurman, Jean-Claude Van Damme, Demi Moore, and Tom Cruise. Interns assist staff in preparing press releases, sending out mailings, and running errands.

PERKS
Free passes to film screenings; attendance welcome at PMK events; star-gazing opportunities.

FYI
Former interns warn that PMK staff are particularly wary about accepting interns who seem to be star-struck . . . A rarity in the entertainment/public relations business, PMK is owned by three female partners.

TO APPLY
Open only to students who will receive credit from their college or university. International applicants eligible. Submit resume and cover letter.

Internship Coordinator
PMK Public Relations
1775 Broadway, Suite 701
New York, NY 10019
(212) 582-1111

> The current editor-in-chief of Time, Inc., **Norman Pearlstein** began his career interning while he was an undergrad at Haverford College. He spent two summers in a Dow Jones-sponsored internship at the Allentown, Pennsylvania *Evening Chronicle* and then interned as a police reporter at *The Philadelphia Inquirer*.

SELECTIVITY 🔍🔍
Approximate applicant pool: 1,500; Interns accepted: 225–400 (Interns), 27 (Reps)

COMPENSATION 💲
Interns : None; Reps : $6/hour. College credit only

LOCATION(S)
Interns : Los Angeles, CA; New York, NY; Nashville, TN; Reps : Los Angeles and San Francisco, CA; Marietta, GA; Chicago, IL; Woburn, MA; Greenbelt, MD; Warren, MI; Queens, NY; Dallas, TX

FIELD
Record labels

DURATION
Interns: 8–20 weeks, Summer, Fall, Spring; Reps: one year minimum, ongoing

DEADLINE(S)
Rolling

THE WORK
Founded in 1898 as Deutsche Grammophon Gesellschaft, PolyGram is one of the world's leading record companies. Through such labels as Motown, Mercury, Polydor, Vertigo, Fontana, A&M, Def Jam, Island, Perspective, and Verve, to name a few, PolyGram promotes the likes of Bryan Adams, Sting, Billy Ray Cyrus, Kathy Mattea, U2, Public Enemy, Salt 'n' Pepa, and Luciano Pavarotti. CA and NY interns work in Marketing, Promotion, Sales, Creative Services (i.e., Advertising), Human Resources, Publicity, Product Management, Artists & Repertoire, Video, Classical Music, Inventory Production, and Legal Affairs (NY only). TN interns (six or seven) work in similar departments for Mercury Nashville. Working out of nine regional offices under the auspices of two college-rep programs—one alternative, one urban—Reps set up promotions and in-store contests as well as service college radio, press, and magazines for alternative artists like Gavin Bryars and Joan Osborne, and urban artists like Montell Jordan, Joya, and Lo-Key.

PERKS
Free promotional items (e.g., t-shirts, hats, CDs, and tapes); free concert tickets; attendance welcome at most staff meetings.

FYI
PolyGram's internship was started in 1986 . . . Each year, an average of three to five interns and 30–50 percent of college reps are hired by PolyGram for entry-level positions.

TO APPLY
Interns: open to undergrads and third-year law students (Legal Affairs); must receive academic credit. Reps: open to undergrads. International applicants eligible. Submit resume and cover letter.

Internship Coordinator
Human Resources
PolyGram
825 Eighth Avenue, 23rd Floor
New York, NY 10019
(212) 333-8000

Internship Coordinator
Mercury Nashville
66 Music Square West
Nashville, TN 37203
(615) 320-0110

Internship Coordinator
PolyGram
11150 Santa Monica Blvd., Suite 1100
Los Angeles, CA 90025
(310) 996-7200

Director,
College Representative Program
PolyGram
825 Eighth Avenue, 20th Floor
New York, NY 10019
(212) 333-8000

See General Motors

SELECTIVITY 🔍🔍🔍🔍
Approximate applicant pool: 200; Interns accepted: 8–12

COMPENSATION 💲💲
$1,500/month; medical dental benefits

LOCATION(S)
Washington, DC

FIELD
Health care; Public policy; Women's issues; Environmental issues

DURATION
6 months: Fall, Spring

DEADLINE(S)
Fall : April 15; Spring : September 15

THE WORK
Founded in 1969, The Population Institute (TPI) is the world's largest private nonprofit public awareness organization dedicated to achieving a balance between the world's population and its environmental resources. TPI's activities, supported by over 60,000 members in 172 countries, include lobbying Congress, the United Nations, and foreign governments for family-planning funds; organizing World Population Awareness Week every October; providing 5,000 editors and reporters worldwide with population information; and publishing *POPLINE*, TPI's bimonthly newspaper. Under the auspices of TPI's Future Leaders of the World Program, interns work as public policy assistants, media coordinators, field coordinators, and special projects coordinators.

PERKS
Orientation; networking, entry-level experience in nonprofit sector.

FYI
International fellowships are available upon completion of domestic internships (subject to availability of funds).

TO APPLY
Open to college juniors and seniors, recent college grads, college grads of any age, and grad students no older than 25. International applicants eligible with permission to work in the U.S. Submit resume, cover letter, transcript, and three recommendations (two academic, one employment-related).

Education/Internship Coordinator
The Population Institute
107 Second Street NE
Washington, DC 20002
(202) 544-3300
(202) 544-0068 (Fax)
www.populationinstitute.org

SELECTIVITY 🔍 🔍 🔍 🔍

Approximate applicant pool: 400; Interns accepted: 24—40

COMPENSATION 💲

None

LOCATION(S)

New York, NY; Washington, DC

FIELD

Television

DURATION

8—14 weeks: Summer, Fall, Winter, Spring

DEADLINE(S)

Rolling

THE WORK

Debuting in 1989, ABC News' *PrimeTime Live* is an Emmy award–winning news magazine show anchored by Sam Donaldson and Diane Sawyer. Concentrating on investigative news pieces using hidden cameras, the show has uncovered cheating on college campuses ("Faking the Grade"), fraud in the Government's Supplemental Security Income Program ("Crazy Checks"), and corrupt judges ("Who's Judging the Judges?") as well as profiled people like Rosario Ames and Boris Yeltsin. Six to ten interns per quarter work in all areas of the organization: Research, Production, and Editing.

PERKS

Travel with correspondents on local shoots; attendance welcome at weekly meetings on day of broadcast; summer softball team.

FYI

The intern coordinator says: " . . . [We] attempt to expose each student to all aspects of the broadcast journalism profession . . . on-the-job training with some of the best producers, directors, writers, editors and correspondents in the television news business."

TO APPLY

Open to college juniors and seniors as well as recent college grads. Must receive academic credit. International applicants eligible. Write for application.

Internship Program
PrimeTime Live
ABC News
147 Columbus Avenue, 4th Floor
New York, NY 10023
(212) 456-1600

SELECTIVITY 🔍 🔍 🔍 🔍

Approximate applicant pool: 300; Interns accepted: 40

COMPENSATION 💲

Minimum wage

LOCATION

Cincinnati, OH; other US sites & overseas (see Appendix)

FIELD

Consumer goods

DURATION

9—14 weeks: Summer

DEADLINE(S)

February 1

THE WORK

Founded in 1837 by brothers-in-law William Procter and James Gamble as a soap and candle business, Procter & Gamble has since grown by leaps and bounds. It's now a $30-billion-a-year consumer products empire, with approximately 100,000 employees. P & G recruits interns for the following departments: Brand Management, Product Supply/Engineering, Research & Product Development, Financial & Accounting Management, Market Research, Management Systems, Sales & Accounting Management, and Product Supply/Manufacturing.

PERKS

Dorm housing; social activities; P & G College; car for sales interns.

FYI

It's said that P & G, widely recognized as the world's best marketer of products, spends more on advertising than any other US company . . . P & G is an international company, doing business with 140 countries around the world . . . As part of the regular sales force, each Sales intern gets full use of a company car in which to make his or her rounds.

TO APPLY

Open to college sophomores, juniors, and seniors, and grad students. Some positions require certain fields of study. International applicants eligible. Submit resume and cover letter indicating area of interest.

Procter & Gamble
Internship Program Manager
(Area of Interest)
P.O. Box 599
Cincinnati, OH 45201-0599
(513) 983-1100
www.pg.com

PROCTER & GAMBLE PRODUCTIONS

PROCTER & GAMBLE PRODUCTIONS, INC.

SELECTIVITY 🔍 🔍 🔍 🔍
Approximate applicant pool: 300; Interns accepted: 30

COMPENSATION 💲
Minimum wage

LOCATION(S)
New York, NY

FIELD
Television

DURATION
12–20 weeks; Summer, Fall, Spring

DEADLINE(S)
Summer: March 15; Spring: November 15; Fall: August 1.

THE WORK
Incorporated in 1949, Procter & Gamble Productions (PGP) produces the daytime soap operas *As The World Turns* and *Guiding Light*. These shows are taped in New York City and broadcast nationwide weekdays. Since their founding (1936 for *Guiding Light*, and 1956 for *As The World Turns*), P & G's soaps have won over 60 Emmys. Interns at *Guiding Light* and *As The World Turns* work in Production, Casting, Publicity, and the Writers' offices.

PERKS
Attendance welcome at staff meetings and luncheons; invitations to industry parties; occasional invitations to actor showcases; reservation welcome on the studio floor and in the control room to observe tapings.

FYI
P & G Productions' internship program can lead to permanent employment at one of the soaps for approximately 10 percent of interns . . . America's first soap opera *Oxydol's Own Ma Perkins*, produced by Procter & Gamble, debuted in 1933 on WLW Radio in Cincinnati and was so called because its sponsor (Oxydol) was a soap product . . . *Guiding Light*, airing on radio in 1936 and on television in 1952, was the first program in history to be broadcast on both media simultaneously.

TO APPLY
Open to undergrads, recent college grads, college grads, and graduate students. Submit resume and cover letter.

Internship Coordinator
Procter & Gamble Productions
c/o Tele Vest Daytime Programs
Worldwide Plaza
825 Eighth Avenue—35th Floor
New York, NY 10019
(212) 474-5888
(212) 474-5631 (Fax)

PRO-FOUND SOFTWARE

SELECTIVITY 🔍 🔍 🔍 🔍 🔍
Approximate applicant pool: 500; Interns accepted: 3–5

COMPENSATION 💲 💲 💲 💲
$400–$600/week

LOCATION(S)
Teaneck, NJ

FIELD
Computer software

DURATION
12–24 weeks: Summer, Fall, Spring

DEADLINE(S)
Rolling

THE WORK
Founded in 1989, Pro-Found Software is a New Jersey based custom software company best known for rapid application development in client-server environments. Pro-Found Software's current focus is to leverage the Internet infrastructure to bridge distributed application components across diverse platforms. The company utilizes a modular construction process that entails weaving together custom-created software with off-the-shelf industry-standard software. Interns work in the Software Engineering department, where they help create software and participate in client interviews.

PERKS
Attendance welcome at educational workshops; access to spa/health club; occasional opportunities to co-publish articles; state-of-the-art office minutes from NYC.

FYI
Pro-Found Software hires approximately 50 percent of its interns for full-time employment.

TO APPLY
Open to college juniors and seniors as well as grad students. Must be studying a technical subject and be proficient in C/C++ or JAVA. International applicants eligible. Submit resume and cover letter.

Internship Coordinator
Pro-Found Software
Glenpointe Centre West
500 Frank West Burr Boulevard
Teaneck, NJ 07666
(201) 928-0400
(201) 928-1122 (Fax)

PSYCHOLOGY TODAY

See Sussex Publishers

SELECTIVITY 🔍 🔍 🔍
Approximate applicant pool: 1,000 (Allies); Interns accepted: 116 (Allies)

COMPENSATION 💲 💲 💲
None

LOCATION(S)
Wilmington, DE; Chicago, IL; Durham, NC; Milwaukee, WI; Washington, DC

FIELD
Public service

DURATION
10 months: September to June

DEADLINE(S)
March 30

THE WORK
Since 1991, Public Allies has dedicated itself to nurturing "public service entrepreneurs," placing young adults in ten-month paid positions at community-based, local, state, and national non-profit and government agencies. A high profile and highly praised program, Public Allies was designated "model for national service" by the Commision on National and Community Service. Program participants, or "Allies," have performed such work as founding a Community Development Credit Union for two Latino neighborhoods, constructing low-income housing at Habitat for Humanity, and supervising the activities of young people at "After School Kids."

PERKS
Weekly seminars in leadership, organization, and management; team service project; geographically and racially diverse group of Allies.

FYI
In addition to the ten-month Allies program, Public Allies offers semester-long internships for undergrads, recent college grads, college grads of any age, and grad students. Interns work in Operations or Fundraising at the Washington, DC headquarters. Call for more information.

TO APPLY
Open to high school grads under 30 years of age, undergrads, recent college grads, college grads under 30 years of age, and grad students under 30 years of age. International applicants eligible. Write for application.

Public Allies
1015 18th Street NW
Suite 200
Washington, DC 20036
(202) 822-1180
E-mail: panational@aol.com

SELECTIVITY 🔍 🔍
Approximate applicant pool: 650–700; Interns accepted: 200

COMPENSATION 💲
None; fellowships may be available

LOCATION
Washington, DC

FIELD
Law

DURATION
12 weeks: Summer, Fall, Spring

DEADLINE(S)
Summer: April 1; Fall & Spring: 3 weeks before start of session

THE WORK
The Public Defender Service (PDS) for the District of Columbia provides legal representation to indigent persons charged with criminal offenses, respondents in civil commitment proceedings, and incarcerated individuals in need of legal assistance. Recently, the Law Enforcement Assistance Administration designated PDS as an "exemplary" office—the only defender office in the country so honored.

PERKS
Special lectures and field trips; extensive training; test prep. discounts.

FYI
PDS accepted only law students when its internship program began in 1976 . . . Interns are taken on a series of tours that would fascinate even Hannibal Lechter . . . Having at least part-time access to a car is an important prerequisite for this internship . . . Interns may work part-time, though PDS prefers students who can commit to 40 hours per week.

TO APPLY
Open to undergrads, recent college grads, grad students. International applicants eligible. Write for application.

Internship Coordinator
Public Defender Service for DC
633 Indiana Avenue, NW
Washington, DC 20004
(202) 626-8327

HANNIBAL LECTER'S TOUR OF DC:

A term interning at the Public Defender Service for DC includes tours of the city's Mobile Crime Unit, the autopsy room at the Chief Medical Examiner's Office, the facility for the criminally insane at St. Elizabeth's Hospital, and the lock down at Lorton Penitentiary.

It Comes Down To Attitude

You have decided to apply to some internships. But your GPA is less than stellar and your college didn't come close to cracking the top colleges list. Add to that the fact that you have taken few courses relating to the industry in which you want to work.

No hope? Should you invest in a spatula and head to the nearest burger joint?

If you were applying to a top grad school, the answer might be a hearty "yes." Grad schools are notoriously interested in their applicants' grades, courses, and college reputation.

But internships are a different bag. Unlike "ivory tower" admissions committees, internship coordinators are more flexible in deciding whom they will select.

To be sure, some internship programs impose a minimum grade-point-average, although such requirements are relatively rare. The CIA, for example, seeks undergraduates with at least a 2.75 GPA, while the Environmental Protection Agency draws the line at a 3.0 GPA. Moreover, a few programs also scrutinize the coursework of their applicants. The auction house Butterfield & Butterfield favors art history majors, and *The Washington Post* seeks out students who have taken classes in journalism. And every now and then, one runs across an internship that seems to have a disproportionately high representation of students from the Ivy League and other top schools.

But with most internships, application requirements are typically looser.

According to the vast majority of internship coordinators, the deciding factor is often an applicant's attitude. Specifically, coordinators use cover letters and interviews to gauge an applicant's motivation and energy. Organizations want interns who are fired-up and who will accept all assignments or ask for more during slow periods. Says the internship coordinator at *Rolling Stone* magazine in New York, "We look for applicants who want to learn every aspect of magazine publishing . . . [ones who are] inquisitive and enthusiastic, even when carrying out clerical work."

Counterbalancing the "go-getter" attitude, applicants must also show they realize that as interns, they will be temporary observers, oftentimes in a sensitive, hierarchical institution. Consequently, coordinators highly prize interns who display diplomacy and discretion. Interns have to know when to check their enthusiasm and assume the role of low-key team-player.

The importance of intern discreetness is best illustrated by the experience of a former intern at the White House. During his summer at the world's most powerful address, the intern kept a small camera in his pocket, just in case he came upon a photo opportunity with a bigwig. As luck would have it, one day the Vice President walked by the office in which the intern was working. Armed with a loaded Minolta, the intern pounced, begging the Vice President to pose with him for a picture. Although he was late for a meeting, the Veep begrudgingly complied. The intern got his way, but days later the story was relayed to his supervisor, who considered it a serious breach of White House protocol. Not surprisingly, the intern lost the faith of his supervisor, who distanced himself from the intern for the rest of the internship.

The key for internship applicants is to play up not only their enthusiasm but also their professionalism and maturity. As the internship coordinator at Lucasfilm in San Rafael, Calif., says, companies "don't want people with pixie dust in their eyes."

It is essential for prospecitve interns to understand the importance of the attitude they display in their cover letters and interviews. It will go a long way—often further than the GPA—toward securing a rewarding internship.

PUBLIC THEATER / NEW YORK SHAKESPEARE FESTIVAL

SELECTIVITY 🔍🔍🔍
Approximate applicant pool: 100–150; Interns accepted: 25

COMPENSATION 💲
$25–$50/week

LOCATION(S)
New York, NY

FIELD
Performing arts

DURATION
12 weeks; Sumer, Fall, Spring

DEADLINE(S)
Rolling

THE WORK
Since 1954, the New York Shakespeare Festival (NYSF) has staged a rich variety of theatrical productions. In addition to running its Shakespeare Marathon, the NYSF has presented award-winning productions such as *A Chorus Line, Hair, The Pirates of Penzance*, and *Twilight: Los Angeles, 1992*. Departments hiring interns include Marketing, Community Affairs, Press, Producer's Office, Production, General Management, Development, Film, and Casting.

PERKS
Access to productions, workshops, readings, and screenings at theater; invitations to social events.

FYI
Former interns have found permanent employment at the NYSF (one assists the Associate Producer) while others have gone on to jobs at Broadway and Off-Broadway productions (e.g., one became an assistant to the director of *The Merry Wives of Windsor*, another assisted the director of *Richard II*).

TO APPLY
Open to high school students (primarily used during summer season at Central Park), undergrads, recent college grads, college grads of any age, and grad students. International applicants eligible. Submit resume, cover letter, and recommendations.

Internship Coordinator
New York Shakespeare Festival
425 Lafayette Street
New York, NY 10003
(212) 598-7100
(212) 598-7161 (Fax)

SELECTIVITY   N/A
Approximate applicant pool: N/A; Interns accepted: 100–160

COMPENSATION $
None

LOCATION(S)
Washington, DC and CA, CO, CT, FL,GA, IL, IN,IA, ME, MD, MA, MI, MO, NJ, NM, NC, OH, OR, PA, TX, VT, WA,WI.

FIELD
Public policy; Environment; Consumer; Government

DURATION
Semester; varies

DEADLINE(S)
Rolling

THE WORK
Founded in 1971, Public Interest Research Groups (PIRGs) is a nationwide network of state PIRGs, each an independent environmental and consumer advocacy organization. Through research, legislative advocacy, media events, and grassroots organizing, PIRGs build campaigns for environmental and consumer protection, including those for clean water, safe energy, recycling, government reform, and voter registration. At the national lobbying office in DC, interns conduct policy and legal research, write briefs on legislative issues, prepare testimony for congressional hearings, investigate and report on environmental and consumer problems, and organize lobbying and public education campaigns. State PIRG interns research problems relating to environmental and consumer issues, draft legislative proposals, coordinate media events, write opinion pieces, and help develop effective grassroots campaign strategies.

PERKS
Attendance welcome at all PIRG meetings, events, and social activities; occasional brown-bag luncheons with leaders from other nonprofits; access to PIRG briefings by Ralph Nader and members of Congress (DC).

FYI
Throughout the year, PIRGs mobilize grassroots support for national causes.

TO APPLY
Open to undergrads and law students. International applicants eligible. Submit resume and cover letter.

College Student or Law Student	Recruitment Director
Internship Coordinator	The State PIRGS
US PIRG	29 Temple Pl.
218 D Street, SE	Boston, MA 02111
Washington, DC 20003	(617) 292-4800
(202) 546-9707	
E-mail: uspirg@pirg.org	
www.pirg.org	

SELECTIVITY   🔍🔍🔍🔍🔍
Approximate applicant pool: 200; Interns accepted: 5

COMPENSATION $ $ $
NY: $287/week; health insurance; Brussels & Geneva: $150–$200/week; free housing

LOCATION(S)
New York, NY; Brussels, Belgium; Geneva, Switzerland

FIELD
Foreign affairs; Public policy

DURATION
NY: 1 year: September–August

DEADLINE(S)
NY: February 11

THE WORK
Created shortly after the United Nations' founding in 1945 the Quaker United Nations Office (QUNO) represents Quaker groups worldwide at the UN in New York and Geneva and at the European Union (EU) in Brussels (the Brussels office is called the Quaker Council for European Affairs [QCEA]). Areas of QUNO and QCEA concern include disarmament, security, human rights, economic justice and development. Interns support QUNO/QCEA staff by monitoring the UN's General Assembly or activities of the EU, researching Quaker issues, preparing mailings, attending to visitors, and writing and editing the QUNO newsletter.

PERKS
Possible speaking and travel opportunities; attendance welcome at QUNO receptions for UN and EU officials; participation in weekly staff meetings.

FYI
Quakers, as members of the Religious Society of Friends are known, embrace nonviolence, a philosophy whose essence is captured in Ephesians 4:3—"Do all you can to preserve the unity of the spirit by the peace that binds you together."

Known across the land as "America's oldest teenager," **Dick Clark** launched his career in entertainment in 1945 by running the office mimeograph machine at WRUN radio in Utica, New York. Smitten by show business, he went on to Syracuse University and a series of jobs in entertainment, before eventually becoming host of *American Bandstand* and the *$100,000 Pyramid.*

TO APPLY

Open to recent college grads, college grads of any age, and grad students. Interns are expected to have some familiarity with Quaker organizations, practices, and beliefs. International applicants eligible. Write for application directly to office of interest.

QUNO Internship Program
Quaker United Nations Office
777 United Nations Plaza
New York, NY 10017
(212) 682-2745
(212) 983-0034 (Fax)
E-mail: qunony@pipeline.com

QCEA Program Assistant
Quaker Council for European Affairs
Quaker House
50 Square Ambiorix
B-1040 Brussels, Belgium
32-2-230-4935
32-2-230-6370 (Fax)

QUNO Internship Program
Quaker United Nations Office
Quaker House
13 Avenue du Mervelet
Geneva, 1209
Switzerland
41-22-733-3397
41-22-734-0015 (Fax)

QUALITY EDUCATION FOR MINORITIES NETWORK

QEM Network

SELECTIVITY 🔍🔍🔍
Approximate applicant pool: 150; Interns accepted: 15

COMPENSATION 💲💲💲
$3,000 stipend for undergraduate students; $4,000 stipend for graduate students. Interns are provided with round-trip transportation to Washington DC, and housing.

LOCATION(S)
Washington, DC; Arlington, VA

FIELD
Education; Public policy; Science policy; Health education and awareness

DURATION
10 weeks: Summer

DEADLINE(S)
February 1

THE WORK
Founded in 1990, the Quality Education for Minorities (QEM) Network is a nonprofit organization dedicated to improving the education of minority children, youth, and adults. QEM has a special focus on mathematics, science, and engineering. Network interns work with mentors at the QEM Network in such areas as community outreach, HIV/AIDS education and awareness, education policy, education research, and legislation analysis. Summer Science Interns learn about science policy formulation with mentors at science-orientated agencies such as the National Science Foundation.

PERKS
Brown-bag luncheons with executives and key policymakers; field trips to federal agencies (e.g., Capitol Hill, and Library of Congress); meetings with QEM members and affiliates.

FYI
The goal of QEM's internship programs is to "develop the potential of minority and nonminority student interns to become leaders and advocates for quality education for minorities."

TO APPLY
Open to college sophomores, juniors, and seniors as well as graduate students. Contact QEM for application.

Internship Program
QEM Network
1818 N Street NW, Suite 350
Washington, DC 20036
(202) 659-1818
(202) 659-5408 (Fax)
E-mail: qemnetwork@qem.org
qemnetwork.qem.org

RAND

SELECTIVITY 🔍🔍🔍🔍
Approximate applicant pool: 350; Interns accepted: 25

COMPENSATION 💲💲💲💲
$750/week; round-trip travel

LOCATION(S)
Santa Monica, CA; Washington, DC; Pittsburgh, PA

FIELD
Public policy research

DURATION
12 weeks: Summer

DEADLINE(S)
February 1

THE WORK
Founded in 1948, Rand is a private, nonprofit institution that helps improve public policy through research and analysis. With a research staff of about 600 resident professionals and some 600 consultants, Rand covers the spectrum of economic and technical disciplines. Summer associates work in Project Air Force, Army, or National Security divisions, where they study policy questions related to national security and military service missions, operations, technology, and resource management; or they work in the Domestic Research Division, where they analyze social and economic problems and policies affecting the nation.

PERKS
Lectures and seminars with staff researchers and distinguished visitors; research library with over 100,000 titles (CA); oceanside location (CA).

FYI
Alumni of the program, started in 1969, include Rand's Senior Vice President.

TO APPLY
Open to grad students with a minimum of two years in a PhD program. International applicants eligible for domestic research. Submit resume, cover letter, and list of three academic references.

Graduate Student Summer Associate Program
Rand
1700 Main Street
Santa Monica, CA 90407-2138
(310) 393-0411 x6546
(310) 393-4818 (Fax)
E-mail: keating@rand.org
www.rand.org/fellowships/gsip

RANDOM HOUSE

SELECTIVITY   🔍 🔍 🔍 🔍
Approximate applicant pool: 1,000; Interns accepted: 30

COMPENSATION   💲 💲 💲
$300/week

LOCATION(S)
New York, NY

FIELD
Publishing

DURATION
10 weeks: Summer

DEADLINE(S)
March 31

THE WORK
In 1925, Random House, Inc., was founded as a publishing house that would print original books "on the side at random." It is now the world's largest general-trade publisher, and its "house" has published authors like John Updike, Toni Morrison, James Joyce, Albert Camus, William Faulkner, Eugene O'Neill, and Dr. Seuss. Interns are placed in one of the company's major publishing groups—Crown, Ballantine, Knopf, Random House, or Children's Publishing, as well as Trade Sales and Marketing Division—but get an in-depth look at publishing by rotating through Publicity, Marketing, Production, and Editorial areas.

PERKS
Youthful staff; discounted books; weekly seminars; trip to Westminster, MD, distribution center.

FYI
The Random House Internship Program was established in the summer of 1990 . . . No two interns ever work in the same department at the same time to eliminate competition between interns.

TO APPLY
Open to college juniors and grad students with one year left in school after completion of the internship. International applicants eligible. Submit a resume demonstrating an interest in publishing, and a cover letter indicating what you want out of a book publishing internship and why.

Random House, Inc.
Internship Coordinator
Human Resources
1540 Broadway
New York, NY 10036
No phone calls

RAYCHEM

Raychem

SELECTIVITY   🔍 🔍 🔍 🔍 🔍
Approximate applicant pool: 2,000; Interns accepted: 40

COMPENSATION   💲 💲 💲 💲
$400–$700/week for undergrads; $600–$1,000/week for grad students; round-trip travel

LOCATION(S)
Menlo Park, CA

FIELD
Material science; High-tech

DURATION
10–12 weeks: Summer

DEADLINE(S)
April 1

Blissful Internship Experiences

- Flying on Air Force One to Disney World for President Reagan's Inaugural (*Newsweek*)

- On the first day of the internship, writing a front page story for the Washington Post; on the second day, getting a call from NBC News' John Chancellor for more details (*The Washington Post*)

- Meeting Mick Jagger during an *MTV News* interview (MTV)

- Delivering the Supreme Court nomination of Ruth Bader Ginsburg to the Senate (The White House)

- Personally selecting and editing the radio programs to include on *The Best of Rush Limbaugh* (*The Rush Limbaugh Show*)

- Escorting swimsuit model Rachel Hunter to media interviews and accompanying her and husband Rod Stewart during an interview (*Sports Illustrated*)

- Writing some of the Captain's lines for *Star Trek: The Next Generation* (Academy of Television Arts & Sciences)

- Being flagged down by ZZ Top and getting taken by them to a sushi dinner (Oscar Mayer Weinermobile)

USING THE INTERNET
TO HELP YOU WIN AN INTERNSHIP

Successful internship seekers are increasingly using the Internet to help them land top internships. Several online sites offer vital information to help prep for internship interviews and find out more information on specific companies.

- **Wall Street Journal Careers (www.careers.wsj.com):** provides general information on the job search and employment trends. The site is distinguished by its panel of career columnists, many of whom are Wall Street Journal reporters.

- **Vault Reports (www.vaultreports.com):** one of the most popular career sites on the Net, Vault Reports provides "insider" information on many of the companies that offer top internships. It's a must-visit before applying to an internship.

- **JobWeb (www.jobweb.org):** maintained by the National Association of Colleges and Employers, JobWeb contains thousands of job and internship postings, as well as links to over 50 other career-related sites. You can't post a resume here, but you can retrieve invaluable information on jobs and the companies that offer them.

- **Newsgroups:** There are endless newsgroups in which one can search "help wanted" ads posted by employers. Many are industry-specific, such as comp.jobs.offered, which lists only computer-related jobs. A general list of internship and job-related newsgroups is available on the Web at www.collegegrad.com/jobs/usenet.html. If you're still partial to wanted ads of newspapers, you can scan through the pages of newspapers across the country through CareerPath.com (www.careerpath.com), which offers ads from, among other publications, The New York Times and the Washington Post.

- **Company Websites:** an often overlooked source of helpful company information is found directly at the source. After identifying the companies at which you want to intern, make sure to visit their websites. Pay special attention to the "recruiting" areas of the websites.

THE WORK

Manufacturer extraordinaire of material science products since 1957, Raychem Corporation is on the cutting edge of scientific discovery. The company has invented more than 10,000 high-performance products, from fiber-optic cable accessories and computer touchscreens to cable TC coaxial-cable connectors and gel sealants. Internship opportunities are available in the areas of Engineering, Research & Development (R&D), Product Design, Manufacturing, Marketing, Finance, Human Resources, and Accounting.

PERKS

Plant tours; intramurals; dedicated employees.

FYI

Raychem's Intern Program dates back to the mid-1970s . . . Spending over 10 percent of sales on R&D annually, Raychem ranks among the top 100 corporations for R&D expenditures . . . Student office accommodations are mixed, ranging from cubicles to private offices. However, most interns spend the majority of their time in the laboratory.

TO APPLY

Open to college juniors and seniors and grad students. Minimum GPA: 3.0. Submit resume and cover letter discussing work experience, leadership activities, and area of interest.

Raychem Corporation
PO Box 9206
Los Angeles, CA 90009-2016
(310) 337-3379 (Fax)
E-mail: raychem@isearch.com

RCA RECORDS

See Bertelsmann Music Group

THE REAL WORLD

SELECTIVITY 🔍 🔍 🔍
Approximate applicant pool: 100; Interns accepted: 15

COMPENSATION 💲
None

LOCATION(S)
Los Angeles, CA

FIELD
Television

DURATION
12 weeks: Summer, Fall, Spring

DEADLINE(S)
Rolling

THE WORK

Established in 1992 by Bunim-Murray Productions, *The Real World* is a reality-based soap opera following the adventures of seven young adults who live together in a house. Broadcast on MTV (see separate entry), the show merges traditional elements of soap opera—strong stories and engrossing characters—with the unmistakable style of MTV—fast pace, quick cuts, rock and roll scores, and contemporary attitudes. Interns assist staff in all phases of production, including helping with casting and post-production editing.

PERKS

Training in off-line video editing (during post-production season); passes to movie screenings; attendance welcome at parties.

FYI

The Real World has been set in New York, Los Angeles, San Francisco, London, Miami, Boston, Seattle, and Honolulu. Co-founder Mary-Ellis Bunim has produced more than 2,500 television episodes as Executive Producer for *Santa Barbara*, *As The World Turns*, *Search for Tomorrow*, and *Loving*.

TO APPLY

Open to undergrads and grad students. International applicants eligible. Submit resume and cover letter.

Internship Coordinator
Bunim-Murray Productions
6007 Sepulveda Blvd.
Van Nuys, CA 91411
(818) 756-5100
(818) 756-5140 (Fax)

REEBOK

SELECTIVITY 🔍 🔍 🔍 🔍 🔍
Approximate applicant pool: 2,500; Interns accepted: 35

COMPENSATION 💲 💲 💲 💲
$500/week for undergraduates; $650+/week for graduates—Averages depending on expenses

LOCATION(S)
Stoughton, MA

FIELD
Athletic shoes and apparel

DURATION
10–12 weeks: Summer

DEADLINE(S)
April 1

THE WORK

Reebok International Ltd. is a sporting good company comprising Reebok, Rockport, Greg Norman, Polo Sport/Ralph Lauren, and Weebok. Reebok holds a large percent of the US market, second only to Nike and is now a $3 billion-per-year operation. Undergrad interns work in the company's Reebok division in areas such as Promotions, Human Resources, Retail, Management Information Systems (MIS), Finance, and Sales. Grad students receive assignments in the marketing or operations unit.

PERKS

Independence; 40 percent discount on shoes; lunchtime basketball games; use of fitness center; interactive chess with management; self enrichment classes.

FYI

The Rhebok is a small South African gazelle. It is extraordinarily aggressive, agile, and fleet-footed, a fine image for the Reebok company . . . Reebok started the College Relations Internship Program in the summer of 1990 . . . Reebok's definition of internship uses words and phrases such as structured, meaningful, and impact upon the business group.

TO APPLY

Open to college juniors and seniors, recent grads, grad students. International applicants eligible. Submit resume and cover letter between January and March. Since all applications will be acknowledged, Reebok asks interested parties not to call their offices.

Reebok
c/o College Relations Program
100 Technology Center Drive
Stoughton, MA 02072
E-mail: college.recruiting@reebok.com

RENAISSANCE MULTIMEDIA

Renaissance Computer Art Center, Inc.

SELECTIVITY 🔍 🔍 🔍
Approximate applicant pool: 30; Interns accepted: 3

COMPENSATION $
None

LOCATION(S)
New York, NY

FIELD
Internet and multimedia development

DURATION
6–12 weeks year round

DEADLINE(S)
Rolling

THE WORK

Established in 1989, Renaissance Multimedia is a full-service digital production firm focused on interactive multimedia and online communication service including internet web sites and events. Production services include project development, scripting, design, illustration, authoring, and software programming online marketing and advertising.

PERKS

Daily contact with principals of company and with clients; office includes high-end computers and a digital video editing suite.

FYI

The president of Renaissance, Andrew Edwards, is an accomplished computer graphics illustrator who has taught seminars in computer design across the country.

TO APPLY

Open to college students, recent college grads, grad students. Submit resume, cover letter, and any work samples (on disk or give URLs).

Internship Coordinator
Renaissance Multimedia
90 John Street
New York, NY 10038
(212) 619–0051
(212) 619–0054 (Fax)
E-mail: info@rcac.com
www.rcac.com

RENEW AMERICA

RENEW AMERICA

SELECTIVITY 🔍 🔍 🔍 🔍 🔍
Approximate applicant pool: 180; Interns accepted: up to 6 per year

COMPENSATION $ $ $ $
$7,500 for interns hired for six months

LOCATION(S)
Washington, DC

FIELD
Environment

DURATION
6 months: ongoing

DEADLINE(S)
Rolling

THE WORK

Founded in 1979, Renew America (RA) is a nonprofit organization that collects and promotes information on successful environmental programs developed by community groups, nonprofit organizations, government agencies, and businesses. RA maintains the "Environmental Success Index" (a clearinghouse of environmental programs), sponsors the National Awards for Environmental Sustainability. Interns spend much of their time working with local grassroots environmental organizations to identify and verify projects for inclusion in the "Index."

PERKS

Attendance at some client meetings and all staff meetings; access to RA gym; possible attendance at in-town conferences.

FYI

The internship program has been running since 1989 . . . More than 1,600 environmental programs have been included in RA's "Environmental Index."

TO APPLY

Open to recent college grads. International applicants eligible. Submit resume and cover letter.

Internship Coordinator
Renew America
1400 16th Street NW, Suite 710
Washington, DC 20036
(202) 232-2252
(202) 232-2617 (Fax)
E-mail: renewamerica@ige.org
www.crest.org/renew.america

While J.R. Ewing might have interned for his daddy's oil company, actor **Larry Hagman** apprenticed with St. John Terrell's theater companies in Florida and New Jersey in 1950.

RHINO RECORDS

See Atlantic Records

RHODE ISLAND STATE GOVERNMENT

SELECTIVITY 🔍
Approximate applicant pool: 600; Interns accepted: 450

COMPENSATION 💲
Summer and Spring: $100/week; Fall: None

LOCATION(S)
Providence and 15 surrounding cities, RI

FIELD
Government; Law; Public service; Ballet; Dance; Arts; Television

DURATION
8 weeks: Summer, Fall, Spring

DEADLINE(S)
Summer: May 15; Fall: rolling; Spring: November 15

THE WORK
Established in 1842 with the adoption of the State Constitution, the Rhode Island State Government (RISG) governs Rhode Island, one of the original thirteen states of the Union. Interns are placed within all areas of state government, legislative, executive, and judicial branches as well as departments and agencies including the Attorney General's Office, Health, Drug Control, Corrections, Labor, Transportation, State Medical Examiner, Juvenile Probation and Family Court, Commission on Human Rights, Environmental Management, Historical Preservation, State Archives, Legislative Research, Library Services, Mental Health, State Budget and Finance, and International Relations. Placements are also available with government-funded theaters, museums, shelters, television stations, and public service groups, such as the Boys and Girls Club, Festival Ballet, Fusionworks Dance Company, Langston Hughes Center for the Arts, and WSBE-TV.

PERKS
Weekly lecture series on government featuring professors from nearby colleges; academic component: papers and exams (spring only).

FYI
RISG's spring internship program dates back to 1969 . . . 60 percent of intern placements are law-related.

TO APPLY
Open to juniors and seniors as well as law school students. For summer, must be a resident of Rhode Island attending an out-of-state school or a disabled student. Minimum GPA: 2.5. Must receive academic credit (fall only). International applicants eligible. Write for application.

Internship Program
Rhode Island State Government
State Capitol, Room 8AA
Providence, RI 02903
(401) 222-6782

RIO GRANDE NATIONAL FOREST

See San Juan/Rio Grande National Forests

THE RIPON SOCIETY

SELECTIVITY 🔍🔍🔍
Approximate applicant pool: 50; Interns accepted: 5

COMPENSATION 💲
Internship bonus possible

LOCATION(S)
Washington, DC

FIELD
Public policy; Magazines; Event management

DURATION
8–12 weeks: ongoing

DEADLINE(S)
Rolling

THE WORK
Founded in 1962, The Ripon Society is a nonprofit research and public policy organization promoting the acceptance of moderate Republican principles in the Republican Party, government, and society. Ripon programs include DC's Breakfast Series with members of Congress, national and regional conferences, and *The Ripon Forum*, the Society's quarterly magazine. Interns assist staff in all capacities, from conducting research and writing for the magazine to organizing conferences.

PERKS
Participation in Ripon public policy events; articles published in quarterly magazine; interact with members of Congress; attendance welcome at Congressional hearings.

FYI
Ripon Republicans bill themselves as fiscally conservative and socially aware, promoting smaller government, individual fiscal responsibility, and respect for differences in religion, gender, race, and sexual orientation.

TO APPLY
Open to undergrads, recent college grads, and grad students. Submit resume and cover letter.

Ashleigh Roberts
The Ripon Society
501 Capitol Court NE, Suite 300
Washington, DC 20002
(202) 546-1292
(202) 547-6560 (Fax)
E-mail: letters@riponsoc.org

Queen Noor al-Hussein of Jordan, while in junior high school at Washington, DC's National Cathedral School, served as an intern-volunteer for Lyndon B. Johnson's 1964 election campaign. She later attended the Chapin School in New York City and the Concord Academy in Massachusetts before enrolling at Princeton to study architecture.

THE ROCKEY COMPANY

SELECTIVITY 🔍🔍🔍
Approximate applicant pool: 75–100; Interns accepted: 6-8/year

COMPENSATION 💲
$500 bonus possible

LOCATION(S)
Portland, OR; Seattle, WA; Spokane, WA

FIELD
Public relations

DURATION
10–12 weeks: Summer, Fall, Spring, Winter

DEADLINE(S)
Rolling

THE WORK
Founded in 1962, The Rockey Company is a full-service public relations firm, providing services in public affairs, investor relations, graphic design, marketing communications, opinion research, video production, and satellite communications. Its clients include some of the Pacific Northwest's largest companies, such as Nintendo, Boeing, Washington Mutual Bank, and Brooks Sports. Interns help service Rockey clients by working directly with account executives and public affairs consultants.

PERKS
Intern luncheon with executives; weekly intern meetings; $500 bonus at end of internship for top interns.

FYI
Rockey's internship program was started in 1984 . . . Says the internship coordinator: "When possible, we try to bring interns on board at the start of projects to enable them to see all aspects of the services we provide our clients."

TO APPLY
Open to college juniors and seniors as well as recent college grads. Submit resume, cover letter, and writing samples.

Internship Coordinator
The Rockey Company
2121 Fifth Avenue
Seattle, WA 98121
(206) 728-1100

MARK TWAIN OWES HIS NAME TO AN APPRENTICESHIP

When **Samuel Clemens** was 22, he set out for South America to make his fortune. On the way, he took a riverboat to New Orleans and became so enamored with riverboats that he convinced the boat's pilot to take him on as an apprentice. Abandoning his travel plans to South America, Clemens spent a few years learning the ropes of riverboating, and in 1859 he became a full-fledged riverboat pilot. Years later, when Clemens started to build what would become a distinguished career as a journalist and an author, he chose to be published under a name that he frequently heard during his apprenticeship—"mark twain," a riverboat pilot's term meaning "two fathoms deep."

ROCKWELL SEMICONDUCTOR SYSTEMS

SELECTIVITY 🔍🔍🔍
Approximate applicant pool: 300; Interns accepted: 40

COMPENSATION 💲💲💲💲
$400/week for undergrads; $800/week for grad students

LOCATION(S)
Newport Beach, CA

FIELD
Microelectronics; Telecommunications

DURATION
12 weeks: Summer

DEADLINE(S)
Rolling

THE WORK
Rockwell Semiconductor systems is a leading developer and manufacturer of fax and modem chipsets and other telecommunications technology. It is a business segment of Rockwell International, a company with sales of $13 billion. Interns work in many of the engineering departments, including Microelectronic Device Engineering, Systems Engineering, Applications Engineering, Process Engineering, Test Engineering, and Production Industrial Engineering, as well as Marketing and Analytical Laboratory.

PERKS
Weekly presentations on parts of the company; barbecue picnic; lunch with executives; social activities; free frisbees, t-shirts.

FYI
Interns have been part of Rockwell for 13 years . . . Approximately 35 percent of interns are hired for full-time positions . . . Applicants should be considering majors in electrical engineering, computer engineering, computer science, industrial engineering, chemistry, or physics.

EXCLUSIVE INTERVIEW WITH
KATHRYN FULLER

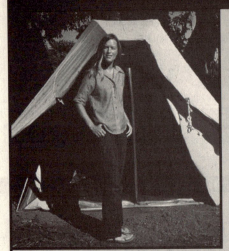

Kathryn Fuller is the President of the World Wildlife Fund in Washington, DC. Before joining WWF, Fuller was the Chief of Wildlife & Marine Resources at the US Justice Department. She earned a B.A. in English and American Literature from Brown University in 1968 and a J.D. from the University of Texas Law School in 1976. At left is Fuller during her internship in Tanzania.

The Internship Informants: When did your internship experiences start?
Fuller: It's fair to say that most everything I did had the look of an internship or an apprenticeship until I got my first real job as a lawyer with the Justice Department. In college, I spent the summer after my junior year working as an apprentice copywriter at the ad agency BBDO. It was great—it was the first time I had the opportunity to be treated as a professional, and I really did write advertising copy. I was assigned to the Pepsi account, so I had my own little cubicle near all the other copywriters. I wasn't writing the big national ads, but I was taking some of the basic themes and writing everything from local radio ads to point-of-purchase display pieces to contests under bottle-cap liners—you name it.

The Internship Informants: What is your most memorable internship experience?
Fuller: A self-created internship, if you will. When I was 25 I was working in the library of the Museum of Comparative Zoology at Harvard, learning a lot about how libraries run and talking with professors and students about their zoology work. I ended up talking a mammologist into letting me come to Tanzania with him and his wife and their very young son to share with his wife child care and research assistant duties.

The Internship Informants: How did you finance the trip?
Fuller: The professor's work at that point was funded by National Geographic, and he said, "Well, I've got enough money, so if you can get yourself to Tanzania, I can cover your costs while you are there."

The Internship Informants: What did you do over there?
Fuller: I studied wildebeest behavior, living in a tent on the floor of the Ngorongoro Crater for about two months. In some respects, it really changed my life. I met all sorts of people in the wildlife conservation community. I spent all that time out there in the bush.

The Internship Informants: It must have required some adjustment being over there.
Fuller: It was just thrilling. We were living in a tent in the middle of a place where the only other people were Masai warriors. The Masai are so tall and lean—they are very striking. There they are, out walking across the plains barefoot with a cloth draped around them and a spear. They're out there tending their cattle but prepared to ward off lions and so forth. And there were researchers coming through, and that was fascinating to talk to some of them. Even in just a few short months, this internship provided me with a huge amount of background, a kind of storehouse of impressions that are still with me.

The Internship Informants: What came next?
Fuller: I went to law school, and while there, I had a sort of ongoing legal internship with the State of Texas doing consumer protection work, anti-trust work, and civil rights work. It gave me experience of being in court, and doing legal writing and research—it was a chance to be the equivalent of a lawyer while still in law school.

The Internship Informants: Looking back, was serving so many internships worth it?
Fuller: Absolutely. All of these internships that I had along the way added up to my view of the world and the workplace. [The internships] were like different puzzle pieces, and each has been valuable to me in what I now do.

TO APPLY

Open to college juniors, and seniors as well as grad students. International applicants eligible. Write for application.

Rockwell Semiconductor Systems
Mail Stop 501-377, Dept. SH
4311 Jamboree Road, PO Box C
Newport Beach, CA 92658-8902
(714) 221-4984
E-mail: intern.program@nb.rockwell.com

RODALE INSTITUTE EXPERIMENTAL FARM

 RODALE INSTITUTE

SELECTIVITY
Approximate applicant pool: 150; Interns accepted: varies depending on needs and funding

COMPENSATION
$6.50/hour

LOCATION(S)
Kutztown, PA

FIELD
Agriculture; Horticulture

DURATION
3–9 months: generally starting March, April, May, or June

DEADLINE(S)
February 1

THE WORK
The Rodale Institute Experimental Farm (RIEF) is a 333-acre research farm located in Berks County, PA. It maintains a Demonstration Garden, a research and test facility for regenerative gardening visited by nearly 20,000 people every year; and conducts scientific research on low-input regenerative agriculture, including applied weed ecology, nitrogen cycling, soil biology, compost utilization, and tree-based cropping systems. Interns work in Demonstration Garden, Outreach Department, Farm Operations, Dairy Network Partnership and Soil Health.

PERKS
Attendance welcome at RIEF meetings, conferences, and guest lectures; training in the use of complex equipment used in agricultural research; two-month training program in April and May (Outreach Department); weekly seminars, and staff discussions.

FYI
Unpaid internships for college credit or paid internships funded by outside grants can be arranged throughout the year.

TO APPLY
Open to recent college grads and grad students. Must have a background in biology, ecology, or agriculture (Agronomy/Farming Systems only). International applicants eligible. Write for application.

Internship Program
Rodale Institute Experimental Farm
611 Siegfriedale Road
Kutztown, PA 19530
(610) 683-1400
(610) 683-8548 (Fax)
E-mail: info@rodaleinst.org

ROLL CALL

 THE NEWSPAPER OF CAPITOL HILL

SELECTIVITY
Approximate applicant pool: 50 per season; Interns accepted: 3 per season

COMPENSATION
None

LOCATION(S)
Washington, DC

DURATION
16–20 weeks: Summer, Fall, Spring

FIELD
Newspapers

DEADLINE(S)
Summer: last week of February; Fall: last week of July; Spring: last week of November

THE WORK
The only publication of its kind, *Roll Call* is a twice-weekly newspaper written specifically for members of Congress and their staffs. In existence since 1955, *Roll Call* provides an "insider's perspective" on Congress and the people who run it. Interns work in the Editorial department.

PERKS
Lunches with members of Congress; attendance welcome at editorial meetings; free copies of newspaper.

FYI
Says the internship coordinator: "We especially encourage interns to develop their own stories . . . We've had students who show initiative and ability come back for full-time positions."

TO APPLY
Open to undergrads, recent college grads, and grad students. International applicants eligible. Submit resume, cover letter, and writing samples.

Internship Coordinator
Roll Call
50 F Street, NW
7th Floor
Washington, DC 20001
(202) 824-6800
(202) 824-6843 (Fax)

RollingStone

SELECTIVITY 🔍 🔍 🔍 🔍 🔍

Approximate applicant pool: 600–750; Interns accepted: 12–18

COMPENSATION Ⓢ

None

LOCATION(S)

New York, NY

FIELD

Music journalism; Magazines

DURATION

12 weeks: Summer, Fall, Spring

DEADLINE(S)

Summer: March 30; Fall: August 1; Spring: December 15

THE WORK

Beginning in 1967 as a grassroots publication distributed mostly in Northern California, *Rolling Stone* has become the world's premier music magazine, grossing more than $110 million annually and reaching upwards of 1.2 million readers per issue. Published biweekly, and issued 24 times a year, it features incisive interviews and photographs of the music world's hottest performers. Part gofers and part research assistants, interns do not write articles but do gain exposure to all aspects of magazine publishing.

PERKS

Hip culture; sleek offices; promotional freebies.

FYI

Typing and basic computer skills are essential for *Rolling Stone* interns . . . Several former interns have made their mark in the publishing world, including one who's a former editor of *Sassy* magazine and another who's the music editor at *Vibe*.

TO APPLY

Open to undergrads and recent grads. International applicants eligible. Submit resume, cover letter stating the session to which the student is applying and the reasons for wanting to work at *Rolling Stone*, transcript, and a letter of recommendation.

*R*olling *Stone* interns Jennifer Manette, Christina Vegiard, and Laurie Trombley (l-r) working the *Rolling Stone* booth at the CMJ Music Marathon, New York City.

Rolling Stone
Internship Coordinator
1290 Avenue of the Americas
New York, NY 10104
(212) 484-1616

SELECTIVITY 🔍 🔍 🔍 🔍 🔍

Approximate applicant pool: 300–400; Interns accepted: 10

COMPENSATION Ⓢ

None

LOCATION(S)

Philadelphia, PA

FIELD

Corporate travel management

DURATION

10–15 weeks: Summer, Fall, Spring

DEADLINE(S)

August/September for Fall; December/January for Spring; April/May for Summer

THE WORK

Rosenbluth International is a worldwide travel management firm, arranging the travel for over 1,500 corporate clients, including DuPont, SmithKline, and Phillips. Rosenbluth's motivated workplace has helped make it one of the nation's largest travel companies. Rosenbluth leads the pack in associate satisfaction and was named one of the *Top 100 Best Companies to Work For* by *Fortune* magazine. Internships are available in a variety of areas, including Accounting, Human Resources, Information Technology, Learning and Development, Marketing, Supplier Relations, and Travel Reservations.

PERKS

Quality of Life; friendly, upbeat culture; unique orientation; intern events.

FYI

Rosenbluth chose a salmon as its mascot to reflect the company's willingness to buck tradition. One example is their policy of putting the employee first, the customer second. Interns begin their internship with an involved, two-day New Associate Orientation Program.

TO APPLY

Open to undergrads, recent college grads, and grad students. International applicants eligible. Submit resume, with a cover letter and a writing sample.

Internship Coordinator
Rosenbluth International
2401 Walnut Street
Philadelphia, PA 19103-4390
(215) 977-5429
www.rosenbluth.com

ROY A. SOMLYO PRODUCTIONS

SELECTIVITY 🔍🔍🔍🔍
Approximate applicant pool: 50; Interns accepted: 4

COMPENSATION 💲
None

LOCATION(S)
New York, NY

FIELD
Theater; Television

DURATION
12–24 weeks: Summer, Fall, Spring

DEADLINE(S)
Rolling

THE WORK
Since 1983, Roy A. Somlyo Productions has produced and managed plays on Broadway and Off-Broadway, on tour, and in London. It also produces television specials and the Tony Awards. Interns read and evaluate scripts, assist staff members in business and production duties, and perform clerical work.

PERKS
Passes to Broadway, Off-Broadway, and Off-Off-Broadway productions, readings, and auditions; attendance welcome at parties; star-gazing opportunities.

FYI
In existence since 1982, the internship program counts among its alumni two playwrights, one filmmaker, three television executives, one radio executive, one entertainment union area supervisor, one casting director, one regional theatre artistic director, one stage manager and one assistant at the League of American Theatre and Producers.

TO APPLY
Open to high school grads, undergrads, recent college grads, college grads of any age, and grad students. International applicants eligible. Submit resume and cover letter.

Internship Coordinator
Roy A. Somlyo Productions
234 West 44th Street
(212) 764-6080
(212) 764-6363 (Fax)

In the summer of 1959, after graduating from the University of Florida, **Senator Bob Graham** (D-FL) interned for Rep. Dante Fascell (D-FL), chairman of the House Foreign Affairs Committee. (Pictured at far left, intern Graham confers with Fascell). Reflecting on the internship, Sen. Graham said: "I will admit to having a low-grade political infection prior to that summer, but Dante hyped it to full-scale addiction. Dante gave me challenging work to do from day one. My first assignment was to track down why the John Birch Society thought that spies within the US were sending good red-blooded Americans to a mental hospital in Alaska as a prelude to a communist takeover. Now that's a research assignment."

It's Good to Be Here, Jim... or Was it Tim?

During the first week of your internship, it is a good idea to discreetly take notes on the names and positions of the people you meet, from custodians to the CEO. The first days on the job will likely find you bombarded with dozens of names and faces, many of which will slip from your memory faster than it takes to make five photocopies.

HELLO! My name is... ~~Jim~~ Tim

RUDER · FINN

SELECTIVITY 🔍🔍🔍🔍🔍
Approximate applicant pool: 200; Interns accepted: 6–15

COMPENSATION 💲💲💲
Prorated weekly on a $19,000 per year salary

LOCATION(S)
New York, NY (HQ); Washington, DC

FIELD
Public relations

DURATION
16 weeks: Summer, Fall/Winter, Winter/Spring

DEADLINE(S)
Summer: April 1; Fall/Winter: June 1; Winter/Spring: November 1

 THE WORK
Since 1948, the privately held family-owned firm of Ruder·Finn has excelled in corporate communications, science and health-based campaigns, investor relations marketing support, event planning environmental marketing, and corporate support of the arts. As New York's third largest public relations agency, Ruder·Finn handles such clients as Citibank, Seagram and Novartis. Interns/trainees are assigned to one or two account groups or serve as "floaters" to assist groups in need. Some of the account groups are Marketing Communications, Product Marketing, Investor Relations, Health Care, Corporate Technology & Public Affairs, High Tech, Arts & Communications Counselors, Visual Technology, Environmental Communications, Strategic Communications, Corporate communications, Entertainment Event Marketing, Planned Television Arts, and Travel & Tourism.

PERKS
Educational curriculum; field trips.

 FYI
Ruder·Finn established its internship program in 1978 . . . During the first week, trainees attend all-day classes on the public relations profession . . . An average of 50 percent of interns are hired as permanent employees.

TO APPLY
Open to college seniors (part-time in summer) and college grads of any age. For application packet:

RuderFinn
Trainee Coordinator
301 East 57th Street
New York, NY 10022
(212) 593-6332

SELECTIVITY 🔍🔍🔍🔍
Approximate applicant pool: 50; Interns accepted: 3

COMPENSATION 💲
None

LOCATION(S)
New York, NY

FIELD
Radio

DURATION
12–16 weeks: Summer, Fall, Spring

DEADLINE(S)
Rolling

THE WORK
Since 1988, *The Rush Limbaugh Show* has been rallying conservatives and frustrating liberals with more impact than any other radio show in broadcasting history. Carried nationwide by almost 700 stations to 20 million listeners a week, it is the most listened-to talk-radio program in the country. Interns work in Administration or Production, where duties range from gofering and opening fan mail to editing tape.

PERKS
Opportunities to watch tapings of Limbaugh television show; "family-like" office atmosphere; attendance welcome at company parties; free t-shirts, sweatshirts, or other gift items.

FYI
Says a former intern: "When you're an intern with Rush Limbaugh, you're tapped into everything that's going on in the political scene . . . As for working with Rush, I can talk to him like anyone else . . . He's surprisingly down-to-earth and professional."

TO APPLY
Open to high school seniors, undergrads, and grad students. Must receive academic credit. International applicants eligible. Submit resume, cover letter, and recommendations.

Internship Coordinator
The Rush Limbaugh Show
Excellence in Broadcasting Network-WABC Radio
2 Penn Plaza, 17th Floor
New York, NY 10121

> **"W**hen you're an intern with Rush Limbaugh, you're tapped into everything that's going on in the political scene."
> —former intern with The Rush Limbaugh Show

> **W**hile in high school in 1966, talk-show host **Rush Limbaugh** served an apprenticeship at KGMO, the local radio station in his hometown of Cape Girardeau, Missouri. Working at the station before and after school, he eventually moved up from gofer to disc jockey.

ST. PAUL'S SCHOOL

SELECTIVITY 🔍🔍
Approximate applicant pool: 175; Interns accepted: 35

COMPENSATION $$$$
$350/week; free room and board

LOCATION(S)
Concord, NH

FIELD
Teaching

DURATION
5 weeks: Summer; 10 months: Academic year

DEADLINE(S)
January 20

THE WORK
Established in 1855, St. Paul's School is one of the world's finest boarding schools, known as much for its illustrious alumni as it is for its 2,000 wooded acres and top-flight facilities. During the summer, interns teach and tutor students in St. Paul's Advanced Studies Program, a program that offers college-level courses to academically talented juniors from New Hampshire high schools. Interns also teach recreational activities and supervise dormitories.

PERKS
Use of libraries and athletic facilities; mentors; hiking, skiing, and other nearby recreational opportunities.

FYI
During the academic year, St. Paul's accepts up to four recent college grads as Teaching Fellows. Serving ten-month tenures, Fellows spend fall term observing different classes and teachers; during winter and spring terms, they take on responsibility for all teaching activities in at least one class.

TO APPLY
Open to college juniors, seniors, and recent college grads. International applicants eligible. Write for application.

Apprentice Teaching Programs
St. Paul's School
325 Pleasant Street
Concord, NH 03301-2591
(603) 229-4777
(603) 229-4767 (Fax)
E-mail: asp@sps.edu

SAKS FIFTH AVENUE

SELECTIVITY 🔍
Approximate applicant pool: 1,500; Interns accepted: 50

COMPENSATION $$$
$375/week

LOCATION(S)
Corporate Offices, New York; Flagship Store, New York; More than 50 stores in 23 states throughout US; More than 40 Offices throughout US

FIELD
Fashion; Speciality retailer

DURATION
10–14 weeks: Summer, Fall, Spring

DEADLINE(S)
Spring: November; Summer: March; Fall: June

THE WORK
Participants engage in a full-time program that encompasses all aspects of store-line retail; customer service, operations, merchandising, and management. Interns work directly with an experienced Department Manager. In addition to a specific department assignment, weekly seminars conducted by the senior management team are a key component of the internship program. The responsibilities are diverse and require problem solving and decision making abilities. Upon successful completion of the Internship Program, many interns become candidates for positions within stores and for Saks Fifth Avenue's corporate executive training program.

PERKS
Weekly seminars conducted by the senior management team, generous employee discount, field trips to a vendor showroom, branch store, and one of the off 5th stores.

FYI
Saks is a public company. Possible internships at branch stores across the country (call for more information).

TO APPLY
Open to undergrads, recent college grads, college grads of any age, and grad students. International applicants eligible. Submit resume and cover letter.

Internship Coordinator
Saks Fifth Avenue
611 Fifth Avenue
New York, NY 10022
(212) 753-4000

EXCLUSIVE INTERVIEW WITH NANCY HOGSHEAD

At the 1984 Olympics in Los Angeles, Nancy won three gold medals and one silver in swimming. Currently studying for her law degree at Georgetown, she finds time to serve as a motivational speaker, a spokesperson on overcoming asthma for the American Lung Association, an author (Asthma and Exercise, 1990), a contributing editor to Fitness, and a regular on ESPN's exercise show, Bodyshaping. Nancy graduated with honors in political science and women's studies from Duke in 1986.

The Internship Informants: You were first an intern at the Women's Sports Foundation. How did that come about?

Hogshead: While I was at the Olympics in '84, Donna DeVarona, who had won two Gold medals in the 1964 Olympics, came to the team and talked about Title IX, which I didn't know anything about [Title IX makes it unlawful for colleges and universities receiving federal funds of any sort to discriminate against women's sports]. Since I was up in front of the newspapers a lot, she and Ken Bastian [one of Nancy's mentors, he put on the first Goodwill Games] got me up to speed on Title IX so I could go on *Larry King Live* and ABC and on the *Tonight Show*, talking about how important this legislation was. I thought I had got a college scholarship because I was good, and then I saw that—wow—people gave up a large hunk of their lives to make sure that I had the opportunity [to swim competively]...so Ken Bastian was the one who more than firmly suggested "you've got to get out there [promoting Title IX]" and that I become an intern at the Foundation.

The Internship Informants: Was it any different interning as an already-famous athlete?

Hogshead: I remember my first day. I went in, and Leslie Evans was the director of the interns, and she pulls me aside...and says "now just because you've won Olympic Gold medals doesn't mean that you're going to get any special treatment," and I remember kind of thinking "oh, yeah, right."... I mean, people were still naming parades after me and giving me keys to cities. And, no joke, she handed me a mop, and that was all I did when I first got there.

The Internship Informants: After things warmed up, how was it?

Hogshead: I really, really learned a lot. We had two executive directors at the time—one was Eva Auchincloss, the other was Holly Turner—and they both let us be executive director for the day. We got to sit right beside them, and we got to make all the phone calls they did. I also wrote letters to people like Nancy Reagan, asking her if she would attend various functions. I also learned a lot, and got in touch with [WSF members], answering the phone, talking with people from middle America...about the plight of young girls who get taunted and teased for no other reason because they're a girl playing a sport...to irate fathers who were so angry at [the local high school] cutting the women's basketball team while giving the men's football team brand new uniforms. You get to learn, sort of hands-on, what's legal, what's not legal.

The Internship Informants: How important is it for a person who doesn't play high-level sports but who wants to get into the sports business to do a sports-related internship?

Hogshead: I would say that with sports, almost more than any other career, it's who you know...and at the Foundation [or other sports internships], you really get a lot of experience with the NBA, with the Players Assocation for the NFL, with events-management people, etc. so that you leave with a rolodex of names. For example, during the Dinner [WSF's annual event], you get to meet 90 of the top athletes around the country. So you don't have to play sports but you need to have a passion for sports.

The Internship Informants: What's the environment at WSF like?

Hogshead: [As an intern], I felt right at home at the Women's Sports Foundation. And I would say that the women there go out of their way to make sure that the guys feel really comfortable, too. Everybody likes each other a lot. And the people that you're working side by side with could have a very different interest than you do, so it's not like you're in direct competition for one particular job with the person who's right next to you. Some people want to get into coaching, some into administration, some want to represent athletes. The business of sports is very broad.

The Internship Informants: Was your ascension to the WSF presidency a direct result of your internship there?

Hogshead: I doubt seriously that I would have become president of the Foundation [where she served until January 1995] if I hadn't been an intern there. I think being an intern laid the groundwork for me to be an effective advocate, so I'm in law school to learn how to be an even more effective advocate, but it's where I got my beginnings—and also it's not just where I learned how to be one, it's where I got the idea of what one was and what a good advocate was. So whether I'm advocating for asthmatics or whatever, I'm very grateful to the Women's Sports Foundation.

The Internship Informants: By the way, where did you get your last name?

Hogshead: A hogshead is a large barrel, so it's like having the last name Cooper [i.e. one who makes or repairs wooden casks], and actually most people with the last name changed their name to Cooper, so it's like you're a barrel maker. It's British—I guess [my ancestors were] very prestigious barrel makers.

EXCLUSIVE INTERVIEW WITH DIANNE FEINSTEIN

The Mayor of San Francisco from 1978 to 1988, Dianne Feinstein is a U.S. Senator from California. She received a B.A. in history from Stanford University in 1955.

The Internship Informants: Let's start with your year-long, multi-internship experience with The Coro Foundation.

Feinstein: I did the Coro Fellowship in 1955-56 in San Francisco. It was a very frustrating year for me because I like to know ahead of time exactly what I'm getting into, and I found that there was very little predictability with the Coro program. In the long run, that turned out to be very helpful. We had a number of assignments—I was assigned to the DA's office, to labor unions, to Pan American Airlines. I did a preliminary master-plan study for the City of South San Francisco. I interviewed downtown business leaders on planning needs. I did a team study on the post-conviction phases of the administration of criminal justice. I served an internship in the Department of Industrial Relations with the Industrial Welfare Board—that led to my first job following Coro, which was in that department.

The Internship Informants: So what about Coro's lack of predictability?

Feinstein: Coro would do things like—"Okay interns, get into a bus," and we'd ask, "Where are we going?" and they'd say, "You'll see." Then, we'd drive to Sacramento, and [we'd ask] "Where are we going?," [and they'd say] "You'll see." We'd go in the Capitol [and ask] "Where are we going?" and [they'd say,] "You'll see." We'd walk into the Governor's office and sit down—with no preparation, and then you're supposed to ask questions. So it taught me to think on my feet and to think fast.

The Internship Informants: Overall, it sounds like Coro was a positive experience for you.

Feinstein: You make a lot of contacts that someone just out of college would not ordinarily make. You begin to learn that the streets are very different from the ivory tower from which you have just emerged. You begin to temper ideology with reality, history with the present, the present with what the future might be. And it did have a practical dividend for me because I got my first job [through Coro], and after that, I got my second job [through Coro]. I sent Pat Brown, who was then Governor, a copy of our team project . . . and he appointed me to the California Women's Board of Terms and Parole, where I became the youngest parole board member in America at the time. It was then that I really began to develop my portfolio of expertise in the criminal justice area. So it was very valuable. One thing did lead to another.

The Internship Informants: If you could take three months off from the Senate right now, where would you like to serve an internship?

Feinstein: It would probably be in the Middle East, on the peace process . . . I would like to study how the peace process is going, what the impediments to peace are, and how realistic Islamic fundamentalism is as a number-one threat. Or I'd like to be in China, [serving an internship] on human rights. I would study the transition that will be taking place in government, who the new leaders will be, what is their agenda, and where that agenda takes China. I think these are two very important relationships.

The Internship Informants: What would you tell young adults on the threshold of a career?

Feinstein: One of the things that I've learned about bright, young people is that they don't want to do their apprenticeship. They're interested in building their resume and going up the ladder. I think the biggest thing young people can do is develop a real portfolio of expertise, something about which they know a lot. It takes about four years to do, and it's not done in school. But whatever they do, they should master it. And then they are really ready for the next step. They have proved their worth to their employer, so that they have a glowing recommendation. It's gaining that portfolio of experience, it's doing that apprenticeship.

SELECTIVITY 🔍 🔍 🔍
Approximate applicant pool: 200; Interns accepted: 25

COMPENSATION 💲
None

LOCATION(S)
New York, NY

FIELD
Television

DURATION
12 weeks: Summer, Fall, Winter, Spring

DEADLINE(S)
Rolling

THE WORK
Famous as "the talk show host with the red glasses," Sally Jessy Raphael has hosted one of America's most popular daytime talk shows since 1982. With topics ranging from "Women and Stress" to "I Want to Divorce My Kids," the *Sally Jessy Raphael Show* is seen in almost 200 markets nationwide and in countries throughout the world. Departments accepting interns include Production, Research, Publicity, Travel, and Audience. Schedule is on a rotating basis.

PERKS
Prime networking opportunities; use of company gym; abundant star-gazing opportunities; school credit; good references.

FYI
According to the intern coordinator, most entry-level positions are offered to former interns. Approximately one third of the staff were former interns on the show.

TO APPLY
Open to undergrads and grad students. Communications, Broadcasting majors preferred. Minimum GPA: 2.7. Must receive academic credit. International applicants eligible. Send or fax resume.

Intern Coordinator
Sally Jessy Raphael Show
15 Penn Plaza/OF2
New York, NY 10001
(212) 419-7400 x7416
(212) 244-5329 (Fax)

SELECTIVITY 🔍 🔍 🔍 🔍 🔍
Approximate applicant pool: 300; Interns accepted: 5

COMPENSATION 💲 💲
$275/week, round-trip travel

LOCATION(S)
San Diego, CA

FIELD
Zoos

DURATION
12 weeks, Summer

DEADLINE(S)
March 1

THE WORK
Established in 1916, the San Diego Zoo attracts over 3 million visitors a year. Set in a 100-acre tropical garden, the zoo is home to a Children's Zoo, a Botanical Garden, and 4,000 animals, from lions, bears, and elephants to koalas, Przewalski's horses, and Sichuan takins. At the Center for Reproduction of Endangered Species (CRES), a zoo facility applying modern medical and scientific methods to save exotic animal species from extinction, interns conduct animal research in the areas of behavior, virology/immunology, reproductive physiology, comparative physiology, molecular genetics, cytogenetics, infectious diseases, and endocrinology.

PERKS
Mentors; attendance welcome at departmental meetings; a few free passes to the zoo for family and friends; occasional tours of other areas of the zoo.

FYI
Started in 1975, CRES's internship program offers little opportunity for hands-on animal work (exceptions: interns involved in behavior research do some field observation work and interns in physiology assist in animal surgical procedures).

TO APPLY
Open to college juniors and seniors as well as recent college grads attending grad school in the fall.

Summer Fellowship Committee
Center for Reproduction of
Endangered Species
San Diego Zoo
P.O. Box 551
San Diego, CA 92112-0551

GUARDIAN

SELECTIVITY 🔍🔍🔍
Approximate applicant pool: 200; Interns accepted: 8–10 per program

COMPENSATION 💲
None

LOCATION(S)
San Francisco

FIELD
Newspapers

DURATION
4-month program

DEADLINE(S)
Summer: April 15; Fall: August 15; Spring: December 15

THE WORK
The *San Francisco Bay Guardian* is an independent, alternative weekly newspaper with a strong local focus, specializing in investigative reporting, political commentary, and arts and entertainment coverage. It was a founding member of the Assocation of Alternative Newsweeklies and has been locally owned and edited since its founding in 1966. Interns work in the Editorial department.

PERKS
Opportunities to cover press conferences; attendance welcome at parties; free t-shirts.

FYI
In existence since 1977, the internship program counts among its alumni Bill Ristow, an editor at *The Seattle Times* . . . Says the internship bulletin: "Eventually interns develop short articles of their own, like 'On Guards.' . . . Toward the end of their [internship], some interns may write longer news features and, if their interests lean more toward arts and entertainment, lifestyle articles, and/or short entertainment pieces."

TO APPLY
Open to high school students, undergrads, recent college grads, college grads of any age, and grad students. International applicants eligible. Write for application.

Internship Coordinator
San Francisco Bay Guardian
520 Hampshire Street
San Francisco, CA 94110
E-mail: mandy@sfbayguardian.com

SELECTIVITY 🔍🔍🔍🔍🔍
Approximate applicant pool: 1,000; Interns accepted: varies

COMPENSATION 💲💲💲💲
Summer Internship: $535/week; 2-year Internship: approximately $35,000 the first year and $40,000 the second year plus health benefits

LOCATION(S)
San Francisco, CA

FIELD
Newspapers

DURATION
Summer internship: 12 weeks; 2-year Internship: starts June

DEADLINE(S)
October 1–November 15, 2000

THE WORK
Founded by two teenagers in 1865, *The San Francisco Chronicle* has grown to become the nation's eleventh largest newspaper, with a daily circulation of almost 500,000. *Chronicle* interns are hired as copy editors, reporters, photographers, infographic artists, and librarians.

FYI
Says the internship coordinator: "If an intern's work deserves to be on Page One, that is where it will run."

TO APPLY
Internships are available to current college students (undergraduate and graduate) and recent college grads who have been out of school no longer than one year prior to start of the internship. Applicants must submit a resume, cover letter, at least one letter of recommendation, and the names of at least three references.

Summer Internship or Two-year Internship
The San Francisco Chronicle
901 Mission Street
San Francisco, CA 94103-2988
(415) 777-8485

SAN FRANCISCO

SELECTIVITY 🔍
N/A

COMPENSATION 💲
None; credit

LOCATION(S)
San Francisco, CA

FIELD
Magazines

DURATION
3 months, 3 days a week

DEADLINE(S)
Rolling

THE WORK
San Francisco is a monthly city/Bay Area magazine. Interns work on research, fact checking, some writing, and copyediting depending on ability.

PERKS
Attendance welcome at issue planning meetings; field trips to the library in San Francisco; flexible schedule.

FYI
San Francisco Focus was sold by KQED last year to a private publisher.

Lights... Camera... *Intern!*
Interns in film and on television:

During an episode of Fox TV's *Melrose Place*, Allison (played by **Courtney Thorne-Smith**) has lunch with an ambitious former advertising exec named Brooke, who is looking for work. When Allison makes it known that there is an internship opening at her agency, D&D, Brooke responds: "Are you serious? I would kill to intern at D&D."

TO APPLY
Open to (public TV/radio station) journalism undergraduate students and graduate students or those interested in writing and editorial work. Submit resume, cover letter, and writing samples.

Research Editor
San Francisco Magazine
243 Vallejo Street
San Francisco, CA 94111
(415) 398-6777 (Fax)

SELECTIVITY 🔍🔍🔍🔍🔍
Approximate applicant pool: 200; Interns accepted: 3

COMPENSATION 💲
None

LOCATION(S)
Santa Clara, CA

FIELD
Sports

DURATION
16–20 weeks: Season (July–January); Off-season (March–July)

DEADLINE(S)
Rolling

THE WORK
Founded in 1946, the San Francisco 49ers have won five Super Bowl championships, tied for the most in NFL history. Past 49er greats include quarterback Joe Montana, coach Bill Walsh, quarterback John Brodie, defensive back Jimmy Johnson, and wide receiver Dwight Clark. Current stars include quarterback Steve Young, wide receiver Jerry Rice, defensive tackle Bryant Young, and running back Garrison Hearst. Interns work in Public Relations, where they answer phones, prepare press releases, and coordinate player interviews.

PERKS
Work in pressbox on game days; attendance welcome at media and social events.

FYI
The 49ers hold the NFL record for the most touchdown passes (6) in a Super Bowl . . . In 1994, Steve Young recorded the highest single season quarterback rating in the history of the league . . . Jerry Rice holds 14 NFL records, including career receptions, career receiving yards, and career touchdowns.

TO APPLY
Open to undergrads and grad students going to school in the local Bay Area only. Must receive academic credit. International applicants eligible. Submit resume and cover letter.

Internship Coordinator
San Francisco 49ers
4949 Centennial Boulevard
Santa Clara, CA 95054
(408) 562-4949
(408) 727-2760 (Fax)

SAN FRANCISCO OPERA

SELECTIVITY 🔍🔍🔍
Approximate applicant pool: 100; Interns accepted: 10–12

COMPENSATION Ⓢ
None

LOCATION(S)
San Francisco, CA

FIELD
Opera

DURATION
12 weeks: Fall, Spring, Summer

DEADLINE(S)
Rolling

THE WORK
Founded in 1932, the San Francisco Opera is the second largest opera company in North America. Housed in an elegant concert hall, the Opera produces a 14-week season of international opera and regularly presents premiers of new operas and commissioned works. Internships are available in the following departments: Artistic and Musical Administration, Costume Shop, Development, Education/Training, Finance/Accounting, Guild Activities and Events, Human Resources/Labor Relations, Information Systems, Marketing, Orchestra Administration, Production, and Public Relations.

PERKS
Attendance welcome at dress rehearsals; tours of various departments.

FYI
Where did the character played by Richard Gere in *Pretty Woman* take his call-girl/girlfriend on their big date? To his private balcony at the San Francisco Opera . . . The stately, Beaux Arts-style Opera House seats 3,200 people.

TO APPLY
Open to undergrads, recent college grads, college grads of any age, and grad students. International applicants eligible. To receive an application, please send a self-addressed, stamped envelope to:

Internship Program Coordinator
San Francisco Opera
301 Van Ness Avenue
San Francisco, CA 94102
(415) 861-4008
(415) 621-7508 (Fax)

For Sweden's celebrated filmmaker **Ingmar Bergman**, it all started with an unpaid internship at Stockholm's Royal Opera House in 1941. Bergman would eventually emerge as the "thinking filmgoer's favorite writer-director," creating such provocative classics as *The Virgin Spring*, *The Passion of Anna*, *Cries and Whispers*, and *Fanny and Alexander*.

SAN JUAN/RIO GRANDE NATIONAL FORESTS

SELECTIVITY 🔍
Approximate applicant pool: N/A; Interns accepted: 200–320

COMPENSATION Ⓢ Ⓢ
Some positions pay up to $14/day, offer free room and board, and/or provide vehicles for daily round-trip travel

LOCATION(S)
CO

FIELD
Forest management

DURATION
3–20 weeks: ongoing

DEADLINE(S)
Rolling (April 1 for summer)

THE WORK
Created by Presidential proclamations in 1908, the Rio Grande National Forest is overseen by the US Forest Service. Placed at visitor's centers, monuments, campgrounds, trails, and historical sites, volunteers work as computer programmers, receptionists, mappers, environmental education coordinators, interpreters, botanists, hydrologists, geologists, surveyors, cleanup crew, rangers, campground hosts, archaeologists, and construction workers.

PERKS
Some field supplies (e.g., tent, camera, hard hat); training in skills necessary to complete assigned project; numerous recreational opportunities (e.g., camping, fishing, skiing).

FYI
The forest offers nearly 2 million acres of land for hiking, camping, fishing, hunting, mountain biking, snow skiing, water skiing, horseback riding, and mountain climbing.

TO APPLY
Open to high school students, undergrads, recent college grads, college grads of any age, and grad students. International applicants eligible. Write for application.

Volunteer Program
Rio Grande National Forest
1803 West Highway 160
Monte Vista, CO 81144
(719) 852-5941

SATURDAY NIGHT LIVE

See National Broadcasting Company

SATURN

See General Motors

SAVANNAH RIVER ECOLOGY LABORATORY

See Oak Ridge Institute for Science and Education

SAVE THE SOUND

Save the Sound™

SELECTIVITY 🔍 🔍 🔍 🔍
Approximate applicant pool: 75; Interns accepted: 7

COMPENSATION ⑤
None

LOCATION(S)
Stamford, CT (HQ); Glen Cove, NY

FIELD
Environment

DURATION
12–16 weeks (flexible): Summer, Fall, Spring

DEADLINE(S)
Rolling

THE WORK
Founded in 1972 as the Long Island Sound Task Force, the group changed its name in 1995 to Save the Sound. Its mission has remained the same: to save the Long Island Sound, a 110-mile long estuary that winds through Connecticut, Westchester County, New York City, and Long Island, from an onslaught of pollution—annually, over a billion gallons of contaminated runoff end up in the Sound. Interns work in the Education, Development, Research, Communications, or Advocacy departments. Past intern projects have included setting up the group's website (www.savethesound.org), writing educational materials, and testing water quality in local harbors.

PERKS
Free t-shirt; occasional travel within region and/or attendance at local seminars and conferences; fun working environment; small office; chance to make a difference to the Long Island Sound.

FYI
Former interns have gone on to careers in the Connecticut Department of Environmental Protection, the Connecticut Department of Agriculture, and other environmental protection agencies . . . One of Save the Sound's eight current full-time employees is a former intern.

TO APPLY
Open to high school juniors and seniors, undergrads, recent college grads, high school or college grads of any age, and grad students. International applicants eligible. Write for application or submit resume, cover letter, and writing samples. Applications are accepted by fax, E-mail (savethesound@snet.com), or regular mail.

Internship Coordinator
Save the Sound
185 Magee Avenue
Stamford, CT 06902
(203) 327-9786
(203) 967-2677 (Fax)
www.savethesound.org

SAVVY MANAGEMENT

SELECTIVITY 🔍 🔍 🔍 🔍 🔍
Approximate applicant pool: 200; Interns accepted: 7

COMPENSATION ⑤
$100/week

LOCATION(S)
New York, NY

FIELD
Public relations

DURATION
12 weeks: Summer, Fall, Spring

DEADLINE(S)
Rolling

THE WORK
In existence since 1978, Savvy Management is a small public relations firm that represents clients in such industries as fashion, giftware, home furnishings, housewares, publishing, and special events. Its client roster has included Chantall cookware, Council of Fashion Design Association, and Fortrel EcoSpun recycled clothing. Interns assist account executives in everything from writing press releases to calling media contacts.

PERKS
At departure, interns are given samples of projects on which they have worked; attendance welcome at various events; small, friendly office.

FYI
Says a former intern: "The internship at Savvy is great because you don't just do busywork, you actually get to work directly on accounts. Instead of just watching, you're doing."

TO APPLY
Open to college sophomores, juniors, and seniors as well as recent grads. Submit resume and cover letter.

Internship Coordinator
Savvy Management
80 Fourth Avenue, Suite 800
New York, NY 10003
(212) 477-1717
(212) 477-1736 (Fax)

SCHLUMBERGER

Schlumberger

SELECTIVITY 🔍🔍🔍🔍
Approximate applicant pool: 1,500; Interns accepted: 200

COMPENSATION 💲💲💲💲
$525–$825/week

LOCATION(S)
Atlanta, GA; Austin, Houston, and Sugarland (HQ), TX; AR; Corte Madera, San Jose, and Simi Valley, CA; Ridgefield, CT; KY; LA; MI; New York, NY; PA; AL; WY; Canada; Aracaju, Brazil; Paris, France

FIELD
Electronics; Oil and gas

DURATION
12 weeks: Summer

DEADLINE(S)
March 31

THE WORK
Established in 1927, Schlumberger is a worldwide leader in oilfield services as well as measurements and systems, employing 57,000 people in over 100 countries around the world. Its oilfield services range from oil exploration and offshore drilling to software and hardware development, while its work in measurements and systems focuses on the manufacture of electricity, water, and gas meters. Interns work in Computer Engineering; Mechanical, Electrical, Petroleum, Civil, and Chemical Engineering; Physics; Geology; and Marketing.

PERKS
Tour of on-site oil rig (Sugarland, TX); friendly, "first-name-basis" company culture.

FYI
Schlumberger's internship program has been in existence since 1945 . . . Says the internship coordinator: "Virtually every department in the company is run by engineers. Even the Marketing department is made up of engineers." . . . Schlumberger is pronounced shlum-burr-JAY.

TO APPLY
Open to college seniors, recent college grads, and grad students. International applicants eligible. Write for application.

Recruiting Manager
Schlumberger
300 Schlumberger Drive
Sugarland, TX 77478
(281) 285–7173 (fax)
E-mail: recruiting@slb.com
www.slb.com

SCIENCE

SELECTIVITY 🔍🔍🔍🔍
Approximate applicant pool: 35; Interns accepted: 2

COMPENSATION 💲💲💲
$350–400/week

LOCATION(S)
Washington, DC

FIELD
Magazines

DURATION
6 months: January–June; July–December

DEADLINE(S)
Summer/Fall: April 20; Winter/Spring: November 20

THE WORK
Founded in 1880 by Thomas Edison and published by the American Association for the Advancement of Science, *Science* is the world's largest circulating weekly of scientific research. Interns work as news writers—reporting, writing, researching, and editing technical stories as well as obtaining photos and laying out the magazine's "ScienceScope" section.

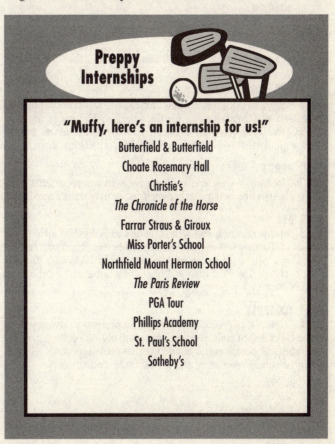

Preppy Internships

"Muffy, here's an internship for us!"

Butterfield & Butterfield

Choate Rosemary Hall

Christie's

The Chronicle of the Horse

Farrar Straus & Giroux

Miss Porter's School

Northfield Mount Hermon School

The Paris Review

PGA Tour

Phillips Academy

St. Paul's School

Sotheby's

PERKS
Attendance welcome at *Science* luncheons between editors and reporters; intern acknowledgment in magazine's masthead; possible travel nationwide as part of story assignments.

FYI
The internship program began in 1990 . . . Interns write an average of five to ten stories with bylines and another ten or so stories without . . . Two of the organization's ten former interns have returned as full-time staff writers.

TO APPLY
Open to recent college grads. International applicants eligible. Submit resume, cover letter, any published writing samples, and references.

Science Internship Program
Science
1333 H Street NW
Washington, DC 20005
(202) 326-6589

SCIENCE NEWS

SELECTIVITY   🔍 🔍 🔍 🔍 🔍
Approximate applicant pool: 80; Interns accepted: 3

COMPENSATION   💲 💲 💲 💲
$1,650/month

LOCATION(S)
Washington, DC

FIELD
Magazines

DURATION
3–4 months: Summer, Fall, Spring

DEADLINE(S)
Summer: February 1; Fall: June 15; Spring: October 15

THE WORK
Science News, a weekly news magazine, was founded over 75 years ago as a news service for the sciences. The magazine now reports the latest research advances to a broad audience. Interns work as journalists—researching, writing, and editing stories.

PERKS
Attendance welcome at *Science News* functions; interns write under their byline and are acknowledged in magazine's masthead.

FYI
Interns research and write one or two published articles per week . . . Former interns include reporters Bill Broad of *The New York Times*, Michael Guillen of ABC News' *Good Morning America*, Rick Weiss of *The Washington Post*, Joanne Silberner of NPR, and Linda Garmon, a producer at *NOVA*.

TO APPLY
Science News prefers journalism grad students studying science writing, but recent college grads, grad students, and college grads of any age are occasionally hired. International applicants eligible. Submit resume, cover letter, and at least three writing samples.

Managing Editor
Science News
1719 N Street, NW
Washington, DC 20036
(202) 785-2255
(202) 659-0365 (Fax)

SCOTT RUDIN PRODUCTIONS

SELECTIVITY   🔍 🔍 🔍 🔍
Approximate applicant pool: 400; Interns accepted: 16

COMPENSATION   💲
None

LOCATION(S)
Los Angeles, CA; New York, NY

FIELD
Film; Theater

DURATION
6–12 weeks: Summer, Fall, Spring

DEADLINE(S)
Rolling

THE WORK
An independent producer at Paramount Pictures, Scott Rudin Productions is a film and theater production house, whose motion picture credits include *The Firm*, *Searching for Bobby Fischer*, *Regarding Henry*, *Flatliners*, *The Addams Family*, *Sister Act*, *Nobody's Fool*, *Ransom*, *First Wives Club*, and *Sabrina*. Broadway plays produced by Rudin include *Passion*. Interns in the New York office work in Film Development, where they help acquire books and plays to be adapted into feature films; Los Angeles interns work in Production, helping with budgets and casting.

PERKS
Occasional free tickets to film screenings and theater productions; opportunities to read and analyze manuscripts, screenplays, and plays.

FYI
Occational opportunities for advancement.

TO APPLY
Open to undergrads, recent college grads, and grad students. Must be fluent in English with computer experience. International applicants eligible. Submit resume and cover letter.

Internship Coordinator
Scott Rudin Productions
Demille 200
5555 Melrose Avenue
Hollywood, CA 90038
(213) 956-4600
(213) 862-0262 (Fax)

Internship Coordinator
Scott Rudin Productions
120 W45th Street, 10 Floor
New York, NY 10036
(212) 704-4600
(212) 869-8557 (Fax)

> "Instead of just watching, you're doing."
> —former intern at Savvy Management

SELECTIVITY 🔍🔍🔍

Approximate applicant pool: 50–100; Interns accepted: 5–8

COMPENSATION 💲💲💲💲

$1,500/month; round-trip travel; health insurance

LOCATION(S)

Washington, DC

FIELD

Public policy; Foreign policy; Arms control; Peace; International security

DURATION

4–6 months: Fall and Spring

DEADLINE(S)

Fall: March 15; Spring: October 15

THE WORK

Established in 1987, the Herbert Scoville Jr. Peace Fellowship Program selects college graduates to work in Washington, DC with a peace, disarmament, or nuclear arms control organization. Scoville Fellows serve as special project assistants on the staff of one of twenty-one participating organizations, including the British American Security Information Council, Union of Concerned Scientists, the National Security Archive, Peace Action, and Women's Action for New Directions. Recent Fellows have focused on such topics as nuclear testing, conventional arms trade, the B-2 Stealth Bomber, UN peacekeeping, and North Korea's nuclear program.

PERKS

Meetings with leaders in the arms control community; periodic lunches and happy-hour gatherings for current and former fellows; mentoring from a member of the Fellowship's Board of Directors.

FYI

Says a former Fellow: "I can't imagine a better way to get started in this line of work . . . I'd be surprised if any graduate program succeeded in teaching me as much as I've learned in the last six months."

TO APPLY

Open to grads and grad students. International applicants eligible. Write for application.

Scoville Peace Fellowship Program
110 Maryland Avenue NE, Suite 211
Washington, DC 20002
(202) 546-0795
(202) 546-5142 (Fax)
E-mail: Scoville@CLW.ORG
www.CLW.Org/PUB/CLW/Scoville/Scoville.HTML

SELECTIVITY 🔍🔍🔍

Approximate applicant pool: 150; Interns accepted: 1

COMPENSATION 💲💲💲💲

$2500 stipend; campus housing; round-trip travel

LOCATION(S)

La Jolla, CA

FIELD

Science research

DURATION

8 weeks: Summer

DEADLINE(S)

March 12

THE WORK

A graduate department of the University of California at San Diego, the Scripps Institution of Oceanography (SIO) is an international leader in oceanographic and earth science research. Major areas of study at SIO include geochemistry, marine geology, geophysics, marine biology, climatology, space science, and physical oceanography. SIO's Summer Undergraduate Research Fellowship enables qualified students to engage in laboratory research with a faculty member.

PERKS

State-of-the-art shore-based laboratory facilities; scientific seminars in the earth sciences; GRE preparation seminars.

TO APPLY

Open to college juniors and seniors who are majoring in applied ocean sciences, astronomy, biological oceanography, climatology, electrical engineering, geochemistry, geological sciences, geophysics, marine biology, marine chemistry, marine geology, math, mechanical engineering, physical oceanography, physics, and space science. Minimum GPA: 3.0. Submit personal statement and personal profile page found on the website, current academic transcript, and two faculty recommendations in sealed envelopes.

Office of Graduate Studies & Research
SURF Program
9500 Gilman Drive
518ERE
La Jolla, CA 92093-0003
(858) 534-3550
(858) 534-3868 (Fax)
E-mail: abynum@ucsd.edu
www-ogsr.ucsd.edu/outreach/surf.html

Sea World
Orlando, Florida

SELECTIVITY 🔍 🔍
Approximate applicant pool: 100–150; Interns accepted: 25

COMPENSATION 💲
Minimum Wage ($5.15/hour)

LOCATION(S)
Orlando, FL

FIELD
Theme parks/Camp program

DURATION
11 weeks: May 21–August 3
10 weeks: May 29–August 3

DEADLINE(S)
March 30

THE WORK
SeaWorld Orlando has two camp programs that are accredited by the American Camping Association—Camp SeaWorld and SeaWorld/Busch Gardens Adventure Camp. Interns will be involved in implementing both camps. Camp SeaWorld is a day camp that focuses on learning about animals and their habitats at SeaWorld and Busch Gardens. In addition to visiting behind the scenes and enjoying our shows and attractions, interns and campers are involved in creative crafts, games, and activities that reinforce information learned about animals. As part of the internship, interns will complete two weeks of training including department orientation, animal information and camp procedures. Adventure Camp programs are multi-day, overnight trips to field locations such as Orlando, the Florida Keys and Florida's east coast. Middle and high school students are immersed in the study of marine science through activities such as snorkeling, canoeing, and exploring the challenges and rewards of working with animals. Interns with current American Red Cross lifeguard certification may serve as assistant counselors for Adventure Camp programs. SeaWorld Orlando has a full-time staff of camp instructors whom interns assist with every aspect of camp. Intern responsibilities may include, but are not limited to, preparing for classes, registering campers, teaching classes and assisting camp management with daily operations. Teaching experience and a basic knowledge of marine life are helpful, since interns must be willing to teach in front of large groups.

PERKS
Free passes for family and friends to SeaWorld, Busch Gardens, and Adventure Island. 30 percent discount on park food and merchandise.

FYI
Launched in 1992, the internship program leads to permanent employment at Sea World for approximately 20 percent of interns. Interns are responsible for providing their own transportation.

TO APPLY
This program is for undergraduates who have completed their sophomore year and are in good standing at a recognized

Top Capitol Hill Internships

As any Washington insider knows, the task of assessing internships in the offices of Members of Congress is difficult because elections ensure that there will be Senators and Congresspeople voted in and out of office every two years. By the time some internship programs have established an excellent reputation, their sponsoring politicians are packing their bags.

There are nevertheless internships on Capitol Hill that have proven themselves rewarding and are currently available. We turned to the Washington Center for Internships and Academic Seminars, which has placed over 20,000 students from more than 750 colleges and universities in Washington internships since 1975. We asked the Washington Center to provide a list of the Members of Congress known to have consistently rewarding internships. Here are the top picks:

US Representatives	US Senators
Sanford Bishop (D-GA)	Dianne Feinstein (D-CA)
Gene Green (D-TX)	Charles Grassley (R-IA)
Richard Gephardt (D-MO)	Tom Harkin (D-IA)
Earl Hilliard (D-AL)	Edward Kennedy (D-MA)
Steny Hoyer (D-MD)	Frank Lautenberg (D-NJ)
Susan Molinari (R-NY)	Richard Lugar (R-IN)
Richard E. Neal (D-MA)	Don Nickles (R-OK)
Donald M. Payne (D-NJ)	Robert Smith (R-NH)
John E. Porter (R-IL)	Arlen Specter (R-PA)
Robert Scott (D-VA)	

For the phone numbers of any of these offices, call the Capitol operator at (202) 224-3121.

academic institution. Applicants must be seeking degrees in education, science, or recreation. Students can arrange to receive academic credit through their school. Submit resume, an official college transcript, a completed recommendation form and a completed application. Only completed applications will be considered. Successful applicants will be contacted for phone interviews. SeaWorld Orlando Adventure Park is an Equal Opportunity Employer.

Camp SeaWorld Internship
Education Department
SeaWorld Orlando
7007 SeaWorld Drive
Orlando, FL 32821
www.seaworld.org

THE SEATTLE TIMES

SELECTIVITY 🔍🔍🔍🔍🔍
Approximate applicant pool: 300–400; Interns accepted: 12

COMPENSATION 💲💲💲💲
Weekly salary

LOCATION(S)
Seattle, WA

FIELD
Newspapers

DURATION
12 weeks: Summer program; 1 year: Blethen family internship

DEADLINE(S)
November 1: Summer program; 3 times/year Blethen Family Internship

THE WORK
Founded in 1896, the Pulitzer Prize–winning *Seattle Times* is one of the top newspapers in the Pacific Northwest. It has a subscriber list of over 250,000 people. Most interns serve as general assignment reporters working off the city desk and in suburban bureaus. Additional positions include business reporter, copy desk editor, photographer, artist/page designer, and sports reporter.

PERKS
Attendance welcome at diversity meetings and computer workshops; summer picnic; espresso machine in cafeteria.

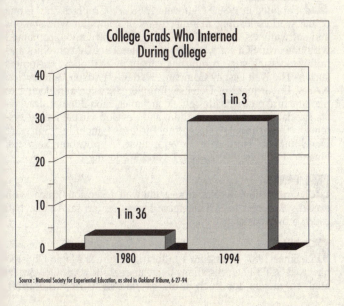

College Grads Who Interned During College

1 in 3 (1994)
1 in 36 (1980)

Source: National Society for Experiential Education, as sited in *Oakland Tribune*, 6-27-94

FYI
The Seattle Times also runs a one-year internship for minorities. Known as the Blethen Family Internship, the program has interns spend four months in training at the *Walla Walla Union-Bulletin*, then four months at the *Yakima Herald*, and the final four months at *The Seattle Times*.

TO APPLY
Summer internships are open to college sophomores, juniors, and seniors as well as recent grads and grad students. Applicants must be journalism majors or have a demonstrated commitment to print journalism. In addition, there are requirements specific to each position (Reporting, Copy Editing, Photojournalism, Graphic Design). For more information contact: Patricia Preciado, Hiring Administrative Assistant ppreciado@seattle-times.com, (206) 464-2414. To apply, send cover letter, resume, and the names of three references familiar with your work to:

Newsroom Intern Coordinator
The Seattle Times
P.O. Box 70
Seattle, WA 98111
(206) 464-3274

SELECT RECORDS

See Atlantic Records

SENIOR PGA TOUR

See PGA Tour

765-ARTS

SELECTIVITY N/A
Approximate applicant pool: N/A; Interns accepted: 5

COMPENSATION 💲
Daily travel expenses reimbursed

LOCATION(S)
New York, NY

FIELD
Performing arts

DURATION
12 weeks: Summer, Fall, Spring

DEADLINE(S)
Rolling

THE WORK
Founded in 1991, 765-ARTS is a nonprofit organization providing area residents and visitors with cultural event information through a free, 24-hour, phone service for the arts. Designed to increase patronage of art and cultural events in New York City, 765-ARTS allows small nonprofit organizations, often struggling with limited publicity funds, to reach a wider audience. Interns work in Arts Administration, Public Relations, Development, and Database Management.

PERKS
Free tickets to various performances; direct contact with Associate Director.

FYI
Says the internship coordinator: "This program is ideal for any young person looking for a foot-in-the-door to the New York City art world. There are excellent opportunities for developing contacts, and learning who's who in New York, national, and international theater, visual arts, music, and dance."

TO APPLY
Open to high school seniors, undergrads, recent college grads, college grads of any age, and grad students. International applicants eligible. Submit resume and cover letter.

Internship Coordinator
765-ARTS (Big Apple Arts and Festivals Information Project)
225 West 57th Street, 8th Floor
New York, NY 10019-2194
(212) 315-4186
(212) 247-4087 (Fax)

SEVENTEEN MAGAZINE

SELECTIVITY 🔍🔍🔍🔍🔍
Approximate applicant pool: 1,000; Interns accepted: 25

COMPENSATION 💲💲
$250/week (Summer only)

LOCATION(S)
New York, NY

FIELD
Magazines

DURATION
6 weeks: Summer; 20 weeks: Fall and Spring

DEADLINE(S)
Rolling

THE WORK
First published in 1944, *Seventeen Magazine* was the first magazine to target the teen market (girls, ages 12 to 24). Devoted to fashion and issues relating to teenage girls, it has a circulation of 1.9 million. Summer interns work in Marketing, Advertising, and various Editorial departments, including Fashion, Style, Beauty, Art, and Lifestyle. Fall and Spring interns work in the Articles department, assisting editors with research, fact checking, and writing.

PERKS
Seminars with editors, publisher, and marketing director; opportunity to help coordinate fashion shows (Marketing interns); "young, hip" office environment; free t-shirts and magazines.

FYI
Says the internship coordinator: "Occasionally we do have male interns, and some of them like to brag to their friends, 'Hey, I work at *Seventeen*!'"

TO APPLY
Open to high school students, undergrads, recent college grads. International applicants eligible. Submit resume and cover letter.

Internship Coordinator
Seventeen Magazine
850 Third Avenue, 9th Floor
New York, NY 10022
(212) 407-9700

"Occasionally we do have male interns, and some of them like to brag to their friends, 'Hey, I work at *Seventeen*!'"
—intern coordinator, *Seventeen Magazine*

SGI

sgi
(formerly known as Silicon Graphics, Inc.)

SELECTIVITY 🔍🔍
Approximate applicant pool: 1,000; Interns accepted: 200

COMPENSATION 💲💲💲💲💲
Approximately $42,000–$60,000 annually (undergrads/grad students)

LOCATION(S)
Mountain View, CA; Chippewa Falls, WI; Egan, MN

FIELD
Computers

DURATION
10–16 weeks: ongoing

DEADLINE(S)
Rolling

THE WORK
Founded in 1982, SGI (formerly Silicon Graphics, Inc.) is one of the world's leading manufacturers of computer workstations and software. Its workstations (e.g., Indy and Onyx), combined with powerful SGI software, provide interactive 3-D graphics and multiprocessing supercomputing capability that allow customers such as The Walt Disney Company, Harley-Davidson Motorcycles, NASA, Department of Defense, Daimler Chrysler, and Boeing to manufacture products, design video games, model molecules, create special effects and animation, and develop virtual reality systems. Departments accepting interns include Software Development, Hardware Development, Application Services, Finance, Facilities, Purchasing, IS, and Marketing.

PERKS
Orientation; welcome and farewell reception/lunch with executives; access to SGI cafeteria; fitness center; sand volleyball court; brown bags.

FYI
Since 1987, Lucasfilm's Industrial Light & Magic Division has used SGI 3-D workstations to create realistic computer-generated characters for such films as *Jurassic Park* (dinosaurs),

Terminator 2: Judgement Day (cyborg), *The Mask* (Jim Carrey's half-man/half-cartoon character), and *The Flintstones* (Dino).

TO APPLY

Open to undergrads and grad students. International applicants eligible. Submit resume online to:

sgiurcampus@resume.isearch.com. For additional information on SGI please visit our website at www.sgi.com.

SGRO PROMO ASSOCIATES/GENERAL MOTORS INTERNSHIP

SELECTIVITY   N/A
Approximate applicant pool: N/A; Interns accepted: 2,000

COMPENSATION $
None

LOCATION(S)
Approximately 110 college campuses in CA, GA, MA, NV, RI, TX, and WA

FIELD
Marketing

DURATION
One quarter or semester: Fall and Spring

DEADLINE(S)
Rolling

THE WORK

A marketing firm, SGRO (rhymes with grow) Promo founded General Motors Internship (GMI) in 1989 so that college students, through their participating college's marketing course or club, could form a marketing team for a specific GM division and a local GM dealership. Interns create marketing campaigns to sell GM cars to college students.

PERKS

Each team receives $2,500 to put its ideas into action; post-program party; free GM t-shirts, hats, and other paraphernalia.

FYI

Over 3,000 students have gone through the GMI program since its inception. Six have been hired by Sgro straight out of the program; those less fortunate may use Sgro Promo Associates' Placement Program in their post-graduation career hunt.

TO APPLY

Open to undergrads. Write for application and list of participating schools.

General Motors Internship
Sgro Promo Associates
5500 Shellmound, Suite 150
Emeryville, CA 94608
(800) 783-9464

SHADOW BROADCAST SERVICES

SELECTIVITY   🔍
Approximate applicant pool: 40–50; Interns accepted: 15–20

COMPENSATION $
$50

LOCATION(S)
East Rutherford and New Brunswick, NJ; Farmingdale, NY

FIELD
Radio

DURATION
13 weeks: Summer, Fall, Spring

DEADLINE(S)
Rolling

THE WORK

Founded in 1980, Shadow Broadcast Services (SBS) originated in 1980 with a few CB radio users who would chat about finding the best routes through traffic. It now broadcasts traffic, news, sports, and weather over sixty-five radio stations and two television stations in the Northeast. Interns work in Traffic, Sports, and News.

PERKS

Opportunity to write broadcast copy for radio stations and "have your name mentioned on several radio stations"; travel throughout tri-state area reporting traffic from the "Shadow Van"; free t-shirts.

FYI

In existence since 1984, the internship program counts among its alumni SBS's Vice President of Operations, Director of Cellular Communications, and several on-air personalities . . . The name "Shadow" comes from the founder's silver "Shadow" Rolls Royce . . . SBS hires nearly half of interns for permanent employment.

TO APPLY

Open to college students and grad students. Minimum GPA: 2.8. International applicants eligible. Preference will be given to students taking internship for college credit. Submit resume, cover letter, and transcript (optional).

Internship Coordinator
Shadow Broadcast Services
201 Route 17 North, 9th Floor
East Rutherford, New Jersey 07070
(201) 939-1888
(201) 939-1043 (Fax)

SHAVER'S CREEK ENVIRONMENTAL CENTER

**SHAVER'S CREEK
ENVIRONMENTAL CENTER**

SELECTIVITY

Approximate applicant pool: 100; Interns accepted: 15

COMPENSATION

$125/week; free housing

LOCATION(S)

Petersburg, PA; 13 miles south of State College and the main campus of Penn State University

FIELD

Education; Environment; Recreation

DURATION

14–17 weeks: Summer, Fall, Spring

DEADLINE(S)

Summer: March 1; Fall: July 1; Spring: November 1

THE WORK

Established in 1976, Shaver's Creek is an environmental education laboratory seeking to "enhance the quality of life of our local and global community" by providing exemplary outdoor learning opportunities. Administered by Penn State's Division of Continuing and Distance Education, the multifaceted center offers environmental education programs for group visits; natural/cultural history exhibits; live amphibians and reptiles; hiking trails; herb gardens; and more. The Raptor Center provides perpetual care and housing for eagles, falcons, hawks, and owls. Interns become an integral part of the staff and are encouraged to participate in all aspects of the center's operation. A two-week orientation and training period is followed by seasonal program opportunities in both a day and residential setting. Interns work with all ages, preschool to adult, as they lead natural and cultural history programs for school and community groups, families, and the general public. Interns also have the opportunity to contribute articles to the member newsletter, lead adventure and team-building programs, participate in the care and handling of the live animal collection, and assist in the general operation of the center.

PERKS

Interns encouraged to participate in professional development workshops and regional conferences; each session includes a three-day staff trip to another environmental center or a facility of interest; Macintosh computers are on site and access to email and the Internet is available through Penn State University; resources on job listings and assistance with resume writing.

FYI

The internship program has been in existence since 1976 . . . Says a former intern: "I've realized I truly can teach kids about almost anything—from the history of Pennsylvania iron processing to the fact that mint plants have square stems; from why it's important to listen and cooperate with your neighbor to the life cycle of a newt."

TO APPLY

Open to undergrads and grads. International applicants eligible. Write for application.

Internship Coordinator
Shaver's Creek Environmental Center
Pennsylvania State University
508 A Keller Building
University Park, PA 16802
(814) 863-2000
(814) 865-2706 (Fax)
E-mail: shaverscreek@cde.psu.edu
www.cde.psu/ShaversCreek

SHERWIN-WILLIAMS

SELECTIVITY

Approximate applicant pool: 800; Interns accepted: 120

COMPENSATION

$7/hour

LOCATION(S)

2,000 stores in all 50 states and Washington, DC

FIELD

Construction; Consumer goods; Retail

DURATION

9 weeks minimum: Summer

DEADLINE(S)

Rolling

THE WORK

Founded in 1866, Sherwin-Williams (S-W) is America's largest independent manufacturer and distributor of architectural and industrial coatings, with sales of nearly $3 billion. Products include paint, wallcoverings, floorcoverings, window treatments, blinds and shades, carpets, paint brushes and rollers, tape, and spray equipment. Assigned to S-W stores throughout the country, interns sell products and learn the operational and financial procedures of the store.

PERKS

Mentors; weekly training sessions; 20 percent discount on S-W products; opportunities to travel to regional offices to meet President, Vice President of Sales, and other interns.

FYI

Contractors make up approximately 80 percent of S-W's business . . . Interns may stay on part time at their S-W stores during the academic year . . . Because they have already completed the field training portion of the manager training program, interns who join the company after graduating from college are a step ahead of other new-hires . . . Nearly 30 percent of interns are hired by S-W as full-time manager trainees.

TO APPLY

Open to college juniors and seniors. Minimum GPA: 2.5. Must be majoring in business, marketing, or management. International applicants studying in the US are eligible. Submit resume and cover letter to region of interest.

EXCLUSIVE INTERVIEW WITH
DR. P. ROY VAGELOS

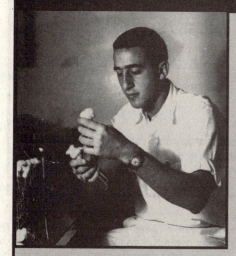

After graduating from Columbia University Medical School in 1954, Roy Vagelos began practicing as a doctor at Massachusetts General Hospital and the NIH, among other places, until 1975. In that year, he joined Merck & Co. as Senior Vice President of Research, becoming CEO and Chairman in 1985 and 1986, respectively. He retired from Merck in October 1994, at the age of 65 and now serves as Chairman at the University of Pennsylvania (where he graduated Phi Beta Kappa in chemistry in 1950) and on the boards of Pepsico and the Prudential Insurance Co. of America. At left, intern Vagelos tinkers in the Merck Lab.

The Internship Informants: Why did you decide to do an internship at Merck?
Vagelos: This was 1951, and I had just finished my first year of medical school. I was looking for a job...the pharmaceutical industry was clearly one that held a great interest to me since it was conducting research in new medicines, and therefore, I wrote to the people at Merck and was delighted to get a positive response. At that time, internships weren't all that plentiful and not many people were doing them.

The Internship Informants: Where were you placed at Merck?
Vagelos: I was fortunate to come into the laboratory of Dr. Harry Robinson, who at that time headed up a laboratory that was interested in antibiotics and the search for new antibiotics, and it came not too long after the development of streptomycin [the drug that kills streptococci bacteria responsible for "strep throat"].

The Internship Informants: What exactly were your responsibilities as a summer intern?
Vagelos: Harry Robinson had done a PhD degree with [the discoverer of streptomycin] and was very much into this new antibiotic era, so I participated that summer in early studies attempting to discover new antibiotics...I did various techniques—working with soil microorganisms and doing both microbiology and some isolation steps, looking for new anti-bacterial agents—and also did some early studies looking at the toxicology of agents that had been found in the laboratory before I arrived.

The Internship Informants: What was the most important thing you learned that summer?
Vagelos: Most of all, I got to know the people in the laboratory, who were very smart and very, very dedicated to what they were doing. There was such enthusiasm and excitement about antibiotics and new drug research at the time that I was very impressed that someone could work in this industry...The dedication to the work and the hope of doing something that was important for mankind was pretty obvious and also infectious, so I learned a great deal. I got to see that one could have an effect on a broad population if one had a real invention.

The Internship Informants: Why, as a medical student, did you do an internship in pharmaceuticals instead of something patient-related?
Vagelos: I had an interest in chemistry, which is different from most people who go into medicine, and I have always been interested in the research side of medicine. So going to the pharmaceutical industry was, in a sense, hanging on to my research interest as well as looking at the patient end of medicine.

The Internship Informants: Should today's pre-meds and medical students do internships in pharmaceuticals?
Vagelos: I think the pharmaceutical industry is a very special place where science, the latest of science, is trying to impact those diseases for which there are no good treatments or preventive therapies . . . . Medical students, or other people as well, would certainly get some idea of the difficulty in drug discovery and the enormous complications that one runs into between the discovery of the drug and the time that it is introduced into large-scale human use. One can understand both the complexity, the time, and the enormous expense in discovering and developing a new drug.

The Internship Informants: What prompted you to return to Merck some twenty-odd years later?
Vagelos: My coming back, of course, was a complete surprise to me because I never expected to come back to Merck. I worked in research and teaching from 1956 to 1975, and they asked me to come back to head up the research division, so I came back to exactly what I had been doing as an intern in research, only this time I was head of the show. Then ten years later, I became CEO and Chairman . . . . . When I came back, I was head of the entire Discovery Group, which had more than a thousand people, and so it had many projects in all fields of medicine. A long list of drugs which catapulted Merck to number one in the industry are drugs that were developed while I was head of research.

The Internship Informants: How has Merck's internship changed since you participated in it?
Vagelos: There is a formal program now, and it has a couple of hundred interns every year . . . . Some of the people come more than once during the course of their education, and of course, we always hope to get them back as staff people.

The Internship Informants: As CEO and Chairman, what role did you play in Merck's internship?
Vagelos: I greeted [the interns] every summer. I met with the students and talked with them about what they might derive from their experience, what they should look for, and what benefits, I thought, they would be able to derive also. It was always fun for me to meet the new ones, and I always told them a little bit about my experience and said, 'You know, we don't know that perhaps someone among you might end up running this company.'

Midwestern Division:
Division Personnel Director
Sherwin-Williams
Great Northern Technology Park II
25221 Country Club Boulevard
Suite 235
North Olmsted, OH 44070

Eastern Division:
Division Personnel Director
Sherwin-Williams
313 Technology Drive
Malvern, PA 19355

Southeastern Division:
Division Personnel Directory
Sherwin-Williams
11 LaVista Perimeter Office Park
Suite 107
Tucker, GA 30084

Southwestern Division:
Division Personnel Director
Sherwin-Williams
10440 Northwest Highway
Dallas, TX 75238

SHIRLEY HERZ ASSOCIATES

SELECTIVITY 🔍🔍🔍
Approximate applicant pool: 100; Interns accepted: 10

COMPENSATION $
Reimbursement for daily lunch and transportation

LOCATION(S)
New York, NY

FIELD
Public relations

DURATION
16 weeks: Summer, Fall, Spring

DEADLINE(S)
Rolling

THE WORK
Founded in 1976, Shirley Herz Associates (SHA) is a public relations agency servicing Broadway and Off-Broadway theater productions, concert events, dance troupes, actors, restaurants, record companies, and nightclub acts. Clients have included such shows as

La Cage aux Folles, Three Penny Opera, Fiddler on the Roof, Peter Pan, and *Other People's Money*; organizations like Takarazuka, the Bolshoi Ballet Academy, Cisne-Negro Danco de Brazil, Ringling Brothers Circus, and the St. Petersburg National Opera; and actors such as Kevin Kline. Interns assist staff with all facets of the business, from contacting media to helping write press releases.

PERKS
Free tickets to shows SHA handles; free CDs and cassettes.

FYI
Approximately 20 percent of SHA's staff once served as SHA interns; many others have gone on to work in the theater as press agents, producers, general managers, and actors.

TO APPLY
Open to undergrads. International applicants fluent in English are eligible. Submit resume and cover letter.

Internship Coordinator
Shirley Herz Associates
165 West 46th Street, Suite 910
New York, NY 10036
(212) 221-8466
(212) 921-8023 (Fax)

SIERRA CLUB

SELECTIVITY 🔍🔍🔍🔍
Approximate applicant pool: N/A; Interns accepted: Varies

COMPENSATION $
None

LOCATION(S)
Washington DC; San Francisco, CA; field offices throughout the US

FIELD
Environment

DURATION
12–15 weeks: Summer, Fall, Winter, Spring

DEADLINE(S)
Flexible

THE WORK
Founded in 1892 by naturalist John Muir, the 500,000-member Sierra Club (SC) seeks to protect and restore the quality of the environment, focusing on such areas as forest protection, clean air and water, international and global water and energy issues, and endangered species. DC interns work in conservation issues, Media, Political, and Legislative internships available.

PERKS
Brown-bag meetings with staff; attendance welcome at hearings on Capitol Hill (DC only), summer softball team. Hands-on experience.

FYI
In the DC office, 10 to 20 percent of interns are hired for full-time positions: at least seven (of 25 staff) once served as interns . . . Current EPA assistant administrator David Gardiner served an internship in SC's San Francisco office in the late 1970s.

TO APPLY
Open to college juniors and seniors, college grads, and grad students. International applicants eligible. Submit resume, cover letter, and two five-page writing samples directly to the office of interest; a list of addresses may be requested from the DC or San Francisco office (HQ).

Internship Coordinator
Sierra Club
85 Second Street
2nd Floor
San Francisco, CA 94105
(415) 977-5500

Internship Coordinator
Sierra Club
408 C Street, NE
Washington, DC 20002
(202) 547-1141
(202) 547-6009 (Fax)

SIGNET CLASSICS

See Penguin Books

SIMON AND GOODMAN PICTURE COMPANY

SIMON & GOODMAN
PICTURE COMPANY

SELECTIVITY
Approximate applicant pool: 150; Interns accepted: 6

COMPENSATION
None

LOCATION(S)
New York, NY

FIELD
Film; Television

DURATION
10–16 weeks: Summer, Fall, Spring

DEADLINE(S)
Rolling

THE WORK
Founded in 1987 by independent filmmakers Kirk Simon and Karen Goodman, Simon and Goodman Picture Company (SGPC) is a documentary film company producing programs broadcast on PBS, HBO, and National Geographic television. Its productions have garnered two Emmy awards and three Oscar nominations. Interns work in Production, Editing, and Research.

PERKS
Direct interaction with the filmmakers; attendance welcome at film shoots; small, friendly office.

FYI
In existence since 1990, the internship program has produced alumni who are now producers and associate producers as well as editors and associate editors.

TO APPLY
Open to film students only, college juniors and seniors only. Interest in documentary film a must. International applicants eligible. Submit resume and cover letter.

Internship Coordinator
Simon and Goodman Picture Company
2095 Broadway, Suite 402
New York, NY 10023
(212) 721-0922 (Fax)
E-mail: SGPIC@aol.com

---
60 MINUTES

See CBS News

SKADDEN, ARPS, SLATE, MEAGHER & FLOM

SKADDEN ARPS SLATE MEAGHER & FLOM

SELECTIVITY
Approximate applicant pool: 150; Interns accepted: 10–15

COMPENSATION
$400/week

LOCATION(S)
Boston, MA; New York, NY (HQ); Washington, DC; Chicago, IL; Los Angeles, CA

FIELD
Law

DURATION
10–12 weeks: Fall, Winter, Spring

DEADLINE(S)
Fall: August 1; Winter: December 1; Spring: February 1

THE WORK
Founded in 1948, Skadden, Arps, Slate, Meagher & Flom, LLP is one of the nation's leading law firms, best known for its corporate and litigation work. With over 1,000 lawyers and nearly 450 legal assistants in thirteen countries, Skadden, Arps represents all twenty of the world's largest banks and about one-third of the Fortune 500 companies. Assisting legal assistants and attorneys, interns at Skadden, Arps work in various departments, including Corporate Finance, Banking, Labor, Intellectual Property, Mergers & Acquisitions, Litigation, Bankruptcy, and Product Liability.

PERKS

Occasional travel to client sites; interaction with attorneys.

FYI
At Skadden, interns are exposed to many aspects of the legal profession and dedicate many hours to high profile assignments. Interns work closely with attorneys and legal assistants and are given assignments ranging in levels of responsibility. One intern reports, "While at Skadden, I have learned a tremendous amount about the legal process and what it takes to make it in a large New York firm."

TO APPLY
Open to college juniors and seniors. International applicants eligible. Submit resume and cover letter.

Hiring Coordinator, Legal Assistant Services
Skadden, Arps, Slate, Meagher & Flom, LLP
919 Third Avenue
New York, NY 10022-3897
(212) 735-3090

SMITHSONIAN INSTITUTION

SELECTIVITY
Approximate applicant pool: N/A; Interns accepted: 700

COMPENSATION $
None, but a few positions may offer stipends

LOCATION(S)
Washington, DC; New York, NY (Cooper Hewitt Museum; National Museum of the American Indian), Boston (Smithsonian Astrophysical observatory); Panama (Smithsonian Tropical Research Institute)

FIELD
Museums and related disciplines

DURATION
2 months–1 year; at least 20 hours/week: Summer, Fall, Spring; Winter

DEADLINE(S)
Summer: February 15; Fall: June 15; Spring: October 15; Dates May Vary

THE WORK
The Smithsonian Institution is the world's largest museum complex, composed of sixteen museums, the National Zoo, and several research facilities. With upwards of 25 million visitors each year, the Smithsonian is a wonderland of things valuable and collectible. Interns are placed among forty museums, administrative offices, and research programs, including the National Zoo, National Portrait Gallery, Hirshhorn Museum, National Museum of Natural History, and Smithsonian Institution Libraries.

PERKS
Seminars and workshops; gift-shop discounts; gym available.

FYI
Interns may apply for a full tuition scholarship to take a Smithsonian Institution summer course. Taught by local professors and museum experts, courses are open to the public and cover topics in areas such as art history, music history, and American history . . . One returning intern reports that the Air and Space museum has the best cafeteria food in the Smithsonian.

TO APPLY

Requirements vary by program. Write for application and brochure.

Internship Coordinator
Smithsonian Center for
Education and Museum Studies
Arts & Industries Building
Suite 2235
Washington, DC 20560-0427
(202) 357-3102
E-mail: interninfo@scems.si.edu

SOLOMON R. GUGGENHEIM MUSEUM

SELECTIVITY   🔍 🔍 🔍
Approximate applicant pool: 300; Interns accepted: 50

COMPENSATION $
$1,000 stipend for grad students (pending funding)

LOCATION(S)
New York, NY

FIELD
Museums

DURATION
8–10 weeks: Summer, Fall, Spring

DEADLINE(S)
Summer: February 1; Fall: August 1; Spring: December 1

THE WORK
Established in 1939 and housed in its dramatic Frank Lloyd Wright–designed building since 1959, the Guggenheim Museum is one of the world's leading museums of twentieth-century art. A New York City landmark, the Guggenheim contains sculpture, figurative painting, modern French masterpieces, and twentieth-century European avant-garde painting, including works by Mondrian, Dubuffet, Modigliani, and Kandinsky. Departments accepting interns include Archives, Conservation, Curatorial, Design, Development, Director's Office, Education, Exhibition Services, Finance, Information Systems, Learning Through Art, Legal, Library, Membership, Personnel, Photography, Public Affairs, Publications, Registrar, Retail Operations, Security, Special Events, and Visitor Services.

PERKS
Museum Culture Day every Thursday (discussion on current trends in museums, lecture by staff members, and field trips to museums, artists' studios, corporate art collections, etc.).

FYI
The Guggenheim has been accepting interns since 1970; former interns include the museum's Curator of Collections and Exhibitions . . . Approximately 20 percent of interns are hired for full-time positions . . . It is often said that the Guggenheim's white spiral-shaped building is the museum's single greatest work of art

TO APPLY
Open to college juniors and seniors as well as grad students (art, law, and business). Must have taken at least one course in modern art. International applicants eligible. Write for application

Internship Coordinator
Solomon R. Guggenheim Museum
1071 Fifth Avenue
New York, NY 10128
(212) 423-3557

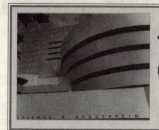

T he cutting-edge modernity of New York City's renowned Guggenheim Museum.

SONY

SELECTIVITY
Approximate applicant pool: 1,000; Interns accepted: 80

COMPENSATION
$250–$500/week; free housing (Japan)

LOCATION(S)
Park Ridge, NJ; Tokyo, Japan

FIELD
Electronics

DURATION
8 weeks–1 year: ongoing

DEADLINE(S)
Rolling

THE WORK
Founded in 1946, Sony is a worldwide leader in the manufacture of electronic products as well as the production and distribution of records, movies, and television programs through Sony Music Entertainment (see separate entry) and Sony Pictures Entertainment (see separate entry). Its core electronics business encompasses everything from CD players, headphone stereos, and televisions to DAT recorders, still-image video cameras, and car navigation systems. Interns work in Engineering, Research, Marketing, and Sales.

PERKS
Subsidized cafeteria; discounts on Sony products.

FYI
Sony gave the world the first consumer VCR and the Walkman. It is now betting on the success of its car navigation systems, lithium-ion batteries, and mini-disc audio systems.

TO APPLY
Open to undergrads and grad students. International applicants eligible. Submit resume and cover letter.

Internship Coordinator
Sony Corporation of America
1 Sony Drive
Park Ridge, NJ 07656-8003
(201) 930-1000
(201) 358-4060 (Fax)

Internship Coordinator
Sony Corporation
6-7-35 Kitashinagawa
Shinagawa-ku, Tokyo, 141
81-3-5448-5770
81-3-5448-5581 (Fax)
E-mail: intlgp@jinji.sony.co.jp

Sony Music

SELECTIVITY
Approximate applicant pool: 200 (credit), 500 (minority); Interns accepted: 100 (credit), 70 (minority)

COMPENSATION N/A
None (credit); Varies with position (minority)

LOCATION(S)
Santa Monica, CA; New York, NY (HQ); and field offices in CA, GA, IL, MA, MD, NY, OH, and TX

FIELD
Music

DURATION
10 weeks: Summer, Fall, Spring (Credit); 10 weeks: Summer (Minority)

DEADLINE
Rolling (Credit); April 1 (Minority)

THE WORK
In 1986, Sony acquired CBS Records, arguably the world's most successful record empire. The resulting division, Sony Music Entertainment, Inc. (SMEI), took over CBS Records' Columbia and Epic record labels and also established new labels such as Chaos Recordings and TriStar Music Group. Now, SMEI has an impossibly rich roster of artists, including the likes of Michael Jackson, Bruce Springsteen, and Pearl Jam. SMEI runs two internships. The Credited Internship is open to undergraduate and graduate students who are able to secure academic credit for their work. The Summer Minority Internship Program is a paid experience for minority undergraduate and graduate students that is augmented by a number of seminars and training sessions. Interns are placed in departments including Promotions, Publicity, Retail Marketing, Artists and Repertoire (A&R), A&R Administration, Business Affairs, Finance, and MIS.

PERKS
Promotional freebies; cafeteria; seminars and trips.

FYI
Invitations to listening parties are a possible perk; one intern reports attending listening parties for Columbia Records stars Kris Kross and Baby Face . . . Located in a skyscraper whose roof is "curved like a scoop," Sony headquarters has the "extremely modern" black-and-white decor one would expect of a Japanese electronics company.

TO APPLY
The Credited Internship Program is open to undergrad and grad students. Participants in this program must receive academic credit for their work. The Minority Internship Program targets minority undergrad and grad students. Minority interns need at least a 3.0 GPA and must be returning to school after their internship. Submit resume and cover letter.

Sony Music Entertainment, Inc.
Credited Internship Program
550 Madison Avenue, 2nd Floor
New York, NY 10022-3211

Sony Music Entertainment, Inc.
Minority Internship Program
550 Madison Avenue, 13th Floor
New York, NY 10022-3211
Attn: Department 13-5

Internship Hotline: (212) 833-7980

TY 🔍 🔍 🔍 🔍
Approximate applicant pool: 700; Interns accepted: 60

COMPENSATION Ⓢ
Credit and/or paid

LOCATION(S)
Culver City, CA (HQ); New York, NY

FIELD
Film; Television

DURATION
12 weeks: Summer, Fall, Spring

DEADLINE(S)
Rolling

THE WORK
Established in 1990, Sony Pictures Entertainment (SPE) is one of the world's largest film and television companies, generating over $3 billion in revenues. At the core of its operations are four film companies—Columbia Pictures, TriStar Pictures, Sony Pictures Classics, and Triumph Releasing Corp.—which have produced such hit films as *Jerry Maguire, Men In Black, Air Force One,* and *My Best Friend's Wedding.* Interns work in Accounting, Human Resources, Marketing, MIS, and Publicity and Promotions.

PERKS
Tours of SPE facilities (e.g., the state-of-the-art Sony Pictures Studios and Culver Studios); free movie passes and promotional materials; free screenings.

FYI
SPE also includes Columbia TriStar Television, Columbia TriStar Television Distribution, Columbia TriStar Home Video, Sony Theatres, Sony Pictures Classics, *The Ricki Lake Show,* and several major in-house technology groups.

TO APPLY
Open to undergrads and grad students. International applicants eligible. Must receive academic credit. Submit resume and cover letter.

Internship Coordinator
Sony Pictures Entertainment
10202 West Washington Boulevard
Culver City, CA 90232-3195
Employment hotline: (310) 280-4436

Internship Coordinator
Sony Pictures Entertainment
550 Madison Ave.
New York, NY 10022-3109
(212) 833-6526
(212) 833-6249 (Fax)

SOTHEBY'S
FOUNDED 1744

SELECTIVITY 🔍 🔍
Approximate applicant pool: 200–250; Interns accepted: 50–60

COMPENSATION Ⓢ
None

LOCATION(S)
New York, NY

FIELD
Auction house

DURATION
8 weeks: Mid-June through mid-August

DEADLINE
February 15

THE WORK
Founded in 1744 so British citizens could exchange property without the burden of face-to-face bargaining, Sotheby's today is known the world over as the place to sell property of great value and interest. Recent Sotheby's auctions have featured the Duchess of Windsor's jewelry collection, Andy Warhol's art collection, and paintings by Georgia O'Keefe. Interns are placed either in a client-service department like the Press Office, Graphic, or Marketing, or in one of thirty-three expert departments like American Paintings or Chinese Works of Art.

PERKS
Wednesday trips and lectures; gallery walks.

FYI
Every Wednesday at Sotheby's is devoted to educating interns about the art world. In the morning, interns receive guided tours of New York art museums and galleries. In the afternoon, interns attend a lecture back at the office.

TO APPLY
Open to college juniors and seniors, and recent grads. International applicants eligible. Submit introductory letter and resume.

Internship Coordinator
Sotheby's Inc., Human Resources
1334 York Avenue, 8th Floor
New York, NY 10021
(212) 606-7000
(212) 606-7028 (Fax)

SELECTIVITY 🔍 🔍 🔍
Approximate applicant pool: 50–75; Interns accepted: 5–8

COMPENSATION 💲
None

LOCATION(S)
New York, NY

FIELD
Magazines

DURATION
12 weeks: Summer, Fall, Spring

DEADLINE(S)
Rolling

THE WORK
Founded in 1988, *The Source* is a monthly magazine covering hip hop music, culture, and politics. Distributed to 150,000 subscribers, the magazine is known for delivering sharp graphics and opinionated writing while retaining a distinctly "street" feel. Interns work in Editorial and Advertising.

PERKS
Attendance welcome at music industry parties; free copies of magazine; free promotional CDs, cassettes, t-shirts, etc.; "laid-back, casual" work environment.

FYI
Says a staff member: "All the big names in hip hop come in here—from RedMan to Tribe to Mary J. Blige."

TO APPLY
Open to high school students, undergrads, recent college grads, college grads of any age, and grad students. International applicants eligible. Submit cover letter, resume, and writing samples (for Editorial internships).

Internship Coordinator
The Source
594 Broadway, Suite 510
New York, NY 10012
(212) 274-0464
(212) 274-8334 (Fax)

SELECTIVITY 🔍
Approximate applicant pool: 40; Interns accepted: 20

COMPENSATION 💲
None

LOCATION(S)
Washington, DC

FIELD
Theater

DURATION
8–10 weeks: Summer

DEADLINE(S)
Summer: May 15; Year round program: rolling

THE WORK
Since 1977, Source Theater Company has been dedicated to producing contemporary plays, reinterpretations of the classics, and new productions. Interns work on the annual Washington Theater Festival, in which Source stages productions of over fifty new plays, ranging from ten-minute plays to full-length productions in locations throughout Washington. Interns work in PR/Marketing, Box Office, Stage Management, Technical Theater, and General Administration.

PERKS
Weekly production workshop with theater professionals; free tickets to all performances; passes to shows at other local theaters; written evaluation at end of internship.

FYI
Says a former intern: "Learning the inner workings of a show made me realize more than ever before how much of a collaborative effort theater is." . . . The internship program has been in existence since 1980.

TO APPLY
Open to high school juniors and seniors, undergrads, recent college grads, college grads of any age, and grad students. International applicants eligible. Submit resume and cover letter.

Internship Coordinator
Source Theatre Company
1835 14th Street NW
Washington, DC 20009
(202) 462-1073
(202) 462-2300 (Fax)

When television talk-show host **Charlie Rose** enrolled at Duke University in 1960, he planned to become a physician. That all changed the summer after his junior year when he served an internship in the office of then-Senator B. Everett Jordan (D-NC). The internship prompted him to change his major to history, where he gained a background in world affairs that would later serve him well as host of the highly praised *Charlie Rose* talk show.

"Young man, you were hired to empty wastebaskets, sharpen pencils, and distribute mail. You were not hired to do funny impressions of me."

Drawing by J. Mirachi; © 1966, 1994 The New Yorker Magazine, Inc.

SOUTH SEAS RESORT

SELECTIVITY
Approximate applicant pool: 150; Interns accepted: 24/year

COMPENSATION
$50/week, free housing; one free meal per day

LOCATION(S)
Captiva Island, FL

FIELD
Hotels

DURATION
15 weeks: Summer, Fall, Spring

DEADLINE(S)
Rolling

THE WORK
Established in 1960, South Seas Resort is a 330-acre luxury resort nestled amidst the towering palms of Captiva Island, a barrier island located off Florida's west coast. Described as "Florida's Tahiti" by *Travel and Leisure Magazine*, South Seas offers twenty-one tennis courts, golfing by the sea, swimming pools, watersports, a marina, and a health and fitness center. Interns work in the Recreation department, where they plan social activities, corporate events, holiday activities, and assist in the coordination of special events such as wine tastings, fun runs, and magic shows.

PERKS
Leisure time access to all recreational facilities; formal exposure to other departments; discounts on watersports (e.g., waverunning, parasailing, and waterskiing) and at retail shops and sister resorts; free uniform shirts and jackets.

FYI
More than a third of the Recreation staff started as interns at South Seas . . . According to legend, the island is called "Captiva" because in the late 1700s the infamous pirate Jose Gaspar kept beautiful women captive there.

TO APPLY
Open to college seniors, recent college grads, college grads of any age, and grad students. International applicants eligible. Write for application.

Internship Coordinator
Recreation Department
South Seas Resort
P.O. Box 194
Captiva Island, FL 33924
(941) 472-5111 ext. 3441
(941) 472-7620 (Fax)

THE SOUTHERN CENTER FOR INTERNATIONAL STUDIES

SELECTIVITY
Applicant Pool: 100; Applicants Selected: 8–12

COMPENSATION
Governor's interns: small stipend

LOCATION(S)
Atlanta, GA

FIELD
International relations; Education

DURATION
High school and governor's interns: 1 semester
Grad Students and PhDs: 1 year

DEADLINE(S)
June 1

THE WORK
The Southern Center for International Studies is a nonprofit educational organization that develops educational programming, conducts research, and advises members on international affairs. The Center's educational programming includes annual policy conferences with national and world leaders.

The Center has three internship tiers: High school student interns, Governor's student interns (primarily college and Master's students), and Southern Center Research Associates (primarily advanced graduate students or PhDs). All interns are expected to maintain the Center's current events files on countries, international issues, international organizations, and specific industries. High school interns are expected to complete a research project on an international policy topic and present their findings at a staff meeting. Governor's interns work extensively on preparing background briefs for upcoming programs while attending the Center's local programming and even assisting in the production of some events.

PERKS
Opportunities to attend events; opportunities to work on Peabody Award-winning conferences; access to library files.

FYI
The SCIS has hosted such distinguished guests as the Dalai Lama, Crown Prince Hassan of Jordan, the Head of the Soviet Information Ministry Gennadi Gerasimov, and other luminaries. In addition, they sponsored the first-ever conference of former US Secretaries of State, which was made into a one-hour television special and aired nationally over the Public Broadcasting Service.

TO APPLY
Minimum GPA requirement 3.0.

For the Governor's internship, contact:

Governor's Intern Program
Office of the Governor
State Capitol
Atlanta, GA 30334
404-656-3804

Minimum GPA requirement 3.0.

For an Associate Position (Grad students and PhDs):

Dr. Christopher L. Brown
Research Director, The Southern Center for International Studies
320 West Paces Ferry Road, NW
Atlanta, GA 30305
404-261-5763 ext. 151

SOUTHERN PROGRESS CORPORATION

SELECTIVITY 🔍 🔍
Approximate applicant pool: 400; Interns accepted: 90

COMPENSATION 💲 💲 💲
$400/week

LOCATION(S)
Birmingham, AL

FIELD
Magazines; Publishing

DURATION
12 weeks: Summer; 16 weeks: Fall; 24 weeks: Spring

DEADLINE(S)
Summer: February 15; Fall: June 15; Spring: October 15

THE WORK
Dating back to 1886, the Southern Progress Corporation is the largest regional magazine and book publisher in the country. A subsidiary of Time Warner, we now publish six magazines: *Southern Living, Southern Accents, Cooking Light, Progressive Farmer, Coastal Living,* and *Weight Watchers* as well as Oxmoor House books. Interns work in Editorial (includes Foods, Homes, Travel, and Copy Desk), Graphic Design, Test Kitchens, Marketing Research, Photography, Advertising, Computer Science, and Accounting.

PERKS
Orientation; career development luncheon; after-work socials; access to on-site chair massages; free fruit daily; discounted gym membership; free parking; casual Fridays.

FYI
All interns are encouraged to participate as a group in one community service project . . . The SPC internship program commenced in 1988 with just one intern.

TO APPLY
Open to college juniors, seniors, recent grads, as well as grad students. International applicants eligible. Submit resume, cover letter, and 1–3 letters of recommendation and samples on 8 1/2 x 11 copies only.

Internship Coordinator
Southern Progress Corporation
P.O. Box 2581
Birmingham, AL 35202

SOUTHFACE ENERGY INSTITUTE

SELECTIVITY 🔍 🔍 🔍 🔍
Approximate applicant pool: 150; Interns accepted: 8–10

COMPENSATION 💲 💲
$335/month stipend; free housing; free transportation (car, bikes, public transportation)

LOCATION(S)
Atlanta, GA

FIELD
Construction; Environment

DURATION
8–12 weeks: ongoing

DEADLINE(S)
Rolling

THE WORK
Established in 1978, the Southface Energy Institute is a nonprofit group promoting sustainable building and community design, water and energy conservation, healthy indoor environments, and clean air/transportation. Southface's activities include publishing a quarterly journal on energy and building technologies; running the Southface Energy and Environmental Resource Center (SEERC), analyzing the energy efficiency of planned construction (Design Review Service); and offering courses on energy-efficient construction, sustainable landscaping, and more. Interns monitor the in-house recycling program, maintain membership databases, do carpentry work, lead workshops, set up exhibits, conduct research for the journal, facilitate the gardening program, and complete an independent project (e.g., create an exhibit relating sun angle to thermal gain in a passive solar house or produce a children's version of the guide book for the SEERC).

PERKS
Opportunities to travel with experts on home audits and reviews; attendance welcome and encouraged at all Southface programs; geographically diverse group of interns; free housing; use of intern car/bikes.

FYI
The SEERC includes over 100 different energy-efficient and environmental technologies and concepts such as innovative insulation systems, solar (PV) roof shingles, low-emissivity windows, geothermal heat pump, passive solar design, low flush toilets, drought-tolerant landscape, solar water heater, and an aggressive daylighting strategy. Southface successfully exhibits overlap of environmental issues.

> Interns who work at the Southface Energy Institute will find that the organization doubles as a model of energy efficiency, sporting insulation systems, solar panels, low-emissivity windows, heat barriers, low-flow showerheads, low-flush toilets, and a drought-tolerant landscape.

TO APPLY

Open to high school students, undergrads, recent college grads, college grads of any age, and grad students. International applicants eligible. Write for application.

Internship Coordinator
Southface Energy Institute
241 Pine Street
Atlanta, GA 30308-5424
(404) 872-3549
(404) 872-5009 (Fax)

THE SOUTHWESTERN COMPANY

SOUTHWESTERN COMPANY

SELECTIVITY
Approximate applicant pool: N/A; Interns accepted: 3,600

COMPENSATION $ $ $ $
Average $7,541/summer

LOCATION(S)
All 50 states; Canada; England

FIELD
Sales

DURATION
12 weeks: Summer

DEADLINE(S)
June 1

THE WORK

Dating back to 1855, the Southwestern Company is one of the oldest publishing and direct selling companies in the nation. Since 1868, Southwestern has been giving students the opportunity to finance their education while building character and life skills through selling family-oriented educational reference books and software each summer in family's homes. The Southwestern salesforce is made up of thousands of students representing hundreds of colleges and universities from North America and Europe.

PERKS

Southwestern allows students the opportunity to be their own boss – from sales to accounting to inventory management! No flipping burgers this summer! The on-going training seminars and sales techniques more than prepare the student with skills in both a career and life. The experience is also a great resume builder for any field of study. Needless to say, the harder a student works, the heftier their profits.

FYI

Most Southwestern salespeople choose to live in their designated territory with several other participants of the program to keep living expenses to a minimum. Many Southwestern alumni move on to Fortune 500 companies and beyond! Some examples include: Fuller Warren, former Governor of FL; minister and best-selling Christian author Max Lucado; U.S. Senator Jeff Sessions of Alabama; and U.S. Independent Counsel Kenneth Starr. Southwestern is also the winner of the Direct Selling Association's Education for Life Award.

TO APPLY

Open to high school seniors, undergrads, recent college grads, college grads of any age and grad students. International applicants are eligible. Please submit resume and cover letter.

Sales Summer Program
The Southwestern Company
P.O. Box 305140
Nashville, TN 37230
800 424 6205
615 391 2875 (Fax)
www.southwestern.com

SPACE NEEDLE CORPORATION

SPACE NEEDLE

SELECTIVITY 🔍 🔍 🔍
Approximate applicant pool: 80; Interns accepted: 10

COMPENSATION $
Free meals; free parking or bus pass

LOCATION(S)
Seattle, WA

FIELD
Restaurant management; Tourism

DURATION
12 weeks: Summer, Fall, Spring

DEADLINE(S)
Summer: March 1; Fall and Spring: rolling

THE WORK

Erected in 1961 as the central structure for the 1962 Seattle World's Fair, the Space Needle is a 50-story tower featuring an observation deck, two restaurants, and banquet facilities. An internationally recognized symbol of Seattle, the Space Needle was inspired by the Stuttgart Tower in Germany. Interns work in Marketing, Human Resources, Restaurants (management), and Finance/Accounting.

PERKS

Free passes and admission coupons to local attractions, movies, and events; the beautiful Northwest is at your feet.

FYI

The Space Needle has been the site of several weddings, one birth, three suicide leaps, and a jump by two parachutists.

TO APPLY

Open to college seniors, recent college grads, college grads of any age, and grad students. Minimum GPA: 2.5. International applicants eligible. Submit resume, cover letter, and transcript.

Internship Coordinator
Space Needle Corporation
203 Sixth Avenue North
Seattle, WA 98108-5005
(206) 443-9700
(206) 441-7415 (Fax)

SELECTIVITY 🔍🔍🔍
Approximate applicant pool: 100; Interns accepted: 8–10

COMPENSATION $
$35/week

LOCATION(S)
Washington, DC

FIELD
The disabled; Public service; Sports

DURATION
8–12 weeks: Summer, Fall, Spring

DEADLINE(S)
Summer: April 1; Fall and Spring: rolling

THE WORK
Founded in 1968 by Eunice Kennedy Shriver, Special Olympics International (SOI) provides year-round sports training and athletic competition in a variety of Olympic-type sports for children and adults with mental retardation. With over 500,000 volunteers in more than 130 countires, SOI strives to provide its participants with improved fitness and motor skills, greater self confidence, a more positive self-image, friendships, and increased family support. Interns work in Sports, Public Affairs, Chapters, Marketing, International Programs, Finance, and Administration.

PERKS
Brown-bag luncheons with department heads; an opportunity to travel to local Special Olympic Games. Free T-shirt, Special Olympic paraphernalia.

FYI
The Special Olympics Oath: "Let me win. But if I cannot win, let me be brave in the attempt."

TO APPLY
Open to college juniors and seniors as well as recent college grads. International applicants eligible. Write for application.

Internship Coordinator
Special Olympics International
1325 G Street NW, Suite 500
Washington, DC 20005
(202) 628-3630
(202) 824-0200 (Fax)

SELECTIVITY N/A
Interns accepted: 4–5 per semester

COMPENSATION $
None

LOCATION(S)
New York, NY

FIELD
Advertising; Marketing

DURATION
16 weeks: Summer, Fall, Spring

DEADLINE(S)
Rolling

THE WORK
In print since 1985, *Spin* is a music-oriented magazine known for its hip, youthful attitude. With a readership that is 90 percent concentrated in the 18-29 age group, *Spin* describes itself as "fifty percent music news and fifty percent social and political coverage." Interns work in Advertising (e.g., Marketing, Promotions, and Publicity) and Editorial.

PERKS
Attendance welcome at staff meetings and *Spin* parties; occasional intern luncheons; free t-shirts, CDs, concert tickets, and magazines.

FYI
In existence since 1985, the internship program counts among its alumni *Spin*'s office manager, music news editor, special events coordinator, all of the editorial assistants, and almost all of the advertising assistants . . . *Spin* is owned by Bob Guccione, Jr., son of the publisher of *Penthouse* magazine.

TO APPLY
Open to undergrads, recent college grads, and college grads of any age. International applicants eligible. Submit resume and cover letter.

Patricia Manley
SPIN
205 Lexington Avenue 3rd Floor
New York, NY 10016
(212) 231-7400
(212) 231-7300 (Fax)

SELECTIVITY 🔍 🔍
Approximate applicant pool: 250–350; Interns accepted: 50–75

COMPENSATION 💲 💲
$225/week; housing

LOCATION(S)
Charleston, SC

FIELD
Performing arts

DURATION
3–4 weeks: Spring

DEADLINE(S)
February 1

THE WORK
Named "the most varied arts festival given on this continent" by *The Washington Post*, Spoleto Festival USA produces and presents world class opera, dance, theater, chamber, symphonic and choral music, jazz, visual arts, and experimental multi-media works of all kinds. Departments hiring interns include: (in Administration) Media Relations, Development, Finance, Box Office, Housing, General Administration, Merchandising, and Orchestra Management; (in Production) Stage Carpenters, Stage Electricians, Sound, Properties, Wardrobe, Wigs, Make-up, and Production.

PERKS
Admission to all festival events; use of College of Charleston gym/facilities; orientation activities.

FYI
A few non-paying, informal internship positions are available in the summer and fall.

TO APPLY
Open to undergrads, recent college grads, college grads of any age, and grad students. International applicants eligible. Write for application.

Apprentice Program
Spoleto Festival USA
P.O. Box 157
Charleston, SC 29402-0157
(803) 722-2764

SELECTIVITY 🔍 🔍 🔍
Approximate applicant pool: 2,000; Interns accepted: 175–225

COMPENSATION 💲 💲 💲 💲 💲
Highly competitive

LOCATION(S)
95 percent of internships located in New York, NY

FIELDS
Accounting; Asset management; Investment banking; Management consulting

DURATION
10 weeks minimum: Summer

DEADLINE(S)
February 15 (candidates are encouraged to submit applications in December)

THE WORK
An approximate combined total of 200 internships are offered each summer in the fields of accounting, asset management, corporate law, investment banking and management consulting. All internships are sponsored by premiere Wall Street firms and other leaders in the financial services industry including corporate law. During the summer of 1998, the Career Program placed a total of 238 interns from over 75 colleges nationwide; 15 firms participated in investment banking, 7 in management consulting, 6 in accounting, 5 in asset management and 17 in corporate law.

PERKS
Comprehensive training and orientation program; summer-long seminar allowing interns to meet with the chief executive officers, senior managers and recruitment officers from each of the participating firms; mentors at each firm; career couseling during summer, school year and beyond; and, upon completion of the internship, membership in the Alumni Association.

FYI
Since its founding in 1980, the Career Program has placed over 1,800 students of color in Summer internships. Seventy-five percent of all interns have accepted full-time positions in the industries in which they have interned. The Career Program has helped to exponentially increase the number of people of color employed in the financial services industry.

TO APPLY
Open to undergraduate students of color. International students of color eligible. To receive an application, visit our website or send a stamped ($1.10), self-addressed 9"x12" manila envelope to:

Sponsors for Educational Opportunity
23 Gramercy Park South
New York, NY 10003
(212) 979-2040
www.seo-NY.org

SPORTS ILLUSTRATED

SELECTIVITY 🔍🔍🔍🔍🔍
Approximate applicant pool: 300; Interns accepted: 10

COMPENSATION 💲
Reimbursement for local travel and $6 per day meal money

LOCATION(S)
New York, NY

FIELD
Magazines; Sports; Public relations

DURATION
12 weeks: Summer, Fall, Spring

DEADLINE(S)
Spring: November 1; Summer: April 1; Fall: July 15

THE WORK
In print since 1954, *Sports Illustrated* (SI) is the nation's premier sports magazine, admired for its lively reporting, striking photography, and vivid design. Owned by Time Warner, SI reaches some 25 million readers each week. Interns typically work in Communications, but a few are sometimes placed in Marketing and Ad Sales. Communications internships also available with *SI For Kids* and *SI For Women*.

PERKS
Free promo items; summer softball team; attendance welcome at magazine events (e.g., Swimsuit Party, Sportsman/Sportswoman of the Year); discounts on merchandise in Time Warner store; contact with sports industry executives, sports celebrities; association with the Olympics; free tickets to NY sporting events.

FYI
Says the internship coordinator: "Interning here gives you a unique taste of both sports and entertainment. One week, interns may work with the NBA, the next they could be doing background research for an athlete's appearance on *The Tonight Show*, [and] the following week they might be working with Major League Baseball." . . . In existence since 1987, the internship program counts among its alumni staff at NIKE, NBA, NHL, ESPN, Disney, Madison Square Garden, and US Weightlifting. Former interns have gone on to work for ESPN, The Boston Bruins, the editorial and photography staff at SI and other Time Inc. magazines.

TO APPLY
Open to college juniors and seniors as well as grad students. Must receive academic credit. International applicants eligible. Submit resume, cover letter, and relevant writing sample (press release, newspaper article, etc.—no term papers).

Internship Coordinator–Rick McCabe
Sports Illustrated
135 West 50th Street
New York, NY 10020-1393
(212) 522-1375
(212) 522-0747 (Fax)

SPY

See Sussex Publishers

STARLIGHT FOUNDATION

SELECTIVITY 🔍🔍🔍
Approximate applicant pool: 25 (NY); Interns accepted: 3 (NY)

COMPENSATION 💲
None

LOCATION(S)
Los Angeles, CA; Atlanta, GA; Chicago, IL; Boston, MA; Scarborough, ME; New York, NY; Redmond, WA; Melbourne and Sydney, Australia; Montreal and Toronto, Canada; London, England

FIELD
Public service

DURATION
12 weeks–1 year: Summer, Fall, Spring

DEADLINE(S)
Rolling

THE WORK
Founded in 1983 by actress Emma Samms and film executive Peter Samuelson, the Starlight Foundation helps brighten the lives of seriously ill children, ages 4 through 18, through the granting of wishes and related programs. With 12 chapters throughout the world and 300 volunteers, Starlight has granted wishes such as meeting Paul McCartney, visiting Disney World, viewing a taping of *Sesame Street*, and having dinner with Cindy Crawford. Departments accepting interns include Children Services, Fundraising, Office Operations, and Public Relations/Marketing.

PERKS
Attendance welcome at galas, sports auctions, and other events; attendance welcome at hospital parties; free promotional items (mug, t-shirts, etc.).

FYI
Says a former intern, "Starlight was my fourth internship and the one that was both the most challenging and most rewarding . . . The thought of the thousands of kids and their families that Starlight has touched is what brought me to New York."

ORIGINS OF THE APPRENTICESHIP

Although use of the term "internship" to refer generally to a program of experiential learning is only a few decades old, the idea of gaining supervised practical experience is rooted in antiquity. The Babylonian Code of Hammurabi, written in 2100 B.C., contains a provision requiring artisans to teach their handicrafts to their sons. Similarly, records of ancient Greece, Egypt, and Rome show that the young learned their trade under the supervision of skilled workers.

In the Middle Ages, the concept of experiential learning evolved further. Skilled craftsmen began to sponsor "apprenticeships" (from the French word aprendre—"to learn"), whereby they would teach the art of their trade to young novices. Such a system was mutually beneficial, offering the apprentice the opportunity for on-the-job training and advancement while providing the master with a source of cheap labor. The details of the apprenticeship were usually formalized with a contract, which was signed not only by the master and his apprentice but also by the apprentice's parents. A guild oversaw the establishment of such an apprenticeship, approving the parameters of its duration and setting the work requirements. Most apprenticeships lasted at least a year, and some, such as those in England, typically spanned five to seven years. Apprenticeships were offered in a wide range of fields, from printing to shoemaking to shipbuilding.

While apprentices did not receive a salary, they were typically offered free room and board at their master's home. On some occasions, an apprentice's family actually paid a small sum to the master in exchange for the training their son would receive. During the apprenticeship, the master served as a kind of father-figure, guiding his young workers and instilling in them a positive work ethic. It was even acceptable for a master to discipline his apprentices if they stepped out of line. Because such authority created the possibility of abuse by the master, however, guilds and civil authorities were empowered to supervise the relations between master and apprentice.

Apprenticeships became so common in subsequent centuries that many countries sought to regulate them on a national basis. In 1562, for example, England enacted the Statute of Artificers, mandating that apprentices work at least seven years and serve until they were at least 24 years of age. Interestingly, apprenticeships during this time were not the sole province of one socio-economic class—both the well-off and the poor served as apprentices. But with whom they apprenticed differed greatly. The sons of prosperous townsmen were often apprenticed to workers in high-end trades, such as printing and silversmithing. Conversely, poor children would find apprenticeships in less lucrative areas like craft-making and agriculture. For some children, it was the only way to keep off the streets.

SOME APPRENTICES IN HISTORY
(AND WHERE THEY APPRENTICED)

Benedict Arnold, famous "traitor" and military leader (apothecary's shop)

Captain James Cook, sailor, explorer, and discoverer of the Hawaiian Islands (shipping firm of John Walker in North Yorkshire, 1747)

Elevthère Irénée du Pont de Nemours, founder of Du Pont (French chemist Antoine Lavoisier, 1790)

Benjamin Franklin, scientist and politician (printer's shop of brother James, 1718-1723)

Samuel Gompers, labor leader, (shoemaker, 1860)

Alexander Hamilton, Secretary of the Treasury and author of the Federalist Papers (merchant on St. Croix)

Thomas Hardy, author (architect, 1856)

Andrew Johnson, 17th President of the United States (tailor in Raleigh, NC, 1820-1826)

John Paul Jones, renowned naval officer (shipowner in Whitehaven, England, 1761-1764)

Alfred Nobel, Swedish philanthropist, originator of the Nobel prizes (Swedish ship designer, 1860)

Terence Powderly, labor leader (machinist shop, 1866-1869)

Paul Revere, courier and political activist (gold and silversmith shop, 1753)

Benjamin Rush, signer of the Declaration of Independence and renowned medical researcher (Dr. John Redman of Philadelphia, PA, 1761)

Frederick Taylor, the "father of scientific management" (Enterprise Hydraulic Works in Philadelphia, PA, 1874)

Mark Twain, author and journalist (printer's shop, 1846 & riverboat, 1857)

Martin Van Buren, 8th President of the United States (NY law offices of Francis Silvester, 1796-1801)

The apprentice system remained a significant force in subsequent centuries, but not without facing new challenges. The Industrial Revolution of the nineteenth century posed the greatest threat to apprenticeships, as the growth of factories during this time diminished the need for skilled workers. Those who pursued trades that still demanded intensive training, such as engineering and pharmacology, were gradually turning to newly established graduate and trade schools for training. Such schools provided more thorough training than on-the-job experience, especially in fields like engineering that were growing increasingly complex. By the beginning of the twentieth century, the impersonality of industry had rendered the apprentice system outmoded. Whereas one would have once apprenticed himself to a shoemaker, he was now employed on the production line of a shoe factory.

Although apprenticeships as a widespread labor system gradually disappeared, the spirit of apprenticeships lives on today. Occupations in which production remains unstandardized, such as custom tailoring and glassblowing, require their new initiates to undergo years of apprenticeship-like supervision and training. But the idea of the medieval apprentice system, with its mutually beneficial pairing of master and novice, lives on in the practice of modern-day internships.

TO APPLY
Open to undergrads, grad students, and grads. International applicants eligible. Call New York for Starlight contacts in other cities. Write for application.

Internship Coordinator
Starlight Foundation
1560 Broadway, Suite 600
New York, NY 10036
(212) 354-2878
(212) 354-2977 (Fax)

STATE TEACHERS RETIREMENT SYSTEM OF OHIO

SELECTIVITY 🔍🔍🔍🔍
Approximate applicant pool: 500; Interns accepted: 16

COMPENSATION 💲💲💲💲
$650–$750/week for undergrads; $750–$1,000/week for grad students

LOCATION(S)
Columbus, OH

FIELD
Business

DURATION
3 months: Summer, Fall, Spring

DEADLINE(S)
Rolling

THE WORK
State Teachers Retirement System of Ohio (STRS-Ohio) provides Ohio's schoolteachers with a variety of benefits, including retirement planning and health care coverage. With $53 billion in assets, STRS is one of the largest pension funds in Ohio and the eighteenth largest in the U.S. Interns are placed in Finance, Equities, Real Estate, Fixed Income, International Investments, Information Technology Services, and Member Services.

PERKS
Free housing; fitness center; participation welcome on company sports teams; occasional brown bag luncheons and a summer picnic; other summer events for interns only, such as attending sporting events, dinners, and cookout.

FYI
STRS's internship program, begun in 1997; to date, STRS–Ohio has hired five former interns as full-time employees.

TO APPLY
Open to college juniors and seniors majoring in business, recent college grads, and grad students (MBA preferred). Submit resume and cover letter. International applicants eligible.

State Teachers Retirement System of Ohio
Attn: Internship Coordinator
275 East Broad Street
Columbus, OH 43215
(614) 227-2908
(614) 227-2952 (Fax)
E-mail: resumes@strsoh.org

STATEN ISLAND ZOO

SELECTIVITY 🔍🔍🔍
Approximate applicant pool: 30; Interns accepted: 4

COMPENSATION 💲💲
Summer: $250/week; September–June: $375/week

LOCATION(S)
Staten Island, NY

FIELD
Education; Zoos

DURATION
12 weeks: Summer; 10 months: Fall–Spring

DEADLINE(S)
Summer: February 1; Fall–Spring: July 1

THE WORK
Established in 1936, the Staten Island Zoo calls itself the "biggest little zoo" in the New York City Area. Attracting some 300,000 visitors each year, the Zoo features a tropical forest, an aquarium, a children's center, a serpentarium, and outdoor

exhibits. Under the auspices of the Zoo's ZOOFARI Day Camp for pre-sixth graders, interns work as instructors of art, outdoor recreation, and science.

PERKS
Attendance welcome at staff meetings; attendance welcome at weekend educational programs; 50 percent discount on food and gifts.

FYI
The internship program has been running since 1986 . . . Says the internship coordinator: "For our size, we have the strongest education department of any zoo in the area. We are the only zoo in the region that offers outreach programs."

TO APPLY
Open to recent college grads, college grads of any age, and grad students. International applicants eligible. Write for full job description. Send resume and cover letter.

Internship Coordinator
Staten Island Zoo
614 Broadway
Staten Island, NY 10310
(718) 442-3174
(718) 981-8711 (Fax)

STATUE OF LIBERTY

See National Park Service

STENNIS SPACE CENTER

See National Aeronautics and Space Administration

STEPPENWOLF THEATRE COMPANY

steppenwolf
theatre company

SELECTIVITY
Approximate applicant pool: 400; Interns accepted: 25

COMPENSATION
Small stipends or college credit

LOCATION(S)
Chicago, IL

FIELD
Theater administration; Theater production

DURATION
3–12 months

DEADLINE(S)
July 1 for Fall; November 1 for Winter/Spring; March 1 for Summer

THE WORK
Founded in 1975, the Tony Award–winning Steppenwolf Theatre Company is one of Chicago's leading regional theatres. Internships are available in the following areas: Artistic, Arts Exchange, Costumes, Development, Finance Office, Electrics, Marketing, Production Management, Properties, Scenic Art, Sound, Technical Production Publicity, and Stage Management.

PERKS
Performance attendance; discounts at Steppenwolf store; attendance at workshops and seminars.

FYI
Says the internship coordinator: "Our internships attempt to bridge the gap between an academic and a professional career in the theater. Interns here have the opportunity to work closely with industry professionals and are exposed to the inner workings of one of the country's top theaters."

TO APPLY
Open to undergrads, recent college grads, college grads of any age, and grad students. International applicants eligible. Applications available on the website.

Kimberly Senior
Steppenwolf Theatre Company
758 West North Avenue, 4th Floor
Chicago, IL 60610
(312) 335-1888
(312) 335-0808 (Fax)
E-mail: ksenior@steppenwolf.org
www.steppenwolf.org

STUDENT CONSERVATION ASSOCIATION

SELECTIVITY
Approximate applicant pool: 3,000; Interns accepted: 1,300 (interns), 200 (CCDP), 450 (CWC)

COMPENSATION
Interns: $50/week, round-trip travel, free housing, accident insurance; CCDP, CWC: free tent & food

LOCATION(S)
Interns at CWC: 50 states in the US

FIELD
Archaeology; Environment; Resource and Wildlife Management; Recreation; Biology; Botany; Ecology; Landscape Architecture; Paleontology; Visitor/Youth Education; History; Engineering; and Forestry.

DURATION
Interns: 12 weeks to 12 months, Year round; CWC: 4–5 weeks, summer, fall

DEADLINE(S)
Interns: Rolling (at least 2 months before start date preferred); CCDP: Rolling; CWC: March 1

THE WORK
Founded in 1957, the Student Conservation Association, Inc. (SCA) is a national nonprofit organization that fosters stewardship of the environment. In addition to offering education and leadership programs, SCA marshals interns and volunteers of all ages to perform public service in natural resource management, endangered species protection, and ecological restoration on America's public lands. Under the auspices of SCA Conservation Internship Program, Conservation Career Development Program (CCDP), and the Conversation Work Crew (CWC) for high school students, interns and volunteers work in national parks, forests, wildlife refuges, and conservation centers.

PERKS
Stunning natural beauty; intensive, on-site training (Interns); mentors & career counseling (CCDP).

FYI
Interns get numerous and unparalleled opportunities to explore the wilderness. One intern in Alaska "found that [her supervisors] were always encouraging [her] to go out and take trips" on days off, resulting in camping expeditions to Denali National Park and the Kenai Peninsula Wildlife Refuge . . . 25 percent of interns return to their sponsoring agencies for full-time entry-level employment.

TO APPLY
The CCDP program is open to minority high school students and undergrads from urban centers. The CWC program is open to 16–18 year-old high school students. The internship program is open to any high school graduate over 18. International applicants are eligible for most positions. Write call, fax, e-mail, or visit our website to request an application.

Student Conservation Association (SCA)
P.O. Box 550, 689 River Road
Charlestown, NH 03603
(603) 543-1700
(603) 543-1828 (Fax)
E-mail: internships@sca-inc.org
www.sca-inc.org

STUDENT WORKS PAINTING

SELECTIVITY 🔍🔍🔍🔍🔍
Approximate applicant pool: 12,000; Interns accepted: 570

COMPENSATION 💲💲💲💲
$700/week average

LOCATION(S)
CA; CO; MI; OH; OR; WA; TX; UT; ID; NC; Alberta; British Columbia; Manitoba; Ontario.

FIELD
Business/Management

DURATION
Part-time Spring, Full-time Summer (12 weeks)

DEADLINE(S)
March 30

THE WORK
Founded in 1981, the summer management program with Student Works Painting hires high achieving college students and trains them how to manage a business from start to finish. Each selected manager will oversee the marketing, sales, management and customer relations of a house painting business in their hometown. Interns are provided with the tools and training, the systems and support, and the licenses and insurance necessary to manage a successful business during the summer. The requirements are confidence, leadership skills and motivation. Earnings range from $2,500 to $30,000. Full information available at www.studentworks.com.

PERKS
Intense training program, continual support, average summer earnings of $9,200. Bi-weekly company events, reward dinners with executives, alumni interaction, limousine night, whitewater rafting and an end of the year trip to Mexico.

FYI
Top performers receive an all-expenses paid Cabo San Lucas vacation with the company. Student Works is the largest residential paint contractor in California. There are many career opportunities available within the company (for above average performers) and also with several affiliated organizations who actively recruit Student Works alumni. In 1998, a Student Works alumnus, Mark Moses of Platinum Capital Group, received the "Ernst and Young Entrepreneur of the Year Award" and was listed #10 on the "Inc. 500, fastest growing businesses in America." Another alumnus' business, AutoWeb interactive, went public and hit a market cap of $910 million.

TO APPLY
Open to undergrads, recent college grads, college grads of any age, and grad students. International applicants eligible (undergrads only). Write for application.

Southern California, Colorado, Texas and the Pacific Northwest
1505 East 17th Street, Suite 210
Santa Ana, CA 92705
(800) 394-6000
(714) 564-7900

Northern California
1802 Tice Valley Blvd.
Walnut Creek, CA 94595
(800) 295-9675
(925) 937-0434

Alberta and British Columbia
Suite 4, 1037 West Broadway
Vancouver
V6H 1E3
(800) 665-4992
(604) 733-6110

Top-performing interns from Student Works Painting pose for a picture after hauling in a 50-pound sailfish on their all-expenses-paid trip to Cabo San Lucas.

Students For
Central & Eastern Europe
INCORPORATED

SELECTIVITY
Approximate applicant pool: 290; Interns accepted: 95

COMPENSATION
Approximately $50/week; free housing (apartment or dorm room); free meals (in some placements)

LOCATION(S)
Bulgaria; Czech Republic; Slovakia; Poland

FIELD
Teaching

DURATION
10–16 weeks: Summer, Fall, Spring

DEADLINE(S)
Summer: April 30; Fall: May 31; Spring: November 10

THE WORK
Founded in 1990, Students for Central & Eastern Europe (SFCEE) is a nonprofit, student-run teaching organization that provides English language instruction to the people of Europe's emerging democratic nations. Funded by the Rockefeller Foundation, SFCEE uses interns as teachers in schools, universities, and summer camps in cities and towns throughout Central and Eastern Europe.

PERKS
Orientation support in Washington, DC and Prague; access to college facilities (varies); possible deferment of student loans.

FYI
While visiting Georgetown University in 1990, Czech President Vaclav Havel was asked by a student what Americans could do to assist Europe's new democracies. The response given by a Czech student accompanying Havel—stirred the GU student and a few of his peers to establish SFCEE that night— "You can learn us English."

TO APPLY
Open to undergrads, recent college grads, college grads of any age, and grad students. International applicants eligible (native English speakers only). Write for application. Application fee: $20.

Students for Central & Eastern Europe
3421 M Street NW, Suite 1720
Washington, DC 20007
(202) 625-1901
(202) 333-1147 (Fax)

SUCCESS

See MacDonald Communications Corp.

WHAT MAKES A "BAD INTERN," ACCORDING TO "THE ROCK N' ROLL MADAME"

Jo Maeder, a veteran disc jockey known to millions of listeners as "The Rock n' Roll Madame," has spun discs at some of the country's top radio stations, including WXRK (K-ROCK) in New York and Y-100 in Miami. Because she has come in contact with hundreds of interns over the years, we asked her to name three things that make "a bad intern." Here's what she said:

• A bad intern is undependable. If the intern is supposed to show up at nine o'clock, he or she has got to be there at nine.

• A bad intern has a bad attitude, like "I am above this—I don't want to be here doing this." This is not to say that if someone asks you to do something that's unreasonable, then you don't have a right to say something. If your boss says, 'OK, I want you to pick up my laundry,' then if he or she is really in a bind, it's fine. But that kind of thing should be spelled out initially, before you start work.

• A bad intern has no idea of presentability. You should always ask [your supervisor] 'How do you want me to dress?' and so on. I interviewed somebody once and she had a great resume and was very intelligent but she had dirty fingernails . . . I know when you're young you sometimes don't think about these things. But they can make a difference.

SUMMERBRIDGE NATIONAL

SELECTIVITY
Approximate applicant pool: 1,500; Interns accepted: 850

COMPENSATION
$750 stipend & up to $1,250 aid available for undergrads; $500 stipend for HS students

LOCATION(S)
Nationwide (see Appendix)

FIELD
Education

DURATION
8 weeks: Summer

DEADLINE(S)
February 2

THE WORK

Founded in 1978 at San Francisco University High School, Summerbridge enables high school students and college students to fully experience the challenges, exhilaration, and realities of teaching During the eight-week summer program, Summerbridge interns teach elemetary and middle school students with limited educational opportunities the academic skills necessary to succeed in college preparatory high school programs. Interns not only teach the classes but also manage the entire program.

PERKS

Independence; creative environment; workshops on teaching; mentoring.

FYI

Teachers work from 7:30 am to 6:00 pm on campus and then well into the evening to correct homework assignments . . . "We give them hope and direction and excite them about the possibility of going to college," said a teacher.

TO APPLY

Open to high school sophomores, juniors, seniors, and college undergrads. International applicants eligible. For an application please visit our homepage located at www.summerbridge.org. All applications are now submitted on-line. For further questions call or write:.

Summerbridge National
361 Oak St.
San Francisco, CA 94102
(415) 865-2970
(415) 865-2979 (Fax)
E-mail: sbnation@aol.com
www.summerbridge.stanford.edu

SUNDAY MORNING

See CBS News

Lights... Camera... *Intern!*

Interns in film and on television:

In the comedy film *Spanking the Monkey*, pre-med student Ray (played by **Jeremy Davies**) must give up his summer internship in order to take care of his injured mother.

SUPREME COURT OF THE UNITED STATES

SELECTIVITY   🔍 🔍 🔍 🔍 🔍
Approximate applicant pool: 80; Interns accepted: 2

COMPENSATION $
None; $1,000 scholarship may be available

LOCATION(S)
Washington, DC

FIELD
Government

DURATION
3–4 months; Summer, Fall, Spring

DEADLINE(S)
Summer: March 10; Fall: June 10; Spring: October 20

THE WORK

The US Supreme Court is America's highest judicial body. The nine justices of the Court meet to discuss and issue decisions on our nation's most important jurisprudential issues. To give college students a chance to experience parts of this process, there is the Judicial Internship Program, enabling students to work under the auspices of the administrative assistant, who serves as the chief justice's right-hand man or woman.

PERKS

Law-clerk luncheons; cafeteria/gym.

FYI

The program was established in 1972 by the Office of the Administrative Assistant to the Chief Justice . . . "You may be a small fish, but you are one of two small fish in a prestigious, marble-lined pond," said an intern. "With a little luck, you'll gain great insight into the inner workings of the judiciary." . . . Past interns stress the importance of the applicant's personal statement: "Use it to explain why you can offer the Supreme Court something extraordinary. Cite examples. Don't exaggerate."

TO APPLY

Open to college juniors and seniors, and recent grads. Constitutional law coursework required. Submit resume, transcript, a statement explaining your reasons for seeking the internship, a short writing sample, three letters of recommendation, and a two-page essay on the American constitutional system.

Supreme Court of the United States
Judicial Internship Program
Office of the Administrative Assistant
to the Chief Justice
Room 5
Washington, DC 20543
(202) 479-3415

SELECTIVITY
Approximate applicant pool: 25; Interns accepted: up to 4 per year quarter

COMPENSATION Ⓢ
None

LOCATION(S)
San Clemente, CA

FIELD
Environmental activism

DURATION
Winter: January 1–March 31; Spring: April 1–June 30; Fall: October 1–December 31; duration flexible depending on project and intern's availability

DEADLINE(S)
Applications are accepted during the quarter preceding the internship. Decisions are made 6 weeks prior to the internship start date.

THE WORK
Fed up with Southern California's increasingly polluted waters, a circle of surfers banded together in 1984 to create a group dedicated to the preservation of coastal waters and beaches. Today, Surfrider is an international organization with over 25,000 members. Over the past few years, Surfrider has made a concerted effort to have interns carry out important projects. There is a lot of busywork to be done, but that's normal for a nonprofit group.

PERKS
Easygoing culture; participation in Surfrider events.

FYI
When the surf is unusually good, it's acceptable for staff to take time out to hit the waves . . . Interns say there is a positive energy at Surfrider and some of it is directed their way: "The staff bends over backward to show that they think interns are important. Working hours, for example, are flexible. If you come in late because you're working on your project at the library, no problem . . . They trust you."

TO APPLY
Open to high school students, undergrads, recent college grads, and grad students. International applicants eligible. Submit resume and cover letter explaining the reasons for wanting to work at Surfrider.

Surfrider Foundation
Internship Program
122 South El Camino Real
PMB #67
San Clemente, CA 92672
(800) 743-SURF

SELECTIVITY
Approximate applicant pool: 100; Interns accepted: 5 per season

COMPENSATION Ⓢ
$25–$50/week, depending on hours

LOCATION(S)
New York, NY

FIELD
Magazines

DURATION
10–14 weeks; Summer, Fall, Spring, and Winter

DEADLINE(S)
Rolling

THE WORK
Founded in 1991, Sussex publishes *Psychology Today*, a magazine covering issues and trends in psychology since 1967, *Mother Earth News*, a country/outdoors lifestyle magazine started in 1970, and *Country Music*, a music magazine based in Nashville. Interns at each magazine work in Editorial, Photo/Art, and Advertising/Marketing.

PERKS
Interns write at least one story with byline; intern acknowledgment in magazine's masthead.

LINDA DAVIS'S "INTERNSHIP" WITH REBA McENTIRE

When country singer **Linda Davis** moved to Nashville in 1982, she cut some demo records and sang the jingles for a few television commercials, but nothing hit big. Her luck changed in 1989, however, when she hired as her manager Narvel Blackstock, the husband of country music great **Reba McEntire**. Through Blackstock, Davis was able to sing her way into what she likened to a "paid internship with McEntire." She ended up singing back-up vocals on the country star's concert tour, and in time she proved so talented that she was invited to sing the lead during some of McEntire's many costume changes. Soon after, McEntire and Davis teamed up to do duets, notably "Does He Love You," a song that won them a Grammy and Davis a record deal with Arista Nashville. Said Davis in *The News Tribune*: "I feel fortunate having been taken under the wing of such a sweet, classy lady . . . I've been around a long time. It's a really good feeling."

FYI
Sussex's intimate office environment encourages interns at each magazine to pitch story ideas to the other magazines.

TO APPLY
Open to undergrads, recent college grads, college grads of any age, and grad students. International applicants eligible. Submit resume, cover letter, and writing samples.

Internship Coordinator
Sussex Publishers
49 East 21st Street, 11th Floor
New York, NY 10010
(212) 260-7210

SYMANTEC CORPORATION

SELECTIVITY
Approximate applicant pool: 1,000; Interns accepted: 20–30

COMPENSATION
$500–$700/week for undergrads; $700/week for grad students

LOCATION(S)
Cupertino, Sunnyvale, and Santa Monica, CA; Eugene, Beaventon, OR; Toronto, Canada

FIELD
Computer software

DURATION
12 weeks: Summer; Part-time positions available year-round

DEADLINE(S)
Rolling

THE WORK
Symantec Corporation was founded in 1982 by Dr. Gary Hendrix. Symantec develops, markets, and supports a complete line of application and system software products designed to enhance individual and workgroup productivity as well as manage networked computing environments. Interns work as members of the following departments: Engineering (Development & SQA), Human Resources, Finance, Marketing, Sales, and Management Information Services.

PERKS
Free munchies; paid holidays; fitness center (Cupertino only).

FYI
"We hire F-1 and J-1 students! The majority of our interns convert to full-time employees!"

TO APPLY
Open to college undergrads as well as grad students. Students must currently be enrolled in a program of interest to Symantec. International applicants encouraged to apply. Submit resume and cover letter.

Internship Coordinator
Symantec Corporation
10201 Torre Avenue
Cupertino, CA 95014-2132
(408) 253-9600
(408) 366-5972 (Fax)
E-mail: jobs@symantec.com
www.symantec.com

TADA!

SELECTIVITY
Approximate applicant pool: 35; Interns accepted: 12

COMPENSATION
Stipends for some production interns

LOCATION(S)
New York, NY

FIELD
Dance; Theater

DURATION
8 weeks–6 months: Summer, Fall, Spring

DEADLINE(S)
Summer: April 1; Fall and Spring: rolling

THE WORK
Founded in 1984, TADA! is New York's premiere youth theater company offering theater and dance productions performed by children for family audiences. Guided by a staff of experienced theater professionals, the performance group is made up of 55 children ages 8 to 18 who rehearse after school and on weekends. Interns work in Production (Technical Director, Theater Electrician, Wardrobe Seamstress, Box Office, House Manager) and as Production Assistants, and in Arts Administration.

PERKS
Training sessions in technical departments; attendance welcome at all performances; participation in fundraising events (cocktail parties, benefits, etc.).

FYI
In existence since 1989, the internship program leads to permanent employment at TADA! for about 20 percent of Interns.

TO APPLY
Open to undergrads, recent college grads, college grads of any age, and grad students. Submit resume and cover letter.

Internship Coordinator
TADA!
120 West 28th Street, 2nd Floor
New York, NY 10001
(212) 627-1732
(212) 243-6736 (Fax)

Sports Team Contacts

Most major sports teams offer internships, typically in the areas of public relations, sales, finance, and operations. Here are contacts for the teams in the National Basketball Association, National Football League, Major League Baseball, and National Hockey League.

NATIONAL BASKETBALL ASSOCIATION
(see separate entry)

Atlanta Hawks (see separate entry)

Boston Celtics
151 Merrimac Street
Boston, MA 02114
(617) 523-6050

Charlotte Hornets
One Hive Drive
Charlotte, NC 28217
(704) 357-0252

Cleveland Cavaliers (see separate entry)

Dallas Mavericks
Reunion Arena
777 Sports Street
Dallas, TX 75207
(214) 748-1808

Denver Nuggets
McNichols Sports Arena
1635 Clay Street
Denver, CO 80204
(303) 893-6700

Detroit Pistons
The Palace of Auburn Hills
Two Championship Drive
Auburn Hills, MI 48326
(313) 377-0100

Golden State Warriors
Oakland Coliseum Arena
7000 Coliseum Way
Oakland, CA 94621
(510) 638-6300

Houston Rockets
The Summit
Ten Greenway Plaza
Houston, TX 77046
(713) 627-0600

Indiana Pacers
300 E. Market Street
Indianapolis, IN 46204
(317) 263-2100

Los Angeles Clippers
LA Memorial Sports Arena
3939 S. Figueroa Street
Los Angeles, CA 90037
(213) 748-8000

Los Angeles Lakers (see separate entry)

Miami Heat
Miami Arena
Miami, FL 33136-4102
(305) 557-4328

Milwaukee Bucks
Bradley Center
1001 N. Fourth Street
Milwaukee, WI 53203-1312
(414) 227-0500

Minnesota Timberwolves
600 First Ave. N.
Minneapolis, MN 55403
(612) 673-1600

New Jersey Nets
Meadowlands Arena
East Rutherford, NJ 07073
(201) 935-8888

New York Knickerbockers (see separate entry)

Orlando Magic
One Magic Place
Orlando Arena
Orlando, FL 32801
(407) 649-3200

Philadelphia 76ers
Veterans Stadium
P.O. Box 25040
Philadelphia, PA 19147-0240
(215) 339-7600

Phoenix Suns
201 E. Jefferson
Phoenix, AZ 85004
(602) 379-7900

Portland Trail Blazers
700 NE Multnomah Street
Suite 600
Portland, OR 97232
(503) 234-9291

Sacramento Kings
One Sports Parkway
Sacramento, CA 95834
(916) 928-0000

San Antonio Spurs
Alamodome
100 Montana Street
San Antonio, TX 78203
(210) 554-7787

Seattle Supersonics
190 Queen Anne Ave. N., Suite 200
Seattle, WA 98109
(206) 281-5800

Utah Jazz
Delta Center
301 W. South Temple
Salt Lake City, UT 84101
(801) 325-2500

Washington Bullets
USAir Arena
Landover, MD 20758
(301) 773-2255

NATIONAL
FOOTBALL LEAGUE

(see separate entry)

Arizona Cardinals
8701 South Hardy
Tempe, AZ 85284
(602) 379-0101

Atlanta Falcons
One Falcon Place
Suwanee, GA 30024

BILLS

Buffalo Bills
Rich Stadium
One Bills Drive
Orchard Park, NY 14127
(716) 648-1800

BEARS

Carolina Panthers
800 South Mint Street
Charlotte, NC 28202

Chicago Bears
Hallis Hall at Conway Park
Lake Forest, IL 60045
(708) 295-6600

Cincinnati Bengals
One Bengals Drive
Cincinnati, OH 45204
(513) 621-3550

COWBOYS

Dallas Cowboys (see separate entry)

Denver Broncos
13655 Broncos Parkway
Englewood, CO 80112
(303) 649-9000

Detroit Lions
Pontiac Silverdome
1200 Featherstone Road
Pontiac, MI 48342
(313) 335-4131

Green Bay Packers
1265 Lombardi Avenue
Green Bay, WI 54304
(414) 496-5700

Indianapolis Colts
P.O. Box 535000
Indianapolis, IN 46253
(317) 297-2658

Jacksonville Jaguars
One Alltel Stadium Place
Jacksonville, FL 32202
(904) 633-6000

Kansas City Chiefs
Arrowhead Stadium
One Arrowhead Drive
Kansas City, MO 64129
(816) 924-9300

Miami Dolphins
7500 S.W. 30th Street
SDavie, FL 33314
(305) 650-5000

Minnesota Vikings
9520 Viking Drive
Eden Prairie, MN 55344
(612) 828-6500

New England Patriots
Foxboro Stadium
60 Washington Street
Foxboro, MA 02035
(508) 543-8200

New Orleans Saints
5800 Airline Highway
Metairie, LA 70003
(504) 733-0255

New York Giants
Giants Stadium
East Rutherford, NJ 07073
(201) 935-8111

New York Jets
1000 Fulton Avenue
Hempstead, NY 11550
(516) 538-6600

Oakland Raiders
1220 Harbor Bay Parkway
Alameda, CA 94502

Philadelphia Eagles
Veterans Stadium
3501 S. Broad Street
Philadelphia, PA 19148
(215) 463-2500

Pittsburgh Steelers
Three Rivers Stadium
300 Stadium Circle
Pittsburgh, PA 15212
(412) 323-1200

San Diego Chargers
Qualcomm Stadium
P.O. Box 609609
San Diego, CA 92160
(619) 280-2111

San Francisco 49ers (see separate entry)

Seattle Seahawks
11220 N.E. 53rd St.
Kirkland, WA 98033
(206) 827-9777

ST. Louis Rams
One Rams Way
St. Louis, MO 63045

Tennessee Oilers
Baptist Sports Park
7640 Highway 70 South
Nashville, TN 37221

Tampa Bay Buccaneers
One Buccaneer Place
Tampa, FL 33607
(813) 870-2700

Washington Redskins
21300 Redskin Park Drive
Ashburn, VA 20147
(703) 478-8900

MAJOR LEAGUE BASEBALL

Atlanta Braves (see separate entry)

Baltimore Orioles
Oriole Park at Camden Yards
333 W. Camden St.
Baltimore, MD 21201
(410) 685-9800

Boston Red Sox
Fenway Park
4 Yawkey Way
Boston, MA 02215-3496
(617) 267-9440

California Angels
Anaheim Stadium
2000 Gene Autry Way
Anaheim, CA 92806
(714) 937-7200

Chicago Cubs
1060 W. Addison St.
Chicago, IL 60613
(312) 404-CUBS

Chicago White Sox
Comiskey Park
333 W. 35th St.
Chicago, IL 60616
(312) 924-1000

Cincinnati Reds
100 Riverfront Stadium
Cincinnati, OH 45202
(513) 421-4510

Cleveland Indians
Indians Park
2401 Ontario St.
Cleveland, OH 44115
(216) 861-1200

Colorado Rockies
1700 Broadway, Suite 2100
Denver, CO 80290
(303) 292-0200

Detroit Tigers
Tiger Stadium
Detroit, MI 48216
(313) 962-4000

Florida Marlins
Joe Robbie Stadium
2267 N.W. 199th St.
Miami, FL 33056
(305) 626-7400

Houston Astros
P.O. Box 288
Houston, TX 77001-0288
(713) 799-9500

Kansas City Royals
Royals Stadium
P.O. Box 419969
Kansas City, MO 64141
(816) 921-2200

Los Angeles Dodgers
1000 Elysian Park Ave.
Los Angeles, CA 90012-1199
(213) 224-1500

Milwaukee Brewers
Milwaukee County Stadium
Milwaukee, WI 53214
(414) 933-4114

Minnesota Twins
The Metrodome
501 Chicago Ave., South
Minneapolis, MN 55415
(612) 375-1366

Montreal Expos
P.O. Box 500
Station "M"
Montreal, Quebec
CANADA H1V 3P2
(514) 253-3434

New York Mets
126th St. & Roosevelt Ave.
Flushing, NY 11368
(718) 507-METS

New York Yankees
Yankee Stadium
Bronx, NY 10451
(718) 293-4300

Oakland Athletics
Oakland-Alameda County Coliseum
Oakland, CA 94621
(510) 638-4900

Philadelphia Phillies
P.O. Box 7575
Philadelphia, PA 19101
(215) 463-6000

Pittsburgh Pirates
P.O. Box 7000
Pittsburgh, PA 15212
(412) 323-5000

St. Louis Cardinals
250 Stadium Plaza
St. Louis, MO 63102
(314) 421-3060

San Diego Padres
P.O. Box 2000
San Diego, CA 92112-2000
(619) 283-4494

San Francisco Giants
Candlestick Park
San Francisco, CA 94124
(415) 468-3700

Seattle Mariners
The Kingdome
P.O. Box 4100
Seattle, WA 98104
(206) 628-3555

Texas Rangers
The Ballpark in Arlington
P.O. Box 90111
Arlington, TX 76004-3111
(817) 273-5222

Toronto Blue Jays
SkyDome
Bremner Blvd.
Toronto, Ontario M5V 1J1
(416) 341-1000

NATIONAL HOCKEY LEAGUE

Anaheim Mighty Ducks
Arrowhead Pond of Anaheim
2695 Katella
P.O. Box 61077
Anaheim, CA 92803
(714) 704-2700

Boston Bruins
150 Causeway Street
Boston, MA 02114
(617) 227-3206

Buffalo Sabres
Memorial Auditorium
140 Main Street
Buffalo, NY 14202
(716) 856-7300

Calgary Flames
Olypic Saddledome
Box 1540—Station M
Calgary, Alberta T2P 3B9
(403) 261-0475

Chicago Blackhawks
1901 W. Madison
Chicago, IL 60612
(312) 455-7060

Dallas Stars
901 Main St., Suite 2301
Dallas, TX 75202
(214) 712-2807

Detroit Red Wings
Joe Louis Arena
600 Civic Center Drive
Detroit, MI 48226
(313) 396-7535

Edmonton Oilers
Northlands Coliseum
7824—118 Avenue
Edmonton, Alberta T5B 4M9
(403) 474-8561

Florida Panthers
100 N.E. Third Avenue, 10th Floor
Fort Lauderdale, FL 33301
(305) 768-1912

Hartford Whalers
242 Trumbull Street, 8th Floor
Hartford, CT 06103
(203) 728-3366

Los Angeles Kings
The Great Western Forum
3900 West Manchester Boulevard
Inglewood, CA 90305
(310) 419-3150

Montreal Canadiens
2313 Ste. Catherine West
Montreal, Quebec H3H 1N2
(514) 989-2803

New Jersey Devils
Meadowlands Arena
50 Route 20 North
East Rutherford, NJ 07073
(201) 935-9502

New York Islanders
Nassau Coliseum
Uniondale, NY 11553
(516) 542-9314

New York Rangers (see separate entry)

Ottawa Senators
301 Moodie Drive, Suite 200
Nepean, Ontario K2H 9C4
(613) 721-4327

Philadelphia Flyers
The Spectrum
3601 South Broad Street
Philadelphia, PA 19148
(215) 389-9553

Pittsburgh Penguins
Civic Arena, Gate 9
Pittsburgh, PA 15219
(412) 642-1812

Quebec Nordiques
Colisee de Quebec
2205 Ave. du Colisee
Quebec, PQ G1L 4W7
(418) 529-4676

St. Louis Blues
1401 Clark Avenue
St. Louis, MO 63103
(314) 622-2521

San Jose Sharks
San Jose Arena
525 West Santa Clara Street
San Jose, CA 95113
(408) 999-5712

Tampa Bay Lightning
501 E. Kennedy Boulevard, Suite 175
Tampa, FL 33602
(813) 276-7392

Toronto Maple Leafs
Maple Leaf Gardens
60 Carlton Street
Toronto, Ontario M5B 1L1
(416) 596-3096

Vancouver Canucks
Pacific Coliseum
100 North Renfrew Street
Vancouver, BC V5K 3N7
(604) 251-0575

Washington Capitals
USAir Arena
Landover, MD 20785
(301) 350-3400

Winnipeg Jets
1661 Portage Avenue, 10th Floor
Winnipeg, MB R3J 3T7
(204) 982-5313

TALK OF THE NATION

See National Public Radio

TBS

See Turner Broadcasting System

TBWA/CHIAT DAY

SELECTIVITY 🔍🔍🔍
Approximate applicant pool: 900; Interns accepted: 24–36

COMPENSATION Ⓢ
$75–225/week

LOCATION(S)
New York, NY; Overseas

FIELD
Advertising

DURATION
10 weeks: Summer

DEADLINE(S)
March 1

THE WORK
The mighty Absolut Vodka bottle has been etched into the minds of millions of consumers, thanks to an ingenius advertising campaign featuring the sleek Absolut bottle in over 300 different ads. The mastermind behind this campaign is TWBA/Chiat Day, a high quality, medium-sized advertising house in New York. With $1.2 billion in billings, TWBA/Chiat Day ranks among the world's top twenty advertising agencies. Besides Absolut, its clients include such high-profile companies as Wonderbra, Apple, ABC Television, Taco Bell, Nissan, Phillips van Heusen, Prodigy Internet and Nivea skin cream and Levis. Each intern is assigned a job in one of four work areas: Strategic Planning, Creative, Account Management, or Media.

In 1994, **Robert Rosenthal** completed a four-month culinary/production internship at the TV Food Network, a required part of his coursework at Peter Kump's New York Cooking School. Not a feat in itself, until you learn that Rosenthal interned at the network while serving as Senior VP and Director of Business Planning of TBWA Advertising where he was responsible for strategic planning for top accounts. "The show I worked on—*Robin Leach Talking Food*—was taped live at 10 pm," he recalled. "That allowed me to intern after I finished work at TBWA around 6 or 6:30 until 11:30 at night. I remember how odd it felt to pitch $100 million ad accounts by day only to be followed by cooking gourmet concoctions at night."

PERKS
Hip atmosphere; luncheon seminars; international flavor; parties/picnic.

FYI
TBWA/Chiat Day has offices and internships in over 60 countries, with the strongest opportunities in Amsterdam, Barcelona, Frankfurt, London, Paris, and Johannesburg . . . Interns also participate in a marketing project where teams of five or six interns develop complete marketing and communications plans for a TBWA/Chiat Day client. Each team presents its work to the senior management of TBWA/Chiat Day and then shows it to representatives of the actual client. It is the highlight of the internship.

TO APPLY
Open to college juniors and seniors. International applicants eligible. Submit resume and cover letter explaining your reasons for seeking the job.

Internship Program
TBWA/Chiat Day
180 Maiden Lane
New York, NY 10038
(212) 804-1000 (phone)
(212) 804-1200 (fax)

TEACH FOR AMERICA

TEACHFORAMERICA

SELECTIVITY 🔍🔍
Approximate applicant pool: 4,000; 30–35 percent accepted

COMPENSATION Ⓢ Ⓢ Ⓢ
$20,000–$34,500/year depending on location

LOCATION(S)
Urban placement in: Baltimore, the Bay Area, Greater New Orleans, Houston, Los Angeles, New Jersey, New York City, Phoenix, Atlanta, Chicago, and Washington, DC. Rural placement in: The Mississippi Delta, North Carolina, the Rio Grande Valley, and Southern Louisiana.

FIELD
Teaching

DURATION
Two years minimum

DEADLINE(S)
October 30; February 20

THE WORK
Teach for America is the national teacher corps of outstanding recent college graduates of all academic majors and cultural backgrounds who commit two years to teach in under-resourced urban and rural public schools. Teach for America recruits from August through February, interviews applicants in December, March, and April, trains them for five weeks at a summer institute, places them in selected placement sites in August, and then coordinates an ongoing support network throughout their two-year commitment.

PERKS
Possibility of gaining a state teaching certificate; possibility of receiving an education reward that can be used for past loans or future education and/or loan deferment.

TO APPLY

Open to undergrads and grad students. Must receive academic credit (Account Service only). International applicants eligible. Submit resume, cover letter, writing samples (Public Relations only), and five to seven nonreturnable samples of copywriting or art direction (Creative only).

Internship Coordinator
Temerlin McClain
P.O. Box 619200
Dallas/Forth Worth Airport, TX 75261
(214) 830-2655
(214) 830-2655 (Fax)

TEXAS INSTRUMENTS

SELECTIVITY

Approximate applicant pool: 500–600; Interns accepted: 75

COMPENSATION

$240/week for high school students; $520–$600/week for undergrads; $3,000/month for grad students; round-trip travel; employee benefits

LOCATION(S)

Attleboro, MA; Austin, Dallas, Houston, Lubbock, and Sherman, TX

FIELD

Electronics; Defense; Computers

DURATION

Summer: 3 months; Fall and Spring: 4–5 months

DEADLINE(S)

Summer: March 1; Fall: June 1; Spring: October 1

THE WORK

Founded in 1930, Texas Instruments (TI) is an electronics company responsible for the invention of the integrated circuit, the LCD digital watch, and the single-chip microprocessor as well as the development of the first commercial transistor radio, the first hand-held calculator, and the first speech synthesizer (Speak & Spell™). Its 70,000 employees generate over $7 billion annually in TI products, from radar and weapons systems to notebook computers. Interns work in Corporate Services, Defense Systems & Electronics, Semiconductor, Finance, Facilities, Materials & Controls, Legal, and Research.

PERKS

Access to TI recreational facility; mentors; tours (e.g., TI clean room) and demos (e.g., manufacturing techniques); intern social events (e.g., picnic, bowling, ball game) and luncheons.

FYI

Organized in the early 1960s, TI's Intern/Co-op Program offers 80–95 percent of interns full-time employment.

TO APPLY

Open to high school seniors, college sophomores, juniors, and seniors, and engineering grad students. Minimum GPA: 3.0. Submit resume, cover letter, and transcript.

Internship Coordinator
Texas Instruments
P.O. Box 655012 M/S 70 or
P.O. Box 655303 M/S 8333
Dallas, TX 75265

TEXAS MONTHLY

TexasMonthly.

SELECTIVITY

Approximate applicant pool: 100; Interns accepted: 35

COMPENSATION

None

LOCATION(S)

Austin, Dallas, and Houston, TX

FIELD

Magazines

DURATION

10–12 weeks: Summer, Fall, Spring

DEADLINE(S)

Rolling (preferably 2 months before start date)

THE WORK

Proclaimed by locals the "National Magazine of Texas," *Texas Monthly* has been the leading cultural magazine of the Lone Star state since 1973. It has over 300,000 subscribers and a readership of approximately 2.25 million people. Departments accepting interns include Marketing Services, Sales Development/Advertising, Editorial, Production, Publisher's Office, Circulation, General Administration, and Custom Publishing.

PERKS

Free one-year subscription to *Texas Monthly*; letter of recommendation from publisher.

FYI

Says a former intern: "I received valuable insight into the rich oral tradition and folk tales of Texas [and also] had a boot-stomping good time!"

TO APPLY

Open to undergrads, grads, and grad students. Submit resume and cover letter stating desired session and department.

Internship Coordinator
Texas Monthly
P.O. Box 1569
Austin, TX 78767

THEATER DE LA JEUNE LUNE

SELECTIVITY
Approximate applicant pool: 100; Interns accepted: 3 Fall and Spring.

COMPENSATION S
None

LOCATION(S)
Minneapolis, MN

FIELD
Performing arts

DURATION
A four and one half month commitment in Fall and Spring

DEADLINE(S)
One month prior to start date depending on slot availability.

THE WORK
Founded in 1979, Theater de la Jeune Lune is a professional, nonprofit theater company with a national reputation for innovative productions and a distinct, physical performance style. Production internships are available in Properties, Directing, Set & Costume Design, Lighting, Stage Management & Technical Direction, with occasional opportunities in other departments such as Music or Dramaturgy. Administrative positions are available in Development, Business, Office Management, and Front-of-House.

PERKS
Complimentary tickets to Jeune Lune and other theaters.

FYI
Theater de la Jeune Lune, which is French for "theater of the young moon," is housed in the former Minneapolis Van and Warehouse building in the city's hip warehouse district.

TO APPLY
Open to high school seniors, undergrads, recent college grads, college grads of any age, and grad students. International applicants eligible. Write for application.

Internship Program
Theater de la Jeune Lune
105 First Street North
Minneapolis, MN 55401
(612) 332-3968
(612) 332-0048 (Fax)

THIRTEEN/WNET

SELECTIVITY
Approximate size of applicant pool: 300–400; Interns accepted: 100

COMPENSATION S
$10/day

LOCATION(S)
New York, NY

FIELD
Production

DURATION
8–40 weeks: Summer, Fall, Winter, Spring

DEADLINE(S)
Summer: second Friday in April; Fall: second Friday in July; Winter: second Friday in October; Spring: second Friday in December

THE WORK
Established twenty years ago, Channel Thirteen's internship program gives students entry-level employment experience relating to business administration and the broadcast communications industry. Internships are available in all departments, including Advertising, American Masters, Art, Research, Business Affairs, Information Systems, Design/Graphics, Development, Educational Outreach, Educational Video Service, Foundation/Government Underwriting, Human Resources, Library, Music Services, New Media Group, Operations, Dance Programming, Music Programming, Drama Programming, Photography, Premiers/Pledge, Promotional & Events, Science & Nature, and Program Funding/Underwriting.

PERKS
Placement of interns is in coordination with the student's academic and career goals.

FYI
5–10 percent of interns are later hired for full-time positions; Channel Thirteen's viewing area encompasses New York, New Jersey, and Connecticut.

TO APPLY
College juniors, seniors, and grad students should submit a resume and a cover letter. In addition, a letter from their school should be sent confirming that the student will receive college credit: Students working for college credit are given preference over those who are not. Open to international students who will receive college credit.

College Internship Program Thirteen/WNET
450 West 33rd Street
New York, NY 10001
(212) 560-2047
(212) 560-6865
www.thirteen.org/jobs/index.html

SELECTIVITY 🔍
Approximate applicant pool: 50; Interns accepted: 20

COMPENSATION 🆂
None

LOCATION(S)
New York, NY

FIELD
Art

DURATION
1 month minimum

DEADLINE(S)
Rolling

THE WORK
Established in 1992, the Thread Waxing Space (TWS) is a nonprofit visual arts and performance organization incorporated under the University of the State of New York. Dedicated to displaying the works of emerging artists and artists who deserve greater visibility, TWS presents media and performance art, poetry readings, dance performances, film screenings, lectures, and panel discussions. Interns work in Development, Art-in-Education, Installation, General Administration, and Curation.

PERKS
Studio visits with contemporary artists; attendance welcome at all lectures and special events; free publications; cool SoHo location.

FYI
The internship program has been in existence since 1992 . . . The name "Thread Waxing Space" comes from the organization's location in an abandoned thread waxing factory . . . Interns are supplied with a guide on intern procedures and responsibilities.

TO APPLY
Open to high school juniors and seniors, undergrads, recent college grads, college grads of any age, and grad students. International applicants eligible. Write or call for application.

Internship Coordinator
Thread Waxing Space
476 Broadway, 2nd Floor
New York, NY 10013
(212) 966-9520
(212) 274-0792 (Fax)

SELECTIVITY 🔍🔍🔍🔍
Approximate applicant pool: 4,000; Interns accepted: 200

COMPENSATION 🆂🆂🆂
$440–$540/week for undergraduates; $550–$680/week for graduate students

LOCATION(S)
St. Paul, MN; Austin, TX; and 80 plants nationwide (see Appendix)

FIELD
Consumer; Health care; Commercial; Industrial goods

DURATION
14 weeks: Summer

DEADLINE
December 31

THE WORK
Founded in 1902 as a maker of sandpaper, 3M now manufactures more than 60,000 products. Innovative inventions such as 3M Post-it notes, masking tape, and Scotch Brand transparent tape have made 3M a world-recognized company with yearly sales of over $15 billion. The Summer Intern Program places students in laboratory, engineering, and manufacturing positions, where they help improve old products and create new ones. Interns are also placed in finance, marketing, and administrative positions.

PERKS
Employee comraderie; social activities; 3M Center.

FYI
3M stands for Minnesota Mining and Manufacturing . . . 3M started its summer program in 1951, making it one of the oldest internship programs in corporate America . . . Approximately 50 percent of graduating interns receive full-time employment with 3M.

TO APPLY
Open to college sophomores, juniors, and seniors, and grad students. Minimum 3.0 GPA. International applicants eligible. Submit resume and cover letter.

3M
Staffing & College Relations
224-1W-02
3M Center
St. Paul, MN 55144-1000
(800) 328-1343

See Turner Broadcasting System

See National Broadcasting Company

SELECTIVITY 🔍🔍🔍🔍🔍
Approximate applicant pool: 500; Interns accepted: 5

COMPENSATION $
Credit

LOCATION(S)
New York, NY

FIELD
Record labels

DURATION
12 weeks: Summer, Fall, Spring

DEADLINE(S)
Rolling

THE WORK
Established in 1981, Tommy Boy Music is one of the nation's largest independent distributors of hip hop, rap, and dance music. The label features artists such as De La Soul, Everlast, Joydrop, and Amber. Interns work in Promotion, Publicity, Artists & Repertoire, Accounting, and Business.

PERKS
Free CDs, cassettes, and posters; occasional free tickets to concerts; upbeat, informal work environment.

FYI
Inspiration for the company's name came when the grandfather of CEO Tom Silverman rummaged through his basement and found a crate of oranges labeled "Tommy Boy."

TO APPLY
Open to undergrads and grad students. International applicants eligible. Submit resume and cover letter.

Internship Coordinator
Tommy Boy Music
902 Broadway, 13th Floor
New York, NY 10010
(212) 388-8300
(212) 388-8413 (Fax)

SELECTIVITY 🔍🔍
Approximate applicant pool: 60–80; Interns accepted: 10

COMPENSATION $
None

LOCATION(S)
Burbank, CA

FIELD
Television

DURATION
12–16 weeks: Summer, Fall, Spring

DEADLINE(S)
Summer: July 1; Fall: November 1; Spring: April 1

THE WORK
Established in 1992, *The Tonight Show With Jay Leno* is the successor to the long-running American institution, *The Tonight Show With Johnny Carson*. Hosted by former stand-up comic Jay Leno, it is produced by the National Broadcasting Company (see separate entry) and features Leno monologues, celebrity interviews, and comedy sketches. First broadcast in 1953, *The Tonight Show* starred Steve Allen (1953-56) and Jack Paar (1956-62) before Carson and then Leno took the reins. Interns work in the General Office and the Writing department.

PERKS
Free tickets to show for family and friends; attendance welcome at remote shoots around Los Angeles; opportunities to attend show rehearsals and tapings.

FYI
Since establishing its internship program in 1992, *The Tonight Show* has hired seven interns for full-time positions . . . Says the internship coordinator: "We work our interns very hard, but they leave our show qualified for nearly any entry-level position in the entertainment industry."

TO APPLY
Open to college juniors and seniors as well as grad students. Must be majoring in broadcasting, communications, or television/film. International applicants eligible. Submit resume, cover letter, and recommendations.

Internship Coordinator
The Tonight Show With Jay Leno
NBC
3000 West Alameda Avenue
Burbank, CA 91523
(818) 840-2222
(818) 840-2240 (Fax)

SELECTIVITY 🔍
Approximate applicant pool: N/A; Interns accepted: 25–35

COMPENSATION $ $ $
$12.50/hour

LOCATION(S)
Los Angeles, CA

FIELD
Automobiles

DURATION
12 weeks

DEADLINE(S)
Apply between January 15–February 28

THE WORK

Founded in 1926, Toyota manufactures more than 4 million cars and trucks a year, over half of which are sold outside of Japan. Its vehicles, which bring the company nearly $100 billion in revenues annually, include Toyota Tercel, Cressida, Paseo, Celica, Camry, Avalon, Tacoma, and Corolla as well as the Lexus line of luxury automobiles. Interns work at Toyota Motor Sales in CA, in Advertising, Business Processes and Controls, Corporate Used Vehicle Operations, Distribution Operations, Financial Planning, Toyota Industrial Equipment (forklift division), Toyota Marine Division. Interns should be pursuing a Business Administration, Marketing, Management or related degree.

PERKS

Luncheon featuring department heads (e.g., BBQ, volleyball, basketball); access to Toyota fitness centers.

FYI

Interns are offered the opportunity to apply for the Management Trainee Program just prior to the completion of their internship.

TO APPLY

Open to college students the summer before their senior year. MBA internships are also available. Submit resume and cover letter.

College Relations – A134
Toyota Motor Sales
19001 South Western Avenue
Torrance, CA 90509

TRACY WATTS MILLINERY

tracywatts

SELECTIVITY   N/A
Approximate applicant pool: N/A; Interns accepted: 6

COMPENSATION $
Free lunch daily

LOCATION(S)
New York, NY

FIELD
Hats (millinery)

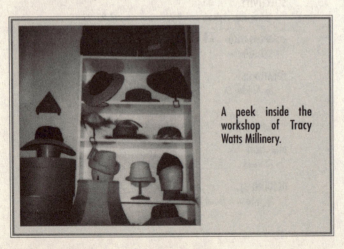

A peek inside the workshop of Tracy Watts Millinery.

DURATION
12 weeks: Summer, Fall, Spring

DEADLINE(S)
Rolling

THE WORK

Established in 1992, Tracy Watts Millinery produces hats that are carried by Neiman Marcus stores and upscale boutiques across the country. Featured in magazines such as *Elle*, *Mademoiselle*, and *Condé Nast Traveler*, Tracy Watts's hats range from sporty berets and simple soft cloches wrapped with ribbon to elegant toppers trimmed with ribbon and buckles. Interns assist in all aspects of the business, from dealing with buyers to carrying out millinery techniques.

PERKS

Direct contact with owner/designer Tracy Watts; exposure to a wide range of buyers, designers, and editors; free hats.

FYI

Ms. Tracy Watts studied millinery under the guidance of the renowned milliner Janine Galimard, one of the handful of milliners still active. Says Watts: "There are very few milliners out there, especially in America. I use all the old techniques. Interning here is the opportunity to learn a dying art."

TO APPLY

Open to undergrads, recent college grads, college grads of any age, and grad students. Must have design or art background. International applicants eligible. Submit resume, cover letter, recommendations, and any work samples (e.g., hats or garments).

Internships
TracyWatts, Inc.
305 West 20th Street
New York, NY 10011
(212) 727-7349
(212) 229-0471 (Fax)

from Dave Barry, *Claw Your Way to the Top*

Intern Tattler continued from page 264 . . .

Aural SEX

A former *LA Times* intern admitted to making more than 100 dial-a-porn calls from Orange County Supervisor Bruce Nestande's office. The district attorney's office declined to prosecute the former intern, and he made restitution of $236.49 for the calls.

Under "Covers" Intern

In 1990, a New Hampshire high school teacher was charged with persuading three of her students, one of whom was her lover, to murder her husband. An audio tape of the teacher admitting to arranging the murder was made by her intern, who wore a hidden recording device.

Perks With The President

Four former interns of James B. Holderman, then president of the University of South Carolina, alleged that Holderman asked them for sexual favors. Holderman was fond of taking his interns on trips to such places as Washington, Paris, Tokyo, and New York, where the group rode in limousines and bedded down in posh hotels.

TRIBECA FILM CENTER

SELECTIVITY 🔍🔍🔍
Approximate applicant pool: 150; Interns accepted: 18

COMPENSATION $
None

LOCATION(S)
New York, NY

FIELD
Film

DURATION
12–16 weeks: Summer, Fall, Spring

DEADLINE(S)
Rolling

THE WORK
Founded in 1990, Tribeca Film Center houses some of the most influential film production companies in show business. In addition to Robert De Niro's Tribeca Productions, the Center contains Miramax Films (producer of *Pulp Fiction*), and several independent commercial and industrial film companies. Interns work in Executive Services, assisting staff with greeting clients, administrative duties, and general production work.

PERKS
Attendance welcome at "First Look" film screenings; star gazing.

FYI
Says a former intern: "At Tribeca you get to see all the stages of film production, from scripts to casting to production to editing." . . . Former interns report that there is great potential to network with staff from the Center's various production companies . . . Actor Robert De Niro co-owns the Tribeca Film Center.

TO APPLY
Open to undergrads and grad students. Must receive academic credit. International applicants eligible. Submit resume and cover letter with availability date and semester applying for.

Internship Coordinator
Tribeca Film Center
375 Greenwich Street
New York, NY 10013
(212) 941-4000
(212) 941-3997 (Fax)
www.tribecafilm.com

TRISTAR PICTURES

See Sony Pictures Entertainment

TUCSON CHILDREN'S MUSEUM

SELECTIVITY
Approximate applicant pool: 25; Interns accepted: 5

COMPENSATION
None

LOCATION(S)
Tucson, AZ

FIELD
Education

DURATION
12–24 weeks, year-round

DEADLINE(S)
Rolling

THE WORK
The Tucson Children's Museum (TCM) is a non-profit organization providing fun, interactive and educational exhibits for children ages 2 to 11. The mission of the museum is: to excite children about learning, inspire them to set goals important ot their futures and challenge them to reach their full potential. TCM accomplishes this mission by providing hands-on exhibits that make learning a little more exciting, while supporting what the children are already receiving in the classroom. The museum focuses on electricity, the body, science and has implemented a careers exhibit that allows children to role-play a chosen career through the entire museum, so that they actually start wondering what it might be like to really be a paramedic, or an entomologist, or a writer, or whatever they want to be. The museum also offers art and science craft activities on the weekends, special events on holidays and different programs that bring the children visiting the museum and youth from the community together for storytelling and cultural education. School groups come to the museum for guided tours during the week. The following departments will accept interns: Education, Art, Graphic Arts and Marketing/Public Relations.

PERKS
Free passes to museum events, baseball games, and movies; free t-shirts.

FYI
Approximately 25 percent of interns are hired for full-time positions.

TO APPLY
Open to undergrads, recent college grads, college grads of any age, and grad students. International applicants eligible. Write for application.

Internship Coordinator
Tucson Children's Museum
200 South Sixth Avenue
P.O. Box 2609
Tucson, AZ 85702-2609
(520) 792-9985 .x102
(520) 792-0639 (Fax)

TURNER BROADCASTING SYSTEM

SELECTIVITY
Approximate applicant pool: 1,000; Interns accepted: 250–300

COMPENSATION
None

LOCATION(S)
Atlanta, GA (HQ); CNN bureaus in Chicago, IL; Dallas, TX; Detroit, MI; Los Angeles and San Francisco, CA; Miami, FL; New York, NY; Washington, DC; Belgium; Brazil; Chile; China; Egypt; England; France; Germany; India; Israel; Italy; Japan; Jordan; Kenya; South Korea; Nicaragua; Philippines; Russia; Thailand

FIELD
Television; Sports; Entertainment; Corporate

DURATION
12 weeks: Summer, Fall, Winter/Spring; 4–6 week holiday-break internship available at CNN DC bureau

DEADLINE(S)
Summer: March 1; Fall: July 1; Winter/Spring: November 1

THE WORK
Turner Broadcasting System, Inc. is a dynamic entertainment and news company headquartered in Atlanta, GA, with offices around the world. They are an integral part of the world's leading media company, Time Warner Inc. Turner consists of several diverse groups who all work together under the Turner Broadcasting System, Inc. umbrella: Corporate, News, Entertainment, Sports, Teams, Domestic Sales & Distribution, and International. Our companies include: CNN, TNT, Cartoon Network, Atlanta Braves, CNN en Espanol, CNN/Sports Illustrated, Atlanta Thrashers, Turner Sports, WCW, and many more. Atlanta headquarters internship opportunities include Creative Services, Public Relations, Photo & Video Services, CNN Newsroom, Sports Production, Philips Arena Video, Headline News, CNN Medical Unit, Latin America Public Relations/Marketing, CNN Business News, and many others. CNN Bureaus outside of Atlanta manage their own internship programs.

PERKS
CNN offers interns a seminar series in which employees from CNN talk about the broadcasting industry. Past topics and guests have included ethics in journalism, field producing, CNN News Group Chairman and CEO Tom Johnson, and CNN Anchor Leon Harris. We also offer interns newsroom computer system training, control room and studio classes, broadcast writing class and videotape editing training. In the control room and studio classes, interns learn the technical aspect of getting a newscast on the air, as well as operating a studio camera, computer teleprompting and floor directing. They also write packages for CNN Newsroom Show and CNN Student Bureau.

FYI
In the Atlanta headquarters, interns are allowed to train and work with cameras and other technical equipment, depending on which department they are interning with.

TO APPLY
Open to college juniors and seniors as well as grad students. International applicants eligible. Write for "Student Internship Information Packet" (includes a CNN address list, since each CNN bureau has its own application packet).

Internship Coordinator
Turner Broadcasting System
One CNN Center
P.O. Box 105366
Atlanta, GA 30348-5366
(404) 827-0844

TWENTIETH CENTURY FOX

See Fox

20/20

SELECTIVITY 🔍🔍
Approximate applicant pool: 150; Interns accepted: 20

COMPENSATION Ⓢ
None

LOCATION(S)
New York, NY

FIELD
Television

DURATION
10–18 weeks: Summer, Fall, Spring

DEADLINE(S)
Rolling

THE WORK
On the air since 1977, ABC News's *20/20* is a news magazine show anchored by Barbara Walters and Hugh Downs. Winner of over 250 Emmy Awards, *20/20* produces health, lifestyle, and consumer-oriented segments (e.g., "Attention Deficit Disorder in Adults," "Persian Gulf War Sickness," and "Defective Baby Formulas") as well as personality profiles on people such as Desiree Washington, Mike Tyson's rape accuser. 10-20 interns in the Spring, Summer, Fall and Winter work in production, where they pitch story ideas, do research, go on field shoots, attend script meetings, and observe studio tapings.

PERKS
"Open-door" policy at other ABC News programs; interaction with ABC News anchors and correspondents.

FYI
The internship program has been going strong since 1979 ... About 10 percent of interns are later hired for full-time positions.

TO APPLY
Open to undergrads who will be receiving college credit. International applicants eligible. Submit resume and cover letter.

Internship Coordinator
20/20
ABC News
147 Columbus Avenue
New York, NY 10023
(212) 456-2020

SELECTIVITY 🔍🔍🔍🔍🔍
Approximate applicant pool: 150; Interns accepted: 1–2 per semester

COMPENSATION Ⓢ
None

LOCATION(S)
Washington, DC

FIELD
Environment; Peace studies; Civic participation

DURATION
Summer, Fall, Spring

DEADLINE(S)
Rolling for Fall and Spring; Summer deadline: March 31

THE WORK
20/20 Vision is a national non–profit organization dedicated to protecting the environment and promoting peace through grassroots lobbying and citizen education. 20/20 Vision's simple and effective model for citizen activism—$20 a year, 20 minutes a month—inspires over 30,000 concerned citizen's to make their voices heard on a regular basis on issues from safe drinking water to nuclear war. Interns work in legislation, Media, Field, Development, Promotion, and Membership.

PERKS
"Beautiful, bright office with skylights and deck in historic town house." Young, fun, progressive staff with monthly social activities.

FYI
"If you can handle it, the task is yours. It's not just copying and filing," says the internship coordinator. "A great foot in the door to non-profit, political work in Washington D.C."

TO APPLY
Open to undergrads, recent college grads, college grads and grad students. International applicants eligible. Submit resume, cover letter, and three references.

Internship Coordinator
20/20 Vision
1828 Jefferson Place NW
Washington, DC 20036
(212) 833-2020
(212) 833-5307 (Fax)
E-mail: vision@2020vision.org
www.2020vision.org

> 20/20 Vision has a young, progressive office with a monthly fun coordinator who organizes regular staff events.

TYCO®

SELECTIVITY 🔍 🔍 🔍 🔍 🔍
Approximate applicant pool: 100–150; Interns accepted: 4–6

COMPENSATION Ⓢ
None

LOCATION(S)
Mt. Laurel, NJ

FIELD
Consumer goods (toys)

DURATION
12–16 weeks: Summer, Fall, Spring

DEADLINE(S)
Rolling

THE WORK
Founded in 1926, Tyco Toys is the nation's third largest toy company, with annual sales of nearly $800 million and over 2,000 employees worldwide. Its playthings include Matchbox cars, Looney Tunes action figures, Travel Jeopardy games, Magic 8 Balls, Viewmaster Viewers, Magna Doodle dolls, Watch It Bake Ovens, and magnetic drawing pads. Interns work in Marketing, Advertising, and Research & Development.

PERKS
Orientation; mentors; occasional training sessions.

FYI
In recent years, Tyco has hired two to three interns a year for full-time positions.

TO APPLY
Open to undergrads, recent college grads, and MBA students. International applicants eligible. Submit resume and cover letter.

Internship Coordinator
Tyco Toys
6000 Midlantic Drive
Mt. Laurel, NJ 08054
(609) 234-7400

SELECTIVITY 🔍 🔍 🔍 🔍
Approximate applicant pool: 75; Interns accepted: 5

COMPENSATION Ⓢ
None

LOCATION(S)
Riverside, CA

FIELD
Museum; Photography

DURATION
10 weeks: Summer, Fall, Spring

DEADLINE(S)
Rolling

THE WORK
Established in 1973 by the University of California a[t] Riverside, the California Museum of Photography (CMP) is one o[f] the nation's leading photographic museums, housing nearl[y] 10,000 pieces of historic and contemporary photographic equip[-]ment and over 350,000 negatives, prints, and videos. Collection[s] include a walk-in camera, an Interactive Gallery featuring hands[-]on displays, and works by such masters as Ansel Adams, Walke[r] Evans, and Barbara Morgan. Interns work in Education, Publi[c] Relations, Exhibition Design, Curatorial, Development, or in ou[r] new Digital Studio.

PERKS
Intern meetings featuring curators; attendance welcome a[t] UCR/CMP speeches, openings, performances, etc.

FYI
UCR/CMP's Network Exhibitions, showcasing the work o[f] artists such as Lisa Bloomfield and Kevin Boyle, are accessible o[n] the Internet.

TO APPLY
Open to high school students, high school grads, unde[r]grads, and grad students. International applicants eligible. Subm[it] resume and cover letter.

Internship Coordinator
UCR/California Museum of Photography
University of California at Riverside
Riverside, CA 92521
(909) 787-4787
www.cmpl.ucr.edu

SELECTIVITY 🔍
Approximate applicant pool: 75–100; interns accepted: 9

COMPENSATION 💲💲
Free housing

LOCATION(S)
San Francisco, CA

FIELD
AIDS; Mental health care

DURATION
12 months: begins in July

DEADLINE(S)
April 15

THE WORK
Since 1984, the University of California, San Francisco AIDS Health Project (AHP) has provided services to more than 20,000 people who face the challenges of AIDS. At low cost to San Francisco residents and organizations, AHP offers mental health services to people with HIV disease, runs an AIDS antibody counseling and testing program, organizes training and educational programs on AIDS topics, and publishes newsletters and books for AIDS professionals. Interns work in Publications, Psychosocial Services, HIV Testing, Operations, HIV Prevention, and Behavioral Research.

PERKS
Access to library and athletic facility at UCSF; "relaxed, friendly, very San Franciscan" office environment.

FYI
Says the internship coordinator: "Interns will have a window on what's happening on the cutting edge of AIDS and mental health work."

TO APPLY
Open to recent college grads, college grads of any age, and grad students. International applicants eligible. Write for application.

Staffing Coordinator
UCSF AIDS Health Project
Box 0884
San Francisco, CA 94143-0884
(415) 476-3890
(415) 476-3613 (Fax)
E-mail: ssunshi@itsa.ucsf.edu
www.ucsf-aihp.org

SELECTIVITY 🔍🔍🔍
Approximate applicant pool: 1,000; Interns accepted: 135–150

COMPENSATION 💲💲💲💲
$1,730/month for recent h.s. grads; $2,150-$3,230/month for undergrads; $3,345–$3,545/month for grad students; round-trip travel; housing benefits; health & life insurance

LOCATION(S)
Danbury, CT; New Orleans, LA; Bound Brook & Somerset, NJ; Cary, NC; Houston, Texas City, & Victoria, TX; South Charleston, WV

FIELD
Chemicals

DURATION
12 weeks, Summer, Fall, Spring

DEADLINE
Summer: March 31; Fall: May 31; Spring: November 30

THE WORK
Union Carbide is one of the world's leading manufacturers of chemicals and polymers, with over 13,000 employees and annual sales of approximately $5 billion. Founded in 1917, it is also the world's largest producer of ethylene oxide, which is used to make ethylene glycol, a component of polyester and antifreeze. Union Carbide offers internship and co-op positions in Production, Technology Improvements, Distribution, Engineering, Management Information Systems, Finance, Research and Development, and Sales.

PERKS
Brown-bag luncheons; organized social activities; city survival kits; orientation.

FYI
Union Carbide's Student Employment Program was established in 1990 . . . Union Carbide has an astounding 90 percent rehire rate from its internship program . . . Many interns prize the fact that they often work on several projects over the summer. "A lot of companies give you only one assignment, but at Carbide when they give you three or four . . . you get a real sense of responsibility. You feel like you're a full-time engineer," said an Engineering intern.

TO APPLY
Open to recent high school graduates, undergrads, and grad students with a BS in engineering who are working on an MS or MBA. Minimum GPA of 3.0. Submit resume.

Internship Coordinator
Union Carbide Corporation
Eastern Region Skill Center
P.O. Box 8004
South Charleston, WV 25303

SELECTIVITY
Approximate applicant pool: 40; interns accepted: 6

COMPENSATION S
None

LOCATION(S)
Washington, DC

FIELD
Public policy

DURATION
8–12 weeks: Summer, Fall, Spring

DEADLINE(S)
Rolling

THE WORK
The Union Institute's Office for Social Responsibility is a university-based applied research and social action office that houses a Center for Public Policy dedicated to nonprofit sector issues and a Center for Women that focuses on collaborative work between feminist academics and activists. In addition, the OSR develops programs and initiatives aimed at fostering and exploring issues concerning the social responsibility of universities and the work of scholar activists. Founded in 1964, The Union Institute is a university of highly motivated adults concerned with social, economic, and political justice in society. Interns assist staff in researching issues on OSR or Center projects and other duties such as planning conferences and workshops.

PERKS
Attendance welcome at meetings with policymakers and area activists.

FYI
The mission of The Union Institute's Office for Social Responsibility is to develop innovative approaches and program models through which higher education can benefit society as powerfully as it does individual learners. Such approaches include: conducting research and service efforts that better connect theory and practice, academy and community; bringing fresh, critical perspectives to contemporary problems and providing commentary on key issues; helping people work collaboratively to better serve the common good; and working for synthesis of teaching, research, and service in creating new directions for higher education. For additional information see the website.

TO APPLY
Open to high school grads, undergrads, recent college grads, college grads of any age, and grad students. International applicants eligible. Submit cover letter and resume.

Internship Coordinator
The Union Institute
1710 Rhode Island Avenue, Suite 1100
Washington, DC 20036-3007
(202) 496-1630
(202) 496-1635 (Fax)
www.tui.edu
http://www.tui.edu/osr/internship/internship.html

UNITED ARTISTS

See Metro-Goldwyn-Mayer/United Artists

SELECTIVITY
Approximately one-sixth of those who apply are accepted (160 graduate students each session)

COMPENSATION S
None

LOCATION(S)
New York, NY

FIELD
Economics; Humanitarian and environmental affairs; Information systems; International law; International relations; Journalism; Library science; Political science; Population studies; Public administration; Public policy; Social affairs; Translation amd terminology; Women's studies.

DURATION
Three two-month periods throughout the year: mid-January to Mid-March, early June to early August and mis-September to mid-November.

DEADLINE(S)
At least 6 months prior to start date)

THE WORK
Founded in 1945, the United Nations (UN) is an organization of over 185 member-countries working for world peace, friendly relations among nations, human rights, and eradication of world hunger, disease, and illiteracy. Its work is carried out through six major "organs"—the Security Council, a fifteen-member group that deals with questions of peace and security; the Economic and Social Council, a fifty-four member group concerned with such issues as trade, industrialization, population, drug trafficking, and the environment; the Trusteeship Council, made up of the UN's five permanent members (China, France, Russia, UK, and US), who watch over non-self-governing territories; International Court of Justice, a fifteen-judge panel that issues international legal judgments; Secretariat, the UN staff headed by the Secretary-General; and the General Assembly, the UN's central organ in which every member-country is represented by one delegate and one vote. In New York, interns work in Offices of the UN Secretariat.

PERKS
Mentors; attendance welcome at General Assembly meetings (NY, fall only), UN briefings/meetings, and speeches by heads of state; guided tour; subsidized cafeterias.

FYI
The land and buildings of the UN headquarters in New York are located in an international zone, which permits the UN to make its own laws, keep its own flag, maintain its own security force, and issue its own postage stamps.

TO APPLY
Open to matriculated grad students only. Must be fluent in English and proficient in one foreign language. International applicants eligible. See website: www.un.org for eligibility.

Coordinator of the Internship Programme
United Nations, Room S-2570E
New York, NY 10017
(212) 963-7522
(212) 963-3683 (Fax)

UNITED NATIONS ASSOCIATION OF THE UNITED STATES OF AMERICA

SELECTIVITY 🔍🔍🔍
Approximate applicant pool: 100; Interns accepted: 15 (summer), 5 (fall/winter)

COMPENSATION 💲
Paid fellowships and unpaid positions

LOCATION(S)
New York, NY; Washington, D.C.

FIELD
International affairs

DURATION
10–12 weeks: Summer, Fall, Spring

DEADLINE
Summer: March 15; Fall: August 15; Spring: November 15

THE WORK
A private, nonprofit organization, the UNA dedicates itself to enhancing US participation in the UN system through programs in public outreach, policy analysis, and international dialogue. Though not officially a part of the UN, it is a bastion of information about and analysis on the UN. Internships are available in Communications, Corporate Affairs, Education Programs, and Policy Studies Programs.

PERKS
Access to UN; summer brown-bag lunches; free books/posters.

FYI
As one intern commented, "although it's in New York, UN headquarters feels like a world unto itself." Indeed it should, for the compound is an international zone, complete with its own laws, flag, and postage stamps. Armed with a prized UN pass, interns are free to roam through the 39-story glass and marble Secretariat tower and the low-domed General Assembly Building.

TO APPLY
Open to HS Model U.N. Students, undergrads, recent college grads, and grad students. International applicants eligible. Write for application.

United Nations Association of the USA
Intern Coordinator
801 Second Avenue
New York, NY 10017
(212) 907-1300
E-mail: unahq@unausa.org
www.unausa.org

UNITED NATIONS VOLUNTEER PROGRAM

SELECTIVITY 🔍🔍
Approximate applicant pool: 5,000; volunteers accepted: 1,000 (25–50 US citizens) per year

COMPENSATION 💲💲💲💲
$600–$1,900/month living stipend; round-trip travel; housing included in stipend; health and life insurance

LOCATION(S)
Any non-industrialized UN member country

FIELD
Public service in over 12 fields (see THE WORK)

DURATION
2 weeks–2 years

DEADLINE(S)
Rolling (at least 6 months before start date)

THE WORK
Established in 1971 by the UN General Assembly, the United Nations Volunteer (UNV) Program works with governments, UN agencies, development banks, and nongovernmental organizations to support development and humanitarian relief projects in Africa, Asia, Eastern Europe, and Latin America. Volunteers work as water sanitation engineers, land managers, HIV/AIDS careworkers, food monitors, information officers, logisticians, radio technicians, election planners, human rights monitors and lawyers, peace advisors, doctors, paramedics, epidemiologists, policy analysts, accountants, and business advisors. Short-term positions (three to six months) are available in humanitarian relief and disaster assistance.

PERKS
Occasional volunteer conferences and training; possible language training in country.

FYI
On average, volunteers are in their early forties, with at least a Bachelor's degree and 15 or more years of experience in their field.

TO APPLY
Must be at least 25 years old, have a bachelor's, and have at least two years of post-graduation work experience as well as professional experience in developing countries. Must be fluent in local language for some posts. International applicants eligible. Write for application, please include resume.

US citizens contact:

United Nations Volunteers
c/o Peace Corps
1111 20th Street NW
Washington, DC 20526
(800) 424-8580, x2256 or (202) 692-2256

For short-term positions:
United Nations Volunteers
Attn: Humanitarian Relief Unit
Palais des Nations
1211 Geneva 10, Switzerland
41-22-979-9065 (Fax)

NonUS citizens contact:

United Nations Volunteers/UNDP
1775 K Street NW
Washington, DC 20006

UNITED STATES AGENCY FOR INTERNATIONAL DEVELOPMENT

SELECTIVITY 🔍🔍🔍
Approximate applicant pool: 500; Iinterns accepted: 50

COMPENSATION 💲💲💲
None

LOCATION(S)
US AID headquarters is in Washington, D.C. with various overseas locations in third world developing nations

FIELD
Government

DURATION
6 weeks to several months

DEADLINE(S)
January 15

THE WORK
The principal vehicle for American foreign aid, the US Agency for International Development (USAID) carries out programs of economic and technical assistance to developing nations. Operating in over 100 missions worldwide, USAID provides over $6 billion (out of a total US foreign aid budget of $12 billion) to programs in areas such as health, the environment, economic growth, humanitarian assistance, and post-crisis transition. Interns—assigned to the year-round Co-op, Volunteer Intern (VI), and Stay in School (SIS) programs as well as the Summer Employment (SE) Program—work in overseas missions as well as all bureaus and offices in DC, including Africa Bureau, Asia and the Near East Bureau, Human Resources, Financial Management, Legislative and Public Affairs, Equal Opportunity Programs, and the Office of the Inspector General and General Counsel.

PERKS
Weekly brown-bag luncheons with USAID assistant administrators; attendance welcome at meetings, workshops, and speeches; access to State Department gym (approximately $50).

FYI
Interns must pass a background investigation . . . USAID's Director, Brian Atwood, was a USAID intern in the 1960s . . . Serving as a USAID intern increases one's chances of landing a position with USAID's two-year International Development Intern Program or the Federal Government's two-year Presidential Management Intern Program.

TO APPLY
Open to students 16 years or older who maintain a 3.0 average in their respective schools. Applicant must recieve security clearance before start date. Forward application to:

USAID
Student Programs Coordinator
1300 Pennsylvania Avenue, NW
Washington, DC 20523-2700
(202) 663-3340
(202) 663-3295 (Fax)
(202) 663-2400 (for address list of overseas missions)

UNITED STATES AND FOREIGN COMMERCIAL SERVICE

SELECTIVITY 🔍
Approximate applicant pool: 250; Interns accepted: 100

COMPENSATION 💲
None

LOCATION(S)
132 posts in 69 countries overseas (See Appendix)

FIELD
Trade

DURATION
10–12 weeks: ongoing

DEADLINE(S)
Rolling

THE WORK
A division of the International Trade Administration, the US and Foreign Commercial Service (US & FCS) is a federal marketing office promoting American goods and services overseas. Assisting primarily small and medium-sized businesses, US & FCS gathers and disseminates trade information, sponsors trade fairs, identifies overseas business agents, runs credit checks on prospective trading partners, and obtains information on foreign import requirements. Interns work at overseas posts as junior-level commercial specialists, conducting market research, preparing reports, drafting replies to correspondence, and recruiting exhibitors for trade missions, shows, and seminars.

PERKS
Mentors; attendance welcome at all post social and trade events.

FYI
According to the internship coordinator, interns are prohibited from handling classified information . . . US & FCS's DC interns are placed by the International Trade Administration (see separate entry).

TO APPLY
Open to undergrads, recent college grads attending grad school the semester following the internship, and grad students. Must be proficient in local language. Submit resume and cover letter directly to post of interest. Contact US & FCS headquarters in DC for a list of addresses and phone numbers.

Madeleine Albright, the Secretary of State, got her start as an intern with the *Denver Post* in 1957. While at the *Post* she met another intern, newspaper heir Joseph Albright, who would become her husband three days after she graduated from Wellesley.

Overseas Work-Study Internship Program Coordinator
Office of Foreign Service Personnel
US and Foreign Commercial Service
US Department of Commerce
Room 3224
Washington, DC 20230
(202) 482-4717

UNITED STATES ARMY ENVIRONMENTAL HYGIENE AGENCY

See Oak Ridge Institute for Science and Education

UNITED STATES BUREAU OF MINES

See Oak Ridge Institute for Science and Education

UNITED STATES CHAMBER OF COMMERCE

SELECTIVITY

Approximate applicant pool: 300–400; Interns accepted: 60–70

COMPENSATION

None; Transportation allowance provided

LOCATION(S)

Washington, DC

FIELD

Business; Policy

DURATION

8–12 weeks: Summer, Fall, Spring

DEADLINE(S)

Rolling

THE WORK
Its primary mission to promote private enterprise, the US Chamber of Commerce is the world's largest business federation, with 215,000 businesses, 3,000 state and local chambers of commerce, 1,300 trade and professional associations, and 80 American Chambers of Commerce Abroad as members. Interns work in the following areas: Accounting, Center for Workforce Preparation and Quality Education, Congressional Affairs, International, Media Relations, Personnel, Environment and Energy, Labor and Employee Benefits, Small Business Institute, Statistics and Research Center, Membership Programs and Services, Corporate Development Institute for Organizational Management, Office of Association Relations, Office of Chamber of Commerce Relations, Corporate Communications.

PERKS
Intern orientation; White House tour and ice-cream social.

FYI
Internship assignments vary considerably, depending on area of interest.

TO APPLY
Open to college juniors, seniors, and currently enrolled graduate students. International applicants eligible. Submit resume, cover letter, writing sample, and recommendation.

Internship Coordinator
US Chamber of Commerce
1615 H Street NW
Washington, DC 20062-2000
(202) 463-5731

UNITED STATES DEPARTMENT OF AGRICULTURE

SELECTIVITY

Approximate applicant pool: 300; Interns accepted: 100

COMPENSATION

Varies by position and department. $240–$600/week

LOCATION(S)

Washington, DC; Sacramento, CA; Fort Worth, TX; Memphis, TN; Lenexa, KS; St. Paul, MN; Corpus Christi, TX; Harlingen, TX; New Orleans, LA; Portland, OR; Fayetteville, NC; League City, TX; Raleigh, NC; Harrisburg, PA; Riverdale, MD; Frankfort, KY; Auburn, AL; Gastonia, NC; Fort Collins, CO; Lincoln, NE; Gulfport, MS; Gainesville, FL; Carrollton, TX; Ames, IA; Detroit, MI; Kansas City, MO; Jamaica, NY; Philadelphia, PA; Newark, NJ; Beltsville, MD; Columbia, SC; Destrehan, LA; Alexandria, VA; San Francisco, CA

FIELD

Agricultural services

DURATION

Length varies for each position: Summer

DEADLINE(S)

February 15

THE WORK
The US Department of Agriculture (USDA) was established by President Abraham Lincoln in 1862. Lincoln established USDA "to acquire and to diffuse among the people of the United States useful information on subjects connected with agriculture in the most general and comprehensive sense of that word." Internships are available in many of the service areas of the USDA: Farm and Foreign Agricultural Services; Food, Nutrition, and Consumer Services; National Resources and Environment; and Departmental Administration.

PERKS
Government car may be provided; some positions require outdoor field work.

FYI
Chiseled into the stone of the USDA building in Washington, DC are these words: "Dedicated to the Service of Agriculture for the Public Welfare." . . . The USDA recently completed organizational changes to streamline the agency . . . One in six working Americans has a job in some aspect of the food and fiber economy.

TO APPLY
Open to high school students, college undergrads, grad students. Must be enrolled in a qualified education program. Write for "Summer Intern Program" brochure.

United States Department of Agriculture
Office of the Secretary
Office of Personnel
Washington, DC 20250

SELECTIVITY 🔍
Approximate applicant pool: N/A; Interns accepted: 500–1,000

COMPENSATION 💲💲
Volunteer: None; Co-op and SE: $275–$500/week

LOCATION(S)
Washington, DC

FIELD
International trade and economics; Business administration and related fields

DURATION
Volunteer: 2 weeks–4 months: ongoing; Co-op: at least 640 hours in 1 or more sessions: ongoing; SE: 1–4 months: ongoing

DEADLINE(S)
Rolling

THE WORK
Founded in 1903, the US Department of Commerce (DOC) is the federal agency that promotes, protects, and develops America's international trade, economic growth, and technological advancement. Under the auspices of the Volunteer, Co-op, and Student Employment (SE) Programs, interns work in all seventeen of DOC's agencies, including the International Trade Administration (see separate entry), US and Foreign Commercial Service (see separate entry), Bureau of the Census, National Oceanic & Atmospheric Administration, Patent & Trademark Office, National Institute of Standards & Technology, and Office of Inspector General as well as the Office of the Secretary, and agencies whose personnel matters fall under its jurisdiction—Bureau of Economic Analysis, Bureau of Export Administration, Economics & Statistics Administration, Economic Development Administration, Minority Business Development Agency, National Technical Information Service, National Telecommunications & Information Administration, Technology Administration, and US Travel & Tourism Administration.

PERKS
Occasional brown-bag luncheons featuring guest speakers; field trips to local cultural sites; access to fitness center (approximately $7/month); mentors; attendance at post social and trade events.

FYI
Interns are usually placed in nonsensitive positions. Approximately 30 percent of co-op interns receive offers of permanent employment from DOC.

Considered one of the century's most talented Japanese architects, **Arata Isozaki** studied at the University of Tokyo, where in 1954 he began an apprenticeship with the famed architect Kenzo Tange. He went on to design such buildings as the full-scale replica of Shakespeare's Globe Theater in Tokyo, the Gunma Prefectural Museum of Fine Arts in Takasaki, and the Museum of Contemporary Art in Los Angeles.

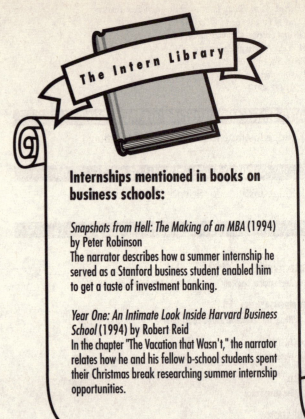

The Intern Library

Internships mentioned in books on business schools:

Snapshots from Hell: The Making of an MBA (1994) by Peter Robinson
The narrator describes how a summer internship he served as a Stanford business student enabled him to get a taste of investment banking.

Year One: An Intimate Look Inside Harvard Business School (1994) by Robert Reid
In the chapter "The Vacation that Wasn't," the narrator relates how he and his fellow b-school students spent their Christmas break researching summer internship opportunities.

TO APPLY
Open to high school students, undergrads, and grad students. Proficiency in local language recommended. Must receive academic credit (Volunteer Program only). Submit resume and cover letter to agency of interest directly. Contact the US and Foreign Commercial Service (see separate entry) for contact names and phone numbers (limit of three).

Office of Personnel Operations
Room 1069
Office of the Secretary
US Department of Commerce
14th and Constitution Avenue NW
Washington, DC 20230
(202) 482-2560

Personnel Office
Patent & Trademark Office
2011 Crystal Drive
Crystal Park One, Suite 700
Washington, DC 22202
(703) 305-8434

Personnel Office
Office of Inspector General
Room 7713 HCHB
Washington, DC 20230
(202) 482-3006

Personnel Office
National Oceanic & Atmospheric
*   Administration*
SSMC #2 OA215 Room 01230
Silver Spring, MD 20910
(301) 713-0534

Personnel Office
Bureau of the Census
Federal Building 3, Room 3124
Suitland, MD 20233
(301) 457-3371

Personnel Office
Administration Building
Room A-123
National Institute of Standards
*   & Technology*
Gaithersburg, MD 20899
(301) 975-3026

UNITED STATES DEPARTMENT OF DEFENSE

SELECTIVITY 🔍 🔍 🔍 🔍
Approximate applicant pool: 4,000; Interns accepted: 325–375

COMPENSATION 💲 💲 💲 💲
None for SVP; $240–$275/week for high school students; $350–$400/week for undergrads; $450–$575/week for grad students

LOCATION(S)
Washington, DC

FIELD
Government; Defense

DURATION
SEP: 12–16 weeks: Summer; SVP: 2 weeks–1 year: ongoing; OGC: 10 weeks: Summer

DEADLINE(S)
SVP and SEP: Rolling (at least 4 months in advance of start date); OGC: first-year law students (January 10), second-year law students (November 18)

THE WORK
Established in 1947 by Congress, the US Department of Defense (DOD) is the Executive department responsible for overseeing the national security of the United States. Headquartered at the Pentagon, it manages an annual budget on the order of $260 billion and employs 900,000 civilians as well as 1.4 million troops in the Army, Air Force, Navy, and Marine Corps. Under the auspices of the Summer Employment Program (SEP) and Student Volunteer Program (SVP), 300 and 30 interns, respectively, work within the Office of the Secretary of Defense (OSD) in departments such as Ballistic Missile Defense Operations, Staffing, Budget & Finance, Real Estate & Facilities, Executive Classification, Military Personnel, Personnel Systems & Evaluation, and Equal Employment Opportunities. Law students (ten positions) work in the Office of General Counsel (OGC) in Acquisition & Logistics, Fiscal, Inspector General, International Affairs & Intelligence, Legal Counsel, Legislative Reference, Standards of Conduct, and Personnel & Health Policy.

PERKS
Training seminars; mentors; specially arranged tours of DOD departments, the U.S. Supreme Court, the Court of Appeals of the Armed Forces, Senate Armed Services Committee's General Counsel, Department of Justice.

FYI
Many DOD internships require security clearances that can take about five months to obtain . . . DOD's Staffing Division also places one or two interns with the Joint Chiefs of Staff, and up to forty interns in OSD departments as part of the Stay-In-School Program, which allows students (usually from MD, VA, and DC) to work part time at DOD while attending school.

TO APPLY
Open to high school students, undergrads, college grads within one year of graduation (SEP only), law students (OGC), and other grad students. Must receive academic credit (SVP only). Submit resume and cover letter (for OGC). Write for application.

Student Volunteer Program
Employee Career Development
 & Training Division
Washington Headquarters Services
Personnel & Security Directorate
1155 Defense Pentagon
Washington, DC 20301-1155

Summer Employment Program
 or Stay-In-School Program
 Staffing Division
Personnel and Security Directorate
1155 Defense Pentagon
Washington, DC 20301-1155

Honors Legal Internship Program

Ambassador **George Moose**, currently the Assistant Secretary of State for African Affairs, became interested in the Foreign Service after serving two summer internships at the State Department—the first in 1966 with the Bureau of African Affairs, the second in 1967 at the embassy in Mexico City.

UNITED STATES DEPARTMENT OF STATE

SELECTIVITY 🔍 🔍
Approximate applicant pool: 3,000; Interns accepted: 900

COMPENSATION 💲 💲 💲
95 percent of all interns are volunteers

LOCATION(S)
Washington, DC; New York, NY; and overseas

FIELD
Foreign policy

DURATION
Summer: 10 weeks; Fall/Spring: one semester or quarter; Fellowships: 1 year or more

DEADLINE
Varies (see brochure)

THE WORK
Established in 1789 by President George Washington, the State Department engineers the fair treatment of Americans abroad, issues visas and passports, negotiates treaties and trade agreements, controls the proliferation of nuclear weapons, combats drug trafficking, and helps foreign nations establish viable political and economic systems, among other endeavors. The department administers seven major student-employment programs including the Student Intern Program, the largest. Interns in this program can choose from a wide list of areas: Art in Embassies Program, Consular Affairs, Diplomatic Security, Information Management, Economic and Business Affairs,

ropean and Canadian Affairs, Human Rights and Humanitarian Affairs, Intelligence and Research, International Narcotics Matters, Office of the Legal Advisor, Near Eastern and South Asian Affairs, Oceans & International Environmental and Scientific Affairs, and Politico-Military Affairs.

PERKS
Embassy tours; free housing at most overseas posts; gym available (DC); access to events.

FYI
The US Department of State makes its home in Washington's Foggy Bottom district, home also to the World Bank and George Washington University.

TO APPLY
Open to undergrads, recent grads, and grad students (see brochure for details). Write for application or visit the Department's website.

U.S. Department of State
Office of Recruitment
Student Programs
P.O. Box 9317
Arlington, VA 22219
www.STATE.gov

Art Spinner, once a director at 11 companies, is a founding partner of Hambro International Venture Fund, which financed Tylan General, a $50-million-a-year instrumentation company in San Diego; Vertex Semiconductor Corp. in Silicon Valley; and Rasna, a San Jose-based developer of design optimization software for mechanical engineers. He worked as a summer intern at the White House in 1972.

UNITED STATES ENVIRONMENTAL PROTECTION AGENCY

U.S. Environmental Protection Agency

SELECTIVITY
Approximate applicant pool: 300; Interns accepted: 75–100

COMPENSATION
Approximately $5,000–$9,000 for a 3-month, full-time fellowship. Amount varies depending on level of education and duration/location of research project.

LOCATION(S)
Nationwide

FIELD
Environmental policy, regulation, and law; Environmental science; Environmental management and administration; Public relations and communications; and Computer programming and development

DURATION
10–14 weeks: Fall, Spring, Summer; 1-year grants and part-time available

DEADLINE(S)
December

THE WORK
The US Environmental Protection Agency (EPA) was created by President Nixon in 1970 to enforce government environmental mandates. Today, the EPA's enforcement—capable of implementing a host of penalties, from fines to criminal lawsuits—extends to fourteen major laws, including the Clean Air Act, the Clean Water Act, and Superfund. Interns may work in the following areas: Environmental Policy, Regulations, and Law; Environmental Management and Administration; Environmental Science; Public Relations and Communications; and Computer Programming and Development.

PERKS
Some travel; stipends; possible presentation of paper.

FYI
One intern tells this story: "I attended an EPA meeting half a year later to answer questions about my paper, which by this time had been widely distributed around the agency. After I finished, one person came up to thank me for getting the ball rolling." . . . Another reports: "If you're looking to save the world, you won't. But you can make an impact."

TO APPLY
Open to undergrads and grad students. Undergrads are required to have taken at least four courses in environmental studies. For more information write:

US Environmental Protection Agency
NNEMS National Program Manager
US EPA (1704A)
1200 Pennsylvania Avenue NW
Washington, DC 20460
www.epa.gov/enviroed/students.html

UNITED STATES HOLOCAUST MEMORIAL MUSEUM

SELECTIVITY
Approximate applicant pool: 350; Interns accepted: 34

COMPENSATION
$250/week stipend, not all internships carry stipends

LOCATION(S)
Washington, DC

FIELD
Museums; Modern European history

DURATION
12 weeks: Summer, Fall, Spring

DEADLINE(S)
Summer: March 15; Fall: June 15; Spring: October 15

THE WORK
Established in 1993, the US Holocaust Memorial Museum is dedicated to presenting the history of the persecution and murder of 6 million Jews and millions of other victims of Nazi tyranny from 1933 to 1945. Housed in a fortress-like building, the Museum contains a three-floor permanent exhibition of photographs, films

and eyewitness testimony as well as a sky-lit Hall of Remembrance, an exhibition for children, a learning center, and a Center for Advanced Holocaust Studies. Interns work in Education, Development, Communications, Exhibitions, Collections, Community Programs, and the Center for Advanced Holocaust Studies, whose departments comprise: Archive, Library, Photo Archive, Oral History Archive, Film & Video Archive, and the National Registry of Holocaust Survivors.

PERKS
Attendance welcome at special lectures, readings, and films; ten free tickets to museum.

FYI
Upon entering the exhibition, each visitor receives an identity card bearing the name and picture of a Holocaust victim of the same gender, and similar in age to the visitor . . . As the experience unfolds, the identity card is updated and the fate of the visitor's silent companion is gradually revealed.

TO APPLY
Open to undergrads, recent college grads, college grads of any age, and grad students. International applicants eligible. Write for application, or visit the website.

Internship Coordinator
US Holocaust Memorial Museum
100 Raoul Wallenberg Place SW
Washington, DC 20024-2150
(202) 488-0400 or intern office #:(202) 479–9738
(202) 488-6568 (Fax)
www.ushmm.org

UNITED STATES NATIONAL ARBORETUM

SELECTIVITY
Approximate applicant pool: 50; Interns accepted: 10–15

COMPENSATION $ $ $
$8.47/hour

LOCATION(S)
Washington, DC

FIELD
Horticulture

DURATION
Varies: 3–12 months

DEADLINE(S)
February 8

THE WORK
Established in 1927 by Congress as a division of the US Department of Agiculture, the US National Arboretum is America's horticultural museum, dedicated to improving the environment by conducting plant research, offering educational programs to the public, and displaying horticulturally significant trees, shrubs, and flowers. Its collections include the National Herb Garden, Friendship Garden, Fern Valley, and the Gotelli Dwarf Conifer, Bonsai, and Asian collections. Interns work in Plant Sciences, Garden Unit, Research, and Education.

PERKS
Workshops/demonstrations on horticultural issues: Bi-weekly tours of the Arboretums collections and some off-sight collections.

The Intern Library

Interns mentioned in modern literature:

A Slip of the Tong (1991) by Charles Goodrum
A murder mystery in which Kit Chang, a student-intern with the Werner-Bok research library, helps an investigative team unearth foul play in the library's Asian Division.

American Psycho (1991) by Bret Easton Ellis
In the chapter entitled "Harry's," investment banker Patrick Bateman describes himself sarcastically as a "boy next door who...let a British corporate finance intern" have his way with him.

Bicycle Days (1989) by John Burnham Schwartz
Follows the story of a college grad interning at a Tokyo computer firm.

Bright Days, Stupid Nights (1992) by Norma Fox Mazer and Harry Mazer
Follows four teens from disparate circumstances through their summer internship at a small-town newspaper.

Loving Edith (1995) by Mary Tannin
Relates the story of two twentysomethings who move to Manhattan, where one of them, Edith, snags an internship with *Ubu* magazine.

Love & Memory (1992) by Amy Oleson
Describes how soccer-playing computer whiz Liz Edwards redeems a dismal summer internship at a computer firm by streamlining the firm's accounting procedures.

You Bet Your Life (1993) by Julie Reece Deaver
Follows the story of Bess, a high school senior who dreams of becoming a comedy writer and finally lands an internship on the *Les Comack Show*, a Chicago-based TV program.

FYI
The arboretum's internship program was launched in 1985 . . . Interns find themselves planting, pruning, weeding, mulching, watering, raking, controlling pests, maintaining plant records, and answering public inquiries . . . Recent interns have been hired by the arboretum for full-time positions as technicians.

TO APPLY
Open to undergrads, graduate students, or college graduates of any age. Some international applicants eligible. For more

detailed information on individual internships or an application check our website or write to:

Internship Coordinator
US National Arboretum
3501 New York Avenue NE
Washington, DC 20002
(202) 245-5898
www.ars-grin.gov/na

> "The internship coordinator pulls me aside . . . and says 'now just because you've won Olympic Gold medals doesn't mean that you're going to get any special treatment,' and I remember kind of thinking 'oh, yeah, right.' . . . I mean, people were still naming parades after me and giving me keys to cities. And, no joke, she handed me a mop, and that was all I did when I first got there."
> —*Olympic swimming champ Nancy Hogshead, on her first day as an intern for the Women's Sports Foundation*

UNITED STATES OLYMPIC COMMITTEE

SELECTIVITY 🔍🔍🔍🔍
Approximate applicant pool: 250–300 (Fall, Spring), 500–600 (Summer); Interns accepted: 30–35

COMPENSATION 💲💲
$78/week, plus room & board

LOCATION(S)
Colorado Springs, CO; Lake Placid, NY; San Diego, CA

FIELD
Sports

DURATION
Winter/Spring: 18 weeks; Summer: 10 weeks; Fall: 15 weeks

DEADLINE
Spring: October 1; Summer: February 15; Fall: June 1

THE WORK
The United States Olympic Committee (UCOC) is a multi-faceted organization headquartered in Colorado Springs, Colo., that provides leadership and guidance for the Olympic Movement in the United States. The USOC also maintains Training Centers at Colorado Springs, Colo., Lake Placid, New York; and San Diego, California. Internships are available in the areas of: Accounting, Broadcasting, Computer Science, Journalism, Marketing/Fund Raising, Sports Administration and Sport Science. For more information on the USOC, visit their website at www.olympic-usa.org.

PERKS
Intern seminars; stunning recreational facilities; excellent food; freebies.

FYI
Interns have a unique opportunity to interact with athletes and coaches from around the country because they are housed in athlete dormitories and eat at athlete dining halls. Interns may also use Olympic Training Facilities; gymnasiums, weightrooms, swiming pools, etc.

TO APPLY
Open to college juniors and seniors and grad students. Write for application.

United States Olympic Committee
Manager, Intern Program
One Olympic Plaza
Colorado Springs, CO 80909-5760
(719) 632-5551, ext. 2597
(719) 578-4817 (Fax)
E-mail: internprog@usoc.org

UNITED STATES PRISON

See Federal Bureau of Prisons

Fun in the Sun

Get a great tan at these internships:

Amelia Island Plantation

Aspen Center for Environmental Studies

Camp Counselors USA

Chincoteague National Wildlife Refuge

City of New York Parks & Recreation

Hawk Mountain Sanctuary

Hawthorne Valley Farm

Land Between The Lakes

Long Lake Conservation Center

Mystic Seaport Museum

National Park Service

The Nature Conservancy

North Cascades Institute

Outward Bound/Voyageur School

Sea World

Sierra Club

South Seas Plantation

Yosemite National Park

UNITED STATES SECRET SERVICE

SELECTIVITY 🔍 🔍 🔍
Approximate applicant pool: 1,500; Interns accepted: 200 (Nationwide)

COMPENSATION 💲
None

LOCATION(S)
Washington, D.C.; various field offices nationwide

FIELD
Government; Criminal justice; Business administration; Political science

DURATION
10–16 weeks: Summer, Fall, Spring

DEADLINE(S)
Fall Term: April 14; Spring: August 15; Summer: January 10

THE WORK
Established in 1865 as a bureau of the Department of the Treasury, the US Secret Service (USSS) is responsible for suppressing the counterfeiting of US and foreign currency and securities; investigating the fraud and forgery of checks, bonds, identification documents, credit and debit cards, and computer transactions; and protecting the president and vice president and their families, visiting heads of state, former presidents, and presidential and vice presidential candidates. Interns at headquarters (twenty-five to fifty each year) work in Counterfeit, Financial Crimes, Forensic Services, Special Agent Training & Employee Development, Intelligence, Technical Security, Public Affairs and Administrative Operations. Interns in the field offices (four to nine per year in each office) conduct research and do clerical work for the local forgery, counterfeit, and fraud units.

PERKS
Mentors; tours of USSS and White House facilities (DC).

FYI
Prior to starting the internship, interns undergo a background investigation that takes approximately 100 days to complete . . . According to former interns, intern duties never involve protecting high-level government officials, conducting surveillance, or interviewing witnesses and suspected criminals. . . During [W...] USSS was assigned by the President to guard the De[...] Independence, the US Constitution, and the Gutenberg B[...]

TO APPLY
Open to undergrads and grad students. Write for application. Call DC headquarters for contacts in field offices.

Student Volunteer (Intern) Program
Personnel Division
US Secret Service
1800 G Street NW, Room 912
Washington, DC 20223
(202) 435-5800

UNITED STATES SECURITIES AND EXCHANGE COMMISSION

SELECTIVITY 🔍 🔍 🔍
Approximate applicant pool: 300; Interns accepted: 35

COMPENSATION 💲
None for summer honors program; some paid positions in headquarters and field offices

LOCATION(S)
Atlanta, GA; Boston, MA; Chicago, IL; Denver, CO; Fort Worth, TX; Los Angeles and San Francisco, CA; Miami, FL; New York, NY; Philadelphia, PA; Salt Lake City, UT; and Washington, DC (HQ).

FIELD
Government; Law; Finance

DURATION
8–16 weeks: Summer, Fall, Spring

DEADLINE(S)
Summer: March 15; Fall and Spring: rolling

THE WORK
After the Wall Street crash that caused the Great Depression, Congress established the US Securities and Exchange Commission (SEC) to protect the public from such abuses as insider trading and stock price manipulation, administer and enforce the Securities Act of 1933 and the Securities Exchange Act of 1934, and regulate the securities markets, stock brokers, investment companies, and investment advisers. Every year, 20 Summer Honors interns work in the Office of the General Counsel and the Division of Enforcement. Volunteer positions are available during the fall and spring for all law students.

PERKS
Weekly brown-bag luncheons on federal securities laws (HQ); field trips to NYSE, an investment bank, and the HQ of NASD (HQ); "mock testimony" workshop (HQ); attendance welcome at SEC meetings, oral arguments, and federal trials (HQ).

FYI
The Summer Honors Program was started in 1978 . . . Intern duties include gathering evidence, assisting in discovery, observing negotiations, and preparing trial briefs. There are also opportunities in the legal offices in Headquarters and the field to work on important securities industry issues and investigations.

Lights... Camera... *Intern!*
Interns in film and on television:

In an episode of the television sitcom *Wings*, Roy, the stout manager of AeroMass Airlines, arranges an internship for Marty, an earnest college student. To Marty's frustration, the internship turns out to be a busywork trap, requiring him to do little more than fetch Roy's dry-cleaning and build a tool shed.

TO APPLY

Summer Honors Program: open to first- and second-year law and JD/MBA students. Clerical positions: open to high school students and undergrads. Some international applicants eligible. Please inquire with OAPM. Submit resume, cover letter, transcript, writing sample, and references. Call DC headquarters or directory information for contacts in other cities.

Summer Honors Program
US Securities and Exchange Commission
Mail Stop 4-1
450 Fifth Street NW
Washington, DC 20549
(202) 942-4150

UNITED STATES SENATE YOUTH PROGRAM

United States Senate Youth Program

SELECTIVITY 🔍 🔍 🔍
2 from each state for a total of 104 delegates

COMPENSATION 💲 💲 💲 💲
Round-trip travel; hotel and meals; $2,000 college scholarship

LOCATION(S)
Washington, DC

FIELD
Government

DURATION
1 week: first week in March

DEADLINE(S)
Late September or early October; Varies by state

THE WORK

Supported by funds from the William Randolph Hearst Foundation, the US Senate established the US Senate Youth Program in 1962. The program arranges for two student delegates from each state, DC, and Department of Defense Education. Activity schools overseas to spend a week visiting the Senate, House, Supreme Court, and Pentagon as well as listening to major policy addresses by senators, cabinet members, and officials from the Departments of State and Defense.

PERKS

Field trips to Smithsonian museums; nurse and physician on call 24 hours a day; supervision by officers from the armed services.

FYI

A certificate representing the $2,000 scholarship is often personally presented to each delegate by his or her senator.

TO APPLY

Open to high school juniors and seniors. Must be student-body or class president, vice president, secretary, or treasurer, student council representative or student representative to district, regional, or state-level civic or educational organization. Must be attending a US high school or an overseas Department of Defense Education Activity school. Contact your high school principal or

---

the address below for the address and phone number of your state's selection administrator.

United States Senate Youth Program
William Randolph Hearst Foundation
90 New Montgomery Street, Suite 1212
San Francisco, CA 94105-4504
(800) 841-7048 or (415) 543-4057
(415) 243-0760 (Fax)

UNITED STATES TRAVEL AND TOURISM ADMINISTRATION

U.S. Department of Commerce
United States Travel and Tourism Administration

See US Department of Commerce

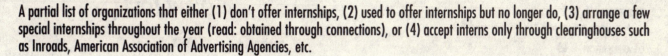

Internship Wish List

A partial list of organizations that either (1) don't offer internships, (2) used to offer internships but no longer do, (3) arrange a few special internships throughout the year (read: obtained through connections), or (4) accept interns only through clearinghouses such as Inroads, American Association of Advertising Agencies, etc.

Allure	Good Housekeeping	Royal & Ancient Golf Club of St. Andrews
Amerada Hess	GQ	Safeway Stores
American Airlines	Greater Media	Scotland Yard
American Hawaii Cruises	Harper's Bazaar	Sega
Anti-Defamation League	Hasbro	Simon & Schuster
Architectural Digest	Hershey Foods	Soros Fund Management
Arnold Palmer Golf Management	Honda Motor Co.	Southwest Airlines
Ben & Jerry's	International Development Association	Specialized Bicycle Co.
Berkshire Hathaway	International Finance Corporation	Thorn EMI
Beverly Hills, 90210	Johnson & Johnson	Town & Country
Blockbuster Entertainment	Lego Systems	Toys "R" Us
Brooks Brothers	Leo Burnett	Trump Organization
Bulova Watch	Lufthansa Airlines	U-Haul International
Caesars Palace	Mademoiselle	United Airlines
Trojan Condoms/Carter Wallace	McGraw-Hill	United Negro College Fund
Colt Guns	Melrose Place	United Parcel Service (UPS)
Cosmopolitan	N.A.A.C.P.	United Way of America
Details	Nintendo	Vanity Fair
Esquire	Organization of Petroleum	Virgin Airlines
Estee Lauder	Exporting Countries (OPEC)	Vogue
Fender Musical Instruments Corp.	Pepperidge Farm	World Bank
Fruit of the Loom	Popular Mechanics	
Glamour	Radio Free Europe/Radio Liberty	
Glaxo	Redbook	

UNITED TALENT AGENCY

SELECTIVITY 🔍🔍🔍🔍🔍
Approximate applicant pool: 1,000; Interns accepted: 40–45

COMPENSATION 💲💲
$350 a week

LOCATION(S)
Beverly Hills, CA

FIELD
Talent and literary agency

DURATION
2–4 years: ongoing

DEADLINE(S)
Rolling

THE WORK
Founded in 1991, United Talent Agency (UTA) is a talent and literary agency representing actors, producers, directors, and writers. Clients include Harrison Ford, Johnny Depp, Madonna, Claire Danes, Jim Carrey, Ben Stiller, Janeane Garofalo, and Vince Vaughn. Trainees work in the mailroom from two to eight months, where they deliver mail, organize scripts for agents, run errands, and dub videotapes, followed by a year or more of services as assistants to agents.

PERKS
Occasional meetings or luncheons with agents; building relationships with people in the entertainment industry; tickets to film screenings.

FYI
As one of the fastest growing talent and literary agencies in the motion picture, television industry, and new media, UTA provides great opportunity and growth.

TO APPLY
Open to college grads. International applicants eligible. Submit resume and cover letter:

Trainee Coordinator
United Talent Agency
9560 Wilshire Boulevard
Beverly Hills, CA 90212
(310) 273-6700
(310) 247-1111 (Fax)

UNITEL

![UNITEL WIRELESS COMMUNICATIONS SYSTEMS]

SELECTIVITY
Approximate applicant pool: N/A; Interns accepted: N/A

COMPENSATION $
$100/week

LOCATION(S)
Atlantic City, NJ

FIELD
Telecommunications; Marketing

DURATION
15 weeks (flexible): Summer, Fall, Spring

DEADLINE(S)
Rolling

THE WORK
Unitel Wireless Marketing Solutions (UWMS) is a unique marketing resource for wireless service providers. UWMS is staffed by a team of professionals with nearly two decades of in-depth experience and a strong track record of success in marketing for wireless systems throughout the United States. Interns perform duties for all facets of marketing including advertising, public relations, direct marketing, market research, special events planning, Internet marketing, and data analysis.

PERKS
Exposure to a rapidly growing industry.

FYI
The wireless communications industry is directly responsible for more 155,000 jobs in the US and the industry is indirectly responsible for than 1 million jobs nationwide.

TO APPLY
Open to college undergrads, recent grads, and grad students. Send resume and cover letter.

Unitel
Internship Coordinator
P.O. Box 1000
Pleasentville, NJ 08232
(609) 646-9400
(609) 646-1350 (Fax)

UNIVERSAL PICTURES
See MCA/Universal

UNIVERSAL STUDIOS
See MCA/Universal

UP TO THE MINUTE
See CBS News

URBAN FELLOWS/GOVERNMENT SCHOLARS PROGRAMS

The City of New York

SELECTIVITY 🔍🔍🔍🔍
Approximate applicant pool: 200 (UF), 200 (GS); Interns accepted: 25 (UF), 25 (GS)

COMPENSATION $ $ $
Government Scholars: $3,000 taxable stipend; Urban Fellows: $21,000 taxable stipend

LOCATION(S)
New York, NY

FIELD
City government

DURATION
GS: 10 weeks, Summer; UF: 9 months, Academic Year

DEADLINE
Government Scholars: January 12; Urban Fellows: January 19

THE WORK
The Urban Fellows Program is a nine-month internship in city management run by the city of New York. Interns are exposed to over 100 meaningful jobs, ranging from assistants to the city commissioner, budget director, and desk jobs, to "street work" positions involving daily contact with people.

PERKS
High-powered atmosphere; weekly seminars.

FYI
The program originated in 1969. During the four week orientation Fellows receive training in interview techniques, learn about the structure of City government and explore the 5 boroughs of the City. Fellows interview for job placements in City agencies and offices including some mayoral placements.

TO APPLY
Open to GS: college sophomores, juniors, and graduating seniors. UF: Class of '98, '99 or '00. Write for application, or apply online.

City of New York
Department of Cityside Administrative Services
Fellowship Programs
1 Centre Street, Room 2425
New York, NY 10007
(212) 669-3695
www.ci.nyc.us/html/dcas/html/intern.html

US-ASIA INSTITUTE

US-ASIA

SELECTIVITY 🔍🔍🔍🔍
Approximate applicant pool: 80; Interns accepted: 4

COMPENSATION 💲
None

LOCATION(S)
Washington, DC

FIELD
Foreign affairs

DURATION
12 weeks: Summer, Fall, Spring

DEADLINE(S)
Summer: March 15; Fall: July 15; Spring: November 15

THE WORK
Founded in 1979, the US-Asia Institute is a nonprofit organization working to foster understanding between the people and governments of the United States and Asia. Through conferences, research, symposia, international exchanges, and publications, the US-Asia Institute promotes the examination of the economic, political, and culture issues vital to US-Asian relations. Interns assist staff in researching issues, coordinating congressional staff trips overseas, and preparing for congressional briefings.

PERKS
Attendance welcome at Institute conferences and symposia; opportunity to attend congressional hearings on Asian issues; attendance welcome at receptions and exhibits sponsored by Asian embassies.

FYI
Says a former intern: "It's refreshing to know that nestled among our nation's bevy of bureaucratic buildings is an organization . . . committed to the advancement of international progress at the one-on-one level." . . . Interns have conducted research on such subjects as China's "Most Favored Nation Status," the impact of telecommunications in trade, the US withdrawal of troops from Korea, Japan trade issues, and North Korean nuclear issues.

TO APPLY
Open to college juniors and seniors as well as grad students. International applicants eligible. Submit resume, cover letter, writing sample, and college transcript.

Internship Coordinator
US-Asia Institute
232 East Capitol Street NE
Washington, DC 20003
(202) 544-3181
(202) 543-1748 (Fax)

UTAH STATE LEGISLATURE

SELECTIVITY 🔍
Approximate applicant pool: 85; Interns accepted: 60

COMPENSATION 💲💲💲
$1,800

LOCATION(S)
Salt Lake City, UT

FIELD
Government

DURATION
6 weeks: Fall

DEADLINE(S)
November 15

THE WORK
Established in 1896, the year Utah was admitted into the Union, the Utah State Legislature is Utah's legislative branch, divided into a seventy-five–member House and a twenty-nine–member Senate. Assigned to specific legislators by the Legislature's Office of Legislative Research and General Counsel, interns write to constituents, draft amendments, conduct research, and provide general support related to bills and debate during the Legislature's 45-day General Session.

PERKS
Orientation; 12 quarter-units of academic credit.

FYI
The Utah State Legislature's internship program was established in 1971 . . . Former interns include Rob W. Bishop, former Legislature's Speaker of the House.

TO APPLY
Open to college juniors and seniors. Must be attending one of Utah's five universities. Must receive academic credit. Contact the campus Coordinator of Legislative Programs in the Political Science Department.

Student Internship Program
Office of Legislative Research and General Counsel
436 State Capitol Building
Salt Lake City, UT 84114
(801) 538-1032
(801) 538-1712 (Fax)

EXCLUSIVE INTERVIEW WITH BOB COHN

The former White House Correspondent for Newsweek, Bob Cohn won the American Bar Association's Silver Gavel Award in 1992 for his coverage of the Supreme Court nomination process. He just finished a four-year stint as editor-in-chief of Stanford magazine. He graduated Phi Beta Kappa with a B.A. in political science from Stanford in 1985 and received a Masters degree in law from Yale in 1990.

The Internship Informants: Let's start with a chronology of your internships.
Cohn: In the summer of 1983, I interned at the Nuclear Information and Resource Service in DC, an anti-nuclear power organization. Then, in the summer of 1984 I interned with the *San Francisco Examiner* working at the Democratic National Convention (which was held in San Francisco that year). And because that was only a one-week internship, I spent the rest of the summer interning at the *Peninsula Times Tribune*, which has since closed.

The Internship Informants: And your internship at *Newsweek*?
Cohn: I started an internship at *Newsweek* in May of 1985. I had actually finished my coursework during the winter quarter of my senior year at Stanford, so before graduation I flew out to work at the DC bureau of *Newsweek*. By the time I flew back to Stanford for graduation, I had already covered a bunch of stories and even ridden on Air Force One.

The Internship Informants: You rode on Air Force One as an intern?
Cohn: Well, [*Newsweek*'s] Washington bureau is pretty small, and there were only two interns there that summer. The celebrations for [President] Reagan's second inaugural, which would have been in January of '85, had been rescheduled to Memorial Day Weekend because of cold weather. So when the time came for Reagan to fly down to Disney World for the celebrations, our two regular White House correspondents—since it was during Memorial Day Weekend—weren't available to fly down. But they sent me—the intern—to fly down on Air Force One to cover the event and attend a fund-raiser for Reagan in Miami.

The Internship Informants: What was it like on Air Force One?
Cohn: The press sits in a rear compartment, and we come up the back stairs—the same stairs the Secret Service and most of the staff use. The President sits in one of the forward compartments, along with the senior staff.

The Internship Informants: Were there any other highlights to your *Newsweek* internship?
Cohn: One day the office got word that there would be a briefing at the White House on the results of the President's medical checkup. As this was a pretty common occurrence and because everyone else was busy, they sent me over to the news conference at the White House on a Friday afternoon. At the conference they announced that [the President] had cancer and that he would have surgery the next day. There were all sorts of Latin terms that were being thrown around about his medical condition. I called back to the office and said, 'It's Bob, the intern, and it was announced that the President has cancer and he's having surgery tomorrow.' And everyone was like, 'Oh my God!" So it turned out that I had a hand in that story. I went to the hospital the next day, along with another *Newsweek* reporter, and I helped to cover the results of the surgery. We obviously did a cover story, which we finished after midnight on Saturday night. So just by chance, I walked into the middle of the story because I was around on a Friday afternoon.

The Internship Informants: How did your internship lead to a permanent job?
Cohn: I was hired on as a *Newsweek* reporter in Washington after six months as an intern. For the next three years, I covered labor and business issues. Then after studying one year at the Kennedy School of Government, and another in a program for journalists at Yale Law School, I returned to Newsweek to cover the legal affairs week. I was there for almost three years, and then, after the Clinton election, I switched over to the White House beat.

STUDENT PAINTERS
www.varsitystudent.com

SUMMER MANAGEMENT PROGRAM

SELECTIVITY
Approximate applicant pool: 5,000; Interns accepted: 125

COMPENSATION
$760/week average, $420/week minimum

LOCATION(S)
Nationwide U.S.

FIELD
Business; Management

DURATION
3 months: Summer, full time; Spring, part time

DEADLINE(S)
March 31

 THE WORK
The Varsity Student Painters summer management program hires high-achieving college students and trains them to manage a business from start to finish. Each selected manager will oversee the marketing, sales, and management of a house painting business in their hometown. Interns are provided with the tools, training, systems, and support they will need to manage a successful business during the summer. The requirements are confidence, leadership skills, and motivation. Earnings range from $5,000–30,000. Full information available at www.varsitystudent.com.

PERKS
Intense training program, continual support, average summer earnings of $9,200. Bi-weekly company events, reward dinners with executives, limousine night, and whitewater rafting.

FYI
Top performers receive an all-expenses paid Cabo San Lucas vacation with the company. Many career opportunities are available within the company (for above-average performers) and also with several affiliated organizations who actively recruit Varsity Alumni.

TO APPLY
Open to undergraduates (freshman–senior).

The Varsity Summer Management Program
1802 Tice Valley Blvd.
Walnut Creek, CA 94595
Website: www.varsitystudent.com
E-mail: roly@varsitystudent.com
Toll free: (888) 295-9675
(925) 937-0434
(925) 937-0499 (Fax)
www.varsitystudent.com

VAULT.com

SELECTIVITY
Approximate applicant pool: 600; Interns accepted: 30

COMPENSATION
Stipend

LOCATION(S)
New York, NY

FIELD
Internet; New media

DURATION
12–16 weeks (flexible): Summer, Fall, Spring

DEADLINE(S)
Rolling

THE WORK
Vault.com, the premier source of career information on the Web, is a popular destination for young professionals as well as the companies that recruit them. While it offers a broad array of resources and tools for career management, Vault.com's core concern has always been providing the most accurate and timely information culled through independent research in addition to input from actual company insiders. In addition to its career guides to popular industries (Investment Banking, Law, Consulting, High Tech) and employers (you name it, they probably cover it), Vault.com boasts an interactive community that attracts the nation's most ambitious students and professionals. Clearly, a smart way to kick-start your own career is to intern at the company that knows the most about high-powered professions.

PERKS
A major benefit of working at Vault.com, say interns, is the opportunity to learn how companies and careers really work. In addition to learning about what Vault.com does, they get that trademark "inside look" at every industry and career issue the company covers. Interns may speak and correspond with hundreds of employees from various industries, as well as recruiters and executives at those firms. This means that when it's time for interns to enter the working world, they will not only be intimately familiar with the best companies and how to interview; they will know that Vault.com is an impressive line on their resumes.

FYI
All interns work in Vault.com's sunny headquarters in the Chelsea section of Manhattan. The "airy," window-filled" office takes up three floors of a converted industrial loft. The company uses an open seating plan, and employees bring in their favorite CDs to play in the office. Says one former intern: "they play everything from Beck, to the Beastie Boys, to the soundtrack from *Strictly Ballroom*."

TO APPLY
Open to high school, college, and graduate students, as well as recent college graduates. In the past, most interns have come from top colleges and high schools, with majors ranging from English to computer science. Prospective interns should send a resume, cover letter, and two references.

Moby Van Romsey
Internship Coordinator
Vault.com
150 W 22nd St., 5th Floor
New York, NY 10011

VEREINSBANK CAPITAL CORPORATION

SELECTIVITY 🔍🔍
Approximate applicant pool: 90; Interns accepted: 8

COMPENSATION 💲💲
$1,000/month

LOCATION(S)
New York, NY

FIELD
Investment banking

DURATION
3 months minimum, 6 months preferred

DEADLINE(S)
November 1

THE WORK
Established in 1981, Vereinsbank Capital Corp. (VCC) is the US investment banking arm of Bayerische Vereinsbank, a bank based in Munich, Germany. Interns work in Accounting, Mergers & Acquisitions, Equity Sales, and Fixed Income Sales.

PERKS
Tours of NYSE, Federal Building, etc.; participation welcome in spring Corporate Challenge (sports and dinner).

FYI
Only forty employees work in VCC's New York office . . . Interns from Germany, under the auspices of BV's internship program, work at VCC throughout the year . . . The intern coordinator describes BV as "like a Morgan Guaranty."

TO APPLY
Open to graduate students in business and finance. Must be bilingual in German and English. International applicants eligible. Submit resume and cover letter.

Internship Coordinator
Vereinsbank Capital Corporation
150 East 42nd Street
New York, NY 10017
(212) 672-6000

VERTIGO RECORDS

See PolyGram

VERVE RECORDS

See PolyGram

VH-1

See MTV: Music Television

VIBE

SELECTIVITY 🔍🔍🔍🔍
Approximate applicant pool: 250; Interns accepted: 18

COMPENSATION 💲
Possible stipend in summer

LOCATION(S)
New York, NY

FIELD
Magazines

DURATION
16 weeks: Summer, Fall, Spring

DEADLINE(S)
Rolling

THE WORK
In print since 1993, *Vibe* is a monthly magazine featuring the music, movies, and trends of urban and hip hop culture. Owned by Vibe Ventures, *Vibe* is more than just an entertainment magazine; it is as comfortable covering political issues as it is profiling the rapper DMX. Interns work in Editorial and Business.

PERKS
Attendance welcome at occasional parties and events; intern acknowledgment in magazine's masthead; "loose" work atmosphere; free copies of the magazine.

FYI
Vibe was founded by ace music producer Quincy Jones.

TO APPLY
Open to college sophomores, juniors, and seniors as well as recent college grads, and grad students. International applicants eligible. Submit resume, cover letter, and any journalism clips (Editorial department).

Internship Coordinator
Vibe
215 Lexington Avenue, 6th Floor
New York, NY 10016
(212) 448-7300
(212) 448-7400 (Fax)

VICTIM-WITNESS ASSISTANCE PROGRAM - OFFICE OF THE DISTRICT ATTORNEY, COUNTY OF LOS ANGELES

SELECTIVITY 🔍
Approximate applicant pool: 200; Interns accepted: 100

COMPENSATION 💲
None

LOCATION(S)
Los Angeles County, CA

FIELD
Law; Human services

DURATION
16–24 weeks, ongoing

DEADLINE(S)
Apply the season before start date

THE WORK

The District Attorney's Victim-Witness Assistance Program began in 1977, in recognition of the need to provide court-based information and assistance to victims/witnesses coming to court. Today, the program continues as a part of a network of state-wide local assistance centers. Interns may work in any of the local branch and area offices or in special units such as Family Violence, Sex Crimes, and Gang Crimes.

PERKS

Invited to Program training seminars and social activities; recognized with certificates and/or awards.

FYI

The volunteer program began in late 1977, actively recruiting both student and community volunteers . . . The Los Angeles District Attorney Internship Program formally began in 1985 . . . Approximately 5 percent of interns are hired for full-time positions.

TO APPLY

Open to college undergrads, recent grads, and college grads of any age. Applicants must sign authorization for and pass a Criminal Record Background Check. International applicants eligible, but must possess a US Social Security number. Write for application. Call Volunteer Coordinator at (626) 572-6364 for telephone interview and application. For further information contact:

Victim-Witness Assistance Program
3220 Rosemead Blvd. 2nd Floor
El Monte, CA 91731
Attn: Volunteer Services
(626) 572-6364

VIKING BOOKS

See Penguin Books

THE VILLAGE VOICE

SELECTIVITY 🔍 🔍 🔍 🔍
Approximate applicant pool: 250; Interns accepted: 20

COMPENSATION $
None

LOCATION(S)
New York, NY

FIELD
Newspapers

DURATION
12 weeks: Summer, Fall; Winter, Spring

DEADLINE(S)
Summer: March 30; Fall: August 10; Winter: November 1; Spring: November 11

THE WORK

In print since 1955, *The Village Voice* is the largest weekly alternative newspaper in the country. Self-described as "outspoken, opinionated, and left-wing," the *Voice* reaches over half a million readers every week. Interns work in the Editorial department.

PERKS

An in-house library; free t-shirt, movie passes, CDs, and tapes; casual office environment.

FYI

Alumni of the internship program include staff writers at the *New York Post*, *New York Daily News*, *Miami Herald*, *Entertainment Weekly*, *New York Observer*, *New York Newsday*, *The New York Times*, and a former speechwriter for former Mayor David Dinkins.

TO APPLY

Open to high school students, high school grads, undergrads, recent college grads, college grads of any age, and grad students. International applicants eligible. Write for application.

Internship Coordinator
The Village Voice
36 Cooper Square
New York, NY 10003
(212) 475-3300
(212) 475-8944 (Fax)

The Governor of Massachusetts, **William F. Weld**, got his start in politics as an intern during the summer of 1969 with Martin Linsky, a former Massachusetts state representative and now Counselor to Governor Weld.

—*Governor Weld (right) and Martin Linsky review a map outlining Massachusetts' congressional districts.*

SELECTIVITY
Approximate applicant pool: 200 (US), 300 (London); Interns accepted: 25–45 (US), 10–20 (London)

COMPENSATION
Interns: None; Reps: $200/month and reimbursement of expenses for postage, gas, photocopies, phone, etc.

LOCATION(S)
Interns: Los Angeles, CA; New York, NY; London, England; Reps: 38 cities in 23 states (AZ, CA, CO, DC, FL, GA, IL, KS, LA, MA, MD, MI, MN, NY, NC, OH, OR, PA, TN, TX, UT, WA, WI) and Washington, DC

FIELD
Record label

DURATION
Interns (US): 10–14 weeks, Summer, Fall, Spring; Interns (London): 2 weeks, on-going; Reps: 1 year minimum, ongoing

DEADLINE(S)
Rolling

THE WORK
Virgin Records (VR) was launched in 1973 by Richard Branson, the maverick British entrepreneur who later founded Virgin Airlines. Its first release, Mike Oldfield's "Tubular Bells," went multi-platinum. Purchased in 1992 by Thorn EMI, a London-based entertainment company, VR records such artists as Paula Abdul, Lenny Kravitz, Tina Turner, UB40, the Rolling Stones, Smashing Pumpkins, Soul II Soul, Simple Minds, Boy George, and Janet Jackson. Interns work in the New York, Los Angeles, and London offices in Advertising, Artists & Repertoire, Promotions, Publicity, Sales, Computers (London only), and Finance (London only). College Representatives, under the auspices of the College Promotions Department, promote Virgin's new artists on their college campuses.

PERKS
Free CDs, cassettes, and concert tickets; attendance welcome at listening parties and promotions.

FYI
College Rep duties include providing campus radio stations with CDs and posters, arranging listening parties, monitoring stock at record stores, and escorting visiting bands to radio stations and record stores for public appearances and interviews.

TO APPLY
US: open to undergrads. London: open to high school students 16 and up, undergrads, recent college grads, and grad students. Must receive academic credit (US Interns only). International applicants eligible. Submit resume and cover letter.

College Intern Program or
National College Representative Program
Personnel Department
Virgin Records America
338 North Foothill Road
Beverly Hills, CA 90210
(310) 288-2451
(310) 288-2433 (Fax)

Personnel Administrator
Virgin Records
553-579 Harrow Road
London W10 4RH
44-181-964-6000

VIRGINIA SYMPHONY
JOANN FALLETTA MUSIC DIRECTOR

SELECTIVITY
Approximate applicant pool: N/A; Interns accepted: N/A

COMPENSATION
None

LOCATION(S)
Norfolk, Virginia

FIELD
Performing Arts

DURATION
10–16 weeks: Summer, Fall, Spring

DEADLINE(S)
Rolling

THE WORK
Once the only professional orchestra between Baltimore and Atlanta, the current Virginia Symphony was founded in 1979 by the merger of the Peninsula Symphony Orchestra, the Virginia Beach Pops Symphony, and the Virginia Orchestra Group. The symphony is also one of the few with a female music director: JoAnn Falletta, under whose direction the group performs over 140 concerts a year. Internships are offered in five areas—Development, Finance, Marketing, Production, and the Executive Office—and in three tracks: Area Specific, Job Specific, and Comprehensive. More information about the departments and tracks is available in the orchestra's internship handbook.

PERKS
Free admission to concerts; attendance at staff meetings.

FYI
According to the New York Times, the orchestra's recent Carnegie Hall debut was a "remarkable" performance, "energetic, committed, and . . . finely polished" . . . Over 50 percent of the Symphony's interns are later hired full-time.

TO APPLY
Open to college undergrads, recent graduates, and grad students. Write for application.

Virginia Symphony
Attn: Internship Coordinator
880 N. Military Highway, Suite 1064
Norfolk, VA 23502
(757) 466-3060
(757) 466-3046 (Fax)
www.virginiasymphony.org

VOICE OF AMERICA

SELECTIVITY
Approximate applicant pool: 200; Interns accepted: 50

COMPENSATION 💲
None

LOCATION(S)
Washington, DC

FIELD
Radio

DURATION
6–12 weeks: Summer, Fall, Spring

DEADLINE(S)
Rolling

THE WORK
Established in 1942 as a department of the US Information Agency (see separate entry), the Voice of America (VOA) is one of the largest broadcasting systems in the world, reaching more than 130 million listeners through worldwide programming in over 49 languages. Departments accepting interns include the English Divisions (Newsroom, Current Affairs, and Worldwide English), Audience Mail, External Affairs, Affiliate Relations, and Language Program Divisions (African, American Republics, Central Asia, East Asia, Eurasia, North Africa, Near East, South Asia, and North and South European).

PERKS
Access to gym.

FYI
VOA is legendary for broadcasting in times of crisis . . . For example, immediately after the August 1990 Iraqi invasion of Kuwait, VOA established a 24-hour network for Middle East listeners who needed current and accurate news.

TO APPLY
Open to undergrads and grad students. International applicants eligible. Write for application.

Internship Coordinator
Voice of America
Room 1543
HHS-N Building
330 Independence Avenue SW
Washington, DC 20547
(202) 619-3117
(202) 205-8427 (Fax)

VOLUNTEERS FOR ISRAEL

SELECTIVITY 🔍
Approximate applicant pool: N/A; Interns accepted: 100–800

COMPENSATION 💲
Volunteers responsible for their own transportation to Israel; In addition, there is a $100 application fee; $75 program fee ($50 for students) to cover all meals and accomodations.

LOCATION(S)
Israel

FIELD
Public service

DURATION
18 days: ongoing

DEADLINE(S)
Rolling: Specific dates throughout the year

THE WORK
Volunteers for Israel (VFI) is a nonprofit, nonpolitical, nondenominational organization taking its basic ideology from Zionist precepts. VFI was founded in 1982 in response to the critical manpower shortage in Israel due to the Peace for Galilee operation. VFI provides aid to Israel through short-term volunteer work. Assigned to army bases and hospitals throughout Israel, volunteers are involved in work such as patient care, kitchen duties, manual labor, repair jobs, and gardening.

PERKS
Two sight-seeing tours; evening lectures on topics related to Israel.

FYI
In addition to the eighteen-day program, VFI offers a five-week volunteer/touring program, archaeology digs, volunteering opportunities in botanical gardens, and programs for graduate students, high school students, and young professionals . . . Says the Volunteer Coordinator: "We'll accept applications a day before a departure, if there's room available, and they fulfill all the application requirements."

TO APPLY
Programs are open to those 18 years and older.

Volunteer Coordinator
Volunteers for Israel
330 West 42nd Street, Suite 1618
New York, NY 10036-6029
(212) 643-4848
(212) 643-4855 (Fax)
E-mail: vol4israel@aol.com
www.vfi-usa.org

Fashion designer **Donna Karan** got her start in design as a summer intern in 1968 for Anne Klein. Karan later became chief designer at Anne Klein & Company, where she worked until 1984, the year she launched her $100-million-a-year Donna Karan New York company.

Volunteers For Peace, INC.

SELECTIVITY
Approximate applicant pool: N/A; Interns accepted: 1,400

COMPENSATION
None

LOCATION(S)
21 states in the US; Washington, DC; 70 countries overseas (see Appendix)

FIELD
Public service; At least 5 fields (see THE WORK)

DURATION
2–3 weeks: Summer, Fall, Spring

DEADLINE(S)
Summer: late March to late May; Fall and Spring: rolling

THE WORK
Founded in 1981, Volunteers For Peace (VFP) is a nonprofit volunteer organization, part of a network of such organizations that has been coordinating work camps since the early 1920s. VFP volunteers work on community projects, which are sanctioned by the United Nations, under the auspices of over 1,500 programs in more than 70 countries worldwide. Projects are available in a variety of fields, particularly construction (historic preservation or low-income housing), ecology, social work, agriculture, and archaeology.

PERKS
Field trips to local cultural sites; recreational activities; geographically diverse group of volunteers.

FYI
Over 90 percent of work camp opportunities occur between July and September and over 20 percent of volunteers register for several work camps in the same or different countries in order to spend several months abroad . . . According to a VFP staffer: "Work camps are a lot of fun but require an open mind and willingness to face new challenges."

TO APPLY
Open to individuals age 18 and up (age 16 and up in France and Germany). US citizens, nonUS citizens residing in the US, or Canadians residing in Canada: write, call, or e-mail VFP for our free newsletter, application, and International Workcamp Directory (published April 1, it costs $20. NonUS citizens living outside the US: contact CCIVS for address and phone number of organization in your country that runs the work camp programs.

Volunteers For Peace
43 Tiffany Road
Belmont, VT 05730
(802) 259-2759
(802) 259-2922 (Fax)
E-mail: vfp@vfp.org
www.vfp.org

CCIVS
UNESCO
1 Rue de Miollis
75015 Paris, France
33-14-568-2731

SELECTIVITY
Approximate applicant pool: 75; Interns accepted: 30–40

COMPENSATION
Fee: $950–$1,425; living stipend that covers housing, roundtrip airfare, basic health insurance, language training, in-country orientation

LOCATION(S)
China; Indonesia; Laos; Vietnam

FIELD
Teaching; working with nongovernmental organizations on a wide range of environmental and social issues

DURATION
Undergrads: 6 weeks or 1 year; Recent college grads: 1 or 2 years; starting late June

DEADLINE(S)
February (varies from year to year)

THE WORK
Started in 1963 by Stanford University students, Volunteers in Asia (VIA) is a small, nonprofit organization that provides Asian communities with volunteer teachers. VIA's goal is to stimulate long-term interest in Asia and further communication between Americans and Asians. Volunteers teach English in colleges and at community organizations or assist women's or environmental organizations with English translation and editing.

PERKS
Advising sessions from returning volunteers and alumni; three-month training program at Stanford University from March to May; arranged housing (guesthouse, faculty apartment, dorm, etc.). Volunteers are VIA, no bureaucracy to get lost in.

FYI
Over three decades, VIA has placed more than 1,300 volunteers throughout Asia. Partial scholarships are available.

TO APPLY
Open to undergrads from Bay area schools and recent college grads nationwide. International applicants eligible. Write for application.

Volunteers in Asia
P.O. Box 20266
Stanford, CA 94309
(650) 723-3228
(650) 725-1805 (Fax)
E-mail: volasia@volasia.org
www.volasia.org

SELECTIVITY
Approximate applicant pool: 65; Interns accepted: 40

COMPENSATION Ⓢ
None

LOCATION(S)
Hartford, CT

FIELD
Museums

DURATION
10 weeks: Summer, Fall, Spring

DEADLINE(S)
Summer: April 30; Fall: August 1; Spring: December 31

THE WORK
Founded in 1842, the Wadsworth Atheneum is the oldest public museum in the United States. It houses a fine arts collection with particular strengths in nineteenth-century American painting, Renaissance and Baroque European painting, European and American decorative arts, African American art and artifacts, and colonial American furniture. Interns work in Curatorial, Development, Design and Installation, Photographic Services, Business Office, Museum Shop, Education, Library, Registrar, Membership, and Public Information.

PERKS
Weekly seminar on museum studies; 10 percent discount at museum shop and cafe; free admission to educational programs.

TO APPLY
Open to college juniors and seniors, recent college grads, and grad students. International applicants eligible. Write for application or e-mail request.

Internship Coordinator
The Martin Office of Museum Education
Wadsworth Atheneum
600 Main Street
Hartford, CT 06103
E-mail: kendra.dowd@wadsworthatheneum.org.

THE WALL STREET JOURNAL.

SELECTIVITY   🔍🔍🔍🔍🔍
Approximate applicant pool: 600–800; Interns accepted: 15–18

COMPENSATION   Ⓢ Ⓢ Ⓢ Ⓢ
$600/week

LOCATION(S)
New York, NY, and various major cities (including Chicago, Atlanta, Dallas, and Washington, DC)

FIELD
Newspapers

DURATION
10 weeks: Summer

DEADLINE
Thanksgiving

THE WORK
Founded in 1889 as a four-page bulletin pledging to offer "a faithful picture of the rapidly shifting panorama of [Wall] Street," the *Journal* has grown into an international daily with a circulation larger than that of any other US newspaper. Despite this stature, it strives to adhere to old values, namely "accuracy, independence, and fairness." The internships begin fast and furious, doing "the kind of work a regular reporter does. . . . [They] expect you to write from day one," says one intern.

PERKS
Demanding pace; formal dress; low-key newsroom.

FYI
One the average, the *Journal* hires one former intern about every other year . . . About half of the internships go to minority applicants . . . Derek Dingle, a former intern, eventually became managing editor of *Black Enterprise* magazine and now runs a company that makes comic books featuring black superheroes.

TO APPLY
Open to undergrads, graduating seniors, and grad students. Previous journalism internships and/or college newspaper experience. International applicants eligible. Submit resume, cover letter, and clips of journalistic work.

The Wall Street Journal
Internship Program
c/o Carolyn Phillips, Assistant Managing Editor
200 Liberty Street
New York, NY 10281

SELECTIVITY
Approximate applicant pool: 200; Interns accepted: 8

COMPENSATION
None

LOCATION(S)
Southfield, MI

FIELD
Record labels

DURATION
12 weeks: Summer, Fall, Winter, Spring

DEADLINE(S)
Rolling

THE WORK
Founded in 1985 by Joseph Sanders, a music manager and producer, and Tim Rochon, a video and music producer, Wall Street Music (WSM) began producing music for Fortune 500 Clients including Corvette, MCI, Disney, IBM, and Johnson & Johnson to name a few. In 1993, Wall Street launched its record label producing and distributing urban hip-hop and rap music to 13 countries. Three interns per quarter work in the field of Promotion, Marketing, Public Relations, and Audio Production.

PERKS
Interaction with entertainment companies worldwide, free CDs (all labels) and concert tickets; opportunities to attend trade association conferences.

FYI
The work environment at Wall Street is that of an empowered, open office. Interns have the opportunity to lead a campaign as if head of their own department. The intern's area of interest is matched with tasks that put them in control of a project, responsibile for its end result.

TO APPLY
Open to undergrads, recent college grads, college grads of any age, and grad students. International applicants eligible. Write for appliation.

Internship Coordinator
Wall Street Music
19111 W. 10 Mile Road
Suite 205
Southfield, NI 48075-2472
(248) 353-0700
(248) 353-5985 (Fax)
E-mail: tim@wallstreetmusic.com

SELECTIVITY
Approximate applicant pool: 16,000; Interns accepted: 1,900–2,100 (varies by season)

COMPENSATION
$6/hour; (guaranteed at least 30 hours per week); transportation to/from work; housing in Disney-owned apartments

LOCATION(S)
Lake Buena Vista, FL

FIELD
Vacation resort; Theme parks; Resort operations; Retail; Recreation and hospitality management

DURATION
10–18 weeks; Summer, Fall, Spring

DEADLINE(S)
Rolling

THE WORK
Walt Disney World College Program interns will experience the Walt Disney World Resort through attractions, food and beverages, housekeeping, merchandise, or resort operations. Interns will work with visiting guests from around the world and learn the Guest Service Guidelines that make Walt Disney World a leader in the hospitality and entertainment industry. Additional opportunities are also available in areas such as Engineering, Marine Biology, Horticulture, Animal Programs, and many more.

PERKS
Corporate training program; free business seminars; resource libraries; free admission to the parks and discounts within Walt Disney World Resort.

FYI
Disney World is home to the largest number of theme parks in the world. Students from more than 1,000 colleges and universities from across the United States have experienced a semester at the Walt Disney World Resort and the opportunity to learn from a Fortune 100 company.

TO APPLY
Open to full- and part-time students who have completed at least one semester of college. Grad students and international students also eligible.

Walt Disney World
College Relations Program
P.O. Box 10090
Lake Buena Vista, FL 32830
(407) 828-3091
(407) 934-3943 (Fax)
www.wdwcollegeprogram.com

W A R W I C K ▪ B A K E R ▪ O ▪ N E I L L

SELECTIVITY 🔍 🔍 🔍 🔍
Approximate applicant pool: 200; Interns accepted: 2–5

COMPENSATION 💲
$150/week

LOCATION(S)
New York, NY

FIELD
Advertising

DURATION
6 weeks: Summer

DEADLINE(S)
April 30

 THE WORK
Established in 1939, Warwick Baker O'Neill (WBO) is a privately owned full-service ad agency, with nearly $200 million in billings in 1994. Clients have included US Tobacco, Schering-Plough, Fruit of the Loom, Federal Express, AT&T, Bausch & Lomb, Liz Claiborne, McGraw-Hill, and Van Munching (importers of Heineken and Amstel Light beer). Interns work in Account Management, Creative, New Business, Strategic Planning & Research, and Media.

PERKS
Occasional luncheons with executives; attendance welcome at client meetings; summer picnic; softball team.

FYI
WBO's internship program was started in 1986 . . . Approximately one-third of the agency's interns are hired for full-time employment.

TO APPLY
Open to college seniors. Submit resume and cover letter.

Internship Coordinator, Human Resources
Warwick Baker O'Neill
100 Avenue of the Americas
New York, NY 10013
(212) 941-4469
(212) 941-4459 (Fax)
www.warwick.com

Jurassic Internships

Internships that have stood the test of time:
AIESEC (1948)
Arena Stage Theater (1959)
Arthur Andersen (1950)
AT&T Bell Laboratories (1945)
Brethren Volunteer Service (1948)
Brookhaven National Laboratory (1949)
Brooklyn Botanic Garden (1944)
California State Assembly (1957)
The Coro Foundation (1943)
Ford Motor Company (1953)
Glen Helen Outdoor Education Center (1957)
Gould Farm (1914)
Hewlett-Packard (1955)
Historic Deerfield (1956)
Kimberly-Clark (1957)
McDonnell Douglas (1945)
McLean Hospital (1958)
Merck (1951)
National Aeronautics and Space Administration (1958)
National Security Agency (1952)
Overseas Service Corps of the YMCA, Japan (1880)
PERA Club (1951)
The Southwestern Company (1868)
Schlumberger (1945)
St. Paul's School (1958)
3M (1951)
US Department of State (1959)
Wadsworth Atheneum (1954)
Weyerhaeuser (1955)
William Morris Agency (1945)

THE WASHINGTON CENTER

For Internships and Academic Seminars

SELECTIVITY
Approximate applicant pool: 1,600; Interns accepted: 1,400 annually.

COMPENSATION
Program and housing fees vary per internship program/seminar and per semester; approximately 68 percent of students receive some form of financial aid that varies based on students' geographic region and program initiative. Accepted students are eligible to receive up to $2,000 in assistance applied toward housing. The Washington Center awards more than two million dollars per year in financial assistance to interns.

LOCATION(S)
Greater Washington D.C. and surrounding areas

FIELD
All fields, all majors. Programs include Woman in Public Policy; The Environment; Nonprofit Leaders; Mass Communications; Minority Leaders Fellowship Program; Diversity in Congress; College Plus One, Law Plus One, and the NAFTA Internship Program

DURATION
Internship program: 10–15 weeks: Fall, Winter, Spring, Summer
Academic seminars: Range from 1 to 2 weeks; Seminars are held in January and May

DEADLINE(S)
Consult application for program deadlines

THE WORK
The Washington Center for Internships and Academic Seminars realizes that Success Starts with Experience™. The program seeks to provide students with that experience. Founded in 1975, The Washington Center brings students to the nation's capital to complete an internship and participate in a three-credit academic course. Students receive college credit for the internship experience. Participants have interned everywhere from the US Senate, US Department of Labor, and the US Information Agency to the Folger Shakespeare Theatre, United Way, Amnesty International, and the American Association of University Women. In addition to its regular internship program, The Washington Center administers two internship programs for minority students and another for recent college grads and first-year law students.

PERKS
Presidential lecture series; embassy visits; brown-bag lunches; workshops; Congressional Breakfasts; tours of government offices; alumni network; secure housing in Arlington, VA at fully furnished apartments; academic credit from students' home institution; small student to staff ratio; expert faculty teach evening courses.

FYI
The Washington Center's Academic Seminars offer students the opportunity to meet and interact directly with national leaders and policy makers, such as Senators Connie Mack (R-FL) and Robert G. Torricelli (D-NJ); CNN Correspondent Charles Bierbauer; ABC News Anchor Sam Donaldson; C-SPAN Chairman Brian Lamb; Department of Health and Human Services Secretary Donna Shalala; *The Chicago Sun Times* journalist Robert Novak. It is the largest, most diverse full-time internship program of its kind in Washington, D.C.

TO APPLY
Write for an application and for more information on dates, fees, program initiatives, and financial aid.

The Washington Center for Internships and Academic Seminars
2000 M Street #750
Washington, DC 20036-3307
(800) 486-8921 or (202) 336-7600
(202) 336-7609 (Fax)
E-mail: Info@twc.edu
www.twc.edu

WASHINGTON CENTER FOR POLITICS & JOURNALISM

SELECTIVITY
Approximate applicant pool: 300; Interns accepted: 26 annually (13 per semester)

COMPENSATION
$2,500 stipend

LOCATION(S)
Washington, DC

FIELD
Newspapers; Radio; Television

DURATION
16 weeks: Fall and Spring

DEADLINE(S)
Fall: end of first week of April; Spring: end of first week of November

THE WORK
Founded in 1988, The Washington Center for Politics & Journalism is a nonprofit, nonpartisan foundation whose mission is "to promote greater understanding of politics by journalists and journalism by politicians." Under The Politics & Journalism Semester, interns work as reporters at major Washington news bureaus for organizations like CNN, *Houston Chronicle*, *The Wall Street Journal*, the *Chicago Tribune*, ABC News, Knight-Ridder, and National Public Radio.

PERKS
Twice-weekly seminars on campaign, governance, and interest group politics, featuring political practioners and political journalists; "Lunch-time Mentors" meet individually with students during the semester (e.g., Tom Brokaw, Diane Sawyer, Mike McCurry); alumni newsletter.

FYI
Interns at newspapers publish from a dozen to several dozen stories with bylines during the program . . . Scores of well-known politicos and journalists have addressed P&J interns at the twice-weekly seminars—from Lynn Martin, Mary Matalin, George McGovern, and Norm Ornstein to David Broder, Eleanor Clift, Cokie Roberts, and Judy Woodruff . . . Of the more than 275 former P&J interns, over three-fourths are working in the field of journalism.

TO APPLY
Open to second-semester college juniors and college seniors recent college grads (within one year of graduation), and grad stu

dents. Academic credit at the discretion of an intern's university; not required by the center. International applicants eligible. Obtain application at campus career center, write for application, or visit website.

Washington Center for Politics & Journalism
P.O. Box 15201
Washington, DC 20003-0201
(202) 296-8455
(800) 858-8365 (Fax)
E-mail: pol-jrn@wcpj.org
www.wcpj.org

WASHINGTON INTERNSHIPS FOR STUDENTS OF ENGINEERING

SELECTIVITY 🔍🔍🔍🔍
Approximate applicant pool: 175; Interns accepted: 15

COMPENSATION 💲💲💲
$2,700 stipend plus round-trip travel allowance

LOCATION(S)
Washington, DC

FIELD
Technological policy research

DURATION
10 weeks: Summer

DEADLINE
December 10

THE WORK
In 1973, University of Washington Engineering Professor Barry Hyman served a one-year tenure as a Congressional Fellow. Through this experience, he realized that undergraduate engineering students would benefit from a similar experience and founded WISE in 1978. Interns are introduced to the technical public policy of DC and asked to think about the ways science contributes to society.

PERKS
Independence; meetings with political big-wigs; dorm housing; faculty-in-residence.

FYI
Interns write a required research paper as part of their learning experience . . . As a WISE alumnus puts it: "If you are an engineer interested in the broader implications of engineering, in understanding how technology plays a role in public policy, then WISE up—this program is for you."

TO APPLY
Open to college seniors in engineering. International applicants eligible. Write for application.

Washington Internships for Students
of Engineering
1899 L Street NW, Suite 500
Washington, DC 20036
(202) 466-8744

THE WASHINGTON OFFICE ON AFRICA

SELECTIVITY 🔍🔍🔍
Approximate applicant pool: 30; Interns accepted: 2

COMPENSATION 💲
None

LOCATION(S)
Washington, DC

FIELD
Public policy; Foreign affairs

DURATION
Negotiable: normally 12 weeks Summer, Fall, Spring

DEADLINE(S)
Rolling

THE WORK
The Washington Office on Africa is a church-sponsored advocacy organization seeking to articulate and promote a just American policy toward Africa. Founded in 1972 to support the movement for freedom from white-minority rule in southern Africa, WOA now has an expanded mission, which seeks to address issues affecting grassroots African interests throughout the continent. We monitor Congressional legislation and executive policies and actions and issue action alerts to advance progressive legislation and policy. We seek to work in partnership with colleagues in Africa, the Africa advocacy community in the United States, and grassroots organizations concerned with various aspects of African affairs. WOA publishes *Washington Notes on Africa* three times a year as well as periodic updates and action alerts, which urge action by the Congress or the administration.

PERKS
WOA works in solidarity with a wide range of progressive advocacy groups. Interns have the opportunity to participate in the Advocacy Network for Africa and various issue or region specific working groups.

TO APPLY
Open to college juniors and seniors, recent college grads, college grads of any age, and grad students. International applicants eligible. Write for application.

Internship Coordinator
The Washington Office on Africa
212 East Capitol Street
Washington, DC 20013
(202) 547-7503
(202) 547-7505 (Fax)
E-mail: woa@igc.org
www.woaafrica.org

WASHINGTON OFFICE ON LATIN AMERICA

SELECTIVITY 🔍🔍🔍🔍🔍
Approximate applicant pool: 150; Interns accepted: 7 per semester term

COMPENSATION 💲
None

LOCATION(S)
Washington, DC

FIELD
Human rights, International affairs; U.S. foreign policy

DURATION
10–16 weeks: Summer, Fall, Spring

DEADLINE(S)
Summer: March 15; Fall: open; Spring: open

THE WORK
Founded in 1974, the Washington Office on Latin America (WOLA) is a nonprofit organization advancing human rights, democracy, and equitable economic growth in Latin America. Striving to inform US policymakers and the public of the economic and political developments in the region, WOLA briefs congressional aides, disseminates reports, organizes press conferences, addresses academic audiences, and writes op-ed pieces. Interns provide clerical support and help monitor events in Latin America.

PERKS
Luncheons with staff and visiting human rights activists; attendance at Capitol Hill hearings.

FYI
WOLA's internship program commenced in 1980 . . . Former interns include several WOLA staffers as well as a few prominent human rights activists.

TO APPLY
Open to undergrads and recent college grads. Must show a demonstrated interest in human rights issues and Latin America. International applicants eligible. Check out website for application procedures or call.

Internship Recruitment Coordinator
Washington Office on Latin America
1630 Connecticut Ave, NW
Washington, DC 20009
(202) 797-2171
(202) 797-2172 (Fax)
E-mail: wola@wola.org
www.wola.org

THE WASHINGTON POST

The Washington Post

SELECTIVITY 🔍🔍🔍🔍🔍
Approximate applicant pool: 400–800; Interns accepted: 20

COMPENSATION 💲💲💲💲💲
Reporters $790/week; copy editors $897/week

LOCATION(S)
Washington, DC; VA; MD

FIELD
Newspapers

DURATION
12 week: Summer

DEADLINE
November 1

THE WORK
Pick up a copy of *Power, Privilege, and the Post* in your bookstore to read about the story of Katharine Graham, a woman who helped build a spectacularly profitable, internationally renowned newspaper empire—*The Washington Post*. One of the world's most respected newspapers, *The Washington Post* is a locus of power in the United States, reporting on, and in some instances shaping, the course of American history. *The Washington Post* assigns its interns to the National, Metro, Business, Sports, Style, Photo, and News Art departments.

PERKS
Speaker luncheons; mentors; strenuous workload.

FYI
More than 80 current staffers launched their careers as *Post* interns, including the newspaper's executive and former managing editor . . . There's no busywork. "[*The Post*] assumes you are there to be a reporter—photocopying, answering phones, and the like are unheard of," a former intern reported.

TO APPLY
Open to college juniors and seniors, and grad students. Previous journalism experience required. International applicants eligible. Write for application or see www.washingtonpost.com/intern.

Summer News Program
The Washington Post
1150 15th Street NW
Washington, DC 20071-5508
(202) 334-6000
www.washingtonpost.com/intern

Judith Martin, a.k.a. "Miss Manners," launched her journalism career in the summer of 1958 as a copy girl at *The Washington Post*. When she graduated from Wellesley a year later, she was hired by the *Post* as a reporter and society columnist. Since then, she has become one of the nation's most respected authorities on etiquette.

Uncovering the Watergate Coverup

Carl Bernstein (at right), who together with **Bob Woodward** at The *Washington Post* broke the story on the Watergate scandal, launched his career at the age of sixteen as a copy boy for *The Washington Star*.

THE WASHINGTONIAN

SELECTIVITY
Approximate applicant pool: 200–400; Interns accepted: 3

COMPENSATION
$6.15/hour

LOCATION(S)
Washington, DC

FIELD
Magazines

DURATION
Summer: June 1–August 15; School year: September–May

DEADLINE(S)
Summer: February 1; Fall: July 1;

THE WORK
Started in 1965, *The Washingtonian* is a general interest magazine focusing on the people and issues of Washington, DC. It reaches more than 165,000 readers per issue. Departments accepting interns include Editorial.

PERKS
Weekly meetings with department heads; free copies of magazine; promotional freebies.

FYI
All interns get to do some writing for the magazine; most write short pieces for the "Capital Comment" column, but the talented are allowed to write 1,000 to 1,500-word stories.

TO APPLY
Open to college juniors and seniors, recent college grads, and grad students. Submit resume, cover letter, and writing samples (published articles).

Ellen Ryan, Managing Editor
The Washingtonian
1828 L Street NW, Suite 200 Washington, DC 20036-5169
(202) 296-3600

WAXQ-Q104.3

NEW YORK'S ONLY CLASSIC ROCK STATION

SELECTIVITY
Approximate applicant pool: 75; Interns accepted: 15

COMPENSATION
None; credit

LOCATION(S)
New York, NY

FIELD
Radio

DURATION
12–18 weeks: Summer, Fall; Winter, Spring

DEADLINE(S)
Rolling

THE WORK
One of the best rock radio stations in the country according to *Rolling Stone* magazine, WAXQ-Q104.3 specializes in "classic" with a minimum of radio frills. In existence since 1996, it is owned by AMFM Broadcasting Corp. Interns work in Promotions and Marketing.

PERKS
Attendance at all station events such as concerts, sporting events, and club appearances; promotional freebies (t-shirts, hats, posters, etc.).

TO APPLY
Open to undergrads. International applicants eligible. Send cover letter and resume to:

Internship Coordinator
WAXQ-Q104.3
1180 Avenue of the Americas
New York, NY 10036
(212) 575-1043
(212) 302-7814 (Fax)

An outdoor concert with the band "Stick" sponsored by WAXQ-Q104.3 in New York.

WCHS-TV NEWS 8

SELECTIVITY
Approximate applicant pool: 30; Interns accepted: 25

COMPENSATION
None; credit

LOCATION(S)
Charleston; Huntington, WV

FIELD
Television

DURATION
6–10 weeks: Summer, Fall, Spring, Winter

DEADLINE(S)
Rolling

THE WORK
WCHS-TV and WVAH-TV are two of the 61 television stations owned or operated by Sinclair Broadcast Group Inc. We produce 24 hours of news a week on our two ABC and FOX affiliate channels. Interns get a broad base of experience from working the assignment desk to working with individual "show" producers to assisting video tape editors to working with sports and weather. Basic work includes research for producers and reporters. It also includes taking satellite feeds and doing other basic news gathering research in this union shop.

PERKS
Opportunities to accompany reporters on shoots; possible opportunities for permanent employment. Well over 80 percent of newsroom staff interned at WCHS-TV or elsewhere.

FYI
Interns have been a part of WCHS-TV's staff since 1984 . . . According to WCHS-TV's station manager, more Charleston viewers tune in to WCHS-TV than to any other local station.

TO APPLY
Open to undergrads, recent college grads, college grads of any age, and grad students. International applicants eligible. Submit resume, cover letter, and recommendations. Arrange for phone or in-person interview.

Lisa Bradley
Internship Coordinator
WCHS/WVAH-TV
1301 Piedmont Road
Charleston, WV 25301
(304) 346-4115
(304) 345-1849 (Fax)
lbradley@wchstv.com
or
byuna@sbgnet.com

Behold, the Cyber Intern!

These companies let interns spin their wheels on the information superhighway:

Apple Computer

AT&T Bell Laboratories

B.U.G.

Cybergrrl

Dell Computer

Geffen Records

Hewlett-Packard

Intel

The Kitchen

Lucasfilm/LucasDigital

Microsoft

Raychem

Renaissance Computer Art Center

Silicon Graphics

Texas Instruments

Trilogy Development Group

Weyerhaeuser

Wired

Not described in this, but also worth looking into:

Amazon.com (WA)

At Home (CA)

CNET (CA)

Double Click (NY)

Ebay (CA)

Excite (CA)

Infoseek IGO (CA)

PCOrder.com (TX)

Yahoo (CA)

SELECTIVITY 🔍 🔍 🔍 🔍 🔍
Approximate applicant pool: 1,200; Interns accepted: 35–55

COMPENSATION 💲 💲 💲 💲
$540/week for undergrads; $900/week for grad students

LOCATION(S)
Los Angeles, San Francisco, San Jose, CA; Dallas, TX.

FIELD
Banking and Financial Services

DURATION
10–12 weeks: Summer

DEADLINE(S)
March 1

THE WORK
Wells Fargo (WF) was founded in 1852 as an express company to transport goods around the country. With assets of over $100 billion and 33,000 employees, WF is the tenth largest bank holding company in the nation. Interns work in Finance, Lending, Marketing, Accounting/Auditing, Operations, Technology, and Human Resources.

PERKS
Weekly seminars/luncheons on networking, business ethics, etc.; intern lunch with the CEO of the company; trip to Oakland A's baseball game.

FYI
CEO Hazen writes in 1994's issue of *Summer Intern News*: "We encourage you to analyze and question our policies and procedures, in an attempt to improve the Bank's operations." . . . 36 to 53 percent of the interns receive full-time job offers.

TO APPLY
Open to college seniors and grad students. Call 1–800–541–8980.

SELECTIVITY 🔍 🔍 🔍
Approximate size of applicant pool: N/A ; Interns accepted: 1–2

COMPENSATION 💲
Gas money

LOCATION(S)
Los Angeles, CA

FIELD
Film and television productions

DURATION
3–6 months: ongoing

DEADLINE(S)
Rolling

THE WORK
Wessler Entertainment, a motion picture development and production company, recently established an internship program for both film majors and nonfilm majors. Interns will take part in many aspects of the company, from script-reading and brainstorming sessions to the not-so-glamorous duties of office work.

PERKS
Meet producers/talent; possible attendance at movie premiers and parties; lunches.

FYI
Wessler Entertainment places an emphasis on comedies, as evidenced by Producer Charles Wessler's recent project *Dumb and Dumber*.

TO APPLY
Undergrad and grad students should submit a resume, cover letter, and one to three recommendations. In addition, a writing sample—preferably script coverage or analytical writing sample—should be sent. Open only to students with a G.P.A. of 3.0 and above; open to international students who are juniors, seniors, or grad students.

Wessler Entertainment
9056 Santa Monica Boulevard, Suite 300
Los Angeles, CA 90069
(310) 248-6035
(310) 848-0464 (Fax)
E-mail: Lali_Kagan@newline.com

WESTIN HOTELS & RESORTS

SELECTIVITY 🔍 🔍
Approximate applicant pool: 400; Interns accepted: 70–90

COMPENSATION ⑤
One complimentary meal per day

LOCATION(S)
Dallas, Houston, TX; Los Angeles, Rancho Mirage, San Francisco, CA; Tucson, AZ; Maui, HI; New York, NY; Seattle, WA (HQ); Waltham, MA

FIELD
Hotels

DURATION
10–12 weeks: Summer, Fall, Spring

DEADLINE(S)
Rolling

THE WORK
Founded in 1930, Westin Hotels & Resorts operates over 100 hotels in 23 countries worldwide. Interns work at the corporate headquarters in Seattle or directly at a Westin Hotel, including The Westin La Paloma in Tucson, The Westin Mission Hills Resort in Rancho Mirage, The Westin Bonaventure and The Century Plaza Hotel in Los Angeles, The Westin St. Francis in San Francisco, The Westin Maui in Hawaii, The Westin Hotel in Waltham, The Westin Hotel in Dallas, The Westin Galleria & Oaks in Houston, and The Westin Hotel in Seattle. Depending on location, interns may work in Public Relations/Marketing, Special Events, or Promotions.

The futuristic Westin Bonaventure Hotel in Los Angeles, famous for appearing in scenes from *L.A. Law* and for offering an excellent internship program.

PERKS
Access to recreational facilities; employee discounts on food and orientation.

FYI
A gleaming assemblage of mirrored, cylindrical buildings, the futuristic Westin Bonaventure Hotel in Los Angeles was deemed the world's tenth most photographed building by *Fortune* magazine. It has made cameos in a slew of movies and television shows, including *True Lies, Rainman, In the Line of Fire, Lethal Weapon II, L.A. Law,* and *It's A Living.*

TO APPLY
Open to undergrads, recent college grads, and grad students. International applicants eligible. Submit resume, cover letter, writing samples, and recommendations. Call Seattle headquarters for contacts at Westin Hotels.

Internship Coordinator
Westin Hotels & Resorts
2001 Sixth Avenue, 13th Floor
Seattle, WA 98121
(206) 443-5000
(206) 443-8997 (Fax)

THE WESTWOOD ONE RADIO NETWORK

SELECTIVITY 🔍
Approximate applicant pool: 20; Interns accepted: 6

COMPENSATION ⑤
$50 stipend at end of internship

LOCATION(S)
New York, NY

FIELD
Radio

DURATION
8 weeks: Summer; 12–15 weeks: Fall and Spring

DEADLINE(S)
Rolling (preferably 2 weeks before start date)

THE WORK
The nation's largest producer of syndicated radio programming, The Westwood One Radio Network creates shows that encompass every major radio format and reach all parts of the world. Westwood One's programs include *Larry King Live, Imus in The Morning, The Weekly Country Music Countdown, The G. Gordon Liddy Show,* and *Casey's Top 40.* Interns work in either the programming department or the Production Department, where they attain hands-on experience in artist relations or studio recording

PERKS
Full use of broadcast equipment; use of facilities to create personal demo tapes.

FYI
Says the intern coordinator: "Some interns have and will get to engineer celebrity interviews, and work with nationally known disc-jockeys and personalities."

Open to college juniors and seniors as well as grad students. Must receive academic credit. International students eligible. Submit resume, two letters of recommendation (one from a faculty member), and proof that school will grant credit.

Internship Coordinator
The Westwood One Radio Network
1675 Broadway
New York, NY 10019
(212) 641-2000

WEYERHAEUSER

 Weyerhaeuser

SELECTIVITY 🔍🔍🔍
Approximate applicant pool: 1,000; Interns accepted: 100

COMPENSATION 💲💲💲💲
$560–$680/week for undergrads; $700–$900/week for grad students; company benefits

LOCATION(S)
Federal Way, WA; 250 offices and plants nationwide (see Appendix)

FIELD
Technology and business areas of Forest Products company

DURATION
3–6 months: Spring/Summer, Summer/Fall, Fall/Winter

DEADLINE
Winter/Spring: October 10; Summer/Fall: January 20

THE WORK
The company offers interns experiences in Information Technology, Accounting, Engineering and Forestry. Information Technology, the largest intern program, offers over 60 positions annually for computer science and information systems majors. With nearly 50 years experience managing intern programs, Weyerhaeuser does it best! Caring supervisors and mentors ensure interns successfully contribute to projects of value to the company. Weyerhaeuser grooms its interns for future professional careers with the company through carefully planned developmental activities, training and learning events, and individual guidance.

PERKS
Mentors; seminars/tours; social activities.

FYI
Weyerhaeuser recently celebrated its 100-year anniversary. The company has grown to be the world's premier forest products company, with 45,000 employees and over $12 billion in annual sales. Weyerhaeuser has been managing forestlands since 1900 and is committed to continuously improving its strong performance as a responsible steward of environmental quality.

TO APPLY
Requirements vary by internship area. Visit their website for specific program information:
http://www.weyerhaeuser.com/careers/college/.
Submit resume and cover letter.

College Relations CCB5D7
Weyerhaeuser
PO Box 9777
Federal Way, WA 98063-9777
E-mail: college@weyerhaeuser.com
www.weyerhaeuser.com

WGN-CHICAGO

SELECTIVITY 🔍🔍🔍🔍🔍
Approximate applicant pool: 600; Interns accepted: 25
Summer extremely selective, better prospects for fall, winter, and spring applicants

COMPENSATION 💲
$75/week

LOCATION(S)
Chicago, IL

FIELD
Radio

DURATION
14 weeks: Summer, Fall, Winter, Spring

DEADLINE(S)
Rolling

THE WORK
Established in 1924, WGN-Chicago is one of the top-grossing AM-radio station in the nation. Voted "America's Most Respected and Admired Radio Station" by the radio industry, the 50,000-watt station reaches much of the midwest by day, and thirty-eight states, along with parts of Canada and Mexico, by night. Interns work in Programming, Promotions, Sports, or News.

PERKS
Attendance welcome at all social and volunteer activities; published or broadcasted credit for work; free tickets to Cubs and Northwestern games; star-gazing opportunities; full use of equipment and access to facilities.

FYI
In existence since 1964, the internship program counts among its alumni the actor Robert Urich, star of *Vegas* and *Spenser For Hire*, and Mary Ann Childers, news anchor with Chicago's WBBM-TV, as well as WGN's assistant program director and promotions manager . . . Approximately 20 percent of interns are hired by WGN for full-time employment . . . Says the internship coordinator: "This is a very 'hands-on' internship where a regular schedule of duties and assignments are completed by the interns as they learn. These are 'make-a-difference' duties, not 'copy and file.'"

TO APPLY
Open to college juniors and seniors, recent college grads, college grads of any age, and grad students. International applicants eligible. Submit resume and cover letter.

Internship Coordinator
WGN-Chicago
435 North Michigan Avenue
Chicago, IL 60611
E-mail: Reccles@tribune.com

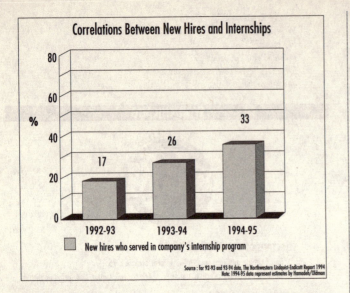

Correlations Between New Hires and Internships

- 1992-93: 17
- 1993-94: 26
- 1994-95: 33

New hires who served in company's internship program

Source: for 92-93 and 93-94 data, The Northwestern Lindquist-Endicott Report 1994
Note: 1994-95 data represent estimates by Hamadeh/Oldman

THE WHITE HOUSE

SELECTIVITY 🔍🔍🔍
Approximate applicant pool: 1,200; Interns accepted: 200

COMPENSATION 💲
None

LOCATION(S)
Washington, DC

FIELD
Government

DURATION
Summer: 15 weeks full-time (minimum 10-week commitment); Fall and Spring: 3 days and 25 hours

DEADLINE
Summer: March 1; Fall: June 25; Spring: November 2

THE WORK
The White House Internship Program responds to the President's call for active participation in government by providing students with an opportunity to learn through service in the Executive Office of the President. In addition, the program enables interns to contribute to work in over 30 offices in the White House Office, Office of the Vice President, and Office of Policy Development on behalf of the Administration. The White House Internship Program is designed to challenge and reward a select number of students from across the country with an opportunity to work in the Executive Office of the President. The goal of the program is to provide an outstanding educational experience within the offices of the White House. The program is intended to provide knowledge, tools, skills, and experiences that an intern can readily apply to future challenges and professional pursuits.

PERKS
Speaker series; farewell reception; athletic and service opportunities; tour series; group photo with the president.

FYI
Says the intern coordinator: "We are looking for a wide variety of enthusiastic students with a commitment to community and public service." . . . Few interns actually work in the White House itself. Most are situated next door in the Old Executive Office Building.

TO APPLY
Open to undergrads, recent grads, and grad students. Write for application.

The White House
Intern Program
Old Executive Office Building
Room 84
Washington, DC 20502
(202) 456-2742
www.whitehouse.gov/internship

Interns at the White House in 1994 designed the White House's Internet site (address: www.whitehouse.gov), which catalogs documents and press releases from government agencies such as the EPA and the Small Business Administration. According to *Time*, the database also boasts "a spiffy Peter Max rendition of the White House, a Camelot-ish photo of the President on horseback, and recorded meows from Socks."

WHITNEY MUSEUM OF AMERICAN ART

Whitney Museum of American Art

SELECTIVITY 🔍🔍
Approximate applicant pool: 125; Interns accepted: 25

COMPENSATION 💲
$500 + 2 monthly Metrocards

LOCATION(S)
New York, NY; and Stamford, CT

FIELD
Art museums

DURATION
Summer: 9 weeks (full time); Fall and Spring: 10–16 weeks (part time)

DEADLINE
Summer: March 1; Fall and Spring: rolling

THE WORK
The Whitney is arguably the world's most comprehensive museum of the twentieth century American art. Its permanent collection of over 12,000 works reads like a who's who of modern American artists, including Edward Hopper, Georgia O'Keefe, and Andy Warhol. Interns are placed in the following departments: Administration, Communications, Curatorial, Development, Education, Film and Video, Marketing, Publications and New Media, and Registration.

PERKS
Cozy atmosphere; weekly trip & lectures; exhibition openings; Sarabeths.

FYI
An intern's ID card is good for free admission to most New York museums . . . Housed in an angular building designed by Marcel Breuer, the Whitney has five floors of galleries and an office annex devoted to administration. Interns work in the new annex offices.

TO APPLY

Open to college juniors and seniors, and grad students. Applicants should have "a strong background and interest in American art and/or museum studies." International applicants eligible. The application procedure is eight parts: resume, a letter of recommendation, transcript, a list of three museum departments in order of work preference, proposed beginning and ending dates of internship, housing arrangements, availability for an in-person interview (give dates), and a one-page statement of purpose stating one's reasons for requesting the internship and what one hopes to gain from and contribute to the experience.

Whitney Museum of American Art
Internship Program
Human Resources
945 Madison Avenue
New York, NY 10021
(212) 570-3600
(212) 570-1807 (Fax)

WHO CARES: THE TOOL KIT FOR SOCIAL CHANGE

who cares
the tool kit for social change

SELECTIVITY 🔍🔍🔍🔍
Approximate applicant pool: 50; Interns accepted: 4

COMPENSATION Ⓢ
None

LOCATION(S)
Washington, DC

FIELD
Magazines; Public service

DURATION
10–12 weeks: Summer, Fall, Spring

DEADLINE(S)
Spring 2000: November 1, 1999; Summer 2000: March 27, 2000; Fall 2000: July 24, 2000; Spring 2001: November 6, 2000

THE WORK

Who Cares is a national business magazine for people who do good works, issued six times a year. Our 50,000 readers are primarily managers and staff in nonprofit social change organizations (average age: 32) who seek information that will help them do their jobs better.

The philosophy that drives our editorial content is that a desire to "do good" is not good enough. Inefficient and ill-informed people can't save the world. Positive social change—which we define as change that makes society more equal, just, and free—occurs when do-gooders are entrepreneurial, pragmatic, and well-informed. Our editorial goals include: reporting news and trends that define the vanguard of positive social change; strengthening the leadership, management, and entrepreneurship skills of our readers; promoting communication and understanding between the nonprofit, for-profit, and government sectors; creating a greater sense of community among people engaged in positive social change. The magazine was founded in 1993 and is published by Who Cares, Inc., a nonprofit organization.

PERKS

Interns are encouraged to write and publish articles; the office is located in one of the "hippest neighborhoods in America" (according to the Utne Reader)—the U Street corridor, home to Washington's hip-hop scene; small, young staff.

FYI

Says the *Boston Globe*, "From the generation raised on MTV and *Details*, [*Who Cares*] puts a stylish spin on doing good."

TO APPLY

To apply, send a cover letter, resume, and your best writing samples to:

Editorial Internship Coordinator
Who Cares Magazine
1436 H Street, NW #201
Washington, DC 20009
(202) 628-1691
(202) 628-2063 (Fax)

THE WIDMEYER BAKER GROUP

SELECTIVITY 🔍🔍🔍🔍🔍
Approximate applicant pool: 200; Fellows accepted: 10

COMPENSATION Ⓢ Ⓢ Ⓢ
Fellowship: $300/week; Senior Fellowship: $368/week plus health benefits

LOCATION(S)
Washington, DC

FIELD
Public relations

DURATION
12–16 weeks: Summer, Fall, Winter/Spring

DEADLINE
Summer: April 15; Fall: August 1; Winter/Spring: December 1

THE WORK

As Washington's fastest-growing independent public relations agency, the Widmeyer–Baker Group creates media strategies for leading corporations, foundations, and nonprofit advocacy groups. The realm of public policy and government is one of Widmeyer Baker's specialties, for it has developed strategies, written speeches and produced graphic materials for government agencies and officials. Fellows receive a broad public relations experience, including research, writing press releases, and attending events and press conferences.

PERKS

Upbeat, tightknit culture; youthful staff; strategy meetings.

FYI

Widmeyer has the dubious distinction of being situated only paces away from the Washington Hilton, the hotel were President Ronald Reagan was shot . . . The company is mid-sized, around 75 employees, including the fellows.

EXCLUSIVE INTERVIEW WITH KAY BAILEY HUTCHISON

A U.S. Senator from Texas, Kay Bailey Hutchison is the first woman to represent her state in the Senate. Formerly the Lone Star State's Treasurer, she holds a B.A. and J.D. from the University of Texas.

The Internship Informants: Tell us about your internship on Capitol Hill.
Hutchison: I interned with Congressman Clark Thompson, who was the Congressman from my home district, after my freshman year at the University of Texas. It was just a wonderful experience. For someone who came from a hometown smaller than the University of Texas, the opportunity to spend part of a summer in Washington was one of the great experiences of a lifetime.

The Internship Informants: How did you like living in DC?
Hutchison: Well, I shared a house with four other girls who were just out of college. It was close to the Capitol, so I walked to work. I went to the Texas State Society and other Texas events where I met other young people who were doing internships . . . It was just terrific.

The Internship Informants: How much busywork was involved in your internship?
Hutchison: It was a lot of busywork. But I don't want to downgrade the importance of busywork. I know interns want to come in and do meaningful work, but even if it's mostly busywork, you can absorb so much and see so much. For instance, with my own interns now, I try to take my interns with me to committee hearings and speeches. Congressman Thompson did that [for me] as well, and that enriches the experience. But a lot of my interns now do the busywork things, whether it's working in the mailroom or [in] other support roles. This work gives them an experience they can build on for the future. Of course, everything in life is part busywork. It's part of life. [laughs]

The Internship Informants: How important are internships to those interested in public service?
Hutchison: People who have the opportunity to be interns have a heightened awareness of the importance of public service. And even if they go into other walks of life, they still understand the importance of what goes on in Washington and in Congress . . . Also, the percentage of people in public office who started as interns is very high. Once you see and enjoy being in the Capitol group, many people gravitate back to it.

The Internship Informants: I imagine many of the interns in your office are from Texas. Is there something unique about your Texan interns, in terms of their outlook or personalities?
Hutchison: Well, certainly I think the people who are drawn to internships in Congress are the outgoing, bright, and energetic types. I give preference to Texans because a Texan only has two chances [to intern with a Texas senator]; that is, there's Phil Gramm and me. But I do employ people from other parts of the country as interns, particularly during the academic year. [Nevertheless,] most of the interns here are Texans. [Laughs] And, of course, all Texans have wonderful personalities!

TO APPLY

Fellowship is open to recent college grads or grad students with public relations experience. International applicants eligible. Submit resume, cover letter, and a few brief writing samples.

Paul Stilp, Fellowship Coordinator
The Widmeyer–Baker Group
1825 Connecticut Avenue NW
5th Floor
Washington, DC 20009
(202) 667-0901
(202) 667-0902 (Fax)
E-mail: fellowships@twbg.com

WILDLIFE PRAIRIE PARK

Wildlife Prairie Park
PEORIA, ILLINOIS

SELECTIVITY 🔍🔍🔍🔍

Approximate applicant pool: 100; Interns accepted: 7

COMPENSATION 💲

Summer interns: minimum wage; volunteers: none

LOCATION(S)

Peoria, IL

FIELD

Environment

DURATION

12 weeks: Summer, Fall, Winter, Spring

DEADLINE(S)

Summer: February 28; Fall, Winter, Spring: rolling

THE WORK

Opened in 1978 and run by the Forest Park Foundation, Wildlife Prairie Park (WPP) is a 2,000-acre zoological park featuring such animals as wolves, bison, waterfowl, black bear, elk, cougar, bald eagles, and otter as well as a butterfly garden, restored prairie, Pioneer Farmstead, and sight-seeing train. Two paid interns (summer) and one nonpaid intern per quarter (academic year) work in the Education Department, where they greet visitors, present programs to the public, and monitor trails.

PERKS

Two free guest passes for every month of employment; free admission to the park during nonworking hours; fishing privileges intern and one guest per session).

FYI

Since 1979 when the internship program was founded, approximately 30 percent of its interns have been hired for full-time positions.

TO APPLY

Open to college juniors and seniors, recent college grads, and grad students (PhD in Biology or Education). Minimum GPA: .0. International applicants eligible. Submit resume and cover etter.

Internship Coordinator
Wildlife Prairie Park
3826 North Taylor Road
R.R. #2, Box 50
Peoria, IL 61615-9617
(309) 676-0998
(309) 676-7783 (fax)

THE WILDLIFE SOCIETY

SELECTIVITY 🔍🔍🔍

Approximate applicant pool: 20; Interns accepted: 2 per year

COMPENSATION 💲💲

$250/week

LOCATION(S)

Bethesda, MD

FIELD

Environmental policy

DURATION

24 weeks: January–June or July–December

DEADLINE(S)

January–June: December 5; July–December: June 5

THE WORK

Established in 1937, The Wildlife Society is a nonprofit organization dedicated to enhancing the scientific, technical, managerial, and educational capability of wildlife professionals. In addition to its lobbying activities, it holds meetings, symposia, and an annual conference for wildlife professions. Interns work in the Wildlife Policy department, where they research conservation issues, prepare background information for use in testimony or comments, and assist with the preparation of Society publications.

PERKS

Private office; attendance welcome at Capitol Hill meetings; opportunities to meet government officials.

FYI

In existence since 1982, the internship counts among its alumni the chief of staff for US Senator Murkowski, the assistant wildlife program manager for the US Forest Service, and the environmental affairs specialist for Pioneer Hi-Bred International.

TO APPLY

Open to undergrads, recent college grads, college grads of any age, and grad students. Submit resume, cover letter, two writing samples, transcript, and three recommendations.

Internship Coordinator
The Wildlife Society
5410 Grosvenor Lane, Suite 200
Bethesda, MD 20814
(301) 897-9770
(301) 530-2471 (Fax)
E-mail: tws@wildlife.org

WILLIAMSTOWN THEATER FESTIVAL

SELECTIVITY 🔍🔍🔍
Approximate applicant pool: 650; Interns accepted: 85

COMPENSATION 💲
No stipend; housing costs are $500/summer; limited scholarships available

LOCATION(S)
Williamstown, MA

FIELD
Performing arts

DURATION
10–12 weeks: Summer

DEADLINE(S)
Rolling

THE WORK
A "favorite hangout of many of America's finest actors" according to the *New York Post*, the Williamstown Theater Festival (WTF) has produced nationally renowned performances since 1955. Situated on the idyllic campus of Williams College in Massachusetts, the Festival stages about ten plays each season. Interns work in Design, Tech Production, Publicity, Directing, Box Office, General/Company Management, Stage Management, Production Management, House Management, Photography, Literary Management, and Publications Management. One Management internship is available in New York City each spring.

PERKS
Opportunity to develop own projects; attendance welcome at all performances and working with industry professionals; lovely forested setting.

FYI
For those primarily interested in acting, WTF offers an Apprentice Workshop, in which participants take acting classes, attend seminars with artists, rotate through various production assignments, and audition for roles in WTF productions. Open to anyone 17 years or older, the Apprentice Workshop runs the ten-week summer theater season and charges $2,700 for room and board and tuition. Write WTF for more details . . . WTF's stellar roster of former apprentices includes George C. Wolfe, Sigourney Weaver, Christopher Reeve, Dick Cavett, Keifer Sutherland, John Badham, and Tony Goldwyn.

TO APPLY
Open to high school students 17 years or older, high school grads, undergrads, recent college grads, college grads of any age, and grad students. International applicants eligible. Write for application.

Alumni of the apprenticeship program at the Williamstown Theater Festival include **Sigourney Weaver**, Santo Loquasto, Austin Pendleton, John Badham, George C. Wolfe, and Tony Goldwyn.

Internship Coordinator
Williamstown Theater Festival
100 East 17th Street, 3rd Floor
New York, NY 10003
(212) 228-2286
(212) 228-9091 (Fax)

THE WILMA THEATER

SELECTIVITY 🔍🔍🔍
Approximate applicant pool: 50; Interns accepted: 5–7

COMPENSATION 💲
None

LOCATION(S)
Philadelphia, PA

FIELD
Theater

DURATION
16–36 weeks: (seasonal—winter, spring, summer, fall)

DEADLINE(S)
Rolling

THE WORK
Founded in 1973, The Wilma Theater presents a variety of original plays, new adaptations and translations, and classic works. Productions include works by such playwrights as Eugene Ionesco, Romulus Linney, Tom Stoppard, and Athol Fugard. Interns work in Marketing, Development, Literary, Management, and Education.

PERKS
Attendance welcome at symposia, script readings, and preview performances; free tickets to Wilma productions and other local theaters; small, friendly staff; discounts on studio school classes.

FYI
The Wilma prides itself on being a "socially conscious" theater, staging productions that "often focus on topical political and social issues."

TO APPLY
Open to undergrads, recent college grads, and grad students. International applicants eligible. Submit resume and cover letter.

THE APPRENTICES SUTHERLAND

Prolific actor **Donald Sutherland** began his thespian career with apprenticeships in repertory theater companies in the English towns of Nottingham, Chesterfield, Sheffield, Perth, and Stratford. Sutherland's actor son, **Kiefer**, opted to stay in the States for his apprenticeship, participating in Williamstown Theatre Festival's apprenticeship program in Williamstown, MA.

Attn: Char Vandermeer
The Wilma Theater
265 S. Broad Street
Philadelphia, PA 19107
(215) 893-9456
(215) 893-0895 (Fax)
www.wilmatheater.org

THE WILSON QUARTERLY

SELECTIVITY 🔍 🔍 🔍 🔍 🔍
Approximate applicant pool: 300; Interns accepted: 9

COMPENSATION Ⓢ
$100/week

LOCATION(S)
Washington, DC

FIELD
Magazines

DURATION
12–14 weeks: Summer, Fall, Spring

DEADLINE(S)
Summer: March 15; Fall: July 15; Spring: October 15

THE WORK
Founded in 1976, *The Wilson Quarterly* is a general interest, nonprofit publication dedicated to the latest critical scholarly research on a variety of humanities-oriented topics. Recent topics covered in the magazine include the information superhighway, the decline of the American passenger train, and the world population crisis. Interns work in the Editorial Department.

PERKS
Attendance welcome at lectures and colloquia sponsored by the Woodrow Wilson International Center for Scholars; 20 percent discount at Smithsonian Museum shops.

FYI
Alumni of the internship program, started in 1976, include journalists with the *New York Review of Books* and the *New Republic.*

TO APPLY
Open to undergrads, recent college grads, college grads of any age, and grad students. International applicants eligible. Submit resume, cover letter, three writing samples, and three recommendations.

Internship Coordinator
The Wilson Quarterly
901 D Street, SW Suite 704
Washington, DC 20024
(202) 287-3000

WINANT-CLAYTON VOLUNTEERS

SELECTIVITY 🔍 🔍
Approximate applicant pool: 75; Interns accepted: 20

COMPENSATION Ⓢ
Free room and board

LOCATION(S)
New York, NY; United Kingdom

FIELD
Public service

DURATION
9 weeks

DEADLINE(S)
January 31

THE WORK
Since 1948, Americans known as Winant Volunteers have traveled to Britain to provide community service. In like fashion, British volunteers, the Claytons, have come to the United States since 1959. Volunteers work with trained social workers on projects dealing with people of all ages and with a variety of needs: on playgrounds, settlement houses, rehabilitation centers, and neighborhood associations. Most volunteers are placed in inner-city London, and volunteer 40 hours a week.

PERKS
Winant volunteers receive ample amounts of leisure time, in which they explore the full spectrum of British life, from high culture to the every day, from the historic to the contemporary.

FYI
Says a former Winant volunteer: "My placement not only encouraged me to pursue a job working with the homeless; it also showed me how to be a 'master of goodwill.'"

TO APPLY
Winant Volunteers must be citizens of the United States. Clayton Volunteers must be citizens of the United Kingdom. Minimum age of 18.

American applicants:
Volunteer Coordinator
Winant-Clayton Volunteers
109 East 50th Street
New York, NY 10022
(212) 378-0271

British applicants:
Volunteer Coordinator
Winant-Clayton Volunteers
Davenant Centre
179 Whitechapel Road
London E1 1DU England
011-441-71-375-0547

WIRED

SELECTIVITY 🔍🔍🔍
Approximate applicant pool: 80; Interns accepted: 4–8

COMPENSATION Ⓢ
$25/week

LOCATION(S)
San Francisco, CA

FIELD
Magazines

DURATION
12 weeks: Summer, Fall, Spring

DEADLINE(S)
Rolling

THE WORK
Founded in 1993, *Wired* is a hip and vividly designed magazine covering "the most important phenomenon of our times, the Digital Revolution, for the people who are making it happen." With a circulation of almost 200,000 readers, *Wired* features the movers and shakers, companies, issues, and trends of the Computer Age. Interns work in Editorial, Advertising Sales, Production, and *Hot Wired* (online magazine).

PERKS
Attendance welcome at *Wired* staff meetings, parties, and social events; intern acknowledgement in magazine's masthead; young, casual office culture; free copies of the magazine.

FYI
Says a former intern: "At *Wired*, I felt like part of the cultural and digital revolution. [Interning at *Wired*] allows one to work among the minds that are at the forefront of the revolution." . . . *Wired* won the 1994 National Magazine Award for General Excellence.

TO APPLY
Open to high school students, high school grads, undergrads, recent college grads, college grads of any age, and grad students. International applicants eligible. Submit resume and cover letter.

Internship Coordinator
Wired
520 3rd Street, 4th Floor
San Francisco, CA 94107
(415) 276-5000
(415) 276-5100 (Fax)
E-mail: hotjobs@hotwired.com

WISH-TV 8
24 HOUR NEWS

SELECTIVITY 🔍🔍🔍
Approximate applicant pool: 350; Interns accepted: 40

COMPENSATION Ⓢ
None

LOCATION(S)
Indianapolis, IN

FIELD
Television

DURATION
3 terms: Summer, Fall, Winter, Spring

DEADLINE(S)
Rolling

THE WORK
A CBS affiliate, WISH-TV 8 broadcasts throughout central Indiana and ranks first in the region in news according to the Nielsen ratings. Interns work as News Writers/Reporters, Video Photographers, Production Assistants, and Graphic Artists as well as in Sports, Promotion, Sales, Engineering, Investigative-Team, and Marketing.

PERKS
Attendance welcome at employee functions and parties; tickets to station-sponsored events; access to major sporting event (Sports interns).

FYI
WISH-TV 8's internship program was created in 1974 . . . Interns in news, sports, photography, and production on all shifts including weekends, early mornings, or nights . . . Many former WISH-TV 8 interns are now working at the station—including reporters and one anchor.

TO APPLY
Open to college juniors and seniors as well as grad students. Must receive academic credit. Submit resume, cover letter, at least one writing sample, and videotapes of any television work (available).

Internship Coordinator
WISH-TV 8
1950 North Meridian Street
Indianapolis, IN 46202
(317) 923-8888
(317) 926-1144 (Fax)

WNBC-TV

See National Broadcasting Company

WNYC

AM820　FM93.9　TV31

SELECTIVITY 🔍🔍
Approximate applicant pool: 100; Interns accepted: 25

COMPENSATION
Stipend for daily transportation

LOCATION(S)
New York, NY

FIELD
Radio

DURATION
12–16 weeks: Summer, Fall, Spring

DEADLINE(S)
Rolling

 THE WORK

A nonprofit, public radio station, WNYC has been broadcasting to the New York Metropolitan Area since 1924. Over 500,000 people tune in each week to WNYC AM (820) and WNYC FM (93.9), to hear music programming, talk shows, news, and NPR segments. Interns work in Radio and TV Programming, Marketing, Radio Operations and Engineering, Facilities and Construction (i.e., architecture), Public Relations, and Membership.

PERKS
Orientation; upbeat, supportive staff.

FYI
WNYC's internship program was started in 1992 and has yet to hire any former interns . . . WNYC's internship brochure states: "Interns assume tasks commensurate with their abilities and take on higher level functions as skills are sharpened and new ones developed."

TO APPLY
Open to undergrads and grad students. International applicants eligible. Write for application.

Volunteer Internship Program
WNYC
1 Centre Street, 26th Floor
New York, NY 10007
(212) 669-7800
(212) 669-8986 (Fax)

WOLF TRAP FOUNDATION FOR THE PERFORMING ARTS

WOLF TRAP FOUNDATION
FOR THE PERFORMING ARTS

SELECTIVITY 🔍🔍🔍
Approximate applicant pool: 200; Interns accepted: 25

COMPENSATION
$1,800 (full time); $1,000 (part time)

LOCATION(S)
Vienna, VA

FIELD
Theater production; Arts management

DURATION
12 weeks: Summer (full time); Fall & Spring (part time)

DEADLINE
Summer: March 1; Fall: July 1; Spring: November 1

THE WORK

Situated on an expanse of Virginia farmland, the Wolf Trap Foundation for the Performing Arts is a little different than most major performance centers. Since its founding in 1968, the organization has attracted performers of every kind, including Bob Dylan, Ray Charles, Seal, and Tony Bennett. Interns are placed in the following departments: the Wolf Trap Opera (directing, administrative, stage management, technical), education, development special projects, communications, and marketing (advertising/marketing, graphic design ,publications, media relations, photography), human resources, accounting, box office/group sales, information systems, internet programs, special events/development events, associates, food and beverage/catering.

PERKS
Park setting; free tickets; brown-bags; diverse intern class.

FYI
The Wolf Trap Foundation for the Performing Arts is a large performing arts organization that presents a wide spectrum of the performing arts: music, dance, theatre, opera and related education programs. Wolf Trap presents over 200 performances year-round, Attracting more than 500,000 audience members annually. Wolf Trap's internship program provides meaningful hands-on training and experience in arts administration and technical theatre. The Josie A. Bass career development program is designed to provide intern experience in arts administration for qualified African American students.

TO APPLY
Open to college sophomores, juniors, seniors, recent grads, and grad students. Some programs have prerequisites. International applicants eligible. Submit resume, cover letter, two references, and two contrasting samples of writing.

Wolf Trap Foundation for the Performing Arts
Intern Coordinator
1624 Trap Road
Vienna, VA 22182
(703) 255-1933
(703) 255-1924 (fax)
www.wolf-trap.org

SELECTIVITY
Approximate applicant pool: 25; Interns accepted: 20

COMPENSATION
None, but workstudy available in special situations

LOCATION(S)
Boston, MA

FIELD
Public service

DURATION
12 weeks minimum: ongoing

DEADLINE(S)
Rolling

THE WORK
Women Express, Inc. is a nonprofit organization whose mission is to further social and economic justice by empowering teenage and young adult women through the publication of *Teen Voices*, an educational magazine by, for and about teenage women. Internship positions are available in Public Relations, Publishing, Fundraising, Editorial, Graphic Design, Advertising, Business and Accounting, and Office Management. Interns are expected to work at least 12 hours per week.

PERKS
Training in leadership skills and those specific to the department in which the intern works; opportunity to work with a dynamic and diverse group of women.

FYI
Writes a former intern: "It probably goes without saying, but Women Express provides an extremely supportive atmosphere for the women who work here."

TO APPLY
Open to women 18 years of age and older. Must be fluent in written English. International applicants eligible. Submit resume, cover letter, writing samples (for Editorial).

Internship Coordinator
Women Express, Inc.
P.O. Box 120-027
Boston, MA 02112-0027
(617) 426-5505
(617) 426-5577 (Fax)

SELECTIVITY
Approximate applicant pool: 60; Interns accepted: 15–20

COMPENSATION
None; paid transportation to and from office

LOCATION(S)
New York, NY

FIELD
Film; Video

DURATION
12 weeks: Summer, Fall, Spring

DEADLINE(S)
Rolling

THE WORK
Women Make Movies (WMM) is a nonprofit media arts organization dedicated to the production, promotion, distribution, and exhibition of films and videotapes by and about women. Founded in 1972 to address the under-representation and misrepresentation of women in the media, WMM is the leading distributor of women's films and videotapes in North America with a collection of more than 300 titles. Internship positions include Distribution/Promotions Assistant, General Office Intern, Production Assistant/Membership Services, and Special Project Intern.

PERKS
Free student membership (use of resource center, job board, screening room, discounts on workshops, advance notice of WMM events).

FYI
Alumni of the internship program include Debra Zimmerman, WMM's executive director.

TO APPLY
Open to high school students "on a case by case basis," high school grads, undergrads, recent college grads, college grads of any age, and grad students. International applicants eligible. Write for application.

Internship Coordinator
Women Make Movies
462 Broadway, 5th Floor
New York, NY 10013
(212) 925-0606
(212) 925-2052 (Fax)
E-mail: info@wmm.com
www.wmm.com

Women Express Director Alison Amoroso, teen members, and interns putting together an issue of *Teen Voices*.

WOMEN'S INSTITUTE FOR FREEDOM OF THE PRESS

SELECTIVITY 🔍
Approximate applicant pool: 10; Interns accepted: 6–8

COMPENSATION 💲
None

LOCATION(S)
Washington, DC

FIELD
Magazines; Women's studies

DURATION
Summer, Fall, Spring

DEADLINE(S)
Rolling

THE WORK
Founded in 1972, the Women's Institute for Freedom of the Press (WIFP) is a nonprofit organization seeking to increase communication among women and with the general public. It has published a monthly magazine, *Media Report to Women*. It now publishes an international directory of women's media, and a booklet series about media issues of special concern to women. Interns work in Research, Writing, Graphic Arts, Publications, and Archives.

PERKS
Trips to congressional hearings, Executive Department press conferences, State Department briefings, US Supreme Court arguments, and the Library of Congress.

FYI
According to the internship bulletin: "Approximately 50 percent of [interns'] time is spent on a project mutually agreeable to both intern and the Institute that will advance the studies and/or career of the intern."

TO APPLY
Open to high school students, high school grads, undergrads, recent college grads, college grads of any age, and grad students. International applicants eligible. Submit resume and cover letter. Encouraged to visit website first.

Internship Coordinator
Women's Institute for Freedom of the Press
1940 Clavert Street, NW
Washington, DC 20004
(202) 265-6707
(202) 966-7783 (Fax)
E-mail: director@wifp.org
www.wifp.org

WOMEN'S INTERNATIONAL LEAGUE FOR PEACE AND FREEDOM

SELECTIVITY 🔍🔍🔍🔍
Approximate applicant pool: 200; Interns accepted: 3–6 (NY), 7–12 (PA), 2 (Geneva)

COMPENSATION 💲💲
NY and PA: None; Geneva: SFr 600/month (approximately $450/month); round-trip travel, free housing

LOCATION(S)
Philadelphia, PA; New York, NY; Geneva, Switzerland

FIELD
Environment; Human rights; Peace studies; Women's issues

DURATION
NY: 12 weeks, ongoing (except for July and August); PA: 10–15 weeks, ongoing; Geneva: 11 months, starting in January

DEADLINE(S)
Geneva: May 15; NY and PA: rolling

THE WORK
Founded in 1915 by over 1,000 women, two of whom later won Nobel Peace Prizes, the Women's International League for Peace and Freedom (WILPF) is the world's oldest international women's organization, promoting political rather than military solutions to conflicts. Focusing on the impact of disarmament, environmentally sustainable development, racism, and human rights policies on women, WILPF publishes informational brochures and journals as well as collaborates with the UN agencies ECOSOC, UNCTAD, UNESCO, FAO, ILO, and UNICEF. Interns in NY and Geneva monitor UN meetings and briefings, prepare oral and written reports, and assist with administrative tasks. PA interns work in Publications (as editorial assistants for *Peace and Freedom*), Program, Fundraising, Membership, and Resources.

PERKS
Attendance welcome at WILPF press conferences; attendance at United Nations and NGO meetings; geographically diverse group of interns in Geneva.

FYI
WILPF launched its New York and Geneva internship programs in 1985 and 1981, respectively.

TO APPLY
Open to female high school students and high school grads (PA only), undergrads, and grad students. International applicants eligible. Submit resume, cover letter, writing sample (PA), letter of intention (NY), recommendations (Geneva), and 1,500–2,000 word essay describing reasons for wanting internship, area of interest (disarmament or human rights), and plans after the internship (Geneva).

Director
WILPF Office at the United Nations
777 United Nations Plaza, 6th Floor
New York, NY 10017
(212) 682-1265
(212) 286-8211 (Fax)
E-mail: wilpfnatl@igc.org
Director
WILPF International Secretariat
1, rue de Varembé, CP 28
CH-1211 Geneva 20, Switzerland
41-22-733-615
41-22-740-1063 (Fax)

Internship Coordinator
WILPF National Office
1213 Race Street
Philadelphia, PA 19107
(215) 563-7110
(215) 563-5527 (Fax)

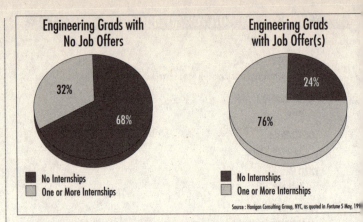

Source : Hanigan Consulting Group, NYC, as quoted in *Fortune 5 May, 199*

WOMEN'S PROJECT & PRODUCTIONS

SELECTIVITY 🔍 🔍 🔍
Approximate applicant pool: 200; Interns accepted: 15–20

COMPENSATION Ⓢ
None

LOCATION(S)
New York, NY

FIELD
Theater; Women's issues

DURATION
Minimum 12 weeks

DEADLINE(S)
Accept interns continually throughout the year.

THE WORK
Founded in 1978, Women's Project & Productions (WPP) is an Off-Broadway theater in its 21st Anniversary Season that develops the work of women playwrights and directors. Along with staging three mainstage productions annually, WPP offers a Director's Forum, a Playwright's Lab, a high school outreach playwriting program, rehearsed readings, and staged readings. Interns work in Administration, Development, Marketing, Education, Production, and Literary Management.

PERKS
Attendance welcome at all WPP productions, readings, and seminars; free tickets to other productions and readings.

FYI
In existence since 1987, the internship program counts among its alumni the playwrights Kate Moira Ryan, Kia Corthron, and Chiori Miyagawa.

TO APPLY
Open to high school grads, college and graduate students of any age. Men are welcome. Write for application:

Internship Coordinator
Women's Project & Productions
55 West End Avenue
New York, NY 10023
(212) 765-1706
(212) 765-2024 (Fax)

WOMEN'S SPORTS FOUNDATION

25 Years of Making a Difference

SELECTIVITY 🔍 🔍
Approximate applicant pool: 200/year; Interns accepted: 45/year

COMPENSATION Ⓢ Ⓢ
Full time: $450–700/month stipend; part time: $5/day transportation reimbursement; Zina Garrison and Jackie Joyner Kersee interns: $1,000/month stipend

LOCATION(S)
East Meadow, Long Island, NY

FIELD
Sports education

DURATION
3–6 months or more: Summer, Fall, Winter, Spring

DEADLINE(S)
Rolling

THE WORK
The Women's Sports Foundation (WSF) was founded in 1974 by Billie Jean King and other elite women athletes to improve the physical and emotional well-being of females through sports and fitness participation. Interns work in Education, Public Relations, Advocacy, Special Events, Marketing, Administration, Publications, and Athlete Services. Some students intern at WSF under the auspices of the Zina Garrison and Jackie Joyner-Kersee minority programs.

PERKS
Out of office meetings with staff, especially Donna Lopiano. All former interns receive *The Women's Sports Experience* free; and attendance is welcome at WSF Annual Conference and New York Dinner.

FYI
Academic-year interns receive an extra $100/month . . . Since the internship program's inception in 1982, over 350 interns have worked at WSF, including Nancy Hogshead, a three-time Olympic Gold Medal swimmer and former president of WSF's Board of Trustees, and Julie Croteau, the first woman to play intercollegiate baseball.

TO APPLY

Open to undergrads, recent college grads, college grads of any age, and grad students. International applicants (students only) eligible. Call for application or visit the website..

Internship Coordinator
Women's Sports Foundation
Eisenhower Park
East Meadow, NY 11554
(516) 542-4700 or (800) 227-3988
www.womenssportsfoundation.org

WOODROW WILSON INTERNATIONAL CENTER FOR SCHOLARS

SELECTIVITY 🔍🔍🔍🔍
Approximate applicant pool: 700–800; Interns accepted: 60

COMPENSATION 💲
For credit; $5/hour, 16 hours/week

LOCATION(S)
Washington, DC

FIELD
Academic research; Social sciences; Public policy

DURATION
12 weeks: Summer; 9 months: Fall/Spring

DEADLINE(S)
Summer: March 20; Fall/Spring: August 1

THE WORK

Established by Congress in 1968, the Woodrow Wilson International Center for Scholars is the nation's official "living memorial" to the 28th president. The Center awards approximately 35 residential fellowships to scholars in the social sciences and humanities and invites a number of Public Affairs scholars to carry on research. Interns serve as research assistants to one or two Center Fellows or staff members.

PERKS

Attendance welcome at discussions, colloquia, and seminars; access to center library and area libraries.

FYI

The center is independently housed in the Reagan Building in Washington, DC.

TO APPLY

Open to college juniors and seniors, recent college grads, and grad students. Minimum GPA: 3.0. International applicants eligible when they are registered US college students (1-F student visa). Submit cover letter, transcript, and two faculty recommendations.

Internship Office
Woodrow Wilson International Center for Scholars
One Woodrow Wilson Plaza
1300 Pennsylvania Avenue NW
Washington, DC 20004-3027
(202) 691-4000
(202) 691-4001 (Fax)
E-mail: benamin@wwic.si.edu

Striving to break into the radio business after graduating from Eureka College in 1932, **Ronald Reagan** journeyed to Chicago and begged the major stations there for an entry-level sports announcer's position. They all said no, citing his lack of experience. But one woman recommended that he start in "the sticks," her name for small radio stations outside of Chicago. Heeding this advice, he headed to station WOC in Davenport, Iowa, where the program director asked him on the spot to announce an imaginary football game. A college football player, Reagan began describing a football game in which he had played. The director loved Reagan's impassioned performance and hired the young man as a sportscasting intern to announce the next four U. of Iowa games for $35. A few months after the internship ended, WOC hired Reagan as a full-time announcer, a job he held for the next four years.

WORK EXPERIENCE OUTBOUND

SELECTIVITY
Interns accepted: 400 per program.

COMPENSATION
Regular work wages—will vary depending on job type

LOCATION(S)
Australia and New Zealand

FIELD
Any

DURATION
New Zealand: Summer June–September
Australia: 4 months, year-round

DEADLINE(S)
Australia: rolling deadline

THE WORK

Work Experience Outbound provides sponsorship for work/travel experiences in Australia and New Zealand. Participants live independently and are able to work legally and travel throughout the country.

PERKS

The opportunity to visit another country and experience life abroad. Orientation, supportive home office, emergency hotline.

FYI

Work Experience Outbound is designated an Exchange Visitor Program sponsored by the United States Information Agency.

TO APPLY

New Zealand: 18–30 years of age and full-time students. Australia: 18–25 years of age. E-mail or call for an application:

Work Experience, Outbound Program
2330 Marinship Way, Suite 250
Sausalito, CA 94965
(800) 999-2267
Email: Outbound@workexperienceusa.com
www.workexperienceoutbound.com

WORKING MOTHER

See MacDonald Communications Corp.

WORKING WOMAN

See MacDonald Communications Corp.

WORLD FEDERALIST ASSOCIATION

SELECTIVITY   🔍 🔍 🔍
Approximate applicant pool: 200; Interns accepted: 20

COMPENSATION   Ⓢ
$10/day

LOCATION(S)
Washington, DC (HQ)

FIELD
Environment; Foreign affairs

DURATION
Summer, Fall, Spring

DEADLINE(S)
Rolling

THE WORK
The World Federalist Association (WFA) is a nonprofit organization dedicated to the empowerment of the United Nations so it is capable of preventing war, protecting the global environment, and ending international terrorism. WFA's accomplishments include stimulating debate on the proposal for an International Criminal Court, participating in the Rio de Janeiro Earth Summit, sponsoring the Global Structures Convocation on Human Rights, and authoring legislation proposed in both houses of Congress. Interns work on WFA's national activist program, The Partners for Global Change, as well as policy research, communications, fundraising, and student outreach. WFA was founded in 1947 and has 10,000 members.

PERKS

Field trips to cultural sites in DC; lots of responsibility.

FYI
WFA's DC headquarters is located seven blocks from the US Capitol building . . . The founders of WFA include Albert Einstein, former US Supreme Court Justice William O. Douglas, and US Senator Alan Cranston.

TO APPLY
Open to undergrads and recent college grads. International applicants eligible. Submit resume, cover letter, and writing samples.

Internship Coordinator
World Federalist Association
418 7th Street SE
Washington, DC 20003-2796
(202) 546-3950
(202) 546-3749 (Fax)

WORLDNET

SELECTIVITY   🔍 🔍
Approximate applicant pool: 100; Interns accepted: 25

COMPENSATION   Ⓢ
None

LOCATION(S)
Washington, DC

FIELD
Television

DURATION
6–12 weeks: Summer, Fall, Spring

DEADLINE(S)
Rolling

THE WORK

As the television counterpart to Voice of America (see separate entry), the federal government's radio broadcasting system, Worldnet is the television broadcasting arm of the US Government. It acquires, produces, and distributes television programs to countries across the world. Worldnet's television programs cover art and literature, current events, entertainment, human rights, language telecourses, science and technology, and US society. Interns work in the Production department.

PERKS
Access to gym.

FYI
Worldnet began in 1983, when it broadcast an interactive press conference on the Grenada rescue mission. The conference

---

As a sophomore at Tennessee State University in 1974, **Oprah Winfrey** probably knew that she had sufficient oratorial skill and charisma to appear on television. She was majoring in speech and drama. In her freshman year, she had been crowned Miss Black Tennessee. And at 16 had won an Elks Club speaking contest, providing her with a full scholarship to college. But Winfrey wanted to become a producer and applied for an internship at Nashville's CBS affiliate, WTVF-TV. "She was absolutely cute as a button", Harold Crump, then WTF's station managr, told us. "I mean a real doll. She had a nice voice and nice personality, so the news director and I attempted to persuede her to go on camera." But Winfrey protested. "She had no desire to be infront of the camera at all," said Crump.

For the next four months, intern Winfrey wrote stories, answered the phones, and dubbed tapes. But Crump didn't give up on trying to put her on the air. "I made her an offer", he said. "I would pay for her to see a [television and voice] coach...for a few months and cut an audition tape". Winfrey relented and, upon returning to the station, decided she would give being on air a try. Crump couldn't have been more pleased: "I looked at that tape and thought, 'Boy, this is wonderful.'" So Winfrey moved from intern to co-anchor on WTVF's weekend news, a year later moving to WTVF's weekday evening news. Crump never had a doubt that she would one day be successgul. "I had a hunch...," he says," and this is the one time in my life that it worked.

linked Jeane Kirkpatrick, then-US Ambassador to the United Nations, with two Caribbean prime ministers in the Bahamas and journalists in six European capitals.

TO APPLY
Open to undergrads and grad students. International applicants eligible. Write for application.

Internship Coordinator
Worldnet
Room 1543
HHS-N Buiding
330 Independence Avenue SW
Washington, DC 20547
(202) 619-3117

WORLDTEACH

SELECTIVITY 🔍
Approximate applicant pool: 800; Interns accepted: 300

COMPENSATION 💲
Stipend covering daily living expenses; fee: $3,990–$5,990; limited financial aid available

LOCATION(S)
China; Costa Rica; Ecuador; Namibia; Mexico; Honduras; Thailand; South Africa

FIELD
Teaching

DURATION
1 year, 6 months, and summer

DEADLINE(S)
Rolling admissions; see website for departure information.

THE WORK
A nonprofit organization based at Harvard University, WorldTeach places volunteers as teachers in developing countries around the world. Working in both rural and urban areas, volunteers serve as full-time, professional teachers at elementary schools, high schools, teaching colleges, universities, technical institutes, and adult education programs. Volunteers either live with a local family, share a house with other teachers, or have their own apartments, depending on the country.

PERKS
Country-specific information sent before departure; in-country orientation; mid-year and end-year conferences; reference provided upon completion of program.

FYI
Summer teaching opportunities in China for undergrads are also available. Call WorldTeach for more details.

TO APPLY
Open to college grads; summer teaching program open to undergraduates as well. International applicants eligible. Write or visit website to print application.

WorldTeach Center
c/o Harvard Institute for International Development
79 JFK Street
Cambridge, MA 02138
(617) 495–5527
(617) 495–1599(Fax)
E-mail: info@worldteach.org
www.worldteach.org

WRITERS GUILD OF AMERICA, WEST

SELECTIVITY   N/A
Approximate applicant pool: 100; Interns accepted: 60

COMPENSATION 💲💲💲💲
$672/week

LOCATION(S)
Los Angeles, CA

FIELD
Television

DURATION
6–20 weeks

DEADLINE(S)
Rolling

THE WORK
The Writers Guild of America (WGA), West is the sole collective bargaining representative for writers in the motion picture, television, and radio industries. Interns (called "writer trainees" by WGA) arrange to work as writers with any Guild-member company or studio that produces episodic, prime-time television programming in its second or subsequent season (e.g., *Beverly Hills, 90210, Dream On, Star Trek, Frasier,* and *Seinfeld*).

PERKS
Mentors (professional TV/film writers); interaction with producers, directors, and actors.

FYI
Founded in 1987, WGA's trainee program is "so far, the best vehicle for providing employment opportunities for women and minorities who have historically been underrepresented as industry writers." . . . Approximately 60 percent of former trainees land jobs as writers; former trainees include writers on *The Cosby Show, In Living Color,* and *Family Matters.*

TO APPLY
Open to high school students 18 years and older, high school grads, undergrads, recent college grads, college grads of any age, and grad students. Must be a woman, Latino, African American, Asian American, American Indian, Eskimo, disabled, or over 40 years of age. International applicants eligible. Write or call for an information letter.

Writers Guild of America, West
Employment Access Department
7000 W Third Street
Los Angeles, CA 90048
(323) 782-4648

XEROX

SELECTIVITY 🔍🔍🔍🔍🔍
Approximate applicant pool: 3,500; Interns accepted: 100–250

COMPENSATION 💲💲💲💲
$450–$725/week for undergrads; $700–$900/week for grad students

LOCATION(S)
El Segundo, Palo Alto, San Diego, CA; Rochester, Webster (HQ), NY

FIELD
Consumer goods (photocopiers); Computers

DURATION
Intern: 10–12 weeks, Summer; Co-op: at least two 3–6 month sessions, ongoing

DEADLINE(S)
Intern: March 1; Co-op: rolling

THE WORK

Founded in 1906 as Haloid, Xerox is a global company in the document processing business. Xerox Corporation offers the widest array of products and consulting services in the industry: publishing systems, copiers, printers, scanners, fax machines and document management software, along with related products and services. Xerox products and services are all designed to help customers master the flow of information from paper to electronic form and back again. The Xerox customer is anyone who uses documents: Fortune 500 corporations and small companies; public agencies and universities; businesses run from home. CA interns (summer only) work in the Production Systems Group, Document Systems Group, Office Systems Group, Corporate Strategic Services, Office Document Systems, Xerox Special Information Systems, Xerox Research and Technology as well as the Xerox Palo Alto Research Center (see separate entry). Interns in NY (summer and co-op) work in nine divisions including Customer Operations, Production Systems Group, Document Systems Group, Office Systems Group, Corporate Strategic Services, Office Document Systems and Xerox Research and Technology.

PERKS

Weekly seminars on resume writing, succeeding in corporate America, leadership through quality, etc.; tours of Xerox facilities; access to Xerox fitness centers; organized social activities (e.g., banquets, picnic, beach luau).

Paul A. Allaire, Chairman and CEO of Xerox, tests a handwriting recognition experiment devised by Xerox PARC intern Cate Richardson. Intern Mike Hopcroft looks on.

TO APPLY

Must be currently enrolled as a full-time student in an accredited degree program; must be enrolled as a full-time student in the quarter/semester immediately following the summer. Majors accepted include computer science, computer engineering, electrical engineering, industrial engineering and mechanical engineering for our technical positions and business administration, marketing, finance and accounting for our non-engineering positions. The timeframe for internships is based on student availability, generally May through September. Submit resume and cover letter directly to the website at www.xerox.com/employment.

XEROX PALO ALTO RESEARCH CENTER

SELECTIVITY 🔍🔍🔍
Approximate applicant pool: 500; Interns accepted: 50

COMPENSATION 💲💲💲💲
$700–$1,000/week

LOCATION(S)
Palo Alto, CA

FIELD
Computer research

DURATION
13 weeks: Summer, Fall

DEADLINE(S)
February 14

THE WORK

Established in 1970, the Xerox Palo Alto Research Center (Xerox PARC) is one of Xerox' four crystalized research centers engaged in pioneering computer science and microelectronics physics research. Its inventions include the optical "mouse," bit-mao graphics, display-list graphics, windows, icons, the ethernet, the first graphics oriented monitor, the first layperson's word processing program, the first laser printer, the Alto, the first personal computer and diode lasers. Generally considered one of the most influential research labs, Xerox PARC is investigating the social and organizational effects of computers, conducting research on smart matter, workscapes of the future and the next generation HTTP and developing blue laser diodes, intelligent white boards, and computers the size of key tags. Assigned to one of the several work teams, interns work alongside PhDed scientists in all PARC's research areas.

PERKS

Luncheons with scientific thought leaders; field trips to other local research centers; access to company gym and subsidized cafeteria.

FYI

Xerox PARC's internship program commenced in 1973 . . . Says the internship coordinator: "Interns have a chance to make real contributions in their fields and see their work taken seriously by world-famous researchers. They may even have a hand in inventing technologies."

TO APPLY

Open to grad students in Computer Science, Electrical Engineering, physics, or math. International applicants eligible. Submit application via the Web at the following URL.

www.parc.xerox.com/parc/summerterns
or
Call Lorna Fear, Program Coordinator
(650) 812–4813
Email: fear@parc.xerox.com

YELLOWSTONE NATIONAL PARK

See National Park Service

Y.E.S. TO JOBS

SELECTIVITY 🔍 🔍
Approximate applicant pool: 1,300; Interns accepted: 300

COMPENSATION 💲 💲 💲 💲
$215/week

LOCATION(S)
Atlanta, GA; Chicago, IL and surrounding suburbs; Dallas, TX; Detroit, MI; Los Angeles and San Francisco, CA; Miami, FL; Eden Prairie, MN; New York, NY; Nashville, TN; Seattle, WA; Washington D.C.

FIELD
Film; Law; Public relations; Record labels; Television

DURATION
10 weeks: Summer

DEADLINE(S)
April 1

THE WORK
Founded in 1987 by A&M Records, Y.E.S. To Jobs provides summer employment in the entertainment industry—including public relations of entertainment law firms—for minority high school students. Over fifty companies participate, including A&M, Blockbuster, Capitol Records, CNN, E! Entertainment, HBO, MTV, Sony Pictures, Ticketmaster, and Warner Music Groups. Interns work in Publicity, Marketing, Finance, Sales, Development, Promotion, Artist Development, Graphics, MIS, Creative, Telecommunications, Personnel, and Legal.

PERKS
Biweekly enrichment seminars and career workshops; intern newsletter "YES Press" and culmination activities.

FYI
Approximately 20 percent of former interns land full-time jobs in the entertainment industry after graduating from high school or college. Former interns include Eric Reed, a jazz pianist; Michael Koger, Manager of traffic- FOX Broadcasting; Keri Cooper, MTV Networks; Morgan Fouch, Turner Classic Movies; Enrique Maitland, Anslem Samuels, and *The Source* magazine.

TO APPLY
Open to minority high school students 16–18 years of age. Requirements are minimum GPA 2.5 and 90 percent percent attendance in school. Interested students can pick-up an application from the career counselor at your high school or write to Y.E.S. TO JOBS for an application.

Y.E.S. To JOBS
P.O. Box 3390
Los Angeles, CA 90078-3390
E-mail: yestojobs@aol.com
www.yestojobs.org

HIGH SCHOOL STUDENTS INTERESTED IN ENTERTAINMENT: SAY Y.E.S. TO Jobs

Eric Reed, a jazz pianist, is a former member of the Wynton Marsalis Septet and now the leader of the Eric Reed Trio. His albums include *The Swing And I* and *It's All Right To Swing* (both on MoJazz, a division of Motown).
Eric's story:

"I was a junior at Westchester High School in Los Angeles, in the choir, when one day, I got this form from Y.E.S. to Jobs. I filled it out, did an interview, and landed a placement at A&M Records. This was the summer of 1987. I worked in Sales for A&M's classical label, Nimbus, and did mostly promotional things, like send out CDs or information on the label to radio stations . . . When I was interning, I saw a side of entertainment—the business—that I never saw as a performer. I learned how music is marketed and promoted. So now, when I look at my own product and I see a typo on a CD or I get some line on how something can't be done, I know what really happened and what to do to get it done. The departments are pretty isolated and when there's a glitch somewhere, say in a picture, I know which department to go to."

Terrance Quaites (top right corner) is the lead singer for the R&B a cappella group, Coming of Age. The bands records include "Coming of Age" (Zoo Entertainment) and "Comin' Correct" (Holland Dozier Holland).
Terrance's story:

"In the summer of '92, after my junior year in high school, Y.E.S. to Jobs placed me at A&M Records, and every seminar, I would ask the speaker, "How do you get a record deal?" even when the seminar had nothing to do with records. That didn't get me very far, but a few months into my senior year, I contacted this connection I had made at Y.E.S. to Jobs, the president of Platinum Plus in Los Angeles. It turned out that she had a group in Atlanta who needed a lead singer, so I sang for her over the phone. She loved it, and we proceeded to call her partner in Atlanta—at 2 am. I sang to him, and he loved it, so I became their lead singer."

EXCLUSIVE INTERVIEW WITH TOM LEHMAN

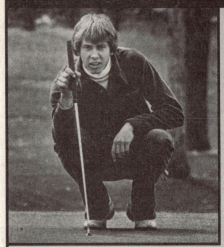

Tom Lehman is a professional golfer whose achievements include winning the The Memorial Tournament in Dublin, Ohio and placing second at both The Masters in Augusta, GA and The Hawaiian Open in Honolulu. Winner of the 1996 British Open, he was named PGA Player of the Year. He graduated with a B.A. from the University of Minnesota in 1982. At left, a young Lehman takes time off from his internship to shoot a round.

The Internship Informants: We read that you served an internship in the athletic department of the University of Minnesota. How did this internship come about?

Lehman: During the '81-'82 academic year, my [athletic] eligibility was finished. Being an athlete, I knew the fundraising head of the athletic department, Tom Barron, pretty well. So I asked him if I could work as his intern, and [I] ended up assisting him with organizing fund-raisers and sending out mailings. The year that I worked, it was the 100th anniversary of the University of Minnesota's football program, so we put together a big yearbook for it. I was also in charge of all of the direct sales of the yearbook.

The Internship Informants: What did you get out of this internship?

Lehman: It was good to see how a major university's athletic department works. When you're a [college] athlete, you take for granted that there's money to pay for the trips and money to pay for the training. But when you work on the inside, you see how the money has to be raised, and you realize that a lot depends on alumni and other people who support the program. Raising money like that is not always an easy task. To see it in action was an eye-opener.

The Internship Informants: Has the internship influenced your relationship with the school and the athletic department now that you're an alum?

Lehman: Oh, definitely. At the time [of the internship], I didn't have any money at all, so I wasn't involved with the giving part of it. As I've gotten older and a little more successful, I realize that it's people who are in my position now who make [college athletic] programs work...It's like a revolving door. I realize that it's my obligation to reach back down to where I was and support those kids who are just starting out.

The Internship Informants: Are there things you do in golf that are applicable to doing well on the job, doing well in an internship?

Lehman: Sure. First of all, you have to have belief in your ability. You have to feel that the way you do the job is good enough to get the job done and done well, so that you aren't changing your method all of the time. Believing in yourself and sticking to what you think works is very important. More than that, if money is your only motivation, I don't think you'll ever do the job properly. But if your motivation is to provide the best service or do the best job you can, then the money part of it should follow. That's one thing I learned from [my internship] with Tom Barron. He really knew how to do things properly. He had a passion for his job and always gave people their money's worth.

YMCA

SELECTIVITY 🔍
Approximate applicant pool: N/A; Interns accepted: 300–500

COMPENSATION 💲
None

LOCATION(S)
Cities in all 50 states of the US

FIELD
Education; Recreation

DURATION
8 weeks minimum: ongoing

DEADLINE(S)
Rolling

THE WORK
An American institution immortalized by the Village People, the YMCA was founded in 1844 to offer community programs promoting Christian values. Accepting people of all faiths, races, abilities, ages, and incomes, the Y operates in 122 countries, servicing over 30 million men, women, and children annually with swimming lessons, youth basketball games, exercise classes, day camps, child care, substance abuse prevention programs, family nights, and job training. Many of the 2,100 Y's in the US offer internships and volunteer positions in recreation, child development, health & fitness, camping, job training, youth mentoring, and family programs. At the YMCA of Greater New York, for example, twelve to sixteen interns work in UN Projects, Educational Programs, and Educational Travel and Tourism, Communications, Marketing, Fundraising, and as Small Group Facilitators and Airport Greeters for the International Camp Counselor Program (see separate entry).

PERKS
Orientation; attendance welcome at Y staff meetings and activities; free t-shirts and other Y paraphernalia.

FYI
The Overseas Service Corps of the YMCA places college grads as English teachers at Y's throughout Japan and Taiwan . . . YMCA is an acronym for Young Men's Christian Association . . . The YMCA of Greater New York's Multinational Leadership Training Program places nonUS citizens 18 and older in internships in education, social service, camp or hotel management, finance, and health care throughout the United States.

TO APPLY
Open to undergrads and recent college grads. International applicants eligible. Submit resume and cover letter directly to Y of interest. Contact the nearest Y or YMCA's US headquarters for addresses and phone numbers.

YMCA of the USA
101 North Wacker Drive
Chicago, IL 60606
(800) 872-9622 or (312) 977-0031

Internship Coordinator
YMCA of Greater New York
71 West 23rd Street, Suite 1904
New York, NY 10010
(212) 727-8800
(212) 727-8814 (Fax)

YOSEMITE NATIONAL PARK

SELECTIVITY 🔍🔍🔍
Approximate applicant pool: 300; Interns accepted: 25–30

COMPENSATION 💲💲💲
$50/week stipend; $1,000 scholarship on successful completion of program; free housing (from tent cabins to shared houses); round-trip travel not to exceed $300; uniforms provided

LOCATION(S)
Yosemite National Park, CA

FIELD
Park management

DURATION
12 weeks: summer, spring

DEADLINE(S)
February 1

THE WORK
Yosemite National Park comprises nearly 800,000 acres of wilderness in California and welcomes nearly 4 million visitors from all over the world each year. The Yosemite Association, a nonprofit organization that provides financial support to the park, sponsors the intern program. Positions are available in natural and cultural resources interpretation and in wilderness management. Interns in interpretation prepare and lead nature walks and campfire programs on such topics as geology, plant or forest ecology, astronomy, and pioneer history. Interns in wilderness management issue backcountry permits and discuss weather conditions, equipment, and trail conditions with hikers.

PERKS
Enrollment in one Yosemite Association seminar free of charge; books, maps, and other materials about Yosemite; privilege card offering discounts with the park concessioner.

FYI
An internship through the Yosemite Association improves the odds of gaining seasonal employment with the National Park Service.

TO APPLY
Open to college juniors and seniors. International applicants eligible. Preference is given to applicants who work through their colleges or universities to obtain credit for the internship and who have major professor involvement.

Yosemite Association Student Internship Coordinator
National Park Service
P.O. Box 2027
Wawona, CA 95389
(209) 375-9505

Youth For Understanding
International Exchange

SELECTIVITY
Approximate applicant pool: 250; Interns accepted: 85

COMPENSATION
Reimbursement of daily travel expenses

LOCATION(S)
Boston, MA; Bridgeport, MI; Columbus, OH; Des Moines, IA; Edmonds, WA; Glen Ellyn, IL; Houston, TX; Indianapolis, IN; Los Altos, CA; Washington, DC (HQ)

FIELD
Education

DURATION
6–10 weeks: ongoing

DEADLINE(S)
Rolling

THE WORK
Established in 1951, Youth For Understanding International Exchange (YFU) is a nonprofit organization offering exchange programs in 40 countries to over 5,000 high school students every year. YFU programs include academic exchanges and Sport for Understanding, a sports-oriented homestay program for high school athletes wishing to compete against sports teams overseas. DC interns/volunteers work in Marketing & Recruitment, Public Affairs & Development, Information Systems, Finance, International Publications, and Human Services. Interns in regional offices (approximately two to three per office) help select families for visiting non-American students, make presentations to local high schools, and conduct administrative tasks.

FYI
Established in 1982, the internship program counts among its alumni YFU's Director of Outbound Programs.

TO APPLY
Open to high school juniors and seniors, high school grads, undergrads, recent college grads, college grads of any age, and grad students. International applicants eligible. Submit resume, cover letter, and writing sample (DC only). Call 1-800-TEENAGE to be connected to the nearest US regional office.

Internship Coordinator
Youth For Understanding International Exchange
3501 Newark Street NW
Washington, DC 20016
(800) 424-3691, x116
(202) 895-1104 (Fax)

YSB (YOUNG SISTERS & BROTHERS)

See Black Entertainment Television

ZOO ENTERTAINMENT

See Bertelsmann Music Group

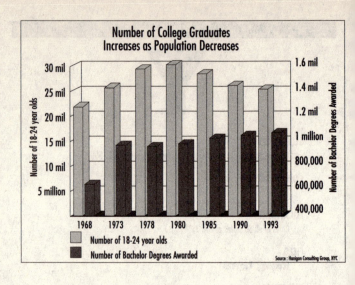

Number of College Graduates Increases as Population Decreases

- Number of 18-24 year olds
- Number of Bachelor Degrees Awarded

Source: Hanigan Consulting Group, NYC

THE TOP TEN INTERNSHIPS IN AMERICA FOR THE YEAR 2001

Academy of Television Arts & Sciences

❦

The Coro Foundation

❦

CNN

❦

Hewlett Packard

❦

Inroads

❦

Northwestern Mutual Life

❦

Procter & Gamble

❦

Summerbridge International

❦

The Supreme Court of the United States

❦

The Washington Post

❦

❦

Source: Mark Oldman and Samer Hamadeh, *The Best 106 Internships*
(Random House/Princeton Review)

APPENDIX

INTERNSHIPS WITH THE HIGHEST COMPENSATION

Abbott Laboratories
Aetna Life Inc.
The Boston Globe
BP
Chevron
Citibank
Deloitte & Touche
Dow Chemical Company
Du Pont
Eastman Kodak Company
Exxon
The Ford Foundation
Ford Motor Company
Frito-Lay
General Mills
GMC Truck
GTE
Hallmark Cards
Hewitt Associates
Hewlett-Packard
Inroads
Intel
J.P. Morgan & Co.
Kraft Foods, Inc.
Lawrence Livermore National Laboratory
Lincoln Center for the Performing Arts
Mattel Toys
Merck & Company
Microsoft
Miller Brewing Company
Morrison & Foerster
Nabisco
National Consortium for Graduate Degrees for Minorities in Engineering and Science
National Security Agency
The New York Times
Newsday/New York Newsday
Newsweek
Octel Communications
Office of Job Corps
Oldsmobile
Oscar Mayer Wienermobile
Peace Corps
Peggy Guggenheim Collection
Pella
Pfizer
The Philadelphia Inquirer
Pro-Found Software
Rand
Raychem
Reebok
Renew America
St. Paul's School
San Francisco Chronicle
Schlumberger
SGI
The Southwestern Company
Sponsors for Educational Opportunity
State Teachers Retirement System of Ohio
Student Works Painting
Symantec Corporation
Tellabs
Texas Instruments
Union Carbide
United States Senate Youth Program
Varsity Student Painters
The Wall Street Journal
The Washington Post
Weyerhauser
Writers Guild of America, West
Xerox
Xerox Palo Alto Research Center

MOST SELECTIVE INTERNSHIPS

Abbott Laboratories
The Academy for Advanced and Strategic Studies
Academy of Television Arts & Sciences
Actors Theatre of Louisville
Advocates for Children of New York
Aigner Associates
American Bar Association
American Civil Liberties Union
American Committee on Africa/The Africa Fund
American Forests
Anchorage Daily News
Anheuser-Busch
Aperture Foundation
Apple Computer
Assistant Directors Training Program
Association of Trial Lawyers of America
Bernstein-Rein
Betsey Johnson
Black Enterprise
The Blade
Boeing
Bozell Public Relations
Brooklyn Museum
Brown·Miller Communications
Bucks County Courier Times
California State Senate
The Callaghan Group
Callaway Advanced Technology

Center for Coastal Studies
Chicago Bulls
The Citizens Network for Foreign Affairs
The Conservative Caucus
Council on Hemispheric Affairs
Creamer Dickson Basford
Crown Capital
Dallas Cowboys
Davis Hays & Co.
DesignTech International
Du Pont
Dykeman Associates
Edelman Public Relations Worldwide
Federal Bureau of Investigation
Federal Reserve Bank of New York
Forbes
The Ford Foundation
Forty Acres and a Mule Filmworks
Gensler
GTE
Hallmark Cards
Hill and Holiday Advertising, Inc.
Hoffman-La Roche
Insurance Services Office
International Creative Management
The International Foundation for Education & Self-Help
The Jim Henson Company
John Wiley & Sons
KCSA Public Relations
Lake Charles American Press
Late Show with David Letterman
The Library of Congress
Lincoln Center for the Performing Arts
Lucasfilm/LucasDigital
Maine State Music Theatre
Makovsky & Company
Manhattan Theater Club
Merck & Company
Merrill Lynch
Miller Brewing Company
The Milwaukee Journal Sentinel
Miss Porter's School
Mother Jones
The Nation
The National Audobon Society
National Center for Fair and Open Testing
National Collegiate Athletic Association
National Endowment for the Humanities
National Football League
National Journal
National Review
National Wildlife Federation
National Women's Health Network
The New Republic
The Newshour with Jim Lehrer
Newsweek
The New York Times
Nightline

NIKE
Northwestern Mutual Financial Network
NOW Legal Defense and Education Fund
Octel Communications
Oklahoma Redhawks Baseball Club
Open City Films
Oscar Mayer Wienermobile
Ove Arup & Partners
The Paris Review
Pella
Pittsburgh Post-Gazette
Playhouse on the Square
PMK Public Relations
Pro-Found Software
Quaker United Nations Office
Raychem
Reebok
Renew America
Rolling Stone
Rosenbluth International
Ruder-Finn
San Diego Zoo
San Francisco Chronicle
San Francisco 49ers
Savvy Management
Science News
The Seattle Times
Student Works Painting
Supreme Court of the United States
Symantec Corporation
Tellabs
Tyco Toys
United Talent Agency
Varsity Student Painters
The Wall Street Journal
Wall Street Music
Washington Office on Latin America
The Washington Post
Wells Fargo Bank
WGN-Chicago
The Widmeyer Baker Group
The Wilson Quarterly
Xerox

SEPTEMBER

Central Intelligence Agency

OCTOBER

Dow Chemical Company

NOVEMBER

Assistant Directors Training Program
The Boston Globe (Editorial Summer program only)
Central Intelligence Agency
The Dow Jones Newspaper Fund
Essence
Exxon
Federal Bureau of Investigation
International Radio and Television Society
The Milwaukee Journal Sentinel
National Security Agency
San Francisco Chronicle
The Seattle Times
Teach for America (early admission)
The Wall Street Journal
The Washington Post

DECEMBER

American Society of Magazine Editors
Assistant Directors Training Program
Association for Education in Journalism
AT&T Bell Laboratories (SRP program only)
Du Pont
The Gazette Company
Inroads
Japanese Exchange and Teaching Program
Lawrence Livermore National Laboratory
Longwood Gardens
Los Angeles Times
Magazine Publishers of America
The Milwaukee Journal
National Aeronautics and Space Administration
National Consortium for Graduate Degrees for Minorities in
   Engineering and Science
National Review
The New York Times
Newsweek
NOW Legal Defense and Education Fund (1st-year law students)
Peggy Guggenheim Collection
The Philadelphia Inquirer
Pittsburgh Post-Gazette
3M
United States Environmental Protection Agency
Washington Internships for Students of Engineering

JANUARY

American Association for the Advancement of Science
American Association of Advertising Agencies
The American-Scandinavian Foundation
Anchorage Daily News
AT&T Bell Laboratories (UR program only)
The Blade
Boeing
Brookhaven National Laboratory
Carnegie Endowment for International Peace
Center for Coastal Studies
Chevron
Congressional Hispanic Caucus Institute
The Coro Foundation
Death Valley
Duke University Talent Identification Program
Ernst & Young
Everglades
Federal Emergency Management Agency
Federal Reserve Bank of New York
Foreign Policy
GAP, Inc.
Gettysburg Battlefield
Good Morning America
Grand Canyon
Hallmark Cards
IAESTE
Inroads
Institute of Government
International Management Group (London only)
Joshua Tree
Klondike Gold Rush
Mass Media Science and Engineering Fellows Program
The Metropolitan Museum of Art
Mount Rushmore
National Aeronautics and Space Administration
National Park Service
New York City Government
Newsday/New York Newsday
NIKE
St. Paul's School
Statue of Liberty
Teach for America
United States Agency for International Development
Urban Fellows/Government Scholars Programs
Weyerhaeuser
Winant-Clayton Volunteers
Yellowstone National Park

FEBRUARY

AFS Intercultural Programs
Amelia Island Plantation
American-Arab Anti-Discrimination Committee (congressional
   placement only)
American Dance Festival

American Indian Science & Engineering Society
Amway
Anacostia Museum
Anchorage Daily News
Argonne National Laboratory
Arthritis Foundation—Northern California Chapter
Arthur Andersen
Atlanta Junior Golf Association
Bermuda Biological Station for Research (WSP only)
Bernstein-Rein
Black Enterprise
The Boston Globe (Business Summer and Minority programs only)
Brookfield Zoo
Bucks County Courier Times
Buick
Burson-Marsteller
Cadillac
California State Senate
Callaway Gardens
The Catholic University of America
Center for Talented Youth (TA & LA positions)
Chemical Industry Institute of Toxicology
Chevrolet
Children's Defense Fund
Conservation Analytical Laboratory
Cooper-Hewitt Museum
David Leadbetter Golf Academy
Duke University Talent Identification Program
Eastman Kodak Company
Economic Research Service
Fenton Communications
The Ford Foundation
Freer Gallery of Art
The Gazette Company
General Mills
General Motors Marketing Internship
Gensler
Georgia Governor's Office (law students)
The Gesher Summer Internship Program
GMC Truck
Golf Digest
The Hansard Society for Parliamentary Government
Harper's Magazine
Hill and Knowlton
Hillel
Hirshhorn Museum and Sculpture Garden
Hoffman-LaRoche
Illinois General Assembly
Insurance Services Office
The International Foundation for Education & Self-Help
International Management Group
International Telecommunications Satellite Organization
John Wiley and Sons
Joint Chiefs of Staff
Korean American Coalition
Kraft Foods, Inc.
Lincoln Center for the Performing Arts
Los Angeles Magazine

LPGA Junior Golf Program
Lunar and Planetary Institute
Maine State Music Theater
Merck & Company
Morris Arboretum
The Museum of Modern Art, New York
National Aeronautics and Space Administration
National Air and Space Museum
National Asian Pacific American Legal Consortium
National Association of Professional Surplus Lines Offices
National Foundation for the Improvement of Education
National Institutes of Health
National Museum of African Art
National Museum of American Art
National Museum of American History
National Museum of Natural History
National Portrait Gallery
National Starch and Chemical Company
National Zoo
Nick Bollettieri Tennis Academy
NIKE Tour
Northfield Mount Hermon School
NOW Legal Defense and Education Fund (second-year law students)
Oldsmobile
Oscar Mayer Wienermobile
The Pentagon
PGA Tour
Pontiac
Procter & Gamble
Quality Education for Minorities Network
Rand
Rodale Institute Research Center
Saturn
Science News
Scripps Institution of Oceanography
Senior PGA Tour
Smithsonian Institution
Solomon R. Guggenheim Museum
Spoleto Festival USA
Sponsors for Educational Opportunity (investment banking, consulting, & asset management)
Summerbridge National
Tellabs
United States Department of Defense
United States Olympic Committee
Volunteers in Asia
The Washingtonian
Wildlife Prairie Park
Xerox Palo Alto Research Center
Yosemite National Park

MARCH

Abbott Laboratories
Academy of Television Arts & Sciences
Accuracy in Academia
Accuracy in Media
Advertising Club of New York

Aetna Life Inc.
AIFS-London
All Things Considered
American-Arab Anti-Discrimination Committee (national & regional offices only)
American Civil Liberties Union
American Federation of Teachers
American Friends Service Committee
American Heart Association (Louisiana only)
American Institute for Foreign Study
American Rivers
Arena Stage
The Arizona Republic
Aspen Center for Environmental Studies
Associaton of Trial Lawyers of America
Baxter International
Berkeley Repertory Theater (Stage Management only)
Boston University International Programs
Breckenridge Outdoor Education Center
The Brooklyn Museum
Bucks County Courier Times
Butterfield & Butterfield
California State Assembly
The Callaghan Group
Callaway Gardens
Canadian Embassy
Capital Gang
The Carter Center
The Cartoon Network
CBS News
Center for Talented Youth (RA positions)
Central Newspapers/The Indianapolis News
Chemical Industry Institute of Toxicology
Choate Rosemary Hall
Cinemax
The Citizens Network for Foreign Affairs
CNN
Corporation for National Service
The Conservative Caucus
Council of Energy Resource Tribes
Creamer Dickson Basford
Creede Repertory Theatre
Crossfire
Crow Canyon Archaeological Center
D.C. Booth Historic Fish Hatchery
Discovery Communications
Economic Research Service
The Economist
Edelman Public Relations Worldwide
Education Programs Abroad
Entenmann's
Entertainment Weekly
ESPN
Face the Nation
Federal Reserve Board
Fellowship of Reconciliation
Foreign Affairs
48 Hours
Foundation for Contemporary Mental Health

Friends Committee on National Legislation
Genentech
General Foods
Goodman Theatre
Habitat for Humanity International
Harley-Davidson
HBO
Headline News
The Heritage Foundation
Hewitt Associates
Hill and Holliday Advertising
Hispanic Association of Colleges and Universities
Historic Deerfield
Hoffman-La Roche
Home Box Office
IBM
IES—The Institute for the International Education of Students
The Indianapolis News
The Indianapolis Star
Institute of International Education
Insurance Services Office
Interhemispheric Resource Center
The International Center
International Foundation of Employee Benefit Plans
The J. Paul Getty Trust (undergrad program only)
Jacob's Pillow Dance Festival
John Wiley & Sons
J.P. Morgan & Co.
The Kennedy Center
Lake Charles American Press
Lamont-Doherty Earth Observatory
Late Show with David Letterman
Lawyers Alliance for World Security/Committee for National Security
Liz Claiborne
Lovelace Respiratory Research Institute
The Lowell Whiteman School
Lucasfilm
Manhattan Theater Club
Manice Education Center
Mattel, Inc.
Merrill Lynch
Miss Porter's School
Ms.
Museum of Contemporary Art, Chicago
Nabisco
National Aeronautics and Space Administration
National Basketball Association
National Center for Fair & Open Testing
National Endowment for the Humanities
National Journal
The National Partnership for Women and Families
National Public Radio
National Trust for Historic Preservation
New Canaan Country School
The New Republic
Nightline
NIKE
North Carolina Botanical Garden

NOW Legal Defense and Education Fund
Organization of Chinese Americans
Oscar Mayer
Outward Bound/Voyageur School
Pacific Investment Management Company
People to People International
Performance Today
Phillips Academy
The Phoenix Gazette
Public Allies
Quaker United Nations Office
Reebok
Roll Call
Rolling Stone
San Diego Zoo (CRES only)
Schlumberger
Sea World
Shaver's Creek Environmental Center
Sierra Club
60 Minutes
Sotheby's
Southern Progress Corporation
Space Needle Corporation
Special Olympics International
Sponsors for Educational Opportunity (corporate law and
   accounting only)
Student Conservation Association
Student Works Painting
Students for Central & Eastern Europe
Sunday Morning
Supreme Court of the United States
Talk of the Nation
TBS
Texas Instruments
TNT
Turner Broadcasting System
Union Carbide
United States Secret Service
United States Securities and Exchange Commission
Up to the Minute
US-Asia Insitute
Varsity Student Painters
Washington Center for Internships and Academic Seminars
Washington Office on Latin America
Wells Fargo Bank
The White House
Whitney Museum of American Art
The Wilson Quarterly
Wolf Trap Foundation for the Performing Arts
Woodrow Wilson International Center for Scholars
Work Experience USA
Xerox

APRIL

Academic Study Associates
Alaska State Parks
American Committee on Africa
American Conservatory Theater

American Enterprise Institute
American Friends Service Committee
American Israel Public Affairs Committee
American Management Association
American Symphony Orchestra League
Anasazi Heritage Center
Australian Embassy
Ballantine Books
Beacon Press
Berkeley Repertory Theater
Bet Tzedek Legal Services
The Brookings Institution
Brooklyn Botanic Garden
Business Executives for National Security
Camp Counselors USA
Center for Defense Information
Chicago Bulls
Citibank
The Citizen's Network for Foreign Affairs
Clarke & Company
Comedy Central
Common Cause
Corporation for National Service
Cromarty & Co.
Crown Books
Dell Computer
The Discovery Channel
Discovery Communications
Educational Programs Abroad
Forbes
Ford Motor Company
Franklin D. Roosevelt Library
Frito-Lay
Georgia Governor's Office
Global Exchange
Greater Media Cable
GTE
Harper's Magazine
The Hermitage
Hewlett-Packard
Historic Deerfield
The History Factory
Hostelling International—American Youth Hostels
Houghton Mifflin Company
IES—The Institute for the International Education of Students
International Creative Management
International Voluntary Services
International Volunteer Projects
JC Penney
Jewish Vocational and Career Counseling Service
KCSA Public Relations
KIRO
Knopf Books
Late Night with Conan O'Brien
The Learning Channel
Legacy International
Leo Castelli Gallery
The Library of Congress
Lighthouse Production

Los Angeles Magazine
Madison Square Garden
The Martin Agency
The Maternal & Child Health Institute
Makovsky & Company
Michael Phillips Productions
Middle East Institute
Miniwanca Education Center
Museum of Fine Arts, Boston
Mystic Seaport: The Museum of America & the Sea
The Nation
National Aeronautics and Space Administration
National Aquarium in Baltimore
National Asian Pacific American Legal Consortium
National Audubon Society
National Broadcasting Company
National Football League
National Journalism Center
National Organization for Women
National Space Society
National Wildlife Federation (July–December internship)
National Women's Health Network
NBC Nightly News
New Stage Theatre
New York Knicks
New York Rangers
New York State Bar Association
Norfolk Chamber Music Festival
Pediatric AIDS Foundation
Penguin Books
Plume Books
Public Defender Service for DC
Random House
Renew America
Rio Grande National Forest
Ruder-Finn
Sally Jessy Raphael Show
San Juan/Rio Grande National Forests
Saturday Night Live
Science
Signet Classics
Sony Music Entertainment (Minority Internship only)
Staten Island Zoo
TADA!
TBWA
Thirteen/WNET
The Today Show
Toyota (Toyota Sales only)
United Nations Association of the United States of America
United States Holocaust Museum
United States National Arboretum
Viking Books
Volunteers For Peace
Wadsworth Atheneum
Warwick Baker O'Neill
The White House
Who Cares
WNBC-TV
Y.E.S. to Jobs

AFS Intercultural Programs (Team Mission only)
American Conservatory Theater
American Red Cross
Arms Control Association
ASHOKA: Innovators for the Public
Boston Magazine
The Brooklyn Museum
Brown-Miller Communications
Cabrillo National Monument
Cairns & Associates
Camp Counselors USA
Center for Investigative Reporting
Center for Marine Conservation
Chicago Children's Museum
Elkman Advertising & Public Relations
Foreign Student Service Council
Frito-Lay
Geffen Records
Global Exchange
Haft/Nasatir
Hostelling International: American Youth Hostels
KGO-TV
Lightstorm Entertainment
Liz Claiborne
Los Angeles Lakers
Los Angeles Municipal Art Gallery
MacDonald Communications Corporation
Mad Magazine
Manhattan Theatre Club
Marina Maher Communications
Mixed media
Ms.
Museum of Fine Arts, Boston
North Cascades Institute
Octel Communications
Physicians for Social Responsibility
Reebok
Rhode Island State Government
Saks Fifth Avenue
San Francisco Bay Guardian
Success
Temerlin McClain
The Tonight Show With Jay Leno
Volunteers For Peace
The Widmeyer Baker Group
Women's Project & Productions
Working Mother
Working Woman

E! Entertainment Television Networks
The Juilliard School
Little Keswick School
Lutheran Volunteer Corps
The Southwestern Company
The Wildlife Society (July–December internship)

See also Rolling Deadlines

(INCLUDES FALL, SPRING, AND SUMMER INTERNSHIPS)

A&M Records
Abrams Artists Agency
The Academy for Advanced and Strategic Studies
Ackerman McQueen
Actors Theater of Louisville
Adrienne Vittadini
Advocates for Children of New York
A.E. Schwartz & Associates
Affiliated Sante Group
Agora, Inc.
Agora Publishing
AIESEC
Aigner Associates
AIM for the Handicapped
The Algonquin
Alliance of Residence Theaters
Alper International
America West Airlines
American Association of University Women Educational
  Foundation
American & International Designs
American Association of Overseas Studies
American Bar Association
American Committee on Africa/The Africa Fund
American Forests
American Friends Service Committee
The American Geographical Society
American Hockey League
American Jewish Congress
American Judicature Society
American Management Association
The American Place Theatre
American Repertory Theatre
American Rivers
American School for the Deaf
American University in Moscow
American Wind Energy Association
American Woman's Economic Development Corp.
American Youth Work Center
AMIDEAST
Amnesty International
Amtrak
The Andy Warhol Museum
Angel Records
Anheuser-Busch
Annie Leibovitz Studio
Another World
The Antarctica Project
Aperture Foundation
Apple Computer
Arab American Institute
Archive Films
Arden Theatre Company
A.R.I.Q. Footage
Arista Records

Artists Space
The Arts & Education Council of Greater St. Louis
As The World Turns
Asian American Arts Centre
Asian American Journalists Association
ASSIST
Association for International Practical Training
Association of Hispanic Arts
Association of Trial Lawyers of America
Asylum Records
Atlanta Ballet
Atlantic Council of the United States
Atlantic Records
BalletMet
Baltimore Zoo
Barneys New York
Barry-Haft-Brown Artists Agency
Barwood Productions
Baywatch
Beach Associates
Bechtel
Bellevue Hospital Center
Benetton USA Corp.
Berkshire Public Theatre
Bermuda Biological Station for Research (grad students only)
Bertelsmann Music Group
Best Buddies International
Betsey Johnson
Bike-Aid
Black Entertainment Television
Blair Television
Blue Corn Comics
The Boston Globe (Co-op program only)
Boys Hope Girls Hope
Bozell Public Relations
BP
Brethren Volunteer Service
Brick Wall Management
Buffalo Bill Historical Center
B.U.G.
California Governor's Office
California Museum of Photography
Callaway Advanced Technology
Camphill Soltane
Canaan Public Relations
Capitol Records
CARE
Carolyn Ray
CAVS/Gund Arena Company
CDS International/CDG
Census Bureau
The Center for Human Rights Advocacy
Center for Strategic & International Studies
Center for the Study of Conflict
Central Park SummerStage
Centro para los Adolescentes de San Miguel de Allende

Chamber Music America
Chanticleer Films
Charlesbridge Publishing
Charlie Rose
Chevron
Chicago Botanic Garden
Chicago Bulls
Child's Play Touring Theatre
Children's Museum of Indianapolis
The Chronicle of the Horse
Chrysalis Records
CityArts
City Limits
City of New York Parks & Recreation
Classic Stage Company
College Light Opera Company
Columbia Journalism Review
Columbia Pictures
Community Service Volunteer Programme
Concrete Marketing
Congressional Research Service
Connecticut Judicial Branch
Connecticut Magazine
Consumers for World Trade
The Corporate Response Group
Council on Foreign Relations
Council on Hemispheric Affairs
Council on International Educational Exchange
Creative Artists Agency
Creative Time
Crown Capital
C-SPAN
Cushman School
Cybergrrl
Dallas Cowboys
Davis Hays & Co.
Decatur House Museum
Deloitte & Touche
Denver Art Museum
DesignTech International
DHL Worldwide Express
Donna Maione
The Drawing Center
Dublin Internships, Ireland
Duffey Communications
Dykeman Associates
E-Systems
E/The Environmental Magazine
Earle Palmer Brown
The Ecco Press
Economic Development Administration
Elektra Entertainment Group
Elektra Records
Elite Model Management
Elizabeth Dow
Emerge
EMI Records
EMI Records Group North America

EMILY's List
Energy Records
Entertainment Design/Lighting Dimensions
The Environmental Careers Organization
Exxon
Faber and Faber
FAIR
Families USA Foundation
Fantagraphics Books
Farm Sanctuary
Farrar Straus & Giroux
Federal Bureau of Prisons
Federal Reserve Board (academic year only)
The Feminist Majority
First Business
Fisher-Price Toys
Focus on Women
Food for the Hungry
Ford Models
Foreign Policy Research Institute
Forty Acres and a Mule Filmworks
Fourth World Movement
Fox
Fox FX
The Franklin Life Insurance Co.
French Embassy
The French-American Center
Frontier Nursing Service
Glen Helen Outdoor Education Center
Global Volunteers
The Gothard Group
Gould Farm
The Government Affairs Institute
Great Projects Film Company
Grubb & Ellis
Guiding Light
Gund Arena
Halstead Communications/College Connections
HALT: Americans for Legal Reform
Hawk Mountain Sanctuary
Hawthorne Valley Farm
Health & Environmental Sciences Group
Healthy Mothers, Healthy Babies
HERE
Hewitt Associates
Hewlett-Packard
High Country News
High Museum of Art
Hill and Knowlton
Historic Films
H.O.M.E.
Houston International Protocol Alliance
The Howard Stern Show
Howard Talent West
H.S.I. Productions
Hudson Institute
Human Service Alliance
Hunter House

Independent Sector
Indianapolis Zoological Society
Institute of Cultural Affairs
Institute for International Cooperation and Development
Institute for Policy Studies
Institute for Unpopular Culture
Intel
Interactive Public Relations
Interhemispheric Resource Center
Interior Design Collections
Interlocken Center for Experimental Living
The International Center of Photography
International Creative Management
International Labor Organization
International Sculpture Center
International Trade Administration
Internships International
Iowa Film Office
Island Records
It's Your Business
Japan-America Society of Washington
The Jim Henson Company
Jones & Bartlett
JUSTACT: Youth Action for Global Justice
Karl Lagerfeld
The Kitchen
Korff Enterprises
KQED-FM
KRCB
Land Between the Lakes
Leavenworth Prison
Levine/Schneider Public Relations
Lobsenz-Stevens
Longlake Conservation Center
Mallory Factor
Mammoth Records
Manus & Associates Literary Agents
Marvel Comics
Matador Records
MCA/Universal
McDonald's
MCT Management/Bold! Records
Mercury Records
MetLife
Metro-Goldwyn-Mayer/United Artists
Microsoft
Middle Earth
Middle East Research & Information Project
Miller Brewing Company
Minority Business Development Agency
Mixed Media
Mobility International
Montgomery County Community Corrections
Morrison & Foerster
Mote Marine Laboratory
Mother Jones
MTV
My Sister's Place

Nation's Business
National Association for Female Executives
National Association of College Broadcasters
National Committee for Responsive Philanthropy
National Institute of Standards & Technology
National Oceanic & Atmospheric Administration
National Technical Information Service
National Telecommunications & Information Administration
The Nature Conservancy
NETWORK
New Dramatists
The New York Hospital-Cornell Medical Center
New York Shakespeare Festival
New York State Theatre Institute
Northwestern Mutual Financial Network
Office of Inspector General
Office of Job Corps
Open City Films
Oracle
Overland Entertainment
Overseas Private Investment Corporation
The Paris Review
The Partnership for Service-Learning
Patent & Trademark Office
Peace Corps
Pella
Pendulum Records
PERA Club
Perspective Records
Pfizer
The Philadelphia Center
Physicians for Human Rights
Playboy
Playhouse on the Square
PMK Public Relations
PolyGram
PrimeTime Live
Pro-Found Software
Procter & Gamble Productions
Psychology Today
Public Interest Research Groups
RCA Records
The Real World
Renaissance Computer Art Center
Renew America
Rhino Records
The Ripon Society
The Rockey Company
Rockwell Semiconductor Systems
Rosenbluth International
Roy A. Somlyo Productions
The Rush Limbaugh Show
San Diego Zoo (PR only)
San Francisco Focus
San Francisco 49ers
Save the Sound
Savvy Management
SBK Records

Scott Rudin Productions
Select Records
765-ARTS
Seventeen Magazine
Sgro Promo Associates/General Motors Internship
Shadow Broadcast Services
Sherwin-Williams
Shirley Herz Associates
Sierra Club (academic year only)
SGI
Simon & Goodman Picture Company
Sony
Sony Music Entertainment (Credited Internship only)
Sony Pictures Entertainment
The Source
South Seas Plantation
Southface Energy Institute
Spin
Sports Illustrated
Spy
Starlight Foundation
State Teacher's Retirement System of Ohio
Steppenwolf Theatre Company
Surfrider Foundation
Sussex Publishers
Technology Administration
Teen Voices
Texas Monthly
Theater de la Jeune Lune
Tommy Boy Music
Toyota (Toyota Technical Center only)
Tracy Watts Millinery
Tribeca Film Center
TriStar Pictures
Tucson Children's Museum
Food Network
Twentieth Century Fox
Twentieth Television
20/20
20/20 Vision
Tyco Toys
UCSF AIDS Health Project
The Union Institute for Social Responsibility for Social
   Responsibility
United Artists
United Nations
United States and Foreign Commercial Service
United States Chamber of Commerce
United States Department of Commerce
United States Prison
United States Travel & Tourism Administration
United Talent Agency
Unitel
Universal Pictures
Universal Studios
Vault.com
Vereinsbank Capital Corp.
Vertigo Records
Verve Records

VH-1
Vibe
Village Voice
Virginia Symphony
Virgin Records
Voice of America
Volunteers for Israel
Wall Street Music
The Washington Office on Africa
WAXQ - Q104.3
WCHS-TV
Wessler Entertainment
Westin Hotels & Resorts
The Westwood One Radio Network
Weyerhaeuser (Company-wide program only)
WGN-Chicago
Whitney Museum of American Art
Wildlife Prairie Park (academic year only)
Williamstown Theater Festival
The Wilma Theater
Wired
WISH-TV 8
WNYC
Women Express
Women Make Movies
Women's Institute for Freedom of the Press
Women's International League for Peace and Freedom
Women's Sports Foundation
World Federalist Association
Worldnet
Writers Guild of America, West
YMCA
Youth for Understanding International Exchange
YSB (Young Sisters & Brothers)
Zoo Entertainment

INTERNSHIPS OPEN TO HIGH SCHOOL STUDENTS

Abrams Artists Agency
The Academy for Advanced and Strategic Studies
Accuracy in Education
Accuracy in Media
Ackerman McQueen
Actors Theatre of Louisville
Aetna Life & Casualty (CT students only)
Affiliated Sante Group
AFS Intercultural Programs
AIM for the Handicapped
American Association of Overseas Studies
American Civil Liberties Union
American Friends Service Committee
American Heart Association
American Management Association
The American Place Theatre
American Repertory Theatre
American Woman's Economic Development Corp.
Ames Research Center
Amnesty International
The Andy Warhol Museum
Angel Records
Arden Theatre Company
Arms Control Association
Arthritis Foundation—Northern California Chapter
Artists Space
Asian American Arts Centre
Asian American Journalists Association
ASSIST
Association of Hispanic Arts
Association of Trial Lawyers of America
AT&T Bell Laboratories
Atlantic Records
Baywatch
Beacon Press
Bellevue Hospital Center
Benetton USA Corp.
Berkshire Public Theatre
Betsey Johnson
Bike-Aid
Black Entertainment Television
Blue Corn Comics
Brick Wall Management
Brooklyn Botanic Garden
Bureau of Economic Analysis
Bureau of Export Administration
California Museum of Photography
Capitol Records
Carolyn Ray
Census Bureau
Center for Defense Information
Center for Investigative Reporting
Centro para los Adolescentes de San Miguel de Allende

Child's Play Touring Theatre
Chrysalis Records
City of New York Parks & Recreation
CityArts
College Light Opera Company
Concrete Marketing
Congressional Hispanic Caucus Institute
Connecticut Magazine
The Conservative Caucus
Council on Economic Priorities
Council on Hemispheric Affairs
Donna Maione
Economic Development Administration
Elizabeth Dow
Emerge
EMI Records
EMI Records Group North America
Entertainment Design/Lighting Dimensions
Farm Sanctuary
Federal Bureau of Prisons
Federal Reserve Bank of New York
Federal Reserve Board
The Feminist Majority
Fisher-Price Toys
Foreign Policy Research Institute
Forty Acres and a Mule Filmworks
Freer Gallery of Art
Global Volunteers
Goddard Space Flight Center
Grubb & Ellis
Habitat for Humanity International
HALT: Americans for Legal Reform
Harley-Davidson (Milwaukee, WI students only)
HERE
Hewlett-Packard
High Museum of Art
H.O.M.E.
H.S.I. Productions
Human Service Alliance
Indianapolis Zoo
Inroads
Institute for International Cooperation and Development
Institute for Unpopular Culture
Interior Design Collections
Interscope Records
Iowa Film Office
Japan-America Society of Washington
Jet Propulsion Laboratory
Johnson Space Center
Joint Chiefs of Staff
JUSTACT: Youth Action for Global Justice
Kennedy Space Center
KRCB
Langley Research Center
Lawrence Livermore National Laboratory

Leavenworth Prison
Legacy International
Levine/Schneider Public Relations
Lewis Research Center
Liberty Records
Los Angeles Municipal Art Gallery
MacDonald Communications
Maine State Music Theatre
Mammoth Records
Manhattan Theatre Club
Marina Maher Communications
Marion Penitentiary
Marshall Space Flight Center
Matador Records
Middle East Research & Information Project
Minority Business Development Agency
Mixed Media
Mobility International
Ms.
MTV: Music Television
National Aeronautics and Space Administration
National Association of College Broadcasters
National Institute of Standards & Technology
National Institutes of Health
National Oceanic & Atmospheric Administration
National Organization for Women
National Space Society
National Technical Information Service
National Telecommunications & Information Administration
New Dramatists
New Stage Theatre
New York City Government
New York Shakespeare Festival
New York State Theatre Institute
Office of Inspector General
Overland Entertainment
The Partnership for Service-Learning
Patent & Trademark Office
Pediatric AIDS Foundation
Pendulum Records
The Pentagon
PERA Club
Rhino Records
Rio Grande National Forest
The Rush Limbaugh Show
Sally Jessy Raphael Show
San Diego Zoo
San Francisco Bay Guardian
San Juan/Rio Grande National Forests
Save the Sound
SBK Records
Scott Rudin Productions
Select Records
765-ARTS
Seventeen Magazine
Smithsonian Institution
The Source
The Source Theater Company

The Southern Center for International Studies
Southface Energy Institute
The Southwestern Company
Spin
Stennis Space Center
Student Conservation Association
Success
Summerbridge National
Surfrider Foundation
TADA!
Teach for America (Employment Dept. only)
Technology Administration
Teen Voices
Texas Instruments
Texas Monthly
Theater de la Jeune Lune
Thread Waxing Space
Tommy Boy Music
United Nations Association of the United States of America
United States Agency for International Development
United States Department of Commerce
United States Department of Defense
United States Holocaust Museum
United States Prison
United States Senate Youth Program
United States Travel & Tourism Administration
VH-1
Village Voice
Virgin Records
Volunteers for Israel
Volunteers For Peace
Weyerhaeuser
Williamstown Theater Festival
Wired
Women Express
Women Make Movies
Women's Institute for Freedom of the Press
Women's International League for Peace and Freedom
Working Mother
Working Woman
Writers Guild of America, West
Vault.com
Y.E.S. to Jobs
Youth For Understanding International Exchange
YSB (Young Sisters & Brothers)

A&M Records
Abrams Artists Agency
The Academy for Advanced and Strategic Studies
Access: A Security Information Service
Accuracy in Education
Accuracy in Media
Ackerman McQueen
Actors Theatre of Louisville
Adrienne Vittadini
A.E. Schwartz & Associates
Affiliated Sante Group
AFS Intercultural Programs
Agency for Toxic Substances and Disease Registry
Agora, Inc.
AIESEC
Aigner Associates
AIM for the Handicapped
Alaska State Parks
The Algonquin
Alliance of Residence Theaters
Alper International
Amelia Island Plantation
America West Airlines
American Association of University Women Educational
  Foundation
American Association for the Advancement of Science
American Association of Overseas Studies
American Bar Association
American Civil Liberties Union
American Committee on Africa/The Africa Fund
American Dance Festival
American Enterprise Institute
American Federation of Teachers
American Friends Service Committee
The American Geographical Society
American Heart Association
American Hockey League
American Israel Public Affairs Committee
American Jewish Congress
American Judicature Society
American Management Association
The American Place Theatre
American Red Cross
American Repertory Theatre
American Rivers
American School for the Deaf
American Symphony Orchestra League
American University in Moscow
American Wind Energy Association
American Woman's Economic Development Corp.
American Youth Work Center
Ames Research Center
AMIDEAST
Amnesty International
Amtrak
Anacostia Museum
Anchorage Daily News

The Andy Warhol Museum
Angel Records
Another World
Aperture Foundation
Arab American Institute
Archive Films
Arden Theatre Company
Arena Stage
Arista Records
Arms Control Association
Arthritis Foundation—Northern California Chapter
Artists Space
The Arts & Education Council of Greater St. Louis
As The World Turns
ASHOKA: Innovators for the Public
Asian American Arts Centre
Asian American Journalists Association
ASSIST
Association of Hispanic Arts
Association of Trial Lawyers of America
Asylum Records
The Atlanta Ballet
Atlantic Records
BalletMet
Baltimore Zoo
Barneys New York
Barry-Haft-Brown Artists Agency
Barwood Productions
Baywatch
Beacon Press
Bellevue Hospital Center
Benetton USA Corp.
Berkeley Repertory Theater
Berkshire Public Theatre
Bertelsmann Music Group
Best Buddies International
Bet Tzedek Legal Services
Betsey Johnson
Bike-Aid
Black Enterprise
Black Entertainment Television
The Blade
Blue Corn Comics
The Boston Globe
Boston Magazine
Boston University International Programs
Bozell Public Relations
Brethren Volunteer Service
Brick Wall Management
Bucks County Courier Times
Buffalo Bill Historical Center
B.U.G.
Bureau of Economic Analysis
Bureau of Export Administration
Business Executives for National Security
Cabrillo National Monument
Cairns & Associates
California Governor's Office

California Museum of Photography
Callaway Advanced Technology
Camp Counselors USA
Camphill Soltane
Canaan Public Relations
Capitol Records
Carolyn Ray
CAVS/Gund Arena Company
CBS Records
CDG/CDS International
Census Bureau
Center for Defense Information
Center for Investigative Reporting
Center for Marine Conservation
Center for Strategic & International Studies
Center for Talented Youth
Central Park SummerStage
Centro para los Adolescentes de San Miguel de Allende
The Century Plaza Hotel
Chamber Music America
Chanticleer Films
Charlesbridge Publishing
Charlie Rose
Chevron
Chicago Botanic Garden
Child's Play Touring Theatre
Children's Defense Fund
Children's Museum of Indianapolis
The Chronicle of the Horse
Chrysalis Records
Cinemax
City of New York Parks & Recreation
CityArts
Classic Stage Company
Cleveland Cavaliers
The Cloisters
College Connections
College Light Opera Company
Student Works Painting
The Public Forum Institute
Columbia Journalism Review
Columbia Pictures
Columbia Records
Comedy Central
Common Cause
Community Service Volunteer Programme
Concrete Marketing
Congressional Hispanic Caucus Institute
Congressional Management Foundation
Connecticut Magazine
Conservation Analytical Laboratory
The Conservative Caucus
Consumers for World Trade
Continuous Electron Beam Accelerator Facility
Cooper-Hewitt Museum
Corporation for National Service
Council on Economic Priorities
Council on Foreign Relations

Council on Hemispheric Affairs
Council on International Educational Exchange
Creative Time
Creede Repertory Theatre
Cromarty & Co.
Cushman School
Cybergrrl
Dallas Cowboys
David Leadbetter Golf Academy
Davis Hays & Co.
D.C. Booth Historic Fish Hatchery
Death Valley
Decatur House Museum
Def Jam Records
Dell Computer
Donna Maione
The Drawing Center
Duke University Talent Identification Program
Dykeman Associates
E/The Environmental Magazine
Eastman Kodak Company
EastWest Records
The Ecco Press
Economic Development Administration
Elektra Entertainment Group
Elektra Records
Elite Model Management
Elizabeth Dow
Emerge
EMI Records
EMI Records Group North America
Emily's List
Energy Records
Entertainment Design/Lighting Dimensions
Entertainment Weekly
The Environmental Careers Organization (DIP only)
Epic Records
ESPN
Everglades
Exxon
Faber and Faber
Fantagraphics Books
FAIR
Farm Sanctuary
Farrar Straus & Giroux
Federal Bureau of Prisons
Federal Reserve Board
The Feminist Majority
Fenton Communications
Fisher-Price Toys
Fontana Records
Forbes
Ford Models
Ford Motor Company
Foreign Policy Research Institute
Foreign Student Service Council
Forty Acres and a Mule Filmworks
Fourth World Movement

Fox
Franklin D. Roosevelt Library
Freer Gallery of Art
The French-American Center
French Embassy
Frontier Nursing Service
Gettysburg Battlefield
Global Exchange
Global Volunteers
Goddard Space Flight Center
Gould Farm
The Government Affairs Institute
Grand Canyon
Great Projects Film Company
Greater Media Cable
Grubb & Ellis
GTE
Guiding Light
Gund Arena
Habitat for Humanity International
Haft/Nasatir
HALT: Americans for Legal Reform
Harper's Magazine
The Hastings Center
Hawk Mountain Sanctuary
Hawthorne Valley Farm
HBO
Healthy Mothers, Healthy Babies
HERE
The Heritage Foundation
High Museum of Art
H.O.M.E.
Home Box Office
Hostelling International—American Youth Hostels
Houghton Mifflin Company
Houston International Protocol Alliance
The Howard Stern Show
Howard Talent Agency
I.S.I. Productions
Hudson Institute
Human Service Alliance
Hunter House
IES – The Institute for the International Education of Students
Indianapolis Zoo
Inroads
Institute for International Cooperation and Development
Institute for Unpopular Culture
Intel
Interhemispheric Resource Center
Interactive Public Relatons
Interior Design Collections
Interlocken
The International Center of Photography
International Creative Management
International Labor Organization
International Management Group
International Telecommunications Satellite Organization
International Trade Administration

International Volunteer Projects
Interscope Records
Iowa Film Office
Island Records
Jacob's Pillow Dance Festival
Japan-America Society of Washington
Jet Propulsion Laboratory
The Jim Henson Company
Johnson Space Center
Joint Chiefs of Staff
Jones & Bartlett
Joshua Tree
The Juilliard School
JUSTACT: Youth Action for Global Justice
Karl Lagerfeld
The Kennedy Center
Kennedy Space Center
Klondike Gold Rush
KRCB
Lake Charles American Press
Langley Research Center
Late Night with Conan O'Brien
Late Show with David Letterman
Lawrence Livermore National Laboratory
Lawyers Alliance for World Security/Committee for National
  Security
Leavenworth Prison
Legacy International
Leo Castelli Gallery
Levine/Schneider Public Relations
Lewis Research Center
Liberty Records
Little Keswick School
Liz Claiborne
Longwood Gardens
Los Angeles Lakers
Los Angeles Municipal Art Gallery
Los Angeles Times
MacDonald Communications
Madison Square Garden
Maine State Music Theatre
Makovsky & Company
Mallory Factor
Mammoth Records
Manhattan Theatre Club
Manice Education Center
Manus & Associates Literary Agency
Marina Maher Communications
Marion Penitentiary
Marshall Space Flight Center
The Martin Agency
Matador Records
Mattel Toys
MCT Management/Bold! Records
Mercury Records
MetLife
Metro-Goldwyn-Mayer/United Artists
Middle Earth

Middle East Institute
Middle East Research & Information Project
Minority Business Development Agency
Miss Universe
Miss USA
Mixed Media
Mobility International
Morris Arboretum
Morrison & Foerster
Mote Marine Laboratory
Mother Earth News
Motown Records
Mount Rushmore
Ms.
MSG Network
MTV: Music Television
Museum of Contemporary Art, Chicago
Museum of Fine Arts, Boston
The Museum of Modern Art, New York
My Sister's Place
Nabisco
The Nation
National Aeronautics and Space Administration
National Air and Space Museum
National Aquarium in Baltimore
National Association for Female Executives
National Association of College Broadcasters
National Broadcasting Company
National Center for Fair & Open Testing
National Center for Toxicological Research
National Football League
National Institute of Standards & Technology
National Institutes of Health
National Journalism Center
National Museum of African Art
National Museum of American History
National Museum of Natural History
National Oceanic & Atmospheric Administration
National Organization for Women
National Park Service
The National Partnership for Women and Families
National Portrait Gallery
National Security Agency
National Space Society
National Technical Information Service
National Telecommunications & Information Administration
National Women's Health Network
National Zoo
The Nature Conservancy
Naval Training Systems Center
NBC Nightly News
New Dramatists
New Stage Theatre
The New York Hospital-Cornell Medical Center
New York Knicks
New York Rangers
New York Shakespeare Festival
New York State Theatre Institute

Nick Bollettieri Tennis Academy
North Carolina Botanical Garden
North Cascades Institute
Northwestern Mutual Financial Network
Oak Ridge Institute for Science and Education
Oak Ridge National Laboratory
Office of Inspector General
Office of Job Corps
Office of House Speaker
Open City Films
Oracle
Organization of Chinese Americans
Outward Bound/Voyageur School
Overland Entertainment
Overseas Private Investment Corporation
The Partnership for Service-Learning
Patent & Trademark Office
Pediatric AIDS Foundation
Peggy Guggenheim Collection
Pendulum Records
Penguin Books
The Pentagon
PERA Club
Perspective Records
The Philadelphia Inquirer
Pittsburgh Energy Technology Center
Playboy
Plume Books
PMK Public Relations
PolyGram
Procter & Gamble Productions
Psychology Today
Public Allies
Public Defender Service for DC
Public Interest Research Groups
RCA Records
The Real World
Renew America
Rhino Records
Rhode Island State Government
Rio Grande National Forest
The Ripon Society
Roll Call
Rolling Stone
Rosenbluth International
Roy A. Somlyo Productions
The Rush Limbaugh Show
Saks Fifth Avenue
Sally Jessy Raphael Show
San Diego Zoo
San Francisco Bay Guardian
San Francisco Chronicle
San Francisco 49ers
San Francisco Opera
San Juan/Rio Grande National Forests
Saturday Night Live
Savannah River Ecology Laboratory
Save the Sound

SBK Records
Scott Rudin Productions
Select Records
765-ARTS
Seventeen Magazine
Sgro Promo Associates/General Motors Internship
Shaver's Creek Environmental Center
Shirley Herz Associates
Signet Classics
SGI
Simon & Goodman Picture Company
Smithsonian Institution
Sony
Sony Music Entertainment
Sony Pictures Entertainment
The Source
The Southern Center for International Studies
The Source Theater Company
Southface Energy Institute
The Southwestern Company
Spin
Spoleto Festival USA
Spy
Starlight Foundation
Statue of Liberty
Stennis Space Center
Steppenwolf Theatre Company
Student Conservation Association
Student Works Painting
Students for Central & Eastern Europe
Success
Summerbridge National
Surfrider Foundation
Sussex Publishers
TADA!
Teach for America (Employment Dept. only)
Technology Administration
Teen Voices
Temerlin McClain
Texas Monthly
Theater de la Jeune Lune
Thread Waxing Space
The Today Show
Tommy Boy Music
Tracy Watts Millinery
Tribeca Film Center
TriStar Pictures
Tucson Children's Museum
Twentieth Century Fox
Twentieth Television
20/20
20/20 Vision
Tyco Toys
UCSF AIDS Health Project
The Union Institute for Social Responsibility
United Artists
United Nations
United Nations Association of the United States of America

United States Agency for International Development
United States and Foreign Commercial Service
United States Army Environmental Hygiene Agency
United States Bureau of Mines
United States Department of Commerce
United States Department of Defense
United States Environmental Protection Agency
United States Holocaust Museum
United States National Arboretum
United States Prison
United States Secret Service
United States Securities and Exchange Commission
United States Travel & Tourism Administration
Unitel
Varsity Student Painters
Vault.com
Vereinsbank Capital Corp.
Vertigo Records
Verve Records
VH-1
Viking Books
Village Voice
Virgin Records
Virginia Symphony
Voice of America
Volunteers For Peace
Volunteers for Israel
Volunteers in Asia
Wall Street Music
Washington Office on Latin America
WAXQ - Q104.3
WCHS-TV
Westin Hotels & Resorts
Weyerhaeuser
The White House
Who Cares
The Widmeyer Baker Group
The Wildlife Society
Williamstown Theater Festival
The Wilma Theater
The Wilson Quarterly
Winant-Clayton Volunteers
Wired
WNBC-TV
WNYC
Women Express
Women Make Movies
Women's Institute for Freedom of the Press
Women's International League for Peace and Freedom
Women's Sports & Fitness Magazine
Women's Sports Foundation
Work Experience USA
Working Mother
Working Woman
World Federalist Association
Worldnet
Writers Guild of America, West
Yellowstone National Park

Youth For Understanding International Exchange
YSB (Young Sisters & Brothers)
Zoo Entertainment

INTERNSHIPS OPEN TO COLLEGE SOPHOMORES

A&M Records
Abrams Artists Agency
The Academy for Advanced and Strategic Studies
Academy of Television Arts & Sciences
Access: A Security Information Service
Accuracy in Education
Accuracy in Media
Ackerman McQueen
Actors Theatre of Louisville
Adrienne Vittadini
A.E. Schwartz & Associates
Affiliated Sante Group
AFS Intercultural Programs
Agency for Toxic Substances and Disease Registry
Agora, Inc.
AIESEC
Aigner Associates
AIM for the Handicapped
Alaska State Parks
The Algonquin
Alliance of Residence Theaters
Alper International
Amelia Island Plantation
America West Airlines
American-Arab Anti-Discrimination Committee
American Association for the Advancement of Science
American Association of Overseas Studies
American Association of University Women Educational
  Foundation
American Bar Association
American Civil Liberties Union
American Committee on Africa/The Africa Fund
American Conservatory Theater
American Dance Festival
American Enterprise Institute
American Federation of Teachers
American Forests
American Friends Service Committee
The American Geographical Society
American Heart Association
American Hockey League
American Indian Science & Engineering Society
American Israel Public Affairs Committee
American Jewish Congress
American Judicature Society
American Management Association
The American Place Theatre
American Red Cross
American Repertory Theatre
American Rivers
American School for the Deaf
American Symphony Orchestra League
American University in Moscow

American Wind Energy Association
American Woman's Economic Development Corp.
American Youth Work Center
Ames Research Center
AMIDEAST
Amnesty International
Amtrak
Anacostia Museum
Anchorage Daily News
The Andy Warhol Museum
Angel Records
Another World
Aperture Foundation
Apple Computer
Arab American Institute
Archive Films
Arden Theatre Company
Arena Stage
Arista Records
Arms Control Association
Arthritis Foundation—Northern California Chapter
Artists Space
The Arts & Education Council of Greater St. Louis
As The World Turns
ASHOKA: Innovators for the Public
Asian American Arts Centre
Asian American Journalists Association
ASSIST
Association for Education in Journalism
Association of Hispanic Arts
Association of Trial Lawyers of America
Asylum Records
AT&T Bell Laboratories (SRP only)
The Atlanta Ballet
Atlantic Records
BalletMet
Baltimore Zoo
Barneys New York
Barry-Haft-Brown Artists Agency
Barwood Productions
Baywatch
Beacon Press
Bechtel
Bellevue Hospital Center
Benetton USA Corp.
Berkeley Repertory Theater
Berkshire Public Theatre
Bertelsmann Music Group
Best Buddies International
Bet Tzedek Legal Services
Betsey Johnson
Bike-Aid
Black Enterprise
Black Entertainment Television
The Blade
Blue Corn Comics
The Boston Globe
Boston Magazine

Boston University International Programs
Boys Hope/Girls Hope
Bozell Public Relations
BP
Brethren Volunteer Service
Brick Wall Management
Bucks County Courier Times
Buffalo Bill Historical Center
B.U.G.
Buick
Bureau of Economic Analysis
Bureau of Export Administration
Business Executives for National Security
Cabrillo National Monument
Cadillac
Cairns & Associates
California Governor's Office
California Museum of Photography
Callaway Advanced Technology
Camp Counselors USA
Camphill Soltane
Canaan Public Relations
Capitol Records
Carolyn Ray
CAVS/Gund Arena Company
CBS News
CBS Records
CDG/CDS International
Census Bureau
Center for Defense Information
Center for Investigative Reporting
Center for Marine Conservation
Center for Strategic & International Studies
Center for Talented Youth
Central Park SummerStage
Centro para los Adolescentes de San Miguel de Allende
The Century Plaza Hotel
Chamber Music America
Chanticleer Films
Charlesbridge Publishing
Charlie Rose
Chevrolet
Chevron
Chicago Botanic Garden
Child's Play Touring Theatre
Children's Defense Fund
Children's Museum of Indianapolis
The Chronicle of the Horse
Chrysalis Records
Cinemax
City of New York Parks & Recreation
CityArts
Classic Stage Company
Cleveland Cavaliers
The Cloisters
College Connections
College Light Opera Company
Student Works Painting

The Public Forum Institute
Columbia Journalism Review
Columbia Pictures
Columbia Records
Comedy Central
Common Cause
Community Service Volunteer Programme
Concrete Marketing
Congressional Hispanic Caucus Institute
Congressional Management Foundation
Congressional Research Service
Connecticut Magazine
Conservation Analytical Laboratory
The Conservative Caucus
Consumers for World Trade
Continuous Electron Beam Accelerator Facility
Cooper-Hewitt Museum
Corporation for National Service
Council of Energy Resource Tribes
Council on Economic Priorities
Council on Foreign Relations
Council on Hemispheric Affairs
Council on International Educational Exchange
Creative Time
Creede Repertory Theatre
Cromarty & Co.
Cushman School
Cybergrrl
Dallas Cowboys
David Leadbetter Golf Academy
Davis Hays & Co.
D.C. Booth Historic Fish Hatchery
Death Valley
Decatur House Museum
Def Jam Records
Dell Computer
DHL Worldwide Express
Donna Maione
Dow Chemical Company
The Drawing Center
Duke University Talent Identification Program
Dykeman Associates
E-Systems
E/The Environmental Magazine
Eastman Kodak Company
EastWest Records
The Ecco Press
Economic Development Administration
The Economist
Elektra Entertainment Group
Elektra Records
Elite Model Management
Elizabeth Dow
Emerge
EMI Records
EMI Records Group North America
Emily's List
Energy Records

Entenmann's
Entertainment Design/Lighting Dimensions
Entertainment Weekly
The Environmental Careers Organization (DIP only)
Epic Records
ESPN
Everglades
Exxon
Faber and Faber
Face the Nation
FAIR
Fantagraphics Books
Farm Sanctuary
Farrar Straus & Giroux
Federal Bureau of Prisons
Federal Reserve Board
The Feminist Majority
Fenton Communications
Fisher-Price Toys
Fontana Records
Forbes
Ford Models
Ford Motor Company
Foreign Policy Research Institute
Foreign Student Service Council
Forty Acres and a Mule Filmworks
48 Hours
Fourth World Movement
Fox
Franklin D. Roosevelt Library
Freer Gallery of Art
French Embassy
The French-American Center
Frontier Nursing Service
The Gazette Company
Genentech
General Foods
General Mills
General Motors Marketing Internship
Gensler and Associates/Architects
The Gesher Summer Internship Program
Gettysburg Battlefield
Global Exchange
Global Volunteers
GMC Truck
Goddard Space Flight Center
Good Morning America
Gould Farm
The Government Affairs Institute
Grand Canyon
Great Projects Film Company
Greater Media Cable
Grubb & Ellis
GTE
Guiding Light
Gund Arena
Habitat for Humanity International
Haft/Nasatir

HALT: Americans for Legal Reform
The Hansard Society for Parliamentary Government
Harley-Davidson
Harper's Magazine
The Hastings Center
Hawk Mountain Sanctuary
Hawthorne Valley Farm
HBO
Healthy Mothers, Healthy Babies
HERE
The Heritage Foundation
Hewlett-Packard
High Museum of Art
Hill, Holliday, Connors, Cosmopulos Advertising
Hispanic Association of Colleges and Universities
Historic Deerfield
H.O.M.E.
Home Box Office
Hostelling International—American Youth Hostels
Houghton Mifflin Company
Houston International Protocol Alliance
The Howard Stern Show
Howard Talent West
H.S.I. Productions
Hudson Institute
Human Service Alliance
Hunter House
IBM
IES – The Institute for the International Education of Students
Indianapolis Zoo
Inroads
Institute for International Cooperation and Development
Institute for Unpopular Culture
Institute of Government
Intel
Interhemispheric Resource Center
Interactive Public Relations
Interior Design Collections
Interlocken
The International Center
The International Center of Photography
International Creative Management
International Labor Organization
International Management Group
International Telecommunications Satellite Organization
International Trade Administration
International Voluntary Services
International Volunteer Projects
Interscope Records
Iowa Film Office
Island Records
The J. Paul Getty Trust
Jacob's Pillow Dance Festival
Japan-America Society of Washington
Jet Propulsion Laboratory
Jewish Vocational and Career Counseling Service
Jim Henson Productions
John Wiley & Sons

Johnson Space Center
Joint Chiefs of Staff
Jones & Bartlett
Joshua Tree
The Juilliard School
JUSTACT: Youth Action for Global Justice
Karl Lagerfeld
KCSA Public Relations
The Kennedy Center
Kennedy Space Center
Klondike Gold Rush
Korean American Coalition
KPIX-TV
Kraft Foods, Inc.
KRCB
Lake Charles American Press
Langley Research Center
Late Night with Conan O'Brien
Late Show with David Letterman
Lawrence Livermore National Laboratory
Lawyers Alliance for World Security/Committee for National
   Security
Leavenworth Prison
Legacy International
Leo Castelli Gallery
Levine/Schneider Public Relations
Lewis Research Center
Liberty Records
Little Keswick School
Liz Claiborne
Long Lake Conservation Center
Longwood Gardens
Los Angeles Lakers
Los Angeles Municipal Art Gallery
Los Angeles Times
Lunar and Planetary Institute
MacDonald Communications
MAD Magazine
Madison Square Garden
Maine State Music Theatre
Makovsky & Company
Mallory Factor
Mammoth Records
Manhattan Theatre Club
Manice Education Center
Manus & Associates Literary Agency
Marina Maher Communications
Marion Penitentiary
Marshall Space Flight Center
The Martin Agency
Matador Records
Mattel Toys
MCT Management/Bold! Records
Mercury Records
MetLife
Metro-Goldwyn-Mayer/United Artists
Microsoft
Middle Earth

Middle East Institute
Middle East Research & Information Project
Minority Business Development Agency
Miss Universe
Miss USA
Mixed Media
Mobility International
Morris Arboretum
Morrison & Foerster
Mote Marine Laboratory
Mother Earth News
Motown Records
Mount Rushmore
Ms.
MSG Network
MTV: Music Television
Museum of Contemporary Art, Chicago
Museum of Fine Arts, Boston
The Museum of Modern Art, New York
My Sister's Place
Nabisco
The Nation
National Aeronautics and Space Administration
National Aquarium in Baltimore
National Air and Space Museum
National Association for Female Executives
National Association of College Broadcasters
National Basketball Association
National Broadcasting Company
National Center for Fair & Open Testing
National Center for Toxicological Research
National Football League
National Institute of Standards & Technology
National Institutes of Health
National Journalism Center
National Museum of African Art
National Museum of American History
National Museum of Natural History
National Oceanic & Atmospheric Administration
National Organization for Women
National Park Service
The National Partnership for Women and Families
National Portrait Gallery
National Security Agency
National Space Society
National Technical Information Service
National Telecommunications & Information Administration
National Trust for Historic Preservation
National Women's Health Network
National Zoo
The Nature Conservancy
Naval Training Systems Center
NBC Nightly News
New Dramatists
New Stage Theatre
New York City Government
The New York Hospital-Cornell Medical Center
New York Knicks

New York Rangers
New York Shakespeare Festival
New York State Theatre Institute
Newsday/New York Newsday
Nick Bollettieri Tennis Academy
North Carolina Botanical Garden
North Cascades Institute
Northwestern Mutual Financial Network
Oak Ridge Institute for Science and Education
Oak Ridge National Laboratory
Office of House Speaker
Office of Inspector General
Office of Job Corps
Oldsmobile
Open City Films
Oracle
Organization of Chinese Americans
Oscar Mayer
Outward Bound/Voyageur School
Overland Entertainment
Overseas Private Investment Corporation
The Partnership for Service-Learning
Patent & Trademark Office
Pediatric AIDS Foundation
Peggy Guggenheim Collection
Pella
Pendulum Records
Penguin Books
The Pentagon
PERA Club
Perspective Records
The Philadelphia Center
The Philadelphia Inquirer
Physicians for Human Rights
Pittsburgh Energy Technology Center
Playboy
Plume Books
PMK Public Relations
PolyGram
Pontiac
Procter & Gamble
Procter & Gamble Productions
Psychology Today
Public Allies
Public Defender Service for DC
Public Interest Research Groups
RCA Records
The Real World
Renew America
Rhino Records
Rhode Island State Government
Rio Grande National Forest
The Ripon Society
Roll Call
Rolling Stone
Rosenbluth International
Roy A. Somlyo Productions
The Rush Limbaugh Show

Saks Fifth Avenue
Sally Jessy Raphael Show
San Diego Zoo
San Francisco Bay Guardian
San Francisco Chronicle
San Francisco 49ers
San Francisco Opera
San Juan/Rio Grande National Forests
Saturday Night Live
Saturn
Savannah River Ecology Laboratory
Save the Sound
Savvy Management
SBK Records
Scott Rudin Productions
The Seattle Times
Select Records
765-ARTS
Seventeen Magazine
Sgro Promo Associates/General Motors Internship
Shaver's Creek Environmental Center
Shirley Herz Associates
Signet Classics
SGI
Simon & Goodman Picture Company
60 Minutes
Smithsonian Institution
Sony
Sony Music Entertainment
Sony Pictures Entertainment
The Source
The Source Theater Company
The Southern Center for International Studies
Southface Energy Institute
The Southwestern Company
Spin
Spoleto Festival USA
Sponsors for Educational Opportunity
Spy
Starlight Foundation
Statue of Liberty
Stennis Space Center
Steppenwolf Theatre Company
Student Conservation Association
Student Works Painting
Students for Central & Eastern Europe
Success
Summerbridge National
Sunday Morning
Surfrider Foundation
Sussex Publishers
TADA!
TBWA
Teach for America (Employment Dept. only)
Technology Administration
Teen Voices
Temerlin McClain
Texas Instruments

Texas Monthly
Theater de la Jeune Lune
Thread Waxing Space
3M
The Today Show
Tommy Boy Music
Tracy Watts Millinery
Tribeca Film Center
TriStar Pictures
Tucson Children's Museum
Twentieth Century Fox
Twentieth Television
20/20
20/20 Vision
Tyco Toys
UCSF AIDS Health Project
Union Carbide
The Union Institute for Social Responsibility
United Artists
United Nations
United Nations Association of the United States of America
United States Agency for International Development
United States and Foreign Commercial Service
United States Army Environmental Hygiene Agency
United States Bureau of Mines
United States Department of Commerce
United States Department of Defense
United States Environmental Protection Agency
United States Holocaust Museum
United States National Arboretum
United States Prison
United States Secret Service
United States Securities and Exchange Commission
United States Travel & Tourism Administration
Unitel
Up to the Minute
Urban Fellows/Government Scholars Programs
Varsity Student Painters
Vault.com
Vereinsbank Capital Corp.
Vertigo Records
Verve Records
VH-1
Vibe
Viking Books
Village Voice
Virgin Records
Virginia Symphony
Voice of America
Volunteers For Peace
Volunteers for Israel
Volunteers in Asia
The Wall Street Journal
Wall Street Music
Warwick Baker O'Neill
Washington Center for Internships and Academic Seminars
Washington Office on Latin America
WAXQ - Q104.3

WCHS-TV
Wessler Entertainment
Westin Hotels & Resorts
Weyerhaeuser
The White House
Who Cares
The Widmeyer Baker Group
The Wildlife Society
Williamstown Theater Festival
The Wilma Theater
The Wilson Quarterly
Winant-Clayton Volunteers
Wired
WNBC-TV
WNYC
Wolf Trap Foundation for the Performing Arts
Women Express
Women Make Movies
Women's Institute for Freedom of the Press
Women's International League for Peace and Freedom
Women's Project & Productions
Women's Sports & Fitness Magazine
Women's Sports Foundation
Work Experience USA
Working Mother
Working Woman
World Federalist Association
Worldnet
Writers Guild of America, West
Yellowstone National Park
Yosemite National Park
Youth For Understanding International Exchange
YSB (Young Sisters & Brothers)
Zoo Entertainment

INTERNSHIPS OPEN TO COLLEGE JUNIORS

A&M Records
Abbott Laboratories
Abrams Artists Agency
Academic Study Associates
The Academy for Advanced and Strategic Studies
Academy of Television Arts & Sciences
Access: A Security Information Service
Accuracy in Education
Accuracy in Media
Ackerman McQueen
Actors Theatre of Louisville
Adrienne Vittadini
Advertising Club of New York
A.E. Schwartz & Associates
Aetna Life & Casualty
Affiliated Sante Group
AFS Intercultural Programs
Agency for Toxic Substances and Disease Registry
Agora, Inc.
AIESEC
Aigner Associates
AIM for the Handicapped

Alaska State Parks
The Algonquin
All Things Considered
Alliance of Residence Theaters
Alper International
Amelia Island Plantation
America West Airlines
American-Arab Anti-Discrimination Committee
American Association for the Advancement of Science
American Association of Overseas Studies
American Association of University Women Educational
  Foundation
American Bar Association
American Civil Liberties Union
American Committee on Africa/The Africa Fund
American Conservatory Theater
American Dance Festival
American Enterprise Institute
American Federation of Teachers
American Forests
American Friends Service Committee
The American Geographical Society
American Heart Association
American Hockey League
American Indian Science & Engineering Society
American Institute for Foreign Study
American Israel Public Affairs Committee
American Jewish Congress
American Judicature Society
American Management Association
The American Place Theatre
American Red Cross
American Repertory Theatre
American Rivers
American School for the Deaf
American Society of Magazine Editors
American Symphony Orchestra League
American University in Moscow
American Wind Energy Association
American Woman's Economic Development Corp.
American Youth Work Center
Ames Research Center
AMIDEAST
Amnesty International
Amtrak
Anacostia Museum
Anasazi Heritage Center
Anchorage Daily News
The Andy Warhol Museum
Angel Records
Anheuser-Busch
Another World
The Antarctica Project
Aperture Foundation
Apple Computer
Arab American Institute
Archive Films
Arden Theatre Company

Arena Stage
Argonne National Laboratory
Arista Records
Arms Control Association
Arthritis Foundation—Northern California Chapter
Arthur Andersen
Artists Space
The Arts & Education Council of Greater St. Louis
As The World Turns
ASHOKA: Innovators for the Public
Asian American Arts Centre
Asian American Journalists Association
Aspen Center for Environmmental Studies
ASSIST
Association for Education in Journalism
Association of Hispanic Arts
Association of Trial Lawyers of America
Asylum Records
AT&T Bell Laboratories
The Atlanta Ballet
Atlantic Council of the United States
Atlantic Records
Australian Embassy
Ballantine Books
BalletMet
Baltimore Zoo
Barneys New York
Barry-Haft-Brown Artists Agency
Barwood Productions
Baxter International
Baywatch
Beach Associates
Beacon Press
Bechtel
Bellevue Hospital Center
Benetton USA Corp.
Berkeley Repertory Theater
Berkshire Public Theatre
Bermuda Biological Station for Research
Bertelsmann Music Group
Best Buddies International
Bet Tzedek Legal Services
Betsey Johnson
Bike-Aid
sBlack Enterprise
Black Entertainment Television
The Blade
Blue Corn Comics
Blair Television
Boeing
The Boston Globe
Boston Magazine
Boston University International Programs
Boys Hope/Girls Hope
Bozell Public Relations
BP
Brethren Volunteer Service
Brick Wall Management

Brookfield Zoo
Brookhaven National Laboratory
The Brookings Institution
Brooklyn Botanic Garden
Brown-Miller Communications
Bucks County Courier Times
Buffalo Bill Historical Center
B.U.G.
Buick
Bureau of Economic Analysis
Bureau of Export Administration
Business Executives for National Security
Butterfield & Butterfield
Cabrillo National Monument
Cadillac
Cairns & Associates
California Governor's Office
California Museum of Photography
The Callaghan Group
Callaway Advanced Technology
Callaway Gardens
Camp Counselors USA
Camphill Soltane
Canaan Public Relations
Canadian Embassy
Capital Gang
Capitol Records
Carolyn Ray
The Carter Center
The Cartoon Network
The Catholic University of America
CAVS/Gund Arena Company
CBS News
CBS Records
CDG/CDS International
Census Bureau
Center for Coastal Studies
Center for Defense Information
Center for Investigative Reporting
Center for Marine Conservation
Center for Strategic & International Studies
Center for Talented Youth
Central Intelligence Agency
Central Park SummerStage
Centro para los Adolescentes de San Miguel de Allende
The Century Plaza Hotel
Chamber Music America
Chanticleer Films
Charlesbridge Publishing
Charlie Rose
Chemical Industry Institute of Toxicology
Chevrolet
Chevron
Chicago Botanic Garden
Chicago Children's Museum
Child's Play Touring Theatre
Children's Defense Fund
Children's Museum of Indianapolis

Chincoteague National Wildlife Refuge
Chote Rosemary Hall
Christie's
The Chronicle of the Horse
Chrysalis Records
Cinemax
The Citizens Network for Foreign Affairs
City Limits Magazine
City of New York Parks & Recreation
CityArts
Clarke & Company
Classic Stage Company
Cleveland Cavaliers
The Cloisters
CNN
College Connections
College Light Opera Company
The Public Forum Institute
Columbia Journalism Review
Columbia Pictures
Columbia Records
Comedy Central
Common Cause
Community Service Volunteer Programme
Concrete Marketing
Congressional Hispanic Caucus Institute
Congressional Management Foundation
Congressional Research Service
Connecticut Judicial Branch
Connecticut Magazine
Conservation Analytical Laboratory
The Conservative Caucus
Consumers for World Trade
Continuous Electron Beam Accelerator Facility
Cooper-Hewitt Museum
The Corporate Response Group
Corporation for National Service
Council of Energy Resource Tribes
Council on Economic Priorities
Council on Foreign Relations
Council on Hemispheric Affairs
Council on International Educational Exchange
Creative Time
Creede Repertory Theatre
Cromarty & Co.
Crossfire
Crow Canyon Archaeological Center
Crown Books
Crown Capital
C-SPAN
Cushman School
Cybergrrl
Dallas Cowboys
David Leadbetter Golf Academy
Davis Hays & Co.
D.C. Booth Historic Fish Hatchery
Death Valley
Decatur House Museum

Def Jam Records
Dell Computer
Deloitte & Touche
DesignTech International
DHL Worldwide Express
The Discovery Channel
Discovery Communications
Donna Maione
Dow Chemical Company
The Dow Jones Newspaper Fund
The Drawing Center
Dublin Internships, Ireland
Duke University Talent Identification Program
Dykeman Associates
E! Entertainment Television Networks
E-Systems
E/The Environmental Magazine
Earle Palmer Brown
Eastman Kodak Company
EastWest Records
The Ecco Press
Economic Development Administration
Economic Research Service
The Economist
Educational Programs Abroad
Elektra Entertainment Group
Elektra Records
Elite Model Management
Elizabeth Dow
Elkman Advertising & Public Relations
Emerge
EMI Records
EMI Records Group North America
Emily's List
Energy Records
Entenmann's
Entertainment Design/Lighting Dimensions
Entertainment Weekly
The Environmental Careers Organization
Epic Records
ESPN
Everglades
Faber and Faber
Face the Nation
FAIR
Families USA Foundation
Fantagraphics Books
Farm Sanctuary
Farrar Straus & Giroux
Federal Bureau of Prisons
Federal Reserve Board
The Feminist Majority
Fenton Communications
First Business
Fisher-Price Toys
Focus on Women
Fontana Records
Food for the Hungry

Forbes
Ford Models
Ford Motor Company
Foreign Policy Research Institute
Foreign Student Service Council
Forty Acres and a Mule Filmworks
48 Hours
Fourth World Movement
Fox
Franklin D. Roosevelt Library
Freedom Theatre
Freer Gallery of Art
French Embassy
The French-American Center
Frito-Lay
Frontier Nursing Service
fX
Gap
The Gazette Company
Geffen Records
Genentech
General Foods
General Mills
General Motors Marketing Internship
Gensler and Associates/Architects
Georgia Governor's Office
The Gesher Summer Internship Program
Gettysburg Battlefield
Glen Helen Outdoor Education Center
Global Exchange
Global Volunteers
GMC Truck
Goddard Space Flight Center
Good Morning America
The Gothard Group
Gould Farm
The Government Affairs Institute
Grand Canyon
Great Projects Film Company
Greater Media Cable
Grubb & Ellis
GTE
Guiding Light
Gund Arena
Habitat for Humanity International
Haft/Nasatir
HALT: Americans for Legal Reform
The Hansard Society for Parliamentary Government
Harley-Davidson
Harper's Magazine
The Hastings Center
Hawk Mountain Sanctuary
Hawthorne Valley Farm
HBO
Headline News
Health & Environmental Sciences Group
Healthy Mothers, Healthy Babies
HERE

The Heritage Foundation
The Hermitage
Hewitt Associates
Hewlett-Packard
High Country News
High Museum of Art
Hill, Holliday, Connors, Cosmopulos Advertising
Hirshhorn Museum and Sculpture Garden
Hispanic Association of Colleges and Universities
Historic Deerfield
The History Factory
Hoffman-La Roche
H.O.M.E.
Home Box Office
Hostelling International—American Youth Hostels
Houghton Mifflin Company
Houston International Protocol Alliance
The Howard Stern Show
Howard Talent West
H.S.I. Productions
Hudson Institute
Human Service Alliance
Hunter House
IBM
IES – The Institute for the International Education of Students
Indianapolis Zoo
Inroads
Institute for International Cooperation and Development
Institute for Policy Studies
Institute for Unpopular Culture
Institute of Government
Institute of International Education
Insurance Services Office
Intel
Interhemispheric Resource Center
Interactive Public Relations
Interior Design Collections
Interlocken
The International Center
The International Center of Photography
International Creative Management
International Foundation of Employee Benefit Plans
International Labor Organization
International Management Group
International Radio and Television Society
International Sculpture Center
International Telecommunications Satellite Organization
International Trade Administration
International Voluntary Services
International Volunteer Projects
Internships in Francophone Europe
Interscope Records
Iowa Film Office
Island Records
It's Your Business
The J. Paul Getty Trust
Jacob's Pillow Dance Festival
Japan-America Society of Washington

J.C. Penney
Jet Propulsion Laboratory
Jewish Vocational and Career Counseling Service
Jim Henson Productions
John Wiley & Sons
Johnson Space Center
Joint Chiefs of Staff
Jones & Bartlett
Joshua Tree
The Juilliard School
JUSTACT: Youth Action for Global Justice
Karl Lagerfeld
KCSA Public Relations
The Kennedy Center
Kennedy Space Center
KGO-TV
KIRO
The Kitchen
Klondike Gold Rush
Knopf Books
Korean American Coalition
Korff Enterprises
KPIX-TV
Kraft Foods, Inc.
KRCB
Lake Charles American Press
Lamont-Doherty Earth Observatory
Land Between The Lakes
Langley Research Center
Larry King Live
Late Night with Conan O'Brien
Late Show with David Letterman
Lawrence Livermore National Laboratory
Lawyers Alliance for World Security/Committee for National Security
The Learning Channel
Leavenworth Prison
Legacy International
Leo Castelli Gallery
Levine/Schneider Public Relations
Lewis Research Center
Liberty Records
The Library of Congress
Lightstorm Entertainment
Little Keswick School
Liz Claiborne
Lobsenz-Stevens
Long Lake Conservation Center
Longwood Gardens
Los Angeles Lakers
Los Angeles Magazine
Los Angeles Municipal Art Gallery
Los Angeles Times
Lucasfilm
Lunar and Planetary Institute
MacDonald Communications
MacNeil/Lehrer News Hour
MAD Magazine

Madison Square Garden
Maine State Music Theatre
Makovsky & Company
Mallory Factor
Mammoth Records
Manhattan Theatre Club
Manice Education Center
Manus & Associates Literary Agency
Marina Maher Communications
Marion Penitentiary
Marshall Space Flight Center
The Martin Agency
Marvel Comics
Matador Records
The Maternal & Child Health Institute
Mattel Toys
MCA Records
MCA/Universal
McDonald's
McLean Hospital
MCT Management/Bold! Records
Mercury Records
MetLife
Metro-Goldwyn-Mayer/United Artists
The Metropolitan Museum of Art
Microsoft
Middle Earth
Middle East Institute
Middle East Research & Information Project
The Milwaukee Journal
Miniwanca
Minority Business Development Agency
Miss Universe
Miss USA
Mixed Media
Mobility International
Montgomery County Community Corrections
Morris Arboretum
Morrison & Foerster
Mote Marine Laboratory
Mother Earth News
Mother Jones
Motown Records
Mount Rushmore
Ms.
MSG Network
MTV: Music Television
Museum of Contemporary Art, Chicago
Museum of Fine Arts, Boston
The Museum of Modern Art, New York
My Sister's Place
Mystic Seaport Museum
Nabisco
The Nation
Nation's Business
National Aeronautics and Space Administration
National Air and Space Museum
National Aquarium in Baltimore
National Asian Pacific American Legal Consortium

National Association for Female Executives
National Association of College Broadcasters
National Association of Professional Surplus Lines Offices
National Audubon Society
National Basketball Association
National Broadcasting Company
National Center for Fair & Open Testing
National Center for Toxicological Research
National Consortium for Graduate Degrees for Minorities in Engineering and Science
National Endowment for the Humanities
National Football League
National Foundation for the Improvement of Education
National Institute of Standards & Technology
National Institutes of Health
National Journalism Center
National Museum of African Art
National Museum of American History
National Museum of Natural History
National Oceanic & Atmospheric Administration
National Organization for Women
National Park Service
The National Partnership for Women and Families
National Portrait Gallery
National Public Radio
National Security Agency
National Space Society
National Technical Information Service
National Telecommunications & Information Administration
National Trust for Historic Preservation
National Women's Health Network
National Zoo
The Nature Conservancy
Naval Training Systems Center
NBC Nightly News
NETWORK
New Dramatists
New Stage Theatre
New York City Government
The New York Hospital-Cornell Medical Center
New York Knicks
New York Rangers
New York Shakespeare Festival
New York State Bar Association
New York State Theatre Institute
Newsday/New York Newsday
Nick Bollettieri Tennis Academy
Nightline
Norfolk Chamber Music Festival
North Carolina Botanical Garden
North Cascades Institute
Northwestern Mutual Financial Network
NOW Legal Defense and Education Fund
Oak Ridge Institute for Science and Education
Oak Ridge National Laboratory
Office of House Speaker
Office of Inspector General
Office of Job Corps
Oldsmobile

Open City Films
Oracle
Organization of Chinese Americans
Oscar Mayer
Outward Bound/Voyageur School
Overland Entertainment
Overseas Private Investment Corporation
The Paris Review
The Partnership for Service-Learning
Patent & Trademark Office
Pediatric AIDS Foundation
Peggy Guggenheim Collection
Pella
Pendulum Records
Penguin Books
The Pentagon
People to People International
PERA Club
Performance Today
Perspective Records
The Philadelphia Center
The Philadelphia Inquirer
Physicians for Human Rights
Physicians for Social Responsibility
Pittsburgh Energy Technology Center
Playboy
Plume Books
PMK Public Relations
PolyGram
Pontiac
The Population Institute
PrimeTime Live
Pro-Found Software
Procter & Gamble
Procter & Gamble Productions
Psychology Today
Public Allies
Public Defender Service for DC
Public Interest Research Groups
Quality Education for Minorities Network
Random House
Raychem
RCA Records
The Real World
Reebok
Renew America
Rhino Records
Rhode Island State Government
Rio Grande National Forest
The Ripon Society
The Rockey Company
Roll Call
Rolling Stone
Rosenbluth International
Roy A. Somlyo Productions
The Rush Limbaugh Show
Saks Fifth Avenue
Sally Jessy Raphael Show

San Diego Zoo
San Francisco Bay Guardian
San Francisco Chronicle
San Francisco 49ers
San Francisco Opera
San Juan/Rio Grande National Forests
Saturday Night Live
Saturn
Savannah River Ecology Laboratory
Save the Sound
Savvy Management
SBK Records
Scott Rudin Productions
Scripps Institution of Oceanography
Sea World
The Seattle Times
Select Records
765-ARTS
Seventeen Magazine
Sgro Promo Associates/General Motors Internship
Shadow Broadcast Services
Shaver's Creek Environmental Center
Sherwin-Williams
Shirley Herz Associates
Sierra Club
Signet Classics
SGI
Simon & Goodman Picture Company
60 Minutes
Skadden, Arps, Slate, Meagher & Flom
Smithsonian Institution
Solomon R. Guggenheim Museum
Sony
Sony Music Entertainment
Sony Pictures Entertainment
Sotheby's
The Source
The Source Theater Company
The Southern Center for International Studies
Southern Progress Corporation
Southface Energy Institute
The Southwestern Company
Special Olympics International
Spin
Spoleto Festival USA
Sponsors for Educational Opportunity
Sports Illustrated
Spy
Starlight Foundation
State Teachers Retirement System of Ohio
Statue of Liberty
Stennis Space Center
Steppenwolf Theatre Company
Student Conservation Association
Student Works Painting
Students for Central & Eastern Europe
Success
Summerbridge National

Sunday Morning
Supreme Court of the United States
Surfrider Foundation
Sussex Publishers
TADA!
Talk of the Nation
TBS
TBWA
Teach for America (Employment Dept. only)
Technology Administration
Teen Voices
Tellabs
Temerlin McClain
Texas Instruments
Texas Monthly
Theater de la Jeune Lune
Thirteen/WNET
Thread Waxing Space
3M
TNT
The Today Show
Tommy Boy Music
The Tonight Show With Jay Leno
Toyota
Tracy Watts Millinery
Tribeca Film Center
TriStar Pictures
Tucson Children's Museum
Turner Broadcasting System
Food Network
Twentieth Century Fox
Twentieth Television
20/20
20/20 Vision
Tyco Toys
UCSF AIDS Health Project
Union Carbide
The Union Institute for Social Responsibility
United Artists
United Nations
United Nations Association of the United States of America
United States Agency for International Development
United States and Foreign Commercial Service
United States Army Environmental Hygiene Agency
United States Bureau of Mines
United States Chamber of Commerce
United States Department of Commerce
United States Department of Defense
United States Department of State
United States Environmental Protection Agency
United States Holocaust Museum
United States National Arboretum
United States Olympic Committee
United States Prison
United States Secret Service
United States Securities and Exchange Commission
United States Travel & Tourism Administration
Unitel

Universal Pictures
Universal Studios
Up to the Minute
Urban Fellows/Government Scholars Programs
US-Asia Institute
Utah State Legislature
Varsity Student Painters
Vault.com
Vereinsbank Capital Corp.
Vertigo Records
Verve Records
VH-1
Vibe
Viking Books
Village Voice
Virgin Records
Virginia Symphony
Voice of America
Volunteers For Peace
Volunteers for Israel
Volunteers in Asia
Wadsworth Atheneum
The Wall Street Journal
Wall Street Music
Warwick Baker O'Neill
Washington Center for Internships and Academic Seminars
Washington Center for Politics & Journalism
The Washington Office on Africa
Washington Office on Latin America
The Washington Post
The Washingtonian
WAXQ - Q104.3
WCHS-TV
Wessler Entertainment
Westin Hotels & Resorts
The Westwood One Radio Network
Weyerhaeuser
WGN-Chicago
The White House
Whitney Museum of American Art
Who Cares
The Widmeyer Baker Group
Wildlife Prairie Park
The Wildlife Society
Williamstown Theater Festival
The Wilma Theater
The Wilson Quarterly
Winant-Clayton Volunteers
Wired
WISH-TV 8
WNBC-TV
WNYC
Wolf Trap Foundation for the Performing Arts
Women Express
Women Make Movies
Women's Institute for Freedom of the Press
Women's International League for Peace and Freedom
Women's Project & Productions

Women's Sports & Fitness Magazine
Women's Sports Foundation
Woodrow Wilson International Center for Scholars
Work Experience USA
Working Mother
Working Woman
World Federalist Association
Worldnet
Writers Guild of America, West
Xerox
Yellowstone National Park
Yosemite National Park
Youth For Understanding International Exchange
YSB (Young Sisters & Brothers)
Zoo Entertainment

INTERNSHIPS OPEN TO COLLEGE SENIORS

A&M Records
Abbott Laboratories
Abrams Artists Agency
Academic Study Associates
The Academy for Advanced and Strategic Studies
Academy of Television Arts & Sciences
Access: A Security Information Service
Accuracy in Education
Accuracy in Media
Ackerman McQueen
Actors Theatre of Louisville
Adrienne Vittadini
Advertising Club of New York
A.E. Schwartz & Associates
Aetna Life & Casualty
Affiliated Sante Group
AFS Intercultural Programs
Agency for Toxic Substances and Disease Registry
Agora, Inc.
AIESEC
Aigner Associates
AIM for the Handicapped
Alaska State Parks
The Algonquin
All Things Considered
Alliance of Residence Theaters
Alper International
Amelia Island Plantation
America West Airlines
American-Arab Anti-Discrimination Committee
American Association for the Advancement of Science
American Association of Advertising Agencies
American Association of Overseas Studies
American Association of University Women Educational
   Foundation
American Bar Association
American Civil Liberties Union
American Committee on Africa/The Africa Fund
American Conservatory Theater
American Dance Festival
American Enterprise Institute

American Federation of Teachers
American Forests
American Friends Service Committee
The American Geographical Society
American Heart Association
American Hockey League
American Indian Science & Engineering Society
American Institute for Foreign Study
American Israel Public Affairs Committee
American Jewish Congress
American Judicature Society
American Management Association
The American Place Theatre
American Red Cross
American Repertory Theatre
American Rivers
The American-Scandinavian Foundation
American School for the Deaf
American Symphony Orchestra League
American University in Moscow
American Wind Energy Association
American Woman's Economic Development Corp.
American Youth Work Center
Ames Research Center
AMIDEAST
Amnesty International
Amtrak
Amway
Anacostia Museum
Anasazi Heritage Center
Anchorage Daily News
The Andy Warhol Museum
Angel Records
Anheuser-Busch
Another World
The Antarctica Project
Aperture Foundation
Apple Computer
Arab American Institute
Archive Films
Arden Theatre Company
Arena Stage
Argonne National Laboratory
Arista Records
Arms Control Association
Arthritis Foundation—Northern California Chapter
Arthur Andersen
Artists Space
The Arts & Education Council of Greater St. Louis
As The World Turns
ASHOKA: Innovators for the Public
Asian American Arts Centre
Asian American Journalists Association
Aspen Center for Environmmental Studies
ASSIST
Association for Education in Journalism
Association of Hispanic Arts
Association of Trial Lawyers of America

Asylum Records
AT&T Bell Laboratories
The Atlanta Ballet
Atlanta Junior Golf Association
Atlantic Council of the United States
Atlantic Records
Australian Embassy
Ballantine Books
BalletMet
Baltimore Zoo
Barneys New York
Barry-Haft-Brown Artists Agency
Barwood Productions
Baywatch
Beach Associates
Beacon Press
Bechtel
Bellevue Hospital Center
Benetton USA Corp.
Berkeley Repertory Theater
Berkshire Public Theatre
Bermuda Biological Station for Research
Bernstein-Rein
Bertelsmann Music Group
Best Buddies International
Bet Tzedek Legal Services
Betsey Johnson
Bike-Aid
Black Enterprise
Black Entertainment Television
The Blade
Blair Television
Blue Corn Comics
Boeing
The Boston Globe
Boston Magazine
Boston University International Programs
Boys Hope/Girls Hope
Bozell Public Relations
Brethren Volunteer Service
Brick Wall Management
Brookfield Zoo
Brookhaven National Laboratory
The Brookings Institution
Brooklyn Botanic Garden
Brown-Miller Communications
Bucks County Courier Times
Buffalo Bill Historical Center
B.U.G.
Buick
Bureau of Economic Analysis
Bureau of Export Administration
Burson-Marsteller
Business Executives for National Security
Butterfield & Butterfield
Cabrillo National Monument
Cadillac
Cairns & Associates

California Governor's Office
California Museum of Photography
The Callaghan Group
Callaway Advanced Technology
Callaway Gardens
Camp Counselors USA
Camphill Soltane
Canaan Public Relations
Canadian Embassy
Capital Gang
Capitol Records
Carolyn Ray
The Carter Center
The Cartoon Network
The Catholic University of America
CAVS/Gund Arena Company
CBS News
CBS Records
CDG/CDS International
Census Bureau
Center for Coastal Studies
Center for Defense Information
The Center for Human Rights Advocacy
Center for Investigative Reporting
Center for Marine Conservation
Center for Strategic & International Studies
Center for the Study of Conflict
Center for Talented Youth
Central Intelligence Agency
Central Park SummerStage
Centro para los Adolescentes de San Miguel de Allende
The Century Plaza Hotel
Chamber Music America
Chanticleer Films
Charlesbridge Publishing
Charlie Rose
Chemical Industry Institute of Toxicology
Chevrolet
Chevron
Chicago Botanic Garden
Chicago Children's Museum
Child's Play Touring Theatre
Children's Defense Fund
Children's Museum of Indianapolis
Chincoteague National Wildlife Refuge
Choate Rosemary Hall
Christie's
The Chronicle of the Horse
Chrysalis Records
Cinemax
Citibank
The Citizens Network for Foreign Affairs
City Limits Magazine
City of New York Parks & Recreation
CityArts
Clarke & Company
Classic Stage Company
Cleveland Cavaliers

The Cloisters
CNN
College Connections
College Light Opera Company
Student Works Painting
Columbia Journalism Review
Columbia Pictures
Columbia Records
Comedy Central
Common Cause
Community Service Volunteer Programme
Concrete Marketing
Congressional Hispanic Caucus Institute
Congressional Management Foundation
Congressional Research Service
Connecticut Judicial Branch
Connecticut Magazine
Conservation Analytical Laboratory
The Conservative Caucus
Consumers for World Trade
Continuous Electron Beam Accelerator Facility
Cooper-Hewitt Museum
Corporation for National Service
Council of Energy Resource Tribes
Council on Economic Priorities
Council on Foreign Relations
Council on Hemispheric Affairs
Council on International Educational Exchange
Creamer Dickson Basford
Creative Time
Creede Repertory Theatre
Cromarty & Co.
Crossfire
Crow Canyon Archaeological Center
Crown Books
Crown Capital
C-SPAN
Cushman School
Cybergrrl
Dallas Cowboys
David Leadbetter Golf Academy
Davis Hays & Co.
D.C. Booth Historic Fish Hatchery
Death Valley
Decatur House Museum
Def Jam Records
Dell Computer
Deloitte & Touche
Denver Art Museum
DesignTech International
DHL Worldwide Express
The Discovery Channel
Discovery Communications
Donna Maione
Dow Chemical Company
The Dow Jones Newspaper Fund
The Drawing Center
Dublin Internships, Inc.

Duffey Communications
Du Pont
Duke University Talent Identification Program
Dykeman Associates
E! Entertainment Television Networks
E/The Environmental Magazine
Earle Palmer Brown
Eastman Kodak Company
EastWest Records
The Ecco Press
Economic Development Administration
Economic Research Service
The Economist
Educational Programs Abroad
Elektra Entertainment Group
Elektra Records
Elite Model Management
Elizabeth Dow
Elkman Advertising & Public Relations
Emerge
EMI Records
EMI Records Group North America
Emily's List
Energy Records
Entenmann's
Entertainment Design/Lighting Dimensions
Entertainment Weekly
The Environmental Careers Organization
Epic Records
Ernst & Young
ESPN
Essence
Everglades
Exxon
Faber and Faber
Face the Nation
FAIR
Families USA Foundation
Fantagraphics Books
Farm Sanctuary
Farrar Straus & Giroux
Federal Bureau of Investigation
Federal Bureau of Prisons
Federal Reserve Bank of New York
Federal Reserve Board
The Feminist Majority
Fenton Communications
First Business
Fisher-Price Toys
Focus on Women
Fontana Records
Food for the Hungry
Forbes
Ford Models
Ford Motor Company
Foreign Policy Research Institute
Foreign Student Service Council
Forty Acres and a Mule Filmworks

48 Hours
Foundation for Contemporary Mental Health
Fourth World Movement
Fox
Franklin D. Roosevelt Library
The Franklin Life Insurance Company
Freedom Theatre
Freer Gallery of Art
French Embassy
The French-American Center
Frito-Lay
Frontier Nursing Service
fX
The Gazette Company
Geffen Records
Genentech
General Foods
General Mills
General Motors Marketing Internship
Gensler and Associates/Architects
Georgia Governor's Office
The Gesher Summer Internship Program
Gettysburg Battlefield
Glen Helen Outdoor Education Center
Global Exchange
Global Volunteers
GMC Truck
Goddard Space Flight Center
Golf Digest
Good Morning America
Goodman Theatre
The Gothard Group
Gould Farm
The Government Affairs Institute
Grand Canyon
Great Projects Film Company
Greater Media Cable
Grubb & Ellis
GTE
Guiding Light
Gund Arena
Habitat for Humanity International
Haft/Nasatir
Hallmark Cards
HALT: Americans for Legal Reform
The Hansard Society for Parliamentary Government
Harley-Davidson
Harper's Magazine
The Hastings Center
Hawk Mountain Sanctuary
Hawthorne Valley Farm
HBO
Headline News
Health & Environmental Sciences Group
Healthy Mothers, Healthy Babies
HERE
The Heritage Foundation
The Hermitage

Hewitt Associates
Hewlett-Packard
High Country News
High Museum of Art
Hill, Holliday, Connors, Cosmopulos Advertising
Hirshhorn Museum and Sculpture Garden
Hispanic Association of Colleges and Universities
Historic Deerfield
The History Factory
Hoffman-La Roche
H.O.M.E.
Home Box Office
Hostelling International—American Youth Hostels
Houghton Mifflin Company
Houston International Protocol Alliance
The Howard Stern Show
Howard Talent West
H.S.I. Productions
Hudson Institute
Human Service Alliance
Hunter House
IBM
IES – The Institute for the International Education of Students
Indianapolis Zoo
Institute for International Cooperation and Development
Institute for Policy Studies
Institute for Unpopular Culture
Institute of Government
Institute of International Education
Intel
Interhemispheric Resource Center
Interactive Public Relations
Interior Design Collections
Interlocken
The International Center
The International Center of Photography
International Creative Management
International Labor Organization
International Management Group
International Radio and Television Society
International Sculpture Center
International Telecommunications Satellite Organization
International Trade Administration
International Voluntary Services
International Volunteer Projects
Internships in Francophone Europe
Interscope Records
Iowa Film Office
Island Records
It's Your Business
The J. Paul Getty Trust
Jacob's Pillow Dance Festival
Japan-America Society of Washington
J.C. Penney
Jet Propulsion Laboratory
Jewish Vocational and Career Counseling Service
The Jim Henson Company
Johnson Space Center

Joint Chiefs of Staff
Jones & Bartlett
Joshua Tree
J.P. Morgan & Co.
The Juilliard School
JUSTACT: Youth Action for Global Justice
Karl Lagerfeld
KCSA Public Relations
The Kennedy Center
Kennedy Space Center
KGO-TV
KIRO
The Kitchen
Klondike Gold Rush
Knopf Books
Korean American Coalition
Korff Enterprises
KPIX-TV
KQED-FM
Kraft Foods, Inc.
KRCB
Lake Charles American Press
Lamont-Doherty Earth Observatory
Land Between The Lakes
Langley Research Center
Larry King Live
Late Night with Conan O'Brien
Late Show with David Letterman
Lawrence Livermore National Laboratory
Lawyers Alliance for World Security/Committee for National
  Security
The Learning Channel
Leavenworth Prison
Legacy International
Leo Castelli Gallery
Levine/Schneider Public Relations
Lewis Research Center
Liberty Records
The Library of Congress
Lightstorm Entertainment
Little Keswick School
Liz Claiborne
Lobsenz-Stevens
Long Lake Conservation Center
Longwood Gardens
Los Angeles Lakers
Los Angeles Magazine
Los Angeles Municipal Art Gallery
Los Angeles Times
LPGA Junior Golf Program
Lucasfilm
Lunar and Planetary Institute
Lutheran Volunteer Corps
MacDonald Communications
MacNeil/Lehrer News Hour
MAD Magazine
Madison Square Garden
Maine State Music Theatre

Makovsky & Company
Mallory Factor
Mammoth Records
Manhattan Theatre Club
Manice Education Center
Manus & Associates Literary Agency
Marina Maher Communications
Marion Penitentiary
Marshall Space Flight Center
The Martin Agency
Marvel Comics
Matador Records
The Maternal & Child Health Institute
Mattel Toys
MCA Records
MCA/Universal
McLean Hospital
MCT Management/Bold! Records
Merck & Company
Mercury Records
Merrill Lynch
MetLife
Metro-Goldwyn-Mayer/United Artists
The Metropolitan Museum of Art
Michael Phillips Productions
Microsoft
Middle Earth
Middle East Institute
Middle East Research & Information Project
The Milwaukee Journal
Miniwanca Education Center
Minority Business Development Agency
Miss Universe
Miss USA
Mixed Media
Mobility International
Montgomery County Community Corrections
Morris Arboretum
Morrison & Foerster
Mote Marine Laboratory
Mother Earth News
Mother Jones
Motown Records
Mount Rushmore
Ms.
MSG Network
MTV: Music Television
Museum of Contemporary Art, Chicago
Museum of Fine Arts, Boston
The Museum of Modern Art, New York
My Sister's Place
Mystic Seaport Museum
Nabisco
The Nation
Nation's Business
National Aeronautics and Space Administration
National Air and Space Museum
National Aquarium in Baltimore

National Asian Pacific American Legal Consortium
National Association for Female Executives
National Association of College Broadcasters
National Association of Professional Surplus Lines Offices
National Audubon Society
National Basketball Association
National Broadcasting Company
National Center for Fair & Open Testing
National Center for Toxicological Research
National Consortium for Graduate Degrees for Minorities in
  Engineering and Science
National Endowment for the Humanities
National Football League
National Foundation for the Improvement of Education
National Institute of Standards & Technology
National Institutes of Health
National Journal
National Journalism Center
National Museum of African Art
National Museum of American Art
National Museum of American History
National Museum of Natural History
National Oceanic & Atmospheric Administration
National Organization for Women
National Park Service
The National Partnership for Women and Families
National Portrait Gallery
National Public Radio
National Review
National Security Agency
National Space Society
National Technical Information Service
National Telecommunications & Information Administration
National Trust for Historic Preservation
National Women's Health Network
National Zoo
The Nature Conservancy
Naval Training Systems Center
NBC Nightly News
NETWORK
New Dramatists
The New Republic
New Stage Theatre
New York City Government
The New York Hospital-Cornell Medical Center
New York Knicks
New York Rangers
New York Shakespeare Festival
New York State Bar Association
New York State Theatre Institute
The New York Times
Newsday/New York Newsday
Newsweek
Nick Bollettieri Tennis Academy
Nightline
NIKE
NIKE Tour
Norfolk Chamber Music Festival

North Carolina Botanical Garden
North Cascades Institute
Northfield Mount Hermon School
Northwestern Mutual Financial Network
NOW Legal Defense and Education Fund
Oak Ridge Institute for Science and Education
Oak Ridge National Laboratory
Octel Communications
Office of House Speaker
Office of Inspector General
Office of Job Corps
Oldsmobile
Open City Films
Oracle
Organization of Chinese Americans
Oscar Mayer
Outward Bound/Voyageur School
Overland Entertainment
Overseas Private Investment Corporation
The Paris Review
The Partnership for Service-Learning
Patent & Trademark Office
Pediatric AIDS Foundation
Peggy Guggenheim Collection
Pella
Pendulum Records
Penguin Books
The Pentagon
People to People International
PERA Club
Performance Today
Perspective Records
Pfizer
PGA Tour
The Philadelphia Center
The Philadelphia Inquirer
Phillips Academy
Physicians for Human Rights
Physicians for Social Responsibility
Pittsburgh Energy Technology Center
Pittsburgh Post-Gazette
Playboy
Plume Books
PMK Public Relations
PolyGram
Pontiac
The Population Institute
PrimeTime Live
Pro-Found Software
Procter & Gamble
Procter & Gamble Productions
Psychology Today
Public Allies
Public Defender Service for DC
Public Interest Research Groups
Quality Education for Minorities Network
Random House
Raychem

RCA Records
The Real World
Reebok
Renaissance Computer Art Center
Renew America
Rhino Records
Rhode Island State Government
Rio Grande National Forest
The Ripon Society
The Rockey Company
Roll Call
Rolling Stone
Rosenbluth International
Roy A. Somlyo Productions
Ruder-Finn
The Rush Limbaugh Show
St. Paul's School
Saks Fifth Avenue
Sally Jessy Raphael Show
San Diego Zoo
San Francisco Bay Guardian
San Francisco Chronicle
San Francisco 49ers
San Francisco Opera
San Juan/Rio Grande National Forests
Saturday Night Live
Saturn
Savannah River Ecology Laboratory
Save the Sound
Savvy Management
SBK Records
Schlumberger
Scott Rudin Productions
Scripps Institution of Oceanography
Sea World
The Seattle Times
Select Records
Senior PGA Tour
765-ARTS
Seventeen Magazine
Sgro Promo Associates/General Motors Internship
Shadow Broadcast Services
Shaver's Creek Environmental Center
Sherwin-Williams
Shirley Herz Associates
Sierra Club
Signet Classics
SGI
Simon & Goodman Picture Company
60 Minutes
Skadden, Arps, Slate, Meagher & Flom
Smithsonian Institution
Solomon R. Guggenheim Museum
Sony
Sony Music Entertainment
Sony Pictures Entertainment
Sotheby's
The Southern Center for International Studies

Southern Progress Corporation
The Source
The Source Theater Company
South Seas Plantation
Southface Energy Institute
The Southwestern Company
Space Needle Corporation
Special Olympics International
Spin
Spoleto Festival USA
Sponsors for Educational Opportunity
Sports Illustrated
Spy
Starlight Foundation
State Teachers Retirement System of Ohio
Statue of Liberty
Stennis Space Center
Steppenwolf Theatre Company
Student Conservation Association
Student Works Painting
Students for Central & Eastern Europe
Success
Summerbridge National
Sunday Morning
Supreme Court of the United States
Surfrider Foundation
Sussex Publishers
TADA!
Talk of the Nation
TBS
TBWA
Teach for America
Technology Administration
Teen Voices
Tellabs
Texas Instruments
Texas Monthly
Theater de la Jeune Lune
Thirteen/WNET
Thread Waxing Space
3M
TNT
The Today Show
Tommy Boy Music
The Tonight Show With Jay Leno
Toyota
Tracy Watts Millinery
Tribeca Film Center
TriStar Pictures
Tucson Children's Museum
Turner Broadcasting System
Food Network
Twentieth Century Fox
Twentieth Television
20/20
20/20 Vision
Tyco Toys
UCSF AIDS Health Project

Union Carbide
The Union Institute for Social Responsibility
United Artists
United Nations
United Nations Association of the United States of America
United States Agency for International Development
United States and Foreign Commercial Service
United States Army Environmental Hygiene Agency
United States Bureau of Mines
United States Chamber of Commerce
United States Department of Commerce
United States Department of Defense
United States Department of State
United States Environmental Protection Agency
United States Holocaust Museum
United States National Arboretum
United States Olympic Committee
United States Prison
United States Secret Service
United States Securities and Exchange Commission
United States Travel & Tourism Administration
Unitel
Universal Pictures
Universal Studios
Up to the Minute
Urban Fellows/Government Scholars Programs
US-Asia Institute
Utah State Legislature
Varsity Student Painters
Vault.com
Vereinsbank Capital Corp.
Vertigo Records
Verve Records
VH-1
Vibe
Viking Books
Village Voice
Virgin Records
Virginia Symphony
Voice of America
Volunteers For Peace
Volunteers for Israel
Volunteers in Asia
Wadsworth Atheneum
The Wall Street Journal
Wall Street Music
Washington Center for Internships and Academic Seminars
Washington Center for Politics & Journalism
Washington Internships for Students of Engineering
The Washington Office on Africa
Washington Office on Latin America
The Washington Post
The Washingtonian
WAXQ - Q104.3
WCHS-TV
Wells Fargo Bank
Wessler Entertainment
Westin Hotels & Resorts

The Westwood One Radio Network
Weyerhaeuser
WGN-Chicago
The White House
Whitney Museum of American Art
Who Cares
The Widmeyer Baker Group
Wildlife Prairie Park
The Wildlife Society
Williamstown Theater Festival
The Wilma Theater
The Wilson Quarterly
Winant-Clayton Volunteers
Wired
WISH-TV 8
WNBC-TV
WNYC
Wolf Trap Foundation for the Performing Arts
Women Express
Women Make Movies
Women's Institute for Freedom of the Press
Women's International League for Peace and Freedom
Women's Project & Productions
Women's Sports Foundation
Woodrow Wilson International Center for Scholars
Work Experience USA
Working Mother
Working Woman
World Federalist Association
Worldnet
Writers Guild of America, West
Xerox
Yellowstone National Park
Yosemite National Park
Youth For Understanding International Exchange
YSB (Young Sisters & Brothers)
Zoo Entertainment

Abrams Artists Agency
The Academy for Advanced and Strategic Studies
Academy of Television Arts & Sciences
Access: A Security Information Service
Accuracy in Education
Accuracy in Media
Ackerman McQueen
Actors Theatre of Louisville
Adrienne Vittadini
A.E. Schwartz & Associates
Affiliated Sante Group
Agora, Inc.
AIESEC
AIM for the Handicapped
Association for International Practical Training
Alaska State Parks
The Algonquin
Alliance of Residence Theaters
Alper International
Amelia Island Plantation
American & International Designs
American-Arab Anti-Discrimination Committee
American Association for the Advancement of Science
American Association of Advertising Agencies
American Association of Overseas Studies
American Association of University Women Educational
  Foundation
American Bar Association
American Civil Liberties Union
American Committee on Africa/The Africa Fund
American Conservatory Theater
American Dance Festival
American Enterprise Institute
American Federation of Teachers
American Forests
American Friends Service Committee
The American Geographical Society
American Hockey League
American Institute for Foreign Study
American Israel Public Affairs Committee
American Jewish Congress
American Judicature Society
American Management Association
The American Place Theatre
American Red Cross
American Repertory Theatre
American Rivers
American Symphony Orchestra League
American University in Moscow
American Wind Energy Association
American Woman's Economic Development Corp.
American Youth Work Center
AMIDEAST
Amnesty International
Anasazi Heritage Center
Anchorage Daily News
The Andy Warhol Museum

Another World
The Antarctica Project
Aperture Foundation
Archive Films
Arden Theatre Company
Arena Stage
Argonne National Laboratory
Arista Records
The Arizona Republic
Arms Control Association
Arthritis Foundation—Northern California Chapter
Artists Space
The Arts & Education Council of Greater St. Louis
As The World Turns
ASHOKA: Innovators for the Public
Asian American Arts Centre
Asian American Journalists Association
Aspen Center for Environmental Studies
ASSIST
Assistant Directors Training Program
Association of Hispanic Arts
Association of Trial Lawyers of America
The Atlanta Ballet
Atlantic Council of the United States
Australian Embassy
Baltimore Zoo
Barneys New York
Barry-Haft-Brown Artists Agency
Barwood Productions
Baywatch
Beach Associates
Beacon Press
Bellevue Hospital Center
Benetton USA Corp.
Berkeley Repertory Theater
Berkshire Public Theatre
Bermuda Biological Station for Research
Bertelsmann Music Group
Bet Tzedek Legal Services
Betsey Johnson
Bike-Aid
Black Enterprise
The Blade
Blair Television
Blue Corn Comics
The Boston Globe
Boston Magazine
Boston University International Programs
Boys Hope/Girls Hope
Bozell Public Relations
Breckenridge Outdoor Education Center
Brethren Volunteer Service
Brick Wall Management
Brookfield Zoo
Brooklyn Botanic Garden
The Brooklyn Museum
Brown-Miller Communications
Buffalo Bill Historical Center

B.U.G.
Business Executives for National Security
Butterfield & Butterfield
Cabrillo National Monument
Cairns & Associates
California Governor's Office
California Museum of Photography
California State Assembly
California State Senate
The Callaghan Group
Callaway Advanced Technology
Camp Counselors USA
Camphill Soltane
Canaan Public Relations
Canadian Embassy
Carnegie Endowment for International Peace
Carolyn Ray
The Carter Center
CBS News
CDG/CDS International
Center for Coastal Studies
Center for Defense Information
The Center for Human Rights Advocacy
Center for Investigative Reporting
Center for Strategic & International Studies
Center for the Study of Conflict
Central Newspapers/The Indianapolis News
Central Park SummerStage
Centro para los Adolescentes de San Miguel de Allende
The Century Plaza Hotel
Chamber Music America
Chanticleer Films
Charlesbridge Publishing
Charlie Rose
Chemical Industry Institute of Toxicology
Chevron
Chicago Botanic Garden
Chicago Bulls
Chicago Children's Museum
Child's Play Touring Theatre
Children's Defense Fund
Children's Museum of Indianapolis
Chincoteague National Wildlife Refuge
Choate Rosemary Hall
Christie's
The Chronicle of the Horse
Cinemax
The Citizens Network for Foreign Affairs
City Limits Magazine
City of New York Parks & Recreation
Classic Stage Company
College Connections
College Light Opera Company
The Public Forum Institute
Columbia Journalism Review
Community Service Volunteer Programme
Concrete Marketing
Congressional Hispanic Caucus Institute

Congressional Management Foundation
Congressional Research Service
Connecticut Judicial Branch
Connecticut Magazine
The Conservative Caucus
Consumers for World Trade
The Coro Foundation
The Corporate Response Group
Council of Energy Resource Tribes
Council on Economic Priorities
Council on Foreign Relations
Council on Hemispheric Affairs
Creamer Dickson Basford
Creative Artists Agency
Creative Time
Creede Repertory Theatre
Cromarty & Co.
C-SPAN
Cushman School
Dallas Cowboys
Davis Hays & Co.
D.C. Booth Historic Fish Hatchery
Death Valley
Decatur House Museum
Denver Art Museum
DesignTech International
Donna Maione
The Drawing Center
Duffey Communications
Du Pont
Duke University Talent Identification Program
Dykeman Associates
E/The Environmental Magazine
Earle Palmer Brown
The Ecco Press
Educational Programs Abroad
Elizabeth Dow
Elkman Advertising & Public Relations
Energy Records
Entertainment Design/Lighting Dimensions
Entertainment Weekly
The Environmental Careers Organization
Everglades
Faber and Faber
Face the Nation
Families USA Foundation
Fantagraphics Books
Farm Sanctuary
Farrar Straus & Giroux
Federal Bureau of Prisons
Fellowship of Reconciliation
Fenton Communications
Florida Grand Opera
Focus on Women
Food for the Hungry
Foreign Affairs
Foreign Policy
Foreign Policy Research Institute

Foreign Student Service Council
48 Hours
Fourth World Movement
The Franklin Life Insurance Company
Freedom Theatre
French Embassy
The French-American Center
Friends Committee on National Legislation
Frontier Nursing Service
The Gesher Summer Internship Program
Gettysburg Battlefield
Glen Helen Outdoor Education Center
Global Exchange
Global Volunteers
Goodman Theatre
The Gothard Group
Gould Farm
Grand Canyon
Great Projects Film Company
Greater Media Cable
Grubb & Ellis
Guiding Light
Habitat for Humanity International
Haft/Nasatir
HALT: Americans for Legal Reform
The Hansard Society for Parliamentary Government
Harper's Magazine
Hawk Mountain Sanctuary
Hawthorne Valley Farm
HBO
Health & Environmental Sciences Group
Healthy Mothers, Healthy Babies
HERE
The Heritage Foundation
The Hermitage
High Country News
High Museum of Art
Hillel
The History Factory
H.O.M.E.
Home Box Office
Hostelling International—American Youth Hostels
Houghton Mifflin Company
Houston International Protocol Alliance
Howard Talent West
H.S.I. Productions
Hudson Institute
Human Service Alliance
Hunter House
Illinois General Assembly
Independent Sector
The Indianapolis News
The Indianapolis Star
Indianapolis Zoo
Institute for International Cooperation and Development
Institute for Policy Studies
Institute for Unpopular Culture
Institute of Cultural Affairs

Institute of International Education
Interhemispheric Resource Center
Interactive Public Relations
Interior Design Collections
Interlocken
The International Center
International Creative Management
The International Foundation for Education and Self-Help
International Labor Organization
International Telecommunications Satellite Organization
International Voluntary Services
International Volunteer Projects
Internships in Francophone Europe
Internships International
Iowa Film Office
The J. Paul Getty Trust
Jacob's Pillow Dance Festival
Japanese Exchange and Teaching Program
Joint Chiefs of Staff
Joshua Tree
The Juilliard School
JUSTACT: Youth Action for Global Justice
Karl Lagerfeld
The Kennedy Center
The Kitchen
Klondike Gold Rush
Korff Enterprises
KQED-FM
KRCB
Land Between The Lakes
Lawyers Alliance for World Security/Committee for National
   Security
Leavenworth Prison
Legacy International
Leo Castelli Gallery
The Library of Congress
Little Keswick School
Long Lake Conservation Center
Longwood Gardens
Los Angeles Lakers (within 2 years of graduation)
Los Angeles Magazine
Los Angeles Municipal Art Gallery
Los Angeles Times
The Lowell Whiteman School
Lunar and Planetary Institute
Lutheran Volunteer Corps
The MacNeil/Lehrer NewsHour
Maine State Music Theatre
Makovsky & Company
Mallory Factor
Manhattan Theatre Club
Manice Education Center
Manus & Associates Literary Agency
Marina Maher Communications
Marion Penitentiary
The Maternal & Child Health Institute
McLean Hospital
MCT Management/Bold! Records

MetLife
Metro-Goldwyn-Mayer/United Artists
The Metropolitan Museum of Art
Michael Phillips Productions
Middle Earth
Middle East Institute
Middle East Research & Information Project
The Milwaukee Journal
Miniwanca Education Center
Miss Porter's School
Mixed Media
Mobility International
Montgomery County Community Corrections
Morris Arboretum
Morrison & Foerster
Mote Marine Laboratory
Mother Earth News
Mother Jones
Mount Rushmore
Museum of Contemporary Art, Chicago
Museum of Fine Arts, Boston
The Museum of Modern Art, New York
My Sister's Place
Mystic Seaport Museum
National Asian Pacific American Legal Consortium
National Association for Female Executives
National Association of College Broadcasters
National Association of Professional Surplus Lines Offices
National Audubon Society
National Broadcasting Company
National Center for Fair & Open Testing
National Collegiate Athletic Association
National Committee for Responsive Philanthropy
National Consortium for Graduate Degrees for Minorities in
    Engineering and Science
National Foundation for the Improvement of Education
National Institutes of Health
National Journal
National Journalism Center
National Organization for Women
National Park Service
The National Partnership for Women and Families
National Review
National Space Society
National Trust for Historic Preservation
National Wildlife Federation
National Women's Health Network
National Zoo
The Nature Conservancy
NETWORK
New Canaan Country School
New Dramatists
The New Republic
New Stage Theatre
New York City Government
The New York Hospital-Cornell Medical Center
New York Shakespeare Festival
New York State Theatre Institute

The New York Times
Newsweek
Norfolk Chamber Music Festival
North Carolina Botanical Garden
North Cascades Institute
Northfield Mount Hermon School
Office of House Speaker
Office of Job Corps
Organization of Chinese Americans
Oscar Mayer Wienermobile
Outward Bound/Voyageur School
Ove Arup & Partners
Overland Entertainment
Overseas Service Corps of the YMCA
The Paris Review
The Partnership for Service-Learning
Peace Corps
Peggy Guggenheim Collection
Pella
Penguin Books
The Pentagon
People to People International
The Philadelphia Inquirer
Phillips Academy
The Phoenix Gazette
Physicians for Human Rights
Physicians for Social Responsibility
Pittsburgh Post-Gazette
Playhouse on the Square
Plume Books
PMK Public Relations
The Population Institute
PrimeTime Live
Procter & Gamble Productions
Psychology Today
Public Allies
Public Defender Service for DC
Quaker United Nations Office
RCA Records
Reebok
Renaissance Computer Art Center
Renew America
Rio Grande National Forest
The Ripon Society
The Rockey Company
Rodale Institute Research Center
Roll Call
Rolling Stone
Rosenbluth International
Roy A. Somlyo Productions
Ruder-Finn
St. Paul's School
Saks Fifth Avenue
San Diego Zoo
San Francisco Bay Guardian
San Francisco Chronicle
San Francisco Opera
San Juan/Rio Grande National Forests

Save the Sound
Savvy Management
Schlumberger
Science
Science News
Scott Rudin Productions
Scoville Peace Fellowship Program
The Seattle Times
765-ARTS
Seventeen Magazine
Shadow Broadcast Services
Shaver's Creek Environmental Center
Sierra Club
Signet Classics
60 Minutes
Smithsonian Institution
Sotheby's
The Source
The Source Theater Company
South Seas Plantation
The Southern Center for International Studies
Southface Energy Institute
The Southwestern Company
Space Needle Corporation
Special Olympics International
Spin
Spoleto Festival USA
Sponsors for Educational Opportunity (Corporate Law program only)
Spy
Starlight Foundation
Staten Island Zoo
State Teachers Retirement System of Ohio
Statue of Liberty
Steppenwolf Theatre Company
Student Conservation Association
Student Works Painting
Students for Central & Eastern Europe
Summerbridge National
Sunday Morning
Supreme Court of the United States
Surfrider Foundation
Sussex Publishers
TADA!
Teach for America
Teen Voices
Temerlin McClain
Texas Monthly
Theater de la Jeune Lune
Thread Waxing Space
Tommy Boy Music
Tracy Watts Millinery
Tucson Children's Museum
Twentieth Century Fox
20/20 Vision
Tyco Toys
UCSF AIDS Health Project
The Union Institute for Social Responsibility

United Artists
United Nations Association of the United States of America
United Nations Volunteer Program
United States and Foreign Commercial Service
United States Department of Defense
United States Holocaust Museum
United States National Arboretum
United States Olympic Committee
United States Prison
United Talent Agency
Unitel
Up to the Minute
Urban Fellows/Government Scholars Programs
Vault.com
Vibe
Viking Books
Village Voice
Virginia Symphony
Virgin Records
Volunteers for Israel
Volunteers For Peace
Volunteers in Asia
Wadsworth Atheneum
The Wall Street Journal
Wall Street Music
Washington Center for Internships and Academic Seminars
Washington Center for Politics & JournalismThe Washington Office on Africa
Washington Office on Latin America
The Washingtonian
WCHS-TV
Westin Hotels & Resorts
WGN-Chicago
The White House
Who Cares
The Widmeyer Baker Group
Wildlife Prairie Park
The Wildlife Society
Williamstown Theater Festival
The Wilma Theater
The Wilson Quarterly
Winant-Clayton Volunteers
Wired
Wolf Trap Foundation for the Performing Arts
Women Express
Women Make Movies
Women's Institute for Freedom of the Press
Women's International League for Peace and Freedom
Women's Project & Productions
Women's Sports Foundation
Woodrow Wilson International Center for Scholars
World Federalist Association
WorldTeach
Work Experience USA
Writers Guild of America, West
Yellowstone National Park
Youth For Understanding International Exchange
Zoo Entertainment

Abbott Laboratories
Abrams Artists Agency
Academic Study Associates
The Academy for Advanced and Strategic Studies
Access: A Security Information Service
Accuracy in Education
Accuracy in Media
Ackerman McQueen
Actors Theatre of Louisville
Adrienne Vittadini
Advocates for Children of New York
A.E. Schwartz & Associates
Affiliated Sante Group
AFS Intercultural Programs
Agency for Toxic Substances and Disease Registry
Agora, Inc.
Aigner Associates
AIM for the Handicapped
Alaska State Parks
The Algonquin
All Things Considered
Alliance of Residence Theaters
Alper International
A&M Records
Amelia Island Plantation
America West Airlines
American-Arab Anti-Discrimination Committee
American Association for the Advancement of Science
American Association of Advertising Agencies
American Association of Overseas Studies
American Association of University Women Educational
  Foundation
American Bar Association
American Civil Liberties Union
American Dance Festival
American Enterprise Institute
American Federation of Teachers
American Forests
American Friends Service Committee
The American Geographical Society
American Heart Association
American Hockey League
American Indian Science and Engineering Society
American Institute for Foreign Study
American Israel Public Affairs Committee
American Jewish Congress
American Judicature Society
American Management Association
The American Place Theatre
American Red Cross
American Repertory Theatre
American Rivers
The American-Scandinavian Foundation
American University in Moscow
American Wind Energy Association
American Woman's Economic Development Corp.
American Youth Work Center

Ames Research Center
AMIDEAST
Amnesty International
Amtrak
Amway
Anacostia Museum
Anasazi Heritage Center
Anchorage Daily News
The Andy Warhol Museum
Angel Records
Anheuser-Busch
Another World
The Antarctica Project
Aperture Foundation
Apple Computer
Archive Films
Arden Theatre Company
Arena Stage
Argonne National Laboratory
Arista Records
Arms Control Association
Artists Space
The Arts & Education Council of Greater St. Louis
As The World Turns
ASHOKA: Innovators for the Public
Asian American Arts Centre
Asian American Journalists Association
Aspen Center for Environmental Studies
ASSIST
Assistant Directors Training Program
Association of Hispanic Arts
Association of Trial Lawyers of America
AT&T Bell Laboratories (UR only)
The Atlanta Ballet
Atlanta Junior Golf Association
Atlantic Council of the United States
Atlantic Records
Australian Embassy
Ballantine Books
Baltimore Zoo
Barneys New York
Barry-Haft-Brown Artists Agency
Barwood Productions
Baywatch
Beacon Press
Bechtel
Bellevue Hospital Center
Benetton USA Corp.
Berkeley Repertory Theater
Berkshire Public Theatre
Bermuda Biological Station for Research
Bertelsmann Music Group
Best Buddies International
Bet Tzedek Legal Services
Betsey Johnson
Bike-Aid
Black Enterprise
Black Entertainment Television

The Blade
Blue Corn Comics
The Boston Globe
Boston Magazine
Boston University International Programs
Boys Hope/Girls Hope
Bozell Public Relations
Breckenridge Outdoor Education Center
Brethren Volunteer Service
Brick Wall Management
Brookfield Zoo
Brooklyn Botanic Garden
The Brooklyn Museum
Brown-Miller Communications
Buffalo Bill Historical Center
B.U.G.
Buick
Bureau of Economic Analysis
Bureau of Engraving and Printing
Bureau of Export Administration
Business Executives for National Security
Butterfield & Butterfield
Cabrillo National Monument
Cadillac
California Governor's Office
California Museum of Photography
The Callaghan Group
Camp Counselors USA
Camphill Soltane
Canadian Embassy
Capital Gang
Capitol Records
Carolyn Ray
The Carter Center
The Cartoon Network
The Catholic University of America
CAVS/Gund Arena Company
CBS News
CBS Records
CDG/CDS International
Census Bureau
Center for Coastal Studies
Center for Defense Information
The Center for Human Rights Advocacy
Center for Investigative Reporting
Center for Marine Conservation
Center for the Study of Conflict
Center for Strategic & International Studies
Center for Talented Youth
Central Intelligence Agency
Central Park SummerStage
Centro para los Adolescentes de San Miguel de Allende
The Century Plaza Hotel
Chamber Music America
Chanticleer Films
Charlesbridge Publishing
Charlie Rose
Chemical Industry Institute of Toxicology

Chevrolet
Chevron
Chicago Botanic Garden
Chicago Children's Museum
Child's Play Touring Theatre
Children's Defense Fund
Children's Museum of Indianapolis
Chincoteague National Wildlife Refuge
Choate Rosemary Hall
The Chronicle of the Horse
Chrysalis Records
Citibank
The Citizens Network for Foreign Affairs
City Limits Magazine
City of New York Parks & Recreation
Clarke & Company
Classic Stage Company
Cleveland Cavaliers
CNN
College Light Opera Company
The Public Forum Institute
Columbia Journalism Review
Columbia Pictures
Columbia Records
Community Service Volunteer Programme
Concrete Marketing
Congressional Hispanic Caucus Institute
Congressional Management Foundation
Congressional Research Service
Connecticut Judicial Branch
Connecticut Magazine
Conservation Analytical Laboratory
The Conservative Caucus
Consumers for World Trade
Continuous Electron Beam Accelerator Facility
Cooper-Hewitt Museum
The Corporate Response Group
Corporation for National Service
Council of Energy Resource Tribes
Council on Economic Priorities
Council on Hemispheric Affairs
Council on International Educational Exchange
Creamer Dickson Basford
Creative Time
Creede Repertory Theatre
Cromarty & Co.
Crossfire
Crow Canyon Archaeological Center
Crown Books
C-SPAN
Cushman School
Dallas Cowboys
David Leadbetter Golf Academy
Davis Hays & Co.
D.C. Booth Historic Fish Hatchery
Death Valley
Decatur House Museum
Def Jam Records

Dell Computer
Deloitte & Touche
Denver Art Museum
DesignTech International
DHL Worldwide Express
The Discovery Channel
Discovery Communications
Donna Maione
Dow Chemical Company
The Dow Jones Newspaper Fund
Dublin Internships, Ireland
Duffey Communications
The Drawing Center
Duke University Talent Identification Program
Dykeman Associates
E! Entertainment Television Networks
E/The Environmental Magazine
Earle Palmer Brown
Eastman Kodak Company
The Ecco Press
Economic Development Administration
Economic Research Service
The Economist
Educational Programs Abroad
Elizabeth Dow
Elkman Advertising & Public Relations
Emerge
EMI Records
EMI Records Group North America
Energy Records
Entenmann's
Entertainment Design/Lighting Dimensions
Entertainment Weekly
The Environmental Careers Organization
Epic Records
Ernst & Young
Everglades
Exxon
Face the Nation
Families USA Foundation
Fantagraphics Books
Farm Sanctuary
Farrar Straus & Giroux
Federal Bureau of Investigation
Federal Bureau of Prisons
Federal Emergency Management Agency
Federal Reserve Bank of New York
Federal Reserve Board
The Feminist Majority
Fenton Communications
Fisher-Price Toys
Focus on Women
Fontana Records
Food for the Hungry
Forbes
The Ford Foundation
Ford Motor Company
Foreign Policy Research Institute

Foreign Student Service Council
Forty Acres and a Mule Filmworks
48 Hours
Foundation for Contemporary Mental Health
Fourth World Movement
Fox
Franklin D. Roosevelt Library
Freedom Theatre
Freer Gallery of Art
French Embassy
The French-American Center
Friends Committee on National Legislation
Frito-Lay
Frontier Nursing Service
Geffen Records
Genentech
General Foods
General Mills
General Motors Marketing Internship
Gensler and Associates/Architects
Georgia Governor's Office
The Gesher Summer Internship Program
Gettysburg Battlefield
Glen Helen Outdoor Education Center
Global Exchange
Global Volunteers
GMC Truck
Goddard Space Flight Center
Golf Digest
Good Morning America
Goodman Theatre
Gould Farm
The Government Affairs Institute
Grand Canyon
Great Projects Film Company
Greater Media Cable
Grubb & Ellis
GTE
Guiding Light
Gund Arena
Habitat for Humanity International
Haft/Nasatir
Hallmark Cards
HALT: Americans for Legal Reform
The Hansard Society for Parliamentary Government
Harley-Davidson
Harper's Magazine
The Hastings Center
Hawk Mountain Sanctuary
Hawthorne Valley Farm
Headline News
Health & Environmental Sciences Group
Healthy Mothers, Healthy Babies
HERE
The Heritage Foundation
The Hermitage
Hewlett-Packard
High Country News

High Museum of Art
Hill and Knowlton
Hill, Holliday, Connors, Cosmopulos Advertising
Hirshhorn Museum and Sculpture Garden
Hispanic Association of Colleges and Universities
The History Factory
Hoffman-La Roche
H.O.M.E.
Hostelling International—American Youth Hostels
Houghton Mifflin Company
Howard Hughes Medical Institute (medical students only)
The Howard Stern Show
H.S.I. Productions
Hudson Institute
Human Service Alliance
Hunter House
IBM
The New York Times
Independent Sector
Indianapolis Zoo
Institute for International Cooperation and Development
Institute for Policy Studies
Institute for Unpopular Culture
Institute of Cultural Affairs
Institute of International Education
Intel
Interhemispheric Resource Center
Interactive Public Relations
Interior Design Collections
Interlocken
The International Center
The International Center of Photography
International Creative Management
The International Foundation for Education and Self-Help
International Labor Organization
International Management Group
International Telecommunications Satellite Organization
International Trade Administration
International Voluntary Services
International Volunteer Projects
Internships in Francophone Europe
Internships International
Interscope Records
Iowa Film Office
Island Records
The J. Paul Getty Trust
Jacob's Pillow Dance Festival
Japan-America Society of Washington
J.C. Penney
Jet Propulsion Laboratory
The Jim Henson Company
Johnson Space Center
Joint Chiefs of Staff
Joshua Tree
The Juilliard School
JUSTACT: Youth Action for Global Justice
Karl Lagerfeld
The Kennedy Center

Kennedy Space Center
KGO-TV
KIRO
The Kitchen
Klondike Gold Rush
Knopf Books
Korff Enterprises
KPIX-TV
KQED-FM
Kraft Foods, Inc.
KRCB
Land Between The Lakes
Langley Research Center
Larry King Live
Late Show with David Letterman
Lawrence Livermore National Laboratory
Lawyers Alliance for World Security/Committee for National
   Security
The Learning Channel
Leavenworth Prison
Leo Castelli Gallery
Lewis Research Center
Liberty Records
The Library of Congress
Lightstorm Entertainment
Lincoln Center for the Performing Arts
Little Keswick School
Liz Claiborne
Long Lake Conservation Center
Los Angeles Municipal Art Gallery
LPGA Junior Golf Program
Lucasfilm
Lutheran Volunteer Corps
The MacNeil/Lehrer NewsHour
Madison Square Garden
Maine State Music Theatre
Makovsky & Company
Mallory Factor
Mammoth Records
Manhattan Theatre Club
Manice Education Center
Manus & Associates Literary Agency
Marina Maher Communications
Marion Penitentiary
Marshall Space Flight Center
Mass Media Science and Engineering Fellows Program
Matador Records
The Maternal & Child Health Institute
Mattel Toys
MCA Records
MCA/Universal
McLean Hospital
Merck & Company
Mercury Records
MetLife
Metro-Goldwyn-Mayer/United Artists
The Metropolitan Museum of Art
Michael Phillips Productions

Middle Earth
Middle East Research & Information Project
Miller Brewing Company
The Milwaukee Journal
Miniwanca Education Center
Minority Business Development Agency
Miss Universe
Miss USA
Mixed Media
Mobility International
Montgomery County Community Corrections
Morris Arboretum
Morrison & Foerster
Mote Marine Laboratory
Mother Earth News
Mother Jones
Motown Records
Mount Rushmore
MSG Network
MTV: Music Television
Museum of Contemporary Art, Chicago
Museum of Fine Arts, Boston
Mystic Seaport Museum
The Museum of Modern Art, New York
My Sister's Place
Nabisco
The Nation
National Aeronautics and Space Administration
National Air and Space Museum
National Association for Female Executives
National Audubon Society
National Center for Fair & Open Testing
National Center for Toxicological Research
National Football League
National Foundation for the Improvement of Education
National Institute of Standards & Technology
National Institutes of Health
National Journal
National Journalism Center
National Museum of African Art
National Museum of American Art
National Museum of American History
National Museum of Natural History
National Oceanic & Atmospheric Administration
National Organization for Women
National Park Service
The National Partnership for Women and Families
National Portrait Gallery
National Public Radio
National Security Agency
National Space Society
National Technical Information Service
National Telecommunications & Information Administration
National Trust for Historic Preservation
National Wildlife Federation
National Women's Health Network
The Nature Conservancy
NETWORK

New Canaan Country School
New Dramatists
The New Republic
New Stage Theatre
New York Knicks
New York Rangers
New York Shakespeare Festival
New York State Theatre Institute
Newsday/New York Newsday
Newsweek
Nick Bollettieri Tennis Academy
NIKE
NIKE Tour
Norfolk Chamber Music Festival
North Carolina Botanical Garden
North Cascades Institute
Northfield Mount Hermon School
Northwestern Mutual Financial Network
NOW Legal Defense and Education Fund
Oak Ridge Institute for Science and Education
Oak Ridge National Laboratory
Octel Communications
Office of House Speaker
Office of Inspector General
Office of Job Corps
Oldsmobile
Organization of Chinese Americans
Oscar Mayer
Oscar Mayer Wienermobile
Outward Bound/Voyageur School
Overland Entertainment
Overseas Private Investment Corporation
The Paris Review
The Partnership for Service-Learning
Patent & Trademark Office
Peace Corps
Pediatric AIDS Foundation
Peggy Guggenheim Collection
Pendulum Records
Penguin Books
The Pentagon
People to People International
PERA Club
Performance Today
Perspective Records
PGA Tour
The Philadelphia Inquirer
Phillips Academy
Physicians for Human Rights
Physicians for Social Responsibility
Pittsburgh Energy Technology Center
Pittsburgh Post-Gazette
Playhouse on the Square
Plume Books
PMK Public Relations
PolyGram
Pontiac
The Population Institute

Pro-Found Software
Procter & Gamble
Procter & Gamble Productions
Psychology Today
Public Allies
Public Defender Service for DC
Public Interest Research Groups
Quaker United Nations Office
Quality Education for Minorities Network
Rand (minimum 2 years in PhD program)
Random House
Raychem
RCA Records
The Real World
Reebok
Renaissance Computer Art Center
Renew America
Rhino Records
Rhode Island State Government
Rio Grande National Forest
The Ripon Society
Rodale Institute Research Center
Roll Call
Rosenbluth International
Roy A. Somlyo Productions
The Rush Limbaugh Show
Saks Fifth Avenue
Sally Jessy Raphael Show
San Diego Zoo
San Francisco Bay Guardian
San Francisco Chronicle
San Francisco 49ers
San Francisco Opera
San Juan/Rio Grande National Forests
Saturn
Savannah River Ecology Laboratory
Save the Sound
SBK Records
Schlumberger
Science News
Scott Rudin Productions
Scoville Peace Fellowship Program
The Seattle Times
Select Records
Senior PGA Tour
65-ARTS
Seventeen Magazine
Shadow Broadcast Services
Sierra Club
Signet Classics
SGI
60 Minutes
Smithsonian Institution
Solomon R. Guggenheim Museum
Sony
Sony Music Entertainment
Sony Pictures Entertainment
The Source

The Source Theater Company
South Seas Plantation
The Southern Center for International Studies
Southern Progress Corporation
Southface Energy Institute
The Southwestern Company
Space Needle Corporation
Spin
Spoleto Festival USA
Sports Illustrated
Spy
Starlight Foundation
Staten Island Zoo
State Teachers Retirement System of Ohio
Statue of Liberty
Stennis Space Center
National Asian Pacific American Legal Consortium
Steppenwolf Theatre Company
Student Conservation Association
Student Works Painting
Students for Central & Eastern Europe
Sunday Morning
Surfrider Foundation
Sussex Publishers
TADA!
Talk of the Nation
TBS
Technology Administration
Teen Voices
Tellabs
Temerlin McClain
Texas Instruments
Texas Monthly
Theater de la Jeune Lune
Thirteen/WNET
Thread Waxing Space
3M
TNT
Tommy Boy Music
The Tonight Show With Jay Leno
Toyota
Tracy Watts Millinery
Tribeca Film Center
TriStar Pictures
Tucson Children's Museum
Turner Broadcasting System
Food Network
Twentieth Century Fox
Twentieth Television
20/20 Vision
Tyco Toys
UCSF AIDS Health Project
Union Carbide
The Union Institute for Social Responsibility
United Artists
United Nations
United Nations Association of the United States of America
United States Agency for International Development

United States and Foreign Commercial Service
United States Army Environmental Hygiene Agency
United States Bureau of Mines
United States Department of Commerce
United States Department of Defense
United States Enviromental Protection Agency
United States Holocaust Museum
United States National Arboretum
United States Olympic Committee
United States Prison
United States Secret Service
United States Securities and Exchange Commission
United States Travel & Tourism Administration
Unitel
Universal Pictures
Universal Studios
Up to the Minute
US-Asia Institute
Vault.com
Vertigo Records
Verve Records
VH-1
Vibe
Viking Books
Village Voice
Virginia Symphony
Voice of America
Volunteers For Peace
Volunteers for Israel
Wadsworth Atheneum
The Wall Street Journal
Wall Street Music
Washington Center for Internships and Academic Seminars
Washington Center for Politics & Journalism
The Washington Office on Africa
Washington Office on Latin America
The Washington Post
The Washingtonian
WCHS-TV
Wells Fargo Bank
Wessler Entertainment
Westin Hotels & Resorts
The Westwood One Radio Network
Weyerhaeuser
WGN-Chicago
The White House
Whitney Museum of American Art
Who Cares
The Widmeyer Baker Group
Wildlife Prairie Park
The Wildlife Society
Williamstown Theater Festival
The Wilma Theater
The Wilson Quarterly
Winant-Clayton Volunteers
Wired
WISH-TV 8
WNYC

Wolf Trap Foundation for the Performing Arts
Women Express
Women Make Movies
Women's Institute for Freedom of the Press
Women's International League for Peace and Freedom
Women's Project & Productions
Women's Sports Foundation
Woodrow Wilson International Center for Scholars
Work Experience USA
World Federalist Association
Worldnet
WorldTeach
Writers Guild of America, West
Xerox
Xerox Palo Alto Research Center
Yellowstone National Park
Yosemite National Park
Youth For Understanding International Exchange
YSB (Young Sisters & Brothers)
Zoo Entertainment

Abrams Artists Agency
The Academy for Advanced and Strategic Studies
Accuracy in Education
Accuracy in Media
Ackerman McQueen
Actors Theatre of Louisville
Adrienne Vittadini
Affiliated Sante Group
AIM for the Handicapped
American Association of Overseas Studies
American Association of University Women Educational
   Foundation
American Friends Service Committee
American Management Association
The American Place Theatre
American Repertory Theatre
American University in Moscow
Amnesty International
The Andy Warhol Museum
Aperture Foundation
Archive Films
Arden Theatre Company
Asian American Arts Centre
Asian American Journalists Association
ASSIST
Association of Hispanic Arts
Baltimore Zoo
Barry-Haft-Brown Artists Agency
Baywatch
Beacon Press
Bellevue Hospital Center
Berkshire Public Theatre
Betsey Johnson
Bike-Aid
Blue Corn Comics
Breckenridge Outdoor Education Center
Brethren Volunteer Service
Brick Wall Management
California Governor's Office
California Museum of Photography
Camphill Soltane
CARE
Carolyn Ray
CDG/CDS International
Center for Defense Information
Central Park SummerStage
Centro para los Adolescentes de San Miguel de Allende
Child's Play Touring Theatre
City of New York Parks & Recreation
Classic Stage Company
Community Service Volunteer Programme
Concrete Marketing
Connecticut Magazine
The Conservative Caucus
Council on Economic Priorities
Council on Hemispheric Affairs
Creede Repertory Theatre

D.C. Booth Historic Fish Hatchery
Donna Maione
Elizabeth Dow
Energy Records
Entertainment Design/Lighting Dimensions
Farm Sanctuary
Federal Bureau of Prisons
Fourth World Movement
Freedom Theatre
Frontier Nursing Service
Global Exchange
Global Volunteers
Grubb & Ellis
Habitat for Humanity International
Haft/Nasatir
HALT: Americans for Legal Reform
Hawthorne Valley Farm
HERE
High Museum of Art
H.O.M.E.
H.S.I. Productions
Human Service Alliance
Institute for International Cooperation and Development
Institute for Unpopular Culture
Institute of Cultural Affairs
International Volunteer Projects
Iowa Film Office
Jacob's Pillow Dance Festival
The Juilliard School
JUSTACT: Youth Action for Global Justice
KRCB
Leavenworth Prison
Long Lake Conservation Center
Los Angeles Municipal Art Gallery
Lutheran Volunteer Corps
Maine State Music Theatre
Marina Maher Communications
Marion Penitentiary
Metro-Goldwyn-Mayer/United Artists
Mixed Media
Mobility International
Morrison & Foerster
Museum of Contemporary Art, Chicago
My Sister's Place
National Organization for Women
National Space Society
The Nature Conservancy
New Stage Theatre
New York State Theatre Institute
North Carolina Botanical Garden
The Partnership for Service-Learning
Peace Corps
Public Allies
Renew America
Rio Grande National Forest
Roll Call
Roy A. Somlyo Productions
San Diego Zoo

San Francisco Bay Guardian
San Juan/Rio Grande National Forests
Save the Sound
Scott Rudin Productions
Seventeen Magazine
Shaver's Creek Environmental Center
The Source
The Source Theater Company
The Southern Center for International Studies
Southface Energy Institute
The Southwestern Company
Spoleto Festival USA
Starlight Foundation
Steppenwolf Theatre Company
Student Conservation Association
TADA!
Teen Voices
Theater de la Jeune Lune
Tommy Boy Music
The Union Institute for Social Responsibility
United Artists
United States Holocaust Museum
United States Prison
Village Voice
Virgin Records
Volunteers For Peace
Volunteers for Israel
Williamstown Theater Festival
Winant-Clayton Volunteers
Wired
Women Express
Women Make Movies
Women's Institute for Freedom of the Press
Women's International League for Peace and Freedom
Women's Project & Productions
Writers Guild of America, West
Youth For Understanding International Exchange

INTERNSHIPS OPEN TO COLLEGE GRADS OF ANY AGE

Abrams Artists Agency
The Academy for Advanced and Strategic Studies
Accuracy in Education
Accuracy in Media
Ackerman McQueen
Actors Theatre of Louisville
Adrienne Vittadini
A.E. Schwartz & Associates
Aetna Life & Casualty
Affiliated Sante Group
Agora, Inc.
AIM for the Handicapped
Alaska State Parks
Alliance of Residence Theaters
Alper International
American-Arab Anti-Discrimination Committee
American Association of Overseas Studies
American Association of University Women Educational
  Foundation

American Civil Liberties Union
American Committee on Africa/The Africa Fund
American Conservatory Theater
American Dance Festival
American Federation of Teachers
American Forests
American Friends Service Committee
The American Geographical Society
American Management Association
The American Place Theatre
American Repertory Theatre
American Rivers
American University in Moscow
American Woman's Economic Development Corp.
Amnesty International
Anasazi Heritage Center
The Andy Warhol Museum
Aperture Foundation
Archive Films
Arden Theatre Company
Arena Stage
Arista Records
Artists Space
Asian American Arts Centre
Asian American Journalists Association
ASSIST
Assistant Directors Training Program
Association of Hispanic Arts
Baltimore Zoo
Barry-Haft-Brown Artists Agency
Barwood Productions
Baywatch
Beacon Press
Bellevue Hospital Center
Benetton USA Corp.
Berkeley Repertory Theater
Berkshire Public Theatre
Bertelsmann Music Group
Bet Tzedek Legal Services
Betsey Johnson
Bike-Aid
Blair Television
Blue Corn Comics
Boston University International Programs
Boys Hope/Girls Hope
Breckenridge Outdoor Education Center
Brethren Volunteer Service
Brick Wall Management
Brookfield Zoo
Buffalo Bill Historical Center
Butterfield & Butterfield
Cabrillo National Monument
California Governor's Office
California Museum of Photography
California State Assembly
California State Senate
The Callaghan Group
Camp Counselors USA

Camphill Soltane
CARE
Carolyn Ray
CBS News
CDG/CDS International
Center for Defense Information
The Center for Human Rights Advocacy
Center for Investigative Reporting
Center for the Study of Conflict
Central Park SummerStage
Centro para los Adolescentes de San Miguel de Allende
Chanticleer Films
Charlesbridge Publishing
Charlie Rose
Chevron
Chicago Children's Museum
Child's Play Touring Theatre
Children's Defense Fund
Cinemax
The Citizens Network for Foreign Affairs
City of New York Parks & Recreation
CityArts
Classic Stage Company
The Public Forum Institute
Community Service Volunteer Programme
Concrete Marketing
Congressional Research Service
Connecticut Judicial Branch
Connecticut Magazine
The Conservative Caucus
The Coro Foundation
The Corporate Response Group
Council on Economic Priorities
Council on Hemispheric Affairs
Creamer Dickson Basford
Creative Artists Agency
Creede Repertory Theatre
Cromarty & Co.
Cushman School
Davis Hays & Co.
D.C. Booth Historic Fish Hatchery
Death Valley
Decatur House Museum
Denver Art Museum
DesignTech International
Donna Maione
Duffey Communications
Duke University Talent Identification Program
Dykeman Associates
Earle Palmer Brown
The Ecco Press
Educational Programs Abroad
Elizabeth Dow
Energy Records
Entertainment Design/Lighting Dimensions
The Environmental Careers Organization
Everglades
Face the Nation
Farm Sanctuary

Federal Bureau of Prisons
Fellowship of Reconciliation
Focus on Women
Food for the Hungry
The Ford Foundation
Foreign Affairs
48 Hours
Fourth World Movement
Freedom Theatre
Friends Committee on National Legislation
Frontier Nursing Service
Gettysburg Battlefield
Glen Helen Outdoor Education Center
Global Exchange
Global Volunteers
Goodman Theatre
Gould Farm
Grand Canyon
Great Projects Film Company
Grubb & Ellis
Habitat for Humanity International
Haft/Nasatir
HALT: Americans for Legal Reform
The Hansard Society for Parliamentary Government
Harper's Magazine
Hawthorne Valley Farm
HBO
Health & Environmental Sciences Group
Healthy Mothers, Healthy Babies
HERE
High Country News
High Museum of Art
The History Factory
H.O.M.E.
Home Box Office
H.S.I. Productions
Hudson Institute
Human Service Alliance
Hunter House
Illinois General Assembly
Indianapolis Zoo
Institute for International Cooperation and Development
Institute for Unpopular Culture
Institute of Cultural Affairs
Interactive Public Relations
Interlocken
International Creative Management
International Volunteer Projects
Iowa Film Office
The J. Paul Getty Trust
Jacob's Pillow Dance Festival
Japanese Exchange and Teaching Program
Joshua Tree
The Juilliard School
JUSTACT: Youth Action for Global Justice
KCSA Public Relations
The Kitchen
Klondike Gold Rush
KQED-FM

KRCB
Land Between The Lakes
Leavenworth Prison
Long Lake Conservation Center
Longwood Gardens
Los Angeles Municipal Art Gallery
Lutheran Volunteer Corps
Maine State Music Theatre
Makovsky & Company
Manice Education Center
Marina Maher Communications
Marion Penitentiary
Metro-Goldwyn-Mayer/United Artists
Middle Earth
Middle East Research & Information Project
Mixed Media
Mobility International
Montgomery County Community Corrections
Morris Arboretum
Morrison & Foerster
Mother Earth News
Mother Jones
Mount Rushmore
Museum of Contemporary Art, Chicago
My Sister's Place
Mystic Seaport Museum
National Broadcasting Company
National Collegiate Athletic Association
National Consortium for Graduate Degrees for Minorities in
   Engineering and Science
National Journal
National Journalism Center
National Organization for Women
National Park Service
The National Partnership for Women and Families
National Space Society
The Nature Conservancy
New Canaan Country School
New Dramatists
The New Republic
New Stage Theatre
New York State Theatre Institute
Norfolk Chamber Music Festival
North Carolina Botanical Garden
North Cascades Institute
Office of Job Corps
Organization of Chinese Americans
Outward Bound/Voyageur School
Overland Entertainment
Overseas Service Corps of the YMCA
The Partnership for Service-Learning
Peace Corps
Penguin Books
People to People International
Physicians for Human Rights
Playhouse on the Square
Plume Books
PMK Public Relations

Psychology Today
Public Allies
Quaker United Nations Office
RCA Records
Renaissance Computer Art Center
Renew America
Roll Call
Roy A. Somlyo Productions
San Diego Zoo
San Francisco Bay Guardian
San Francisco Opera
Save the Sound
Science News
Scott Rudin Productions
Scoville Peace Fellowship Program
Seventeen Magazine
Shadow Broadcast Services
Shaver's Creek Environmental Center
Sierra Club
Signet Classics
60 Minutes
Smithsonian Institution
The Source
The Southern Center for International Studies
Southface Energy Institute
The Southwestern Company
Spoleto Festival USA
Spy
Starlight Foundation
Staten Island Zoo
Statue of Liberty
Steppenwolf Theatre Company
Student Conservation Association
Students for Central & Eastern Europe
Sunday Morning
Sussex Publishers
TADA!
Teach for America
Teen Voices
Texas Monthly
Theater de la Jeune Lune
Tommy Boy Music
Tracy Watts Millinery
20/20 Vision
UCSF AIDS Health Project
The Union Institute for Social Responsibility
United Artists
United Nations Volunteer Program
United States Holocaust Museum
United States Prison
United Talent Agency
Up to the Minute
Viking Books
Village Voice
Volunteers For Peace
Volunteers for Israel
Wall Street Music
The Washington Office on Africa

WCHS-TV
WGN-Chicago
Who Cares
The Wildlife Society
Williamstown Theater Festival
The Wilson Quarterly
Winant-Clayton Volunteers
Wired
Women Express
Women Make Movies
Women's Institute for Freedom of the Press
Women's International League for Peace and Freedom
Women's Project & Productions
Women's Sports Foundation
Work Experience USA
WorldTeach
Writers Guild of America, West
Yellowstone National Park
Youth For Understanding International Exchange
Zoo Entertainment

INTERNSHIPS OPEN TO INTERNATIONAL APPLICANTS

(NON-US CITIZENS)
A&M Records
Abrams Artists Agency
Academic Study Associates
The Academy for Advanced and Strategic Studies
Access: A Security Information Service
Accuracy in Education
Accuracy in Media
Ackerman McQueen
Actors Theatre of Louisville
Adrienne Vittadini
Advocates for Children of New York
A.E. Schwartz & Associates
Aetna Life & Casualty
Affiliated Sante Group
AFS Intercultural Programs
Agora, Inc.
AIESEC
Aigner Associates
AIM for the Handicapped
Alaska State Parks
The Algonquin
Alper International
Amelia Island Plantation
America West Airlines
American-Arab Anti-Discrimination Committee
American Association for the Advancement of Science
American Association of Overseas Studies
American Association of University Women Educational
  Foundation
American Bar Association
American Civil Liberties Union
American Committee on Africa/The Africa Fund
American Dance Festival
American Federation of Teachers

American Forests
American Friends Service Committee
The American Geographical Society
American Hockey League
American Institute for Foreign Study
American Israel Public Affairs Committee
American Judicature Society
American Management Association
The American Place Theatre
American Repertory Theatre
American Rivers
The American-Scandinavian Foundation
American School for the Deaf
American Symphony Orchestra League
American University in Moscow
American Woman's Economic Development Corp.
American Youth Work Center
AMIDEAST
Amnesty International
Amtrak
Amway
Anasazi Heritage Center
Anchorage Daily News
The Andy Warhol Museum
Angel Records
The Antarctica Project
Aperture Foundation
Arab American Institute
Archive Films
Arden Theatre Company
Arena Stage
The Arizona Republic
Arthritis Foundation—Northern California Chapter
Artists Space
The Arts & Education Council of Greater St. Louis
ASHOKA: Innovators for the Public
Asian American Arts Centre
Asian American Journalists Association
ASSIST
Assistant Directors Training Program
Association for Education in Journalism
Association of Hispanic Arts
Asylum Records
The Atlanta Ballet
Atlanta Junior Golf Association
Atlantic Council of the United States
Australian Embassy
BalletMet
Baltimore Zoo
Barneys New York
Barry-Haft-Brown Artists Agency
Barwood Productions
Baywatch
Beach Associates
Beacon Press
Bellevue Hospital Center
Benetton USA Corp.
Berkshire Public Theatre

Bermuda Biological Station for Research
Best Buddies International
Bet Tzedek Legal Services
Betsey Johnson
Bike-Aid
Black Entertainment Television
The Blade
Blue Corn Comics
The Boston Globe
Boston Magazine
Boston University International Programs
Breckenridge Outdoor Education Center
Brethren Volunteer Service
Brooklyn Botanic Garden
The Brooklyn Museum
Brown-Miller Communications
Bucks County Courier Times
Buffalo Bill Historical Center
B.U.G.
Buick
Burson-Marsteller
Business Executives for National Security
Cadillac
Cairns & Associates
California Governor's Office
California Museum of Photography
California State Assembly
California State Senate
Callaway Advanced Technology
Camp Counselors USA
Camphill Soltane
Canaan Public Relations
Canadian Embassy
Capital Gang
Capitol Records
CARE
Carnegie Endowment for International Peace
Carolyn Ray
The Cartoon Network
CAVS/Gund Arena Company
CBS News
CDG/CDS International
Center for Coastal Studies
Center for Defense Information
The Center for Human Rights Advocacy
Center for Marine Conservation
Center for Strategic & International Studies
Center for the Study of Conflict
Central Newspapers/The Indianapolis News
Central Park SummerStage
Centro para los Adolescentes de San Miguel de Allende
The Century Plaza Hotel
Chanticleer Films
Charlesbridge Publishing
Chevrolet
Chevron
Chicago Botanic Garden
Chicago Children's Museum
Child's Play Touring Theatre

Children's Defense Fund
Children's Museum of Indianapolis
Choate Rosemary Hall
Chrysalis Records
Cinemax
The Citizens Network for Foreign Affairs
City Limits Magazine
City of New York Parks & Recreation
CityArts
Clarke & Company
Classic Stage Company
Cleveland Cavaliers
CNN
College Connections
College Light Opera Company
The Public Forum Institute
Student Works Painting
Columbia Journalism Review
Comedy Central
Common Cause
Community Service Volunteer Programme
Concrete Marketing
Congressional Hispanic Caucus Institute
Congressional Management Foundation
Congressional Research Service
Connecticut Judicial Branch
Consumers for World Trade
The Corporate Response Group
Council on Economic Priorities
Council on Foreign Relations
Council on Hemispheric Affairs
Creamer Dickson Basford
Creative Artists Agency
Creative Time
Creede Repertory Theatre
Crossfire
C-SPAN
Cushman School
Dallas Cowboys
David Leadbetter Golf Academy
D.C. Booth Historic Fish Hatchery
Def Jam Records
Dell Computer
Deloitte & Touche
Denver Art Museum
DesignTech International
DHL Worldwide Express
The Discovery Channel
Discovery Communications
Donna Maione
Dow Chemical Company
The Drawing Center
Dublin Internships, Ireland
Duke University Talent Identification Program
Dykeman Associates
E! Entertainment Television Networks
E/The Environmental Magazine
Earle Palmer Brown
Eastman Kodak Company

EastWest Records
The Ecco Press
The Economist
Educational Programs Abroad
Elektra Entertainment Group
Elektra Records
Elizabeth Dow
Elkman Advertising & Public Relations
Emerge
EMI Records
EMI Records Group North America
Energy Records
Entertainment Design/Lighting Dimensions
Ernst & Young
ESPN
Essence
Face the Nation
Families USA Foundation
Farm Sanctuary
Farrar Straus & Giroux
Federal Reserve Board
First Business
Fisher-Price Toys
Focus on Women
Fontana Records
Forbes
The Ford Foundation
Ford Models
Ford Motor Company
Foreign Affairs
Foreign Policy
Foreign Policy Research Institute
Foreign Student Service Council
48 Hours
Foundation for Contemporary Mental Health
Fourth World Movement
Fox
Franklin D. Roosevelt Library
French Embassy
Friends Committee on National Legislation
fX
The Gazette Company
General Motors Marketing Internship
Georgia Governor's Office
Glen Helen Outdoor Education Center
Global Exchange
Global Volunteers
GMC Truck
Golf Digest
Good Morning America
Goodman Theatre
The Gothard Group
Gould Farm
Great Projects Film Company
Grubb & Ellis
Gund Arena
Habitat for Humanity International
Haft/Nasatir

HALT: Americans for Legal Reform
The Hansard Society for Parliamentary Government
Harper's Magazine
The Hastings Center
Hawk Mountain Sanctuary
Hawthorne Valley Farm
HBO
Headline News
Health & Environmental Sciences Group
Healthy Mothers, Healthy Babies
HERE
The Heritage Foundation
High Country News
High Museum of Art
Hillel
Historic Deerfield
The History Factory
Hoffman-La Roche
H.O.M.E.
Home Box Office
Hostelling International—American Youth Hostels
Houghton Mifflin Company
Houston International Protocol Alliance
Howard Hughes Medical Institute
The Howard Stern Show
Howard Talent West
H.S.I. Productions
Human Service Alliance
IES – The Institute for the International Education of Students
Illinois General Assembly
The Indianapolis News
The Indianapolis Star
Indianapolis Zoo
Institute for International Cooperation and Development
Institute for Policy Studies
Institute for Unpopular Culture
Institute of Cultural Affairs
Institute of International Education
Insurance Services Office
Interactive Public Relations
Interior Design Collections
Interlocken
The International Center
The International Center of Photography
International Foundation of Employee Benefit Plans
International Labor Organization
International Management Group
International Radio and Television Society
International Telecommunications Satellite Organization
International Voluntary Services
International Volunteer Projects
Internships in Francophone Europe
Internships International
Iowa Film Office
Island Records
It's Your Business
The J. Paul Getty Trust
Jacob's Pillow Dance Festival

Japan-America Society of Washington
Japanese Exchange and Teaching Program
The Jim Henson Company
The Juilliard School
JUSTACT: Youth Action for Global Justice
Karl Lagerfeld
KCSA Public Relations
KIRO
The Kitchen
Korean American Coalition
Korff Enterprises
KQED-FM
KRCB
Land Between The Lakes
Larry King Live
Late Night with Conan O'Brien
Lawyers Alliance for World Security/Committee for National
  Security
The Learning Channel
Legacy International
Leo Castelli Gallery
Levine/Schneider Public Relations
Liberty Records
Lightstorm Entertainment
Little Keswick School
Lobsenz-Stevens
Long Lake Conservation Center
Longwood Gardens
Los Angeles Lakers
Los Angeles Municipal Art Gallery
The Lowell Whiteman School
LPGA Junior Golf Program
Lunar and Planetary Institute
Lutheran Volunteer Corps
MacDonald Communications
MAD Magazine
Madison Square Garden
Maine State Music Theatre
Makovsky & Company
Manhattan Theatre Club
Manice Education Center
Manus & Associates Literary Agency
Marina Maher Communications
The Martin Agency
Mass Media Science and Engineering Fellows Program
The Maternal & Child Health Institute
Mattel Toys
MCA Records
MCA/Universal
McLean Hospital
MCT Management/Bold! Records
Merck & Company
Mercury Records
Merrill Lynch
Metro-Goldwyn-Mayer/United Artists
Michael Phillips Productions
Middle Earth
Middle East Institute
Middle East Research & Information Project

Miller Brewing Company
The Milwaukee Journal
Miniwanca Education Center
Miss Porter's School
Miss Universe
Miss USA
Mixed Media
Mobility International
Montgomery County Community Corrections
Morris Arboretum
Morrison & Foerster
Mote Marine Laboratory
Mother Earth News
Mother Jones
Motown Records
Ms.
MSG Network
Museum of Contemporary Art, Chicago
Museum of Fine Arts, Boston
The Museum of Modern Art, New York
My Sister's Place
Mystic Seaport Museum
Nation's Business
National Aquarium in Baltimore
National Asian Pacific American Legal Consortium
National Association for Female Executives
National Association of College Broadcasters
National Association of Professional Surplus Lines Offices
National Broadcasting Company
National Center for Fair & Open Testing
National Committee for Responsive Philanthropy
National Football League
National Foundation for the Improvement of Education
National Journal
National Journalism Center
National Organization for Women
The National Partnership for Women and Families
National Review
National Space Society
National Trust for Historic Preservation
National Women's Health Network
The Nature Conservancy
NBC Nightly News
NETWORK
New Canaan Country School
New Dramatists
The New Republic
New Stage Theatre
The New York Hospital-Cornell Medical Center
New York Knicks
New York Rangers
New York Shakespeare Festival
New York State Bar Association
New York State Theatre Institute
Newsday/New York Newsday
Newsweek
Nick Bollettieri Tennis Academy
NIKE Tour
Norfolk Chamber Music Festival

North Carolina Botanical Garden
North Cascades Institute
Northfield Mount Hermon School
NOW Legal Defense and Education Fund
Octel Communications
Office of Job Corps
Oldsmobile
Organization of Chinese Americans
Outward Bound/Voyageur School
Ove Arup & Partners
Overland Entertainment
Overseas Service Corps of the YMCA
The Paris Review
The Partnership for Service-Learning
Pediatric AIDS Foundation
Peggy Guggenheim Collection
Pendulum Records
Penguin Books
People to People International
PERA Club
Perspective Records
PGA Tour
The Philadelphia Center
The Philadelphia Inquirer
The Phoenix Gazette
Physicians for Human Rights
Pittsburgh Post-Gazette
Playhouse on the Square
Plume Books
PMK Public Relations
PolyGram
Pontiac
The Population Institute
PrimeTime Live
Pro-Found Software
Psychology Today
Public Allies
Public Defender Service for DC
Public Interest Research Groups
Quaker United Nations Office
Rand
The Real World
Renew America
Rhode Island State Government
Rio Grande National Forest
The Ripon Society
Rodale Institute Research Center
Roll Call
Roy A. Somlyo Productions
St. Paul's School
Saks Fifth Avenue
Sally Jessy Raphael Show
San Diego Zoo
San Francisco Bay Guardian
San Francisco 49ers
San Francisco Opera
San Juan/Rio Grande National Forests
Saturday Night Live
Saturn

SBK Records
Schlumberger
Science
Science News
Scott Rudin Productions
Scoville Peace Fellowship Program
Scripps Institution of Oceanography
The Seattle Times
Senior PGA Tour
765-ARTS
Seventeen Magazine
Shadow Broadcast Services
Shaver's Creek Environmental Center
Sherwin-Williams
Shirley Herz Associates
Sierra Club
Signet Classics
SGI
Simon & Goodman Picture Company
60 Minutes
Skadden, Arps, Slate, Meagher & Flom
Solomon R. Guggenheim Museum
Sony
The Source
The Source Theater Company
South Seas Plantation
The Southern Center for International Studies
Southern Progress Corporation
Southface Energy Institute
The Southwestern Company
Special Olympics International
Spin
Spoleto Festival
Sports Illustrated
Spy
Starlight Foundation
Staten Island Zoo
State Teachers Retirement System of Ohio
Steppenwolf Theatre Company
Student Conservation Association
Student Works Painting
Students for Central & Eastern Europe
Success
Sunday Morning
Sussex Publishers
TADA!
TBS
Teach for America
Teen Voices
Temerlin McClain
Theater de la Jeune Lune
Thread Waxing Space
TNT
The Today Show
Tommy Boy Music
The Tonight Show With Jay Leno
Toyota
Tracy Watts Millinery
Tribeca Film Center

Tucson Children's Museum
Turner Broadcasting System
Food Network
Twentieth Century Fox
Twentieth TelevisionGap
20/20
20/20 Vision
Tyco Toys
UCSF AIDS Health Project
Union Carbide
The Union Institute for Social Responsibility
United Artists
United Nations
United Nations Volunteer Program
United States Chamber of Commerce
United States Holocaust Museum
United States National Arboretum
United States Securities and Exchange Commission
United Talent Agency
Universal Pictures
Universal Studios
Up to the Minute
US-Asia Institute
Varsity Student Painters
Vereinsbank Capital Corp.
Vertigo Records
Verve Records
Vibe
Viking Books
Village Voice
Virgin Records
Voice of America
Volunteers For Peace
Volunteers for Israel
Volunteers in Asia
Wadsworth Atheneum
Wall Street Music
Washington Center for Internships and Academic Seminars
Washington Center for Politics & Journalism
The Washington Office on Africa
Washington Office on Latin America
The Washingtonian
WAXQ-Q104.3
WCHS-TV
Wells Fargo Bank
Westin Hotels & Resorts
The Westwood One Radio Network
WGN-Chicago
Who Cares
Wildlife Prairie Park
Williamstown Theater Festival
The Wilma Theater
The Wilson Quarterly
Winant-Clayton Volunteers
Wired
WNBC-TV
WNYC
Women Express

Women Make Movies
Women's Institute for Freedom of the Press
Women's International League for Peace and Freedom
Women's Project & Productions
Women's Sports Foundation
Woodrow Wilson International Center for Scholars
Work Experience USA
Working Mother
Working Woman
World Federalist Association
Worldnet
WorldTeach
Writers Guild of America, West
Xerox
Xerox Palo Alto Research Center
Y.E.S. to Jobs
Yosemite National Park
Youth For Understanding International Exchange
YSB (Young Sisters & Brothers)

INTERNSHIPS WITH MINORITY PROGRAMS

(M = MINORITY INTERNSHIP IS THE ONLY PROGRAM AVAILABLE)
American Association of Advertising Agencies (M)
American Indian Science & Engineering Society (M)
American Red Cross (M)
American Wind Energy Association
Ames Research Center
Anchorage Daily News
Arena Stage
Association for Education in Journalism (M)
AT&T Bell Laboratories
Atlanta Junior Golf Association
The Boston Globe
Bucks County Courier Times (M)
Buffalo Bill Historical Center
CBS Records
Central Intelligence Agency
Columbia Records
Council of Energy Resource Tribes (M)
C-SPAN
The Dow Jones Newspaper Fund
The Environmental Careers Organization
Epic Records
Exxon
Frito-Lay (M)
Goddard Space Flight Center
Golf Digest
Hallmark Cards
Inroads (M)
Intel
Jet Propulsion Laboratory
Jewish Vocational and Career Counseling Service (M)
Johnson Space Center
Kennedy Space Center
Langley Research Center
Lawyers Alliance for World Security/Committee for National
   Security

Lewis Research Center
LPGA Junior Golf Program
Marshall Space Flight Center
Mass Media Science and Engineering Fellows Program
Merck & Company
The Milwaukee Journal
National Aeronautics and Space Administration
National Collegiate Athletic Association (M)
National Consortium for Graduate Degrees for Minorities in
  Engineering and Science (M)
National Zoo
The New York Times (M)
NIKE (M)
NIKE Tour
Oak Ridge Institute for Science and Education
PGA Tour
The Philadelphia Inquirer
Scripps Institution of Oceanography (M)
The Seattle Times
Senior PGA Tour
Sony Music Entertainment
Sponsors for Educational Opportunity (M)
Stennis Space Center
Student Conservation Association (M)
3M
Washington Center for Internships and Academic Seminars
Women's Sports Foundation
Writers Guild of America, west (M)
Y.E.S. to Jobs

FREE HOUSING

Abbott Laboratories
Academic Study Associates
The Academy for Advanced and Strategic Studies
Aetna Life & Casualty
Alaska State Parks
American Indian Science & Engineering Society
American School for the Deaf
Anasazi Heritage Center
Argonne National Laboratory
Aspen Center for Environmental Studies
Bermuda Biological Station for Research
Boys Hope/Girls Hope
Breckenridge Outdoor Education Center
Brethren Volunteer Service
Brookhaven National Laboratory
Callaway Gardens
Camp Counselors USA
Camphill Soltane
Center for Coastal Studies
Center for Talented Youth
Centro para los Adolescentes de San Miguel de Allende
Chincoteague National Wildlife Refuge
Choate Rosemary Hall
College Light Opera Company
Council of Energy Resource Tribes
Creede Repertory Theatre
Crow Canyon Archaeological Center
D.C. Booth Historic Fish Hatchery
DesignTech International
Duke University Talent Identification Program
Farm Sanctuary
Fellowship of Reconciliation
Florida Grand Opera
Ford Motor Company
Fourth World Movement
Freedom Theatre
Frontier Nursing Service
Glen Helen Outdoor Education Center
Gould Farm
Habitat for Humanity International
Hawk Mountain Sanctuary
Hawthorne Valley Farm
The Hermitage
H.O.M.E.
Hostelling International—American Youth Hostels
Human Service Alliance
Interhemispheric Resource Center
Interlocken
International Radio and Television Society
International Volunteer Projects
Jacob's Pillow Dance Festival
Lamont-Doherty Earth Observatory
Land Between The Lakes

Long Lake Conservation Center
Longwood Gardens
The Lowell Whiteman School
Lutheran Volunteer Corps
Maine State Music Theatre
Manice Education Center
Microsoft
Miller Brewing Company
Miniwanca Education Center
Miss Porter's School
Montgomery County Community Corrections
Mystic Seaport Museum
National Aeronautics and Space Administration
National Park Service
The Nature Conservancy
Norfolk Chamber Music Festival
North Cascades Institute
Northfield Mount Hermon School
Oak Ridge Institute for Science and Education
Oscar Mayer Wienermobile
Outward Bound/Voyageur School
Ove Arup & Partners
Overseas Service Corps of the YMCA
Peace Corps
Phillips Academy
Playhouse on the Square
Quaker United Nations Office
Rio Grande National Forest
St. Paul's School
San Juan/Rio Grande National Forests
Shaver's Creek Environmental Center
South Seas Plantation
Southface Energy Institute
Spoleto Festival USA
State Teachers Retirement System of Ohio
Student Conservation Association
Students for Central & Eastern Europe
Summerbridge National
UCSF AIDS Health Project
Union Carbide
United Nations Volunteer Program
United States Olympic Committee
United States Senate Youth Program
Winant-Clayton Volunteers
Women's International League for Peace and Freedom
Yosemite National Park

HOUSING ARRANGEMENTS AVAILABLE

AIESEC
American Association of Overseas Studies
American Friends Service Committee
American Institute for Foreign Study
The American-Scandinavian Foundation
ASSIST
Association for Education in Journalism

AT&T Bell Laboratories
Baltimore Zoo
Berkshire Public Theatre
Bermuda Biological Station for Research
Boeing
Boston University International Programs
The Catholic University of America
Central Intelligence Agency
Community Service Volunteer Programme
Council on International Educational Exchange
Dow Chemical Company
Dublin Internships, Ireland
Educational Programs Abroad
Exxon
Federal Bureau of Investigation
The Hansard Society for Parliamentary Government
Hewitt Associates
High Country News
Historic Deerfield
IBM
IES – The Institute for the International Education of Students
Institute for International Cooperation and Development
Institute of Government
Intel
The Juilliard School
Lawrence Livermore National Laboratory
Lincoln Center for the Performing Arts
Merck & Company
Microsoft
Mobility International
National Security Agency
New Canaan Country School
New Stage Theatre
The New York Times
NIKE Tour
The Partnership for Service-Learning
Pella
People to People International
PGA Tour
The Philadelphia Center
Procter & Gamble
Rand
Senior PGA Tour
Tellabs
3M
Volunteers For Peace
Volunteers for Israel
Volunteers in Asia
Washington Center for Internships and Academic Seminars
Washington Internships for Students of Engineering
Williamstown Theater Festival
WorldTeach

FREE MEALS

Academic Study Associates
The Academy for Advanced and Strategic Studies
Aetna Life & Casualty
The Algonquin

Amelia Island Plantation
American School for the Deaf
Aspen Center for Environmental Studies
Bellevue Hospital Center
Bermuda Biological Station for Research
Boys Hope/Girls Hope
Breckenridge Outdoor Education Center
Brethren Volunteer Service
Camp Counselors USA
Camphill Soltane
Center for Talented Youth
The Century Plaza Hotel
Chicago Bulls
Choate Rosemary Hall
Christie's
College Light Opera Company
Council on Hemispheric Affairs
Crow Canyon Archaeological Center
Duke University Talent Identification Program
Food Network
Frontier Nursing Service
Glen Helen Outdoor Education Center
Gould Farm
Hawthorne Valley Farm
HERE
The Hermitage
H.O.M.E.
H.S.I. Productions
Human Service Alliance
Interlocken
International Volunteer Projects
Jacob's Pillow Dance Festival
J.P. Morgan & Co.
Little Keswick School
Long Lake Conservation Center
The Lowell Whiteman School
Maine State Music Theatre
Manice Education Center
Middle Earth
Miniwanca Education Center
Miss Porter's School
Montgomery County Community Corrections
Norfolk Chamber Music Festival
North Cascades Institute
Northfield Mount Hermon School
Oscar Mayer Wienermobile
Outward Bound/Voyageur School
Phillips Academy
Rio Grande National Forest
St. Paul's School
San Juan/Rio Grande National Forests
Shirley Herz Associates
South Seas Plantation
Student Conservation Association
Students for Central & Eastern Europe
Summerbridge National
Tracy Watts Millinery
United States Olympic Committee

United States Senate Youth Program
Westin Hotels & Resorts
Winant-Clayton Volunteers

VEHICLES PROVIDED

Frontier Nursing Service
Intel
Microsoft
Miller Brewing Company
National Aeronautics and Space Administration (Goddard's Summer Institute)
Oscar Mayer Wienermobile
Procter & Gamble
Rio Grande National Forest
San Juan/Rio Grande National Forests

ROUND-TRIP TRAVEL COVERED

Abbott Laboratories
Academic Study Associates
Academy of Television Arts and Sciences
American Indian Science & Engineering Society
Amway
Apple Computer
Argonne National Laboratory
AT&T Bell Laboratories
Atlanta Junior Golf Association
Boeing
Boys Hope/Girls Hope
BP
Brethren Volunteer Service
Brookhaven National Laboratory
Buick
Cadillac
Chemical Industry Institute of Toxicology
Chevrolet
Chevron
Congressional Hispanic Caucus Institute
Council of Energy Resource Tribes
Dell Computer
Dow Chemical Company
The Dow Jones Newspaper Fund
Du Pont
Eastman Kodak Company
Exxon
Florida Grand Opera
Ford Motor Company
Frito-Lay
General Motors Marketing Internship
GMC Truck
Golf Digest
GTE
Hewlett-Packard
Hispanic Association of Colleges and Universities
IBM
Intel
The International Foundation for Education and Self-Help
International Radio and Television Society

Lamont-Doherty Earth Observatory
Lawrence Livermore National Laboratory
LPGA Junior Golf Program
Lunar and Planetary Institute
Lutheran Volunteer Corps
Mass Media Science and Engineering Fellows Program
Microsoft
National Aeronautics and Space Administration
National Association of Professional Surplus Lines Offices
National Collegiate Athletic Association
National Consortium for Graduate Degrees for Minorities in Engineering and Science
National Space Society
The New York Times
NIKE Tour
Oldsmobile
Ove Arup & Partners
Overseas Service Corps of the YMCA
Peace Corps
Pella
PGA Tour
Pontiac
Procter & Gamble
Rand
Raychem
San Diego Zoo
Saturn
Scoville Peace Fellowship Program
Senior PGA Tour
Texas Instruments
Union Carbide
United Nations Volunteer Program
United States Senate Youth Program
Washington Internships for Students of Engineering
Weyerhaeuser
Women's International League for Peace and Freedom
Yosemite National Park

SCHOLARSHIPS/FINANCIAL AID AVAILABLE

American Indian Science & Engineering Society
AT&T Bell Laboratories
Boston University International Programs
The Coro Foundation
Council on International Educational Exchange
C-SPAN
The Dow Jones Newspaper Fund
Frito-Lay
Gensler and Associates/Architects
Hewlett-Packard
Hispanic Association of Colleges and Universities
Historic Deerfield
Howard Hughes Medical Institute
IES – The Institute for the International Education of Students
Institute for International Cooperation and Development
International Volunteer Projects
J.C. Penney
McDonald's
MetLife

National Collegiate Athletic Association
Peace Corps
Public Defender Service for DC
Student Conservation Association
Summerbridge National
Supreme Court of the United States
United States Senate Youth Program
Volunteers in Asia
Washington Center for Internships and Academic Seminars
WorldTeach

LET'S GET PHYSICAL—FITNESS FACILITIES AVAILABLE

Abbott Laboratories
Academic Study Associates
Aetna Life & Casualty
Agency for Toxic Substances and Disease Registry
The Algonquin
Amelia Island Plantation
American Association of Overseas Studies
American Institute for Foreign Study
Ames Research Center
Amtrak
Amway
Anacostia Museum
Association of Trial Lawyers of America
AT&T Bell Laboratories
Atlanta Junior Golf Association
Beach Associates
Boeing
The Boston Globe
BP
Breckenridge Outdoor Education Center
Brookhaven National Laboratory
Bureau of Economic Analysis
Bureau of Engraving and Printing
Bureau of Export Administration
Cairns & Associates
Camp Counselors USA
Canadian Embassy
Census Bureau
Center for Talented Youth
Central Intelligence Agency
The Century Plaza Hotel
Chevron
Choate Rosemary Hall
CIGNA
Cinemax
Citibank
Conservation Analytical Laboratory
Continuous Electron Beam Accelerator Facility
DHL Worldwide Express
Dow Chemical Company
E-Systems
Eastman Kodak Company
Economic Development Administration
Educational Programs Abroad
Federal Bureau of Investigation
Federal Reserve Board

Fisher-Price Toys
Forbes
The Ford Foundation
Foreign Policy Research Institute
Freer Gallery of Art
Frito-Lay
Frontier Nursing Service
Genentech
General Foods
General Mills
Glen Helen Outdoor Education Center
Goddard Space Flight Center
Golf Digest
GTE
Hallmark Cards
The Hansard Society for Parliamentary Government
Harley-Davidson
HBO
Hill, Holliday, Connors, Cosmopulos Advertising
Hirshhorn Museum and Sculpture Garden
Home Box Office
Howard Hughes Medical Institute
Insurance Services Office
Intel
International Telecommunications Satellite Organization
International Trade Administration
Jet Propulsion Laboratory
Johnson Space Center
Kennedy Space Center
Kraft Foods, Inc.
Langley Research Center
Lawrence Livermore National Laboratory
Lewis Research Center
Long Lake Conservation Center
Los Angeles Times
LPGA Junior Golf Program
Lucasfilm
Lunar and Planetary Institute
Marshall Space Flight Center
Mattel Toys
Merck & Company
Microsoft
Miller Brewing Company
Minority Business Development Agency
Miss Porter's School
National Aeronautics and Space Administration
National Air and Space Museum
National Center for Toxicological Research
National Collegiate Athletic Association
National Institute of Standards & Technology
National Museum of African Art
National Museum of American Art
National Museum of American History
National Museum of Natural History
National Oceanic & Atmospheric Administration
National Portrait Gallery
National Security Agency
National Technical Information Service

National Telecommunications & Information Administration
Naval Training Systems Center
New Canaan Country School
NIKE
NIKE Tour
Northfield Mount Hermon School
Oak Ridge Institute for Science and Education
Oak Ridge National Laboratory
Octel Communications
Office of Inspector General
Office of Job Corps
Oracle
Oscar Mayer
Overseas Private Investment Corporation
Patent & Trademark Office
PERA Club
PGA Tour
Phillips Academy
Pittsburgh Energy Technology Center
Pro-Found Software
Procter & Gamble
Reebok
Savannah River Ecology Laboratory
Senior PGA Tour
Smithsonian Institution
Sony
South Seas Plantation
Southern Progress Corporation
Special Olympics International
Spoleto Festival USA
State Teachers Retirement System of Ohio
Stennis Space Center
National Institutes of Health
Supreme Court of the United States
Technology Administration
Tellabs
Texas Instruments
Toyota
United States Agency for International Development
United States Army Environmental Hygiene Agency
United States Bureau of Mines
United States Department of Commerce
United States Olympic Committee
United States Travel & Tourism Administration
Voice of America
Westin Hotels & Resorts
Weyerhaeuser
Worldnet
Xerox
Xerox Palo Alto Research Center

GOOD CHANCE FOR PERMANENT EMPLOYMENT
(APPROX. 50%+ FORMER INTERNS OFFERED JOBS)

Academy of Television Arts & Sciences
Advertising Club of New York
Aetna Life & Casualty
American Association of University Women Educational
  Foundation

Atlantic Records
Ballantine Books
Baywatch
Bertelsmann Music Group
Boeing
Buick
Cadillac
Callaway Advanced Technology
Chevrolet
Chevron
Crown Books
Dell Computer
Deloitte & Touche
Dow Chemical Company
Du Pont
E-Systems
Eastman Kodak Company
Elizabeth Dow
Entenmann's
Ernst & Young
Federal Reserve Bank of New York
Ford Motor Company
Frito-Lay
Gap
General Foods
General Mills
General Motors Marketing Internship
GMC Truck
Great Projects Film Company
Habitat for Humanity International
International Radio and Television Society
Hewlett-Packard
Inroads
Intel
J.C. Penney
Knopf Books
Kraft Foods, Inc.
Marvel Comics
McDonald's
MetLife
Miller Brewing Company
Mother Earth News
National Association of Professional Surplus Lines Offices
National Security Agency
Octel Communications
Oldsmobile
Oscar Mayer
Outward Bound/Voyageur School
Ove Arup & Partners
Pella
Pontiac
Pro-Found Software
Procter & Gamble
Psychology Today
Random House
Reebok
Ruder-Finn
Saturn

Sponsors for Educational Opportunity
Spy
Sussex Publishers
Teach for America
Texas Instruments
3M
Trilogy Development Group
Union Carbide
Virginia Symphony
Wells Fargo Bank
Weyerhaeuser
Writers Guild of America, West

ACCOUNTING

Abbott Laboratories
Aetna Life & Casualty
AIESEC
Ames Research Center
Amway
Arthur Andersen
Boeing
The Boston Globe
CDG/CDS International
Chevron
Cinemax
Council on International Educational Exchange
Deloitte & Touche
Dow Chemical Company
E-Systems
Ernst & Young
Exxon
Federal Bureau of Investigation
Fisher-Price Toys
Forty Acres and a Mule Filmworks
The French-American Center
Georgia Governor's Office
Goddard Space Flight Center
GTE
Hallmark Cards
HBO
Hewlett-Packard
Hill, Holliday, Connors, Cosmopulos Advertising
Hispanic Association of Colleges and Universities
Home Box Office
Inroads
Intel
International Management Group
Internships International
Jet Propulsion Laboratory
Johnson Space Center
J.P. Morgan & Co.
Kennedy Space Center
KIRO
Langley Research Center
Lewis Research Center
Lucasfilm
Marshall Space Flight Center
Mattel Toys
Nabisco
National Aeronautics and Space Administration
National Organization for Women
National Space Society
NIKE
Pella
People to People International
The Philadelphia Center
Procter & Gamble
Raychem

Reebok
Sponsors for Educational Opportunity
Stennis Space Center
United Nations Volunteer Program
United States Chamber of Commerce
United States Olympic Committee
Vereinsbank Capital Corp.
Weyerhaeuser
Wolf Trap Foundation for the Performing Arts
Note: Many corporations and organizations listed in this book offer positions in their Accounting departments.

ADVERTISING

Ackerman McQueen
Advertising Club of New York
American Association of Advertising Agencies
American Institute for Foreign Study
ASSIST
Association for Education in Journalism
Bernstein-Rein
Boston University International Programs
Blue Corn Comics
Bozell Public Relations
Council on International Educational Exchange
Earle Palmer Brown
Educational Programs Abroad
Elkman Advertising & Public Relations
The French-American Center
The Gesher Summer Internship Program
Hill, Holliday, Connors, Cosmopulos Advertising
International Radio and Television Society
Internships International
The Martin Agency
People to People International
The Philadelphia Center
TBWA
Temerlin McClain
Warwick Baker O'Neill

See Public Relations/Marketing Agencies

AEROSPACE

American Association of Overseas Studies
Ames Research Center
Boeing
CDG/CDS International
Council on International Educational Exchange
Goddard Space Flight Center
Inroads
Internships International
Jet Propulsion Laboratory
Johnson Space Center
Kennedy Space Center
Langley Research Center

Lewis Research Center
Lunar and Planetary Institute
Marshall Space Flight Center
National Aeronautics and Space Administration
National Air and Space Museum
National Space Society
The Philadelphia Center
Stennis Space Center

AGRICULTURE

American Friends Service Committee
The American-Scandinavian Foundation
Brethren Volunteer Service
CARE
CDG/CDS International
Economic Research Service
Farm Sanctuary
Food for the Hungry
Global Volunteers
Hispanic Association of Colleges and Universities
IAESTE
International Volunteer Projects
Peace Corps
The Philadelphia Center
Rodale Institute Research Center
United Nations Volunteer Program
United States Department of Agriculture
Volunteers For Peace

AIDS (POLICY OR RESEARCH)

Abbott Laboratories
American Civil Liberties Union
American Red Cross
Boston University International Programs
Brethren Volunteer Service
The Ford Foundation
Genentech
Georgia Governor's Office
Healthy Mothers, Healthy Babies
Internships International
National Institutes of Health
Peace Corps
Pediatric AIDS Foundation
The Philadelphia Center
UCSF AIDS Health Project
United Nations Volunteer Program
Urban Fellows/Government Scholars Programs

See Health Care

AIRLINES

See Transportation

ANIMAL RIGHTS

See Environment/Nature

APPAREL

See Clothing

AQUARIUMS

National Aquarium in Baltimore

ARCHAEOLOGY

Anasazi Heritage Center
Crow Canyon Archaeological Center
Death Valley
Everglades
The French-American Center
Gettysburg Battlefield
Grand Canyon
The Hermitage
International Volunteer Projects
Joshua Tree
Klondike Gold Rush
Mount Rushmore
National Park Service
The Philadelphia Center
Rio Grande National Forest
San Juan/Rio Grande National Forests
Statue of Liberty
Student Conservation Association
Volunteers for Peace
Yellowstone National Park

ARCHITECTURE

American Association of Overseas Studies
Argonne National Laboratory
Bechtel
Boston University International Programs
Council on International Educational Exchange
Educational Programs Abroad
The French-American Center
Gensler & Associates/Architects
Historic Deerfield
IAESTE
Internships International
NIKE Tour
Oak Ridge Institute for Science and Education
Oak Ridge National Laboratory
Ove Arup & Partners
Peace Corps
People to People International
PGA Tour
The Philadelphia Center
Senior PGA Tour

See Construction

ART GALLERIES

Boston University International Programs
CDG/CDS International
Council on International Educational Exchange

Educational Programs Abroad
The French-American Center
Internships International
Leo Castelli Gallery
People to People International
The Philadelphia Center

See Museums

ARTS MANAGEMENT

The Arts & Education Council of Greater St. Louis

See Performing Arts
See Talent Agencies

ASTRONOMY

Yosemite National Park

See Aerospace

AUCTION HOUSES

American Association of Overseas Studies
Boston University International Programs
Butterfield & Butterfield
Christie's
Council on International Educational Exchange
Educational Programs Abroad
The French-American Center
IES -- The Institute For the International Education of Students
Internships International
The Philadelphia Center
Sotheby's

AUTOMOBILES/MOTORCYCLES

AIESEC
Buick
Cadillac
Callaway Advanced Technology
CDG/CDS International
Chevrolet
Council on International Educational Exchange
Ford Motor Company
General Motors Marketing Internship
GMC Truck
Harley-Davidson
Internships International
Oldsmobile
People to People International
The Philadelphia Center
Pontiac
Saturn
Sgro Promo Associates/General Motors Internship
Toyota

BALLET

The Atlanta Ballet
BalletMet
The Philadelphia Center
Rhode Island State Government

BANKING

AIESEC
American Association of Overseas Studies
American Institute for Foreign Study
ASSIST
Boston University International Programs
CDG/CDS International
Citibank
Council on International Educational Exchange
Educational Programs Abroad
Federal Reserve Bank of New York
Federal Reserve Board
The French-American Center
The Gesher Summer Internship Program
IES -- The Institute For the International Education of Students
Inroads
Internships International
J.P. Morgan & Co.
Merrill Lynch
Overseas Private Investment Corporation
People to People International
The Philadelphia Center
Sponsors for Educational Opportunity
United States Chamber of Commerce
Vereinsbank Capital Corp.
Wells Fargo Bank

See Investment Management

BEER

See Consumer Goods

BIOLOGY

See Science

BIOMEDICAL RESEARCH

See Health Care/Medicine

BIOTECHNOLOGY

Ames Research Center
Argonne National Laboratory
Council on International Educational Exchange
Genentech
Goddard Space Flight Center
Inroads
Internships International
Jet Propulsion Laboratory
Johnson Space Center
Kennedy Space Center

Langley Research Center
Lewis Research Center
Marshall Space Flight Center
National Aeronautics and Space Administration
The Philadelphia Center
Stennis Space Center
Washington Internships for Students of Engineering (policy)

BOTANY

See Environment/Nature

BUSINESS

AIESEC
American Indian Science & Engineering Society
American University in Moscow
American Woman's Economic Development Corp.
Blue Corn Comics
CARE
Student Works Painting
The Public Forum Institute
Food for the Hungry
The French-American Center
Hispanic Association of Colleges and Universities
Peace Corps
The Philadelphia Center
State Teacher's Retirement System of Ohio
Student Works Painting
United Nations Volunteer Program
United States Chamber of Commerce
United States Department of Commerce
Varsity Student Painters

See Accounting
See Banking

CARTOONS

See Television

CHAMBER MUSIC

See Symphony/Chamber Music

CHEMICALS

AIESEC
BP
CDG/CDS International
Chevron
Council on International Educational Exchange
Dow Chemical Company
Du Pont
Exxon
Internships International
People to People International
The Philadelphia Center
Union Carbide

CHEMISTRY

See Science

CIVIL RIGHTS

See Human/Civil Rights

CLOTHING

Adrienne Vittadini
Alper International
American Association of Overseas Studies
Benetton USA Corp.
Betsey Johnson
Council on International Educational Exchange
Donna Maione
Educational Programs Abroad
The French-American Center
Gap
Inroads
Internships International
J.C. Penney
Karl Lagerfeld
Liz Claiborne
NIKE
People to People International
The Philadelphia Center
Reebok
Saks Fifth Avenue
Tracy Watts Millinery

COMICS

Blue Corn Comics
Fantagraphics Books
Marvel Comics

COMMUNICATIONS

See Journalism
See Public Relations/Marketing
See Radio
See Television

COMPUTERS

The Academy for Advanced and Strategic Studies
Agency for Toxic Substances and Disease Registry
AIESEC
American Association of Overseas Studies
American Institute for Foreign Study
Apple Computer
Argonne National Laboratory
AT&T Bell Laboratories
B.U.G.
Bureau of Engraving and Printing
CDG/CDS International
Continuous Electron Beam Accelerator Facility
Council on International Educational Exchange
Dell Computer

Educational Programs Abroad
Food for the Hungry
The Gazette Company
The Gesher Summer Internship Program
GTE
Hewlett-Packard
IAESTE
IBM
Internships International
Inroads
Intel
Microsoft
National Center for Toxicological Research
National Consortium for Graduate Degrees for Minorities in
  Engineering and Science
Naval Training Systems Center
Oak Ridge Institute for Science and Education
Oak Ridge National Laboratory
Oracles
Office of House Speaker
Peace Corps
People to People International
The Philadelphia Center
Pittsburgh Energy Technology Center
Pro-Found Software
Raychem
Renaissance Computer Art Center
Savannah River Ecology Laboratory
SGI
Tellabs
Texas Instruments
United States Army Environmental Hygiene Agency
United States Bureau of Mines
Weyerhaeuser
Xerox
Xerox Palo Alto Research Center
*Note: Many organizations in this book offer experience in computer or
  information systems.*

CONSTRUCTION

American Friends Service Committee
American Institute for Foreign Study
Argonne National Laboratory
Bechtel
Brethren Volunteer Service
CARE
Global Volunteers
Habitat for Humanity International
H.O.M.E.
Institute for International Cooperation and Development
International Volunteer Projects
Peace Corps
The Philadelphia Center
Rio Grande National Forest
San Juan/Rio Grande National Forests
Sherwin-Williams
Southface Energy Institute
Student Conservation Association
Volunteers For Peace

CONSUMER GOODS

Amway
Anheuser-Busch
CDG/CDS International
Council on International Educational Exchange
DesignTech International
Eastman Kodak Company
Entenmann's
Fisher-Price Toys
Frito-Lay
General Foods
General Mills
The Gesher Summer Internship Program
Hallmark Cards
Harley-Davidson
IES – The Institute for the International Education of Students
Inroads
J.C. Penney
Kraft Foods, Inc.
Mattel Toys
Miller Brewing Company
Nabisco
Oscar Mayer
Oscar Mayer Wienermobile
People to People International
Pella
The Philadelphia Center
Procter & Gamble
Sherwin-Williams
3M
Tyco Toys
Weyerhaeuser
Xerox

CORRECTIONS

Federal Bureau of Prisons
Leavenworth Prison
Marion Penitentiary
Montgomery County Community Corrections
United States Prison

CRIMINAL JUSTICE

See Corrections

DANCE

American Dance Festival
Jacob's Pillow Dance Festival
The Philadelphia Center
Rhode Island State Government
TADA!

DEFENSE

AIESEC
Bureau of Export Administration
Center for Defense Information
Council on International Educational Exchange

E-Systems
GTE
Internships International
Joint Chiefs of Staff
Lawrence Livermore National Laboratory
National Security Agency
The Pentagon
People to People International
The Philadelphia Center
Texas Instruments
United States Department of Defense

DESIGN (ART, GRAPHIC, INTERIOR AND/OR TEXTILE)

The Academy for Advanced and Strategic Studies
American & International Designs
American Institute for Foreign Study
Apple Computer
Blue Corn Comics
California Museum of Photography
Carolyn Ray
CDG/CDS International
Chicago Botanic Garden
Educational Programs Abroad
Elizabeth Dow
fX
Habitat for Humanity International
Hallmark Cards
Houghton Mifflin Company
Interior Design Collections
Internships International
KPIX-TV
Lucasfilm
Marvel Comics
NIKE
Mother Earth News
Nation's Business
National Zoo
The New York Times
Newsday/New York Newsday
People to People International
The Philadelphia Center
Psychology Today
Reebok
Renaissance Computer Art Center
Spy
Sussex Publishers
Teen Voices
WISH-TV 8
Y.E.S. to Jobs

See Architecture

DISABLED

Affiliated Sante Group
AIM for the Handicapped
Best Buddies
Breckenridge Outdoor Education Center
Brethren Volunteer Service

Camphill Soltane
Community Service Volunteer Programme
Foundation for Contemporary Mental Health
Gould Farm
Little Keswick School
Mobility International
Special Olympics International

ECONOMICS

AIESEC
American Association of Overseas Studies
American Institute for Foreign Study
Boston University International Programs
Bureau of Economic Analysis
Census Bureau
Council on Economic Priorities
Economic Development Administration
Economic Research Service
The French-American Center
Hispanic Association of Colleges and Universities
International Trade Administration
Internships in Francophone Europe
Internships International
Minority Business Development Agency
National Institute of Standards & Technology
National Technical Information Service
People to People International
The Philadelphia Center
Technology Administration
United Nations
United States Department of Commerce

See Banking
See Investment Management
See Trade
Note: Many organizations in this book offer positions in their Finance or Economics departments.

EDUCATION

Academic Study Associates
The Academy for Advanced and Strategic Studies
Accuracy in Education
Advocates for Children of New York
AFS Intercultural Programs
American Association for the Advancement of Science
American Federation of Teachers
American University in Moscow
Brethren Volunteer Service
CDG/CDS International
Center for the Study of Conflict
Community Service Volunteer Programme
Dublin Internships, Ireland
Foreign Student Service Council
Fourth World Movement
Georgia Governor's Office
Internships International
Jewish Vocational and Career Counseling Service
Miniwanca Education Center

Mobility International
Morris Arboretum
National Center for Fair & Open Testing
National Foundation for the Improvement of Education
Peace Corps
Youth For Understanding International Exchange

See Teaching/Education

ELECTRONICS

AIESEC
CDG/CDS International
Council on International Educational Exchange
Du Pont
Internships International
People to People International
The Philadelphia Center
Schlumberger
Sony
Texas Instruments

ENGINEERING

The Academy for Advanced and Strategic Studies
American Association for the Advancement of Science
American Indian Science & Engineering Society
The American-Scandinavian Foundation
The Gesher Summer Internship Program
IAESTE
National Consortium for Graduate Degrees for Minorities in
    Engineering and Science
National Institutes of Health
Peace Corps
United Nations Volunteer Program
Washington Internships for Students in Engineering

See Aerospace
See Architecture
See Automobiles/Motorcycles
See Biotechnology
See Chemicals
See Computers
See Construction
See Consumer Goods
See Defense
See Electronics
See Environment/Nature
See Government (research laboratories, United States Dept. of Energy, etc.)
See Pharmaceuticals
See Telecommunications
See Utilities

ENTERTAINMENT

See Comics
See Events Management
See Film
See Magazines/Journals

See Music
See Radio
See Record Labels/Record Industry
See Sports
See Talent Agencies
See Television

ENVIRONMENT/NATURE

American Forests
American Institute for Foreign Study
American Rivers
The American-Scandinavian Foundation
American Wind Energy Association
The Antarctica Project
Argonne National Laboratory
Atlantic Council of the United States
Boston University International Programs
Brethren Volunteer Service
Corporation for National Service
Council of Energy Resource Tribes
Council on International Educational Exchange
Dublin Internships, Ireland
Educational Programs Abroad
The Environmental Careers Organization
Farm Sanctuary
Food for the Hungry
The Ford Foundation
The French-American Center
Georgia Governor's Office
High Country News
Hispanic Association of Colleges and Universities
International Volunteer Projects
Internships International
Lamont-Doherty Earth Observatory
Morris Arboretum
National Audubon Society
National Wildlife Federation
The Nature Conservancy
New York City Government
Oak Ridge Institute for Science and Education
Oak Ridge National Laboratory
The Partnership for Service-Learning
Peace Corps
People to People International
The Philadelphia Center
Physicians for Social Responsibility
Public Interest Research Groups
Renew America
Rodale Institute Research Center
Savannah River Ecology Laboratory
Save the Sound
Sierra Club
Smithsonian Institution
Student Conservation Association
Surfrider Foundation
20/20 Vision
United Nations Volunteer Program
United States Army Environmental Hygiene Agency

United States Environmental Protection Agency
Urban Fellows/Government Scholars Programs
Volunteers For Peace
Washington Center for Internships and Academic Seminars
Washington Internships for Students of Engineering
Weyerhaeuser
Wildlife Prairie Park
The Wildlife Society
Women's International League for Peace and Freedom
World Federalist Association

See Agriculture
See Horticulture
See Parks/Forests
See Oceanography
See Outdoor Education Centers
See Recreation
See Zoos

ETHICS

The Hastings Center
MANAGEMENT
International Management Group
Korff Enterprises
Overland Entertainment

EVENTS MANAGEMENT

International Management Group
Korff Enterprises
Overland Entertainment

FILM

American Association of Overseas Studies
Archive Films
Assistant Directors Training Program
Barwood Productions
Boston University International Programs
Chanticleer Films
Cinemax
Columbia Pictures
Council on International Educational Exchange
Forty Acres and a Mule Filmworks
Fox
The French-American Center
Great Projects Film Company
Haft/Nasatir
HBO
Home Box Office
Iowa Film Office
The Jim Henson Company
Lightstorm Entertainment
Lucasfilm
MCA/Universal
Metro-Goldwyn-Mayer/United Artists
Michael Phillips Productions
Open City Films
People to People International

The Philadelphia Center
Scott Rudin Productions
Simon & Goodman Picture Company
Sony Pictures Entertainment
Tribeca Film Center
TriStar Pictures
Twentieth Century Fox
United Artists
Universal Pictures
Universal Studios
Wessler Entertainment
Women Make Movies
Y.E.S. to Jobs

FINANCE

AIESEC
American Association of Overseas Studies
American Institute for Foreign Study
CARE
Hispanic Association of Colleges and Universities
IES – The Institute for the International Education of Students
Overseas Private Investment Corporation
The Philadelphia Center
United States Securities and Exchange Commission

See Banking
See Economics
See Investment Management
See Trade
Note: Many organizations in this book offer positions in their Finance or Economics departments, and in those cases aren't listed above.

FINE ARTS (PAINTING, SCULPTURE, ETC.)

The Academy for Advanced and Strategic Studies
CityArts
Council on International Educational Exchange
Creative Time
Fisher-Price Toys
The French-American Center
Institute for Unpopular Culture
International Sculpture Center
Mattel Toys
People to People International
The Philadelphia Center

FLOWERS/GIFTS

See Consumer Goods

FOODS

See Consumer Goods

FOREIGN AFFAIRS

Access: A Security Information Service
American-Arab Anti-Discrimination Committee
American Committee on Africa/The Africa Fund
American Israel Public Affairs Committee

AMIDEAST
Arms Control Association
Atlantic Council of the United States
The Brookings Institution
Carnegie Endowment for International Peace
The Carter Center
Center for Defense Information
Center for Strategic & International Studies
Center for the Study of Conflict
Central Intelligence Agency
The Citizens Network for Foreign Affairs
Consumers for World Trade
Council on Foreign Relations
Council on Hemispheric Affairs
The Ford Foundation
Foreign Policy
Foreign Policy Research Institute
The French-American Center
Houston International Protocol Alliance
Interhemispheric Resource Center
The International Center
Japan-America Society of Washington
Lawyers Alliance for World Security/Committee for National
 Security
Legacy International
Middle East Institute
Middle East Research & Information Project
The Nation
People to People International
The Philadelphia Center
Quaker United Nations Office
Scoville Peace Fellowship Program
The Southern Center for International Studies
United Nations
United Nations Association of the United States of America
United Nations Volunteer Program
United States Chamber of Commerce
US-Asia Institute
Washington Center for Internships and Academic Seminars
The Washington Office on Africa
World Federalist Association

FORESTS

See Parks/Forests

GEOGRAPHY

The American Geographical Society
The Philadelphia Center
Rio Grande National Forest
San Juan/Rio Grande National Forests

GOVERNMENT AGENCIES/OFFICES

Agency for Toxic Substances and Disease Registry
American Association of Overseas Studies
Ames Research Center
Argonne National Laboratory

Australian Embassy
Boston University International Programs
Brookhaven National Laboratory
Bureau of Economic Analysis
Bureau of Engraving and Printing
Bureau of Export Administration
California Governor's Office
California State Assembly
California State Senate
Canadian Embassy
The Catholic University of America
Census Bureau
Central Intelligence Agency
Congressional Research Service
Continuous Electron Beam Accelerator Facility
The Coro Foundation
Council on International Educational Exchange
Economic Development Administration
Educational Programs Abroad
The Environmental Careers Organization
Federal Bureau of Investigation
Federal Reserve Board
French Embassy
The French-American Center
Georgia Governor's Office
Goddard Space Flight Center
The Government Affairs Institute
The Hansard Society for Parliamentary Government
Hispanic Association of Colleges and Universities
IES – The Institute for the International Education of Students
Illinois General Assembly
International Trade Administration
Internships in Francophone Europe
Internships International
Japanese Exchange and Teaching Program
Jet Propulsion Laboratory
Johnson Space Center
Joint Chiefs of Staff
Kennedy Space Center
Langley Research Center
Lawrence Livermore National Laboratory
Lewis Research Center
The Library of Congress
Marshall Space Flight Center
Minority Business Development Agency
National Aeronautics and Space Administration
National Center for Toxicological Research
National Endowment for the Humanities
National Institute of Standards & Technology
National Institutes of Health
National Oceanic & Atmospheric Administration
National Security Agency
National Technical Information Service
National Telecommunications & Information Administration
Naval Training Systems Center
New York City Government
Oak Ridge Institute for Science and Education

Oak Ridge National Laboratory
Office of House Speaker
Office of Inspector General
Office of Job Corps
Overseas Private Investment Corporation
Patent & Trademark Office
The Pentagon
People to People International
The Philadelphia Center
Pittsburgh Energy Technology Center
Quality Education for Minorities Network
Rhode Island State Government
Rio Grande National Forest
San Juan/Rio Grande National Forests
Savannah River Ecology Laboratory
Stennis Space Center
Supreme Court of the United States
Technology Administration
United States Agency for International Development
United States Army Environmental Hygiene Agency
United States Bureau of Mines
United States Department of Commerce
United States Department of Defense
United States Environmental Protection Agency
United States National Arboretum
United States Secret Service
United States Securities and Exchange Commission
United States Senate Youth Program
United States Travel & Tourism Administration
Urban Fellows/Government Scholars Programs
Utah State Legislature
Washington Center for Internships and Academic Seminars
The White House

HEALTH CARE/MEDICINE

Abbott Laboratories
Aetna Life & Casualty
Affiliated Sante Group
Agency for Toxic Substances and Disease Registry
American Friends Service Committee
American Heart Association
American Institute for Foreign Study
American Red Cross
Ames Research Center
Argonne National Laboratory
Arthritis Foundation—Northern California Chapter
Baxter International
Bellevue Hospital Center
Boston University International Programs
Brethren Volunteer Service
CARE
CDG/CDS International
Centro para los Adolescentes de San Miguel de Allende
Chemical Industry Institute of Toxicology
Chicago Botanic Garden
Community Service Volunteer Programme
Council on International Educational Exchange
Educational Programs Abroad

Families USA Foundation
Food for the Hungry
The Ford Foundation
Foundation for Contemporary Mental Health
The French-American Center
Frontier Nursing Service
Genentech
Georgia Governor's Office
Global Volunteers
Goddard Space Flight Center
Gould Farm
Health & Environmental Sciences Group
Healthy Mothers, Healthy Babies
Hispanic Association of Colleges and Universities
Hoffman-La Roche
Howard Hughes Medical Institute
Human Service Alliance
Institute for International Cooperation and Development
Internships International
Jet Propulsion Laboratory
Jewish Vocational and Career Counseling Service
Johnson Space Center
Kennedy Space Center
Langley Research Center
Lewis Research Center
Lobsenz-Stevens
Marshall Space Flight Center
The Maternal & Child Health Institute
McLean Hospital
National Aeronautics and Space Administration
National Center for Toxicological Research
National Institutes of Health
National Organization for Women
National Women's Health Network
New York City Government
The New York Hospital-Cornell Medical Center
Oak Ridge Institute for Science and Education
Oak Ridge National Laboratory
The Partnership for Service-Learning
Peace Corps
Pediatric AIDS Foundation
People to People International
Pfizer
The Philadelphia Center
Physicians for Human Rights
The Population Institute
Stennis Space Center
3M
UCSF AIDS Health Project
United Nations Volunteer Program
United States Army Environmental Hygiene Agency
Urban Fellows/Government Scholars Programs
Washington Center for Internships and Academic Seminars
The White House

See Pharmaceuticals

HIGH TECHNOLOGY

National Institute of Standards & Technology
National Technical Information Service
Technology Administration

See Engineering

HISTORIC PRESERVATION

Historic Deerfield
National Park Service
National Trust for Historic Preservation

HISTORY

Anacostia Museum
Death Valley
Everglades
Georgia Governor's Office
Gettysburg Battlefield
Grand Canyon
Hispanic Association of Colleges and Universities
The History Factory
Houghton Mifflin Company
Joshua Tree
Klondike Gold Rush
Mount Rushmore
National Museum of American History
National Museum of Natural History
National Park Service
The Philadelphia Center
Rio Grande National Forest
San Juan/Rio Grande National Forests
Smithsonian Institution
Statue of Liberty
Student Conservation Association
Yellowstone National Park
Yosemite National Park

HORTICULTURE

Brooklyn Botanic Garden
Callaway Gardens
Chicago Botanic Garden
Longwood Gardens
Morris Arboretum
National Zoo
North Carolina Botanical Garden

See Environment/Nature

HOSPITALITY

The Gesher Summer Internship Program
McDonald's

See Hotels/Resorts
See Tourism

HOTELS/RESORTS

The Algonquin
Amelia Island Plantation
American Institute for Foreign Study
Boston University International Programs
CDG/CDS International
The Century Plaza Hotel
Council on International Educational Exchange
The French-American Center
Hostelling International—American Youth Hostels
PGA Tour
The Philadelphia Center
South Seas Plantation
Walt Disney World
Westin Hotels & Resorts

See Hospitality

HUMAN/CIVIL RIGHTS

American-Arab Anti-Discrimination Committee
American Association of Overseas Studies
American Civil Liberties Union
American Committee on Africa/The Africa Fund
American Friends Service Committee
American Jewish Congress
Amnesty International
Bet Tzedek Legal Services
Brethren Volunteer Service
The Center for Human Rights Advocacy
Council on International Educational Exchange
The Ford Foundation
The French-American Center
Georgia Governor's Office
International Labor Organization
Internships International
National Organization for Women
The Partnership for Service-Learning
People to People International
The Philadelphia Center
Physicians for Human Rights
Quaker United Nations Office
The Southern Center for International Studies
United Nations
United Nations Volunteer Program
Washington Office on Latin America
Women's International League for Peace and Freedom

HUMAN RESOURCES

International Foundation of Employee Benefit Plans
Note: Many organizations in this book offer human resources or person-nel experience.

IMAGING

See Consumer Goods
See Photography

INFORMATION SYSTEMS

See Computers
See Telecommunications

INSURANCE

Aetna Life & Casualty
AIESEC
American Institute for Foreign Study
Council on International Educational Exchange
The Franklin Life Insurance Company
Insurance Services Office
Internships International
MetLife
National Association of Professional Surplus Lines Offices
Northwestern Mutual Financial Network
People to People International
The Philadelphia Center

INTERIOR DESIGN

See Architecture
See Design

INTERNATIONAL RELATIONS

See Foreign Affairs

INVESTMENT BANKING

See Banking

INVESTMENT MANAGEMENT

Aetna Life & Casualty
American Association of Overseas Studies
Merrill Lynch

See Banking

JOURNALISM

Accuracy in Media
Asian American Journalists Association
ASSIST
Association for Education in Journalism
Boston University International Programs
Brookhaven National Laboratory
DG/CDS International
Council on International Educational Exchange
FAIR
Food for the Hungry
The French-American Center
Internships International
Jewish Vocational and Career Counseling Service
Mass Media Science and Engineering Fellows Program
National Journalism Center
Washington Center for Internships and Academic Seminars

See Magazines/Journals
See Newspapers

See Radio
See Television

JOURNALS

See Magazines/Journals

LATIN AMERICAN STUDIES

See Foreign Affairs
See Human/Civil Rights
See Public Policy

LAW

American Association of Overseas Studies
American Bar Association
American Civil Liberties Union
American Institute for Foreign Study
American Judicature Society
Association of Trial Lawyers of America
Bet Tzedek Legal Services
Boston University International Programs
The Center for Human Rights Advocacy
Children's Defense Fund
Connecticut Judicial Branch
Council on International Educational Exchange
Educational Programs Abroad
The Environmental Careers Organization
HALT: Americans for Legal Reform
Morrison & Foerster
National Asian Pacific American Legal Consortium
The National Partnership for Women and Families
New York State Bar Association
NOW Legal Defense and Education Fund
The Philadelphia Center
Public Defender Service for DC
Rhode Island State Government
Skadden, Arps, Slate, Meagher & Flom
Sponsors for Educational Opportunity
Supreme Court of the United States
United Nations
United States Securities and Exchange Commission
Washington Center for Internships and Academic Seminars
Y.E.S. to Jobs
Note: Many of the organizations in this book have Legal departments that accept interns.

See AIDS
See Environment/Nature
See Foreign Affairs
See Government
See Human/Civil Rights
See Public Policy
See Public Service

LEADERSHIP

See Education

LIBRARIES

The Academy for Advanced and Strategic Studies
Congressional Research Service
Council on International Educational Exchange
Franklin D. Roosevelt Library
International Labor Organization
The J. Paul Getty Trust
The Library of Congress
Newsday/New York Newsday
The Philadelphia Center
United Nations

LITERARY AGENCIES

See Talent Agencies

MAGAZINES/JOURNALS

American Association of Overseas Studies
American Forests
American Society of Magazine Editors
Black Enterprise
Blue Corn Comics
Boston Magazine
Boston University International Programs
Center for Investigative Reporting
The Chronicle of the Horse
City Limits Magazine
Columbia Journalism Review
Common Cause
Connecticut Magazine
Cybergrrl
The Discovery Channel
Discovery Communications
E/The Environmental Magazine
The Ecco Press
The Economist
Educational Programs Abroad
Emerge
Entertainment Design/Lighting Dimensions
Entertainment Weekly
Essence
Forbes
Foreign Affairs
Foreign Policy
Foreign Policy Research Institute
Harper's Magazine
IES – The Institute for the International Education of Students
International Sculpture Center
Los Angeles Magazine
MacDonald Communications Corp.
MAD Magazine
Middle East Institute
Middle East Research & Information Project
Mother Earth News
Mother Jones
Ms.
The Nation
Nation's Business

National Journal
National Review
National Space Society
National Wildlife Federation
Newsweek
The Paris Review
People to People International
Playboy
Psychology Today
The Ripon Society
Rolling Stone
Rosenbluth International
Science
Science News
Seventeen Magazine
Sierra Club
The Source
Southern Progress Corporation
Spin
Sports Illustrated
Spy
Success
Sussex Publishers
Teen Voices
Texas Monthly
Vibe
The Washingtonian
Who Cares
The Wilson Quarterly
Wired
Women's Institute for Freedom of the Press
Working Mother
Working Woman
YSB (Young Sisters & Brothers)

Note: Many of the organizations in this book publish in-house magazines that use interns.

MANAGEMENT CONSULTING

A.E. Schwartz & Associates
AIESEC
American University in Moscow
The Corporate Response Group
Council on International Educational Exchange
Deloitte & Touche
Ernst & Young
Hewitt Association
Internships International
The Philadelphia Center
Sponsors for Educational Opportunity

MANAGEMENT—GENERAL

American Management Association
Congressional Management Foundation

MANUFACTURING

See Consumer Goods
See Engineering

MARINE STUDIES

See Oceanography

MARKETING

See Advertising
See Public Relations/Marketing Agencies
Note: Many of the organizations in this book offer marketing experience.

MATHEMATICS

The Academy for Advanced and Strategic Studies
Agency for Toxic Substances and Disease Registry
Argonne National Laboratory
Brookhaven National Laboratory
Bureau of Engraving and Printing
Continuous Electron Beam Accelerator Facility
Corporation for National Service
E-Systems
Federal Reserve Board
GTE
Hispanic Association of Colleges and Universities
Insurance Services Office
Lamont-Doherty Earth Observatory
Lunar and Planetary Institute
National Center for Toxicological Research
National Security Agency
Naval Training Systems Center
Oak Ridge Institute for Science and Education
Oak Ridge National Laboratory
The Philadelphia Center
Pittsburgh Energy Technology Center
Savannah River Ecology Laboratory
United Nations
United States Army Environmental Hygiene Agency
United States Bureau of Mines
Xerox Palo Alto Research Center

MEDICINE

See Health Care/Medicine
See Pharmaceuticals

MENTAL HEALTH

See Disabled
See Health Care/Medicine

MILLINERY

See Clothing

MODELING AGENCIES

Elite Model Management
Ford Models
International Management Group

MOTORCYCLES

See Automobiles/Motorcycles

MUSEUMS

American Association of Overseas Studies
Anacostia Museum
Anasazi Heritage Center
The Andy Warhol Museum
Artists Space
Asian American Arts Centre
Boston University International Programs
The Brooklyn Museum
Buffalo Bill Historical Center
California Museum of Photography
Chicago Children's Museum
Children's Museum of Indianapolis
The Cloisters
Conservation Analytical Laboratory
Cooper-Hewitt Museum
Council on International Educational Exchange
D.C. Booth Historic Fish Hatchery
Decatur House Museum
Denver Art Museum
The Drawing Center
Educational Programs Abroad
Freer Gallery of Art
The French-American Center
Georgia Governor's Office
HERE
High Museum of Art
Hirshhorn Museum and Sculpture Garden
Historic Deerfield
IES – The Institute for the International Education of Students
The International Center of Photography
Internships International
The J. Paul Getty Trust
Los Angeles Municipal Art Gallery
The Metropolitan Museum of Art
Museum of Contemporary Art, Chicago
Museum of Fine Arts, Boston
The Museum of Modern Art, New York
Mystic Seaport Museum
National Air and Space Museum
National Museum of African Art
National Museum of American Art
National Museum of American History
National Museum of Natural History
National Portrait Gallery
Peggy Guggenheim Collection
People to People International
The Philadelphia Center
Rhode Island State Government
Smithsonian Institution
Solomon R. Guggenheim Museum
Tucson Children's Museum
United States Holocaust Museum
Wadsworth Atheneum
Whitney Museum of American Art

See Auction Houses

MUSIC

See Audio Recording
See Performing Arts
See Radio
See Record Labels/Record Industry

NATURE

See Environment/Nature

NEWSPAPERS

American Association of Overseas Studies
American Youth Work Center (Youth Today)
Anchorage Daily News
The Arizona Republic
The Blade
The Boston Globe
Boston University International Programs
Bucks County Courier Times
Center for Investigative Reporting
Central Newspapers/The Indianapolis News
Council on International Educational Exchange
The Dow Jones Newspaper Fund
Educational Programs Abroad
The Gazette Company
High Country News
IES – The Institute for the International Education of Students
The Indianapolis News
The Indianapolis Star
Lake Charles American Press
Los Angeles Times
The Milwaukee Journal
The New York Times
Newsday/New York Newsday
People to People International
The Philadelphia Center
The Philadelphia Inquirer
The Phoenix Gazette
Pittsburgh Post-Gazette
Roll Call
San Francisco Bay Guardian
San Francisco Chronicle
The Seattle Times
Village Voice
The Wall Street Journal
Washington Center for Politics & Journalism
The Washington Post

OCEANOGRAPHY

Bermuda Biological Station for Research
Center for Coastal Studies
Center for Marine Conservation
Mote Marine Laboratory
National Oceanic & Atmospheric Administration
Scripps Institution of Oceanography

See Environment/Nature

OIL AND GAS

AIESEC
BP
CDG/CDS International
Chevron
Council on International Educational Exchange
Du Pont
Exxon
Internships International
Schlumberger

OPERA

College Light Opera Company
Council on International Educational Exchange
Florida Grand Opera
The Philadelphia Center
San Francisco Opera

OUTDOOR EDUCATION CENTERS

Aspen Center for Environmental Studies
Breckenridge Outdoor Education Center
Glen Helen Outdoor Education Center
Hawk Mountain Sanctuary
Land Between The Lakes
Long Lake Conservation Center
Manice Education Center
North Cascades Institute
Pittsburgh Energy Technology Center
Shaver's Creek Environmental Center
Southface Energy Institute

See Environment/Nature

PAINTING

Student Works Painting
Sherwin-Williams
Student Works Painting
Varsity Student Painters

See Fine Arts

PARKS/FORESTS

Alaska State Parks
Cabrillo National Monument
Chincoteague National Wildlife Refuge
City of New York Parks & Recreation
Death Valley
Everglades
Gettysburg Battlefield
Grand Canyon
Joshua Tree
Klondike Gold Rush
Mount Rushmore
National Park Service
Rio Grande National Forest
San Juan/Rio Grande National Forests

Statue of Liberty
Student Conservation Association
Yellowstone National Park
Yosemite National Park

See Environment/Nature

PEACE STUDIES

American Friends Service Committee
Brethren Volunteer Service
Fellowship of Reconciliation
United Nations
United Nations Volunteer Program
Women's International League for Peace and Freedom

See Foreign Affairs
See Human/Civil Rights
See Public Policy

PERFORMING ARTS

American Association of Overseas Studies
American Institute for Foreign Study
Asian American Arts Centre
Association of Hispanic Arts
Central Park SummerStage
Creative Time
Educational Programs Abroad
Freedom Theatre
The French-American Center
HERE
Institute of Government
The Juilliard School
The Kennedy Center
The Kitchen
Lincoln Center for the Performing Arts
Longwood Gardens
Madison Square Garden
Miss Universe
Miss USA
People to People International
765-ARTS
Spoleto Festival USA
Thread Waxing Space
Virginia Symphony
Wolf Trap Foundation for the Performing Arts

See Ballet
See Dance
See Opera
See Symphony/Chamber Music
See Talent Agencies
See Theater

PERSONAL CARE/PAPER PRODUCTS

See Consumer Goods

PETROLEUM

See Oil and Gas

PHARMACEUTICALS

Abbott Laboratories
AIESEC
Council on International Educational Exchange
Du Pont
Genentech
The Gesher Summer Internship Program
Hoffman-La Roche
Inroads
Internships International
Merck & Company
Pfizer

PHILANTHROPY

National Committee for Responsive Philanthropy

See Public Service

PHOTOGRAPHY

American Dance Festival
Aperture Foundation
The Boston Globe
Butterfield & Butterfield
California Museum of Photography
Central Intelligence Agency
Council on International Educational Exchange
Habitat for Humanity International
IES – The Institute for the International Education of Students
The International Center of Photography
The Library of Congress
Los Angeles Times
National Basketball Association
National Zoo
The New York Times
Newsday/New York Newsday
Rio Grande National Forest
San Juan/Rio Grande National Forests
Smithsonian Institution
Sotheby's
United States Chamber of Commerce
The White House
WISH-TV 8
Wolf Trap Foundation for the Performing Arts

PHYSICS

American Association of Overseas Studies
E-Systems
Xerox Palo Alto Research Center

See Science

PLANETARIUMS

See Astronomy
See Art Galleries
See Museums

POLITICS

American Association of Overseas Studies
American Institute for Foreign Study
Boston University International Programs
The Conservative Caucus
Educational Programs Abroad
Emily's List
The French-American Center
IES – The Institute for the International Education of Students
Internships International
People to People International
The Philadelphia Center
The Ripon Society
The Southern Center for International Studies
United Nations Volunteer Program

See Government
See Public Policy

PRISONS

See Corrections

PSYCHIATRY/PSYCHOLOGY

See Health Care/Medicine

PUBLIC POLICY

The Academy for Advanced and Strategic Studies
Advocates for Children of New York
American-Arab Anti-Discrimination Committee
American Association for the Advancement of Science
American Association of Overseas Studies
American Civil Liberties Union
American Committee on Africa/The Africa Fund
American Enterprise Institute
American Federation of Teachers
American Jewish Congress
American Youth Work Center
Arab American Institute
Association of Trial Lawyers of America
Atlantic Council of the United States
Bernstein-Rein
The Brookings Institution
Business Executives for National Security
The Carter Center
CDG/CDS International
Center for Defense Information
Center for Strategic & International Studies
Children's Defense Fund
The Citizens Network for Foreign Affairs
Common Cause
Congressional Hispanic Caucus Institute

Congressional Management Foundation
The Conservative Caucus
The Coro Foundation
Corporation for National Service
Council of Energy Resource Tribes
Council on Economic Priorities
Educational Programs Abroad
Emily's List
The Environmental Careers Organization
FAIR
Families USA Foundation
The Feminist Majority
The Ford Foundation
The French-American Center
Friends Committee on National Legislation
Georgia Governor's Office
The Hansard Society for Parliamentary Government
The Hastings Center
The Heritage Foundation
Hillel
Hudson Institute
Institute for Policy Studies
Institute of Government
International Labor Organization
Internships in Francophone Europe
Internships International
Jewish Vocational and Career Counseling Service
Korean American Coalition
The Maternal & Child Health Institute
Middle East Institute
Middle East Research & Information Project
My Sister's Place
National Asian Pacific American Legal Consortium
National Audubon Society
The National Partnership for Women and Families
National Wildlife Federation
National Women's Health Network
NETWORK
Organization of Chinese Americans
Overseas Private Investment Corporation
People to People International
The Philadelphia Center
Physicians for Social Responsibility
The Population Institute
Public Interest Research Groups
Quaker United Nations Office
Quality Education for Minorities Network
Rand
The Ripon Society
Scoville Peace Fellowship Program
Surfrider Foundation
20/20 Vision
The Union Institute for Social Responsibility
United Nations
United Nations Association of the United States of America
United Nations Volunteer Program
United States Chamber of Commerce
United States Environmental Protection Agency
Urban Fellows/Government Scholars Programs

Washington Center for Internships and Academic Seminars
Washington Internships for Students in Engineering
The Washington Office on Africa
The White House
Woodrow Wilson International Center for Scholars

See Environment/Nature
See Women's Studies

PUBLIC RELATIONS/MARKETING

Aigner Associates
American Association of Overseas Studies
American Institute for Foreign Study
Association for Education in Journalism
Beach Associates
Blue Corn Comics
Boston University International Programs
Bozell Public Relations
Brown-Miller Communications
Burson-Marsteller
Cairns & Associates
The Callaghan Group
Canaan Public Relations
Clarke & Company
College Connections
Concrete Marketing
Council on International Educational Exchange
Creamer Dickson Basford
Cybergrrl
Davis Hays & Co.
Duffey Communications
Dykeman Associates
Elkman Advertising & Public Relations
Fenton Communications
The French-American Center
The Gothard Group
Hill and Knowlton
The History Factory
Interactive Public Relations
Internships International
KCSA Public Relations
Korff Enterprises
Levine/Schneider Public Relations
Lobsenz-Stevens
Makovsky & Company
Mallory Factor
Marina Maher Communications
Mixed Media
Office of House Speaker
Pella
People to People International
The Philadelphia Center
PMK Public Relations
The Rockey Company
Ruder-Finn
Savvy Management
Sgro Promo Associates/General Motors Internship
Shirley Herz Associates

Temerlin McClain
Vault.com
The Widmeyer Baker Group
Y.E.S. to Jobs

See Advertising
Note: A majority of the organizations in this book offer public relations experience.

PUBLIC SERVICE

Affiliated Sante Group
AFS Intercultural Programs
American Association of Overseas Studies
American Friends Service Committee
American Institute for Foreign Study
American Red Cross
American Woman's Economic Development Corp.
AMIDEAST
ASHOKA: Innovators for the Public
Best Buddies International
Bet Tzedek Legal Services
Bike-Aid
Boys Hope/Girls Hope
Brethren Volunteer Service
The Carter Center
Centro para los Adolescentes de San Miguel de Allende
Children's Defense Fund
CityArts
Community Service Volunteer Programme
The Coro Foundation
Corporation for National Service
Fellowship of Reconciliation
Food for the Hungry
Fourth World Movement
The French-American Center
Georgia Governor's Office
Global Exchange
Global Volunteers
Habitat for Humanity International
Hillel
H.O.M.E.
Human Service Alliance
IES – The Institute for the International Education of Students
Inroads
Institute for International Cooperation and Development
Institute of Cultural Affairs
The International Foundation for Education and Self-Help
International Voluntary Services
International Volunteer Projects
Jewish Vocational and Career Counseling Service
JUSTACT: Youth Action for Global Justice
Lutheran Volunteer Corps
Office of Job Corps
The Partnership for Service-Learning
Peace Corps
People to People International
The Philadelphia Center
Public Allies

Rhode Island State Government
Special Olympics International
Starlight Foundation
Teen Voices
Urban Fellows/Government Scholars Programs
Volunteers for Israel
Volunteers For Peace
Washington Center for Internships and Academic Seminars
The White House
Who Cares
Winant-Clayton Volunteers
Women Express

PUBLISHING

Agora, Inc.
American Association of Overseas Studies
American Institute for Foreign Study
ASSIST
Association for Education in Journalism
Ballantine Books
Beacon Press
Blue Corn Comics
Boston University International Programs
Charlesbridge Publishing
Council on International Educational Exchange
Crown Books
The Ecco Press
Educational Programs Abroad
Faber and Faber
Farrar Straus & Giroux
The French-American Center
Houghton Mifflin Company
Hunter House
International Management Group
Internships International
John Wiley & Sons
Jones & Bartlett
Knopf Books
Penguin Books
People to People International
The Philadelphia Center
Plume Books
Random House
Signet Classics
Southern Progress Corporation
Vault.com
Viking Books

RADIO

All Things Considered
Boston University International Programs
Brethren Volunteer Service
Center for Investigative Reporting
Council on International Educational Exchange
Educational Programs Abroad
The Howard Stern Show
IES – The Institute for the International Education of Students
International Radio and Television Society

KIRO
KQED-FM
KRCB
National Association of College Broadcasters
National Public Radio
People to People International
Performance Today
The Philadelphia Center
The Rush Limbaugh Show
Shadow Broadcast Services
Talk of the Nation
United Nations Volunteer Program
Voice of America
Washington Center for Politics & Journalism
WAXQ - Q104.3
The Westwood One Radio Network
WGN-Chicago
WNYC
Y.E.S. to Jobs

RAILROAD

See Transportation

REAL ESTATE

Council on International Educational Exchange
Crown Capital
Grubb & Ellis

RECORD LABELS/RECORD INDUSTRY

A&M Records
American Association of Overseas Studies
Angel Records
Arista Records
Asylum Records
Atlantic Records
Bertelsmann Music Group
Brick Wall Management
Capitol Records
CBS Records
Chrysalis Records
Columbia Records
Concrete Marketing
Council on International Educational Exchange
Def Jam Records
EastWest Records
Elektra Entertainment Group
Elektra Records
EMI Records
EMI Records Group North America
Energy Records
Epic Records
Fontana Records
Geffen Records
Interscope Records
Island Records
Liberty Records
Mammoth Records
Matador Records

MCA Records
MCT Management/Bold! Records
Mercury Records
Motown Records
Pendulum Records
Perspective Records
The Philadelphia Center
PolyGram
RCA Records
Rhino Records
SBK Records
Select Records
Sony Music Entertainment
Tommy Boy Music
Vertigo Records
Verve Records
Virgin Records
Wall Street Music
Y.E.S. to Jobs
Zoo Entertainment

RECREATION

AIM for the Handicapped
Alaska State Parks
Boys Hope/Girls Hope
Breckenridge Outdoor Education Center
Brethren Volunteer Service
Camp Counselors USA
Camphill Soltane
City of New York Parks & Recreation
The French-American Center
Gould Farm
Hawthorne Valley Farm
Interlocken
Land Between The Lakes
Long Lake Conservation Center
Manice Education Center
Mobility International
North Cascades Institute
Outward Bound/Voyageur School
The Partnership for Service-Learning
PERA Club
The Philadelphia Center
Shaver's Creek Environmental Center

RELIGIOUS AFFILIATION

American Friends Service Committee
American Jewish Congress
Brethren Volunteer Service
Fellowship of Reconciliation
Food for the Hungry
Friends Committee on National Legislation
Jewish Vocational and Career Counseling Service
Habitat for Humanity International
Hillel
Quaker United Nations Office
YMCA

RESORTS

See Hotels/Resorts

RESTAURANT MANAGEMENT

See Hospitality

RETAIL

Barney's New York
Sherwin-Williams

See Clothing
See Consumer Goods

SALES

A&M Records
Abbott Laboratories
AIESEC
America West Airlines
Angel Records
Apple Computer
Archive Films
The Boston Globe
Buick
Cadillac
Capitol Records
Chevrolet
Chicago Bulls
Chrysalis Records
Comedy Central
Council on International Educational Exchange
Def Jam Records
EMI Records
EMI Records Group North America
Entenmann's
Exxon
Fontana Records
Ford Motor Company
Fox
Frito-Lay
fX
General Foods
General Mills
General Motors Marketing Internship
GMC Truck
GTE
Hallmark Cards
Hewlett-Packard
International Radio and Television Society
International Telecommunications Satellite Organization
Internships International
Island Records
J.C. Penney
KIRO
Kraft Foods, Inc.
Liberty Records
Liz Claiborne
Merck & Company

Mercury Records
Middle East Research & Information Project
Motown Records
Nabisco
National Broadcasting Company
Northwestern Mutual Financial Network
Oldsmobile
Oscar Mayer
Pendulum Records
People to People International
Perspective Records
The Philadelphia Center
PolyGram
Pontiac
Procter & Gamble
Reebok
Saturn
SBK Records
The Southwestern Company
Food Network
Twentieth Century Fox
Twentieth Television
Union Carbide
Vertigo Records
Verve Records
Weyerhaeuser
Whitney Museum of American Art
WISH-TV 8
Y.E.S. to Jobs

SCIENCE

American Association for the Advancement of Science
American Association of Overseas Studies
American Institute for Foreign Study
Council of Energy Resource Tribes
Educational Programs Abroad
The Gesher Summer Internship Program
IAESTE
Morris Arboretum
National Consortium for Graduate Degrees for Minorities in Engineering and Science
Science
Science News
Washington Center for Internships and Academic Seminars
See Aerospace
See Astronomy
See Biotechnology
See Chemicals
See Computers
See Consumer Goods
See Environment/Nature
See Government (research laboratories, United States Dept. of Energy, etc.)
See Health Care/Medicine
See Oceanography
See Pharmaceuticals
See Telecommunications
See Utilities
See Zoos

SCULPTURE

International Sculpture Center

See Fine Arts

SPORTS

American Association of Overseas Studies
American Hockey League
ASSIST
Atlanta Junior Golf Association
CAVS/Gund Arena Company
Chicago Bulls
Cleveland Cavaliers
Council on International Educational Exchange
Dallas Cowboys
David Leadbetter Golf Academy
ESPN
Golf Digest
Gund Arena
International Management Group
Korff Enterprises
Los Angeles Lakers
LPGA Junior Golf Program
Madison Square Garden
MSG Network
National Basketball Association
National Collegiate Athletic Association
National Football League
New York Knicks
New York Rangers
Nick Bollettieri Tennis Academy
NIKE
NIKE Tour
People to People International
PGA Tour
The Philadelphia Center
Reebok
San Francisco 49ers
Senior PGA Tour
Special Olympics International
Sports Illustrated
United States Olympic Committee
Women's Sports Foundation
Youth For Understanding International Exchange

See Newspapers
See Television

STATISTICS

See Economics
See Mathematics

SYMPHONY/CHAMBER MUSIC

American Symphony Orchestra League
Chamber Music
Council on International Educational Exchange
Norfolk Chamber Music Festival
The Philadelphia Center

TALENT AGENCIES

Abrams Artists Agency
Barry-Haft-Brown Artists Agency
Council on International Educational Exchange
Creative Artists Agency
Howard Talent West
International Creative Management
Manus & Associates Literary Agency
MCT Management/Bold! Records
United Talent Agency

TEACHING/EDUCATION

AIM for the Handicapped
American Institute for Foreign Study
American School for the Deaf
Aspen Center for Environmental Studies
Boston University International Programs
Boys Hope/Girls Hope
Brethren Volunteer Service
Camp Counselors USA
Camphill Soltane
Center for Talented Youth
Choate Rosemary Hall
The Cloisters
Council on International Educational Exchange
Crow Canyon Archaeological Center
Cushman School
Duke University Talent Identification Program
Educational Programs Abroad
Food for the Hungry
The Ford Foundation
The French-American Center
Frontier Nursing Service
Glen Helen Outdoor Education Center
Global Volunteers
IES – The Institute for the International Education of Students
Institute for International Cooperation and Development
Institute of International Education
Japanese Exchange and Teaching Program
Land Between The Lakes
Legacy International
Little Keswick School
Long Lake Conservation Center
The Lowell Whiteman School
Manice Education Center
Middle Earth
Miss Porter's School
New Canaan Country School
North Cascades Institute
Northfield Mount Hermon School
Overseas Service Corps of the YMCA
The Partnership for Service-Learning
Peace Corps
People to People International
The Philadelphia Center
Phillips Academy
Quality Education for Minorities Network

Rio Grande National Forest
St. Paul's School
San Juan/Rio Grande National Forests
Sea World
Shaver's Creek Environmental Center
Staten Island Zoo
Students for Central & Eastern Europe
Summerbridge National
Teach for America
Volunteers in Asia
WorldTeach

TELECOMMUNICATIONS

The Academy for Advanced and Strategic Studies
AIESEC
AT&T Bell Laboratories
CDG/CDS International
Council on International Educational Exchange
GTE
Inroads
International Telecommunications Satellite Organization
Internships International
National Telecommunications & Information Administration
Octel Communications
People to People International
Tellabs
The Philadelphia Center
Raychem
Unitel

TELEVISION

Academy of Television Arts & Sciences
American Association of Overseas Studies
Another World
Archive Films
As The World Turns
Assistant Directors Training Program
Barwood Productions
Baywatch
Black Entertainment Television
Blair Television
Boston University International Programs
Capital Gang
The Cartoon Network
CBS News
Center for Investigative Reporting
Charlie Rose
Cinemax
CNN
Columbia Pictures
Comedy Central
Council on International Educational Exchange
Crossfire
C-SPAN
The Discovery Channel
Discovery Communications
E! Entertainment Television Networks
Educational Programs Abroad

ESPN
Face the Nation
First Business
Food Network
48 Hours
Fox
The French-American Center
fX
The Gazette Company
Good Morning America
Greater Media Cable
Guiding Light
Haft/Nasatir
HBO
Headline News
Home Box Office
H.S.I. Productions
IES – The Institute for the International Education of Students
International Management Group
International Radio and Television Society
Internships International
It's Your Business
The Jim Henson Company
KGO-TV
KIRO
KPIX-TV
KRCB
Larry King Live
Late Night with Conan O'Brien
Late Show with David Letterman
The Learning Channel
Lucasfilm
The MacNeil/Lehrer NewsHour
MCA/Universal
Michael Phillips Productions
MSG Network
MTV: Music Television
National Association of College Broadcasters
National Broadcasting Company
NBC Nightly News
Nightline
Open City Films
People to People International
The Philadelphia Center
PrimeTime Live
Procter & Gamble Productions
The Real World
Rhode Island State Government
Roy A. Somlyo Productions
Sally Jessy Raphael Show
Saturday Night Live
Simon & Goodman Picture Company
60 Minutes
Sony Pictures Entertainment
Sunday Morning
TBS
TNT
The Today Show

The Tonight Show With Jay Leno
Thirteen/WNET
TriStar Pictures
Turner Broadcasting System
Twentieth Television
20/20
Up to the Minute
VH-1
Washington Center for Politics & Journalism
WCHS-TV
WISH-TV 8
WNBC-TV
WNYC
Worldnet
Writers Guild of America, West
Y.E.S. to Jobs

THEATER

Actors Theatre of Louisville
Alliance of Residence Theaters
American Conservatory Theater
The American Place Theatre
American Repertory Theatre
Arden Theatre Company
Arena Stage
Berkeley Repertory Theater
Berkshire Public Theatre
Boston University International Programs
Child's Play Touring Theatre
Classic Stage Company
College Light Opera Company
Council on International Educational Exchange
Creede Repertory Theatre
Cromarty & Co.
The French-American Center
Georgia Governor's Office
Goodman Theatre
Maine State Music Theatre
Manhattan Theatre Club
New Dramatists
New Stage Theatre
New York Shakespeare Festival
New York State Theatre Institute
People to People International
The Philadelphia Center
Playhouse on the Square
Rhode Island State Government
Roy A. Somlyo Productions
Scott Rudin Productions
The Source Theater Company
Steppenwolf Theatre Company
TADA!
Theater de la Jeune Lune
Williamstown Theater Festival
The Wilma Theater
Women's Project & Productions

THEME PARKS

See Tourism

THINK TANKS

See Foreign Affairs
See Public Policy

TOURISM

ASSIST
Hostelling International—American Youth Hostels
The Philadelphia Center
Rosenbluth International
Sea World
Space Needle Corporation
United States Travel & Tourism Administration
Walt Disney World

TOYS

See Consumer Goods

TRADE

Bureau of Export Administration
Consumers for World Trade
Economic Development Administration
International Trade Administration
Minority Business Development Agency
Office of Inspector General
Patent & Trademark Office
Technology Administration
United States and Foreign Commercial Service
United States Department of Commerce

TRANSPORTATION

America West Airlines
Amtrak
Boston University International Programs
Council on International Educational Exchange
DHL Worldwide Express
Internships International
People to People International
The Philadelphia Center

TRAVEL MANAGEMENT

See Tourism

URBAN PLANNING

See Architecture

UTILITIES

CDG/CDS International
Council on International Educational Exchange

Internships International
People to People International
The Philadelphia Center

VIDEO GAMES

Fox
SGI

VIDEO PRODUCTION

Beach Associates

See Film
See Television

WILDLIFE MANAGEMENT

See Aquariums
See Environment/Nature
See Zoos

WOMEN'S STUDIES/WOMEN'S ISSUES

American Association of Overseas Studies
American Association of University Women Educational
  Foundation
American Civil Liberties Union
American Committee on Africa/The Africa Fund
American Jewish Congress
American Woman's Economic Development Corp.
Council on International Educational Exchange
The Feminist Majority
Focus on Women
The Ford Foundation
The French-American Center
Georgia Governor's Office
Healthy Mothers, Healthy Babies
International Labor Organization
Internships International
MacDonald Communication
The Maternal & Child Health Institute
Ms.
My Sister's Place
National Association for Female Executives
National Organization for Women
The National Partnership for Women and Families
NOW Legal Defense and Education Fund
The Partnership for Service-Learning
People to People International
The Philadelphia Center
The Population Institute
Quaker United Nations Office
Teen Voices
Washington Center for Internships and Academic Seminars
Women Express
Women's Institute for Freedom of the Press
Women's International League for Peace and Freedom
Women's Project & Productions

Women's Sports & Fitness Magazine
Working Mother
Working Woman

ZOOS

Baltimore Zoo
Brookfield Zoo
Indianapolis Zoo
National Zoo
The Philadelphia Center
San Diego Zoo
Staten Island Zoo

ALABAMA

AIESEC
American Civil Liberties Union
The American-Scandinavian Foundation
Boeing
Camp Counselors USA
CDG/CDS International
Council on International Educational Exchange
Du Pont
The Environmental Careers Organization
Ernst & Young
Gap
Habitat for Humanity International
Hispanic Association of Colleges and Universities
Howard Hughes Medical Institute
Inroads
International Foundation of Employee Benefit Plans
International Volunteer Projects
Marshall Space Flight Center
National Aeronautics and Space Administration
National Consortium for Graduate Degrees for Minorities in
  Engineering and Science
National Park Service
The Nature Conservancy
Northwestern Mutual Financial Network
Oak Ridge Institute for Science and Education
Oscar Mayer Wienermobile
Pediatric AIDS Foundation
Procter & Gamble
Schlumberger
Sherwin-Williams
Sierra Club
Southern Progress Corporation
The Southwestern Company
Student Conservation Association
3M
United States Secret Service
Weyerhaeuser
Writers Guild of America, West

ALASKA

Alaska State Parks
American Civil Liberties Union
The American-Scandinavian Foundation
Anchorage Daily News
CDG/CDS International
The Environmental Careers Organization
Federal Bureau of Prisons
Habitat for Humanity International
Hispanic Association of Colleges and Universities
Howard Hughes Medical Institute
Interlocken
International Foundation of Employee Benefit Plans
International Volunteer Projects

National Consortium for Graduate Degrees for Minorities in
  Engineering and Science
National Park Service
The Nature Conservancy
Northwestern Mutual Financial Network
Oak Ridge Institute for Science and Education
Oscar Mayer Wienermobile
Pediatric AIDS Foundation
Physicans for Social Responsibility
Public Interest Research Groups
Sherwin-Williams
Sierra Club
The Southwestern Company
Student Conservation Association
Volunteers For Peace
Writers Guild of America, West

ARIZONA

AIESEC
America West Airlines
American Civil Liberties Union
The American-Scandinavian Foundation
The Arizona Republic
Atlantic Records
Boeing
Boys Hope/Girls Hope
Brethren Volunteer Service
Camp Counselors USA
CDG/CDS International
Central Newspapers/The Indianapolis News
Chrysalis Records
Council on International Educational Exchange
The Dow Jones Newspaper Fund
EMI Records
Ernst & Young
Federal Bureau of Prisons
Ford Models
Frito-Lay
Gap
Grand Canyon
Grubb & Ellis
Habitat for Humanity International
Hillel
Hispanic Association of Colleges and Universities
Howard Hughes Medical Institute
Inroads
Institute of Cultural Affairs
Intel
Interlocken
International Foundation of Employee Benefit Plans
International Volunteer Projects
Interscope Records
Mammoth Records
Matador Records
McDonald's

National Audubon Society
National Consortium for Graduate Degrees for Minorities in
   Engineering and Science
National Park Service
The Nature Conservancy
Northwestern Mutual Financial Network
Oak Ridge Institute for Science and Education
Oscar Mayer Wienermobile
Pediatric AIDS Foundation
PERA Club
The Phoenix Gazette
Physicans for Social Responsibility
Procter & Gamble
Rhino Records
SBK Records
Select Records
Sherwin-Williams
Sierra Club
The Southwestern Company
Student Conservation Association
Teach for America
3M
Tucson Children's Museum
Virgin Records
Westin Hotels & Resorts
Writers Guild of America, West

ARKANSAS

American Civil Liberties Union
American Heart Association
The American-Scandinavian Foundation
CDG/CDS International
Council on International Educational Exchange
The Dow Jones Newspaper Fund
The Environmental Careers Organization
Ernst & Young
Federal Bureau of Prisons
Gap
Global Volunteers
Habitat for Humanity International
Hispanic Association of Colleges and Universities
Howard Hughes Medical Institute
International Foundation of Employee Benefit Plans
International Volunteer Projects
National Center for Toxicological Research
National Consortium for Graduate Degrees for Minorities in
   Engineering and Science
National Park Service
The Nature Conservancy
Northwestern Mutual Financial Network
Oak Ridge Institute for Science and Education
Oscar Mayer Wienermobile
Pediatric AIDS Foundation
Procter & Gamble
Schlumberger
Sherwin-Williams
The Southwestern Company
Student Conservation Association

Teach for America
3M
Weyerhaeuser
Writers Guild of America, West

CALIFORNIA

Abrams Artists Agency
Academic Study Associates
Academy of Television Arts & Sciences
Aetna Life & Casualty
AFS Intercultural Programs
AIESEC
A&M Records
American-Arab Anti-Discrimination Committee
American Civil Liberties Union
American Conservatory Theater
American Friends Service Committee
American Heart Association
American Israel Public Affairs Committee
American Jewish Congress
The American-Scandinavian Foundation
American Society of Magazine Editors
American Woman's Economic Development Corp.
Ames Research Center
Amnesty International
Amtrak
Apple Computer
Arista Records
Arthritis Foundation—Northern California Chapter
Arthur Andersen
Assistant Directors Training Program
Asylum Records
Atlantic Records
Baxter International
Baywatch
Bechtel
Berkeley Repertory Theater
Bertelsmann Music Group
Best Buddies International
Bet Tzedek Legal Services
Bike-Aid
Blue Corn Comics
Boeing
Boys Hope/Girls Hope
Bozell Public Relations
Brethren Volunteer Service
Brown-Miller Communications
Butterfield & Butterfield
Cabrillo National Monument
California Governor's Office
California Museum of Photography
California State Assembly
California State Senate
Camp Counselors USA
CARE
CBS News
CBS Records
CDG/CDS International

Center for Investigative Reporting
Center for Marine Conservation
Center for Talented Youth
The Century Plaza Hotel
Chanticleer Films
Chevron
Chrysalis Records
Citibank
CNN
Columbia Pictures
Columbia Records
The Coro Foundation
Council on International Educational Exchange
Creative Artists Agency
Crown Capital
Death Valley
Def Jam Records
Deloitte & Touche
DHL Worldwide Express
Dow Chemical Company
The Dow Jones Newspaper Fund
E! Entertainment Television Networks
EastWest Records
Elektra Entertainment Group
Elektra Records
Elite Model Management
EMI Records
Energy Records
The Environmental Careers Organization
Epic Records
Ernst & Young
F.A.O. Schwarz
Farm Sanctuary
Federal Bureau of Prisons
Feminist
Fisher-Price Toys
Fontana Records
Ford Models
Fox
The French-American Center
Frito-Lay
Gap
Geffen Records
Genentech
General Mills
Gensler and Associates/Architects
Global Exchange
Grubb & Ellis
GTE
Habitat for Humanity International
Haft/Nasatir
Hallmark Cards
Hewlett-Packard
Hillel
Hispanic Association of Colleges and Universities
Howard Hughes Medical Institute
H.S.I. Productions
Hunter House

IBM
Inroads
Institute for Unpopular Culture
Intel
Interactive Public Relations
Interlocken
International Creative Management
International Foundation of Employee Benefit Plans
International Management Group
International Telecommunications Satellite Organization
International Volunteer Projects
Interscope Records
Island Records
The J. Paul Getty Trust
Jet Propulsion Laboratory
Jewish Vocational and Career Counseling Service
Joshua Tree
JUSTACT: Youth Action for Global Justice
KGO-TV
Korean American Coalition
Korff Enterprises
KPIX-TV
KQED-FM
KRCB
Lawrence Livermore National Laboratory
Levine/Schneider Public Relations
Lightstorm Entertainment
Los Angeles Lakers
Los Angeles Magazine
Los Angeles Municipal Art Gallery
Los Angeles Times
LPGA Junior Golf Program
Lucasfilm
Mammoth Records
Manus & Associates Literary Agency
Mass Media Science and Engineering Fellows Program
Matador Records
Mattel Toys
MCA Records
MCA/Universal
McDonald's
Mercury Records
Metro-Goldwyn-Mayer/United Artists
Michael Phillips Productions
Miss Universe
Miss USA
Morrison & Foerster
Mother Jones
Motown Records
MTV: Music Television
National Aeronautics and Space Administration
National Association of Professional Surplus Lines Offices
National Audubon Society
National Broadcasting Company
National Consortium for Graduate Degrees for Minorities in
    Engineering and Science
National Park Service
The Nature Conservancy

Nick at Nite
Northwestern Mutual Financial Network
Oak Ridge Institute for Science and Education
Octel Communications
Office of Job Corps
Oscar Mayer Wienermobile
Pacific Investments Management Company
Pediatric AIDS Foundation
Perspective Records
Physicans for Social Responsibility
Playboy
PolyGram
Procter & Gamble
Public Interest Research Groups
Raychem
RCA Records
The Real World
Reebok
Rhino Records
San Diego Zoo
San Francisco Bay Guardian
San Francisco Chronicle
San Francisco 49ers
San Francisco Opera
SBK Records
Schlumberger
Scott Rudin Productions
Scripps Institution of Oceanography
Select Records
Sgro Promo Associates/General Motors Internship
Sherwin-Williams
Sierra Club
SGI
60 Minutes
Sony Music Entertainment
Sony Pictures Entertainment
The Southwestern Company
Starlight Foundation
Student Conservation Association
Student Works Painting
Summerbridge National
Surfrider Foundation
Teach for America
3M
The Tonight Show With Jay Leno
Toyota
TriStar Pictures
Food Network
Twentieth Century Fox
Twentieth Television
UCSF AIDS Health Project
United Artists
United States Environmental Protection Agency
United States Secret Service
United States Securities and Exchange Commission
United Talent Agency
Universal Pictures
Universal Studios

Vertigo Records
Verve Records
VH-1
Virgin Records
Volunteers For Peace
Wells Fargo Bank
Wessler Entertainment
Westin Hotels & Resorts
Weyerhaeuser
Wired
Writers Guild of America, West
Xerox
Xerox—Palo Alto Research Center
Y.E.S. to Jobs
Youth For Understanding International Exchange
Zoo Entertainment

COLORADO

Academic Study Associates
AIESEC
American Civil Liberties Union
The American-Scandinavian Foundation
Amnesty International
Anasazi Heritage Center
Arista Records
Arthur Andersen
Aspen Center for Environmental Studies
Atlantic Records
Bertelsmann Music Group
Boys Hope/Girls Hope
Breckenridge Outdoor Education Center
Brethren Volunteer Service
Camp Counselors USA
CARE
CDG/CDS International
The Center for Human Rights Advocacy
Chrysalis Records
Council of Energy Resource Tribes
Council on International Educational Exchange
Creede Repertory Theatre
Crow Canyon Archaeological Center
Denver Art Museum
The Dow Jones Newspaper Fund
EastWest Records
Elektra Records
EMI Records
Ernst & Young
Federal Bureau of Prisons
Gap
Gensler and Associates/Architects
Grubb & Ellis
Habitat for Humanity International
Hewlett-Packard
High Country News
Hispanic Association of Colleges and Universities
Howard Hughes Medical Institute
IBM
Inroads

Institute of Cultural Affairs
Interlocken
International Foundation of Employee Benefit Plans
International Management Group
International Volunteer Projects
Interscope Records
The Lowell Whiteman School
The MacNeil/Lehrer NewsHour
Mammoth Records
Mass Media Science and Engineering Fellows Program
Matador Records
Morrison & Foerster
National Association of Professional Surplus Lines Offices
National Consortium for Graduate Degrees for Minorities in
   Engineering and Science
National Park Service
The Nature Conservancy
Northwestern Mutual Financial Network
Oak Ridge Institute for Science and Education
Office of Job Corps
Oscar Mayer Wienermobile
Pediatric AIDS Foundation
Pfizer
Physicans for Social Responsibility
Procter & Gamble
Public Interest Research Groups
RCA Records
Rhino Records
Rio Grande National Forest
San Juan/Rio Grande National Forests
SBK Records
Select Records
Sherwin-Williams
Sierra Club
The Southwestern Company
Student Conservation Association
Student Works Painting
Summerbridge National
3M
United States Environmental Protection Agency
United States Olympic Committee
United States Secret Service
United States Securities and Exchange Commission
Virgin Records
Women's Sports & Fitness Magazine
Writers Guild of America, West
Yosemite National Park
Zoo Entertainment

CONNECTICUT

Aetna Life & Casualty
American Civil Liberties Union
American Heart Association
The American-Scandinavian Foundation
American School for the Deaf
American Woman's Economic Development Corp.
Arthur Andersen
Association for Education in Journalism

Atlantic Records
Best Buddies International
Callaway Advanced Technology
Camp Counselors USA
CDG/CDS International
Choate Rosemary Hall
Connecticut Judicial Branch
Connecticut Magazine
Council on International Educational Exchange
Deloitte & Touche
Dow Chemical Company
The Dow Jones Newspaper Fund
Du Pont
E! Entertainment Television Networks
E/The Environmental Magazine
The Environmental Careers Organization
Ernst & Young
ESPN
Federal Bureau of Prisons
Gap
Golf Digest
GTE
Habitat for Humanity International
Hillel
Hispanic Association of Colleges and Universities
Howard Hughes Medical Institute
Inroads
International Foundation of Employee Benefit Plans
International Volunteer Projects
Interscope Records
Mammoth Records
Matador Records
Miss Porter's School
Mystic Seaport Museum
National Audubon Society
National Consortium for Graduate Degrees for Minorities in
   Engineering and Science
National Park Service
The Nature Conservancy
New Canaan Country School
Norfolk Chamber Music Festival
Northwestern Mutual Financial Network
Oak Ridge Institute for Science and Education
Oscar Mayer Wienermobile
Pediatric AIDS Foundation
Pfizer
Physicans for Social Responsibility
Public Interest Research Groups
Rhino Records
Save the Sound
Schlumberger
Select Records
Sherwin-Williams
The Southwestern Company
Student Conservation Association
Summerbridge National
Union Carbide
Virgin Records

Volunteers For Peace
Wadsworth Atheneum
Whitney Museum of American Art
Writers Guild of America West

DELAWARE

American Civil Liberties Union
American Heart Association
The American-Scandinavian Foundation
Camp Counselors USA
CDG/CDS International
Council on International Educational Exchange
Du Pont
The Environmental Careers Organization
Federal Bureau of Prisons
Gap
Habitat for Humanity International
Hewlett-Packard
Hispanic Association of Colleges and Universities
Howard Hughes Medical Institute
International Foundation of Employee Benefit Plans
International Volunteer Projects
Lutheran Volunteer Corps
National Consortium for Graduate Degrees for Minorities in Engineering and Science
National Park Service
The Nature Conservancy
Northwestern Mutual Financial Network
Oak Ridge Institute for Science and Education
Oscar Mayer Wienermobile
Pediatric AIDS Foundation
Public Allies
Sherwin-Williams
The Southwestern Company
Writers Guild of America, West

FLORIDA

Aetna Life & Casualty
Agora, Inc.
AIESEC
Amelia Island Plantation
American & International Designs
American Civil Liberties Union
American Forests
American Heart Association
American Jewish Congress
The American-Scandinavian Foundation
Arista Records
Arthur Andersen
Atlantic Records
Bertelsmann Music Group
Best Buddies International
Boeing
Boys Hope/Girls Hope
Brethren Volunteer Service
Camp Counselors USA
CBS News

CDG/CDS International
Center for Marine Conservation
Chrysalis Records
CNN
Council on International Educational Exchange
Cushman School
David Leadbetter Golf Academy
Deloitte & Touche
The Dow Jones Newspaper Fund
Du Pont
E-Systems
Earle Palmer Brown
Elite Model Management
EMI Records
The Environmental Careers Organization
Ernst & Young
Everglades
Federal Bureau of Prisons
Florida Grand Opera
Ford Models
Gap
The Gothard Group
Grubb & Ellis
GTE
Habitat for Humanity International
Hillel
Hispanic Association of Colleges and Universities
Howard Hughes Medical Institute
IBM
Inroads
International Foundation of Employee Benefit Plans
International Management Group
International Volunteer Projects
Interscope Records
Kennedy Space Center
Mammoth Records
Matador Records
Mote Marine Laboratory
MTV: Music Television
National Aeronautics and Space Administration
National Audubon Society
National Consortium for Graduate Degrees for Minorities in Engineering and Science
National Park Service
The Nature Conservancy
Naval Training Systems Center
Nick Bollettieri Tennis Academy
NIKE Tour
Northwestern Mutual Financial Network
Oak Ridge Institute for Science and Education
Oscar Mayer Wienermobile
Pediatric AIDS Foundation
PGA Tour
Physicans for Social Responsibility
Procter & Gamble
Public Interest Research Groups
RCA Records
Rhino Records

SBK Records
Sea World
Select Records
Senior PGA Tour
Sherwin-Williams
Sierra Club
The Southwestern Company
Student Conservation Association
Summerbridge National
United States Environmental Protection Agency
United States Secret Service
United States Securities and Exchange Commission
VH-1
Virgin Records
Writers Guild of America, West
Xerox
Y.E.S. to Jobs
Zoo Entertainment

GEORGIA

A&M Records
Aetna Life & Casualty
Agency for Toxic Substances and Disease Registry
AIESEC
American Civil Liberties Union
American Friends Service Committee
American Heart Association
The American-Scandinavian Foundation
Arista Records
Arthur Andersen
The Atlanta Ballet
Atlanta Junior Golf Association
Atlantic Records
Bertelsmann Music Group
Best Buddies International
Brethren Volunteer Service
Callaway Gardens
Camp Counselors USA
CARE
The Carter Center
The Cartoon Network
CBS Records
CDG/CDS International
Chrysalis Records
Citibank
CNN
Columbia Records
Council on International Educational Exchange
Def Jam Records
Deloitte & Touche
Duffey Communications
Du Pont
EastWest Records
Elektra Records
Elite Model Management
EMI Records
The Environmental Careers Organization
Epic Records

Ernst & Young
Federal Bureau of Prisons
Fontana Records
Frito-Lay
Gap
General Mills
Georgia Governor's Office
Grubb & Ellis
GTE
Habitat for Humanity International
Hallmark Cards
Headline News
Hewlett-Packard
High Museum of Art
Hispanic Association of Colleges and Universities
Howard Hughes Medical Institute
Inroads
International Foundation of Employee Benefit Plans
International Volunteer Projects
Interscope Records
Island Records
Mammoth Records
Mass Media Science and Engineering Fellows Program
Matador Records
The Maternal & Child Health Institute
Merck & Company
Mercury Records
Motown Records
MTV: Music Television
National Consortium for Graduate Degrees for Minorities in
    Engineering and Science
National Park Service
The Nature Conservancy
Nick at Nite
Northwestern Mutual Financial Network
Oak Ridge Institute for Science and Education
Oscar Mayer Wienermobile
Pediatric AIDS Foundation
Perspective Records
Physcians for Social Responsibility
PolyGram
Procter & Gamble
RCA Records
Reebok
Rhino Records
SBK Records
Schlumberger
Select Records
Sgro Promo Associates/General Motors Internship
Sherwin-Williams
Sierra Club
Sony Music Entertainment
The Southern Center for International Studies
Southface Energy Institute
The Southwestern Company
Summerbridge National
TBS
Teach for America
3M

TNT
Turner Broadcasting System
United States Environmental Protection Agency
United States Prison
United States Secret Service
United States Securities and Exchange Commission
Vertigo Records
Verve Records
VH-1
Virgin Records
The Wall Street Journal
Writers Guild of America, West
Y.E.S. to Jobs
Zoo Entertainment

HAWAII

AIESEC
American Civil Liberties Union
American Heart Association
The American-Scandinavian Foundation
CDG/CDS International
Council on International Educational Exchange
The Environmental Careers Organization
Ernst & Young
Federal Bureau of Prisons
Gap
Habitat for Humanity International
Hispanic Association of Colleges and Universities
Howard Hughes Medical Institute
International Volunteer Projects
National Consortium for Graduate Degrees for Minorities in
   Engineering and Science
National Park Service
The Nature Conservancy
Northwestern Mutual Financial Network
Oak Ridge Institute for Science and Education
Oscar Mayer Wienermobile
Pediatric AIDS Foundation
Physicans for Social Responsibility
Procter & Gamble
Sherwin-Williams
The Southwestern Company
Student Conservation Association
Summerbridge National
Westin Hotels & Resorts
Writer's Guild of America, West

IDAHO

American Civil Liberties Union
The American-Scandinavian Foundation
Camp Counselors USA
CDG/CDS International
Council on International Educational Exchange
The Dow Jones Newspaper Fund
The Environmental Careers Organization
Federal Bureau of Prisons
Habitat for Humanity International

Hewlett-Packard
Hispanic Association of Colleges and Universities
Howard Hughes Medical Institute
International Foundation of Employee Benefit Plans
International Volunteer Projects
National Consortium for Graduate Degrees for Minorities in
   Engineering and Science
National Park Service
The Nature Conservancy
Northwestern Mutual Financial Network
Oak Ridge Institute for Science and Education
Oscar Mayer Wienermobile
Pediatric AIDS Foundation
Physicans for Social Responsibility
Sherwin-Williams
The Southwestern Company
Student Conservation Association
Writers Guild of America, West

ILLINOIS

A&M Records
Abbott Laboratories
Aetna Life & Casualty
AFS Intercultural Programs
AIESEC
American-Arab Anti-Discrimination Committee
American Bar Association
American Civil Liberties Union
American Friends Service Committee
American Heart Association
American Israel Public Affairs Committee
American Jewish Congress
American Judicature Society
The American-Scandinavian Foundation
Amnesty International
Amtrak
Argonne National Laboratory
Arista Records
Arthur Andersen
Atlantic Records
Baxter International
Bertelsmann Music Group
Best Buddies International
Boys Hope/Girls Hope
Brethren Volunteer Service
Brookfield Zoo
Buick
Cadillac
Camp Counselors USA
CARE
CBS Records
CDG/CDS International
Chevrolet
Chicago Botanic Garden
Chicago Bulls
Chicago Children's Museum
Child's Play Touring Theatre

Chrysalis Records
Citibank
CNN
Columbia Records
Council on International Educational Exchange
Def Jam Records
Deloitte & Touche
Du Pont
EastWest Records
Elektra Records
Elite Model Management
EMI Records
Energy Records
Entenmann's
The Environmental Careers Organization
Epic Records
Ernst & Young
F.A.O. Schwarz
Federal Bureau of Prisons
Fontana Records
Food Network
Frito-Lay
Gap
General Mills
General Motors Marketing Internship
GMC Truck
Goodman Theatre
Grubb & Ellis
GTE
Habitat for Humanity International
Hallmark Cards
Henri Bendel
Hewitt Associates
Hillel
Hispanic Association of Colleges and Universities
Howard Hughes Medical Institute
Illinois General Assembly
Inroads
Institute of Cultural Affairs
International Foundation of Employee Benefit Plans
International Management Group
International Volunteer Projects
Interscope Records
Island Records
Kraft Foods, Inc.
Lutheran Volunteer Corps
Mammoth Records
Mass Media Science and Engineering Fellows Program
Matador Records
Mercury Records
Merrill Lynch
Motown Records
MTV: Music Television
Museum of Contemporary Art, Chicago
National Association of Professional Surplus Lines Offices
National Consortium for Graduate Degrees for Minorities in
   Engineering and Science
National Park Service
The Nature Conservancy

Northwestern Mutual Financial Network
Oak Ridge Institute for Science and Education
Office of Job Corps
Oldsmobile
Oscar Mayer
Oscar Mayer Wienermobile
Pediatric AIDS Foundation
Perspective Records
Physicans for Social Responsibility
Playboy
PolyGram
Pontiac
Prairie Park
Procter & Gamble
Public Allies
Public Interest Research Groups
RCA Records
Reebok
Rhino Records
Saturn
SBK Records
Select Records
Sherwin-Williams
Sony Music Entertainment
The Southwestern Company
Starlight Foundation
Steppenwolf Theatre Company
Student Conservation Association
Tellabs
3M
United States Environmental Protection Agency
United States Secret Service
United States Securities and Exchange Commission
Vertigo Records
Verve Records
VH-1
Virgin Records
Volunteers For Peace
The Wall Street Journal
WGN-Chicago
Writers Guild of America, West
Y.E.S. to Jobs
Youth For Understanding International Exchange
Zoo Entertainment

INDIANA

AIESEC
American Civil Liberties Union
American Heart Association
The American-Scandinavian Foundation
Arthur Andersen
Atlantic Records
Brethren Volunteer Service
Buick
Cadillac
Camp Counselors USA
CDG/CDS International

Central Newspapers/The Indianapolis News
Chevrolet
Children's Museum of Indianapolis
Council on International Educational Exchange
The Dow Jones Newspaper Fund
The Environmental Careers Organization
Ernst & Young
Federal Bureau of Prisons
Gap
General Motors Marketing Internship
GMC Truck
GTE
Habitat for Humanity International
Hispanic Association of Colleges and Universities
Howard Hughes Medical Institute
Hudson Institute
The Indianapolis News
The Indianapolis Star
Indianapolis Zoo
Inroads
International Foundation of Employee Benefit Plans
International Volunteer Projects
Interscope Records
Mammoth Records
Matador Records
National Consortium for Graduate Degrees for Minorities in
    Engineering and Science
National Park Service
The Nature Conservancy
Northwestern Mutual Financial Network
Oak Ridge Institute for Science and Education
Oldsmobile
Oscar Mayer Wienermobile
Pediatric AIDS Foundation
Pfizer
Physicans for Social Responsibility
Pontiac
Procter & Gamble
Rhino Records
Saturn
Select Records
Sherwin-Williams
The Southwestern Company
Student Conservation Association
3M
Volunteers For Peace
WISH-TV 8
Writers Guild of America, West
Y.E.S. to Jobs
Youth For Understanding International Exchange

IOWA

American Civil Liberties Union
American Friends Service Committee
American Heart Association
The American-Scandinavian Foundation
Brethren Volunteer Service
Camp Counselors USA

CDG/CDS International
Council on International Educational Exchange
Du Pont
Ernst & Young
Federal Bureau of Prisons
Gap
The Gazette Company
General Mills
Habitat for Humanity International
Hispanic Association of Colleges and Universities
Howard Hughes Medical Institute
International Foundation of Employee Benefit Plans
International Volunteer Projects
Iowa Film Office
National Consortium for Graduate Degrees for Minorities in
    Engineering and Science
National Park Service
The Nature Conservancy
Northwestern Mutual Financial Network
Oak Ridge Institute for Science and Education
Oscar Mayer Wienermobile
Pediatric AIDS Foundation
Pella
Physicans for Social Responsibility
Procter & Gamble
Sherwin-Williams
The Southwestern Company
3M
Volunteers For Peace
Writers Guild of America, West
Youth For Understanding International Exchange

KANSAS

AIESEC
American Civil Liberties Union
The American-Scandinavian Foundation
Atlantic Records
Boeing
Brethren Volunteer Service
Camp Counselors USA
CDG/CDS International
Council on International Educational Exchange
Duke University Talent Identification Program
Federal Bureau of Prisons
Gap
Habitat for Humanity International
Hallmark Cards
Hispanic Association of Colleges and Universities
Howard Hughes Medical Institute
International Foundation of Employee Benefit Plans
International Volunteer Projects
Interscope Records
Leavenworth Prison
Mammoth Records
Matador Records
National Collegiate Athletic Association
National Consortium for Graduate Degrees for Minorities in
    Engineering and Science

National Park Service
The Nature Conservancy
Northwestern Mutual Financial Network
Oak Ridge Institute for Science and Education
Oscar Mayer Wienermobile
Pediatric AIDS Foundation
Physicans for Social Responsibility
Procter & Gamble
Rhino Records
Select Records
Sherwin-Williams
The Southwestern Company
United States Environmental Protection Agency
Virgin Records
Volunteers For Peace
Writers Guild of America, West

KENTUCKY

Actors Theatre of Louisville
American Civil Liberties Union
The American-Scandinavian Foundation
Brethren Volunteer Service
Camp Counselors USA
CDG/CDS International
Council on International Educational Exchange
The Dow Jones Newspaper Fund
Du Pont
The Environmental Careers Organization
Ernst & Young
Federal Bureau of Prisons
Frontier Nursing Service
Gap
Habitat for Humanity International
Hispanic Association of Colleges and Universities
Howard Hughes Medical Institute
International Foundation of Employee Benefit Plans
International Volunteer Projects
Land Between The Lakes
National Audubon Society
National Consortium for Graduate Degrees for Minorities in
  Engineering and Science
National Park Service
The Nature Conservancy
Northwestern Mutual Financial Network
Oak Ridge Institute for Science and Education
Oscar Mayer Wienermobile
Pediatric AIDS Foundation
Physicans for Social Responsibility
Procter & Gamble
Schlumberger
Sherwin-Williams
The Southwestern Company
Student Conservation Association
Summerbridge National
3M
Toyota
Writers Guild of America, West

LOUISIANA

AIESEC
American Civil Liberties Union
American Heart Association
The American-Scandinavian Foundation
Arthur Andersen
Atlantic Records
Boys Hope/Girls Hope
BP
CDG/CDS International
Chevron
Council on International Educational Exchange
Dow Chemical Company
Du Pont
The Environmental Careers Organization
Ernst & Young
Exxon
Federal Bureau of Prisons
Fourth World Movement
Gap
Habitat for Humanity International
Hispanic Association of Colleges and Universities
Howard Hughes Medical Institute
Inroads
International Foundation of Employee Benefit Plans
International Volunteer Projects
Interscope Records
Lake Charles American Press
Mammoth Records
Matador Records
National Consortium for Graduate Degrees for Minorities in
  Engineering and Science
National Park Service
The Nature Conservancy
Northwestern Mutual Financial Network
Oak Ridge Institute for Science and Education
Oscar Mayer Wienermobile
Pediatric AIDS Foundation
Procter & Gamble
Rhino Records
Schlumberger
Select Records
Sherwin-Williams
The Southwestern Company
Student Conservation Association
Summerbridge National
Teach for America
Union Carbide
United States Secret Service
Virgin Records
Writers Guild of America, West

MAINE

American Civil Liberties Union
The American-Scandinavian Foundation
Brethren Volunteer Service
Camp Counselors USA

CDG/CDS International
Council on International Educational Exchange
The Environmental Careers Organization
Federal Bureau of Prisons
Gap
Habitat for Humanity International
Hispanic Association of Colleges and Universities
H.O.M.E.
Howard Hughes Medical Institute
International Foundation of Employee Benefit Plans
International Volunteer Projects
Maine State Music Theatre
National Audubon Society
National Consortium for Graduate Degrees for Minorities in
    Engineering and Science
National Park Service
The Nature Conservancy
Northwestern Mutual Financial Network
Oak Ridge Institute for Science and Education
Oscar Mayer Wienermobile
Pediatric AIDS Foundation
Physicans for Social Responsibility
Sherwin-Williams
Sierra Club
The Southwestern Company
Starlight Foundation
Student Conservation Association
Volunteers For Peace
Writers Guild of America, West

MARYLAND

A&M Records
Affiliated Sante Group
AFS Intercultural Programs
Agora, Inc.
AIESEC
American Civil Liberties Union
American Friends Service Committee
American Jewish Congress
The American-Scandinavian Foundation
Association for International Practical Training
Atlantic Records
Baltimore Zoo
Bechtel
Brethren Volunteer Service
Camp Counselors USA
CBS Records
CDG/CDS International
Center for the Study of Conflict
Center for Talented Youth
Columbia Records
Council on International Educational Exchange
Def Jam Records
The Discovery Channel
Discovery Communications
E-Systems
Earle Palmer Brown
The Environmental Careers Organization

Epic Records
Ernst & Young
Federal Bureau of Prisons
Fontana Records
Foundation for Contemporary Mental Health
Gap
Goddard Space Flight Center
Habitat for Humanity International
Hispanic Association of Colleges and Universities
Howard Hughes Medical Institute
Inroads
International Foundation of Employee Benefit Plans
International Volunteer Projects
Interscope Records
Island Records
The Learning Channel
Lutheran Volunteer Corps
Mammoth Records
Matador Records
Mercury Records
Montgomery County Community Corrrections
Motown Records
National Aeronautics and Space Administration
National Aquarium in Baltimore
National Consortium for Graduate Degrees for Minorities in
    Engineering and Science
National Institutes of Health
National Park Service
National Security Agency
The Nature Conservancy
Northwestern Mutual Financial Network
Oak Ridge Institute for Science and Education
Oscar Mayer Wienermobile
Pediatric AIDS Foundation
Perspective Records
Physicans for Social Responsibility
PolyGram
Procter & Gamble
Public Interest Research Groups
Quality Education for Minorities Network
Rhino Records
Select Records
Sherwin-Williams
Sierra Club
Sony Music Entertainment
The Southwestern Company
Student Conservation Association
Teach for America
Tellabs
3M
United States Army Environmental Hygiene Agency
United States Secret Service
Vertigo Records
Verve Records
Volunteers For Peace
The Washington Post
The Wildlife Society
Writers Guild of America, West

A&M Records
Academic Study Associates
A.E. Schwartz & Associates
Aetna Life & Casualty
AFS Intercultural Programs
AIESEC
Aigner Associates
American Civil Liberties Union
American Friends Service Committee
American Hockey League
American Jewish Congress
American Repertory Theatre
The American-Scandinavian Foundation
Amnesty International
Arista Records
Arthur Andersen
Atlantic Records
Beacon Press
Berkshire Public Theatre
Bertelsmann Music Group
The Boston Globe
Boston Magazine
Brethren Volunteer Service
Camp Counselors USA
CARE
CBS Records
CDG/CDS International
Center for Coastal Studies
Center for Talented Youth
Charlesbridge Publishing
Chrysalis Records
Clarke & Company
College Light Opera Company
Columbia Records
Council on International Educational Exchange
Creamer Dickson Basford
Def Jam Records
Deloitte & Touche
The Dow Jones Newspaper Fund
Du Pont
EastWest Records
Elektra Records
EMI Records
Energy Records
The Environmental Careers Organization
Epic Records
Ernst & Young
Faber and Faber
Federal Bureau of Prisons
Fontana Records
Gap
Gould Farm
Greater Media Cable
Grubb & Ellis
GTE
Habitat for Humanity International
Henri Bendel

Hewlett-Packard
Hill, Holliday, Connors, Cosmopulos Advertising
Hillel
Hispanic Association of Colleges and Universities
Historic Deerfield
Houghton Mifflin Company
Howard Hughes Medical Institute
Inroads
International Foundation of Employee Benefit Plans
International Management Group
International Volunteer Projects
Interscope Records
Island Records
Jacob's Pillow Dance Festival
Jones & Bartlett
Mammoth Records
Manice Education Center
Mass Media Science and Engineering Fellows Program
Matador Records
McLean Hospital
Mercury Records
Motown Records
Museum of Fine Arts, Boston
National Center for Fair & Open Testing
National Consortium for Graduate Degrees for Minorities in Engineering and Science
National Park Service
The Nature Conservancy
Northfield Mount Hermon School
Northwestern Mutual Financial Network
Oak Ridge Institute for Science and Education
Office of Job Corps
Oscar Mayer Wienermobile
Pediatric AIDS Foundation
Perspective Records
Phillips Academy
Physicans for Social Responsibility
Physicians for Human Rights
PolyGram
Procter & Gamble
Public Interest Research Groups
RCA Records
Reebok
Rhino Records
SBK Records
Select Records
Sgro Promo Associates/General Motors Internship
Sherwin-Williams
Sierra Club
Skadden, Arps, Slate, Meagher & Flom
Sony Music Entertainment
The Southwestern Company
Starlight Foundation
Student Conservation Association
Summerbridge National
Teen Voices
Texas Instruments
Tellabs

3M
United States Environmental Protection Agency
United States Secret Service
United States Securities and Exchange Commission
Vertigo Records
Verve Records
Virgin Records
Volunteers For Peace
Westin Hotels & Resorts
Williamstown Theater Festival
Women Express
Writers Guild of America, West
Youth For Understanding International Exchange
Zoo Entertainment

MICHIGAN

A&M Records
AIESEC
American-Arab Anti-Discrimination Committee
American Civil Liberties Union
The American-Scandinavian Foundation
Amway
Arista Records
Arthur Andersen
Atlantic Records
Bertelsmann Music Group
Boys Hope/Girls Hope
Bozell Public Relations
Buick
Cadillac
Camp Counselors USA
CDG/CDS International
Chevrolet
Chrysalis Records
CNN
Council on International Educational Exchange
Def Jam Records
Deloitte & Touche
Dow Chemical Company
The Dow Jones Newspaper Fund
Du Pont
EastWest Records
Elektra Records
EMI Records
The Environmental Careers Organization
Ernst & Young
Federal Bureau of Prisons
Focus on Women
Fontana Records
Ford Motor Company
Gap
General Motors Marketing Internship
GMC Truck
Grubb & Ellis
Habitat for Humanity International
Hispanic Association of Colleges and Universities
Howard Hughes Medical Institute
Inroads

International Foundation of Employee Benefit Plans
International Management Group
International Volunteer Projects
Interscope Records
Island Records
Mammoth Records
Mass Media Science and Engineering Fellows Program
Matador Records
Mercury Records
Miniwanca Education Center
Motown Records
MTV: Music Television
National Consortium for Graduate Degrees for Minorities in Engineering and Science
National Park Service
The Nature Conservancy
Northwestern Mutual Financial Network
Oak Ridge Institute for Science and Education
Oldsmobile
Oscar Mayer Wienermobile
Pediatric AIDS Foundation
Perspective Records
Physicans for Social Responsibility
PolyGram
Pontiac
Procter & Gamble
Public Interest Research Groups
RCA Records
Rhino Records
Saturn
SBK Records
Select Records
Sherwin-Williams
The Southwestern Company
Student Conservation Association
Student Works Painting
3M
Toyota
United States Environmetal Protection Agency
United States Secret Service
Vertigo Records
Verve Records
VH-1
Virgin Records
Volunteers For Peace
Wall Street Music
Weyerhaeuser
Writers Guild of America, West
Y.E.S. to Jobs
Youth For Understanding International Exchange
Zoo Entertainment

MINNESOTA

AFS Intercultural Programs
AIESEC
American Civil Liberties Union
The American-Scandinavian Foundation
Arista Records

Arthur Andersen
Atlantic Records
Bertelsmann Music Group
Bozell Public Relations
Brethren Volunteer Service
Camp Counselors USA
CARE
CDG/CDS International
Chrysalis Records
Council on International Educational Exchange
Deloitte & Touche
The Dow Jones Newspaper Fund
EastWest Records
Elektra Entertainment Group
Elektra Records
EMI Records
Energy Records
Ernst & Young
Federal Bureau of Prisons
Gap
General Mills
Habitat for Humanity International
Hispanic Association of Colleges and Universities
Howard Hughes Medical Institute
IBM
Inroads
International Foundation of Employee Benefit Plans
International Volunteer Projects
Interscope Records
Long Lake Conservation Center
Lutheran Volunteer Corps
Mammoth Records
Matador Records
National Consortium for Graduate Degrees for Minorities in
   Engineering and Science
National Park Service
The Nature Conservancy
Northwestern Mutual Financial Network
Oak Ridge Institute for Science and Education
Oscar Mayer Wienermobile
Outward Bound/Voyageur School
Pediatric AIDS Foundation
Physicans for Social Responsibility
Procter & Gamble
Public Interest Research Groups
RCA Records
Rhino Records
SBK Records
Select Records
Sherwin-Williams
The Southwestern Company
Student Conservation Association
Theater de la Jeune Lune
3M
United States Environmental Protection Agency
Virgin Records
Writers Guild of America, West
Xerox

Y.E.S. to Jobs
Zoo Entertainment

MISSISSIPPI

American Civil Liberties Union
The American-Scandinavian Foundation
Camp Counselors USA
CDG/CDS International
Chevron
Council on International Educational Exchange
Du Pont
Ernst & Young
Federal Bureau of Prisons
Gap
Global Volunteers
Habitat for Humanity International
Hispanic Association of Colleges and Universities
Howard Hughes Medical Institute
International Foundation of Employee Benefit Plans
International Volunteer Projects
National Aeronautics and Space Administration
National Consortium for Graduate Degrees for Minorities in
   Engineering and Science
National Park Service
The Nature Conservancy
New Stage Theatre
Northwestern Mutual Financial Network
Oak Ridge Institute for Science and Education
Oscar Mayer Wienermobile
Pediatric AIDS Foundation
Public Interest Research Groups
Schlumberger
Sherwin-Williams
The Southwestern Company
Stennis Space Center
Teach for America
Virgin Records
Writers Guild of America, West

MISSOURI

AIESEC
American Civil Liberties Union
American Heart Association
American Jewish Congress
The American-Scandinavian Foundation
Anheuser-Busch
Arista Records
Arthur Andersen
Atlantic Records
Bernstein-Rein
Bertelsmann Music Group
Boeing
Boys Hope/Girls Hope
Camp Counselors USA
CARE
CDG/CDS International
Chrysalis Records

The Coro Foundation
Council on International Educational Exchange
Deloitte & Touche
The Dow Jones Newspaper Fund
EMI Records
Ernst & Young
Federal Bureau of Prisons
Gap
Habitat for Humanity International
Hallmark Cards
Hillel
Hispanic Association of Colleges and Universities
Howard Hughes Medical Institute
Inroads
International Foundation of Employee Benefit Plans
International Management Group
International Volunteer Projects
Interscope Records
Mammoth Records
Matador Records
National Consortium for Graduate Degrees for Minorities in
   Engineering and Science
National Park Service
The Nature Conservancy
Northwestern Mutual Financial Network
Oak Ridge Institute for Science and Education
Office of Job Corps
Oscar Mayer Wienermobile
Pediatric AIDS Foundation
Pfizer
Physicans for Social Responsibility
Public Interest Research Groups
RCA Records
Rhino Records
SBK Records
Select Records
Sherwin-Williams
The Southwestern Company
Student Conservation Association
Summerbridge National
3M
United States Secret Service
Writers Guild of America, West
Zoo Entertainment

MONTANA

American Civil Liberties Union
American Israel Public Affairs Committee
The American-Scandinavian Foundation
Camp Counselors USA
CDG/CDS International
Council on International Educational Exchange
Federal Bureau of Prisons
Habitat for Humanity International
Hispanic Association of Colleges and Universities
Howard Hughes Medical Institute
International Foundation of Employee Benefit Plans
International Volunteer Projects

National Consortium for Graduate Degrees for Minorities in
   Engineering and Science
National Park Service
The Nature Conservancy
Northwestern Mutual Financial Network
Oak Ridge Institute for Science and Education
Oscar Mayer Wienermobile
Pediatric AIDS Foundation
Physicans for Social Responsibility
Public Interest Research Groups
Sherwin-Williams
Sierra Club
The Southwestern Company
Student Conservation Association
Writers Guild of America, West

NEBRASKA

AIESEC
American Civil Liberties Union
American Heart Association
The American-Scandinavian Foundation
Arthur Andersen
Bozell Public Relations
Camp Counselors USA
CDG/CDS International
Council on International Educational Exchange
Deloitte & Touche
The Dow Jones Newspaper Fund
Federal Bureau of Prisons
Gap
Habitat for Humanity International
Hispanic Association of Colleges and Universities
Howard Hughes Medical Institute
International Foundation of Employee Benefit Plans
International Volunteer Projects
National Consortium for Graduate Degrees for Minorities in
   Engineering and Science
National Park Service
The Nature Conservancy
Northwestern Mutual Financial Network
Oak Ridge Institute for Science and Education
Oscar Mayer Wienermobile
Pediatric AIDS Foundation
Sherwin-Williams
The Southwestern Company
3M
Volunteers For Peace
Writers Guild of America, West

NEVADA

American Civil Liberties Union
The American-Scandinavian Foundation
Atlantic Records
Camp Counselors USA
CDG/CDS International
Council on International Educational Exchange
Deloitte & Touche
Ernst & Young

Federal Bureau of Prisons
Gap
Habitat for Humanity International
Hispanic Association of Colleges and Universities
Howard Hughes Medical Institute
International Foundation of Employee Benefit Plans
International Volunteer Projects
Interscope Records
Mammoth Records
Matador Records
National Consortium for Graduate Degrees for Minorities in
  Engineering and Science
National Park Service
The Nature Conservancy
Northwestern Mutual Financial Network
Oak Ridge Institute for Science and Education
Oscar Mayer Wienermobile
Pediatric AIDS Foundation
Rhino Records
Select Records
Sgro Promo Associates/General Motors Internship
Sherwin-Williams
Sierra Club
The Southwestern Company
Student Conservation Association
United States Environmental Protection Agency
Writers Guild of America, West

NEW HAMPSHIRE

AIESEC
American Civil Liberties Union
American Heart Association
The American-Scandinavian Foundation
Camp Counselors USA
CDG/CDS International
Council on International Educational Exchange
The Environmental Careers Organization
Ernst & Young
Federal Bureau of Prisons
Gap
Habitat for Humanity International
Hewlett-Packard
Hispanic Association of Colleges and Universities
Howard Hughes Medical Institute
Interlocken
International Foundation of Employee Benefit Plans
International Volunteer Projects
National Consortium for Graduate Degrees for Minorities in
  Engineering and Science
National Park Service
The Nature Conservancy
Northwestern Mutual Financial Network
Oak Ridge Institute for Science and Education
Oscar Mayer Wienermobile
Pediatric AIDS Foundation
Physicians for Social Responsibility
St. Paul's School
Sherwin-Williams

The Southwestern Company
Student Conservation Association
Summerbridge National
Volunteers For Peace
Writers Guild of America, West

NEW JERSEY

AIESEC
American Civil Liberties Union
American Heart Association
American Jewish Congress
The American-Scandinavian Foundation
Arthur Andersen
Association for Education in Journalism
AT&T Bell Laboratories
Atlantic Records
Camp Counselors USA
CDG/CDS International
Council on International Educational Exchange
Davis Hays & Co.
Deloitte & Touche
The Dow Jones Newspaper Fund
Du Pont
The Ecco Press
The Environmental Careers Organization
Ernst & Young
Exxon
Federal Bureau of Prisons
The French-American Center
Gap
Habitat for Humanity International
Hewlett-Packard
Hillel
Hispanic Association of Colleges and Universities
Hoffman-La Roche
Howard Hughes Medical Institute
Inroads
International Foundation of Employee Benefit Plans
International Management Group
International Telecommunications Satellite Organization
International Volunteer Projects
Interscope Records
Korff Enterprises
Liz Claiborne
Mammoth Records
Matador Records
Merck & Company
Nabisco
National Basketball Association
National Consortium for Graduate Degrees for Minorities in
  Engineering and Science
National Park Service
The Nature Conservancy
Northwestern Mutual Financial Network
Oak Ridge Institute for Science and Education
Oscar Mayer Wienermobile
Pediatric AIDS Foundation
Pfizer

Physicans for Social Responsibility
Pro-Found Software
Procter & Gamble
Public Interest Research Groups
Rhino Records
Select Records
Shadow Broadcast Services
Sherwin-Williams
Sony
The Southwestern Company
Student Conservation Association
Teach for America
3M
Tyco Toys
Union Carbide
United States Secret Service
Unitel
Volunteers For Peace
Writers Guild of America, West
Y.E.S. to Jobs

NEW MEXICO

American Civil Liberties Union
The American-Scandinavian Foundation
Brethren Volunteer Service
Camp Counselors USA
CDG/CDS International
Council on International Educational Exchange
Duke University Talent Identification Program
Federal Bureau of Prisons
Gap
General Mills
Habitat for Humanity International
Hispanic Association of Colleges and Universities
Howard Hughes Medical Institute
Intel
Interhemispheric Resource Center
International Foundation of Employee Benefit Plans
International Volunteer Projects
Mass Media Science and Engineering Fellows Program
National Audubon Society
National Consortium for Graduate Degrees for Minorities in
    Engineering and Science
National Park Service
The Nature Conservancy
Northwestern Mutual Financial Network
Oak Ridge Institute for Science and Education
Oscar Mayer Wienermobile
Pediatric AIDS Foundation
Physicans for Social Responsibility
Public Interest Research Groups
Sherwin-Williams
The Southwestern Company
Student Conservation Association
Writers Guild of America, West

NEW YORK

A&M Records
Abrams Artists Agency
Adrienne Vittadini
Advertising Club of New York
Advocates for Children of New York
AFS Intercultural Programs
AIESEC
The Algonquin
Alliance of Residence Theaters
Alper International
American & International Designs
American Association of Advertising Agencies
American Association of Overseas Studies
American Civil Liberties Union
American Committee on Africa/The Africa Fund
American Friends Service Committee
The American Geographical Society
American Heart Association
American Jewish Congress
American Management Association
The American Place Theatre
The American-Scandinavian Foundation
American Society of Magazine Editors
American Woman's Economic Development Corp.
Angel Records
Another World
Aperture Foundation
Archive Films
Arista Records
Arthur Andersen
Artists Space
As The World Turns
Asian American Arts Centre
ASSIST
Association for Education in Journalism
Association of Hispanic Arts
Asylum Records
Atlantic Records
Ballantine Books
Barry-Haft-Brown Artists Agency
Barwood Productions
Bellevue Hospital Center
Benetton USA Corporation
Bertelsmann Music Group
Betsey Johnson
Black Enterprise
Blair Television
Boys Hope/Girls Hope
Bozell Public Relations
Brethren Volunteer Service
Brick Wall Management
Brookhaven National Laboratory
Brooklyn Botanic Garden
The Brooklyn Museum
Buick
Burson-Marsteller
Business Executives for National Security

Cadillac
Cairns & Associates
The Callaghan Group
Camp Counselors USA
Canaan Public Relations
Capitol Records
CARE
Carolyn Ray
CBS News
CBS Records
CDG/CDS International
Center for Talented Youth
Central Park SummerStage
Chamber Music America
Charlie Rose
Chevrolet
Christie's
Chrysalis Records
Cinemax
Citibank
City Limits Magazine
City of New York Parks & Recreation
CityArts
Classic Stage Company
The Cloisters
CNN
College Connections
Columbia Journalism Review
Columbia Pictures
Columbia Records
Comedy Central
Cooper-Hewitt Museum
The Coro Foundation
Council on Economic Priorities
Council on Foreign Relations
Council on International Educational Exchange
Creamer Dickson Basford
Cromarty & Company
Crown Books
Cybergrrl
Def Jam Records
Deloitte & Touche
The Discovery Channel
Discovery Communications
Donna Maione
The Dow Jones Newspaper Fund
The Drawing Center
Du Pont
E! Entertainment Television Networks
Earle Palmer Brown
Eastman Kodak Company
EastWest Records
Elektra Entertainment Group
Elektra Records
Elite Model Management
Elizabeth Dow
EMI Records
EMI Records Group North America

Energy Records
Entenmann's
Entertainment Design/Lighting Dimensions
Entertainment Weekly
The Environmental Careers Organization
Epic Records
Ernst & Young
ESPN
Essence
Farm Sanctuary
Farrar Straus & Giroux
Federal Bureau of Prisons
Federal Reserve Bank of New York
Fellowship of Reconciliation
Fontana Records
Food Network
Forbes
The Ford Foundation
Ford Models
Foreign Affairs
Forty Acres and a Mule Filmworks
48 Hours
Fourth World Movement
Franklin D. Roosevelt Library
The French-American Center
fX
Gap
Geffen Records
General Foods
General Mills
General Motors Marketing Internship
Gensler and Associates/Architects
GMC Truck
Good Morning America
Great Projects Film Company
Grubb & Ellis
Guiding Light
Habitat for Humanity International
Haft/Nasatir
Hallmark Cards
Harper's Magazine
The Hastings Center
Hawthorne Valley Farm
HBO
HERE
Hill and Knowlton
Hillel
Hispanic Association of Colleges and Universities
Home Box Office
Howard Hughes Medical Institute
The Howard Stern Show
H.S.I. Productions
IBM
Inroads
Insurance Services Office
Interior Design Collections
The International Center of Photography
International Creative Management

International Foundation of Employee Benefit Plans
International Labor Organization
International Management Group
International Radio and Television Society
International Volunteer Projects
Interscope Records
Island Records
John Wiley & Sons
J.P. Morgan & Co.
The Juilliard School
Karl Lagerfeld
KCSA Public Relations
The Kitchen
Knopf Books
Kraft Foods, Inc.
Lamont-Doherty Earth Observatory
Late Night with Conan O'Brien
Late Show with David Letterman
The Learning Channel
Leo Castelli Gallery
Liberty Records
Lincoln Center for the Performing Arts
Liz Claiborne
MacDonald Communications Corp.
MAD Magazine
Madison Square Garden
Makovsky & Company
Mallory Factor
Mammoth Records
Manhattan Theatre Club
Manus & Associates Literary Agency
Marina Maher Communications
Marvel Comics
Mass Media Science and Engineering Fellows Program
Matador Records
MCT Management/Bold! Records
Mercury Records
Metro-Goldwyn-Mayer/United Artists
The Metropolitan Museum of Art
Morrison & Foerster
Mother Earth News
Motown Records
Ms.
MSG Network
MTV: Music Television
The Museum of Modern Art, New York
Music Television
Nabisco
The Nation
National Association of Professional Surplus Lines Offices
National Audubon Society
National Basketball Association
National Broadcasting Company
National Consortium for Graduate Degrees for Minorities in
   Engineering and Science
National Football League
National Park Service
National Review

The Nature Conservancy
NBC Nightly News
New Dramatists
New York City Government
The New York Hospital-Cornell Medical Center
New York Knicks
New York Rangers
New York Shakespeare Festival
New York State Bar Association
New York State Theatre Institute
The New York Times
Newsday/New York Newsday
Newsweek
Northwestern Mutual Financial Network
NOW Legal Defense and Education Fund
Oak Ridge Institute for Science and Education
Office of Job Corps
Oldsmobile
Open City Films
Oscar Mayer Wienermobile
Overland Entertainment
The Paris Review
Pediatric AIDS Foundation
Pendulum Records
Penguin Books
Perspective Records
Pfizer
Physicians for Social Responsibility
Playboy
Plume Books
PMK Public Relations
PolyGram
Pontiac
PrimeTime Live
Procter & Gamble
Procter & Gamble Productions
Psychology Today
Public Interest Research Groups
Quaker United Nations Office
Random House
RCA Records
Renaissance Computer Art Center
Renew America
Rhino Records
Rolling Stone
Roy A. Somlyo Productions
Ruder-Finn
The Rush Limbaugh Show
Saks Fifth Avenue
Sally Jessy Raphael Show
Saturday Night Live
Saturn
Save the Sound
Savvy Management
SBK Records
Schlumberger
Scott Rudin Productions
Select Records

765-ARTS
Seventeen Magazine
Shadow Broadcast Services
Sherwin-Williams
Shirley Herz Associates
Sierra Club
Signet Classics
Simon & Goodman Picture Company
60 Minutes
Skadden, Arps, Slate, Meagher & Flom
Solomon R. Guggenheim Museum
Sony Music Entertainment
Sony Pictures Entertainment
Sotheby's
The Source
The Southwestern Company
Spin
Sponsors for Educational Opportunity
Sports Illustrated
Spy
Starlight Foundation
Staten Island Zoo
Statue of Liberty
Student Conservation Association
Success
Summerbridge National
Sunday Morning
Sussex Publishers
TADA!
TBWA
Teach for America
Tellabs
Thirteen/WNET
Thread Waxing Space
3M
The Today Show
Tommy Boy Music
Tribeca Film Center
TriStar Pictures
Twentieth Century Fox
20/20
Union Carbide
United Artists
United Nations
United Nations Association of the United States of America
United States Environmental Protection Agency
United States Olympic Committee
United States Secret Service
United States Securities and Exchange Commission
Up to the Minute
Urban Fellows/Government Scholars Programs
Vault.com
Vereinsbank Capital Corp.
Vertigo Records
Verve Records
VH-1
Vibe
Viking Books

Village Voice
Virgin Records
Volunteers For Peace
The Wall Street Journal
Warwick Baker O'Neill
WAXQ - Q104.3
Westin Hotels & Resorts
Whitney Museum of American Art
Winant-Clayton Volunteers
WNBC-TV
WNYC
Women's International League for Peace and Freedom
Women's Project & Productions
Women's Sports Foundation
Working Mother
Working Woman
World Federalist Association
Writers Guild of America, West
Xerox
Y.E.S. to Jobs
Zoo Entertainment

NORTH CAROLINA

AIESEC
American Civil Liberties Union
American Dance Festival
American Heart Association
The American-Scandinavian Foundation
American Society of Magazine Editors
Arista Records
Arthur Andersen
Atlantic Records
Bertelsmann Music Group
Brethren Volunteer Service
Camp Counselors USA
CDG/CDS International
Chemical Industry Institute of Toxicology
Chrysalis Records
Council on International Educational Exchange
Deloitte & Touche
Du Pont
Duke University Talent Identification Program
EMI Records
The Environmental Careers Organization
Ernst & Young
Federal Bureau of Prisons
Gap
Habitat for Humanity International
Hispanic Association of Colleges and Universities
Howard Hughes Medical Institute
Human Service Alliance
IBM
Inroads
Institute of Government
International Foundation of Employee Benefit Plans
International Management Group
International Volunteer Projects
Interscope Records

Mammoth Records
Mass Media Science and Engineering Fellows Program
Matador Records
National Consortium for Graduate Degrees for Minorities in
    Engineering and Science
National Park Service
The Nature Conservancy
North Carolina Botanical Garden
Northwestern Mutual Financial Network
Oak Ridge Institute for Science and Education
Oscar Mayer Wienermobile
Pediatric AIDS Foundation
Physicans for Social Responsibility
Procter & Gamble
Public Allies
RCA Records
Rhino Records
SBK Records
Select Records
Sherwin-Williams
The Southwestern Company
Student Conservation Association
Summerbridge National
Teach for America
3M
Union Carbide
United States Environmental Protection Agency
United States Secret Service
Virgin Records
Weyerhaeuser
Writers Guild of America, West
Zoo Entertainment

NORTH DAKOTA

American Civil Liberties Union
American Heart Association
The American-Scandinavian Foundation
CDG/CDS International
Council on International Educational Exchange
Federal Bureau of Prisons
Gap
Habitat for Humanity International
Hispanic Association of Colleges and Universities
Howard Hughes Medical Institute
International Foundation of Employee Benefit Plans
International Volunteer Projects
National Consortium for Graduate Degrees for Minorities in
    Engineering and Science
National Park Service
The Nature Conservancy
Northwestern Mutual Financial Network
Oak Ridge Institute for Science and Education
Oscar Mayer Wienermobile
Pediatric AIDS Foundation
Sherwin-Williams
The Southwestern Company
Student Conservation Association
3M
Writers Guild of America, West

OHIO

AIESEC
AIM for the Handicapped
American Civil Liberties Union
American Heart Association
American Jewish Congress
The American-Scandinavian Foundation
Arthur Andersen
BalletMet
The Blade
Boys Hope/Girls Hope
BP
Brethren Volunteer Service
Buick
Cadillac
Camp Counselors USA
CAVS/Gund Arena Company
CBS Records
CDG/CDS International
Chevrolet
Chrysalis Records
Cleveland Cavaliers
Columbia Records
Council on International Educational Exchange
Deloitte & Touche
Dow Chemical Company
The Dow Jones Newspaper Fund
Du Pont
EMI Records
Energy Records
The Environmental Careers Organization
Epic Records
Ernst & Young
Federal Bureau of Prisons
Gap
General Mills
General Motors Marketing Internship
Glen Helen Outdoor Education Center
GMC Truck
Grubb & Ellis
Gund Arena
Habitat for Humanity International
Henri Bendel
Hillel
Hispanic Association of Colleges and Universities
Howard Hughes Medical Institute
Inroads
International Foundation of Employee Benefit Plans
International Management Group
International Volunteer Projects
Lewis Research Center
Marion Penitentiary
Mass Media Science and Engineering Fellows Program
National Aeronautics and Space Administration
National Consortium for Graduate Degrees for Minorities in
    Engineering and Science
National Park Service
The Nature Conservancy

Northwestern Mutual Financial Network
Oak Ridge Institute for Science and Education
Oldsmobile
Oscar Mayer Wienermobile
Pediatric AIDS Foundation
Physicans for Social Responsibility
Pontiac
Procter & Gamble
Public Interest Research Groups
Saturn
SBK Records
Sherwin-Williams
Sony Music Entertainment
The Southwestern Company
State Teachers Retirement System of Ohio
Student Conservation Association
Student Works Painting
Summerbridge National
3M
United States Secret Service
Virgin Records
Writers Guild of America, West
Y.E.S. to Jobs
Youth For Understanding International Exchange

OKLAHOMA

Ackerman McQueen
American Civil Liberties Union
American Heart Association
The American-Scandinavian Foundation
Camp Counselors USA
CDG/CDS International
Council on International Educational Exchange
The Environmental Careers Organization
Ernst & Young
Federal Bureau of Prisons
Gap
Habitat for Humanity International
Hispanic Association of Colleges and Universities
Howard Hughes Medical Institute
International Foundation of Employee Benefit Plans
International Volunteer Projects
National Consortium for Graduate Degrees for Minorities in
  Engineering and Science
National Park Service
The Nature Conservancy
Northwestern Mutual Financial Network
Oak Ridge Institute for Science and Education
Oscar Mayer Wienermobile
Pediatric AIDS Foundation
Sherwin-Williams
The Southwestern Company
Student Conservation Association
3M
United States Environmental Protection Agency
Weyerhaeuser
Writers Guild of America, West

OREGON

AFS Intercultural Programs
AIESEC
American Civil Liberties Union
American Heart Association
The American-Scandinavian Foundation
Arista Records
Bertelsmann Music Group
Brethren Volunteer Service
Camp Counselors USA
CDG/CDS International
Chrysalis Records
Council on International Educational Exchange
Deloitte & Touche
The Dow Jones Newspaper Fund
EMI Records
Energy Records
The Environmental Careers Organization
Federal Bureau of Prisons
Gap
Grubb & Ellis
Habitat for Humanity International
Hewlett-Packard
Hispanic Association of Colleges and Universities
Howard Hughes Medical Institute
Intel
International Foundation of Employee Benefit Plans
International Volunteer Projects
Mobility International
National Consortium for Graduate Degrees for Minorities in
  Engineering and Science
National Park Service
The Nature Conservancy
NIKE
Northwestern Mutual Financial Network
Oak Ridge Institute for Science and Education
Oscar Mayer Wienermobile
Pediatric AIDS Foundation
Physicans for Social Responsibility
Procter & Gamble
Public Interest Research Groups
RCA Records
The Rockey Company
SBK Records
Sherwin-Williams
The Southwestern Company
Student Conservation Association
Summerbridge National
3M
United States Environmental Protection Agency
Volunteers For Peace
Weyerhaeuser
Writers Guild of America, West
Zoo Entertainment

AIESEC
American Civil Liberties Union
American Friends Service Committee
American Heart Association
American Jewish Congress
The American-Scandinavian Foundation
The Andy Warhol Museum
Arden Theatre Company
Arista Records
Arthur Andersen
AT&T Bell Laboratories
Atlantic Records
Bertelsmann Music Group
Best Buddies International
Boeing
Boys Hope/Girls Hope
BP
Brethren Volunteer Service
Bucks County Courier Times
Camp Counselors USA
Camphill Soltane
CARE
CDG/CDS International
Center for Talented Youth
Chrysalis Records
Council on International Educational Exchange
Creamer Dickson Basford
Deloitte & Touche
The Dow Jones Newspaper Fund
Du Pont
E-Systems
Earle Palmer Brown
EastWest Records
Elektra Records
Elkman Advertising & Public Relations
EMI Records
The Environmental Careers Organization
Ernst & Young
Federal Bureau of Prisons
Foreign Policy Research Institute
Freedom Theatre
Gap
Gettysburg Battlefield
Grubb & Ellis
Habitat for Humanity International
Harley-Davidson
Hawk Mountain Sanctuary
Hillel
Hispanic Association of Colleges and Universities
Howard Hughes Medical Institute
Inroads
International Foundation of Employee Benefit Plans
International Management Group
International Volunteer Projects
Interscope Records
Mammoth Records
Matador Records

Merck & Company
Middle Earth
National Consortium for Graduate Degrees for Minorities in
    Engineering and Science
National Park Service
The Nature Conservancy
Northwestern Mutual Financial Network
Oak Ridge Institute for Science and Education
Office of Job Corps
Oscar Mayer Wienermobile
Pediatric AIDS Foundation
The Philadelphia Center
The Philadelphia Inquirer
Physicans for Social Responsibility
Pittsburgh Energy Technology Center
Pittsburgh Post-Gazette
Procter & Gamble
Public Interest Research Groups
RCA Records
Rhino Records
Rodale Institute Research Center
Rosenbluth International
SBK Records
Schlumberger
Select Records
Shaver's Creek Environmental Center
Sherwin-Williams
The Southwestern Company
Student Conservation Association
Summerbridge National
United States Bureau of Mines
United States Environmental Protection Agency
United States Secret Service
United States Securities and Exchange Commission
Virgin Records
Volunteers For Peace
The Wilma Theater
Winant-Clayton Volunteers
Women's International League for Peace and Freedom
Writers Guild of America, West
Zoo Entertainment

AIESEC
American Civil Liberties Union
The American-Scandinavian Foundation
Camp Counselors USA
CDG/CDS International
Council on International Educational Exchange
EastWest Records
Elektra Records
The Environmental Careers Organization
Ernst & Young
Federal Bureau of Prisons
Gap
Habitat for Humanity International
Hillel
Hispanic Association of Colleges and Universities

Howard Hughes Medical Institute
International Foundation of Employee Benefit Plans
International Volunteer Projects
Mixed Media
National Association of College Broadcasters
National Consortium for Graduate Degrees for Minorities in
    Engineering and Science
National Park Service
The Nature Conservancy
Northwestern Mutual Financial Network
Oak Ridge Institute for Science and Education
Oscar Mayer Wienermobile
Pediatric AIDS Foundation
Rhode Island State Government
Sgro Promo Associates/General Motors Internship
Sherwin-Williams
Sierra Club
The Southwestern Company
Summerbridge National
Volunteers For Peace
Writers Guild of America, West

SOUTH CAROLINA

American Civil Liberties Union
The American-Scandinavian Foundation
Atlantic Records
Camp Counselors USA
CDG/CDS International
Council on International Educational Exchange
The Dow Jones Newspaper Fund
Du Pont
Ernst & Young
Federal Bureau of Prisons
Gap
Habitat for Humanity International
Hispanic Association of Colleges and Universities
Howard Hughes Medical Institute
International Foundation of Employee Benefit Plans
International Volunteer Projects
Interscope Records
Mammoth Records
Matador Records
National Audubon Society
National Consortium for Graduate Degrees for Minorities in
    Engineering and Science
National Park Service
The Nature Conservancy
Northwestern Mutual Financial Network
Oak Ridge Institute for Science and Education
Oscar Mayer Wienermobile
Pediatric AIDS Foundation
Physicans for Social Responsibility
Procter & Gamble
Rhino Records
Savannah River Ecology Laboratory
Select Records
Sherwin-Williams
The Southwestern Company
Spoleto Festival USA

Student Conservation Association
3M
Virgin Records
Writers Guild of America, West

SOUTH DAKOTA

American Civil Liberties Union
The American-Scandinavian Foundation
Camp Counselors USA
CDG/CDS International
Council on International Educational Exchange
D.C. Booth Historic Fish Hatchery
The Dow Jones Newspaper Fund
Federal Bureau of Prisons
Habitat for Humanity International
Hispanic Association of Colleges and Universities
Howard Hughes Medical Institute
International Foundation of Employee Benefit Plans
International Volunteer Projects
Mount Rushmore
National Consortium for Graduate Degrees for Minorities in
    Engineering and Science
National Park Service
The Nature Conservancy
Northwestern Mutual Financial Network
Oak Ridge Institute for Science and Education
Oscar Mayer Wienermobile
The Partnership for Service-Learning
Pediatric AIDS Foundation
Physicans for Social Responsibility
Sherwin-Williams
The Southwestern Company
Student Conservation Association
3M
Writers Guild of America, West

TENNESSEE

American Civil Liberties Union
The American-Scandinavian Foundation
Arthur Andersen
Asylum Records
Atlantic Records
Buick
Cadillac
Camp Counselors USA
CDG/CDS International
Chevrolet
Council on International Educational Exchange
The Dow Jones Newspaper Fund
Du Pont
The Environmental Careers Organization
Ernst & Young
Federal Bureau of Prisons
Gap
General Motors Marketing Internship
GMC Truck
Habitat for Humanity International
The Hermitage

Hispanic Association of Colleges and Universities
Howard Hughes Medical Institute
Inroads
International Foundation of Employee Benefit Plans
International Volunteer Projects
Mercury Records
National Consortium for Graduate Degrees for Minorities in
  Engineering and Science
National Park Service
The Nature Conservancy
Northwestern Mutual Financial Network
Oak Ridge Institute for Science and Education
Oak Ridge National Laboratory
Oldsmobile
Oscar Mayer Wienermobile
Pediatric AIDS Foundation
Physicans for Social Responsibility
Playhouse on the Square
Pontiac
Procter & Gamble
Saturn
Sherwin-Williams
The Southwestern Company
Student Conservation Association
Virgin Records
Writers Guild of America, West
Y.E.S. to Jobs

TEXAS

A&M Records
Ackerman McQueen
AFS Intercultural Programs
AIESEC
American Bar Association
American Civil Liberties Union
American Heart Association
American Israel Public Affairs Committee
American Jewish Congress
The American-Scandinavian Foundation
Arista Records
Arthur Andersen
Atlantic Records
Bechtel
Bertelsmann Music Group
Best Buddies International
Boeing
BP
Brethren Volunteer Service
Camp Counselors USA
CARE
CBS News
CBS Records
CDG/CDS International
Chevron
Chrysalis Records
Citibank
Columbia Records
Council on International Educational Exchange

Dallas Cowboys
Def Jam Records
Dell Computer
Deloitte & Touche
Dow Chemical Company
The Dow Jones Newspaper Fund
Du Pont
Duke University Talent Identification Program
Dykeman Associates
E-Systems
EastWest Records
Elektra Records
EMI Records
Energy Records
The Environmental Careers Organization
Epic Records
Ernst & Young
Exxon
Federal Bureau of Prisons
Fontana Records
Frito-Lay
Gap
Gensler and Associates/Architects
Global Volunteers
Grubb & Ellis
GTE
Habitat for Humanity International
Hispanic Association of Colleges and Universities
Houston International Protocol Alliance
Howard Hughes Medical Institute
IBM
Inroads
International Foundation of Employee Benefit Plans
International Management Group
International Volunteer Projects
Interscope Records
Island Records
Johnson Space Center
Lunar and Planetary Institute
Mammoth Records
Mass Media Science and Engineering Fellows Program
Matador Records
Mercury Records
Motown Records
National Aeronautics and Space Administration
National Consortium for Graduate Degrees for Minorities in
  Engineering and Science
National Park Service
The Nature Conservancy
Northwestern Mutual Financial Network
Oak Ridge Institute for Science and Education
Office of Job Corps
Oscar Mayer Wienermobile
Outward Bound/Voyageur School
Pediatric AIDS Foundation
Perspective Records
Physicans for Social Responsibility
PolyGram

Procter & Gamble
RCA Records
Rhino Records
SBK Records
Schlumberger
Select Records
Sgro Promo Associates/General Motors Internship
Sherwin-Williams
Sierra Club
Sony Music Entertainment
The Southwestern Company
Student Conservation Association
Summerbridge National
Teach for America
Tellabs
Temerlin McClain
Texas Instruments
Texas Monthly
3M
Twentieth Century Fox
Union Carbide
United States Environmental Protection Agency
United States Secret Service
United States Securities and Exchange Commission
Vertigo Records
Verve Records
Virgin Records
The Wall Street Journal
Westin Hotels & Resorts
Writers Guild of America, West
Y.E.S. to Jobs
Youth For Understanding International Exchange
Zoo Entertainment

UTAH

American Civil Liberties Union
The American-Scandinavian Foundation
Atlantic Records
Camp Counselors USA
CDG/CDS International
Chrysalis Records
Council on International Educational Exchange
Deloitte & Touche
The Dow Jones Newspaper Fund
EMI Records
Ernst & Young
Federal Bureau of Prisons
Gap
Habitat for Humanity International
Hispanic Association of Colleges and Universities
Howard Hughes Medical Institute
International Foundation of Employee Benefit Plans
International Volunteer Projects
Interscope Records
Korff Enterprises
Mammoth Records
Matador Records
National Consortium for Graduate Degrees for Minorities in

Engineering and Science
National Park Service
The Nature Conservancy
Northwestern Mutual Financial Network
Oak Ridge Institute for Science and Education
Oscar Mayer Wienermobile
Pediatric AIDS Foundation
Physicans for Social Responsibility
Rhino Records
SBK Records
Select Records
Sherwin-Williams
Sierra Club
The Southwestern Company
Student Conservation Association
3M
United States Securities and Exchange Commission
Utah State Legislature
Virgin Records
Writers Guild of America, West

VERMONT

American Civil Liberties Union
The American-Scandinavian Foundation
Atlantic Records
Camp Counselors USA
CDG/CDS International
Council on International Educational Exchange
The Environmental Careers Organization
Federal Bureau of Prisons
Gap
Habitat for Humanity International
Hispanic Association of Colleges and Universities
Howard Hughes Medical Institute
IBM
National Park Service
International Foundation of Employee Benefit Plans
International Volunteer Projects
Interscope Records
Mammoth Records
Matador Records
National Consortium for Graduate Degrees for Minorities in
  Engineering and Science
The Nature Conservancy
Northwestern Mutual Financial Network
Oak Ridge Institute for Science and Education
Oscar Mayer Wienermobile
Pediatric AIDS Foundation
Physicans for Social Responsibility
Public Interest Research Groups
Rhino Records
Select Records
Sherwin-Williams
The Southwestern Company
Student Conservation Association
Volunteers For Peace
Writers Guild of America, West

Ackerman McQueen
AIESEC
American Civil Liberties Union
American Heart Association
The American-Scandinavian Foundation
ASHOKA: Innovators for the Public
Atlantic Records
Beach Associates
Brethren Volunteer Service
Camp Counselors USA
CDG/CDS International
Center for Marine Conservation
Central Intelligence Agency
Chincoteague National Wildlife Refuge
The Chronicle of the Horse
The Conservative Caucus
Continuous Electron Beam Accelerator Facility
Council on International Educational Exchange
Deloitte & Touche
DesignTech International
The Dow Jones Newspaper Fund
Du Pont
Duke University Talent Identification Program
E-Systems
Earle Palmer Brown
Ernst & Young
Federal Bureau of Investigation
Federal Bureau of Prisons
The Feminist Majority
Foundation for Contemporary Mental Health
Gap
The Government Affairs Institute
Habitat for Humanity International
Hispanic Association of Colleges and Universities
Howard Hughes Medical Institute
Inroads
International Foundation of Employee Benefit Plans
International Volunteer Projects
Interscope Records
Langley Research Center
Legacy International
Little Keswick School
Mammoth Records
The Martin Agency
Mass Media Science and Engineering Fellows Program
Matador Records
Merck & Company
National Aeronautics and Space Administration
National Consortium for Graduate Degrees for Minorities in
    Engineering and Science
National Park Service
National Zoo
The Nature Conservancy
Northwestern Mutual Financial Network
Oak Ridge Institute for Science and Education
Oscar Mayer Wienermobile
Pediatric AIDS Foundation

Physicans for Social Responsibility
Procter & Gamble
Quality Education for Minorities Network
Rhino Records
Select Records
Sherwin-Williams
The Southwestern Company
Student Conservation Association
Summerbridge National
Tellabs
United States Secret Service
Virginia Symphony
Virgin Records
Volunteers For Peace
The Washington Post
Winant-Clayton Volunteers
Wolf Trap Foundation for the Performing Arts
Writers Guild of America, West

AIESEC
American Civil Liberties Union
American Friends Service Committee
American Heart Association
The American-Scandinavian Foundation
Arista Records
Arthur Andersen
Atlantic Records
Bertelsmann Music Group
Boeing
Brethren Volunteer Service
Camp Counselors USA
CARE
CDG/CDS International
Chrysalis Records
Congressional Management Foundation
Council on International Educational Exchange
Deloitte & Touche
The Dow Jones Newspaper Fund
EastWest Records
Elektra Records
EMI Records
Energy Records
The Environmental Careers Organization
Ernst & Young
Fantagraphics Books
Federal Bureau of Prisons
Gap
Grubb & Ellis
Habitat for Humanity International
Hewlett-Packard
Hispanic Association of Colleges and Universities
Howard Hughes Medical Institute
Institute of Cultural Affairs
Interlocken
International Foundation of Employee Benefit Plans
International Volunteer Projects
Interscope Records

KIRO
Klondike Gold Rush
Lutheran Volunteer Corps
Mammoth Records
Matador Records
Microsoft
National Consortium for Graduate Degrees for Minorities in
  Engineering and Science
National Park Service
The Nature Conservancy
Northwestern Mutual Financial Network
Oak Ridge Institute for Science and Education
Office of Job Corps
Oscar Mayer Wienermobile
Pediatric AIDS Foundation
Physicans for Social Responsibility
Procter & Gamble
Public Interest Research Groups
RCA Records
Rhino Records
The Rockey Company
SBK Records
The Seattle Times
Select Records
Sgro Promo Associates/General Motors Internship
Sherwin-Williams
Sierra Club
The Southwestern Company
Starlight Foundation
Student Conservation Association
Teach for America
3M
United States Environmental Protection Agency
United States Secret Service
Virgin Records
Westin Hotels & Resorts
Weyerhaeuser
Writers Guild of America, West
Youth For Understanding International Exchange
Zoo Entertainment

WASHINGTON, D.C.

The Academy for Advanced and Strategic Studies
Access: A Security Information Service
Accuracy in Education
Accuracy in Media
Agora, Inc.
AIESEC
All Things Considered
American-Arab Anti-Discrimination Committee
American Association for the Advancement of Science
American Association of University Women Educational
  Foundation
American Bar Association
American Civil Liberties Union
American Enterprise Institute
American Federation of Teachers
American Forests

American Indian Science & Engineering Society
American Israel Public Affairs Committee
American Jewish Congress
American Red Cross
American Rivers
The American-Scandinavian Foundation
American Society of Magazine Editors
American Symphony Orchestra League
American University in Moscow
American Wind Energy Association
American Woman's Economic Development Corp.
American Youth Work Center
AMIDEAST
Amtrak
Anacostia Museum
The Antarctica Project
Arab American Institute
Arena Stage
Arista Records
Arms Control Association
Arthur Andersen
Asian American Journalists Association
Association of Trial Lawyers of America
Atlantic Council of the United States
Australian Embassy
Beach Associates
Bertelsmann Music Group
Best Buddies International
Bike-Aid
Black Entertainment Television
The Boston Globe
Boston University International Programs
Brethren Volunteer Service
The Brookings Institution
Bureau of Economic Analysis
Bureau of Engraving and Printing
Bureau of Export Administration
Business Executives for National Security
California Governor's Office
Camp Counselors USA
Canadian Embassy
Capital Gang
CARE
Carnegie Endowment for International Peace
CBS News
Census Bureau
Center for Defense Information
Center for Marine Conservation
Center for Strategic & International Studies
Central Intelligence Agency
Children's Defense Fund
Chrysalis Records
The Citizens Network for Foreign Affairs
CNN
The Public Forum Institute
Common Cause
Congressional Hispanic Caucus Institute
Congressional Management Foundation

Congressional Research Service
Conservation Analytical Laboratory
Consumers for World Trade
The Corporate Response Group
Corporation for National Service
Council on Hemispheric Affairs
Council on International Educational Exchange
Crossfire
C-SPAN
Decatur House Museum
Deloitte & Touche
The Dow Jones Newspaper Fund
EastWest Records
Economic Development Administration
Economic Research Service
Elektra Records
Emerge
EMI Records
Emily's List
The Environmental Careers Organization
Ernst & Young
Face the Nation
Families USA Foundation
Federal Bureau of Investigation
Federal Bureau of Prisons
Federal Emergency Management Agency
Federal Reserve Board
Fenton Communications
First Business
Foreign Policy
Foreign Student Service Council
Foundation for Contemporary Mental Health
Fourth World Movement
Freer Gallery of Art
French Embassy
Friends Committee on National Legislation
Gap
Gensler and Associates/Architects
The Government Affairs Institute
Grubb & Ellis
Habitat for Humanity International
HALT: Americans for Legal Reform
Health & Environmental Sciences Group
Healthy Mothers, Healthy Babies
The Heritage Foundation
Hirshhorn Museum and Sculpture Garden
Hispanic Association of Colleges and Universities
The History Factory
Hostelling International—American Youth Hostels
Howard Hughes Medical Institute
Hudson Institute
Independent Sector
Inroads
Institute for Policy Studies
The International Center
International Foundation of Employee Benefit Plans
International Labor Organization
International Sculpture Center
International Telecommunications Satellite Organization

International Trade Administration
International Voluntary Services
It's Your Business
Japan-America Society of Washington
Joint Chiefs of Staff
The Kennedy Center
Larry King Live
Lawyers Alliance for World Security/Committee for National
   Security
The Library of Congress
Los Angeles Times
Lutheran Volunteer Corps
Mass Media Science and Engineering Fellows Program
Middle East Institute
Middle East Research & Information Project
Minority Business Development Agency
Morrison & Foerster
My Sister's Place
The Nation
Nation's Business
National Aeronautics and Space Administration
National Air and Space Museum
National Asian Pacific American Legal Consortium
National Association for Female Executives
National Audubon Society
National Committee for Responsive Philanthropy
National Consortium for Graduate Degrees for Minorities in
   Engineering and Science
National Endowment for the Humanities
National Foundation for the Improvement of Education
National Institute of Standards & Technology
National Journal
National Journalism Center
National Museum of African Art
National Museum of American Art
National Museum of American History
National Museum of Natural History
National Oceanic & Atmospheric Administration
National Organization for Women
National Park Service
The National Partnership for Women and Families
National Portrait Gallery
National Public Radio
National Space Society
National Technical Information Service
National Telecommunications & Information Administration
National Trust for Historic Preservation
National Wildlife Federation
National Women's Health Network
National Zoo
NETWORK
The New Republic
Nightline
Northwestern Mutual Financial Network
NOW Legal Defense and Education Fund
Oak Ridge Institute for Science and Education
Office of House Speaker
Office of Inspector General
Office of Job Corps

Organization of Chinese Americans
Oscar Mayer Wienermobile
Overseas Private Investment Corporation
Patent & Trademark Office
Pediatric AIDS Foundation
The Pentagon
Performance Today
Physicans for Social Responsibility
The Population Institute
PrimeTime Live
Public Allies
Public Defender Service for DC
Public Interest Research Groups
Quality Education for Minorities Network
RCA Records
The Ripon Society
Roll Call
Ruder-Finn
SBK Records
Science
Science News
Scoville Peace Fellowship Program
Sherwin-Williams
Sierra Club
Skadden, Arps, Slate, Meagher & Flom
Smithsonian Institution
The Source Theater Company
The Southwestern Company
Special Olympics International
Student Conservation Association
Supreme Court of the United States
Talk of the Nation
Teach for America
Technology Administration
The Union Institute : Office for Social Responsibility
United States Agency for International Development
United States Chamber of Commerce
United States Department of Commerce
United States Department of Defense
United States Environmental Protection Agency
United States Holocaust Museum
United States National Arboretum
United States Secret Service
United States Securities and Exchange Commission
United States Senate Youth Program
United States Travel & Tourism Administration
US-Asia Institute
Virgin Records
Voice of America
Volunteers For Peace
The Wall Street Journal
Washington Center for Politics & Journalism
Washington Internships for Students of Engineering
The Washington Office on Africa
Washington Office on Latin America
The Washington Post
The Washingtonian
The Westwood One Radio Network

The White House
Who Cares
The Widmeyer Baker Group
The Wilson Quarterly
Woodrow Wilson International Center for Scholars
World Federalist Association
Worldnet
Y.E.S. to Jobs
Youth For Understanding International Exchange
YSB (Young Sisters & Brothers)
Zoo Entertainment

See Maryland
See Virginia

WEST VIRGINIA

American Civil Liberties Union
The American-Scandinavian Foundation
Camp Counselors USA
CDG/CDS International
Council on International Educational Exchange
Du Pont
Ernst & Young
Federal Bureau of Prisons
Gap
Habitat for Humanity International
Hispanic Association of Colleges and Universities
Howard Hughes Medical Institute
Inroads
International Foundation of Employee Benefit Plans
International Volunteer Projects
National Consortium for Graduate Degrees for Minorities in
    Engineering and Science
National Park Service
The Nature Conservancy
Northwestern Mutual Financial Network
Oak Ridge Institute for Science and Education
Oscar Mayer Wienermobile
Pediatric AIDS Foundation
Sherwin-Williams
The Southwestern Company
Student Conservation Association
3M
United States Secret Service
Volunteers For Peace
WCHS-TV
Writers Guild of America, West

WISCONSIN

AIESEC
American Civil Liberties Union
American Heart Association
The American-Scandinavian Foundation
Arthur Andersen
Asylum Records
Atlantic Records
Camp Counselors USA

CDG/CDS International
Council on International Educational Exchange
EastWest Records
Elektra Records
Ernst & Young
Federal Bureau of Prisons
Frito-Lay
Gap
Habitat for Humanity International
Harley-Davidson
Hillel
Hispanic Association of Colleges and Universities
Howard Hughes Medical Institute
Inroads
Interlocken
International Foundation of Employee Benefit Plans
International Volunteer Projects
Interscope Records
Lutheran Volunteer Corps
Mammoth Records
Mass Media Science and Engineering Fellows Program
Matador Records
Miller Brewing Company
The Milwaukee Journal
National Audubon Society
National Consortium for Graduate Degrees for Minorities in
   Engineering and Science
National Park Service
The Nature Conservancy
Northwestern Mutual Financial Network
Oak Ridge Institute for Science and Education
Oscar Mayer
Oscar Mayer Wienermobile
Pediatric AIDS Foundation
Physicans for Social Responsibility
Procter & Gamble
Public Allies
Public Interest Research Groups
Rhino Records
Select Records
Sherwin-Williams
Sierra Club
The Southwestern Company
Student Conservation Association
3M
Virgin Records
Weyerhaeuser
Writers Guild of America, West

WYOMING

American Civil Liberties Union
The American-Scandinavian Foundation
Buffalo Bill Historical Center
Camp Counselors USA
CDG/CDS International
Council on International Educational Exchange
The Dow Jones Newspaper Fund
Federal Bureau of Prisons

Habitat for Humanity International
Hispanic Association of Colleges and Universities
Howard Hughes Medical Institute
International Foundation of Employee Benefit Plans
International Volunteer Projects
National Audubon Society
National Consortium for Graduate Degrees for Minorities in
   Engineering and Science
National Park Service
The Nature Conservancy
Northwestern Mutual Financial Network
Oak Ridge Institute for Science and Education
Oscar Mayer Wienermobile
Pediatric AIDS Foundation
Schlumberger
Sherwin-Williams
Sierra Club
The Southwestern Company
Student Conservation Association
Writers Guild of America, West
Yellowstone National Park

AFRICA

ALGERIA

United States and Foreign Commercial Service
Volunteers For Peace

ANGOLA

CARE

BENIN

Peace Corps
United Nations Volunteer Program
United States Agency for International Development

BOTSWANA

AIESEC
Deloitte & Touche
Habitat for Humanity International
Peace Corps
United Nations Volunteer Program
United States Agency for International Development
United States Department of State

BURKINA FASO

Fourth World Movement
United Nations Volunteer Program
United States Agency for International Development
United States Department of State

BURUNDI

CARE
Habitat for Humanity International
Peace Corps
United Nations Volunteer Program
United States Agency for International Development

CAMEROON

AIESEC
CARE
Deloitte & Touche
Peace Corps
United States Agency for International Development
United States Department of State

CAPE VERDE

Peace Corps
United Nations Volunteer Program
United States Agency for International Development

CENTRAL AFRICAN REPUBLIC

Fourth World Movement

Habitat for Humanity International
Peace Corps
United Nations Volunteer Program
United States Department of State

CHAD

CARE
Peace Corps
United Nations Volunteer Program
United States Agency for International Development

COMOROS

CARE
Peace Corps
United Nations Volunteer Program

CONGO

Peace Corps
United States Agency for International Development
United States Department of State

COTE D'IVOIRE

See Ivory Coast

DJIBOUTI

United Nations Volunteer Program
United States Department of State

EGYPT

See The Middle East

EQUATORIAL GUINEA

Peace Corps
United Nations Volunteer Program
United States Department of State

ERITREA

United States Agency for International Development
United States Department of State

ETHIOPIA

CARE
Habitat for Humanity International
The International Foundation for Education and Self-Help
United Nations Volunteer Program
United States Agency for International Development
United States Department of State

GABON

Peace Corps
United States Department of State

GAMBIA

The International Foundation for Education and Self-Help
Peace Corps
United Nations Volunteer Program
United States Agency for International Development
United States Department of State

GHANA

AFS Intercultural Programs
AIESEC
CARE
Deloitte & Touche
Habitat for Humanity International
IAESTE
International Volunteer Projects
Peace Corps
United States Agency for International Development
United States Department of State
Volunteers For Peace

GUINEA

Peace Corps
United Nations Volunteer Program
United States Agency for International Development
United States Department of State

GUINEA BISSAU

Peace Corps
United Nations Volunteer Program
United States Agency for International Development
United States Department of State

IVORY COAST

AIESEC
Deloitte & Touche
Fourth World Movement
The International Foundation for Education and Self-Help
Peace Corps
United States and Foreign Commercial Service

KENYA

AIESEC
CARE
CNN
Deloitte & Touche
Food for the Hungry
Habitat for Humanity International
Institute of Cultural Affairs
The International Foundation for Education and Self-Help
Peace Corps
People to People International

Procter & Gamble
United States Agency for International Development
United States and Foreign Commercial Service
United States Department of State

LESOTHO

CARE
Deloitte & Touche
Peace Corps
United Nations Volunteer Program
United States Agency for International Development
United States Department of State

LIBERIA

AIESEC
United Nations Volunteer Program
United States Department of State

MADAGASCAR

CARE
Fourth World Movement
Peace Corps
United Nations Volunteer Program
United States Agency for International Development

MALAWI

Deloitte & Touche
Habitat for Humanity International
Peace Corps
United Nations Volunteer Program
United States Agency for International Development
United States Department of State

MALI

CARE
United Nations Volunteer Program
United States Agency for International Development
United States Department of State

MAURITANIA

Deloitte & Touche
Peace Corps
United Nations Volunteer Program
United States Agency for International Development

MAURITIUS

Deloitte & Touche
Fourth World Movement

MOROCCO

AIESEC
AMIDEAST
Deloitte & Touche
International Volunteer Projects

Peace Corps
Procter & Gamble
United States Agency for International Development
United States and Foreign Commercial Service
United States Department of State
Volunteers For Peace

MOZAMBIQUE

CARE
Institute for International Cooperation and Development
Peace Corps
United Nations Volunteer Program
United States Agency for International Development

NAMIBIA

Deloitte & Touche
Peace Corps
United States Agency for International Development
United States Department of State
WorldTeach

NIGER

CARE
The International Foundation for Education and Self-Help
Peace Corps
United Nations Volunteer Program
United States Agency for International Development
United States Department of State

NIGERIA

AIESEC
Brethren Volunteer Service
Deloitte & Touche
Habitat for Humanity International
IAESTE
The International Foundation for Education and Self-Help
Peace Corps
Procter & Gamble
United States Agency for International Development
United States and Foreign Commercial Service
Volunteers For Peace

REUNION ISLAND

Fourth World Movement

RWANDA

CARE
Food for the Hungry
Peace Corps
United Nations Volunteer Program
United States Agency for International Development

SAO TOME AND PRINCIPE

Peace Corps
United Nations Volunteer Program

SENEGAL

AIESEC
Fourth World Movement
The International Foundation for Education and Self-Help
Peace Corps
United States Agency for International Development
United States Department of State

SEYCHELLES

Peace Corps

SIERRA LEONE

AIESEC
CARE
IAESTE
The International Foundation for Education and Self-Help
Peace Corps
United Nations Volunteer Program
United States Agency for International Development
Volunteers For Peace

SOMALIA

CARE
United Nations Volunteer Program
United States Agency for International Development

SOUTH AFRICA

AIESEC
CARE
Deloitte & Touche
Ernst & Young
Habitat for Humanity International
IAESTE
International Management Group
TBWA
United States Agency for International Development
United States and Foreign Commercial Service
United States Department of State
WorldTeach

SUDAN

CARE
United Nations Volunteer Program
United States Agency for International Development

SWAZILAND

Deloitte & Touche
Peace Corps
United Nations Volunteer Program
United States Agency for International Development
United States Department of State

TANZANIA

CARE
Global Volunteers

Habitat for Humanity International
Peace Corps
United Nations Volunteer Program
United States Agency for International Development
United States Department of State

TOGO

AIESEC
CARE
Peace Corps
United Nations Volunteer Program
United States Department of State
Volunteers For Peace

TUNISIA

AIESEC
AMIDEAST
Deloitte & Touche
IAESTE
International Volunteer Projects
Peace Corps
United States Agency for International Development
Volunteers For Peace

UGANDA

CARE
Food for the Hungry
Habitat for Humanity International
Peace Corps
United Nations Volunteer Program
United States Agency for International Development
United States Department of State

ZAIRE

Food for the Hungry
Habitat for Humanity International
Peace Corps
United Nations Volunteer Program
United States Department of State

ZAMBIA

CARE
Deloitte & Touche
Habitat for Humanity International
Institute of Cultural Affairs
Peace Corps
United Nations Volunteer Program
United States Agency for International Development
United States Department of State

ZIMBABWE

AIESEC
CARE
Deloitte & Touche
Institute for International Cooperation and Development

The International Foundation for Education and Self-Help
Peace Corps
The Population Institute
United States Agency for International Development
United States Department of State

ASIA & PACIFIC (INCLUDING AUSTRALIA AND NEW ZEALAND)

AFGHANISTAN

CARE
United Nations Volunteer Program

AUSTRALIA

AIESEC
Boston University International Programs
CDG/CDS International
Deloitte & Touche
Educational Programs Abroad
Ernst & Young
Habitat for Humanity International
IAESTE
IES – The Institute for the International Education of Students
The International Foundation for Education and Self-Help
International Management Group
People to People International
Procter & Gamble
Starlight Foundation
United States and Foreign Commercial Service
Volunteers For Peace
Work Experience USA

BANGLADESH

CARE
Food for the Hungry
Search Associates International School Intern Program
United Nations Volunteer Program
United States Agency for International Development
United States Department of State
Volunteers For Peace

BHUTAN

United Nations Volunteer Program

BRUNEI

Deloitte & Touche
United States Department of State

CAMBODIA

CARE
Food for the Hungry
United Nations Volunteer Program
United States Department of State

CHINA

AFS Intercultural Programs
Boston University International Programs
Brethren Volunteer Service
CARE
CNN
Deloitte & Touche

Duke University Talent Identification Program
Ernst & Young
Food for the Hungry
Interlocken
Peace Corps
Procter & Gamble
United Nations Volunteer Program
United States and Foreign Commercial Service
United States Department of State
Volunteers in Asia
WorldTeach

See also Hong Kong

COOK ISLANDS

Peace Corps

FIJI

Deloitte & Touche
Habitat for Humanity International
Peace Corps
United States Agency for International Development

GUAM

Deloitte & Touche
National Park Service

HONG KONG

AFS Intercultural Programs
Agora, Inc.
AIESEC
California Governor's Office
Deloitte & Touche
Duke University Talent Identification Program
Elite Model Management
Ernst & Young
Forbes
International Management Group
Procter & Gamble
Summerbridge National
United States and Foreign Commercial Service
United States Department of State

INDIA

AIESEC
CARE
CNN
Deloitte & Touche
Ernst & Young
Habitat for Humanity International
IAESTE
Institute of Cultural Affairs
International Volunteer Projects

The Partnership for Service-Learning
Procter & Gamble
United Nations Volunteer Program
United States Agency for International Development
United States and Foreign Commercial Service
United States Department of State
Volunteers For Peace

INDONESIA

AIESEC
CARE
Deloitte & Touche
Global Volunteers
Habitat for Humanity International
The Population Institute
Procter & Gamble
United Nations Volunteer Program
United States Agency for International Development
United States and Foreign Commercial Service
Volunteers in Asia

JAPAN

AIESEC
Brethren Volunteer Service
B.U.G.
California Governor's Office
CDG/CDS International
CNN
Deloitte & Touche
Duke University Talent Identification Program
Elite Model Management
Food for the Hungry
Ford Models
IAESTE
International Management Group
International Volunteer Projects
Japanese Exchange and Teaching Program
Overseas Service Corps of the YMCA
Procter & Gamble
Sony
United States Agency for International Development
United States and Foreign Commercial Service
United States Department of State
Volunteers For Peace

KIRIBATI

Peace Corps
United Nations Volunteer Program

LAOS

CARE
Food for the Hungry
United Nations Volunteer Program
United States Department of State

MACAU

Deloitte & Touche

MALAYSIA

AIESEC
Deloitte & Touche
Institute of Cultural Affairs
Procter & Gamble
United States and Foreign Commercial Service

MALDIVES

United Nations Volunteer Program

MARSHALL ISLANDS

Peace Corps

MICRONESIA

Peace Corps

MONGOLIA

Peace Corps
United Nations Volunteer Program
United States Agency for International Development

MYANMAR (FORMERLY BURMA)

United Nations Volunteer Program
United States Agency for International Development

NEPAL

CARE
Peace Corps
United Nations Volunteer Program
United States Agency for International Development
United States Department of State

NEW ZEALAND

AIESEC
Council on International Educational Exchange
Deloitte & Touche
Ernst & Young
Habitat for Humanity International
International Management Group
Procter & Gamble
United States and Foreign Commercial Service
Work Experience USA

NORTH KOREA

NORTHERN MARIANA ISLANDS

Deloitte & Touche

PAKISTAN

AIESEC
Deloitte & Touche
Habitat for Humanity International
Procter & Gamble
United Nations Volunteer Program
United States Agency for International Development
United States and Foreign Commercial Service
United States Department of State

PAPUA NEW GUINEA

AIESEC
CARE
Deloitte & Touche
Habitat for Humanity International
Peace Corps
United States Agency for International Development
United States Department of State

PHILIPPINES

AIESEC
CARE
CNN
Deloitte & Touche
Food for the Hungry
Fourth World Movement
Habitat for Humanity International
The Partnership for Service-Learning
Peace Corps
Procter & Gamble
United States Agency for International Development
United States and Foreign Commercial Service
United States Department of State
Volunteers For Peace

SINGAPORE

AIESEC
Deloitte & Touche
International Management Group
Procter & Gamble
United States Agency for International Development
United States and Foreign Commercial Service
United States Department of State

SOLOMON ISLANDS

Habitat for Humanity International
Peace Corps
United Nations Volunteer Program

SOUTH KOREA

AIESEC
Brethren Volunteer Service
CNN
Deloitte & Touche
IAESTE
Procter & Gamble
United Nations Volunteer Program
United States and Foreign Commercial Service
United States Department of State

SRI LANKA

CARE
Habitat for Humanity International
Peace Corps
United Nations Volunteer Program
United States Agency for International Development
United States Department of State

TAIWAN

AIESEC
Deloitte & Touche
Fourth World Movement
Overseas Service Corps of the YMCA
Procter & Gamble
United States Department of State

THAILAND

AIESEC
CARE
CNN
Deloitte & Touche
Food for the Hungry
Fourth World Movement
IAESTE
The International Foundation for Education and Self-Help
International Management Group
Peace Corps
Procter & Gamble
United States Agency for International Development
United States and Foreign Commercial Service
United States Department of State
Volunteers in Asia
WorldTeach

TONGA

Peace Corps

TUVALU

Peace Corps
United Nations Volunteer Program

VANUATU

Peace Corps
United Nations Volunteer Program

VIETNAM

CARE
Deloitte & Touche
Global Volunteers
United Nations Volunteer Program
Volunteers in Asia

WESTERN SAMOA

Peace Corps
United Nations Volunteer Program

EURASIA

ARMENIA

American University in Moscow
CARE
Habitat for Humanity International
Peace Corps
United Nations Volunteer Program
United States Agency for International Development

AZERBAIJAN

American University in Moscow
CARE
United States Agency for International Development
United States Department of State

BELARUS

American University in Moscow
CARE
Peace Corps
United States Agency for International Development
United States Department of State
Volunteers For Peace

ESTONIA

AIESEC
American University in Moscow
CARE
IAESTE
Peace Corps
United Nations Volunteer Program
United States Agency for International Development

GEORGIA

American University in Moscow
CARE
United Nations Volunteer Program
United States Agency for International Development

KAZAKHSTAN

American University in Moscow
CARE
Peace Corps
United Nations Volunteer Program
United States Agency for International Development
United States and Foreign Commercial Service

KYRGHYZSTAN

American University in Moscow
CARE
Peace Corps
United Nations Volunteer Program
United States Agency for International Development

LATVIA

American University in Moscow
CARE
IAESTE
Peace Corps
United Nations Volunteer Program
United States Agency for International Development
Volunteers For Peace

LITHUANIA

AIESEC
American University in Moscow
CARE
IAESTE
International Volunteer Projects
Peace Corps
United Nations Volunteer Program
United States Agency for International Development
United States Department of State
Volunteers For Peace

MOLDOVA

American University in Moscow
CARE
Peace Corps
United Nations Volunteer Program
United States Agency for International Development

RUSSIA

AFS Intercultural Programs
AIESEC
American University in Moscow
ASSIST
Boston University International Programs
Camp Counselors USA
The Center for Human Rights Advocacy
CNN
Deloitte & Touche
Ernst & Young
Global Volunteers
IAESTE
International Volunteer Projects
Peace Corps
People to People International
Procter & Gamble
United States Agency for International Development
United States and Foreign Commercial Service
United States Department of State
Volunteers For Peace
WorldTeach

SLOVAKIA (AKA SLOVAK REPUBLIC)

AIESEC
American University in Moscow
CARE
Deloitte & Touche
IAESTE
International Volunteer Projects
Peace Corps
United Nations Volunteer Program
United States Agency for International Development
United States and Foreign Commercial Service
Volunteers For Peace

SLOVENIA

AIESEC
Deloitte & Touche
IAESTE
International Volunteer Projects
United Nations Volunteer Program
United States Department of State
Volunteers For Peace

TAJIKISTAN

American University in Moscow
CARE
IAESTE
United Nations Volunteer Program
United States Agency for International Development

TURKMENISTAN

American University in Moscow
CARE
Peace Corps
United Nations Volunteer Program
United States Agency for International Development

UKRAINE

AIESEC
American University in Moscow
CARE
Deloitte & Touche
IAESTE
International Volunteer Projects
Peace Corps
United Nations Volunteer Program
United States Agency for International Development
United States and Foreign Commercial Service
United States Department of State
Volunteers For Peace

UZBEKISTAN

American University in Moscow
CARE
Peace Corps
United Nations Volunteer Program
United States Agency for International Development
United States and Foreign Commercial Service

EUROPE (INCLUDING EASTERN EUROPE)

ALBANIA

IAESTE
Peace Corps
United States Agency for International Development

AUSTRIA

AIESEC
CDG/CDS International
Deloitte & Touche
Ernst & Young
IAESTE
IES – The Institute for the International Education of Students
International Management Group
Procter & Gamble
United States Agency for International Development
United States and Foreign Commercial Service
United States Department of State
Volunteers For Peace

BELGIUM

AIESEC
Brethren Volunteer Service
CDG/CDS International
CNN
Deloitte & Touche
Educational Programs Abroad
Ernst & Young
Fourth World Movement
IAESTE
Institute of Cultural Affairs
International Management Group
International Volunteer Projects
Procter & Gamble
Quaker United Nations Office
United States and Foreign Commercial Service
United States Department of State
Volunteers For Peace

BOSNIA-HERZEGOVINA

United Nations Volunteer Program

BULGARIA

AIESEC
Deloitte & Touche
IAESTE
Peace Corps
Students for Central & Eastern Europe
United States Agency for International Development
United States and Foreign Commercial Service
Volunteers For Peace

CHANNEL ISLANDS

Deloitte & Touche

CROATIA

AIESEC
Brethren Volunteer Service
IAESTE
United Nations Volunteer Program
United States Agency for International Development
United States and Foreign Commercial Service
United States Department of State
Volunteers For Peace

CZECH REPUBLIC

AFS Intercultural Programs
AIESEC
Brethren Volunteer Service
CDG/CDS International
Deloitte & Touche
IAESTE
Interlocken
International Volunteer Projects
Peace Corps
People to People International
Procter & Gamble
Students for Central & Eastern Europe
United States Agency for International Development
United States and Foreign Commercial Service
United States Department of State
Volunteers For Peace

DENMARK

AIESEC
The American-Scandinavian Foundation
CDG/CDS International
Deloitte & Touche
Elite Model Management
Ernst & Young
IAESTE
International Volunteer Projects
People to People International
United States and Foreign Commercial Service
United States Department of State
Volunteers For Peace

ENGLAND

Academic Study Associates
AFS Intercultural Programs
AIESEC
American Association of Overseas Studies
American Institute for Foreign Study
Bechtel
Boston University International Programs
Bozell Public Relations
Brethren Volunteer Service
California Governor's Office
Camp Counselors USA

The Catholic University of America
CDG/CDS International
CNN
Council on International Educational Exchange
Deloitte & Touche
Duke University Talent Identification Program
The Economist
Educational Programs Abroad
Elite Model Management
Ernst & Young
Fourth World Movement
The Hansard Society for Parliamentary Government
IAESTE
IES – The Institute for the International Education of Students
Institute of Cultural Affairs
Interlocken
International Management Group
International Volunteer Projects
Internships International
National Association of Professional Surplus Lines Offices
Ove Arup & Partners
The Partnership for Service-Learning
Penguin Books
People to People International
Plume Books
Procter & Gamble
Signet Classics
The Southwestern Company
Starlight Foundation
TBWA
United States Agency for International Development
United States and Foreign Commercial Service
United States Department of State
Viking Books
Virgin Records
Volunteers For Peace
Winant-Clayton Volunteers

FINLAND

AIESEC
The American-Scandinavian Foundation
CDG/CDS International
Deloitte & Touche
Ernst & Young
IAESTE
Procter & Gamble
United States Agency for International Development
United States and Foreign Commercial Service
United States Department of State
Volunteers For Peace

FRANCE

AIESEC
Boston University International Programs
Brethren Volunteer Service
CDG/CDS International
CNN

Council on International Educational Exchange
Deloitte & Touche
Duke University Talent Identification Program
Educational Programs Abroad
Elite Model Management
Ernst & Young
Ford Models
Fourth World Movement
The French-American Center
IAESTE
IES – The Institute for the International Education of Students
Interlocken
International Management Group
International Volunteer Projects
Internships in Francophone Europe
Internships International
The Partnership for Service-Learning
People to People International
Procter & Gamble
Schlumberger
TBWA
United States Agency for International Development
United States and Foreign Commercial Service
United States Department of State
Volunteers For Peace

GERMANY

AIESEC
Brethren Volunteer Service
California Governor's Office
CDG/CDS International
CNN
Council on International Educational Exchange
Deloitte & Touche
Duke University Talent Identification Program
Educational Programs Abroad
Elite Model Management
Ernst & Young
Forbes
Fourth World Movement
IAESTE
IES – The Institute for the International Education of Students
Institute of Cultural Affairs
International Management Group
International Telecommunications Satellite Organization
International Volunteer Projects
Internships International
Oscar Mayer Wienermobile
People to People International
Procter & Gamble
TBWA
United States Agency for International Development
United States and Foreign Commercial Service
United States Department of State
Volunteers For Peace

GIBRALTER

Deloitte & Touche

GREECE

AIESEC
CDG/CDS International
Deloitte & Touche
Ernst & Young
Global Volunteers
IAESTE
Procter & Gamble
United States and Foreign Commercial Service
United States Department of State
Volunteers For Peace

HUNGARY

AFS Intercultural Programs
AIESEC
CDG/CDS International
Deloitte & Touche
Habitat for Humanity International
IAESTE
International Management Group
Internships International
Peace Corps
Procter & Gamble
United States Agency for International Development
United States and Foreign Commercial Service
United States Department of State
Volunteers For Peace

ICELAND

AIESEC
The American-Scandinavian Foundation
CDG/CDS International
Deloitte & Touche
IAESTE

IRELAND

AIESEC
Brethren Volunteer Service
The Catholic University of America
CDG/CDS International
Council on International Educational Exchange
Deloitte & Touche
Dublin Internships, Ireland
Fourth World Movement
IAESTE
International Management Group
International Volunteer Projects
People to People International
Procter & Gamble
United States and Foreign Commercial Service
United States Department of State
Volunteers For Peace

ISLE OF MAN

Deloitte & Touche

ITALY

AIESEC
Bozell Public Relations
CDG/CDS International
CNN
Deloitte & Touche
Duke University Talent Identification Program
Elite Model Management
Ernst & Young
Global Volunteers
IAESTE
IES – The Institute for the International Education of Students
Interlocken
International Management Group
Internships International
Peggy Guggenheim Collection
Procter & Gamble
United States Agency for International Development
United States and Foreign Commercial Service
United States Department of State
Volunteers For Peace

LUXEMBOURG

CDG/CDS International
Deloitte & Touche
Fourth World Movement
IAESTE
Search Associates International School Intern Program

MACEDONIA

AIESEC
United States Agency for International Development

MALTA

AIESEC
Deloitte & Touche
IAESTE
Peace Corps

MONACO

International Management Group

NETHERLANDS

AIESEC
Brethren Volunteer Service
Camp Counselors USA
CDG/CDS International
Deloitte & Touche
Elite Model Management
Ernst & Young
Fellowship of Reconciliation
Fourth World Movement
IAESTE
International Volunteer Projects
Procter & Gamble
TBWA

United States and Foreign Commercial Service
United States Department of State
Volunteers For Peace

NORTHERN IRELAND

See Ireland

NORWAY

AIESEC
The American-Scandinavian Foundation
CDG/CDS International
Deloitte & Touche
Ernst & Young
IAESTE
International Management Group
United States and Foreign Commercial Service
United States Department of State
Volunteers For Peace

POLAND

AIESEC
Brethren Volunteer Service
Deloitte & Touche
Ernst & Young
Global Volunteers
Habitat for Humanity International
IAESTE
International Volunteer Projects
Peace Corps
Procter & Gamble
Students for Central & Eastern Europe
United Nations Volunteer Program
United States Agency for International Development
United States and Foreign Commercial Service
Volunteers For Peace
WorldTeach

PORTUGAL

AIESEC
Deloitte & Touche
Ernst & Young
IAESTE
Institute of Cultural Affairs
Procter & Gamble
United States and Foreign Commercial Service

ROMANIA

AIESEC
Deloitte & Touche
Food for the Hungry
IAESTE
Peace Corps
United States Agency for International Development
United States and Foreign Commercial Service
Volunteers For Peace
Deloitte & Touche

SCOTLAND

AIESEC
CDG/CDS International
Community Service Volunteer Programme
Deloitte & Touche
Fourth World Movement
International Management Group
International Volunteer Projects
The Partnership for Service-Learning
Procter & Gamble
United States Department of State
Volunteers For Peace
Winant-Clayton Volunteers

SERBIA

Brethren Volunteer Service
United Nations Volunteer Program
United States and Foreign Commercial Service

SPAIN

AIESEC
Boston University International Programs
CDG/CDS International
Deloitte & Touche
Educational Programs Abroad
Elite Model Management
Ernst & Young
Fourth World Movement
Global Volunteers
IAESTE
IES – The Institute for the International Education of Students
Interlocken
International Management Group
International Volunteer Projects
Procter & Gamble
TBWA
United States and Foreign Commercial Service
United States Department of State
Volunteers For Peace

SWEDEN

AIESEC
The American-Scandinavian Foundation
CDG/CDS International
Deloitte & Touche
Ernst & Young
IAESTE
International Management Group
People to People International
Procter & Gamble
United States and Foreign Commercial Service
United States Department of State
Volunteers For Peace

SWITZERLAND

AIESEC
Brethren Volunteer Service
Camp Counselors USA
CDG/CDS International
Deloitte & Touche
Elite Model Management
Ernst & Young
Fourth World Movement
IAESTE
International Labor Organization
International Management Group
Procter & Gamble
Quaker United Nations Office
United Nations
United States and Foreign Commercial Service
United States Department of State
Volunteers For Peace
Women's International League for Peace and Freedom

WALES

AIESEC
CDG/CDS International
Community Service Volunteer Programme
Deloitte & Touche
Fourth World Movement
International Volunteer Projects
Procter & Gamble
Volunteers For Peace

YUGOSLAVIA

AIESEC
Brethren Volunteer Service
Deloitte & Touche
IAESTE
United States Agency for International Development

BAHRAIN

AMIDEAST
Deloitte & Touche

CYPRUS

Deloitte & Touche
IAESTE
United States Department of State

EGYPT

AIESEC
AMIDEAST
CARE
CNN
Deloitte & Touche
Ernst & Young
Habitat for Humanity International
IAESTE
Institute of Cultural Affairs
Procter & Gamble
United States Agency for International Development
United States and Foreign Commercial Service
United States Department of State

GAZA/WEST BANK

AMIDEAST
Brethren Volunteer Service
United States Agency for International Development

IRAQ

CARE
United Nations Volunteer Program

ISRAEL

AIESEC
American Association of Overseas Studies
American Israel Public Affairs Committee
American Jewish Congress
Brethren Volunteer Service
CNN
Deloitte & Touche
The Gesher Summer Internship Program
Hillel
IAESTE
Interlocken
The Partnership for Service-Learning
United States and Foreign Commercial Service
United States Department of State
Volunteers for Israel
Volunteers For Peace

JORDAN

AMIDEAST
CARE
CNN
Deloitte & Touche
IAESTE
United States Agency for International Development
United States Department of State

KUWAIT

AMIDEAST
Deloitte & Touche
United Nations Volunteer Program
United States and Foreign Commercial Service
United States Department of State

LEBANON

AMIDEAST
Deloitte & Touche
IAESTE
Procter & Gamble
United Nations Volunteer Program
United States Agency for International Development

MOROCCO

See Africa

OMAN

Deloitte & Touche
United States Agency for International Development
United States Department of State

PAKISTAN

See Asia & Pacific

QATAR

Deloitte & Touche

SAUDI ARABIA

Deloitte & Touche
Ernst & Young
Procter & Gamble
United States and Foreign Commercial Service
United States Department of State

SYRIA

AMIDEAST
Deloitte & Touche
IAESTE
United States Agency for International Development
United States Department of State

TUNISIA

See Africa

TURKEY

AIESEC
Deloitte & Touche
IAESTE
International Volunteer Projects
Procter & Gamble
United States Agency for International Development
United States and Foreign Commercial Service
United States Department of State
Volunteers For Peace

UNITED ARAB EMIRATES

Deloitte & Touche
United States and Foreign Commercial Service
United States Department of State

WEST BANK

See Gaza/West Bank

YEMEN

AMIDEAST
CARE
Deloitte & Touche
Peace Corps
United Nations Volunteer Program
United States Agency for International Development
United States Department of State

ANGUILLA

Deloitte & Touche
Peace Corps
United States Agency for International Development

ANTIGUA/BARBUDA

Peace Corps
United States Agency for International Development

ARUBA

AIESEC
Deloitte & Touche

BAHAMAS

Deloitte & Touche
United States Department of State

BARBADOS

Deloitte & Touche
Peace Corps
United States Agency for International Development
United States Department of State

BELIZE

Deloitte & Touche
Peace Corps
United Nations Volunteer Program
United States Agency for International Development
United States Department of State

BERMUDA

Bermuda Biological Station for Research
Deloitte & Touche

CANADA

AIESEC
Boys Hope/Girls Hope
Council on International Educational Exchange
Deloitte & Touche
Elite Model Management
Ernst & Young
Ford Models
Fourth World Movement
Gap
Habitat for Humanity International
IAESTE
Institute of Cultural Affairs
Interlocken
International Management Group
International Volunteer Projects
Metro-Goldwyn-Mayer/United Artists

Oscar Mayer Wienermobile
Outward Bound/Voyageur School
Procter & Gamble
Sierra Club
The Southwestern Company
Starlight Foundation
Student Conservation Association
Student Works Painting
Tellabs
United Artists
United States and Foreign Commercial Service
United States Department of State
Volunteers For Peace

CAYMAN ISLANDS

Deloitte & Touche

COSTA RICA

AFS Intercultural Programs
AIESEC
CARE
Council on International Educational Exchange
Deloitte & Touche
Global Volunteers
Habitat for Humanity International
International Volunteer Projects
Peace Corps
The Population Institute
United States Agency for International Development
United States and Foreign Commercial Service
United States Department of State
Volunteers For Peace
WorldTeach

CUBA

American Friends Service Committee
Volunteers For Peace

CURACAO

AIESEC
Deloitte & Touche

DOMINICA

Peace Corps
United States Agency for International Development

DOMINICAN REPUBLIC

AIESEC
CARE
Deloitte & Touche
Habitat for Humanity International
The International Foundation for Education and Self-Help
Peace Corps

United Nations Volunteer Program
United States Agency for International Development
United States and Foreign Commercial Service

EL SALVADOR

Brethren Volunteer Service
CARE
Habitat for Humanity International
Peace Corps
The Population Institute
United Nations Volunteer Program
United States Agency for International Development
United States Department of State

GREENLAND

Deloitte & Touche

GRENADA

Peace Corps
United States Agency for International Development

GUADELUPE

GUATEMALA

AIESEC
CARE
Deloitte & Touche
Food for the Hungry
Fourth World Movement
Global Volunteers
Habitat for Humanity International
Peace Corps
Procter & Gamble
United Nations Volunteer Program
United States Agency for International Development
United States and Foreign Commercial Service
United States Department of State
Volunteers For Peace

HAITI

CARE
Fourth World Movement
Habitat for Humanity International
Peace Corps
United Nations Volunteer Program
United States Agency for International Development

HONDURAS

CARE
Food for the Hungry
Fourth World Movement
Habitat for Humanity International
Peace Corps
United Nations Volunteer Program
United States Agency for International Development

United States and Foreign Commercial Service
United States Department of State

JAMAICA

Council on International Educational Exchange
Deloitte & Touche
Global Volunteers
Habitat for Humanity International
IAESTE
The Partnership for Service-Learning
Peace Corps
Procter & Gamble
United States Agency for International Development
United States and Foreign Commercial Service

MARTINIQUE

MEXICO

AIESEC
American Friends Service Committee
California Governor's Office
CDG/CDS International
Centro para los Adolescentes de San Miguel de Allende
Deloitte & Touche
Global Volunteers
Habitat for Humanity International
IAESTE
Institute of Cultural Affairs
Institute of International Education
International Volunteer Projects
Internships International
Oscar Mayer Wienermobile
The Partnership for Service-Learning
The Population Institute
Procter & Gamble
Search Associates International School Intern Program
United States Agency for International Development
United States and Foreign Commercial Service
United States Department of State
Volunteers For Peace

MONTSERRAT

Peace Corps
United States Agency for International Development

NETHERLANDS-ANTILLES

See Aruba
See Curacao
See St. Maarten

NEVIS

Peace Corps
United States Agency for International Development

NICARAGUA

Brethren Volunteer Service
CARE
CNN
Fellowship of Reconciliation
Food for the Hungry
Habitat for Humanity International
Institute for International Cooperation and Development
Peace Corps
United States Agency for International Development
United States Department of State
Volunteers For Peace

PANAMA

AFS Intercultural Programs
AIESEC
Deloitte & Touche
Fellowship of Reconciliation
Peace Corps
United States Agency for International Development
United States and Foreign Commercial Service
United States Department of State

PUERTO RICO

AIESEC
Gap
Interlocken
Mass Media Science and Engineering Fellows Program
Merck & Company
National Park Service
Pediatric AIDS Foundation
Procter & Gamble
United States Secret Service

ST. KITTS

Peace Corps
United States Agency for International Development

ST. LUCIA

Peace Corps
United States Agency for International Development

ST. MAARTEN

Deloitte & Touche
Peace Corps
United States Agency for International Development

ST. VINCENT

Peace Corps
United States Agency for International Development

VIRGIN ISLANDS

Brethren Volunteer Service
Deloitte & Touche

National Park Service
Peace Corps
United States Agency for International Development

SOUTH AMERICA

ARGENTINA

AIESEC
Deloitte & Touche
Ernst & Young
Fellowship of Reconciliation
Ford Models
Habitat for Humanity International
IAESTE
International Management Group
Peace Corps
Procter & Gamble
United States Agency for International Development
United States and Foreign Commercial Service
United States Department of State

BOLIVIA

AFS Intercultural Programs
AIESEC
CARE
Fellowship of Reconciliation
Habitat for Humanity International
International Volunteer Projects
Peace Corps
United States Agency for International Development
United States Department of State
Volunteers For Peace

BRAZIL

AIESEC
CDG/CDS International
CNN
Deloitte & Touche
Elite Model Management
Ernst & Young
Fellowship of Reconciliation
Ford Models
Habitat for Humanity International
IAESTE
Institute for International Cooperation and Development
International Volunteer Projects
Procter & Gamble
Schlumberger
United States Agency for International Development
United States and Foreign Commercial Service
United States Department of State

CHILE

AIESEC
CNN
Deloitte & Touche
Fellowship of Reconciliation
International Volunteer Projects
Peace Corps
Procter & Gamble
United States Agency for International Development
United States and Foreign Commercial Service
United States Department of State
Volunteers For Peace

COLOMBIA

AIESEC
Deloitte & Touche
Fellowship of Reconciliation
IAESTE
The Population Institute
Procter & Gamble
United States Agency for International Development
United States and Foreign Commercial Service

ECUADOR

AIESEC
CARE
Deloitte & Touche
Fellowship of Reconciliation
The Partnership for Service-Learning
Peace Corps
The Population Institute
United States Agency for International Development
United States and Foreign Commercial Service
United States Department of State
Volunteers For Peace
WorldTeach

GUYANA

Deloitte & Touche
United States Department of State

PARAGUAY

Fellowship of Reconciliation
IAESTE
Peace Corps
United States Agency for International Development

PERU

AIESEC
Brethren Volunteer Service
CARE
Deloitte & Touche
Fellowship of Reconciliation
Habitat for Humanity International
Institute of Cultural Affairs
Procter & Gamble
United States Agency for International Development
United States and Foreign Commercial Service

SURINAME

Deloitte & Touche
United States Department of State

TRINIDAD/TOBAGO

Deloitte & Touche

URUGUAY

AIESEC
Deloitte & Touche
Ford Models
IAESTE
Peace Corps
United States Agency for International Development
United States Department of State

VENEZUELA

AIESEC
Deloitte & Touche
Procter & Gamble
United States Agency for International Development
United States and Foreign Commercial Service

The authors and publisher would like to thank the following for their permission to reproduce copyright material:

Amelia Island Plantation
American-Arab Anti-Discrimination Committee
American Institute for Foreign Study
American Forests, Dan Smith,
Amway
Peter Arnett, young shot
Wendy Barrows
Bike Aid
The Buffalo Bill Historical Center
Centro para los Adolescentes de San Miguel de Allende
John Champion
Chincoteague National Wildlife Refuge
Christie's New York
Cleveland Browns
c.1993 CNN, Inc. All Rights Reserved. Photo by George Bennett
Common Cause
Commonwealth of Massachusetts Governor's Office
Donna Karan New York
Elizabeth Dow
Daniel Duff
Egg Pictures
Joan Embery
Nora Ephron
Fellowship Reconciliation
Stuart Flack
Kathryn Fuller-World Wildlife Fund
Greater Media Cable
Mark Green
Timothy Greenfield-Sanders, Mirabella
Julie Hanson
The Hansard Society for Parliamentary Government
Harold Prince Organization
Roald Hoffman
Nancy Hogshead
Human Service Alliance
Institute for International Cooperation and Development
The Institute for Unpopular Culture
International Management Group
IRTS Foundation
Betsey Johnson
Lawrence Berkeley Laboratory
Leo Castelli Gallery, c. Dorothy Zeidman
Jo Maeder
Michael Marsland, Lorimer
Donna Maione
The Martin Agency
Oscar Mayer
photo by Chris McKinney
Morris Arboretum
Mote Marine Laboratory
MTV Networks, Soren
NASA, Harbaugh, Hieb, Voss
National Organization for Women
New Stage Theater
Newsweek, Cohn

NYS Theatre Institute
photo by Malcom Pinckney
Platinum Plus Entertainment, Quaites
George Plimpton
Jane Pratt
Rob Reed
Reuters/Bettmann: Albright, Basketball, Bochco, Chancellor, Eisner, Feinstein, Gates, Geffen, Giuliani, Hutchison, Klein, Lee, Peterson, Petty, Reiner, Weaver, Zemin
Robert Rosenthal, TBWA
Savvy Management
Signature Sports Group, Lehman
c.1992 Solomon R. Guggenheim Foundation. Photo Credit: David Heald
Student Works Painting
Tracy Watts Millinery
Food Network
24/7 Management, Reed
U.S. Senate
University of Minnesota, young Lehman
UPI/The Bettmann Archive: Jacqueline Bouvier, Wright
UPI/Bettmann: Bocuse, Bernstein, Cronauer, Fuller, Lean, Martin, Plimpton (football), Reagan, Rolling Stones, Shields, Straus, Sutherland, Von Furstenberg
UPI/Bettmann Newsphotos: Clark, Eisenhower
P. Roy Vagelos
Christina Vegiard
Volunteers for Peace, Washington Center for Politics and Journalism
WAXQ-Q104.3
photo by Cindy Wehling
Westin Hotels
The White House: Gore, Stephanopoulos
Women Express
Xerox Palo Alto Research Center,

ABOUT THE AUTHORS

Mark Oldman and **Samer Hamadeh** are **The Internship Informants™**, the only nationally recognized experts on the subject of internships. They are authors of *The Best 106 Internships* and *The Internship Bible* as well as nationally syndicated columists on internships and career education. They are also the founders of Vault.com, the leading Internet site for career information.

Mark Oldman (at left) graduated Phi Beta Kappa with a BA and an MA in English from Stanford University as well as a JD from Stanford Law School. At Stanford, he designed and taught an undergraduate course on the US Supreme Court, ran the Stanford Wine Circle, and spent a term at Oxford University. He has completed internships in government, law, television, music, and advertising.

Samer Hamadeh graduated with a BS in Chemistry and an MS in Chemical Engineering from Stanford University. At Stanford, he managed his own printing company, played rugby, and served a teaching assistantship in the Chemistry Department. He has served internships in engineering, management consulting, and public policy.

Address:
150 W. 22nd St., 5th Floor
New York, NY 10011

E-mail:
interninfo@aol.com

CAMPUS SPEECHES

"INTERNSHIPS: SMART STARTS IN A TOUGH JOB MARKET"

Mark Oldman and Samer Hamadeh—The Internship Informants™ —give a lively and encouraging presentation on the hows, wheres, and whys of internships. Named "The Gurus of the Internship Search" by *The Michigan Daily*, they discuss how to find internships and turn them into permanent jobs, insider tips on what companies are looking for, and the best opportunities in specific career fields—from accounting to zookeeping. They also cover the busywork issue, and the pros and cons of serving an internship in school, and after. Their Princeton Review/Random House guides—which *The Houston Chronicle* calls "the latest, neatest reference books for college students"—identify more than 100,000 opportunities for teens to career-changers. Some of the internships they cover pay up to $1,000 per week, and according to the authors, internships pay off: 58 percent of all students who worked as interns got permanent job offers from the organizations where they interned.

To provide inspirational proof of an internship's ability to launch a successful career, Mark and Samer describe in their presentation the exclusive interviews they have conducted with dozens of famous former interns. They engage audiences with the little-known internship experiences of journalist George Plimpton (who calls himself "Mr. Intern"), actress Jodie Foster, MTV's Tabitha Soren, Tipper Gore, Broadway director Harold Prince, as well as astronauts, CEO's, Olympic athletes, and academics.

Recent grads of Stanford University, Mark and Samer have served eleven internships and interviewed more than 3,000 interns at organizations from Microsoft to the CIA to The Late Show with David Letterman. Their seminars run 90 minutes and close with Q&A. The authors have spoken in a wide variety of forums, including dozens of colleges and universities, including UCLA, Ohio State, Emory, and Harvard. Mark and Samer are available to speak together or individually.

To arrange a speech on internships for your campus or organization, please contact The Internship Informants at:

Address:
150 W 22nd St., 5th Floor
New York, NY 10011

E-mail:
interninfo@aol.com

WE WANT TO HEAR FROM YOU!

Please tell us about any internship programs you think we should know about. Then mail this form (feel free to attach additional sheets if necessary) to the address listed below. Thanks!

Name of organization: _____

City in which internship is located: _____

Phone number and contact person (if available):_____
_____

What did you do?_____
_____
_____
_____
_____
_____

Describe any extracurricular activities (seminars, field trips, etc.) and perks:_____
_____
_____

Your name: _____

Phone:_____

School:_____

Year in school during internship: _____

■ The Internship Bible
    150 West 22nd Street
    New York, NY 10011

NOTES

NOTES

NOTES

NOTES

NOTES

NOTES

Expert Advice

Talk About It

Pop Surveys

Paying for it

The Princeton Review

Getting in

Word du Jour

Find-O-Rama School & Career Search

www.review.com

Finding it

Best Schools

FIND US...

International

Hong Kong
4/F Sun Hung Kai Centre
30 Harbour Road, Wan Chai,
Hong Kong
Tel: (011)85-2-517-3016

Japan
Fuji Building 40, 15-14
Sakuragaokacho, Shibuya Ku,
Tokyo 150, Japan
Tel: (011)81-3-3463-1343

Korea
Tae Young Bldg, 944-24,
Daechi- Dong, Kangnam-Ku
The Princeton Review- ANC
Seoul, Korea 135-280,
South Korea
Tel: (011)82-2-554-7763

Mexico City
PR Mex S De RL De Cv
Guanajuato 228 Col. Roma
06700 Mexico D.F., Mexico
Tel: 525-564-9468

Montreal
666 Sherbrooke St.
West, Suite 202
Montreal, QC H3A 1E7 Canada
Tel: (514) 499-0870

Pakistan
1 Bawa Park - 90 Upper Mall
Lahore, Pakistan
Tel: (011)92-42-571-2315

Spain
Pza. Castilla, 3 - 5° A, 28046
Madrid, Spain
Tel: (011)341-323-4212

Taiwan
155 Chung Hsiao East Road
Section 4 - 4th Floor,
Taipei R.O.C., Taiwan
Tel: (011)886-2-751-1243

Thailand
Building One, 99 Wireless Road
Bangkok, Thailand 10330
Tel: (662) 256-7080

Toronto
1240 Bay Street, Suite 300
Toronto M5R 2A7 Canada
Tel: (800) 495-7737
Tel: (716) 839-4391

Vancouver
4212 University Way NE,
Suite 204
Seattle, WA 98105
Tel: (206) 548-1100

National (U.S.)
We have over 60 offices around the U.S. and run courses in over 400 sites. For courses and locations within the U.S. call 1 (800) 2/Review and you will be routed to the nearest office.

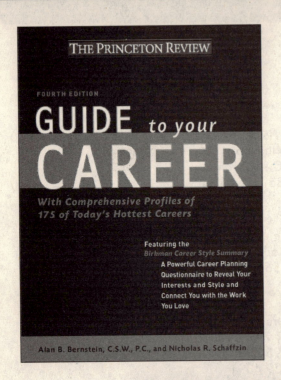
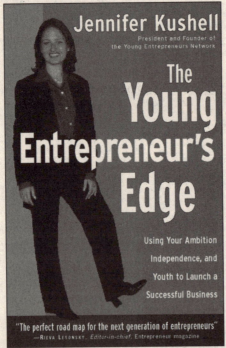